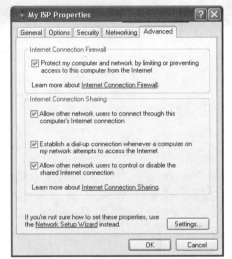

Securing Your PC and Network from Intruders

Let this book show you how to implement all of Windows XP Professional's security features. You'll learn how to encrypt data and prevent anyone from accessing your computer by enabling the Internet Connection Firewall. You'll also learn how to secure your network and to audit your security system to ensure it's airtight. Telecommuting is convenient but risky, so *Mastering Windows XP Professional* teaches you how to secure VPN connections and RAS dial-in sessions so no one can intercept and steal data or impersonate an authorized user. *See Chapters 6, 11, and 18 through 20.*

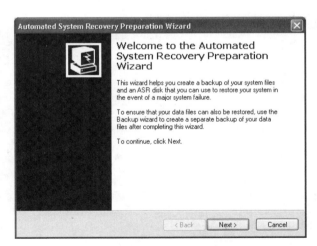

Disaster Prevention and Recovery, and Loads of Troubleshooting Advice

Mastering Windows XP Professional shows you how to fine-tune your system in order to prevent disasters and how to use Windows XP Professional's Recovery Console, System Restore, and backup utilities to recover system data should a disaster occur. This book also includes sections and chapters that will help you diagnose and fix a variety of problems. Troubleshooting topics include problems with installation, Internet connections, notebook PCs, networks, printing, and error messages. *See Chapters 10, 11, 17, and 21 through 25.*

Mastering™
Windows® XP Professional

Mark Minasi

SYBEX®   San Francisco   London

Associate Publisher: Joel Fugazzotto

Acquisitions and Developmental Editor: Ellen L. Dendy

Editor: Kari Brooks

Production Editor: Leslie E.H. Light

Technical Editor: James Kelly

Book Designer: Maureen Forys, Happenstance Type-O-Rama

Graphic Illustrators: Tony Jonick, Elizabeth Creegan, Cuong Le, Inbar Berman

Electronic Publishing Specialist: Franz Baumhackl

Proofreaders: Nelson Kim, Suzanne Stein, Nancy Riddiough

Indexer: Ted Laux

Cover Designer: Design Site

Cover Illustrator/Photographer: Sergie Loobkoff

Library of Congress Card Number: 2002104863

ISBN: 0-7821-4114-5

Manufactured in the United States of America

10 9 8 7 6 5

This book is dedicated to everyone who has ever taken one of my seminars. It's probably true that I've learned more over the years from my students than from anyone else.

—Mark Minasi

Acknowledgments

As YOU CAN TELL by lifting this tome, a lot of work went into creating all these pages about the workings of Windows XP Professional.

First, I'd like to thank Pat Coleman, who worked tirelessly to rework material and add valuable information when needed. Without her dedication and expertise, this book would not be possible. Quite a few others also revised and updated various chapters of this book. My thanks go out to Chris Brooks, Quentin Docter, Michael Jang, and Faithe Wempen.

I would be remiss if I didn't thank those at Sybex who helped get this book out on time. Thanks go to Joel Fugazzotto, Associate Publisher, and Ellen L. Dendy, Acquisitions and Developmental Editor, for helping get the book on the road, and providing guidance throughout the process. Thanks to our Editor, Kari Brooks, for making sure the manuscript was beautiful and for being patient with a strict schedule. Thanks also to James Kelly, Technical Editor, for keeping a technical eye on the book at all times. Thanks to Leslie Light, Production Editor, for keeping the book on schedule and making sure everything was in order, and to Franz Baumhackl, Electronic Publishing Specialist, for making the pages look so good! Lastly, thanks go to the graphic artist, Tony Jonick, who contributed to the wonderful illustrations enhancing this book; the proofreaders, Nelson Kim, Suzanne Stein, and Nancy Riddiough; and Ted Laux, the indexer.

Contents at a Glance

Introduction . . . . *xxviii*

Essential Skills for Windows XP Professional **1**

Part 1 • Windows XP Professional Basics **97**

    Chapter 1 • Introducing Windows XP Professional 99

    Chapter 2 • Installing Windows XP Professional (and Automating Installation) . 123

    Chapter 3 • Using the Desktop and Getting Help 159

    Chapter 4 • Customizing the Interface 197

    Chapter 5 • Installing, Running, and Managing Applications 231

    Chapter 6 • Managing Files and Folders 265

    Chapter 7 • Installing and Working with Printers and Fonts 299

    Chapter 8 • Installing and Configuring Hardware 327

    Chapter 9 • Media Player and Movie Maker 357

    Chapter 10 • Using Windows XP Professional on Notebook PCs 399

Part 2 • Communications and the Internet **421**

    Chapter 11 • Connecting to the Internet 423

    Chapter 12 • Web Browsing with Internet Explorer 457

    Chapter 13 • Using the Communications Programs 493

    Chapter 14 • Using Outlook Express for E-mail and News 541

Part 3 • Networking Windows XP Professional **561**

    Chapter 15 • Windows XP Professional Networking and
Network Design Primer 563

Chapter 16 • Setting Up and Configuring a Peer-to-Peer Network . . . . • 591

Chapter 17 • Connecting to Domains . . . . • 631

Chapter 18 • Living with Windows XP Professional Strict Security . . . . • 651

Chapter 19 • Auditing Security . . . . • 671

Chapter 20 • Secure Telecommuting . . . . • 681

**Part 4 • Diagnosing, Administering, Automating
and Troubleshooting Windows XP . . . . • 695**

Chapter 21 • Administrative and Diagnostic Tools . . . . • 697

Chapter 22 • Understanding and Using the Registry . . . . • 723

Chapter 23 • Using Scripts to Automate Windows XP . . . . • 737

Chapter 24 • Disaster Prevention And Recovery . . . . • 757

Chapter 25 • Advanced Troubleshooting Methodology . . . . • 787

Part 5 • Advanced Topics . . . . • **805**

Chapter 26 • The Microsoft Management Console . . . . • 807

Chapter 27 • Manage Windows XP Professional Services . . . . • 825

Chapter 28 • Hosting Web/FTP Servers . . . . • 841

Appendix A • Web Publishing with Windows XP Professional . . . . • 875

Appendix B • Connecting to Novell NetWare Networks . . . . • 885

Appendix C • Active Directory Essentials . . . . • 901

Index . . . . • *917*

Contents

Introduction . . . . *xxviii*

Essential Skills for Windows XP Professional 1

Part 1 • Windows XP Professional Basics 97

   Chapter 1 • Introducing Windows XP Professional 99
      What Is Windows XP Professional? 99
      What's New in Windows XP Professional? 101
         The "Evil" Windows Product Activation 101
         Easier Installation and Updating 101
         Effective Multiuser Capabilities 103
         Enhanced User Interface 103
         Taskbar Changes and Enhancements 105
         Better Audio and Video Features 106
         CD Burning 107
         Compressed Folders 108
         Search Companion 108
         Easy Publishing to the Web 108
         A Sane Implementation of Autoplay 108
         More Games 108
         Remote Desktop Connection 109
         A More Useful Winkey 109
         Improvements for Portable Computers 109
         Faxing 109
         More Help 110
         Network Connectivity 112
         Internet Connectivity and Web Browsing 112
         Multiple Monitor Support—for Both Desktops and Laptops 113
         Advanced Features 113
         What's Hiding under the Hood? 114
      Should You Upgrade to Windows XP Professional? 116
         Windows 9*x* 116
         Windows 3.1 116
         Windows 2000 Professional 117
         Intended Usage 117
      How Is Windows XP Professional Different from Other Operating Systems? 117
         Windows XP Professional Compared with OS/2 117
         Windows XP Professional Compared with Unix 117
         Windows XP Professional Compared with the Macintosh OS 118
      What Are the Features of Windows XP Professional Architecture? 118
         Kernel Mode 118
         User Mode 121
      Summary 122

**Chapter 2 • Installing Windows XP Professional
(and Automating Installation)** **123**

The Order of Business 124
Will Your Computer Be Able to Run Windows XP Professional? 124
    Processor 124
    RAM 124
    Free Disk Space 125
    SVGA-Capable Video Adapter and Monitor 125
    CD Drive or DVD Drive 126
Checking System Compatibility 126
Choosing an Installation Method 127
Preparing for Installation 128
    Back Up All Your Data Files 128
    Write Down Internet Connection Information 128
    Plug In and Switch On All Hardware 128
    Use the Files and Settings Transfer Wizard to Transfer Settings 128
    Stop Any Antivirus Software or Disk Utilities 131
Upgrading to Windows XP 132
Performing a New Installation of Windows XP 135
Performing a Clean Install of Windows XP 139
    Choosing a Hard Disk Partition 139
    Converting the Partition to NTFS 140
    Choosing Regional and Language Options 140
    Entering Your Name and Organization 142
    Entering Your Product Key 142
    Entering the Computer Name 142
    Entering the Modem Dialing Information 142
    Checking the Date and Time 142
    Specifying Networking Settings 142
The Installation Paths Converge 144
    Setting Up Your Internet Connection 144
    Creating User Accounts 146
    Activating Windows 146
Applying Your Files and Settings 147
Uninstalling Windows XP and Reverting to a Previous Version of Windows 149
Removing Your Old Version of Windows 149
Keeping Windows Updated 149
    When Windows Update Runs 150
    Configuring Windows Update 150
    Running Windows Update Manually 151
Automating the Installation of Windows XP 152
Summary 157

Chapter 3 • Using the Desktop and Getting Help **159**

Logging On and Logging Off 160
    Logging On 161
    Logging Off 162

Logging On to a Domain 163
Using the Desktop and Start Menu 163
Switching to Another User 165
Locking the Computer 165
Checking Which User Is Currently Active 166
Seeing Who Else Is Logged On to the Computer 166
Seeing Which Programs the Other Users Are Running 166
Logging Another User Off 169
Sending a Message to Another User 170
Using the Winkey 171
Shutting Down Windows 172
Help and Support Center 173
    Starting Help and Support Center 173
    Finding Your Way around Help and Support Center 174
    Browsing for Help 178
    Creating and Using Favorites in Help 181
    Using Views 182
    Navigating with Help History 182
    Printing Out Help Information 182
Using Remote Assistance 183
    Security Considerations 183
    Enabling Remote Assistance 184
    Setting Limits for Remote Assistance 184
    Sending a Remote Assistance Invitation via E-mail 185
    Viewing the Status of Your Invitations 188
    Receiving Remote Assistance 189
    Responding to a Remote Assistance Invitation 191
Microsoft Online Support (Get Help from Microsoft) 194
Windows Newsgroups (Go to a Windows Web Site Forum) 194
Using the Troubleshooters 194
Finding Help on the Internet and Web 195
    Help on the Web 195
    Help in Newsgroups 196
Summary 196

Chapter 4 • Customizing the Interface **197**
Working with the XP Control Panel 197
Changing the Date and Time 199
Adjusting Video Settings 201
    Installing Video and Monitor Drivers 201
    Setting Resolution, Color Depth, and Refresh Rate 203
    Setting Monitor Controls 206
    Troubleshooting Video Problems 207
Customizing the Windows XP Display 208
    Working with Themes 208
    Customizing the Desktop 208
    Working with Screen Savers 213
    Changing Color and Appearance Options 213

Customizing the Taskbar 215
    Setting Taskbar Options 215
    Working with Taskbar Toolbars 216
    Customizing the Notification Area 217
Setting Start Menu Options 218
    Customizing the Windows XP Start Menu 218
    Customizing the Classic Start Menu 220
Adjusting the Keyboard and Mouse 220
    Keyboard Properties 221
    Mouse Properties 221
Choosing System Sounds 222
Using Accessibility Options 222
    Using the Accessibility Wizard 223
    Accessibility Options in Control Panel 223
    Using Magnifier 227
    Running Narrator 228
    Using the On-Screen Keyboard 228
    Using Utility Manager 228
Summary 229

Chapter 5 • Installing, Running, and Managing Applications **231**
Multiuser Considerations 232
    Who Can Install Programs? 232
    Who Is the Program Available To? 233
    What Happens When Multiple Users Open the Same File at the Same Time? 233
    What Happens When Multiple Users Run the Same Program at the Same Time? . . . 234
Installing a Program 235
    Installing and Running Multiple Versions of the Same Application 236
    Making Programs Run at Startup 236
Removing a Program 237
Adding and Removing Windows Components 240
Running Programs 242
Dealing with Unresponsive Programs 242
Program Compatibility Issues 245
    Programs You Shouldn't Even Try to Run on Windows XP 247
    Running Programs in Compatibility Mode 248
Exchanging Data Between Programs 255
    Clipboard Basics 256
    For Office 2000/XP Users: The Enhanced Microsoft Office Clipboard 256
    Using the ClipBook Viewer 257
    Object Linking and Embedding 258
Organizing the Start Menu 262
    Editing Pinned Shortcuts 263
    Editing the All Programs List 263
Summary 264

Chapter 6 • Managing Files and Folders **265**

Using Explorer 266
   Opening vs. Exploring 266
   Branches 267
   Views 267
   Working with Shortcut Menus 271
Organizing Your Files and Folders 272
   Creating New Folders 272
   Moving Items 272
   Copying Items 273
   Saving Files and Folders to the Desktop 273
   Dragging with the Right Mouse Button 273
   Renaming Files and Folders 274
   Deleting Files and Folders 274
Understanding the Multiuser Environment 276
Customizing the Explorer Interface 277
   Setting Folder Options 277
   Customizing an Individual Folder 279
   Customizing the Toolbar 280
Setting File and Folder Properties 280
Searching for Files and Folders 281
Working with Compressed Files and Folders 283
   Using Zip Compression 283
   Using NTFS Compression 283
Using Encrypting File System (EFS) 285
   Backing Up Your Certificates 285
   Encrypting and Decrypting 286
   Sharing Encrypted Files with Other Local Users 287
   Transferring Encrypted Files to Another PC 288
Working with Offline Files 288
   Turning Off Fast User Switching 288
   Configuring the Offline Files Feature 289
   Selecting Files and Folders to Be Available Offline 290
   Working Offline 290
   Synchronizing 290
Setting File Associations 291
Creating CDs 293
   Copying the Files to the Storage Area 293
   Checking the Files in the Storage Area 294
   Writing the Files to CD 294
   When Things Go Wrong Writing the CD 296
   Clearing the Storage Area 297
Summary 297

Chapter 7 • Installing and Working with Printers and Fonts . . . . • • • • **299**
How Windows XP Handles Printing 299
Installing Local Printers 301
    Installing a Local Printer Driver 301
    Installing Multiple Drivers for the Same Printer 303
    Sharing a Local Printer 305
    Setting Permissions for a Shared Printer 306
    Installing Multiple OS Support for a Shared Local Printer 308
Installing Remote Printers 309
    Setting Up a Remote Printer 309
    Installing a Printer on a TCP/IP Port 310
    Installing a Printer Through a Unix Host 311
Managing Installed Printers 311
    Removing a Printer Driver 311
    Working with Printer Properties 311
Managing the Printing Process 315
    Managing a Print Queue 315
    Taking a Printer Out of Service with Pending Print Jobs 316
    Using Separator Pages 316
    Setting Print Server Properties 318
Managing Fonts 319
    Installing Fonts 320
    Managing Your Font Collection 320
    Using Other Types of Fonts 322
    Working with the Font Substitution Table 324
    Selecting a Different Display Font 324
    Enabling ClearType for the Display Font 325
Summary 325

Chapter 8 • Installing and Configuring Hardware **327**
How Hardware Interacts with Windows XP 327
    Device Drivers 327
    System Resources 329
    What Happens When You Install a Device in Windows? 330
Using Hot-Pluggable Devices 331
Using the Hardware Wizards 332
    Installing a Driver from a Specific Location 333
    Running the Add Hardware Wizard 336
Disabling a Device 338
Uninstalling a Device 339
Working with Device Properties 339
    Viewing Device Properties 339
    Viewing and Changing Drivers 340
    Viewing and Changing Resource Assignments 341
    Configuring a Modem 342
    Configuring a CD Drive 345
    Configuring a Removable Drive 347

Configuring a Video Card 348
Viewing USB Hub Usage 349
Using Multiple Monitors 350
Configuring Windows to Use an Uninterruptible Power Supply 352
What Is a UPS? 352
Choosing a UPS 352
Installing a UPS 353
Summary 356

Chapter 9 • Media Player and Movie Maker **357**
Getting Started with Windows Media Player 357
Using the Media Guide 358
Working with Player Controls 358
Working with Audio and Video Clips 359
Cataloging Media Files on Your PC 359
Playing Audio and Video Clips 360
Creating Playlists 360
Using the Graphic Equalizer and Sound Effects 360
Editing MP3 and WMA Tags 361
Setting Media Library Options 362
Working with Audio CDs and DVD Movies 364
Playing a CD 364
Copying (Ripping) a CD 365
Setting Copying Options 367
Playing a DVD 372
Tuning into Internet Radio 373
Connecting to an Internet Radio Station 374
Searching for a Radio Station 375
Creating and Editing Presets 375
Applying Skins 375
Choosing Visualizations 376
Backing Up and Restoring Licenses 377
Backing Up Your Licenses 379
Restoring Your Licenses 380
Working with Portable Devices 380
Making Media Player Recognize Your Device 381
Copying Audio Files to a Portable Player 381
Setting Media Player Options 382
Setting Output Volume and Recording Volume 383
Displaying the Volume Control in the Notification Area 383
Setting Volume from the Sounds and Audio Devices Properties Dialog Box 384
Setting Speaker Balance 385
Setting Advanced Audio Properties 385
Using the Volume Control Program 386
Recording Audio Files with Sound Recorder 389
Starting Sound Recorder 389
Recording a Sound File with Sound Recorder 390
Converting a File to Another Format 390

Using Windows Movie Maker 391
Creating Collections 392
Importing Content 392
Recording Content 393
Creating a Movie Project 395
Exporting a Project to a Movie File 396
Summary 397

Chapter 10 • Using Windows XP Professional on Notebook PCs . . . . • **399**
How Notebook PCs are Physically Different 399
Using Built-In and External Monitors 400
Working with PC Cards 401
Working with Hardware Profiles 402
Monitoring and Optimizing Battery Usage 404
Choosing a Power Scheme 404
Setting Power Alarms 405
Working with the Power Meter 406
Choosing Advanced Power Options 407
Enabling and Disabling Hibernation 408
Using Multiple Dialing Locations 409
Synchronizing Files with Other PCs 410
Working with Offline Files 411
Using Briefcase 414
Troubleshooting Notebook PC Problems 417
Problems with PC Cards under Windows XP 417
Problems with a Wheel-Style PS/2 Mouse 417
Power Management Problems 418
Summary 420

Part 2 • Communications and the Internet **421**

Chapter 11 • Connecting to the Internet **423**
Types of Internet Connections 424
Connecting to the Internet with an Analog Modem 424
Connecting to the Internet with a Cable Modem 428
Cable Internet Access—How Does It Work? 428
How Fast Is It? 428
Cable Internet Access—Advantages and Disadvantages 429
Getting Hooked Up 430
Configuring Your Connection 431
Connecting to the Internet with DSL 432
DSL—How Does It Work? 432
How Fast Is It? 432
DSL—Advantages and Disadvantages 433
Getting Hooked Up 433
Connecting to the Internet with Satellite 434
Satellite: How Does It Work? 434

Satellite: Advantages and Disadvantages 435
Satellite: Getting Hooked Up 435
Protecting Your System 435
Connecting to the Internet with ISDN 436
ISDN—How Does It Work? 437
ISDN—Advantages and Disadvantages 437
Getting Hooked Up 438
Using the Network Setup Wizard to Share an Internet Connection 439
Set Up the Computer That Will Share the Connection 440
Setting Up a Client Computer 444
What ICS Does 448
NAT Improvements in Windows XP 448
Configuring ICS Manually 450
Specifying Which Programs and Services Can Use the Shared Connection 451
Setting the IP Addresses of Connected Computers 454
Turning Off ICS 454
Using a Shared Internet Connection 455
Troubleshooting Internet Connectivity Problems 455
Dial-Up Modem Problems 455
Cable/DSL Problems 456
Satellite Problems 456
Summary 456

Chapter 12 • Web Browsing with Internet Explorer **457**
Starting Internet Explorer 457
Moving around the Web 458
Working with the Links Bar 460
Keeping Track of Your Favorite Sites 460
Working with the History List 463
Using the Media Bar 464
Accessing E-Mail and Newsgroups from Internet Explorer 465
Sending a Link or Page via E-Mail 465
Saving and Printing Web Pages 466
Working with Offline Favorites 468
Finding Exactly What You Want on the Internet 470
Performing a Simple Search 470
Expanding a Search 472
Other Ways to Search 472
Downloading Files 473
Customizing Internet Explorer 473
Configuring the General Tab 474
Looking at the Security Tab 475
Using the Privacy Tab 477
Using the Content Tab 479
Setting Up the Connections Tab 481
Looking at the Programs Tab 481
Configuring the Advanced Tab 482

Customizing the Internet Explorer Toolbar 482
Changing Text Size 483
MSN Explorer 484
Using Built-In Internet Utilities 486
    Address Resolution Display and Control (ARP) 486
    File Transfer Protocol (FTP) 486
    Trivial File Transfer Protocol (TFTP) 488
    Finger 488
    Ping 488
    Protocol Statistics (Netstat) 489
    Remote File Copy (RCP) 490
    Remote Program Execution (REXEC) 490
    Remote Shell/Script (RSH) 490
    Remote Terminal (Telnet) 490
    Route 491
    Trace Route (tracert) 491
Summary 491

Chapter 13 • Using the Communications Programs **493**
Using the Windows XP Professional Fax Service 493
    Installing Fax 494
    Configuring Windows XP Professional Fax 494
    Sending Faxes in Windows XP Professional 498
    Creating a Cover Page 500
    Using the Fax Console 504
Connecting with HyperTerminal 505
    Creating a New HyperTerminal Connection 505
    Sending and Receiving Files 506
Communicating and Sharing with NetMeeting 507
    Installing NetMeeting 507
    Making a Call 509
    Using the Chat Application 510
    Using Directory Servers 511
    Hosting a Meeting 511
    Using Video 512
    Sharing Applications 512
Using Windows Messenger 512
    Starting Messenger 513
Configuring Messenger 513
    Personal Tab Options 514
    Phone Tab Options 514
    Preferences Tab Options 514
    Privacy Tab Options 516
    Connection Tab Options 517
    Running the Audio and Video Tuning Wizard 517
Signing Out and Signing Back In 520

Adding a Contact 520
   Adding a Contact by E-mail Address or Passport Sign-In 520
   Adding a Contact by Searching for Them 521
   Adding a Contact when Someone Adds You to Their Contacts List 522
Removing a Contact from Your Contacts List 522
Chatting 522
   Adding More People to a Conversation 524
   Setting Font, Style, and Color for Text You Send 524
Adding Voice to a Conversation 524
Adding Video to a Conversation 525
Blocking and Unblocking Users 525
Changing Your Status 526
Transferring Files 526
   Sending a File 526
   Receiving a File 528
Using Remote Desktop Connection 528
   Remote Desktop Connection Terminology and Basics 529
   Setting the Remote Computer to Accept Incoming Connections 530
   Choosing Settings for Remote Desktop Connection 531
   Connecting via Remote Desktop Connection 536
   Working via Remote Desktop Connection 538
   Returning to Your Local Desktop 539
   Disconnecting the Remote Session 539
   Logging Off the Remote Session 540
Summary 540

Chapter 14 • Using Outlook Express for E-mail and News **541**
Using Outlook Express As Your Mail Reader 541
   A Quick Tour 542
   Retrieving Your Mail 543
   Reading and Processing Messages 543
   Creating and Sending Messages 548
   Creating E-mail Messages with HTML 549
   Attaching Files to Your Messages 553
   Applying Message Rules 554
   Adding and Managing Identities 555
Using Outlook Express As Your Newsreader 556
   Setting Up a Newsgroup Account 557
   Connecting to Newsgroups 558
   Finding a Newsgroup of Interest 558
   Subscribing to a Newsgroup 558
   Reading a Newsgroup 559
   Posting to a Newsgroup 559
Customizing Outlook Express 559
Summary 560

Part 3 • Networking Windows XP Professional **561**

**Chapter 15 • Windows XP Professional Networking and
Network Design Primer** **563**
What is a Network? 563
    Early Networking: Sneakernet 564
    LAN: The Alternative 564
Networking Vocabulary 568
A Little Theory 569
    OSI Model 569
    Protocol Stacks 571
    TCP/IP Network Protocols 572
    IP Addressing 573
Network Relationships 578
    Master/Slave 579
    Peer-to-Peer 579
    Client-Server 579
    Servers 580
    What Type of Network is Best? 581
The Look and Feel of a Network 582
Building Your Own Network 583
    Selecting Ethernet Hardware 583
    Network Cards 584
    Cables 585
    Wireless Considerations 587
    Hubs 587
    Routers 588
    Installation 589
Summary 590

Chapter 16 • Setting Up and Configuring a Peer-to-Peer Network **591**
Setting Up a Network 591
Connecting Your Ethernet Network 593
Configuring Your Network 594
    Using the Network Setup Wizard 594
    Configuring Windows 95/NT Workstation Machines 597
    Identification 599
    File and Printer Sharing for Microsoft Networks 599
    Configuring Windows XP Manually 600
    Network Bridging 602
Creating Shares 604
Attaching to Network Resources 607
    Browsing My Network Places 607
    Mapping a Network Drive 607
    Making a Direct Connection via a UNC 608
Using Profiles 610
    Creating Hardware Profiles 610

Managing Hardware Profiles 612
Managing User Profiles 613
Connecting to Non-Microsoft Networks 615
Entering the Dark Place that Is Unix 615
Macintosh Networks 617
Troubleshooting Windows XP Professional Networking 618
Is It Plugged In? 618
Configuration Testing 619
Is Anybody Out There? 620
How Do You Troubleshoot Windows XP Professional Network Architecture? 626
Quick Advice 629
Summary 629

Chapter 17 • Connecting to Domains **631**
Setting Up a Domain 632
Requirements on the Domain Server 633
User Account 634
Computer Account 634
Profiles 634
Name of Domain 634
Connecting to a Domain 635
Configuring Windows XP for a Domain 635
Attaching to Network Resources 642
Browsing My Network Places 642
Mapping a Network Drive 643
Making a Direct Connection via a UNC 644
Using Profiles 646
Creating Hardware Profiles 646
User Profiles 646
Attaching to Network Resources Using Login Scripts 647
Troubleshooting Domains 647
Receiving the Error Message "No Domain Server Was Available" 647
Identification 649
Summary 649

Chapter 18 • Living with Windows XP Professional Strict Security **651**
Understanding User Accounts in Windows XP Professional 652
Understanding User Rights 653
Creating a User Account 655
Creating a Group Account 658
Setting Permissions 659
Setting Share-Level Permissions 659
Types of File and Folder Permissions 661
Assigning File and Folder Permissions 664
Auditing Files and Folders 664
Understanding Ownership 668
Defining Ownership 668
Taking Ownership 669
Summary 670

Chapter 19 • Auditing Security **671**

Deciding What to Audit 671
    Benefits of Auditing 672
    The Dark Side of Auditing 673
Setting up Auditing in Windows XP 673
Monitoring Security 677
Summary 679

Chapter 20 • Secure Telecommuting **681**

Telecommuting Overview: Risks and Rewards 681
Protecting Against the Interception of Data 682
    Securing RAS Dial-In Sessions 682
    Virtual Private Networking Connections 684
    VPN Performance Considerations 687
Protecting Against the Impersonation of a User 688
    Common Sense Guidelines 689
    Encrypted Authentication 689
    Caller-ID/Callback Security 690
    Third-Party Products: SecurID, SafeWord 691
Protecting Against the Abduction of Data 692
    Encrypting Files with EFS 692
Summary 694

**Part 4 • Diagnosing, Administering, Automating
and Troubleshooting Windows XP** **695**

Chapter 21 • Administrative and Diagnostic Tools **697**

Running Disk Management 697
    Deciding Which File System Is Best 698
    Setting Up a New Disk Drive in Windows XP Professional 700
Running Event Viewer 704
Monitoring Performance 708
    Adding a Counter in Graph View 711
    Using Alerts 712
    Using Counter Log View 713
    Using Report View 714
    Running System Information 715
Running Task Manager 719
Summary 722

Chapter 22 • Understanding and Using the Registry **723**

What Is the Registry and What Does It Do? 723
Why Work with the Registry? 724
Preparing to Access the Registry 725
Running Registry Editor 725
    Backing Up Your Registry 726
    Restoring Your Registry 727

Working in the Registry 727
 The Five Subtrees of the Registry 727
 Keys, Subkeys, and Value Entries 727
 Registry Data Types 729
 Where the Registry Is Stored 730
 Finding Information in the Registry 731
 Editing a Value Entry 732
 Adding a Key or a Value Entry 733
 Deleting a Key or a Value Entry 734
 Copying a Key Name 734
An Example: Changing Your Windows Name and Organization 734
Using Registry Favorites to Quickly Access Keys 735
Summary 735

Chapter 23 • Using Scripts to Automate Windows XP **737**
What Is Scripting? 737
Shell Scripting with BAT and CMD Files 738
 Tools for Scripting 738
 Your First Shell Script 739
 Adding Logic to Shell Scripts 740
Introduction to the Windows Script Host 744
 The WScript and CScript Executables 744
 Script File Languages 745
 XML-based Scripts 746
 Your First WSH 2.0 Script 746
 Adding Logic to Your Scripts 748
Advanced Concepts 750
 Objects 750
 Scheduling Scripts 751
Scripts for Common Administrative Chores 751
 AddUser.wsf 752
 ChangeRole.wsf 753
 LogEvent.vbs 755
Summary 756

Chapter 24 • Disaster Prevention And Recovery **757**
Avoiding Windows XP Professional Crashes 758
 Buy Reliable Hardware 758
 Guard Against Environmental Hazards 759
 Install Windows XP Professional Properly 760
 Obtain Tested, Certified Drivers for Your Hardware 760
 Always Shut Down Windows XP Professional Properly 760
 Back Up Your Disk Regularly 760
 Be Sure You're Authorized to Do Something Before Doing It 761
An Ounce of Prevention 761
 Defragmenting Files 761

Cleaning Up Disks 762
Checking Disks for Errors 763
Restoring a Configuration 764
Using the Last Known Good Configuration 764
Using System Restore 765
Creating and Using the Automated System Recovery Disk 768
The Recovery Console 770
Installing the Recovery Console 771
Using the Recovery Console 771
The Driver Verifier—a Babysitter for Your Drivers 777
Running the Driver Verifier 778
System File Checker 779
Running the SFC 779
The Registry Entry That Lets You Force a Blue Screen (Core Dump) 780
Backing Up and Restoring 781
Making a Backup 781
Restoring a Backup 785
Summary 786

Chapter 25 • Advanced Troubleshooting Methodology **787**
The Tao of Troubleshooting 787
Define the Problem: "It's Broken." 788
Explore the Boundaries 788
Brainstorm and Document 788
Test Your Ideas 789
Repair the Problem 789
Clean Up After Yourself 789
Provide Closure 789
Document the Situation 790
Troubleshooting Printing 790
Troubleshooting Scenario 1: Printer Is Unplugged 791
Troubleshooting Scenario 2: Nothing in the Print Queue Will Print 791
Other Print Troubleshooting Steps 792
Troubleshooting Windows XP Professional Setup 794
Planning and Text Mode Setup 794
Troubleshooting Scenario 3: Drives Not Found 795
SCSI Troubleshooting 796
Troubleshooting Text Mode to GUI Mode 797
Addressing GUI Mode and Initial Boot Issues 798
Troubleshooting Stop Errors 799
Common Stop Errors 800
Responding to Stop Errors 802
Fixing Stop Errors 802
Boot Process Troubleshooting 803
Summary 804

Part 5 • Advanced Topics **805**

Chapter 26 • The Microsoft Management Console **807**
The Basic Features of MMC 807
MMC Terms to Know 808
The MMC Console 809
    What Are Snap-Ins? 810
    Working In Author Mode and Adding Snap-Ins 811
    Customizing MMC Views 814
    User Mode-Full Access 815
    User Mode-Limited Access, Multiple Window 816
    User Mode-Limited Access, Single Window 817
The Computer Management Console 817
Additional Customization Options 819
    File 820
    Action 820
    Taskpad 821
    View 824
    Favorites 824
Summary 824

Chapter 27 • Manage Windows XP Professional Services **825**
The Purpose of a Service 825
The Service Management Console 826
Windows XP Professional Services 827
    Automatic Services 827
    Manual Services 830
    Disabled Services 832
    Additional Services 833
Configuring Services 833
    General Startup 833
    Log On 834
    Recovery 835
    Dependencies 836
    Service Commands 837
Troubleshooting Service Issues 839
Summary 839

Chapter 28 • Hosting Web/FTP Servers **841**
Installing Internet Information Server 841
Windows XP Professional Limits on IIS 844
The Internet Information Service Console 844
    Connecting to Remote IIS Services 845
    Basic Configuration Management 845
Configuring the Web Server 846
    Generic Web Site Configuration 847
    Specific Web Site Configuration 852

Configuring the FTP Server 862
    FTP Site 863
    Security Accounts 863
    Messages 864
    Home Directory 865
    Virtual Directories 866
Configuring the SMTP Server 867
    Basic SMTP Configuration 868
    Access 869
    Messages 870
    Delivery 871
    LDAP Routing 872
    Security 873
Troubleshooting IIS 873
    Log Files 873
Summary 874

Appendix A • Web Publishing with Windows XP Professional 875
What Will You Publish? 875
    Understanding Copyright Issues 875
    Controlling Quality 877
Where Will You Publish Your Content? 878
How Will You Publish Your Content? 878
    Using FTP 878
    Using WebDAV 878
    Using Network Places to Access an FTP Site or Web Folder 879
    FTP via Internet Explorer 883
    FTP via an FTP Client 884
Summary 884

Appendix B • Connecting to Novell NetWare Networks 885
CSNW Features 885
Novell Directory Services Versus Bindery-Based Servers 886
Using Novell Administration Utilities 887
    Accessing a NetWare Server 889
Running NetWare and Windows Networking Together 891
    Configuring Windows XP Professional to Run in Parallel with NetWare 891
Printing to Novell Printers 894
Enabling Long Filename Support on the Novell Server 896
Choosing a Novell Client Solution 896
Installing the Novell Client 897
Configuring the Novell Client 898
Summary 899

Appendix C • Active Directory Essentials **901**
Security: Keeping Track of Who's Allowed to Use the Network and Who Isn't 902
   Maintaining a "Directory" of Users and Other Network Objects 903
   Centralizing the Directory and Directories: a "Logon Server" 903
Searching: Finding Things on the Network 905
   Finding Servers: "Client-Server Rendezvous" 905
   Name Resolution and DNS 905
Creating New Types of Subadministrators 906
Delegation: Subdividing Control over a Domain 907
Satisfying Political Needs 908
Connectivity and Replication Issues 909
Scalability: Building Big Networks 910
Simplifying Computer Names or Unifying the Namespace 910
Satisfying the Lust for Power and Control 912
Connecting a Windows XP Professional Machine to an AD Domain 912
   Checklist 912
   Connecting to AD 913
Summary 915

Index. *917*

Introduction

WHAT YOU HAVE IN your hands is a soup-to-nuts, beginner-to-expert, end-user-to-administrator handbook—the all-in-one guide to using and supporting Windows XP Professional, Microsoft's latest release in the NT family of operating systems.

This book is for you if you are upgrading from a previous version of Windows or if you're coming to the Windows world from another operating system. This book is also for you if you are new to networking or if you're thinking about setting up a network at home or in your business. In addition, this book is for you if you use a corporate client-server Windows 2000 (or, in the near future, Windows .NET Server) network at the office. In other words, if you use Windows XP Professional in any environment, including a stand-alone system at home, you'll find here information you can use—all the way from installing Windows XP Professional to network-troubleshooting techniques.

What I Cover in This Book

This book is divided into four parts, building in a logical order from setting up your system to configuring advanced features.

Essential Skills Section

The visual Essential Skills section will teach you some of the most important Windows XP Professional skills through a series of easy-to-follow screens, step-by-step instructions, to-the-point tips and tricks, and expert advice segments. You'll find references in the main text of the book to indicate when a process is covered in the Essential Skills section. The Essential Skills section begins with a table of contents to help you quickly find what you're looking for.

Part I: Windows XP Professional Basics

Part I consists of 10 chapters.

Chapter 1 is an overview of Windows XP Professional—what's new since the last incarnation (plenty!), what makes it different from other operating systems and other versions of Windows (including what makes it different from Windows 9x), and what its main features are. Don't be misled if it seems there's a lot of jargon in this first chapter. I figured that power users who are already familiar with other operating systems will be looking to this chapter just to get an idea of what's different in Windows XP Professional; if you're not a power user on another system, you won't miss anything if you simply skim these comparisons.

In Chapter 2, I take up the topic of *installing* Windows XP Professional, on your own as well as for other users. This chapter discusses how to install Windows XP Professional in these three ways:

◆ As an upgrade to a previous version of Windows

◆ As a new installation on a computer that already has installed an operating system that you want to keep

◆ As a clean installation on a computer that doesn't have an operating system installed.

I'll also show you how you can reduce the amount of work needed to install the system—by means of an automatic, "unattended" installation.

Chapter 3 shows you how to get started using the newly redesigned Desktop and Start menu. It also includes information about the radically different Help system, Help and Support Center, and about how to get remote assistance help from a colleague or co-worker.

Chapter 4 shows you how to customize Windows XP so it's specifically suited to your needs. You'll learn how to use the XP Control Panel to adjust your video settings and display, customize and snaz up your desktop, set systems sounds, and adjust your keyboard and mouse. Chapter 4 also shows you how to customize the Taskbar and Start menu so you can work more efficiently. Readers with disabilities will want to read the section on using Windows XP's accessibility features.

Chapter 5 covers how to install, run, and remove programs, including how to set up an application for multiple users. You'll learn how to use Compatibility mode to run non-native Windows XP applications, and you'll read about which types of programs you shouldn't install on Windows XP. Terminating an unresponsive application using Task Manager is also covered, as well as exchanging data between programs.

Chapter 6 shows you how to work with and manage your files and folders. The chapter information includes searching, compressing, encrypting, using the Offline Files feature, and burning CD-ROMs.

Chapter 7 is all about printers, printing, and fonts. Step-by-step instruction is provided on installing and configuring local and remote printers, sharing a local printer, and managing a print queue. Fonts are tied closely to printers, so this chapter also shows you how to install and manage fonts.

Chapter 8 covers installing and configuring specific types of hardware, how to assign and manage hardware resources, how to disable a device, and how to update hardware drivers. You'll also learn how to set up multiple monitors to your desktop system.

Chapter 9 concerns the latest version (version 8) of Windows Media Player, which you can use to play audio and video files, listen to Internet radio stations, and so on. Windows Media Player will be new to you if you were previously a user of Windows NT Workstation or Windows 2000 Professional. Previous users of Windows Me, which included version 7, will find version 8 much improved and providing much more functionality.

If you need to run Windows XP Professional on a portable computer, you'll definitely want to read Chapter 10. Topics cover using external monitors, PC cards, setting hardware profiles, managing battery usage, saving dial-up profiles for multiple locations, and troubleshooting. No discussion of portables would be complete without coverage of file synchronization.

Part II: Communications and the Internet

The chapters in Part II cover how to use the communications tools included with Windows XP Professional.

Chapter 11 includes instructions for installing and configuring an Internet connection (including broadband connections) and for setting up Internet Connection Sharing.

Chapter 12 covers all you need to know to use the Internet Explorer Web browser.

Chapter 13 explains the communications programs: Fax, HyperTerminal, NetMeeting, Windows Messenger, and Remote Desktop Sharing.

Chapter 14 is an overview of Outlook Express, the news and mail client that's included with Windows XP Professional.

NOTE *Be sure to check out Appendix A, which shows you how to publish information to the Web.*

Part III: Networking Windows XP Professional

If you're a networking newbie, you'll definitely want to read the chapters in Part III.

Chapter 15 preps you for planning and setting up your Windows XP Professional network.

In Chapter 16, I show you how to set up and configure a Windows XP Professional peer-to-peer network. You'll learn how to create shares, attach to network resources, and utilize user and hardware profiles. Chapter 16 wraps up with a section on network troubleshooting.

Chapter 17 shows you how to connect Windows XP Professional machines to a domain, how to connect domain-based documents and printers, how to create user and hardware profiles, and how to troubleshoot your domain.

One of the ways that Windows XP Professional is radically different from every other operating system is that it is *secure*; in fact, Windows XP Professional has been certified by the U.S. government as meeting the requirements for C2-level security. Security is a great thing to have, for obvious reasons, but it can also cause problems—the first time you can't access a file on your own computer, you'll want to know why! Chapter 18 takes you through the details of security so that you can address problems quickly and directly.

Chapter 19 shows you how to use Windows XP Professional's security and monitoring tools to audit your security system. Apply what you learn in this chapter, and you'll be able to see if someone logged on or off, changed security settings, created or modified users, or accessed system resources.

Chapter 20 is about Virtual Private Networks (VPNs). A VPN is a tunnel through the Internet that connects your computer to a network. When you're on the road, you can dial up almost any ISP and set up a VPN session to your network over the Internet. If you're a road warrior, you shouldn't skip this chapter.

NOTE *If you're one of the many network administrators who need to connect to a Novell Network, be sure to read Appendix B.*

NOTE *Windows 2000/.NET Server administrators will want to check out Appendix C on Active Directory.*

Part IV: Diagnosing, Administering, Automating, and Troubleshooting Windows XP Professional

The chapters in Part IV provide you with the tools and skills you need to work more efficiently and to keep your Windows XP Professional system in tip-top shape.

Chapter 21 shows you how to monitor and optimize your system using Windows XP Professional's administrative and diagnostic tools including Disk Management, Event Viewer, and Task Manager.

Chapter 22 explains how and when to use the Registry to change Windows applications and hardware settings. Also covered in Chapter 22 is the important topic of backing up and restoring the Registry.

Creating scripts that automate everyday tasks is explained in Chapter 23, as well as how to schedule your scripts to run at specific times.

Chapter 24 shows you how to prevent system crashes and other system disasters, how to restore a configuration, and how to recover lost data, among other topics.

Chapter 25 looks at advanced troubleshooting principles and procedures. It also provides specific techniques for troubleshooting your Windows XP setup, printing, and error messages.

Part V: Advanced Topics

Part V comprises three chapters for true power users.

Chapter 26 discusses the Microsoft Management Console, an all-in-one administrative tool that can be set up to include everything you need to administer Windows XP Professional.

You'll learn how to configure and manage services—programs that run in the background to support basic activities—in Chapter 27.

Chapter 28 addresses the three basic services you can set up and configure with Internet Information Server (IIS): Web service, FTP service, and SMTP service.

Appendixes

You'll learn important issues about publishing your own Web pages in Appendix A. Topics discussed include what you can legally publish and the importance of performing quality control; where to publish your material; and how to get the material from your computer to the Web host.

Appendix B and Appendix C are for network administrators. Appendix B deals with the very likely scenario using your Windows XP Professional workstations over a Novell NetWare network. Microsoft has worked with Novell to provide Windows XP Professional users with Client Service for Novell NetWare tools to make it easy to operate over such systems. In Appendix B, you'll learn the idiosyncrasies of those tools. In Appendix C, I introduce you to Active Directory and how it provides better, more flexible administration options, and significant control to network administrators. You'll also learn how to connect your Windows XP Professional workstation to an Active Directory domain.

Typesetting Conventions Followed in This Book

As much as I could, I attempted to be consistent throughout the book with the capitalization of menu commands and dialog-box options. And all program-level filenames and command names appear in a `special font` to help distinguish them from the natural grammar of the sentence.

I've *italicized* terms for emphasis or as needed to avoid confusion. For example, key terms being defined for the first time are in italics. Furthermore, when I'm presenting the syntax of a command (yes, system administrators will still occasionally be dealing with command-line entry), placeholders and variables will be represented in italics.

Finally, anything I instruct you to type into an entry field or command line will be shown in **`boldface type`**.

Stay in Touch!

I hope you find the answers to all your Windows XP Professional questions here. But if you have questions I didn't cover, or if you have a comment on the book, or if I made a mistake, I'd love to hear from you. Just e-mail `help@minasi.com` with questions, comments, or suggestions for future editions. I try to answer all of the e-mail I get, but you can help me with that by doing a couple of things. First, please don't send me receipted mail. For various reasons that I won't go into here, I've set up my mail handler to automatically delete receipted mail. Sorry. Second, if you're asking for advice, please try to keep the problem statement to a few paragraphs. If it gets any more involved than that, then, well, we're sort of moving into the field of network consulting, which is partially how I make my living, so I'm afraid your request will be slotted to be dealt with *after* those of my contracted clients. As you've probably guessed by now, I *do* receive a lot of mail. Much of it is highly complimentary, and I am very thankful to all of you who have corresponded! I *will* try to reply to all mail I get—and thanks again for reading!

Mastering™
Windows XP Professional

Essential Skills

The Essential Skills for Windows XP Professional

Welcome to the Windows XP Professional Essential Skills section! This incredibly visual section will teach you the most important Windows XP Professional skills through a series of easy-to-follow screens, step-by-step instructions, to-the-point tips and tricks, and expert advice segments. These simple numbered steps show you exactly what you'll see on your screen at every step along the way as you learn, hands-on, the skills that will enable you to take control of your computer quickly and effectively. In a matter of minutes, you'll learn how to perform important tasks ranging from using the Taskbar to sharing folders on a network to changing hardware drivers. Whenever possible, we've highlighted the on-screen elements you'll need to click, select, or perform some action on, in order to eliminate any guess work on your part.

These handy directions are so easy to understand and follow that you may want to simply walk through the procedures in the entire Essential Skills section all at once. Or you may prefer to flip to the Essential Skills section each time you need to perform a key task. You'll find references in the main text of the book to indicate when a process is covered in the Essential Skills section; you can then easily move from the detailed discussion of a topic to the graphical coverage of the steps involved.

Keep in mind that none of the procedures covered in this section involve long textual explanations. Those discussions occur in later sections of the book, along with thorough explanations, background information, and troubleshooting. In this section, you'll learn the important tasks that empower you to use Windows XP most efficiently—everything from handy window-arranging shortcuts, to listening to an audio CD, to encrypting files and folders. So sit down at your PC with this section and master the most important Windows XP Professional skills, hands-on! The page that follows provides a table of contents for the entire Essential Skills section.

Contents

Arranging Windows by Using the Taskbar 5

Unlocking, Resizing, and Moving the Taskbar 7

Displaying and Using Desktop Toolbars 8

Customizing the Start Menu 10

Customizing the Notification Area 13

Navigating in Explorer 14

Using Views in Explorer 16

Creating a Folder 18

Renaming a File or Folder 19

Copying or Moving a File or Folder 20

Copying or Moving by Using Copy, Cut, and Paste 21

Copying Files to a Floppy Disk or Removable Disk 22

Copying Files or Folders to a Recordable CD 23

Deleting a File or Folder 25

Recovering a Deleted File or Folder from the Recycle Bin 26

Searching for Files 27

Adding an Address Bar to the Taskbar 30

Creating a Shortcut on Your Desktop 31

Setting Up a Dial-Up Internet Connection 33

Using a Dial-Up Internet Connection 36

Listening to an Audio CD 38

Installing a Program 39

Removing a Program 41

Keeping Windows Up-to-Date with Windows Update 42

Installing a Printer 44

Sharing a Printer 48

Connecting to a Shared Printer 49

Setting Printer Properties 50

Setting Print Server Properties 52

Enabling Offline Files Synchronization 54

Making a File or Folder Available Offline 55

Backing Up Your Certificates 56

Encrypting and Decrypting Folders and Files 58

Sharing Encrypted Files 59

Defragmenting Your Hard Disk 60

Running Disk Cleanup 62

Scheduling a Task to Run Automatically 63

Setting System Restore Points 66

Restoring Your System 68

Sharing Files or Folders with Other Users of the Computer 70

Keeping a Folder Private 71

Sharing a Folder on the Network 72

Connecting to a Network Drive 73

Creating a User Account 75

Creating a Group Account 77

Setting Share-Level Permissions 78

Setting Security Permissions 79

Changing a Driver 80

Rolling Back a Driver 84

Enabling Remote Desktop Connection on the Remote Computer 85

Enabling Remote Desktop Connection on the Home Computer 86

Enabling Internet Connection Firewall 87

Securing RAS Dial-In Sessions 88

Setting Up a Virtual Private Networking Connection 89

Joining a Domain 91

Enabling Compatibility Mode for an Application 93

Setting Up Fax Services 95

ARRANGING WINDOWS BY USING THE TASKBAR

Windows provides the following automated commands for arranging windows easily:

◆ Cascade Windows: Displays the nonminimized windows overlapping each other so you can see the title bar of each

◆ Undo Cascade: Restores the windows to the positions they were in before cascading

◆ Tile Windows Horizontally: Implements a horizontal tiling scheme for all nonminimized windows

◆ Tile Windows Vertically: Implements a vertical tiling scheme for all nonminimized windows

◆ Undo Tile: Restores the windows to the positions they were in before tiling

◆ Show the Desktop: Displays the Desktop by minimizing all nonminimized windows

◆ Show Open Windows: Restores the windows to the positions they were in before minimization via the Show the Desktop command

1. Right-click the notification area or open space in the Taskbar. Windows displays the shortcut menu.

Choose the appropriate command for the action you want to take.

2. Issuing a Show the Desktop command minimizes all windows.

To restore the windows to their previous positions, issue the Show Open Windows command.

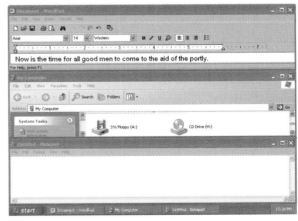

3. Issuing a Tile Windows Horizontally command tiles the windows in a horizontal pattern.

To restore the windows to their previous positions, issue the Undo Tile command.

ARRANGING WINDOWS BY USING THE TASKBAR *(continued)*

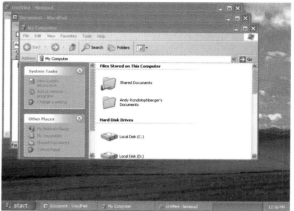

4. Issuing a Tile Windows Vertically command tiles the windows in a vertical pattern.

To restore the windows to their previous positions, issue the Undo Tile command.

5. Issuing a Cascade Windows command arranges the windows in an overlapping pattern with their title bars visible.

To restore the windows to their previous positions, issue the Undo Cascade command.

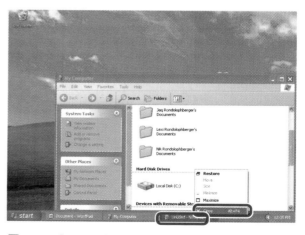

6. To maximize a window, right-click its Taskbar button and choose Maximize from the shortcut menu.

7. To close a window, right-click its Taskbar button and choose Close from the shortcut menu.

UNLOCKING, RESIZING, AND MOVING THE TASKBAR

By default, the Taskbar is locked so that it cannot be resized or moved, and so that you cannot display any Desktop toolbars.

By unlocking the Taskbar, you can resize it, move it to another edge of the screen, and display and use the Desktop toolbars.

1. To unlock the Taskbar, right-click the notification area. Windows displays the shortcut menu.

Choose the Lock the Taskbar item. Windows unlocks the Taskbar and removes the check mark from the shortcut menu item.

2. To resize the Taskbar, move the mouse pointer over its border so that the pointer becomes a double-headed arrow.

Drag the border to enlarge or reduce the Taskbar.

3. To move the Taskbar to another edge of the screen, click open space in it and drag it to the edge you want. Windows moves the Taskbar.

To lock the Taskbar at its new size or position, right-click the notification area and choose Lock the Taskbar.

DISPLAYING AND USING DESKTOP TOOLBARS

To give you quick access to programs and features, Windows provides four Desktop toolbars: the Quick Launch toolbar, the Desktop toolbar, the Address toolbar, and the Links toolbar.

You can display any or all of these toolbars. Most people find the Quick Launch toolbar and the Desktop toolbar more useful than the Address toolbar or the Links toolbar.

When you've displayed a Desktop toolbar, you can resize or reposition it by dragging the dotted handle at its left or upper end. (Unlock the Taskbar first.)

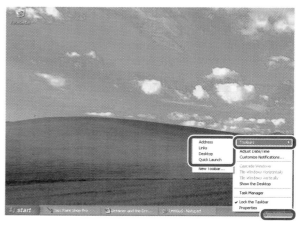

1. Right-click the notification area. Windows displays the shortcut menu.

Select the Toolbars item. Windows displays the submenu.

Select the toolbar name from the list. Windows displays the toolbar you chose.

2. The Quick Launch toolbar contains shortcuts for launching Internet Explorer, showing the Desktop, and launching Windows Media Player (from left to right).

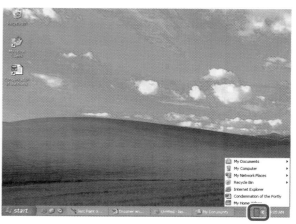

3. The Desktop toolbar contains shortcuts to the items on your Desktop, to key items on the Start menu, and to Internet Explorer.

This toolbar is usually most useful with just its title and >> button displayed.

DISPLAYING AND USING DESKTOP TOOLBARS *(continued)*

4. The Address toolbar contains an address box and a Go button. Enter an URL or a network location and click the Go button to open an Internet Explorer window to that site or folder.

5. The Links toolbar displays your links from Internet Explorer. (You can customize these links in Internet Explorer.)

Click a link to display it in Internet Explorer.

6. To customize the Quick Launch toolbar, unlock the Taskbar, right-click the Quick Launch toolbar's handle and choose Open Folder from the shortcut menu. Windows displays the Quick Launch folder.

7. To add a shortcut to the Quick Launch toolbar, right-drag an item to the folder and drop it there.

Windows displays the shortcut menu.

Choose Create Shortcuts Here. Windows creates a shortcut for the item.

CUSTOMIZING THE START MENU

You can customize the Start menu so that it contains the items you need. Because the Start menu is such a vital part of Windows XP, you can save time and make computing easier by customizing it. Besides, each user with a separate user account can customize the Start menu without affecting other users.

The easiest way to customize the Start menu is to "pin" an item to it, nailing that item in place permanently—or until you choose to "unpin" it. You can also easily remove an item from the Start menu's recently used–programs area. With a little more effort, you can customize the Start menu extensively.

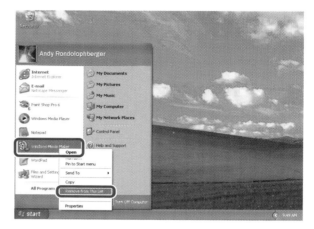

1. Click the Start button. Windows displays the Start menu.

To remove an item from the recently used–programs area, right-click it and choose Remove from This List from the shortcut menu.

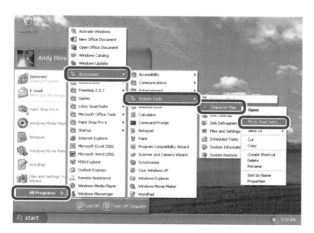

2. To pin an item to the Start menu, right-click it and choose Pin to Start Menu from the shortcut menu.

Some items are not available for pinning to the Start menu.

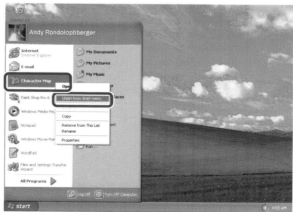

3. To remove a pinned item, unpin it by right-clicking it and choosing Unpin from Start Menu from the shortcut menu.

CUSTOMIZING THE START MENU *(continued)*

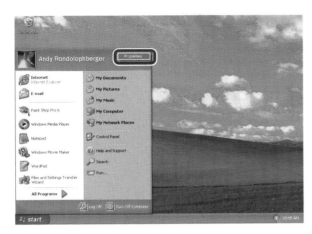

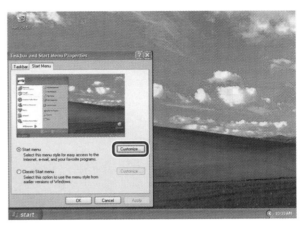

4. To perform further customizations, right-click the Start button or open space on the Start menu and choose Properties from the shortcut menu.

Windows displays the Start Menu tab of the Taskbar and Start Menu Properties dialog box.

5. Click the upper Customize button.

Windows displays the General tab of the Customize Start Menu dialog box.

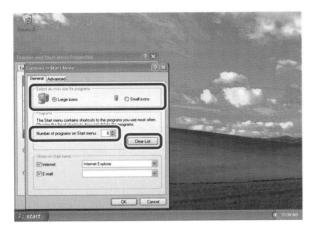

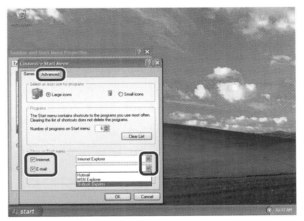

6. Choose an icon size for programs.

Specify the number of programs to show on the Start menu (or clear the list).

7. To remove the Internet item or e-mail item from the Start menu, clear its check box.

To change the program for the item, use the drop-down list.

Click the Advanced tab. Windows displays the Advanced tab of the Customize Start Menu dialog box.

CUSTOMIZING THE START MENU *(continued)*

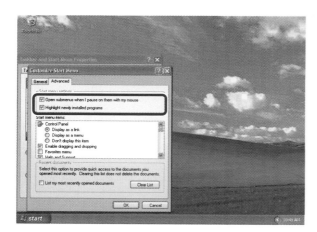

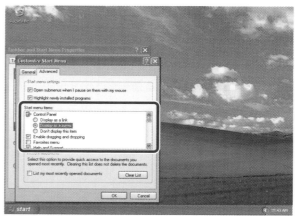

8. Choose whether to open submenus when you hover the mouse over them (rather than clicking them) and whether to display a highlight for newly installed programs.

9. Choose which items to display on the Start menu and which features to enable (for example, dragging and dropping).

For some items, you can choose between displaying the item as a link (the default), as a menu, or not displaying it at all.

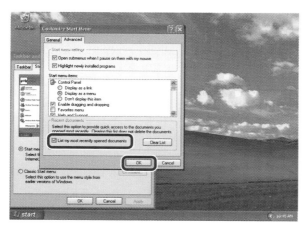

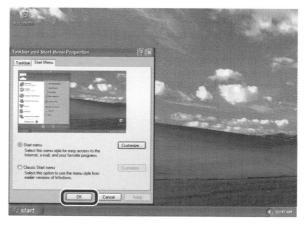

10. Select the List My Most Recently Opened Documents check box if you want the Start menu to include a menu of recently used documents (as in previous versions of Windows).

Click the OK button. Windows closes the Customize Start Menu dialog box.

11. Click the OK button. Windows closes the Taskbar and Start Menu Properties dialog box and applies your changes.

CUSTOMIZING THE NOTIFICATION AREA

· ·

The notification area (also known as the System Tray) appears at the right end of the Taskbar. The notification area contains items that it's useful to have displayed all the time (such as the clock, which is displayed by default), together with information and alerts (which are displayed at appropriate times).

By default, Windows XP collapses the notification area so that only the icons you've used most recently are displayed. To display the other icons in the notification area, click the < button at the left end of the notification area.

1. Right-click the notification area and choose Customize Notifications from the shortcut menu.

Windows displays the Taskbar and Start Menu Properties dialog box and, in front of it, the Customize Notifications dialog box.

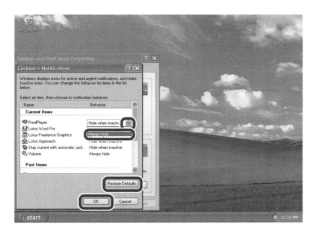

2. Use the Behavior drop-down list to specify when to display an item. Choose Hide when Inactive, Always Hide, or Always Show as appropriate.

Click the Restore Defaults button if you want to apply default settings to the notification area.

Click the OK button. Windows closes the Customize Notifications dialog box.

3. Select or clear the Show the Clock check box.

If you don't want Windows to hide inactive icons, clear the Hide Inactive Icons check box.

Click the OK button. Windows closes the Taskbar and Start Menu Properties dialog box.

NAVIGATING IN EXPLORER

Windows Explorer is a program for viewing and manipulating the contents of the drives and folders on your computer.

You can use Explorer for a wide variety of tasks including creating, deleting, and renaming files and folders; copying and moving files and folders; and finding files and folders you've lost.

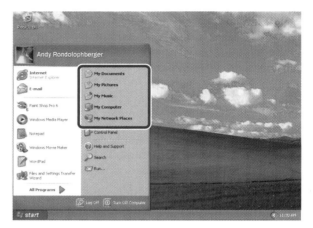

1. Click the Start button. Windows displays the Start menu.

Choose one of the five circled links from it. If your computer isn't connected to a network, you won't have a My Network Places link.

2. The My Documents link displays the My Documents folder, in which Windows automatically places files you create other than graphics, music, or video files. This folder contains the My Pictures folder, the My Music folder, and the My Videos folder.

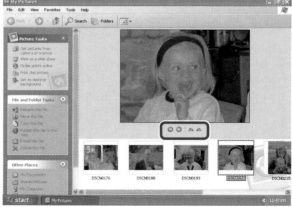

3. The My Pictures link displays the My Pictures folder, in which Windows automatically places picture files you create and download. This folder contains features and links for manipulating pictures.

NAVIGATING IN EXPLORER *(continued)*

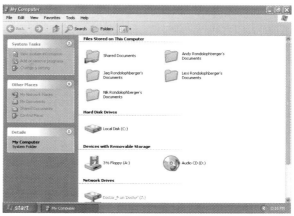

4. The My Music link displays the My Music folder, in which Windows automatically places music files you create and download. This folder contains features and links for working with music files.

5. The My Computer link displays a list of document folders and drives on the computer.

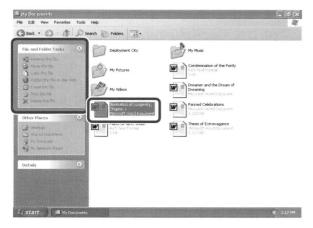

6. To perform a task on a file or folder, select it and use the File and Folder Tasks list.

7. To navigate to other frequently used places and folders, use the Other Places list.

   To open a folder or file, double-click it.

USING VIEWS IN EXPLORER

Explorer provides five views for looking at the contents of most files and folders, together with a specialized view for folders containing graphics. The various views are designed to make it easy to work with different types of folder contents.

Some custom folders also have other views. You can apply these views from the View menu.

1. Display the View menu, then choose one of the views from it.

2. Thumbnails view displays a large icon for each file or folder. For graphics files, Thumbnails view displays a miniature version of each graphic.

3. Tiles view displays a medium-sized icon for each file or folder. It's good for viewing folders that contain relatively few files or folders.

USING VIEWS IN EXPLORER *(continued)*

4. Icons view displays a smallish icon for each file or folder. It's good for viewing folders that contain a moderate number of files or folders.

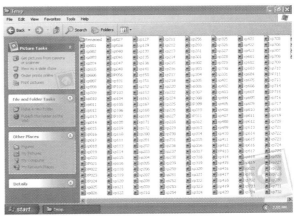

5. List view displays a list of folders and files, showing only the filename or folder name and a small icon for each. It's good for viewing folders that contain a large number of files or folders.

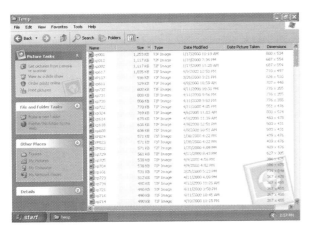

6. Details view displays a list of files and folders, including the filename or folder name, a small icon, the file size, the file type, and the date on which it was modified. You can sort by any of the columns displayed.

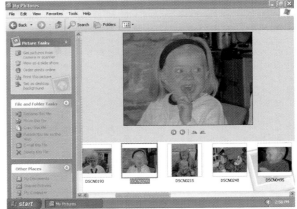

7. The My Pictures folder and the Shared Pictures folder also have a Filmstrip view designed for scrolling through a folder of images.

CREATING A FOLDER

Windows lets you create an almost unlimited number of folders in which to store your files. By using separate folders, you can group your files by category such as subject, type, or date, keeping the files organized and making it easy to find the ones you need.

You can create folders on your Desktop as well by using the technique shown here.

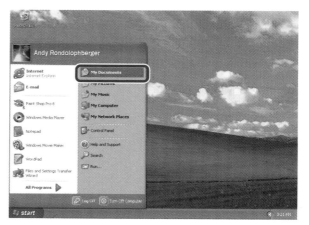

1. Open an Explorer window to the folder in which you want to create the new folder. For example, choose Start ➤ My Documents if you want to create the new folder in the My Documents folder.

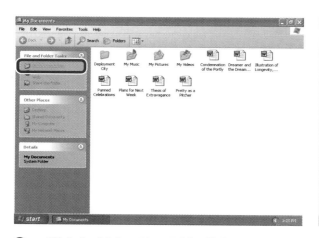

2. Click the Make a New Folder link.

Windows creates a new folder named New Folder or a similar name (New Folder 1, New Folder 2, and so on) and displays an edit box around the name.

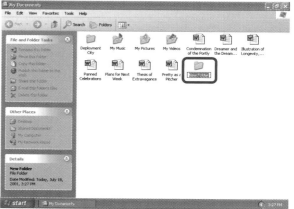

3. Type the name for the folder and press Enter. Windows renames the folder.

RENAMING A FILE OR FOLDER

Often, you'll need to rename a file or folder, to make its name shorter, longer, more explicit, or simply different from the names of other files or folders in the same folder. Including the drive and folder path to it, a filename can be up to 255 characters long, so you can get verbose if necessary.

Filenames can't contain the following characters: forward slashes (/), backslashes (\), colons (:), asterisks (*), question marks (?), double quotation marks ("), less-than (<) and greater-than (>) signs, or pipe characters (|).

To rename a file or folder, open an Explorer window to the appropriate folder and follow these steps:

1. Select the file or folder you want to rename.

   Click the Rename This File link or the Rename This Folder link.

   Windows displays an edit box around the name.

Expert Advice

- Instead of clicking the Rename This File link or the Rename This Folder link, you can display an edit box around the filename or folder name by clicking it again a moment or two after selecting it.

- This two-click technique works on the Desktop and in common dialog boxes as well as in Explorer windows.

- If you can't get the hang of clicking twice slowly enough, select the file or folder and press F2, or right-click it and choose Rename from the context menu.

2. Type the name you want, and then press the Enter key.

   Windows applies the new name to the file or folder.

COPYING OR MOVING A FILE OR FOLDER

Often, you'll need to copy files or folders—for example, so that you can store copies in a safe location, or so that you can share the files or folders with someone else.

Similarly, you'll frequently need to move files or folders from their current location to a different location. For example, you might need to move a folder of files from your My Documents folder to the Shared Documents folder so that other users can work with it.

Windows provides several ways to copy or move a file or folder. This page shows you the easiest and most consistent way of performing each operation.

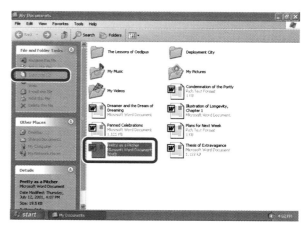

1. Select the file or folder.

To copy it, click the Copy This File link or the Copy This Folder link. Proceed to step 2.

To move it, click the Move This File link or the Move This Folder link. Proceed to step 3.

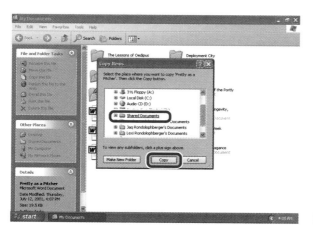

2. Navigate to the folder in which you want Windows to place the copy of the file or folder.

Click the Copy button. Windows closes the Copy Items dialog box and copies the file or folder.

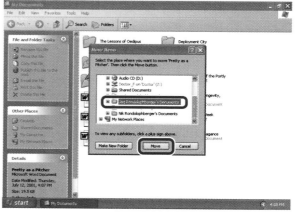

3. Navigate to the folder to which you want Windows to move the file or folder.

Click the Move button. Windows closes the Move Items dialog box and moves the file or folder.

COPYING OR MOVING BY USING COPY, CUT, AND PASTE

You can also copy a file or folder by using the Copy and Paste commands, and move a file or folder by using the Cut and Paste commands.

The Copy, Cut, and Paste commands are most useful for copying and moving files and folders when you have two Explorer windows open, one showing the source folder and the other the destination folder. You can then quickly copy or move files or folders from the source folder to the destination folder. But you can also use the Copy, Cut, and Paste commands in a single window if you find them easy or convenient.

1. Open two Explorer windows and arrange them so that you can see both.

In one Explorer window, navigate to the source folder.

In the other Explorer window, navigate to the destination folder.

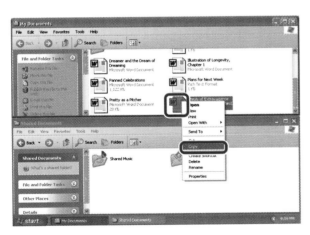

2. In the source folder, right-click the file or folder you want to copy or move.

From the shortcut menu, choose Copy (to copy the item) or Cut (to move it).

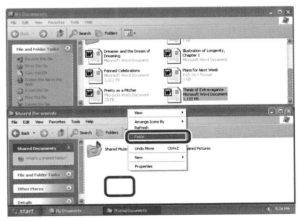

3. Right-click in open space in the destination folder.

From the shortcut menu, choose Paste.

Windows pastes the copy of the file or folder, or the folder itself, into the destination folder.

COPYING FILES TO A FLOPPY DISK OR REMOVABLE DISK

Because you'll often need to copy files to a floppy disk or another removable disk (such as a Zip drive), Windows provides a convenient way of doing so.

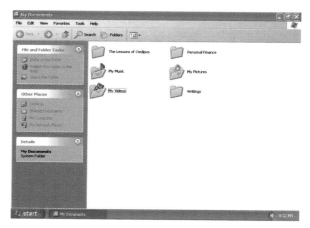

1. Open an Explorer window to the folder that contains the file or folder you want to copy.

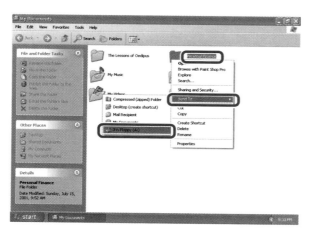

2. Right-click the file or folder. Windows displays the shortcut menu.

Choose Send To. Windows displays the submenu.

Select the item for the floppy disk or removable disk. Windows copies the file or folder.

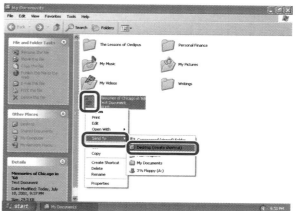

3. You can also create a shortcut on the Desktop to the file or folder by using a similar technique.

Right-click the file or folder and choose Send To ➤ Desktop.

Windows creates a shortcut on the Desktop.

COPYING FILES OR FOLDERS TO A RECORDABLE CD

If you have a recordable CD drive (CD-R) or a rewritable CD drive (CD-RW), you can copy files or folders to a recordable CD.

Because recordable CDs are capacious, inexpensive, durable, and (at least in theory) relatively long lasting, they're good for backup and archiving. Even if the CDs turn out not to last, they're good for transferring files from point A to point B in the short term, because most computers have CD drives.

Windows also provides features for recording an audio CD that you can play on most CD players—audio CD players as well as computer CD drives.

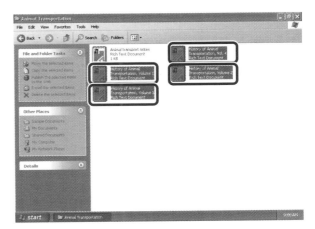

1. Load a blank CD in your recordable CD drive.

Open an Explorer window to the appropriate folder.

Select the files or folders you want to copy to the CD.

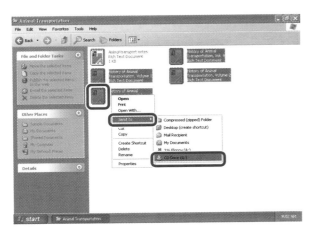

2. Right-click one of the selected files or folders and choose Send To ➢ CD Drive.

Windows copies the files or folders to a queue for writing to the CD drive and displays a notification-area icon and pop-up.

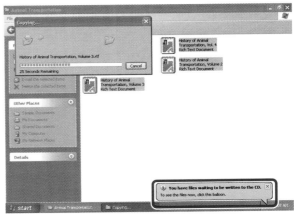

3. Add further files or folders to the CD list as necessary.

Click the notification-area pop-up to open an Explorer window showing the CD drive. (If the pop-up disappears, choose Start ➢ My Computer, and then double-click the CD drive.)

COPYING FILES OR FOLDERS TO A RECORDABLE CD *(continued)*

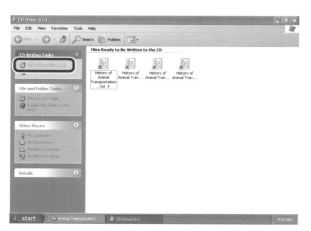

4. Click the Write These Files to CD link.
Windows starts the CD Writing Wizard.

5. Change or improve the name for the CD. (The Wizard suggests the current date for the CD's name.)

Click the Next button. The Wizard starts writing the files to the CD.

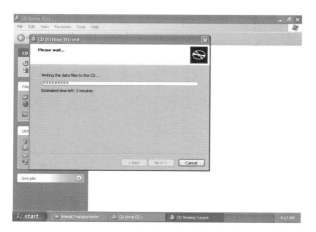

6. When the Wizard has finished writing the CD, it ejects the CD and displays the Completing the CD Writing Wizard page.

7. If you want to create another CD containing the same files, select the Yes, Write These Files to Another CD check box.

Click the Finish button. The Wizard closes or restarts, as appropriate.

DELETING A FILE OR FOLDER

When you no longer need a file, you can delete it to remove it from your disk. By default, deleting a file on your hard disk sends the file to the Recycle Bin, from which you can retrieve it if necessary. Deleting a file on a removable disk, a floppy disk, or a network drive gets rid of the file immediately.

Don't try to delete any Windows files. Doing so can prevent Windows from running. Usually, though, Windows simply reinstalls the files when it discovers they're missing, so deleting them achieves nothing.

Similarly, it's best not to delete any program files manually. Instead, use Windows' Remove Programs feature to remove the program, as discussed on page 41.

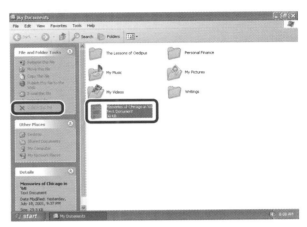

1. Select a file that you're sure you don't need.

Click the Delete This File link.

Windows displays the Confirm File Delete dialog box.

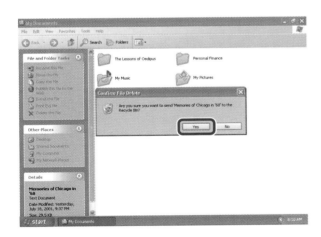

2. Click the Yes button.

Depending on where the file is stored, Windows moves the file to the Recycle Bin or deletes it.

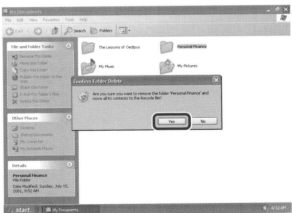

3. To delete a folder, select it and click the Delete This Folder link.

Windows displays the Confirm Folder Delete dialog box, asking if you want to remove the folder and all its contents.

Click the Yes button.

RECOVERING A DELETED FILE OR FOLDER FROM THE RECYCLE BIN

If you move a file or folder to the Recycle Bin and subsequently wish you hadn't, you may be able to recover the file or folder.

Files or folders stay in the Recycle Bin until the Recycle Bin gets full or you empty it manually. When the Recycle Bin gets full, Windows discards the oldest files or folders to make space for new files or folders you delete.

Once Windows has deleted a file or folder from the Recycle Bin, you may be able to recover it using a specialized undelete utility, but there's no guarantee that this will work. So when you delete a file or folder by mistake, it's best to recover it immediately. When you recover a file or folder, Windows removes it from the Recycle Bin and restores it to the folder that previously contained it.

1. Double-click the Recycle Bin icon on the Desktop.

Windows opens an Explorer window showing the contents of the Recycle Bin.

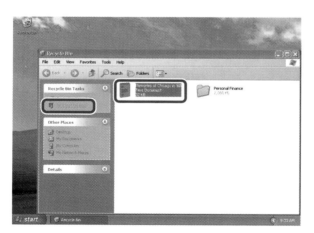

2. Select the file or folder.

Click the Restore This Item link.

To restore all the files and folders in the Recycle Bin, click the Restore All Items link without selecting a file or folder.

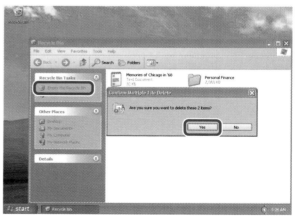

3. To get rid of the files and folders in the Recycle Bin again, click the Empty the Recycle Bin link.

Windows displays the Confirm Multiple File Delete dialog box.

Click the Yes button.

SEARCHING FOR FILES

If you create a lot of files, you'll probably forget before too long where one or more files are located.

Windows provides a feature called Search Companion for searching for files. You can search by all or part of a file's name, by its approximate size, by the date it was created, or even by a word or phrase contained in the body of the file.

Search Companion offers different features for searching for specific types of files. This example shows how to search for all file types, because this gives the most flexible search.

1. Choose Start ➤ Search.

Windows displays a Search Results window.

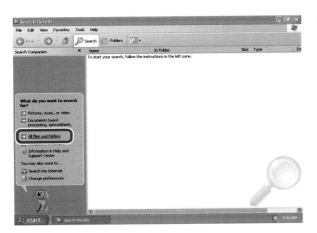

2. Click the All Files and Folders link.

Search Companion displays a panel of search options.

3. To search by filename, enter a distinctive part of the filename in the All or Part of the Filename text box.

SEARCHING FOR FILES *(continued)*

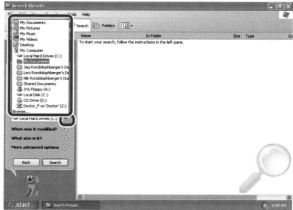

4. To search by contents, or to narrow a search by other criteria, you can enter a distinctive word or phrase in the A Word or Phrase in the File text box.

5. Specify the drives or folders to search.

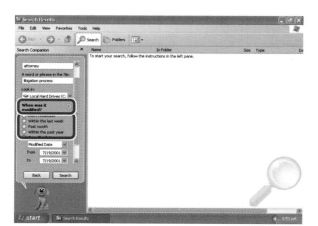

6. To specify a range of dates when the file was modified, click the When Was It Modified? heading.

Use the options for specifying a time period.

7. To search only for files of a specified size, click the What Size Is It? heading.

Use the options for specifying an approximate size.

SEARCHING FOR FILES *(continued)*

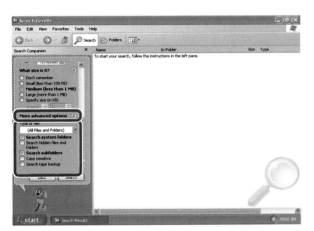

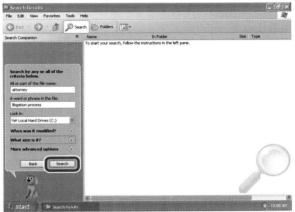

8. To specify advanced options, such as searching a tape backup, click the More Advanced Options heading.

By default, Search Companion searches system folders and subfolders.

9. Click the Search button. Search Companion performs the search and returns a list containing any matches it finds.

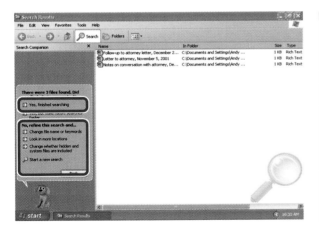

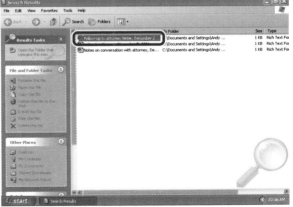

10. If Search Companion didn't find the right match, use the No, Refine This Search And... links to search again.

Otherwise, click the Yes, Finished Searching link to close Search Companion.

11. Select a file to display its details.

Double-click a file to open it.

Select a file and click the Open the Folder That Contains This Item link to open the folder.

ADDING AN ADDRESS BAR TO THE TASKBAR

Users experienced with Windows NT Workstation or Windows 2000 Professional are familiar with how to use the command line to quickly access programs, files, folders, and so on. But you can easily add an Address bar to the Taskbar that you can use to type and execute a command, open a folder, display a Web page, and more.

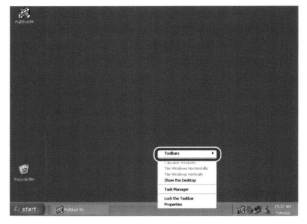

1. Right-click an empty area of the Taskbar to display the shortcut menu.

2. Click Toolbars to display a submenu.

3. Click Address to display the Address bar on the Taskbar.

CREATING A SHORTCUT ON YOUR DESKTOP

If you need quick access to a program or file, place a shortcut to it on your Desktop or in another convenient place. The shortcut acts as a pointer, making it easy to access the program or file. You can create any number of shortcuts to any given program or file.

You can create a shortcut in several different ways. This section shows two of the easiest ways to create a shortcut.

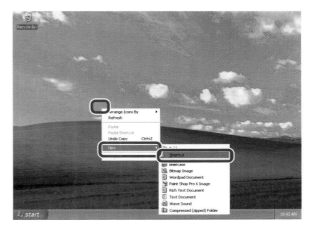

1. Right-click open space on the Desktop. Windows displays the shortcut menu.

Choose New ➣ Shortcut.

Windows starts the Create Shortcut Wizard.

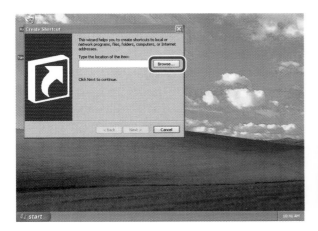

2. Click the Browse button.

Windows displays the Browse for Folder dialog box.

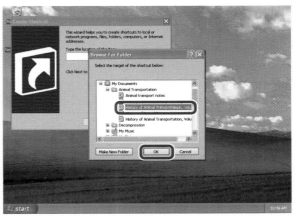

3. Navigate to the program or file and select it.

Click the OK button. Windows closes the Browse for Folder dialog box and enters the path and filename in the Create Shortcut Wizard.

CREATING A SHORTCUT ON YOUR DESKTOP *(continued)*

4. Click the Next button.

The Wizard displays the Select a Title for The Program screen and suggests the file or program's name as the name for the shortcut.

5. Change the name if necessary.

Click the Finish button.

The Wizard creates the shortcut, names it, and places it on your Desktop.

6. You can also create a shortcut from an Explorer window.

Select the file. Then choose File ➢ Send To ➢ Desktop (Create Shortcut).

Windows creates a shortcut on the Desktop.

7. Change the name of the shortcut if necessary.

Windows names shortcuts created this way *Shortcut to* and the filename.

SETTING UP A DIAL-UP INTERNET CONNECTION

In order to connect to the Internet via a dial-up connection, you need to give Windows the details of the connection: what technology to use, which number to call, and so on.

You can choose whether to set up the connection as the computer's default connection, whether to store the username and password or require each user to provide them, and whether to make a stored username and password available to all users.

Before starting to set up a dial-up Internet connection, make sure that your modem is connected to the computer, that it's connected to a working phone line, and that it's powered on (if it has its own power controls).

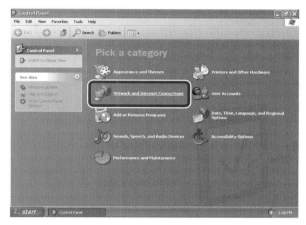

1. Choose Start ➤ Control Panel.

Click the Network and Internet Connections link.

Windows displays the Network and Internet Connections screen.

2. Click the Network Connections link.

Windows displays the Network Connections screen.

3. Click the Create a New Connection link.

Windows starts the New Connection Wizard.

SETTING UP A DIAL-UP INTERNET CONNECTION *(continued)*

4. Click the Next button.

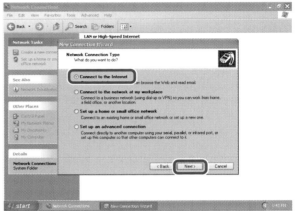

5. Make sure the Connect to the Internet option button is selected.

Click the Next button.

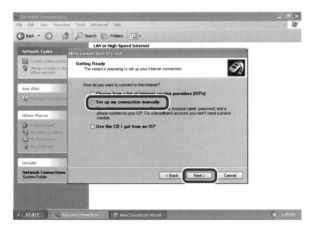

6. Select the Set Up My Connection Manually option button.

Click the Next button.

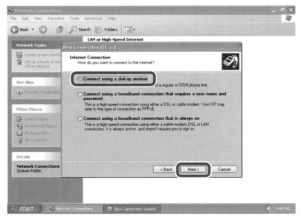

7. Select the Connect Using a Dial-Up Modem option button.

Click the Next button.

SETTING UP A DIAL-UP INTERNET CONNECTION *(continued)*

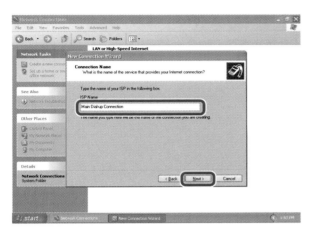

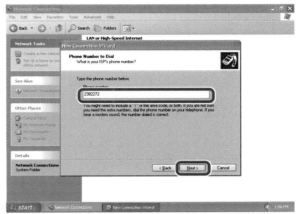

8. Enter the name you want to use for the connection. (This name doesn't have to be the ISP's name, but that may be clearest.)

Click the Next button.

9. Enter the phone number for your ISP, including the area code and long-distance code if appropriate.

Click the Next button.

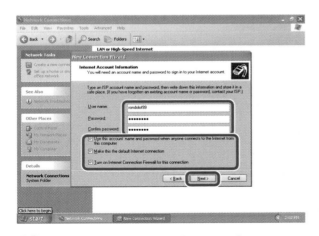

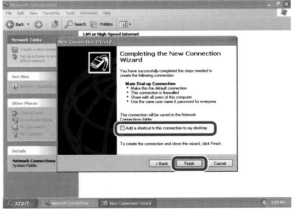

10. Enter the username and password.

Select or clear the first two check boxes as appropriate.

Leave the Turn On Internet Connection Firewall for This Connection check box selected.

Click the Next button.

11. Select the Add a Shortcut to This Connection to My Desktop check box if appropriate.

Click the Finish button. The Wizard creates the connection, closes itself, and displays the Connect dialog box for the connection. Connect as described in the next section.

USING A DIAL-UP INTERNET CONNECTION

When you set up a dial-up Internet connection (as described on the previous pages), Windows stores the details of the connection so that you can reconnect to it quickly.

If you didn't store the username and password in the Internet connection, you'll need to enter them each time you use the connection. Storing this information can compromise your security, but it makes establishing the connection significantly quicker.

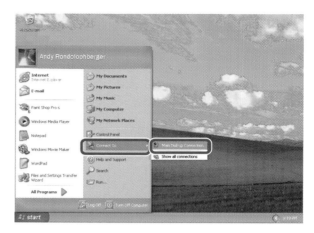

1. Choose Start ≻ Connect To.

Select the Internet connection from the Connect To submenu.

Windows displays the Connect dialog box for the connection.

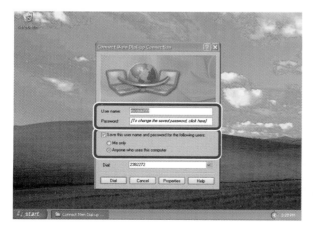

2. Enter the username and password if necessary.

Select the Save This User Name and Password for the Following Users check box if appropriate. If you do, select the Me Only option button or the Anyone Who Uses This Computer option button.

3. Click the Dial button. Windows dials the connection.

USING A DIAL-UP INTERNET CONNECTION *(continued)*

4. If Windows is able to establish the connection, it displays a notification-area icon for the connection and a notification-area pop-up showing the connection speed.

5. To view brief information on the status of the connection, hover the mouse pointer over the notification-area icon.

Windows displays a pop-up of statistics.

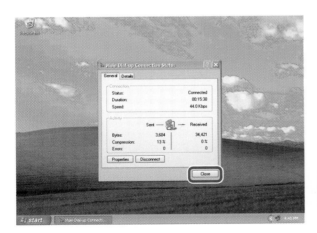

6. To view detailed information about the status of the connection, click the notification-area icon.

Windows displays the Status dialog box for the connection.

Click the Close button to dismiss the Status dialog box.

7. To disconnect the connection, right-click the notification-area icon and choose Disconnect from the shortcut menu.

LISTENING TO AN AUDIO CD

Windows Media Player is a capable multimedia player that you can use for listening to music and for watching video files. You can also watch DVDs with Windows Media Player if you add a DVD decoder to Windows.

If your computer has a CD drive, you can use it to listen to an audio CD or to copy the audio from a CD to your hard drive as Windows Media Audio (WMA) files.

If your computer has a sound card, connect the speakers or headphones to the output jack. If your computer doesn't have a sound card, connect the speakers or headphones to the output jack on your CD drive.

If Autoplay is disabled on your computer, the CD won't start playing automatically. Instead, start Windows Media Player manually by choosing Start ➣ All Programs ➣ Windows Media Player.

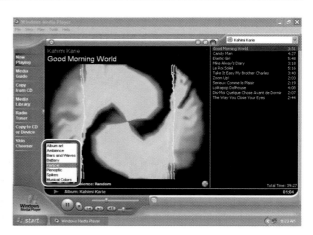

1. Load the CD in your CD drive. Windows Media Player opens automatically, starts playing the CD, and displays a visualization on the Now Playing screen.

Use the visualization buttons to change the visualization.

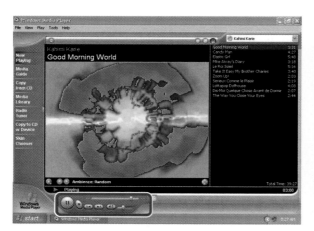

2. Use the play controls to control the play.

Drag the Volume slider to control the volume.

Click the Mute/Sound button to mute and unmute the sound.

3. To jump to a track, double-click it in the playlist.

INSTALLING A PROGRAM

Windows comes with a modest selection of mostly limited programs (such as Notepad, WordPad, and Paint), but you'll probably want to add various programs to supplement them.

If you got the program on a physical medium, such as a floppy disk, a CD-ROM, a DVD, or a removable disk, load the disk in the appropriate drive. If you downloaded the file, you need only know where you saved it.

Before installing a program, it's a good idea to close all open programs. This isn't always necessary, but it's possible for the files you're installing to conflict with files that are being used by open programs.

1. Choose Start ➢ Control Panel. Windows displays Control Panel.

2. Click the Add or Remove Programs link. Windows displays the Add or Remove Programs window.

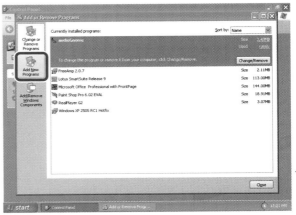

3. Click the Add New Programs button. Windows displays the Add New Programs screen.

INSTALLING A PROGRAM (continued)

4. Click the CD or Floppy button. Windows displays the Install Program from Floppy Disk or CD-ROM screen.

5. If the program is on a CD or a floppy, and you haven't inserted the disk already, do so now.

Click the Next button. Windows searches your floppy drives and CD drives for a setup file and displays the Run Installation Program dialog box.

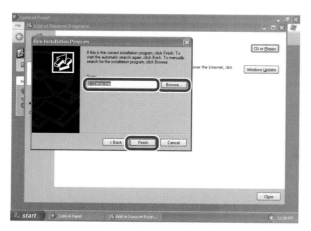

6. If Windows found a setup file, it lists it in the Open text box. Make sure this is the right file. If not, or if Windows didn't find the file, click the Browse button and use the Browse dialog box to locate the setup file.

Click the Finish button. Windows starts the setup routine for the program.

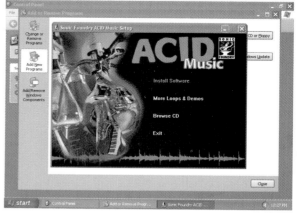

7. Follow the prompts, supplying decisions and information as necessary.

REMOVING A PROGRAM

If you cease to find a program useful, or if you replace it with a better program, you can remove the program to reclaim the space it occupied on your disk.

To remove a program, always use the procedure shown on this page. If you try to remove a program by deleting its files, you'll usually be able to remove only part of it, so it'll still take up some space on the disk. Worse, Windows won't know that you've disabled the program, which may cause problems.

Before you remove a program, make sure that no other user still needs it. Make doubly sure that no other user is currently using it.

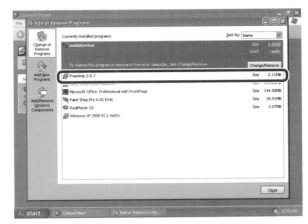

1. Take steps 1 and 2 of the previous item to display the Change or Remove Programs page of the Add or Remove Programs window.

Select the program. The window displays information about the program and buttons for changing it or removing it.

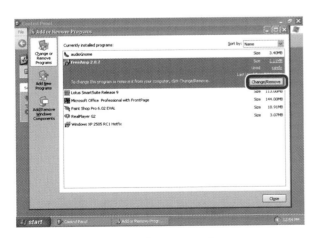

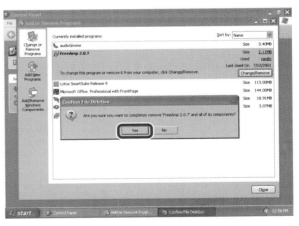

2. Click the Remove button or the Change/Remove button. Windows starts the uninstall routine for the program.

Most uninstall routines display some kind of confirmation dialog box.

3. Choose the confirmation button in any confirmation message box.

You may also need to choose uninstall options and confirm the removal of some files.

KEEPING WINDOWS UP-TO-DATE WITH WINDOWS UPDATE

Windows Update keeps your copy of Windows up-to-date and secure by downloading and installing the latest updates, additions, and security patches that Microsoft releases. In order to use Windows Update, your computer needs to be connected to the Internet.

By default, Windows Update runs itself periodically, downloads update files you might want to install, and prompts you to install them. If you prefer, you can run Windows Update manually as described in this section. You can also run Windows Update from Help and Support Center.

Because Windows Update is implemented via the Microsoft Web site, the interface may have changed from the screens shown here.

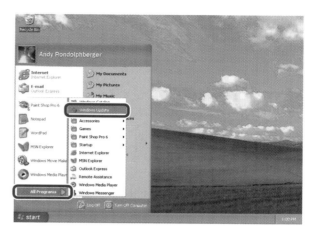

1. Choose Start ➤ All Programs ➤ Windows Update. Windows opens an Internet Explorer window to the Windows Update Web site.

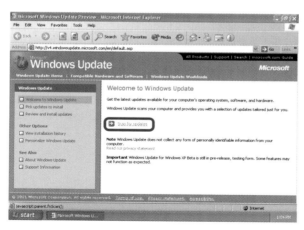

2. Click the Scan for Updates link. Windows scans the available updates and presents a list.

   If you see a Security Warning dialog box asking you to install controls signed by Microsoft Corporation, choose the Yes button.

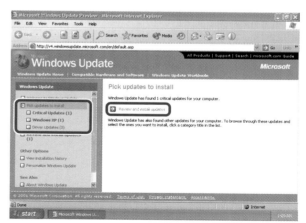

3. Click the Review and Install Updates link. Windows displays information on the updates.

   If there are no critical updates, you can choose other updates in the Pick Updates to Install area.

KEEPING WINDOWS UP-TO-DATE *(continued)*

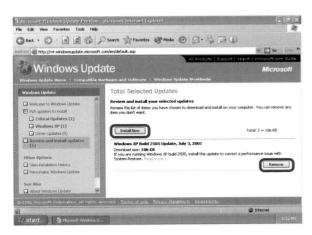

4. Click the Remove button to remove any update you don't want to install.

Click the Install Now button. Windows may display a license agreement.

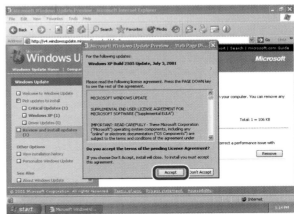

5. Click the Accept button if the license is acceptable.

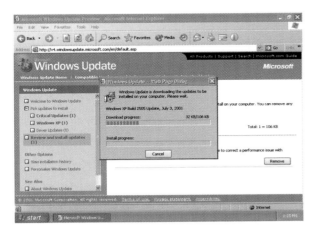

6. Wait while Windows downloads and installs the updates. When it has finished, it may display the Installation Complete screen or may require you to shut down your computer (as shown in the next figure).

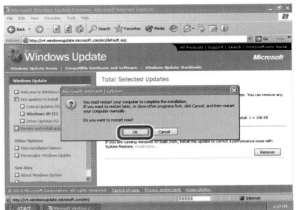

7. Click the OK button to restart your computer. Windows restarts your computer and finishes installing the update.

INSTALLING A PRINTER

In order to print documents on a printer, you need to install the printer on your computer. Installing the printer lets Windows know that the printer is there, what type of printer it is, and which driver (software) to use for it.

You can install a printer locally (as described in this section) or connect to a shared printer on another computer to which your computer is networked (as described in "Connecting to a Shared Printer" on page 49).

Windows may detect a local printer when you connect it to your computer. If so, it installs the driver if it can; otherwise, it prompts you to start the installation process. If Windows does not detect your printer, you can install it manually as described here.

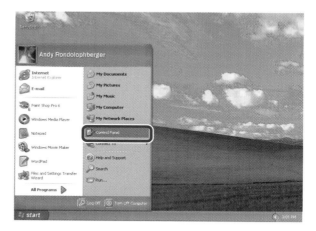

1. Choose Start ➤ Control Panel. Windows displays Control Panel.

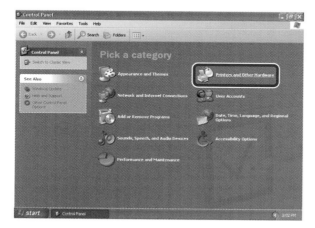

2. Click the Printers and Other Hardware link. Windows displays the Printers and Other Hardware screen.

3. Click the Add a Printer link. Windows starts the Add Printer Wizard, which displays its first screen.

INSTALLING A PRINTER *(continued)*

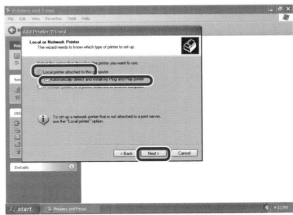

4. Click the Next button. The Wizard displays the Local or Network Printer screen.

5. Make sure the Local Printer Attached to This Computer option button is selected.

Make sure the Automatically Detect and Install My Plug and Play Printer check box is selected.

Click the Next button. If the Wizard finds the printer, go to step 12.

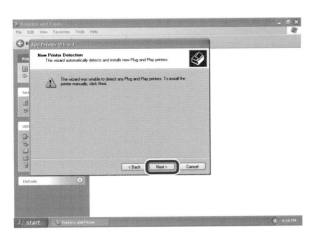

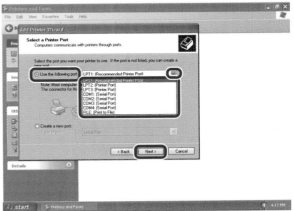

6. Click the Next button. The Wizard displays the Select a Printer Port page.

7. Select the port in the Use the Following Port drop-down list.

Click the Next button. The Wizard displays the Install Printer Software screen.

INSTALLING A PRINTER *(continued)*

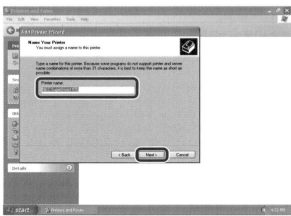

8. Select the manufacturer and printer model.

Click the Next button. The Wizard displays the Name Your Printer screen.

9. Change the name for the printer if you want to.

Click the Next button. The Wizard displays the Printer Sharing page.

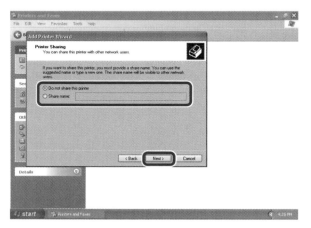

10. If you want to share the printer with other computers, select the Share Name option button and enter the name in the text box.

Click the Next button. The Wizard displays the Print Test Page page.

11. Select the Yes option button or the No option button as appropriate.

Click the Next button. The Wizard displays the Completing the Add Printer Wizard page, which summarizes the choices you made.

INSTALLING A PRINTER *(continued)*

12. Click the Finish button. The Wizard installs the files for the printer.

If you chose to print a test page, the Wizard prints the page and displays a dialog box checking that it printed okay.

13. Click the OK button to close the dialog box. (If the page didn't print correctly, click the Troubleshoot button and follow the Printing Troubleshooter.)

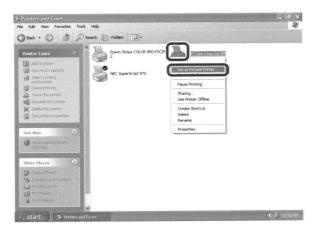

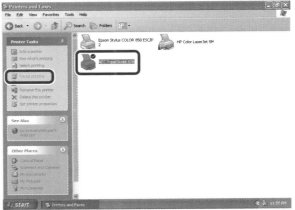

14. The default printer is designated by a black circle containing a white check mark.

To set a different default printer, right-click the printer and choose Set As Default Printer from the shortcut menu.

15. To pause printing on a printer, select it and click the Pause Printing link in the Printer Tasks list.

To resume printing, click the resulting Resume Printing link in the Printer Tasks list.

SHARING A PRINTER

Windows XP lets you share a printer with other users so that they can use it as if it were attached to their computer.

If you didn't set up your printer for sharing while installing it by using the Add Printer Wizard, you can set it up for sharing as described in this section.

1. Display the Printers and Other Hardware screen as described in steps 1 and 2 on page 44.

Click the View Installed Printers or Fax Printers link. Windows displays the Printers and Faxes screen.

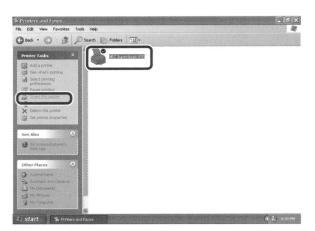

2. Select the printer you want to share.

Click the Share This Printer item in the Printer Tasks list. Windows displays the Sharing tab of the Properties dialog box for the printer.

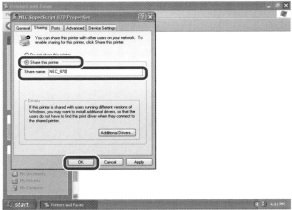

3. Select the Share This Printer option button.

Check—and if necessary, change—the name Windows suggests for the shared printer.

Click the OK button. Windows shares the printer and closes the Properties dialog box.

CONNECTING TO A SHARED PRINTER

Instead of installing a local printer, you can connect to a printer shared by a computer to which your computer is networked. Such a printer is called a *network printer*. Provided that the computer to which the network printer is attached is running, you can print to the network printer as you would to a local printer.

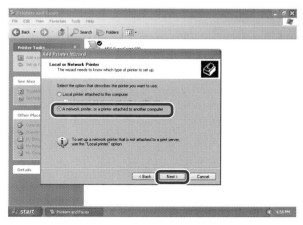

1. Display the Local or Network Printer tab of the Add Printer Wizard by following steps 1 to 4 on pages 44–45.

   Select the A Network Printer, or a Printer Attached to Another Computer option button. Click the Next button.

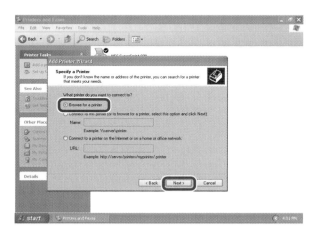

2. Make sure the Browse for a Printer option button is selected.

   Click the Next button. The Wizard displays the Browse for Printer screen.

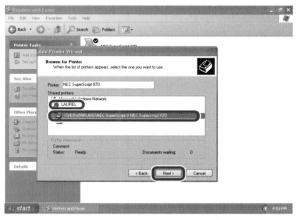

3. Expand the appropriate workgroup and computer, then select the shared printer.

   Follow through the remaining steps of the Wizard for specifying whether this is the default printer and finishing the Wizard (see pages 45–47).

SETTING PRINTER PROPERTIES

Through a printer's properties, you can adjust almost every aspect of the way it works, from the print quality to the paper feed.

    The properties for a printer vary widely depending on the printer model. Because the printer drivers are supplied by the printer manufacturer, the options available for changing may be different for your printer than for the one shown here. However, a few of the tabs, such as General, will be the same for any printer.

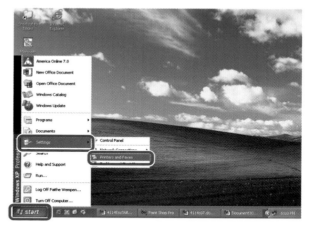

1. To display the Printers and Faxes folder, choose Start Settings ➤ ➤ Printers and Faxes.

2. To display the properties for a certain printer, right-click the printer and choose Properties.

3. In the General tab, change the name, location, and/or comments for the printer.

To test the printer, click the Print Test Page button.

SETTING PRINTER PROPERTIES (continued)

4. To share the printer with network users, click the Sharing tab.

Click Share This Printer, and then enter a share name in the text box.

To make drivers available for other operating systems, click Additional Drivers and install other drivers.

5. Click the Advanced tab, and then change any of the advanced settings there.

To change the defaults for the printer such as orientation and number of copies, click the Printing Defaults button.

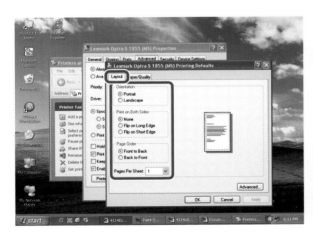

6. After clicking the Printing Defaults button, make any desired changes to the defaults.

Click OK to return to the Advanced tab of the Printer Properties box.

7. Click the Device Settings tab, and then make any changes to the options there. The options will be different for every printer depending on its features.

SETTING PRINT SERVER PROPERTIES

Print server properties are global settings that affect all the installed printers. You can set them for a server functioning as a print server and also for individual PCs that happen to have more than one PC attached to them.

Setting print server properties is especially handy when you share multiple printers with other network users because it enables you to control the parameters for that sharing.

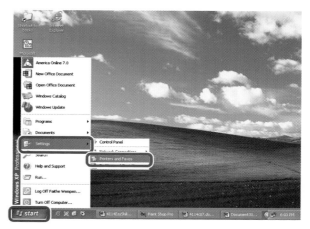

1. To display the Printers and Faxes folder, choose Start ➤ Settings ➤ Printers and Faxes.

2. Right-click a blank area of the Printers and Faxes folder and choose Server Properties.

3. In the Forms tab, create or delete form definitions for use on all printers. These could include descriptions of custom forms that your company uses to print invoices, receipts, statements, or other business paperwork.

Choose Metric or English to define how form measurements will appear to users.

SETTING PRINT SERVER PROPERTIES *(continued)*

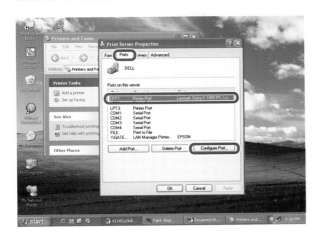

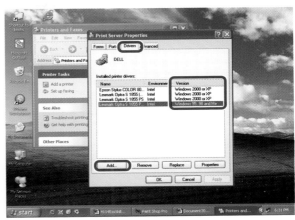

4. In the Ports tab, review the port assignments for the installed printers. Add or delete ports as needed.

To change the options for a port, click the port and click Configure Port. The dialog box that appears depends on the port type.

5. In the Drivers tab, review the installed drivers for each printer. You might need additional drivers so users running other operating systems can access a shared printer.

If needed, click Add and work through the Add Printer Driver Wizard to add other drivers.

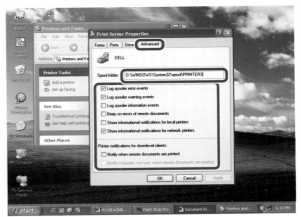

6. To review the driver files installed for a particular printer and operating system, click it and then click Properties.

Review the list of files installed. When you are finished reviewing the list of files, click OK to return to the Drivers tab.

7. In the Advanced tab, mark or clear any check boxes for advanced settings as desired.

To change the location of the print spooler file, enter a new location in the Spool Folder box.

When you have finished setting properties, click OK.

ENABLING OFFLINE FILES SYNCHRONIZATION

Offline Files, a new feature in Windows XP Professional, enables you to easily keep files synchronized between a portable and a desktop PC via a network connection.

In order to use it, you must first turn off Fast User Switching in the User Accounts section of the Control Panel. Then you can enable the feature as described next.

1. From any Explorer window, choose Tools ➤ Folder Options.

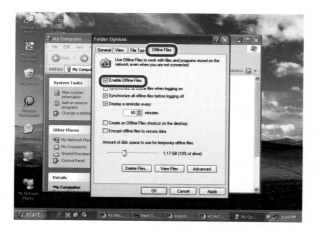

2. Click the Offline Files tab and mark the Enable Offline Files check box. The synchronization settings become available.

Change any synchronization settings. Many of these can also be set through the Offline Files Wizard that runs when you select files for later offline use.

Click OK to apply the new setting.

Expert Advice

You can return to the Offline Files tab at any time. In this tab, you might wish to

♦ Delete offline files (Delete Files button) to save space on your hard disk.

♦ View offline files (View Files button) to see what files are being cached on your hard disk (perhaps before you delete them).

♦ Set properties for the Offline Files feature (Advanced button), such as configuring the behavior for when a connection to another PC is lost.

MAKING A FILE OR FOLDER AVAILABLE OFFLINE

After turning on the Offline Folders feature, you can select individual network files and folders to be available offline. Doing so caches them on your local hard drive, so they'll always be available to you even if the network or Internet connection is down. Then just use the files and folders normally. When originals are available, the originals will be accessed; when originals are not available, the cached copy will be accessed. An icon appears in the notification area to let you know you are working offline.

When network access is once again available after having worked offline, you must synchronize your cached copies with the online originals. If you have set the configuration options to synchronize automatically at logon and/or logoff, this process is automatic.

1. Locate a file or folder in My Network Places that you want to cache, and then right-click it and choose Make Available Offline.

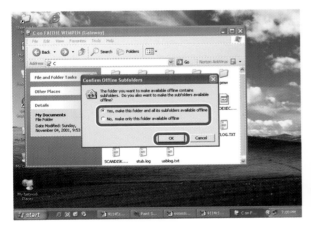

2. If a Confirm Offline Subfolders dialog box appears, choose to make subfolders available or not. Then click OK.

3. If you ever need to synchronize manually, choose Start ➤ All Programs ➤ Accessories ➤ Synchronize. Then in the Items to Synchronize dialog box, deselect any items you don't want to synchronize and click Synchronize.

BACKING UP YOUR CERTIFICATES

Certificates are an important part of NTFS file-encryption security, but if you lose your certificates due to a hard disk failure or accidental deletion, you can lose access to your important files. That's why it's important to back up your certificates.

The first time you use NTFS encryption, Windows generates your personal encryption certificate. This certificate includes a public key and a private key. You will want to back up your private key using the following procedure.

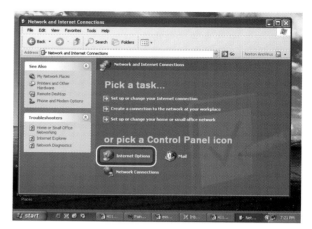

1. Make sure you are logged in using the user account that needs its certificate backed up.

From the Control Panel, choose Network and Internet Connections, and then choose Internet Options to open the Internet Properties dialog box.

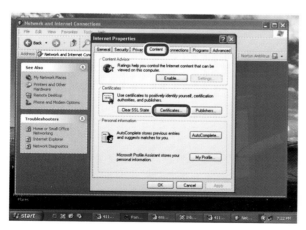

2. In the Content tab, click the Certificates button to open the Certificates dialog box.

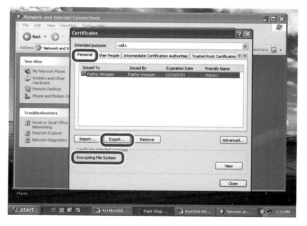

3. In the Personal tab, select the certificate that shows Encrypting File System in the Certificate Intended Purposes area.

Click Export. The Certificate Export Wizard starts.

BACKING UP YOUR CERTIFICATES *(continued)*

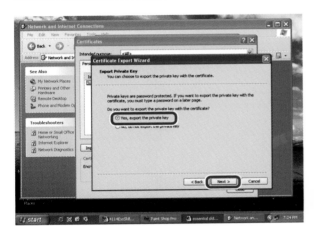

4. Choose Yes, Export Private Key, and click Next. Click Next to accept the defaults on the next screen.

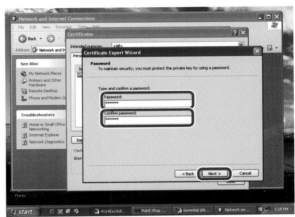

5. When prompted for a password, make one up and enter it in the first field. Confirm it in the second field. Then click Next.

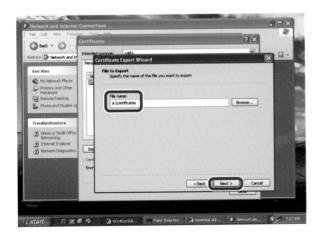

6. Enter a path and name for the exported file. You might want to export to a floppy, for example. Then click Next.

Click Finish.

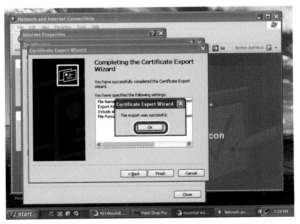

7. A box appears telling you it was a success; click OK.

Click Close to close the Certificates dialog box.

Click OK to close the Internet Properties dialog box.

ENCRYPTING AND DECRYPTING FOLDERS AND FILES

EFS (Encrypting File System) works only on NTFS drives. It is different from network permissions because it deals with security on a local level. It's based on the logged-in user on the machine. When the user who encrypted the folder or file is logged in, it's transparent; but when anyone else is logged in, the file or folder is inaccessible. This is handy when multiple users share a PC and must work with sensitive data.

EFS uses the logged-in user's public key to generate a file-encryption key that the encrypted file or folder must pass through in order to be accessed. When you are logged in as the same user who did the encrypting, Windows automatically accesses the needed keys; but when anyone else is logged in, there is a different public key in use so the decryption doesn't happen.

To encrypt or decrypt a file or folder, follow these steps:

1. Right-click the file or folder and choose Properties.

In the General tab, click the Advanced button to open the Advanced Attributes dialog box.

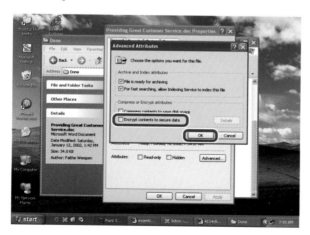

2. Mark or clear the Encrypt contents to secure data check box to encrypt or decrypt.

Click OK to close the Advanced Attributes box, and then click OK again to close the Properties box.

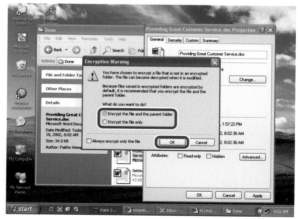

3. If you are encrypting a file, a warning appears enabling you to choose to encrypt the parent folder as well as the individual file. Choose Encrypt the File and Parent Folder or Encrypt the File Only, and then click OK.

SHARING ENCRYPTED FILES

This is a brand-new feature in Windows XP. In Windows 2000, EFS-encrypted files were accessible locally only to the user who encrypted them.

You can set up sharing for individual encrypted files only; however, you can't do it for folders or multiple files at once. ("Encrypted files" here includes both files that have been individually encrypted and files that are encrypted because they reside in an encrypted folder.)

To share a file with a user, that user must have an encryption certificate on that PC. To set one up, create a user account for the person and then log in as that person and encrypt a file. (You can decrypt it later if you wish.) Encrypting a file creates a certificate. Then log in as yourself and complete the following steps.

1. If the file is not already encrypted, encrypt it as described on the preceding page or place it in an encrypted folder.

Right-click the file and choose Properties.

In the General tab, click Advanced. Then in the Advanced Attributes dialog box, click Details.

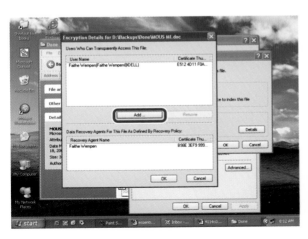

2. In the Encryption Details box, click Add.

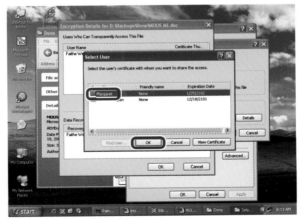

3. Select the user with whom you want to share access and click OK.

Click OK twice more to close the open dialog boxes.

DEFRAGMENTING YOUR HARD DISK

To keep your hard disk in good shape, and to improve disk performance, defragment it regularly by using Disk Defragmenter. How frequently you need to run Disk Defragmenter depends on how actively you use your computer and how often you create, modify, or delete files. Try running Disk Defragmenter once a week and see if it recommends defragmenting your disks. If not, decrease the frequency with which you run Disk Defragmenter.

Defragmenting a volume (a drive) can take several hours, and it's best not to use the computer during defragmentation. Set Disk Defragmenter running when you don't need to use the computer for a few hours—for example, at night.

Before defragmenting a disk, close all open programs and make sure no one else is logged on to the computer.

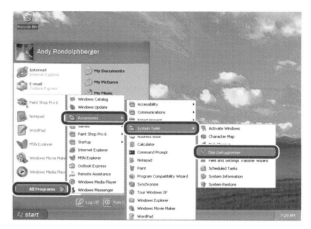

1. Choose Start ➤ All Programs ➤ Accessories ➤ System Tools ➤ Disk Defragmenter. Windows starts Disk Defragmenter.

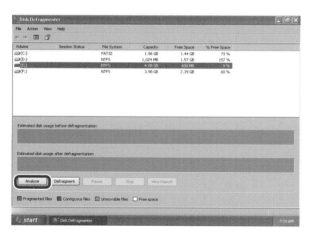

2. Select the volume you want to defragment. Click the Analyze button. Disk Defragmenter analyzes the volume and displays a summary.

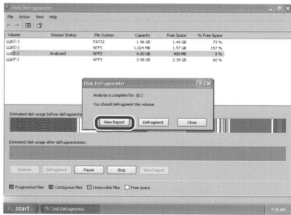

3. If the volume needs defragmentation, click the View Report button. Disk Defragmenter displays the Analysis Report dialog box.

If the volume doesn't need defragmentation, click the Close button and go to step 7.

DEFRAGMENTING YOUR HARD DISK *(continued)*

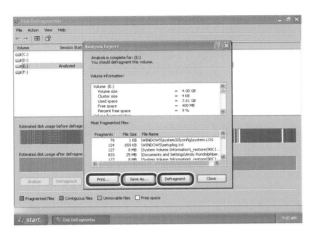

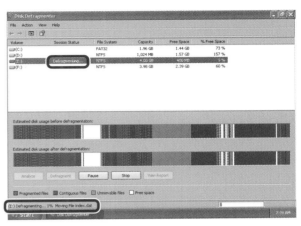

4. If you want, click the Print button to print the analysis report, or click the Save As button to save it.

Click the Defragment button to start defragmentation.

5. Defragmenter displays its status and its progress.

You can pause defragmentation by clicking the Pause button or stop it by clicking the Stop button.

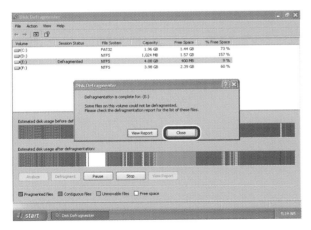

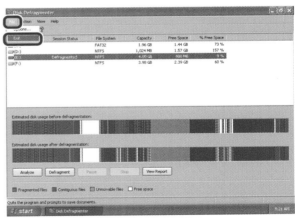

6. When defragmentation is complete, Disk Defragmenter displays another Disk Defragmenter dialog box telling you so.

Click the View Report button to display the defragmentation report on the volume's status, or click the Close button to close the dialog box.

7. Defragment other volumes as necessary.

Choose File ➤ Exit. Disk Defragmenter closes.

You can now resume computing as normal.

RUNNING DISK CLEANUP

Windows' Disk Cleanup feature lets you keep your hard disk in order by removing temporary files, emptying the Recycle Bin, and compressing old files. By getting rid of old files, you can reclaim disk space.

It's a good idea to run Disk Cleanup once every few weeks. If you find it hard to remember to run Disk Cleanup, you can schedule it to run automatically at a convenient time, as described in the next section.

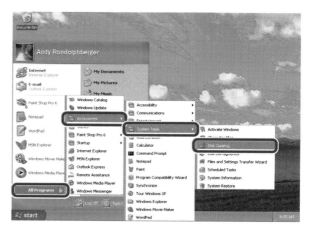

1. Choose Start ➤ All Programs ➤ Accessories ➤ System Tools ➤ Disk Cleanup. Windows starts Disk Cleanup, which displays the Select Drive dialog box.

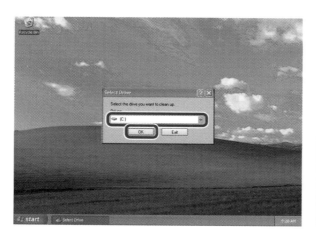

2. Select the drive to clean up.

Click the OK button. Disk Cleanup scans the drive and displays the Disk Cleanup dialog box.

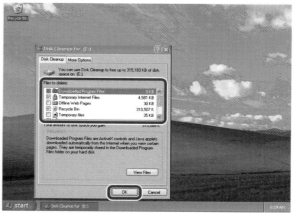

3. Select the items you want to delete.

Click the OK button. Windows removes the items and closes the Disk Cleanup dialog box.

SCHEDULING A TASK TO RUN AUTOMATICALLY

You can schedule tasks to run automatically at times and frequencies that suit you. Scheduling tasks can be useful for tasks that are best run automatically, when no one is using the computer, at an antisocial hour, or on a regular schedule that makes them hard to remember. You can also schedule tasks that you need to run only once at some point in the future—either at a specific point in time or when a particular event occurs, such as a user's logging on.

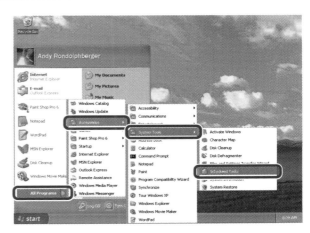

1. Choose Start ➤ All Programs ➤ Accessories ➤ System Tools ➤ Scheduled Tasks.

Windows displays the Scheduled Tasks folder.

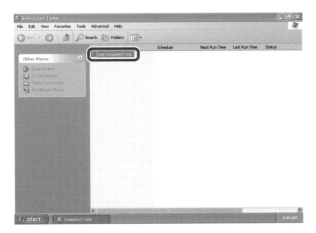

2. Double-click the Add Scheduled Task icon. Windows starts the Scheduled Task Wizard.

3. Click the Next button. The Wizard displays the next page.

SCHEDULING A TASK TO RUN AUTOMATICALLY *(continued)*

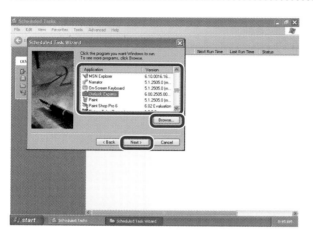

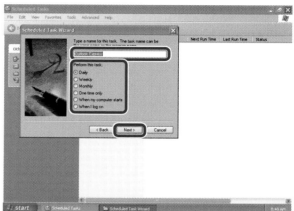

4. Select the program in the list.

If the program isn't in the list, click the Browse button and use the Select Program to Schedule dialog box to select the program.

Click the Next button.

5. Change the name for the task if necessary.

Select the frequency or occasion for the task.

Click the Next button. If the schedule involves times or dates, the Wizard displays a screen of options.

6. Choose schedule options as appropriate.

Click the Next button. The Wizard displays the name and password screen.

7. Specify the username and password under which to run the task. The Wizard suggests your username.

Click the Next button. The Wizard displays its final screen.

SCHEDULING A TASK TO RUN AUTOMATICALLY *(continued)*

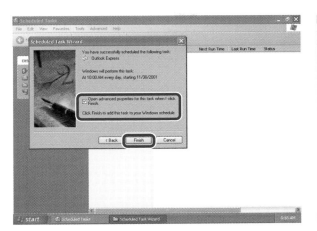

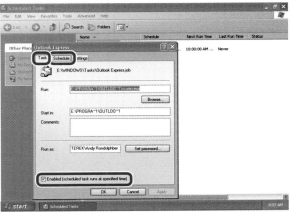

8. Select the Open Advanced Properties for This Task when I Click Finish check box.

Click the Finish button. The Wizard adds the task to your schedule and displays the Properties dialog box for the task.

9. You can turn the task on or off by selecting or clearing the Enabled check box.

Click the Schedule tab. Windows displays the Schedule tab.

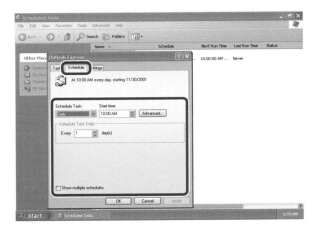

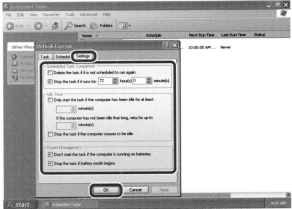

10. Choose further settings in the Schedule tab as necessary.

Click the Settings tab. Windows displays the Settings tab.

11. Choose further settings in the Settings tab as necessary.

Click the OK button. Windows closes the Properties dialog box and applies your changes.

SETTING SYSTEM RESTORE POINTS

The System Restore feature lets you roll back your computer's software state following a change of software that doesn't turn out satisfactorily. For example, you might update a device driver but find that the new driver didn't work correctly. Or you might install a program that doesn't work as it should—and which won't uninstall correctly.

System Restore lets you return your computer to a system restore point created in the past. Windows automatically creates system restore points both periodically and when you use Windows Update, and you can create them manually whenever you want—for example, before installing or updating software. With typical settings, Windows retains two to three weeks' worth of restore points, giving you good flexibility in recovering from software and hardware mishaps.

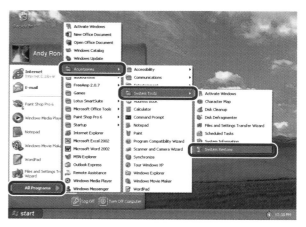

1. Choose Start ➤ All Programs ➤ Accessories ➤ System Tools ➤ System Restore. Windows starts System Restore.

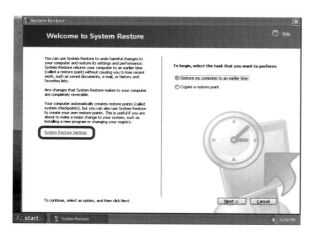

2. Click the System Restore Settings link. System Restore displays the System Restore tab of the System Properties dialog box.

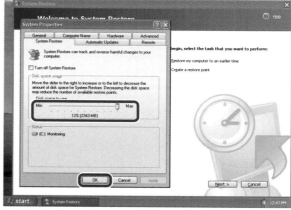

3. If necessary, use the Disk Space to Use slider to adjust the amount of space System Restore uses. (If your system has multiple drives, click the Settings button and use the Settings dialog box.)

Click the OK button.

SETTING SYSTEM RESTORE POINTS *(continued)*

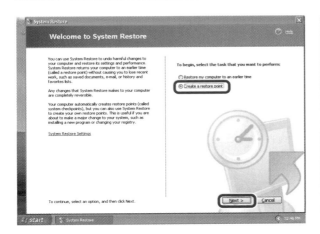

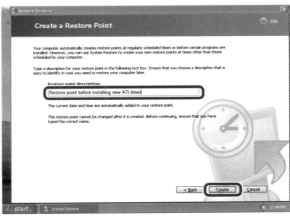

4. Select the Create a Restore Point option button.

Click the Next button. System Restore displays the Create a Restore Point screen.

5. Enter the name for the restore point.

Click the Create button. System Restore creates the restore point and displays the Restore Point Created screen.

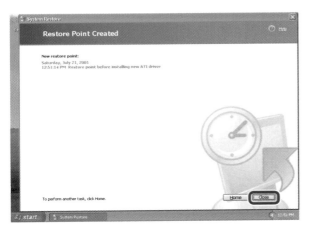

6. Click the Close button. System Restore closes.

Expert Advice

◆ You can turn off System Restore by selecting the Turn Off System Restore check box (or the Turn Off System Restore on All Drives check box, if you have multiple drives) on the System Restore page of the System Properties dialog box, but doing so isn't a good idea: Although Windows XP is reliable and stable, badly written software or drivers can still prevent it from running. But you may be able to save disk space by reducing the amount of space System Restore can take up. System Restore needs at least 200MB of space.

◆ If you have multiple hard drives, you can save disk space by turning off System Restore for data-only drives. Keep System Restore turned on for the drive that contains your Windows files and your program files.

RESTORING YOUR SYSTEM

When a software installation or a driver upgrade doesn't work as planned, you can use System Restore to return Windows to one of the restore points that you or Windows created.

Because System Restore changes the software configuration of your computer, it's best to use it only when your software goes seriously wrong. If you experience a problem that you can solve by changing a driver or rolling back a driver to the previously installed driver, it's better to solve the problem that way than by using System Restore.

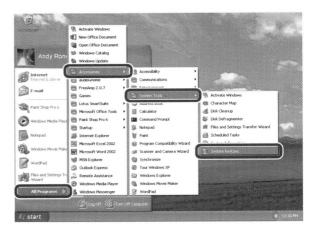

1. Choose Start ➤ All Programs ➤ Accessories ➤ System Tools ➤ System Restore. Windows starts System Restore.

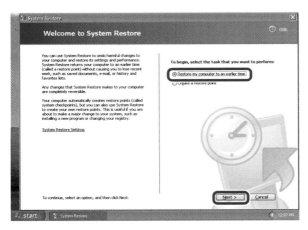

2. Make sure the Restore My Computer to an Earlier Time option button is selected.

Click the Next button. System Restore displays the Select a Restore Point screen.

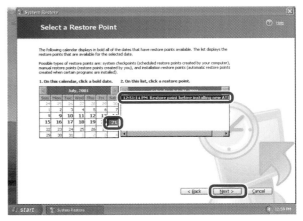

3. Use the calendar to select the date to which you want to restore the computer. Boldface dates indicate restore points.

Select a restore point in the list for the date.

Click the Next button. System Restore displays the Confirm Restore Point Selection screen.

RESTORING YOUR SYSTEM *(continued)*

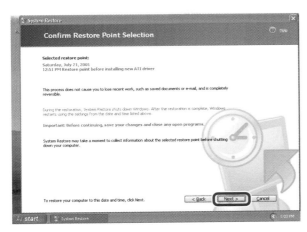

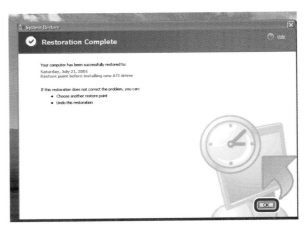

4. Close any other open programs.

Click the Next button. System Restore restores your system to the restore point you chose, then restarts Windows and displays the Restoration Complete screen after you log on.

5. Click the OK button. System Restore closes.

Check your system to see if it's running properly.

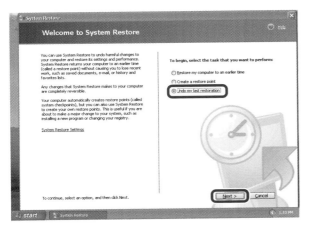

6. If the restoration didn't produce the effect you wanted, run System Restore again. You can either choose a restore point further in the past or undo your last restoration.

Expert Advice

◆ System Restore stores several weeks' worth of restore points, depending on how much space you've allocated to it.

◆ Restoring your system affects only your system files—it doesn't affect your data files. So any data files that you've created since the restore point to which you're restoring Windows will still be there after the restoration.

◆ Conversely, this also means that you can't use System Restore to rescue a data file that you've deleted or damaged. For example, if you delete the contents of an Excel workbook and then save it, you can't recover an earlier version of the file by using System Restore.

SHARING FILES OR FOLDERS WITH OTHER USERS OF THE COMPUTER

To share a file or folder with other users of your computer, copy or move it to the Shared Documents folder or one of its subfolders. Windows provides the Shared Documents folder for shared documents, the Shared Music folder for shared music files, the Shared Pictures folder for shared pictures, and the Shared Videos folder (when you start working with video) for shared video files.

If you copy the file or folder (as described here), you can keep the original to yourself. If you move the file or folder, anyone can change the original.

1. Open an Explorer window to the folder that contains the file or folder.

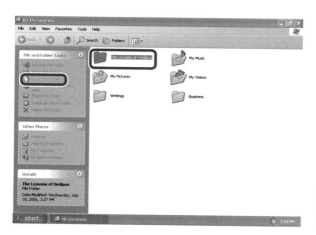

2. Select the file or folder.

Click the Copy This File link or the Copy This Folder link. Windows displays the Copy Items dialog box.

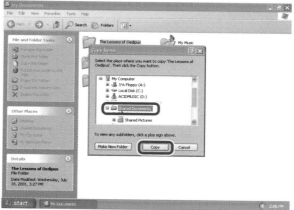

3. Select the Shared Documents icon.

Click the Copy button.

Windows copies the file or folder to the Shared Documents folder.

KEEPING A FOLDER PRIVATE

Even if you don't share a folder under your My Documents folder, other Computer Administrator users of your computer can access it. To prevent them from doing so, you need to mark the folder as private.

If you don't have a password on your user account, you need to set one. (Otherwise, other users can log on as you and see your folders.)

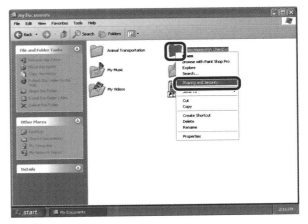

1. Right-click the folder and choose Sharing and Security from the shortcut menu. Windows displays the Sharing tab of the Properties dialog box.

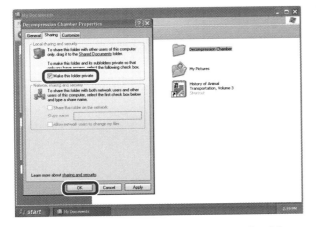

2. Select the Make This Folder Private check box. Click the OK button. Windows closes the Properties dialog box and makes the folder private.

Expert Advice

◆ If you don't have a password on your user account, Windows displays the Sharing dialog box warning you that because you don't have a password, anyone can log in as you and then access the folder you've made private.

◆ Click the Yes button in the Sharing dialog box. Windows displays the Create a Password for Your Account screen of User Accounts.

◆ Enter the password in the top two text boxes.

◆ If you want, enter a cryptic word or phrase for a password hint.

◆ Click the Create Password button. Windows applies the password to your account. The folder is then securely private.

SHARING A FOLDER ON THE NETWORK

Instead of sharing a folder only with other users of your computer, you can share it with them and with other users of computers networked to yours.

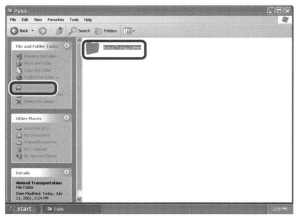

1. Select the folder.

Click the Share This Folder link. Windows displays the Sharing tab of the Properties dialog box for the folder.

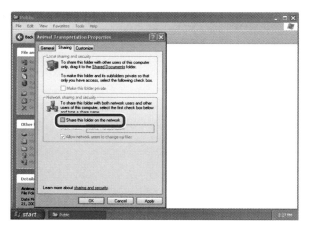

2. Select the Share This Folder on the Network check box. Windows enables the other sharing options.

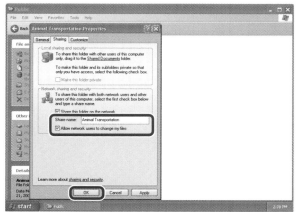

3. Adjust the share name if you want to.

Select or clear the Allow Network Users to Change My Files check box as appropriate.

Click the OK button. Windows shares the folder.

CONNECTING TO A NETWORK DRIVE

If your computer is connected to a network, you can connect to any drive that a computer on the network has shared. You can then work with the files and folders on that network drive as if it were a drive on your computer.

1. From an Explorer window, choose Tools ➢ Map Network Drive. Windows displays the Map Network Drive dialog box.

2. Specify the drive letter to use for the network drive. Windows starts with the letter Z, the last letter used.

Click the Browse button. Windows displays the Browse for Folder dialog box.

3. Expand the Microsoft Windows Network item.

Expand the appropriate workgroup item.

CONNECTING TO A NETWORK DRIVE *(continued)*

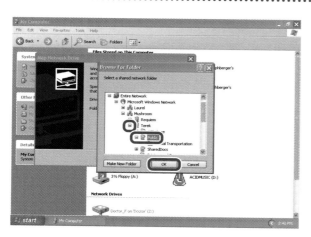

4. Expand the item for the computer that contains the shared folder.

Select the shared folder.

Click the OK button. Windows closes the Browse for Folder dialog box and enters the folder path and name in the Folder text box.

5. To automatically connect this network drive each time you log on, select the Reconnect at Logon check box.

To specify a different username for connecting to the network drive, click the Connect Using a Different User Name link.

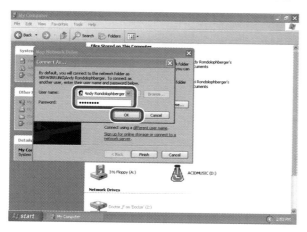

6. Enter your username. If necessary, preface it with the computer name and a backslash.

Enter your password.

Click the OK button. Windows closes the Connect As dialog box.

7. Click the Finish button. Windows closes the Map Network Drive dialog box and maps the drive.

CREATING A USER ACCOUNT

By setting up multiple user accounts on your PC, you can enable different settings for different users. On page 71, you saw one use for user accounts: keeping files and folders secure. Other uses include defining custom screen-appearance settings and installing applications accessible by only one user.

When you set up a user account, you can give the user either Computer Administrator or Guest privileges. Guest is a limited type of account that permits only running programs and accessing files. Computer User gives the user full privileges to make changes, delete files, install and remove programs, and so on.

You can set up new users through the User Accounts section of the Control Panel or through Computer Management. The following steps show how to do it through the Control Panel. Before performing these steps, make sure you have logged in with a Computer Administrator account.

1. Choose Start ➤ Control Panel to open Control Panel, and then click User Accounts to open User Accounts.

Click the Create a New Account link to open the Name the New Account screen.

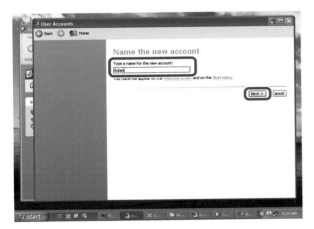

2. Enter a username for the person. The name can be up to 20 characters. Then click Next.

3. Specify the type of account you want this user to have: Computer Administrator or Guest. Then click Create Account.

CREATING A USER ACCOUNT (continued)

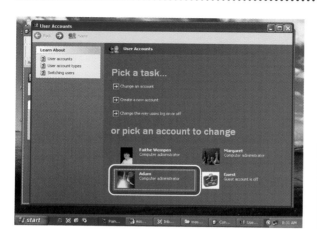

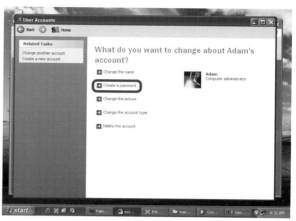

4. Back in User Accounts, click the account you just created to open the options for that account.

5. Click Create Password to open the screen on which you can create a password for the account.

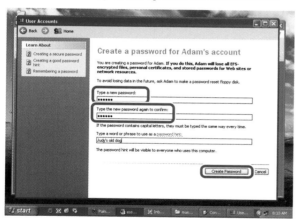

Click Create Password to establish the password for the new user account.

If needed later, you can return here and click Change the Password or Remove the Password.

You can also change the name, change the picture, change the account type (Computer Administrator or Guest), and Delete the Account.

6. In the Type a New Password box, enter a password, and then enter it again in the Type the New Password Again to Confirm box. If you want, you can then type a hint (which can be seen by anyone using this computer) to trigger your memory of the password if you forget it in the future.

A password can be up to 127 characters, but if you have Windows 9x PCs on your network, limit the password to 14 characters. Passwords are case-sensitive.

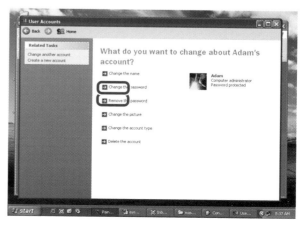

CREATING A GROUP ACCOUNT

Local groups are useful for assigning permissions to resources. For example, suppose you want to assign the same local permissions to each of the part-time workers who use a certain PC; you could set up a group called Part-Time and then add all those users to the group. You could then share files or offer other permissions to that group.

When creating a group, you type the usernames you want to add to it. You can't select them from a list; you must know them. However, you can click the Check Names button after entering a name to make sure that username does exist.

The group name you choose can contain any numbers or letters and can be a maximum of 256 characters. The name must be unique in the local database.

1. In Control Panel, click Performance and Maintenance, click Administrative Tools, and then click Computer Management.

Expand System Tools, expand Local User and Groups, right-click Groups, and choose New Group.

2. Type a name for the group in the space provided.

Enter some text in the Description field that will describe the membership and purpose of this group.

Click the Add button to open the Select Users dialog box.

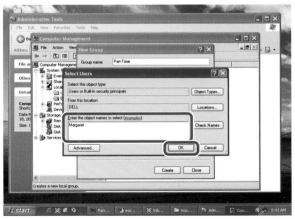

3. In the Enter the Object Name to Select box, enter the name of the user you want to add to the group. Enter multiple names, if desired. Then click OK.

Click the Create button to create the new group, and then click Close.

SETTING SHARE-LEVEL PERMISSIONS

You assign share-level permissions to determine what other network users can access on your hard drive and if they can view/edit your files and folders. This is a separate issue from local-user security, which affects only users who work at your local PC and relies on NTFS.

By default, Simple File Sharing is turned on for Windows XP Professional; however, this feature severely limits your options for setting file-sharing permissions. To turn it off, choose Tools ➤ Folder Options from any file management window, and then in the View tab, scroll to the bottom of the list of options and deselect Use Simple Sharing (Recommended). After doing so, you can use the following steps.

(Note that the default shared permission in Windows XP Professional is for the Everyone group to have Full Control. In a secure environment, be sure to remove this permission before assigning specific permissions to users and groups.)

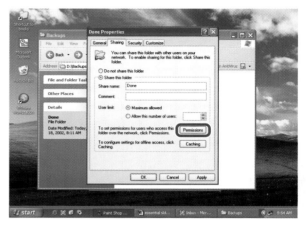

1. In Explorer, right-click the shared resource and choose Sharing and Security. The Properties dialog box opens at the Sharing tab.

Click the Permissions button to open the Permissions dialog box. Click Add to open the Select Users or Groups dialog box.

2. In the Enter the Object Name to Select box, enter the name of the user or group to whom you are granting permission, and then click OK.

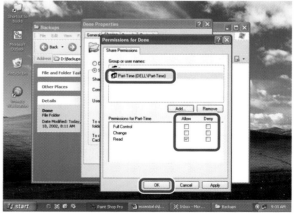

3. In the Permissions section, click Allow or Deny to specify the type of permission you want to grant this user or group.

When you've granted the permissions, click OK.

SETTING SECURITY PERMISSIONS

Security permissions are separate from sharing permissions. The Security tab is available only on drives that use the NTFS file system. With Security permissions you can be much more specific about which users and groups have access and what permissions they have. Security permissions also affect local users as well, whereas sharing permissions affect only users accessing the PC from the network.

If a file or folder does not have a Security tab, it may be because that drive does not use the NTFS file system, or it may be because simple file sharing is enabled. See the explanation before the steps on the preceding page if you need to disable simple sharing.

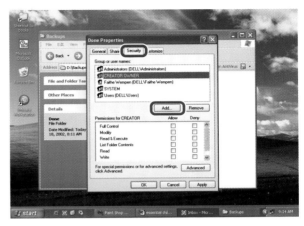

1. In Explorer, right-click the file or folder for which you want to establish permissions, and then choose Properties from the shortcut menu to open the Properties dialog box for that file or folder.

In the Security tab, click Add to open the Select Users or Groups dialog box.

2. In the Enter the Object Name to Select box, enter the name of the user or group to whom you are granting permission, and then click OK.

3. Mark or clear the check boxes for each type of permission you want to grant.

Click OK.

CHANGING A DRIVER

You can often improve a device's performance by updating its driver, the software that enables Windows to communicate with it. Most hardware manufacturers release updated drivers periodically for their hardware to remove bugs and add new features. Once you've downloaded the driver, you can install it as described in this section.

If a new driver doesn't work satisfactorily, you can roll the driver back (as described in the next section) or use the System Restore feature to restore your system's state to before you installed the driver.

1. Choose Start ➤ Control Panel. Windows displays Control Panel.

(Alternatively, press Winkey+Break and go directly to step 4.)

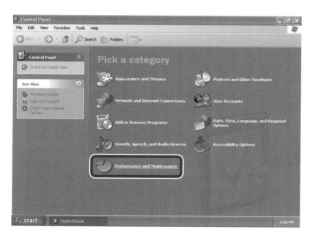

2. Click the Performance and Maintenance link. Windows displays the Performance and Maintenance screen.

3. Click the System link. Windows displays the System Properties dialog box.

CHANGING A DRIVER *(continued)*

4. Click the Hardware tab. Windows displays the Hardware tab.

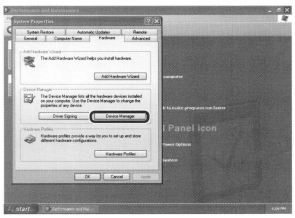

5. Click the Device Manager button. Windows displays Device Manager.

6. Select the device for which you want to change the driver.

Click the Update Driver button. Windows starts the Hardware Update Wizard.

7. Select the Install from a List or Specific Location option button.

Click the Next button. The Wizard displays the Please Choose Your Search and Installation Options screen.

CHANGING A DRIVER *(continued)*

8. Select the Don't Search. I Will Choose the Driver to Install option button.

Click the Next button.

The Wizard Displays the Select the Device Driver You Want to Install for This Hardware screen.

9. Click the Have Disk button. The Wizard displays the Install from Disk dialog box.

10. Click the Browse button. The Wizard displays the Locate File dialog box.

11. Navigate to and select the file containing the driver information.

Click the Open button. The Wizard closes the Locate File dialog box and enters the driver name in the Install from Disk dialog box.

CHANGING A DRIVER *(continued)*

12. Click the OK button. The Wizard closes the Install from Disk dialog box and enters the driver name on the Select the Device Driver You Want to Install for This Hardware screen.

13. Click the Next button. The Wizard installs the software and displays the final screen of the Wizard.

14. Click the Finish button. The Wizard closes.

15. Click the Close button to close Device Manager.

Click the Close button to close the System Properties dialog box.

Click the Close button to close the Performance and Maintenance window.

ROLLING BACK A DRIVER

In case a driver upgrade doesn't work correctly, Windows stores information about the previous driver used for the hardware in question so that you can easily restore that driver. Windows calls this process *rolling back* the new driver to the previous driver.

1. Follow steps 1 to 5 of the previous section to display Device Manager.

Select the device whose driver you want to roll back.

Click the Properties button. Windows displays the Properties dialog box for the driver.

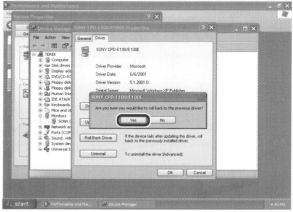

2. Click the Driver tab. Windows displays the Driver tab of the dialog box.

Click the Roll Back Driver button. Windows displays a confirmation dialog box.

3. Click the Yes button. Windows restores the previous driver.

Click the OK button. Windows closes the Properties dialog box.

Close all of the open dialog boxes.

ENABLING REMOTE DESKTOP CONNECTION ON THE REMOTE COMPUTER

You use Remote Desktop Connection to take control of another computer via a dial-up connection, a local area network, or the Internet. You might want to use Remote Desktop Connection, for example, to connect to your office computer from home if you forget to take home some files you need to work on.

When you're setting up Remote Desktop Connection, your computer is known as the home computer, and the other computer is known as the remote computer. The first order of business is to set up the remote computer to accept incoming connections.

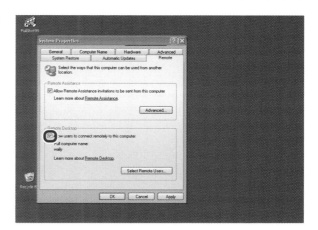

1. Click Start, right-click My Computer, and choose Properties from the shortcut menu to open the System Properties dialog box.

Click the Remote tab, and select the Allow Users to Connect Remotely to This Computer check box.

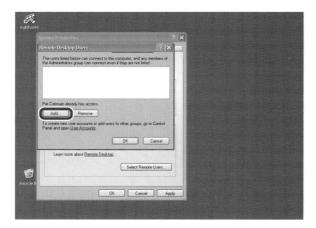

2. Click the Select Remote Users button to open the Remote Desktop Users dialog box.

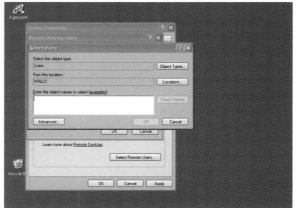

3. Click the Add button to open the Select Users dialog box.

In the Enter the Object Names To Select box, enter a user's name, and then click OK.

Click OK twice.

ENABLING REMOTE DESKTOP CONNECTION ON THE HOME COMPUTER

After you enable Remote Desktop Connection on the remote computer, you need to set up your computer (the home computer). After you set up the following options, click the Connect button in the General tab of the Remote Desktop Connection dialog box to establish a connection to the remote computer. You can then take charge of the remote computer and use it as you would your own Desktop.

1. Choose Start ➣ All Programs ➣ Accessories ➣ Communications ➣ Remote Desktop Connection to open the Remote Desktop Connection dialog box in a reduced state.

Click Options to display the entire Remote Desktop Connection dialog box.

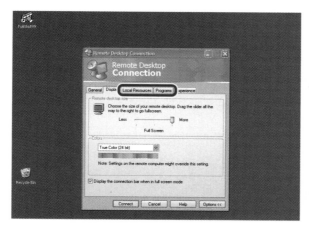

2. Use the options on the Display tab to specify how you want to display the remote Desktop.

Click the Local Resources tab and use its options to specify how sound, the keyboard, disk drives, printers, and serial ports will be handled.

On the Programs tab, specify that Windows run a particular program when you connect.

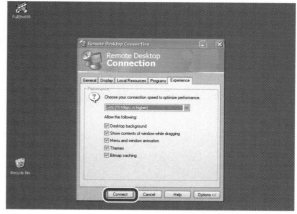

3. On the Experience tab, select your connection speed, and choose display options.

Click the Connect button to connect, or back on the General tab, click the Save As button if you want to save your settings.

ENABLING INTERNET CONNECTION FIREWALL

A *firewall* is a security system that prevents would-be mischief makers from accessing your computer system when you are connected to the Internet. Windows XP Professional includes a personal firewall system called Internet Connection Firewall. If you have an Internet connection that is always on, such as a DSL or a cable modem, you'll want to be sure that Internet Connection Firewall is enabled, although it certainly doesn't hurt to have firewall protection if you have a dial-up connection. The information on your computer system is important to you, or it wouldn't be there in the first place. You don't want to take chances with it.

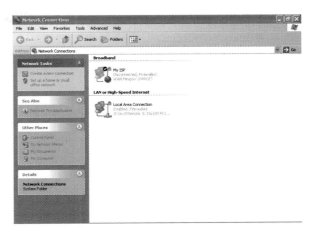

1. Choose Start ➢ Connect To ➢ Show All Connections to open the Network Connections folder.

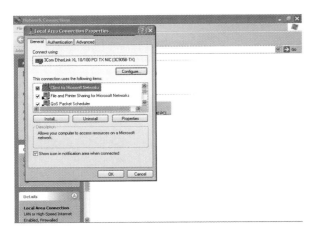

2. Right-click the icon for your Internet connection, and then choose Properties from the shortcut menu to open the Properties dialog box for your connection.

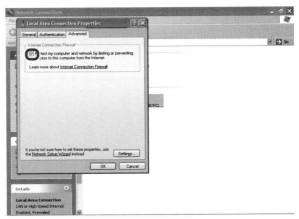

3. Click the Advanced tab.

Click the check box in the Internet Connection Firewall section, and then click OK.

SECURING RAS DIAL-IN SESSIONS

Dialing into a network through a dial-up networking connection is relatively secure, but it still could be compromised: someone could tap into your phone line and record the data conversations traveling back and forth between your computer and the remote computer. Therefore, the primary means to protect RAS (remote access server) dial-in sessions is via encryption. Windows XP Professional makes it easy to implement (and require) encryption on any dial-up networking connection.

Start with a working dial-up networking connection and then follow these steps to enable encryption for it.

1. Choose Start ➤ Connect To ➤ Show All Connections to open the Network Connections folder.

Right-click the icon for your dial-up connection, and choose Properties from the shortcut menu.

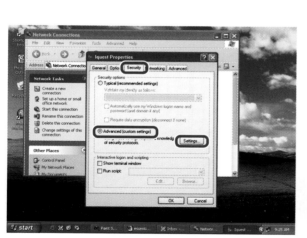

2. In the Security tab, click the Advanced (Custom Settings) option button.

Click the Settings button to open the Advanced Security Settings dialog box.

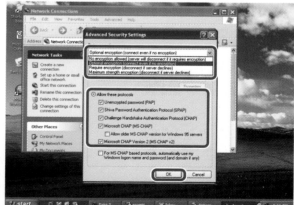

3. Select a Data Encryption setting from the Data Encryption drop-down list.

Under Allow These Protocols, clear the check boxes for any protocols you do not wish to use. Then click OK.

If you see a warning, click Yes. Then click OK to close the Properties box.

SETTING UP A VIRTUAL PRIVATE NETWORKING CONNECTION

A virtual private network (VPN) connection enables you to connect securely and privately from one PC to another by using the Internet as a conduit. Before you can set one up you must first have a functional Internet connection.

1. Choose Start ≻ Connect To ≻ Show All Connections to open the Network Connections folder.

In the Network Tasks bar, click the Create a New Connection link to start the New Connection Wizard.

Click Next to open the Network Connection Type screen.

2. Select the Connect to the Network at My Workplace option, and then click Next to open the Network Connection screen.

3. Click the Virtual Private Network Connection option, and then click Next to open the Connection Name screen.

SETTING UP A VIRTUAL PRIVATE NETWORKING CONNECTION *(cont.)*

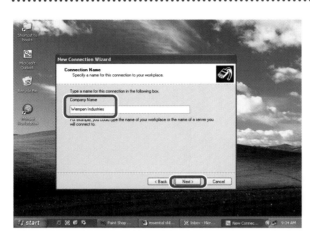

4. Enter a name for your connection, and then click Next to open the Public Network screen.

5. If your Internet connection is always on, click Do Not Dial the Initial Connection.

If you use dial-up service, choose Automatically Dial This Initial Connection, and then select the dial-up service from the list. Then click Next.

6. Enter the IP address or DNS name to connect with, and then click Next.

At the final screen of the Wizard, specify whether you want a shortcut to this connection on your Desktop, and then click Finish.

7. A Connect dialog box opens for your new connection; enter your username and password for that system and click Connect to establish the connection.

JOINING A DOMAIN

If you work on a small peer-to-peer network, you probably connect to a workgroup, but if you work on a larger client-server network, you may well need to connect to a domain to access the network. In order to connect to a domain, you will need the following information: your username, your password, the name of the domain that you will join, your computer name, and the name of your computer's domain.

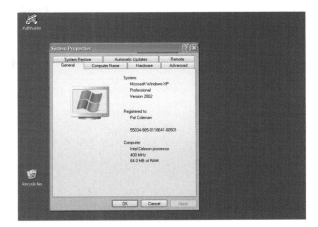

1. Click Start, right-click My Computer, and then choose Properties from the shortcut menu to open the System Properties dialog box. Click the Computer Name tab.

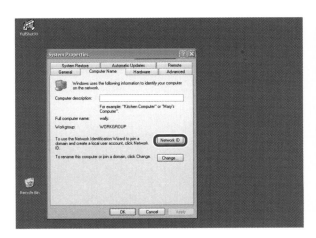

2. Click the Computer Name tab.

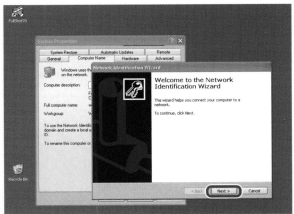

3. Click the Network ID button to start the Network Identification Wizard.

4. Click the Next button to run the Network Identification Wizard.

JOINING A DOMAIN *(continued)*

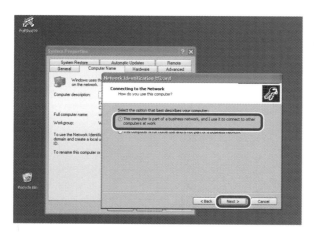

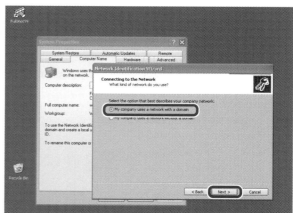

5. Click Next to open the Connecting to the Network screen, click the option that tells Windows XP this is a business network, and then click Next.

6. In the Connecting to the Network screen, click the option that tells Windows XP that your network has a domain, and then click Next.

Be sure that you have all the information listed on the Network Information screen, and then click Next.

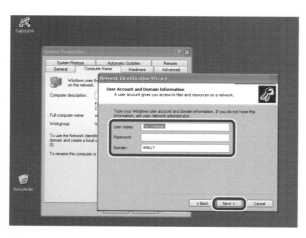

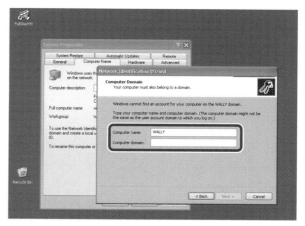

7. On the User Account and Domain Information screen, enter your username, your password, and your domain name, and then click Next.

8. On the Computer Domain screen, enter your information, and click Next.

In the Domain User Name and Password dialog box, enter your information, and click OK twice.

In the Access Level Wizard, select the type of access you want, and then click Next twice.

ENABLING COMPATIBILITY MODE FOR AN APPLICATION

Windows XP includes a feature called Compatibility mode that lets you tell Windows XP to emulate Windows 95, Windows 98, Windows NT 4, or Windows 2000 so that you can run a program that was written for one of those operating systems. Being able to run programs written for previous versions of Windows can be especially valuable when a new operating system is released and not many applications have been developed to run on it.

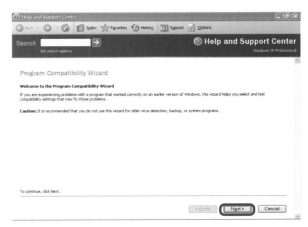

1. Choose Start ➤ All Programs ➤ Accessories ➤ Program Compatibility Wizard to start the Wizard. Click Next.

2. On this screen, tell the Wizard how you want to locate the program you want to run. Click Next.

3. Regardless of the option you choose to find the program, you'll need to tell the Wizard which operating system you want to use. In the Select a Compatibility Mode for the Program screen, select the operating system and click Next.

ENABLING COMPATIBILITY MODE FOR AN APPLICATION *(continued)*

4. In the Select Display Settings for the Program screen, select the number of colors and resolution and select to disable visual themes, if necessary. Normally, you need to set these options only for games or educational programs. Click Next.

5. In the Test Your Compatibility Settings screen, click Next to see how the program will run with the settings you've selected.

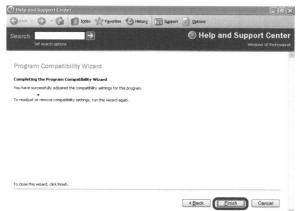

6. If the program ran correctly, click Next.

If the program did not run correctly, click No, Try Different Compatibility Settings, and click Next.

If the program did not run correctly click one of the other options as appropriate.

7. In the final screen of the Wizard, click Finish.

SETTING UP FAX SERVICES

If you want to use the Fax Services in Windows XP, you will need to install this feature using the Add or Remove Program applet in Control Panel because Fax Services are not installed by default. Once you install Fax Services, you will see a Fax icon with a hand under it in your Printers and Faxes folder if you are on a network. (Fax is shared by default if you are working on a network.)

Before you can send and receive faxes, however, you will need to configure Fax Services.

1. Choose Start ➤ Printers and Faxes to open the Printers and Faxes folder.

   Double-click Fax to start the Fax Configuration Wizard.

   Click Next to open the Sender Information screen.

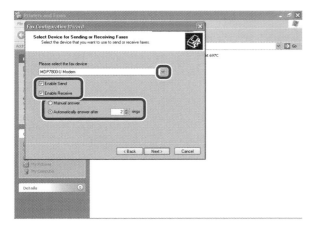

2. Enter the information you want on your cover sheet, and then click Next to open the Select Device for Sending or Receiving Faxes screen.

   Click the drop-down list to select the modem you want to use. If you want to both send and receive faxes, click those check boxes.

   Specify whether you want to answer manually or automatically.

3. Enter the information for your TSID (Transmitting Subscriber Identification) and click Next.

SETTING UP FAX SERVICES (*continued*)

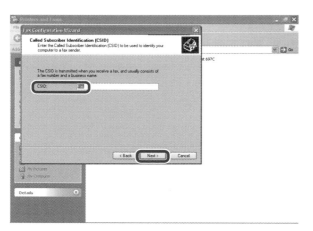

4. In the CSID box, enter the identifying text you want, and then click Next to open the Routing Options screen.

5. Specify whether and where you want a received fax printed and where you want to store fax files, and click Next to open the summary screen.

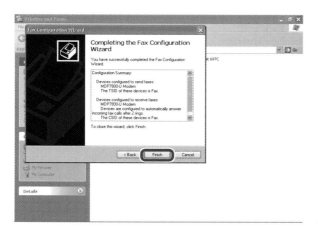

6. If the summary information is satisfactory, click Finish; if not, click Back and correct what you want changed.

7. Clicking Finish opens the Fax Console, which you use to monitor faxes, access the Fax Configuration Wizard, create personal cover pages, and administer Fax Services.

Chapter 1

Introducing Windows XP Professional

SINCE THE ADVENT OF the personal computer, users have wanted three things in an operating system: power, stability, and usability. Windows XP Professional has all these and more in abundance. It features an indefatigable 32-bit architecture, complete with built-in networking and the capability to run almost every piece of Windows software on the market, as well as a new interface.

What does all this mean to the consumer, the person sitting at a desk 52 weeks a year who just wants to be a productive computer user? It means a lot. It means a fast, up-to-date operating system with a slew of advanced features that ensure the computer will almost never crash. It means an operating system that can host the emerging multitude of 32-bit software applications, some of which offer amazing facilities for professional audio and video recording, editing, and broadcasting. It means a new interface, which gives users tremendous control over how the system performs its tasks and how it maintains its connections to peripherals and to other computers.

In this chapter, I'll give you an overview of Windows XP Professional: what's new, what's different, and what's under the hood. I'll compare Windows XP Professional with its sibling, Windows XP Home, and with previous versions of Windows. In later chapters, I'll expand on most of the topics I'll introduce in this chapter, but you'll find a lot here to whet your appetite.

- ◆ What is Windows XP Professional?
- ◆ What's new in Windows XP Professional?
- ◆ Should you upgrade to Windows XP Professional?
- ◆ How is Windows XP Professional different from other operating systems?
- ◆ What are the features of Windows XP Professional architecture?

What Is Windows XP Professional?

In a nutshell: Windows XP Professional is the latest version of the Windows NT family of operating systems (which includes Windows 2000). Windows XP Professional comprises a feature set designed for business users, while its less powerful (and less expensive) sibling Windows XP Home offers features designed for consumers, or home users.

If you've used Windows before, or if you're currently using Windows, you may wonder what the big deal is. The good news is that Windows XP *is* a big deal, especially if you've had less than satisfactory experiences with Windows in the past. Windows XP isn't the be-all and end-all of operating systems, but it's a great improvement on its predecessors.

As you probably know, in the past Microsoft offered two main categories of Windows versions for 32-bit personal computers: the Windows 95 family and the Windows NT family. In the Windows 95 family were Windows 95 itself, naturally enough; Windows 98; Windows 98 Second Edition, which (despite its unassuming name) was a major upgrade to Windows 98; and Windows Millennium Edition, also known as Windows Me. In the Windows NT family were Windows NT versions 3.1, 3.5, 3.51, and 4, each of which came in a Workstation version and a Server version, and then Windows 2000, which came in a Professional version and several Server versions.

The Windows 95 family, widely referred to as Windows 9x in a brave attempt to simplify Microsoft's inconsistent nomenclature, offered impressive compatibility with older hardware ("legacy hardware," as it's sometimes politely termed) and software ("legacy software"), including full (or full-ish) DOS capabilities for running games and character-based applications. These versions of Windows kept their hardware demands to a reasonable minimum. They were aimed at the consumer market. When things went wrong (which happened regrettably often), they became unstable. And they crashed. Frequently.

Many of those people—both professionals and home users—who couldn't stand or afford to lose their work because of Windows 9x's frequent crashes migrated to Windows NT instead. (Others tried OS/2 while it lasted, then returned disconsolately to Windows. Others went to Linux and mostly stayed there.) NT, which stands for New Technology, had a completely different underpinning of code than Windows 9x. NT was designed for stability, and as a result, it crashed much less frequently than Windows 9x. Unfortunately, though, NT wasn't nearly as compatible as Windows 9x with legacy hardware and software. Most games and much audio and video software wouldn't run on NT, and it was picky about the hardware on which it would run. (Actually, this wasn't "unfortunate" at all—it was deliberate on Microsoft's part and probably wise. But the result was far from great for many users.)

So for the last half-dozen years, users have essentially had to decide between stability and compatibility. This led to a lot of unhappy users, some of whom couldn't run the software they wanted, and others who kept losing work or at least having to reboot their computers more than they should have had to.

The Windows 9x line culminated in Windows Me, which tacked some stability and restoration features on to the Windows 9x code base. NT culminated in Windows 2000 Professional, which featured increased compatibility with applications over NT (which wasn't saying all that much—many games still didn't run on Windows 2000 Professional), a smooth user interface, and usability enhancements.

Windows 2000 Professional was arguably the most stable operating system that Microsoft had produced until Windows XP came along. (Some old-timers reckoned Windows NT 3.51 was more stable.) But Windows 2000 Professional's stability came at a price: It had no interest in running any games or other demanding software that wouldn't conform to its stringent requirements. And while it was compatible with quite an impressive range of legacy hardware, many items still wouldn't work. Even up-to-date hardware could be problematic, especially if it connected via USB.

Since the late 1990s, Microsoft had been promising to deliver a consumer version of Windows that melded the stability of NT and the compatibility of Windows 9x. In Windows XP Home Edition, that version of Windows is finally here. According to Microsoft, Windows XP Professional is a strict superset of Home Edition, as well as of all the desktop clients that preceded Professional.

NOTE *A third flavor of Windows XP is planned for release in the not too distant future—Windows .NET Server. Windows .NET Server will do everything that Windows XP Professional does and will add a comprehensive set of tools for managing and administering a network. It is designed to run on a network file server or application server.*

What's New in Windows XP Professional?

This section outlines the most striking and appealing new features in Windows XP, starting with installation and upgrading, moving through the user interface and visible features, and ending up with the features hidden under the hood.

Some of these new features fall into convenient categories, and this section presents them in categories. Others don't; this section presents these features individually.

The "Evil" Windows Product Activation

The notion behind this controversial new feature of Windows XP is really rather simple—to prevent piracy. In a nutshell, Windows Product Activation (WPA) ties each copy of Windows XP to a specific computer. Although activation is mandatory, it is anonymous. Your Product Key is coupled to a computer hardware ID that is nonunique and cannot be traced back to a specific computer.

WPA is not the same as product registration, and you can take care of it over the Internet or by phone. After installation, you are asked if you want to activate the product. If you don't do it then, you'll have a certain number of days to do so. If you still haven't activated your copy of Windows XP within that time, you'll be able to boot the system, but you won't be able to get beyond the opening screen until you activate.

NOTE *Corporate users who purchase volume licenses for Windows XP don't have to worry about product activation. Their versions of Windows XP won't include Windows Product Activation.*

Easier Installation and Updating

Windows XP includes several features designed to make it easier to install and to keep up-to-date. These include Windows Update; the Files and Settings Transfer Wizard; more Wizards for a variety of tasks; a wider selection of device drivers; simplified installation for multifunction devices; and an effective way to uninstall and revert to your previous version of Windows.

WINDOWS UPDATE

Windows Update runs periodically after setup and offers to download the latest patches, packages, and fixes and install them so that your copy of Windows is as up-to-date, secure, and compatible as possible. (You can also run Windows Update manually whenever you want to.)

FILES AND SETTINGS TRANSFER WIZARD

Making its debut in Windows XP is the Files and Settings Transfer Wizard, a feature that Windows users have been demanding for a good 10 years. The Files and Settings Transfer Wizard provides a way of transferring designated files and settings from one computer to another or from one installation of Windows to another on the same computer. You'll still need to reinstall all your programs on the new computer or new installation of Windows, but you can transfer your data and a good amount of information about your work environment easily.

If you're migrating from an old computer to a new computer, or if you're installing Windows XP as a dual-boot with an existing version of Windows, you can use the Files and Settings Transfer Wizard to clone your existing Desktop and files and transfer them to the new computer or new version of Windows.

MORE WIZARDS TO MAKE TASKS EASIER

Windows XP includes a slew of Wizards designed to walk you through complicated processes (and some that aren't so complicated). Perhaps most welcome are the improvements to the Network Setup Wizard, which provides effective configuration of simple networks and Internet connection sharing, and the Add Hardware Wizard.

On the less useful front, Windows XP also includes Wizards such as the Desktop Cleanup Wizard, which pops out periodically like the neighborhood dog and tries to persuade you to let it herd the stray icons on your Desktop into a folder where they'll be available but less obtrusive. If you refuse, it wags its tail and goes away for a while.

MORE DEVICE DRIVERS

Windows XP comes complete with drivers for a large number of devices, including scanners, digital still cameras, digital video cameras, printers, and so on. So there's a better chance than with another version of Windows (say, Windows Me or Windows 2000) that when you plug in a new device, Windows XP will be able to load a driver for it and get it working without any fuss.

You'll probably want to take this improvement with a grain of salt. To enjoy the latest features and the best performance from a new device, you'll probably want to install the driver that comes with the device or (better) download the latest version from the manufacturer's Web site.

SIMPLIFIED INSTALLATION FOR MULTIFUNCTION DEVICES

Apart from having more drivers (as described in the previous section), Windows XP makes it easier to install multifunction devices—for example, a multifunction printer/scanner/fax device (the kind that people sometimes call "hydra" machines), a PC card that combines a network interface card with a modem, or a sound board with extra features.

Previous versions of Windows tended to recognize the component pieces of multifunction devices separately in sequence. If you installed a hydra, Windows would recognize the printer and demand the installation software for it. Once that was done, Windows would recognize the fax and demand the software for *that*. After that, it would recognize the scanner and suggest you might want to install yet more software. Windows XP improves on this social ineptitude by recognizing multifunction devices as such the first time you introduce it to them, and so it demands the installation software only once.

EFFECTIVE UNINSTALL BACK TO WINDOWS 98 AND WINDOWS ME

Windows XP Professional provides an effective uninstall feature for rolling back the Windows XP installation to your previous installation of Windows 98, Windows 98 Second Edition, and Windows Me. However, you can't revert to a previous installation of Windows NT 4 or Windows 2000 Professional.

Effective Multiuser Capabilities

Windows XP provides far better multiuser capabilities than Windows 9x and requires an existing account and password in order to log on. Like NT and Windows 2000, Windows XP provides features for preventing one user from seeing another user's files. Windows XP keeps each user's files separate so that no user can see another user's files unless they have been shared deliberately.

Windows XP goes further than NT and Windows 2000, though, in that it lets multiple users be logged on at the same time, each with applications running. Only one user can be actually *using* the computer, or can be *active*, in Windows XP parlance, at any one time, but the other user sessions continue running in the background (*disconnected*, in Windows XP parlance). When you've finished with the computer for the time being, you can log off Windows, just as you did in previous versions of Windows. Logging off closes all the applications you were using and frees up the memory they took up. But if you stop using the computer only temporarily, you may prefer to "switch user," which leaves your applications running but lets someone else use the computer in the interim. Further encouraging you to switch user, Windows' default screen saver setting is to display the Welcome screen after 15 minutes of inactivity, performing the equivalent of a Switch User command as it disconnects the user and leaves their session running hidden in the background.

Enhanced User Interface

Windows XP has a completely revamped user interface with a large number of visual enhancements and improved functionality. Some of the visual enhancements improve usability, while others are mere eye candy. But the overall effect is mostly easy to use and mostly looks good—and if you don't like the look, you can restore the "classic" Windows look with minimal effort.

The following sections discuss the main changes to the user interface.

REDESIGNED START MENU

Windows XP sports a redesigned Start menu that's supposedly easier and quicker to use. Whether you find it so depends on your experience with the Start menu in Windows 9x and Windows 2000. But don't worry if you like the "classic" Start menu—you can restore it easily enough with a few clicks of the mouse.

The Start menu appears as a panel containing two columns (shown in Figure 1.1). The right-hand column remains the same unless you customize it. The lower part of the left-hand column automatically reconfigures itself to show your most used applications. You can pin an item to the Start menu to prevent it from moving and keep it available.

As you can see in the figure, the current user's name appears in a bar across the top of the Start menu, and the Log Off button and Turn Off Computer button appear at the bottom of the menu.

FIGURE 1.1

The redesigned Start menu contains a static column of choices on the right and a variable column of choices on the left.

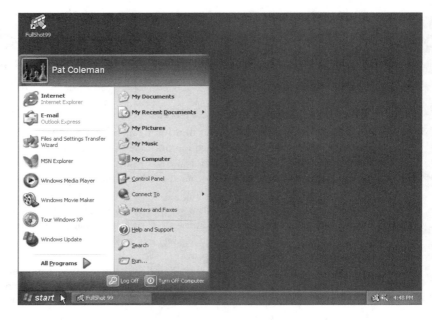

REDESIGNED CONTROL PANEL

Windows XP also has a redesigned Control Panel (shown in Figure 1.2) that presents Control Panel as categories of items and actions you can take with them.

FIGURE 1.2

Control Panel divides its bevy of icons into categories. You can use the Classic view to see all the icons at once.

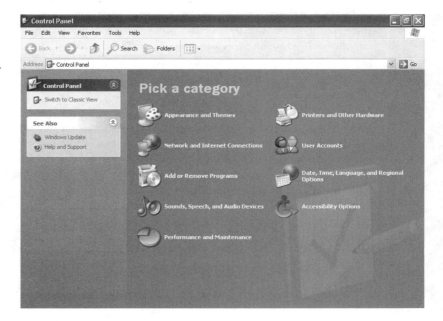

New users will likely find the Category view of Control Panel easy to use. Power users who are familiar with the regular manifestation of Control Panel in Windows 9*x*, Windows NT 4, and Windows 2000 will probably prefer to use the Classic view. (I know I do.)

EYE CANDY

To complement its highly graphical interface, Windows XP includes a dangerous amount of eye candy. Most people will like at least some of it. Some users will love it all. And no doubt some people will claim to detest every pixel of it.

The prime example of eye candy is the My Pictures Slideshow screen saver, which lets you set up an automated (or mouse-controlled) slideshow of designated pictures instead of a regular screen saver. This feature seems destined to be widely popular.

Less assured of a rapturous welcome are the staggering amounts of adornment in the interface, such as shadows under the mouse pointer and under menus, the color gradient in the title bar of windows, and the effect of sliding icons, controls, and Taskbar buttons. This overbearing emphasis on graphics places heavy demands on your graphics board and processor, and if your computer's hardware tends to the lukewarm rather than hot, you may find the eye candy exacts an unacceptable performance penalty. Microsoft has had the sense to let you set performance options to balance the demands of appearance against your need for performance, so you can turn off the least necessary effects and speed up your computer. (Chapter 21 discusses how to set performance options.)

Taskbar Changes and Enhancements

Windows XP includes a number of tweaks to the Taskbar. These seem designed for beginners, so if you're an experienced Windows user, you may find some good and others bad. Fortunately, you can change the Taskbar's behavior back to how it was in previous versions of Windows.

TASKBAR LOCKING

By default, the Taskbar is locked in Windows XP Professional. Presumably this is intended to prevent users from dragging their Taskbar to an inaccessible area at the edge of the screen. You can, however, easily unlock the Taskbar so that it can be resized or moved.

TASKBAR SCROLLING

If you read the previous paragraph, you probably started raising objections: If the Taskbar is a fixed size, the buttons for the running applications must become tiny and useless as soon as you've got 10 or more applications running.

Two other changes come into play here, of which the first is Taskbar scrolling. When the Taskbar is locked, it keeps the buttons bigger than a minimum size. To accommodate the buttons, it increases the depth of the Taskbar, but displays only its top row. On the displayed portion of the Taskbar, it puts scroll buttons so that you can scroll the Taskbar up and down one row of buttons at a time.

TASKBAR BUTTON GROUPING

The second change that makes Taskbar locking reasonable is Taskbar button grouping.

By default, Windows XP displays only one button per application on the Taskbar, whereas other versions of Windows displayed multiple buttons. For example, if you open nine Internet Explorer windows in Windows 98, it displays nine Internet Explorer buttons in the Taskbar. Having all these buttons can make it easy to find the window you want, but the buttons take up a lot of space (or each button on the Taskbar gets shrunk to a tiny size to fit them all in).

In Windows XP, if the application has multiple open windows, the Taskbar button displays the number of windows, the title of the current active window or last active window, and a drop-down arrow. To access one of the other open windows, click the Taskbar button. Windows displays a list of the windows by title. Select the window you want, and Windows displays it.

NOTIFICATION AREA

By default, Windows XP Professional collapses the notification area (formerly known as the *system tray* or the *status area*) so that only the icons you've used most recently are displayed.

Better Audio and Video Features

Windows XP includes a slew of new features and improvements for audio and video. These include a new version of Windows Media Player, better features for grabbing and handling images from digital input devices such as scanners and cameras, and Windows Movie Maker, a modest video-editing application.

WINDOWS MEDIA PLAYER VERSION 8

Front and center among the improved audio and video features of Windows XP is Windows Media Player version 8, which combines a video and DVD player, a CD player, an Internet radio tuner, and a jukebox for playing and organizing digital-audio files such as Windows Media Audio (WMA) files and MP3 files. Windows Media Player 8 comes with a number of visually interesting skins (graphical looks) that you can apply at will, and you can even create your own skins if you have the time and talent to invest.

All in all, Windows Media Player 8 is a huge improvement over the 98-pound weakling version of Windows Media Player shipped with all previous versions of Windows except Windows Me. (Me included Windows Media Player 7, which offered many of the features of version 8.) Windows Media Player can even burn audio CDs at the full speed of your CD-R or CD-RW drive.

MY MUSIC FOLDER AND MY PICTURES FOLDER

Like several of its predecessors, Windows XP uses custom folders for music (the My Music folder) and pictures (the My Pictures folder). Again like its predecessors, it tries none too subtly to persuade you to save your music in these folders. But Windows XP goes further, in that it makes these folders much more useful than they were in earlier versions of Windows.

The My Music folder and the My Pictures folder present customized lists of actions you can take with music files and picture files. Some of these actions tend to the commercial—for example, the Order Prints Online link in the Picture Tasks list, and the Shop for Music Online link in the Music Tasks list. But others are solidly useful—for example, the Play All link in the Music Tasks list, which lets you play all the music in a folder without spelunking into it, or the View As a Slide Show link in the Picture Tasks list, which lets you set a whole folder of pictures running as a slide show with a single click.

Not surprisingly, the My Music folder works hand-in-hand (or is it glove?) with Windows Media Player. Windows Media Player is definitely happy for you to keep your music in the My Music folder, though it will let you keep it elsewhere as well. Better yet, Windows Media Player's features for cataloging music tracks are flexible enough to keep track of music files even when you move them from one folder to another.

The My Pictures folder works closely with Windows Image Acquisition, Image Preview, and Paint (all three of which are discussed in the next section). The folder includes a slideshow applet and a filmstrip view, and it can publish your pictures to the Web.

BETTER IMAGE ACQUISITION AND HANDLING

Windows XP provides strong features for capturing images from scanners, still cameras, and video cameras. It also provides better throughput for video streams, though unless you had a duplicate computer running an older version of Windows to use as a benchmark, you could be forgiven for failing to go into raptures over the improvement. Less cynically, the improvement in throughput is unquestionably a good thing, and on decent hardware, Windows XP delivers adequate to impressive video performance; but the chances of your confusing your PC with your GameCube remain poor.

One of the central tools for image acquisition and handling is the Scanner and Camera Wizard. This Wizard has a variety of duties, including transferring image files from still cameras and digital media (for example, CompactFlash cards and SmartMedia cards) to the computer. Most of its capabilities stay on the useful side of the esoteric. For example, you can scan multiple pages into a single image file, an ability that can come in handy in both home and business settings.

Windows XP provides some basic tools for handling still images. As mentioned, the My Pictures folder acts as a default repository for images and provides some basic image-handling abilities, such as rotating an image. The Image Preview feature lets you examine an image (and annotate a fax). And Paint, the basic image-manipulation and drawing package that's been included with Windows since Windows 3.*x*, has been beefed up as well. Paint can now open—and save—JPEG, GIF, TIFF, and PNG images as well as Windows bitmap (BMP) files, making it about five times as useful as before.

WINDOWS MOVIE MAKER

Windows XP includes Windows Movie Maker, a basic package for capturing video, editing video and audio, and creating video files in the Windows Media format. You won't find yourself making the next *Timecode* or *Traffic* with Windows Movie Maker, but it's good enough for home-video editing. You can also create video slide shows with still images for those family occasions on rainy weekends or holidays.

CD Burning

Windows XP comes with built-in CD-burning capabilities. You can burn CDs from an Explorer window with minimal effort. You can also burn CDs directly from Windows Media Player, which lets you easily create CDs containing music files.

Compressed Folders

Windows XP has built-in support for compressed folders in both the ubiquitous Zip format and the Microsoft Cabinet (CAB) format. You can create Zip folders containing one or more files or folders. Better still, you can view the contents of a Zip or CAB folder seamlessly in Explorer as if it were a regular folder.

Search Companion

Windows XP includes Search Companion, an enhanced search feature for finding information both on your PC and in the wider world. You can use Search Companion to search for files, for computers or people online, or for information in Help and Support Center. Search Companion brokers the search requests that you enter and farms them out to the appropriate search mechanisms.

You can choose between having Search Companion appear in a straightforward and unexceptional window and having it manifest itself using one of various animated characters reminiscent of the Office Assistant.

Easy Publishing to the Web

Windows XP makes it easier to publish files or folders to a Web site by using a Web-hosting service. Windows XP includes a feature called Web Digital Authoring and Versioning (WebDAV for short) that lets you save information to the Web from any application rather than having to use the regular Web-publishing protocols.

A Sane Implementation of Autoplay

If you've used Windows 9x, NT 4, or Windows 2000, you'll know all about the Autoplay feature and how it used to drive people crazy. You remember Autoplay—the moment you insert a CD, it starts playing the music from it or installing any software it contains. By default, Autoplay was enabled, so you had to switch it off (or override it by holding down the Shift key while closing the CD tray) to prevent it from occurring.

Windows XP includes a new version of Autoplay that's improved in several ways. First, you can customize it. Second, you can configure it to take different actions depending on what the CD (or other medium) contains. For example, you might want Windows to play your audio CDs automatically when you insert them (okay, you don't—but you *might*), or you might want Windows to display a slideshow automatically when you insert a CD containing nothing but pictures.

What's that about "other medium"? That's the third thing: In Windows XP, Autoplay works for CDs, DVDs, assorted flash cards (including CompactFlash, Memory Stick, and Smart Media), PC Cards, Zip and other removable disk drives, and FireWire hot-plug external drives.

More Games

Windows XP includes more games than previous versions of Windows. Some of these are single-player games (for example, Spider Solitaire). Others are multiplayer games that you can play across the Internet via MSN's Zone.com Web site.

Remote Desktop Connection

Windows XP Professional includes Remote Desktop Connection, a technology that lets you use your computer to access a remote computer (for example, your computer at the office) that's running Windows XP Professional. Once you've connected to the remote computer, you can control it as if you were sitting at it.

A More Useful Winkey

A what? "Winkey," pronounced "Win-key" rather than as the diminutive of "wink," is the Windows key on the keyboard—the key with the Windows logo. Most keyboards have one or two Winkeys, usually located next to the Alt or Ctrl keys.

Windows XP includes more functionality for the Winkey. You can still press the Winkey to open or close the Start menu, but you can also use it in a number of key combinations. For example, pressing Winkey+M issues a Minimize All command, and pressing Winkey+Shift+M issues an Undo Minimize All command.

For the full list of Winkey combinations, see the section "Using the Winkey" in Chapter 3.

Improvements for Portable Computers

Windows XP includes several improvements for portable computers.

First, Windows XP supports processor power control, which lets the computer make use of features in chips such as Intel's SpeedStep, in which the processor runs at full speed when the computer is plugged into the main power supply (or told that it's plugged in) but at a lower speed to save power when it's running on battery power (or told that it is).

Throttling back the processor like this reduces the computer's power usage a bit, improving battery life, but in most portables, the screen consumes far more power than the processor. Windows XP also targets the screen, providing a couple of features designed to reduce power use when the computer is running on battery power. First, Windows XP turns off the display when the user closes the computer's lid, on the basis that the user probably isn't looking at the display. Second, it runs the screen at a dimmer brightness when the computer is running off the battery. The cynical among you will point out that most sentient portables implement both these functions already in hardware. Still, it shouldn't do any harm to have Windows help out for the manufacturers who design their machines a little less carefully.

Windows XP also includes some other less obvious visual enhancements, such as support for ClearType, a Microsoft text-display technology that improves the look of fonts on LCD screens that have digital interfaces. While these screens aren't strictly confined to portables, that's where the bulk of the market is.

Faxing

Windows XP Professional contains a built-in fax client that's more than adequate for most home needs and many home office needs. You can send faxes from any application that supports printing and you can specify whether to print out incoming faxes automatically or store them in a folder. You can even configure different fax/modems to take different roles. For example, if you use faxes extensively, you might want to keep separate incoming and outgoing fax lines. You'll need a modem for each of the phone lines involved, but that's about as difficult as it gets.

More Help

Windows XP delivers more Help—and more different types of Help—than any other version of Windows. If you've searched fruitlessly for information in the past, you'll be aware that Windows' Help files have never exactly delivered the ultimate in user satisfaction. Digging information out of Help often felt so difficult that if you knew Windows well enough to find Help on the right topic, you could probably solve the problem without Help's assistance.

Windows XP takes a new approach to Help. There are Help files on your hard drive still, but they're integrated into an application called Help and Support Center. Help and Support Center not only works with the Help files but also with the Microsoft Knowledge Base (a database of support queries) and other online sources of information. For example, if you run a query within Help and Support Center to find information on hardware, it might return some information from local files, some information from the Microsoft Web site, and some information from hardware manufacturers' Web sites, all packaged into one window so that you can access them conveniently.

Help and Support Center also provides a gateway to other areas of support, including Microsoft Assisted Support and Support Communities, and to applications that you can use to get help from other users (such as Remote Assistance) and troubleshoot your computer (such as System Configuration Utility and System Restore).

The following sections discuss some of the Help and Support Center features.

MICROSOFT ONLINE ASSISTED SUPPORT

Windows XP's Microsoft Online Assisted Support feature lets you automatically collect information on a problem you're having and submit it to Microsoft electronically. A Microsoft technician then sends a solution, which appears as a pop-up in your notification area. You can read the response in the Help and Support Center window and apply the wisdom it contains to fix the problem.

Microsoft Online Assisted Support is designed to bypass the problems inherent with tech support via phone call, namely: that it's difficult for the user to tell the Help technician what's wrong with their computer; that it's even harder for the technician to get a good idea of what's going wrong without knowing a fair bit of technical information about the computer; and that waiting on hold for tech support is nobody's idea of fun, especially if you're paying for any part of the privilege.

SUPPORT COMMUNITIES

Instead of contacting a Microsoft technician via Microsoft Online Assisted Support, you can try to get support from one of the Windows Newsgroups, which are Microsoft-hosted newsgroups dedicated to Windows.

REMOTE ASSISTANCE

Remote Assistance is an ingenious feature by which you can get assistance from a friend or other knowledgeable person remotely by computer.

Here's the brief version of how Remote Assistance works. You send out an invitation file via e-mail or via Windows Messenger instant messaging. Your helper receives the invitation and responds to it. Remote Assistance sets up a secure connection between their computer and yours, using a password to verify their identity. Your helper can then view your screen remotely and chat with you (via text chat and voice). If you trust your helper, you can even let them control your computer so that they can take actions directly.

TOOLS SECTION

Help and Support Center includes a Tools section that gives you quick access to information about your computer (My Computer Information and Advanced System Information) and its configuration (System Configuration Utility), network diagnostic tools (Network Diagnostics), the System Restore feature, and more. In addition to the tools that Microsoft makes available in the Tools section, OEMs can add tools of their own, so you may also find custom tools provided by your computer manufacturer.

Many of the tools accessible through the Tools section are also accessible in other ways through the Windows interface. For example, Windows XP includes an improved version of Disk Defragmenter, which you can use to keep your hard disk from becoming fragmented (fragmentation decreases performance). You can run Disk Defragmenter from the Tools section, but you can also run it from the System Tools submenu of the Start menu (Choose Start ➢ All Programs ➢ Accessories ➢ System Tools ➢ Disk Defragmenter.); you can also schedule Disk Defragmenter to run automatically at convenient times.

FIXING A PROBLEM TOOL

Help and Support Center includes an area called Fixing a Problem that contains a number of troubleshooters for walking you through the steps of diagnosing and curing various common problems. Fixing a Problem isn't a panacea, but it's a good place to start, and it can save you a call to a guru or even a trip to your local computer shop.

DEVICE DRIVER REFERRAL SITE

Help and Support Center contains a system for referring searches for drivers that don't come with Windows or with the hardware device. When you plug in a new hardware device, and Windows finds that it doesn't have a driver for it and you can't supply a driver, Windows invites you to send information about the hardware to Microsoft. Once you've sent the information, you can take a variety of actions depending on what information is available. For example, you might be able to view a list of compatible devices (if any), search for information on compatible devices or Knowledge Base articles about the hardware, or find a link to the vendor's Web site.

OTHER HELP IMPROVEMENTS

Help and Support Center includes assorted other Help improvements that can save you time. For example, you can print out a whole chapter of Help information at once instead of having to slog through it screen by screen. And you can open multiple Help and Support Center windows at the same time. This makes it easier to pursue different avenues of exploration for the information you need. When you find useful information, you can create a favorite for it so that you can access it quickly again at need.

Network Connectivity

Windows XP provides various improvements in network connectivity, from creating a home or office network to joining a computer to two separate networks. There are also great improvements in Internet connectivity, discussed in the next section.

NETWORK SETUP WIZARD

The Network Setup Wizard simplifies the process of creating a network, sharing printers, Internet connections, and other resources, and configuring protocols and security.

ALTERNATIVE TCP/IP CONFIGURATION

Windows XP provides an alternative TCP/IP configuration that allows you to connect to a network that has a DHCP server and to a network that doesn't without changing your TCP/IP settings. For example, you might use a laptop at work (where the network has a DHCP server) and at home (where your network doesn't).

NETWORK BRIDGING

Windows XP's network-bridging capability lets you use a computer with two or more network adapters to join two separate networks. You're perhaps unlikely to have two (or more) networks at home or in a small office—unless you have a wired network to which you've added a wireless component to provide roaming capabilities for some of the computers.

Internet Connectivity and Web Browsing

Windows XP provides a number of enhanced features for Internet connectivity and Web browsing, from favorites for Internet connections through to a new version of Internet Explorer.

INTERNET CONNECTION FAVORITES

Windows XP lets you create favorites for your Internet connections. By using favorites, you can switch easily from one Internet connection to another. This is a great time-saver if you use multiple ISPs or (perhaps more likely) travel frequently and need to use different dial-up numbers from different locations.

INTERNET CONNECTION SHARING AND INTERNET CONNECTION FIREWALL

Like Windows 98 Second Edition, Windows Me, and Windows 2000, Windows XP includes an Internet Connection Sharing feature that lets you share an Internet connection on one computer with one or more networked computers. Windows XP's version of Internet Connection Sharing has some tweaks, such as that you can disconnect the shared Internet connection from another PC if necessary—for example, if you need to use the phone line that the connection is using. Windows XP includes a Quality of Service Packet Scheduler that works to optimize the utilization of a shared Internet connection.

Internet Connection Sharing is a great convenience, particularly if you have a high-speed connection such as a DSL or a cable modem—but it lays your network open to assault from the Internet. Windows XP goes one better than its predecessors by including a personal firewall (called Internet Connection Firewall) to protect the Internet connection (whether shared or not).

New Version of Internet Explorer

Windows XP includes Internet Explorer 6, the latest version of Internet Explorer. Even if you feel you've already had it up to there with new versions of Internet Explorer, stifle your impatience, because Internet Explorer 6 offers a number of welcome innovations, including the following:

◆ You can save images, music, and videos more easily to your computer.

◆ The new Media bar makes it easier to listen to streaming audio directly in Internet Explorer.

◆ Internet Explorer provides better handling of cookies and digital certificates for securing information transfer and authenticating content.

◆ Internet Explorer can automatically resize an image you've displayed directly. If you've ever used Internet Explorer to open a digital photo and found it displayed bigger than your screen so that you could see only part of it, you may appreciate this feature. (But you'd be better off opening the photo in Paint in the first place.)

◆ Internet Explorer 6 has more integrated functionality for handling different file types. This won't strike you over the head; you'll simply find that more file types open without your being prodded to download and install extra components. For example, Internet Explorer 6 has built-in support for Macromedia Flash and Shockwave animations and support for Cascading Style Sheets Level 1 (CSS1). The net result is that more animations will play without your needing to add software, and documents formatted with CSS1 style sheets will be displayed as their authors intended. (They may still look horrible, but at least you'll know that they're meant to look that way.)

MSN Explorer

Windows XP includes MSN Explorer, an Internet client dedicated to MSN. If you don't have an ISP, you may want to use MSN Explorer to connect to the Internet.

Multiple Monitor Support—for Both Desktops and Laptops

Several versions of Windows have had multiple monitor support for desktops: By installing two or more graphics cards, each hooked up to a monitor, you can spread your Desktop across two or more monitors, giving you far more space to view multiple applications. Windows XP Professional includes multiple monitor support like its predecessors. Windows XP Professional also includes a new technology called DualView, which lets you hook up two monitors to a single graphics card that supports two interfaces. Relatively few AGP and PCI graphics cards support two interfaces, though you'll find a number of cards with digital outputs (for LCD panels) that have a regular VGA connection as well.

Most of the excitement here is for laptops, most of which have a connector for an external display as well as the internal connector for the built-in screen. Instead of using the external display to display the same image as the built-in screen, you can use DualView to make the external display an extension of your Desktop. This is a wonderful feature for laptop users who crave more screen space.

Advanced Features

Just so you know, most of the new features I've described so far apply to both Windows XP Professional and Windows XP Home. Those that follow are specific to Professional.

BACKUP AND AUTOMATED SYSTEM RECOVERY (ASR)

Windows XP Professional includes a Backup utility and an Automated System Recovery (ASR) feature that can be activated from bootup to restore a damaged system.

OFFLINE FILES

Offline files let you cache (store) copies of files located on network drives on your local drive so that you can work with them when your computer is no longer connected to the network. Windows XP Professional can encrypt the Offline Files database to help keep the information in the files secure.

REMOTE DESKTOP

Remote Desktop is a little confusing because of the terminology. The Remote Desktop component lets you make a computer available for remote control. The Remote Desktop Connection component lets you use a computer to access a remote computer that's running Remote Desktop. Both Professional and Home have Remote Desktop Connection. So you can use a computer running Home to access a computer running Professional, but not the other way around. If you need to be able to connect to your computer remotely via Remote Desktop Connection, you need Professional rather than Home.

NETWORKING FEATURES

Windows XP Professional has many networking features, including the Simple Network Management Protocol (SNMP), the Client Services for NetWare, Simple TCP/IP Services, and the Multiple Roaming feature. If you need to connect to a NetWare server, or if you need to use roaming profiles, you'll need Windows XP Professional rather than Windows XP Home.

NOTE   *One other thing—there will be a 64-bit version of Windows XP Professional for the Intel Itanium processor.*

IMPROVED SYSPREP

SYSPREP is a tool used to prepare a system for drive imaging. It allows you to make a complete image of a hard drive and load it onto another system, thus facilitating the installation of the operating system on a large number of computers. In Windows XP Professional, SYSPREP has been modified so that you can more quickly and efficiently install the operating system on multiple computers. These modifications reduce startup and imaging time and minimize restarts.

What's Hiding under the Hood?

The features mentioned so far catch the eye—some even on a cursory scan of the Windows XP Desktop and interface.

Less glamorous, but more important in the long run, are the enhancements hiding under Windows XP's hood. This section discusses the major enhancements that you probably *won't* see.

PROTECTED MEMORY MANAGEMENT

Windows XP offers fully protected memory management. With protected memory management, Windows XP can handle memory errors with more aplomb. When an application tries to access memory that doesn't belong to it, Windows XP can close the application without affecting any other running application. You still lose any unsaved work in the guilty application, but all your other applications continue running.

While Windows XP is dealing with the misbehaving application, you can move the application's window so that it doesn't obstruct your view of any other applications you have open.

SYSTEM FILE PROTECTION

Windows XP offers a feature called System File Protection that protects your system files from ill-advised actions on your part.

Windows XP tries to persuade you not to view the contents of folders that you probably shouldn't be messing with by refusing to show them to you until you demand it display them. You can then delete system files if you want (except for any file that's actively in use, which is locked automatically). But the next time that Windows boots, or if it catches the damage you've done before you reboot it, it replaces the files you deleted without notifying you.

SYSTEM RESTORE

Windows XP offers a System Restore feature similar to but more effective than the System Restore feature in Windows Me. System Restore automatically creates restore points both periodically and each time you make a change to the system—for example, by installing an application or a driver. When one of your changes leads to an unwelcome result, such as your computer failing to boot, you can use System Restore to roll back the change to an earlier point at which the system was working properly.

DEVICE DRIVER ROLLBACK

Device drivers have long been the bane of Windows—okay, *one* of the banes of Windows. By installing the wrong driver, or a buggy driver, you could render your computer useless until you reinstalled Windows (or turned in frustration to another operating system).

Windows XP tracks the drivers you install and lets you roll back the installation of the driver—in other words, you can revert to the driver you were using before.

Better yet, Windows XP stores details of the previous driver in what's called the Last Known Good Configuration—the configuration used the last time the computer seemed to be running okay. This means that if installing a new driver prevents your computer from booting as normal, you can boot into Safe mode and use the Last Known Good Configuration to restore the previous driver.

COMPATIBILITY WITH WINDOWS 9x APPLICATIONS

Windows XP aims to be able to run all applications that would run on Windows 9x, Windows NT, and Windows 2000. As you'll know if you've struggled to run a Windows 9x application on NT or Windows 2000, this is quite a challenge. NT-based operating systems (including Windows XP) handle memory and hardware access in a different way than Windows 9x operating systems. These differences mean that applications designed for Windows 9x often won't run satisfactorily on NT and Windows 2000.

Being able to run these legacy applications is a big feature of Windows XP—but because Microsoft has implemented this feature very successfully, it remains hidden most of the time. Usually, you can simply install a legacy application and run it without complications. Behind the scenes, Windows XP may be running the application in its Compatibility mode or applying one of its new AppFixes to the application (to prevent it from detecting the wrong operating system and from causing problems such as referencing memory once it's been freed up), but you often won't know about it. You may need to specifically run some applications in Compatibility Mode, and you may see Windows Update automatically downloading new information for AppFixes to keep your copy of Windows up-to-date, but most of the time your old applications will simply work—which of course is the way it should be.

Should You Upgrade to Windows XP Professional?

Whether you should upgrade to Windows XP Professional depends on your needs, how well your current version of Windows is fulfilling them, and whether your hardware is up to the test. The decision is wholly yours (of course), but the following sections offer some suggestions, depending on where you're coming from.

Windows 9x

If you're using one of the versions of Windows 9x—Windows 95, Windows 98, Windows 98 Second Edition, or Windows Me—the main attractions of Windows XP Professional are much greater stability, the enhanced user interface, the extra features that Windows XP includes, and security.

Exactly which extra features Windows XP includes depends—obviously enough—on which version of Windows 9x you have. Not surprisingly, later versions of Windows 9x offer more features than earlier versions. For example, the Internet Connection Sharing feature debuted in Windows 98 Second Edition, so ICS might be a reason to upgrade to Windows XP if you have Windows 95 or Windows 98 (first edition), but not if you have Windows 98 Second Edition or Windows Me. (The Internet Connection Firewall feature, however, is new.) Likewise, Windows Me includes Windows Media Player 7, a version that greatly improved on the earlier, anemic versions of Windows Media Player but isn't as capable as Windows Media Player 8, the version included in Windows XP. From Windows Me, the new version of Windows Media Player provides only a modest incitement to upgrade, whereas from earlier versions of Windows 9x, it provides much more encouragement—assuming you're interested in multimedia, that is.

Whichever version of Windows 9x you're using, you'll need to make sure that your hardware is up to scratch for Windows XP. Very generally speaking, if your computer is capable of running Windows 98 or Windows Me at a decent clip, it should be able to run Windows XP without much trouble (though you might need to add memory). You'll find details of Windows XP's hardware requirements in Chapter 2.

Windows 3.1

If you're still using Windows 3.1 and DOS as your main operating system, Windows XP Professional represents a considerable upgrade. There are two major considerations in taking this step:

◆ First, unless you've installed Windows 3.1 on a modern system (as you might have done for backward compatibility with ancient applications), you'll almost certainly need to get a new PC to run Windows XP.

◆ Second, if you will need to continue running DOS applications and 16-bit Windows applications (rather than upgrading to 32-bit applications that provide similar functionality), check to make sure that these applications are compatible with Windows XP before upgrading. As mentioned earlier, Windows XP runs older 32-bit Windows applications quite impressively, but it has problems with some 16-bit applications.

Windows 2000 Professional

If you're currently using Windows 2000 Professional and are happy with it, stick with it for the time being. The "natural" upgrade path from Windows 2000 Professional is to Windows XP Professional, but make this upgrade only after carefully evaluating the benefits that Windows XP Professional will provide. If Windows 2000 Professional is currently fulfilling all your computing needs, stick with it.

Intended Usage

As its name suggests (and is designed to suggest), Windows XP Professional is geared toward use in a "professional" setting—for example, in an office or in a corporate setting. That doesn't mean you can't use it at home if you want, just that it has features designed for use in office and corporate settings. For example, it's designed to connect to Windows 2000 servers running Active Directory, and it has features for being managed remotely by administrators.

How Is Windows XP Professional Different from Other Operating Systems?

I've discussed the differences and advantages of Windows 2000 Professional compared with Windows 95/98, but how does it stack up against other popular operating systems?

Windows XP Professional Compared with OS/2

Both Windows XP Professional and OS/2 are 32-bit operating systems that also run 16-bit Windows applications and DOS applications in separate memory addresses. In terms of robustness, Windows XP Professional and OS/2 are on about even footing. Past that, OS/2 gets left in the dust. OS/2 is not a secure environment, and it lacks native networking capability—you must buy additional software so OS/2 can talk to its network brethren. Furthermore, it won't run 32-bit Windows applications. Because only about three native OS/2 applications are available, this is a serious shortcoming.

Windows XP Professional Compared with Unix

Of all the operating systems under discussion here, Unix is probably the most similar to Windows XP Professional in terms of architecture. There are many different flavors of Unix, however. Each flavor has a different user interface, and not all of them are graphical. As a group, Unix operating systems are 32-bit, secure, and capable of running on Intel, RISC, and DEC Alpha processors.

In the past, artists and designers have used high-end Unix-based workstations to create special effects for films. Windows XP Professional, however, supports high-end 3-D protocols such as Raydream. Running Windows XP Professional on a high-powered *x*86 processor such as the Pentium Pro or Pentium II or III will give you equal processing power to those Unix workstations, with the added punch of Windows XP Professional, for a fraction of the price. And running Windows XP Professional on a high-end Pentium IV processor will pretty much leave every other workstation in the dust.

Windows XP Professional Compared with the Macintosh OS

Like Windows XP Professional, the Macintosh operating system (OS) is a 32-bit environment with built-in networking capabilities. Despite its well-known and intuitive interface, the Macintosh OS lacks many of the powerful features found in Windows XP Professional. Object linking and embedding (OLE), MAPI, and TAPI are all unfamiliar to Apple users. The Mac OS supports only a limited sort of cooperative multitasking, and you can switch between programs only with the mouse; there's no equivalent to the mighty Alt+Tab key combination in Windows. There is also a relatively limited amount of software available to the Macintosh market as compared with the Windows market.

What Are the Features of Windows XP Professional Architecture?

I've already discussed some of the Windows XP Professional architecture. In this section, I'll analyze it a little more closely to see what makes Windows XP Professional tick and why it is different from other operating systems.

From a programmer's perspective, Windows XP Professional is divided into two layers. These are actually two separate operating modes. The *kernel mode* is where Windows XP Professional performs its internal tasks and controls interaction between programs and the operating system, and between programs themselves. It is generally protected from end users fiddling with it. The *user mode*, which is usually described as sitting above the kernel mode because it is closer to the end user, is where your applications run. The area is considered nonprotected because you have access to it through your applications.

Kernel Mode

Nothing happens in the Windows XP Professional universe without the operating system knowing about it and giving its blessing. The kernel is the core of Windows XP Professional. It acts as a "gofer" between the operating system and the computer's processor. As such, it is responsible for scheduling all the operating system's interactions with your computer. The kernel also manages all the interrelationships between the different kernel mode operations. It does this by means of *threads*. A thread is a series of instructions that are attached to a command that is executed by a program. Threads include memory addresses, scheduling for the amount of time the process will take, and anything else that describes the process.

The kernel mode is divided into three subsections: the HAL, the kernel, and Executive Services. Executive Services is subdivided further into its own component parts; more on those parts shortly.

THE HAL AND THE KERNEL

The HAL (hardware abstraction layer) controls the interaction between the kernel and the system hardware. One of the design goals of Windows XP Professional was the capability to be easily ported from one type of computer to another. To this end, the HAL *abstracts* the hardware from the kernel so that the kernel does not need to know what type of hardware is installed in the computer. This extends to running multiple processors in your computer. Windows XP Professional is one of the only PC-based operating systems that can take advantage of symmetric multiprocessing. The abstraction provided by the HAL gives Windows XP Professional greater stability.

Because of the abstraction provided by the HAL, software that attempts to directly access the hardware is not permitted to run. The HAL, working with the kernel, stops those programs dead in their tracks. For performance reasons, many DOS programs—particularly games—use direct hardware access. Programs written for Windows XP Professional don't need to worry about how to access the hardware; they just ask the operating system for support, and Windows XP Professional takes care of the rest.

Windows XP Professional does have some communication that bypasses the HAL and goes directly to the hardware. In each of these cases, the communication is between the Executive Services and the individual drivers for hardware devices such as the video card and network card. But the concept of hardware abstraction is still maintained.

EXECUTIVE SERVICES

Executive Services is a set of separate components that complete the underpinnings of the Windows XP Professional kernel mode. Each Executive Service controls a specific function. The following is a brief overview of each of those functions.

I/O Manager

I/O Manager handles all communication between your applications and your hard disk. Additionally, it manages drivers for different file formats (FAT, NTFS) and keeps the Windows XP Professional kernel informed of the hard drive's status. I/O Manager also manages network cards and modems. In short, this manager controls any device that delivers data to or from the computer. Its components are illustrated in Figure 1.3.

FIGURE 1.3

I/O Manager is built to simultaneously control multiple devices and drivers.

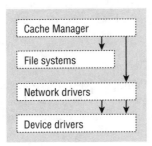

I/O Manager is divided into the following sections:

Cache Manager   Monitors your use of disk cache and disk pages.

File systems   Manages the file systems you have installed on your computer.

Network drivers   Controls your network cards and network protocols.

Device drivers   Manages the hardware you have in your computer. This includes everything from your hard drive(s) and modem to your keyboard and mouse.

Object Manager

Object Manager manages all the system objects that are used by Windows XP Professional. An object is a piece of data used by the operating system to create system events. Objects are acted upon by processes. Every object has a handle (yes, that's the technical term) that a process connects to in order to complete its job. The Object Manager is extensible, meaning that it can be expanded and added to as new object types are developed.

Security Reference Monitor

Security Reference Monitor is the "watchdog" for Windows XP Professional. Security Reference Monitor assigns security tokens and authenticates users each time they execute a task.

Process Manager

Process Manager is the complement to Object Manager. Process Manager manages the creation and deletion of processes. A *process* is a set of threads combined with a memory address and the necessary objects needed to complete a system task. The Process Manager works in conjunction with the Security Reference Monitor to ensure that every process is assigned a security token.

Local Procedure Call Facility

Local Procedure Call facility acts as a negotiator between user mode and kernel mode. From an internal standpoint, Windows XP Professional uses a client-server model to administer itself. Just as Windows XP Professional connects to a server and requests services from it, the Windows XP Professional user mode requests services from the Windows XP Professional kernel mode. Those requests are handled by local procedure calls. Local procedure calls are also used in standard client-server networks.

Virtual Memory Manager

Virtual Memory Manager oversees how Windows XP Professional uses virtual memory. To increase the amount of usable memory space, Windows XP Professional uses hard-disk space as memory when it runs out of memory (which can happen fairly quickly with some high-powered programs). The disk memory is known as *virtual* memory.

Win32K and GDI

The Win32K and Graphics Device Interface (GDI) are the graphics subsystem of Windows XP Professional. The graphics functions in earlier versions of Windows NT were provided by the Win32 subsystem in user mode. Microsoft moved the graphics subsystem into Executive Services for version 4 to give the graphics functions a performance boost. In fact, this resulted in the single greatest increase in the apparent speed of Windows NT 4.

User Mode

In the Windows XP Professional user mode, each of your programs runs in a separate memory space, an arrangement that protects each program from the others in case one should crash. This is true for 32-bit and 16-bit programs, both Windows and DOS.

The user mode is divided into subsystems. Each subsystem handles a different type of application and can report directly to the kernel mode. The subsystems are described briefly in Table 1.1.

TABLE 1.1: USER MODE SUBSYSTEMS

SUBSYSTEM	DESCRIPTION
Win32	Administers 32-bit and 16-bit Windows programs.
OS/2	Administers character-based OS/2 programs.
POSIX	Administers POSIX programs, which are Unix hybrids that can be run on any POSIX-compliant system, including Windows XP Professional. They are written to a series of application programming interfaces (APIs) that are platform independent. They control interaction with system components such as hard drives and memory.
Security	Administers system security and manages security tokens, monitors, and passwords. The user mode portion of the Security subsystem runs only during a user logon.

In addition to the subsystems noted in Table 1.1, user mode may also contain VDMs (video display metafiles). A VDM simulates a computer running MS-DOS 5, with 16MB of RAM and conventional, expanded, and extended memory. As stated earlier in this chapter, this simulation makes it possible to run MS-DOS programs on Windows XP Professional. It also enables you to run 16-bit Windows applications by simulating Windows 3.1 running on that MS-DOS computer with 16MB of memory. By default, Windows XP Professional starts all 16-bit Windows applications in the same Win16 on Win32 or *WOW* environment. This simulates exactly the environment the programs were written to operate in under Windows 3.1. However, Windows XP Professional gives you the ability to start the application in a separate memory space, which creates another WOW for each 16-bit Windows application.

Remember that the WOW environment imitates Windows 3.1 so well that it even hangs just like the old Windows did! That means that if one of your 16-bit Windows applications crashes, it will take all the other 16-bit applications with it—unless you have chosen to start them in their own memory spaces, in which case the other 16-bit programs will keep running without a problem.

TIP   *If a 16-bit application crashes, it will also crash any other program running in the same memory space. If this happens, you can stop the WOW by using Task Manager and restart the 16-bit program. All 32-bit applications will be unaffected by the crash and continue to run normally.*

Summary

This chapter has discussed what you need to know about Windows XP Professional in order to decide whether to upgrade to it or stay with your current version of Windows.

Chapter 2

Installing Windows XP Professional (and Automating Installation)

THIS CHAPTER DISCUSSES HOW to install Windows XP Professional in each of the three ways in which you may want to install it: as an upgrade to Windows 9x, Windows NT, or Windows 2000 Professional; as a new installation on a computer that already has installed an operating system that you want to keep; and as a clean installation on a computer that doesn't have an operating system installed (or a computer whose operating system you want to wipe).

At the end of the chapter, you'll find a discussion of how to perform an unattended installation, which can be useful if you need to install the same operating system multiple times.

◆ Making sure your computer can run Windows XP Professional

◆ Choosing a method of installing Windows XP Professional

◆ Preparing for installation

◆ Upgrading Windows 9x or Windows 2000 Professional to Windows XP

◆ Performing a new installation of Windows XP Professional

◆ Performing a clean installation of Windows XP Professional

◆ Using the Files and Settings Transfer Wizard to transfer files and settings

◆ Uninstalling Windows XP Professional and reverting to Windows 9x

◆ Removing your old version of Windows

◆ Keeping Windows updated

◆ Automating the installation of Windows XP

The Order of Business

Here's the order of business for installing Windows XP successfully:

1. First, make sure that your computer will be able to run Windows XP Professional. Start by comparing your system specifications with the minimum requirements, and see if you need to upgrade any components.

2. Then, assuming your computer has an operating system loaded already, load the Windows XP CD in your computer and run the Windows Upgrade Advisor.

3. If you want to perform a clean installation of Windows XP rather than an upgrade, but you want your new installation to pick up your current settings and some of your files, run the Files and Settings Transfer Wizard to save the settings from your current version of Windows.

4. Then perform the upgrade, new installation, or clean installation.

5. If you ran the Files and Settings Transfer Wizard, run it again to apply your files and settings.

Will Your Computer Be Able to Run Windows XP Professional?

First, make sure that your computer will be able to run Windows XP Professional. The following sections discuss the main requirements.

Processor

Windows XP requires a minimum of a Pentium II processor running at 233MHz. But realistically, you'll want a 600MHz or faster processor for the kind of performance you'll need in a business setting.

If you don't know what processor your computer has, watch the information that comes up as it boots. This will give you at least the processor speed, though it may give an incorrect classification of the chip. For example, some systems classify Celeron chips as Pentium III chips. (Mid-range Celeron chips *are* in fact cut-down Pentium III chips, but your system should really know the difference.)

RAM

Windows XP requires a minimum of 64MB of RAM to install and run. This too is an absolute minimum and delivers poor performance unless your processor is extremely fast (in which case the lack of RAM cannibalizes processor performance). You'll get good performance for one concurrent user session if you have 128MB of RAM. For multiple concurrent user sessions, get 256MB or more RAM. (At this writing, 256MB RAM modules are selling for prices as low as $45, so upgrading your RAM is relatively painless.)

NOTE   *Windows XP Professional can access a maximum of 4GB of RAM.*

If you don't know how much RAM your computer has, watch the count of RAM when you boot. If the number is in kilobytes, divide by 1024 to get the number in megabytes. Alternatively, click Start, right-click My Computer, and choose Properties from the shortcut menu. Windows displays the System Properties dialog box open at the General tab. At the bottom of the tab is a readout of the amount of RAM in the computer.

GET PLENTY OF RAM

Everyone knows that you need plenty of RAM to run Windows. That's true—up to a point. But most people still have too little RAM on their computers.

Windows XP Professional will run—well, more like stagger along—on 64MB RAM. If the computer has a fast processor, and if you don't use any large applications or large files, performance may be tolerable. But the hard disk will be kept busy as Windows continually uses virtual memory to store the information that won't fit in the RAM.

If you're buying a new computer, you'll be much better off saving a little money on the processor and putting it into RAM. Unless you're running the latest 3-D games or performing terrain mapping or other advanced imaging, you'll notice little benefit from having a few hundred extra megahertz on your computer. But another 128MB (better, another 256MB) of RAM will make a huge difference over 64MB on a system with just about any processor.

Windows XP runs adequately on an antiquated processor such as a Pentium II 266 provided the computer has enough RAM—128MB for a single user session running a "normal" number of applications, 192MB for a single user session running a heavy number of applications, and 256MB or more for multiple user sessions running concurrently.

Given this, it's sad to see that many companies that should really know better—including IBM, Dell, and Compaq—are plugging computers with gigahertz-plus processors and 64MB RAM. (They'll happily sell you as much extra memory as you specify, of course—but the implication is that a computer with 64MB RAM is adequately configured to run Windows, which it isn't.)

Free Disk Space

Windows XP Professional requires approximately 650MB of free disk space to install on a 2GB hard drive. If you're installing over a network, you'll need more free space. In addition, there has to be room for your paging file (by default, 1.5 times the amount of RAM in your computer) and for your hibernation file (the same size as the amount of RAM) if your computer supports hibernation. On top of that, you'll need space for any applications you want to install and any files you want to create.

In practice, it's a good idea to have at least 1GB of free space on the drive on which you install Windows XP, plus space for your applications and files. To see how much space is free on a drive, right-click the drive in an Explorer window and choose Properties from the shortcut menu. The General tab of the resulting Properties dialog box for the drive shows how much free space it has.

SVGA-Capable Video Adapter and Monitor

Your video adapter and monitor need to be capable of SVGA resolution (800×600 pixels) with 256 or more colors for you to enjoy Windows XP in all its glory. Beyond that, just about any PCI or AGP video adapter should work (drivers permitting, of course), as should any CRT or LCD monitor.

CD Drive or DVD Drive

You need a CD drive or DVD drive, or access to one or the other, to install Windows XP. If the drive is on another computer, you can install across a network or copy the files to your local drive and run them from there.

Checking System Compatibility

To check whether Windows XP thinks your computer will be able to run it, run the Windows Upgrade Advisor program by following these steps:

1. Insert the Windows XP CD. If your computer doesn't automatically start running the CD, open an Explorer window, navigate to the CD, and double-click the `setup.exe` program.

2. On the opening screen, click the Check System Compatibility link. Setup offers the choices Check My System Automatically and Visit the Compatibility Web Site.

3. Click the Check My System Automatically link.

4. If an Internet connection is available, Setup runs Dynamic Update to download any new files that may help with the installation. It then runs the Windows Upgrade Advisor program and displays the Upgrade Report screen of the Microsoft Windows Upgrade Advisor. Figure 2.1 shows an example of an upgrade report.

FIGURE 2.1

Use the Microsoft Windows Upgrade Advisor to check whether your computer will be able to run Windows XP.

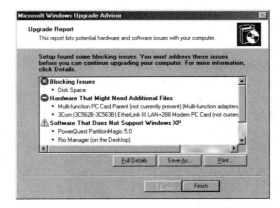

5. If your computer seems to be fit for Windows XP, the report tells you that the check found no incompatibilities or problems. Any problems are listed in the list box in summary form. Click the Full Details button to view the details (broken up into categories such as Blocking Issues, Warnings, and Helpful Information) and advice on what to do about the problems. (Click the resulting Summary button to return to the summary view.) Click the Save As button to save the information to file, or click the Print button to print a copy of it.

6. Click the Finish button. Windows closes the Microsoft Windows Upgrade Advisor.

Follow the Upgrade Advisor's advice to get your computer ready for upgrading to Windows XP. In particular, you need to take care of any blocking issues that the Advisor has identified. An example of a blocking issue is not having enough disk space to install Windows XP. You might need to remove some existing files or reconfigure your partitions (for example, by using a tool such as PartitionMagic), in order to resolve such an issue.

Choosing an Installation Method

Once you've decided to install Windows XP, your next decision is how to install Windows XP on your computer. You can install Windows XP in three ways:

Upgrade   If you have Windows 9x, Windows NT 4 Workstation (including service packs), or Windows 2000 Professional (including service packs), you can perform an upgrade, essentially overwriting the previous version of Windows with Windows XP. Upgrading like this transfers all your files, settings, and applications to Windows XP, so (in theory) you can pick up your work or play straight away in Windows XP where you left off.

New installation   A new installation of Windows replaces your current version of Windows or installs Windows XP on a new disk or a separate partition. You can use the Files and Settings Transfer Wizard to copy your files and settings from your previous version of Windows to Windows XP.

Clean installation   You can install Windows XP from scratch on your computer, setting it up as the only operating system but not upgrading from your current operating system. Again, you can use the Files and Settings Transfer Wizard to copy your files and settings from your previous version of Windows to Windows XP. You'll need to install all the applications you want to use after you install Windows XP.

Which type of installation to perform can be a tricky decision. The longer you've been running Windows on this computer since installing it, the stronger the arguments are for both an upgrade and a clean installation:

◆   By now, you've probably installed all the applications you need and got them working together. By upgrading, you can transition your whole work environment to Windows XP, so that your Desktop, Start menu, and folder structure retain their current settings and your applications all work as before.

◆   Then again, you probably have applications that you no longer use, or applications that no longer work. By performing a clean install, you can strip your system down to only the software you need. It'll take longer, but the result may be better. Similarly, your data folders could probably do with some cleaning out and archiving.

If you need to install a new hard drive as your main hard drive, you'll need to perform a clean install. (The exception is if you use a hard-drive cloning or migration package such as DriveImage or Ghost. These packages are often used for upgrading the hard drives in laptops, where the lack of expansion room forces you to replace the current hard drive rather than add a drive, but some of them work for desktops as well.)

Preparing for Installation

Once you've established that your computer should be able to run Windows XP, prepare for installation by taking those of the following steps as are applicable to the type of installation you're planning (upgrade, new installation, or clean installation).

Back Up All Your Data Files

For safety, back up all your data files shortly before installation, using your usual backup medium.

Write Down Internet Connection Information

If you're planning a new installation or clean installation rather than an upgrade, and you use a dial-up Internet connection, write down the information you need to create the connection: your ISP account username, your password, your ISP's phone number, and your ISP's primary DNS server and secondary DNS server.

Plug In and Switch On All Hardware

Make sure that all the hardware you intend to use with the computer is attached to it and powered on. For example, if you'll use a printer and scanner with the computer, make sure these devices are attached to the computer and powered on, so that Setup can detect them if it's smart enough.

Use the Files and Settings Transfer Wizard to Transfer Settings

Windows XP includes a Wizard for transferring files and settings from one computer or operating system to another. You don't need to use this Wizard, which is called the Files and Settings Transfer Wizard, if you're upgrading Windows 9x to Windows XP, because Windows automatically transfers all your settings when you perform an upgrade. But the Wizard can save you a great deal of time when you want to transfer files and settings either to a new computer that's running Windows XP or to a new installation of Windows XP on the same computer on which you've kept your previous installation of Windows as a dual-boot. For example, if you choose to test Windows XP on a new partition before committing yourself to it, you can use the Files and Settings Transfer Wizard to transfer your work environment to the new partition so that you can use your regular settings and files.

Before you use the Files and Settings Transfer Wizard, make sure you've connected any network drive you want to use, or that you have a removable disk or recordable CD ready. To transfer files and settings, you'll need plenty of storage. You can save settings files to a floppy drive, but most data files will be too big.

To use the Files and Settings Transfer Wizard, follow these steps:

1. Insert the Windows XP CD. If your computer doesn't automatically start running the CD, open an Explorer window, navigate to the CD, and double-click the `setup.exe` program. Windows displays the Welcome to Microsoft Windows XP screen.

2. Click the Perform Additional Tasks link.

3. On the next screen, click the Transfer Files and Settings link. Setup starts the Files and Settings Transfer Wizard.

4. Click the Next button. If this computer is running Windows XP, the Wizard displays the Which Computer Is This? screen. If it does, select the Old Computer option button and click the Next button. (If this computer isn't running Windows XP, the Wizard knows it's the old computer.) The Wizard then displays the Select a Transfer Method screen (shown in Figure 2.2).

FIGURE 2.2

On the Select a Transfer Method screen of the Files and Settings Transfer Wizard, specify how you want to transfer files and settings from the old computer to the new computer.

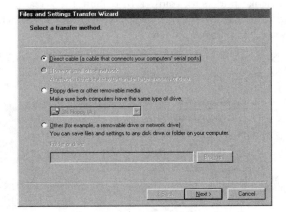

5. Select the Direct Cable option button, the Home or Small Office Network option button (if it's available), the Floppy Drive or Other Removable Media option button, or the Other option button as appropriate. The Other option button lets you use the Browse button and the resulting Browse for Folder dialog box or the Folder or Drive text box to specify a removable drive or a network drive.

6. Click the Next button. The Wizard displays the What Do You Want to Transfer? screen (shown in Figure 2.3).

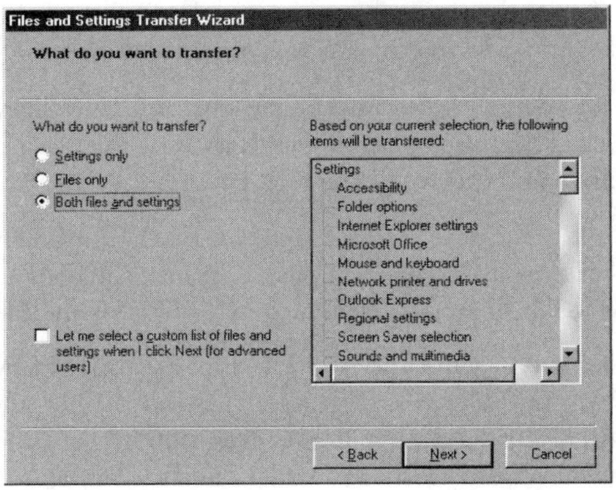

FIGURE 2.3

On the What Do You Want to Transfer? screen of the Files and Settings Transfer Wizard, specify which settings and files you want to transfer to the new computer (or to Windows XP).

7. In the What Do You Want to Transfer? list, select the Settings Only option button, the Files Only option button, or the Both Files and Settings option button as appropriate. The list box on the right side of the dialog box lists the types of settings and files that will be affected.

8. If you want to customize the list of settings, files, or both, select the Let Me Select a Custom List of Files and Settings When I Click Next check box. Customizing the list of files lets you specify particular folders for transfer. By default, the Wizard transfers the Desktop folder, the Fonts folder, the My Documents folder, the My Pictures folder, the Shared Desktop folder, and the Shared Documents folder.

9. Click the Next button. If you selected to customize, the Wizard displays the Select Custom Files and Settings screen (shown in Figure 2.4).

FIGURE 2.4

On the Select Custom Files and Settings screen of the Files and Settings Transfer Wizard, choose the files and settings to transfer.

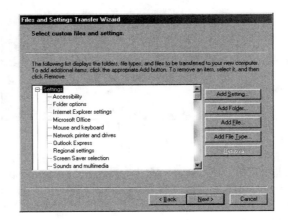

10. Select the files and settings to transfer:

- ◆ To add a setting, click the Add Setting button. The Wizard displays the Add a Setting dialog box. Select the setting or settings in the list box and click the OK button. The Wizard closes the Add a Setting dialog box and adds the setting or settings to the list.

- ◆ To add a folder, click the Add Folder button. The Wizard displays the Browse for Folder dialog box. Select the folder and click the OK button. The Wizard closes the Browse for Folder dialog box and adds the folder to the list.

- ◆ To add a file, click the Add File button. The Wizard displays the Add a File dialog box (a common Open dialog box in disguise). Select the file and click the Open button. The Wizard closes the Add a File dialog box and adds the file to the list.

- ◆ To add a file type, click the Add File Type button. The Wizard displays the Add a File Type dialog box (shown in Figure 2.5). Select the file type in the Registered File Types list box; if it's not listed there, enter its extension in the Other text box. Then click the OK button. The Wizard closes the Add a File Type dialog box and adds the file type to the list.

◆ To remove a setting, folder, file, or file type, select it in the list box and click the Remove button.

FIGURE 2.5

Use the Add a File Type dialog box to add a file type to the list of file types to transfer.

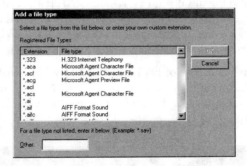

11. Click the Next button. The Wizard may display the Install Programs on Your New Computer screen, suggesting some programs that you may want to install on your new computer (or new installation of Windows) before transferring settings. If so, note these suggestions.

12. The Wizard then displays the Collection in Progress screen (shown in Figure 2.6) while it collects your files and settings. It then displays the Completing the Collection Phase screen.

FIGURE 2.6

The Wizard collects the files.

13. Click the Finish button. The Wizard closes itself.

For details of how to apply your saved files and settings to your new installation of Windows, see "Applying Your Files and Settings" later in this chapter.

Stop Any Antivirus Software or Disk Utilities

Stop any antivirus software or disk utilities before running the Windows installation, because the installation process needs direct access to your hardware.

Upgrading to Windows XP

When you upgrade, the installation procedure copies the settings from your current version of Windows and applies them to the installation of Windows XP. If the installation doesn't work correctly, or if you find Windows XP doesn't suit you, you can uninstall it and revert to your previous installation of Windows unless you are upgrading from Windows NT or Windows 2000 Professional.

To perform an upgrade, follow these steps:

1. Insert the CD in a CD drive or DVD drive. If Autoplay is enabled on your computer, Windows displays the introductory screen (shown in Figure 2.7). If not, open an Explorer window and double-click the CD. This should trigger the Autoplay action. If it doesn't, double-click the SETUP.EXE file on the CD to run it.

FIGURE 2.7

To start the upgrade, select the Install Windows XP link.

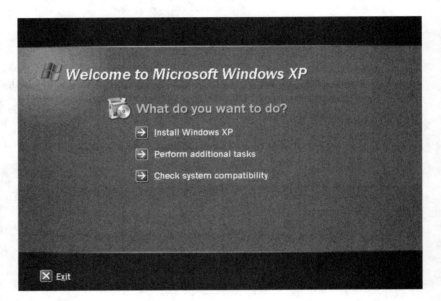

2. Click the Install Windows XP link. Setup displays the Welcome to Windows Setup screen (shown in Figure 2.8).

3. In the Installation Type drop-down list, choose the Upgrade item.

4. Click the Next button. Setup displays the License Agreement screen. Read it.

5. If you agree to the license, select the I Accept This Agreement option button and click the Next button. (If you don't agree to the license, Setup exits.) Setup displays the Your Product Key screen.

FIGURE 2.8

On the Welcome to Windows Setup screen, choose the Upgrade item in the Installation Type drop-down list.

6. Enter your product key and click the Next button. Setup displays the Upgrade Report screen (shown in Figure 2.9).

FIGURE 2.9

On the Upgrade Report screen of Setup, choose the type of upgrade report you want for this computer.

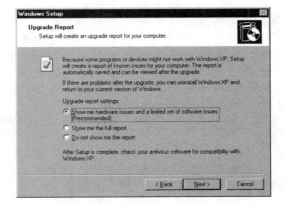

7. Choose the type of upgrade report you want by selecting the Show Me Hardware Issues Only option button, the Show Me the Full Report option button, or the Do Not Show Me the Report option button.

8. Click the Next button. Setup displays the Get Updated Setup Files screen (shown in Figure 2.10), which lets you choose whether to use Dynamic Update to download any new Setup files that Microsoft may have released since your copy of Windows XP was pressed.

9. To download any available files, leave the Yes, Download the Updated Setup Files option button selected, as it is by default. To skip Dynamic Update, select the No, Skip This Step and Continue Installing Windows option button.

FIGURE 2.10

On the Get Updated Setup Files screen of Setup, choose whether to let Dynamic Update download the latest Setup files.

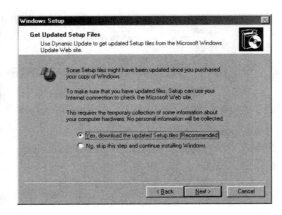

NOTE   You can download any updated files by using Windows Update after you finish installing Windows XP. The only advantage to Dynamic Update comes if the new files are needed for any of the hardware on your computer during installation.

10. Click the Next button. If you chose to use Dynamic Update, Setup contacts the Microsoft Web site and downloads any relevant files. Setup then starts analyzing your computer for possible problems in upgrading to Windows XP.

◆ If you don't have enough space to install Windows XP, you'll see a Windows XP Setup dialog box such as that shown in Figure 2.11 warning you of the problem. Click the Quit Setup button, retire disconsolately from the fray, and return when you've made more space available.

FIGURE 2.11

Setup warns you if you don't have enough space available to install Windows XP.

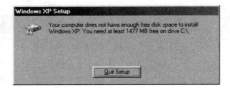

11. If you have any incompatible hardware or software, Setup displays the Upgrade Report screen (of which Figure 2.12 shows a sample). You can click the Full Report button to view the details of the hardware and software, click the Save As button to save the information to file, or click the Print button to print a copy of it. If you don't select one of these options, Setup displays the Windows XP Setup dialog box, which warns you that some devices on your computer may not work with Windows XP and offers you a View Report button, a Continue button, and a Quit Setup button. Click the Continue button if you want to continue.

12. Click the Next button. Setup continues running the setup routine, reboots your computer, and takes the installation all the way to the Welcome to Microsoft Windows screen. Skip ahead to "The Installation Paths Converge" later in the chapter.

FIGURE 2.12

The Upgrade Report screen of Setup summarizes any potential hardware and software upgrade problems you may face.

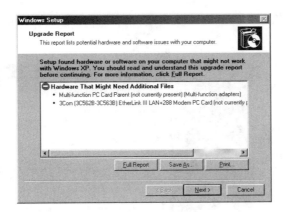

Performing a New Installation of Windows XP

To perform a new installation of Windows XP (without upgrading your current version of Windows), follow these steps:

1. Insert the CD in a CD drive or DVD drive. If Autoplay is enabled on your computer, Windows displays the introductory screen (shown in Figure 2.13). If not, open an Explorer window and double-click the CD. This should trigger the Autoplay action. If it doesn't, double-click the SETUP.EXE file on the CD to run it.

FIGURE 2.13

To start installing, select the Install Windows XP link.

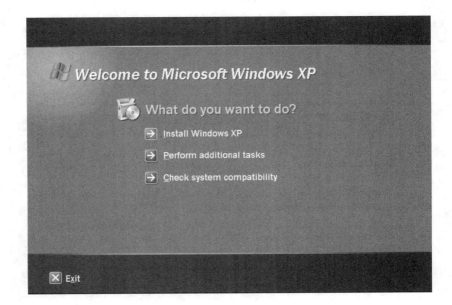

2. Click the Install Windows XP link. Setup displays the Welcome to Windows Setup screen (shown in Figure 2.14).

FIGURE 2.14

On the Welcome to Windows Setup screen, choose the New Installation item in the Installation Type drop-down list.

3. In the Installation Type drop-down list, choose the New Installation item.

4. Click the Next button. Setup displays the License Agreement screen. Read it.

5. If you agree to the license, select the I Accept This Agreement option button and click the Next button. (If you don't agree to the license, Setup exits.) Setup displays the Your Product Key screen.

6. Enter your product key and click the Next button. Setup displays the Setup Options screen (shown in Figure 2.15). From this screen, you can choose language options, installation options, and accessibility options.

7. To change the language used, select the language in the Select the Primary Language and Region You Want to Use drop-down list. If you want to install support for East Asian languages, select the Install Support for East Asian Languages check box.

FIGURE 2.15

When you perform a new installation, Setup displays the Setup Options screen, on which you can choose advanced options and accessibility options.

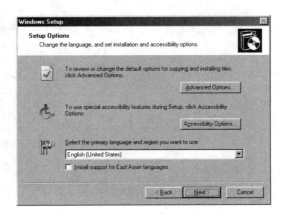

8. To set the advanced options, which let you control the installation folder and specify that you want to select the installation partition, click the Advanced Options button on the Setup Options screen. Setup displays the Advanced Options dialog box (shown in Figure 2.16), which offers the following options:

FIGURE 2.16

In the Advanced Options dialog box, you can specify the installation folder and tell Setup that you want to choose the installation partition.

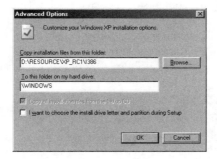

◆ The Copy Installation Files from This Folder text box lists the path from which you ran the Setup program (or it ran itself). Usually, you won't need to change this path, but you can if necessary.

◆ The To This Folder on My Hard Drive text box shows the location to which Setup is planning to install Windows XP: your current Windows folder. If you don't want Windows XP to overwrite your current version of Windows, choose a different folder. For example, you may want to create a dual-boot setup so that you can compare Windows XP to your current version of Windows without yet removing the latter from your computer.

◆ The Copy All Installation Files from the Setup CD check box enables you to force Setup to copy all its files to the hard drive rather than leaving them on the CD. Use this option when installing Windows XP from a CD that will not be available after Setup reboots the computer. For example, when installing Windows XP on a laptop computer using an external CD drive (such as a parallel-port drive, a USB drive, or a PC Card–connected drive), you'll probably need to copy all setup files to the hard drive because the CD drive will not be available from the reboot until Setup is complete. You may also need to use this option if your CD drive will not read the Windows XP CD reliably during the setup routine after the reboot. (This shouldn't happen, but it does. After the reboot, Setup uses a different CD driver that apparently disagrees with some CD drives.) By default, this check box is cleared unless you're installing from a network drive, in which case it's not available (as in Figure 2.16).

◆ The I Want to Choose the Install Drive Letter and Partition During Setup check box lets you tell Setup to display the partitioning screen so that you can specify the partition on which to install Windows XP. If you're performing a new installation of Windows XP, you don't need to select this check box, because Setup automatically displays the partitioning screen so that you can specify where to install Windows XP.

9. Click the OK button. Setup closes the Advanced Options dialog box.

10. During Setup, Windows XP offers two accessibility options, Magnifier and Narrator. Magnifier is designed for people with limited but viable vision and displays an enlarged version of the selected portion of the screen. Narrator is designed for the blind and those with more limited vision. It reads the contents of the screen aloud. To use these options, click the Accessibility Options button on the Setup Options screen. Setup displays the Accessibility Options dialog box (shown in Figure 2.17). Select the Use Microsoft Magnifier During Setup check box or the Use Microsoft Narrator During Setup check box as appropriate. Then click the OK button. Setup closes the Accessibility Options dialog box and applies your choices.

FIGURE 2.17

Setup offers Magnifier and Narrator accessibility options for those with limited vision and the blind.

11. Once you've finished choosing special options, click the Next button on the Setup Options screen. Setup displays the Get Updated Setup Files screen (shown in Figure 2.18), which lets you choose whether to use Dynamic Update to download any new Setup files that Microsoft may have released since your copy of Windows XP was pressed.

12. To download any available files, leave the Yes, Download the Updated Setup Files option button selected, as it is by default. To skip Dynamic Update, select the No, Skip This Step and Continue Installing Windows option button.

FIGURE 2.18

On the Get Updated Setup Files screen of Setup, choose whether to let Dynamic Update download the latest Setup files.

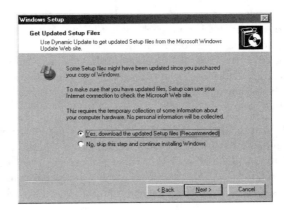

13. Click the Next button. If you chose to use Dynamic Update, Setup contacts the Microsoft Web site and downloads any relevant files. Setup then continues running the setup routine, reboots your computer, and displays the partitioning screen. Go to the "Choosing a Hard Disk Partition" section in the "Performing a Clean Install of Windows XP" section, a little later in this chapter.

WHY IS THE FOLDER CALLED "I386"?

If you're looking at the Advanced Options dialog box, the Copy Installation Files from This Folder text box is probably listing a path that ends in i386. What's this all about?

i386 stands for Intel 386. The 386, as you'll remember if you've been computing for a while, was Intel's hottest processor at the end of the 1980s. But it's also the descriptor for the entire family of chips that has continued through the 486 chips and Pentium chips (renamed from 586, which wasn't trademarkable) to the Pentium IV chips of today.

But why is i386 there? Why is the folder not called something intuitive like "Files"? It's because NT was originally written to be processor independent so that it could run on various types of processors without major rebuilding.

The early version of NT ran on Intel chips, Alpha chips, MIPS chips, and PowerPC chips. The installation CD came with a separate folder for each of these. Over the years (or, more correctly, over the versions of NT), Microsoft gradually dropped support for processors other than the Intel 386 family. But the i386 folder survives as a hold over of the old days.

Performing a Clean Install of Windows XP

To perform a clean installation of Windows XP, put the Windows XP CD in your CD-ROM drive or DVD drive and boot from it. (You may have to change the boot settings in your computer's BIOS to boot from the CD.) Windows Setup automatically launches itself.

First, Setup displays the Welcome to Setup screen. From here, press the Enter key to start the installation. (Press the F3 key if you've reached this stage by mistake and need to quit.) Setup displays the partitioning screen.

Choosing a Hard Disk Partition

The partitioning screen lets you create and delete partitions as well as specify the installation partition. The screen lists the current partitions on the disk, their label, their type (for example, NTFS for an NTFS partition, FAT32 for a FAT partition, and Raw for a new, unformatted partition), their size, and the amount of space free on each. Any unpartitioned space is listed as such. Any space you've deliberately left unpartitioned will of course be free, but there will often be a few megabytes of unpartitioned space left over after you've tried to allocate all the space on the disk.

To choose an existing partition for the installation, use the up and down arrows to move the highlight to it. Then press the Enter key.

To create a new partition, select some unpartitioned space and press the C key. Setup displays a Details screen. Specify the size of the partition in megabytes and press the Enter key.

If you want to install Windows XP and use up the full amount of unpartitioned space, you don't need to explicitly create a partition first. Just select the Unpartitioned Space item and press the Enter key to start the installation.

To delete an existing partition, select it in the list and press the D key. Setup displays a screen confirming the action. Press the L key. If the partition is a system partition, Setup displays a more extensive warning. And if the partition is the partition on which Setup has installed its temporary files for carrying out the installation of Windows, Setup refuses to delete the partition.

Once you've chosen a partition, Setup proceeds. If the partition is a new partition, Setup offers you the choice of formatting it with NTFS or with FAT. For each, there's the option of a quick format. A full format includes a scan of the disk for bad sectors; a quick format skips this scan. Unless you're in a tearing hurry and have checked the disk recently for bad sectors, go with the full format.

NOTE *If you choose to install Windows XP on a partition that already contains another operating system, Setup displays a screen warning you that this may cause problems. Press the C key if you're prepared to continue. Press the Esc key to return to the partitioning screen and select another partition.*

Converting the Partition to NTFS

If you're installing Windows XP on an existing partition that uses FAT, Setup offers you the option of converting the installation partition to NTFS. Think seriously about doing so, because NTFS is one of the major improvements in Windows XP Professional over Windows 9x.

NTFS offers two compelling advantages over FAT. First, NTFS has security features (including auditing and file-level permissions), while FAT does not. And second, NTFS keeps a log of activities so that it can restore the disk to order after a hardware or power failure; FAT simply loses your data instead.

WARNING *If you are creating a dual-boot configuration with a version of Windows 9x, be aware that NTFS can access FAT partitions but Windows 9x cannot access NTFS partitions. If this doesn't matter to you, go ahead and convert the partition to NTFS.*

Next, you see the license agreement. Read it and press the F8 key if you agree and want to proceed. Press the Esc key to cancel installation.

Choosing Regional and Language Options

After this, Setup entertains itself for a few minutes as it performs part of the installation. Next, you see the Regional and Language Options screen. From here, you can change the computer's standards and formats setting so that it displays numbers, currencies, and dates in the appropriate formats for the country or user. You can also change the default keyboard layout.

To change the standards and formats setting, click the Customize button. Setup displays the Regional and Language Options dialog box with the Region Options tab foremost, as shown in Figure 2.19. In the Standards and Formats group box, select the language and locale you want to use. The text boxes in the Samples area show samples of a number, a currency, a time, a short date, and a long date for that language and locale. (You can change these by clicking the Customize button and working in the Customize Regional Options dialog box.) In the Location drop-down list, select your

PERFORMING A CLEAN INSTALL OF WINDOWS XP | 141

geographical location so that Windows knows which part of the world you're in when its services try to present you with local information. Click the OK button. Setup closes the Regional and Language Options dialog box.

FIGURE 2.19

On the Region Options tab of the Regional and Language Options dialog box, specify the standards and formats setting to use and tell Windows your location.

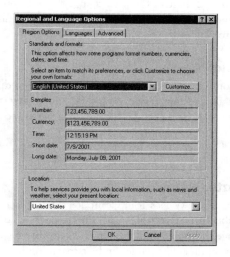

To change the keyboard layout, click the Details button. Setup displays the Text Services and Input Languages dialog box (shown in Figure 2.20). Select the language in the Default Input Language drop-down list. To add an input language, click the Add button and use the resulting Add Input Language dialog box to specify the input language and keyboard layout. For example, if you use the Dvorak layout for your keyboard, set it as the default keyboard layout. Then click the OK button. Setup closes the Text Services and Input Languages dialog box.

Click the Next button to continue the setup process.

FIGURE 2.20

Use the Text Services and Input Languages dialog box to change your default input language.

Entering Your Name and Organization

Next, Setup displays the Personalize Your Software screen, which demands your name and your organization's name. Enter these with due care and consideration, as they get deeply buried within the Windows Registry. (Chapter 22 discusses how to change them if you get them wrong.) You have to enter some text in the Name text box, but you can leave the Organization text box empty if you want.

Click the Next button to proceed.

Entering Your Product Key

Next, for a clean installation (but not for a new installation), Setup displays the Your Product Key screen. Enter the 25-character product key (it should be on a yellow sticker on the back of the folder or CD box your Windows CD came in) and click the Next button to proceed.

TIP   *If there's any risk of your misplacing your product key, write it on the Windows CD using a permanent pen.*

Entering the Computer Name

Next, Windows Setup displays the What's Your Computer's Name? screen. By default, Setup suggests a complex and unmemorizable name that starts with the first part of the first name you entered in the previous dialog box. Change this name to something descriptive that you'll be able to remember and associate easily with this computer. The name can be a maximum of 63 characters, but you'd do well to keep it shorter than this to make it manageable. Names of more than 15 characters will be visible to other computers only via TCP/IP; via other network protocols, they won't be visible.

Click the Next button once again.

Entering the Modem Dialing Information

Next, if the computer has a modem that Setup was able to detect, Setup displays the Modem Dialing Information screen. Specify your country or region (for example, United States of America), your area code (which is compulsory), any number you dial to get an outside line, and whether the phone system uses tone dialing or pulse dialing. Then click the Next button to proceed.

Checking the Date and Time

Next, Setup displays the Date and Time Settings screen. Check the date, time, and time zone, and select or clear the Automatically Adjust Clock for Daylight Saving Changes check box as appropriate. Then click the Next button.

Specifying Networking Settings

Next, Setup installs some networking components and attempts to detect any network cards installed in your computer. Setup then displays the Networking Settings screen, which offers you the choice of Typical Settings or Custom Settings.

The Typical Settings option installs the Client for Microsoft Networks, the QoS Packet Scheduler, File and Print Sharing for Microsoft Networks, and TCP/IP with automatic addressing. You can install other services after Setup completes (or remove these services), of course, but usually you'll be better off choosing the Custom Settings option and specifying suitable settings as described in the rest of this section.

If you select the Custom Settings option button and click the Next button, Windows Setup displays the Networking Components screen.

You can adjust the default settings by adding other services, uninstalling the default services, or choosing not to apply the selected services to this network adapter. When you remove a service, you make it unavailable to any of the network or dial-up adapters on your computer. So if you need to install a service but not use it for your primary network connection, let Setup install it, but clear its check box on the Networking Components screen.

UNINSTALLING A SERVICE

To uninstall one of the services, select it and click the Uninstall button. Setup displays a confirmation message box warning you that uninstalling the component removes it from all network connections. Click the Yes button if you want to remove the service.

ADDING A SERVICE

To add other services to the default services, follow these steps:

1. Click the Install button. Setup displays the Select Network Component Type dialog box.

2. Select the type of component you want to add—Client, Service, or Protocol—and click the Add button. Setup displays the Select Network Client dialog box, the Select Network Service dialog box, or the Select Network Protocol dialog box, as appropriate.

3. Select the client, service, or protocol in the list box. To add an unlisted client, service, or protocol that you have on disk, click the Have Disk button and use the resulting Install from Disk dialog box to identify the file.

4. Click the OK button. Windows Setup installs the client, service, or protocol and closes the Select Network Component Type dialog box.

CONFIGURING TCP/IP

Some of the network components have parameters you can configure. Of these, the key component is TCP/IP, the Internet protocol suite. If you don't run Internet Connection Sharing (ICS) on this computer, connect to the Internet through a computer running ICS, or connect to a DHCP server, you'll probably want to configure TCP/IP manually.

To configure your TCP/IP settings for the primary network card, follow these steps:

1. Select the Internet Protocol (TCP/IP) item in the list box on the Networking Components tab.

2. Click the Properties button to open the Internet Protocol (TCP/IP) Properties dialog box.

3. On the General tab, select the Use the Following IP Address option button.

4. Enter the IP address in the IP Address text box (for example, **192.168.0.11**).

5. Enter the subnet mask in the Subnet Mask text box (for example, **255.255.255.0**). Setup automatically enters a suggested subnet mask appropriate to the IP address you enter, but you may need to change it.

6. Enter the IP address of the default gateway in the Default Gateway text box.

7. Select the Use the Following DNS Server Addresses option button.

8. Enter the IP address of your primary DNS server in the Preferred DNS Server text box.

9. Enter the IP address of your secondary DNS server (if you have one) in the Alternate DNS Server text box.

10. Click the OK button. Setup closes the Internet Protocol (TCP/IP) Properties dialog box and applies your settings.

NOTE   *If necessary, you can also set advanced TCP/IP settings by clicking the Advanced button on the General tab of the Internet Protocol (TCP/IP) dialog box and working in the resulting Advanced TCP/IP Settings dialog box.*

Click the Next button to proceed with the installation. You've now chosen all the custom options.

CHANGING DISPLAY SETTINGS

If Setup detects that your screen has a recommended resolution (for example, if it is an LCD panel) or if it detects that you are using the 640 × 480 screen resolution, Setup displays the Display Settings dialog box, which announces that Windows will automatically adjust your screen resolution to improve the appearance of visual elements. Click the OK button. Windows adjusts the resolution and displays a Monitor Settings dialog box asking if you want to keep the change. Click the OK button if you do. If not, click the Cancel button or (if the screen isn't legible after the change) wait 30 seconds, after which Windows restores the previous screen resolution.

The Installation Paths Converge

The installation paths converge at the Welcome to Microsoft Windows screen, at which Setup starts playing active elevator music while an animated help logo struts its stuff. Click the Next button to move along.

Setting Up Your Internet Connection

Setup then tries to get you connected to the Internet. It tests any detected network adapter to see if it can find an Internet connection. If it detects an Internet connection, Setup displays the How Will This Computer Connect to the Internet? screen, which offers three options: the Telephone Modem option button, the Digital Subscriber Line (DSL) or Cable Modem option button, and the Local Area Network (LAN) option button.

Select the appropriate option button. If you don't want to configure an Internet connection at the moment—for example, you don't have your ISP or network information—click the Skip button.

The following sections describe what happens when you select each of these options.

TELEPHONE MODEM

If your computer connects with a telephone modem, select the Telephone Modem option button, then click the Next button. Setup displays the Ready to Activate Windows? screen.

After the step of activating Windows (or your turning down the invitation to do so), Setup displays the Do You Want to Set Up Internet Access Now? screen. Select the Yes, Help Me Connect to the Internet option button or the No, Not at This Time option button as appropriate.

If you choose the Yes option button, Setup displays the Let's Get on the Internet screen. This offers three choices: the Get Online with MSN option button, the Use My Existing Internet Account with Another Service Provider (ISP) option button, and the Create a New Internet Account after I Finish Setting Up Windows option button. Select the appropriate option button and click the Next button to proceed.

If you choose Get Online with MSN and click Next, you'll see the Ready to Get an Internet Account? screen, which tells you that Setup will make a call to sign you up for an Internet account. Click Next to dial in to MSN. When you're connected, follow the instructions on the screen to set up an account.

If you chose to use your existing Internet account, Setup displays the Do You Want Help Finding an Internet Service Provider? screen. If you don't have your connection information available, click the Yes, I Need Help Finding Information about My Account option, and click Next. Setup dials the Microsoft Referral Service to locate an ISP in your area. If you do have your connection information available, click the No, I Have My Username, Password, and My ISP's Name and Phone Number Handy option, and click Next. Windows displays the Set Up Your Internet Account screen.

Enter your username, password, and ISP phone number. By default, Windows selects the Obtain IP Automatically (DHCP) check box and the Obtain DNS Automatically check box. If you need to specify a static IP address rather than have the IP address be assigned automatically, clear the Obtain IP Automatically (DHCP) check box and enter the IP address in the Static IP Address text box. Similarly, if your ISP does not supply DNS information automatically, clear the Obtain DNS Automatically check box and enter the IP addresses of the primary and secondary DNS servers in the Preferred DNS text box and the Alternate DNS text box.

When you click the Next button, Setup displays a Congratulations screen telling you that you can connect to the Internet using your phone line. Bear in mind that this isn't necessarily true—you've entered the information, but Windows hasn't checked that it works.

DIGITAL SUBSCRIBER LINE (DSL) OR CABLE MODEM

If your computer connects with a DSL or cable modem, select the Digital Subscriber Line (DSL) or Cable Modem option button, then click the Next button. Setup displays the Do You Use a Username and Password to Connect to the Internet? screen. Select the Yes, I Use a Username and Password to Connect option button or the No, This Computer Is Always Connected to the Internet option button as appropriate. Click the Next button to display the Do You Use a Username and Password to Connect to the Internet? screen. If you select the Yes, I Use a Username and Password to Connect option and then click Next, you'll see the Let's Set Up Your Internet Account screen. Enter your username, password, and the name of your ISP and click Next. Setup displays the Ready to Activate Windows? screen.

If you select the No, This Computer Is Always Connected to the Internet option and click Next, you'll see the Setting Up a High Speed Connection screen.

If your network is set up to automatically supply an IP address and Domain Name System (DNS) information, this screen is easy: Select the Obtain IP Automatically check box and the Obtain DNS Automatically check box, and you're all set. If your network isn't set up to deliver the goods, leave these check boxes cleared and enter your static IP address, your subnet mask, and your default gateway in the left stack of text boxes; your primary DNS server's IP address in the Preferred DNS text box; and your secondary DNS server's IP address (if you have one) in the Alternate DNS text box.

Click the Next button to proceed. Setup displays the Ready to Activate Windows? screen.

LOCAL AREA NETWORK (LAN)

If your computer connects through a local area network (LAN), select the Local Area Network (LAN) option button, then click the Next button. Setup displays the Setting Up a High Speed Connection screen.

If your network is set up to automatically supply an IP address and Domain Name System (DNS) information, this screen is easy: Select the Obtain IP Automatically check box and the Obtain DNS Automatically check box, and you're all set. If your network isn't set up to deliver the goods, leave these check boxes cleared and enter your static IP address, your subnet mask, and your default gateway in the left stack of text boxes; your primary DNS server's IP address in the Preferred DNS text box; and your secondary DNS server's IP address (if you have one) in the Alternate DNS text box.

Click the Next button to proceed. Setup displays the Ready to Activate Windows? screen.

Creating User Accounts

Next, Setup displays the Who Will Use This Computer? screen, which provides an easy way of setting up accounts for one to five users. This screen contains five text boxes. The first is named Your Name; the rest are numbered 2nd User through 5th User.

NOTE *When you're upgrading from Windows 9x, Setup creates an account for the username under which you upgraded if you yourself forget to do so.*

Enter the names of the users in the text boxes. Each name can be up to 20 characters long, and each must be unique. Names cannot use the characters " * + , / : ; < = > ? [ ] \ or |, and no name can consist of all spaces, all periods, or a combination of the two.

Click the Next button. Setup displays the Thank You! screen telling you you're ready to start using Windows.

Click the Finish button. Setup completes a few odds and ends, and then displays the Welcome screen for you to log in.

Activating Windows

When Windows starts, you'll see a message about activating Windows in the lower right of your Desktop.

Activation is a one-time procedure that you need to perform within a certain number of days of installing Windows. If you don't activate Windows, it stops working. The activation procedure is intended to reduce software piracy. A side-effect is to increase the annoyance of legitimate software users.

Activating Windows now is convenient because you get the activation out of the way once and for all. But I recommend you wait until you're sure that all your hardware works before activating Windows. This needn't take long, and it's much better than needing to get your activation revoked because you need to install Windows on another computer instead. If you don't activate Windows now, it reminds you every few days, so the chances of your forgetting are slim and none.

Activation is a little creepy, even though it doesn't involve supplying any personal information. Windows creates what it calls "a unique hardware configuration that represents the configuration of the PC at the time of activation." At this writing, it's hard to tell how many problems upgrading your PC will cause if you need to reinstall Windows.

The Windows Product Activation Privacy Statement reassures you that "Windows can detect and tolerate minor changes to your PC configuration" and that only a complete overhaul will need reactivation. But you have to wonder: if you upgrade, say, the BIOS, the processor, and the network card, how will Microsoft be able to tell that it's the same computer? Doubtless there will be plenty of horror stories about activation going wrong—and pirates will offer hacks and cracks for circumventing activation.

If you want to activate Windows now, click the icon in the message box. You'll see the Let's Activate Windows screen. You can activate Windows over the Internet or by phone. Click the appropriate option and click Next. If you want to wait to activate Windows, you can do so later. Choose Start ➤ All Programs ➤ Activate Windows.

REGISTERING WINDOWS

During activation, you're heavily encouraged to register your copy of Windows XP with Microsoft.

If you've already registered on Microsoft's Web site, your Windows registration information gets merged into your current information. If you haven't registered, Microsoft creates a new profile for you with a personal information number (PIN) and adds the PIN to your hard drive in a cookie file. When you then visit the Microsoft Web site, it prompts you to create a Registration ID (not usually acronymed to RID). You can keep a profile with personal information—and you can opt out of the communications that Microsoft and the other companies it "occasionally" allows to offer its customers information will bombard you with.

Applying Your Files and Settings

To apply the files and settings you saved by using the Files and Settings Transfer Wizard to your new installation of Windows, take the following steps:

1. Choose Start ➤ All Programs ➤ Accessories ➤ System Tools ➤ Files and Settings Transfer Wizard.

2. Click the Next button. The Wizard displays the Which Computer Is This? screen.

3. Select the New Computer option button.

4. Click the Next button. The Wizard displays the Do You Have a Windows XP CD? screen, which offers to create a Wizard disk that you can use to collect the information from your old computer.

5. Select the I Don't Need the Wizard Disk. I Have Already Collected My Files and Settings from My Old Computer option button.

6. Click the Next button. The Wizard displays the Where Are the Files and Settings? screen (shown in Figure 2.21).

FIGURE 2.21

On the Where Are the Files and Settings? screen of the Files and Settings Transfer Wizard, tell the Wizard where you saved the files and settings.

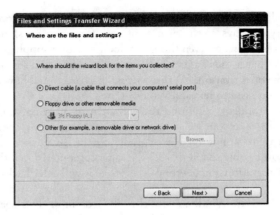

7. Select the Direct Cable option button, the Floppy Drive or Other Removable Media option button, or the Other option button as appropriate.

   ◆ If you select the Floppy Drive or Other Removable Media option button, select the drive in the drop-down list.

   ◆ If you select the Other option button, use the text box and (if necessary) the Browse button and the resulting Browse for Folder dialog box to specify the location of the files and settings.

8. Click the Next button. The Wizard displays the Transfer in Progress screen (shown in Figure 2.22) as it transfers the files and settings.

FIGURE 2.22

The Files and Settings Transfer Wizard transfers the files and settings.

9. If the Wizard displays a dialog box telling you that you need to log off for the settings to take effect and inviting you to log off now, choose the Yes button. The Wizard logs you off and finishes applying the settings.

10. Log back in, and your files and settings are available.

Uninstalling Windows XP and Reverting to a Previous Version of Windows

If you upgraded from Windows Me or Windows 98 to Windows XP, you can uninstall Windows XP and revert to your previous version of Windows if necessary. To do so, take the following steps:

1. Choose Start ➤ Control Panel. Windows displays Control Panel.

2. Click the Add or Remove Programs link. Windows displays the Add or Remove Programs window with the Add or Remove Programs page foremost.

3. Select the Windows XP Uninstall item. Windows displays its details, including a Change/Remove button.

4. Click the Change/Remove button. Windows displays the Uninstall Windows XP dialog box (shown in Figure 2.23).

FIGURE 2.23

In the Uninstall Windows XP dialog box, choose whether to uninstall Windows XP or to remove the backup of your old version of Windows.

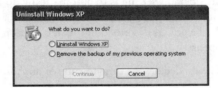

5. Select the Uninstall Windows XP option button.

6. Click the Continue button. Windows displays a confirmation dialog box checking that you're absolutely sure.

7. Click the Yes button. Windows closes, runs the uninstall procedure, and automatically restarts your computer with your previous version of Windows.

NOTE   *You cannot revert to a previous installation of Windows NT 4 Workstation or Windows 2000 Professional.*

Removing Your Old Version of Windows

If you decide to stick with Windows XP after upgrading to it, you can reclaim the space taken up by the backup of your old version of Windows. To do so, follow the first four steps in the previous section but then select the Remove the Backup of My Previous Operating System option button in the Uninstall Windows XP dialog box. Click the Continue button, confirm your choice, and Windows deletes the backup of your previous operating system.

Keeping Windows Updated

Windows XP includes a feature called Windows Update that's designed to keep Windows up-to-date by automatically downloading Windows updates, such as patches and fixes for security holes, and offering to install them. If you need to run old applications that have compatibility problems, Windows Update may be of particular interest because it also includes new fixes for applications to run on Windows XP.

You should know several things about Windows Update before you find it springing into action: how it works, how to configure it, and what to do when an update presents itself.

When Windows Update Runs

By default Windows Update runs automatically, but only when an Administrator user is logged in. (Microsoft assumes that you don't want Limited users—let alone guests—to install or refuse updates.) If multiple Administrator users are logged on to the computer at the same time, Windows Update runs for only one of them.

You can also run Windows Update manually by choosing Start ➤ All Programs ➤ Windows Update. (If you prefer to run Windows Update manually, you may also want to turn off automatic updating. Read on.)

Windows Update's default setting is to automatically download updates when they're available (and an Administrator user is logged on) and then invite the Administrator to install them. You can change this default behavior, as described in the next section.

Here's what happens:

1. Windows Update decides it's time to run (or an Administrator runs it manually).

2. Windows Update goes online and checks which updates are available and then compares the list to those that have already been applied to the computer and those that have been offered to the computer but refused by an Administrator.

3. If update files are available, Windows Update downloads them in the background, using bandwidth-throttling technology to make sure it doesn't prevent you from using your Internet connection by grabbing all bandwidth when you need it. ("Bandwidth-throttling" means that Windows Update throttles back the amount of bandwidth the download is taking up, not that it throttles your bandwidth.) If you're not using your Internet connection, Windows Update downloads the update files as fast as possible.

4. Once the update files are downloaded, Windows Update notifies you (assuming you're an Administrator) that they're available and invites you to install them.

Configuring Windows Update

To configure Windows Update, follow these steps:

1. Press Winkey+Break. Windows displays the System Properties dialog box. (Alternatively, click the Start button to display the Start menu, then right-click the My Computer item and choose Properties from the shortcut menu.)

2. Click the Automatic Updates tab (shown in Figure 2.24).

FIGURE 2.24

You can configure Windows Update on the Automatic Updates tab of the System Properties dialog box.

3. In the Notification Settings section, choose one of the three option buttons:

    Download the Updates Automatically and Notify Me When They Are Ready to Be Installed   The default, this setting is convenient if you want to use automatic updating and you have a fast Internet connection.

    Notify Me Before Downloading Any Updates and Notify Me Again Before Installing Them on My Computer   Use this setting if you want to use automatic updating but you want to be aware of when Windows Update is downloading updates. You might want to know this because your Internet connection isn't fast enough to support your surfing (or downloading MP3s) at the same time as Windows is trying to squeeze a large update through it, or because you don't like unexplained activity across your Internet connection.

    Turn Off Automatic Updating. I Want to Update My Computer Manually   Select this option button if you prefer to control not only when Windows Update downloads and installs updates but when it checks for them—or if you don't want to use Windows Update at all.

4. If you have previously declined updates that Windows has offered you, you can click the Restore Declined Updates button in the Previous Updates section to make them available again. (Until you've declined an update, the Restore Declined Updates button is unavailable.)

5. Click the OK button. Windows closes the System Properties dialog box.

Running Windows Update Manually

If you don't want to wait for Windows Update to run automatically on schedule, or if you don't like to have your computer calling Microsoft secretly in the wee hours of dark and stormy nights, you can run Windows Update manually. You can do so either from the Start menu (Start ➤ All Programs ➤ Windows Update) or from the Help and Support Center window.

See page 42 of "Essential Skills for Windows XP Professional" for a visual guide to running Windows Update.

Automating the Installation of Windows XP

The installation procedure described in this chapter is effective and relatively straightforward once you know what the options mean. But it still takes between 45 and 90 minutes to complete, depending on the speed of your computer, and requires you to be there at odd moments to answer prompts, so it's a bit of a waste of time.

Still, you only need to run the installation procedure once on any computer. Or do you? Some people find that they need to install Windows multiple times on the same computer. Every installation of Windows gradually accumulates unneeded programs, files, and settings. These can cause Windows to slow down or even become unstable. Windows 98 was so notorious for this that the joke went that the name specified the number of days that you could reasonably run it before expecting enough trouble to set in that would require a reinstall to fix.

Windows XP improves your chances of not needing to reinstall by providing tools such as System Restore, Roll Back Driver, and Disk Cleanup and Disk Defragmenter (all discussed later in this book) to keep your system in working order. But even these can't fix every problem. If you need a fresh start, or if you maintain a test computer, you may want to blow away all the old files and settings and virtual dust-bunnies by performing a new installation.

To help you do so, Windows XP includes a tool for performing an unattended installation. (You can of course use these tools to set up Windows XP the first and only time, but most people don't find it worth their while to do so.)

If you had to guess at how the procedure works, you'd probably figure that it consists of creating a file ahead of time that gives Windows the information for which it normally prompts you during setup, and then feeding that file to the Setup procedure. That's just how it works. The file is called an *answer file* for obvious enough reasons. There's a Wizard to help you create the answer file, but then you have to edit it a bit by hand.

To perform an unattended installation, follow these steps:

1. Extract the tools from the `Support\Tools\Deploy.cab` folder on the CD to a convenient location. If you already have Windows XP installed on one of your computers, you can extract these files by using Explorer. If you have an earlier version of Windows, use a Zip program (for example, WinZip) from Windows or the `EXTRACT` command from a command prompt instead.

2. Open an Explorer window to the folder to which you extracted the files.

3. Double-click the `SETUPMGR.EXE` program. Windows starts the Windows XP Setup Manager Wizard, which displays its first screen.

4. Click the Next button. The Wizard displays the New or Existing Answer File screen.

5. Leave the Create a New Answer File option button selected (as it is by default) unless you already have an answer file that you want to tweak. In that case, select the Modify an Existing Answer File option button and enter the path and file name in the text box, either by typing or by clicking the Browse button and using the resulting Open dialog box.

6. Click the Next button. The Wizard displays the Product to Install screen:

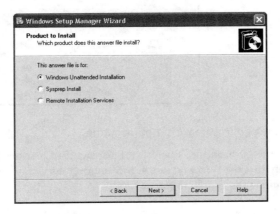

7. Make sure the Windows XP Unattended Installation option button is selected.

8. Click the Next button. The Wizard displays the Platform screen:

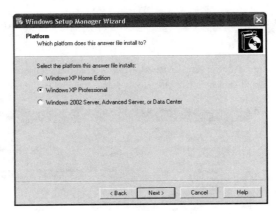

9. Select the Windows XP Professional option button.

10. Click the Next button. The Wizard displays the User Interaction Level screen:

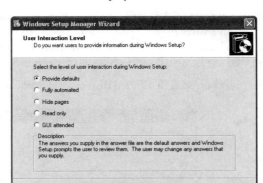

11. Select the Fully Automated option button.

12. Click the Next button. The Wizard displays the Distribution Folder screen, which lets you specify that the Wizard create a distribution folder on your computer or on a networked drive containing the Windows source files.

NOTE   *Creating a distribution folder lets you not only install without the CD but also add extra files (such as device drivers) to the custom installation. If you like unattended installation so much that you'd like to buy the company that made it—that is, if you want to run unattended installations frequently and you have a convenient drive or folder—you'll probably want to try this option. For the moment, we'll stick with installing from the CD.*

13. Select the No, This Answer File Will Be Used to Install from a CD option button.

14. Click the Next button. The Wizard displays the License Agreement screen.

15. Select the I Accept the Terms of the License Agreement check box and click the Next button. The Wizard displays the Windows XP Setup Manager screen:

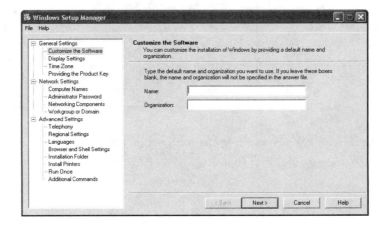

16. Select each screen in turn and specify those settings applicable to your installation. Browsing through the screens feels like a sort of Redmond Roulette, because you must fill in any required fields (such as the Name text box on the Customizing the Software screen) before leaving any given screen. If you don't, the Wizard halts you in your tracks with a peremptory message box pointing out your involuntary omission. So it's best to deal with the screens in order.

Customize the Software screen   Enter your name on the Name text box (compulsory). If appropriate, enter the organization in the Organization text box.

Display Settings screen   You can use the Colors drop-down list, the Screen Area drop-down list, and the Refresh Frequency drop-down list to specify the colors, screen area, and refresh rate to use instead of accepting the Windows defaults. For custom settings, click the Custom button and specify them in the Custom Display Settings dialog box.

Time Zone screen   Select the time zone in the Time Zone drop-down list.

Providing the Product Key screen   Enter the product key on this screen. (This is compulsory for creating a fully automated answer file.)

Computer Names screen   Enter the computer name in the Computer Name text box (compulsory).

Administrator Password screen   Enter the password for the Administrator account in the Password text box and the Confirm Password text box. Select the Encrypt Administrator Password in Answer File check box if you want to do just that. If you want Windows to log the Administrator on automatically, you can select the When the Computer Starts, Automatically Log On As Administrator check box and specify the number of times in the Number of Times to Auto Logon text box. (Auto-logon can be useful for the first boot, but beyond that, it's a severe security threat.)

Networking Components screen   Select the Typical Settings option button or the Customize Settings option button as appropriate. If you select the latter, customize the settings as discussed in "Specifying Network Settings" earlier in the chapter.

Workgroup or Domain screen   Leave the Workgroup option button selected and enter the name of the workgroup in the Workgroup text box.

17. Click the Next button. Windows displays the Windows Setup Manager dialog box telling you that it has created an answer file and inviting you to specify the location for it:

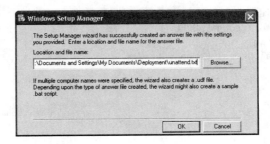

18. Enter the appropriate location and change the file name from its default UNATTEND.TXT to WINNT.SIF. Click the OK button. Windows XP Setup Manager creates the file and saves it under that name.

19. Choose File ➣ Exit. Windows XP Setup Manager closes itself.

Now you've created the basic file. It's ready to go—but before you run it, you probably want to take a look at the contents. (You might also want to add extra parameters. Consult the Setup Manager Help file for possibilities.) Right-click the file in an Explorer window, choose Open With from the shortcut menu, select Notepad in the Open With dialog box, and click the OK button. Windows opens the file in Notepad. Depending on the options you chose, it should look something like this:

```
;SetupMgrTag
[Data]
    AutoPartition=1
    MsDosInitiated="0"
    UnattendedInstall="Yes"
[Unattended]
    UnattendMode=FullUnattended
    OemSkipEula=Yes
    OemPreinstall=No
    TargetPath=\WINDOWS
[GuiUnattended]
    AdminPassword=*
    EncryptedAdminPassword=NO
    OEMSkipRegional=1
    TimeZone=85
    OemSkipWelcome=1
[UserData]
    ProductID=NNNNN-NNNNN-NNNNN-NNNNN-NNNNN
    FullName="Andy Rondolophberger"
    OrgName="Rondolophberger Pharmaceuticals"
    ComputerName=Verwirrung
[Display]
    BitsPerPel=32
    Xresolution=800
    YResolution=600
    Vrefresh=85
[Identification]
    JoinWorkgroup=LAUREL
[Networking]
    InstallDefaultComponents=Yes
```

If you've chosen other options—for example, customizing networking or choosing language settings—you'll see further lines covering them. You can also add other lines as necessary to take other actions, such as specifying that the installation repartition the hard drive or convert the file system to NTFS. You'll find details of the possibilities in the Help files contained in `DEPLOY.CAB`.

If you make any changes, save the file, close it, and copy it to a floppy disk. Then boot the computer from the Windows XP CD and put the floppy disk in the floppy drive. Windows installs automatically using the settings you specified.

Summary

This chapter has discussed how to install Windows, as a clean install, an upgrade to your current version of Windows, or as an entirely new installation. You've also learned how to use the Windows Update feature to keep your copy of Windows updated, compatible, and secure, and how to create an answer file to perform an unattended installation.

Chapter 3

Using the Desktop and Getting Help

IN THE FIRST PART of this chapter, I'll discuss how to get started with Windows XP Professional. I'll cover how to log on and log off; how to switch from one user session to another; and how to exit Windows. I'll also discuss how you can find out who else is logged on to the computer when you're working at it; how you can get an idea of which programs the other users are running; and how you can log off another user (or all other users) in order to reclaim the resources they're using.

In the second part of this chapter, I'll discuss how to find the help you need to use Windows XP most effectively. XP includes a greater amount of help than previous versions of Windows and presents that help in a new interface, the Help and Support Center program. I'll describe how to use Help and Support Center and the various areas it offers. I'll also mention other resources that you may need to turn to when you run into less tractable problems.

- ◆ Logging on and off
- ◆ Using the Desktop and the Start menu
- ◆ Switching users
- ◆ Seeing what other users are doing
- ◆ Using the Winkey
- ◆ Shutting down Windows
- ◆ Using the Help and Support Center
- ◆ Using the Support Options
- ◆ Using Remote Assistance
- ◆ Using the Troubleshooters
- ◆ Finding help on the Internet

NOTE   *Before we start, here's something you need to know. Windows XP Professional supports three types of users: Computer Administrator users, Limited users, and the Guest user. By default, all named users are set up as Computer Administrator users, which gives them full authority to configure and customize the computer. Limited users, which you create manually, can perform only minimal configuration and customization. The Guest user, an account that's created automatically by Windows, can perform no configuration or customization. In the first part of this chapter, I'll assume you're logging on as a Computer Administrator user, because that's most likely to be the case. Chapter 18 discusses how to create and manage user accounts.*

Logging On and Logging Off

Logging on and off in Windows XP work differently from previous versions of Windows. Logging on and off could hardly be easier, but it's important to understand what happens when you log on and off, and how logging on and off differ from switching users.

In earlier versions of Windows, only one user at a time could be logged on to a computer running Windows. For a second user to log on, the first user needed to log off. Logging off involved closing all the open programs and files: either the user could close the programs and files manually before logging off, or Windows would close them automatically when the user issued the Log Off command (and confirmed that they wanted to log off).

Once all the programs and files were closed, and all network and Internet connections were closed as well, Windows displayed the Log On to Windows dialog box or the Enter Network Password dialog box, depending on whether the computer was attached to a network. Another user could then log on to Windows, run programs, open files, establish network and Internet connections, and so on.

In Windows XP, multiple users can be logged on at the same time, though of course only one user can actually be using the computer. Each of those users who is logged on can have programs running and files open. Windows XP lets you switch quickly between users without closing the programs and files.

Only one user can be *active*—actually using the computer—at any time. (Given that most computers have only one keyboard, mouse, and monitor, this may seem too obvious to mention—but things are very different in Unix and Linux, in which multiple users can be actively using the same computer at the same time, some locally and some remotely.) A user who is logged on but not active is said to be *disconnected*.

This means that, for example, Jane and Jack can keep their programs open while Ross is using the computer. When Jane logs back on (in the process disconnecting Ross, who perhaps stepped away for a cup of coffee), Windows resumes her session from where she left off, displaying the programs she had running and the files she had open. Windows reestablishes any of Jane's persistent network connections, including any Internet connection that's set to connect automatically.

Being able to leave multiple users up and running is great—up to a point. But it has serious implications for performance and file integrity. The following sections discuss these considerations briefly.

FAST USER SWITCHING, PERFORMANCE, AND FILE INTEGRITY

Having multiple users logged on to Windows at the same time affects performance because each user who's logged on takes up some of the computer's memory. Having a user logged on itself takes up relatively little memory, but each program that the user has running, and each file that they have open, adds to the amount being used.

Windows XP needs a minimum of 64MB of RAM to run at an acceptable speed. For each light user, reckon another 32MB of RAM; for each moderate user, 64MB; and for each heavy user, 128MB. If you have 256MB of RAM, you should be able to have two or three users logged on and running several programs each without running short of memory.

Having multiple users logged on at once can also affect file integrity. For example, what happens when two users try to change the same file at the same time? The short answer is: It depends.

Some programs are smart enough to realize that someone else has a copy of the file open. For example, if you try to open in Word 2002 the same document that another user has open, Word displays the File in Use dialog box to warn you that the document is locked for editing and to offer you ways to work with the document (open a read-only copy; create a local copy and merge your changes later; or receive notification when the original copy is available).

Other programs aren't smart enough to spot the problem. For example, WordPad (Windows XP's built-in word processing program) lets you open a document that another user has open, change it, and save the changes. The other user can then save *their* changes to the same file, which can end up with some of the changes you've made and some that the other user has made. And this is assuming that only two users are editing the document at the same time. For all WordPad knows, half the people in Delaware could be editing the document at the same time and wiping out each other's changes.

If your computer has a modest amount of RAM—say, 64MB, 96MB, or 128MB—or if you're having problems with users opening files at the same time, turn off the Fast User Switching feature. Choose Start ➢ Control Panel to open Control Panel, click the User Accounts link to open the User Account screen, click the Change the Way Users Log On or Off link, clear the Use Fast User Switching check box, and then click Apply Options. When you turn off Fast User Switching, only one user can be logged on to the computer at any given time, and that user must log off before another user can log on. This reduces the amount of memory needed and avoids most problems with shared files.

Logging On

To start using Windows, log on from the Welcome screen. Figure 3.1 shows an example of the Welcome screen, which displays a list of the users who have accounts set up on the computer. Any programs a user has running appear listed under the username, together with the number of e-mail messages waiting for them. If a user is logged on but has no programs running, the Welcome screen displays *Logged on* beneath their name.

FIGURE 3.1

The Welcome screen lists the users with accounts on this computer, any tasks the user has running, and any unread e-mail messages they have.

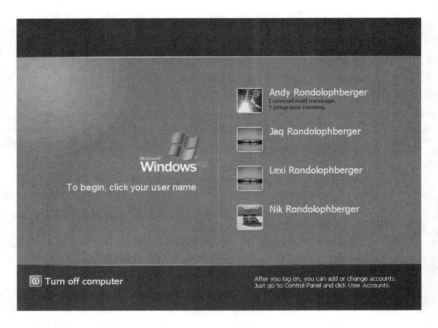

By default, user accounts are set up without passwords, so you log on by clicking the username under which you want to log on. (If an administrator has set up Windows to require passwords, you'll need to enter the password for the account as well.)

When it accepts your logon, Windows displays your Desktop with its current settings. (The section "Using the Desktop and Start Menu" a little later in this chapter discusses the basics of the Desktop and Start menu.)

The first time you log on, Windows creates your folders and sets up program shortcuts for you—so the logon process takes a minute or two. Subsequent logons are much quicker.

Logging Off

The counterpart to logging on is (unsurprisingly) logging off. When you log off, Windows closes all the programs and files you've been using. If the files contain unsaved changes, Windows prompts you to save them.

To log off, display the Start menu by clicking the Start button, and click the Log Off button. Windows displays the Log Off Windows dialog box (shown in Figure 3.2). Click the Log Off button to log off.

NOTE   If you leave your computer unattended for a while, the screen saver usually kicks in—unless you have something open that prevents the screen saver from starting (or you've disabled the screen saver). For example, a dialog box open on-screen usually prevents the screen saver from starting. The default setting is for the screen saver to start after 10 minutes and to display the Welcome screen. The screen saver gives you some protection against prying eyes (particularly if you're using passwords for logging on), but it also makes it harder to see who's doing what on the computer.

FIGURE 3.2

The Log Off Windows dialog box lets you log off, cancel the command, or switch to another user.

Logging On to a Domain

If your Windows XP Professional computer is connected to a domain, when you power on the computer it will boot to a Windows Log On screen. You'll need to press Ctrl+Alt+Del to get to the Log On to Windows dialog box. You must supply a valid username and password that has domain access privileges. If you do not have this information, contact your domain administrator.

Before clicking OK, check that the Log On To entry has your domain name listed. If it does not, use the drop-down arrow and select your domain name. If the Log On To entry does not appear, click the Options button. Click OK, and you will log on to the domain. You can only access information in the domain to which you have privileges.

If you want multiuser support, you cannot be joined to a domain. If you were joined to a domain and now are part of a Workgroup and want to enable multiuser support, follow these steps:

1. Choose Start ➢ Control Panel to open Control Panel, and then click the User Accounts link to open the User Accounts screen.

2. Click the Change the Way Users Log On or Off link to open the Select Logon and Logoff Options screen.

3. Click the Use the Welcome Screen check box, and then click the Use Fast User Switching check box.

4. Click Apply Options. Close all open windows, and then restart your system.

Using the Desktop and Start Menu

Once you've logged on successfully, Windows displays the Desktop. Figure 3.3 shows what the Desktop looks like the first time you start Windows and start a couple of programs. Because you can customize the Desktop extensively, your Desktop might not look anything like the Desktop shown in the figure: the wallpaper might be different; the Taskbar could be located at a different side of the screen; or various toolbars might be displayed. About the one unchanging thing about the Desktop is the Start menu button—but even this might not be displayed if someone has chosen to hide the Taskbar (of which the Start button is part).

FIGURE 3.3

The components of the Windows Desktop

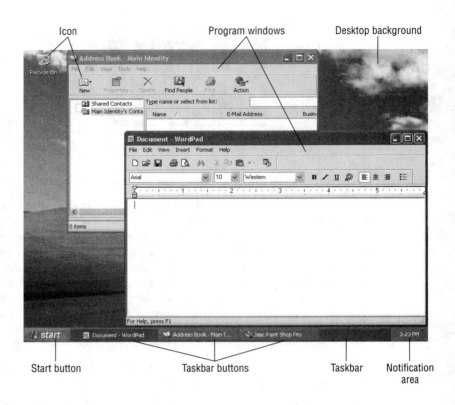

We'll examine the Desktop in more detail in the forthcoming chapters, but these are the basic actions for navigating it:

- ◆ The Desktop contains one or more shortcuts to items. Usually, there's an icon for the Recycle Bin, if nothing else. Double-click an icon to run the program associated with it.

- ◆ The Start menu provides access to the full range of programs and features currently installed on Windows. Click the Start button to display the Start menu. Choose one of the items that appears on it, or click the All Programs button to display a cascading menu containing further items.

- ◆ The Taskbar gives you quick access to each program that's currently running. The Taskbar displays a button for each active program window. To display that window in front of all other windows, click its button. To minimize the program, click its Taskbar button again.

See pages 5–9 of "Essential Skills for Windows XP Professional" for a visual guide to how to use the Taskbar.

◆ The notification area contains items that are useful to have displayed all the time (such as the clock, which is displayed by default), together with information and alerts (which are displayed at appropriate times).

◆ The Desktop background is a graphic that you can change at will.

Switching to Another User

As you saw in Figure 3.2, the Log Off Windows dialog box also contains a button called Switch User. When you click the Switch User button, Windows keeps your programs running (instead of closing them, as it does when you log out) and displays the Welcome screen so that you can log on as another user or (more likely) other users can log on as themselves.

USING THE CONNECT COMMAND TO SWITCH USERS QUICKLY

Switching users as described above is easy but takes a few clicks. There's a quicker way of switching—by using Task Manager as follows:

1. Right-click open space in the Taskbar and choose Task Manager from the shortcut menu. Windows opens Task Manager.

2. Click the Users tab (shown in Figure 3.4, later in this chapter).

3. Right-click the user that you want to connect as and choose Connect from the shortcut menu. If the user's account has a password, Windows displays the Connect Password Required dialog box. When you enter the password correctly (or if the account has no password), Windows disconnects your session and connects you as the user you selected.

Locking the Computer

To leave your current session running but display the Welcome screen quickly, press Winkey+L. (If you're not using the Welcome screen, Windows displays the Log On to Windows dialog box instead.)

NOTE   If you're connected to a domain, pressing Winkey+L locks the computer.

Microsoft calls this action *locking* the computer, though the term is neither accurate nor helpful with Windows XP's default settings. The computer isn't locked in any useful sense unless all user accounts are protected with effective passwords.

However, if you turn off the Welcome screen and Fast User Switching, Windows manages a semblance of locking. When the current user disconnects their session, Windows displays a blank background topped by the Unlock Computer dialog box, which tells the user that the computer is in use, that it has been locked, and that only the current user or an administrator can unlock it. If you've applied passwords, this is true; if you haven't, anyone can click the OK button in the Unlock Computer dialog box to unlock the computer and log on as the current user.

Checking Which User Is Currently Active

If you're in any doubt as to which user is currently active, display the Start menu (by clicking the Start button or pressing the Winkey) and check the username displayed at the top.

Seeing Who Else Is Logged On to the Computer

As you saw a page or two ago, the Welcome screen displays details of each user logged on to the computer and the number of programs they're running. But if you don't want to display the Welcome screen (and disconnect your session by doing so), you can find out which other users are logged in by using Task Manager as follows:

1. Right-click the Taskbar and choose Task Manager from the shortcut menu. Windows displays Task Manager.

2. Click the Users tab (shown in Figure 3.4), which lists the users and their status.

FIGURE 3.4

The Users tab of Task Manager shows you which other users are logged on to the computer. You can send them messages, switch to their sessions, or log them off forcibly.

NOTE   *Limited users and the Guest user can't see which other users are logged on or which processes they're running. As a result, Limited users and the Guest user can't switch directly to another user's session by using Task Manager, though they can disconnect their own session or log themselves off by using Task Manager.*

Seeing Which Programs the Other Users Are Running

It's not easy to see exactly which programs the other users of the computer are running unless you know the names of the executable files for the programs, but you can get an idea by using the Processes tab of Task Manager. This tab also shows you how much memory each program is using, which helps you establish whether—or why—your computer is running short of memory.

Follow these steps to start Task Manager and display its Processes tab:

1. Right-click the Taskbar and choose Task Manager from the shortcut menu to open Task Manager.

2. Click the Processes tab, which lists the processes you're running.

3. Select the Show Processes from All Users check box. (This check box is cleared by default.) Task Manager adds to the list all the processes that the other users are running as well. Figure 3.5 shows an example of the Processes tab. You can sort the list of processes by any column by clicking the column heading. In the figure, the processes are sorted by the User Name column so that it's easy to see which process belongs to which user.

FIGURE 3.5

Use the Processes tab of Task Manager to see which programs the other users are running.

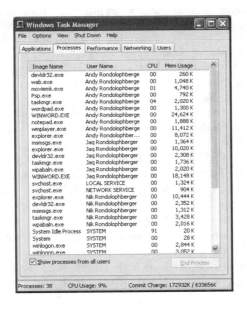

As you can see in the figure, three of the Rondolophbergers are running programs, and between them they're using quite a chunk of memory: the Commit Charge counter in the lower-right corner of the Processes tab shows that 172932K (about 169MB) out of 633656K (about 619MB) of memory has been used up. In the list, you can see some of the principal offenders: copies of WINWORD.EXE (Microsoft Word) that Andy and Jaq are running (24,624K and 18,148K, respectively), several instances of EXPLORER.EXE, and some programs with unpronounceable names such as DEVLDR32.EXE and WPABALN.EXE.

Some of the other names are readily identifiable. For example, WMPLAYER.EXE is the executable for Windows Media Player, as you'd expect, and TASKMGR.EXE is the executable for Task Manager itself. You don't need to memorize the mapping of each executable filename to its program, but if you look at Task Manager now and then, you'll learn to scan the list of processes and see which is running. This will help you decide whether you should go ahead and log another user off Windows (as described in the next section) or whether doing so will trash their work and ruin their life.

WHICH NAME CORRESPONDS TO WHICH PROGRAM?

To find out which program corresponds to each executable file, display the Applications tab of Task Manager. Right-click a program and choose Go to Process from the shortcut menu. Task Manager displays the Processes tab and selects the process for that program.

That's easy enough—but there are many more processes running than programs. Try closing all the programs listed on the Applications tab of Task Manager, and you'll see that there's still a goodly list of processes left. Try stopping any obvious services that you can temporarily dispense with, and see if an associated process disappears. For instance, try closing your Internet connection or stopping your PC Cards. Did either of those actions lose you a process? Then you have an idea of what that process does.

If you're desperate to find out which function or service an executable runs, try searching for the executable. The folder that contains the executable may give you a clue as to the program, or there may be a comment on the executable that reveals its purpose. Then again, the executable may prove to be one of the mysterious system files stored in the Windows folder or the `Windows\System32` folder. If the latter is the case, figure it's something unknowable and leave it alone.

While you're looking at Task Manager, there are a couple of other things you might as well know. First, you can also see in the figure that it's not just the Rondolophbergers who are using memory like there was no tomorrow—Windows also has a number of processes open on its own account. The LOCAL SERVICE account is running `SVCHOST.EXE` (service host), as is the NETWORK SERVICE account. The SYSTEM account is running a dozen or more processes, of which you can see only the top few in the figure. Of these, the first, the System Idle Process, is consuming 91 percent of the processor cycles. (This is actually good news. When the System Idle Process is taking up most of the processor cycles like this, the computer is idling along—goofing off until the user does something that presses it into action.)

Second, you may have noticed that the numbers in the Mem Usage column don't add up to anything like the 172932K listed as being committed (even though you can't see the whole column). That's because that committed figure is both physical memory (RAM) used and virtual memory (hard disk space being used to simulate more RAM). If you want to see how much virtual memory each process is taking up, follow these steps:

1. In Task Manager, choose View ➣ Select Columns to open the Select Columns dialog box (shown in Figure 3.6).

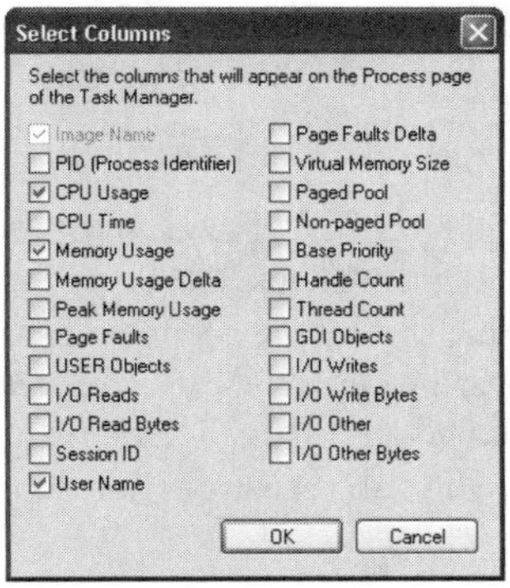

FIGURE 3.6

Use the Select Columns dialog box to add further columns of information to Task Manager's Processes tab.

2. Select the Virtual Memory Size check box.

◆ Also select the check boxes for any other information you want to see in Task Manager. Many of the items here are somewhat arcane, but you might want to look at CPU Time or Peak Memory Usage.

3. Click the OK button. Task Manager closes the Select Columns dialog box and adds the columns you chose to the Processes tab.

Figure 3.7 shows the Processes tab of Task Manager with the Virtual Memory Size column added and the processes sorted by that column. Notice that the two copies of Word have very heavy memory usage indeed (when you add the Mem Usage column and the VM Size column). SVCHOST.EXE also shows itself as a heavyweight, using a little over 11MB of virtual memory in addition to its 10MB of RAM.

FIGURE 3.7

If you want to see virtual memory usage, add the Virtual Memory Size (VM Size) column to the Processes tab in Task Manager.

Logging Another User Off

If necessary, any Computer Administrator user can log another user off the computer.

Logging someone else off isn't usually a great idea, because while you can use Task Manager to see which processes they're running (as described in the previous section), you can't see whether they have any unsaved work in them. If you don't use passwords to log on to Windows, it's much better to log on as the other user and close the programs and documents manually. Then log off (as the other user) and log back on as yourself. If you do use passwords, you'll need to know the other user's password to log on as them, which kinda defeats the point of having passwords in the first place.

That said, you may need to log another user off if they are running enough programs to affect the computer's performance or if they have open a single-user program or a document that you need to use. If you do so, you may want to send them a message as described in the next section so that they know what's happened.

To log another user off, follow these steps:

1. Right-click the Taskbar and choose Task Manager from the shortcut menu to display Task Manager.

2. Click the Users tab (shown in Figure 3.8).

FIGURE 3.8

From the Users tab of Windows Task Manager, you can log another user off the computer.

3. Select the user and click the Logoff button. (Alternatively, right-click the user and choose Log Off from the shortcut menu.) Windows displays the Windows Task Manager dialog box (shown in Figure 3.9), asking if you want to log the selected user off.

FIGURE 3.9

You can log another user off the computer—but be aware that doing so will cost them any unsaved work.

4. Click the Yes button. The other user's session is toast—as is any unsaved work they had open.

Sending a Message to Another User

You can send a message to another user logged in to this computer. Because the other user can't be using the computer at the same time as you, this feature is not useful for real-time communication—it's not exactly instant messaging—but it can be useful for making sure a family member or a colleague gets a message the next time they use the computer. (For example, you might ask them not to shut down the computer because you're still using it.) It's also useful for notifying another user that you've had to terminate a program that they were using.

To send a message to another user, follow these steps:

1. Right-click the Taskbar and choose Task Manager from the shortcut menu to display Windows Task Manager.

2. Click the Users tab.

3. Right-click the user and choose Send Message from the shortcut menu. Windows displays the Send Message dialog box (shown in Figure 3.10).

FIGURE 3.10

Use the Send Message dialog box to send a message to another user logged on to this computer.

4. Enter the message title in the Message Title text box and the message in the Message text box.

◆ To start a new line, press Ctrl+Enter. (Pressing the Enter key on its own registers a click on the OK button, sending the message.)

◆ To type a tab, press Ctrl+Tab. (Pressing the Tab key on its own moves the focus to the next control.)

5. Click the OK button to send the message.

The next time the user logs on to Windows, they receive the message as a screen pop. Figure 3.11 shows an example.

FIGURE 3.11

When you send a message, the user receives a screen pop like this when they start using the computer.

Using the Winkey

As I mentioned in Chapter 1, Windows XP provides a number of keyboard combinations for the Winkey, the key (or keys) with the Windows logo on the keyboard. If you're comfortable leaving your hands on the keyboard, these combinations are doubly convenient, because not only can you avoid reaching for the mouse, but you can also display with a single keystroke a number of windows and dialog boxes that lie several commands deep in the Windows interface.

Table 3.1 lists the Winkey combinations.

TABLE 3.1: WINKEY COMBINATIONS

WINKEY COMBINATION	WHAT IT DOES
Winkey	Toggles the display of the Start menu
Winkey+Break	Displays the System Properties dialog box
Winkey+Tab	Moves the focus to the next button in the Taskbar
Winkey+Shift+Tab	Moves the focus to the previous button in the Taskbar
Winkey+B	Moves the focus to the notification area
Winkey+D	Displays the Desktop
Winkey+E	Opens an Explorer window showing My Computer
Winkey+F	Opens a Search Results window and activates Search Companion
Winkey+Ctrl+F	Opens a Search Results window, activates Search Companion, and starts a Search for Computer
Winkey+F1	Opens a Help and Support Center window
Winkey+M	Issues a Minimize All Windows command
Winkey+Shift+M	Issues an Undo Minimize All command
Winkey+R	Displays the Run dialog box
Winkey+U	Displays Utility Manager
Winkey+L	Locks the computer

Shutting Down Windows

You can shut down Windows in several ways:

◆ By clicking the Turn Off Computer button at the bottom of the default Start menu or by choosing Start ➢ Turn Off Computer from the classic Start menu. (If you're connected to a domain, Turn Off Computer becomes Shut Down.)

◆ By clicking the Turn Off Computer button on the Welcome screen and then clicking the Turn Off button on the Turn Off Computer screen (shown in Figure 3.12).

FIGURE 3.12

To turn off the computer, click the Turn Off button on the Turn Off Computer screen.

- ◆ By choosing Shut Down ➤ Turn Off from Windows Task Manager.
- ◆ By pressing Alt+F4 with the Desktop active and then clicking the Turn Off button on the Turn Off Computer screen.

From the Turn Off Computer screen, you can also click the Hibernate button to make your computer hibernate or the Restart button to restart the computer and Windows. If your computer doesn't support hibernation, the Hibernate button doesn't appear on the Turn Off Computer screen.

POWERING DOWN YOUR COMPUTER WHEN WINDOWS HAS CRASHED

If Windows won't shut down because it has crashed, you'll need to shut it down the hard way. To do so, press the power button on the computer. On ACPI-compliant computers, you may need to hold the power button down for four seconds or more to shut the system down—short presses of the power button may have no effect.

On some computers, a short press of the power button may make Windows display the Turn Off Computer screen so that you can specify whether to hibernate, turn off the computer, or restart it. Under normal circumstances, catching the power signal like this is pretty smart, helping to dissuade users from powering down the computer without exiting Windows first. But if Windows has crashed, you won't be able to do anything from the Turn Off Computer screen.

Help and Support Center

Help and Support Center is the latest in Microsoft's efforts to provide help resources powerful enough to silence the ringing of the phones on its costly support lines. Windows XP's Help and Support Center builds on the improvements introduced in the Help and Support Center in Windows Me, which introduced a Web-style interface to replace the old-style Help-file interface in earlier versions of Windows, by integrating many more external resources. For example, you can now search the Microsoft Knowledge Base, an online database of questions and answers, directly from Help and Support Center instead of having to access it separately by using Internet Explorer. And many hardware manufacturers are now providing product-support information that's accessible through Help and Support Center.

Starting Help and Support Center

Choose Start ➤ Help and Support to open Help and Support Center at the Home page. You should see something like Figure 3.13, except that it will contain some updated information. (Your hardware manufacturer may also have customized Help and Support Center by adding content to it or by adapting its interface.)

FIGURE 3.13

The Home page in Help and Support Center provides links to the many different areas of Help and Support Center.

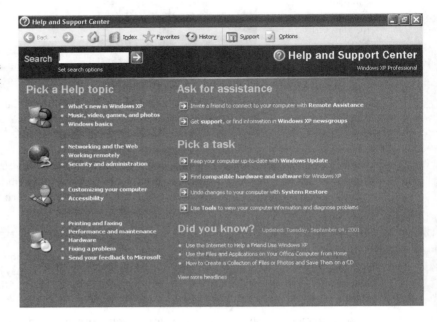

As you can see in Figure 3.13, the Help and Support Center window has a toolbar (at the top, starting with the Back button) for primary navigation rather than a menu bar. This toolbar is called the *navigation bar*. Below the navigation bar appears the Search bar.

TIP   You can open multiple Help and Support Center windows at once, which can be a help when you're searching for different pieces of help information or navigating different routes in search of the same piece of information.

Finding Your Way around Help and Support Center

Help and Support Center has access to a large amount of information in Help files that Windows installs on your hard drive, together with troubleshooters for stepping you through the process of finding solutions to common problems and links for running Windows programs (such as Remote Assistance and the System Configuration Utility) that may help you solve or eliminate problems. But Help and Support Center's strongest feature is that it also provides a gateway to information resources on the Web and Internet.

Because of the amount of information and resources that Help and Support Center offers, you may find that it takes you a while to get the hang of navigating around Help and Support Center. This section highlights the main ways of finding the information you need: searching, browsing, using the History feature, and using the Index.

SEARCHING FOR HELP

If you don't see an immediately appropriate link on the Help and Support Center Home page, the easiest way to find information on a particular topic is to search for it.

To search, enter the search term or terms in the Search text box and click the Start Searching button or press Enter. Help and Support Center displays the Search Results pane on the left side and adds a toolbar containing four buttons (Add to Favorites, Change View, Print, and Locate in Contents) under the right side of the Search bar.

The Search Results list box breaks up the results into three categories:

Suggested Topics   Suggested topics are keyword matches—one or more of your search terms match a keyword in each of these topics. These topics are further broken up into subcategories such as Pick a Task and Overviews, Articles, and Tutorials.

Full-Text Search Matches   Full-text matches are topics that contain one or more of your search terms in the body text of the help topic rather than in the keywords.

Microsoft Knowledge Base   These results are from the Microsoft Knowledge Base (see the next sidebar). Use them to glean extra or extraneous information beyond that offered by the topics listed in the Suggested Topics and Full-Text Search Matches lists.

To display a category, click its heading. Then click a search result to display it in the right pane, as in the example in Figure 3.14. By default, Windows highlights the word or words you searched for, as in the figure. If there are one or two instances this can be a help, but if there are many instances, this highlighting appears as more of a defacement than an enhancement. But you can get rid of it, as described after the sidebar.

FIGURE 3.14

Click a search result in the Search Results pane to display the page in the right pane.

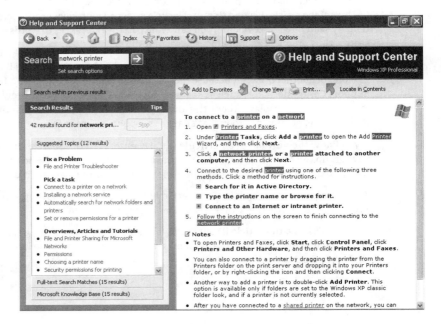

NOTE *You can also start searching for help from Search Companion by clicking the Information in Help and Support Center link. There's no advantage to starting to search this way unless you happen to have Search Companion displayed when you want help.*

Making the Most of the Microsoft Knowledge Base

The Microsoft Knowledge Base is an online repository of knowledge and wisdom accumulated by Microsoft about its products. Given that the Knowledge Base is one of the main tools that Microsoft's support engineers use for troubleshooting customer problems with Windows, it's a great resource for searching for solutions to problems that Windows' local help resources don't know about.

The disadvantage to the Knowledge Base, and perhaps the reason it's not more heavily emphasized in Microsoft's battery of help solutions, is the way it's arranged and the necessarily scattershot nature of its coverage. The Knowledge Base consists of a large number of answers that Microsoft's support engineers and other experts have written to questions that frustrated users and developers have submitted. The answers vary greatly in length, depending on the complexity of the problem and user level, ranging from beginner topics to super-advanced (developer-level) topics. Coverage is patchy, because the questions tend to be answered only when they're not covered in the Help files and other more accessible resources. This is why the Help and Support Center Search Results pane presents the Microsoft Knowledge Base list after the Suggested Topics list and the Full-Text Search Matches list: the Knowledge Base's offerings may be helpful, but they may equally well be completely irrelevant to your needs.

Each article is identified by an Article ID number, which consists of the letter Q followed by a six-digit number (for example, Q201950). Each article has a title that describes the problem it covers, information on which products and versions it covers, a summary that you can scan to get an idea of the contents, and the full text of the article. Beyond this, each article is tagged with keywords describing the main areas of its content. By searching for keywords, you can avoid passing references to words you might have included in the search, thus producing a more focused set of results.

For power use, you may get better results by searching the Knowledge Base directly by using Internet Explorer or another browser, because the Knowledge Base's Web interface offers extra options that Help and Support Center does not, such as searching for what's new in the last few days on a particular product and being able to display either titles and excerpts from hits found or just titles. To search the Knowledge Base directly, point your browser at `search.support.microsoft.com/kb/c.asp`.

If you know the number of a particular query, enter it in the Search text box. For example, if you read newsgroups on Microsoft-related subjects, you'll often see references to particular queries (or, more accurately, to the *answers* to particular queries) mentioned as the place to find a fix for a given problem.

You can also use the Article ID to retrieve the article by e-mail by sending a message to `mshelp@microsoft.com` with the Article ID number in the Subject line.

If you don't know the Article ID but think you can locate it by searching article titles, you can get an index of Knowledge Base articles by e-mail by sending a message to `mshelp@microsoft.com` with the word "Index" in the Subject line.

SETTING SEARCH OPTIONS

Help and Support Center lets you specify how you want it to search. To set search options, take the following steps:

1. Click the Options button on the navigation bar. Help and Support Center displays the Options screen.

2. In the Options list in the left pane, click the Set Search Options link. Help and Support Center displays the Set Search Options screen (shown in Figure 3.15).

FIGURE 3.15

Choose search options on the Set Search Options screen in Help and Support Center.

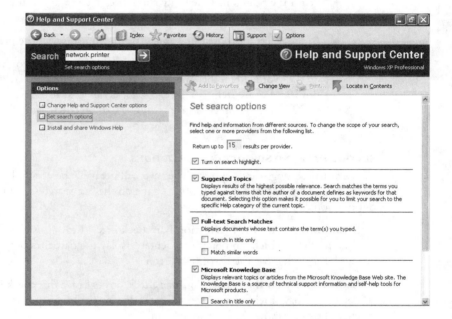

3. In the Return Up to *NN* Results per Provider text box, enter the number of search results you want Help and Support Center to get at once from each source of help. The default setting is 15, but you may want to increase this number if you find 15 doesn't give you the information you need. The disadvantage to returning more search results is that it takes longer to download those that come across your Internet connection.

4. Clear the Turn On Search Highlight check box if you don't want Help and Support Center to highlight your search terms in each result it displays.

5. If you don't want to use the Suggested Topics category, clear the Suggested Topics check box. (Usually, this category is well worth using, but in some circumstances you might want to set up Help and Support Center to search only the Knowledge Base.)

6. If you don't want to use full-text searching, clear the Full-Text Search Matches check box. If you do use full-text searching, you can refine it by selecting the Search in Title Only check box

to limit full-text searches to the titles of documents instead of including their body text, or the Match Similar Words check box to have full-text searching include matches with words it thinks are similar to (instead of identical to) your search terms.

7. Clear the Microsoft Knowledge Base check box if you don't want to search the Knowledge Base. You might want to avoid searching the Knowledge Base if you find its suggestions too esoteric or if you're working offline. If you continue to search the Knowledge Base, you can set the following search options to target the results:

◆ Select the Search in Title Only check box if you want to limit searches to the titles of documents instead of including their body text.

◆ In the Select a Product or Topic drop-down list, select the product or topic to search for.

◆ In the Search For drop-down list, choose the search method you want by selecting the All of the Words item, the Any of the Words item, the The Exact Phrase item, or the The Boolean Phrase item. (A *Boolean phrase* is one that uses terms such as AND, OR, or NOT—for example, "Internet NOT Explorer" to search for documents that contain *Internet* but do not contain *Explorer*.)

SETTING HELP AND SUPPORT CENTER OPTIONS

While you're setting search options, your eye will probably be caught by the Change Help and Support Center Options link in the Options pane on the Set Search Options screen. These are the options you can set:

Show Favorites on the Navigation Bar check box   Leave this check box selected (as it is by default) to have Help and Support Center display the Favorites button on the toolbar. Clear this check box to remove the Favorites button.

Show History on the Navigation Bar check box   Leave this check box selected (as it is by default) to have Help and Support Center display the History button on the toolbar. Clear this check box to remove the History button.

Font Size Used for Help Content list   Select the Small option button, the Medium option button, or the Large option button to set a font size you find comfortable.

Options for Icons in the Navigation Bar list   Specify whether Help and Support Center should display text on the navigation bar buttons by selecting the Show All Text Labels option button, the Show Only Default Text Labels option button, or the Do Not Show Text Labels option button.

Browsing for Help

As you saw in Figure 3.13, Help and Support Center provides a list of a dozen or so *help topics* on the left side of its Home page. You can browse any of these help topics by clicking its link. Figure 3.16 shows an example of a help topic. Click one of the links in the topic area to display the links or information available.

FIGURE 3.16

Follow the links in the Pick a Help Topic list to reach help topic areas.

Similarly, Help and Support Center provides a list of key support topics on the right side of its Home page. The Ask for Assistance list provides links to Remote Assistance, Support (from Microsoft), and Windows XP Newsgroups. The Pick a Task list includes links to tools such as Windows Update and System Restore, the Tools area of Help and Support Center for help-specific tools, and Help and Support Center's features for finding XP-compatible hardware and software.

SUPPORT PAGE

The Support page (shown in Figure 3.17 with Remote Assistance information displayed) offers a variety of support tools, some of the items that actually provide support (such as Remote Assistance—accessed via the Ask a Friend to Help link—and Microsoft Online Support) and some that are just links to Windows utilities (such as My Computer Information and System Configuration Utility).

WINDOWS UPDATE PAGE

The Windows Update page provides an alternative method of accessing Windows Update. (You can also access Windows Update from the Start menu.)

COMPATIBLE HARDWARE AND SOFTWARE PAGE

The Compatible Hardware and Software page (shown in Figure 3.18) provides a mechanism for searching for information on whether particular products are compatible with Windows XP. To open the Compatible Hardware and Software page, click Find Compatible Hardware and Software for Windows XP in the Pick a Task section.

FIGURE 3.17

The Support area contains tools and links to Windows utilities.

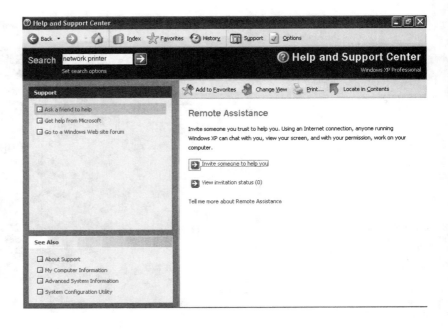

FIGURE 3.18

Use the Compatible Hardware and Software page to search for compatibility information for a specific product.

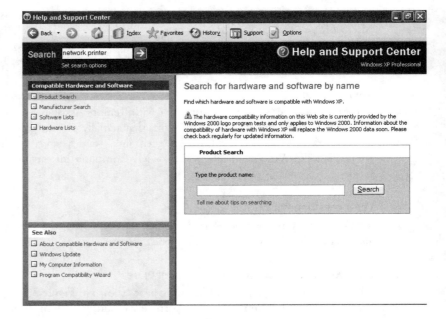

TOOLS PAGE

To access the Tools page, in Help and Support Center click the Use Tools to View Your Computer Information and Diagnose Problems in the Pick a Task section. The Tools page (shown in Figure 3.19 with the Advanced System Information screen displayed) contains the Tools Center, which provides access to a number of tools for configuring and troubleshooting Windows. You'll notice that some of these tools have already popped up on other Help and Support Center pages you've seen so far. This illustrates the large number of redundant paths deliberately built into Help and Support Center to make it easier for you to find the information and tools you need to solve a problem.

FIGURE 3.19

The Tools page provides links to a large handful of system tools.

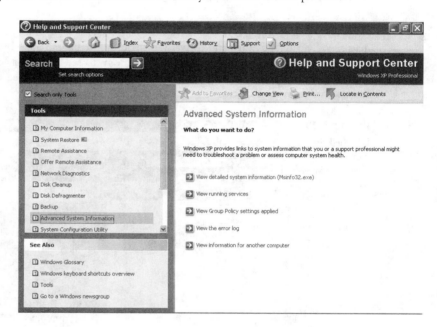

Creating and Using Favorites in Help

You can create favorites in Help and Support Center so that you can access pages of information quickly whenever you need to.

To add the current page to your favorites, click the Add to Favorites button. Help and Support Center adds the favorite to your Favorites list and displays a message box telling you that it is doing so.

To access a favorite, click the Favorites button on the toolbar. Help and Support Center displays the Favorites pane. Select the favorite you want to display and click the Display button.

To rename a favorite, click it in the Favorites pane, and then click the Rename button. Help and Support Center displays an edit box around the favorite's name. Type the new name and press the Enter key.

To delete a favorite, select it in the Favorites pane and click the Remove button.

Using Views

Designed to display a serious amount of information and options at the same time, the Help and Support Center window can threaten visual overload or simply swamp a small screen. To help you retain your sanity and your screen estate, the Help and Support Center window has a reduced view as well.

Click the Change View button to toggle between the full Help and Support Center window (including the left navigation pane, the Search bar, and the toolbar) and the reduced window, which contains only the content page.

Navigating with Help History

You can navigate backward and forward in the chain of pages you've browsed by using the Back button and Forward button on the toolbar. If you want to see the history of where you've been, click the History button. Help and Support Center displays the History pane (shown in Figure 3.20). Click the topic you want to access.

FIGURE 3.20

Use the History pane to return to topics you've visited recently.

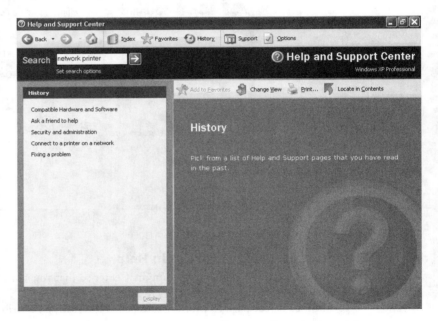

Printing Out Help Information

It goes without saying that you can print out help information if you want a hard copy of it handy: To print the current topic, click the Print button, and then click the Print button in the Print dialog box that Help and Support Center displays.

But it's worth pointing out that, instead of printing just an individual screen at a time, you can print a whole section of help by selecting the Print All Linked Documents check box on the Options tab of the Print dialog box. You can also select the Print Table of Links check box if you want to print a table of linked pages.

Using Remote Assistance

Remote Assistance lets you permit a designated helper to connect to your computer, see what's going on, and help you out of trouble. The helper—a friend or an administrator; whomever you choose— can control the computer directly if you give them permission, or you can simply chat with them and apply such of their advice as you deem fit.

To use Remote Assistance, both your computer and your helper's must be running Windows XP. You send an invitation via e-mail or via Windows Messenger, or save it as a file (for example, to a network location designated for Remote Assistance request files, or on a floppy or CD that you then pop in the snail mail). When your helper responds, you decide whether to accept their help.

Each of the three methods of requesting Remote Assistance has its advantages and disadvantages. An e-mail invitation lets you include details of the Windows problem with which you need help— but you don't know when the recipient will check their e-mail. A Windows Messenger invitation will be received immediately (because you can't send an invitation to someone who isn't online), but you can't include details of the problem. A file invitation, like an e-mail invitation, lets you include details of the problem, but you have no idea of when you'll receive a response to it (if ever).

On the other end of the wire, you can offer Help via Remote Assistance. All you need is for someone to send you an invitation.

Security Considerations

Like all remote-control technologies, Remote Assistance has serious security implications that you need to consider before using it.

If you give another person control of your computer, they can take actions almost as freely as if they were seated in front of the computer. You can watch these actions, and you can take back control of the computer at any time, but you may already be too late: it takes less than a second to delete a key file, and little longer to plant a virus or other form of malware.

Even if you *don't* give your helper control and instead simply chat, keep your wits about you when deciding which of their suggestions to implement. Malicious or ill-informed suggestions can do plenty of damage if you apply them without thinking. Never take any actions that could compromise your security or destroy your data. Above all, treat any incoming files with the greatest of suspicion and virus-check them using an up-to-date antivirus program before using them.

One particular problem is that you can't tell that the person at the other computer is who they claim to be. For this reason alone, you should always protect your Remote Assistance connections with a strong password known only to the person from whom you're requesting help. That way, if someone else is at their computer or has identity-jacked them, they won't be able to respond to the Remote Assistance invitation you send.

Enabling Remote Assistance

Remote Assistance is enabled by default. To find out if Remote Assistance is enabled on your computer, follow these steps:

1. Display the System Properties dialog box (for example, by pressing Winkey+Break or clicking the System link on the Performance and Maintenance screen of Control Panel).

2. Click the Remote tab:

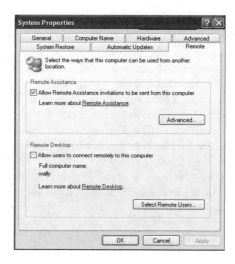

3. Check the status of the Allow Remote Assistance Invitations to Be Sent from This Computer check box. If this check box isn't selected, select it.

4. Click the OK button. Windows closes the System Properties dialog box.

Setting Limits for Remote Assistance

To set limits for Remote Assistance:

1. In the Remote Assistance section of the Remote tab, click the Advanced button to open the Remote Assistance Settings dialog box:

2. In the Remote Control section, clear the Allow This Computer to Be Controlled Remotely check box if you don't want your helpers to be able to control the computer. (This check box is selected by default.) Even when this check box is selected, you need to approve each request for control of the PC manually.

3. In the Invitations section, use the two drop-down lists to specify an expiration limit for Remote Assistance invitations that your computer sends out. The default setting is 30 days; you might want to shorten this period considerably for security.

4. Click the OK button. Windows closes the Remote Assistance Settings dialog box, returning you to the System Properties dialog box.

5. Click the OK button. Windows closes the System Properties dialog box.

You're now ready to start sending out invitations for Remote Assistance.

Sending a Remote Assistance Invitation via E-mail

To send a Remote Assistance invitation as an e-mail message via your existing e-mail account, follow these steps:

1. Choose Start ➤ All Programs ➤ Remote Assistance. Windows opens a Help and Support Center window to the Remote Assistance topic.

2. Click the Invite Someone to Help You link. Help and Support Center displays the Pick How You Want to Contact Your Assistant screen of Remote Assistance (shown in Figure 3.21).

   ◆ The first time you go through these steps, Help and Support Center displays a screen bearing Important Notes. If you want to skip this page in the future, leave the Don't Show This Page Again check box selected (as it is by default) and click the Continue button.

FIGURE 3.21

On the Pick How You Want to Contact Your Assistant screen of Remote Assistance, specify which type of Remote Assistance invitation to send.

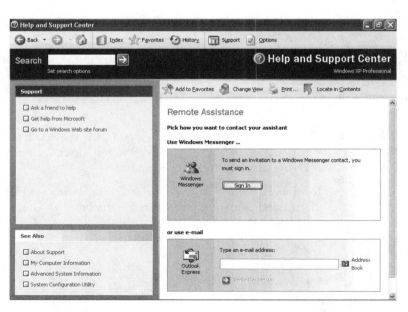

3. In the Or Use E-mail area, enter your putative assistant's e-mail address in the Type an E-mail Address text box. Either type in the address or click the Address Book button and use Address Book to specify the address.

4. Click the Invite This Person link. Help and Support Center displays the Provide Contact Information screen (shown in Figure 3.22).

FIGURE 3.22

On the Provide Contact Information screen of Remote Assistance, check your name and enter a message detailing the problem you're having.

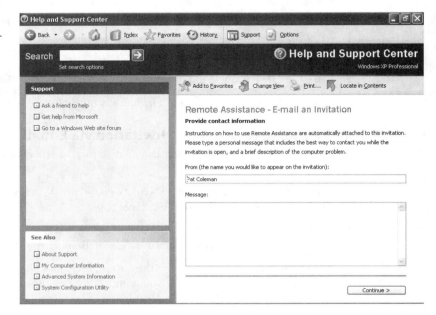

5. Change the name in the From text box if you want.

6. In the Message text box, enter a description of the problem and any blandishments necessary to get the help you want.

7. Click the Continue button. Help and Support Center displays the Set the Invitation to Expire screen (shown in Figure 3.23).

8. In the Set the Invitation to Expire area, specify the time limit for the recipient to accept the invitation. Choose a number in the first drop-down list and a time period—Minutes, Hours, or Days—in the second drop-down list.

9. To set a password, make sure the Require the Recipient to Use a Password check box is selected, and then enter the password in the Type Password text box and the Confirm Password text box.

FIGURE 3.23

On the Set the Invitation to Expire screen of Remote Assistance, set the expiration period for the invitation and enter a password.

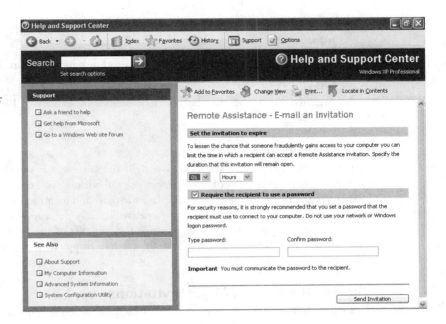

10. Click the Send Invitation button. Help and Support Center creates a file named rcBuddy.MsRcIncident containing the invitation and sends it via your default e-mail client with a message explaining how to use it. Help and Support Center then displays a screen telling you that the invitation has been sent successfully.

   ◆ If Help and Support Center can't send the file—for example, if your ISP's mail server is down—it invites you to save the file and send it manually.

   ◆ If you've set Outlook Express to warn you if other programs attempt to send mail in your name, Outlook Express will display an Outlook Express dialog box, warning you that a program (Help and Support Center) is trying to send a message. Click the Send button.

SENDING AN INVITATION VIA WINDOWS MESSENGER

To send an invitation via your existing Messenger account, follow these steps:

1. Start Messenger as usual, or activate it from the notification area.

2. Choose Tools ➤ Ask for Remote Assistance and choose either a contact name or the Other item from the submenu.

   ◆ If you choose Other, Messenger displays the Send an Invitation dialog box. Enter the person's e-mail address in the text box and click the OK button.

   ◆ You can also send an invitation to an existing contact by right-clicking them in the Online list and choosing Ask for Remote Assistance from the shortcut menu.

3. Messenger opens an Instant Message window with the specified user and displays a note saying that you've invited the user to start Remote Assistance.

◆ To cancel the invitation, click the Cancel link in the Instant Message window, or press Alt+Q.

4. Wait for a response, then proceed as described in "Receiving Remote Assistance," later in this chapter.

SAVING AN INVITATION AS A FILE

Saving an invitation as a file works in essentially the same way as sending an invitation as an e-mail message, except that instead of specifying an e-mail address, you click the Save Invitation As a File link, create the invitation, and then specify a filename and location in the Save File dialog box. For example, your company might designate a network folder as a drop-box for Remote Assistance requests. Administrators would then examine the contents of the folder and respond to the requests accordingly. Alternatively, you could save the file to a floppy disk or other mobile medium and mail it to a helper.

Viewing the Status of Your Invitations

To view the status of the Remote Assistance invitations you've sent (or saved), display the Remote Assistance screen in Help and Support Center.

Click the View Invitation Status link. Windows displays the View or Change Your Invitation screen of Remote Assistance. Figure 3.24 shows an example.

FIGURE 3.24

Viewing the status of invitations you've sent

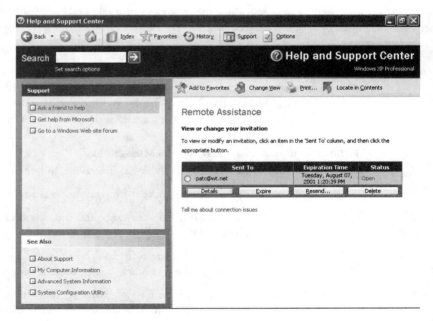

From here, you can view the details of an invitation by clicking the Details button, kill off an open invitation by clicking the Expire button, resend an invitation by clicking the Resend button, or delete an invitation by clicking the Delete button.

Receiving Remote Assistance

The following sections describe what happens when you receive a response to your Remote Assistance request.

E-MAIL INVITATION

When a helper responds to an e-mail invitation, Windows displays a Remote Assistance dialog box such as that shown in Figure 3.25, telling you that the person has accepted the invitation and asking if you want to let them view your screen and chat with you. Click the Yes button to start the Remote Assistance session.

FIGURE 3.25

Remote Assistance dialog box indicating an accepted invitation

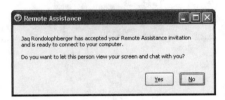

NOTE   If you don't take any action for a few minutes, Windows assumes you're not in the market for Remote Assistance and times out the connection.

WINDOWS MESSENGER INVITATION

When an invitee responds to a Messenger request for Remote Assistance, Windows displays a Remote Assistance dialog box such as that shown in Figure 3.25.

FILE INVITATION

When a helper responds to a Remote Assistance request saved in a file, Windows displays a Remote Assistance window telling you that the person has accepted the invitation and asking if you want to let them view your screen and chat with you. Click the Yes button to start the Remote Assistance session.

RECEIVING ASSISTANCE

Once the Remote Assistance session is established, Remote Assistance displays the Remote Assistance window shown in Figure 3.26, which provides a chat pane and control buttons.

FIGURE 3.26

During a Remote Assistance session, this Remote Assistance window provides a chat pane and control buttons.

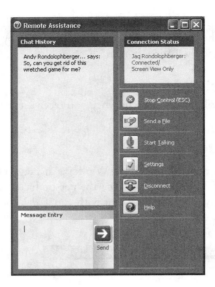

Chatting with Your Helper

◆ Type a message in the Message Entry text box and press the Enter key or click the Send button to send it.

◆ To start voice transmission, click the Start Talking button. Your helper then sees a dialog box asking if they want to use a voice connection. If they click the Yes button, Remote Assistance establishes the voice connection. Talk as usual, and then click the Stop Talking button when you want to stop using the voice connection.

NOTE *The first time you use the talk feature, Remote Assistance runs the Audio and Video Tuning Wizard if you haven't run it before.*

◆ To choose voice settings, click the Settings button. Windows displays a Remote Assistance Settings dialog box. Choose the Standard Quality option button or the High Quality option button as appropriate. Alternatively, click the Audio Tuning Wizard button (if it's available) to run the Audio and Video Tuning Wizard to optimize your speaker and microphone settings. Close the Remote Assistance Settings dialog box when you've finished.

Giving Your Helper Control of Your Computer

If your helper requests control of your computer, Windows displays the Remote Assistance dialog box (shown in Figure 3.27). Click the Yes button or the No button as appropriate.

You can regain control by pressing the Esc key, by pressing Alt+C, or by clicking the Stop Control button.

FIGURE 3.27

When your helper requests control of the computer, decide whether you trust them or not.

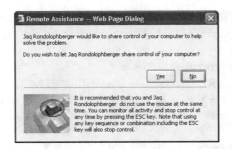

Disconnecting Your Helper

To disconnect your helper, click the Disconnect button. Remote Assistance closes the connection and restores your Desktop to its full complement of colors (if you chose to optimize performance for your helper).

When your helper disconnects themselves, Windows displays a Remote Assistance dialog box telling you so. Click the OK button to close this dialog box, then close the Help and Support Center window.

Responding to a Remote Assistance Invitation

This section discusses how to respond to a Remote Assistance invitation that someone sends you. As you'd expect, the specifics vary depending on whether it's an e-mail invitation, a Messenger invitation, or a file invitation.

E-MAIL INVITATION

When someone sends you a Remote Assistance invitation via e-mail, you receive an e-mail message with the subject line YOU HAVE RECEIVED A REMOTE ASSISTANCE INVITATION FROM and the username. The message comes with explanatory text augmenting whatever message text the requester entered, and an attached file with a name such as rcBuddy.MsRcIncident.

Open the file by double-clicking it. Alternatively, in Outlook Express, click the Attachment icon, select the file from the drop-down menu, select the Open It button in the Open Attachment Warning dialog box, and click the OK button. Windows displays a Remote Assistance window such as that shown in Figure 3.28, giving the details of the Remote Assistance invitation: who it's from, and when it expires.

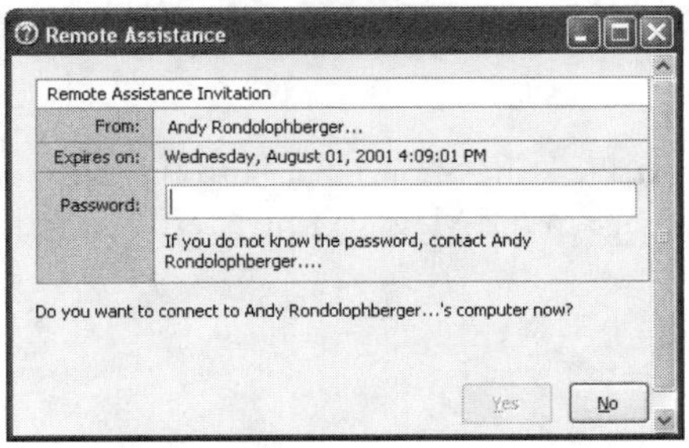

FIGURE 3.28

Double-click the file you receive to open the Remote Assistance invitation.

Enter the password (if the window is displaying a Password text box) and click the Yes button to start the help session. Windows tries to contact the remote computer.

WINDOWS MESSENGER INVITATION

When someone sends you a Remote Assistance invitation via Messenger, you see a Conversation window such as that shown in Figure 3.29. Click the Accept link (or press Alt+T) to accept it or click the Decline link (or press Alt+D) to decline it.

FIGURE 3.29

Receiving a Remote Assistance invitation in Messenger

If the user chose to specify a password, you'll need to enter it in a Help and Support Center window after the user accepts the incoming Remote Assistance connection.

FILE INVITATION

If you find a file invitation waiting for you or receive one on a physical medium, double-click the file to open it. The rest of the procedure is the same as for an e-mail invitation, discussed in the section before last.

PROVIDING REMOTE ASSISTANCE

If Windows is able to contact the remote computer, and if the user accepts the Remote Assistance connection, Windows displays the Remote Assistance window, which features a chat pane, a view panel that shows the user's Desktop, and assorted command buttons.

Chatting with the User

To chat with the user via text, click the Show Chat button to display the chat pane if it's not currently displayed. Type a message in the Message Entry text box and press the Enter key or click the Send button to send it.

To hide the chat pane so that you can see more of the remote screen, click the Hide button.

To chat via voice, click the Start Talking button. Remote Assistance displays a dialog box asking the person at the other end whether they want to use voice. If they click the Yes button, Remote Assistance activates the audio hardware. Click the Stop Talking button to stop using voice to chat.

Scaling the Display

You can scale the remote display to fit the area available on your screen by clicking the Scale to Window button, and restore it to its actual size by clicking the Actual Size button. Depending on the resolution you and the remote user have set, scaling the display may make the fonts illegible, but viewing the whole screen at once may make it easier for you to see what's happening on the computer than viewing only a partial screen and having to scroll to its outer reaches.

Taking Control of the Remote Computer

To request control of the remote computer, click the Take Control button. Windows displays a Remote Assistance dialog box on the remote screen asking the user if they want to give you control. If they click the Yes button, you get a Remote Assistance dialog box telling you so. When you dismiss this dialog box, you have control of the computer and can take any action with it as if you were working directly on it. To release control, click the Release Control button or press the Esc key.

WARNING *Avoid pressing the Esc key when taking keyboard actions on the remote computer. Even combinations that use the Esc key will release control.*

Transferring Files to and from the Remote Computer

To transfer a file to the remote computer, click the Send a File button. Windows displays a Remote Assistance dialog box. Use the Browse button to locate the file, and then click the Send File button to send it. The remote user then gets to decide whether to keep the file and in which folder to save it. (If you have control of the computer, you can make these decisions.)

To transfer a file from the remote computer to your computer, have the user click the Send a File button in their Remote Assistance window. Alternatively, if you have control of the computer, you can do this yourself.

Disconnecting from the Remote Computer

To disconnect from the remote computer, click the Disconnect button. Then close the Remote Assistance Services window manually. Unless you expect you'll need to reconnect to the remote computer to help the user further during the time remaining before the Remote Assistance invitation expires, delete the invitation file before you forget.

If the person you're helping disconnects the connection, Windows displays a Remote Assistance dialog box telling you so.

Microsoft Online Support (Get Help from Microsoft)

Microsoft Online Support lets you automatically collect information on a problem you're having and submit it to Microsoft electronically. A Microsoft technician then sends a solution, which appears as a pop-up in your notification area. You can read the response in the Help and Support Center window and apply the wisdom it contains to fix the problem.

Microsoft Online Support lets you avoid both long waits on hold and the difficulty of explaining complex problems and system configuration over the phone.

To use Microsoft Online Support, you need a Microsoft Passport or a Hotmail account. If you don't have one, Help and Support Center walks you through the process of getting one.

To connect to Microsoft Online Support, click the Get Help from Microsoft link in the Support pane and follow through the steps the Help and Support Center presents. For obvious reasons, your computer needs a working Internet connection to use this feature.

Windows Newsgroups (Go to a Windows Web Site Forum)

The Windows Newsgroups are an assortment of Windows-related online newsgroups that you can access through a Web-based front end. Though these newsgroups are run under the auspices of Microsoft, they suffer to some extent from the problems of noise and irrelevance that characterize public newsgroups. (See Chapter 14 for a discussion of newsgroups and how to use Outlook Express to access them.)

To access the Windows Newsgroups, take the following steps:

1. Display the Support page of Help and Support Center.

2. In the Support pane, click the Go to a Windows Web Site Forum link. Help and Support Center displays the Windows Newsgroups screen.

3. Click the Go to Windows Newsgroups link. Help and Support Center activates or launches Internet Explorer (or your default browser) and displays the Windows XP Newsgroups home page, which lists the newsgroups.

4. Click one of the newsgroup links. Internet Explorer activates or launches Outlook Express (or your default newsreader) and opens that newsgroup in it.

Using the Troubleshooters

Windows XP includes a number of *troubleshooters* for troubleshooting common problems with hardware and software configuration. Help and Support Center provides a central starting point for running these tools, though Windows also offers you the chance to run the appropriate troubleshooter when it detects that you've run into a configuration problem.

To run one of the troubleshooters, follow these steps:

1. From the Help and Support Center Home page, click the Fixing a Problem link. Help and Support Center displays the Fixing a Problem screen.

2. In the Fixing a Problem list, click a link to display a list of troubleshooters for that problem.

3. Click a Troubleshooter, and then follow the onscreen instructions. Figure 3.30 shows the Printing Troubleshooter.

FIGURE 3.30

Windows XP includes trouble-shooters that attempt to walk you through the steps of solving a problem.

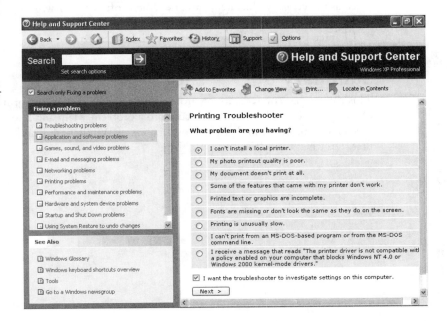

Finding Help on the Internet and Web

If you can't find the information you need through Help and Support Center, try the Internet and the Web.

Help on the Web

With earlier versions of Windows, the first port of call when looking for help on the Web was the Microsoft Web site, which offered all sorts of resources from the latest patches and drivers to the Knowledge Base. But now that Help and Support Center both seamlessly searches the Microsoft Web site and provides links to some hardware and software manufacturers' offerings, and Windows Update can automatically download and prompt you to install updates and patches to Windows, there's less reason to access the Microsoft Web site manually unless you need, say, the extra search capabilities that the Knowledge Base Web site offers.

To find information from hardware and software manufacturers not partnered closely enough with Microsoft to rate inclusion in Help and Support Center's repertoire, to download the latest drivers, or to find other sources of information, the Web can be either more or less valuable, depending on your luck and your persistence in searching.

Chapter 12 discusses how to surf the Web with Internet Explorer.

Help in Newsgroups

Another good source of information and help are the many computer-related public newsgroups (such as the `comp.sys` hierarchy) and the Microsoft public newsgroups (in the `microsoft.public` hierarchy).

Chapter 14 discusses how to use Outlook Express to read news.

Summary

This chapter has covered a lot of ground, but now you have the information you need to navigate the Desktop and to get help when you run into a problem. Help and Support Center gives you access to much more information that previous versions of Windows did, and it's easy to make using it your first step when trying to solve a problem.

Chapter 4

Customizing the Interface

WINDOWS XP CAN BE CUSTOMIZED in an amazing number of ways. You can move, resize, tweak, or change the color of just about everything. In this chapter, you'll learn about some of the most important interface adjustments you can make for usability, convenience, and just plain old personal preference.

This chapter covers the following topics:

◆ Working with the XP Control Panel

◆ Changing the date and time

◆ Adjusting video settings

◆ Customizing Windows XP display

◆ Customizing the desktop

◆ Working with screen savers

◆ Customizing the Taskbar

◆ Setting Start menu options

◆ Adjusting the keyboard and mouse

◆ Choosing system sounds

◆ Using Accessibility options

Working with the XP Control Panel

To open Control Panel, simply click Start ➤ Control Panel.

TIP   In previous versions of Windows there was a Control Panel icon in the My Computer window, but it doesn't appear there in XP by default. If you want an icon for Control Panel to appear there, open My Computer and choose Tools ➤ Folder Options. On the View tab, mark the Show Control Panel in My Computer check box.

In previous versions of Windows, the number of icons in Control Panel had gotten rather large, so Windows XP organizes them into categories rather than simply showing all the icons at once. This new view, called Category view, is the default view in Control Panel. See Figure 4.1.

FIGURE 4.1

Control Panel in Category view

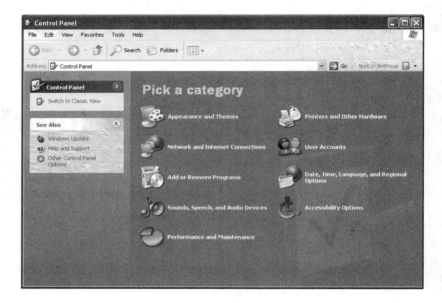

If you would prefer the traditional Control Panel layout, you can click the Switch to Classic View hyperlink to switch to it, as in Figure 4.2.

FIGURE 4.2

Control Panel in Classic view

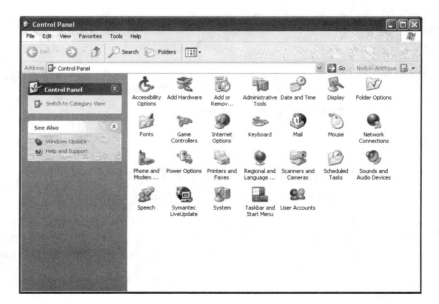

This book uses Category view in its figures and steps, but experienced users will probably prefer Classic view because it involves fewer mouse clicks and because the category in which an item resides is not always obvious.

If there are any items that don't have a category assigned (such as applets added by some third-party program), you can access them from Category view by clicking Other Control Panel Options in the Explorer bar, or by switching to Classic view.

TIP   Sometimes adding new hardware or software to your PC will add Control Panel applets. If the Setup program that placed the applet in Control Panel was written prior to Windows XP, it will not assign the applet to a category. You'll need to view Control Panel in Classic view to have access to that icon. If you would like for that icon to be assigned to a category, use the Registry Editor (see Chapter 22) to alter the DWORD *value for the applet in the* HKEY_LOCAL_MACHINE\SOFTWARE\Microsoft\Windows\CurrentVersion\Control Panel\Extended Properties\{305CA226-D286-468e-B848-2B2E8E697B74} 2 *section of the Registry. If the applet appears on the list there, change its current* DWORD *value (probably 0) to that of an existing applet that is already in the category in which you want to place it. You can also do this to change the category of any applet on the list, not just third-party applets.*

Changing the Date and Time

The system clock in your PC keeps track of the date and time; you can set the date and time through your BIOS setup program. You can also set it from within Windows for the same effect. Double-click the clock in the notification area, or go through Date and Time in Control Panel. See Figure 4.3.

FIGURE 4.3

You can adjust the date and time from within Windows XP.

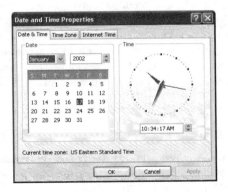

TIP   Point at the clock in the notification area to see today's date.

On the Time Zone tab, you can select your time zone. It's just a simple drop-down list with all the zones in the world.

One problem many people have had with PC clocks over the years is their tendency to lose time. To combat this problem, Windows XP introduces a new feature that automatically synchronizes the system clock with a time server on the Internet. It's turned on by default, and updates your system clock periodically. You can turn it off, or update it immediately, in the Internet Time tab shown in Figure 4.4.

FIGURE 4.4

Choose whether to update time automatically, and which time server to use.

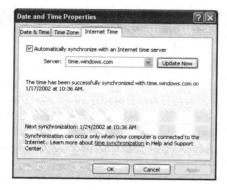

NOTE *When you update the time online, it relies on the Time Zone setting you have selected to know how to adjust the server's time to fit the correct time in your zone. The server is not necessarily in the same time zone as you, after all! That's why the Time Zone setting in the Time Zone tab is important.*

Here are a couple of useful Registry tweaks for working with the Internet Time feature.

By default, Windows checks the time against the time server once a week (that's every 604,800 seconds). If you want to use some other interval, go to HKEY_LOCAL_MACHINE\SYSTEM\ControlSet001\ Services \W32Time\TimeProviders\NtpClient and set the decimal value of the *SpecialPolInterval* key to some other value in seconds. There are 86,400 seconds in a day, just FYI.

There are only two servers available by default time.windows.com and time.nist.gov. To add more, just add them in the registry key HKEY_LOCAL_MACHINE\SOFTWARE\Microsoft\Windows\CurrentVersion\ DateTime\Servers. Not sure what other time servers are available? Check out www.eecis.udel.edu/ ~mills/ntp/clock1.htm.

ADDING MULTIPLE TIME SERVERS AT ONCE

One easy way to add a lot of time servers to the Registry at once is to create a REG file containing them in Notepad. For example, you could create the following text file in Notepad and save it as timesrvr.reg (or whatever name you want, as long as it has a .reg extension):

```
Windows Registry Editor Version 5.00
[HKEY_LOCAL_MACHINE\SOFTWARE\Microsoft\Windows\CurrentVersion\DateTime\Servers]
@="1"
"1"="time.windows.com"
"2"="time.nist.gov"
"3"="clock.isc.org"
"4"="timekeeper.isi.edu"
```

You can keep going ad infinitum with the list, giving each time server you want to add a consecutive number. Then save your work and close Notepad. Locate the file in Windows Explorer, right-click it, and choose Merge.

Adjusting Video Settings

Video settings are the settings and options for both your video card and monitor and their drivers that affect overall display appearance in Windows. These are separate from the color schemes, fonts, and other appearance features you might choose (covered later in this chapter). The following sections review some important information about video.

Installing Video and Monitor Drivers

Windows XP is fairly good at detecting the video card during Setup, so the correct video drivers should already be installed. (It's somewhat less adept at detecting monitors.) You can check by doing the following:

1. Right-click the desktop and choose Properties.

2. On the Settings tab, notice the video card and monitor names that appear under the Display heading. If these match your actual hardware, Windows has accurately detected them. See Figure 4.5.

If either is incorrect, see the following sections to change them.

FIGURE 4.5

The Settings tab reports what video card and monitor Windows thinks you have.

UPDATING THE VIDEO CARD DRIVER

Having the right video card driver is important because the driver tells Windows what display resolutions, color depths, refresh rates, and other performance settings should be available. If Windows cannot detect your video card type, it will install a driver for a standard VGA card, which will limit the display options to 640×480 and 16 colors. In addition, the standard VGA video driver does not support power management, so you will not be able to use features like Suspend or Hibernate (see Chapter 8).

An outdated or corrupted video driver can also be a problem, although there is not a simple test to look for this. If you suspect a video driver problem, your best bet is to go to the card manufacturer's Web site and download a driver designed specifically for Windows XP and for your exact model of card.

To install a video driver, do the following:

1. Right-click the desktop and choose Properties; then click the Settings tab.

2. Click the Advanced button. This opens a Properties box for your video card and monitor.

3. Click the Adapter tab, and then click the Properties button. This opens a separate Properties box just for the video card.

4. Click the Driver tab, and then click the Update Driver button. The Hardware Update Wizard runs.

5. Click Install from a List or Specific Location, and then click Next.

6. If Windows already knows the video card name, choose Search for the Best Driver in These Locations and then make sure the location of the updated driver is included in the search locations. Then click Next and go on to step 7.

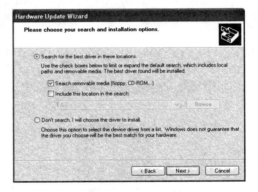

Or, if Windows does not currently report the correct video card, choose Don't Search, and then click Next. You'll see a list of compatible hardware with only one item on it.

If you have a specific driver you want to use, click Have Disk and point to the desired driver. If you don't, clear the Show Compatible Hardware check box to see a larger list of models.

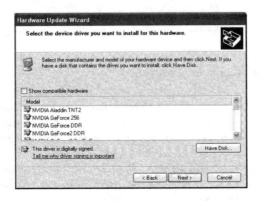

7. Continue working through the Wizard to install your chosen driver. (It's fairly self-explanatory from this point on.)

UPDATING THE MONITOR DRIVER

The procedure for updating the monitor driver is very similar to that for a video card. Monitor drivers are very simple; they're basically just INF files that tell Windows what the monitor's capabilities are (resolution, refresh rate, and so on). They don't actually do anything much within Windows. So if Windows reports that your monitor is standard VGA when in fact it's something better, the worst thing that happens is that you're limited to a lower refresh rate than you would normally be.

TIP   Most high-end monitors come with their own setup disk containing the INF files needed to set them up in Windows. However, since most people keep a monitor much longer than they do a PC, you will likely run into some fairly old monitors out there with unsigned drivers. That just means that the drivers have not been certified to work with Windows XP. For some devices this is a big deal, but the monitor driver does so little in terms of close interaction with Windows XP that it doesn't matter in this case. So if you see a dire warning about not using an unsigned driver, feel free to bypass it with a shrug.

To let Windows know you have a different monitor than the one currently chosen:

1. Right-click the desktop and choose Properties, and then click the Settings tab.
2. Click the Advanced button, and then choose the Monitor tab.
3. Click the Properties button, and then choose the Driver tab.
4. Click the Update Driver button. The Hardware Update Wizard runs.
5. Click Install from a List or Specific Location, and click Next.
6. Click Don't Search, and then click Next.
7. Clear the Show Compatible Hardware check box. Then locate the monitor make and model on the list, as in Figure 4.6, or click Have Disk to use your own driver on disk.
8. Continue working through the Wizard to its finish.

FIGURE 4.6

Select your monitor's correct make and model from the list.

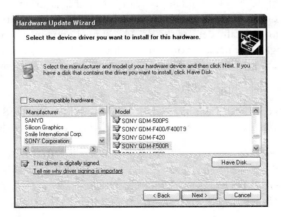

Setting Resolution, Color Depth, and Refresh Rate

If you are not familiar with the terms resolution, color depth, and refresh rate, review the following information before you get started changing those settings in Windows.

Resolution refers to the number of unique pixels that make up the display. It's expressed in two numbers: width and height. For example, standard VGA is 640×480.

Windows XP no longer runs in 640×480 resolution except in Safe Mode; the minimum it supports is 800×600 unless a video driver is loaded that supports only standard VGA. From there the resolution can go up to whatever the maximum is that the video card and monitor can both support. On a high-end monitor, this could be as high as 2048×1536 or more. The higher the resolution, the smaller icons, windows, and text will appear on the screen. The video card has a maximum resolution it can support, and so does the monitor. The overall maximum resolution for the system is the one that both can agree on.

NOTE *Why does everything onscreen get smaller as the resolution goes up? It's because each item—an icon, for example—is a fixed number of pixels in size. When you switch to a higher resolution, that number of pixels takes up less space onscreen in proportion to the total screen area.*

Color depth refers to the number of digital bits needed to accurately describe the color of each pixel. For example, in 4-bit color, there are 4 binary digits to work with, from 0000 to 1111. There are a total of 16 combinations of 0s and 1s in 4 digits, so 4-bit color supports 16 colors. Standard VGA is 4-bit color. Windows XP supports only the much higher color depths (again, except for in Safe Mode), such as 16-bit and 32-bit. Color depth is an issue only for the video card; most monitors can support any color depth.

Refresh rate is the speed at which the monitor is able to refresh each pixel of the display. As soon as the monitor's electron gun hits a pixel, it immediately begins to decay, so each pixel must be refreshed many times a second. Refresh rates are expressed in Hertz (Hz). At low refresh rates, such as 65Hz, the monitor appears to flicker because the pixel light is decaying faster than the monitor is refreshing it. At high refresh rates (85Hz or above), flicker is not noticeable. Refresh rate is primarily an issue for the monitor; most video cards can support any refresh rate that the monitor is capable of. The maximum refresh rate for a monitor goes down as the screen resolution goes up; a monitor that supports 120MHz at 800×600 might support only 85MHz at 2048×1536.

The amount of memory on the video card determines the resolutions and color depths you can use. Windows automatically detects the RAM installed on your video card and adjusts its available settings accordingly. To calculate how much video RAM a particular resolution and color depth combination will require, use this formula:

Width × Height × Number of bits ÷ 8

Dividing by 8 converts bits into bytes. So, for example, 1024×768 resolution with 32-bit color depth would be 1024×768×32÷8, or 3,145,728 bytes (approximately 3.1MB).

TIP *Since most video cards come with at least 16MB of RAM these days, you really don't need to worry about having a video card with a huge amount of memory on it unless you have an extra-large monitor that you plan to run in some very high resolution. And even then you don't need a monster video card with 64MB of RAM on it. For example, my high-end Sony 21-inch monitor goes up to 2048×1536. At 32-bit color, it would require only about 12.6MB of video RAM.*

CHANGING THE RESOLUTION AND COLOR DEPTH

After all that theoretical build-up, changing the resolution and color depth is really simple:

1. Right-click the desktop and choose Properties.

2. Click the Settings tab.

3. Drag the Screen Resolution slider to the right or left to adjust the resolution.

4. Open the Color Quality drop-down list and choose a color depth.

5. Click OK.

TIP   As I mentioned earlier, the lowest resolutions and color depths are not available in Windows XP by ordinary means. However, there's a way to get to them. From the Settings tab shown in Figure 4.5, click Advanced; then go to the Adapter tab and click the List All Modes button. Select the video mode you want (each is a unique combination of refresh rate, color depth, and resolution).

CHANGING THE REFRESH RATE

As noted earlier, the refresh rate is more of a function of the monitor since it depends on the physical ability of the monitor's electron guns to keep up with the pixel refreshing. Therefore, as you would expect, you adjust it in the monitor properties:

1. Right-click the desktop and choose Properties.

2. Click the Settings tab, and then click the Advanced button.

3. Click the Monitor tab.

4. Open the Screen Refresh Rate drop-down list and select a refresh rate. Or, if there is an Optimal setting available, choose that to select the highest refresh rate that the monitor and video card can collectively support in the current screen resolution.

5. Click OK. If you see a message asking if you want to keep the current settings, click Yes. You will see this only the first time that you choose a particular setting.

6. Click OK again to close the Properties box.

TIP With refresh rate, higher is better; but do not exceed the maximum for your monitor, or damage to the monitor could result. This is where having the correct driver loaded for your exact model of monitor is handy; the driver knows your monitor's capabilities. If you don't have the right driver for your monitor and are using a driver for some other model instead, look up your monitor's capabilities on the manufacturer's Web site to be sure. A refresh rate of 85Hz is supported by most monitors and results in a decent display.

Setting Monitor Controls

Most monitors today have external controls for adjusting the size and positioning of the image. These adjustments can help you remove a black ring from around the outside of the picture and help you center the picture precisely. The positioning is sometimes called *phase*. Each monitor is different, so check the manual that came with yours.

You might have controls on your monitor for adjusting other factors, such as the straightness of the sides. Some monitor images bow out at the middle; some constrict at the middle. This adjustment is called *pincushioning*. Another adjustment you might be able to make is to tilt the entire image to the left or right slightly.

Many good-quality monitors also have controls for convergence. *Convergence* refers to the alignment of each red, green, and blue pixel. Display a pure white page in Windows (such as a blank word-processing document); if you notice a red, green, or blue tint, making a convergence adjustment may correct it.

Troubleshooting Video Problems

If you still have display problems after ensuring that the right drivers are loaded and compatible resolution, color depth, and refresh rate settings have been chosen, try the Display Troubleshooter feature:

1. Right-click the desktop and choose Properties. Then click the Setting tab.

2. Click the Troubleshoot button. The Video Display Troubleshooter starts.

3. Work through the troubleshooter by answering the questions and trying the fixes suggested. See Figure 4.7.

FIGURE 4.7

Try the Video Display Troubleshooter if you need further help with video drivers or settings.

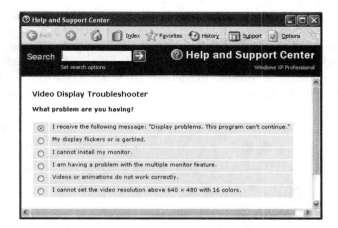

If you are having problems only with a specific program, the Video Display Troubleshooter may be able to offer some suggestions. You might also try the DirectX Diagnostic Tool, for troubleshooting problems related to DirectX technology (which is used in many of the most popular games today). To run it, choose Start ➢ Run and type **dxdiag**; then click OK. Figure 4.8 shows the Display tab, which may be helpful for display-related problems.

FIGURE 4.8

For problems with a game, the DirectX Diagnostic Tool may be helpful.

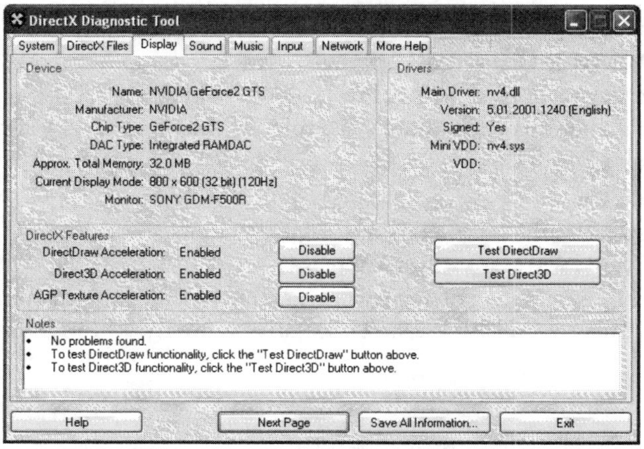

Customizing the Windows XP Display

Now we get into the "fun" display settings, the ones that affect the color choices, backgrounds, shapes, icons, and so on. Some of these settings will be old hat to experienced Windows users, but others are welcome surprises new to Windows XP.

Working with Themes

A *theme* is a collection of settings with complementary colors, icons, sounds, background, and so on. Rather than changing each individual aspect of the appearance separately, you can apply a theme to make a group of selections that work well together.

Themes were part of the Plus Pack for Windows 95 released back in the mid 1990s. They came standard with Windows 98 and Me. Now in Windows XP, the Themes feature is alive and well, but there are only two to choose from: Windows XP and Windows Classic. You can get more themes by buying the Plus Pack for Windows XP, or get free themes from www.themexp.org.

The Windows XP theme is the default. The Windows Classic theme sets Windows' appearance to resemble Windows 2000. If you (or users you support) are more comfortable in Windows 2000, you might want to set up that theme as a transition helper.

To select a theme, follow these steps:

1. Right-click the desktop and choose Properties; then click the Themes tab.

2. Open the Theme drop-down list and choose the theme you want.

3. Click OK.

Applying a theme changes many different settings at once. In the next several sections, you will learn how to change many of these settings manually. After you have made your selections of these settings, you might want to return to the Themes tab and save your set of settings under a new theme name. To do so, from the Themes tab, click the Save As button.

NOTE   *Changing to the Windows Classic theme does not affect the Start menu; it remains in the new Windows XP two-column layout. If you want to change the Start menu so it looks more like the Windows 2000 Start menu, do so from the Start menu's Properties. See "Setting Start Menu Options" later in the chapter for details.*

Customizing the Desktop

The next few sections show you how to set individual appearance attributes for the desktop. Most of these are set automatically when you apply a theme, but you can also adjust them individually.

BACKGROUND

The *background* is the image (or solid color) that appears as the desktop surface. In some previous versions of Windows it was called wallpaper.

You can use a variety of formats of graphics, including bitmap (.bmp or .dib), GIF (.gif), JPEG (.jpg or .jpeg), and PNG (.png). You can also use any HTML file, even though it's not necessarily a graphic; if you do that, the hyperlinks on the Web page remain active, and you can use them as short-cuts to your favorite Web locations.

If you do not choose a background image, the desktop will appear in whatever solid color you specify. The solid color is actually there all the time, even when a background picture obscures it; if you use a small picture, you will see the background color around the edges.

To select a background, complete the following steps:

1. Right-click the desktop and choose Properties; then click the Desktop tab.

2. Select a background image from the Background list. If the image you want doesn't appear on the list, use Browse to locate it.

3. Set a position for the image from the Position drop-down list. Stretch enlarges the image to fill the whole desktop. Center places one normal-size copy in the middle. Tile repeats the image as needed to fill the desktop.

4. Choose a color from the Color list. This color appears behind the image if the image does not fill the desktop, or if you choose None for the image.

5. Click OK.

CHANGING DESKTOP ICONS AND PROPERTIES

If you used previous versions of Windows, you probably remember that there were several system icons on the desktop, for things such as My Computer, My Documents, and so on. Windows XP has only one system icon on the desktop: Recycle Bin. If you miss those old-style icons, you can reinstate them. You can also change their appearance.

1. Right-click the desktop and choose Properties; then click the Desktop tab.

2. Click the Customize Desktop button. This opens the Desktop Items dialog box.

3. In the Desktop Items section, mark the check box for any icons you want to appear on the desktop.

4. Optionally, to change the look for an icon, select its picture in the middle section of the dialog box and then click Change Icon. The Change Icon dialog box opens.

5. Select a different icon for that item and click OK.

TIP *You can click Browse to pick up an icon from a different source; you aren't limited to the ones shown initially in the Change Icon dialog box.*

6. Click OK.

CLEANING UP THE DESKTOP

Over time, you may end up with a clutter of icons on your desktop that were placed there by programs you install or shortcuts you create yourself for various purposes. To organize and tidy up this clutter, use the Desktop Cleanup Wizard.

From the General tab of the Desktop Items dialog box, click the Clean Desktop Now button to start the Desktop Cleanup Wizard.

This Wizard presents a list of the shortcuts on the desktop with a check box next to each one (see Figure 4.9). Clear the check box for any that you want to remain on the desktop; all others will be moved to a new folder on the desktop called Unused Desktop Shortcuts.

FIGURE 4.9

Clean up the desktop.

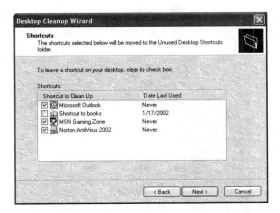

USING WEB CONTENT ON THE DESKTOP

Back when Windows 98 was first introduced, desktop Web content was heavily hyped. Microsoft thought it was going to be the biggest thing ever. But as it turned out, most people don't find it all that useful, so the feature has faded into obscurity. It's still around, however, and you can still play with it.

Here's the basic idea: you can make your desktop "active" and place items on it that get automatically updated from the Web whenever you are connected to the Internet. These items can include normal Web pages as well as special mini-applications such as stock tickers and weather maps.

TIP *You can also place an HTML file on the desktop as a background image, as you learned earlier in the chapter.*

To turn on Web content on the desktop, get back to the Desktop Items dialog box (right-click the desktop, choose Properties, click Desktop, click Customize Desktop) and select the Web tab. This tab lists any Web content that you have already set up. See Figure 4.10. To turn on an item, mark its check box.

FIGURE 4.10

Turn on Web content for the desktop.

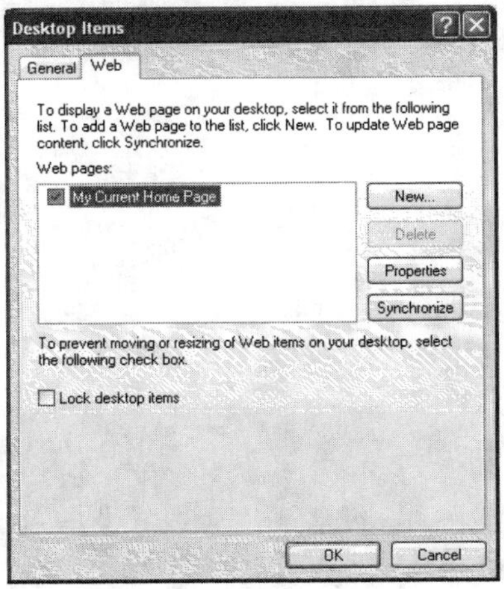

You will probably want to add some items. To add one, click the New button to open the New Desktop Item dialog box, shown in Figure 4.11. Enter the URL for a Web page or other item to use, or click the Visit Gallery button if you want to peruse the items that Microsoft provides free of charge. (It's a pretty cool side trip; give it a try.)

FIGURE 4.11

Enter the URL for the Web item to display on the desktop, or click Visit Gallery.

If you choose Visit Gallery, a Web page opens in Internet Explorer offering various mini Web applications for your desktop. Select one and follow the prompts to install it.

Each desktop Web item is synchronized with the Web according to a specified schedule. You can go with the default schedule for an item, or you can click the Properties button for it (on the Web tab) to customize its settings.

You can also set properties directly from the desktop for an item. For example, Figure 4.12 shows a weather map on the desktop. When you point to a desktop control, a thin gray title bar appears on it, with a down-pointing arrow on the left end. Click that arrow for a menu from which you can manage that item. Using that same title bar, you can turn the item off (with the Close button at the right end).

FIGURE 4.12

Click the arrow to display a menu for the desktop item.

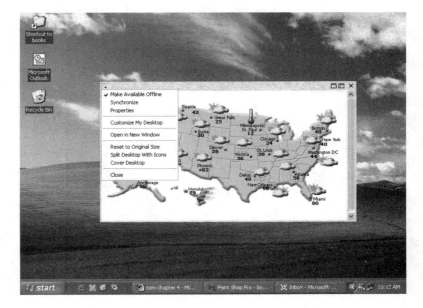

Working with Screen Savers

Screen savers are another once-hot feature that has fallen by the wayside. Put simply, people have gotten bored with seeing images dance across their screens. The practical need for screen savers has also diminished. Originally they were designed to keep images from burning into a monitor when a PC sat idle for a long time, but with today's monitors, burn-in is not an issue, so screen savers are just for decoration and amusement.

Using a screen saver can provide a small amount of local security, because you can set it to return to the Welcome screen when resuming out of the screen saver display. If you have set up a password for yourself for logging in on the Welcome screen, that password must be retyped to regain entry. This can prevent casual passers-by from tampering with the system.

To set up a screen saver:

1. Right-click the desktop and choose Properties; then click the Screen Saver tab.

2. Select a screen saver from the Screen Saver drop-down list. If you want to preview it, click the Preview button.

3. Enter a number in the Wait box for the number of minutes that should elapse before the screen saver starts.

4. If you want to return to the Welcome screen when resuming after the screen saver, mark the On Resume, Display Welcome Screen check box.

5. Optionally, click the Settings button if you want to change any of the settings for the chosen screen saver. The box that appears is different for each screen saver because each has different options.

6. When finished, click OK.

Changing Color and Appearance Options

Windows users have always loved having the ability to express themselves through color choices, and Windows XP offers a full array of settings in this area.

Right-click the desktop and choose Properties; then click the Appearance tab. See Figure 4.13.

FIGURE 4.13

Choose appearance options such as color here.

From here you have three choices to make:

◆ **Windows and buttons:** Your choices are Windows XP Style or Windows Classic Style. The latter makes Windows look like earlier versions.

TIP If you want more choices for window and button styles, check out a program called WindowBlinds at www
.windowblinds.net.

◆ **Color Scheme:** If you chose Windows XP Style in the Windows and Buttons drop-down list, there are only a few choices here: Default (blue), Olive Green, or Silver. If you chose Windows Classic Style in the Windows and Buttons drop-down list, however, you get a huge array of color scheme choices here, as in earlier Windows versions.

◆ **Font Size:** Your choices are Normal, Large, and Extra Large.

TIP Some people like to set the display resolution fairly high, so that everything is really small onscreen, and then use Large or Extra Large font size to make the text more readable. This can result in some odd but harmless display quirks in some programs, such as in cases where the dialog box size is fixed and the large-size text overflows it.

But wait—there's more. Click the Effects button for an Effects dialog box where you can turn on/off various visual effects, as in Figure 4.14. Generally speaking, the more of these you can turn off, the better the video performance you'll get.

FIGURE 4.14

Choose which visual effects you want in Windows.

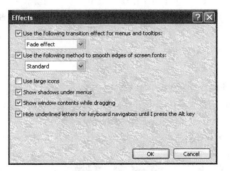

We're not done yet. Back on the Appearance tab, click the Advanced button to open the Advanced Appearance dialog box. Here's where you can customize the chosen color scheme, item by item, as in earlier Windows versions. (This works only for Windows Classic Style windows and buttons.) For example, you could choose Active Title Bar from the Item list, and then select a color, size, and font for it, as shown in Figure 4.15.

NOTE You can't save your custom color schemes in Windows XP, although you could in earlier Windows versions.

FIGURE 4.15

You can customize each aspect of a color scheme.

Customizing the Taskbar

The Taskbar is your gateway to all sorts of programs and windows, both those that are already running and those that you can run. In the following sections you'll learn how to control its appearance and functionality.

Setting Taskbar Options

To set Taskbar options, right-click the Taskbar and choose Properties; then click the Taskbar tab. See Figure 4.16.

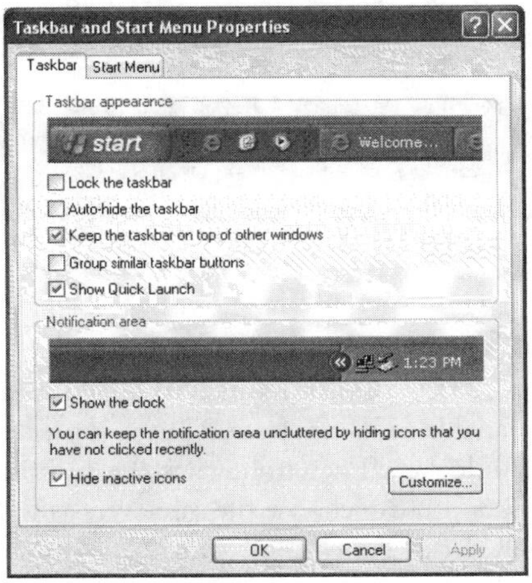

FIGURE 4.16

The Taskbar and Start Menu Properties dialog box

In the Taskbar Appearance section of the Taskbar tab, you have the following options:

Lock the Taskbar   The Taskbar is locked at its current position by default so that a user cannot move it to another location. Another way to access this same setting is to right-click the Taskbar and click Lock the Taskbar to toggle it on/off.

TIP   Another way to lock or unlock the Taskbar is to right-click the Taskbar and choose Lock the Taskbar from the shortcut menu.

Auto-Hide the Taskbar   Hides the Taskbar until you move your mouse pointer to where the Taskbar is hidden. Auto-hiding the Taskbar is useful if you have limited screen space or if you just don't like the look of the Taskbar.

Keep the Taskbar on Top of Other Windows   Keeps the Taskbar visible at all times. This is the default setting. (Screen saver programs ignore this setting, however, as they cover the entire screen.)

Group Similar Taskbar Buttons   Groups together buttons for files opened by the same program. This is a new feature in Windows XP and is on by default.

If you unlock the Taskbar, you can then drag it to one of the other sides of the screen; it need not be on the bottom.

See page 7 of "Essential Skills for Windows XP Professional" for a visual guide to unlocking, resizing, and moving the Taskbar.

You can also make the Taskbar appear in multiple rows. (Unlock it first.) This is useful if you keep a lot of windows open at once and you would like to be able to see them more easily from the Taskbar. To do so, position the mouse pointer over the top edge of the Taskbar and drag upward. Figure 4.17 shows the Taskbar with two rows.

FIGURE 4.17

A Taskbar with two rows

Working with Taskbar Toolbars

In Windows 98 and Windows 2000, a Quick Launch toolbar appeared by default next to the Start button. This toolbar is still available in Windows XP but it is turned off by default. To display it, first make sure the Taskbar is unlocked. Then right-click the Taskbar and choose Toolbars ➤ Quick Launch. There are other toolbars you can choose the same way as well, but Quick Launch is the most useful. Figure 4.18 shows the Quick Launch toolbar.

FIGURE 4.18

The Quick Launch
toolbar is displayed.

See pages 8–9 of "Essential Skills" for a visual guide to displaying and using desktop toolbars.

You can customize the Quick Launch toolbar (or any other Taskbar toolbar) by dragging short-cuts directly onto it and dropping them there. To remove an icon from a toolbar, right-click it and choose Delete.

Here are some things you can do to a toolbar:

◆ Add icons to it by dragging shortcuts onto it from the desktop or Start menu.

◆ Delete icons by right-clicking them and choosing Delete.

◆ Resize it by dragging the dotted "handle." If you don't see any dots at the left end of a tool-bar, the Lock the Taskbar setting is probably turned on.

◆ Drag it into the center of the screen to make it a floating toolbar, in its own window.

◆ Drag it to a different side of the screen to dock it there as its own separate bar.

You can also make your own toolbars, although not out of thin air. First you create a folder; then you right-click the Taskbar and choose Toolbars ➤ New Toolbar to make that folder into a toolbar. Then any files you put into that folder will appear as shortcuts on the toolbar.

Customizing the Notification Area

The notification area, also called the system tray, is at the far right of the Taskbar and displays icons for programs and tasks that are running in the background. These might include drivers or managers for devices such as a PDA interface or satellite Internet service.

To control which programs load at startup, see Chapter 5. If you just want to control which icons appear in the notification area, however, you can right-click the Taskbar and choose Customize Notifications. Then set notification options in the Customize Notifications dialog box. See Figure 4.19.

FIGURE 4.19

You can specify
which icons appear
in the notification
area and which are
hidden.

See page 13 of "Essential Skills" for a visual guide to customizing notifications.

When some icons are hidden in the notification area, a left-pointing arrow appears to the left of the area; you can click that arrow to see the hidden icons. Click it again to hide them again.

Setting Start Menu Options

The Start menu's options are found in the same Taskbar and Start Menu Properties dialog box as the previous section covered, but on the Start Menu tab.

Windows XP has a new look for the Start menu, but you can revert to the old-style ("Classic") Start menu if you prefer it. Each has its own separate set of customization options. To switch between them:

1. Right-click the Start button and choose Properties.

2. Click Start Menu or Classic Start Menu, whichever you prefer. See Figure 4.20.

Then, to customize the appearance of the Start menu you chose, click the Customize button beside it.

FIGURE 4.20

The Start Menu tab

NOTE *This chapter's coverage of the Start menu focuses on its overall appearance and settings; in Chapter 5 you will learn how to add, remove, and arrange shortcuts on the Start menu for the programs you want to run.*

Customizing the Windows XP Start Menu

Clicking the Customize button for the regular (that is, the Windows XP) Start menu brings up the Customize Start Menu dialog box, containing two tabs.

In the General tab, you can:

◆ Choose an icon size for programs. This controls the icons on the Start menu only.

◆ Set the number of programs to appear on the Start menu. This controls the area on the left side of the Start menu, where recently or frequently used program shortcuts appear. The higher this setting, the taller the Start menu will be.

◆ Choose whether to have an Internet and/or e-mail link in the top left section of the Start menu, and if so, which programs they should represent.

In the Advanced tab, you can:

◆ Choose whether submenus should open automatically when you pause on them with the mouse. If you turn this off, you must click each submenu level to open it.

◆ Choose whether to highlight newly installed programs. This is on by default and makes newly installed programs and their submenus a different color.

◆ Choose and customize Start menu items. This is a list of various items that can appear on the Start menu if you like, such as the Favorites menu. Some of them have additional options, such as displaying them as a link versus a menu. The Control Panel in Figure 4.21 is like that, for example.

FIGURE 4.21

Choose what will appear on the Start menu and in what way.

See pages 10–11 of "Essential Skills" for a step-by-step guide to customizing the XP Start menu.

TIP *When you install a new program, it doesn't find its place in the alphabetical Start menu hierarchy right away; it hangs out at the bottom for awhile. If you're using the Classic Start menu, you can re-alphabetize it manually by right-clicking the Taskbar and choosing Properties, clicking the Customize button next to Classic Start Menu, and clicking the Sort button. There is no equivalent button if you use the Windows XP style of Start menu, however. To have Windows always alphabetize the list, remove the permissions from the Registry key that controls the sort order for the Start menu. To do so, in the Registry Editor, go to HKEY_CURRENT_USER\Software\Microsoft\Windows\CurrentVersion\Explorer\MenuOrder. Then choose Edit, Permissions, and click the Advanced button. Deselect Inherit from Parent, and then click Copy in the Security dialog box. Then click OK and clear the Full Control entry for your account and all security groups you are a member of. Leave only Read permission.*

Customizing the Classic Start Menu

The Classic Start menu has customization options similar to those for earlier versions of Windows. See Figure 4.22.

FIGURE 4.22

Set options for the Classic Start menu here.

The Add, Remove, and Advanced buttons enable you to add, remove, and arrange content on the Start menu. You'll learn more about changing the Start menu content in Chapter 5.

The Sort button re-sorts the Start menu content in alphabetical order. When you install a new program, it appears at the bottom of the menu at first; this Sort feature places it in its rightful alphabetical location.

The Clear button erases the historical usage records for the Start menu; it clears the My Documents menu and also the Personalized Menus feature if you are using it.

The Personalized Menus feature is available only when you use the Classic Start menu. It keeps track of which programs you use the most and displays them first on the Start menu; after a few seconds' pause or when you click the down-pointing arrow at the bottom of the Start menu (present when the feature is on), the complete list appears. To turn Personalized Menus on/off, mark or clear its check box in the Advanced Start Menu Options section.

Speaking of that section, there are many other fine-tune settings you can adjust for the Start menu there. Some of these options are "Display" this or that; mark such a check box to add a certain special-purpose folder or utility to the Start menu. Others are "Expand" something; turn these on to make certain features display as a submenu rather than opening a window when you select them.

Adjusting the Keyboard and Mouse

Your mouse should work automatically in Windows XP Professional, with no special drivers or adjustments. However, the default settings are not optimal for everyone; some people prefer a faster or slower mouse pointer, greater or lesser sensitivity, or for the buttons to be switched for left-hand operation.

The adjustments for both keyboard and mouse are made through Control Panel. (If you're using Category view, you'll find them in the Printers and Other Hardware category.)

Keyboard Properties

The keyboard properties are rather simple. They let you adjust these features:

◆ **Repeat delay:** the amount of time between holding down a key and the key starting to repeat (that is, repeatedly type the character quickly onscreen).

◆ **Repeat rate:** the speed at which repeating occurs once it begins.

◆ **Cursor blink rate:** the speed at which the insertion point (vertical line) flashes in a text-editing program.

Mouse Properties

There are a surprising number of adjustments possible for the average mouse. You can control what the buttons do, how fast the pointer moves across the screen, what that pointer looks like, and whether any special features are applied to its movement. Table 4.1 lists the mouse adjustments you can make.

TABLE 4.1: MOUSE PROPERTIES

TAB	SETTING	PURPOSE
Buttons	Switch primary and secondary buttons	Useful for left-handed people to enable the index finger to control the primary button.
	Double-click speed	Adjusts the sensitivity for double-clicks. Useful for users who have a difficult time double-clicking fast enough.
	ClickLock	Makes the mouse button into an on/off toggle. Useful for people who have mobility problems that hinder normal dragging.
Pointers	Scheme	Enables you to select a predefined set of mouse pointers.
	Customize	Enables you to select a specific image for an individual pointer in a scheme.
Pointer Options	Select a pointer speed	Controls the distance the pointer moves onscreen when you move the mouse.
	Enhanced pointer precision	Enables more precise control of the pointer through little enhancements such as assisted deceleration.
	Snap to	Automatically moves the mouse pointer to the default option in a dialog box.
	Display pointer trails	Turns on a trail for the mouse pointer to make it easier to see, especially for people with vision impairment.
	Hide pointer while typing	Makes the mouse pointer vanish while you are working in a text editing application, so you don't get it confused with the insertion point.
	Show location of pointer when Ctrl key is pressed	Just what the name says. Useful for people who "lose" the pointer onscreen due to visual impairment.

Continued on next page

TABLE 4.1: MOUSE PROPERTIES *(continued)*		
Wheel	Scrolling	Controls how much the display scrolls for every notch movement of the wheel (if present).
Hardware	Troubleshoot	Helps troubleshoot mouse problems.
	Properties	Displays properties for the mouse device installed.

Choosing System Sounds

If you have a sound card and speakers, you hear sounds when certain system events occur, such as Windows startup and shutdown, an error message, and so on. You can change these sounds individually, or you can apply an entirely different sound scheme.

To do so, go to Control Panel and choose Sounds, Speech, and Audio Devices ➤ Change the Sound Scheme. Then pick a scheme from the Sound Scheme drop-down list or click an individual sound on the Program Events list and assign a sound to it from the Sounds list or with the Browse button. See Figure 4.23. To play a sound, click the button that looks like a right-pointing arrow.

FIGURE 4.23

Select different system sounds.

Using Accessibility Options

Accessibility features in Windows XP help people with hearing, vision, or mobility impairments to use their PCs more easily. There's an Accessibility Wizard that sets up several of the settings automatically based on questions you answer; you can also set up each of the settings manually.

There are other display settings that aren't specifically classifiable as Accessibility features, but are nevertheless useful for people with vision impairments. For example, in the Display Properties, you can choose Large or Extra Large font size on the Appearance tab, and you can click the Advanced button (still on the Appearance tab) to specify a color and size for an individual screen element.

TIP   The CompTIA A+ Certification Operating Systems Technologies exam contains some questions about accessibility in Windows, so you may wish to familiarize yourself with the accessibility features if you plan on taking that exam.

Using the Accessibility Wizard

Running the Accessibility Wizard is a great way to gain a general familiarity with the accessibility capabilities of Windows XP; it's also a useful tool for an end user who wants to set up accessibility without learning about every setting individually.

To run it, choose Start ➤ All Programs ➤ Accessories ➤ Accessibility ➤ Accessibility Wizard. Then click Next and work through the Wizard, answering its questions, to configure your system. The Wizard will then enable the needed features to carry out your wishes.

TIP   You can also run the Accessibility Wizard through Control Panel. From Category view, choose Accessibility Options. Then choose Configure Windows to work for your vision, mobility, and hearing needs.

For example, in Figure 4.24, you're asked about the size of type you can read. If you choose Use Large Window Titles and Menus, it will switch to the Large setting for fonts (which you learned to do manually earlier in this chapter, in the Display Properties). If you choose Use Microsoft Magnifier, the Magnifier feature will be turned on. (More about it later in this chapter.)

FIGURE 4.24

The Accessibility Wizard helps you find the right size of on-screen type for your vision ability.

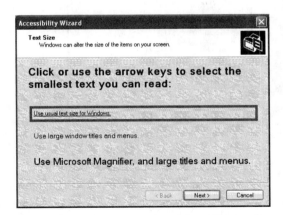

Accessibility Options in Control Panel

The Accessibility Options dialog box, accessible from Control Panel, contains dozens of features you can turn on to help with vision, hearing, or mobility limitations. Check out the following sections that apply to your situation.

FOR VISUALLY IMPAIRED USERS

Here are some settings that people who have difficulty seeing the default Windows display might appreciate. All of these are in the Display tab (Figure 4.25):

◆ Turn on a high-contrast display theme by marking the Use High Contrast check box. You can then click the Settings button to select a high-contrast color scheme that includes large fonts. Note that these are Windows Classic color schemes, and if you choose one, the button and window style will change to Windows Classic. Once you enable High Contrast, you can toggle it on/off by pressing Alt+Left Shift+Print Screen.

NOTE Turning on High Contrast in the Accessibility Options is different from simply selecting a high-contrast or large-font color scheme in the regular Display Properties. When you turn it on via Accessibility Options, the on/off toggle with Alt+Left Shift+Print Screen is available, whereas normally it would not be.

◆ Adjust the cursor blink rate to blink faster or slower—whatever is best for you to be able to see it.

◆ Drag the Width slider to make the cursor wider so it's easier to see.

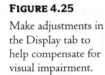

FIGURE 4.25

Make adjustments in the Display tab to help compensate for visual impairment.

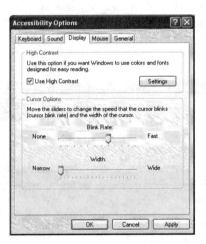

Vision-impaired users may also be interested in the Magnifier program, which magnifies a section of the screen, and/or the Narrator program, which reads the text in dialog boxes aloud. These are covered later in this chapter, in their own separate sections, because they are applications rather than Control Panel options.

FOR DEAF OR HEARING-IMPAIRED USERS

In most programs, deaf or hearing-impaired users should have no problem with the default Windows settings. That's because Windows is primarily a visual operating system, and the sound cues are of minimal importance. However, such users might miss out on the warning beep that accompanies an error message or the system sound that alerts the user to incoming mail or some other event.

Here are some features that might be of interest to users with a hearing disability. Both are in the Sound tab (Figure 4.26):

◆ Turn on SoundSentry to generate a visual cue onscreen when a system sound plays. You can then choose what you want this visual cue to be, such as flashing the desktop or the active window.

◆ Turn on ShowSounds to turn on captioning for any programs that support it. When used in a supported program, this works somewhat like closed captioning on a television.

FIGURE 4.26

Make adjustments in the Sound tab to help compensate for hearing impairment.

FOR MOBILITY-IMPAIRED USERS

Windows XP contains many adjustments for people who have difficulty performing common keyboard and/or mouse activities.

In real-world usage, the biggest help is Windows' ability to accept alternative input devices called SerialKey devices. These attach to the PC's serial port (most models; newer ones may be USB) and are specifically designed to help mobility-impaired people. You can turn on access to a SerialKey device, and set up which port it uses, on the General tab.

There are also numerous features that assume you're using the standard keyboard or mouse but make them work in a non-standard way.

If you have trouble using a standard keyboard, try some of these options, all of which are in the Keyboard tab (Figure 4.27):

◆ Turn on StickyKeys to make the Shift, Ctrl, Alt, and Windows logo keys into on/off toggles by pressing them twice in succession. You can also turn this feature on/off at any time without going through Accessibility Options by pressing the Shift key five times in a row. Click Settings to adjust the properties for the StickyKeys feature.

◆ Turn on FilterKeys to have Windows ignore brief or repeated keystrokes. This is useful for someone who might have a hard time zeroing in on a single key and releasing it quickly. Another way to turn on this feature is to hold down the Shift key for 8 seconds. Click Settings to adjust the feature's properties.

◆ Turn on ToggleKeys if you want a sound to play when the Caps Lock, Num Lock, or Scroll Lock key is pressed. This is useful for someone who might accidentally press one of those keys and turn on the Lock toggle without realizing it.

FIGURE 4.27

Make adjustments in the Keyboard tab to enable features helpful for users with limited mobility or dexterity.

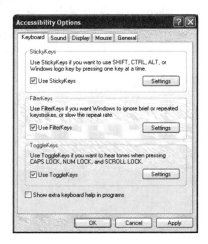

If you have trouble using a mouse but can successfully use a keyboard, you might want to turn on the MouseKeys feature on the Mouse tab. This enables you to move the pointer onscreen with the arrow keys on the keyboard. To turn this feature on you can also press Alt+Left Shift+Num Lock.

If you can use a mouse but not a keyboard, you might be interested in the On-Screen Keyboard application, discussed later in this chapter.

FOR ALL USERS

No matter which accessibility options you choose, you will probably want to take control of the general configuration settings for them so they don't become obtrusive or a nuisance. Check out these settings in the General tab (Figure 4.28):

◆ **Automatic Reset:** You can disable all accessibility features after a certain interval of idle time; this is useful if a person with disabilities shares a computer with someone who does not need or want any of the accessibility features.

◆ **Give Warning Message When Turning a Feature On:** This makes sure that nobody turns on an accessibility option accidentally.

◆ **Make a Sound When Turning a Feature On or Off:** This plays a sound whenever the status of an option changes.

◆ **Apply All Settings to Logon Desktop:** This applies the chosen accessibility options so that the same preferences will be loaded again the next time Windows restarts.

◆ **Apply All Settings to Defaults for New Users:** This makes the chosen accessibility options the default for any new user profiles you might later create.

FIGURE 4.28

The General tab provides settings that affect all accessibility options.

Using Magnifier

The Magnifier application can be very useful for people who are not totally blind but have some degree of visual impairment. It magnifies in a special panel at the top of the screen whatever portion of the screen the mouse pointer passes over. To turn it on, choose Start ➤ All Programs ➤ Accessories ➤ Accessibility ➤ Magnifier.

As long as Magnifier is running, a Magnifier Settings dialog box appears, as shown in Figure 4.29. You can minimize it and keep Magnifier open; however, if you click Exit in that box, the entire Magnifier program will terminate.

FIGURE 4.29

Magnifier focuses in on the current location of the mouse pointer.

Running Narrator

Narrator is useful for people who have a hard time reading text in dialog boxes. When enabled, it reads the text in the active dialog box or window. To turn it on, choose Start ➤ All Programs ➤ Accessories ➤ Accessibility ➤ Narrator.

When you turn on Narrator, a dialog box describing it appears. Read the info, and then click OK to clear it; a Narrator window appears containing options for narration. You must leave this window open for Narrator to continue to work, but you can minimize it. See Figure 4.30.

FIGURE 4.30

Narrator reads the content of the active window aloud.

You can then switch to any other program, and it will attempt to read whatever text appears in it. It works in Microsoft Word, for example, and can read the letters that you type as you type them.

Using the On-Screen Keyboard

The On-Screen Keyboard is an application that displays a facsimile of a keyboard in a window onscreen. You can click the letters you want to type. This might be useful for someone who can use a mouse but cannot type on a keyboard. To turn it on, choose Start ➤ All Programs ➤ Accessories ➤ Accessibility ➤ On-Screen Keyboard. When you're finished with it, close its window. Figure 4.31 shows it in action.

FIGURE 4.31

The On-Screen Keyboard lets you simulate a keyboard by using the mouse.

Using Utility Manager

The Utility Manager is a one-stop shop for controlling the three applications you just learned about: the Magnifier, the Narrator, and the On-Screen Keyboard. You can open it by pressing Winkey+U or by selecting it from the Start menu (Start ➤ All Programs ➤ Accessories ➤ Accessibility ➤ Utility Manager).

The Utility Manager is very handy because it can be accessed quickly with a shortcut key combination so you don't have to wade through multiple levels of the Start menu to turn on an accessibility application. Figure 4.32 shows its interface. Just select the application and click Start or Stop.

FIGURE 4.32

The Utility Manager makes it easier to turn accessibility programs on/off.

Summary

In this jam-packed chapter, you learned how to customize the Windows interface—how it looks, how it sounds, and how it behaves. You also learned about some of the Accessibility features in Windows XP Professional. In the next chapter, we'll take a look at installing and running applications. You'll not only find out how to add and remove programs, but also how to make old programs work well under Windows XP and how to control what programs run automatically.

Chapter 5

Installing, Running, and Managing Applications

HOWEVER WONDERFUL THE FEATURES built into Windows XP—and some of them *are* pretty wonderful; some less so; see the rest of the book for details—they're not the be-all and end-all of computing. The programs bundled with Windows XP let you perform a few basic tasks, from creating simple documents to playing music and video to creating simple video movies of your own. But sooner or later, you're going to want to install a third-party program and run it so that you can carry on with your business and your life.

On the assumption that this is probably going to happen sooner rather than later, this chapter discusses how to install, configure, remove, and run programs—and how to shut them down when they fail to respond to conventional stimuli.

This chapter uses various programs as examples, ranging from the latest (and supposedly greatest) programs specially designed for Windows XP to Windows 9*x* programs to DOS programs that are still only just starting to suspect that graphical environments exist. The odds are overwhelmingly against these programs being those you want to use with your copy of Windows XP, but these programs provide examples of many of the issues you'll encounter with installing, running, and removing programs.

This chapter covers:

- Multiuser considerations

- Installing and removing programs

- Adding and removing Windows components

- Running programs

- Dealing with unresponsive programs

- Program compatibility issues

- Sharing data between applications

- Organizing the Start menu

NOTE   If you performed an in-place upgrade of your previous version of Windows to Windows XP, the installation processes should have configured all your programs for use already, so you shouldn't need to reinstall them. However, if you have old programs that you find don't run properly on Windows XP, you may need to run them in Compatibility mode. If so, turn to the section "Running Programs in Compatibility Mode" later in this chapter.

Multiuser Considerations

As you saw earlier in the book, Windows XP offers strong multiuser capabilities. From the start, Windows XP encourages you to set up your computer for multiple users, allowing each their own custom settings. And multiple users can be logged on to the computer at the same time (though only one user can be active). Some users can be running programs in the background (as it were) while the current user is working away unaware of them.

Windows XP's multiuser capabilities raise some issues for programs and files, as discussed in the next section.

Who Can Install Programs?

Windows XP Professional supports three types of user accounts: Computer Administrator, Limited, and Guest. Only Computer Administrator users can install and remove programs. Limited users and the Guest user cannot install or remove programs. (You'll learn how to set up user accounts and control their type in Chapter 18.)

If a Limited user or the Guest user tries to install a program, Windows displays the Install Program As Other User dialog box (shown in Figure 5.1), telling them that they'll need administrator rights to do so. The user must specify a valid Computer Administrator username in the User Name text box and the appropriate password in the Password text box in order to proceed with administrative privileges.

FIGURE 5.1

To install or uninstall a program, you need to have Computer Administrator rights. If you don't, Windows stops you in your tracks with a warning such as this one.

If the user tries to continue with the installation without supplying Computer Administrator credentials, they usually run into an error message and abrupt termination of the setup routine.

Who Is the Program Available To?

In some operating systems, you can install a program for some users but not for others. By contrast, Windows XP Professional by default makes any program you install available to all users of the computer—provided that the program's setup routine does things in the right way. For example, if you install Office XP, the setup routine automatically creates shortcuts for all users to use the programs, so the next time any user logs on, they'll have a swath of new programs that they can use from the Start menu.

Office XP of course knows all about Windows XP (it's experienced, you might say), because they're both Microsoft products and they're roughly the same vintage. Eudora Pro 4.2, on the other hand, is a couple of years old at this writing and hasn't heard of Windows XP. But it installs fine and is available to all users after installation because its setup routine was (presumably) constructed along Microsoft's guidelines.

If the program's setup routine is deficient, you may need to install the program to an explicitly shared location or create shortcuts for it manually. For example, if you install Lotus SmartSuite Millennium Edition on Windows XP by using its setup routine, the user who installs SmartSuite gets the full set of shortcuts for it (plus a slew of shortcuts clogging the notification area, plus the indescribably wretched SmartCenter program-launcher and general menace). Other users get none of these—except for shortcuts to Net-It Now! Starter Edition, the little-known Web-publishing companion software that was included with SmartSuite. This isn't useful, helpful, or even amusing.

TIP Windows expects all programs to be installed into the Program Files folder. Putting them there seems to help make them available for all users, though it's not a guarantee of success. Putting them in another folder is usually not a good idea, though if you need to make small programs easily accessible to all users, you might be tempted to put them in the Documents and Settings\All Users *folder.*

What Happens When Multiple Users Open the Same File at the Same Time?

Problems arise with some programs when different users have the same file open. For example, multiple users can open the same WordPad file at the same time, and each can save their changes into (or through) the other's changes. The result is pretty horrible.

Of course, some files are *designed* to be accessed by multiple users at the same time. For example, most database files are designed so that they can routinely be accessed by dozens, hundreds, or even thousands of users at the same time. The program prevents any *record* from being accessed by more than one user at a time. Some database programs prevent users from accessing records adjacent to any record being accessed by another user to avoid the problems that can occur when records are added to or deleted from the database, either of which action changes the numbering of records. But as long as each user is (virtually) cordoned off from all other users in the recordset, all is well. Similarly, Excel lets you explicitly share workbooks with other users.

At the risk of generalizing absurdly, more complex (or perhaps more sentient) programs use some form of locking mechanism so that they can tell when another user has a file open. This locking mechanism can consist of flags on the file in question, but often it's implemented as a separate file that's created when the file is opened and is deleted when the file is safely closed. You can see this easily enough with Word, which creates a locking file in the same folder as the document you've opened (or just saved, in the case of a new document) *and* sets a flag on the document. The locking file replaces the first two characters of the file's name with the characters ~$, so that a document named Penguins.doc would generate a locking file named ~$enguins.doc. (Before you ask what happens with two-character filenames—if the file's name is six characters or fewer, Word *adds* the ~$ to the beginning of the filename. Seven characters, it replaces the first character. Eight characters, it replaces the first two.) If you open the locking file in a text editor (such as Notepad), you'll see that it contains the name of the current user (several times over, with variations in the spacing), some extended characters, and a variety of spaces.

NOTE *Word's locking files are hidden, so you won't see them in Explorer or in common dialog boxes unless you've selected the Show Hidden Files and Folders option button in the Advanced Settings list box in the View tab of the Folder Options dialog box (choose Tools ➤ Folder Options) in Explorer.*

When you go to open a file, Word takes a quick look through the folder that contains the file to see if there's a locking file for it. If there is, it displays the File in Use dialog box to let you know about the problem and offer you options for proceeding. When you close the file that was open, Word deletes the locking file. But if you delete the locking file while the file is open, Word still knows that the file is open because the flag is still set on the file, locking file or no.

As you might imagine, any program that doesn't use a locking mechanism so that it can tell when its files are open is going to have problems with multiple users accessing the same file. Very generally speaking, the less complex the program, the less likely it is to check that a file is open, and the more likely you are to have a problem with multiple users opening a file at the same time.

This problem also arises with files that can be opened with two or more different programs that are available on the computer. For example, if you use WordPad to open a Word document, it opens the document without any locking. You can then open the same document in Word while it's still open in WordPad. Word then locks the document, and you won't be able to save changes to the original file from WordPad.

What Happens When Multiple Users Run the Same Program at the Same Time?

By and large, having two or more users open the same document file at the same time (in the same program or in different programs) is more of a problem than having two or more users run the same program at the same time.

The brief answer to this question is as follows:

◆ Some programs are designed to be used by multiple users simultaneously, so they don't cause problems.

◆ Some programs are too dumb to notice that they're being used by multiple users at once, so each session is happy enough. Some of these programs are designed to run multiple instances for any given user anyway, so they're in good shape to run multiple instances for multiple users.

◆ Some programs notice there's a problem with multiple sessions and deal with it gracefully.

◆ Some programs notice there's a problem and sulk conspicuously.

With most programs, the problem comes not with the executable files and libraries (DLLs) but with the settings files. Windows XP handles the executables and libraries, running each in a separate memory space and segregating each user's programs from all other users' programs. But if a program is designed to use a central settings file rather than to implement a separate settings file for each user, the settings file can cause problems. If the program locks the settings file when the first user runs it (the program), the settings file won't be available when the second user runs the program. The same goes if the settings information is stored in a central location in the Registry.

Perhaps the easiest way around this, of course, is to use a separate settings file for each user or to keep separate Registry entries. As you'd imagine, that's what the Microsoft Office programs do. For example, if you're familiar with Word, you probably know that it stores a lot of information in the global template, which is saved in the file `Normal.dot`. The global template is always loaded when you're running Word, so Word maintains a separate global template for each user. This way, it avoids problems when users in separate sessions of the same installation of Word change their settings at the same time.

Problems also arise when separate instances of a program try to use the same hardware resources on the computer at the same time—for example, the COM ports, the audio output, or the microphone input—or the same set of data files.

How a program handles a problem gracefully depends on what the program does and what the problem is. In a program that can manage only one instance running on the computer at the same time, when you start a new instance in another user session, you'll typically see a warning dialog box that lets you choose to either cancel running the new instance of the program or forcibly terminate the other user's session of the program.

As you'd expect, some programs are smarter than others. In particular, it shouldn't come as a shattering surprise to learn that current Microsoft programs are much more aware of Windows XP's multiuser functionality than earlier Microsoft programs or programs from other software companies.

For example, Windows Media Player lets you switch users while you're still playing music or video or copying a CD. The music (or video) continues to run even while the Welcome screen is displayed. If you then log back on as the same user, Windows Media Player simply keeps going without interruption. Only when you log on as another user does Windows Media Player stop playing the music or video (or copying the CD). And—perhaps more important—it exits the instance that was playing or copying for the other user, freeing up the sound and video circuitry together with whatever system resources it was using. (Before you ask—Windows Media Player quits when you switch to another user even if it wasn't playing.)

TIP   If you're experiencing problems with programs that can't run multiple instances successfully at the same time, or with shared documents being opened by multiple users at once, turn off Fast User Switching, as discussed in Chapter 3. All these problems should disappear in a quick puff of logic.

Installing a Program

You have probably already installed programs, so you don't need a full-blown explanation of it. Most programs these days come on CD-ROM, and if you have Autoplay enabled for your CD-ROM drive, the Setup program usually starts automatically when you insert the CD. If it doesn't, you can browse the CD's content, locate the SETUP.EXE file, and double-click it to start the ball rolling.

TIP   If you get an error when installing a program from a CD that started Setup using Autoplay, try opening My Computer, right-clicking the CD-ROM drive, and choosing Explore. This lets you browse the CD's content. (Double-clicking won't work in this case; it'll just re-launch the Autoplay.) Perhaps you can find a file on the CD that will run the Setup program correctly; sometimes the bug is with the Autoplay file rather than with the Setup program itself.

You can also use the Add or Remove Programs applet in Control Panel. This method is advantageous if there is no SETUP.EXE file in the root folder of the setup disk, because it locates the Setup program automatically, even if it's not named SETUP.EXE. However, since it takes longer to get the ball rolling this way, advanced users seldom employ this method. To do so:

1. From Control Panel, choose Add or Remove Programs.

2. Click Add New Programs.

3. Insert the setup disk for the program in your PC; then click the CD or Floppy button and follow the prompts.

See pages 39–40 of "Essential Skills for Windows XP Professional" for a visual guide to installing a program.

What happens when you run the Setup program depends on the whims of the setup routine's programmers or (more commonly) on which of the two commonly used Windows installers they used—InstallShield or WISE. Suffice it to say that the usual steps for installing a program include agreeing to its license agreement, choosing which of the program's components to install, selecting a Start Menu folder (often still called a Program Group, in an embarrassing hangover from Windows 3.x days), and twiddling your thumbs (or fetching a fresh cup of wheat grass). For some programs, you'll have to reboot as well.

Installing and Running Multiple Versions of the Same Application

In previous versions of Windows, any program that you wanted to run needed to be installed on that operating system, even if you dual-booted two different operating systems. For example, if you dual-booted Windows 2000 Professional and Windows 98 and had Office 2000 installed on the Windows 98 partition, you still had to install Office on the Windows 2000 Professional partition in order to run it.

No longer. Now if you dual-boot, for example, Windows XP Professional and Windows 98, and have Office 2000 installed on the Windows 98 partition, you can access that program while running Windows XP Professional. In some cases, the program will appear on the All Programs menu in Windows XP Professional. If it does not, you can locate its executable file in an Explorer-type window and double-click its shortcut to start the program.

This ability to run multiple versions of applications installed on other partitions can save you a tremendous amount of disk space. On one system in my setup, the savings was about 3GB.

Making Programs Run at Startup

If you want a program to start every time you log on to Windows, place a shortcut to it in your Startup folder. Starting programs automatically like this can save you a few seconds each time you start Windows if you always need to use the same programs.

Your Startup folder is the `Documents and Settings\`*Username*`\Start Menu\Programs\Startup` folder. Navigating to this folder usually takes nearly as long as placing in it the shortcuts you want.

TIP   To make a program start automatically each time any user of your computer logs on to Windows, place a shortcut to the program in the Startup folder for All Users. As you'd guess, this folder is the `Documents and Settings\User-name\Start Menu\Programs\Startup` *folder.*

To prevent a program from running at startup, obviously enough, you remove its shortcut from the Startup folder.

Some programs run automatically at startup even though they don't appear in the Startup folder. Some of them run for a good reason, such as applications that start certain Windows services. Others are optional. If you think you can tell the difference, try using the System Configuration Editor (type **msconfig** from the Run command) to disable certain items from loading at startup. See Figure 5.2. Simply deselect the check box in the Startup tab for whatever you want to disable the next time Windows starts. When you do so, Selective Startup in the General tab automatically becomes selected. If undesirable results occur, return to the System Configuration Editor (in Safe mode if need be) and re-select that item, or to reselect all items go to the General tab and choose Normal Startup.

FIGURE 5.2

You can use the System Configuration Utility (`msconfig`) to selectively disable certain items that load at startup.

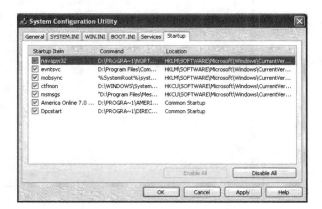

If you decide you want to permanently prevent that item from loading at startup, you can edit the Registry to make that so. Go to `HKEY_LOCAL_MACHINE\SOFTWARE\Microsoft\Windows\CurrentVersion\RUN` and `HKEY_CURRENT_USER\SOFTWARE\Microsoft\Windows\CurrentVersion\RUN` and delete any unwanted items.

Removing a Program

You should always remove a program through its Uninstall routine or through Windows' Add or Remove Programs applet in Control Panel. This keeps your Registry tidy by deleting references in it to that program; it also deletes any files in the `Winnt` folder and any other non-program-specific folders that were used only for that program. If you try to delete a program by removing its folder from the hard disk and deleting its shortcuts from the Start menu and desktop, you will not have removed all the pieces.

To remove a program:

1. From Control Panel, choose Add or Remove Programs. If the Change or Remove Programs page of the window isn't displayed, click its button.

2. In the Currently Installed Programs list box, select the entry for the program you want to remove. The Add or Remove Programs window displays information about the program—its size (the amount of space it's taking up on disk), a rough description of how often you've used it over the last 30 days (Frequently, Occasionally, or Rarely), and the date you used it last—together with a Change/Remove button (or separate Change and Remove buttons, depending on the program). Figure 5.3 shows these details.

FIGURE 5.3

Click the Change or Remove Programs button on the Add or Remove Programs dialog box to uninstall a 32-bit program.

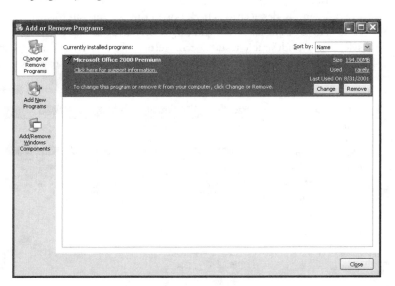

TIP   If you have a lot of programs installed, use the Sort By drop-down list to sort the programs. You can sort by Name, Size, Frequency of Use, and Date Last Used. Obviously enough, the Name category is useful for finding programs by name. The Size category *is good for determining which programs are hogging disk space when you need to free some up in a hurry. And the Frequency of Use category and Date Last Used category are useful for rooting out the programs you installed on a whim and have used hardly at all.*

3. Click the Change/Remove button. Windows checks to see if other users are using the computer (because they might be using the program that you're about to remove).

4. If any other user is logged on, Windows displays a Warning dialog box. At this point, you can click the Switch User button to display the Welcome screen, then log on as each user from there and log them off. But usually you'll find it easier to use the Users tab of Task Manager

to either switch to the other users or simply log them off. When you're ready, click the Continue button if the Warning dialog box is still displayed. (If it's not, click the Change/Remove button in the Add or Remove Programs dialog box instead.)

Once you've cleared the Warning hurdle, Windows invokes the uninstall routine for the program. The next steps vary depending on the program (or on its programmers or the tool they chose), but in most cases, you either specify which parts of the program to uninstall (if the program contains discrete components) or simply confirm that you want to get rid of the program.

If the uninstall routine tells you that it was unable to remove some parts of the program that you've asked to uninstall completely, it usually lets you know which parts are left. For example, unInstallShield provides a Details button that you can click to display a dialog box such as that shown in Figure 5.4. In this case, it's easy enough to delete these folders manually by using Explorer.

See page 41 of "Essential Skills" for a visual guide to removing a program.

TIP *If a program still shows up on the Installed Programs list after you have removed it, you can remove it from the list by going to* HKEY_LOCAL_MACHINE\SOFTWARE\Microsoft\Windows\CurrentVersion\Uninstall *in the Registry and deleting the key for that program.*

FIGURE 5.4

If unInstallShield can't remove all the components of a program, it provides details in the Details dialog box.

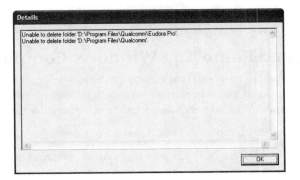

REMOVING 16-BIT WINDOWS PROGRAMS AND DOS PROGRAMS

Windows' Add or Remove Programs feature tracks all 32-bit programs installed on the computer, and it's able to track many 16-bit programs as well. But some 16-bit Windows programs and most DOS programs don't show up in the Add or Remove Programs dialog box, so you can't remove them that way.

The preferred way of removing a program that doesn't show up in the Add or Remove Programs window is to run its uninstall routine manually. Some Windows programs add a shortcut to their uninstall routine to the program folder (or, in Windows XP, to the Start menu) that contains their other shortcuts. If there's no shortcut, you'll need to dig through the folder that contains the program to see if it has one. The file might be an EXE file, but it might also be a BAT (batch) file.

Continued on next page

REMOVING 16-BIT WINDOWS PROGRAMS AND DOS PROGRAMS *(continued)*

If the program doesn't have an uninstall routine, you'll need to remove it manually. (If you've only just installed the program, you *could* use the System Restore feature to return your system to its state before you installed the program—but usually you'll have made other changes to your computer since installing the program. Chapter 24 discusses how to use System Restore.) This usually means deleting the folder (or folders) that contains the program and removing any references to it that you can find.

There are two problems with removing a program manually like this. First, you don't necessarily know where the program has put all its files. This is usually more of a problem with Windows programs, which (following Microsoft's own recommendations) often put shared files into the Windows folder or one of its subfolders, than with DOS programs (which probably don't know that the Windows folder exists, and certainly don't care about it even if they do know). So if you simply delete the folder or folders the program created, it may leave detritus in other folders. (This is why uninstall routines exist, of course.)

The second problem is that the program may also have added commands to configuration files of their era (such as AUTOEXEC.BAT or WIN.INI) that will cause errors when you've deleted its files. You'll need to discover these additions manually (usually when you get an error message) and delete them or comment them out manually. Because Windows XP uses these configuration files only for compatibility, these errors are likely to cause you annoyance rather than grief—unlike in the old days, when a command for a missing program could make Windows 3.1 refuse to load.

Adding and Removing Windows Components

Many of the accessory programs that come with Windows XP are optional. You can remove them if disk space is tight, or if you simply don't want them taking up space on your Start menu.

To add or remove Windows accessories and other optional components:

1. In Control Panel, choose Add or Remove Programs.

2. Click the Add/Remove Windows Components button. A window appears showing various individual components and component categories. See Figure 5.5.

FIGURE 5.5

Select an item or category to add or remove.

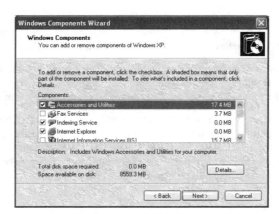

3. Place or remove the check mark next to an item to install or remove it. Some of the items on the list are for single features, such as MSN Explorer; others are for entire categories. If you choose a category, you can then click the Details button to see a list of accessories in that category, and then select each one individually. For some categories there are multiple levels; for example, opening the Accessories and Utilities category produces two sub-categories: Accessories and Games.

4. After you have made all your selections, click OK. If prompted for the Windows XP CD-ROM, insert it and click OK to continue.

TIP   Don't want to keep the Windows XP CD-ROM handy? If you copy the contents of its i386 folder to your hard disk (create a folder for it there), you can then browse to that folder whenever a Setup program such as Add/Remove Windows Components asks for access to the Windows XP CD-ROM. The downside—it takes up some space on your disk (a couple hundred megabytes).

Depending on what you're installing, you might be asked to restart the PC at the end of the procedure; do so if needed. When Windows reboots, any items you added will be available, and any items you removed will not.

REMOVING HIDDEN WINDOWS COMPONENTS

You might be disappointed when you look at the Accessories category of things you can add or remove—not all of the accessories on the Start menu's Accessories submenu appear here. Many of them are actually removable, but by default Windows hides them from the Add/Remove Windows Components screen. Windows Messenger is one example.

However, there's a great little tweak that will make Windows Messenger, and many other "hidden removal" programs, available for removal. Here's what to do:

1. In Notepad, open the text file SYSOC.INF, which is located in your Windows\Inf folder.

2. Notice there's a Components section, and under it, lines for various applets. Windows Messenger's name is msmsgs, for example. Find the line for the program you want to remove. For example:

    msmsgs=msgrocm.dll,OcEntry,msmsgs.inf, hide, 7

3. Edit the line to remove the word *hide* and the comma and space preceding it. For example, if you are doing Windows Messenger, the line might look like this after editing:

    msmsgs=msgrocm.dll,OcEntry,msmsgs.inf,7

4. Close Notepad, saving the changes.

5. Now go to Add or Remove Programs in Control Panel and click Add/Remove Windows Components. The previously hidden program should now be available for removal.

Running Programs

In Windows, you can start a program in any of several ways. If you've used a previous version of Windows, you'll probably be familiar with these ways. They break down into two categories: starting a program directly by opening it, and starting a program indirectly by opening a file whose file type is associated with the program.

You can start a program directly in any of the following ways:

◆ Click its shortcut on the Start menu

◆ Double-click a shortcut on the Desktop or in an Explorer window. (Chapter 6 discusses how to create shortcuts wherever you want.)

◆ Click a shortcut on the Quick Launch toolbar or another Desktop toolbar. (Chapter 4 discusses the Desktop toolbars and how to customize them.)

◆ Choose Start ➤ Run. Windows displays the Run dialog box. Enter the name of the program in the Open text box, either by typing or by clicking the Browse button, using the resulting Browse dialog box to identify the file, and clicking the Open button. Then click the OK button.

NOTE   *Using the Run dialog box seems a clumsy way of running a program, but it's useful for running Windows utilities for which Windows doesn't provide a Start menu entry (for example, the Registry Editor, discussed in Chapter 22) and for running programs for which you don't want to create a shortcut but whose path and filename you can type (or otherwise enter) without undue effort.*

◆ Double-click the icon or listing for the program in an Explorer window (or on the Desktop). You can also use the Search Companion (Start ➤ Search) to locate the program you want to run.

Almost all setup routines create shortcuts to their programs automatically. Usually, the setup routine puts a shortcut on the Start menu or in a subfolder of the Start menu. Some setup routines place a shortcut directly on the Desktop; some consult you first, others don't. Some setup routines offer to also put a shortcut in the Quick Launch toolbar and/or notification area; other setup routines do so without consulting you.

An icon in the Quick Launch toolbar is simply an alternative shortcut to one on the desktop; an icon in the notification area indicates that some portion of the program is already running automatically. You can right-click an icon in the notification area to see a menu of choices for dealing with that running program. If there's a Properties, Setup, Options, or some similar command, it might open a dialog box in which you can prevent the program from loading automatically at startup.

Dealing with Unresponsive Programs

Programs run pretty well on Windows XP—but not all programs run well all the time. Sooner or later, a program will hang or crash on you.

When this happens, first make sure the program hasn't got an open dialog box that you can't see. When you're working with multiple programs, you can easily get an open dialog box stuck behind another open window. If the dialog box is application modal, it prevents you from doing anything else in the program until you dismiss it. (Dialog boxes can also be *system modal*, in which case they prevent you from doing anything else on your computer until you deal with them.)

Minimize all other open windows and see if the dialog box appears. If not, you'll probably have the program that's not responding still displayed on your screen, probably with only some parts of the window correctly drawn. For example, typically the areas of the program that were covered by other programs or windows will not be redrawn (or not redrawn correctly).

TIP   *To quickly minimize all open windows, click the Show Desktop button on the Quick Launch toolbar (if present) or right-click an empty area of the Taskbar and choose Minimize All Windows from the shortcut menu.*

Next, try using Alt+Tab to switch to the program and bring out from behind it any dialog box that's hiding. Chances are that this won't work either, but it's worth a try. If the dialog box appears, deal with it as usual, and the program should come back to life.

If that didn't work, try using Task Manager to switch to the program:

1. Right-click an empty area of the Taskbar and choose Task Manager from the shortcut menu. Windows displays Task Manager. Or, if you can't get to the Taskbar, press Ctrl+Alt+Delete.

2. If the Applications tab isn't displayed, click it. The Applications tab (shown in Figure 5.6) lists each running program and its status. The status can be either Running (all is well with the program, as far as Windows is concerned) or Not Responding (Windows believes that the program is not responding to conventional stimuli).

FIGURE 5.6

The Applications tab of Task Manager lists all running programs and their status: Running or Not Responding.

3. Select the program that's not responding.

4. Click the Switch To button. Task Manager attempts to switch to it, and minimizes itself in the process.

If that didn't work either, it's probably time to kill the program. Take the following steps:

1. Restore Task Manager by clicking its button on the Taskbar.

2. Decide whether the program has hung or crashed. (See the nearby sidebar "'Not Responding' Status Isn't Always Terminal" for advice on determining whether the program is still viable.)

3. Select the task in the Task list.

4. Click the End Task button. Windows displays the End Program dialog box (shown in Figure 5.7).

5. Click the End Now button. Windows terminates the program and frees up the memory it contained.

FIGURE 5.7

To terminate the program, click the End Now button in the End Program dialog box.

If killing the program like this doesn't work, you have several options. Here they are, in descending order of preference:

◆ Close all other programs that are responding. Then log off Windows. Doing this should shut down any programs you're running.

◆ If you can't close the program and can't log off Windows, but Task Manager is still working (apart from not being able to kill the program), use Task Manager to switch to another user, then log off the user session with the crashed program.

◆ At this point, you're pretty much out of options. Reach for the Reset button on your computer. When Windows restarts, check the disk for errors. (See "Checking Disks for Errors" in Chapter 24.)

"NOT RESPONDING" STATUS ISN'T ALWAYS TERMINAL

When you see a program listed as having Not Responding status in the Programs tab of Task Manager, you may be tempted to kill it off right away. But you'd do better to stay your hand for a minute or two. Why? Because Not Responding status doesn't necessarily mean that a program has hung or crashed:

◆ First, Not Responding may mean nothing more than that program is responding more slowly than Windows expects; if you give it a few seconds, or perhaps a few minutes, it may start responding normally again. If your computer seems unresponsive overall, back off and give it a few minutes to sort itself out.

Continued on next page

> **"Not Responding" Status Isn't Always Terminal** *(continued)*
>
> ◆ Second (and often related to the first point), Not Responding may mean that Windows is struggling to allocate enough memory to the program; this often causes the program to run slowly. Task Manager is a little harsh in this respect—it's Windows' fault that the program isn't responding, but Task Manager points the finger at the program.
>
> ◆ Third, VBA-enabled programs (for example, Microsoft Word and Microsoft PowerPoint) are often listed as Not Responding when they're running a VBA routine or macro. In this case, Not Responding means only that VBA temporarily has control over the program. When VBA releases control of the program—in other words, when the routine ends—Task Manager lists the program as Responding again. (If the program shouldn't be running a macro, try pressing Ctrl+Break to stop it.)

Program Compatibility Issues

If you've used of the versions of Windows NT, or if you've used Windows 2000, you'll know that program compatibility has been a major issue for the NT code base. In order to make NT stable and crash-proof, the designers made heavy sacrifices in compatibility. Many Windows 9*x* programs flat out wouldn't run on NT. Games and other programs that tried to access hardware directly were particularly problematic: Windows 9*x* lets a program access hardware directly, whereas NT's hardware abstraction layer (HAL) forces all hardware requests to be brokered by the operating system.

In Windows 2000 Professional, Microsoft greatly increased the number of programs that would run on the NT code base—but some Windows 9*x* programs still wouldn't run, and many DOS-based games wouldn't run either. Direct hardware access was still a problem, because the HAL was still there. Briefly, if the program could run in protected mode, letting the HAL handle the communications with the hardware, it would usually run, though it might run a bit more slowly than on other versions of Windows (or on DOS). If the program insisted on trying to communicate with the hardware directly, HAL gave it grief. (Fill in your own *2001* joke here: "I'm sorry, Doom, I'm afraid I can't do that," and so on.)

On this front, Windows XP brings very welcome news: XP is able to run most 32-bit Windows programs without problems. It can also run many 16-bit Windows programs. And it can run a number of DOS programs. Most of this happens transparently: You install the program by running its setup routine or installation routine as usual; you run the program as usual; and that's that. Behind the scenes, Windows XP provides more flexibility in providing the program with the type of environment it needs. On the surface, all is serene.

That's for many programs—perhaps most programs. But some programs don't run properly like this. For some, you need to explicitly use Windows XP's Compatibility mode to fool the program into thinking that it's running on the version of Windows that it expects. Windows XP then mimics the environment of that version of Windows for that program, sustaining the illusion that things are to the program's liking. For example, if a program expects Windows 95 and won't run without it, Compatibility mode tells the program that it's running on Windows 95 and tries to prevent it from finding out the truth. Usually the program then runs fine, though you may notice some loss of performance as Windows XP soft-soaps the program to keep it happy.

NOTE *If you're familiar with the Mac, you might be wondering how Windows XP's Compatibility mode compares with Mac OS X and its Classic technology for running programs that won't run on OS X. Basically, there are similarities between Compatibility mode and Classic, but Compatibility mode is both less gruesome conceptually and far lighter on the memory. Classic essentially loads a hefty chunk of System 9.1 (on top of OS X, which isn't exactly svelte itself) and uses it to run the program, whereas Windows XP essentially dupes the program into a false sense of security by giving it the cues it expects. This duping requires a bit more memory and system resources, but nothing like the overhead that the Mac needs to run a program in Classic mode. But then Windows XP is less of a drastic change from its predecessors than OS X, which is essentially mutated Unix with a gooey (sorry, GUI) interface.*

16-BIT PROGRAMS AND 32-BIT PROGRAMS

Okay, time out. What *is* a 16-bit program, and what's a 32-bit program? Where does the number of bits come from, and what does it mean?

A layperson's answer to the first question might be that 16-bit programs are programs designed to run on 16-bit versions of Windows (for example, Windows 3.1) and 32-bit programs are programs designed to run on 32-bit versions of Windows (Windows 9x, Windows NT, Windows 2000, and Windows XP).

Actually, it's not quite that simple. To get a fraction more technical, 16-bit programs are written to the Win16 application programming interface (API) and 32-bit programs are written to the Win32 API. The APIs are sets of rules that tell programmers how they can access the functionality that an operating system exposes to them and how a program should behave so that it gets along with the operating system and other programs running on it.

Normally, 32-bit programs *are* written for 32-bit operating systems, and 16-bit programs *are* (or, you might hope, *were*) written for 16-bit operating systems (which have largely gone the way of the dodo). But by using the Win32s extensions—a 32-bit operating system extension that sat on top of the 16-bit Windows 3.1 operating environment (which in turn sat on top of the 16-bit DOS operating system)—you could run a 32-bit program on Windows 3.1. So some 32-bit programs were written for a 16-bit operating system. (Well, sort of.) And because 32-bit operating systems can normally run 16-bit programs, many 16-bit programs are used to this day, running more or less happily in virtual machines on 32-bit operating systems. The 32-bit operating system may have to perform a process called *thunking*, essentially gearing down to run a 16-bit program. Thunking typically involves some overhead and a slight loss of performance. But if the 16-bit program ran at an acceptable speed on Windows 3.1 with, say, a 486 processor, it should run at a decent speed on even a modest Celeron or Duron processor, even with any thunking needed.

Just as 32 valves are better than 16 (for making a satisfactory engine growl if not for reaching the speed limit ahead of that pickup in the next lane at the traffic signal), 32 bits are better than 16. The advantage of 32 bits is that you can move more information at once—*much* more information. Thirty-two bits can represent a range of more than 4 billion integer values (4,294,967,296, to be precise), whereas 16 bits can represent only 65,536 integer values. Sixty-four bits can represent correspondingly more than 32 bits, and 64-bit PC operating systems are on their way. In fact, Windows XP Professional and Windows .NET Server will have 64-bit versions for the forthcoming 64-bit Itanium processor from Intel.

Continued on next page

16-BIT PROGRAMS AND 32-BIT PROGRAMS *(continued)*

That still hasn't answered the second question: Where does the number of bits come from, and what does it mean? The *bit-ness* of a program essentially comes from the word size of the computer it's running on. The *word size* is the biggest number that the computer can handle in one operation. Those fire-breathing speed demons of the mid 1980s, 286 systems, used a 16-bit word size, enabling them to handle much more data at once than the (exhaust-breathing) 8-bit systems that preceded them. Then, 386 systems upped the ante to a 32-bit word size, at which it has stayed for several generations of chips: even Pentium IV and Athlon systems use 32-bit words. The Itanium processor will have a 64-bit word size, enabling it to handle impressively large chunks of data in a single operation.

When you're installing programs on Windows XP, you seldom need to worry about how many bits they're going to use, because Windows XP handles any necessary transitions between 32-bit and 16-bit code seamlessly. You *do* sometimes have to worry about *where* you install older programs so that all users of the computer can use them—but more on this a little later in this chapter.

Once you've set up Compatibility mode for a program, that program runs in Compatibility mode each time, so you shouldn't need to tweak it any further unless some of its features misbehave.

Compatibility mode is very impressive, and it's great when it works. But some ancient programs (particularly DOS programs) may never work, even with Compatibility mode. In these cases, your choices of course of action are approximately (a) give up on the program, (b) dual-boot your system with the version of Windows with which the program was last known to work, or (c) use emulation software such as VMware to run on top of Windows XP. Create a session of the version of Windows with which the program works.

Programs You Shouldn't Even *Try* to Run on Windows XP

No matter how impressive Windows XP's compatibility with programs designed for earlier versions of Windows (or for DOS), there are some types of programs you should never try to run on Windows XP. These include the following:

Operating systems   Obviously, you can't install DOS, an earlier version of Windows, or another operating system or operating environment on top of Windows XP—at least, not without using some kind of PC-emulation software (such as VMware).

Old antivirus programs   Antivirus programs designed for previous versions of Windows, including Windows 2000 Professional, don't know how to deal with Windows XP. You may be able to update the program. More likely, you'll need to get a whole new version.

WARNING   *Attempting to install some of these antivirus programs may crash your Windows XP computer.*

Old troubleshooting and cleanup utilities   Most troubleshooting and cleanup utilities designed for earlier versions of Windows will give XP nothing but grief. So will disk utilities (for example, Norton Utilities) designed for earlier versions. As with the antivirus programs, these utilities don't know how Windows XP works—in fact, most of them assume that Windows works in a completely different way. So despite Windows XP's ability to restore your system after bad software goes on the rampage, it's a mistake to let old troubleshooting and cleanup utilities loose on your system in the first place. Where you still need the added functionality to supplement Windows XP's capabilities, invest in a new utility specifically designed for Windows XP.

Some potential offenders are smart enough to figure out the problem and quit on their own. Figure 5.8 shows the Incorrect Operating System dialog box that an old version of Network Associates' VirusScan displays if you try to install it on Windows XP without using Compatibility mode.

FIGURE 5.8

This old version of VirusScan is smart enough to refuse to be installed on Windows XP.

Running Programs in Compatibility Mode

Compatibility mode lets you tell Windows XP to emulate Windows 95, Windows 98, Windows NT 4, or Windows 2000 so that a program thinks it's running on the operating system it knows and likes.

TIP   Often the program's setup utility will need to be run in Compatibility mode. Then run the program itself in Compatibility mode as well after installation.

Windows XP comes with the Microsoft AppCompat database of compatibility problems known about programs. AppCompat is automatically updated by Windows Update, which gives you another incentive to accept Windows Update's offers to download every update available—at least until your computer's hardware and all your software are working as perfectly as you could wish.

NOTE   You can set Compatibility mode only on files on local drives. You can't set Compatibility mode on a program located on a network drive, on a CD drive or other removable drive, or on a floppy drive. But you can create a shortcut on a local drive to a program located elsewhere, and then specify Compatibility mode for the shortcut.

Windows provides two ways of setting up a program to run in Compatibility mode. The first way is formal and cumbersome, but it lets you test whether the Compatibility mode you chose works for the program. The second way is much quicker, but you run the risk of getting a program comprehensively hung if Compatibility mode doesn't work.

THE FORMAL WAY OF SETTING COMPATIBILITY MODE

Here's the formal way to run a program in Compatibility mode:

1. Choose Start ➤ All Programs ➤ Accessories ➤ Program Compatibility Wizard. Windows displays a Help and Support Center window and starts the Program Compatibility Wizard in it.

2. Read the information and cautions on the Welcome to the Program Compatibility Wizard screen and click the Next button. Windows displays the How Do You Want to Locate the Program That You Would Like to Run with Compatibility Settings? screen (shown in Figure 5.9).

FIGURE 5.9

On the How Do You Want to Locate the Program That You Would Like to Run with Compatibility Settings? screen in Help and Support Center, choose how to select the program you want to run in Compatibility mode.

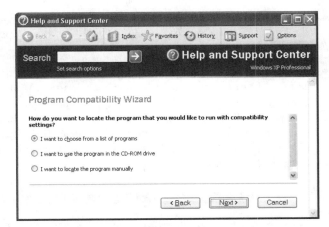

3. Use one of the following three ways to locate the program:

   ◆ To set Compatibility mode for a program that's already installed, select the I Want to Choose from a List of Programs option button and click the Next button. The Wizard scans your hard drive and displays a list of programs (Figure 5.10 shows an example). Select the program and click the Next button.

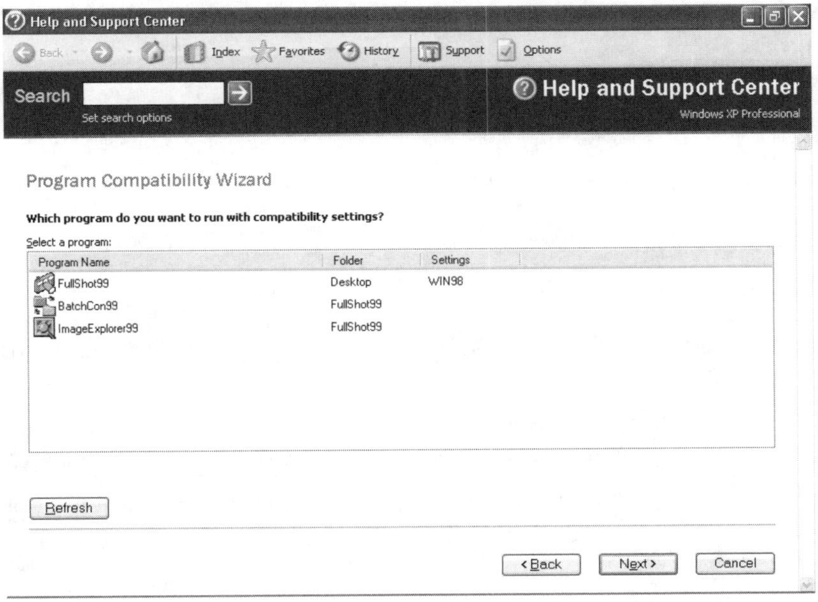

FIGURE 5.10

Select a program from the list that the Program Compatibility Wizard assembles.

◆ To set Compatibility mode for a program you're installing from CD, insert the CD, select the I Want to Use the Program in the CD-ROM Drive option button, and click the Next button.

◆ To set Compatibility mode for a program that isn't installed and whose installation medium isn't on CD, or if you're just feeling ornery, select the I Want to Locate the Program Manually option button and click the Next button. The Wizard displays the Which Program Do You Want to Run with Compatibility Settings? screen (shown in Figure 5.11). Enter the path in the text box, either by typing or by clicking the Browse button and using the resulting Please Select Application dialog box (a common Open dialog box) to select the program. Click the Next button.

FIGURE 5.11

If necessary, or if you prefer, you can identify the program manually on the Which Program Do You Want to Run with Compatibility Settings? screen of the Program Compatibility Wizard.

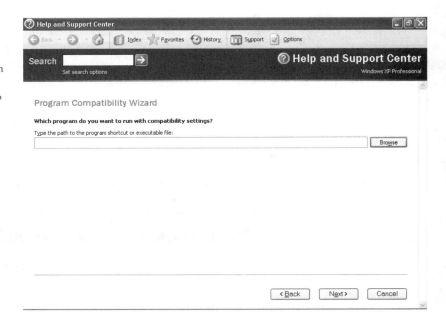

The Wizard displays the Select a Compatibility Mode for the Program screen (shown in Figure 5.12).

4. Select the option button for the operating system you think the program needs: Windows 95, Windows NT 4 (Service Pack 5), Windows 98/Windows Me, or Windows 2000.

5. Click the Next button. The Wizard displays the Select Display Settings for the Program screen (shown in Figure 5.13).

FIGURE 5.12

On the Select a Compatibility Mode for the Program screen of the Program Compatibility Wizard, select the Compatibility mode you want to use.

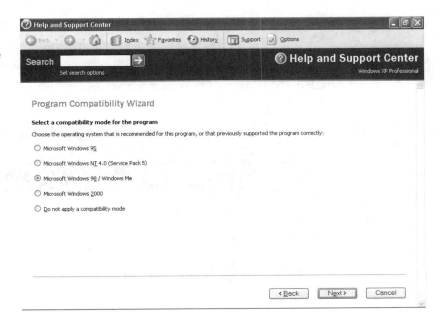

FIGURE 5.13

On the Select Display Settings for the Program screen of the Program Compatibility Wizard, you can apply limitations to the display settings used for the program.

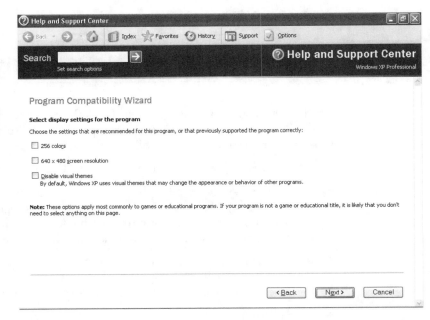

6. If you know the program needs display limitations, select the 256 Colors check box, the 640×480 Screen Resolution check box, or the Disable Visual Themes check box.

   ◆ For most programs, you don't need to select any of these display limitations.

7. Click the Next button. The Wizard displays the Test Your Compatibility Settings screen (shown in Figure 5.14).

FIGURE 5.14

On the Test Your Compatibility Settings screen of the Program Compatibility Wizard, check through the settings you've chosen, and then click the Next button to test them.

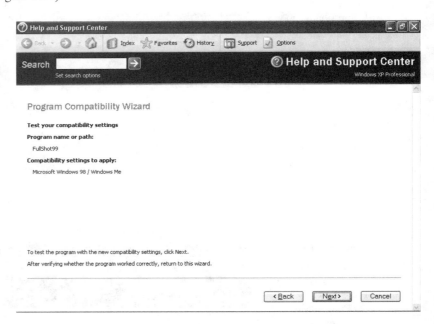

8. Check the settings you've chosen, and then click the Next button. The Wizard launches the program with the compatibility settings you specified and displays the Did the Program Work Correctly? screen (shown in Figure 5.15).

9. Choose the appropriate option button:

   ◆ If the program ran okay, select the Yes, Set This Program to Always Use These Compatibility Settings option button. The Wizard displays the Program Compatibility Data screen (shown in Figure 5.16), on which you can choose whether to send Microsoft information on the program, the settings you chose, and whether they solved the problem.

   ◆ If the program didn't run correctly, but you want to try other settings, select the No, Try Different Compatibility Settings option button. Click the Next button. The Wizard returns to the Select a Compatibility Mode for the Program screen. Return to step 5 and try again.

   ◆ When no compatibility settings seem to work, select the No, I Am Finished Trying Compatibility Settings option button. Click the Next button. The Wizard displays the Program Compatibility Data screen (discussed previously). In this case, you have more incentive for sending Microsoft information, as it may help them fix the problem with this program in the future.

FIGURE 5.15

On the Did the Program Work Correctly? screen, tell the Program Compatibility Wizard whether the program launched correctly with the computer settings.

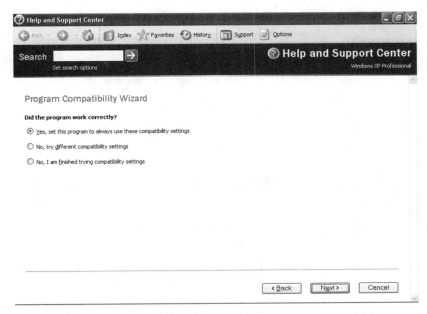

FIGURE 5.16

On the Program Compatibility Data screen of the Program Compatibility Wizard, you can choose whether to send Microsoft information on a program that you couldn't get to work.

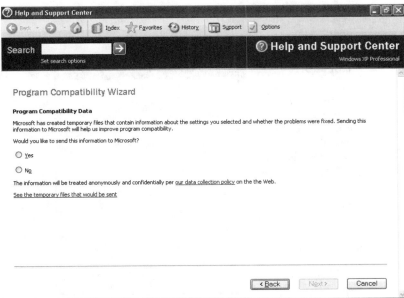

10. Choose the Yes button or the No button as appropriate.

11. Click the Next button. If you chose the Yes button, the Wizard sends the compatibility data. Either way, it displays the Completing the Program Compatibility Wizard screen.

12. Click the Finish button. The Wizard closes itself.

You remember that old version of VirusScan from earlier in the chapter that didn't want to install on Windows XP? It was happy to install in Compatibility mode for Windows 95—but parts of it wouldn't run on Windows XP (see Figure 5.17).

FIGURE 5.17

VirusScan decided it really didn't like Windows XP after all.

See pages 93–94 of "Essential Skills" for a visual guide to enabling Compatibility mode for an application.

THE QUICK WAY OF SETTING COMPATIBILITY MODE

The quick way of setting Compatibility mode is as follows:

1. Right-click the shortcut for the program and select Properties from the shortcut menu. Windows displays the Properties dialog box for the shortcut.

2. Click the Compatibility tab, which is shown in Figure 5.18.

3. Select the Run This Program in Compatibility Mode For check box if it's not already selected.

4. In the drop-down list, select the mode you want to use.

FIGURE 5.18

You can also choose Compatibility mode settings in the Compatibility tab of the Properties dialog box for the shortcut.

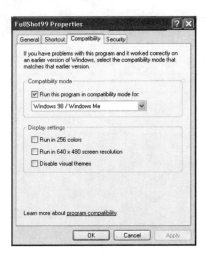

5. In the Display Settings section, select the Run in 256 Colors check box, the Run in 640×480 Screen Resolution check box, or the Disable Visual Themes check box as necessary. (Again, for most programs, you won't need to set these options.)

6. Click the OK button. Windows applies your choice and closes the Properties dialog box.

This method of specifying Compatibility mode settings has the advantage that you can specify different Compatibility mode settings for different shortcuts for the same program or even for the shortcuts to different documents of the same file type.

TIP   If you want to use Compatibility Mode for a shortcut that points directly to a file on CD-ROM, you won't be able to access the Compatibility tab for the shortcut while there is a CD in the drive. Remove it, and then open the properties for the shortcut. Then you can replace the CD in the drive before you run the program to test the settings.

Even with Compatibility Mode, Some Programs Don't Work

Some programs plain don't work even when you use Compatibility mode. For example, Lotus Smart-Suite 96 won't install on Windows XP, no matter whether you try to run it from the CD or copy its files to a local drive and use Compatibility mode. When you run the SmartSuite 96 installation routine on Windows XP, you get to specify the program folder and the type of installation (typical, minimal, custom). Then the installation crashes with the Output message box shown in Figure 5.19. This message box mentions an overflow (trying to put more information in a memory register than will fit), but beyond that, it tells you next to nothing useful.

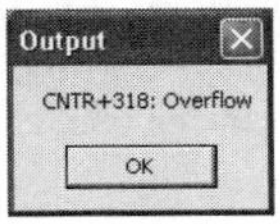

FIGURE 5.19

The Lotus SmartSuite 96 installation routine crashes with an Output CNTR+318 Overflow message box.

After this message box, the program terminates. If you're feeling determined, and you lather, rinse, and repeat, exactly the same thing happens again.

NOTE   Microsoft may have fixed this problem with SmartSuite 96 by the time you read this book. But given that Lotus used to be a major competitor of Microsoft's in the programs field, and that IBM (which owns Lotus) used to make OS/2, and that this version of SmartSuite is a good five years out of date, they may not have gotten around to bothering.

Exchanging Data Between Programs

Ever since the early versions of Windows, one of its great advantages has been its ability to transfer data between programs via its Clipboard.

The Clipboard can transfer data of different types that would not normally be compatible with one another. For example, suppose you are writing a letter in a simple word processor such as Word-Pad that does not support the import of very many types of graphics. You have a graphic in some odd format that you want to include; it will open in a Windows-based drawing program, but not in WordPad. You can copy the graphic to the clipboard in the drawing program, and then paste it into WordPad, bypassing the whole import/export hassle entirely.

But wait—there's more. In addition to the simple copy (or cut) and paste of the Clipboard, you can also maintain links between the original material and the copy. That's Object Linking and Embedding (OLE).

Clipboard Basics

You're probably already familiar with basic Clipboard operation. Almost all Windows programs have an Edit menu containing commands for Cut, Copy, and Paste. These commands place and retrieve things on the Clipboard. There may be several shortcuts for these commands, depending on the program. Here are the most common ones:

◆ Cut: Ctrl+X or the Cut button on the toolbar

◆ Copy: Ctrl+C or the Copy button

◆ Paste: Ctrl+V or the Paste button

 See page 21 of "Essential Skills" for a visual guide to copying, cutting, and pasting.

The Clipboard is not designed to be permanent storage. It holds only one clip at a time, so when you cut or copy something else, whatever was there before is erased. (In Microsoft Office 2000 or Office XP you have an expanded Clipboard available, which is discussed in the next section.) If you want to store something from the Clipboard for later use, check out the Clipboard Viewer, discussed later in this chapter.

TIP   You can capture all or part of a screen image to the Clipboard, and then paste it into a graphics program such as Paint to save it. To do so, press Shift+PrtScn for the entire screen or Alt+PrtScn for the active window.

For Office 2000/XP Users: The Enhanced Microsoft Office Clipboard

In Microsoft Office 2000, an enhanced clipboard called Office Clipboard was introduced that enabled you to copy multiple selections to the Clipboard without losing whatever content was already there. Office XP expanded on this idea to enable even more clips at a time (up to 24). Figure 5.20 shows the Office Clipboard in Microsoft Word XP.

When you use the Office Clipboard, the last item you place on it also appears in the Windows XP Clipboard, so the two Clipboards are related. The Copy, Cut, and Paste commands in all applications, including Office applications, apply to the most recently used clip as well. The only difference is that in the Office Clipboard, when you replace the Windows XP Clipboard contents with something else, instead of that old content being deleted, it simply moves down one slot on the Office Clipboard. When the Office Clipboard fills up completely, the oldest items start scrolling off. Like the Windows Clipboard, the Office Clipboard is cleared when you exit Windows.

As long as an Office application is open, the Office Clipboard is available, and whatever you copy or cut to the regular Clipboard appears there. However, when it comes to pasting from the Clipboard, you can paste the full range of clips only into Office applications; in any other application you are limited to whatever is currently on the regular Windows Clipboard.

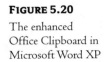

FIGURE 5.20

The enhanced Office Clipboard in Microsoft Word XP

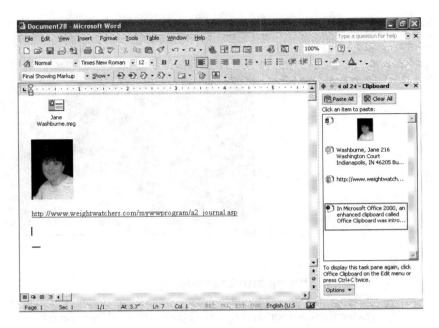

Using the ClipBook Viewer

If you ever forget what's on the Clipboard, you can bring up the ClipBook Viewer by running the program `clipbrd.exe` with the Run command. If you find yourself doing that often, you might want to create a shortcut to it on the desktop or Start menu.

The ClipBook Viewer program comes in handy in a variety of other ways as well. If you're on a network, you can use it to connect to a ClipBook on a remote PC, to share clips with others. You can also use it to save Clipboard contents to a file, and then open that file whenever you want to reuse that content on the Clipboard. This is sort of like the Office Clipboard in that it enables you to retain multiple clips. However, it has some important differences. The clips stored in the ClipBook Viewer are permanently held in saved files (at least until you choose to delete them), so shutting off the PC does not affect them. Also, to paste from the ClipBook Viewer, you must enter the ClipBook Viewer program and copy a saved clip to the Windows XP Clipboard first. Figure 5.21 shows the ClipBook Viewer with the current Windows Clipboard content showing.

TIP   Don't panic if the image shown in ClipBook Viewer is not as high quality as the clip you copied to the Clipboard, or if the image appears distorted. The ClipBook Viewer is simply not as adept at displaying all file types to best advantage as other programs. Rest assured that when you save the clip and then open it later from ClipBook Viewer, it will retain all its original quality.

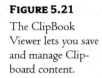

FIGURE 5.21

The ClipBook Viewer lets you save and manage Clipboard content.

Object Linking and Embedding

Object Linking and Embedding (OLE) could be the subject of an entire chapter by itself; it's a very rich technology for creating links between original data and copies of it, or between original data and the program in which it was created. We'll try to keep the discussion succinct here, however, focusing on the facts that an end user would need to know.

NOTE *You may have heard of Dynamic Data Exchange, or DDE, an older version of the same basic technology as OLE. It was used in Windows versions prior to 3.1, and some 16-bit programs still employ it as opposed to OLE. Windows XP includes a DDE driver called NetDDE that helps applications that require DDE to interface with those that use OLE.*

When you share data between applications with the Clipboard (either the standard Windows version or the Office Clipboard), the resulting pasted copy is static. When the original from which it came changes, the copy does not change. In addition, the pasted copy becomes part of the destination document (or whatever data file type it is), and no connection is maintained between that pasted item and the program from which it came.

There are two main features in OLE: linking and embedding. *Linking* refers to creating a link between the original data file and the new location, so that when the original changes, the pasted copy changes too. *Embedding* refers to creating a link between the pasted data and the application in which it was created, so that you can double-click the pasted data to reopen it in its native application for further editing.

Not all programs support OLE, and those that do support it may access it in slightly different ways. Most Microsoft Office applications support it through two separate commands: Edit ➤ Paste Special and Insert ➤ Object.

OLE WITH THE PASTE SPECIAL COMMAND

The Paste Special method is useful when you want to embed a fragment of data from some other program. Embedding works whether or not the data has been saved in that other program; Linking requires that it be saved (since the link must refer to a specific file name). To link or embed with Paste Special:

1. Copy the data to the Clipboard normally in its native program.

2. Switch to the program into which you want to paste it, and choose Edit ➤ Paste Special. The Paste Special dialog box appears.

3. If you want to embed only, leave Paste selected. If you want to link, choose Paste Link. See Figure 5.22.

FIGURE 5.22

Pasting content with Paste Special

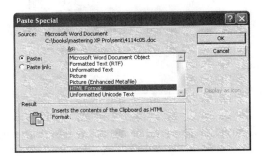

4. Select the type of object you want it to be pasted as. If you want embedding, make sure you choose a type that ends with the word "object" such as Microsoft Word Document Object in Figure 5.22.

TIP It is possible to do regular pasting with the Paste Special dialog box. If you choose Paste rather than Paste Link, and then do not choose an object type that supports embedding, the net result will be the same as if you had used the regular Paste command. You might occasionally want to do such a thing if you wanted it pasted as a particular non-embeddable data type other than the default one.

5. Click OK. Your new link or embedded object is created.

OLE WITH THE INSERT OBJECT COMMAND

The Insert Object method is useful when you want to insert the entire file, not just a fragment of it. You can also use Insert Object to create a new embedded object within a document, of any type for which you have an installed Windows application. For example, suppose you want a drawing in a Word document but you find Word's drawing tools too rudimentary. You could embed a Paint Shop Pro drawing in the document and have access to all of Paint Shop Pro's graphics tools from within Word.

To insert an existing object:

1. Start in the application and document into which you want to insert the object. Then choose Insert ➤ Object.

2. Click the Create from File tab.

3. Type the path to the file, or browse for it with Browse.

4. If you want it to be linked, mark the Link to File check box. (Embedding happens automatically this way, whether you choose linking or not.) See Figure 5.23.

FIGURE 5.23

Inserting an existing file with Insert Object

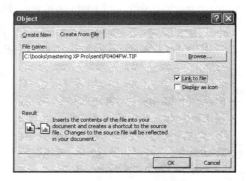

5. If you want the object to appear as a clickable icon in the document, rather than in its native format, mark the Display as Icon check box.

TIP *You probably won't want to use Display as Icon in most cases; most people want embedded/linked content to appear seamless with the rest of the file. An exception might be if you are embedding a large graphic file that takes a long time to draw onscreen, and you didn't want it to always be visible while you are editing the rest of the document.*

6. Click OK. The file is inserted.

If you want to create a new embedded object, you won't be able to link it, of course, since it won't exist outside of the host document. To create a new embedded object:

1. Start in the application and document into which you want to insert the object. Then choose Insert ➤ Object.

2. Click the Create New tab if it is not already on top. Then select the program with which you want to associate the new object. See Figure 5.24.

FIGURE 5.24

Creating a new embedded object

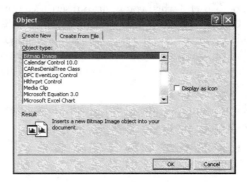

3. If you want the object to appear as a clickable icon in the document, rather than in its native format, mark the Display as Icon check box.

4. Click OK. The application opens, and you can create your new object.

What happens at this point depends on the application. If it is fully compatible with the host application, its menus and tools may appear directly in the same window as the host application. If that happens, you can click away from the embedded object to return to the host application at any time; it's seamlessly saved.

Some applications do not support full integration, so they appear in their own separate window for you to create the object. In such programs, there will be a special command on the File menu that isn't normally present, such as Exit and Return to [application]. Choose it to go back to the host application.

EDITING AN EMBEDDED OBJECT

Any time you want to edit an embedded object, just double-click it. It will reopen in the application with which it is associated.

MANAGING LINKED OBJECTS

Most OLE-enabled applications have a link manager built into them. Microsoft Word is like that; to manage the links in a document, choose Edit ➤ Links. This opens a Links dialog box, as shown in Figure 5.25.

FIGURE 5.25

Managing links in Microsoft Office XP; other programs may have a different-looking dialog box.

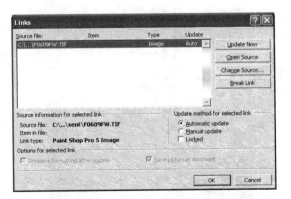

Links are updated automatically by default whenever the file is opened or closed. You can change to Manual updating from the Links dialog box. You can also break a link, terminating the connection to the original so that the copy is no longer updated when the original changes. You can also change the source of the link. This might be useful if you have moved the original file to another folder, for example, and need for the link to point to the new location.

Organizing the Start Menu

In Chapter 4 you learned about customizing the way the Start menu works in general; you can also customize it by selecting which shortcuts appear on it and in what positions.

The Windows XP Start menu has several sections containing program shortcuts, pointed out in Figure 5.26:

◆ The pinned shortcuts area, at top left, shows Internet and E-mail shortcuts by default. You can add shortcuts here for whatever programs you like as well.

◆ The frequently used programs list, at bottom left, contains shortcuts for the programs you use most often or have used most recently. This list is managed automatically by Windows; you cannot edit it manually.

◆ The All Programs menu, accessible when you click All Programs, lists folders and shortcuts for all installed programs. You can add and remove shortcuts from here freely, as well as create and remove folders and rearrange items.

FIGURE 5.26

Shortcuts appear on the Start menu in several places.

Notice in Figure 5.26 at the top of the All Programs menu is a special area containing four short-cuts. When you use the Classic Start menu, there is a section at the top of the top-level Start menu that is much like the pinned shortcuts area on the XP Start menu. Some programs released prior to Windows XP will place shortcuts for themselves there; Windows itself also places a few shortcuts there as well. There's nothing sacred about that area; you can move programs into and out of that area freely.

Editing Pinned Shortcuts

To add a shortcut to the pinned shortcuts area, drag-and-drop it directly onto the Start button without opening the Start menu. Or, drag it onto the Start menu and pause a moment, waiting for the Start menu to appear, and then drag it into the exact spot you want.

To remove the Internet or E-mail shortcut, or change what program either one of those points to, right-click the Start button and choose Properties; then click Customize. Clear the check marks next to Internet and/or E-mail to get rid of them completely, or select other programs to be represented by them from their respective drop-down lists. See Figure 5.27.

FIGURE 5.27

Change the Internet and/or E-mail shortcuts in the pinned shortcut area.

To remove a pinned shortcut other than Internet or E-mail, right-click it and choose Delete.

Editing the All Programs List

The All Programs list is really just a set of folders nested within one another, so you can edit the structure of the All Programs menu by adding, moving, and/or deleting shortcuts and folders within it. For easy access to it, right-click the Start button and choose Open for a My Computer-like Window, or Explore for a Windows Explorer-like Window. Then work with it as you would any other file-management window.

One quirk with Windows XP is that the Start menu structure for all users of the PC is stored separately from that for the current user. When the Start menu actually displays, the two are combined into one Start menu, but you edit them separately. This enables any user to customize the Start menu, even if they do not have the needed permissions to change the settings for the PC as a whole. When you right-click the Start button and choose Open or Explore, you get the version for the current user. If you want to edit the version for all users, right-click and choose Open All Users or Explore All Users instead. Figure 5.28 shows the Programs menu for All Users being explored.

NOTE *If you are new to file management, you may want to refer to Chapter 6 for some help.*

FIGURE 5.28

The contents of the
All Programs menu
for All Users in
Windows Explorer.

Another way to edit the All Programs menu is to use drag-and-drop. This method has several advantages. For one, it is quicker. For another, it works with the Start menu structure as an integrated whole, so you don't need to worry whether the shortcut you want to work with is part of the current user or All Users configuration. With drag-and-drop, you can:

◆ Drag a shortcut from the desktop or a file-management window into the menu system. To do so, drag it to the Start menu and pause, holding the mouse button down, until the Start menu opens. Then pause on All Programs; then continue your way through until the desired location is displayed.

◆ Drag an item from one folder to another on the menu. To make a folder open, drag the item to it and pause, still holding the mouse button down; the folder will open after a few seconds.

◆ Delete an item from the menu by right-clicking it and choosing Delete.

Summary

This chapter has discussed how to install programs, how to run them—using Compatibility mode if necessary—and how to remove them when you tire of them. It's also touched on the types of programs you shouldn't even try to install on Windows XP, and it's shown you how to use Task Manager to kill a program that's crashed. Finally, you learned how to exchange data between programs and how to edit the Start menu's content.

Chapter 6

Managing Files and Folders

ALMOST ALL USERS, AT some point, are called upon to work with files, even if it's just to copy an important document to a floppy disk or unzip a compressed archive. For those who understand how files and folders are organized on a disk, file management is not that difficult, but the learning curve can be fairly steep for rank beginners.

This chapter offers something for both beginning and advanced users. Beginners will want to start with the basics of Windows Explorer; advanced users will likely skip ahead to the sections that cover more advanced operations, such as burning CDs and working with NTFS features.

This chapter covers:

◆ Using Explorer

◆ Organizing your files and folders

◆ Understanding the multiuser environment

◆ Customizing the Explorer interface

◆ Setting file and folder properties

◆ Searching for files and folders

◆ Working with compressed files and folders

◆ Using Encrypting File System (EFS)

◆ Working with offline files

◆ Creating CDs

Using Explorer

Windows Explorer, often just called Explorer for short, is the formal name for the file-management window from which you can perform operations on files like moving, copying, deleting, renaming, and so on. If you're a relative newcomer to Windows, the following sections explain some basics of working with files in Windows Explorer for your benefit.

Opening vs. Exploring

One thing you'll notice right away when you use Explorer is a difference between *opening* a Desktop object and *exploring* a Desktop object. Figures 6.1 and 6.2 show the difference. When you open the My Computer window, for example, you'll see its contents in the pane on the right and an Explorer bar on the left. However, if you right-click My Computer and choose Explore from the shortcut menu, the window that opens displays a Folders bar on the left and a right pane for displaying the contents of whatever you select in the left pane. These are the telltale features of Explorer. If you already know where you want to go, that is, the location of the file or object you want to access, Open is the way to go. But, as the name suggests, Explorer functions best when you want to "explore" the computer for the file or application you want to use.

FIGURE 6.1

Opening My Computer

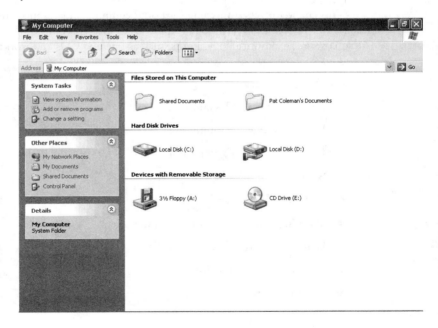

TIP *To switch quickly from the "opening" view to the "exploring" view and vice versa, simply click the Folders button on the toolbar.*

FIGURE 6.2

Exploring My
Computer

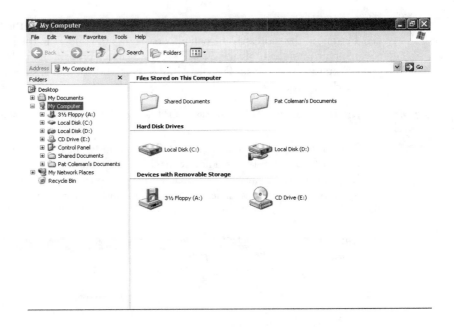

Branches

It's easy to think of Windows Explorer as the filing system of Windows XP Professional. It may be more accurate, though, to describe it as a window to the filing system of Windows XP Professional. The views in Windows Explorer depict an upside down tree with its root being My Computer. It branches down from there showing the various connected drives and other resources. When you open Explorer, you'll notice two panes: on the left is a view of the tree structure of your system; on the right is a group of icons and names representing all the main branches or resources of your computer.

TIP   Each item that appears in Explorer is considered an object. Every object has its own properties, many of which you can modify to suit your needs, regardless of whether you're working with a file, a folder, a program, or a network computer. Although Explorer is often thought of as a method to view or locate objects, you could just as easily think of it as the glue that holds this diverse environment together.

Views

You can arrange objects in Explorer in many ways, all of which are called *views*. The View menu not only controls how objects in the right Explorer pane appear, but also how Explorer itself can be configured to work best for you.

The view that you choose affects only the right Explorer pane. The left pane, the Folders pane, always looks the same—an expandable list of the folders and files—but you can eliminate it in

Windows XP Professional by clicking its Close button. (To restore the Folders pane, click the Folders button on the toolbar.) The default view shows the folders in the left pane, but if you click the Search button in the toolbar, you will see the Search Companion on the left instead of the Folders pane. You can choose from five views in Explorer, and you can arrange the icons in five ways after you've chosen your view.

See page 16 of "Essential Skills for Windows XP Professional" for a visual guide to using views in Explorer.

Tiles is the default view, and Figure 6.2 shows this view. To select a view, click the View menu and then select from Thumbnails, Tiles, Icons, List, and Details.

Icons view (see Figure 6.3) is probably the view you're most familiar with. In this view, the icons are small but easily recognizable, and it is significantly easier to see all the files in a folder—particularly if there are a lot of them.

FIGURE 6.3

Icons view

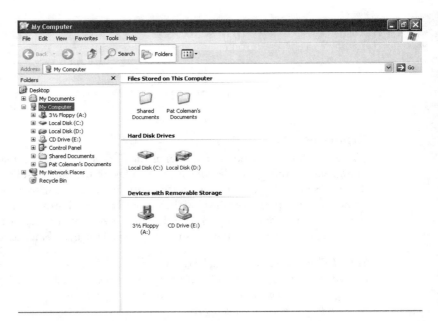

Thumbnails view (see Figure 6.4) is particularly useful for sorting through graphic files. With this view, the graphic files are displayed as miniatures that you can sort through quickly to find just the picture you need. But another view is available for graphic files, Filmstrip, which is shown in Figure 6.5. In Filmstrip view, select a thumbnail from the filmstrip at the bottom of the screen to display it in a larger size. You can then use the tools in the middle of the screen to move forward and backward through the filmstrip and to rotate a graphic.

FIGURE 6.4

Thumbnails view

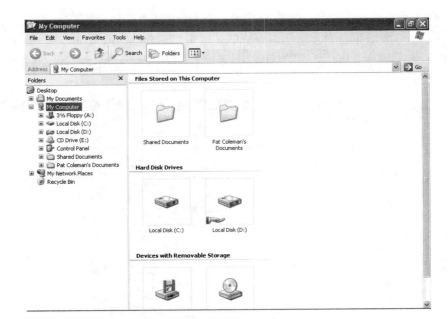

FIGURE 6.5

Filmstrip view

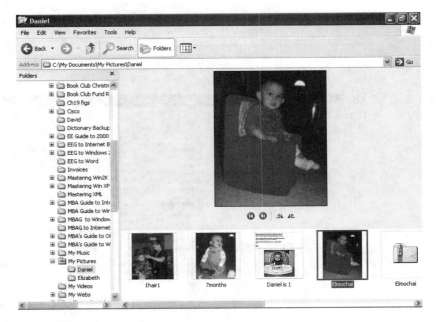

List view (see Figure 6.6) looks much like Icons view except that the objects are displayed in columns. Folders appear first, arranged alphabetically along the left side of the pane, and then the rest of the files appear, also arranged alphabetically.

Details view (see Figure 6.7) moves all the icons to the left-most column and uses the other columns for file/object information. This information includes the file type (which is determined by how the file is associated), the size of the file, and the date the file was last modified or saved. If you can't see all these columns, move the horizontal scroll bar to the right.

FIGURE 6.6

List view

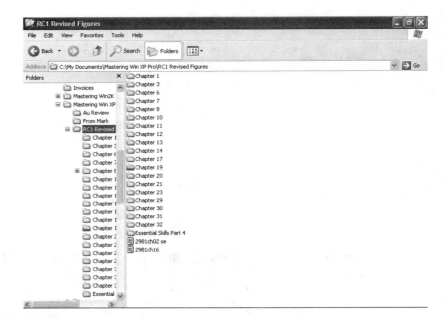

FIGURE 6.7

Details view

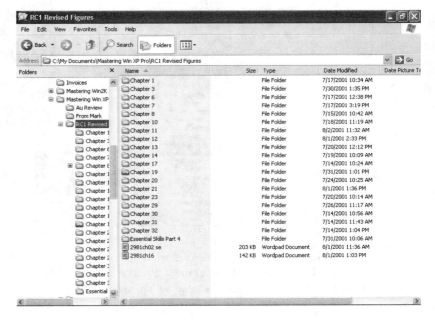

So why do you care about all this organizing? What if you can't remember the name of a file you need, but you do remember the date it was created? Or what if you know which application created the file and what the file extension is? With Explorer, you can arrange the items in the right pane so that they are sorted or organized by name, size, date, or file type. You can then see at a glance what is and isn't inside the folder.

To rearrange the order of your files in Explorer's right pane, choose View ➤ Arrange Icons By, and then select an option from the submenu. Name is self-explanatory; size refers to the size of the file in bytes, kilobytes, or megabytes, whichever is appropriate. Type refers to the three-character extension at the end of the filename (for example, this book was written as a DOC file); and Modified refers to the date. You can also display a Date Picture Taken column and a Dimensions column for digital photos.

TIP   When you're working in Details view, you can click a column heading to sort by that column. For example, you could sort by the Size column, or the Date Modified. Click a column heading again to shift between ascending and descending sort.

You can also set the View using the Views button on the toolbar, and you can arrange the icons by right-clicking anywhere in the right pane, clicking Arrange Icons By, and selecting an order from the submenu.

TIP   Select Auto Arrange if you want the folders to always arrange automatically.

Working with Shortcut Menus

Right-clicking objects throughout the Windows XP Professional interface displays a shortcut menu that contains options pertaining to the objects at hand. The same options are typically available from the main menus but are more conveniently reached with the right-click.

Which commands appear on a shortcut menu depends on such factors as the current folder's location, the current file or folder type, user privileges, and which programs are installed on your computer.

Here are some of the commands that most commonly appear on shortcut menus:

◆ New

◆ Cut, Copy, and Paste

◆ Map Network Drive

◆ Send To

◆ Rename

◆ Delete

◆ Create Shortcut

◆ Properties

Of these commands, most are equivalent to what you'd find on the application's File or Edit menu. Choosing Properties, which usually appears at the bottom of a shortcut menu, generally takes you to the object's Properties dialog box.

Organizing Your Files and Folders

Managing your files in Explorer is easy and logical. After you learn a few commands, you can use them over and over for a variety of tasks. After a short time using Explorer, you'll wonder how you ever did it any other way.

Creating New Folders

To create a new folder in Explorer, follow these steps:

1. Choose where you want to create a new folder. You can create a folder on the Desktop, at the root of a hard drive or a floppy drive, or inside another folder.

2. In Explorer, choose New ➤ Folder, or right-click the item in which you want to create the folder, and choose New ➤ Folder from the shortcut menu. To create a folder on the Desktop, right-click an empty area, and choose New ➤ Folder from the shortcut menu.

3. The folder is created with the default name New Folder. By default the name is highlighted. To give a new name to the folder, type it now. You can always rename a folder by selecting it and choosing File ➤ Rename or by right-clicking the folder and choosing Rename from the shortcut menu. (I'll discuss renaming in detail later in this chapter.)

See page 18 of "Essential Skills" for a visual guide to creating a folder.

Moving Items

You can move files and folders anywhere on your computer or over the network as long as you have permission to do so. To move a file or folder, follow these steps:

1. Select the file or folder you want to move. To select more than one object, hold down Ctrl while you click each one. If the objects constitute an uninterrupted group, hold down Shift while you click the first object and the last.

2. Choose Edit ➤ Cut (or press Ctrl+X).

3. Select the destination, and choose Edit ➤ Paste (or press Ctrl+V).

You can also drag items from one place to another:

◆ Drag from the right Explorer pane to the left.

◆ Drag from either Explorer pane to another Explorer or Explorer-type window.

◆ Drag from either Explorer pane to the Desktop. (Optionally, if you hold down the right mouse button while you drag, you can create a shortcut or shortcuts on the Desktop for the object or objects you are dragging.)

◆ Drag from the Desktop to an Explorer folder.

TIP *If you drag a folder from the right Explorer pane to the left on a* different *drive, Windows XP Professional defaults to copying the file instead of moving it. (As long as you are dragging the object to the* same *drive, Windows XP Professional moves the file or folder by default.) If you don't want Windows XP Professional to copy the file, hold down the Shift key while you drag the object to another drive. That way it will be moved rather than copied.*

Copying Items

You can also copy files and folders anywhere on your computer or the network as long as you have permission to do so. To copy a file or folder, follow these steps:

1. Select the file or folder you are going to copy. To select more than one object, hold down Ctrl while you click each object. To select objects that constitute an uninterrupted group, hold down Shift, click the first object, and then click the last object.

2. Choose Edit ➤ Copy (or press Ctrl+C).

3. Select the destination, and choose Edit ➤ Paste (or press Ctrl+V).

You can also drag the items from one place to another, as described in the previous section, with one difference: to ensure that the objects you are dragging are copied and not moved, hold down the Ctrl key while you are dragging.

TIP   If you drag a folder from the right Explorer pane to the left on the same drive, Windows XP Professional defaults to moving the file instead of copying it. (As long as you are dragging the object to a different drive, Windows XP Professional copies the file or folder by default.) If you don't want Windows XP Professional to move the file, hold down the Ctrl key while you drag the object to another drive. It will be copied, not moved.

See page 20 of "Essential Skills" for a visual guide to copying and moving a file or a folder.

Saving Files and Folders to the Desktop

You can keep files on your Desktop for quick and easy access. To store files and folders on the Desktop, do one of the following:

◆ Drag a file from Explorer to the Desktop.

◆ If you are saving the file from within an application, select Desktop (it's at the very top of your local drive hierarchy) in the application's Save As dialog box.

Dragging with the Right Mouse Button

When you right-click a file, drag it, and then release the button, you'll see a shortcut menu with the following options:

Copy Here   Copies the file to the new location.

Move Here   Moves the file to the new location.

Create Shortcut(s) Here   Creates a shortcut to the file at the new location. As I've discussed, a shortcut is a pointer to the real file or folder and can be stored anywhere on your computer.

Cancel   Cancels the operation.

TIP   If you are new to Windows XP Professional or are confused about when to use Ctrl or Shift when moving or copying files, the safest thing to do is to drag the file with the right mouse button. This way, you are always presented with a choice of whether to move or copy the file.

Renaming Files and Folders

You can quickly and easily rename files and folders. Because Windows XP Professional keeps track of file associations, you don't have to worry about including the three-character file extensions.

WARNING   *The sentence above is true only if you have not turned off the Hide Extensions for Known File Types setting in Folder Options. When a file's extension is hidden, it is not involved in the renaming process. However, for a file that does show the extension onscreen, you must retype the extension when renaming the file.*

To rename a file or folder, follow these steps:

1. In Explorer, select the file or folder you want to rename.

2. Choose File ➤ Rename, or right-click the file and choose Rename from the shortcut menu.

3. When only the name of the file (the text associated with the icon) becomes highlighted, do one of the following:

   ◆ If you want to simply replace the entire name, start typing the new name; the old name disappears the moment you start typing.

   ◆ If you want to make only a correction or two to the existing name, use the arrow keys to move to specific characters within the existing name. The highlight disappears the moment you start moving within the name, enabling you to insert or delete specific characters without deleting the entire name.

4. To accept the name, press Enter or click outside the name area. If you make a mistake, press Escape.

TIP   *You can also rename files and folders with two single-clicks (but don't click so fast that Windows XP Professional interprets it as a double-click) on the name of the object so that it is highlighted. Then follow steps 3 and 4.*

See page 19 of "Essential Skills" for a visual guide to renaming a file or a folder.

Deleting Files and Folders

If you decide that you don't want a file or a folder, you can easily delete it. By default, the file is not actually deleted when you tell Windows XP Professional to delete it: instead, it is compressed and sent to the Recycle Bin folder. A file in the Recycle Bin hasn't been removed from your hard drive, only placed on inactive duty, so to speak. (You can periodically delete items within the Recycle Bin to *actually* remove them entirely, or you can empty the Recycle Bin to delete everything in it.)

The Recycle Bin is a good intermediate place to keep files you're pretty sure you want to delete, because if you change your mind after "deleting" them to the Recycle Bin, you can always open the Recycle Bin and resurrect the object. Mutter your apologies for treating the item so shabbily, and it's ready for use once more.

TIP   *If you're the kind of person who hates being pestered by second thoughts, and you'd prefer to avoid the nice little safeguard of the Recycle Bin, you can really delete an item by selecting it and pressing Shift+Delete.*

TIP   You can turn off the Recycle Bin so that no deleted files go there at all. Just right-click the Recycle Bin icon and choose Properties; then mark the Do Not Move Files to the Recycle Bin check box in the General tab.

SENDING ITEMS TO THE RECYCLE BIN

You can send a file or a folder to the Recycle Bin in several ways:

- ◆ Select the item, and then press the Delete key.

- ◆ Select the item, and then choose File ➤ Delete.

- ◆ Right-click the file or folder, and then choose Delete from the shortcut menu.

- ◆ Select the item, and then drag and drop it on the Recycle Bin icon.

EMPTYING THE RECYCLE BIN

By default, the size of the Recycle Bin folder is set at 10 percent of your hard drive. If you have more than one hard drive or if you have a dual-partitioned drive, you will have a Recycle Bin folder for each drive, and the size of the folder is set at 10 percent for each drive. For example, if drive C is 3.44GB, the Recycle Bin folder is 353MB; and if drive D is 6.09MB, its Recycle Bin folder is 624MB.

When the Recycle Bin folder is full, Windows XP Professional automatically deletes enough items, starting with the oldest, to accommodate whatever you are currently sending to it. When an item is removed from the Recycle Bin, it is gone forever.

To better control the Recycle Bin and maintain its intended functionality (which is to provide second chances), you can periodically empty it manually. You can delete all the items it contains or only selected items.

- ◆ To delete selected items, double-click the Recycle Bin to open the Recycle Bin folder. Now delete items as you would in Explorer.

- ◆ To totally empty the Recycle Bin, right-click its icon, and choose Empty Recycle Bin from the shortcut menu.

WARNING   When a file is deleted in Windows XP Professional, it is really deleted. Other operating systems such as MS-DOS or Windows 9x delete only the first byte from a file and mark the space as available. Windows XP Professional is much more thorough because of its secure nature. When you delete a file in Windows XP Professional, all the bytes in the file are set to a zero value. This is like formatting the space where the file was so it can be reclaimed.

RESTORING ITEMS FROM THE RECYCLE BIN

To restore items from the Recycle Bin you can do one of the following:

- ◆ Open the Recycle Bin folder, select an item, and drag it to the folder of your choice.

- ◆ Open the Recycle Bin, select the item you want to restore, and click Restore This Item in the Recycle Bin Tasks bar. The item is restored to its original location.

 See page 25 of "Essential Skills" for a visual guide to deleting a file or a folder.

Understanding the Multiuser Environment

From the ground up, Windows XP Professional is designed as a multiuser-networking environment. Because security is so integral to the way that Windows XP Professional operates, it is possible for two or more users to use the same workstation without stepping on each other's toes. That is, one user can log in and do the work they want to do without necessarily knowing who else has access to the computer or without having access to another user's files.

When a user logs on to a Windows XP Professional workstation, the operating system assigns that user a security token. The Windows XP Security Manager portion of the Executive Services manages security tokens. Each time that user attempts to do something in Windows XP Professional, be it open a file, send e-mail, or change the way the Desktop looks, the Security Manager checks that person's token to see if they have the rights and permissions to perform the task they've requested. See Chapter 18 for a more thorough discussion of security.

As a result of the token-based security system, Windows XP Professional administers multiuser environments logically. User profile information is stored in the user's folder in the Documents and Settings folder on the drive where Windows XP Professional is installed. Inside the Documents and Settings folder is a folder for each user that logs in to a workstation, and inside each user's folder is a set of folders that customize the Windows XP Professional environment for that user.

Following is a list and a description of some of the folders commonly found inside each user's folder.

NOTE   *Some of these folders are hidden folders. To display hidden folders, choose Tools ➤ Folder Options to open the Folder Options dialog box. Select the View tab, and then in the Advanced Settings list, click Show Hidden Files and Folders.*

Cookies   Contains any cookies that you may have stored from Web sites. Cookies are a small bit of text information that enables a Web site to customize its appearance just for you.

Desktop   Contains any files that a user stores on the Desktop. This does not include the Recycle Bin.

Favorites   Stores your favorite programs, files, and Web sites. You can add files to this folder and delete files from it as you would with any other folder.

Local Settings   Contains a portion of the user-specific information of the Registry, as well as some personal settings for your History, Temporary Internet Files, and a system Temp folder.

Your User Name **Documents**   Keeps files that you don't want any other users to access, even though the users may share other aspects of your workstation. The My Documents folder is empty by default, except for subfolders Your User Name Pictures, Your User Name Music, and Your User Name Videos. Your Pictures folder is the default location for storing your picture files, your Music folder is the default location for storing music files, and your Videos folder is the default location for storing movie files.

NetHood   This folder contains some cached information that normally appears in My Network Places. This is where you will store the browse list for your local network and any persistent network connections.

PrintHood   Stores the mappings for any network printers you have installed. Network printers are actually part of the user profile and are not part of the overall system configuration.

My Recent Documents   Stores files and folders you have accessed recently.

Send To   Stores customizations to your Send To menu.

Start Menu   Stores configurations and customizations you have made to your Start menu. For example, it shows all the shortcuts you have added to your Start menu.

Templates   This folder stores the system templates for various applications that can be installed on Windows XP Professional.

Customizing the Explorer Interface

There are many ways to change the way the Explorer window looks and acts. In the following sections I'll outline some of the most important ones.

Setting Folder Options

The Folder Options dialog box is a rich source for customizing the Explorer interface. Changes made there affect all Explorer windows, regardless of what drive or folder's content appears there. To access it, choose Tools ➤ Folder Options.

In the General tab (shown in Figure 6.8), you can:

◆   Turn off the Common Tasks pane to the left of the file listing by choosing Use Windows Classic folders.

◆   Choose to open each folder in a separate window, instead of the default of having the next-chosen location replace the preceding one.

◆   Choose to have Windows (the Explorer window and the desktop) work more like a Web page, wherein you single-click to activate something and point at it to select it.

FIGURE 6.8

Folder options apply to all Explorer windows.

NOTE *When Windows 98 was in beta testing, the default was this single-click-to-activate behavior, but it drove most people crazy because it was so different from what they were used to. Therefore in the final version, and in all versions since, the double-click-to-select method has been the default and this single-click one has been just an alternative.*

In the View tab, you can:

◆ Set a particular View option to apply to all folder listings. By default, when you change the View setting, it applies to that folder only.

◆ Select or deselect a wide variety of Advanced Settings for how files should be displayed. Table 6.1 lists the complete set.

The File Types tab, covered later in the chapter, lets you change file associations for an extension. The Offline Files tab, covered in Chapter 10, lets you cache copies of files available through a connection that may only be available sporadically.

TABLE 6.1: ADVANCED SETTINGS IN THE VIEW TAB OF THE FOLDER OPTIONS DIALOG BOX

SETTING	PURPOSE/NOTES
Automatically search for network folders and printers	On by default. Allows Windows to re-query the network periodically to see whether any new resources are available.
Display file size information in folder tips	On by default. Includes file size in the ScreenTip that appears when you hover the mouse pointer over a file.
Display simple folder view in Explorer's folder list	On by default. Collapses any branches open in the folder list when you move to a different branch of the folder tree.
Display the content of system folders	Off by default. Displays a warning when you try to view a system folder; you must click the warning to continue.
Display the full path in the address bar	Off by default. Shows the full path rather than just the folder's name.
Display the full path in the title bar	Off by default. Same as above but for title bar.
Do not cache thumbnails	Off by default. When viewing a folder in Thumbnail view, thumbnail images of the content are created. Turn this option on to save them so they need not be regenerated each time you view that folder, saving a little time.
Hidden files and folders	By default set to Do Not Show Hidden Files and Folders. Power Users generally change this to Show Hidden Files and Folders, so that hidden items appear in file listings (but ghosted, to distinguish them from normal files).
Hide extensions for known file types	On by default. Power Users generally turn this off, so that all file extensions appear.
Hide protected operating system files	On by default. Excludes files with the System attribute from file listings.
Launch folder windows in a separate process	Off by default. Launches each folder window in a separate memory space, increasing stability but decreasing performance.

Continued on next page

TABLE 6.1: ADVANCED SETTINGS IN THE VIEW TAB OF THE FOLDER OPTIONS DIALOG BOX *(continued)*

Managing pairs of Web pages and folders	Specifies how Windows should treat Web page files that have associated folders in a file management window.
Remember each folder's view settings	On by default. Opens each folder to the same View setting as was previously selected for it.
Restore previous folder windows at logon	On by default. When Windows shuts down with open folder windows, they are redisplayed when Windows restarts.
Show Control Panel in My Computer	Off by default. In previous Windows versions this was on by default. Adds a Control Panel icon to My Computer.
Show encrypted or compressed NTFS files in color	On by default. Changes the text color for any files that use NTFS compression or NTFS encryption (covered later in this chapter).
Show pop-up description for folder and desktop items	On by default. Displays a pop-up ScreenTip when you hover over an item.
Use simple file sharing	On by default. Limits the capability to assign complex permissions to files and folders in the interest of simplicity.

Customizing an Individual Folder

In addition to the global settings, you can also specify settings for each folder. As you have already seen, by default Windows remembers your choice of View setting for each folder individually. You can also do the following to further customize the folder:

1. Choose View ➤ Customize This Folder. A Properties box for the folder appears.

2. Click the Customize tab, and then choose a different folder type from the Use This Folder Type As a Template list if desired. See Figure 6.9. For example, if the folder will be holding pictures, you might choose that. The folder type template sets several default options appropriate for that content type, including a view.

FIGURE 6.9

Properties for the current folder affect how it appears in Explorer.

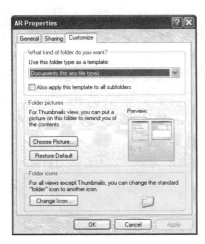

3. If you want a picture thumbnail to appear for the folder in Thumbnails view, click the Choose Picture button and add one.

4. If you want a different icon to appear for the folder whenever icons are shown, click the Change Icon button and select an icon.

5. Click OK when finished.

Customizing the Toolbar

You might want to add, remove, or rearrange the buttons on the toolbar in Explorer. Changes you make apply to Explorer in general, not just to the current folder.

To customize the Explorer toolbar, follow these steps:

1. Choose View ➤ Toolbars ➤ Customize to open the Customize Toolbar dialog box:

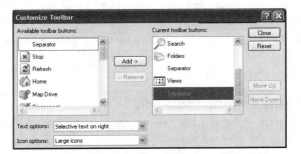

2. To add a button, select it from the list on the left and click Add.

3. To remove a button, select it from the list on the right and click Remove.

4. To change the order of the buttons on the toolbar, click the Move Up or Move Down button until the arrangement is to your liking.

5. Click the drop-down lists to take a look at text and icon options.

6. When you're finished, click Close.

Setting File and Folder Properties

Right-click any file or folder and choose Properties to display its Properties box. Files typically have two tabs in their Properties: General and Summary. Some types of data files, such as Word documents, may also have a Custom tab.

The General tab lists information about the file and lets you turn on/off three attributes for the file:

◆ Read-only prevents the file from being modified or deleted.

- ◆ Hidden excludes the file from file listings (unless the Show hidden files and folders option is chosen in Folder Options).

- ◆ Archive marks the file as having been changed since the last time a backup operation turned off the archive attribute.

The Summary tab contains a variety of text boxes into which you can enter information about the file for classification purposes.

For folders, the Properties box contains a General tab, the same as with files, but also a Customize tab (which you saw in "Customizing an Individual Folder" earlier in the chapter) and a Sharing tab for setting up network sharing permission for the folder. You'll learn about networking features in Part III of this book.

On NTFS volumes, the General tab also has an Advanced button, which you can use to set NTFS options such as encryption and compression. On NTFS volumes there is also no Archive attribute in the General tab; to set that attribute you must click the Advanced button and then mark the Folder is ready for archiving check box.

Searching for Files and Folders

The Search Companion feature in Windows XP is built into Explorer. You can turn it on from any Explorer window by clicking the Search button in the toolbar. You can also start it up by choosing Start ➢ Search.

By default, an animated character called the Search Companion appears in the Search pane, guiding you through a search operation. See Figure 6.10.

FIGURE 6.10

The Search Companion, shown here with an animated character

Just follow the prompts to build a set of search criteria. The All Files and Folders option will be the most familiar choice for experienced users; it offers up a wide array of search criteria. In addition to filename, file content, and location to specify, there are three other categories, as shown in Figure 6.11: When Was It Modified?, What Size Is It?, and More Advanced Options. Each of these has a down arrow next to it; clicking that arrow will expand the full range of options for that choice.

FIGURE 6.11

The All Files and Folders search enables searching based on many possible criteria.

The other choices, such as Pictures, Music, or Video, automatically filter for certain file extensions. With each of these other choices you can click a Use Advanced Options hyperlink to use the full array of search criteria available with All Files and Folders.

The Search feature allows the use of wildcards, just like in MS-DOS file specifications. Use ? for a single character or * for any number of characters. For example, to find all files that end in **.doc** or **.dot**, you might use ***.do?**.

When you click the Search button, the search begins, and the found files and folders appear in the right-hand pane. See Figure 6.12. The list appears in Detail view by default so you can compare the locations, sizes, dates modified, and so on. You can work with this list of found items the same as with any other file listing.

FIGURE 6.12

The results of a search for *.do?

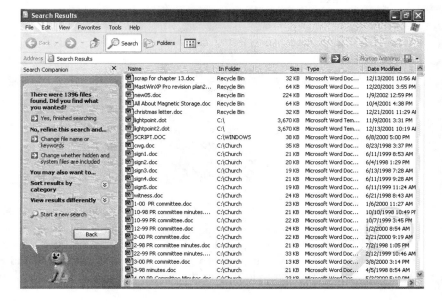

Working with Compressed Files and Folders

There are two kinds of compressed files and folders available in Windows XP. You can use Zip compression to create compressed archives of multiple files in a single ZIP file that Windows XP can work with as if it were a folder; you can also compress files with NTFS compression if you are using the NTFS file system on the drive. The following sections look at these compression features.

Using Zip Compression

If you have limited disk space on your computer or on your network, or if you often need to transfer files over the Internet and have a slow connection, you have probably used a compression utility. Windows XP Professional includes its own version of a compression utility called WinZip, a popular program that has been widely distributed in stand-alone versions for many years.

When you compress, or "zip," a file or a folder in Windows XP Professional, that file or folder can be uncompressed, or "unzipped," by almost any other compression utility. In addition, Windows treats ZIP files like folders, so you can open and browse them just like you would a normal folder.

A compressed folder has a zipper on it.

Compressing a file or a folder is fast and easy. You simply right-click the file or folder in an Explorer-type window, choose Send To on the shortcut menu, and click Compressed Folder on the submenu. A compressed copy of the file or folder is placed in the folder that contains the original file. The filename is the same as that of the original file or folder, but with a .zip extension. If you selected more than one file or folder for zipping into a single ZIP file, the ZIP file will bear the name of the last file or folder in the selected group.

Once a ZIP file exists, you can open it in Explorer and compress other files or folders by simply dragging them to the compressed folder. When you then move the file or folder out of the compressed folder, it is uncompressed.

You can also compress files in Windows applications, and in Chapter 14, we'll look at how to do so in Outlook Express.

WARNING   *Even though a ZIP file appears to be a normal folder when opened in Explorer, it has limitations. For example, if a Setup program and its helper files are contained in a ZIP file, the Setup program probably won't run correctly from its ZIP file location; you will likely need to extract the contents of the ZIP file to a real folder on your hard disk before you can run it. And if you open a document from a ZIP file, it will be read-only and you'll need to save it under a different name.*

Using NTFS Compression

As you learned earlier in the book, the NTFS file system has many advantages over FAT32 under Windows XP. One of these is the capability of compressing a folder to save disk space. Retrieving files from a compressed folder takes slightly longer than a normal folder; other than that the compression is totally invisible. You might want to compress folders that you don't use frequently if disk space is an issue. NTFS compression does not compress as dramatically as Zip-type compression, but is less obtrusive.

On an NTFS drive, files and folders have an Advanced button in the General tab of their properties box. It's your gateway to the NTFS properties for the item:

1. From the file or folder Properties box, click the General tab.

2. Click the Advanced button. The Advanced Attributes dialog box opens (Figure 6.13).

3. Mark the Compress Contents to Save Disk Space check box to compress the item, and then click OK.

4. Choose Apply Changes to This Folder Only, or choose Apply Changes to This Folder, Subfolders, and Files. Then click OK.

NTFS compressed folders and files appear with their names in blue rather than black to differentiate them from normal ones. To decompress them, follow the same steps but clear the check box.

FIGURE 6.13

Set NTFS compression here.

When you move or copy a compressed file or folder onto a non-NTFS drive, it is automatically uncompressed. Here are some additional rules:

◆ Any new files/folders created in a compressed folder become compressed.

◆ Any files/folders copied into a compressed folder become compressed.

◆ Any files/folders moved from another NTFS drive into a compressed folder become compressed.

◆ Any files/folders moved from another location on the same NTFS drive into a compressed folder retain the compression settings from the original location.

◆ Any compressed files/folders moved into an uncompressed location on the same NTFS drive remain compressed.

◆ Any compressed files/folders moved into an uncompressed location on a different NTFS drive become uncompressed.

TIP   NTFS compression and NTFS encryption (covered in the following section) are mutually exclusive; you can use one or the other but not both. If you need NTFS compression, consider using some other method of protection such as network security; if you need NTFS encryption, consider some other method of compression such as Zip compression.

Using Encrypting File System (EFS)

You might have noticed in Figure 6.13 that NTFS encryption is also available, in addition to compression. This encryption is sometimes referred to as Encrypting File System, or EFS.

EFS encryption is different from network permissions because it deals with security on a local level. It's based on the logged-in user on the machine. When the user who encrypted the folder or file is logged in, it's transparent, but when anyone else is logged in, the file or folder is inaccessible. This is handy when multiple users share a PC and must work with sensitive data.

NOTE   Encryption is not limited to local machines only; there is also encryption between a Web browser and a server using Secure Socket Layers and encryption between computers on Virtual Private Networks (VPN) and e-mail. However, this chapter will limit the discussion to local EFS.

It works like this: EFS encryption uses the logged-in user's public key to generate a file-encryption key that the encrypted file or folder must pass through in order to be accessed. When you are logged in as the same user who did the encrypting, Windows automatically accesses the needed keys, but when anyone else is logged in, there is a different public key in use so the decryption doesn't happen.

Backing Up Your Certificates

Before you start using NTFS encryption, you should make a backup copy of the certificates needed to access encrypted files, and store them on a removable disk. There is virtually no way to hack into an encrypted file if you lose the needed certificates/keys.

The first time you use NTFS encryption, Windows generates your personal encryption certificate. This certificate includes a public key and a private key. Windows can also create another certificate, for a designated recovery agent, which will also permit access to the user's encrypted files. You'll want to back up these two certificates separately. The personal encryption certificate should be stored in a safe location that you can personally access; the recovery agent certificate should be given to your system administrator.

To back up your personal encryption certificate:

1. Make sure you are logged in using the user account for which you want to back up the certificate.

2. Display the Internet Options dialog box, either from Control Panel or from Internet Explorer (Tools ➤ Internet Options).

3. In the Content tab, click the Certificates button to open the Certificates dialog box.

4. In the Personal tab, select the certificate that shows Encrypting File System in the Certificate Intended Purposes area. See Figure 6.14.

FIGURE 6.14

Manage certificates, including backing them up, from here.

5. Click Export. The Certificate Export Wizard starts.

6. Click Next, and then click Yes, Export Private Key.

7. Click Next to accept the defaults on the next screen.

8. When prompted for a password, make one up and enter it/confirm it. Then click Next.

9. Enter a path and name for the exported file. You might want to export to a floppy, for example. Then click Next.

10. Click Finish. A box appears telling you it was a success; click OK.

Encrypting and Decrypting

Windows allows you to encrypt both folders and files, but most experts recommend that you encrypt only folders. Any files you place in an encrypted folder become encrypted while they are there, but if you move them out of the folder they become decrypted. However, if you encrypt an individual file, it remains encrypted no matter where you move it.

TIP   Some programs generate temporary files as they operate that store parts of your data file. Even though you may be storing the data file in an encrypted folder, these temp files are not encrypted because they are stored someplace else—for example, in `C:\Windows\Temp` *or some other location. If you can determine where the program stores its temporary working files, you might want to encrypt that folder for added security.*

To encrypt a folder:

1. From the folder's Properties, click Advanced in the General tab.

2. Mark the Encrypt contents to secure data check box. Refer back to Figure 6.13.

3. Click OK, and then OK again. The folder's name turns green to indicate it is encrypted.

When you encrypt a file, rather than a folder, you are asked whether you also want to encrypt the parent folder of the file; you don't get a prompt like that when encrypting a folder.

To decrypt, repeat the process but clear the Encrypt Contents To Secure Data check box. Obviously, you must do this while logged in with the same user account as you used to encrypt. A dialog box asks whether you want to decrypt only the folder or the folder and its contents. If you choose to decrypt the contents too, it will only decrypt the files for which the current user account has valid certificates.

When moving or copying, the following rules apply:

◆ If you move or copy an unencrypted file into an encrypted folder, it becomes encrypted.

◆ If you move or copy a file from an encrypted folder into an unencrypted folder, encryption is removed.

◆ If you have encrypted a file itself (not just the folder in which it resides), it retains its encryption no matter where it is moved or copied.

◆ If you try to move an encrypted file or folder to a non-NTFS drive, encryption is removed.

◆ If you delete an encrypted file or folder to the Recycle Bin, it remains encrypted in the Recycle Bin.

WARNING   *Beginners can get themselves into a fair amount of trouble by using EFS encryption without really understanding it, so don't experiment with EFS on important files, and don't use EFS unless you are confident that you understand its risks and limitations.*

Sharing Encrypted Files with Other Local Users

This is a brand-new feature in Windows XP; in Windows 2000 EFS-encrypted files were accessible locally only to the user who encrypted them.

You can set up sharing for individual encrypted files only; you can't do it for folders or multiple files at once. ("Encrypted files" here includes both files that have been individually encrypted and files that are encrypted because they reside in an encrypted folder.)

NOTE   *This sharing does not have anything to do with sharing files and folders via network. EFS is for local access only. If you want to share an encrypted file or folder via network, place it in your Shared Documents folder or set up its network sharing permission as explained in Chapter 18.*

To share an encrypted file:

1. Right-click the file and choose Properties.

2. In the General tab, click Advanced. Then, in the Advanced Attributes dialog box, click Details.

3. In the Encryption Details box, click Add. The Select User dialog box appears.

4. Select the user that you want to have access, and click OK.

NOTE   *Only other local users of this PC who have an EFS certificate appear here. If the person you want to designate does not appear, have him or her log into the local PC and encrypt a file or folder.*

Transferring Encrypted Files to Another PC

To work with an encrypted file on another PC, you must export your personal encryption certificate on the original PC and then import it on the other one.

1. Back up your personal encryption certificate using the steps in "Backing Up Your Certificates" earlier in this section.

2. On the computer that is to receive the certificate, open the Internet Options dialog box (Tools ➤ Internet Options from within IE) and display the Content tab.

3. Click the Certificates button, and then click Import. The Certificate Import Wizard runs. Click Next to Continue.

4. Browse to locate the exported certificate, which has a `.pfx` extension. Then click Next.

5. Enter the password you assigned when you exported it, and then click Next.

6. Click Place All Certificates in the Following Store. Then click Browse to open the Select Certificate Store dialog box, choose Personal, and click OK.

7. Click Next, and then click Finish.

Working with Offline Files

The Offline Files feature is useful if you need access to files and folders that are not always available 24/7, such as files on a network that periodically goes down for maintenance or files on a desktop PC while you are traveling with your laptop. It takes the place of the My Briefcase feature from Windows 9x and Windows Me.

TIP   The Briefcase feature is still available in Windows XP, although most people will prefer Offline Files. My Briefcase does offer one feature that Offline Files does not: it enables synchronization and transfer via floppy or other removable disk. The Offline Files feature works only with a network.

Offline Files is available only in Windows XP Professional, not Windows XP Home Edition. However, only the computer that needs to maintain and synchronize the offline file access needs Windows XP Professional; the computer where the originals are maintained can be running any operating system.

NOTE   Don't confuse the Offline Files feature with the ability in Windows Explorer to cache Web sites for offline reading by subscribing to them. That capability is covered in Chapter 12.

Turning Off Fast User Switching

To use Offline Files, you must first turn off the Fast User Switching feature in Windows XP. To do so:

1. In Control Panel, open up User Accounts.

2. Click Change the Way Users Log On or Off.

3. Deselect the Use Fast User Switching check box, and then click Apply Options. Then close the Control Panel window.

Configuring the Offline Files Feature

Now you are ready to set up the Offline Files feature. To do so:

1. From any Explorer window, choose Tools ➤ Folder Options.

2. Click the Offline Files tab, and then mark the Enable Offline Files check box. See Figure 6.15.

FIGURE 6.15

Set configuration options for Offline Files.

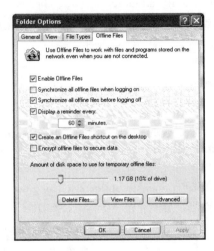

3. Change any synchronization settings. They're described in Table 6.2. Many of these can also be set through the Offline Files Wizard that runs when you select offline files, so you don't have to pay close attention to them now.

4. Click OK to apply the new setting.

TABLE 6.2: OFFLINE FILES SETTINGS

SETTING	PURPOSE/NOTES
Synchronize all offline files when logging on	If the source is available when you log on, it will be checked for updates, and your locally cached copies will be updated as needed.
Synchronize all offline files before logging off	Same as above, except it occurs when you shut down Windows or log off.
Display a reminder every	Specifies the interval at which a notification will appear when you are not connected to the network.
Create an Offline Files shortcut on the desktop	Places a desktop shortcut through which you can easily manage your offline files.
Encrypt offline files to secure data	Allows EFS encryption for the offline files, as discussed earlier in this chapter.
Amount of disk space to use for temporary offline files	Limits the amount of space that offline files can occupy, as a percentage of the total drive space.

You can return to the Offline Files tab at any time to delete offline files (Delete Files button), view offline files (View Files button), or configure the behavior for when a connection to another PC is lost (Advanced button).

Selecting Files and Folders to Be Available Offline

Next, you select certain networked files and folders to be cached to your local hard drive. To do so:

1. Locate a file or folder in My Network Places that you want to cache.

2. Right-click it and choose Make Available Offline.

NOTE   If you have made files or folders available online before, and if there are no subfolders in the folder you chose, you are finished at step 2.

3. The first time you do this procedure, the Offline Files Wizard runs. Work through it, setting any configuration options desired. These configuration options are a subset of the ones that you saw in Table 6.2.

4. If you selected a folder that contains subfolders, a dialog box appears. Choose whether you want to include the subfolders and click OK.

Working Offline

When Offline Files is enabled, the files/folders you have set up appear as if they were online even when they are not actually available. You access them in the same way you normally do—for example, through My Network Places or via shortcuts to them. If they are available via network, you get the "live" copy; if they are not available, you get the cached, offline copy. An icon appears in the notification area to let you know you are working offline.

Synchronizing

When network access is once again available after having worked offline, you must synchronize your cached copies with the online originals. If you have set the configuration options to synchronize automatically at logon and/or logoff, this process is automatic.

You can also manually synchronize by choosing Start ➢ All Programs ➢ Accessories ➢ Synchronize. This opens the Items to Synchronize dialog box, shown in Figure 6.16. Clear the check boxes for any resources you don't want to synchronize, and click the Synchronize button.

FIGURE 6.16

Synchronizing files manually with the Synchronize command.

What happens when you synchronize? It depends on what changes have been made. If your copy has changed but the original has not, the original is updated with your changes. If vice versa (your copy not changed, the original changed), then your copy is updated with the original's changes. If both have changed, a dialog box appears asking what you want to do. You can keep your copy, keep the original as is, or keep both under different names.

Setting File Associations

File extensions are the primary way in which Windows determines what program to use to open a particular data file. For example, Microsoft Word opens DOC files, Paint opens BMP files, Notepad opens TXT files, and so on. The extension also signals the file's format, so a program that can open more than one type of file knows how to treat that particular file.

Sometimes when you install a new application, it commandeers a particular file extension without asking permission. For example, you might install a graphics-editing program that takes the `.bmp` extension away from Paint and assigns it to itself.

To change a file extension association:

1. From an Explorer window, choose Tools ➢ Folder Options and click the File Types tab.

2. Find and select the extension you want to change. See Figure 6.17.

FIGURE 6.17

Manage file extensions and their associated applications here.

3. Click the Change button. The Open With dialog box opens.

4. Select another program with which to associate the extension. Recommended programs appear at the top of the list. See Figure 6.18. Then click OK.

5. Click Close to close the Folder Options dialog box.

FIGURE 6.18

Select a different program for the extension.

Creating CDs

The recordable CD is without doubt the most cost-effective backup and transfer medium available. If you bought your computer recently, it may have come with a recordable CD drive, and you'll be interested to know that Windows XP Professional includes CD-writing (also known as "burning") capability.

Burning CDs from Explorer is an easy, three-step process:

1. Copy the files to the storage area.

2. Check the files in the storage area to make sure that they're the right files and that there aren't too many of them.

3. Write the files to CD.

See pages 23–24 of "Essential Skills" for a visual guide to copying files to a CD.

Copying the Files to the Storage Area

The first step in burning files (or folders) to CD is to copy them to the storage area. You can do so in several ways, of which these three are usually the easiest:

◆ Select the files in an Explorer window or in a common dialog box. Then right-click in the selection and choose Send To ➢ CD Drive from the shortcut menu. (Alternatively, choose File ➢ Send To ➢ CD Drive.) This technique is the most convenient when you're working in Explorer or in a common dialog box.

◆ Drag the files and drop them on the CD drive in an Explorer window or on a shortcut to the CD. For example, you could keep a shortcut to the CD on your Desktop so that you could quickly drag files and folders to it. This technique is good for copying to CD files or folders that you keep on your Desktop.

◆ Open an Explorer window to the storage area, and then drag files to it and drop them there. This technique is mostly useful for adding files when you're checking the contents of the storage area. When you insert a blank CD in your CD drive, Windows displays a CD Drive dialog box offering to open a folder to the writable CD folder.

When you take one of these actions, Windows copies the files to the storage area and displays a notification area pop-up telling you that you have files waiting to be written to the CD.

Either click the pop-up or (if it has disappeared) open a My Computer window and double-click the icon for the CD drive. Windows opens an Explorer window showing the storage area, which appears as a list called Files Ready to Be Written to the CD. (For a CD-RW that already contains files, the storage area also contains a list of Files Currently on the CD.) Figure 6.19 shows an example of the storage area. As you can see in the figure, Windows displays a downward-pointing arrow on the icon for each file or folder to indicate that it's a temporary file destined to be burned to CD and then disposed of.

While Windows copies the files, the CD drive will appear to be busy, but it won't actually be writing any information to CD yet.

FIGURE 6.19

The storage area holds the copies of files to be copied to the CD. The downward-pointing arrow on each file icon and folder icon indicates that the item is temporary and will be deleted after being burned to CD.

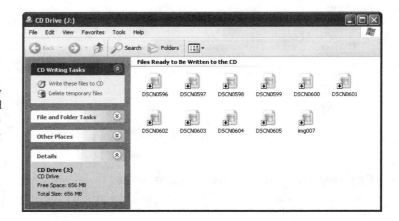

Checking the Files in the Storage Area

Once you've copied to the storage area all the files that you want to burn to the CD, activate the window that Explorer opened to the storage area and check that the files are all there, that you don't want to remove any of them, and that there aren't too many to fit on the CD. (If you closed the window showing the storage area, you can display the storage area again by opening an Explorer window to My Computer and double-clicking the icon for the CD drive.)

NOTE   By default, the storage area is located in the `Local Settings\Application Data\Microsoft\` `CD Burning\` *folder under the folder for your account in the* `Documents and Settings\` *folder.*

To check the size of files in the storage area, select them all (for example, by choosing Edit ➢ Select All), and then right-click and choose Properties from the shortcut menu. Windows displays the Properties dialog box for the files. Check the Size readout in the General tab.

Writing the Files to CD

Once you've looked at the files in the storage area and are satisfied all is well, start the process of writing the files to CD. Take the following steps:

1. Click the Write These Files to CD link in the CD Writing Tasks list. Windows starts the CD Writing Wizard, which displays its first screen (shown in Figure 6.20).

FIGURE 6.20

On the first screen of the CD Writing Wizard, specify the name for the CD and choose whether the Wizard should close itself when the CD is finished.

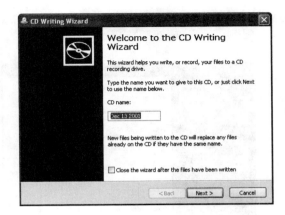

2. Enter the name for the CD in the CD Name text box. CD names can be a maximum of 16 characters.

3. If you want the Wizard to close itself when the CD is finished, select the Close the Wizard after the Files Have Been Written check box. If you select this check box, you won't have the option of creating another CD containing the same files because the Wizard automatically clears the storage area.

4. Click the Next button. The CD Writing Wizard displays the screen shown in Figure 6.21 as it burns the CD. The burning goes through three stages: Adding Data to the CD Image, Writing the Data Files to the CD, and Performing Final Steps to Make the CD Ready to Use.

NOTE *If the PC seems to be locked up during the CD burning process, wait. Sometimes the mouse will stop responding while a CD is being written. This is normal.*

FIGURE 6.21

The CD Writing Wizard shows you its progress in burning the CD.

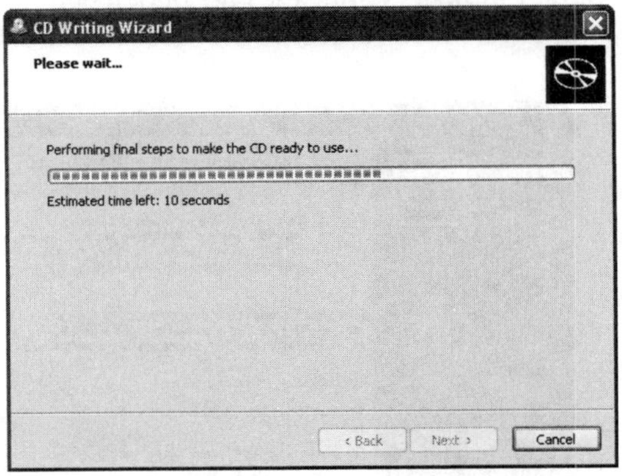

5. When the Wizard has finished burning the CD, it displays the Completing the CD Writing Wizard screen (shown in Figure 6.22) and ejects the CD.

FIGURE 6.22

The CD Writing Wizard displays the Completing the CD Writing Wizard screen when it has finished creating the CD.

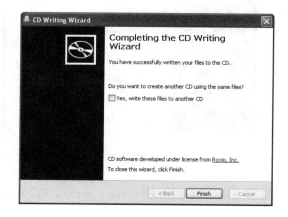

6. If you want to create another CD containing the same files, select the Yes, Write These Files to Another CD check box.

7. Click the Finish button. The Wizard closes itself and deletes the files from the storage area unless you selected the Yes, Write These Files to Another CD check box.

When Things Go Wrong Writing the CD

If you try to write more files to a CD than will fit on it, the CD Writing Wizard displays the Cannot Complete the CD Writing Wizard screen (shown in Figure 6.23). You can remove some files from the storage area, then select the Retry Writing the Files to CD Now option button, and click the Finish button if you want to try to fix the problem while the CD is open; but, in most cases you'll do best to leave the Close the Wizard without Writing the Files option button selected and click the Finish button. Then you can return to the storage area, fix the problem, and restart the writing process.

FIGURE 6.23

The CD Writing Wizard displays the Cannot Complete the CD Writing Wizard screen to warn you that the files won't fit on the CD.

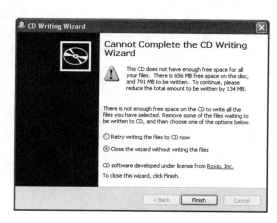

The CD Writing Wizard may also warn you that there was an error in the recording process, and the disc may no longer be usable. This is the other reason that people like the term "burning" for recording CDs—when things go wrong, you get burned and the disc is toast. In this case, you'll probably want to try writing the files to another CD.

When you've finished creating the CD, test it immediately (preferably on a different computer) by opening an Explorer window to its contents and opening some of the files. Make sure all is well with the CD before archiving it or sending it on its way.

TIP   If the CD you create won't read or play properly, it may have suffered recording errors. Try reducing the burning speed by using the Select a Recording Speed drop-down list in the Recording tab of the Properties dialog box for the drive.

Clearing the Storage Area

If you end up deciding not to create the CD after all, clear the storage area by deleting the files in it. To do so, click the Delete Temporary Files link in the Tasks list. Windows displays the Confirm Delete dialog box (shown in Figure 6.24) to make sure you know the files haven't yet been written to CD. Click the Yes button. Windows deletes the files and removes the Files to Add to the CD heading from the Explorer window.

FIGURE 6.24

Windows displays the Confirm Delete dialog box to make sure you want to delete all the files from the storage area.

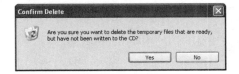

Summary

In this chapter, you learned how Windows XP handles files and folders, and how to manage them on your own system. You not only reviewed the basics of moving, copying, deleting, and so on, but also learned about searching, compression, encryption, and the Offline Files feature. You also learned how to use Windows XP's built-in capability for burning CD-ROMs.

In the next chapter, we'll discuss printers and fonts. The two topics are integrally tied together, since the main purpose of a font is as a formatting device for printouts. Even if you have been using printers and fonts for a long time, you might want to review this chapter to pick up some additional pointers and timesaving tips.

Chapter 7

Installing and Working with Printers and Fonts

WINDOWS XP MAKES PRINTING SEEM so easy that it's easy to overlook the printing subsystem. You simply issue a Print command in an application, select a printer, and out comes your hard copy. But if you need to step beyond the daily end-user routine and install or configure printers, you might need a little help. It's not always obvious what settings are best for network versus local printers, for PostScript versus PCL operating modes, and any number of other operating details.

In this chapter, you'll learn how to install and configure printers and how to manage Windows fonts. This chapter covers the following topics:

◆ How Windows XP handles printing

◆ Installing local printers

◆ Sharing a local printer

◆ Installing remote printers

◆ Working with printer properties

◆ Managing a print queue

◆ Creating and using separator pages

◆ Installing and managing fonts

◆ Changing the display font

How Windows XP Handles Printing

If you're interested in the theory behind Windows XP printing, check out the following explanation; if you just want to learn the practical stuff, feel free to skip it.

To understand why Windows XP's printing subsystem is effective, you need to know something about how printing worked prior to Windows.

MS-DOS applications each interacted directly with the printer through their own proprietary drivers. You needed a separate driver for each printer and each application. Applications typically came with at least one disk full of printer drivers, covering the bases for dozens of the most popular models, but someone with a less popular printer could be out of luck unless that printer happened to emulate one of the more popular ones. Some of the less popular printers came with driver disks for the most popular applications, so you could sometimes acquire the needed driver from that end of the equation instead of from the application side.

Most applications did not include a print spooler, so when you issued the Print command, you had to wait until the print job was finished printing before you could resume using the application.

Not only did the application need a printer driver, but it also needed font files. Most printers had only one or two typefaces built in; if you wanted anything else, the application had to send font files to the printer before a print job. There was a separate font file for each combination of size, typeface, and attribute. So, for example, 16-point bold Helvetica was a separate file from 16-point italic Helvetica or 14-point bold Helvetica. These font files took up space on the hard disk, and if you were going to print a document containing many fonts, the printing was delayed while the fonts were transferred to the printer's memory. To compound matters further, if you had two printers, you had to have a separate set of font files for each of them in some applications. Programs like Ventura Publisher would generate the needed font files during setup, and if you got a new printer, you needed to rerun the setup to generate a new set of fonts for it.

NOTE *Back in this era, add-on cartridges for some laser printers were popular; you could plug a cartridge in to add several typefaces to the printer that some applications could then use in addition to the software fonts (a.k.a., soft fonts).*

Windows solved the problem of needing a different driver for each application by taking over the printing process itself. All Windows-based applications that needed to print sent their requests to the Windows printing subsystem. Since the applications did not interact with the printer, you did not need a separate printer driver for each one. All you needed was a Windows driver for each of your printers.

Windows uses the term *printer* to mean a printer driver. When you set the properties for a printer, you are actually setting up the behavior of the driver and not the printer itself. You can have multiple drivers installed for a single physical printer, each set up for a different behavior. For example, you might have one driver set up to use separator pages between print jobs and another one set up not to do so. Windows would consider each of these separate printers, and it would look from an application's Print dialog box as though you had two printers installed.

The printer drivers tells Windows a variety of things about the printer, including what its paper handling capabilities are, how much RAM is has installed, and what *Page Description Language (PDL)* it speaks. There are several PDLs popular today; two of the most popular are PCL (by Hewlett-Packard) and PostScript (by Adobe).

TIP *Almost all laser printers support either PCL or PostScript, so if you don't have the exact driver you need for a laser printer you can usually hobble through using a driver for some other laser printer that uses the same version of PCL or PostScript.*

Having Windows handle the printing rather than the individual application also frees up the application for continued work more quickly after you issue the Print command. The application quickly prints the entire job to the Windows *print spooler*, basically a holding tank for print jobs. Then Windows spoon-feeds the print job to the printer as the printer can accommodate it.

Remember that the other big hassle with MS-DOS printing was the need for separate font files for each typeface, size, and attribute combination. Starting with Windows 3.1, Windows began offering generic, scaleable typefaces called TrueType. These font files have several advantages:

◆ A TrueType font file contains an outline of each letter, rather than a fixed size, so a single font file can produce any size of text.

◆ TrueType fonts work with the Windows printing subsystem, so they work with any Windows application.

◆ TrueType fonts work with almost any printer, so you need only one set of TrueType fonts no matter what printers you have.

Windows XP continues to support TrueType, but introduces an improved variant of it called OpenType. The improvements are behind-the-scenes and not significant for an end user, but you need to be aware of the two different names because when you start working with fonts (later in this chapter) you'll see two different icons for them.

Installing Local Printers

A *local printer* is one that is directly attached to your PC. It could be attached through a parallel, serial, USB, infrared, or some other port type. With a local printer, you have complete control; you can install and remove drivers for it, share it, control the permissions for the sharing, and so on. (In contrast, you might not always be able to have your way completely with a network printer, discussed later in this chapter.) The following sections explain how to install and share a local printer.

Installing a Local Printer Driver

Most printers these days come with a setup disk of their own. Running the Setup program on the disk installs the needed Windows drivers. If you have such a disk available, you should use it because some Setup programs install a proprietary print spooler for the printer. For example, many of the Epson ink-jet printers have their own spooler. If you install the printer manually using the Add Printer Wizard described next, you will miss out on any special utilities such as that.

If you do not have a setup disk for the printer, or if the Setup program will not run under Windows XP, the next most preferable path is to download a setup utility from the printer manufacturer's Web site. (Actually, this is not a bad idea even if you do have a setup disk already, because the setup disk might have been created prior to Windows XP's introduction and might not have XP-specific drivers on it.)

If no setup files are available from the printer manufacturer, you can try the Add Printer Wizard in Windows. Windows XP provides drivers for hundreds of different printers, so it's possible that it includes a driver for your printer.

NOTE *If no Windows XP driver is available for your model, try the Windows 2000 driver. If no 2000 driver is available, try the one for NT 4.0. Still no luck? Check the printer's manual to find out whether it emulates any other printers; perhaps Windows XP includes a driver for one of them. You might also be able to kludge through with a driver for a similar model by the same manufacturer. For example, all the Lexmark Optra S models are basically the same except for their feature set, so you could print with a different driver using the default settings even if you couldn't reliably set printing properties.*

In earlier versions of Windows there used to be an Add Printer icon in the Printers folder, but not in Windows XP; instead there's an Add a Printer link in the Printer Tasks bar.

To add a local printer with the Add Printer Wizard:

1. Choose Start ➤ Printers and Faxes.

2. Click the Add a Printer link in the Printer Tasks bar.

3. The Add Printer Wizard runs; then click Next.

4. Click Local Printer Attached to This Computer.

5. If you want Windows to try to detect the printer, mark the Automatically Detect and Install My Plug and Play Printer check box. Otherwise clear it.

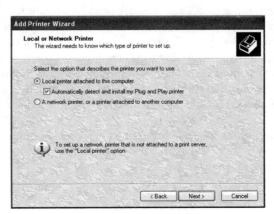

6. Turn the printer's power on if you want Windows to detect it, and then click Next.

   At this point, if Windows finds the printer, a bubble pops up in the notification area and the Wizard reports that the printer has been installed and offers to print a test page.

NOTE *If Windows doesn't find the printer, see the next section, "Installing Multiple Drivers for the Same Printer." Even though you don't actually want multiple drivers in this case, you'll see in that section how to set up a printer without Plug and Play.*

7. Click Yes, and then click Next to print the test page; then click Finish.

8. A box pops up asking whether the test page printed okay; click OK if it did, or click Troubleshoot if it did not; then work through the Printing Troubleshooter.

Installing Multiple Drivers for the Same Printer

As I mentioned earlier, one of the advantages in Windows printing is that Windows can accept multiple drivers for a single physical printer. You can use this capability for any number of purposes, such as:

◆ Installing both a PCL and a PostScript driver for a printer that is capable of using either PDL. Sometimes having two separate PDLs can be a boon when troubleshooting a problem; for example, the printer might run out of memory when printing a large graphic using one PDL but manage to print the page using another.

◆ Using different printer properties for certain jobs. For example, you might have one driver set up by default to pull from a paper tray containing letterhead stationery and another driver set up by default to pull plain paper from a different tray.

◆ Turning off the print spooler for one driver while leaving the other one to use the Windows print spooler.

◆ Setting one printer driver to Landscape by default and another one to Portrait so you don't have to switch between the two orientations in the application in which you're printing.

Setting up a second driver for an already-installed printer is just like setting it up initially except you don't allow Windows to detect the printer automatically:

1. Perform steps 1–4 of the preceding section's steps for setting up a new local printer.

2. Make sure the Automatically Detect and Install My Plug and Play Printer check box is *not* marked, and click Next.

3. Choose the port to which the printer is connected, and click Next.

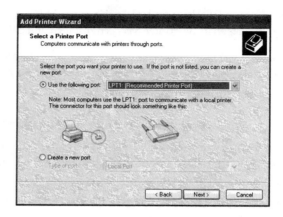

NOTE *The Create a New Port option is useful chiefly for setting up a TCP/IP printer connection; you'll see it in use later in this chapter in the section "Installing a Printer on a TCP/IP Port."*

4. Select the printer from the list of manufacturers and models provided. (Or, if it isn't listed, click Have Disk and point to a location where a driver can be found.) Then click Next.

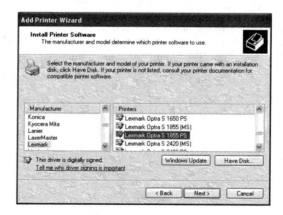

NOTE *The Windows Update button connects to Microsoft's Web site and brings up a list of any updated drivers that have been released since Windows XP came out.*

5. In the Printer Name box, type a name for the printer driver icon. You'll need to give it a different name from any already-installed drivers.

6. Choose Yes or No to set this printer as the default one or not. Then click Next.

7. If you want to set the printer up for sharing now, click Share Name and then type a name by which it should be shared. Then click Next. Or, if you want to skip sharing for now and set it up later, just click Next and skip to step 9.

NOTE *If you use a share name of more than 8 characters, or containing any spaces, it might not be accessible from MS-DOS programs. You'll see a warning to that effect if you enter such a name.*

8. If you chose to share the printer, you're prompted for Location and Comment text. Enter these descriptors if you wish, and then click Next.

9. Click Yes to print a test page or No to skip it; then click Next.

10. Click Finish. You might be prompted for the Windows XP CD-ROM, or not, depending on what driver you chose and whether it was already installed.

When you finish up, you'll have a second driver for the printer in your Printers folder. It will also appear in any applications you print from (at least, any applications that let you specify which printer you want to use).

Sharing a Local Printer

You saw in the preceding section how the Add Printer Wizard can set up printer sharing for you as part of the printer driver installation. (That's an option only if you don't have Windows detect the Plug and Play printer.) But you can also set it up manually.

NOTE *Some printers have built-in network cards so you can attach them directly to a network hub; no particular PC has local control over these printers. You can print to one of these using its IP address. Other printers are not network-capable by themselves, but you can hook them up to a print server that manages their network connection. Then there's the shared local printer. When you share a local printer, you give other network users permission to access it, and when they do use it, the request goes through your own local copy of Windows. If the printer is heavily used, you might notice the drain on your system resources while the print jobs are spooled off to the printer. That's why on busy networks, it is preferable to have printers networked through a print server or their own network address.*

To share one of your local printers, do the following:

1. Right-click the printer in the Printers and Faxes folder and choose Sharing.

2. Enable the Share This Printer option button, and enter a share name for it (or accept the default name).

3. Click OK.

Pretty simple, eh? But see the following section to gain some control over the specifics of the sharing.

Setting Permissions for a Shared Printer

The simple Sharing tab shown in the preceding section might lead you to believe that no options are available for controlling how your printer is shared. However, that's not the case.

First, you can control when the shared printer is available to others in the Advanced tab. You can specify certain times of day when the printer should be available, and you can assign a priority to the print jobs coming in from other people. For example, if you set the priority to 2, and your own print jobs have the default priority of 1, your own jobs will print first, and then anyone else's. See Figure 7.1.

You can set the permissions for the printer—that is, which users can use it and what they can do to it—in the Security tab. See Figure 7.2.

TIP   If you don't have the Security tab in your printer's Properties box, it's probably because Simple File Sharing is turned on. (It's on by default in Windows XP installations.) To turn it off, from any Explorer window choose Tools ➤ Folder Options. In the View tab, scroll down to the bottom of the Advanced Settings list and deselect Use Simple File Sharing.

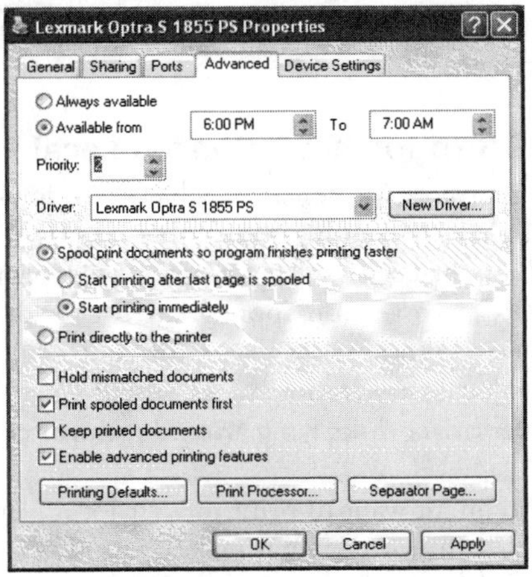

FIGURE 7.1

Control when others
can use your printer
and what priority
should be assigned
to their print jobs

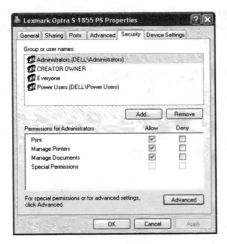

FIGURE 7.2

You can assign dif-
ferent permissions
for the printer to
different users and
groups.

For each listed user or group, you can assign permissions to Print, Manage Printers, and Manage Documents. You'll learn more about users and groups in Chapter 18, but let's look at the printing-specific permissions here:

- **Print:** Can send documents to the printer's queue.

- **Manage Printers:** Can view the print queue and can pause and resume it.

- **Manage Documents:** Can view the print queue and can pause, resume, or delete print jobs in it.

You'll learn about working with print queues later in this chapter, but when you get there keep in mind that the actions explained there can be performed only with the needed permissions to do so.

As with other network resources, you can also click the Advanced button to fine-tune the permission settings, but this is probably beyond the scope of what you want to get into right now. When you learn about advanced permissions in Chapter 18, you might want to come back here and explore the printer's permissions further.

Installing Multiple OS Support for a Shared Local Printer

When others share your local printer, as long as they have Windows XP installed on their PCs, everything works fine. But if they are running some other version of Windows, it's a no-go.

To circumvent this problem, the user wanting to access your printer must install a printer driver for that printer on his own PC, in a version appropriate for his operating system. For example, a Windows 98 user would need a Windows 98 driver for your printer. If he happens to have the needed driver on a disk at his local workstation, he can use it when he sets up the printer. However, most people don't keep printer driver disks lying around for printers they don't own, so the likelihood of this is slim.

As a courtesy to users who might want to print to your local printer over the network, you can pre-install the needed drivers for various operating systems. Then when the person sets up your printer, the needed drivers will be copied from your PC to his as part of the setup process.

To add these drivers, click the Additional Drivers button in the Sharing tab of the printer properties. This opens an Additional Drivers dialog box. See Figure 7.3. Place a check mark next to the drivers you want to install and click OK.

FIGURE 7.3

You might want to provide drivers for other operating systems as a courtesy to other network users.

A dialog box will then appear prompting for the location of the needed driver. If you have a setup CD-ROM for the printer, you might find the driver there; otherwise you can download it from the manufacturer's Web site. Point the dialog box to the needed location with Browse, and then click OK to continue. See Figure 7.4.

FIGURE 7.4

You must have the driver available for each operating system that you wish to support, and you must tell Windows where to find it.

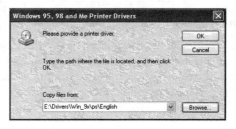

Installing Remote Printers

A *remote* printer is one that is not connected to your PC directly. It could be connected to another individual's PC on the network, connected directly to the network itself, or accessible through the Internet via TCP/IP.

Setting Up a Remote Printer

Before you can print to a remote printer, you must install a driver for it on your local PC. That's actually a good thing, because then you can set your own properties for the printer and not have to rely on someone else's settings for it. For example, perhaps you always print your documents in Landscape orientation, but the printer owner always prints in Portrait. Since you maintain your own copy of the driver, you can have your own default Landscape setting without manually making the change every time.

To install a remote printer, do the following:

1. From the Printers and Faxes folder, click the Add a Printer link. The Add Printer Wizard starts; click Next.

2. Click the A Network Printer, or A Printer Attached to Another Computer option button. Then click Next.

3. If you have an address for the printer already, enter it. It could be a network path (such as \\server\printer) or a URL. If you don't know the address, choose Browse for a Printer, and then click Next and locate it.

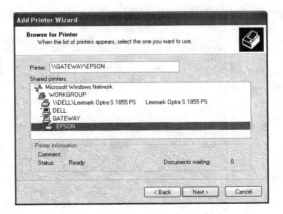

NOTE *If you have an IP address for the printer (a set of four numbers like 198.157.281.2), set up the printer as a local printer and choose the Add Port option to add a TCP/IP port. This is covered in the next section of the chapter.*

If the PC to which the printer is connected is running a different operating system than Windows XP, you might see the following message.

If you see that message, click OK and a list of printer manufacturers and models will appear. If the printer is listed, select it to install the Windows XP driver for it. If it isn't, click Have Disk and then point it to a driver on CD-ROM or downloaded driver.

4. Choose Yes or No to make this printer the default or not; then click Next, and then Finish. The needed drivers are copied to your PC, and the printer is set up.

Installing a Printer on a TCP/IP Port

If a network-capable printer is connected directly to the network, rather than to a print server or some other PC, its built-in network card will have its own unique TCP/IP address. You can use that address to set up the printer.

To do so, start out with the Add Printer Wizard as if it were a local printer, but don't let Windows automatically detect the printer. Then when asked about the printer port, choose Create a New Port, and then choose Standard TCP/IP Port from the list. See Figure 7.5.

FIGURE 7.5

You can print to a printer using its IP address by setting it up as a local printer on a TCP/IP port.

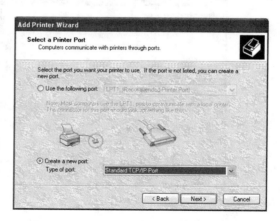

When you click Next after doing this, a whole new Wizard runs: the Add Standard TCP/IP Printer Port Wizard. Follow along with its prompts to install the printer.

Installing a Printer Through a Unix Host

If your network includes Unix-based computers, you can print through the network to a printer attached to them, or to network-capable printers on a Unix network, but you have to do a couple of setup things first:

1. Through Add/Remove Windows Components, install Print Services for Unix.

2. Run the Add Printer Wizard and start setting up a new local printer, but do not automatically detect.

3. Then when asked about the port to use, create a new LPR port.

4. Enter the IP address for that printer's host in the Name or Address of Server Providing LPD box.

5. In the Name of the Printer or Print Queue on That Server box, enter the name of the printer as it is known by the host device.

6. Complete the Wizard normally.

Managing Installed Printers

From the Printers and Faxes window you can view the installed printer drivers. The printer icons are different depending on the printer's status:

A local printer's icon is a regular printer.

A remote printer's icon has a cable beneath it, indicating it's on the network.

The default printer's icon has a check mark on it.

A shared local printer has a hand underneath it.

Removing a Printer Driver

To remove a printer driver, select it and press Delete, just like any other file or folder in Explorer.

Depending on the printer, you might see a message stating that some files were used only by that driver, and asking whether you want to delete them. If you never plan on reinstalling this printer, answer Yes. If you think you might reinstall it, choose No; that way you might not need to reinsert the Windows XP or printer CD-ROM when you reinstall.

Working with Printer Properties

Through a printer's properties, you can adjust almost every aspect of the way it works, from the print quality to the paper feed. To set properties for a printer, right-click it and choose Properties.

The properties for a printer vary widely depending on the printer model. Because the printer manufacturer supplies the printer drivers, there is no real standardization in the options they include or in the layout of the various tabs. However, there are at least a few settings that are available for all printers, regardless of model. The following sections outline some of the broad categories of settings that you might find in the properties for various types of printers.

See pages 50-51 of "Essential Skills for Windows XP Professional" for a visual guide to setting printer properties.

GENERAL PROPERTIES

All printers have a General tab. In it, you can change the printer driver's name, enter comments about the printer, and print a test page. See Figure 7.6.

FIGURE 7.6

The General tab helps you identify the printer.

From the General tab you can also click the Printing Preferences button to open the Printing Preferences dialog box for the printer. The content of this dialog box will vary depending on the printer model; Figure 7.7 shows it for my laser printer.

FIGURE 7.7

Printing Preferences set basic operational parameters such as page orientation.

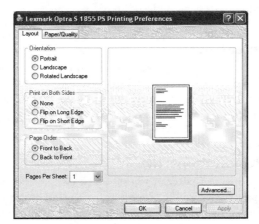

PORTS PROPERTIES

In the Ports tab you can select which port a printer uses. On the surface this seems simple enough: one printer, one port. But if you mark the Enable Printer Pooling check box at the bottom of this tab (see Figure 7.8), you can then choose multiple ports for a single printer driver. This enables you to put multiple identical printers on different ports and have print jobs sent to whichever one happens to be free through a single print driver and print queue.

FIGURE 7.8

In the Ports tab, you can select ports to be associated with the selected printer driver.

Clicking a port and then clicking the Configure Port button brings up a dialog box with options for that type of port. With a parallel port there is only one option: Transmission Retry. However, with a serial (COM) port you can set the communication settings (such as bits per second, parity, stop bits, and so on).

ADVANCED PROPERTIES

In the Advanced tab (Figure 7.9) are a variety of special-purpose settings. You saw earlier about the availability hours, when sharing was discussed. Some of the other options here are:

Spooling: By default a printer uses the Windows print spooler, but you can choose to print directly to the printer instead. If you do that, the application might slow down or lock up entirely while the job prints.

Hold Mismatched Documents: When this is on, the driver checks the document to be printed to make sure it can be successfully printed on the printer (correct page size, etc.) If not, it holds it in the queue.

Print Spooled Documents First: There's a delay between when a document begins being transferred from the application to the print spool. If you have the Spooling setting set so that the document will not start printing until the last page is spooled, the printer will sit idle waiting, even if other documents of a lower priority are completely spooled and waiting. If you mark this check box, however, those lower priority documents will be able to "cut in line" to allow more efficient usage.

Keep Printed Documents: If you turn this on, items in the print spool will not be deleted after they are printed; they'll just go into an inactive status there. This enables you to resubmit the same print job from the spool without having to reprint it in the application.

Enable Advanced Printing Features: When this is on, any special options the printer is capable of, such as booklet printing, page order, and pages per sheet, will be available.

FIGURE 7.9

Advanced properties for the printer control special situations.

DEVICE SETTINGS

Most printer drivers have a Device Settings tab, but the content of it varies dramatically from printer to printer. These are generally the same settings that you can control from the LED panel on the printer itself, but are accessible through the printer driver for convenience. Figure 7.10 shows one for a PostScript/PCL laser printer.

FIGURE 7.10

Device Settings are specific to the printer model.

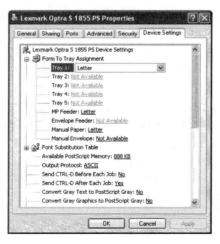

COLOR MANAGEMENT

For color printers only, a Color Management tab may appear, enabling you to select a color profile. A color profile is a configuration file that specifies color fine-tuning for a particular source. This is handy if you are trying to match the colors onscreen more closely with the actual output from the printer, so it's more of a "what you see is what you get" affair.

UTILITIES

Found primarily in ink-jet printer drivers, the Utilities tab offers shortcuts to self-tests, head-cleaning routines, and other utility programs built into the printer. Most of these can also be run by pressing buttons on the printer itself; they're provided in the driver for convenience.

Managing the Printing Process

Once a print job leaves the application, it's at the mercy of the print spooler (a.k.a. the *print queue*), a holding area where print jobs wait to be printed. The bottleneck here is the printer's speed and available memory. The more memory a printer has, the more print jobs can be stacked up in it waiting for the printer's hardware to catch up. The less memory a printer has, the more it relies on the print queue in Windows to hold the excess incoming data.

Managing a Print Queue

To open a print queue, double-click the printer in the Printers and Faxes window. Another way: when a print queue is active (that is, when it contains something to be printed), a printer icon appears in the notification area. Double-click that icon to open the print queue. Figure 7.11 shows a print queue with several print jobs.

FIGURE 7.11

A printer's queue shows what print jobs have been submitted and are waiting to be printed.

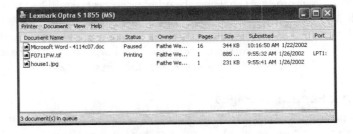

You can control two things from the print queue: the queue itself and individual print jobs within it. As you learned earlier in the chapter, you can grant permissions for these activities separately when assigning sharing permissions to other users.

The overall print queue itself is controlled from the Printer menu. Some of the important commands there are:

◆ **Pause Printing:** Freezes the print queue but leaves all print jobs intact.

◆ **Cancel All Documents:** Clears the entire queue.

◆ **Use Printer Offline**: Pauses the connection between the printer and the queue. The queue stops sending data to the printer temporarily, but the queue itself continues accepting incoming documents.

There are several other commands on the Printer menu, but they're all commands you've already seen in this chapter, such as Sharing and Properties.

Individual print jobs are controlled from the Document menu. The important commands here:

◆ **Pause**: Pauses the print job. If the job is currently printing, it also pauses the printer. If the job is waiting to be printed, it makes other non-paused jobs able to pass the paused job in the queue. So if you submit a big print job and then a small one, and decide you want the small one to print first, you could pause the big one.

◆ **Resume**: Resumes a paused print job.

◆ **Cancel**: Cancels the print job.

TIP   *Occasionally a document might get "stuck" in the print queue. It can't print, and you can't delete it. To fix this, you must stop and restart the Print Spooler service from the Computer Management console (in Administrative Tools in Control Panel). You'll find the print spooler under Services there.*

Taking a Printer Out of Service with Pending Print Jobs

Suppose you have a printer with lots of jobs waiting in its queue and the printer has a blowout that requires you to take it out of service. What happens to all those print jobs? You don't want them to be lost, so you must transfer them to another printer.

To do so, open the print queue for the broken printer, and choose Printer ➤ Properties. In the Ports tab, click the port to which the other printer is assigned and then click OK. You can do this to redirect to any printer on the same print server.

If you need to redirect to a printer on a different print server, you must add a port for it. Click Add Port, click Local Port, and then click New Port. Then enter the name of the other print server and shared printer in this format: *print_server**share_name*.

Using Separator Pages

A separator page is an extra page that prints before each document. It identifies who printed it, the date and time, and so on. On a printer that many users share, this can be a valuable tool for determining whom a print job belongs to, even though it wastes a certain amount of paper.

A separator page also can have another purpose—it can send a printer-specific hexadecimal code to the printer. This is useful for activities such as switching the printer between PCL and PostScript modes.

Separator pages are text files with a `.sep` extension. Windows XP includes four separator page designs:

◆ `Sysprint.sep`: Switches to PostScript and prints a separator page with the account name, job number, date, and time.

◆ `PCL.sep`: Switches to PCL and prints a separator page with the account name, job number, date, and time.

- ◆ `Pscript.sep`: Switches to PostScript but does not print a separator page.

- ◆ `Sysprtj.sep`: Same as Sysprint.sep but uses Japanese fonts if available.

SELECTING A SEPARATOR PAGE

To select a separator page to use with a certain printer, do the following:

1. Open the Properties for the printer and go to the Advanced tab.

2. Click the Separator Page button. The Separator Page dialog box opens.

3. Type the path to the separator page, or click Browse to locate it.

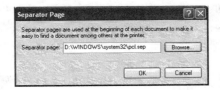

4. Click OK.

DESIGNING YOUR OWN SEPARATOR PAGE

You can design your own separator pages by creating text files in Notepad and saving them with a `.sep` extension. You can modify one of the existing `.sep` files or start fresh.

At the top of the file, type one single character on a line by itself. The `.sep` files that come with Windows XP use the backslash (\) for this but you can use @ or some other character if you prefer. This defines the character that will precede all subsequent commands—the escape character. From there, just start typing your codes. Table 7.1 lists the codes you can use for separator pages. Table 7.1 shows a \ as the escape character, but keep in mind you can use some other character if you prefer.

TABLE 7.1: SEPARATOR PAGE CODES

PAGE CODE	DESCRIPTION
\N	Name of the user who is printing
\I	Job number
\D	Date
\T	Time
\L *message*	Prints a message. Type your message in place of *message*. For example, \L Acme Corporation would print the name "Acme Corporation" on the page. It prints everything that follows the \L code up until the next \ is found or until it runs out of page width. (Messages won't wrap to multiple lines automatically.)

Continued on next page

TABLE 7.1: SEPARATOR PAGE CODES *(continued)*	
\F *pathname*	Prints the content of the specified file. Type your file path and name in place of *pathname*.
\H*nn*	Sends a hexadecimal instruction to the printer. Type the hex code in place of *nn*.
\W*nnn*	Specifies the maximum width of the separator page, in characters. The default is 80; the maximum is 256. Type the width in place of *nnn*.
\B\S	Prints in single-width block letters.
\B\M	Prints in double-width block letters.
\U	Turns off block-letter printing.
n	Skips a number of lines (0 through 9). Type the number of lines in place of *n*.
\E	Ejects the page from the printer.

Make sure that \E is the final code of the file. Then save it with an .sep extension in the %systemroot%/system32 folder.

Setting Print Server Properties

So far you have learned about setting properties for individual printers, but you can also make global printing settings that affect all the installed printers. To do so, right-click an empty area of the Printers and Faxes window and choose Server Properties. This opens the Print Server Properties dialog box.

This dialog box has four tabs:

- **Forms:** This is a master list of the available forms that can be assigned to the various paper trays in the Device Settings tab for an individual printer. You can add new forms here.

- **Ports:** This is the same as the Ports tab in an individual printer's properties.

- **Drivers:** This tab tells what drivers have been installed for which operating systems. For example, if you have added drivers for additional operating systems for some of your shared printers, you'll see them listed here. You can add and remove drivers from here.

- **Advanced:** Here you'll find an assortment of check boxes and other controls for fine-tuning the printing subsystem on your PC. Table 7.2 lists the options here.

See pages 52–53 of the Essential Skills section for a visual guide to setting print server properties.

TIP   *The Spool folder you set in the Advanced tab applies to all printers. If you want to specify a different spool folder location for a specific printer, you must do so by editing the Registry. Go to* HKEY_LOCAL_MACHINE\Software\ Microsoft\Windows NT\CurrentVersion\Print\Printers*printer key, and change the SpoolDirectory to the desired location.*

WARNING   *If you want users to be able to receive notifications when their print jobs are complete, you must start the Alerter service using the Services snap-in in Computer Management. Alerter does not start automatically by default.*

TABLE 7.2: ADVANCED PRINT SERVER PROPERTIES

SETTING	PURPOSE
Spool Folder	Specifies where the print queue's file will be stored.
Log Spooler Error Events	Creates a log file containing any error messages generated. Error messages would include things like Out of Paper.
Log Spooler Warning Events	Creates a log file containing any warning messages generated. Warnings might include things like Toner Low.
Log Spooler Information Events	Creates a log file containing information messages generated. You would not normally want to log these; they're things like Print Job Completed.
Beep on Errors of Remote Documents	Signals the print server to beep when errors occur.
Show Informational Notifications for Local Printers	Makes pop-up bubble messages appear in the notification area for routine events associated with local printers.
Show Informational Notifications for Network Printers	Makes pop-up bubble messages appear for routine events associated with network printers.
Notify When Remote Documents Are Printed	Displays a message when you print to a network printer to let you know the print job has finished. This might be useful if you want to go pick up a printout but don't want to get there too early and have to wait for it to complete.
Notify Computer, Not User, When Remote Documents Are Printed	Normally the user gets the message with the above setting; if you log on as another user, you won't get the message. But if you mark this check box, the message will go to the computer regardless of who is logged on.

Managing Fonts

Whenever you produce anything containing text, you select a font to specify the style of lettering. As you learned earlier in the chapter, Windows versions 3.1 and higher have included a type of font file called TrueType. TrueType revolutionized the desktop publishing industry by providing the average end user with a huge assortment of cheap, scaleable fonts. Windows XP includes support for True-Type fonts, but the fonts that come with Windows XP are of a new type called OpenType.

NOTE *The term font has a somewhat ambiguous meaning. Some people claim it refers to the style of lettering only and is synonymous with typeface. Other people claim a font is a particular typeface at a particular size with a particular set of attributes applied (bold, italic). Usage has been inconsistent over the years in the computer industry, and Windows itself is inconsistent in terminology. In this chapter, I'll use the term font to be synonymous with typeface.*

The Fonts window in Windows XP, accessible through Control Panel, shows all the installed True-Type and OpenType fonts (as well as a few other types of special-purpose fonts that are neither).

Installing Fonts

Most of the fonts you'll acquire will come as part of an application. For example, when you install Microsoft Office XP, the Setup program automatically installs dozens of fonts in Windows. Even when you buy a CD-ROM full of fonts in a computer store, it usually comes with a Setup program for browsing the fonts and choosing the ones you want.

If the font source does not include any installation utility, you can install the fonts from within Windows' Fonts window by doing the following:

1. From Control Panel, click Appearance and Themes, and then in the sidebar area, click Fonts. That's the only way to get to the Fonts applet in Category view; if you're using Classic view, you can simply double-click the Fonts icon.

2. In the Fonts window, choose File ➤ Install New Font.

3. Navigate to the drive and folder where the new font is located. If there are a lot of fonts in that location, it may take a minute for the list to populate. Click the Network button if you need to map a network drive to locate the fonts.

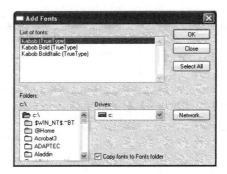

4. Select the font you want. To select multiple fonts, hold down the Ctrl key as you click each one, or hold down Shift to select a block.

NOTE   If you clear the Copy Fonts to Fonts Folder check box, it will save the space on your hard disk by using the fonts from their source location. However, if that source location is ever unavailable, the fonts that are there will be unavailable as well.

5. Click OK to install the fonts.

TIP   You can also drag and drop font files into the Fonts folder instead of going through the process just described.

Managing Your Font Collection

From the Fonts window, shown in Figure 7.12, you can browse the installed fonts, remove any that you don't want, and see previews of the fonts.

FIGURE 7.12

Browse the installed Windows fonts here.

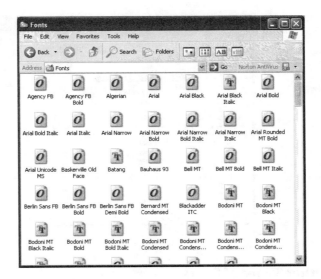

Here are some activities you can perform on fonts:

◆ To see a preview of a font, double-click its icon; when done looking at it, click Close. See Figure 7.13.

◆ To remove a font, delete its icon from the Fonts folder.

◆ To hide variations of the same font, choose View ➤ Hide Variations. This hides any fonts that are exactly like some other font except for being bold or italic.

◆ To sort the fonts by similarity to a chosen font, choose View ➤ List Fonts by Similarity. Then open the List Fonts by Similarity To drop-down list and choose one of the fonts. The other fonts will appear in order from most to least similar to it. This is a great way to trim your font collection by eliminating any identical or virtually identical fonts that have different names. See Figure 7.14.

FIGURE 7.13

A preview of the selected font

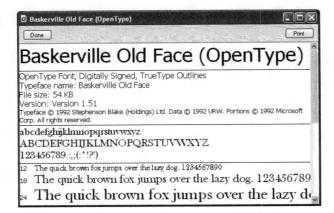

FIGURE 7.14

Listing fonts by similarity helps identify duplicates with different names.

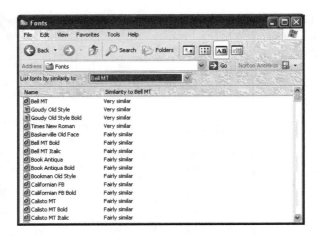

Using Other Types of Fonts

Most people think of TrueType or OpenType fonts only when they hear the term *font*, but there are in fact many different kinds of fonts that Windows applications can use.

TYPE 1 FONTS

These are scaleable soft fonts (that is, fonts contained in software) designed for use with PostScript printers. Type 1 is an Adobe technology that predates TrueType and is still in use today in commercial printing operations.

You install Type 1 fonts the same way you install OpenType or TrueType fonts, as explained earlier in the chapter.

NON-SCALEABLE FONTS

Windows supports several types of fonts that come in fixed sizes, rather than being scaleable. There are two main types:

♦ **Vector fonts:** These are soft fonts designed for use on plotters. Windows XP comes with three vector fonts: Roman, Modern, and Script. These are non-scaleable; they come in a fixed few sizes.

♦ **Raster fonts:** These are soft fonts stored in sets of bitmap images, with one size of lettering per raster file. They're non-scaleable. Before TrueType, almost all PC fonts were of this type.

Both can be installed using the same procedure outlined in "Installing New Fonts" earlier in the chapter.

If you have raster (PCL) printer fonts on a disk and you want to install them into the printer's memory, you would install them from the printer's properties. To do so, go to the Device Settings tab in the printer's Properties box and double-click External Fonts. Then specify the location from which you want to import the fonts. See Figure 7.15. These fonts would be available only for this printer, of course.

FIGURE 7.15

Install raster fonts for a printer.

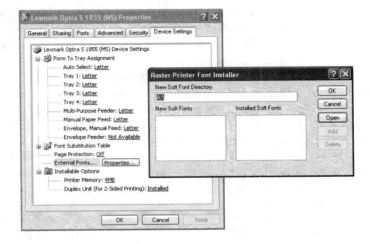

PRINTER-RESIDENT FONTS

Some printers have a number of built-in fonts. Some are scaleable (notably PostScript fonts in a PostScript printer); others are in a few fixed sizes. They are automatically available in applications, but do not show up in the Fonts window. For example, in Figure 7.16, which shows Microsoft Word, notice that some of the fonts have a printer icon next to them; these are printer-resident fonts.

FIGURE 7.16

Printer-resident fonts appear in your font list within an application.

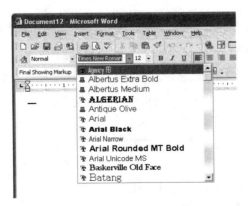

The fonts may be stored in the printer itself, or in an add-on cartridge that plugs into a printer. Back in the early days of Hewlett-Packard LaserJet printers, cartridge fonts were very popular. Today, however, you will seldom see them.

The printer driver knows about any printer-resident fonts automatically, but you may need to tell the printer driver about any cartridges you have installed. If your printer supports cartridges, there will be an Installed Font Cartridges option in the printer's Device Settings tab in its properties. Click it and then select which slot the cartridge is plugged into to make Windows XP recognize the cartridge.

Working with the Font Substitution Table

When a printer has its own resident fonts, you can choose to have them override certain soft fonts that an application might call for in a printout. This makes printing quicker because the soft font does not need to be sent to the printer prior to the print job. The table establishing the rules for which fonts should be substituted, and for what, is the *font substitution table*. Mostly you will find it available on laser printers; ink-jet printers typically don't have resident fonts.

To work with the font substitution table, open the printer's Properties box and go to the Device Settings tab. Then locate the Font Substitutions listing, and click the plus sign next to it, expanding the font list. See Figure 7.17.

This font list consists of all the soft fonts in the Fonts folder in Windows. Click one of them and a drop-down list appears containing all the resident fonts in the printer. Choose one of them, and then whenever a document calls for the chosen soft font, the printer's own font will be used instead.

FIGURE 7.17

You can substitute printer-resident fonts for soft fonts selectively.

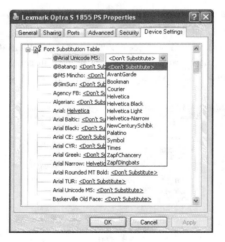

Selecting a Different Display Font

There are two kinds of fonts in Windows XP: printer fonts and display fonts. So far we have been talking only about the printer fonts. Each printer font has a corresponding display font that is used for displaying the font on-screen when you use it in an application (and also when you preview it in the Fonts window).

To change the font used in Windows title bars, dialog boxes, and so on, do the following:

1. Right-click the desktop and choose Properties.

2. In the Appearance tab, click the Advanced button.

3. Select one of the screen elements that contains text, such as Active Title Bar.

4. Open the Font drop-down list and select a different font to use for that element. Change the size, too, if desired, from the Size list.

5. Repeat steps 3 and 4 to change other screen elements if desired; then click OK.

Enabling ClearType for the Display Font

Windows XP comes with a new feature called ClearType that can help with poor on-screen text appearance on LCD monitors. You should not turn it on unless you have an LCD monitor because it can actually make the fonts appear worse on a regular CRT monitor. To turn it on, do the following:

1. Right-click the desktop and choose Properties.

2. Display the Appearance tab, and then click the Effects button.

3. Mark the Use the Following Method to Smooth Edges of Screen Fonts check box.

4. Choose ClearType from the list, and click OK twice.

Summary

This chapter has covered printing and font management. You learned how to set up local and network printers, and how to fine-tune their operation using their Properties. You also learned to manage a print queue, to install and remove fonts, and to change the display font in Windows. In the next chapter, you'll learn how to install and configure hardware devices.

Chapter 8

Installing and Configuring Hardware

WINDOWS XP MAKES IT EASIER than ever to install and configure new hardware. Its full support of Plug and Play, USB, FireWire, and other technologies makes for effortless installation for most new hardware. And for those situations where Plug and Play doesn't work quite right, Windows XP includes several utilities for helping identify and correct the problem.

- ◆ How hardware interacts with Windows XP
- ◆ Using hot-pluggable devices
- ◆ Using the hardware Wizards
- ◆ Disabling a device
- ◆ Uninstalling a device
- ◆ Adding some specific hardware items

How Hardware Interacts with Windows XP

Let's start out this chapter with a little background information about Windows XP's support for hardware devices.

Device Drivers

Each device—whether it's a modem, a sound card, a printer, or whatever—speaks its own language. In order for Windows to communicate with a device, a *device driver* for it needs to be installed. A device driver is a program that translates between Windows and the actual piece of hardware. Most device drivers also include user-adjustable settings that you can use to fine-tune the device's behavior, as you saw in Chapter 7 with printer drivers.

The driver files themselves usually have a `.sys` extension, but there may be helper files associated with them that use other extensions. For example, there might be a `.dll` file (Dynamic Link

Library), an `.hlp` file (a Help file for the device), a `.cpl` file (for Control Panel access to the device's properties), an `.htm` file (a Web document) containing help information, and others.

NOTE *The drivers that come with Windows are stored in the file* `Driver.cab` *on the Windows XP CD or in the* `%Systemroot%\Driver Cache\i386` *folder on your hard disk.*

For the last several years, almost all hardware manufactured has included support for a standard called *Plug and Play* in Windows. It enables Windows to detect the hardware automatically and install the correct driver for it from its own internal database of drivers. Windows XP includes thousands of drivers for popular hardware items. If the correct driver is not available through Windows XP itself, it prompts you to insert the disk provided by the device manufacturer and copies the needed driver from that location to your hard drive. From then on, each time Windows starts up, the driver for that device loads automatically.

DRIVER SIGNING

One reason that earlier versions of Windows could become unstable was because of an outdated or corrupted device driver. This was a problem because not all device manufacturers produced error-free drivers and because sometimes, different devices used driver files of the same name that would over-write one another when you installed a new device. To combat this problem, Microsoft came up with a way of attaching a digital signature to a device driver to certify that it is capable of working with Windows XP and has not been modified since its creation. Drivers that live up to this standard are known as *signed drivers*. When you install a new device, Windows will prefer a signed driver to an unsigned one. If only an unsigned driver is available, you'll see a warning before Windows installs it.

Should you install an unsigned driver? It's a gamble. An unsigned driver could cause system insta-bility, including lockups and blue-screen error messages. On the other hand, the unsigned driver might work just fine. You never know. Try searching the device manufacturer's Web site for a signed driver first; if you can't find one, back up your Windows configuration with System Restore before installing the unsigned driver.

TIP *The default security setting for driver signing is to warn you, but allow you to install an unsigned driver if you confirm the warning. If you want some other setting, such as to always allow unsigned drivers without a warning or never allow them, open the System Properties (by right-clicking My Computer or going through Control Panel) and, in the Hardware Tab, click the Driver Signing button. This opens a dialog box where you can adjust that setting.*

In a few cases, a certain driver may be known to cause problems in Windows XP. If you try to install such a driver, a feature called Windows Driver Protection will kick in and refuse to allow you to install it. Windows XP comes with a database listing the prohibited drivers, and when you use Windows Update, this database gets updated from Microsoft.

.INF FILES

When Windows searches for a driver for a device, it isn't looking directly for the driver file(s); instead it's looking for an information file (`.inf` extension). This is a text file that tells what driver files should be used for the device and what settings for it should be entered into the Registry. Figure 8.1 shows an INF file for an IDE controller card, for example.

FIGURE 8.1

This INF file tells
Windows how to
install the drivers
for an IDE con-
troller card.

For some devices, the INF file is actually all there is to the driver. For example, if you have a driver disk for a monitor, chances are that there aren't any real "drivers" for that monitor; there's just an INF file that describes the monitor to the Registry for the purposes of defining the maximum resolution and refresh rate that should be allowed.

DRIVER VERSIONS

Windows XP works best when all device drivers are written specifically for Windows XP. However, if such a driver is not available for a critical piece of hardware, you may be forced to try a driver written for an earlier version of Windows.

Since Windows XP is based on Windows 2000, the Windows 2000 driver, if available, is your best bet. If that's not available, try the Windows NT 4 driver. Drivers written for Windows 9x or Windows Me will probably not work in Windows XP because the operating systems are too different.

System Resources

Each device requires system resources. These resources can include a range of I/O addresses, an interrupt request line (IRQ), and/or a direct memory access (DMA) channel. Or, to be more precise, the controller through which the device is attached requires the resources. For example, even though you might have two hard disks on an IDE bus, that IDE bus takes up only one set of system resources. Another example: you might have six SCSI or USB devices chained together on a single interface, but that interface would use only one resource.

IRQs

When the CPU communicates with a device, the CPU must initiate the conversation. The device must signal to the CPU, "Hey, I need to talk to you!" and that's the purpose of interrupt request lines (IRQs). A device has an assigned IRQ, and whenever it needs attention it places a message on that bus. The CPU receives it and initiates a conversation. There are 16 IRQs, numbered 0 through 15, but over half of them are pre-assigned to system devices such as the keyboard, system clock, and built-in IDE controllers. When you install a new piece of hardware, an IRQ must be assigned to its controller.

Some devices have a built-in controller that requires the IRQ. An internal modem would fit that description, for example. Other devices share a controller with others—for example, a SCSI device shares a SCSI interface card with up to 6 other devices, and a USB device can share a USB root hub. Therefore it's advantageous to choose USB or SCSI devices when they are available.

So what happens if all the IRQs are taken? It depends on the device. If it's an ISA device, there's not much you can do, because all ISA devices require their own separate IRQ. If it's a PCI device, there should not be a problem because PCI devices can automatically share IRQs. Windows will assign multiple PCI devices to the same IRQ, and no conflict will occur.

I/O ADDRESSES

In addition to the IRQ, the device must have a meeting area for its conversations with the CPU. This assigned area for the device is its I/O address. This is a section of the PC's memory set aside for that device's use. Some devices have a range of memory addresses. Memory addresses are expressed in hexadecimal, so you might have a range like DF68–DF6F. Some devices might have multiple ranges. Since there is more memory to go around than there are IRQs, I/O address conflicts are rare.

DMA CHANNELS

Some devices have a way of working directly with memory, circumventing the CPU, for faster performance. This is called direct memory access, and in order to do it, the device must have a DMA channel assigned to it. This is most common for keyboards and sound cards. Some IDE devices can also use DMA. Each device that uses DMA must have a unique DMA address (0 through 5).

HOW RESOURCES ARE ASSIGNED

Plug and Play also manages the system resource assignments for the devices, ensuring that there are no conflicts. When Windows starts up, it makes a list of the available system resources and then doles them out to devices, trying for a "best fit" so that all devices have what they need.

Devices that are not Plug and Play compatible typically have jumpers on them for manually setting resource assignments. If your system includes one or more such devices, you should make a note of their manually set assignments and then make sure that Windows uses those same assignments in Device Manager (covered later in this chapter).

What Happens When You Install a Device in Windows?

When Windows automatically detects a new device, or when you run the Setup program for a device or install it with Add New hardware, a number of things happen:

- Registry entries are made for the new device.

- If the device requires any drivers, they are copied to your hard drive.

- If the device requires any system resources, Windows claims them on behalf of the device so they won't be assigned to anything else.

Depending on the device, you may see some or all of these tangible signs of the device being installed:

◆ The device appears in the Device Manager listing.

◆ A New Hardware bubble appears briefly in the notification area.

◆ An icon for controlling the new device appears in Control Panel. Some Windows-only modems do this.

◆ An icon for controlling the new device appears in My Computer. Some digital cameras do this, but only when the camera is physically connected to the PC.

NOTE   *If a device's Setup program does add a Control Panel applet, you'll find it only in Classic view, not Category view.*

Using Hot-Pluggable Devices

Hardware devices that use USB, FireWire, and PC Card connections are *hot pluggable*—you can plug in and unplug the device while Windows is running, without any adverse effects. Windows automatically loads and unloads drivers for hot-pluggable devices as needed.

NOTE   *Limited users and Guest users can install hot-pluggable devices. Only Computer Administrator users or users with administrative privileges can install devices that are not hot pluggable.*

When you plug in a hot-pluggable device for the first time, Windows displays a pop-up message in the notification area to let you know that it has noticed the device. Windows then automatically looks for a driver to let Windows and the device communicate with each other. It first checks in its capacious driver cache, which contains a wide variety of preinstalled drivers. If it draws a blank there, and if your computer is connected to the Internet, it checks the Windows Update site for a driver for the device; if it finds a driver, it downloads it and installs it. If Windows is able to find a suitable driver in either the driver cache or Windows Update, it unpacks and installs the driver, displaying a pop-up message identifying the device as it does so.

When the driver is installed and working, Windows displays a pop-up message telling you that the hardware is ready to use.

If Windows can't find a driver for the device, it starts the Found New Hardware Wizard, so that you can supply the driver for the device manually. I'll discuss how to use the Found New Hardware Wizard in just a minute.

Removing a USB device or FireWire device is as simple as unplugging it. Windows notices that you've removed the device and unloads its driver. Any data transfers that were in progress are aborted.

If the device is one through which you are transferring important data, such as an external drive, you might want to use the Safely Remove Hardware feature to ensure that all transfers have completed before you unplug the device. To do so, double-click the Safely Remove Hardware icon in the notification area. The Safely Remove Hardware dialog box opens. Select the device you are going to unplug and click Stop. Then, when a message appears that it has been stopped, you can click Close and then unplug the device.

When you plug a hot-pluggable device in again, Windows notices it and loads the driver without displaying any pop-up message.

Using the Hardware Wizards

For devices that aren't hot pluggable, or for hot-pluggable devices for which Windows can't find a suitable driver, you use Windows' two hardware Wizards, the Found New Hardware Wizard and the Add Hardware Wizard.

When Windows discovers some hardware for which it can't find a suitable driver, it starts the Found New Hardware Wizard. Figure 8.2 shows the first screen of the Found New Hardware Wizard.

FIGURE 8.2

The first screen of the Found New Hardware Wizard

As you can see in the figure, the Wizard lists the type of hardware it has found—in this case, the Multimedia Controller. If the Wizard can't identify the type of hardware, it displays *Unknown Device*. The What Do You Want the Wizard to Do? list gives you two options:

◆ **Install the Software Automatically**: Select this option button (which is usually selected by default) if you want the Wizard to have a go at installing the software needed for the hardware. This is usually a good option: the Wizard often manages to set up the hardware, and if it doesn't, you can easily return to this stage and try the second option. Click the Next button. The Wizard searches for the software and installs it automatically.

◆ **Install from a List or Specific Location**: Select this option button if you want to specify a particular driver for the hardware. Then follow the procedure described in the next section.

If the Found New Hardware Wizard *doesn't* find the driver it needs, it displays the Cannot Install This Hardware screen (shown in Figure 8.3).

FIGURE 8.3

The Found New Hardware Wizard displays the Cannot Install This Hardware screen if it can't find the software needed for the device. Click the Back button if you want to return to the start of the Wizard so that you can try the procedure manually.

At this point, you have three choices:

◆ If you want to give up on installing the software for this hardware completely (or at least for the foreseeable future), make sure the Don't Prompt Me Again to Install This Software check box is selected. Then click the Finish button. The Wizard closes itself and makes a note not to find this piece of hardware again.

◆ If you want to give up on installing the software for the time being, clear the Don't Prompt Me Again to Install This Software check box. Then click the Finish button. Each time you restart Windows (or run the Add New Hardware Wizard), the Found New Hardware Wizard will offer to install the hardware. These offers get old fast, but you may sometimes want to leave the installation of hardware for a day or two while you dig out the driver disk or download a new driver.

◆ To try to identify the necessary software yourself, click the Back button to return to the start of the Wizard. Then follow the steps in the next section.

Installing a Driver from a Specific Location

To install a driver from a specific location, take the following steps:

1. On the first screen of the Found New Hardware Wizard (Figure 8.2), select the Install from a List or Specific Location option button.

2. Click the Next button. The Found New Hardware Wizard displays the Please Choose Your Search and Installation Options screen.

3. Choose whether to let the Wizard search for a driver or to specify a specific driver:

   ◆ To let the Wizard search, leave the Search for the Best Driver in These Locations option button selected. Then select the Search Removable Media (Floppy, CD-ROM) check box if you want the Wizard to search your floppy and CD-ROM drives. (Insert a floppy or CD at this point if appropriate.) Alternatively, or additionally, select the Include This Location in the Search check box and use the text box, drop-down list, or Browse button to specify the location to search.

◆ To specify a driver yourself, select the Don't Search. I Will Choose the Driver to Install option button.

4. Click the Next button.

◆ If you choose to search for a driver, the Wizard searches for one, installs it (if it finds one), and displays the Completing the Found New Hardware Wizard screen.

◆ If you choose to specify a driver, the Wizard displays the Hardware Type screen (shown in Figure 8.4).

FIGURE 8.4

On the Hardware Type screen of the Found New Hardware Wizard, choose the type of hardware you're installing.

5. In the Common Hardware Types list box, select the type of hardware you're installing. The list is extensive, but if the device doesn't fit any of the descriptions, select the Show All Devices item.

TIP *If you're installing a driver from a floppy or a CD, it's not crucial that you get the Hardware Type right. The function of this screen is to display the appropriate list of manufacturers and devices on the Select the Device Driver You Want to Install for This Hardware screen of the Wizard.*

6. Click the Next button. The Found New Hardware Wizard displays the Select the Device Driver You Want to Install for This Hardware screen. Figure 8.5 shows the Select the Device Driver You Want to Install for This Hardware screen with all devices shown.

7. If Windows has a driver for the device, you can select it by selecting the manufacturer in the Manufacturers list box and the device in the Models list box. But usually the Found New Hardware Wizard will have identified the driver if Windows has it already, so you'll be visiting this screen of the Wizard only if you need to install a driver that Windows *doesn't* have. Click the Have Disk button. Windows displays the Install from Disk dialog box.

FIGURE 8.5

On the Select the Device Driver You Want to Install for This Hardware screen, select the manufacturer and device, or click the Have Disk button to identify the driver by its file.

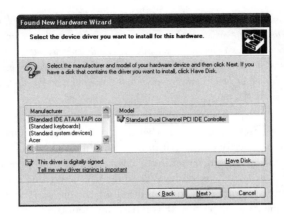

8. If you have the driver on a floppy or a CD, insert it in the appropriate drive and select the drive in the Copy Manufacturer's Files From drop-down list. If you have the driver on a local drive or network drive, click the Browse button, use the resulting Locate File dialog box (a common Open dialog box) to locate the driver file, and click the Open button to enter its name and path in the Copy Manufacturer's Files From text box.

9. Click the OK button. The Wizard displays the Select the Device Driver You Want to Install for This Hardware screen (shown in Figure 8.6) again, this time with the name of the hardware model or models identified by the driver.

FIGURE 8.6

When you specify the driver to use, the Wizard displays the Select the Device Driver You Want to Install for This Hardware screen.

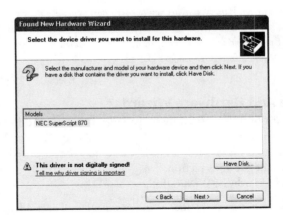

10. Select the driver and click the Next button. If Windows doesn't think the driver is correct for the device, it displays the Update Driver Warning dialog box, warning you that the hardware may not work and that your computer might become unstable or stop working. Click the Yes button if you're sure you want to install this driver. Otherwise, click the No button and select another driver.

NOTE   If the Wizard can't find hardware information in the location you specified, it displays the Select Device message box telling you that the location you specified doesn't contain information about your hardware. The Wizard then displays the Install from Disk dialog box again so that you can specify a different location for the file. If you get to this stage, you're probably stuck. You can click the Cancel button to close the Install from Disk dialog box and return to the Select the Device Driver You Want to Install for This Hardware screen so that you can select a built-in driver, but that's about it. Click the Cancel button to cancel the Wizard.

11. The Wizard checks to make sure that the driver you're installing has passed the Windows Logo testing to verify its compatibility with Windows XP. This is basically the same thing as driver signing, explained earlier in the chapter. If the driver has passed Windows Logo testing, all is well; if it hasn't passed, the Wizard displays a warning box warning you of the problem and strongly discouraging you from installing the driver. If you're sure the driver is okay, click the Continue Anyway button. If you have any doubts about the driver, click the STOP Installation button.

12. If Windows finds no problem with the driver, it installs it and displays the Completing the Found New Hardware Wizard screen.

13. Click the Finish button. Once the Wizard closes, the hardware is ready for use.

If the Found New Hardware Wizard is unable to install the device, it displays the Cannot Install This Hardware screen telling you what the problem was.

NOTE   Help and Support Center contains a system for referring searches for drivers that don't come with Windows or with the hardware device. When you plug in a new hardware device, and Windows finds that it doesn't have a driver for it and you can't supply a driver, Windows invites you to send information about the hardware to Microsoft. Once you've sent the information, you can take a variety of actions depending on what information is available. For example, you might be able to view a list of compatible devices (if any), search for information on compatible devices or Knowledge Base articles about the hardware, or find a link to the vendor's Web site.

Running the Add Hardware Wizard

If Windows doesn't find the new hardware you install, run the Add Hardware Wizard so that you can add the hardware manually. As you'll see, there's considerable overlap between the Add Hardware Wizard and the Found New Hardware Wizard, so don't be surprised if some of the steps in this list duplicate those in the previous section.

To run the Add Hardware Wizard, follow these steps:

1. Choose Start ➤ Control Panel. Windows displays Control Panel.

2. Click the Printers and Other Hardware link. Windows displays the Printers and Other Hardware screen.

3. Click the Add Hardware link in the See Also pane. Windows starts the Add Hardware Wizard, which displays the Welcome to the Add Hardware Wizard screen.

4. Click the Next button. The Wizard searches for new hardware and displays the The Following Hardware Is Already Installed on Your Computer screen (shown in Figure 8.7).

FIGURE 8.7

On the The Following Hardware Is Already Installed on Your Computer screen of the Add Hardware Wizard, select the Add a New Hardware Device item.

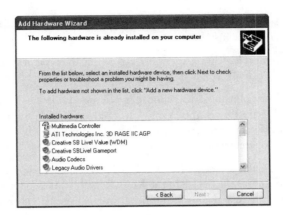

NOTE *If the Add Hardware Wizard doesn't find any hardware it didn't already know about, it displays the Is the Hardware Connected? screen, which asks whether you've already connected the hardware to the computer. Select the Yes, I Have Already Connected the Hardware option button or the No, I Have Not Added the Hardware Yet option button as appropriate. If you select the Yes, I Have Already Connected the Hardware option button, the Wizard displays the "The Following Hardware Is Already Installed on Your Computer" screen. If you select the No, I Have Not Added the Hardware Yet option button, the Wizard displays the Cannot Continue the Add Hardware Wizard screen, which offers to turn off the computer for you so that you can connect the hardware and try the Add Hardware Wizard again.*

5. If the device you want to install is listed in the Installed Hardware list box, select it. If it's not, select the Add a New Hardware Device item in the list box—the last item in the list.

6. Click the Next button. The Wizard displays the The Wizard Can Help You Install Other Hardware screen (shown in Figure 8.8), offering to search for the hardware.

7. Select the Install the Hardware That I Manually Select from a List option button.

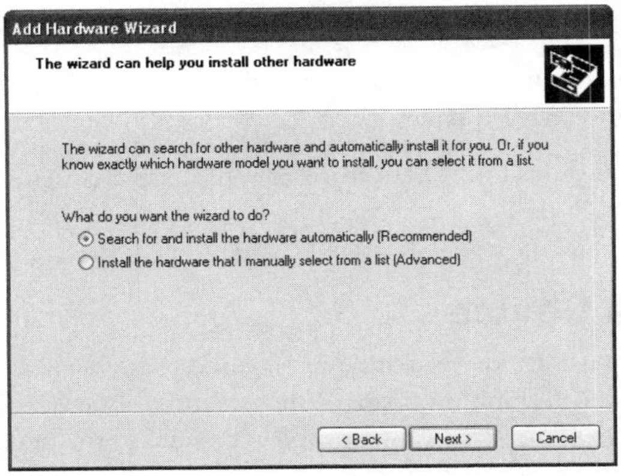

FIGURE 8.8

The Add Hardware Wizard offers to search for the hardware, but usually you'll do better to select it manually.

8. Click the Next button. The Wizard displays the From the List Below, Select the Type of Hardware You Are Installing screen.

9. In the Common Hardware Types list box, select the type of hardware you're installing. Again, if the device doesn't fit any of the descriptions, select the Show All Devices item.

10. Click the Next button. If you choose the Show All Devices item, the Wizard displays the Select the Device Driver You Want to Install for This Hardware screen (shown in Figure 8.9). If you choose a specific type of hardware, the Wizard leads you off on a byway of options appropriate to that type of hardware.

11. If Windows has a driver for the device, select it by selecting the manufacturer in the Manufacturers list box and the device in the Models list box. If you have a new driver, click the Have Disk button and use the resulting Install from Disk dialog box to specify the location of the driver.

12. Click the Next button. The Wizard displays the "The Wizard Is Ready to Install Your Hardware" screen, listing the hardware that's lined up for installation.

FIGURE 8.9

On the Select the Device Driver You Want to Install for This Hardware screen of the Add Hardware Wizard, select the device driver.

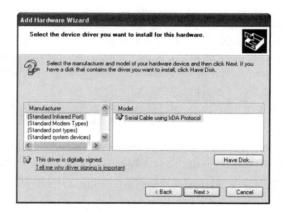

13. Click the Next button. The Wizard installs the hardware and displays the Completing the Add Hardware Wizard screen.

14. Click the Finish button. The Add Hardware Wizard closes itself. The hardware should be ready for use.

Disabling a Device

If you want to stop using a device temporarily, you can disable it. For example, you might want to disable a device that you think is making Windows unstable as a troubleshooting strategy. Or you might want to create multiple hardware profiles (covered in the next section) and disable certain devices in certain profiles.

To disable a device, open Device Manager by clicking Start, right-clicking My Computer to open the System Properties dialog box, clicking the Hardware tab, and then clicking the Device Driver button. Right-click the device, and then choose Disable from the shortcut menu. Windows displays a confirmation message box such as that shown in Figure 8.10. Click the Yes button. Windows closes the message box and disables the device.

FIGURE 8.10

Windows displays a confirmation message box when you instruct it to disable a device.

Uninstalling a Device

If you want to stop using a device permanently and remove it from your computer, uninstall it first. To do so, right-click the device in Device Manager and choose Uninstall from the shortcut menu. Windows displays the Confirm Device Removal dialog box. Click the OK button. Windows closes the dialog box and uninstalls the device.

NOTE *You can also uninstall a device by clicking the Uninstall button on the Driver tab of the Properties dialog box for the device, covered in the next section.*

Working with Device Properties

Device drivers have properties, just like any other files. The properties for the device driver determine how the device behaves, so it's important to know how to set them. In the following sections I'll explain some basics that apply to any type of device and then look at configuring some specific device types.

Viewing Device Properties

Some device types have their own applet in Control Panel, through which you can see all of the installed devices of that type and work with their properties. Modems are like that, for example.

However, you can also work with the Device Manager, which lists all devices of all types. Most people find this the most expedient way to check on multiple device types. To display Device Manager (shown in Figure 8.11), do the following:

1. Right-click My Computer and choose Properties.

2. Click the Hardware tab, and then click the Device Manager button.

Click a plus sign to open a category. In Figure 8.11, the Network Adapters category is open. Then double-click a device to see its properties (or click it once and then click the Properties button in the toolbar).

FIGURE 8.11

Device Manager displays all installed hardware in a single location.

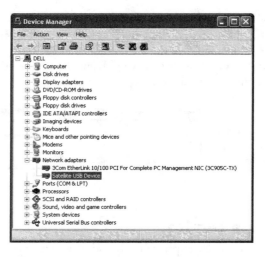

Viewing and Changing Drivers

You can work with a device's drivers in the Drivers tab of its Properties box. Figure 8.12 shows the Drivers tab for a satellite USB device, for example.

FIGURE 8.12

View, change, or remove drivers here.

From the Drivers tab, you can choose:

◆ Driver Details to see exactly what files are being used for the device.

◆ Update Driver to start the Hardware Update Wizard. It's like the Add New Hardware Wizard except it searches for better drivers for an existing device.

◆ Roll Back Driver to revert to a previously used driver after using Update Driver.

◆ Uninstall to completely remove the device's drivers.

See pages 80–83 of "Essential Skills for XP Professional" for a visual guide to changing a driver.

Viewing and Changing Resource Assignments

Plug and Play automatically assigns resources to a device. In earlier versions of Windows, Plug and Play technology was not fully reliable, so it was a rather common occurrence to need to adjust the resource allocations manually. However, in Windows XP, Plug and Play works well nearly every time.

There might still be situations where you would occasionally need to manually adjust resource assignments, however. One might be if you have a very old, non-Plug and Play device. Another might be if you have several ISA devices, since ISA devices don't share IRQs the way PCI and some other types of devices do.

To view a device's resources, display the Resources tab in its properties. See Figure 8.13.

FIGURE 8.13

View resource assignments here, and change them if there are conflicts.

If No Conflicts appears in the Conflicting device list, the current resource assignments are okay. If, on the other hand, you see one or more conflicting devices listed there, you might want to try to resolve the conflict by assigning different resources either to this device or to one of the conflicting ones.

NOTE *If the Use Automatic Settings check box is available, as it is in Figure 8.13, you will be able to try manual resource assignments for the device. In Windows XP, however, for the vast majority of devices this check box will not be available, and you will not be able to manually change resources.*

If a device is working okay, you should not change its resource assignments. Windows XP works best when you allow Plug and Play to handle all resource allocations automatically.

If you do need to change resources, do the following:

1. Deselect the Use Automatic Settings check box in the device's Resources tab. The other controls in the dialog box become available.

2. Open the Setting Based On drop-down list and choose a different configuration. Keep trying configurations until you find one that reports No Conflicts in the Conflicting Devices list.

TIP *If you cannot find one that reports No Conflicts, you can try setting an individual resource manually. To do so, select it from the Resource Settings area and then click Change Setting. For most devices, you won't be allowed to do this; you'll see an error message. However, some devices do allow this, and if it's possible, it's one possible way around an otherwise unresolvable resource conflict.*

3. Click OK to close the device's properties.

TIP *Here's a little-known tweak for all you hard-core techies out there. For more control over manual resource assignments in Windows XP, set the ACPI driver to Standard PC instead of its default of ACPI PC. To do so, view the properties for ACPI in Device Manager (in the Computer category). Go to the Driver tab and choose Update Driver. Then choose Install from a List or Specific Location, and then choose Don't Search. In the list that appears, select Standard PC and then complete the Wizard. Warning: power management features like Standby and Hibernate will no longer work, and you will probably need to reinstall the drivers for some of your devices.*

Configuring a Modem

If your modem is Plug and Play (and it probably is if you acquired your computer recently), Windows XP Professional will recognize and install it automatically. If not, you can use the Add Hardware Wizard as described earlier in the chapter.

NOTE *Windows XP uses a universal modem driver called Unimodem. Unimodem is the software interface between all your computer's 32-bit Windows-compatible communications applications (including the ones that use TAPI) and your modem or other communications hardware. It includes integrated control for port selection, modem initialization, speed, file transfer protocols, and terminal emulation. Because Unimodem handles the modem configuration, you only have to specify setup parameters once.*

After you install your modem, all your TAPI-aware communications programs will use the same configuration settings. When you change them in one application, those changes carry across to all the others.

To change the modem's properties, open up Phone and Modem Options in Control Panel. (It's in the Printers and Other Hardware category if you're using Category view.) Then in the Modems tab, select the modem you want to work with and click Properties. Figure 8.14 displays the Properties dialog box for an MDP 7800-U modem.

FIGURE 8.14

Use this Proper-
ties dialog box to
change your modem
configuration.

Here are some highlights of the modem properties you can set.
In the Modem tab:

◆ **Speaker Volume:** This controls the internal speaker in the modem. It does not affect the sound coming through your speakers.

◆ **Maximum Port Speed:** Leave this at the default in most cases. You might reduce it if your modem is having connection problems at higher speeds and you want to limit its speed for greater reliability.

◆ **Dial Control:** Normally you want the modem to detect a dial tone before dialing; deselect this check box if you don't.

On the Diagnostics tab:

◆ **Query modem:** Click this button if you aren't sure whether the modem is installed correctly. This utility sends some test codes to the modem and shows the modem's response. This is handy because the modem does not have to be connected to a phone line for the test to work. See Figure 8.15.

FIGURE 8.15

The Diagnostics tab of the Modem Properties dialog box lets you test your modem configuration and set logging options.

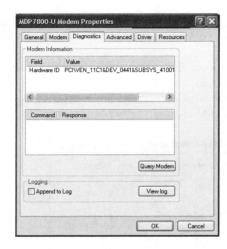

In the Advanced tab (Figure 8.16):

◆ **Extra initialization settings:** You can enter AT commands here if the modem requires any special codes to be sent to it before it dials. For example, some programs like AOL send special initialization strings to the modem, and they can sometimes cause the modem to drop the carrier or have other problems. You could type &FI in this box to tell the modem to use its built-in factory settings instead of the initialization string that a particular program sends.

NOTE   *AT commands, also known as Hayes commands, are codes that tell the modem how to operate. They used to be a lot more common in the days before PPP and TCP/IP Internet connections. To find out more about AT commands, see* www.modems.com/general/extendat.html.

FIGURE 8.16

The Advanced tab of the Modem Properties dialog box

WARNING *You should exercise some caution here, though, and consult the documentation for your modem to verify the actions of the command before using it. If the command isn't right for your modem, using it could cause some real damage to your modem.*

◆ **Advanced Port Settings:** This opens a dialog box where you can turn off/on FIFO buffers (First In, First Out), adjust the size of the Receive and Transmit buffers, and specify which COM port the modem uses. See Figure 8.17. By default the buffers are on and set to the highest settings. Turn them down or off to troubleshoot connection problems.

FIGURE 8.17

The Advanced Settings dialog box

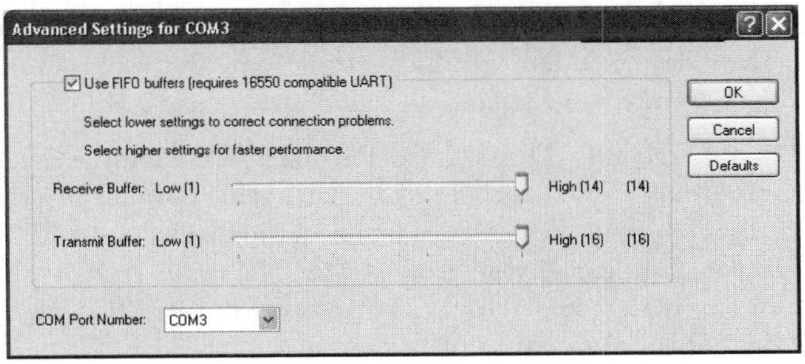

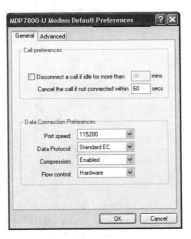

◆ **Change Default Preferences:** This opens a dialog box in which you can set disconnect-when-idle settings and adjust some other low-level modem properties such as compression and flow control. See Figure 8.18.

FIGURE 8.18

The Default Preferences dialog box

Configuring a CD Drive

Windows should detect new CD-ROM drives automatically without having to install any drivers for them. This includes most DVD and CD-RW drives too.

Depending on the model of DVD or CD-ROM drive, Windows may be able to work with it directly with no special software, or you may need to install the software that came with the device to enable its DVD or CD-RW functionality. However, all CD-ROM type drives should at least work as a generic CD-ROM drive with no extra setup.

Once Windows has identified your drive, you can adjust its properties by right-clicking the drive in My Computer and choosing Properties. (You can also access its properties from Device Manager if you prefer.)

The Properties dialog box for a CD-ROM has two settings in its Properties tab (shown in Figure 8.19):

◆ **CD Player Volume slider**: Drag the slider to set the volume you want the CD player to deliver when playing audio CDs. This setting controls the output of the CD drive. You can control the output volume from your sound card by using Volume Control.

◆ **Enable Digital CD Audio for This CD-ROM Device check box**: Select this check box if you want to use digital output rather than analog output from the CD drive for audio CDs. Digital output typically gives you higher audio quality, especially when you're copying audio CDs to your hard drive. Most newer CD-ROM drives and just about all DVD drives support digital output, but some older CD-ROM drives don't. If digital output doesn't work for you, clear this check box to return to analog output.

FIGURE 8.19

On the Properties tab of the Properties dialog box for a CD-ROM drive, you can set the CD's volume and specify whether to use digital CD audio.

TIP   By default, CD-ROM drives are set to AutoRun. That means any CDs play automatically if they have an Autorun.inf file on them. To turn off AutoRun, run the command **GPEDIT.MSC** *at the Run prompt. Then navigate to* Computer Configuration\Administrative Templates\System *and set the Turn Off Autoplay option to Enabled. This Group Policy Editor program is a good place to make other tweaks too; look around while you're there.*

The Properties dialog box for a DVD drive also contains a DVD Region tab, which displays the DVD encoding region currently set for the DVD player. To change the region, select the country you want in the list box and click the OK button.

DVD ENCODING REGIONS

In case you've managed to avoid the question of DVD encoding regions: as far as DVDs are concerned, the world is divided into eight regions, or locales:

◆ Region 1 is the United States, Canada, and U.S. Territories.

◆ Region 2 is Europe, Japan, South Africa, and the Middle East.

◆ Region 3 is Southeast Asia, East Asia, and Hong Kong.

◆ Region 4 is Australia, New Zealand, the Pacific Islands, South America, Central America, Mexico, and the Caribbean.

◆ Region 5 is Eastern Europe, Mongolia, North Korea, the Indian subcontinent, and Africa.

◆ Region 6 is China.

◆ Region 7 is "reserved" (for off-world use, perhaps).

◆ Region 8 is for international vessels such as airplanes and cruise ships.

DVD players are encoded to play only DVDs for their region. Almost all DVDs are encoded for the region in which they're intended to be sold. (There are also all-region DVDs that will play in any region.) So to play a DVD, you need a player with a matching region code.

Most consumer-electronics DVD players are coded for one region only. Some players—typically more expensive ones—can play discs for two, more, or all regions. Other players can be *chipped*—modified—to play DVDs with different regional encoding or even to play any regional encoding.

PC DVD drives are a little more flexible. With most drives, you can switch regions a certain number of times before the drive goes into a locked state in which you can no longer change the region. The DVD Region tab of the Properties dialog box for the DVD drive displays the number of times you can change the region again. Use them sparingly.

Why do DVDs have regional encoding anyway? In theory, it's to let the movie studios control the release of the movie in different countries. For example, U.S.-made movies are usually released in the United States several months before they're released in Europe, and DVDs and videos of the movie are often released in the United States while the movie is still running in Europe. Regional encoding prevents most of the Europeans from viewing the movie on DVD until it's released with Region 2 encoding.

In practice, regional encoding also enables the distributors to charge different prices for DVDs in different countries without being undercut by imported DVDs from the least expensive regions. For example, at this writing, DVDs in Region 2 are substantially more expensive than those in Region 1, and the European Union is investigating whether this constitutes price-fixing.

Configuring a Removable Drive

The first time you plug in a removable drive or a local drive and Windows finds pictures or audio files on it, Windows displays the Removable Disk dialog box or Local Drive dialog box to let you specify whether you want to set a default action to take with files of this type. Figure 8.20 shows an example of the Removable Disk dialog box for a CompactFlash card in a PC Card adapter. The

CompactFlash card contains picture files, so the Removable Disk dialog box contains actions that Windows can take with picture files: Print the Pictures, View a Slideshow of the Images, Copy Pictures to a Folder on My Computer, Open Folder to View Files, or Take No Action.

FIGURE 8.20

In the Local Disk dialog box or Removable Disk dialog box (shown here), you can specify which action you want Windows to take for a particular file type when you add a local disk or removable disk.

Select the action you want to take. If you want Windows to take this action for every disk you add that contains this type of file, select the Always Do the Selected Action check box. Then click the OK button. Windows closes the Local Disk dialog box or Removable Disk dialog box and takes the action you specified.

Configuring a Video Card

When you install a new video card, Windows may detect it on startup and display the Found New Hardware Wizard so that you can install the correct driver for it. Other times, you may have to change the video driver manually by using the Hardware Update Wizard.

After installing the driver for the new video card, you usually need to restart Windows. When you log back in, Windows displays the Display Properties dialog box so that you can test and apply the screen resolution and color quality you want. See Chapter 4 for a discussion of how to choose a suitable screen resolution and color depth.

If you're seeing corrupt images on your monitor, or if the mouse pointer doesn't respond properly to conventional stimuli, or if DirectX isn't working, you may need to change the graphics hardware acceleration on your computer or disable write combining.

NOTE *Write combining is a method of shunting more information from the video card to the monitor at once. It can cause screen corruption by providing the monitor with more information than it can handle.*

To do so, take the following steps:

1. Right-click open space on the Desktop and choose Properties from the shortcut menu to open the Display Properties dialog box.

2. Click the Settings tab.

3. Click the Advanced button to open the Monitor and Graphics Card Properties dialog box.

4. Click the Troubleshoot tab, which is shown in Figure 8.21.

5. Move the Hardware Acceleration slider one notch at a time from Full (or wherever you find it) toward None until the problems disappear. At each setting, click the Apply button, and check your computer to see the effect of the change.

6. Alternatively, or additionally, try clearing the Enable Write Combining check box to prevent screen corruption. Click the Apply button and see the effect of the change.

7. When the screen seems to be behaving as it should, click the OK button. Windows closes the Monitor and Graphics Card Properties dialog box, returning you to the Display Properties dialog box.

8. Click the OK button. Windows closes the Display Properties dialog box.

FIGURE 8.21

If you see corrupt images on the screen, try reducing hardware acceleration or disabling write combining on the Troubleshoot tab of the Monitor and Graphics Card Properties dialog box.

Viewing USB Hub Usage

USB hubs can support multiple devices. Each of these devices appears in Device Manager separately, but with no Resources tab since the device uses no system resources directly. The hub itself also appears there too.

In Device Manager you may see several devices listed in the USB category. The one associated with the motherboard (or add-on USB controller card) will have a Resources tab; it's the only one that directly draws resources. In Figure 8.22 that would be the Intel entry.

FIGURE 8.22

The Universal Serial Bus Controllers section of Device Manager shows the USB management devices.

If you view its Properties, you find an Advanced tab that lists System Reserved as the only user of the device.

You'll also see a USB Root Hub entry, which is the system interface for the above-mentioned controller. It draws no resources directly. Any USB devices that are directly plugged into the USB ports on the PC appear in this device's Power tab.

If you have any expansion hubs connected to the root hub, they also appear in Device Manager. In Figure 8.22 that would be the Generic USB Hub entry, representing a USB hub that's built into the base of my monitor. In its properties is a Power tab that lists the USB devices connected to it. See Figure 8.23.

FIGURE 8.23

View a USB hub's Power tab to see what devices use it.

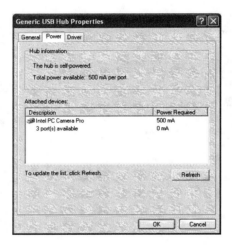

If you have problems with USB devices, the first thing to check is the Power tab for the hub into which it is plugged. If there are many USB devices chained together coming through this hub, there may not be enough power to support them all; this Power tab can tell you how much power is available and how much is used. In Figure 8.23 there is only one device, but a single USB port can support up to 127 devices.

Using Multiple Monitors

Windows XP Professional lets you attach multiple monitors to your computer to increase the amount of Desktop space available to you. This feature can make both work and play much easier—but it can also lead you to loading your desk with more monitors than it can comfortably provide a footing for.

This discussion of using multiple monitors concerns only desktop computers to which you can add one or more extra graphics cards. But Windows XP also includes a feature called DualView that lets you use multiple monitors with portable computers and graphics cards with multiple outputs. Mentioned in Chapter 10, DualView works exactly the same way except with notebook PCs with both a built-in LCD screen and an external VGA port.

WARNING   *Setting up multiple monitors can be a tricky and frustrating business. With some combinations of motherboards and graphics cards, you need to install the graphics cards in the right sequence in order to get them to work. Others work fine immediately. Others never work. Before you try to implement multiple monitors, check the Hardware Compatibility List (HCL) at the Microsoft Web site,* www.microsoft.com, *for details of the graphics cards that are known to work in multiple-monitor configurations with Windows XP.*

To use multiple monitors, you need to make sure that your graphics cards work together (some graphics cards don't) and that your computer's motherboard supports multiple monitors (some motherboards don't). In most cases, you'll want to use an AGP graphics card and one or more PCI graphics cards, but two or more PCI graphics cards without an AGP card can provide a satisfactory solution as well. The monitors, by contrast, don't need to know about each other—each gets its own input, so each can believe it's the only monitor in town if it wants to. So any monitors should do. You can mix CRTs and LCDs provided that the graphics cards in question can handle the monitor to which they're connected.

NOTE   *In the 1990s, large monitors were so expensive that it was much cheaper to buy two, three, or even four small monitors than one large one. That's now changed, at least with cathode-ray tube monitors (LCD monitors are still prohibitively expensive). Nineteen-inch monitors are reasonably affordable, and even 21-inch and 22-inch monitors are worth thinking about if you need a serious amount of Desktop space. But there's no reason why you shouldn't have a monster monitor and a couple of satellite monitors if you want—or even two or more monsters. . .*

To set up multiple monitors, power down your computer and insert the new graphics card. (You *can* install multiple graphics cards and monitors at a time, but unless you're very lucky and everything works, you'll be looking at some doubly confusing troubleshooting.) Connect the second monitor, and then power everything on. Don't be surprised if the bootup display appears on the second monitor rather than your primary one. After you log in to Windows, it should discover the new hardware, which will trigger a Found New Hardware notification-area pop-up followed by the Found New Hardware Wizard. If Windows affects not to have noticed the new hardware, run the Add Hardware Wizard manually to add the graphics card and monitor.

Next, display the Settings tab of the Display Properties dialog box. For each monitor you want to use (hint: all of them), select the monitor and then select the Extend My Windows Desktop onto This Monitor. Once you've done that, let Windows know where the monitors are positioned in relation to each other by dragging the monitor icons into their relative positions. If you get confused as to which monitor is which, click the Identify button to have Windows flash up the number of each monitor on the monitor. Then set the screen resolution, color depth, and refresh rate for each monitor as usual.

Once you close the Display Properties dialog box, you should have a substantially enlarged Desktop. By default, the Taskbar appears on your primary monitor (the one that shows the boot sequence), but you can drag it to any of the other monitors as you see fit.

Maximizing a window maximizes it for the monitor it's currently (or mostly) on. You can extend a "normal" window across two or more monitors by dragging its window border to the appropriate size.

Configuring Windows to Use an Uninterruptible Power Supply

One of the great benefits of a laptop computer is that its battery protects it from data loss when a power outage occurs. To get similar protection in a desktop computer, you need to attach a separate device—an uninterruptible power supply (UPS).

What Is a UPS?

A UPS is essentially a large battery of above-average intelligence that sits between your computer and the electricity supply and ensures a steady power stream to your computer to protect it from blackouts, brownouts, and surges. Different UPSes do this in two different ways.

The simpler way is for the device to monitor power fluctuations and kick in when the power supply falls outside acceptable thresholds. Technically, this type of device is called a *standby power supply* (SPS) rather than a UPS, but you'll often hear SPSes described as UPSes.

The more complicated—and better—way is for the device to feed power to the computer continuously, charging itself when the power supply is running within acceptable parameters. This device is technically a UPS. This way of supplying power is better because the UPS delivers conditioned power to the computer all the time, protecting it better from fluctuations and avoiding the critical moment of changeover from main power to battery power that can be a drawback with an SPS.

Choosing a UPS

If you're looking for a UPS, keep these features in mind:

Operating system support   Make sure the UPS is designed for use with Windows XP. With operating system support and an appropriate system management port (discussed next), the UPS can warn Windows XP when the electricity supply has failed. Windows can then shut itself down automatically if the computer is unattended. (More on this in a moment.)

System management port   Make sure the UPS has an appropriate system management port for your computer. Many UPSes use a serial port connection. Others use a USB connection.

NOTE   If you don't plan on connecting the PC and the UPS, you don't need to worry about a system management port or operating system support. Some people simply ignore their UPS's capability of communicating with the PC and treat it like a dumb battery backup.

Indicators for line voltage and battery power   The UPS should have one indicator to indicate when the incoming power to the UPS is okay and another indicator to indicate when the devices attached to the UPS are running on battery power. (Many UPSes also sound an alarm when battery power is being used.)

Multiple power outlets   Make sure the UPS has enough outlets for all the devices you want to plug into it directly.

Enough power and battery life   Before buying the UPS, work out how much power and battery life you need it to have. Make a list of the computers and devices you'll need to have plugged into the UPS, and then use a power-supply template such as that on the American Power Conversion Corp. Web site (`www.apc.com`) to calculate the number of volt-amps (VA) you'll need to keep the equipment running. (You can simply add up the voltages listed on the equipment, but be aware that the power-supply rating on your computer equipment shows the maximum power rather than typical power usage.) Then decide the amount of time you'll need to shut down the computers once the power alarm goes off. Generally speaking, the more power and battery life you need, the more the UPS will cost. If you just want a few minutes to allow you to shut down Windows under control (or to have Windows shut itself down), a modest and inexpensive UPS may fit the bill.

TIP   Unless you're convinced that you'll need to print during a power outage, don't plan to plug your printer into your UPS. Printers are power hogs. Laser printers are such power hogs that they can kill a UPS.

Installing a UPS

Power down your computer, unplug the computer power source from the wall, and plug it into the UPS. (You might also need to connect a serial or USB cable from the UPS to the computer). Now, bring up the computer again, log on to Windows, and display the UPS tab of the Power Options Properties dialog box (shown in Figure 8.24).

FIGURE 8.24

The UPS tab of the Power Options Properties dialog box

To let Windows know about your UPS, take these steps:

1. Click the Select button to open the UPS Selection dialog box (shown here with American Power Conversion chosen in the Select Manufacturer drop-down list).

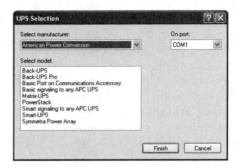

2. In the Select Manufacturer drop-down list, choose the manufacturer of your UPS. If the manufacturer isn't listed, choose the Generic item.

3. If the manufacturer was listed, specify the model of UPS in the Select Model list box, and select the port in the On Port drop-down list. Click the Finish button. Windows closes the UPS Selection dialog box, returning you to the Power Options Properties dialog box.

4. If the manufacturer wasn't listed, select the Custom item in the Select Model list box. Then click the Next button. Windows displays the UPS Interface Configuration dialog box. Consult your documentation, and then choose settings for Power Fail/On Battery, Low Battery, and UPS Shutdown as appropriate. Then click the Finish button. Windows closes the UPS Interface Configuration dialog box, returning you to the Power Options Properties dialog box.

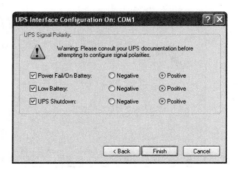

5. In the Power Options Properties dialog box, click the Configure button. Windows displays the UPS Configuration dialog box.

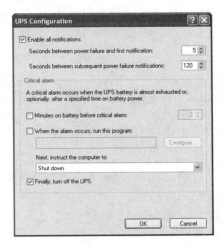

6. Select or clear the Enable All Notifications check box as appropriate. Adjust the value in the Seconds between Power Failure and First Notification text box and the Seconds between Subsequent Power Failure Notifications text box to suit your needs. For example, if your electricity supply suffers from mini-outages of a few seconds each, you might choose to increase the Seconds between Power Failure and First Notification setting to a value such as 20 or 30 seconds so that the UPS raises the alarm only for a more serious outage than usual.

7. In the Critical Alarm group box, specify what actions Windows should take when the UPS sends Windows a critical alarm, warning Windows that the UPS is almost out of battery power.

◆ Minutes on Battery before Critical Alarm check box and text box: Select this check box if you want Windows to sound an alarm after the specified number of minutes running on battery power.

◆ When the Alarm Occurs, Run This Program check box and text box: If you want Windows to run a program when an alarm occurs, select this check box and specify the program in the text box. For example, you might want to run a custom shutdown utility or use a program to send a warning to users of connected computers.

◆ Instruct the Computer To drop-down list: In this drop-down list, choose Shut Down or Hibernate as appropriate.

◆ Turn Off the UPS check box: Leave this check box selected (as it is by default) to have Windows turn off the UPS (and stop the alarm).

8. Click the OK button. Windows closes the UPS Configuration dialog box.

9. Click the Apply button. Windows applies your UPS settings. The Status section shows status information on your UPS, and the Details section shows the UPS's type.

10. Click the OK button.

Summary

This chapter has discussed how to add and support new hardware items in Windows XP Professional. You can use this information when you're having trouble with a device and need to reconfigure it as well as when you get ready to install a new monitor, a DVD drive, or some other hardware device.

In the next chapter, you'll learn about Windows Media Player and Windows Movie Maker, two excellent multimedia tools that come free with Windows XP.

Chapter 9

Media Player and Movie Maker

THIS CHAPTER DISCUSSES HOW to use Windows Media Player, the powerful multimedia player incorporated in Windows XP. A vast improvement on its predecessor of the same name, Windows Media Player not only provides features for enjoying audio and video but also supports copying CDs to your hard disk in WMA (Windows Media Audio) format. It also covers sound volume control and the Sound Recorder, and introduces Windows Movie Maker, a great utility for importing and manipulating video clips. In this chapter, you'll learn about

- ◆ Configuring Windows Media Player
- ◆ Playing music in Windows Media Player
- ◆ Understanding digital rights management
- ◆ Copying a CD to your hard disk
- ◆ Tuning into Internet radio
- ◆ Backing up and restoring digital licenses
- ◆ Using Volume Control to control output and input
- ◆ Recording and converting sounds with Sound Recorder
- ◆ Creating movies with Movie Maker

Getting Started with Windows Media Player

Start Windows Media Player by choosing Start ➤ All Programs ➤ Windows Media Player. By default, Windows Media Player starts on its Media Guide page, which is essentially a browser window that displays the latest news from the WindowsMedia.com Web site.

TIP *If you have used Windows Media Player in earlier Windows versions, you might be skeptical about the capabilities of Windows Media Player 8 (the Windows XP version). Don't be. It's a whole different program than it was in, say, Windows 98. Virtually everything has changed but the name.*

Figure 9.1 shows Windows Media Player in its Full mode, with a track playing. By default, the menu bar and window frame hide themselves automatically when Windows Media Player appears in a normal window (in other words, a window that's not maximized), giving Windows Media Player the irregular effect you see here. You can display the menu bar by moving the mouse pointer over the area it occupies or by clicking the Show Menu Bar button at the left end of the gray bar across the top of the window.

FIGURE 9.1

Windows Media Player 8, shown here in Full mode, rivals many of the best stand-alone media player applications available today.

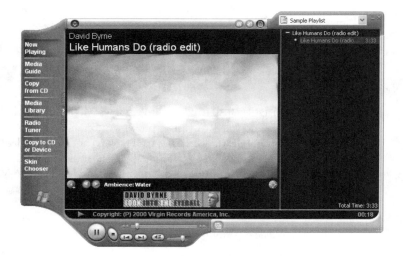

As you can see in Figure 9.1, Full mode takes up a serious chunk of a small screen, even when Windows Media Player isn't maximized and the menu bar and window frame are hidden. For sustained use, you'll be better off using Skin mode, shown in Figure 9.2.

FIGURE 9.2

In Skin mode, Windows Media Player occupies a more reasonable amount of your screen.

Using the Media Guide

When Windows Media Player starts, it goes immediately to the Media Guide tab. If you are connected to the Internet, it loads a start page from WindowsMedia.com containing hyperlinks to various music samples and libraries. You can explore this at your leisure. The content constantly changes.

Working with Player Controls

The player controls at the bottom of the Windows Media Player window are the same as on a cassette deck or audio CD player—you've got your standard Play, Pause, Stop buttons, plus buttons for skipping forward and back among tracks. The slider bar above them can be dragged to rewind or fast forward within the current track. See Figure 9.3.

FIGURE 9.3

The player controls are similar to those found on a home stereo system.

Working with Audio and Video Clips

One of the most common uses for Windows Media Player is to play audio or video clips you have stored on your hard drive. These could come from Internet sites, from audio CDs you have "ripped" (more on that later), or from other sources.

Cataloging Media Files on Your PC

Media Player can store a list of all the media clips on your PC, and display the list in the Media Library tab for easy selection and playback. If you click the Media Library tab before you have done an initial search, it prompts you to search for files. You can also manually initiate the search by doing the following:

1. Choose Tools ➤ Search for Media Files or press the F3 key.

2. In the Search for Media Files dialog box, specify which drives (and if necessary, which folders) to search, and choose any advanced search options needed.

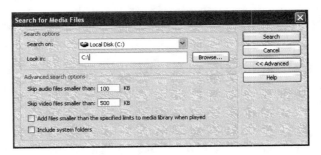

3. Click the Search button to start the search. If you have a hard drive of any size, the search takes a few minutes. Windows Media Player lists the files it found on the Media Library page.

WARNING   *The Media Library is shared with all other users of the computer, including the Guest user. Don't put anything in your Media Library that you don't want other users to see or hear.*

TIP   *In addition to searching for clips, you can also add individual clips. To do so, choose File ➤ Add to Media Library ➤ Add File. Then browse to locate the file and click Open.*

Playing Audio and Video Clips

Once you've let Windows Media Player discover the tracks that you have on your computer and list them in the Media Library, you can play any track by navigating to it and double-clicking it (or by selecting it and clicking the Play button).

There is no difference between audio and video clips as far as Windows Media Player is concerned; both show up in your Media Library, and both play the same way. With a video clip, however, you can change the brightness, contrast, hue, saturation, and size of the image. Choose View ➤ Now Playing Tools ➤ Video Settings and work with the resulting Video Settings tools.

You can also open a file by choosing File ➤ Open (or pressing Ctrl+O) to display the Open dialog box, navigating to and selecting the file, and clicking the Open button.

Creating Playlists

Playing audio files from disk is easy enough, but you can make it even easier by creating playlists of the audio files you like to play together.

To create a new playlist, follow these steps:

1. Click the New Playlist button on the Media Library page to open the New Playlist dialog box.

2. Enter the name for the playlist.

3. Click the OK button. Windows Media Player closes the New Playlist dialog box and creates a new playlist in the My Playlists list.

4. Populate the playlist by dragging tracks to it.

To play a playlist, double-click it on the Media Library page. To switch from one playlist to another, use the drop-down list in the upper-right corner of Windows Media Player.

TIP *Use the File ➤ Import Playlist to Media Library command to import playlists from other users or other PCs.*

Using the Graphic Equalizer and Sound Effects

Windows Media Player includes a minimalist graphic equalizer for improving the sound that emerges from your speakers or headphones. It's minimalist in that, although it comes with a number of preset equalizations and allows you to adjust 10 bands of frequency to your taste, it does not let you save your custom equalizations or load equalizations automatically with tracks.

The Graphic Equalizer appears on the Now Playing page of Windows Media Player when the Equalizer and Settings panel is displayed. If the Equalizer and Settings panel is not displayed, choose View ➤ Now Playing Tools ➤ Show Equalizer and Settings. Then choose View ➤ Now Playing Tools ➤ Graphic Equalizer to display the Graphic Equalizer if one of the other Now Playing tools is displayed. Figure 9.4 shows the Graphic Equalizer.

NOTE *You can also display the Graphic Equalizer by clicking the Previous Setting or Next Setting button on the Equalizer and Settings panel until it appears.*

FIGURE 9.4

Use the Graphic Equalizer to improve the sound of audio.

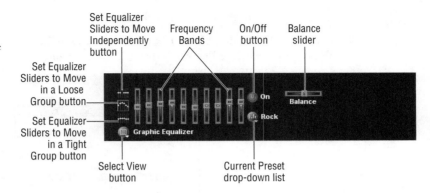

The graphic equalizer is straightforward to use.

◆ To turn the graphic equalizer on and off, click the On/Off button.

◆ To apply a preset equalization, choose it from the Current Preset drop-down list.

◆ To apply custom equalization, drag each frequency-band slider to an appropriate position. The frequency bands start with the lowest frequencies at the left side and progresses to the highest frequencies at the right side.

◆ To specify whether the frequency-band sliders move independently or together, click one of the three buttons on the control to the left of the frequency bands. Click the top button to make the sliders move independently. Click the middle button to make the sliders move together in a loose group. Click the bottom button to make the sliders move together in a tight group.

To apply sound effects, click the Select View button and choose SRS WOW Effects from the shortcut menu. Windows Media Player displays the SRS WOW Effects panel (shown in Figure 9.5). From here, you can use the On/Off button to turn the effects on and off, set bass boosting with the TruBass slider, set the WOW effect with the WOW Effect slider, or choose a different speaker setting.

FIGURE 9.5

Use the SRS WOW Effects panel to apply sound effects to audio.

Editing MP3 and WMA Tags

WMA files and MP3 files include a *tag*—a virtual container with slots for a number of pieces of information such as the artist's name, the track name, the album name, the genre, and so on. By using these tags, not only can you keep your music clearly identified, but you can also sort the tracks by any of the pieces of information. For example, you could sort tracks by artist or by album.

To edit the tag on an MP3 file, follow these steps:

1. In an Explorer window, right-click the file and choose Properties from the shortcut menu. Windows displays the Properties dialog box for the file.

2. Click the Summary tab.

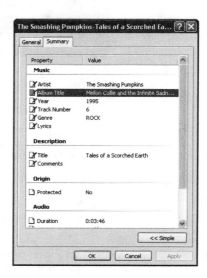

TIP *If the Summary tab is displaying an Advanced button, click it to display the Summary tab in Advanced view. Windows replaces the Advanced button with a Simple button that you can click to return to Simple view.*

3. Edit the tag information as appropriate. You can change any field that has a pen on its icon. You can't change fields such as Duration, Bitrate, and License.

4. Click the OK button. Windows applies the changes to the track's tag and closes the Properties dialog box for the file.

Setting Media Library Options

Choose Tools ➤ Options and click the Media Library tab to adjust media library settings. There are three crucial settings for keeping control of your Media Library, as you see in Figure 9.6. You may want to stay with the default settings, which are suitable for many people, but you should understand these options.

FIGURE 9.6

You can specify access rights to your media library in the Media Library tab of the Options dialog box.

Access Rights of Other Applications   The three option buttons in this group box control whether other programs installed on your computer can access your Media Library. The default setting is the Read-Only Access option button. This setting is useful if you want other programs to be able to read your Media Library (for example, if you use a jukebox other than Windows Media Player to play music sometimes) but not change it. If you want other programs to be able to change your Music Library, select the Full Access option. If you're sure none of your other programs will need to access your Media Library, select No Access.

Access Rights of Internet Sites   The three option buttons in this section control whether Internet sites can access your Media Library. The default setting is the No Access option button. Change this setting to the Read-Only Access option button only if you want Internet sites to be able to access your Media Library to collect information about the audio and video you have.

Media Files   Leave the Automatically Add Purchased Music to My Library check box selected if you want Windows Media Player to automatically add all the music you purchase via online download to your Media Library. This check box is selected by default, and leaving it selected is the easiest way to build your Music Library. If you don't want to add all the music you purchase to your Media Library, clear this check box. You can then add music to your Media Library manually after you purchase it.

On the File Types tab (shown in Figure 9.7) of the Options dialog box, you can select and clear check boxes to specify which file types Windows Media Player is associated with. For example, if Windows Media Player has associated itself with the MP3 file type, but you want to use another player for MP3 files, clear the MP3 Format Sound check box.

FIGURE 9.7

Use the File Types
tab of the Options
dialog box to specify
the file types to asso-
ciate with Windows
Media Player.

Working with Audio CDs and DVD Movies

In addition to playing stored audio and video clips, Windows Media Player can also read media content directly from audio CDs and DVD discs. You can also transfer the content of an audio CD to
your hard disk, in full or in part, for later playback when you don't have the CD handy.

Playing a CD

Unless you turn off Autoplay, Windows Media Player automatically starts playing an audio CD
you insert in your CD drive. If your computer is connected to the Internet, Windows Media Player
attempts to retrieve the CD information by submitting the CD's ID number to the `WindowsMedia.com`
database of information. (According to Microsoft, Windows Media Player doesn't submit any information about you other than the Globally Unique Identifier [GUID] and your IP address, which is
required to get the information about the CD back to your computer.)

If Windows Media Player doesn't automatically display the track names, or if it shows them as
Unknown Artist—Unknown Album, you'll need to retrieve them manually. Click the Get Names
button, and Windows Media Player leads you through a search for the artist and album. The process
is clumsy, but it works well enough if `WindowsMedia.com` has the artist and album listed.

Unfortunately, the `WindowsMedia.com` database isn't very complete at this writing—it's nothing
like as complete as CDDB, the online database of CD information (`www.cddb.org`). The CDDB is
widely used by MP3 rippers and contains impressively accurate information for a very wide range of
CDs. CDDB works in the same way as `WindowsMedia.com`: it uses the unique identifying code that
each commercially released audio CD contains. By submitting this code, a program can download the
CD information: artist name, CD name, and track titles. Most rippers handle this process automatically when you insert a CD.

NOTE *Part of CDDB's wide coverage of CDs is due to its receiving many entries from its users. If a CD you try to look up in CDDB doesn't have an entry, you can submit one. Many MP3 rippers have a built-in mechanism for submitting entries to CDDB.*

If the artist isn't listed, click the Not Found button. Windows Media Player displays a screen that lets you add the CD's information to your local database.

Copying (Ripping) a CD

Windows Media Player provides features for what it calls "copying" an audio CD to your hard drive. This doesn't mean copying each file on the CD bit for bit, but rather extracting the audio data from the CD (a process normally called *ripping*) and encoding it to a compressed format called Windows Media Audio (WMA).

As you probably know, CD-quality audio files are huge, taking up about 9MB per minute. (This is why about 74 minutes of audio fits on a 650-MB CD.) WMA files can be encoded at various bit rates, including the six bit rates that Windows Media Player offers: 48Kbps, 64Kbps, 96Kbps, 128Kbps, 160Kbps, and 192Kbps. Windows Media Player's default bit rate is 64Kbps. This bit rate sounds borderline-okay to many people and is good if you're trying to pack as much music as possible onto a portable device. But to make the files you copy sound good when you play them back on your PC, increase the bit rate to 128Kbps, 160Kbps, or 192Kbps—the higher the better, especially if you're likely to upgrade your sound card or your speakers before you change your taste in music.

Windows Media Player can encode to MP3 if you add a third-party codec. Click the MP3 Information button in the Copy Music tab of the Options dialog box to display an Internet Explorer window containing information on the MP3 Creation Pack for Windows XP and how to get it.

The first time you go to rip a CD with Windows Media Player, it displays the Windows Media Player dialog box shown in Figure 9.8. This dialog box tells you that Windows Media Player is configured to protect your content from "unauthorized use" and that you won't be able to play content that's protected like this on any computer other than this one.

FIGURE 9.8

This Windows Media Player dialog box lets you turn off copy music protection if you claim to understand that the content you're copying is protected by law.

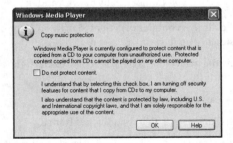

This restriction makes a lot of sense for Microsoft, because it prevents you from violating copyright law in one important way: by preventing you from using illegal copies of these tracks. (See the next sidebar for an explanation of what you can and cannot legally do with digital audio.)

But it doesn't protect you from violating copyright law in one important way: by borrowing a CD from someone else and copying it, or by lending someone one of your CDs so that they can copy it.

If you're fine with this restriction, click the OK button. If you're not, select the Do Not Protect Content check box to disable the protection, and then click the OK button. This means that you'll be able to use the files you copy on other PCs. It also means that you can commit extra copyright violations either intentionally or unintentionally.

WHAT CAN YOU LEGALLY DO WITH DIGITAL AUDIO?

If you're going to enjoy digital audio, you need to know what you can and cannot do with it. Here's what you can legally do:

- Listen to streaming audio from a Web site or an Internet radio station, even if the site or person streaming the audio is doing so illegally.

- Record audio from a medium you own (for example, a CD) to a different medium (for example, a cassette) so you can listen to it at a different time or in a different place.

- Download a digital file that contains copyrighted material from a Web site or FTP site provided that the copyright holder has granted the distributor permission to distribute it.

- Download a digital file from a computer via P2P technology (for example, Napster, audioGnome, or Gnutella) provided that the copyright holder has granted the distributor permission to distribute it.

- Create digital-audio files (for example, WMA files or MP3 files) of tracks on CDs you own for your personal use.

- Distribute a digital-audio file to which you hold the copyright or for whose distribution the copyright holder has granted you permission.

- Download (or copy) MP3 files or other supported digital-audio files to portable audio devices (such as the Diamond Rio or the Creative Labs Nomad).

- Broadcast licensed audio across the Internet.

Here are some of the key things that you cannot legally do with audio:

- Download a digital-audio file that contains copyrighted material if the copyright holder has not granted the distributor permission to distribute it.

- Distribute a digital-audio file that contains copyrighted material if the copyright holder has not granted you permission to distribute it.

- Lend a friend a CD so she can create digital-audio files from it.

- Borrow a CD from a friend and create digital-audio files from it.

- Upload digital-audio files from a portable audio player that supports music uploading, such as the I-JAM or the eGo, to another computer. (In this scenario, you're essentially using the portable player to copy the files from one computer to another.)

To copy a CD, follow these general steps:

1. Load the CD in your CD drive.

2. If Windows Media Player starts playing the CD, stop it.

3. Click the Copy from CD tab. Windows displays the CD Audio page.

4. If Windows Media Player doesn't automatically retrieve the CD information, use the Get Names feature to retrieve the information manually. (If necessary, type in the information.)

5. If necessary, edit the information retrieved. You can edit any of the changeable fields (such as the track names, the artist's name, or the genre) by clicking the field twice (with a pause in between—*not* double-clicking). Windows Media Player displays an edit box around the field. Type the correction and press the Enter key.

6. If necessary, change (or check) the Copy Music at This Quality slider setting in the Copy Music tab of the Options dialog box.

7. Select the check boxes for the tracks you want to copy. Use the check box in the column header to change the status of all the individual check boxes at once.

8. Click the Copy Music button. Windows Media Player starts ripping the music, adding the tracks to the Media Library when they're finished.

If you notice a problem, click the Stop Copy button to stop copying the tracks.

Setting Copying Options

The Copy Music tab of the Options dialog box (shown in Figure 9.9) contains four options that control the "copying" of music from CDs to your hard drive. To display it, choose Tools ➤ Options and click the Copy Music tab.

These options are largely set-and-forget, though you may want to use different music quality settings for different CDs that you copy.

FIGURE 9.9

The Copy Music tab of the Options dialog box

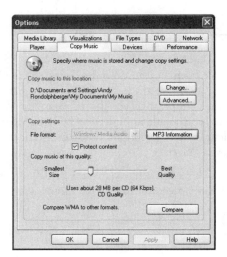

These are the options:

Copy Music to This Location This section contains a label that shows the folder to which Windows Media Player copies music. The default location is your My Music folder, in which Windows Media Player creates folders by artist and, within these, folders by album name. To change the location, click the Change button, use the resulting Browse for Folder dialog box to navigate to and select the location, and then click the OK button. By default, Windows Media Player names the files by track number and track name—for example, 01 Clock without Hands.WMA. To change the naming, click the Advanced button and work in the resulting File Name Options dialog box (shown in Figure 9.10). Select the check boxes for the items you want to include in the filename (track number, song title, artist, album, and so on). Use the Move Up button and Move Down button to shuffle the selected items into order. And use the Separator drop-down list to specify which separator character to use: None, a space, a dash, a dot, or an underline. Then click the OK button. Windows Media Player closes the File Name Options dialog box and applies your choices.

NOTE *Windows Media Player shares the Media Library among all users, so you don't need to use the Shared Documents folder to share music with other users of the computer.*

FIGURE 9.10

Use the File Name Options dialog box to customize the name format that Windows Media Player uses for tracks you copy.

Copy Settings In the File Format drop-down list, select the file format you want to use for the files: Windows Media or MP3. (See the next sidebar for details on how Windows Media and MP3 stack up to each other.) In practice, you'll need to use the Windows Media format for any high-quality recordings unless you add a third-party MP3 encoder to Windows. (If you do add a third-party MP3 encoder, you may well prefer to use its interface for ripping and encoding rather than using Windows Media Player.)

Leave the Protect Content check box selected (as it is by default) if you want to use Windows Media Player's features for personal licensing for CD tracks you copy. See the previous sidebar for a discussion of the advantages and disadvantages of using this feature. Clear this check box if you want more flexibility in what you can do with WMA files.

Use the Copy Music at This Quality slider to specify the quality at which to encode the files you copy. Windows Media Player offers six bit rates (48Kbps, 64Kbps, 96Kbps, 128Kbps, 160Kbps, and 192Kbps) graded from Smallest Size (48Kbps) to Best Quality (192Kbps). Higher bit rates take up more space but sound better. Experiment with this setting on a variety of music and find the bit rate that suits you best:

◆ If you have plenty of hard-disk space for the music you want to copy, choose the 192-Kbps bit rate as a hedge against getting a better sound card or speakers in the future.

◆ If you want to use the files with a portable player with limited memory, use the lowest bit rate that sounds good on the player.

◆ Microsoft describes the 64-Kbps bit rate as "CD Quality." This is optimistic enough to qualify as deluded in most people's terms.

How Do MP3 and WMA Stack Up to Each Other?

Audiophiles, gearheads, and Microsoft-haters have had a long-running argument about whether MP3 or WMA is better. Impressive amounts of research have been done by interested parties, but the resulting articles and papers have drawn such diametrically opposed conclusions that you'd be forgiven for dismissing them all as propaganda. The argument tends to get polarized into a holy war, and neither the crusaders nor the infidels (or heretics, depending on your point of view) have a monopoly on fact, reason, or logic. In fact, each side often seems to have at best a tenuous grasp on all three. If you want to see Microsoft's side of the story, click the Compare button in the Copy Music tab of the Options dialog box.

To really appreciate the nuances of the different sides of the argument, you need to understand a bit about how audio compression works. If you could bear to know some more, try reading *MP3 Complete*, also published by Sybex.

In the meantime, though, you no doubt want some sensible advice. That's easy enough, because from a lay point of view, the situation is very simple. Here's what you need to know:

◆ Even at the highest quality settings they offer, and on the best equipment, neither MP3 nor WMA sounds quite as good as CD-quality audio, which is uncompressed and uses a comprehensive range of samples across the whole area of audio frequencies audible to the human ear. This is because each format uses *lossy* compression to reduce the size of the audio files. As you'd guess from its name, lossy compression involves discarding data from the original in order to compress it. (The opposite of lossy compression is *lossless* compression, which essentially involves squeezing files in such a way that they can be re-expanded to a copy that contains the same information as the original. ZIP files use lossless compression, so the files you extract from a ZIP file are functionally identical to their originals though not actually the same file.)

Continued on next page

HOW DO MP3 AND WMA STACK UP TO EACH OTHER? *(continued)*

◆ Unless you've got amazing ears, very good hi-fi, or perhaps both, the advantages of compression out-weigh the disadvantages. In a nutshell, compressed files are small enough to store in large numbers on computers, to carry in small numbers on ultraportable players, and to transfer easily via removable media, networks, or the Internet.

◆ MP3 and WMA use different encoding methods, but the results are roughly comparable in quality.

◆ MP3 is a more widely used file format than WMA. A wide variety of software MP3 players are available for every conceivable computing platform, and you can get hardware MP3 players in an impressive variety of shapes and sizes. Many software MP3 players and some hardware MP3 players can handle WMA files as well as MP3 files.

◆ In June 2001, Thomson Multimedia (www.thomson-multimedia.com) released a demo version of mp3PRO, a new version of MP3 that delivers better sound quality than MP3 at lower bit rates. mp3PRO is more expensive to license than other MP3 encoders, so it's hard to say how quickly or widely it will be integrated into MP3 solutions—but at this writing, it seems a promising technology.

Whether you choose MP3, WMA, or another format will probably boil down to what you want to do with digital audio, how high your standards are, and how much time, effort, and money you're prepared to invest.

If all you want to do is rip your CDs and store them on your hard disk so that you can play them back from your computer, Windows Media Player and WMA provide an effective solution. Choose a bit rate that delivers satisfactory audio quality through your sound card and speakers, slot the first CD, and you're away. In this case, it may be a good idea to use Windows' licensing features, because they ensure that you can't inadvertently break the law by using the files on another computer. (You can transfer them to another computer, but because it doesn't have the right license information, it won't be able to play them.)

If you want to use digital audio on a portable player, WMA may not be such a suitable choice. Although an increasing number of portable digital-audio players do support WMA as well as MP3, many do not. Even for those players that do support WMA, you may find that MP3 provides more options or simply easier administration. For example, to use WMA files on a portable player that doesn't support the SDMI (Secure Digital Music Initiative) specification, you'll need to turn off Windows Media Player's licensing features; by contrast, with MP3 files, you don't need to worry about digital licenses.

In that same Options dialog box, you'll also find a Devices tab (Figure 9.11). It lets you configure your CD and DVD drives for playing back and copying CDs and any portable devices for downloading tracks from Windows Media Player.

To set properties for a CD drive or DVD drive, select it in the Devices list box and click the Properties button. Windows Media Player displays the Properties dialog box for the drive. Figure 9.12 shows an example of the Properties dialog box for a DVD drive.

FIGURE 9.11

The Devices tab of the Options dialog box lists your CD drives, DVD drives, and portable devices.

FIGURE 9.12

Use the Properties dialog box for a DVD drive or CD drive to specify whether to use analog or digital audio for playback and copying.

In the Playback section and the Copy section, choose between the Digital option button and the Analog option button. Digital audio extraction is preferable to analog audio extraction because it maintains a higher-fidelity signal. The main reason not to use digital audio extraction is if your CD drive does not support it or cannot deliver it successfully. If you choose digital audio extraction, you can select the Use Error Correction check box if you want Windows Media Player to use its error-correction features to try to remove errors that occur during playback or copying. Error correction uses a bit more CPU power than regular playback or copying; it slows down copying considerably; and its effect is often undetectable. You may want to try playing your CDs without error correction and turn it on only if you hear odd noises in the playback. Unless you have a savage degree of impatience encoded in your chromosomes, it's a good idea to use error correction for copying music, because any defects in the copied tracks tend to be much more annoying than spending a few extra minutes copying each CD.

NOTE   *If Windows Media Player finds, when you insert a CD, that your CD drive doesn't support digital playback, it displays a message telling you so and warning you that visualizations, the graphic equalizer, and SRS WOW (Sound Retrieval System WOW) will not work. Windows Media Player then switches to analog mode.*

Click the OK button. Windows Media Player closes the Properties dialog box for the CD drive.

Playing a DVD

Once you've installed a DVD drive and a DVD player, you can play a DVD by putting it in the drive and choosing Play ➤ DVD or CD Audio. Windows Media Player uses the standard Play controls for DVDs and displays a list of the DVD chapters in the playlist area.

NOTE   *If you have a DVD drive but no player for it, consult the DVD Troubleshooter for details of compatible players.*

To make the most of your DVDs, you'll probably want to view them full-screen. To do so, choose View ➤ Full Screen or press Alt+Enter. Windows Media Player switches to full-screen view. You can display pop-up controls on screen by moving the mouse. These disappear after a few seconds when you stop moving the mouse.

To display DVD controls (such as a Variable Play Speed control and a Next Frame control), choose View ➤ Now Playing Tools ➤ DVD Controls.

Choose Tools ➤ Options to set properties for the DVD player feature. The DVD tab offers these options (see Figure 9.13):

FIGURE 9.13

If you have a DVD drive, you can choose parental control and language settings on the DVD tab of the Options dialog box.

Parental Control   To implement parental control on DVDs played on the computer, select the Parental Control check box and use the Select a Rating drop-down list to specify the rating to apply.

Language Settings   Use the Subtitles drop-down list to specify whether you want subtitles and, if so, in which language. Use the Audio drop-down list and the Menu drop-down list to specify the language to use for movie audio and on-screen menus. The default setting for these two controls is Title Default, which gives you the primary language with which the DVD was encoded.

You won't see a DVD tab in the Options dialog box if you do not have a DVD drive and the needed support software for it installed.

If your video playback in Windows Media Player is unsatisfactory, you can try making adjustments to the Video Acceleration setting. On the Performance tab, drag the Video Acceleration slider to improve the speed or smoothness.

For further video acceleration settings, click the Advanced button on the Performance tab. Windows Media Player displays the Video Acceleration Settings dialog box (shown in Figure 9.14). The key settings here are the Digital Video slider, which adjusts the size of the picture and the Display Full-Screen Controls check boxes in the Video Acceleration section and the DVD Video section. The Enable Full-Screen Mode Switch check box, which is cleared by default, attempts to expand the video image for viewing at full-screen size in full-screen mode. This capability typically doesn't work with digital video. The Digital Video (DV) slider (which, as its name suggests, works only for digital video, not for analog video) kicks in when you expand the Windows Media Player window to a larger size than the original video and Windows Media Player needs to stretch the video to fit. The Large setting allows Windows Media Player to interpolate (add) pixels that are not in the original video in order to stretch the picture. The Small setting keeps the video more faithful to the original but requires more CPU power. For best results, experiment with this setting.

If you have both hardware and software DVD decoders installed, you'll be able to choose the Hardware option button or the Software option button in the Preferred Decoder area. Click the OK button. Windows Media Player closes the Video Acceleration Settings dialog box.

FIGURE 9.14

Choose further video settings in the Video Acceleration Settings dialog box. If you don't have a DVD drive and a decoder, you won't see the DVD Video section of the dialog box.

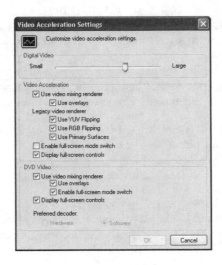

Tuning into Internet Radio

Windows Media Player provides good features for tuning into Internet radio—radio broadcast across the Web via streaming audio servers such as SHOUTcast, icecast, or RealAudio. To listen to Internet radio, click the Radio Tuner tab to display the Radio Tuner page. Figure 9.15 shows the Radio Tuner page with a station playing.

FIGURE 9.15

Use Windows Media Player's Radio Tuner page to listen to radio stations broadcasting across the Internet.

Connecting to an Internet Radio Station

The easiest way to connect to a radio station is to use a preset. Windows Media Player comes with a number of presets built in. You can edit these and create your own presets as you want.

To listen to a preset station, select the category of presets in the Featured Stations drop-down list. Then click the preset you want to listen to. Windows Media Player displays information about the station. Click the Play link.

Windows Media Player displays the message *Connecting to media* while it is connecting to the radio station. Next, it displays the word *Buffering* and a percentage-completed readout as it fills the buffer for the signal. When buffering is complete, Windows Media Player starts playing the station.

NOTE *Windows Media Player sometimes needs to download a codec (a coder/decoder) in order to play back a station. Some codecs may take a minute or two to download—so if you're planning to listen to a broadcast on a station you haven't accessed before, allow time for a codec download. Depending on the settings you've chosen for Windows Media Player, installing a codec may well raise a Security Warning dialog box. Check the publisher's digital certificate if you're in any doubt about the authenticity of the codec.*

Windows Media Player displays a browser window containing information about the radio station. Use this window to learn more about the station and its programming. But if you're listening to radio over a dial-up connection, you may find that this window is taking up bandwidth, especially if it's slow to load or if it runs tickers or animations. If this is happening, close the window so that it doesn't take bandwidth from the signal.

TIP *If you have problems with long pauses while an Internet radio station plays, try adjusting the connection speed and/or network buffering settings. Choose Tools ➤ Options, and then adjust them in the Performance tab.*

Searching for a Radio Station

You can browse for a radio station by following the category links (Country, '80s, Adult Contemporary, and so on) under the Find More Stations heading. Alternatively, click the Find More Stations link and use the screen shown in Figure 9.16 to search by keyword or zip code.

FIGURE 9.16

You can browse for a radio station by genre or search by keyword or zip code.

You can also perform an advanced search. To do so, click the Use Advanced Search link to display the Advanced Search dialog box (shown in Figure 9.17). Specify whichever criteria you want—Genre, Language, Country, State (in the U.S. only), Speed, Band (AM, FM, or the Net), or Keyword, Call Sign, or Frequency—and click the Search button to locate stations that match.

FIGURE 9.17

Use the Advanced Search panel to use multiple criteria in your search for a radio station.

Creating and Editing Presets

You can edit your presets by changing the My Stations list as you need. You cannot change the Featured Stations list.

To add a station to your My Stations list, expand its heading and click its Add to My Stations link.

To remove a station from your My Stations list, expand its heading in the My Stations list and choose Remove from My Stations.

To change the order in which Windows Media Player lists the stations in your My Stations list, use the red up arrow and down arrow buttons to move a station up or down the list.

Applying Skins

You can apply *skins* (custom graphical looks) to Windows Media Player to change its appearance in Skin mode. Windows Media Player comes with a selection of skins built in. To apply a skin, display the Skin Chooser page of Windows Media Player. Select a skin in the list box to see how it looks.

When you find one you like, click the Apply Skin button to apply it. You can also apply a skin quickly by double-clicking its file in an Explorer window or on your Desktop.

To download extra skins, click the More Skins button on the Skin Chooser page. Windows Media Player opens a browser window of the appropriate page of the WindowsMedia.com Web site, which maintains a gallery of skins, some created by Microsoft and others by users. (You'll also find skins in online software archives such as CNET's Download.com, but WindowsMedia.com is a good place to start.)

When you download a skin package, Windows displays the Windows Media Download dialog box. From this, you can click the View Now button to display the skin or the Close button to dismiss the dialog box.

NOTE *Windows Media Player skins can have the file type Windows Media Player Skin File and the WMS extension, but you'll usually find them compressed into files of the Windows Media Player Skin Package file type. These have the WMZ extension.*

To delete a skin from Windows Media Player, select it in the list box and click the Delete button; then click the Yes button in the Confirm Skin Delete dialog box that Windows Media Player displays.

You can create your own custom skins for Windows Media Player. To do so, download the Windows Media Player Software Development Kit from the Microsoft Web site and follow the tutorials on the Microsoft Developer Network (MSDN; `msdn.microsoft.com/workshop/imedia/windowsmedia/wmpskins.asp`). When you've created a skin, store it in the `Program Files\Windows Media Player\Skins` folder, and Windows Media Player will automatically list it on the Skin Chooser page.

Choosing Visualizations

When it's playing audio, Windows Media Player shows visualizations (graphical displays) on the Now Playing page.

To toggle a visualization to full screen, press Alt+Enter or choose View ➤ Full Screen. Press the Esc key (or Alt+Enter again) to toggle off full screen.

To change the visualization, choose View ➤ Visualizations and make a choice from the Ambience, Bars and Waves, Particle, Plenoptic, or Spikes submenu.

You can also set options for visualizations by choosing Tools ➤ Options and clicking the Visualizations tab (see Figure 9.18). Here you can choose the visualization collection to use for enhancing your listening pleasure.

Some visualizations have properties that you can set by selecting the entry in the list box and clicking the Properties button to display a Properties dialog box.

You can add other visualizations that you've downloaded by clicking the Add button, using the resulting Open dialog box to identify the visualizations file, and clicking the Open button.

You can remove some visualizations by selecting them and clicking the Remove button. Other visualizations are built-in and wish to remain so.

FIGURE 9.18

Choose a visualization collection on the Visualizations tab of the Options dialog box.

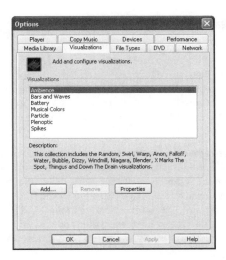

Backing Up and Restoring Licenses

If you download tracks secured with digital licenses, or if you use digital licenses on tracks you copy to disk, back up your licenses in case you have disk trouble. Should you lose the licenses, you won't be able to play the tracks.

DIGITAL RIGHTS MANAGEMENT AND LICENSES

Being able to store audio and video in digital format on a PC, play them back easily, and even transfer them via the Internet or removable media is great for consumers of audio and video content. But it can be way less than great for creators of audio and video content: These computer capabilities pose a severe threat to their livelihoods by compromising their copyrighted works and robbing them of sales.

In the past, audio and video works have largely been distributed on physical media, such as CDs, cassettes, LPs, video cassettes, and DVDs. The tangible nature and physical presence of such media generally makes it clear when a theft has occurred: Physical media can't walk out of stores by themselves. Making unauthorized copies of a work distributed on a physical medium such as a videotape involves cost (for the media, for the copies, and for any duplicating equipment needed), time (typically real-time copying), and effort. Distributing those copies involves further cost, time, and effort. And the illegality of such pirated works is widely known (and recognized, if not exactly appreciated): most consumers are aware that it's illegal to distribute (let alone sell) copies of copyrighted works. Besides, copies of works on analog media (such as videotape or audiotape) are lower fidelity than the originals, so the inauthenticity of late-generation copies is clear.

Continued on next page

DIGITAL RIGHTS MANAGEMENT AND LICENSES *(continued)*

By contrast, any work stored in a digital medium accessible by a PC can be copied in seconds at almost zero cost, and the copies are perfect every time. These perfect copies can be distributed via the Internet, again at negligible cost. And they can be distributed in quantities and over distances unthinkable for physical media. For example, if someone buys a CD in Sioux Falls, makes MP3 files of its tracks, and makes them available on a file-sharing service such as GnutellaNet or Freenet, anyone with Internet connectivity anywhere in the world—from Vladivostok to Tierra del Fuego, from Juneau to Java—can download them and then distribute them further.

At this writing, there are several technologies intended to protect the rights of content creators (and their authorized distributors) while allowing consumers to use the content. For example, most DVDs use an encryption system called Content Scrambling System (CSS), which requires an encryption key in order to be decoded. CSS keys were licensed and tightly controlled by the DVD-Copy Control Association (DVD-CCA)—tightly controlled, that is, until Norwegian hackers in the LiVid (Linux Video group) created a utility called DeCSS by reverse engineering some unencrypted code they discovered in a sloppily constructed software DVD player. Now that DeCSS is widely available, CSS-encrypted content can be deciphered by anyone who has the code.

Perhaps the most promising of the technologies designed to protect content is the digital license. A digital license is encrypted information that links a particular copy of a downloaded work to a particular computer or individual. For example, in the current model of digital licenses for audio, if you download a track that uses a digital license, you buy or are otherwise granted a license to play the track on the computer on which you downloaded it. If you transfer the track to another computer, it won't play, because the computer lacks the necessary license information.

So far, so good. But in order to be viable enough to become widely accepted, digital licenses need not only to be easy and intuitive to use but also compatible with both generally used technology and with the prevailing laws. For example, the First Sale Doctrine laid out in the Copyright Act allows consumers to sell or give a copy they've legitimately acquired of a copyrighted work to another person. Any copyright-protection technology that prevents consumers from doing this effectively (for example, because any subsequent recipient would not be able to view or listen to the work because it was locked by encryption and a non-transferable license to the first purchaser's computer) would be open to heavy-duty legal challenges.

Leaving aside such details for the moment, digital licenses are now being used to secure some copyrighted content. Windows Media Player adopts a two-pronged approach to digital licenses for audio content, supporting digital licenses for both tracks you buy and download and tracks you copy from CD. Windows Media Player automatically issues a license for each track you copy from a CD (unless you set it to copy tracks without licensing them).

At this writing, Windows Media Player lets you choose whether to use digital licenses or to be free, easy, and possibly illegal. As long as you use those tracks on the PC with which you created them, there's no problem with using licenses. But if you want to be able to play the tracks from another computer, you've got a problem, because the license ties the associated digital media file to the PC for which the license is issued: you'll need to acquire a new license or transfer a license from the original computer. Similarly, you may not be able to download a copy of a licensed track to a portable player with licensing gymnastics.

Continued on next page

DIGITAL RIGHTS MANAGEMENT AND LICENSES *(continued)*

Now, simply *playing* a track from another computer should be fine, legally, because it's the same file that you created from the CD. So should be moving the track to another computer that belongs to you and using it on that computer. Only if you create an illegal copy of the track—and particularly if you distribute it—should there be a problem. More on this later in the chapter, but you can see that the implementation of digital licenses tends to be problematic, partly because of the nature of the beast and partly because of the assumption of those who implemented the technology that anything unlicensed will tend to be licentious. There's no good reason for using digital licenses for the tracks you copy from CD unless you can't trust yourself (or other users of your computer) not to take illegal actions with them.

If you choose to use digital licenses for the tracks you copy from CD and the tracks you purchase and download (or download for free), you need to back up your licenses in case you lose them and need to restore them. If your computer crashes, if you reinstall Windows, or if you install another operating system, you'll need to restore your licenses in order to be able to use the tracks.

License files are small, so you can store a good number of them on a floppy disk. If you're not good at keeping your floppy disks in order, or if you want to protect them against local or natural disasters, back them up to an Internet drive instead.

Backing Up Your Licenses

To back up your licenses, follow these steps:

1. Choose Tools ➤ License Management. Windows Media Player displays the License Management dialog box:

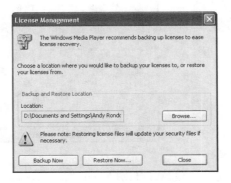

2. Check the folder indicated in the Location text box. If necessary, click the Browse button and use the resulting Browse for Folder dialog box to specify a different folder.

TIP   *For safety, keep the backup on a removable medium, or make a copy of it on an online drive.*

3. Click the Backup Now button. Windows Media Player closes the first License Management dialog box, copies the licenses, and displays the second License Management dialog box:

4. Click the OK button. Windows Media Player closes the second License Management dialog box.

Restoring Your Licenses

To restore your licenses from backup, follow these steps:

1. Choose Tools ➤ License Management. Windows Media Player displays the License Management dialog box.

2. Click the Restore Now button. Windows Media Player displays the License Management dialog box, warning you that the restoration needs Internet access and that Windows Media Player will send your GUID to a Microsoft service.

3. Click the OK button. Windows Media Player contacts the Microsoft site for authorization. If it receives authorization, Windows Media Player copies the licenses and displays the License Management dialog box to let you know the operation has succeeded.

4. Click the OK button. Windows Media Player closes the License Management dialog box.

Working with Portable Devices

Windows Media Player can help you copy audio files to a portable digital audio device. Use the Copy to CD or Device tab to transfer the desired files.

TIP   Most portable devices come with effective software for loading tracks and playlists onto them. Because this software is specifically designed for the portable device, it may offer enhancements that Windows Media Player does not. However, some portable device software packages cannot rip, encode, and load to the portable device in one move, as Windows Media Player can with some of the players it supports.

Making Media Player Recognize Your Device

Media Player will automatically recognize a wide variety of portable devices, so this may not be an issue for you. When you plug in your portable device (usually to a USB port), go to the Copy to CD or Device tab and press F5 to refresh the device list. Then open the Music on Device drop-down list to see whether your device is listed. If it is, select it and you're ready to go. If it doesn't appear on that list, try the following steps to make it noticed:

1. Choose Tools ➢ Options and click the Devices tab.

2. Click the Add button. Windows Media Player opens an Internet Explorer window to the WindowsMedia.com site, which maintains a list of compatible devices and links to the software you can download to make the devices agree with Windows Media Player.

3. Scroll down the Web page to the Driver Downloads section and click the hyperlink for the device you have. If your device is already supported, *Included in Windows XP* will appear next to the device name instead of a hyperlink.

Copying Audio Files to a Portable Player

TIP   You might want to create a playlist containing the files you want to copy to the portable device. If you don't, you'll need to wade through the full list of audio clips to find the files you want.

To copy files to a portable player, follow these steps:

1. Click the Copy to CD or Device tab.

2. Make sure your portable device is plugged in and recognized by Windows XP. (See the preceding section.)

3. In the Music to Copy pane, open the drop-down list and select the source location. If you want to copy from a particular playlist, select it. Otherwise select a musical category or select All Audio.

4. Clear the checkmark from any files you don't want to copy to the device. If you're working with a large list, you might find it easier to click the checkmark at the top of the Music to Copy pane to clear the checkmarks from all entries and then manually select each item you do want.

5. The status for each item will be Ready to Copy. If you select more clips than will fit, some clips will report May Not Fit as the status; deselect clips until none of them display this message. See Figure 9.19.

6. Click the Copy Music button. The clips are copied to the portable device.

When you are tired of those clips and want to delete them from the portable device, you can either use the controls on the device itself or do it through Windows Media Player. To delete through Media Player, simply display the contents of the device on the Copy to CD or Device tab and press the Delete key.

FIGURE 9.19

Select clips to copy to the portable device; keep an eye on the Status column to determine how many will fit.

Setting Media Player Options

There are a few general-purpose Media Player options we haven't looked at yet. Choose Tools ➤ Options and click the Player tab (Figure 9.20) to work with them:

Automatic Updates Select the Once a Month option button (unless you want Windows Media Player to prompt you to upgrade more frequently). Leave the Download Codecs Automatically check box selected (as it is by default) if you want Windows Media Player to download and install any new codecs it needs to play back audio streams or files. Clear this check box if you prefer to have Windows Media Player prompt you before it installs new codecs.

TIP You can force Windows Media Player to check for updates by choosing Help ➤ Check for Player Updates, and then following the Windows Media Component Setup process that ensues.

Internet Settings The Allow Internet Sites to Uniquely Identify Your Player check box sounds like it's threatening to broadcast your personal information all over the Web. In fact, this check box controls whether Windows Media Player passes an identifier to streaming media servers to enable the servers to monitor the connection and adjust the stream to improve playback quality. For best quality of streaming audio, leave this check box selected, as it is by default. The Acquire Licenses Automatically check box controls whether Windows Media Player tries to automatically get a license when a file requires one. (See the sidebar on digital rights management and licenses for a discussion of licenses.)

Player Settings   Choose whether to start the player on the Media Guide page, whether to display the player always on top in Skin mode, whether to display the anchor window (a small reference window) when the player is in Skin mode, and whether to let the Windows screen saver kick in while music or video is playing back. The anchor window is more or less useless, but having the player always on top makes it easy to access. The screen saver seldom improves playback, even of music: visualizations provide better entertainment. Select the Add Items to Media Library when Played check box if you want Windows Media Player to add new tracks to the Media Library when you play them. If you select this check box, you get the choice of selecting the Include Items from Removable Media check box, which controls whether Windows adds tracks from removable media such as CDs or removable disks to the Media Library. (This isn't usually a good idea.)

FIGURE 9.20

The Player tab
of the Options
dialog box

Setting Output Volume and Recording Volume

As you saw earlier in the chapter, you can adjust the output volume by moving the Volume slider in Windows Media Player. If you prefer, you can put a Volume control in the notification area so that it's always at your mouse-tips even when Windows Media Player or your other favorite noisemaker is minimized or hidden behind other windows.

This section starts by showing you how to do that. It then covers the Volume Control program that Windows provides for controlling output volume and recording volume, adjusting the sound balance, choosing input and output, and so on.

Displaying the Volume Control in the Notification Area

For immediate access to a volume control, you can put one in the notification area. Follow these steps:

1. Choose Start ➤ Control Panel to open Control Panel.

2. Click the Sounds, Speech, and Audio Devices link.

3. In the Pick a Task list, click the Adjust the System Volume link. Control Panel displays the Volume tab of the Sounds and Audio Devices Properties dialog box:

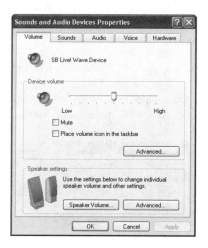

4. Select the Place Volume Icon in the Taskbar check box.

5. Click the OK button. Windows closes the Sounds and Audio Devices Properties dialog box and displays the Volume control in the notification area.

TIP   By default, Windows applies its default notification-area behavior to the Volume control: Hide When Inactive. You'll probably want to change the Volume control's behavior to Always Show so that it's always available.

To set the volume, click the Volume control. Windows displays a pop-up panel bearing a Volume slider and a Mute check box. Drag the slider up and down to set the volume. Windows emits a Ding chord when you release the slider so that you can hear the approximate loudness of that volume. Click anywhere other than the pop-up panel to make the panel disappear.

When you mute the sound by selecting the Mute check box on the pop-up panel, Windows displays a red circle and bar beside the Volume control as a visual reminder.

You can double-click the Volume control, or right-click it and choose Open Volume Control from the shortcut menu, to display the Play Control dialog box. And you can right-click the Volume control and choose Adjust Audio Properties from the shortcut menu to display the Volume tab of the Sounds and Audio Devices Properties dialog box.

Setting Volume from the Sounds and Audio Devices Properties Dialog Box

If you seldom need to change the volume being output by your computer (for example, if you have a physical volume control strapped to your keyboard or elsewhere within reach), you probably won't want to waste notification area space on the Volume control. Instead, you can use the Device Volume slider on the Volume tab of the Sounds and Audio Devices Properties dialog box to set the volume and the Mute check box to mute the sound.

Setting Speaker Balance

To set speaker balance on the signal output by your sound card (as opposed to setting it via your amplifier), click the Speaker Volume button in the Speaker Settings section in the Sounds and Audio Devices Properties dialog box. Windows displays the Speaker Volume dialog box (shown in Figure 9.21). Drag the sliders to suitable positions; select the Move All Slide Indicators at the Same Time check box if you want synchronized sliding. Then click the OK button. Windows closes the Speaker Volume dialog box.

FIGURE 9.21

You can set speaker balance on your sound card's output by using the Speaker Volume dialog box.

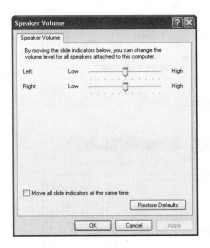

Setting Advanced Audio Properties

Beyond the speaker balance settings, Windows also offers advanced audio settings. You can specify your speaker layout, the degree of hardware acceleration to use on audio playback, and the sample rate conversion quality to use.

To choose advanced audio settings, click the Advanced button in the Speaker Settings section on the Volume tab of the Sounds and Audio Devices Properties dialog box. Windows displays the Advanced Audio Properties dialog box.

The Speakers tab of the Advanced Audio Properties dialog box (shown in Figure 9.22) contains only one setting: the Speaker Setup drop-down list. Choose the appropriate option for your speakers or headphones. Your choices range from Desktop Stereo Speakers through to 7.1 Surround Sound Speakers (seven satellites and a subwoofer).

The Performance tab of the Advanced Audio Properties dialog box (shown in Figure 9.23) contains two settings:

Hardware Acceleration   Drag this slider to set the amount of hardware acceleration you want to use. On most computers, it's best to start with full acceleration and decrease it only if your computer exhibits audio problems.

Sample Rate Conversion Quality   Drag this slider to choose a balance between audio quality and CPU usage. Windows starts you off with a setting of Good. Try improving this, and reduce it only if your computer's performance suffers.

FIGURE 9.22

Specify your speaker setup on the Speakers tab of the Advanced Audio Properties dialog box.

FIGURE 9.23

Choose audio performance settings on the Performance tab of the Advanced Audio Properties dialog box.

Click the OK button. Windows closes the Advanced Audio Properties dialog box.

Using the Volume Control Program

The Volume Control program provides close control over audio output and input.

Volume Control can initially be confusing for several reasons:

◆ First, the window in which it appears isn't even called Volume Control. (See the next objection.)

◆ Second, Volume Control has separate manifestations for output and input. Depending on the sound card installed on your computer, you'll see different names for each. For example, with most Sound Blaster cards, the output manifestation of Volume Control appears as a window named Play Control, and the input manifestation appears as a window named Record Control. With other sound cards, you'll see other names, such as Master Out (which offers assorted BDSM interpretations we shouldn't consider here) and Recording Control.

◆ Third, Volume Control hides Advanced options until you force it to display them.

◆ And fourth, the set of controls that Volume Control displays depends on the capabilities of your sound card.

◆ Oh, and fifth, you can choose which of the available controls are displayed.

USING PLAY CONTROL

To use Play Control (or whatever your sound card calls it), display its window by taking one of the following actions:

1. Choose Start ➤ All Programs ➤ Accessories ➤ Entertainment ➤ Volume Control.

2. If Windows is displaying the Volume control in the notification area, double-click it.

3. Click the Advanced button in the Device Volume section on the Volume tab of the Sounds and Audio Devices Properties dialog box.
   Figure 9.24 shows a typical Play Control window.

FIGURE 9.24

Play Control lets you control the output source and volume for the sound card.

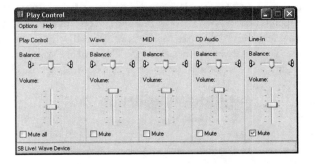

The controls in the Play Control window are intuitive enough to use:

◆ The leftmost set of controls (which appears in Figure 9.24 as Play Control, but which with other sound cards appears with other names such as Master Out) is the master control. Move the Volume slider to control the master volume (doing so manipulates the Volume Control in the notification area directly); move the Balance control to change the master left-right balance; and select the Mute All check box to silence all output from the sound card.

◆ Set the volume, balance, and muting for the other controls as appropriate. Which controls appear depends on your sound card, but typically you'll see entries such as Wave, MIDI, Digital, CD Audio, Line In, and Auxiliary.

◆ Select the Mute check box to mute any given output. Select the Mute All check box to mute all the outputs.

◆ To display any advanced options your sound card supports, choose Options ➤ Advanced Controls. The window displays an Advanced button beneath the master volume controls. Click this button, and Windows displays the Advanced Controls dialog box, which offers bass and treble controls together with any other controls your sound card offers. Figure 9.25 shows an example of the Advanced Controls dialog box.

FIGURE 9.25

Use the Advanced Controls dialog box to set any advanced options your sound card offers.

◆ To change the set of controls displayed, choose Options ➤ Properties. Volume Control displays the Properties dialog box (shown in Figure 9.26). In the Show the Following Volume Controls list box, select the check boxes for the controls you want in the window and clear the check boxes for those you don't want. Then click the OK button. Volume Control closes the Properties dialog box and adjusts the window to show the controls whose check boxes you selected.

FIGURE 9.26

In the Properties dialog box, choose the controls you want the Volume Control window to display.

TIP   *If your computer has multiple sound cards, you can switch between them by using the Mixer Device drop-down list in the Properties dialog box for Volume Control.*

USING RECORD CONTROL

To display the Record Control window (or whatever your sound card calls it), take the following steps:

1. Display Play Control as described in the previous section.

2. Choose Options ➢ Properties. Volume Control displays the Properties dialog box.

3. Select the Recording option button and click the OK button. Volume Control closes the Properties dialog box and displays the Record Control dialog box (shown in Figure 9.27).

FIGURE 9.27

The Record Control window lets you control the input devices, volume, and balance.

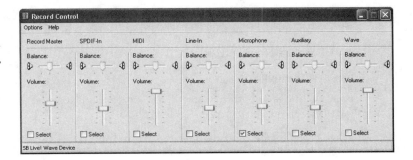

As with Play Control, Record Control has a Balance slider, a Volume slider, and a Select check box for each input device. Select the Select check box for the input device you want to use, and choose appropriate volume and balance settings. (With most sound cards, the Select check boxes actually work like a set of option buttons—selecting one Select check box automatically deselects all the other Select check boxes.)

Recording Audio Files with Sound Recorder

If you need to create some simple WAV files, use Sound Recorder, which comes with Windows. Sound Recorder is a simple program with some severe limitations. The worst limitation is that its maximum file length is a mere 60 seconds, so while it's fine for recording sound effects, short memos, and so on, it's no good for, say, recording a song of even modest length.

You can also use Sound Recorder for converting WAV files to some other formats, including MP3. But Sound Recorder is limited in this, too, offering only bit rates of 56kbps and lower for MP3 files.

Starting Sound Recorder

To start Sound Recorder, choose Start ➢ All Programs ➢ Accessories ➢ Entertainment ➢ Sound Recorder. Figure 9.28 shows Sound Recorder.

FIGURE 9.28

Sound Recorder is useful for recording WAV files.

Recording a Sound File with Sound Recorder

To record a sound file with Sound Recorder:

1. Use Record Control to select the input you want to use. Choose appropriate volume and balance settings.

2. If you currently have a file open in Sound Recorder, choose File ➤ New. Sound Recorder closes the current file, prompting you to save it if it contains unsaved changes, and opens a new file.

3. Get the input ready. For example, bring your microphone within kissing distance of your mouth or throat, or feed in a signal through the Line-In jack.

4. Click the Record button.

5. Start the input.

6. Click the Stop button to stop recording. (Sound Recorder automatically stops recording after 60 seconds.)

7. Save the file by choosing File ➤ Save and specifying the name and path in the Save As dialog box.

Once you've recorded a sound, you can take assorted self-explanatory actions with it:

♦   Click the Play button to play back the file.

♦   Drag the slider to move to a specific position in the file.

♦   To add to the end of a sound file you've created, or to record over part of it and add to the end of it, position the slider at the end or at the position at which you want to start recording over its current contents. Then click the Record button.

♦   To truncate the file, place the slider in the appropriate position and choose Edit ➤ Delete before Current Position or Edit ➤ Delete after Current Position as appropriate.

♦   Apply one of the effects by using the Effects menu: Increase Volume (by 25 percent), Decrease Volume, Increase Speed (by 100 percent), Decrease Speed, Add Echo, and Reverse.

TIP   *Because Sound Recorder doesn't offer an Undo feature, it's a good idea to save the sound file before adding to a file or applying an effect. If you don't like the result, you can then close the file without saving changes.*

Converting a File to Another Format

To convert a WAV file to another format, follow these steps:

1. Open the WAV file.

2. Choose File ➤ Save As. Sound Recorder displays the Save As dialog box.

3. Click the Change button at the bottom of the Save As dialog box. Sound Recorder displays the Sound Selection dialog box (shown in Figure 9.29).

FIGURE 9.29

Use the Sound Selection dialog box to specify the format of the sound file when converting a WAV file to another format.

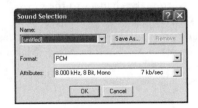

4. Choose the format in the Format drop-down list.

5. Choose any applicable attributes (for example, the bit rate) in the Attributes drop-down list.

6. Click the OK button. Sound Recorder closes the Sound Selection dialog box and returns you to the Save As dialog box.

7. Specify the filename as usual in the Save As dialog box.

8. Click the Save button. Sound Recorder closes the Save As dialog box, converts the file to the specified format, and saves it under the name you chose.

Using Windows Movie Maker

Windows Movie Maker is a tool for combining different kinds of media clips into "movies" that you can share with others via disk, Web, or e-mail. You could combine home video footage from a video camera with voice-over narrative, a musical soundtrack, still photos, and other media types into a single movie file that can be played on any PC with a player that supports the Microsoft movie (.mov) format.

NOTE *If you want to use footage from a video camera, you need a way of getting it into the PC. If it's a digital video camera, that's simple—just hook it up to the PC via whatever interface type it uses. (Most digital video cameras use a FireWire port, which you might need to add on a PCI expansion card.) If it's an analog camera, or you want to transfer from videotape with a VCR, you need a video interface device to convert from analog to digital format.*

Here's the big picture for creating a movie:

1. Create one or more collections. *Collections* are organizational folders for content, and are not specific to a particular movie project; once you import a clip, it can be used again and again in different movies.

2. Import or record the content for the movie into the collection(s).

3. Start a new movie project, and place the media clips into it.

4. Add a soundtrack or voice narration if desired.

5. Save your project.

6. Export your project to a movie file. You cannot edit a movie file; that's why you save the project first, in case you need to make changes to the movie. You can make the changes to the project, and then re-export.

The following sections look at these steps in more detail. Start up Windows Movie Maker (Start ➤ All Programs ➤ Accessories ➤ Windows Movie Maker) and then proceed through these sections.

Creating Collections

Collections are organized beneath a master folder called My Collections. It's a lot like the folder tree in Windows Explorer. To create a collection:

1. Click the collection you want the new one to appear under.

2. Click the New Collection button on the toolbar or choose File ➤ New ➤ Collection.

3. Type a name for the collection and press Enter.

You might want a collection for video clips, another for still photos, one for sound files, and so on. Figure 9.30 shows several collections ready for use. You can have multiple levels in the folder hierarchy; that's the point of clicking the parent collection in step 1.

FIGURE 9.30

Set up your collections for storing incoming clips.

Importing Content

The easiest way to get content into a collection is to import existing content from your hard disk. To do so, follow these steps:

1. Select the collection into which you want to import.

2. Choose File ➤ Import. The Select the File to Import box opens.

3. Locate and select the file you want to import; then click Open to import it.

You can drag clips between collections if you find that you imported it into the wrong folder; it's just like working with files in Windows Explorer.

TIP *You can't import CD audio directly from a CD, but you can use Windows Media Player to convert it to WMA format and then import that WMA file from disk. Or if you want only a portion of a song from a CD, you can use the Record feature, set to Audio Only, to record from the sound card and then play the CD in your PC's CD-ROM drive while it records.*

Recording Content

If you have a digital video camera that can be used while attached to the PC, a microphone, or some other input device, you can record new content directly into Movie Maker.

RECORDING VIDEO CONTENT

You can directly record video content only if you have a supported video device—for example, a digital video camera that can record while it is hooked up to the PC, or another brand of analog-to-digital converter such as Dazzle.

Assuming you do have a supported device, here's how to record with it:

1. Make sure the device is connected to the PC and that your PC recognizes it. You may need to go through the Add Hardware Wizard, as described in Chapter 8.

2. Choose File ➤ Record or click the Record button on the toolbar.

3. The Record dialog box opens. Make sure that Video and Audio is selected in the Record drop-down list if your video camera also records sound, or if you have a microphone you

plan to use separately to record the sound. If you don't want sound, choose Video Only instead.

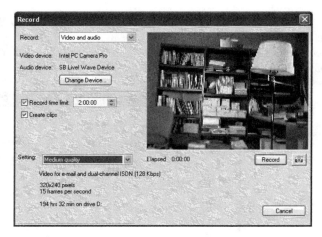

4. Choose a quality level from the Setting drop-down list.

5. Make any other adjustments desired, such as setting a recording time limit or clicking Change Device to configure the properties for your video and audio recorders.

NOTE *Most of the settings are self-explanatory, except maybe Create Clips. If you use Create Clips, it breaks the video into separate clips whenever it detects a different frame (such as when you turn the camera on/off or turn off the Pause feature). Otherwise it records a single, long video clip.*

6. Click Record. When you are done recording, click Stop.

7. In the Save Windows Media File box, enter a file name and click Save.

If you marked Create Clips, it creates a separate folder containing the multiple clips. If you didn't, it creates a single file with the name you specified.

RECORDING A STILL IMAGE WITH A VIDEO CAMERA

If you want a snapshot with the video camera instead of motion video, follow steps 1 and 2 of the preceding procedure. Set Record to Video Only, and then click the Take Photo button below the image preview (the button that looks like a camera). This opens a Save Photo dialog box in which you can save the still photo.

RECORDING AUDIO CONTENT

Recording audio content is the same as video content except you set the Record setting in the Record dialog box to Audio Only.

Creating a Movie Project

Now you're ready to create the movie project. Remember that the clips in collections are available to all movie projects; your collections are entirely separate from any particular project.

When Windows Movie Maker starts, it starts a blank movie project. You can go with this one, or create a new one with the File ➤ New ➤ Project command.

ADDING VISUAL CONTENT TO A PROJECT

Simply start dragging visual content (video or still photos) from collections into the project area at the bottom of the window in the order that you want it to appear in the movie.

There are two project views. Storyboard view is the default; it's the one that looks like a filmstrip. Each clip takes up an equal amount of space in Storyboard view, regardless of its actual length. You can work only with visual clips in Storyboard view; there is no audio track displayed. See Figure 9.31.

FIGURE 9.31

Storyboard view shows visual clips only.

Click here to switch to Timeline view

Timeline view shows each visual clip's size according to the amount of time it will remain onscreen. In Timeline view, you see a soundtrack line below the visual clips, indicating what sounds will play as each visual image appears. See Figure 9.32.

FIGURE 9.32

Timeline view shows both sound and picture, and spaces them out in their actual proportions.

Click here to switch to Storyboard view

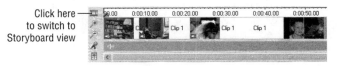

To switch between them, click the Timeline or Storyboard button. It's the button in the top-left corner of the project area.

ADDING A SOUNDTRACK OR NARRATION

To add a soundtrack, you need to be in Timeline view. Then drag any sound clip onto the timeline. You can then drag it to the left or right to adjust its position in the movie.

You will probably want to wait to record narration at the last minute, after you have finalized the order and duration of each clip. To record narration, follow these steps:

1. Make sure your microphone is plugged in to the Mic port on your sound card.

2. Switch to Timeline view and click the Record Narration button to the left of the timeline (it looks like a microphone). Or you can choose File ➤ Record Narration.

3. In the Record Narration Track dialog box, make sure the device and line are correct. The device should be your sound card, and the line should be Microphone.

4. If you want any audio that's stored as part of the video clip to be muted when the narration is going on, mark the Mute Video Soundtrack checkbox.

5. Change the recording level using the Record Level slider if desired. You can practice speaking into the microphone and use the meter on the slider as a guide.

6. Click Record. Your movie displays in the Preview pane. Speak into the microphone to narrate as the movie progresses.

7. Click Stop. A Save box appears.

8. Enter a filename and click Save. The track is saved in WAV format, just like files you create in Sound Recorder.

TIP   If you have added other audio to the movie, you might find that the narration has taken its place, forcing it to move farther to the right on the timeline. Drag them so they overlap to make both play at once.

PREVIEWING THE MOVIE

To preview the movie, click the Play button under the preview pane. If you want to view it full-screen, click the Full Screen button under the preview pane or choose Play ➤ Full Screen.

Exporting a Project to a Movie File

When the movie is exactly the way you want it, save your work on the project (File ➤ Save Project). Then export the movie by doing the following:

1. Choose File ➤ Save Movie.

2. Choose a quality from the Setting drop-down list.

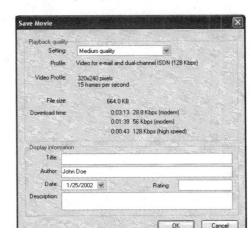

3. Enter any information about the movie as desired. This is optional.

4. Click OK. A Save As dialog box opens.

5. Enter a name for the movie file and click Save.

6. You're asked whether you want to watch the movie now. Click Yes to play it in Windows Media Player or click No to return to Windows Movie Maker.

Summary

This chapter has concentrated on audio and video, discussing how to make the most of Windows Media Player for listening to CDs, copying CDs to your hard disk, and tuning into Internet radio. You've also seen the assorted ways of controlling the volume that Windows outputs, how to record sounds with the distressingly limited tool that Windows provides for the purpose, and how to make your own movies with Windows Movie Maker.

Chapter 10

Using Windows XP Professional on Notebook PCs

WINDOWS XP INCLUDES MANY FEATURES designed to make life easier for notebook PC users. Some of these features work on all PCs but are especially applicable to portables; other features don't even appear when you install Windows XP on a desktop PC. In this chapter, we'll look at some Windows features that people who own notebook computers can use to make their computing experience more trouble-free.

◆ How notebook PCs are physically different

◆ Using built-in and external monitors

◆ Working with PC cards

◆ Working with hardware profiles

◆ Monitoring and optimizing battery usage

◆ Establishing dial-up connections from multiple locations

◆ Synchronizing files with other PCs

◆ Troubleshooting problems with notebook PCs

How Notebook PCs are Physically Different

Besides the obvious of "everything's smaller," notebook PCs have a few important differences from desktop PCs. Here's a quick rundown:

◆ **Fn key:** In addition to the normal keys on a keyboard, most laptops have a key labeled Fn. This is an additional system key, much like Control and Alt. You use it in conjunction with the function keys (F1 through F12) to issue special laptop-specific commands. Figure 10.1 shows several function keys on a notebook PC; notice that they have additional writing on them that shows what they do when combined with the Fn key.

FIGURE 10.1

Some function keys
have extra function-
ality when combined
with the Fn key. For
example, the F7 key
here turns down
screen brightness.

♦ **LCD screens:** Notebooks have built-in LCD monitors; most can also accept an external monitor through a built-in VGA output jack. An Fn key combination switches between the two
monitors when an external one is plugged in.

TIP *Near the end of Chapter 7, you learned about an XP feature called ClearType that can make text on an LCD monitor appear sharper. You will probably want to turn it on for your notebook PC's monitor.*

♦ **Docking station connector:** Most notebooks have a connector on the back for plugging into
a docking station.

♦ **Mouse alternative:** You can connect an external mouse via PS/2 port or serial port, but most
notebook PCs have a built-in mouse alternative. One older style of mouse alternative is called
a pointing stick. (Toshiba calls theirs an Accupoint.) A newer mouse alternative, found on most
laptops sold today, is a touchpad (sometimes called a glidepad).

♦ **PC card slots:** Since laptops do not have expansion slots in the motherboard the way that desktop PCs do, they need a way of accepting expansion cards. The standard for this is the *PC Card*,
also known by its standards organization's name, PCMCIA (Personal Computer Memory Card
International Association). Like USB, PC cards are hot-pluggable.

♦ **Battery:** In addition to using an AC adapter to feed power to your portable computer, you can
choose to run your system with an internal battery. The most common substances used in
computer battery packs are Nickel Cadmium (NiCad), Nickel Metal Hydride (NiMH), and
Lithium Ion (LIon).

These physical features are discussed in more detail later in the chapter, in sections that pertain
to them.

Using Built-In and External Monitors

Most notebook PCs have an external VGA graphics port, and you can switch between using it and
using the built-in LCD display by pressing the Fn key in combination with one of the function keys.
On my Compaq Presario laptop it is Fn+F3, for example. Pressing that combo toggles between
LCD only, external only, and both on at once.

If your notebook supports it, you can also use the DualView feature in Windows XP to extend
the desktop across both monitors. Normally when you enable both monitors at once, both show the

same thing, but with DualView each can show separate content. Microsoft has certified that the following notebook graphic adapters will work with DualView:

◆ S3 Savage MX

◆ Trident 3D

◆ Trident XP

Others may work as well, either by default or with an update from the graphic adapter manufacturer.

TIP   *If you have the ATI Rage Mobility video adapter in your notebook PC, in theory it should be able to support DualView, but it doesn't work with the Rage Mobility driver that ships with Windows XP. By the time you read this, an updated driver may be available through your notebook's manufacturer. Unfortunately ATI does not have a generic Rage Mobility driver available at their Web site.*

DualView is almost exactly like the multiple monitors feature you learned about in Chapter 8 except for the name, and except that on a laptop, the primary monitor is always the built-in one; an attached external monitor is always the secondary one.

Not all laptops support the DualView feature. To determine whether yours does, and try it out if possible, hook up an external monitor to the laptop and enable both displays (with an Fn key combination). They should both show the exact same thing. Then do the following:

1. Right-click the desktop and choose Properties; then click the Settings tab. If your PC supports DualView there will be two separate monitor icons there. If not, there will be only one.

2. If there are two, click the one for the external monitor, and then click Extend My Windows desktop onto this monitor.

3. Click OK. The desktop is now stretched out over both monitors rather than them both showing the same thing.

Working with PC Cards

As mentioned at the beginning of this chapter, notebook PCs use PC Card slots as their primary means of accepting expansion devices. PC Card technology predates USB; today many USB devices are available that take the place of PC Card devices.

PC cards use software known as *socket services* and *card services*. Socket services are similar to device drivers; they handle the interaction between the PC and the card. Card services handle high-level functions and control the transfer of information from the card's memory to the CPU.

Windows XP handles the interface between all types of PC card devices behind-the-scenes, resulting in hot-pluggable functionality. You can insert a PC Card device at any time, and Windows will automatically detect it, as you saw in Chapter 8 when we were talking about adding hardware.

When you remove a PC Card from the system, you are supposed to use the Safely Remove Hardware utility to shut it down first. (You also learned about this in Chapter 8.) However, if you forget and simply remove the card, it'll probably be okay. Using the Safely Remove Hardware feature simply ensures that all the device's activities complete normally rather than being aborted in mid-stream.

When one or more hot-pluggable devices are attached to the PC, an icon appears in the notification area for them. You can click this icon to see the attached devices, and then click the one you want to choose to shut down for safe removal. See Figure 10.2.

FIGURE 10.2

You can stop a PC card or USB device from the notification area by clicking the Safely Remove Hardware icon.

You can also double-click the Safely Remove Hardware icon in the notification area to open a dialog box showing the installed hot-pluggable devices, and stop one from there. See Figure 10.3.

FIGURE 10.3

Double-click the icon to see the Safely Remove Hardware dialog box.

TIP   See the Troubleshooting section at the end of this chapter if you are having problems getting a particular PC Card device to work under Windows XP.

Working with Hardware Profiles

Hardware profiles enable you to have different devices enabled/disabled at different times. This can be useful on any PC, but it is especially so on a notebook PC because you can have different profiles for different usage situations.

For example, suppose you have a built-in network card in your laptop. When you start up the PC, Windows booting takes about 1 minute longer than usual when you aren't connected to a LAN because the adapter has to search for a LAN and time-out before it can continue. You might want to create a hardware profile called No LAN and choose it when you start up while away from the office.

If you have a docking station for your notebook PC, you can also set up separate profiles for docked versus undocked configurations. That way when it's docked, you can take advantage of any extra devices in the docking station such as drives or PCI cards. When it's undocked, the PC will know not to waste time trying to connect to those devices.

NOTE *When you have more than one hardware profile set up, you'll see an extra boot menu when you start Windows XP that asks you to select which profile you want. When you delete all hardware profiles except one, that boot menu goes away.*

To create a hardware profile:

1. Right-click My Computer and choose Properties; then click the Hardware tab.
2. Click the Hardware Profiles button. The Hardware Profiles box appears.

3. Click Copy to copy the current profile. Type a name for the new profile and click OK.
4. Click the Properties button. A Properties box for the new profile opens.

5. If this is a portable computer, mark the This Is a Portable Computer check box and choose an option button to define the docked/undocked state that this profile will represent.

6. If you want this profile to appear on that aforementioned menu at startup so you can select a profile, mark the Always Include This Profile As an Option When Windows Starts check box. Then click OK to close the Properties box.

7. Back in the Hardware Profiles box, select an option in the When Windows Starts section. You can have the startup menu stay onscreen indefinitely until a profile has been selected or specify an amount of time that it should wait before going with the default profile.

8. Click OK. Then reboot the PC and select the new hardware profile.

9. Disable any devices in Device Manager that you won't want to be available in that profile. (See Chapter 8.)

10. If you don't want to continue working in this profile now, restart the PC again and choose your original profile.

Monitoring and Optimizing Battery Usage

Windows XP has several features for helping you make the most of your notebook battery's charge. You don't want the screen going blank every minute that you pause to gather your thoughts, but neither do you want it to remain on using power for a long time if you get called away unexpectedly. Windows XP lets you adjust the settings to come up with your own best compromise between usability and battery life.

Power management is available on both notebooks and desktops, but it's more important on notebooks. In addition, on laptops the controls are more complex, offering separate settings for each profile for when the PC is plugged into AC power versus running on batteries.

NOTE *There are two standards for power management in PCs: Advanced Power Management (APM) and Advanced Configuration and Power Interface (ACPI). ACPI is the more modern one, and works the most smoothly with Windows. If you have an older notebook PC, you might investigate whether a BIOS update is available that would switch it over from APM to ACPI.*

To configure power management, open the Power Options Properties dialog box as follows:

1. Right-click the desktop and choose Properties from the shortcut menu. Windows displays the Display Properties dialog box.

2. Click the Screen Saver tab.

3. Click the Power button to open the Power Options Properties dialog box.

Choosing a Power Scheme

First, choose a power scheme and adjust it as necessary:

1. Display the Power Options Properties dialog box as discussed in the previous section, and click the Power Schemes tab if it is not already on top. See Figure 10.4.

FIGURE 10.4

Choose basic power-management options in the Power Schemes tab of the Power Options Properties dialog box.

NOTE *Figure 10.4 shows the Power Schemes tab for a notebook PC. A laptop PC will have only a single column, rather than separate columns for Plugged In and Running on Batteries. Other tabs vary as well depending on the PC type. A notebook PC will have Alarms and Power Meter tabs; a desktop PC will have a UPS tab.*

2. In the Power Schemes drop-down list, select the power scheme that best describes your computer's role. These are simply sets of settings to begin with; you can customize any of them.

3. Change any of the settings for the chosen power scheme as needed, for both Plugged In and Running on Batteries.

4. Click the Apply button to apply the power scheme to your computer, or click OK to apply the changes and close the dialog box.

NOTE *If you adjust the settings for a power scheme, you can save your custom power scheme by clicking the Save As button and specifying a name for the scheme in the Save Scheme dialog box that Windows displays.*

Setting Power Alarms

An alarm situation occurs when the remaining battery life drops below a certain percentage. In the Alarms tab (Figure 10.5) you can choose what will happen when the battery life crosses two thresholds: Low Battery and Critical Battery. You define for yourself each of these thresholds and the activity that should occur at each.

For example, you might want a warning to appear onscreen when the battery becomes low, and you might define "low" as having 15% of its charge left. You might want the PC to go into Hibernate mode when battery life is critical, and you might define "critical" as having 5% left.

FIGURE 10.5

Specify the power thresholds for low and critical battery alarms.

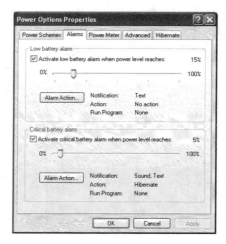

To set the alarm action for a threshold, click the Alarm Action button and choose an action from the dialog box that appears. See Figure 10.6. From here you can choose whether an alarm should sound, choose whether a message should display, and choose what action will occur, if any, when the alarm goes off. You can have the system go into Standby or Hibernate modes, for example, or you could run some external program.

FIGURE 10.6

Specify what should happen when an alarm is triggered.

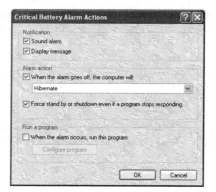

Working with the Power Meter

In the Power Meter tab, use the check box to show the details for each battery. This is an issue only on systems with multiple batteries installed at once. You also can see in this tab how much battery power is left and whether it is currently charging. See Figure 10.7.

FIGURE 10.7

View the remaining battery life in the Power Meter tab.

By default on a laptop, a Power Meter icon appears in the notification area, showing an electrical plug when the PC is running on AC power and showing a battery when it's on battery power. You can double-click that icon at any time to see a Power Meter dialog box telling how much power is left. See Figure 10.8.

FIGURE 10.8

This dialog box appears when you double-click the Power indicator in the notification area.

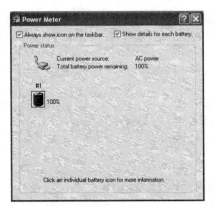

NOTE *Notice in Figure 10.8 the Always Show Icon on the Taskbar check box. If you deselect it, the icon in the notification area will go away. To get it back, mark the Always Show Icon on the Taskbar check box in the Advanced tab of the Power Options dialog box, covered in the next section.*

Choosing Advanced Power Options

The Advanced tab of the Power Options Properties dialog box (shown in Figure 10.9) offers various advanced power-management options. Which of these options you see depends on the hardware configuration of your computer.

FIGURE 10.9

If necessary, choose further power-management options in the Advanced tab of the Power Options Properties dialog box.

Always Show Icon on the Taskbar check box Select this check box to display a power icon in the notification area or not.

Prompt for Password When Computer Resumes from Standby check box Select this check box if you want Windows to make you enter your password when you wake the computer from a standby state.

When I Press the Power Button on My Computer drop-down list In this drop-down list, select the action you want Windows to take when you press the Power button on your computer when Windows is running. The options are Do Nothing, Ask Me What to Do, Sleep, Hibernate, and Shut Down.

When I Press the Sleep Button on My Computer drop-down list In this drop-down list, select the action you want Windows to take when you press the Sleep button on your computer. As for the Power button, the options are Do Nothing, Ask Me What to Do, Sleep, Hibernate, and Shut Down.

Enabling and Disabling Hibernation

First, let's review the difference between Standby and Hibernate. *Standby* places the computer in a low power consumption state. It turns off the display, the drives, the fan—everything possible short of shutting down the PC. Only the memory continues to receive power, to save its contents. Standby can make a battery last a long time—days, even—but it eventually does run down and you lose everything in memory.

Hibernation, on the other hand, copies the content of memory to the hard disk, and then shuts everything down. When you resume from Hibernate, the memory content is transferred back into memory and the system resumes where it left off. With Hibernate, the computer can be shut off for days, weeks, or more, and will resume exactly in the same state regardless of battery power left.

The more RAM you have, the longer it takes for your computer to enter hibernation and to emerge from it again. But using hibernation is usually substantially faster than shutting down the computer and restarting it, especially as hibernation allows you to keep your programs and documents open, so that you can restart your work where you left off.

To enable hibernation, select the Enable Hibernation check box in the Hibernate tab of the Power Options Properties dialog box (shown in Figure 10.10).

FIGURE 10.10

Use the Hibernate tab to enable and disable hibernation.

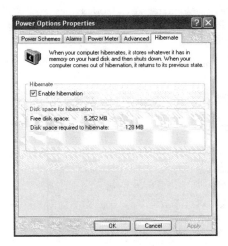

To place the PC in a Standby or Hibernate state, you can:

◆ Choose them as actions in the Advanced tab (Figure 10.9) in the Power Buttons section.

◆ Choose them as Alarm Actions in the Alarms tab.

◆ Choose Start ➤ Turn Off Computer and then click the Stand By button, or press the Shift key to make the Stand By button turn to a Hibernate button, and then click it.

To wake up the PC after entering Standby, press any key. To wake up the PC after entering Hibernate, press the PC's Power button.

TIP   If you have trouble waking the PC up after placing it in Standby or Hibernate, or you get errors or lockups going into or out of those modes, see "Troubleshooting Power Management Problems" later in the chapter.

Using Multiple Dialing Locations

People who travel between cities with a notebook PC often need to connect to the Internet using different dialing settings depending on where they are. For example, in one location you might need to dial a 1 before the number; in another location a 1 plus the area code; in still another it's a local call; and so on.

To make it easier to remember the appropriate settings for each location, Windows XP offers Dialing Rules. Set them up through Control Panel:

1. From Control Panel, open the Phone and Modem Options applet.

2. In the Dialing Rules tab, click New to open a New Location dialog box.

3. Enter all the details about the location you are setting up, as shown in Figure 10.11. Make sure you hit all three tabs: General, Area Code Rules, and Calling Card. The Calling Card tab is useful if you need to punch in the numbers for your calling card or credit card before each call from a certain location.

4. Click OK. Now you have a new location.

FIGURE 10.11

Set up a new dialing location for every city from which you make dial-up connections and need different settings.

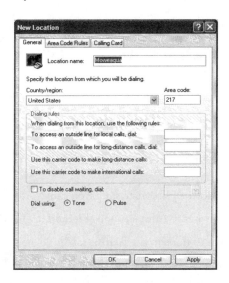

To use your new location, select it from the Dialing Rules tab.

Synchronizing Files with Other PCs

Many people use the "low tech" way of exchanging files between PCs—they copy them onto a floppy for transfer. And there's nothing wrong with that. Others hook the notebook PC into the LAN and copy files over the network. Still another method along those same lines is Direct Cable Connection, a way of creating an impromptu network on PCs that don't have network interface cards.

TIP   To set up a direct cable connection, you could connect the PCs via parallel or serial cable and then run the New Connection Wizard (Start ➤ All Programs ➤ Accessories ➤ Communications ➤ New Connection Wizard) on each PC. Choose Set Up an Advanced Connection on both PCs. Then on one of them, choose Accept Incoming Connections, and on the other, choose Connect Directly to Another Computer. Then finish working through the wizard to set it up. You can also connect directly via other types of connection this way, including modem and infrared.

However, each of those methods has a fundamental problem: What if the copy on the desktop PC or network location has changed too? How do you manage synchronization when it's possible that neither copy is in its original state? To solve this problem, Windows XP offers two different features: Offline Files and Briefcase.

Working with Offline Files

The Offline Files feature is useful if you need access to files and folders that are not always available 24/7, such as files on a network that periodically goes down for maintenance or files on a desktop PC while you are traveling with your laptop. It's designed to be an improvement over the Briefcase feature from previous Windows versions.

TIP   *The Briefcase feature is still available in Windows XP, and is discussed later in this chapter, because Briefcase offers one feature that Offline Files does not: it enables synchronization and transfer via floppy or other removable disk. The Offline Files feature works only with a network.*

Offline Files is available only in Windows XP Professional, not Windows XP Home Edition. However, only the computer that needs to maintain and synchronize the offline file access needs Windows XP Professional; the computer where the originals are maintained can be running any operating system.

NOTE   *Don't confuse the Offline Files feature with the ability in Windows Explorer to cache Web sites for offline reading by subscribing to them. That capability is covered in Chapter 12.*

TURNING OFF FAST USER SWITCHING

To use Offline Files, you must first turn off the Fast User Switching feature in Windows XP. To do so:

1. In Control Panel, open up User Accounts.

2. Click Change the Way Users Log On or Off.

3. Deselect the Use Fast User Switching check box, and then click Apply Options. Then close the Control Panel window.

CONFIGURING THE OFFLINE FILES FEATURE

Now you are ready to set up the Offline Files feature. To do so:

1. From any Explorer window, choose Tools ➤ Folder Options.

2. Click the Offline Files tab and mark the Enable Offline Files check box. See Figure 10.12.

3. Change any synchronization settings. They're described in Table 10.1. Many of these can also be set through the Offline Files Wizard that runs when you select offline files, so you don't have to pay close attention to them now.

4. Click OK to apply the new setting.

FIGURE 10.12

Set configuration options for Offline Files.

TABLE 10.1: OFFLINE FILES SETTINGS

SETTING	PURPOSE/NOTES
Synchronize All Offline Files When Logging On	If the source is available when you log on, it will be checked for updates and your locally cached copies will be updated as needed.
Synchronize All Offline Files Before Logging Off	Same as above, except it occurs when you shut down Windows or log off.
Display a Reminder Every	Specifies the interval at which a notification will appear when you are not connected to the network.
Create an Offline Files Shortcut on the Desktop	Places a desktop shortcut through which you can easily manage your offline files.
Encrypt Offline Files to Secure Data	Allows EFS encryption for the offline files, as discussed earlier in this chapter.
Amount of Disk Space to Use for Temporary Offline Files	Limits the amount of space that offline files can occupy, as a percentage of the total drive space.

You can return to the Offline Files tab at any time to delete offline files (Delete Files button), view offline files (View Files button), or configure the behavior for when a connection to another PC is lost (Advanced button).

SELECTING FILES AND FOLDERS TO BE AVAILABLE OFFLINE

Next, you select certain networked files and folders to be cached to your local hard drive. To do so, follow these steps:

1. Locate a file or folder in My Network Places that you want to cache.

2. Right-click it and choose Make Available Offline.

NOTE   *If you have made files or folders available online before, and if there are no subfolders in the folder you chose, you are finished at step 2.*

3. The first time you do this procedure, the Offline Files Wizard runs. Work through it, setting any configuration options desired. These configuration options are a subset of the ones that you saw in Table 10.1.

4. If you selected a folder that contains subfolders, a dialog box appears. Choose whether you want to include the subfolders and click OK.

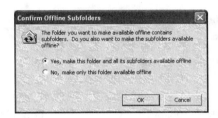

WORKING OFFLINE

When Offline Files is enabled, the files/folders you have set up appear as if they were online even when they are not actually available. You access them in the same way you normally do—for example, through My Network Places or via shortcuts to them. If they are available via network, you get the "live" copy; if they are not available, you get the cached, offline copy. An icon appears in the notification area to let you know you are working offline.

SYNCHRONIZING

When network access is once again available after having worked offline, you must synchronize your cached copies with the online originals. If you have set the configuration options to synchronize automatically at logon and/or logoff, this process is automatic.

You can also manually synchronize by choosing Start ➤ All Programs ➤ Accessories ➤ Synchronize. This opens the Items to Synchronize dialog box, shown in Figure 10.13. Clear the check boxes for any resources you don't want to synchronize, and click the Synchronize button.

What happens when you synchronize? It depends on what changes have been made. If your copy has changed but the original has not, the original is updated with your changes. If vice-versa (your copy not changed, the original changed), then your copy is updated with the original's changes. If both have changed, a dialog box appears asking what you want to do. You can keep your copy, keep the original as-is, or keep both under different names.

FIGURE 10.13

Synchronizing files manually with the Synchronize command.

Using Briefcase

Offline Files works only if you have a network connection between the two PCs. If you must rely on transferring files via removable disk (such as a floppy or rewritable CD-ROM), you might be interested in the Briefcase feature instead.

With Briefcase, you create Briefcase folders on both PCs—the PC containing the originals (probably the desktop PC; in this chapter I'll call it the *main PC*) and the PC on which you will temporarily work with the original files (probably the notebook PC; in this chapter I'll call it the *secondary PC*). Then you synchronize the Briefcase files with one another initially, and then again later when you are ready to return any changes you've made to the original PC.

CREATING A NEW BRIEFCASE FILE

To use Briefcase, you need to have a Briefcase icon on each of the PCs (both the desktop and the notebook). If there isn't already a Briefcase icon on your desktop, you can put one there by right-clicking the desktop and choosing File ➤ New ➤ Briefcase. You can create a Briefcase anywhere, not just on the desktop, but most people prefer to store it there for convenience.

The Briefcase will have the name New Briefcase; you can change its name the same as any other icon (press F2 and type a new name).

COPYING FILES TO A BRIEFCASE

The procedure for copying files to a Briefcase depends on whether you plan on using a floppy disk or a network connection. In reality, if you are going to use a network connection, you're better off using the Offline Files feature instead. However, I'll explain both methods in this chapter.

Copying Files to My Briefcase for Floppy Transfer

1. Start on the main PC. Open a file management window and drag the files you want onto the Briefcase icon on the desktop. This copies those files to the Briefcase folder. You can double-click the Briefcase icon to open the folder and confirm that they are there if desired.

NOTE *The first time you use a Briefcase folder, the Welcome to Windows Briefcase window opens. Read what it has to say, then click Finish.*

2. Insert a blank floppy disk (or other removable disk). Then drag the Briefcase icon from the desktop onto that drive's icon in My Computer. The entire Briefcase is moved there.

3. Take that disk to the secondary PC, and open that drive in My Computer there. Drag the Briefcase folder onto the desktop there.

Now the Briefcase is on the secondary PC's desktop, and you can open the Briefcase folder and work with the files from there.

Copying Files to My Briefcase for Network Transfer

1. Make sure both PCs are logged onto the network and that file sharing is enabled on the main PC.

2. Start on the secondary PC. Open My Network Places and navigate to the files you want to copy.

3. Drag the files from My Network Places and drop them on the Briefcase icon on the desktop. If desired, you can double-click the Briefcase icon to open the folder window and confirm that the files are there.

Now you can work with the files directly from the Briefcase folder on the secondary PC's desktop.

SYNCHRONIZING BRIEFCASE FILES

When you synchronize files, you overwrite the originals with updated versions from the Briefcase. You can update all the files or only selected ones—your choice.

To see which files in the Briefcase need updating, view the Briefcase window in Details view. The Status column tells which files have changed. See Figure 10.14.

FIGURE 10.14

Use Details view to see which files have changed in the Briefcase.

Even if none have changed on the secondary PC, you might still want to synchronize if there is any chance that the originals have changed on the main PC, and if you want to continue to have the most recent versions on the secondary PC.

Once again, the procedures for synchronizing are different depending on whether you are using the floppy disk or network transfer method.

Synchronizing with Floppy Disk Transfer

1. Copy the Briefcase folder from the secondary PC's desktop to a floppy disk, and take that floppy disk to the main PC.

2. Display the floppy disk's content on the main PC, and drag the Briefcase icon onto the desktop there.

3. Double-click the Briefcase icon on the main PC desktop, opening the Briefcase window.

4. To update all files, choose Briefcase ➤ Update All. Or, to update only certain files, select them and choose Briefcase ➤ Update Selection.

5. A report appears. Make sure it lists the actions you want to perform. If you need to change the action for an item, right-click it and choose a different action. See Figure 10.15.

6. Click Update.

FIGURE 10.15

Confirm the update for each changed file.

Synchronizing with Network Transfer

1. Make sure both PCs are connected to the network.

2. On the secondary PC, double-click the Briefcase icon, opening its window.

3. To update all files, choose Briefcase ➤ Update All. Or, to update only certain files, select them and choose Briefcase ➤ Update Selection.

4. A report appears (Figure 10.15). Make sure it lists the actions you want to perform. If you need to change the action for an item, right-click it and choose a different action.

5. Click Update.

Troubleshooting Notebook PC Problems

We'll finish up this chapter by looking at some of the more common problems people experience with notebook PCs in particular, and some possible solutions.

Problems with PC Cards under Windows XP

Windows XP supports most PC Card devices, including very old 16-bit cards designed to work with the ISA interface. These cards are sometimes referred to as R2 cards. You might find that such a device doesn't work under Windows XP, and you see a message like this in Device Manager:

```
This device is either not present, not working properly, or does not have all the
drivers installed. (Code 10)
Try upgrading the device drivers for this device.
```

If this is your predicament, it's probably because the card doesn't support IRQ sharing and there aren't enough free IRQs. To get around this, you can edit the Registry to disable ISA to PCI routing for PCMCIA devices.

Open the Registry Editor, and go to KEY_LOCAL_MACHINE\System\CurrentControlSet\ Services\PCMCIA\Parameters. Choose Edit ➤ Add Value and add a value with the name of **DisableIsaToPciRouting**. Set the type to DWORD and the value to 1. Then reboot.

After you have done the above, you can install 16-bit PC Cards on computers that are low on ISA interrupts by using a shared-PCI interrupt.

If that doesn't work, perhaps the underlying problem is a different one. If you see the black/yellow exclamation point symbol next to the device in Device Manager, perhaps the PC Card device has its configuration information in common memory instead of attribute memory (where the Card information structure and configuration registers are mapped). The Pcmcia.sys driver in Windows XP does not recognize such devices, and because of this, does not allocate resources to the device.

If you think this may be the problem for your situation, contact Microsoft technical support for a fix. A patch is available, but it's intended only to correct this specific problem and not freely available on the Internet. Explain your problem and ask for the updated version of Pcmcia.sys.

NOTE   *There are a few PCMCIA network interface cards that Windows XP does not work with no matter what you try. If you are having trouble with a NIC under Windows XP, the following Knowledge Base article may be helpful:* http://support.microsoft.com/directory/article.asp?ID=KB;EN-US;q315275.

Problems with a Wheel-Style PS/2 Mouse

If you plug a PS/2 wheel mouse into the notebook's PS/2 port, the mouse pointer may jump around onscreen when using that mouse, but the touchpad built into the notebook makes the mouse work fine. Wheel mouse devices may be incompatible with some laptops because the wheel mouse transmits in 4-byte packets, while the touchpad transmits in 3-byte. If the notebook PC does not detect that there are two different pointing devices in use, each sending data in different format, it may misinterpret the data sent from the PS/2 port, causing erratic mouse pointer movement.

To fix this problem, create a hardware profile that disables the touchpad, leaving only the PS/2 mouse. (See the section on Hardware Profiles earlier in the chapter.)

Power Management Problems

One of the biggest complaints I hear from laptop users is that the power management tools don't work correctly. The main problem is that most notebook PCs come with some sort of operating system–independent power-management tool built into the BIOS. Windows itself also has power management tools, and the two often conflict. Another common problem is a non-ACPI-compliant video driver. Many people don't realize it, but Standby and Hibernate work closely with the video card, and if the video driver isn't up for the challenge, problems will ensue.

CAN'T WAKE THE PC UP AFTER PLACING IT IN STANDBY OR HIBERNATE

This is a really scary problem. After placing the PC in Standby or Hibernate, it refuses to resume. Pressing the power button has no effect; pounding your head on the keyboard is in vain.

In the short term, here are some ways to regain control of the PC:

◆ Be a little patient. Some PCs take up to 30 seconds to wake up.

◆ Look for a Suspend or Hibernate key. Some laptops have special keys or buttons for one or both, but the user might not have noticed them if he normally uses some other wakeup method.

◆ Try pressing and holding the PC's power button for 5 seconds or more. On a PC that is configured to suspend or Hibernate with a press of the power button, holding down the Power button will usually reset and reboot.

◆ Look in the PC's documentation for a key combination that might wake it up. Most laptops have an Fn key that you can press in conjunction with other keys to control laptop-specific features.

◆ As a last resort, remove all batteries, wait a few minutes, and then replace the batteries.

After you successfully restart the PC, you need to look for the underlying problem, which is generally a disagreement either between the power management features of the BIOS and those of Windows XP, or between power management and the video card.

To begin troubleshooting, first make sure you have the most recent version of the video driver installed. Download the latest from the manufacturer's Web site and install it. It never hurts, and outdated video drivers have been known to cause power management problems in some systems.

A conflict between the BIOS power management and Windows XP's power management is the most common cause of wakeup failure. Experiment with different settings in the BIOS to see if any can solve the problem. For example, one scenario under which a PC might not wake up is if APM is enabled in the Power Options in Control Panel and the BIOS is configured to suspend the computer and its time-out value is less than the value configured in the Alarms tab in Windows. To correct this, you would set the BIOS time-out higher than the Windows time-out.

If tweaking the BIOS and Windows power settings doesn't help, try visiting the PC manufacturer's Web site to see whether a BIOS update might be available. There are known issues with some PCs regarding failure to resume from Standby; these are corrected by updating the BIOS.

Remember, there are two power management standards that your BIOS can support: Advanced Power Management (APM) and Advanced Configuration and Power (ACPI). ACPI is the more recent and more sophisticated; a BIOS upgrade can add ACPI support to the computer, and can potentially clear up compatibility problems between APM and your hardware or Windows. If you can't upgrade from APM to ACPI in your BIOS, try disabling APM entirely in the BIOS if you continue having wake-up problems.

NOTE   *There's an APM diagnosis tool,* apmstat.exe, *on the Windows XP CD-ROM in the Support/Tools folder in the* Support.cab *archive file. Extract it and then run it with the -v switch for Verbose to get more data.*

If you can't solve the problem from the BIOS, try it from the other side: from Windows. Experiment with Windows Power Management settings to see whether any of them make a difference.

Remember also that you don't necessarily have to use the Windows interface for Standby or Hibernate if your BIOS has direct support for it. On one laptop I worked on, for example, the client finally had to forego the Windows power management and use the Hibernate feature built into the BIOS by pressing the PC's power button.

LOCKUP WHEN ENTERING STANDBY OR HIBERNATION

The symptoms: when you attempt to place the computer in either Standby or Hibernate through Windows XP, the computer locks up, either with a black screen and flashing cursor in the corner or with the Windows desktop locked up.

This is usually a video adapter problem. Try a different video card driver, making sure you have the latest one from the manufacturer's Web site. If the problem occurs only when using Hibernate (not Standby), you might simply have to resort to not using Hibernate on that computer.

It can also result from a COM port being open on some laptops. If you have an open connection through a COM port, such as to a modem or handheld device, close it before entering Standby.

LOCKUP OR ERRORS WHEN RESUMING AFTER HIBERNATION

In this scenario, after resuming from Hibernate, Windows XP doesn't work right. For example, the Start menu might not work anymore, the screen might be totally black, or you might get blue-screen errors.

This is a known bug when using the generic VGA video driver that comes with the OS with a PCI or AGP video card. The generic VGA video driver doesn't support hibernation. You might also see this error with other video drivers too, especially on cheap laptops that use off-brand video drivers not supporting APM or ACPI, or a video driver not designed specifically for your video card and for Windows XP.

If possible, switch to a newer video driver or one designed specifically for the video card. If not, you won't be able to use Hibernate on this PC; go into Power Options in Control Panel and turn off hibernation support.

TIP   *If you need to know how to contact your video adapter manufacturer, check the following lists:*
A through K: http://support.microsoft.com/support/kb/articles/Q65/4/16.ASP
L through P: http://support.microsoft.com/support/kb/articles/Q60/7/81.ASP
Q through Z: http://support.microsoft.com/support/kb/articles/Q60/7/82.ASP

A PROGRAM OR DEVICE PREVENTS STANDBY

Perhaps you try to use Standby but you get an error message instead that goes something like this:

```
The device driver for the device name is preventing the machine from entering
Standby or Hibernation. Please close all applications and try again. If the problem
persists, you may need to update the driver.
```

You close all open programs, but the message still persists.

Some programs or devices, particularly those with outdated drivers or that are not ACPI compliant, can cause this error to occur. You need to determine the root of the problem and then disable the program or device before standing by.

TIP   *Look for a file called* nohiber.txt *in the Windows folder; if present, it will give you clues about what device is preventing hibernation or Standby.*

You can also try looking for the errant device on your own. For example, some models of Epson USB printers have been known to prevent a PC from entering Standby, as well as several models of multi-function devices, particularly those that listen for incoming faxes. Try disconnecting all USB devices and removing all PC cards as part of your troubleshooting process. If that doesn't work, try disabling all USB devices in Device Manager if they do not automatically disappear from Device Manager when disconnected.

Also investigate whether you have any built-in device disabled; this can sometimes cause Standby problems. For example, there are known issues with Intel network cards interfering with Standby when they have been disabled in Device Manager.

A few devices have no workaround, and cannot coexist with Standby or Hibernate. Some versions of the Tseng Labs ET-4000 video adapter are like that. On such computers you cannot use Windows-based Standby or Hibernate; you might try the OS-independent BIOS power management if available.

Summary

In this chapter you learned about the hardware, features, and issues involved in working with Windows XP on a notebook computer. In the next chapter, we'll look at Internet connectivity. There are many ways to connect to the Internet, and also many configuration considerations for modem, network, satellite, and other connection methods.

Part 2

Communications and the Internet

In this section you will learn how to:
- ◆ Connect to the Internet
- ◆ Use Internet Explorer
- ◆ Use Messenger, NetMeeting, and Remote Desktop Connection
- ◆ Use Outlook Express

Chapter 11

Connecting to the Internet

WILL ROGERS ONCE EXPLAINED that the telephone is like a very big dog: when you pulled on its tail in New York, the dog would bark in Los Angeles. Radio, he said, works exactly the same way, but without the dog. In Windows XP Professional, communications functions are integrated into the operating system. Maybe Will Rogers would have said that the dog is now using a keyboard and an Internet connection.

Communications capability has been part of DOS and Windows since the earliest IBM PCs. Windows XP Professional includes an extensive set of communications tools that enable you to exchange electronic mail with other computers, browse the Internet, and use your computer to control telephone calls. In this chapter, I'll discuss the following:

- ◆ Using the Internet Connection Wizard

- ◆ Connecting to the Internet with a cable modem

- ◆ Connecting to the Internet with DSL

- ◆ Connecting to the Internet with Satellite

- ◆ Connecting to the Internet with ISDN

- ◆ Sharing an Internet connection

- ◆ Troubleshooting Internet connections

You can find more specific information about communications applications in the remaining chapters of this part of the book:

- ◆ Chapter 12 covers the Internet Explorer Web browser.

- ◆ Chapter 13 covers Windows Messenger, NetMeeting, and Remote Desktop Connection.

- ◆ Chapter 14 covers Outlook Express, the Windows XP Professional control center for messaging components and news.

Types of Internet Connections

The most common way to connect to the Internet today is through a dial-up modem, but that is also the slowest kind of connection, limited to 56Kbps. People are increasingly finding better, faster ways to gain Internet access, and we'll look at some of them in this chapter along with the traditional dial-up modem.

High-speed Internet connectivity is also known as *broadband*. In theory, connecting through a broadband device can be as much as 1,000 times faster than connecting through a 56Kbps modem. Though only a gleam in our collective browsing and e-mailing eyes in the very recent past, broadband connections are now proliferating. And as you will see in the following sections, they are affordable and, with Windows XP Professional, extremely easy to install and get up and running.

Connecting to the Internet with an Analog Modem

In times past, setting up a connection to the Internet was quite a complex operation, but that is no longer the case. In fact, during installation of Windows XP Professional, you were given an opportunity to configure an Internet connection. If you didn't do so then, you can do so at any later time using the New Connection Wizard, which walks you through the steps. You can use this Wizard to set up a broadband connection as well as an analog modem connection, to connect to your office computer system from a location outside the office, or to set up a local area network.

NOTE   *Chapter 8 covers the installation and configuration of a modem driver.*

If you have a connection that requires you to log on, you'll need your username and password. If you are connecting through an analog modem, you need an account with an Internet Service Provider, your username and password, and the phone number to dial in to your ISP. To start the New Connection Wizard, click Start ➤ All Programs ➤ Accessories ➤ Communications ➤ New Connection Wizard.

To create a new dial-up (modem) connection, follow these steps:

1. At the welcome screen, click Next to open the Network Connection Type screen:

2. Click the Connect to the Internet option, and then click Next to open the Getting Ready screen:

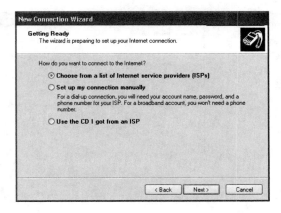

◆ If you don't have an ISP already, click the first option, and then click Next. In the next screen you can choose to set up an account with MSN Explorer or to select from a list of other ISPs. If you choose MSN Explorer, a Wizard will guide you through the steps to getting set up.

◆ If you have an installation CD from an ISP, such as America Online, select the Use the CD I Got from an ISP option, and click Next. Click Finish to close the New Connection Wizard, insert the CD, and follow the on-screen instructions.

◆ If you already have an account with an ISP and have its phone number, your username, and your password, click the Set Up My Connection Manually option, and click Next to open the Internet Connection screen:

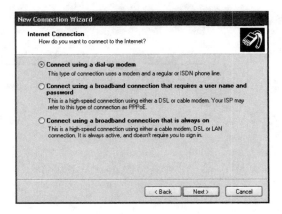

3. Click the Connect Using a Dial-up Modem option, and then click Next to open the Connection Name screen:

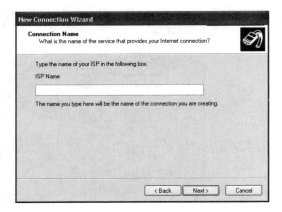

4. In the ISP Name box, enter a name and then click Next to open the Phone Number to Dial screen:

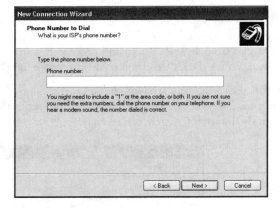

5. Enter the phone number (and area code if necessary), specify whether the modem needs to dial 1 before dialing the phone number, and click Next to open the Internet Account Information screen:

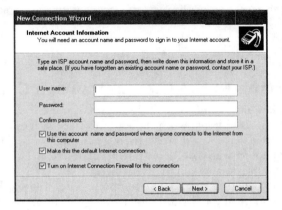

6. Enter your username and password, and enter your password again to confirm it. Leave the three check boxes at the bottom of the screen selected if you want to do the following:

◆ Allow anyone who uses your computer to connect to the Internet using this account and password.

◆ Make the current connection the default.

◆ Enable Internet Connection Firewall.

Clear a check box to disable any of these options. When you've made your selections, click Next to open the final screen of the Wizard.

7. If the summary of your choices is correct, click Finish to close the Wizard. If you want to change anything, click Back to find that screen or screens and make the changes. If you want quick access to this connection, click the Add a Shortcut to This Connection to My Desktop check box before you click Finish.

THE TELEPHONY INTERFACE

Whenever you work with an Internet connection that involves dial-up, you work with TAPI. TAPI (Telephony Application Programming Interface) is a set of software hooks to applications that control the way your computer interacts with the telephone network. TAPI is an internal part of Windows XP Professional rather than a specific application program—it provides a standard way for software developers to access communications ports and devices, such as modems and telephone sets, to control data, fax, and voice calls. Using TAPI, an application can place a call, answer an incoming call, and hang up when the call is complete. TAPI also supports features such as hold, call transfer, voice mail, and conference calls. TAPI-compliant applications work with conventional telephone lines, Private Branch Exchange (PBX), and Centrex systems; these applications also work with specialized services such as cellular and ISDN.

Continued on next page

THE TELEPHONY INTERFACE *(continued)*

End users don't usually work directly with TAPI. The closest you'll get is when you set up Dialing Rules, as you learned in Chapter 10. When you create a set of rules for dialing from a particular location, such as dialing a number for an outside line, you are communicating your preferences to TAPI.

Connecting to the Internet with a Cable Modem

It's amazing how much times have changed. Less than five years ago, everyone wanted the latest and greatest in computer hardware—the fastest processors, the best video, the biggest hard drives. Nowadays, if you offer someone a choice between a computer with all the best hardware on the market or an average computer with a really fast Internet connection, 9 out of 10 people would choose the computer with the Internet connection.

Internet bandwidth is king, and there is no sign that things will change in the near future. So, what can you do when you decide it's time to upgrade from your 56K modem to something a bit faster? One option is to sign up for Internet access over the same cable that brings TV into your home.

That might sound a bit strange at first, but it actually makes good sense. Millions of homes across the country (roughly 100 million) are already wired for cable access. Cable service can bring hundreds of channels of full audio and video content into your home over a single wire. If a cable signal can carry that much content, adding a bit of data into the mix isn't much of a problem.

Cable Internet Access—How Does It Work?

A cable modem has at least two (and maybe more) interfaces on it. The first is a standard F port connector, a coaxial cable connector that is similar to the one on the back of a television or a VCR. Your cable service is connected to that port. The second interface is a 10Base-T (Ethernet) connector, which connects your cable modem to your computer. It uses an RJ-45 plug, which looks like a wider-than-normal telephone plug. If your computer does not have NIC with an RJ-45 plug, or a built-in NIC connector, your cable service provider can probably install one for you.

Once your cable modem is up and running, data comes down to your system on a special channel on your cable signal and, unlike an analog modem, is always on.

How Fast Is It?

Being the techie that I am, I like absolutes. I like to know exactly how things work and exactly how fast something will run. So I did a bit of research to find out how fast cable modem service actually is. What I learned is that you can't find out.

When determining how fast a cable modem will actually run, you must consider a number of factors. Some factors (but not all) are out of the control of the cable Internet service providers, so their common answer—if you really press them on it—will be "it depends." Of course, this doesn't prevent them from bragging that their service is up to 1,000 times faster than a 33.6 modem. In theory, it is.

Let's take a look at that theory. On a typical cable modem installation, a 6MHz analog carrier channel is dedicated to carrying downstream data from the Internet to your computer. Now, the way all the bits and bytes are put together over a cable modem yields a throughput of 36MB on a 6MHz carrier channel. So, in theory, 36,000,000bps is 1,000 times greater than 33,600bps.

Ah, but a few factors get in the way. First, let's start with your computer. Your computer interfaces with your cable modem over a 10Base-T connection. It's called a "10"Base-T connection because the maximum throughput it will support is 10,000,000 bps (10Mbps). That's a bit less than 36Mbps—about 73 percent less. So much for the claim of being 1,000 times faster.

But that's not the only possible bottleneck. The signal that is coming down the 6MHz carrier channel and into your computer is mixed in with other signals headed to other nearby computers. Your cable Internet traffic is traveling across the same cable that connects all the other homes and apartments in your neighborhood. Now, in theory, that cable can carry the entire 36Mbps of signal into your area. But how many users does it take to completely saturate that connection to your neighborhood? Four computers using 9Mbps each? What about 40 users running 900,000 kilobits per second (Kbps) each? What about 400 users running 90Kbps (less than two 56K modems) each? Each combination would saturate the cable signal for your neighborhood and—believe it or not—it is not uncommon for 500 to 2,000 cable TV subscribers to all be running on the same cable (that is, running into the same cable "head-end" or "node"). Hopefully, not all of them are subscribing to cable Internet access as well. If they were, and if everyone were using their cable modems, your connectivity might not be much better than that of two 56K modems, but I admit I'm stretching things a bit to make a point. Simply put, the best neighbor to have is one that doesn't even have a computer.

There is also the potential for a bottleneck from your cable company out to the Internet itself. Now, in all fairness, this is a bottleneck point for any ISP—whether you have dial-up, DSL, cable modem, or whatever. Just as airlines make their money by selling more seats on a plane than they actually have, ISPs make money by selling more bandwidth than they actually have. They wouldn't be able to survive if they didn't.

A close companion who has a cable modem was able to confirm my speed rating of "it depends." In his particular scenario, he was able to see average throughputs of 256Kbps to 512Kbps, with his best connection being about 1.3Mbps—roughly the speed of a T-1 connection. So, cable modems are definitely faster, but don't buy into the hype about their being 1,000 times faster than a regular modem.

Cable Internet Access—Advantages and Disadvantages

A number of advantages and disadvantages are associated with cable modem service in comparison with typical analog modems. I've outlined a few of the positives and negatives for you.

ADVANTAGES OF CABLE MODEM INTERNET ACCESS

Always on   Full-time dedicated Internet access—you'll definitely appreciate this once you have it.

High-speed   Despite the possible bottlenecks I discussed earlier, 99 times out of 100, cable modems will give you far better speed and reliability than analog modems. Once you get connected, you'll never be willing to move somewhere that *doesn't* have high-speed access.

One less phone line required   If you had a dedicated second phone line installed in your house for computer access, you can drop that phone line. This should save you $10–$30 per month, which can offset the cost of the cable modem service.

Affordable   In comparison with other high-speed Internet access options, cable modems are one of the most affordable.

DISADVANTAGES OF CABLE MODEM INTERNET ACCESS

Privacy   Since all systems in a "neighborhood" of cable Internet subscribers use the same connection to send and receive data, someone may be able to intercept your traffic and analyze it—a security risk.

Few choices   Unlike phone companies and Internet service providers, cable companies are more or less a monopoly here in the United States. You usually won't be able to choose from multiple cable Internet providers; you'll have to take whatever is available in your neighborhood.

Getting Hooked Up

OK, so let's assume you've decided to take the plunge and get hooked up to the Internet with a cable modem. Let's take a look at what you might go through, from start to finish.

QUESTIONS TO ASK YOUR PROVIDER

You should definitely ask your cable provider a number of questions before getting hooked up. You might not get answers to all of them, but I would want any provider to be able to answer at least some of the following questions to my satisfaction:

◆ How can you ensure that my neighbors won't be able to intercept my data and read it?

◆ Is yours a two-way service? (Avoid one-way services. One-way means that your computer can receive data quickly from a cable modem, but it must transmit data through an analog modem.)

◆ Will I receive a public IP address? If so, will it be fixed or dynamic? (Fixed IP addresses are better if you need to access your computer remotely; dynamic IP addresses are better from a security point of view.)

◆ How fast can I expect it to be? Can you guarantee a certain level of service? (By all means, e-mail me if you get any provider to actually guarantee a certain level of bandwidth—I'd like to hear about them!)

◆ Are there any speed restrictions on my uplink speed? (*Uplink* refers to data sent from your computer to the Internet. Uploading a large e-mail message, videoconferencing, or transferring a large file to someone are all affected by slow uplink speeds.)

◆ Are there any restrictions on the type of services I can run on my computer?

SERVICE DELIVERY

Once you've talked with your provider and agreed to purchase the service, they will set up a time to send an installer out to your location. Now, I don't have cable modem Internet access, but I would expect the service to be just about as prompt as my regular cable service (meaning: not very prompt). Once they're at your location, they will work with the cables a bit and hook up their cable to a box—the cable modem.

Once the box is hooked up, it is time to hook the computer up. If your computer already has an Ethernet adapter in it, they will most likely connect the cable modem to the Ethernet adapter. If your system doesn't have an Ethernet adapter, they should add one to your computer for you (make sure that you have your original Windows XP Professional software handy, just in case they need it).

Configuring Your Connection

All that remains is to tell Windows XP Professional about your connection, and you do that with the New Connection Wizard. Follow these steps:

1. Choose Start ➤ All Programs ➤ Accessories ➤ Communications ➤ New Connection Wizard to open the Wizard at the welcome screen.

TIP   You can also get to the New Connection Wizard from the Network Connections window; click the Create a New Connection hyperlink in the Network Tasks pane there.

2. In the Welcome screen, click Next to open the Network Connection Type screen.

3. Click the Connect to the Internet option, and then click Next to open the Getting Ready screen.

4. Click the Set Up My Connection Manually option, and then click Next to open the Internet Connection screen.

Now, if your connection doesn't require you to log on, click the Connect Using a Broadband Connection That Is Always On option, click Next, and then click Finish. If you have to supply a username and a password to log on, follow these steps:

1. Click the Connect Using a Broadband Connection That Requires a User Name and Password option, and then click Next to open the Connection Name screen.

2. Enter a name in the ISP Name box, and click Next to open the Internet Account Information screen.

3. Enter your username and password, and then retype your password to confirm it. Leave the three check boxes at the bottom of the screen selected if you want to do the following:

   ◆ Allow anyone who uses your computer to connect to the Internet using this account and password.

   ◆ Make the current connection the default.

   ◆ Enable Internet Connection Firewall.

   Clear a check box to disable any of these options. When you've made your selections, click Next to open the final screen of the Wizard.

4. If the summary of your choices is correct, click Finish to close the Wizard. If you want to change anything, click Back to find that screen or screens and make the changes. If you want quick access to this connection, click the Add a Shortcut to This Connection to My Desktop check box before you click Finish.

Connecting to the Internet with DSL

Another popular high-speed Internet option is Digital Subscriber Line (DSL) service. DSL typically comes in two varieties: Asymmetric DSL (ADSL) and Symmetric DSL (SDSL). Since the two technologies move data in a similar manner, you may also see these commonly referred to as xDSL.

Asymmetric DSL is called asymmetric because the uplink and downlink speeds are different, with more of the speed usually being allocated to the downlink (what you use to download content from the Internet). With Symmetric DSL, the same amount of bandwidth is available in both directions—up and down.

DSL—How Does It Work?

DSL uses the existing copper phone lines already in your house to send a high-speed data signal. Your plain old telephone service (POTS) typically uses a low frequency range for all the types of signals you're accustomed to: voice, fax, and data. DSL operates on the same line—at the same time—by using a higher (inaudible) set of frequencies to transmit data. Since the DSL signal is operating in a different frequency range, you can still use your phone, fax machine, or even a modem at the same time you are using your DSL service to access the Internet.

When you have a DSL modem installed in your home, the device will have at least two or three interfaces on it. The first will be a standard RJ11 phone connector that you're probably very familiar with. Your phone line will be connected to that port. The second interface on your DSL modem will be a 10Base-T connector (also known as an RJ45), which will connect your DSL modem to your computer. Your computer will need a 10Base-T port on the back of it in order to connect the two. If your computer does not have a 10Base-T port, your DSL provider will probably install one for you. The third port that you might have on the back of your DSL modem is another RJ11 jack—this is for connecting your phone to the DSL modem.

How Fast Is It?

Unlike cable modems, DSL service usually has very defined levels of service associated with it, from 1.5 all the way up to 9Mbps. A speed of 1.5Mbps is the same as a T1 Internet access line, the same type of line that many businesses use for their Internet access needs, and it's probably more than enough for the average individual user.

NOTE   *A T1 line is a long-distance circuit that provides 24 channels of 64Kbps each, giving you a total bandwidth of 1.544Mbps.*

You will usually have at least a few providers to choose from. Compare the speed offerings from all the providers able to service your neighborhood and choose what is best for you.

Depending on how your provider's network is configured, the potential for a bottleneck exists from your DSL provider out to the Internet itself. Remember, this is a bottleneck point for any ISP, whether you have dial-up, DSL, a cable modem, or whatever. As I mentioned earlier, ISPs make their money by selling more bandwidth than they actually have, in the expectation that not everyone will use it at once.

Having DSL myself, I can tell you that—in my case—it has lived up to its service speed. I've been able to verify a full 1.1Mbps worth of connectivity on my service, which is exactly what I paid for. Being able to download Windows service packs in five minutes instead of four hours is a definite advantage in my line of business.

DSL—Advantages and Disadvantages

A number of advantages and disadvantages are associated with DSL service in comparison with typical analog modems. I've outlined a few of the positives and negatives for you.

ADVANTAGES OF DSL SERVICE

Always on   Full-time dedicated Internet access—once you've had it, you'll never want to go back. You'll definitely appreciate this once you have DSL.

High-speed   Once you get connected, you'll never be willing to move somewhere that doesn't have high-speed access.

One less phone line needed   If you had a dedicated second phone line installed in your house for computer access, you can drop that phone line because you can still use your DSL line as a voice line—even when you are on the Internet. This should save you $10–$30 per month, which can offset the cost of the DSL service.

DISADVANTAGES OF DSL SERVICE

Limited service area   Due to technical limitations, your location must be within three miles (some providers say anywhere from 12,000 to 20,000 feet) of the phone company's DSL-capable switching location. And that distance is based on the length of cabling between you and the phone company's office, not the "as the crow flies" distance. So, even if you live two miles from a DSL-capable switching location, you won't be able to get DSL if there are more than three miles of cable between you and the switch.

Getting Hooked Up

OK, so let's assume you've decided to take the plunge and get hooked up to the Internet through DSL service. Let's take a look at what you might go through, from start to finish.

QUESTIONS TO ASK YOUR PROVIDER

Before ordering service, you should probably ask any prospective provider a few questions. Although this isn't a complete list of items you may need to consider, it's a good start.

◆ Will I receive a public IP address? If so, will it be fixed or dynamic? (Fixed IP addresses are better if you need to access your computer remotely; dynamic IP addresses are better from a security point of view)

- Do you guarantee the level of service that I am purchasing?

- Are there any speed restrictions on my uplink speed? (*Uplink* refers to data sent from your computer to the Internet—uploading a large e-mail, videoconferencing, or transferring a large file to someone are all affected by slow uplink speeds)

- Are there any restrictions on the type of services I can run on my computer?

SERVICE DELIVERY

Once you've decided on a provider and agreed to a level of service, your provider will set up a time to send an installer out to your location (or, in some areas, they can send you a kit to install the DSL modem yourself—although you should have more technical knowledge than the average casual Internet user does if you're going to do this). Once they're at your location, they may have to work with your phone lines a bit before hooking up your DSL modem, and then they'll hook up your phone line to the DSL modem.

Once the DSL modem is hooked up, it is time to hook up the computer. If your computer already has an Ethernet adapter in it, they will most likely connect the DSL modem to the Ethernet adapter. If your system doesn't have an Ethernet adapter, they should add one to your computer for you (make sure that you have your original Windows XP Professional software handy, just in case they need it).

You may or may not need to run the New Connection Wizard to set up your connection. Your ISP will most likely give you set-up instructions. If you do need to run the New Connection Wizard, follow the steps I gave you earlier in the "Connecting to the Internet with a Cable Modem" section.

Connecting to the Internet with Satellite

Cable and DSL are the preferred methods of broadband connection, but if you live in an area where neither is available, then what? Satellite Internet access may be the answer for you.

Satellite: How Does It Work?

There are two types of satellite Internet access: one-way and two way.

One-way satellite Internet uses a satellite dish for downloads, but uploads are handled with a regular 56-Kbps dial-up modem. Therefore, you need to have two Internet connections—one for the satellite and one dial-up. They must both be active at once for you to surf the Web. The satellite is available all the time, but the dial-up you must connect and disconnect with a dial-up connection. You can use your own dial-up ISP or contract ISP service for the modem through the satellite provider.

Two-way satellite is a much newer technology; it uses a different type of satellite dish, and handles both uploading and downloading through it. Two separate cables run from the satellite dish—one to a Transmit box and one to a Receive box. These boxes hook to one another and then connect to your PC via USB port. The end result—a connection similar in speed and reliability to that of cable or DSL that doesn't require the use of a phone line. As with ADSL, upload speeds are slower than download speeds; you can expect about 128Kbps uploading and between 300Kbps and 600Kbps downloading, on the average.

Satellite: Advantages and Disadvantages

The main advantage of one-way satellite Internet over dial-up is speed. Downloads happen at up to 1Mbps, and since you spend much more of your time downloading than uploading, this results in greater Internet productivity.

Two-way satellite is obviously better than one way because of the higher speed in uploading, and also because you don't need to tie up a phone line or contract with a dial-up ISP. Two-way satellite is also always on, with no per-hour charges.

There are no advantages for satellite over DSL and cable other than broader availability.

All satellite Internet systems have the disadvantage of needing to buy and install a satellite dish. The two-way satellite dish must be professionally installed (by FCC mandate) because of its transmitting capability, and installation will cost $200 or more. The hardware for one-way satellite can be had virtually for free with specials and promotions, but the hardware for a two-way satellite connection will run $500 or more.

Satellite Internet also cannot be shared via router with other PCs in your home or office, unlike cable and DSL. You can share a satellite connection through Internet Connection Sharing, but you can't hook the satellite cable directly into a router.

Setup for satellite Internet on the PC is also a bit more involved. With cable and DSL, you simply plug in the cable and it works; with satellite you must run through a configuration and registration process using an analog modem. (It must be a hardware modem; a software-controlled Winmodem will not work.) You must redo this setup if you ever need to reinstall Windows or if you get a new PC.

WARNING Some people have also run into problems using satellite Internet on a dual-boot system. For example, if you dual-boot with Windows 98 and Windows XP, and you configure the satellite in Windows XP, when you boot to Windows 98 it won't work. So you re-run the Setup program in Windows 98, and it starts working, but then when you go back to Windows XP, it doesn't work anymore and you have to run Setup there again. This is because when you connect to do the configuration, it dynamically assigns you an IP address. You keep that IP address as long as that copy of Windows is installed, but if you run the Setup on a different Windows version it asks for another IP address and locks your user ID onto it instead.

Satellite: Getting Hooked Up

Currently only a few companies are offering satellite Internet service. The largest is Direcway (www .direcway.com). You can place an order for service online, and they will ship your hardware to a professional installer in your area who will come to your home and do the installation.

Depending on the installer you get, he or she may do the PC setup for you, or you may need to do it yourself. You'll receive a CD-ROM containing the Setup program; it is fairly self-explanatory. You will need an analog modem to complete it; you might need to borrow one if you don't have one, just for this one usage.

Protecting Your System

If you have a small business or a home office that's connected to the Internet by cable, DSL, or two-way satellite, you'll want to be sure that Internet Connection Firewall (ICF) is enabled. These types of connections are always on, and thus your computer system is more vulnerable to unauthorized use. A *firewall* is a security system that prevents would-be mischief makers from accessing your computer system through the Internet.

Internet Connection Firewall is included with Windows XP Professional, and by default it is enabled, even if you have an analog modem connection. If you have a cable modem or a DSL modem, be sure that you require passwords to any shared resources, and verify that ICF is enabled. To check on ICF, follow these steps:

1. Click Start ➢ Connect To ➢ Show All Connections to open the Network Connections folder.

2. Right-click your connection, and choose Properties from the shortcut menu to open the Properties dialog box for your connection.

3. Click the Advanced tab:

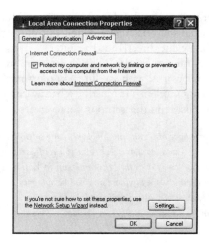

4. Be sure that the Internet Connection Firewall check box is checked, and then click OK.

If you have a larger network or a corporate network, you'll need a more sophisticated firewall. You might start by asking the advice of your ISP. You can also find a wealth of information, vendors, consultants, and so forth on the Internet by searching on "firewall." A good jumping-off place is www.firewall.com.

TIP *Check out the Microsoft Internet Security Advisor check at* www.microsoft.com/technet/mpsa/start.asp *to see how vulnerable to hacking your local PC and network are. You can get the same service with the Shields Up tool available from* www.grc.com.

Connecting to the Internet with ISDN

ISDN is another option for providing high-speed Internet connectivity, but it has taken a back seat to other modern technologies due to two primary factors: cost and speed. Although ISDN can provide high-speed access to the Internet, it is typically slower than other commercial alternatives. In addition to its lack of speed, in some cases it is also more costly than other services, with some providers even charging by the minute. However, ISDN has one advantage over all other high-speed options: it is available almost anywhere. In addition, you aren't tied to an ISP as you usually are with DSL or cable modem. Depending on your situation, ISDN might be a good choice for you.

ISDN—How Does It Work?

ISDN (Integrated Services Digital Network) is an international standard for sending voice, video, and data over normal telephone lines. It works by sending a data signal over a pair of copper wires and then dividing the data signal into three separate channels. A separate function and bandwidth are allocated to each channel.

The first type of channel is a bearer channel, commonly referred to as a *B channel*. A B channel can support data, voice, or fax transmissions and is capable of moving data at 64Kbps. With the exception of commercial-grade circuits, most ISDN lines can support two B channels, yielding a maximum throughput of 128Kbps. As you can see, even a single B channel by itself is already faster than a 56K modem.

The second type of channel is a data channel, commonly referred to as a *D channel*. A D channel typically carries data at 16Kbps and is primarily used for transmitting connection maintenance data such as call signaling and setup information, requests for network services, tearing down a call when it's complete, and so on. Since a D channel is typically used to maintain the connection, it is not typically used for data transmission. Therefore, the most common configuration you will see for an ISDN connection is what's referred to as a 2B+D connection—two bearer channels, one data channel. The maximum data throughput (before compression) allowed through such a circuit is 128Kbps.

ISDN—Advantages and Disadvantages

A number of advantages and disadvantages are associated with ISDN in comparison with typical analog modems.

ADVANTAGES OF ISDN SERVICE

Widely available   ISDN is available almost everywhere. As a matter of fact, only the existing analog phone network has a wider reach. Depending on your location, ISDN might be the only option for high-speed Internet access.

High-speed   With speeds more than 125 percent faster than the fastest 56K analog modems available, you will definitely appreciate the added bandwidth of an ISDN connection.

One less phone line needed   If you had a dedicated second phone line installed in your house for computer access, you can drop that phone line and run your voice and data communications over the same ISDN line. This can help offset some of the cost of your ISDN service.

Multipurpose   You can use the same ISDN line for voice calls, fax, data, and so on.

DISADVANTAGES OF ISDN SERVICE

Cost   ISDN, in some markets, is still expensive in comparison with the additional bandwidth that it provides. Some providers are even charging per-minute fees for ISDN usage, which can add up to some hefty monthly bills if you are a heavy user.

Getting Hooked Up

If you've looked at your connectivity options and decided that ISDN is the best route for you, let's take a look at the process you'll need to go through to get access to the Internet.

ISDN MODEM

The first thing that you will need to install into your system is an ISDN modem. Basically, an ISDN modem is no different from a regular analog modem, except for the fact that it works on an ISDN line instead of an analog line.

NOTE   Although we typically refer to the little box that connects your computer to your DSL, ISDN, or cable line as a modem, it really isn't a modem in the true sense of the word. A modem converts digital signals to analog signals and vice versa. So-called DSL, ISDN, and cable modems transmit and receive all data as digital signals, and so they are really terminal adapters.

Once your ISDN modem is installed (and Windows XP Professional recognizes it correctly), some configuring may be involved.

After you've finished configuring your ISDN modem, the steps to connect to the Internet are amazingly similar to the steps used for connecting to the Internet with an analog modem. That brings us to the next part of the picture.

YOU NEED AN ISP TOO

Unlike other high-speed Internet options, which typically include an ISP account, you will probably have to set up an account with an ISDN-capable ISP. ISPs don't actually run the ISDN line to your location, they just set up banks of ISDN modems at their location to receive calls—just as they do with analog modems. It's up to you to purchase your connection and then to use it to call into them.

This allows you to easily switch from one ISP to another while keeping your high-speed ISDN line. This is also a good option if your existing analog dial-up ISP supports ISDN connections, as you can keep all of your existing e-mail address and other services. The only thing that will change as far as your ISP is concerned is which line you dial in on, the analog or the ISDN.

SERVICE DELIVERY

When you're ready to get started with ISDN, you will need to purchase the service directly from your phone company or, optionally, from your ISP if they offer the service (they will most likely order the line from the phone company on your behalf). A technician from your phone company should arrive at your location to set up your ISDN circuit. Once their work is finished, you should have an ISDN jack installed in your home or office.

At this point, you should refer to your modem manufacturer's directions about how to connect your ISDN modem to your ISDN line. Although most ISDN modems will have a jack for the ISDN connection (and optionally one or two jacks to plug in regular phone equipment), you may need to manually configure some items—such as the ISDN switch type you are connected to, the service profile identifiers (SPIDs), and so on. Although most good ISDN modems autodetect most of these items for you, you may have to configure some of them manually. Results will vary with each modem manufacturer, so follow their directions carefully in conjunction with the paperwork from your ISDN provider.

GETTING CONNECTED

If your ISDN modem is Plug and Play (and it certainly should be), Windows XP Professional will recognize and install it once it is connected to your computer. To configure an ISDN modem, follow these steps:

1. Click Start ➤ Connect To ➤ Show All Connections to open your Network Connections folder.

2. Right-click the dial-up connection that uses ISDN, and choose Properties from the shortcut menu to open the Properties dialog box for your ISDN modem.

3. Click the General tab, select the ISDN device, and then click Configure. (Depending on the type of your ISDN modem, you may open the Modem Configurations dialog box when you click Configure.)

4. In the dialog box that opens, select the type of line you will be using in the Line Type area. If you want to negotiate for a line type, click the Negotiate Line Type check box, and then click OK.

Using the Network Setup Wizard to Share an Internet Connection

As you may know, Windows XP lets you share your Internet connection with other computers on your network. Logically enough, the feature that lets you do this is called *Internet Connection Sharing*, which gets abbreviated to ICS.

ICS can be a great way of saving time and money: instead of needing a modem and phone line (or a DSL or cable modem) for each computer that needs Internet connectivity, you can get by with one modem (or equivalent) and one phone line. ICS is particularly good if you have a fast Internet connection (such as a DSL or a cable modem) that provides enough bandwidth for several computers under normal circumstances. (If someone's perpetually trying to watch streaming video, all bets are off.)

This is all good—provided your Internet connection is fast enough. It goes without saying that ICS doesn't speed up your existing Internet connection. If your connection is slow with one person using it, it'll be glacial once you've connected the whole household or office through it.

Set Up the Computer That Will Share the Connection

Start with the computer that will share the Internet connection. First set up your Internet connection, and then use the Network Setup Wizard to configure the computer by taking the following steps:

1. Choose Start ➤ All Programs ➤ Accessories ➤ Communications ➤ Network Setup Wizard to start Network Setup Wizard.

2. At the Welcome screen, click the Next button. The Wizard displays the Before You Continue screen, which tells you to plug in your devices, turn on all the computers and devices, and connect to the Internet:

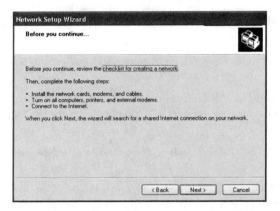

3. Click the Next button. The Wizard displays the Select a Connection Method screen:

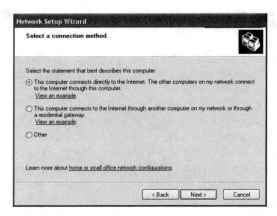

4. Make sure the This Computer Connects Directly to the Internet. The Other Computers on My Network Connect to the Internet through This Computer option button is selected.

5. Click the Next button. The Wizard displays the Select Your Internet Connection screen:

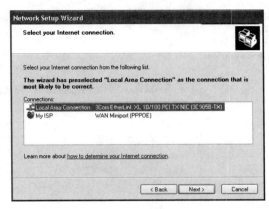

6. In the Connections list box, select your Internet connection. In this example, there's some confusion, as the Wizard is listing a dial-up connection and the local area network connection. If you have configured multiple dial-up connections or broadband connections, you may have to pay a little more attention to this choice. Windows establishes the connection you choose.

7. Click the Next button. The Wizard displays the Give This Computer a Description and Name screen:

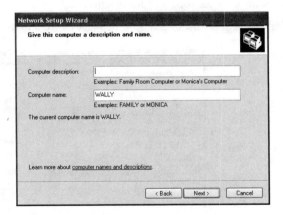

8. Enter the description for your computer in the Computer Description text box. This description is for your benefit and that of other users of the network, so make it concise and descriptive.

9. In the Computer Name text box, enter the name for your computer. Typically, for dial-up connections and DSL connections, you can choose more or less any name that suits you (within Windows' naming conventions). For cable-modem connections, you may have to use a name designated by your ISP.

10. Click the Next button. The Wizard displays the Name Your Network screen:

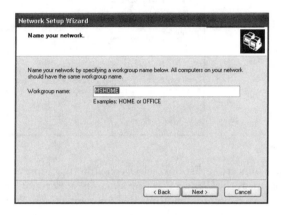

11. In the Workgroup Name text box, enter a name for the network. It's best to use a unique name rather than the default name, MSHome, in case your network or Internet connection puts you on the same network loop as your neighbors.

12. Click the Next button. The Wizard displays the Ready to Apply Network Settings screen:

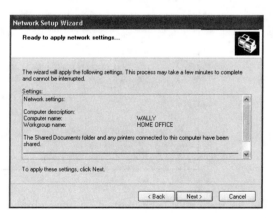

13. Click the Next button. The Wizard starts configuring the home network. While it works, it displays the Please Wait screen:

14. When the Wizard has finished configuring the computer, it displays the You're Almost Done screen, which offers to create a network setup disk for use on non-XP computers connecting to the same computer:

15. If you want to create a network setup disk, select the Create a Network Setup Disk option button. Otherwise, select the Just Finish the Wizard; I Don't Need to Run the Wizard on Other Computers option button. (Selecting the Use the Network Setup Disk I Already Have option button or the Use My Windows XP CD option button displays a screen of instructions for using the network setup disk or the CD.)

16. Click the Next button.

   ◆ If you chose the Create a Network Setup Disk option button, the Wizard displays the Insert the Disk You Want to Use screen:

   ◆ Insert a floppy disk in the floppy drive.

   ◆ If you need to format the floppy disk, click the Format Disk button and use the resulting Format 3-½ Floppy dialog box to format the disk as usual. Then click the Close button. Windows closes the dialog box.

   ◆ Click the Next button. Windows copies files to the floppy and then displays the To Run the Wizard with the Network Setup Disk screen, which contains instructions for using the disk.

   ◆ Click the Next button.

17. The Wizard displays the Completing the Network Setup Wizard screen, which provides links to Help and Support Center topics on sharing files and folders.

18. Click the Finish button. The Network Setup Wizard closes itself.

Setting Up a Client Computer

Next, set up the first of your client computers. Make sure the Internet connection is still open on the computer you set up to share it, and then take the following steps:

1. Start the Network Setup Wizard:

   ◆ On an XP computer, choose Start ➤ All Programs ➤ Accessories ➤ Communications ➤ Network Setup Wizard. The Wizard displays the Welcome to the Network Setup Wizard screen.

◆ On a computer running an earlier version of 32-bit Windows, put the network setup disk you made earlier in the floppy drive. Open an Explorer window to the floppy drive and double-click the file named NETSETUP (or NETSETUP.EXE, if you've set Windows to show file extensions). The Wizard displays three Network Setup Wizard dialog boxes in sequence. The first dialog box tells you that the Wizard needs to install network support files on your computer. Click the Yes button. The second dialog box tells you to remove the floppy and warns you that it will prompt you to restart your computer. Remove the floppy and click the OK button. The third dialog box prompts you to restart your computer. Click the Yes button. After the restart, the Wizard displays the Welcome to the Network Setup Wizard screen.

2. Click the Next button. The Wizard displays the Before You Continue screen, shown earlier.

3. Click the Next button. The Wizard displays the Do You Want to Use the Shared Connection? screen:

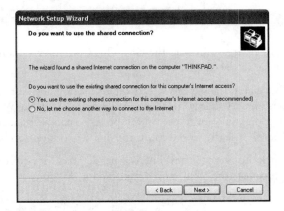

4. If the Wizard has identified the right connection, leave the Yes, Use the Existing Shared Connection for This Computer's Internet Access option button selected. If not, select the No, Let Me Choose Another Way to Connect to the Internet option button.

5. Click the Next button.

◆ If you chose the No, Let Me Choose Another Way to Connect to the Internet option button, Windows displays the Select a Connection Method screen, shown earlier in this chapter.

◆ Make sure the This Computer Connects to the Internet through Another Computer on My Network or through a Residential Gateway option button is selected.

◆ Click the Next button. If your computer has more than one Internet connection, the Wizard displays the Your Computer Has Multiple Connections screen:

(Otherwise, it displays the Give This Computer a Name and Description screen, shown earlier in the chapter).

◆ By default, the Wizard selects the Determine the Appropriate Connections for Me option button. If you leave this option button selected, the Wizard guesses which Internet connection you want to use. If you prefer to choose the connection yourself, select the Let Me Choose the Connections to My Network option button.

◆ Click the Next button. The Wizard displays the Select the Connections to Bridge screen, which lists the connections available for bridging:

◆ Select the check boxes for the connections you want to bridge. Clear the check box for any direct Internet connection. Then click the Next button. (The Wizard displays the Give This Computer a Name and Description screen, shown earlier in this chapter).

6. Enter the description and name for the computer. (See steps 8 and 9 in the previous list.) Because this computer isn't connecting to the Internet directly, you should be free to use any name you want for it even if your ISP requires that you use a specific name for the computer that's directly connected.

7. Click the Next button. (The Wizard displays the Name Your Network screen, shown earlier in this chapter).

8. In the Workgroup Name text box, enter the name you chose earlier for the network.

9. Click the Next button. The Wizard displays the Ready to Apply Network Settings screen, an example of which is shown below:

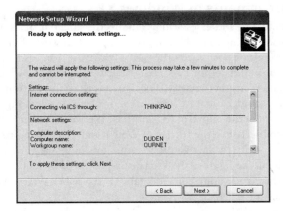

10. Click the Next button. The Wizard displays the Please Wait screen while it configures the computer. It then displays the You're Almost Done screen, shown earlier in this chapter.

11. Select the Just Finish the Wizard; I Don't Need to Run the Wizard on Other Computers option button.

12. Click the Next button. The Wizard displays the Completing the Network Setup Wizard screen.

13. Click the Finish button. The Wizard closes itself and displays the System Settings Change dialog box telling you that you need to restart your computer before the new settings will take effect.

14. Click the Yes button if you want to restart your computer immediately. Click the No button if you want to close some programs and then restart your computer manually.

What ICS Does

In networking terms, ICS combines several elements: a proxy server, a router, and a DHCP server. As such, it's relatively simple—but it comes free with Windows, and it's easy to set up and use.

ICS uses Network Address Translation (NAT), which is also known as *IP masquerading* (particularly in the Linux world). In NAT, the host (in this case, ICS) acts as an intermediary between the client (the PC connected to the network) and the server (the Internet server that is supplying information).

In NAT, the identity of the client submitting a request is hidden: instead, the request appears to come from the host. This can be good and bad. NAT gives you more freedom in the IP addresses you assign within the network. For example, you can use nonroutable internal IP addresses to make sure that incoming packets can reach a computer only through the router. But if someone on your network takes some illegal or offensive action (for example, posting libelous comments or download-ing, uh, *unsuitable* material), the culprit will appear to be the host rather than the individual concerned. (If you had multiple IP addresses, only the specific IP address involved would appear to be guilty.)

NAT Improvements in Windows XP

The nonroutable IP addresses lead us (indirectly, sure, but that's what happens when you're routing requests) to something that's been more of a problem with NAT in the past: computers not being able to communicate with each other across *two* NAT routers.

That might sound complicated, but it really isn't. You see, what usually happens with NAT is one of the computers inside the network originates the conversation with a computer on the Internet. For example, consider Figure 11.1. This shows two simple home networks, unimaginatively named West Network (in the blue trunks) and East Network (in the red). Each network contains a com-puter that's connected to the Internet (West 1 and East 1) and running NAT so that it can provide Internet connectivity to the two other computers in its network (West 2, West 3, East 2, and East 3). In the middle of the figure is the Internet, represented by its traditional cloud of uncertainty. And right below the cloud (quite coincidentally) is the Sybex Web server, represented by a computer the size of a walk-in freezer.

So far, so good. Now, here's the problem that used to occur with NAT. The computers that con-nect through the NAT boxes have only internal IP addresses. That means they can originate a con-versation with a computer on the Internet, but they can't take part in a conversation originated from beyond their NAT box. For example, West 2 can access the Sybex Web server with no problem. It sends its request to the NAT router on West 1, which says the binary equivalent of "ah, an address on the Internet" and shunts the request out through its external connection. The Sybex Web server responds to the request and sends back a response to West 1. The NAT router intercepts this response, matches it to the outgoing request, says "ah, it's for West 2" (again in binary), and passes the data on to West 2. And so it continues: West 2 (and the other internal computers) can access Internet sites provided that it starts the conversation.

But if West 3 wants to start a conversation with East 2, it can't, because it can't see East 2 through the NAT router on East 1. It can get as far as East 1, because that computer has an external IP address. But the computers beyond the NAT router are hidden from view. So you can't access them for a quick DeathMatch, for videoconferencing, for chat—well, for anything. And with NAT routers becoming widely implemented thanks to the rapid spread of broadband availability, that quickly becomes a prob-lem. At one end of the connection, the activity has to take place on the computer running the NAT router rather than on the "inside" machine you want to use.

FIGURE 11.1

Two networks using NAT to connect internal computers to the Internet

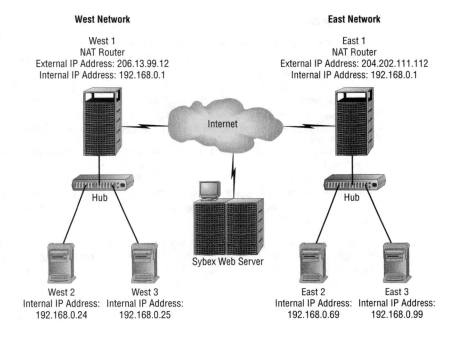

The good news is that Windows XP fixes this problem, letting you communicate across two NAT routers, from one inside machine to another inside machine. This is quite clever, because both the server (the NAT router) and the client (the inside machine) need to understand what's going on and work together. Some of the software has to be reworked in order to make the connection work, but you'll find that many things work.

ALTERNATIVES TO INTERNET CONNECTION SHARING

The preceding description probably makes ICS sound pretty good. And it is—up to a point. But it has two significant limitations:

◆ First, you need to keep the ICS computer running all the time so that it can handle the Internet connection and the sharing.

◆ Second, because of the way ICS is set up, you can share only one Internet connection at the same time on the same network by using ICS. To share two Internet connections, you'll need to set one up manually for sharing via another technology. (Alternatively, you can create two separate networks with an ICS connection in each, but doing so is usually much more work than setting up a second shared connection manually, because those two networks won't be able to talk to each other directly without ICS conflicts.) You can also use unshared Internet connections alongside your shared connections without any problems.

There are better alternatives—*much* better alternatives—to using ICS. Unfortunately, almost all of them require you paying for them and putting some more effort into implementing them than ICS takes. But they're worth a quick mention here in case you're interested.

Continued on next page

ALTERNATIVES TO INTERNET CONNECTION SHARING *(continued)*

Depending on your ISP, you may be able to get multiple IP addresses for your broadband connection without paying more for them. Other ISPs consider supplying multiple IP addresses to involve a different category of service than supplying a single IP address, and charge accordingly. For example, some ISPs charge around $40 a month for "residential" DSL service (which gives just one IP address) and $100–$200 for "business" DSL service (which gives multiple IP addresses—usually between five and twenty). Apart from the IP addresses and the fistful of dollars, the distinctions between the residential and business services tend to be detectable only under sustained scrutiny through an electron microscope.

If you want the residential service but need to be able to connect multiple computers through your single IP address connection, get a cable router or DSL router designed for this purpose. All these routers have NAT built in, and most can run DHCP as well, which means that you don't need to keep one computer running the whole time to handle DHCP and NAT so that other computers can access the Internet. Some routers have firewalls built in as well, which you can use instead of or in addition to Windows XP's Internet Connection Firewall (ICF).

Some models are designed to connect to a network switch or hub and have two ports: an internal port for connecting to the switch or hub and an external port for connecting to the cable modem or DSL splitter. Others have hubs or switches built in, so if you haven't yet bought the hub or switch for your network, you can solve all your connectivity needs with a single box.

Configuring ICS Manually

To configure ICS manually, take the following steps:

1. Choose Start ➢ Connect To ➢ Show All Connections to open the Network Connections window.

2. Right-click the dial-up connection for which you want to implement ICS and choose Properties from the shortcut menu to open the Properties dialog box for the connection.

3. Click the Advanced tab:

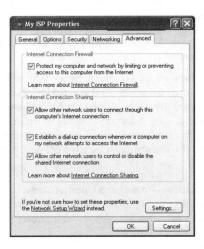

4. Select the Allow Other Network Users to Connect through This Computer's Internet Connection check box.

5. If you want other computers to be able to cause ICS to start up the network connection when it's not running, make sure the Establish a Dial-up Connection Whenever a Computer on My Network Attempts to Access the Internet check box is selected. Clear this check box if you want only the computer with the connection to be able to start the connection.

6. If you want users of the other computers on the network to be able to control the Internet connection, make sure the Allow Other Network Users to Control or Disable the Shared Internet Connection check box is selected. Clear this check box if you don't want them to be able to manipulate the Internet connection directly.

7. If you want to use Internet Connection Firewall on this connection, select the Protect My Computer and Network by Limiting or Preventing Access to This Computer from the Internet check box in the Internet Connection Firewall section.

TIP Unless you're using a separate firewall or you've established that ICF interferes with an Internet program that you must run, it's a good idea to use ICF on your Internet connection.

8. Click the OK button. Windows closes the Properties dialog box for the connection, changes the IP address of your network adapter to the static IP address 192.168.0.1, and starts telling the other computers to get their IP addresses from it (if there's no other DHCP server on the network).

NOTE If you have another computer on the network using the 192.168.0.1 IP address, Windows gives you an angry message telling you to change that IP address on the other computer before it will let you implement ICS on this computer. You're likely to be using this IP address only if you've previously set up ICS on another computer or the stars have decided you're due for a bad-horoscope day. If the other computer is running ICS, display the Properties dialog box for its shared connection and clear the Allow Other Network Users to Connect through This Computer's Internet Connection check box, and then click the OK button. If the other computer isn't running ICS but has the 192.168.0.1 IP address set manually, either set a different address manually or switch to automatic addressing.

At this point, ICS should be up and running. The shared connection appears with a palm-upward hand on its icon to indicate that it's shared. If it's your default connection, the icon has a white check mark in a black circle. And if you're using ICF, the connection has a lock icon in its upper-right quadrant.

Specifying Which Programs and Services Can Use the Shared Connection

Next, if you want, you can specify which programs and services can use the shared connection. This can be useful if you need to manage the shared connection or make sure that only authorized programs are run via it. You may not want to do this, but simply let any program that wants Internet connectivity via the shared connection have it.

To specify which programs and services can use the shared connection, take the following steps:

1. Display the Advanced tab of the Properties dialog box for the network connection in question.

2. Click the Settings button. Windows displays the Advanced Settings dialog box open at the Services tab:

3. In the Services list, select the services running on your network that you want Internet users to be able to access. By default, none of these services are accessible from outside the network—you need to turn them on explicitly.

◆ You can add a service by clicking the Add button and working in the Service Settings dialog box (shown in Figure 11.2). Enter the description of the service, the name or IP address of the computer hosting the service, and the port number and port type (TCP or UDP) of the service, and click the OK button. Windows closes the Service Settings dialog box and adds the service to the Services list box.

FIGURE 11.2

If necessary, you can use the Service Settings dialog box to add a service for sharing.

◆ You can change one of the listed services by selecting it, clicking the Edit button, and working in the resulting Service Settings dialog box.

4. Click the Security Logging tab:

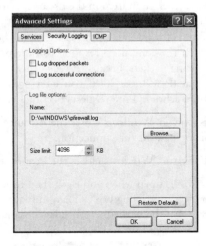

5. Select the Log Dropped Packets check box if you want to log dropped data packets. Select the Log Successful Connections check box if you want to log successful inbound and outbound connections (for example, to see which Internet sites the computers on your network are connecting to and which computers are connecting to your network from the Internet).

6. In the Log File Options section, use the Name text box (and if necessary the Browse button and its resulting Browse dialog box) to specify where to store the log file. If you want, use the Size Limit text box to change the size limit for the security log file. The default setting is 4096KB—in other words, 4MB—which is enough for a large number of successful connections and a few dropped packets.

7. Click the ICMP tab:

8. Select the check boxes for the ICMP (Internet Control Message Protocol) options you want to use. When you select an item in the list box, Windows displays information about it in the Description text box. These options control how the computers on your network respond to incoming requests for information. For example, the Allow Incoming Echo Request check box controls whether the computers respond to Ping packets sent to them. (Usually, it's best not to respond to Ping packets, because it tells other people—including crackers—that there's a computer at that IP address. But if you're trying to establish that your network is alive from a remote location, echoing Ping requests becomes very valuable.)

9. Click the OK button. Windows closes the Advanced Settings dialog box, returning you to the Properties dialog box for the connection.

10. Click the OK button. Windows closes the Properties dialog box.

11. If the connection is open when you close the Properties dialog box, Windows displays the Network Connections dialog box (shown in Figure 11.3) warning you that some changes may not take effect until the next time you start the connection. Click the OK button.

FIGURE 11.3

If the connection is open, Windows displays the Network Connections dialog box to warn you that some settings you changed may not take effect immediately.

Setting the IP Addresses of Connected Computers

If your Windows computers are set to get IP addresses via DHCP, they should automatically get IP addresses from ICS within a few minutes of your implementing ICS. If you're configuring IP addresses manually, you'll need to set each computer to an IP address in the 192.168.0.2 to 192.168.0.254 range.

Turning Off ICS

To turn off ICS on the host computer, clear the Allow Other Network Users to Connect through This Computer's Internet Connection check box on the Advanced tab of the Properties dialog box for the connection, and then click the OK button. Windows closes the Properties dialog box and changes your computer's IP address from using 192.168.0.1 to obtaining an IP address automatically.

If you have a DHCP server on your network, Windows grabs an IP address from it on the next go-around of network polling. If Windows doesn't find a DHCP server (which will be the case if ICS was handling DHCP for you before you turned it off), Windows falls back on its alternate TCP/IP configuration, which uses Automatic Private IP Addressing (APIPA) to automatically assign an IP address in the range 169.254.0.1 to 169.254.255.254.

Using a Shared Internet Connection

Depending on how a shared Internet connection is configured, you can use it in much the same way as you use a regular Internet connection on your computer.

The shared connection appears under the Internet Gateway heading in the Network Connections window with a flashy icon.

To tell Windows to display an icon in the notification area when the connection is connected, take the following steps:

1. Right-click the connection, and choose Properties from the shortcut menu to open the Properties dialog box for the connection.

2. Select the Show Icon in Notification Area When Connected check box.

3. Click the OK button. Windows closes the Properties dialog box and applies the setting.

If the connection is configured to start automatically on demand, you can start the connection by starting a program that attempts to access the Internet. For example, if you start Internet Explorer or Outlook Express, ICS automatically starts the connection.

If the connection is configured to let you control it, you can start it manually by double-clicking its entry on the Network Connections screen, and you can disconnect the connection by right-clicking its notification-area icon and choosing Disconnect from the shortcut menu.

Troubleshooting Internet Connectivity Problems

The following sections provide some solutions for common problems with connecting to the Internet.

Dial-Up Modem Problems

Here are some issues you might encounter with an analog modem:

◆ **No dial tone:** Make sure the phone line is connected to the Line port on the modem, and to the wall outlet. Try plugging a telephone into that jack to confirm that it's working.

◆ **Lots of static on the line/slow connection speeds:** Make sure the phone line is plugged into the Line port on the modem, not the Phone port. It makes a big difference on some modems; on others none at all. Also make sure you are using a good-quality phone cable, and that it isn't overly long (say, over 15 feet), and that it isn't next to any cables or devices emitting electromagnetic interference. Finally, have the phone company run a line quality check on your phone line to make sure there is not undue static interference in general.

◆ **Modem won't dial:** Check the modem through Phone and Modem Options in Control Panel, as you learned to do in Chapter 8. In the Modems tab, click Properties, and then click the Diagnostics tab; then click Query Modem.

◆ **Modem leaves phone off the hook:** Remove and reinstall the driver for the modem. See Chapter 8.

◆ **Frequent disconnects:** Try a different access number if there is more than one in your area. Also you might contact your ISP to see whether there are any special modem settings you need to make in order for the connection to be more reliable. Remember from Chapter 8 that you can add extra initialization AT commands to a modem's Properties.

Cable/DSL Problems

Here are some problems you might face with a cable or DSL connection:

◆ **Blinking lights on cable or DSL box:** If there are no always-on lights on the box, but just one or two blinking ones, the connection is not being made from the box to the Internet. Try turning off or unplugging the box, waiting a few seconds, and turning it on again. Sometimes temporary network outages prevent access and there's nothing you can do about it, so try back in an hour or so. It won't help you after the fact, but if you can catch the cable or DSL box when it's working right, notice which lights are on and which are blinking. Then you'll know what's "normal" for that device.

◆ **After reinstalling Windows, no access:** If the lights on the cable or DSL box indicate it's functioning correctly but you can't get a Web page to come up, the problem is between the box and your PC. You probably don't have the right settings in Windows. Check the IP address for TCP/IP to make sure you are using the assigned IP address (if you have one assigned), and check the computer name in the Computer Name tab of the System Properties dialog box. Some cable or DSL connections require you to use a certain computer name.

TIP   Some people have reported problems with Easy CD Creator 5 software interfering with cable or DSL Internet connections. If connection interruption problems persist, try removing that software if you have it installed.

Satellite Problems

Here are some problems you may encounter with satellite Internet service:

◆ **After upgrading or reinstalling Windows, no access:** You may need to rerun the Setup program again. If you use the Direcway system, you can run WebSetup (Start ➢ All Programs ➢ DIRECWAY ➢ WebSetup) to reconfigure the settings without having to completely reinstall everything.

◆ **Loss of satellite signal:** If you use Direcway, you can double-click the DW icon in the notification area to open a status box for the connection. If the connection strength is poor (under 50%), make sure nobody has bumped your dish out of alignment. Signal strength tends to degrade in rainy or snowy weather. You may need to go out and brush the snow off the dish. (Don't use your hand; use a broom or similar tool.)

Summary

This chapter covered how to install and configure modem and broadband connections to the Internet. It also gave you step-by-step instructions for implementing Internet Connection Sharing, by using the Network Setup Wizard and by setting up this configuration manually.

In the next chapter, you'll learn how to configure and use Internet Explorer to surf the Web.

Chapter 12

Web Browsing with Internet Explorer

OBVIOUSLY, THE MOST IMPORTANT thing about Internet Explorer is not the program itself but all the resources you can access using it. And, to be completely honest about it, Internet Explorer is so easy to use that you hardly need a how-to book, a manual, or even this chapter. If you know how to open any Windows XP Professional program, you know how to open Internet Explorer, and you can start browsing immediately by simply clicking links.

Thus, in this chapter I'm going to move briskly through the tasks you most commonly perform with Internet Explorer. As I proceed, I'll point out some new features of version 6 and show you how to expand on what comes naturally.

- ◆ Starting Internet Explorer
- ◆ Touring Internet Explorer
- ◆ Moving around the Web
- ◆ Finding exactly what you want on the Internet
- ◆ Customizing Internet Explorer

Starting Internet Explorer

When you first start Internet Explorer after installing Windows XP Professional, you'll see the start page shown in Figure 12.1. (The content of the page changes daily, so yours will look different.)

You can start Internet Explorer by doing any of the following:

- ◆ Choose Start ➢ Internet Explorer.
- ◆ Choose Start ➢ All Programs ➢ Internet Explorer.
- ◆ Click the Internet Explorer icon in the Quick Launch toolbar (if displayed).
- ◆ Double-click the icon for a Web page from a file management window or from the desktop.
- ◆ Click a hyperlink in an e-mail message, document, or some other data file.

FIGURE 12.1

You can retain the page at www.msn .com as your start page or select any other page that suits your fancy or interests.

TIP   *If you use both Internet Explorer and some other browser, such as Netscape Navigator, you'll see a dialog box when you start up Internet Explorer if it is not set as the default browser, offering to "fix" the problem. Clear the Always Perform This Check with Starting Internet Explorer check box to prevent it from doing that in the future. You can also control this preference from the Internet Options dialog box's Programs tab. That'll take care of it from the IE side. If you want to also take care of it from Netscape, choose Edit ➤ Preferences in Netscape, expand the Advanced category, and choose Desktop Integration. In the File Types box, you can select file types you want to associate with Netscape. If .htm and .html are not associated with Netscape, Netscape won't think it's the default browser. You can also change file associations from any Windows Explorer window as you learned in Chapter 6.*

Moving around the Web

You probably already use Internet Explorer (or some other Web browser) nearly every day, so we won't dwell on the basics of Web surfing here, other than to run down this quick list of skills:

◆ To open the page represented by a hyperlink, click the hyperlink.

◆ To go to a specific URL, type it in the Address box.

NOTE   *Internet Explorer assumes that when you enter a URL in the Address bar, you want to go to a Web page or some other HTML document. Therefore, whether you enter* http://www.sybex.com *or* www.sybex.com*, you'll reach the Sybex Web site. If you want to access another type of resource, such as an FTP archive, a Telnet host, or a Gopher server, you'll need to enter the full URL, for example,* ftp://ftp.archive.edu*.*

◆ To open a Web page saved locally, use the File ➤ Open command.

◆ To return to a URL you have visited recently, open the Address box's drop-down list and choose it.

◆ To return to a site you have visited in the last several days, click the History button on the toolbar and select it from the History pane (covered in more detail later in this chapter).

◆ To go to a URL you have saved on your Favorites list, open the Favorites menu and select it, or click the Favorites button on the toolbar and then select it from the Favorites pane (also covered in more detail later).

◆ To return to the page you last viewed, click Back. To go back multiple steps, open the drop-down list on the Back button.

◆ After having used Back, click Forward to go forward again to the page you started from when clicking Back. The Forward button has a drop-down list, too, for multiple hops at once.

A LOOK BEHIND THE SCENES: VIEWING HTML PAGES

HTML is the abbreviation for HyperText Markup Language, the language that is used to create Web pages. HTML uses tags to tell the browser how to display the page on the screen. Tags are enclosed in angle brackets, and most come in pairs. For example, the <H1> tag defines a first-level heading, like this:

<H1>This is a level 1 heading.</H1>

An HTML file is really just a plain text file that can be created with a text editor such as Notepad or with a program such as Microsoft FrontPage. To view the HTML behind any page you open in Internet Explorer, choose View ➤ Source. The file is displayed in Notepad and looks similar to the following:

To return to Internet Explorer and the page displayed in the browser, click the Close button in Notepad.

If you're interested in learning more about HTML and creating Web pages, check out the following Sybex titles: *Mastering FrontPage 2002 Premium Edition* and *Mastering HTML 4, Second Edition*.

TIP   If you want to edit only part of an address that's already displayed in the Address bar, place the cursor in the Address bar, hold down Ctrl, and press the right or left arrow to jump forward or backward to the next separator character (\ \ \ . ? - or +).

Working with the Links Bar

One way to keep track of links that you follow and want to revisit is to add them to the Links bar. When you first install Windows XP Professional, the Links bar contains the following:

- ◆ Customize Links, which takes you to a Microsoft page that gives you information on how to add, remove, and rearrange items on the Links bar

- ◆ Free Hotmail, which takes you to a page where you can sign up for a Hotmail e-mail account

- ◆ Windows, which takes you to the Microsoft Windows site

- ◆ Windows Media, which takes you to WindowsMedia.com

The Links bar is locked into place by default, with only its name appearing at the right end of the Address bar. You must click the double arrow on it to display its contents. See Figure 12.2.

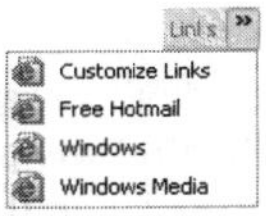

FIGURE 12.2

To view the Links bar's hidden content, click the double arrow.

If you would prefer to have it take up a whole row by itself, or at least a little more room to the right, first unlock it by choosing View ➤ Toolbars ➤ Lock the Toolbars to remove the check mark from that command. Then drag the word *Links* to the left or right, or up or down.

To add a link to the Links bar, simply drag it from the Web page to the Links bar. (You can then rename it if the name is too long by right-clicking and choosing Rename.) To remove a link, right-click it and choose Delete from the shortcut menu. To rearrange items on the Links bar, click the item and then drag it to a new location.

To turn off the Links bar altogether, choose View ➤ Toolbars ➤ Links to remove the check mark from next to its name.

TIP   You can put a link to any file on the Links bar, not just a Web page. If you maintain a log file where you store interesting information you come across on the Web, for example, you could put a link to that text file there.

Keeping Track of Your Favorite Sites

If you add lots of links to the Links bar, it can get really crowded. You might find that you need a more sophisticated method of keeping track of your favorite sites, and the Favorites list is just the thing. To open it, click the Favorites button on the Standard toolbar, or choose Favorites from the menu bar. Figure 12.3 shows the screen you'll see if you click the Favorites button, and Figure 12.4 shows the Favorites menu.

FIGURE 12.3

Click the Favorites button to open the Favorites bar.

FIGURE 12.4

Choose the Favorites menu to see this drop-down list.

ADDING A SITE TO YOUR FAVORITES LIST

To add a site to your Favorites list, follow these steps:

1. Go to the site you want to add.

2. Click Favorites to open the Favorites bar.

3. Click Add to open the Add Favorite dialog box:

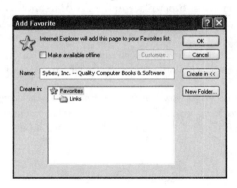

4. If you want to place this page in your top-level Favorites menu, click OK. If you want to add it to an existing folder, click Create In, select a folder, and click OK. If you want to create a new folder for this item, click New Folder, enter a name for the folder, and click OK.

5. In the Add Favorites dialog box, Internet Explorer provides a name for this Favorite site. To give the site another name in your Favorites list, replace the default name with the name you want.

6. Click OK.

NOTE *On some Web pages, you will see a suggestion that you "bookmark" this page. Netscape and some other Web browsers refer to a list of sites that you want to revisit as a* bookmark list *rather than as a Favorites list. If you want to use a Netscape bookmark list in IE, from Netscape, choose Bookmarks ➤ Manage Bookmarks, and then choose File ➤ Export Bookmarks from the window that appears.*

You can also add items to your Favorites list in some other ways:

◆ Right-click a link, and choose Add to Favorites from the shortcut menu.

◆ Right-click on the current page outside a link, and choose Add to Favorites from the shortcut menu to add that page.

◆ Drag and drop a link on a Web page to the Favorites button on the Standard toolbar or to the Favorites bar if displayed.

◆ Press Ctrl+D. This places the item at the top level of the Favorites organizational tree, using the full name of the page.

MAINTAINING YOUR FAVORITES LIST

You'll find out soon enough that your Favorites list will grow quickly, and before too long the titles that seemed patently clear when you added the site to the list will, unfortunately, be meaningless. In addition, you may no longer really care what's happening on the Learn2.com site. To keep your list manageable, you need to do some periodic housekeeping, weeding out what you don't want and rearranging or retitling what you do keep so that it is meaningful.

Deleting a site from your Favorites list is simple: open the Favorites bar, right-click it in the list, and choose Delete from the shortcut menu. You might, however, want to get in the habit of following the link before you right-click—just in case the site is more important than you remembered and you want to keep it in the list.

To move an item to another place in the list or to another folder, simply click and drag it. To rename an item, right-click it and choose Rename from the shortcut menu. Type the new name and press Enter.

You can also do all of this management and more from the Organize Favorites dialog box, shown in Figure 12.5. From here you can rename, delete, move, and so on, plus create new folders.

TIP *If your Favorites list gets very long, it may be difficult to wade through. One way to reduce its size is to turn on the Personalized Favorites Menu option. This hides favorites that have not recently been used, much like the personalized menus feature in Office XP. Choose Tools ➤ Internet Options, click Advanced, and mark the Enable Personalized Favorites Menu check box.*

FIGURE 12.5

Organize your list of favorites.

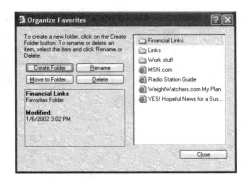

Working with the History List

Yet another way to keep track of where you've been and to quickly revisit sites of interest is the History list. To display it, click the History button on the Standard toolbar. You'll open the History bar, which will look similar to that in Figure 12.6. Simply click a link to go to that page. Click a folder to see pages in that site that have links in the History list.

NOTE *To specify how many days you want to keep links in the History list, choose Tools ➤ Internet Options, and in the General tab change the number in the Days to Keep Pages in History box. You can also clear the history list from there by clicking Clear History.*

FIGURE 12.6

You can use the History bar to see where you went today and in previous days and weeks.

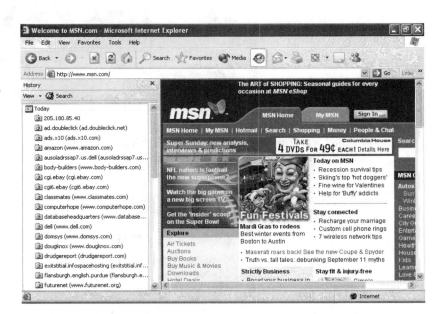

You can display the items in the History list by date, by site, by most visited, and by the order in which you visited sites today. Click the View down arrow to choose an order. If you want to search for something on the History list, click Search, enter a word or a phrase, and click Search Now.

To delete an item from the History list, right-click it, and choose Delete from the shortcut menu. To clear the History list completely, click the Clear History button in the General tab of the Internet Options dialog box.

Using the Media Bar

The Media bar is a new feature in Internet Explorer 6, and you can use it to play music, videos, or multimedia files. You can also use it to listen to Internet radio stations. To open the Media bar, which is shown in Figure 12.7, click the Media button on the Standard toolbar.

FIGURE 12.7

The Media bar in Internet Explorer

The Media bar is a subset of Windows Media Player (see Chapter 9) and has the same controls as Media Player at the bottom of the bar. Point to a control to see a description of what it does. You can use the Media bar features as follows:

◆ Click a link in the Music Videos section to open a page for that item. You can then click a link corresponding to the speed of your Internet connection to play the item.

◆ Click a link in Movie Previews to open a preview and play it.

◆ Scroll down to the More Audio and Video section to display other options for Music, Movies, Radio, and MSN Music.

◆ Click Media Options above the player controls to open a menu from which you can choose More Media (opens the Microsoft Media Web page), Radio Stations (opens the Radio Stations Web page), or Settings.

The quality of your listening and viewing experience will depend on your speakers, your system, and the speed at which you are connected.

TIP *Click the tiny arrow in the upper right corner of the Media Player controls area at the bottom of the Media Bar to undock the controls from the bar. The controls then float in their own window and you can drag them around the screen.*

Accessing E-Mail and Newsgroups from Internet Explorer

To read your e-mail as you're exploring the Internet, you can quickly open your Inbox in Outlook Express by clicking the Mail button on the Standard toolbar and choosing Read Mail. To check a newsgroup, click the Mail button, and choose Read News. To compose an e-mail message, click the Mail button, and choose New Message to open the New Message window. See Figure 12.8.

FIGURE 12.8

Click the Mail button for a menu of mail-related options.

TIP *Outlook Express is one way of reading e-mail and newsgroups; there are other ways too. There are Web-based servers that you can use for e-mail, for example, such as Hotmail. If you have such an e-mail account, you can access it by displaying the Web page for that service (such as* **www.hotmail.com**). *Depending on your ISP, you may be able to use some other Web interface for reading your e-mail. You can also read and post to newsgroups via a Web interface. One of the most famous Web interfaces for newsgroups is Dejanews, found at* **www.deja.com**. *(They were recently bought by Google, so this link will take you to the Google Groups site.) You will learn more about e-mail and newsgroups in Chapter 14.*

Sending a Link or Page via E-Mail

When you find a Web page that someone else you know might enjoy, you can e-mail its link to them. To send a link, follow these steps:

1. Open the page.

2. Click the Mail button, and choose Send a Link. The New Message window opens with the link in the body of the message and the site title in the Subject and Attach lines. (You can also choose File ➤ Send ➤ Link by Email to do the same thing.)

3. Address your message, compose your message, and click Send.

If your recipient is connected to the Internet and has a Web browser, they merely need to click the link in the message to open that page.

Some e-mail programs block the receipt of e-mail links sent in this manner. If the recipient can't read it, try sending the page itself. To send the page itself, follow the same steps but choose Send Page (or Send Page by Email). The current page you are viewing will appear in the body of the message.

WARNING *Before you willy-nilly include Web pages in your e-mail, be sure that your recipient's e-mail program can handle HTML messages. For more information about e-mail and HTML, see Chapter 14.*

Saving and Printing Web Pages

If you always want to see the most current version of a Web page, you probably want to place a link to it on the Links bar or the Favorites bar. However, in some cases, you'll want to save it to your local hard drive or to a drive on your network. For example, I recently wanted easy access to a rather long U.S. government document. In this case, the document had been written and distributed over the Internet and was not going to change. It was what it was, so I saved it to my local network so that I could get to it quickly without being connected to the Internet.

SAVING THE CURRENT PAGE

To save the current page, follow these steps:

1. Choose File ➤ Save As to open the Save Web Page dialog box:

2. Select a folder in which to save the page, and in the File Name box enter a name if you want something different from that which Internet Explorer proposes.

3. In the Save As Type drop-down box, select the format in which you want the page saved.

4. Click Save.

You can also save a Web page without opening it if its link is displayed. Follow these steps:

1. Right-click the link, and choose Save Target As from the shortcut menu. You'll see a dialog box that shows you that the page is being downloaded.

2. In the Save As dialog box, select a folder, and specify a filename.

3. Click Save.

SAVING PORTIONS OF A PAGE

You can also save only a portion of text from a Web page or an image. To save a portion of text to use in another document, select the text, and then press Ctrl+C. Open the other document, place the insertion point where you want the text, and press Ctrl+V.

SAVING AN IMAGE

To save an image, follow these steps:

1. Right-click the image, and choose Save Picture As from the shortcut menu to open the Save Picture dialog box.

2. Select a folder, a filename, and a type, and click Save.

To save an image as wallpaper, right-click the image and choose Set As Background from the shortcut menu. To specify how you want the wallpaper displayed, right-click the image on the Desktop, choose Properties to open the Display Properties dialog box. Click the Desktop tab, and select an option in the Position drop-down box.

PRINTING THE CURRENT PAGE

If you want to quickly print the current page, simply click the Print button on the Standard toolbar. If, however, you want more control over what's printed and how, choose File ➤ Print to open the Print dialog box, as shown in Figure 12.9.

FIGURE 12.9

The Print dialog box, open at the Options tab

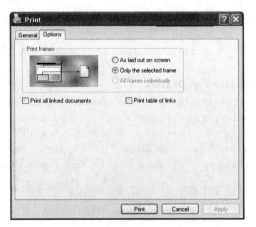

For the most part, this is your standard Windows Print dialog box. (For details about printers and printing in Windows XP Professional, see Chapter 7.) The difference is the Options tab, which you can use to specify how frames and links are printed; it is shown in Figure 12.9. Here are the specifics:

◆ Select the As Laid Out on Screen option in the Print Frames section to print the Web page exactly as it is displayed on your screen.

◆ Select the Only the Selected Frame option to print only a frame you have previously selected. (To select a frame, click inside it in an empty space—in other words, not on a link.)

◆ Select the All Frames Individually option if you want to print each frame on a separate sheet of paper.

◆ Select the Print All Linked Documents option if you want to print the pages that are linked to the current page as well. (Be sure you really want to do this; you could need lots of paper.)

◆ Select the Print Table of Links option if you want to print a table that lists the links for the page at the end of the document.

When you have all your options selected, click the Print button on any tab to print the document.

To print the target of any link, right-click the link, and choose Print Target from the shortcut menu to open the Print dialog box.

TIP   By default, Windows does not print the background colors and background images of Web pages. First, the printed output could be illegible, and, second, unless you have a rather powerful printer, spooling and printing could be really slow. If, for whatever reason, you want or need to print the background, choose Tools ➢ Internet Options to open the Internet Options dialog box. Click the Advanced tab, scroll down to the Printing section in the Settings list, check the Print Background Colors and Images check box, and click OK.

PRINTING YOUR FAVORITES LIST

There is no way to directly print the favorites list in Internet Explorer, but you can do so indirectly like this:

1. Export it to a file (File ➢ Import and Export and use the Wizard).

2. Open that file in Internet Explorer (File ➢ Open).

3. Choose File ➢ Print, and in the Options tab, choose Print Table of Links.

Working with Offline Favorites

If you want to view Web pages when you aren't connected to the Internet, and their currentness is not important, you can simply save them to your local hard drive.

If their currentness is important, you can choose to "work offline." This uses the online version of the page whenever possible, and the offline version whenever the online version is unavailable.

To make the current page available for offline viewing, follow these steps:

1. Right-click in an empty spot on the page, and choose Add to Favorites to open the Add Favorite dialog box.

2. Click the Make Available Offline check box.

3. If you want to view only certain content offline, click the Customize button to start the Offline Favorite Wizard. Otherwise click OK and you're done.

If you are using the Offline Favorite Wizard, follow these steps:

1. From the Offline Favorite Wizard's introductory screen, click Next.

2. If you want the pages that link to the current page to also be available offline, choose Yes, and then set a number of levels deep. Then click Next.

WARNING   *The more levels you choose, the longer it will take to synchronize and the more space it will take up on your hard disk. To limit the amount of disk space a particular item and its associated pages can consume, after you complete the Wizard display the favorite's Properties and in the Download tab, mark the Limit Hard-disk Usage for This Page To check box and specify a limit in kilobytes.*

3. Choose when to synchronize. You can choose manual synchronization only or choose to create a new schedule. Then click Next.

4. If you chose to create a new schedule, choose a certain number of days for an interval and an update time. Then click Next.

5. If the site requires a password, choose Yes and enter the username and password to use. Otherwise leave No marked. Then click Finish.

To view pages offline rather than using the online versions, choose File ➤ Work Offline. To return to online pages, repeat.

TIP   *If you want to take a current favorite and make it available offline, you can select it in the Organize Favorites dialog box and then mark the Make Available Offline check box. This bypasses the Wizard and makes it available with default settings. Click the Properties button to fine-tune those settings if desired.*

If you choose manual updating only, you must choose Tools ➤ Synchronize to update it. Otherwise the updates occur automatically at the interval you specify. When you choose Tools ➤ Synchronize, the Items to Synchronize dialog box appears; you can choose from it which items to synchronize. See Figure 12.10.

FIGURE 12.10

When you synchronize with the Synchronize command, you can choose which pages to update.

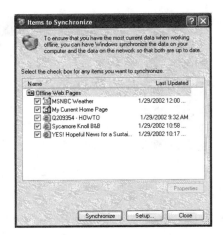

Finding Exactly What You Want on the Internet

The serendipitous experience of clicking and following hyperlinks may suffice while you're polishing off your lunch of tuna sandwich and chips or filling the occasional lazy, rainy afternoon, but most of the time when you connect to the Internet, you have something specific in mind that you want to do or find. Regardless of what you're looking for—information about a topic, an e-mail or mailing address, a business, a Web page, and so on—the way to find it is to use a search service. *Search service* is a relatively new term for what we referred to in the past as a search engine, a program that can search a file, a database, or the Internet for keywords and retrieve documents in which those keywords are found.

Examples of search services that you may have used include Yahoo!, AltaVista, Google, and Hot-Bot Advanced. To search with one of these services, you go to the site (for example, `www.yahoo.com`); optionally, select a category, enter a keyword or phrase, and click Search (or some similar button). You can also access search services within Internet Explorer. Let's do a simple search to see how this works.

Performing a Simple Search

Follow these steps to perform a simple search:

1. In Internet Explorer, click the Search button on the Standard toolbar to open the Search Companion bar:

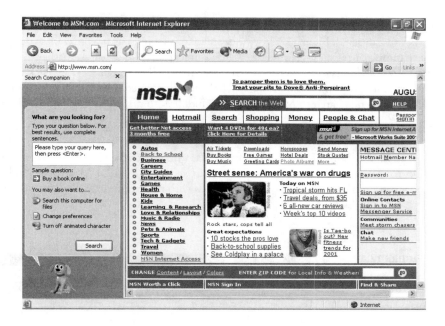

2. Enter a term or a question in the text box, and click Search.

You'll see the results of your search in the pane on the right, as shown in Figure 12.11. Click a link to go to that page.

FIGURE 12.11

The results of a search in Internet Explorer

Expanding a Search

As you can see in Figure 12.11, the Search Companion bar now presents you with options for expanding or refining your search. Click a link to take your search further. By default, MSN Search is your search service. If you'd like to search using other search services, click the Automatically Send Your Search to Other Search Engines link, and then select a search service from those displayed, or click the Send Search to More Search Engines link to display still other search services.

TIP   Click the vertical scroll bar to view all the options in the Search Companion bar.

To modify how the Search Companion bar works, click the Change Preferences link to open the How Do You Want to Use Search Companion? list shown in Figure 12.12. Click a link that corresponds to how you want to search. If you are presented with more options, follow the on-screen instructions.

TIP   You can also do a fast search from the Address bar. Simply enter your search term or phrase and press Enter.

FIGURE 12.12

Setting your search preferences

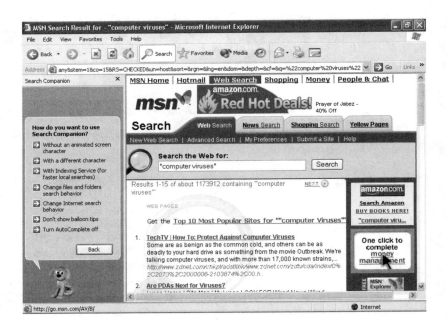

Other Ways to Search

Here are two other ways to search the Web that don't involve the Search Companion:

◆ Type a search string directly into the Address bar. IE passes your search along to the default search engine (probably MSN) and displays the results.

◆ Display the Web site of one of the major search engines on the Internet, such as Google, Ask Jeeves, Excite, Webcrawler, and so on, and use the search tools on that page.

Downloading Files

Sometimes when you click on a hyperlink, it doesn't take you to another Web page; instead it starts a file download, as in Figure 12.13.

If you choose Open, the file is downloaded to a temporary folder and run from there. This is useful if you are downloading a setup program but you don't need to retain that setup program after you run it.

If you choose Save, it prompts you for a folder in which to save the file, but does not run it. When the download is finished, you'll see a box like the one in Figure 12.14. From there you can choose Open to run the program or Open Folder to open the folder into which it was saved.

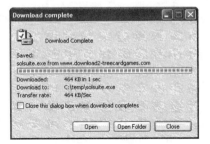

Customizing Internet Explorer

In Windows XP Professional, you can view or change the configuration options relating to Internet Explorer in two ways:

♦ Use Internet Options in Control Panel

♦ Choose Tools ➤ Internet Options from within Internet Explorer

Regardless of which you choose, you open the same dialog box. However, if you open it from Control Panel, it is called Internet Properties, and if you open it from within Internet Explorer, it is called Internet Options. In both cases, the contents of the dialog boxes are identical. In this section, we'll use Internet Explorer. (To open the Internet Properties dialog box, choose Start ➤ Control Panel ➤ Network and Internet Connections ➤ Internet Options.)

The Internet Options dialog box has seven tabs, and in the next few sections, I'll review the most important configuration choices you can make on each of these tabs. I'll start with the General tab.

Configuring the General Tab

The General tab, which is shown in Figure 12.15, contains these groups of settings:

Home Page   Lets you choose which Web page opens each time you connect to the Internet. A home page is the first Web page you see when you start Internet Explorer. Click Use Current to make the current page your home page (if you are online to the Internet), click Use Default to return to the default setting, and click Use Blank to start each Internet session with a blank screen. To use a different Web page as your home page, type the URL in the Address box.

FIGURE 12.15

The General tab in the Internet Options dialog box

Temporary Internet Files   Lets you manage those Web pages that are stored on your hard disk for fast offline access. If these files are occupying too much hard disk space, click the Delete Files button or the Delete Cookies button to remove them. (I'll discuss cookies in detail later in this chapter.) To control how these files are stored on your hard disk, click Settings to open the Settings dialog box. Click the option that applies to when you want Internet Explorer to check for newer versions of these stored Web pages. You can use the slider to specify how much hard disk space is given over to these temporary Internet files. Click Move Folder if you want to use a different folder to hold your temporary Internet files; you must remember to restart your computer after making this change so that the new folder is used in place of the default. Click View Files to open an Explorer window listing all the Web and graphics files in the folder, or click View Objects to open an Explorer window listing all the other Web-related files such as ActiveX controls and Java-related files.

History   Contains a list of the links you have visited so that you can return to them quickly and easily using the History button on the Internet Explorer toolbar. You can specify the number of days you want to keep pages in the History folder; if you are running low on hard disk space, consider reducing this number. To delete all the information currently in the History folder, click the Clear History button.

Colors   Opens the Colors dialog box in which you can choose which colors are used as background, links, and text on those Web pages for which the original author did not specify colors. By default, the Use Windows Colors option is selected.

TIP   You can always change the Windows colors. In Control Panel, click Display, and then select the Appearance tab.

Fonts   Opens the Fonts dialog box in which you can specify the font style and text size to use on those Web pages for which the original author did not make a specification.

Languages   Opens the Language Preference dialog box in which you can choose the character set to use on those Web pages that offer content in more than one language. English is rapidly becoming the most common language in use on the Internet, so you may not use this option often.

Accessibility   Opens the Accessibility dialog box in which you can choose how certain information is displayed in Internet Explorer, including font styles, colors, and text size. You can also specify that your own style sheet is used.

Looking at the Security Tab

When you are connected to the Internet, you immediately have a couple of concerns that are not at issue otherwise: security and privacy. Security concerns involve protecting your computer from unsafe software. Privacy concerns involve protecting your personally identifiable information. To configure the security settings in Internet Explorer, you click the Security tab in the Internet Options dialog box, which we'll look at in this section. To configure privacy settings, you use the Privacy tab, which we'll look at in the next section.

The Security tab, which is shown in Figure 12.16, lets you specify the overall security level for each of four zones. Each zone has its own default security restrictions that tell Internet Explorer how to manage dynamic Web page content such as ActiveX controls and Java applets. The zones are as follows:

Internet   Sites you visit that are not in one of the other categories; default security is set to Medium.

Local Intranet   Sites you can access on your corporate intranet; default security is set to Medium-Low.

Trusted Sites   Web sites in which you have a high degree of confidence will not send you potentially damaging content; default security is set to Low.

Restricted Sites   Sites that you visit but do not trust; default security is set to High.

FIGURE 12.16

The Security tab in the Internet Options dialog box

To change the current security level of a zone, select the zone, click the Default Level button, and then move the slider to the new security level you want to use:

High   Excludes any content capable of damaging your system. Cookies are disabled, and so some Web sites will not work as you might expect. This is the most secure setting.

Medium   Opens a warning dialog box in Internet Explorer before running ActiveX or Java applets on your system. This is a moderately secure setting that is good for everyday use and is selected by default.

Medium-Low   Same as Medium but without the prompts.

Low   Does not issue any warning but runs the ActiveX or Java applet automatically. This is the least secure setting.

Click the Custom Level button to create your own settings in the Security Settings dialog box, which is shown in Figure 12.17. You can individually configure how you want to manage certain categories, such as ActiveX controls and plug-ins, Java applets, scripting, file and font downloads, and user authentication.

FIGURE 12.17

The Security Settings dialog box

Using the Privacy Tab

When you visit a site on the Internet, that site can store information about you in a file that resides on your computer. This file, called a cookie, might contain your name, your e-mail address, any other personal information you supply, and any preferences you established when visiting the site. When you revisit the site, it accesses the cookie in order to personalize the site for your visit. For example, you might get a message that welcomes you by name.

Once a site saves a cookie on your computer, only that Web site can access the cookie; it is not available to other Web sites. In addition, the Web site that created the cookie cannot access any other information that is stored on your computer.

TYPES OF COOKIES

Using the settings on the Privacy tab in the Internet Options dialog box, you can choose to allow all Web sites to store cookies on your computer, to allow only some sites to do so, or to allow none to do so. Before we look at these settings, though, it is helpful to understand the types of cookies:

◆ *Persistent cookies* are stored on your computer and remain there after you close Internet Explorer. You saw earlier in this chapter how to delete cookies using the options in the Temporary Internet Files section in the General tab of the Internet Options dialog box.

◆ *Temporary cookies* are stored on your computer only as long as you have Internet Explorer open. When you close Internet Explorer, these cookies are deleted.

◆ *First-party cookies* originate on or are sent to the Web site you are currently visiting.

◆ *Third-party cookies* originate on or are sent to a Web site that you are not currently viewing. For example, a site that is advertising on the site you are currently viewing might create a cookie to track your Internet usage for marketing purposes.

◆ *Unsatisfactory cookies* allow access to your personal information that can be used without your knowledge or consent.

ESTABLISHING COOKIE PREFERENCES

In the Privacy tab, which is shown in Figure 12.18, you use the slider in the Settings section to specify how you will deal with cookies in the Internet zone. You have the following choices:

◆ Block All Cookies does exactly that. No Web site is allowed to store a cookie on your computer, and any existing cookies that are stored will not be able to be read by the sites that created them.

◆ High blocks all cookies from Web sites that don't have a compact privacy policy and blocks cookies that collect personal information without you knowledge or consent.

NOTE   A compact privacy policy *is a statement in condensed computer-readable form about how a site handles personal information.*

- ◆ Medium High blocks the following:
  - ◆ Third-party cookies from sites that do not have a compact privacy policy
  - ◆ Third-party cookies from sites that use personal information without your knowledge or consent
  - ◆ First-party cookies from sites that use personal information without your knowledge or consent
- ◆ Medium, the default setting, blocks third-party cookies from sites that do not have a compact privacy policy and from sites that use personal information without your knowledge or consent. This setting restricts first-party cookies that use personal information without your knowledge or consent.
- ◆ Low restricts third-party cookies from sites that do not have a compact privacy policy and from sites that use personal information without your knowledge or consent.
- ◆ Accept All Cookies does exactly that. All cookies from all sites are accepted and stored on your computer, and any cookies that are already on your computer can be accessed by the Web sites that created them.

FIGURE 12.18

The Privacy tab in the Internet Options dialog box

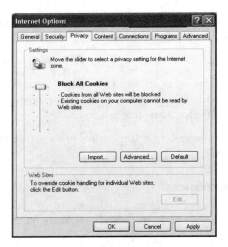

When you use the slider bar to set your preferences, you establish a sort of one-size-fits-all rule that applies to all Web sites that you visit. You can use the other options in the Privacy tab to take a more granular approach and override the settings established using the slider bar.

To apply custom settings that you have stored in a file on your computer, click the Import button to open the Privacy Import dialog box, which is simply an Open dialog box in disguise and works the same as an Open dialog box.

To choose to Accept, Block, or Prompt for first-party and third-party cookies, click the Advanced button to open the Advanced Privacy Settings dialog box:

Click the Override Automatic Cookie Handling check box, and then select the options that you want. If you want to allow session cookies, click that check box, and then click OK.

To establish privacy settings for individual Web sites, click the Edit button in the Web Sites section to open the Per Site Privacy Actions dialog box:

In the Address of Web Site box, type the complete URL for the site you want to allow or block, and then click Block or Allow. The site's domain name and your chosen setting will appear in the Managed Web Sites list. Use the Remove or Remove All button to delete a site from the list.

TIP *To back up your cookies, use the Import/Export Wizard (File ➤ Import and Export.)*

Using the Content Tab

The Content tab, which is shown in Figure 12.19, contains settings you can use to restrict access to sites and specify how you want to manage digital certificates:

Content Advisor Lets you control access to certain sites on the Internet and is particularly useful if children have access to the computer. Click Enable to open the Content Advisor dialog box. Use the tabs in this dialog box to establish the level of content you will allow users to view:

Ratings Lets you use a set of ratings developed by the Recreational Software Advisory Council (RSAC) for language, nudity, sex, and violence. Select one of these categories, and then adjust the slider to specify the level of content you will allow.

Approved Sites Lets you create lists of sites that are always viewable or always restricted regardless of how they are rated.

General Specifies whether people using this computer can view material that has not been rated; users may see some objectionable material if the Web site has not used the RSAC rating system. You can also opt to have the Supervisor enter a password so that users can view Web pages that may contain objectionable material. You can click the Create Password button to create or change the Supervisor password; remember that you have to know the current Supervisor password before you can change it.

Advanced Lets you look at or modify the list of organizations providing ratings services.

Certificates Lets you manage digital certificates used with certain client authentication servers. When you visit a site that has a secure connection, you can choose to verify that site's certificate. Such certificates are stored in a cache until you reboot your computer. To remove these certificates manually, click the Clear SSL State button. (SSL is an abbreviation for Secure Sockets Layer.) Click Certificates to view the personal digital certificates installed on this system, or click Publishers to designate a particular software publisher as a trustworthy publisher. This means that Windows XP Professional applications can download, install, and use software from these agencies without asking for your permission first.

Personal Information Lets you look at or change the settings for Windows AutoComplete and your own personal profile. Click AutoComplete to change the way that this feature works within Windows XP Professional, or click My Profile to create an Address Book entry for yourself that represents your profile or to select an existing Address Book entry to represent your profile. You can then send this information to any Web sites that request information about you when you visit their site.

FIGURE 12.19

The Content tab in the Internet Options dialog box

Setting Up the Connections Tab

The Connections tab, which is shown in Figure 12.20, allows you to specify how your system connects to the Internet. Click the Setup button to run the New Connection Wizard and set up a connection to an Internet Service Provider. (See Chapter 11 for complete details on this.) If you use a modem, click the Settings button to open the My ISP Settings dialog box, where you can specify all aspects of the phone connection to your ISP.

FIGURE 12.20

The Connections tab in the Internet Options dialog box

Looking at the Programs Tab

The Programs tab, which is shown in Figure 12.21, lets you set your default program choices for HTML editor, e-mail, newsgroup reader, Internet call, calendar, and contact list. Finally, you can specify that Internet Explorer check to see if it is configured as the default browser on your system each time it starts running.

FIGURE 12.21

The Programs tab in the Internet Options dialog box

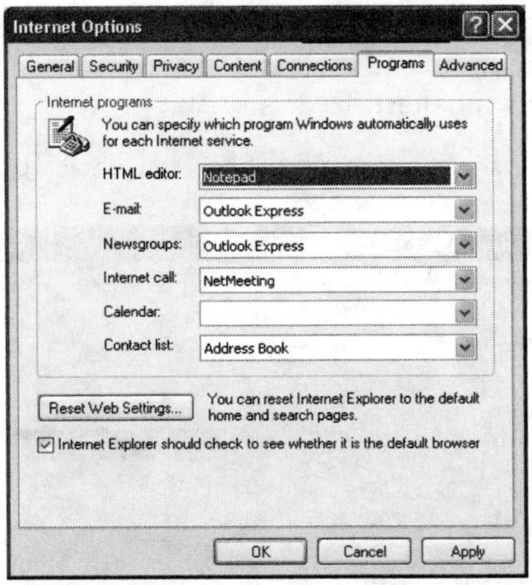

Configuring the Advanced Tab

The Advanced tab, which is shown in Figure 12.22, lets you look at or change a number of settings that control much of Internet Explorer's behavior, including accessibility, browsing, multimedia, security, printing, and searching, and how HTTP 1.1 settings are interpreted. Click a check box to turn an option on; clear the check box to turn the option off.

Changes you make here stay in effect until you change them again, until you download an automatic configuration file, or until you click the Restore Defaults button, which returns the settings in the Advanced tab to their original values.

FIGURE 12.22

The Advanced tab in the Internet Options dialog box

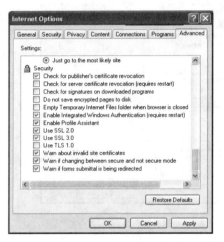

Customizing the Internet Explorer Toolbar

When you unlock the toolbars in Internet Explorer (View ➤ Toolbars ➤ Lock the Toolbars to toggle it on/off), each of the toolbars becomes movable. You can drag it around by its *handle* (the dotted area at its left edge).

You can also customize the Standard toolbar, adding buttons for features you use frequently and removing buttons for features you don't. To do so:

1. Choose View ➤ Toolbars ➤ Customize. The Customize Toolbar dialog box opens.

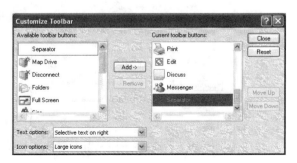

2. To remove a button, click it in the Current toolbar buttons list and click Remove. To add a button, click it in the Available toolbar buttons list and click Add.

3. To rearrange buttons, click one in the Current toolbar buttons list and then click Move Up or Move Down.

4. To control the associated text for each icon, open the Text Options list and select a setting.

5. To control the size of the icons, open the Icon Options list and choose a size.

6. Click OK when finished.

NOTE *The Reset button returns the Standard toolbar to its default configuration. However, if you have installed any add-on programs that add their own buttons to the toolbar, such as an antivirus program or conduit for a PDA, it remains even after you reset.*

Changing Text Size

In addition to the many customizations you have already learned about, you can control how a Web page appears by using commands on the View menu.

One of the handiest ones for people with limited vision is the ability to change the font size for Web page content. To do so, choose View ➤ Text Size and then choose Larger or Largest. This works with all Web pages that have been formatted with standard HTML tags, and are not encoded to use a particular font size. Figure 12.23 shows a Web page set to Largest.

FIGURE 12.23

This Web page is being viewed with the text size set to Largest.

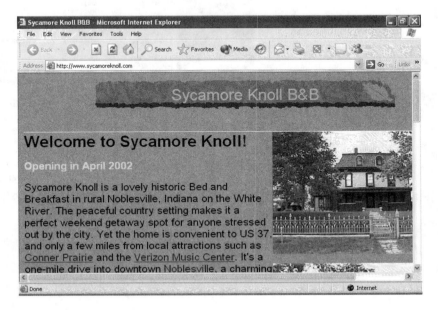

If you have a mouse with a wheel on it, you can use the wheel to change the text size too. Hold down the Ctrl key as you roll the wheel. Rolling forward decreases the text size; rolling backward increases it.

MSN Explorer

Windows XP comes with an alternative to Internet Explorer known as MSN Explorer. It's a custom version of IE for use primarily with the MSN Internet service, but you can use it as your only browser if you prefer it, no matter which ISP you use. It's a "friendlier" interface than IE, and perhaps more suitable for beginners, but serious techies will probably not want to bother with it.

As you can see in Figure 12.24, MSN Explorer is basically just an alternate version of Internet Explorer with larger buttons and closer ties to Microsoft-affiliated Web content such as Hotmail. It's meant to be a competitor to true online communities such as AOL.

FIGURE 12.24

MSN Explorer is an alternative way to surf the Web, well suited for beginners.

To set up MSN Explorer to work with your existing Internet connection:

1. Choose Start ➤ All Programs ➤ MSN Explorer.

   The first time you do, you'll see a question asking whether you want to get on the Internet and write e-mail through the Start menu using MSN Explorer. Answer No unless you want it to replace the program assignments at the top of the Start menu with MSN Explorer for both Web and e-mail.

2. The first time you run MSN Explorer, a Wizard will walk you through its setup. Work through it until you come to the question Do You Want MSN Internet Access? Then make sure you answer No, I already have Internet Access.

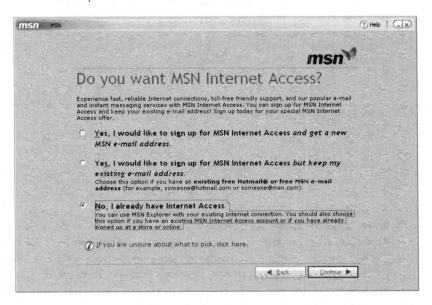

3. Continue through the Wizard until it asks about your e-mail address. To use MSN Explorer, you must have a Hotmail or MSN e-mail address. If you don't have one, you'll need to sign up for one; you can do that through the Wizard.

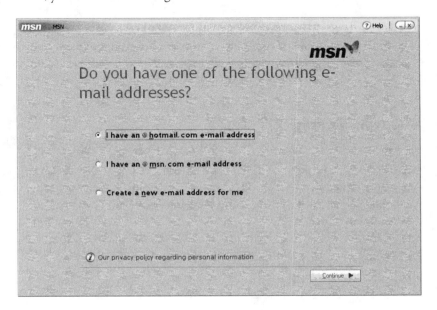

4. Finish working through the Wizard. Eventually a Welcome window for MSN Explorer will appear.

5. From here, just start clicking things to figure out how MSN Explorer works, or click Take the Tour if you want more help.

TIP   When you close the MSN Explorer window, it remains active; to really close it completely you must right-click its icon in the notification area and choose Exit MSN Explorer.

Using Built-In Internet Utilities

Windows XP Professional includes several standard Internet utilities. These programs are in most cases functionally identical to the same programs or commands found on pretty much every flavor of Unix. Although most people are not going to use these nearly as often as they will their Web browsers, I describe each in the following sections so you at least know what they are. It is useful to acquaint yourself, for example, with FTP—if you are ever on a Windows XP Professional system that for some reason does not have a Web browser, knowing how to use FTP to transfer files enables you to connect to Spry, Netscape, or Microsoft and download a browser.

Following this brief rundown of each of the tools, we will look at other Internet applications you can download via the Internet. Note that with each of the following programs, you can get help by typing the program name at the command prompt followed by **-?** (dash, question mark).

To open any of the following utilities, you type a command at a command prompt. To open a command prompt window, do one of the following:

◆ Choose Start ➢ Run, and in the Open text box, type the command (the name of the utility).

◆ Choose Start ➢ All Programs ➢ Accessories ➢ Command Prompt.

Address Resolution Display and Control (ARP)

The ARP program is used to display and/or modify entries in the Internet-to-Ethernet (or Token Ring) address translation tables that are used by the Address Resolution Protocol (ARP). Various command-line switches are documented in the -? option. To use ARP, type **arp** at the command prompt.

File Transfer Protocol (FTP)

FTP is the standard TCP/IP file transfer protocol used for moving text and binary files between computers on the Internet. If you have an account on a distant computer on the Internet, you can use FTP to download files from the other computer to your PC and to upload files from your PC to the host. In addition, there are tens of thousands of *anonymous* FTP archives all over the Internet that accept logins from anybody who wants copies of their files.

TIP   You can do FTP from Internet Explorer; you don't necessarily have to use the command prompt for it. Just type the FTP address in the Address bar, as in `ftp.mysite.com`*. However, the FTP capabilities in IE are rather limited; you can only download with it, for example, not upload.*

The Windows XP Professional FTP program (and the others mentioned here) can be found in the `Winnt\System32` folder, which is included in your search path. Therefore, you don't have to specify the path when you enter an FTP command. To connect to an FTP server, follow these steps:

1. At a command prompt, type the following, and then press Enter:
   `FTP <host name>`

2. Windows XP Professional displays the `ftp>` prompt:

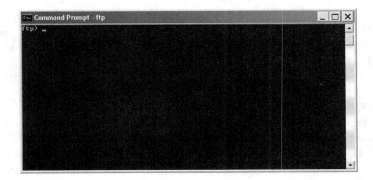

3. After FTP connects to the server, the server asks for your username and password. If you're connecting to an anonymous FTP server, type **anonymous** as your username, and type your e-mail address as your password or leave the password field blank and press Enter. For your password, use the standard *name@address.domain* format.

Most FTP servers use the same system of directories and subdirectories that you may be familiar with from DOS and Windows. To see the contents of the current directory, type **dir** or `ls` at the `ftp>` prompt.

If the FTP server is in UNIX mode, a *d* as the first letter in a listing indicates that the item in that line is a directory. If a dash is the first character, the item is a file. The name of the file or directory is at the extreme right. See Chapter 28 for more info regarding Unix mode.

Use the command **cd** *name* (typing the name of the subdirectory in place of *name*) to move to a subdirectory.

Use the command **cd** `..` to move to the next higher level. (Press the spacebar after you enter the *d* and before you type the first period.)

When you download a file from an FTP server, you must specify that it is either an ASCII text file or a binary file. As a general rule, binary files that you can read on a PC have a DOS file extension (rather than TXT for a text file or PS for a Postscript print file), but you really can't be certain. ASCII text files may or may not have a file extension.

When you initially connect to an FTP server, you're in ASCII mode. Before you try to transfer a binary file, you have to change modes. To switch to binary mode, use the command `binary`. To switch back to ASCII mode, use the command `ascii`. The host acknowledges your mode-change command.

To download a file from the server, use the command **get** *filename* (typing the name of the file in place of *filename*). If you want to store the file on your PC with a different name, use the command get *filename newname* (typing the file you want to get in place of *filename* and the name you want to store the file under in place of *newname*). When the file transfer is complete, the host sends you another message.

When you are finished with your FTP session, type **disconnect** to break the connection to the server. You can connect to another host by typing the new server's address.

To close the FTP utility, type the command **quit**.

TIP *One handy use for the command-line FTP client is automating file transfers. Because FTP accepts scripts (via the* -s:filename *switch), you can easily create a script (which is just a text file of FTP commands) to log on to an FTP server, switch to a particular directory, transfer a long listing of files in one or both directions, and then log off. You can even set this to occur at a given time of day by using the Windows XP Professional* at *command. (For details on using the* at *command, type* **help at** *from any command prompt.)*

Trivial File Transfer Protocol (TFTP)

This program is similar in usage and functionality to the more well-known FTP utility but is used to transfer files to or from a remote computer that is running Trivial File Transfer Protocol (TFTP).

FTP uses the TCP protocol, which guarantees safe delivery of the data. TFTP uses User Datagram Protocol (UDP), which does not provide reliable delivery and hence is somewhat faster. Windows XP Professional does not provide a TFTP server, but some are available for download on the Internet.

Finger

The finger program can be used to retrieve user-supplied information about a user (or host computer). Unfortunately, many users do not have a finger file for others to retrieve and view (or even know about creating one), and some host computers do not provide finger services, so your mileage will vary. On the other hand, some universities and institutions do use finger services, and on these you can find some useful (or at least interesting) information. To use finger, type **finger** *auser@someplace.com*. Enter a valid username or at least a host name, and press Enter, and you may get a listing of information.

Ping

Ping is a useful diagnostic utility that tests your ability to connect your computer to another device through the Internet by sending an echo request and displaying the number of milliseconds required to receive a reply. Whenever you need to diagnose your Internet connection problems, pinging a known host computer is a good first test.

To set up a ping test, follow these steps:

1. At a command prompt, type **ping** *destination*. Use the domain name or the IP address of the host you want to test in place of *destination*. If you do not get a response when using the domain name of the destination, try the IP address of the destination instead.

2. Ping sends four sets of Internet Control Message Protocol (ICMP) echo packets to the host you specify and displays the amount of time it took to receive each reply, as shown here:

The important part of the ping display is the time</>*nnn*ms section of the Reply lines. Ping's capability to connect to the distant host tells you that your connection to the Internet is working properly; the number of milliseconds can tell you if you have an efficient connection to this particular host (anything less than about 500ms is usually acceptable).

Protocol Statistics (Netstat)

Use the netstat command to display a list of currently active Internet connections. At the command prompt, type **netstat**. A list of connections similar to the ones in the following illustration appears:

A netstat report includes the following information:

Proto   Shows the networking protocol in use for each active connection. For PPP or SLIP connections to the Internet, the Proto column always reads TCP, which specifies a TCP/IP connection.

Local Address   Indicates the identity of your PC on the network.

Foreign Address   Shows the address of each distant computer to which a connection is currently active.

State   Shows the condition of each connection.

Remote File Copy (RCP)

If you've ever wanted to copy a file from one directory or drive to another on a remote computer without having the file go through your modem twice (as a normal copy or xcopy would), you understand the purpose of the RCP program. You can also use RCP to copy files from one remote computer to another remote computer without being copied to your computer first. Not all systems permit you to use this command, and if they do, of course you are limited to the directory areas for which you have access rights. Type **-?** for specific usage and option information. To use RCP, open a command prompt, and type **rcp**.

Remote Program Execution (REXEC)

The REXEC program is just as powerful as Remote Shell/Script (RSH; discussed in the next section), if not more so, and likewise is quite restricted by most system administrators. It functions just like RSH, except that it starts binary programs rather than scripts on the remote host. Windows XP Professional stations *do* permit remote execution of programs, provided the system administrator has enabled this and given you the necessary access rights. To run REXEC, type **rexec** at a command prompt.

Remote Shell/Script (RSH)

Another potentially powerful utility, RSH is used to start a script program on a remote host. Again, some host computers do not support this, and of those that do, your access rights may preclude or severely limit what you can do. To use RSH, type **rsh** at a command prompt.

Remote Terminal (Telnet)

Telnet is one of the utilities you are somewhat more likely to use, particularly in university settings or when data you need to access without using HTML is stored on a remote host (a less and less common scenario, thankfully). When you connect through a Telnet connection, your PC becomes a terminal on the distant system. In most cases, a Telnet login requires an account on the host (remote) machine, but many systems accept logins from anybody who wants to connect. Among the most common public Telnet sites are online library catalogs. Other public Telnet sites let you use certain character-based Internet services that may not be available on your computer.

To set up a Telnet connection, type **Telnet *hostname*** at a command prompt (using the domain name or IP address of the computer to which you want to connect in place of *hostname*). Telnet connects your computer to the host whose name you supplied and displays messages from that host in the Telnet window.

Most Telnet hosts display a series of login prompts as soon as you connect. If you're connecting to a public Telnet host, it will probably tell you how to log in.

NOTE   *Telnet is also used to configure most routers. If you are interested in network design and management, you might want to focus some attention on Telnet.*

Route

You can use **route** to view, add to, or modify a routing table on a Windows XP Professional computer with more than one network interface. If you have a *multihomed* computer (one with multiple network cards) and have enabled IP forwarding in the TCP/IP Properties dialog box, you can use the **route** command to view and modify the table of information that tells Windows XP Professional where to direct TCP/IP data from one interface to another. Using this command on a computer with one network interface will also display basic routing information. To use **route**, type **route** at a command prompt.

Trace Route (*tracert*)

In most cases, when you set up a connection to a distant computer through the Internet, your signal path passes through several routers along the way. Because this is all happening in a fraction of a second, these intermediate routers are usually invisible. But when you're having trouble making a connection, the trace route command (`tracert`) can help isolate the source of the problem.

To run a trace route test, type **tracert *target*** at a command prompt. In place of *target*, type the address of the distant system. A trace route report appears in the prompt window.

In many cases, your connection will pass through one or more backbone networks between your connection to the Internet and your ultimate destination.

`Tracert` steps through the connection route, one step at a time. For each step, it shows the amount of time needed to reach that router, in milliseconds. If an intermediate router or a connection between two intermediate routers fails, `tracert` will not display any steps beyond that point in the route. If that happens, you can assume that the failed site is the reason that you are unable to connect to your intended destination.

Summary

Within the space of a very few years, many of us have come to consider access to the Internet an essential component of daily life. It is now the first place I turn when I want information about almost anything, and it's rare that I don't find what I'm looking for.

Internet Explorer is far from the only tool available for communicating on the Internet. In the next chapter, you'll learn about Messenger, NetMeeting, and Remote Desktop Connection; then in Chapter 14 you'll learn about e-mail with Outlook Express.

Chapter 13

Using the Communications Programs

YOU MAY NEVER HAVE an occasion to use the programs I'm going to discuss in this chapter, but I'm including information about them so that you'll know they exist, what each is best suited for, and how to access them when the need arises. I'm guessing that the one you might use the most, especially if you run a small business and have a small network of computers, is Fax.

- ◆ Using Fax
- ◆ Connecting with HyperTerminal
- ◆ Communicating and sharing with NetMeeting
- ◆ Using Windows Messenger
- ◆ Using Remote Desktop Connection

Using the Windows XP Professional Fax Service

If you're in business today, a fax machine is as essential as an office copier or a coffeepot. The most common tool for facsimile communication is still the stand-alone fax machine, but there are some real advantages to using your PC as a personal fax machine instead.

To send a fax through a fax machine you need to: create the document, print a copy on paper, write up a cover sheet, carry the document and cover sheet to the fax machine, wait for your turn to use the machine, dial the recipient's fax number, feed the document and cover sheet through the fax machine, and, finally, walk back to your office. When somebody sends you a fax, it spills out of the machine and waits for you to come get it—meanwhile, everybody who walks past the fax machine has a chance to read your messages before you do.

On the other hand, you can send and receive faxes through your PC and a fax modem without leaving your chair. If you have a home office or a *really* small business with a tight budget, you can do PC-based faxing without spending a hundred dollars or more for a separate machine. And when you're traveling with a portable computer, you can use it to exchange faxes with your office and your customers.

In this section, you will learn how to use Fax to send and receive faxes from your PC just as if you were printing the document or sending e-mail. You'll also learn how to create personalized, custom cover pages for your faxes.

See pages 95–96 of "Essential Skills for Windows XP Professional" for a visual guide to setting up Fax service.

Installing Fax

When you fax a document in Windows XP Professional, you use the same modem you use to connect to the Internet, whether that is an analog modem, a DSL modem, a cable modem, or an ISDN modem. Unless you have a really old analog modem, your modem has fax and data capabilities.

Fax services are not installed by default when you install Windows XP Professional. To install Fax services, choose Start ➤ Printers and Faxes to open the Printers and Faxes folder, and then click Set Up Faxing in the Printer Tasks list. When prompted to do so, insert your Windows XP installation CD in the CD-ROM drive. At the Welcome screen, click the Install Optional Windows Component link, select Fax Services, and then follow the Wizard's instructions.

TIP   To delete a fax printer from the Printers and Faxes folder, select it, and press Delete.

Configuring Windows XP Professional Fax

Once you install the Fax services, you'll see a Fax icon in your Printers and Faxes folder, as shown in Figure 13.1. (To open this folder, choose Start ➤ Printers and Faxes.)

FIGURE 13.1

You'll see a Fax icon in the Printers and Faxes folder after you install the Fax services.

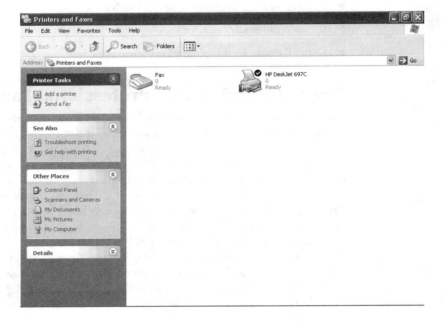

Before you can send and receive faxes, you need to configure the Fax services, and you do so using the Fax Configuration Wizard. Follow these steps:

1. In the Printers and Faxes folder, double-click Fax to start the Fax Configuration Wizard (below left).

2. Click Next to open the Sender Information screen (below right).

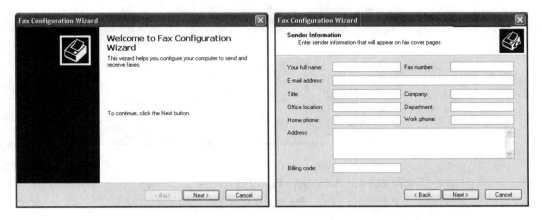

3. Enter the information you want on your cover sheet, and then click Next to open the Select Device for Sending or Receiving Faxes screen:

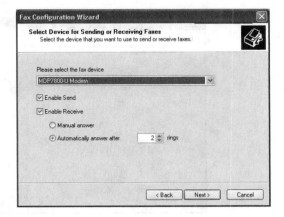

4. Click the drop-down list to select the modem you want to use to send and receive faxes. If you want to both send and receive faxes, click those check boxes. Specify whether you want to answer manually or automatically. If you want to answer automatically, specify the number of rings

before your modem answers in the Rings spin box. Click Next to open the Transmitting Subscriber Identification (TSID) screen:

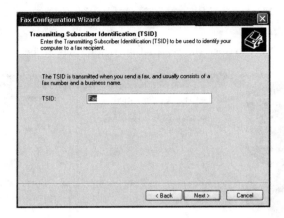

NOTE *The TSID is text that identifies the sending computer and usually includes the name of your business or your fax number. It is automatically displayed in your cover sheet and may also be displayed in the Fax Queue when you are receiving a fax.*

5. Enter the information for your TSID, and click Next to open the Called Subscriber Identification (CSID) screen:

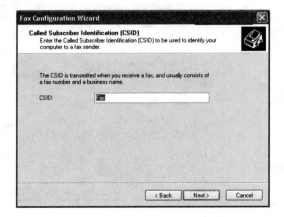

NOTE *The CSID is text that identifies the recipient of a fax, usually the name of your business or your fax number.*

6. In the CSID box, enter the identifying text you want, and then click Next to open the Routing Options screen:

7. Specify whether and where you want a received fax printed and where you want to store fax files, and click Next to open the summary screen:

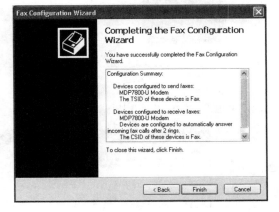

8. If the summary information is satisfactory, click Finish; if not, click Back and correct what you want changed.

9. Clicking Finish opens the Fax Console, which you use to monitor faxes, access the Fax Configuration Wizard, create personal cover pages, and administer Fax Services.

Now when you double-click the Fax icon in the Printers and Faxes folder, you will see the Fax Console. We'll look at the Fax Console in a later section in this chapter.

Sending Faxes in Windows XP Professional

OK, you've read through the entire configuration section, and you're ready to start faxing, so let's get to it. You can fax a document from within any Windows program that contains a Print command. For purposes of example, let's fax a document from WordPad. Follow these steps:

1. Choose Start ➤ All Programs ➤ Accessories ➤ WordPad to open WordPad.

2. Open an existing document, or create a new one.

3. Choose File ➤ Print to open the Print dialog box.

4. Double-click the Fax icon to start the Send Fax Wizard, as shown in Figure 13.2.

FIGURE 13.2

Sending a fax with
the Send Fax Wizard

5. Click Next to open the Recipient Information screen:

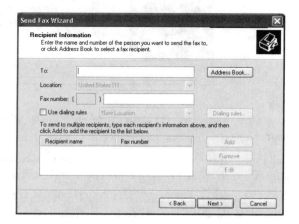

6. Enter the To, Fax Number, and dialing rules information for a single recipient or for multiple recipients, or select this information from your Address Book. Click Next to open the Preparing the Cover Page screen:

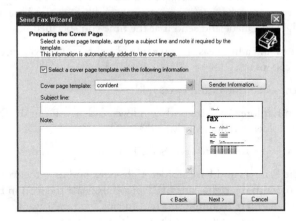

7. Specify a cover page to use for this fax. Four cover page templates are provided with Windows XP Professional: confidential, FYI, generic, and urgent templates. If you have created your own cover pages, they will also appear in the Cover Page Template drop-down list. You can also enter a subject line on this page. Optionally, you can type a message in the Note field that will be sent on the cover page. Often, you just need to send a small bit of text information in a fax; using the Note field lets you do this without adding another page. When you're ready to proceed, click Next to open the Schedule screen:

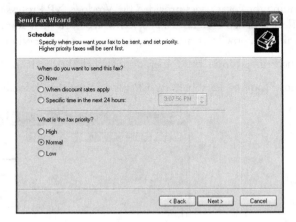

8. In the first section of the Schedule screen, you have three options:

- Now

- When Discount Rates Apply

- Specific Time in the Next 24 Hours

In the lower portion of this screen, you can set a priority for the fax. When you are ready to proceed, click Next.

9. The Completing the Send Fax Wizard screen summarizes your selected options. This gives you one more chance to correct any mistakes you may have made. Click Finish to add your fax to the Fax Queue and send it at the time you specified.

To make faxing a little easier, you can add a shortcut to your fax printer in the Send To menu. Follow these steps:

1. Open your Printers and Faxes folder.

2. Open Explorer and size both windows so that you can see Explorer and your Printers and Faxes folder simultaneously.

3. In Explorer, browse to your Send To folder, and select it.

4. In the Printers and Faxes folder, right-click and drag the icon for your fax printer to the Send To folder in the right pane of Explorer. Release the icon in Explorer, and choose Create Shortcuts Here from the shortcut menu. You might want to rename the shortcut something other than Shortcut to Fax Printer. It's up to you.

5. Close both the Printers and Faxes folder and Explorer, and you're all done.

Now when you right-click a document, you will have an option to send a fax on the shortcut menu. When you use this method, Windows XP Professional opens the Send Fax Wizard to gather the information about your recipient and the cover page you want to use, and then it will send the fax.

Creating a Cover Page

Are you finding the cover pages provided by Windows XP Professional a little dull? They just don't seem to reflect your sense of taste and style? Maybe you want something a little flashier? In this section, you will learn how to create a new custom cover page. Follow these steps:

1. In the Printers and Faxes folder, double-click the Fax icon to open the Fax Console.

2. Choose Tools ➤ Personal Cover Pages to open the Personal Cover Pages dialog box:

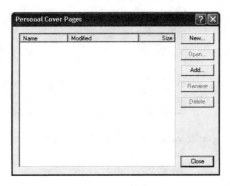

3. Click New to open the Fax Cover Page Editor:

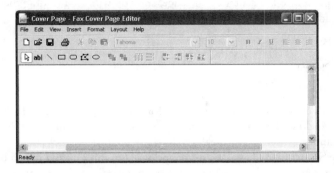

4. Click OK to close the Tips dialog box. The Tips are worth reading through if you are new to Fax and editing cover pages, but we'll pass on them for now.

The Cover Page Editor is now ready to work with a blank document already loaded for use. The Cover Page Editor looks like a simple word processor, such as WordPad, at first glance. But if you browse through the menus and toolbars a little, you'll soon discover that the editor is more akin to a desktop publishing program. The Cover Page Editor is more concerned with placement of fields on the page and the overall layout and appearance of the page than with entering text. Let's take a closer look at some of the capabilities of this editor.

The Basics of Cover Pages

Every cover page needs certain bits of information: the name of the recipient, the fax number of the recipient, the name and phone number of the sender, and so on. Let's start our exploration of the Cover Page Editor with a look at adding these basic fields, and then we'll move on to some of the more advanced features.

First, let's make it easier to place the fields evenly on the page by turning on grid view: choose View ➤ Grid Lines. You'll see something similar to the following:

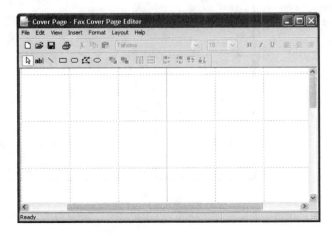

The Insert menu contains commands that place the common fields on your cover page. The fields are dropped into the center of the page, and you will need to drag them to their final destination. The fields are divided into three groups:

◆ Recipient

◆ Sender

◆ Message

The Recipient menu contains fields for the person's name and fax number. You will most likely want to include these in your cover page unless you're certain that the recipient is the only person at that number.

The Sender menu has a few more options. You can mix and match until you find the balance that's right for you. A good minimum might be to include your name and number, though your company name, office location, and department also might be useful.

The Message menu has only four options:

◆ Note

◆ Subject

◆ Date/Time Sent

◆ Number of Pages

At a minimum, include a Subject field and a Date/Time Sent field. Most cover pages include all four of these options as standard practice. Again, you'll have to decide what works best for you.

After you insert the fields that you want to include, you can drag them anywhere you want. In Figure 13.3, you can see that the Subject fields are highlighted with drag handles at the corners. These handles signify that you can move the fields by clicking anywhere in them and dragging them to a new position. You can also use the handles to resize the fields.

FIGURE 13.3

You can easily move any of the fields on your cover page.

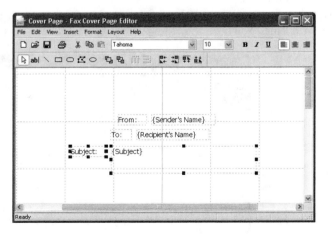

To select multiple fields, click somewhere near the outermost field in the group, and then, holding the mouse button down, drag the cursor until you've selected all the fields in the group. When you let go of the mouse button, all those fields will be selected, and you can move them as a unit.

ADVANCED COVER PAGE EDITING

Well, now you can create a simple cover page that contains all the necessary information. But just having the basic information is, yawn, so dull. You need to spice it up a bit with some graphics.

You can use the tools on the Drawing toolbar to add some visual interest to your cover page. The shapes and text buttons are much like those in the Paint program included with Windows XP Professional, but the Fax Cover Page Editor also includes some tools such as Send to Back and Send to Front that make it simple to create some great layered looks.

Here are the buttons you'll be using in the Fax Cover Page Editor:

	Select	The standard arrow cursor that you can use to select and move items on the page.
	Text	Changes the cursor to a crosshair style and lets you draw a box in which to place text.
	Line	Draws lines of different types based on the Format settings.
	Rectangle	Draws a simple rectangular shape. If you configure the fill settings before drawing, the rectangle can be filled or colored.
	Rounded Rectangle	Draws a rectangle that has rounded corners.
	Polygon	Draws, well, *polygons.* That may not be too clear, but each time you click your mouse button you will define a vertex of a polygon. When you are satisfied with the shape, double-click the last "corner" to stop drawing.
	Ellipse	Draws circles or ovals.
	Send to Front	Moves the selected field or object to the front of the picture or to the top of the stack of images.
	Send to Back	Sends the selected object to the back of the picture.
	Space Across	Evenly spaces the selected objects across the page horizontally.
	Space Down	Evenly distributes the selected objects vertically on the page.
	Align Left	Aligns the selected objects with the left of the page.
	Align Right	Aligns the selected objects with the right side of the page.
	Align Top	Aligns the selected objects with the top of the page.
	Align Bottom	Aligns the selected objects with the bottom of the page.

Using these tools, you can create very complex or very simple cover pages. When you have finished your work of art, be sure to save it so that it will be available in the future.

Using the Fax Console

The Fax Console, shown in Figure 13.4, is the tool you use to manage all fax activities. To open it, choose Start ➤ All Programs ➤ Accessories ➤ Communications ➤ Fax ➤ Fax Console.

FIGURE 13.4

The Fax Console

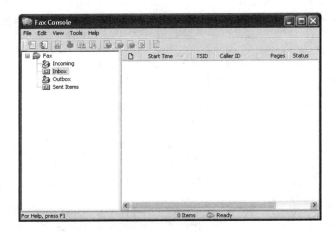

The Fax pane contains the following folders:

Incoming   Stores incoming faxes. When they arrive, they are placed in the Inbox folder.

Inbox   Stores all faxes that have completely arrived.

Outbox   Stores faxes in the process of being sent and faxes that are being held until a certain time to be sent.

Sent Items   Stores faxes that you have sent.

Clicking a folder displays its contents in the pane on the right.

Of particular interest on the menu bar is the Tools menu. It contains the following commands:

Sender Information   Opens the Sender Information dialog box, in which you can change the information you use to fill in the blanks on your cover page.

Personal Cover Pages   Opens the Personal Cover Pages dialog box, which, as you saw earlier, you can use to create customized cover pages.

Fax Printers Status   Opens the Fax Printers Status dialog box, which displays the status of the currently running fax service.

Configure Fax   Starts the Fax Configuration Wizard.

Fax Printer Configuration   Opens the Fax Properties dialog box, which you can use to establish various fax settings.

Fax Monitor   Opens the Fax Monitor dialog box, which displays a diagram that shows faxes in the process of being sent or received.

Connecting with HyperTerminal

HyperTerminal is a utility program you can use to connect to another computer (perhaps one that uses a different operating system such as Unix), to an information service such as the book catalog at your local library, or to a bulletin board. You can use this type of connection to download or transfer files.

TIP   HyperTerminal is a class of program known as terminal emulation software. In other words, it pretends to be a terminal attached to the remote computer. HyperTerminal is not a Web browser and cannot access Web sites on the Internet. For that particular task, see the description of how to use Internet Explorer in Chapter 12.

Creating a New HyperTerminal Connection

To create the phone numbers and specifics for initiating a HyperTerminal connection, follow these steps:

1. Choose Start ➤ All Programs ➤ Accessories ➤ Communications ➤ HyperTerminal to open the Connection Description dialog box in the foreground and the HyperTerminal window in the background. Before these windows open, you'll see a dialog box asking if you want to make HyperTerminal your default Telnet application. Click Yes or No as appropriate.

2. In the Name box, enter the descriptive name you want to assign to this connection, and then choose one of the icons from the selection displayed at the bottom of the dialog box. Click OK to open the Connect To dialog box.

3. Verify the country and area code, type the telephone number you want to use with this connection, and confirm your modem type. Click OK to open the Connect dialog box.

4. Check the phone number for this connection, and if it is incorrect, click Modify to change it. To look at or change any of the settings associated with the phone line or with dialing, click Dialing Properties to open the Phone and Modem Options dialog box. (See Chapter 11 for information about this dialog box.)

5. When you are ready to make the connection, click Call. You will be connected to the other computer, and a named window for the connection will open. If you do not want to call now, click Cancel, and the named window for the connection will be displayed, as shown in Figure 13.5.

The next thing that you see in the window will depend on the service or computer you have connected to; you may be asked to select a terminal type, to enter a password, or to make a selection from a menu. When you are finished, use the appropriate command to log off the remote computer before you close the HyperTerminal window.

FIGURE 13.5

The HyperTerminal
main window

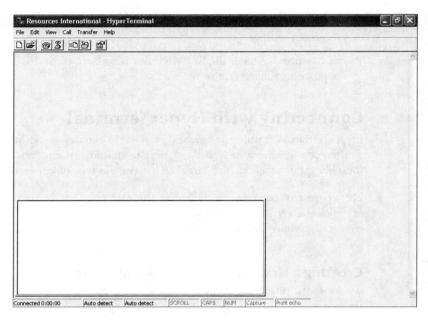

Sending and Receiving Files

While using HyperTerminal, you can send and receive files and capture what you see on your screen to your printer. To send a file, follow these steps:

1. Choose Transfer ➤ Send File to open the Send File dialog box.

2. Enter the name of the file in the Filename box, or click Browse to locate it.

3. In the Protocol box, accept the protocol that HyperTerminal suggests, or click the down arrow to select another protocol from the list.

NOTE *If you know the specific protocol for the system to which you are connected, select that protocol. If you don't know the protocol, stick with Zmodem, which is a generic, commonly used protocol.*

4. Click Send.

To receive a file, follow these steps:

1. Choose Transfer ➤ Receive File to open the Receive File dialog box.

2. Indicate where the received file should be stored, and specify the protocol if necessary.

3. Click Receive.

To capture what you see on your screen to the printer, choose Transfer ➤ Capture to Printer.

Communicating and Sharing with NetMeeting

NetMeeting is an application that you can use to do the following:

- Chat with someone over the Internet, via voice or by typing on the screen
- Audio conference
- Videoconference
- Share applications
- Collaborate on documents
- Transfer files
- Draw on the Whiteboard

Obviously, you need the proper equipment to do some of these, and, as we look at the individual features of NetMeeting, I'll point that out.

Installing NetMeeting

NetMeeting was included with several previous versions of Windows. As of this writing, it is not on any menu in Windows XP Professional, but you can install it by doing the following:

1. Choose Start ➤ Help and Support to open Help and Support Center.

2. In the Search box, type **NetMeeting**, and press Enter.

3. In the Search Results bar, click the What's New in Other Areas of Windows XP Professional link.

4. In the pane on the right, click the plus sign (+) next to NetMeeting, and then click the Using NetMeeting link.

5. In the Using NetMeeting pane, click the NetMeeting link.

6. In the Using NetMeeting screen, click the NetMeeting link to open it. You'll see the following screen, which presents an overview of NetMeeting:

Take a look at it and click Next.

7. Click Next to open a screen in which you enter at least your first name, your last name, and your e-mail address, and then click Next.

8. If you want to log on to a directory server whenever you start NetMeeting, click Log on to a Directory Server When NetMeeting Starts. If you don't want your name to appear in the directory listing for that server, click Do Not List My Name in the Directory. Click Next.

NOTE   *Directory servers are maintained by organizations or companies and provide a list of people who are logged on to the server and have chosen to display their names. If you are connected to the Internet and log on to a directory server, you can click a name in the list to connect to that person. We'll look at exactly how this works later in this chapter and also talk about why you might or might not want to display your name.*

9. In the next screen, specify your modem speed or connection mode, and then click Next.

10. If you want quick access to NetMeeting, leave the options selected in this screen so that you display a shortcut to NetMeeting on your Desktop and an icon on the Quick Launch toolbar. Click Next to start the Audio Tuning Wizard, and then click Next again.

11. If you have sound equipment (speakers and a sound card), click the Test button to sample the volume, and then change it as necessary. Click Next.

12. If you have a microphone, speak into it to ensure that the record volume is correct. Click Next.

13. Click Finish.

You're now ready to start using NetMeeting, which is shown in Figure 13.6. You'll see a Net-Meeting icon on your desktop. Click it to start NetMeeting.

FIGURE 13.6

The opening Net-Meeting window

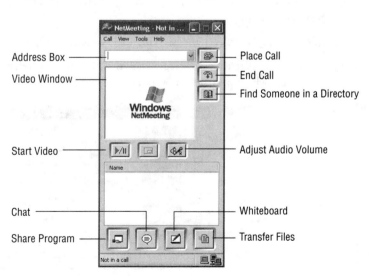

Address Box — Place Call

Video Window — End Call

— Find Someone in a Directory

Start Video — Adjust Audio Volume

Chat — Whiteboard

Share Program — Transfer Files

Making a Call

You can place a call in NetMeeting in the following ways:

◆ By connecting directly to an Internet directory server or to another computer using that computer's name or address.

◆ By using a gateway on your network to connect to a telephone or videoconferencing system.

◆ By using a gatekeeper, which is a computer on your network that locates and connects to people, computers, and gateways.

When you make a call in any of these ways, the person you call does not have to be running NetMeeting.

When you make the connection, you can communicate in several ways, depending on your equipment:

◆ If both people have microphones, sound cards, and speakers, you can talk just as you would over the telephone.

◆ If both people have microphones, sound cards, speakers, video cards, and video cameras, you can talk and be seen on the screen.

◆ If you don't have any of this equipment or just prefer it, you can communicate via the Chat application.

NOTE *You can see video even if you don't have a camera, and you can hear another person who is using a microphone if you have speakers. Video runs in the Video window.*

To make a call, follow these steps:

1. In the Address box, enter one of the following:

◆ An e-mail address

◆ A computer name

◆ A telephone number

◆ An IP (Internet Protocol) address.

2. Click the Place Call button.

If NetMeeting cannot determine how to place the call, it displays the Place a Call dialog box, as shown in Figure 13.7. In the Using box, select the type of connection you are trying to make, and then click Call.

FIGURE 13.7

The Place a Call dialog box

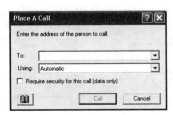

FINDING AN IP ADDRESS

An IP address is a unique number that identifies your computer on the Internet; for example, 209.254.117.155. The first three parts of this number refer to your ISP (Internet Service Provider), and the last three digits refer to your computer. Unless you have a permanent connection to the Internet such as your ISP has, each time you log on you are assigned a different IP address. As I've mentioned, using an IP address is one way to connect through NetMeeting with others who are on the Internet.

To find out what your current IP address is, follow these steps:

1. Choose Start ➢ All Programs ➢ Accessories ➢ Command Prompt to open the Command Prompt window.

2. At the prompt, type **ipconfig** and press Enter.

Now you can share your IP address with someone who wants to call you. I've done this via e-mail before, and it works great. If the person you want to call is not running Windows XP Professional or Windows 2000 Professional, but Windows 9x instead, they can type **winipcfg** to find out their IP address. Remember, though, every time you disconnect from the Internet or lose your connection, you lose that IP address. You'll get another one when you connect again.

Using the Chat Application

If you've visited chat rooms on the Web, you know how to use chat. What you type appears on the screen for you and others to see. Figure 13.8 shows the Chat window. To open Chat, click the Chat button in the main NetMeeting window.

FIGURE 13.8

Chatting in NetMeeting

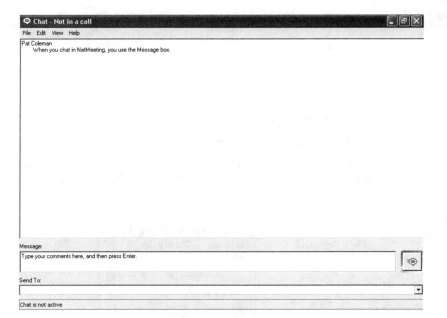

To use Chat, you need to know only the following:

◆ Click in the Message box, type, and press Enter to send your words of wisdom.

◆ If the session involves more than one person, click the down arrow in the Send To box to specify whether to send your chat lines to an individual or to the whole group.

◆ To save the contents of a Chat session, choose File ➤ Save As.

◆ To end a session, close the Chat window.

TIP *To customize the format of the Chat window, such as the fonts used and the display of information, choose View ➤ Options.*

Using Directory Servers

As I mentioned earlier, a directory server is a service maintained by an organization or a company, and when you connect to it, you can see the names, e-mail addresses, and so on of all the others who are logged on and have chosen to display their names. You can also see whether they are available for video and audio transmission.

By default, NetMeeting points you to the Microsoft Internet Directory service. To log on to it, choose Call ➤ Directory, which opens the Find Someone dialog box. Click to log on to Windows Messenger. I'll discuss Windows Messenger in detail later in this chapter.

Hosting a Meeting

You can also use NetMeeting to hold a meeting. To set this up, choose Call ➤ Host Meeting to open the Host a Meeting dialog box, as shown in Figure 13.9. Specify the parameters for the meeting, such as whether only you can place or accept calls, share applications, and so on, and then click OK. Now others can call you or you can call others. The meeting lasts until you end it (or until you or the others lose their connections).

FIGURE 13.9

Setting the guidelines for a meeting

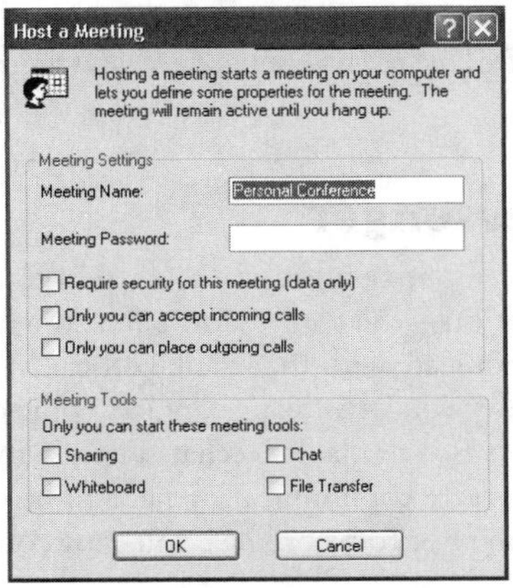

Using Video

When you are receiving or sending video, images are displayed in the video window. To set up video transmissions, choose Tools ➤ Options to open the Options dialog box, and click the Video tab, which is shown in Figure 13.10. You can specify when to send and receive video, the size of the image, its quality (do you want speed or clarity?), and the properties of your camera.

FIGURE 13.10

Setting up video transmission

Sharing Applications

While you are in a call or in a meeting, you can share documents and applications. To do so, open the program you want to share, and then click the Share Program button to open the Sharing dialog box. Specify the program to share and who will control it, and then click Close. Others will now be able to see and interact with you and your application.

NOTE   *To share the Whiteboard, click the Whiteboard button in the main NetMeeting window.*

Using Windows Messenger

Instant messaging (IM) is hot because it's a great way to keep in touch with people. The big advantage to IM is that the communication—the conversation, if you will—takes place in real time. If someone is online, you can communicate with them. Like other IM software, Windows Messenger (hereafter called Messenger) notifies you when your contacts come online (and notifies your contacts when *you* go online), so you know who's available to chat. The disadvantage to IM, of course, is that the person or people with whom you're communicating need to be online at the same time as you. If they're not online (or are pretending not to be online), you can't communicate with them.

Starting Messenger

To start Messenger, choose Start ➤ All Programs ➤ Windows Messenger. Alternatively, if Messenger is displaying an icon in the notification area, double-click it.

If you haven't added a .NET Passport to your Windows XP user account, Messenger displays a Click Here to Sign In link in its window. Clicking this link starts the .NET Passport Wizard, which guides you through the process of adding an existing .NET Passport to Windows XP or getting a new .NET Passport and adding that to Windows. Once you've done that, Messenger signs you in.

Once you've started Messenger, it displays an icon in your notification area. Click this icon to display a menu of actions you can take with Messenger.

When Messenger appears on your screen, chances are that it tells you that you don't have anyone in your contacts list and suggests you click the Add button to start adding contacts. (If you've just set Messenger up, your lack of contacts should be no surprise.) Figure 13.11 shows Messenger with a modest number of contacts added. As you can see in the figure, Messenger tells you the number of new messages you have in your Hotmail account (if you have one).

FIGURE 13.11

Messenger with a number of contacts added

You're probably itching to add some contacts and get on with messaging. But before you do that, configure Messenger by choosing options as described in the next section.

Configuring Messenger

Messenger comes with a raft of configuration options. You don't need to set all of them at once—this section covers them all in case you want to—but you should know about them before using Messenger. At the very least, you should edit your public profile so that you know what information other people can access about you.

Choose Tools ➤ Options to display the Options dialog box, and then configure your choice of the options described in the following sections.

Personal Tab Options

The Personal tab of the Options dialog box (shown in Figure 13.12) contains a couple of important settings and a couple of trivial ones.

FIGURE 13.12

In the Personal tab of the Options dialog box, set your display name and edit your Passport public profile.

My Display Name text box   Enter the name you want Messenger to display for you.

Always Ask Me for My Password When Checking Hotmail or Opening Other .NET Passport-Enabled Web Pages check box   Select this check box (which is cleared by default) if you want to enter your Passport password manually each time it's required by a Web site. Entering the password manually improves your security, but you may find yourself needing to enter the password too often for speedy or comfortable browsing.

Change Font button   Use this button and the resulting Set My Message Font dialog box to specify the font you want to use in IM windows.

Show Graphics (Emoticons) in Instant Messages check box   Clear this check box (which is selected by default) if you want to prevent Messenger from displaying emoticons (for example, ☺).

Phone Tab Options

The Phone tab of the Options dialog box (shown in Figure 13.13) lets you specify your country or region code and your home, work, and mobile phone numbers.

Preferences Tab Options

The Preferences tab of the Options dialog box (shown in Figure 13.14) contains a slew of options that affect Messenger's behavior:

Run This Program When Windows Starts check box   Leave this check box selected (as it is by default) if you want Windows to launch Messenger every time you log on to Windows. Clear this check box if you prefer to run Messenger manually when you need it.

FIGURE 13.13

In the Phone tab of the Options dialog box, specify your country or region code and enter the phone numbers you want Messenger to know.

Allow This Program to Run in the Background check box   Leave this check box selected (as it is by default) if you want Messenger to be able to run in the background and lurk in your notification area when you're not actively using it. Keeping Messenger running in the background lets you know instantly when one of your contacts comes online or sends you a message, but it also means that you need to keep your Internet connection open all the time. If you don't want Messenger to run in the background, clear this check box, and Messenger will exit when you close its window.

Show Me As "Away" When I'm Inactive for *NN* Minutes check box and text box   Leave this check box selected (as it is by default) if you want Messenger to change your status to Away after the specified period of inactivity. (Adjust the number of minutes in the text box as necessary. The default setting is 10 minutes, which is too short for many busy people.) Clear this check box if you don't want Messenger to monitor you in this way.

Display Alerts Near the Taskbar When Contacts Come Online check box   Leave this check box selected (as it is by default) if you want Messenger to pop up an alert above the notification area when one of your contacts comes online.

Display Alerts Near the Taskbar When an Instant Message Is Received check box   Leave this check box selected (as it is by default) if you want Messenger to pop up an alert above the notification area when you receive an instant message.

Play Sound When Contacts Sign in or Send a Message check box   Leave this check box selected (as it is by default) if you want Messenger to play a sound when contacts of yours sign in or send you a message. This audio alert is especially useful if you turn off the two visual alerts. If you use this option, you can click the Sounds button to customize the sounds displayed. Windows displays the Sound and Audio Devices Properties dialog box. In the Program Events list box on the Sounds page, scroll down to the Windows Messenger category. There you can assign sound that you like to these events: the Contact Online event (when a contact signs in), the New Alert event (when Messenger displays an alert), the New Mail event, and the New Message event. Then click the OK button. Windows closes the Sound and Audio Devices Properties dialog box.

File Transfer text box Specify the folder in which you want Messenger to put files that you receive from your contacts. The default setting is in your My Documents\My Received Files folder.

FIGURE 13.14

In the Preferences tab of the Options dialog box, customize Messenger's behavior.

Privacy Tab Options

The Privacy tab of the Options dialog box (shown in Figure 13.15) is where you maintain your Allow List (people who can see your online status and can send you messages) and your Block List (people who can do neither).

FIGURE 13.15

Use the Privacy tab of the Options dialog box to keep your Allow List and your Block List up-to-date.

To move a contact from one list to another, select them in the appropriate list box and click the Allow button or the Block button.

TIP   *By default, Messenger allows all other users to contact you and view your status until you block them. If you want to use Messenger privately, consider blocking all other users until you decide to allow them. To do so, select the All Other Users item in the My Allow List and click the Block button to move it to the My Block List.*

To see which users have added you to their contacts lists, click the View button. Messenger displays the Which Users Have Added You? dialog box, which provides an unadorned list of names. You can right-click a name and choose Add to Contacts from the shortcut menu to add the person to your list of contacts, or choose Properties from the shortcut menu to display a Properties dialog box giving information about the person.

Connection Tab Options

In the Connection tab of the Options dialog box, you can specify proxy server settings if you connect to the Internet through a proxy server (for example, through a company network). If not, leave these settings alone.

Running the Audio and Video Tuning Wizard

If you have speakers (or headphones) and a microphone, you can use them to make voice calls via Messenger. If you have a Webcam or another live video camera, you can make video calls as well. To set Messenger up for making voice and video calls, make sure your sound and video hardware is plugged in and working, and then run the Audio and Video Tuning Wizard by taking the following steps:

1. Choose Tools ➤ Audio and Video Tuning Wizard. Messenger starts the Audio and Video Tuning Wizard, which displays its first screen. This instructs you to make sure that your camera, speakers, and microphone are plugged in and turned on, and to close any other programs that might be using them.

2. Click the Next button. The Wizard displays its second screen (shown in Figure 13.16).

FIGURE 13.16

On the second screen of the Audio and Video Tuning Wizard, choose the video camera to use for video calls.

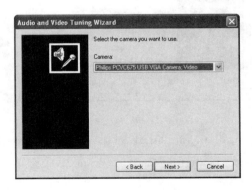

3. In the Camera drop-down list, select the video camera to use.

4. Click the Next button. The Wizard grabs the video feed from the camera and displays it on its third screen (shown in Figure 13.17).

FIGURE 13.17

On the third screen of the Audio and Video Tuning Wizard, adjust your video camera to show the image you want.

5. Adjust the picture until it shows what you want it to.

6. Click the Next button. The Wizard displays its fourth screen with tips on positioning your microphone and speakers.

7. Move your microphone or your speakers if necessary.

8. Click the Next button. The Wizard displays its fifth screen (shown in Figure 13.18).

FIGURE 13.18

On the fifth screen of the Audio and Video Tuning Wizard, choose which microphone and speakers to use.

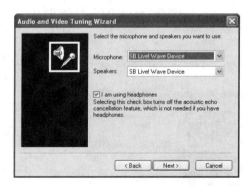

9. In the Microphone drop-down list, select the microphone to use.

10. In the Speakers drop-down list, select the output device (for example, a sound card) connected to the speakers.

11. If you're using headphones, select the I Am Using Headphones check box, which tells the Wizard to turn off echo cancellation. (With headphones, you don't need this because the echoes should be confined to your head.)

12. Click the Next button. The Wizard displays its sixth screen (shown in Figure 13.19).

FIGURE 13.19

On the sixth screen of the Audio and Video Tuning Wizard, test your speakers or headphones.

13. Click the Click to Test Speakers button to play a sound for a volume check. Drag the Speaker Volume slider to adjust the volume as necessary. Click the Stop button (which replaces the Click to Test Speakers button) to stop the sound.

14. Click the Next button. The Wizard displays its seventh screen (shown in Figure 13.20).

FIGURE 13.20

On the seventh screen of the Audio and Video Tuning Wizard, set your microphone volume.

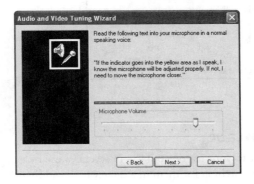

15. Speak into your microphone for 20 to 30 seconds at normal volume. (If you want, read the sample text shown, but it's instructive rather than magical, so declaim poetry or curse fluently if you prefer.) The Audio and Video Tuning Wizard adjusts the Microphone Volume slider to an appropriate level.

16. Click the Next button. You should see the eighth and final screen of the Wizard, telling you that you've completed the Wizard. (If you had a microphone problem, you'll see instead a dialog box telling you that instead. Fix the problem and try setting the microphone volume again.)

17. Click the Finish button. The Wizard closes and applies the settings it helped you choose.

Signing Out and Signing Back In

Messenger automatically signs you in when you start it. But you can sign out manually, leaving Messenger running, by choosing File ➤ Sign Out.

NOTE *The first time you sign out, if you have things going on, Messenger displays a dialog box explaining that signing out will close all your conversations and stop any file transfers. Click the OK button to proceed. After that, Messenger doesn't give you any warning when you sign out.*

To sign back in as the same user, click the Click Here to Sign in As Username link in the Windows Messenger window. Messenger signs you in. To sign in using a different Passport, click the Or, Click Here To Sign In As Someone Else link, or choose File ➤ Sign In, or click the Messenger icon in the notification area and choose Sign In from the menu it displays. Messenger displays the .NET Messenger Service dialog box (shown in Figure 13.21). Enter your sign-in name and password, and then click the OK button.

FIGURE 13.21

Signing back in to Messenger Service

Adding a Contact

You can add a contact to your list of contacts in several ways: by using their e-mail address or Passport sign-in name; by searching for them in a directory; by adding them when they contact you; or by reciprocating when they add you as a contact.

Adding a Contact by E-mail Address or Passport Sign-In

If you know a contact's e-mail address or Passport sign-in name, you can add them to your contacts list as follows:

1. Click the Add button in the Messenger window (or choose File ➤ Add a Contact). Messenger displays the How Do You Want to Add a Contact? screen of the Add a Contact Wizard (shown in Figure 13.22).

2. Leave the By E-mail Address or Sign-In Name option button selected, as it is by default.

3. Click the Next button. Messenger displays the Please Type Your Contact's Complete E-mail Address screen.

FIGURE 13.22

On the How Do You Want to Add a Contact? screen of the Add a Contact Wizard, specify whether to add a contact by e-mail address or Passport sign-in name or to search for them.

4. Enter the e-mail address and click the Next button. Messenger searches for a matching user. If it finds one, it displays a Success screen telling you that it has added the contact to your list. If Messenger doesn't find a match, it offers to send a message to the user inviting them to try Messenger. Take up this request if you like.

Adding a Contact by Searching for Them

You can also add a contact to your contacts list by searching for them:

1. Click the Add button in the Messenger window (or choose File ➢ Add a Contact). Messenger displays the How Do You Want to Add a Contact? screen of the Add a Contact Wizard.

2. Select the Search for a Contact option button.

3. Click the Next button. Messenger displays the Type Your Contact's First and Last Name screen (shown in Figure 13.23).

FIGURE 13.23

To add a contact to your list in Messenger, you can search for them by name.

4. Enter the person's first name and last name. If you're sure of their country or region, specify that in the Country/Region drop-down list.

   ◆ By default, Messenger searches in the Hotmail Member Directory. You may be able to choose another search location, such as your Address Book, in the Search for This Person At drop-down list.

5. Click the Next button. Messenger displays a Search Results screen showing possible matches.

6. Select the right person and click the Next button. Messenger then walks you through the process of having the .NET service send an e-mail to the person and tell them how to install Messenger and contact you. You can add your own message to this e-mail, but Messenger won't give you the person's e-mail address so that you can contact them directly.

Adding a Contact when Someone Adds You to Their Contacts List

You can also add a contact quickly by adding a person who adds you to *their* contacts list (unless you've configured Messenger not to notify you when this happens).

When someone adds you to their contacts list, Messenger displays the Windows Messenger dialog box shown in Figure 13.24, asking whether you want to allow this person or block them. Select the Allow This Person to See When You Are Online and Contact You option button or the Block This Person from Seeing When You Are Online and Contacting You option button as appropriate. If you want to add the person to your contacts list, leave the Add This Person to My Contact List check box selected. If not, clear it. Then click the OK button. Messenger closes the dialog box and takes the actions you specified.

FIGURE 13.24

Messenger displays this Windows Messenger dialog box when someone adds you to their contacts list. Specify whether to allow the contact or block them.

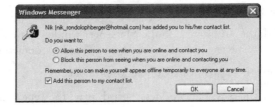

Removing a Contact from Your Contacts List

To remove a contact from your contacts list, select their entry and press the Delete key (or choose File ➤ Delete Contact). Alternatively, right-click the contact and choose Delete Contact from the shortcut menu. Messenger deletes the contact without confirmation.

Chatting

To chat with a Messenger user, double-click the user's entry in the Online list, or right-click the user's entry in the Online list and choose Send an Instant Message from the shortcut menu.

Messenger opens a Conversation window of chat with the user. Figure 13.25 shows an example. Type a message into the text box and press the Enter key (or click the Send button) to send it.

FIGURE 13.25

Starting a conversation in Messenger

The other user receives a screen pop-up (of which Figure 13.26 shows an example) telling them that you've sent them a message and a minimized Conversation window. The user can display the Conversation window by clicking the screen pop-up (if they're quick enough to catch it before it disappears) or by clicking the Conversation window's button on the Taskbar.

FIGURE 13.26

Messenger displays a screen pop-up like this when someone sends you a message.

Figure 13.27 shows a chat getting started in a Conversation window. Note the readout at the bottom that tells you that the other protagonist in the chat is typing a message. This alert helps you avoid sending overlapping messages and having the conversations spiral off into multiple threads.

FIGURE 13.27

Chatting in a Conversation window. The readout at the bottom warns the user that the other participant is typing a message.

Adding More People to a Conversation

To add a third or fourth person to your current conversation, choose File ➤ Invite ➤ To Join This Conversation. From the submenu, select one of your contacts from the context menu. Alternatively, select the Other item, specify the user's e-mail address in the Invite to This Conversation dialog box, and click the OK button. Messenger adds the user to the conversation if they're online.

Setting Font, Style, and Color for Text You Send

If you want to be distinctive, you can change the font, style, and color for text you send to others and that you see on your screen. For the text you see in the Messenger windows, you can change the size as well. (You can't change the size of the text that others see, and they can't change the size that you see.)

To set the font, style, color, and size, choose Edit ➤ Change Font. Messenger displays the Change My Message Font dialog box. Choose settings you like and click the OK button to apply them.

Adding Voice to a Conversation

If both participants have functioning audio hardware, you can add voice to a Messenger conversation between two people. (You can't use voice in a conversation that has three or four people.)

As usual for Internet telephony, the audio that's transmitted is converted from its (spoken) analog form to a digitized version, transmitted digitally, and then converted back to analog output at the sound card, headphones, or speakers on the other end. As a result, the quality tends to suffer compared to a regular phone call, in which the audio stays analog the whole way. That said, you can get intelligible audio quality over a connection as slow as 21.6Kbps, acceptable quality in the 40–53Kbps range, and good quality over faster connections.

NOTE   *If you haven't run the Audio and Video Tuning Wizard, Messenger runs it the first time you click the Talk button.*

To add voice to your current conversation, click the Start Talking heading in the right pane in the Conversation window. Messenger displays a Speakers volume control and a Microphone Mute check box (shown in Figure 13.28) and notifies the person you're chatting with that you want to have a voice conversation. They get to accept this or decline it. If they accept, Messenger establishes the connection.

To hang up the voice portion of the call, click the Stop Talking heading.

FIGURE 13.28

When you add voice to a Messenger conversation, the Conversation window displays a Speakers volume control and a Microphone Mute control.

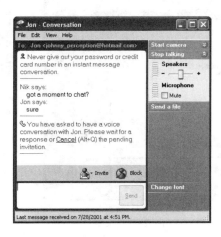

Adding Video to a Conversation

If one or both participants have video hardware installed, you can add video to a Messenger conversation between two people. (As with voice, you can't use video in a conversation that has three or four people.)

To add video to a conversation, click the Start Camera heading. Messenger displays a camera panel on your computer with a picture-in-picture picture of the video you're sending, and invites your victim to take part in the video conversation. If they accept, they receive a larger version of the picture. Figure 13.29 shows a conversation with incoming video.

FIGURE 13.29

You can also add video to a Messenger conversation.

To toggle your picture-in-picture picture on and off, click the Options button and choose Show My Video As Picture-in-Picture from the menu.

To stop transmitting or receiving video, click the Stop Camera heading.

Blocking and Unblocking Users

To block somebody from chatting with you, take one of the following actions:

◆ In a Conversation window with the person you want to block, click the Block button or choose File ➤ Block.

◆ In a Conversation window with multiple people, click the Block button and choose the person from the pop-up menu, or choose File ➤ Block and choose the person from the submenu.

◆ From the Windows Messenger window, right-click the person and choose Block from the context menu.

When you block a user from a Conversation window, Messenger displays the Windows Messenger dialog box shown in Figure 13.30 telling you that the blocked user will not be able to contact you or see your online status. When you unblock a user, Messenger displays a similar dialog box telling you that the other user *will* be able to do these things. In either case, you get an OK button to proceed with the blocking or unblocking, a Cancel button to cancel it, and a Don't Show Me This Message Again check box that you can select to prevent Messenger from telling you what you already know.

FIGURE 13.30

When you block a user, Messenger displays a dialog box to make sure you understand the consequences of your action. Select the Don't Show Me This Message Again check box to prevent Messenger from displaying this dialog box again.

To unblock a user, take one of the following actions:

◆ In a Conversation window, choose File ➤ Unblock.

◆ In a Conversation window with multiple participants, choose File ➤ Block and select the blocked user from the submenu.

◆ In the Windows Messenger window, right-click the blocked user and choose Unblock from the shortcut menu.

Changing Your Status

To let people know what you're up to, you can change the status that Messenger displays for you. To do so, click your icon in the Windows Messenger window and choose Online, Busy, Be Right Back, Away, On the Phone, Out to Lunch, or Appear Offline from the pop-up menu. You can also set your status by choosing File ➤ My Status and selecting the status from the submenu.

Transferring Files

Messenger provides an easy way to transfer files quickly to other Messenger users who are currently online.

Sending a File

To send a file to someone via Messenger, follow these steps:

1. Choose File ➤ Send a File To and select either an existing user or the Other item from the submenu. Messenger displays the Send a File dialog box, which is an Open dialog box in disguise.

◆ If you select the Other item, Messenger displays the Send a File dialog box (shown in Figure 13.31). Enter the person's e-mail address, select the service in the Service drop-down list (if applicable), and click the OK button.

FIGURE 13.31

Use the Send a File dialog box to send a file to a Messenger user who isn't one of your contacts.

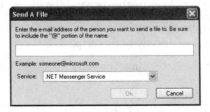

◆ To send a file to a user you're chatting with in a Conversation window, click the Send a File heading or choose File ➤ Send a File. You don't need to identify the user because Messenger knows it already. (If you're chatting with multiple people, Messenger displays the Send a File submenu listing the people in the conversation.)

2. Navigate to the file, select it, and click the Open button. Messenger contacts the user, asking them if they want to accept or decline the file.

◆ You can cancel the transfer by pressing Alt+Q or clicking the Cancel link.

3. If the user accepts the file, Messenger displays a progress readout in the Conversation window. When the file transfer is complete, Messenger lets you know that too. Figure 13.32 shows an example of a successful file-transfer session.

FIGURE 13.32

Messenger keeps you informed at each step of sending a file.

NOTE *If the user does not accept the transfer, or if it fails, Messenger tells you that the user declined the file or the file could not be sent.*

Receiving a File

Receiving a file via Messenger is even easier than sending one. Here's what happens:

1. If you're using pop-ups, Messenger displays a pop-up telling you that someone is trying to send you a file. (Messenger identifies the user and the file by name.)

2. Click the pop-up to display the Conversation window. (If you're already in a messaging session with this user, you'll go directly to this step.)

3. To accept the file, click the Accept link (or press Alt+T). To decline the file, click the Decline link (or press Alt+D).

4. If you choose to accept the file, Messenger displays a Windows Messenger dialog box warning you that files may contain harmful viruses or scripts and advising you to make sure that the file you're receiving is from a trustworthy source. Click the OK button to dismiss this dialog box. You can select the Don't Show Me This Message Again check box before dismissing the dialog box if you're fully aware of malware tricks and you carefully check every file you receive before running it.

5. Messenger transfers the file, stores it in the folder specified in the Preferences tab of the Options dialog box, and displays a link that you can click to open the file. Figure 13.33 shows the anatomy of a successful file-transfer session from the recipient's point of view.

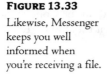

FIGURE 13.33

Likewise, Messenger keeps you well informed when you're receiving a file.

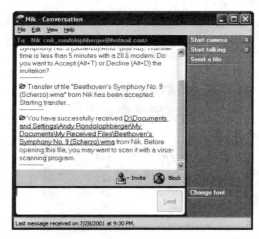

To access your received files folder, choose File ➤ Open Received Files.

Using Remote Desktop Connection

Remote Desktop Connection lets you connect via a dial-up connection, a local area network connection, or across the Internet and take control of somebody's computer (or your own).

Remote Desktop Connection is designed to let you access and control one computer (say, your work computer) from another computer (say, your home computer or your laptop). It's great for catching up with the office when you're at home, or for grabbing the files that you forgot to load on your laptop before you dived into the taxi for the airport.

Remote Desktop Connection Terminology and Basics

Remote Desktop Connection terminology is a little confusing. Here are the terms:

◆ The *home computer* is the computer on which you're working. The home computer needs to have Remote Desktop Connection installed. Remote Desktop Connection is installed by default in Windows XP Professional.

◆ The *remote computer* is the computer that you're accessing from the home computer. The remote computer needs to have Remote Desktop installed. Remote Desktop is separate from Remote Desktop Connection and is included in Windows XP Professional and the (forthcoming, at this writing) versions of Windows .NET Server. Remote Desktop is not included in Windows XP Home.

So the typical scenario is for the home computer to be running Windows XP Home and the remote computer to be running Windows XP Professional. You can also access one Windows XP Professional computer from another Windows XP Professional computer.

NOTE *You can access more than one remote computer at a time from the same home computer. However, unless you have impressive bandwidth, this results in slow sessions.*

In order for you to connect to another computer via Remote Desktop Connection any active session (whether local or connected via Remote Desktop Connection) on that computer needs to be disconnected. You get a warning about this, but the other user doesn't. If you choose to proceed, the remote computer displays the Welcome screen while your Remote Desktop Connection session is going on. There's no easy way for anyone looking at that computer to tell that you're remotely connected to it.

If a user comes back and starts using the remote computer while your Remote Desktop Connection session is going on, your session will be terminated—with a warning on their side, this time, but not on yours. Frankly, this could be more elegant.

In lay terms, Remote Desktop Connection works as follows:

◆ Keystrokes and mouse clicks are transmitted from the home computer to the remote computer via the display protocol. The remote computer registers these keystrokes and clicks as if they came from the keyboard attached to it.

◆ Programs run on the remote computer as usual. (Programs aren't run across the wire—that would be desperately slow.)

◆ Screen display information is passed to the home computer, again via the display protocol. This information appears on the display as if it came from the video adapter (only rather more slowly, and usually in a window).

Sound can be passed to the home computer as well, so that you can hear what's happening at the remote computer. Transferring sound like this enhances the impression of controlling the remote computer, but sound takes so much bandwidth that transferring it isn't a good idea on slow connections. The default Remote Desktop Connection setting is to transfer sound, but you may well want to switch it off.

Setting the Remote Computer to Accept Incoming Connections

The first step in getting Remote Desktop Connection to work is to set the remote computer to accept incoming connections. Remember that this is the computer that's remote from you and that's running Windows XP Professional (or .NET Server).

To set your computer to accept incoming connections, follow these steps:

1. Click the Start button, right-click My Computer, and choose Properties from the shortcut menu to open the System Properties dialog box.

2. Click the Remote tab, which is shown in Figure 13.34.

FIGURE 13.34

The Remote tab of the System Properties dialog box

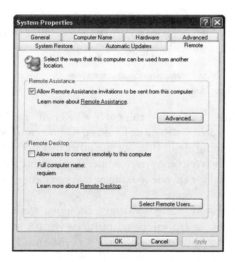

3. To allow users to connect to your computer, select the Allow Users to Connect Remotely to This Computer check box.

4. To specify which users can connect via Remote Desktop Connection, click the Select Remote Users button to open the Remote Desktop Users dialog box (shown in Figure 13.35). The list box shows any users currently allowed to connect to the computer. Below the list box is a note indicating that you (identified by your username) already have access—as you should have.

5. To add users, click the Add button. Windows displays the Select Users dialog box.

FIGURE 13.35

The Remote Desktop Users dialog box

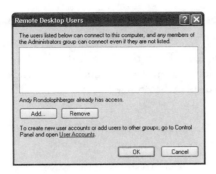

6. Select a user or group, and then click the OK button. Windows adds them to the list in the Remote Desktop Users dialog box.

7. Add further users or groups as necessary.

8. To remove a user or a group, select them in the list box and click the Remove button.

9. Click the OK button to close the Remote Desktop Users dialog box.

10. Click the OK button in the System Properties dialog box. Windows closes the dialog box and applies your changes.

That's the remote computer all set. Leave it up and running and return to the home computer.

Choosing Settings for Remote Desktop Connection

Next, choose settings for Remote Desktop Connection on the home computer. Remote Desktop Connection has a modestly large number of settings, but many of them are set-and-forget. Even better, you can save sets of settings so that you can quickly apply them for accessing different remote computers (or the same remote computer under different circumstances, such as when the cable modem is working and when it's flaked out on you).

To choose settings for Remote Desktop Connection, follow these steps:

1. Choose Start ➤ All Programs ➤ Accessories ➤ Communications ➤ Remote Desktop Connection. Windows starts Remote Desktop Connection and displays the Remote Desktop Connection window in its reduced state (shown in Figure 13.36).

2. Click the Options button. Windows displays the rest of the Remote Desktop Connection window.

FIGURE 13.36

The Remote Desktop Connection window appears first in its reduced state.

3. The General tab of the Remote Desktop Connection window (shown in Figure 13.37) offers these options:

Computer drop-down list   Enter the name or the IP address of the computer to which you want to connect; or select it from the drop-down list; or click the Browse for More item from the drop-down list to display the Browse for Computers dialog box, and then select the computer in that.

User Name text box   Enter the username under which you want to connect to the remote computer. Windows enters your username by default.

Password text box   If you want to store your password (for the remote computer) for the connection, enter it in this text box and select the Save My Password check box. If you don't enter your password here, you get to enter it when logging on to the remote computer.

Domain text box   If the remote computer is part of a domain, enter the domain name here. If the computer is part of a workgroup, you can leave this text box blank.

Save My Password check box   Select this check box if you want to save your password with the rest of the Remote Desktop Connection information. This can save you time and effort, but it compromises your security a bit.

Connection Settings section   Once you've chosen settings for a connection, you can save the connection information by clicking the Save As button and specifying a name for the connection in the Save As dialog box that Windows displays. Remote Desktop Connection connections are saved as files of the file type Remote Desktop File, which by default is linked to the RDP extension, in the My Documents\Remote Desktops folder. You can open saved connections by clicking the Open button and using the resulting Open dialog box.

FIGURE 13.37

The General tab of the expanded Remote Desktop Connection window

NOTE *You'll see a file named* DEFAULT.RDP *in the* My Documents\Remote Desktops *folder. Windows automatically saves your latest Remote Desktop Connection configuration under this name when you click the Connect button. But by explicitly saving your settings under a name of your choice, you can easily maintain different configurations for different Remote Desktop Connection settings.*

4. The Display tab of the Remote Desktop Connection window (shown in Figure 13.38) offers three display options:

Remote Desktop Size section   Drag the slider to specify the screen size you want to use for the remote Desktop. The default setting is Full Screen, but you may want to use a smaller size so that you can more easily access your Desktop on the home computer. When you display the remote Desktop full screen, it takes over the whole of the local Desktop, so that you can't see your local Desktop. (To get to your local Desktop, you use the connection bar, discussed in a moment or two.)

Colors section   In the drop-down list, select the color depth to use for the connection. Choose a low color depth (for example, 256 colors) if you're connecting over a low-speed connection. This choice will be overridden by the display setting on the remote computer if you ask for more colors than the remote computer is using.

Display the Connection Bar When in Full Screen Mode check box   Leave this check box selected (as it is by default) if you want Windows to display the connection bar when the remote Desktop is displayed full screen. The connection bar provides Minimize, Restore/Maximize, and Close buttons for the remote Desktop. (When the remote Desktop is displayed in a window, that window has the control buttons, so the connection bar isn't necessary.)

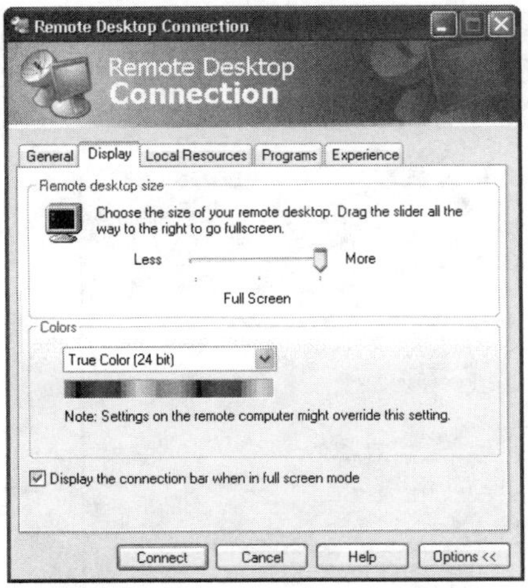

FIGURE 13.38

Choose display settings in the Display tab of the Remote Desktop Connection window.

5. The Local Resources tab of the Remote Desktop Connection window (shown in Figure 13.39) offers the following options:

   Remote Computer Sound section In the drop-down list, specify what you want Windows to do with sounds that would normally be generated at the remote Desktop. The default setting is Bring to This Computer, which transfers the sounds to the home computer and plays them there. This setting helps sustain the illusion that you're working directly on the remote Desktop, but it's heavy on bandwidth, so don't use it over low-speed connections. Instead, choose the Do Not Play setting or the Leave at Remote Computer setting. The Leave at Remote Computer setting plays the sounds at the remote computer and is best reserved for occasions when you need to frighten somebody remotely or pretend to be in your office.

   Keyboard section In the drop-down list, specify how you want Windows to handle Windows key combinations that you press (for example, Alt+Tab or Ctrl+Alt+Delete). Select the On the Local Computer item, the On the Remote Computer item, or the In Full Screen Mode Only item (the default) as suits your needs.

   Local Devices section Leave the Disk Drives, Printers, and Serial Ports check boxes selected (as they are by default) if you want these devices on your home computer to be available from the remote computer. This means that you can save documents from the remote computer to local drives, print them on your local printer, or transfer them via devices attached to serial ports (for example, a PDA). Local disk drives appear in the Other category in Explorer windows, named *Driveletter on COMPUTERNAME*. Local printers appear with *from COMPUTER-NAME* in parentheses after them.

6. The Programs tab of the Remote Desktop Connection window (shown in Figure 13.40) lets you specify that Windows run a designated program when you connect via Remote Desktop Connection. Select the Start the Following Program on Connection check box, then enter the program path and name in the Program Path and File Name text box. If you need to specify the folder in which the program should start, enter that in the Start in the Following Folder text box.

FIGURE 13.39

In the Local Resources tab of the Remote Desktop Connection window, specify how Windows should handle sound, keyboard shortcuts, and devices on the home computer.

FIGURE 13.40

If you need to have a program run on the remote Desktop when you connect, specify it in the Programs tab of the Remote Desktop Connection window.

7. The Experience tab of the Remote Desktop Connection window (shown in Figure 13.41) contains the following options:

   Choose Your Connection Speed to Optimize Performance drop-down list   In this drop-down list, select one of the four listed speeds to apply a preselected set of settings to the five check boxes on this page. The choices in the drop-down list are Modem (28.8Kbps), Modem (56Kbps), Broadband (128Kbps–1.5Mbps), LAN (10Mbps or Higher), and Custom.

   Desktop Background check box   This check box controls whether Remote Desktop Connection transmits the Desktop background. Because Desktop backgrounds are graphical, transmitting them is sensible only at LAN speeds. (If you clear this check box, Remote Desktop Connection uses a blank Desktop background.)

   Show Contents of Window While Dragging check box   This check box controls whether Remote Desktop Connection transmits the contents of a window while you're dragging it, or only the window frame. Don't use this option over a modem connection, because the performance penalty outweighs any benefit you may derive from it.

   Menu and Window Animation check box   This check box controls whether Remote Desktop Connection transmits menu and window animations (for example, zooming a window you're maximizing or minimizing). Don't use this option over a modem connection—it's a waste of bandwidth.

   Themes check box   This check box controls whether Remote Desktop Connection transmits theme information or uses "classic" Windows–style windows and controls. Transmitting theme information takes a little bandwidth, so you can improve performance over a very slow connection by clearing the Themes check box. But bear in mind that Windows will look different enough to unsettle some inexperienced users.

   Bitmap Caching check box   This check box controls whether Remote Desktop Connection uses bitmap caching to improve performance by reducing the amount of data that needs to be sent across the network in order to display the screen remotely. Caching could prove a security threat, so you *might* want to turn it off for security reasons. But in most cases, you're better off using it.

FIGURE 13.41

In the Experience tab of the Remote Desktop Connection window, you can customize which graphical information Remote Desktop Connection transmits in order to balance performance against looks.

8. If you want to save the settings you've chosen under a particular name so that you can reload them at will, click the Save As button in the General tab of the Remote Desktop Connection window.

Connecting via Remote Desktop Connection

Once you've chosen settings as outlined in the previous section, you're ready to connect. If you're connecting via the Internet (rather than a local network) and you have a dial-up connection, make sure it's up and running.

Click the Connect button in the General tab of the Remote Desktop Connection window. Windows attempts to establish a connection to the computer you specified.

If Windows is able to connect to the computer, and you didn't specify your username or password in the Remote Desktop Connection window, it displays the Log On to Windows dialog box (shown in Figure 13.42). Enter your username and password and click the OK button to log in. Windows then displays the remote Desktop. (If you chose to provide your password in the General tab of the Remote Desktop Connection window, you shouldn't need to enter it again.)

FIGURE 13.42

Windows displays the Log On to Windows dialog box for the remote computer.

If you left a user session active on the computer, Remote Desktop Connection drops you straight into it—likewise if you left a user session disconnected and no other user session is active. But if another user *is* active on the remote computer when you submit a successful logon and password, Windows displays the Logon Message dialog box shown in Figure 13.43 to warn you that logging on will disconnect the user's session. Click the Yes button if you want to proceed. Click the No button to withdraw stealthily.

FIGURE 13.43

Windows displays the Logon Message dialog box when you're about to bump a user off the remote computer by logging on.

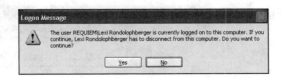

If you click the Yes button, the active user gets a Request for Connection dialog box such as that shown in Figure 13.44. This tells them that you (it specifies your name) are trying to connect to the computer, warns them that they'll be disconnected if you do connect, and asks if they want to allow the connection.

FIGURE 13.44

Windows displays the Request for Connection dialog box to tell the active user of your incoming session.

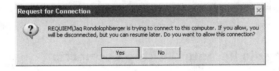

The active user then gets to click the Yes button or the No button as appropriate to their needs and inclinations. If Windows doesn't get an answer within 30 seconds or so, it figures they're not there, disconnects their session, and lets you in.

If the active user clicks the Yes button in the Request for Connection dialog box, Windows logs them off immediately and logs you on. But if the active user clicks the No button, you get a Logon Message dialog box such as that shown in Figure 13.45, telling you that they didn't allow you to connect. Windows displays this Logon Message dialog box for a few seconds, and then closes it automatically, returning you to the Remote Desktop Connection window.

FIGURE 13.45

Windows displays this Logon Message dialog box when the active user decides not to let you interrupt their session on the computer.

If Windows is unable to establish the connection with the remote computer, it displays one of its Remote Desktop Disconnected dialog boxes to make you aware of the problem. Figure 13.46 shows two examples of the Remote Desktop Disconnected dialog box.

FIGURE 13.46

If Windows is unable to connect, you'll see a Remote Desktop Disconnected dialog box.

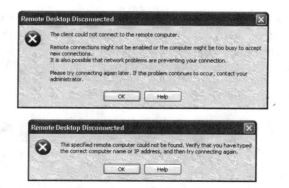

The first example of the Remote Desktop Disconnected dialog box tells you that the client couldn't connect to the remote computer and suggests that you try again later. The second example tells you that the remote computer couldn't be found and suggests checking that the computer name or IP address are correct. This should indeed be your first move—but if that doesn't work, that's about all you can do. If the remote computer has been shut down (or has crashed), or if its network or Internet connection has gone south, or if someone has reconfigured the computer not to accept Remote Desktop Connection connections or has revoked your permission to connect, then you're straight out of luck. No amount of retyping the computer name or IP address will make an iota of difference.

Working via Remote Desktop Connection

Once you've reached the remote Desktop, you can work more or less as if you were sitting at the computer. The few differences worth mentioning are discussed briefly in this section.

USING CUT, COPY, AND PASTE BETWEEN THE LOCAL AND REMOTE COMPUTERS

You can use Cut, Copy, and Paste commands to transfer information between the local computer and the remote computer. For example, you could copy some text from a program on the local computer and paste it into a program on the remote computer.

COPYING FROM REMOTE DRIVES TO LOCAL DRIVES

You can copy from remote drives to local drives by working in Explorer. The drives on your local computer appear in Explorer windows on the remote computer marked as *Driveletter on COMPUTERNAME*. The drives on the remote computer appear as regular drives. You can copy and move files from one drive to another as you would with local drives.

PRINTING TO A LOCAL PRINTER

You can print to a local printer from the remote Desktop by selecting the local printer in the Print dialog box just as you would any other printer.

Printer settings are communicated to the remote Desktop when you access it. If you add a local printer during the remote session, the remote Desktop won't be able to see it. To make the printer show up on the remote Desktop, log off the remote session and log back on.

Returning to Your Local Desktop

If you chose to display the connection bar, it hovers briefly at the top of the screen, and then slides upward to vanish like a docked toolbar with its Auto-Hide property enabled. To pin the connection bar in position, click the pin icon at its left end. (To unpin it, click the pin icon again.) To display the connection bar when it has hidden itself, move the mouse pointer to the top edge of the screen, just as you would do to display a docked toolbar hidden there.

The connection bar provides a Minimize button, a Restore/Maximize button, and a Close button. Use the Minimize button and the Restore button to reduce the remote Desktop from full screen to an icon or a partial screen so that you can access your local Desktop. Maximize the remote Desktop window to return to full-screen mode when you want to work with it again. Use the Close button as discussed in the next section to disconnect your remote session.

Disconnecting the Remote Session

You can disconnect the remote session in either of the two following ways:

◆ On the remote Desktop, choose Start ➤ Disconnect. Windows displays the Disconnect Windows dialog box (shown in Figure 13.47). Click the Disconnect button.

FIGURE 13.47

You can disconnect the remote session by issuing a Start ➤ Disconnect command and clicking the Disconnect button in the Disconnect Windows dialog box.

◆ Click the Close button on the connection bar (if the remote Desktop is displayed full screen) or on the Remote Desktop window (if the remote Desktop is not displayed full screen). Windows displays the Disconnect Windows Session dialog box (shown in Figure 13.48). Click the OK button.

Windows disconnects the remote session but leaves the programs running for the time being. You can then log on again and pick up where you left off.

FIGURE 13.48

The Disconnect Windows Session dialog box appears when you click the Close button on the connection bar. Click the OK button to end your remote session while leaving the programs running.

Logging Off the Remote Session

To log off and end your user session, click the Start button on the remote Desktop and choose Log Off from the Start menu. Windows displays the Log Off Windows dialog box (shown in Figure 13.49). Click the Log Off button.

FIGURE 13.49

To log off from the remote computer, choose Start ➤ Log Off and click the Log Off button in the Log Off Windows dialog box.

When someone else bumps you off the remote Desktop (by logging on locally or remotely), Windows displays the Remote Desktop Disconnected dialog box shown in Figure 13.50, telling you that the remote session "was ended by means of an administration tool."

FIGURE 13.50

This Remote Desktop Disconnected dialog box appears when you log off and when someone logs you off the remote computer.

If the network connection between the home computer and the remote computer is broken, the home computer displays a Remote Desktop Disconnected dialog box such as that shown in Figure 13.51.

FIGURE 13.51

This Remote Desktop Disconnected dialog box indicates that the network connection between the home computer and the remote computer was broken.

Summary

In this chapter, we've taken a quick look at some of the communications programs included with Windows XP Professional: Fax, HyperTerminal, NetMeeting, Windows Messenger, and Remote Desktop Connection. As I said at the outset, you may never have occasion to use any of these applications, or you may need only one of them from time to time. All are easy to learn and use, and if you frequently use any of them, you'll be up to speed with it in no time.

Now let's turn our attention to something you'll probably use every day—Outlook Express.

Chapter 14

Using Outlook Express for E-mail and News

OF ALL THE FEATURES of the Internet, intranets, and local area networks, e-mail is, without question, the most used. Instead of playing phone tag with colleagues at work, you send them e-mail. Millions of extended families stay in touch via e-mail, and an e-mail address has become an expected component of a business card.

Outlook Express is an Internet standards e-mail reader you can use to access an Internet e-mail account. An Internet e-mail account is not the same thing as an account with an online information service. The difference is that an Internet account provides services such as Point-to-Point protocol Internet access and e-mail but does not include services such as chat rooms, access to databases, conferences, and so on. Consequently, you cannot use Outlook Express to access an e-mail account with Hotmail, MS Mail, cc:Mail, CompuServe, America Online, or versions of Microsoft Exchange Server prior to version 5.

In addition to being an e-mail reader, Outlook Express is also a news reader. In the first part of this chapter, I'll look at e-mail features, and in the second part I'll look at how to access newsgroups and post to them.

- ◆ Starting Outlook Express

- ◆ Touring Outlook Express

- ◆ Using Outlook Express to read, compose, and send e-mail

- ◆ Using Outlook Express to read news and post to newsgroups

- ◆ Customizing Outlook Express

Using Outlook Express As Your Mail Reader

To start Outlook Express, choose Start ➤ E-mail Outlook Express or, from within Internet Explorer, click the Mail icon and then select an item from the submenu.

NOTE *Before you can open and use Outlook Express to send and receive e-mail, you need to configure your Internet connection. You'll find information on how to do this in Chapter 11.*

A Quick Tour

When you first open Outlook Express, you'll see a screen similar to that shown in Figure 14.1.

FIGURE 14.1

The opening screen in Outlook Express

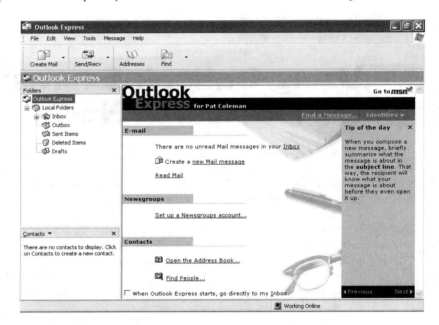

To read your mail, click Read Mail, or click Inbox in the Folders list. Initially the Preview pane is split horizontally; header information is displayed in the upper pane, and the message is displayed in the lower pane.

TIP *To change the arrangement of the Preview pane, choose View ➤ Layout to open the Window Layout Properties dialog box, and select options to show or hide certain parts.*

THE FOLDERS LIST

The Folders list is a tool for organizing messages. Initially, it contains the following folders, although you can create additional folders, as you'll see shortly:

Inbox Contains newly received messages and messages that you have not yet disposed of in some way.

Outbox Contains messages that are ready to be sent.

Sent Items Contains copies of messages that you have sent (a handy device if you send lots of e-mail).

Deleted Items   Contains copies of messages that you have deleted.

Drafts   Contains messages that you are working on but which are not yet ready to be sent.

THE CONTACTS PANE

The Contacts pane contains the names of people in your Address Book. To compose a message to anyone on this list, simply double-click the name.

Retrieving Your Mail

If you are connected to your Internet account, Outlook Express will automatically check the server for new messages and download them when you open Outlook Express. By default, Outlook Express will also check for new mail every 30 minutes, as long as you are connected. To adjust this time interval, follow these steps:

1. Choose Tools ➤ Options to open the Options dialog box:

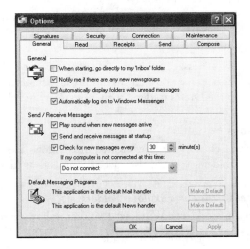

2. In the General tab, click the up or down arrow to change the Check for New Messages Every *x* Minutes option.

3. Click OK.

You can also check for new mail by choosing Tools ➤ Send and Receive ➤ Receive All or by clicking the Send/Recv button on the toolbar in the main window.

Reading and Processing Messages

If you are working in the split Preview pane view, simply click a message header to display the message in a separate window. Otherwise, simply double-click a header to view the message.

PRINTING MESSAGES

For various reasons, it's often handy to have a paper copy of e-mail messages. You can print in a couple of ways:

- ◆ To print a message without opening it, select its header and click the Print icon on the toolbar in the main window.

- ◆ To print an open message, click the Print icon on the toolbar in the message window.

MARKING MESSAGES

If you're like me, you don't always handle each message as you receive it or immediately after you read it, and it's easy to forget that you need to take some action or follow up on a message unless it stands out from the others in the header list. One trick that I use is to mark a message as unread even though I have read it (select the header and choose Edit ➤ Mark As Unread). You can also select the header and choose Message ➤ Flag Message to display a red flag to the left of the message header. To remove the flag, choose Message ➤ Flag Message again.

In addition, you can mark a message as read, and you can mark all messages as read.

MOVING MESSAGES

You can easily move a message from one folder to another by dragging and dropping it. For example, if you receive a message that you want to modify and send to someone else, select the message header and then drag it to the Drafts folder. Open it, revise it, and then send it on its way.

SAVING MESSAGES

You can save messages in folders you created in Windows Explorer, and you can save messages in Outlook Express folders. You can also save attachments as files.

Saving Messages in Windows Explorer Folders

To save messages in a folder in Windows Explorer, follow these steps:

1. Open the message or select its header.

2. Choose File ➤ Save As to open the Save Message As dialog box:

3. Select a folder in which to save the message. Outlook Express places the subject line in the File Name box. You can use this name or type another name.

4. Select a file type in which to save the message, and then click Save.

Saving Messages in Outlook Express Mail Folders

As I've mentioned, you can create your own Outlook Express folders. For example, you might want to create folders for people with whom you regularly correspond, or you might want to create folders for current projects. To create a new folder, follow these steps:

1. In the main Outlook Express window, choose File ➤ New ➤ Folder to open the Create Folder dialog box:

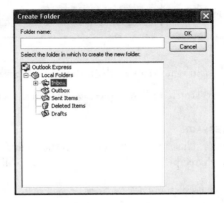

2. In the Folder Name box, type a name for your folder.

3. Select a folder in which to place the new folder, and click OK.

You now have a new folder in your folders list, and you can drag any message to it. You have, however, an even easier and more efficient way to save messages in Outlook Express folders, and I'll look at that in the Apply Message Rules section, later in this chapter.

Saving Attachments

An attachment is a file that is appended to an e-mail message. You'll know that a message has an attachment if the header is preceded by the paper clip icon. When you open the message, you'll see the filename of the attachment in the Attach line in the header. To open an attachment, double-click its filename.

To save an attachment, follow these steps:

1. Open the message, and choose File ➤ Save Attachments to open the Save Attachments dialog box:

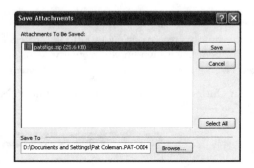

2. Select a folder in which to save the file, and click Save.

I'll discuss how to attach a file to a message later in this chapter.

REPLYING TO A MESSAGE

To reply to a message, click the Reply button on the toolbar in the message window. If the message is addressed to multiple recipients and you want to reply to all of them, click the Reply All button.

TIP *This is a quick and easy way to note the person's e-mail address. By default, Outlook Express automatically places the names of the people you reply to in your Address Book.*

By default, Outlook Express includes the text of the original message in your reply. According to Internet tradition, this squanders bandwidth, and it's better not to include the original message unless it's really necessary. When is it necessary?

◆ When you want to be sure that the recipient understands the nature of your reply and the topic to which it is related

◆ When your message is part of a series of messages that involve some sort of question-and-answer sequence

◆ When it's important to keep track of who said what when

An alternative is to include only the relevant portions of the original message in your reply. To do so, follow these steps:

1. Open the message and click the Reply button.

2. The message is now addressed to the original sender, and the original subject line is preceded by Re:.

3. In the body of the message, edit the contents so that the portions you want are retained, and then enter your response.

4. Click the Send button.

If you don't want to include the original message in your reply, you can simply open the message, click the Reply button, place the insertion point in the body of the message, choose Edit ➤ Select All, and press Delete. If you're sure that you don't want to include the original message, choose Tools ➤ Options, and in the Options dialog box, click the Send tab. Clear the Include Message in Reply check box. If once in a while you need the message included, simply recheck the option.

FORWARDING A MESSAGE

Forwarding an e-mail message is much easier than forwarding a letter through the U.S. mail, and it actually works. To forward a message, follow these steps:

1. Open the message.

2. Click the Forward button on the toolbar in the message window.

3. Enter an address in the To field.

4. Add your own comments if you want.

5. Click Send.

DELETING MESSAGES

To delete a message, you can select its header and click Delete, or you can open it and then click Delete. The message is not yet really deleted, however; Outlook Express has placed it in the Deleted Items folder. And that is where the message stays until you empty the Deleted Items folder or tell Outlook Express to empty it when you close Outlook Express.

If you want to delete items from the Deleted Items folder yourself, follow these steps:

1. Select the Deleted Items folder.

2. Choose Edit ➤ Empty 'Deleted Items' Folder.

3. When Outlook Express asks if you are sure you want to delete these items, click Yes.

To set up automatic deletion of the items in the Deleted Items folder, follow these steps:

1. Choose Tools ➤ Options to open the Options dialog box.

2. Click the Maintenance tab.

3. In the Cleaning Up Messages section, click the Empty Messages from the 'Deleted Items' Folder on Exit check box, and then click OK.

Creating and Sending Messages

In this section, I'll walk you through the steps to create a simple message and send it. You can also create messages in HTML (HyperText Markup Language) and include hyperlinks, pictures, colorful formatting, sounds, and so on. We'll look at that in the next section.

Create Mail

To begin a new message, you can click the Create Mail button in the main window to open the New Message window, as shown in Figure 14.2. Or, if the intended recipient is in your Address Book, you can double-click that person's name in the Contacts pane to open the New Message window; the To line will display the recipient's name.

If your New Message window includes a Formatting toolbar, the message you compose will be formatted as HTML. For my purposes here, I want only plain text. So, if necessary, choose Format ➤ Plain Text before you begin composing your message. Now, follow these steps:

1. If necessary, enter the address of the primary recipient in the To field. If you are sending a message to multiple primary recipients, separate their addresses with semicolons. If you choose multiple recipients from your Address Book, they are automatically separated by semicolons.

2. Optionally, enter e-mail addresses in the Cc (carbon copy) and Bcc (blind carbon copy) fields. To enter a Bcc recipient, click the Cc icon, enter the name in the Select Recipients dialog box, and click Bcc.

3. Enter a subject line for your message.

FIGURE 14.2

You create a new message in the New Message window.

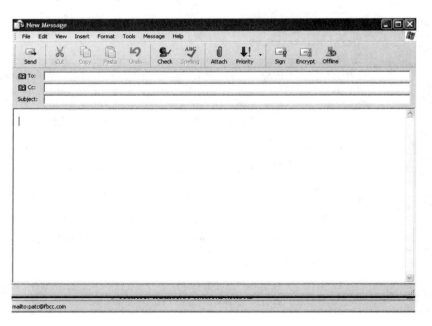

NOTE *If you don't enter a subject line, Outlook Express will ask if you're sure you don't want a subject line. Unless you have a good reason not to do so, enter some text in the subject line. Your recipient will see this text in the header information for the message and will then have a clue as to the nature of your message.*

4. Enter the text of your message.

5. If appropriate, establish a priority for your message. Choose Message ➤ Set Priority, and then choose High, Normal, or Low. The default is Normal.

6. Click Send to start your message on its way.

You can send your message immediately by clicking the Send button, or you can save it in your Outbox to send later by choosing File ➤ Send Later. The message will be sent when you choose Send and Receive All or when you choose Send All.

TIP You can use Copy and Paste in Outlook Express just as you use those commands in other Windows programs. For example, to include a portion of a Word document in a message, open the document, select the text, and press Ctrl+C to copy it to the Clipboard. In Outlook Express, open the New Message window, place the insertion point where you want to copy the text, and press Ctrl+V. Use this same process to copy portions of e-mail messages to other messages or to documents in other applications.

Creating E-mail Messages with HTML

In the previous section, I told you how to create a plain text message, but as I mentioned, you can also compose messages in HTML and include all sorts of neat effects. Before you send a formatted message, be sure that your recipient's e-mail program can display it effectively. When you open the New Message window and choose Format ➤ Rich Text (HTML), the message you compose is essentially a Web page. Newer e-mail programs such as Netscape Messenger and the commercial version of Eudora, Eudora Pro, can read, compose, and send HTML messages, but others cannot. An easy way to find out if your recipient's e-mail program can handle HTML is to send a simple plain text message and ask.

That said, let's look at some bells and whistles you can include in Outlook Express e-mail messages. Click the Create Mail icon to open the New Message window, and be sure that the Rich Text (HTML) option is selected. You'll see the screen shown in Figure 14.3. Notice the Formatting toolbar, which contains many of the same tools you see and use in your Windows word processor. You'll also see the Font and Font Size drop-down list boxes that are present in your word processor.

As you create your message, just pretend that you're using a word processor, and use the Formatting tools to apply emphasis to your message. All the usual design rules apply, including the following:

◆ Don't use a lot of different fonts.

◆ Remember, typing in all capital letters in e-mail is tantamount to shouting.

◆ Don't place a lot of text in italics. It's hard to read on the screen.

◆ Save boldface for what's really important.

To insert a horizontal line that spans the message window, click the Insert Horizontal Line button on the Formatting toolbar.

FIGURE 14.3

You can use the For-
matting toolbar
when creating a mes-
sage in HTML.

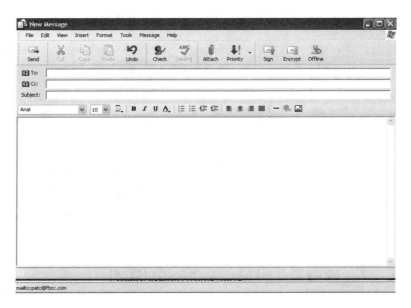

USING STATIONERY

In addition to formatting, you can add some class or some comedy to your e-mail messages in another
way: stationery. In the New Message window, choose Message ➤ New Using, and then choose a predesigned format from the list in the submenu, or click Select Stationery to open the Select Stationery dialog box and select from a larger list. Here's one example of what you'll find:

Continued on next page

USING STATIONERY *(continued)*

To customize stationery, click Create New in the Select Stationery dialog box to start the Stationery Setup Wizard. Follow the on-screen instructions.

To apply HTML styles such as Definition Term or Definition, click the Paragraph Style button on the Formatting toolbar.

ADDING A PICTURE TO YOUR MESSAGES

You can insert a picture in a message in two ways:

- As a piece of art
- As a background over which you can type text

To insert a picture as a piece of art that you can size and move, follow these steps:

1. In the New Message window, click the Insert Picture button on the Formatting toolbar to open the Picture dialog box.

2. Enter the filename of the picture in the Picture Source text box, or click the Browse button to locate it.

3. Optionally, in the Alternate Text box, enter some text that will display if the recipient's e-mail program cannot display the picture, and specify layout and spacing options if you want. (You can also size and move the picture with the mouse once you place it in the message.)

4. Click OK.

To insert a picture as background, follow these steps:

1. In the New Message window, choose Format ➤ Background ➤ Picture to open the Background Picture dialog box.

2. Enter the filename of the picture, or click Browse to select a predesigned stationery background or locate another file.

3. Click Open, and then click OK to insert the background.

ADDING A BACKGROUND COLOR OR SOUND TO YOUR MESSAGE

To apply a color to the background of your message, choose Format ➤ Background ➤ Color, and select a color from the drop-down list. Now type something. Can you see it on the screen? If not, you have probably chosen a dark background and your font is also a dark color—most likely black if you haven't changed it from the default.

To make your text visible, click the Font Color button, and select a lighter color from the drop-down list.

To add a background sound, follow these steps:

1. In the New Message window, choose Format ➤ Background ➤ Sound to open the Background Sound dialog box.

2. Enter the filename of the sound, or click Browse to locate a sound file.

3. Specify the number of times you want the sound to play or whether you want it to play continuously. (In my opinion, a sound that plays continuously while the recipient is reading the message is far more likely to annoy than to entertain.)

4. Click OK.

INCLUDING HYPERLINKS IN YOUR MESSAGE

When you insert a hyperlink in a message, the recipient can go directly to the resource simply by clicking the hyperlink. You can insert a hyperlink in three ways:

- Simply type it in the message body. Be sure to include the entire URL.

- In the New Message window, choose Insert ➤ Hyperlink to open the Hyperlink dialog box, and then enter the URL in the text box.

- In Internet Explorer, choose Tools ➤ Mail and News ➤ Send a Link to open the New Message window. The URL of the current page is automatically inserted in the message body.

ADDING A SIGNATURE TO YOUR MESSAGES

I know people who never sign their e-mail messages. After all, their name is in the From line in the message header. I also know people who append elaborate signatures, touting their accomplishments or advertising their businesses. I usually just sign my first name at the bottom of messages, but what you do depends on your personal style or whether you're sending business or personal correspondence.

To create a signature that's automatically added to all your outgoing messages, follow these steps:

1. Choose Tools ➤ Options to open the Options dialog box.

2. Click the Signatures tab.

3. Click New.

4. To create a text signature, in the Edit Signature section, enter the content in the box next to the Text option button.

5. If you want to use a file you've already created as your signature, click the File option button, and enter the filename or click Browse to locate it.

6. If you have multiple e-mail accounts, click the Advanced button to open the Advanced Signature Settings dialog box, and specify which accounts should use this signature.

7. Click the Add Signatures to All Outgoing Messages check box, and click OK.

If you don't want the signature automatically appended to all outgoing messages, leave the Add Signatures to All Outgoing Messages check box unselected. Then, to add this signature to a message, choose Insert ➤ Signature in the New Message window.

Attaching Files to Your Messages

In Outlook Express, sending a file or multiple files along with your message is painless and simple. Follow these steps:

1. In the New Message window, choose Insert ➤ File Attachment to open the Insert Attachment dialog box:

2. Select a file and click Attach.

Your message now contains the name of the file in the Attach line.

If the file is large or if you know that the recipient has a slow connection, you'll want to compress it. To do so, in the Insert Attachment dialog box, right-click the file, click Send To on the shortcut menu, and then click Compressed Folder. You'll now see a compressed folder for the file in the current folder (the folder displays a zipper). Windows XP Professional uses the WinZip 7 program to compress files and folders, and WinZip 7 is compatible with any compression utility your recipient may have. All the recipient needs to do to uncompress the file or folder is double-click it.

TIP Digital picture files can be quite large, so if your recipient has a compression utility, be sure to compress them before you attach them.

Applying Message Rules

Using the Rules Editor, you can specify where messages go after they are downloaded, block unwanted messages, and, in general, manage incoming messages more efficiently—especially if you deal with a lot of e-mail. In this section, I'll give you a couple of examples that illustrate the possibilities, but, as you will see, there are lots of possibilities, and you'll need to apply the options that make the most sense for your situation.

Let's start by establishing a rule that sends all mail from a particular person to that person's Outlook Express folder. Follow these steps:

1. In the main Outlook Express window, choose Tools ➤ Message Rules ➤ Mail to open the New Mail Rule dialog box:

2. In the Select the Conditions for Your Rule section, click the Where the From Line Contains People check box.

3. In the Select the Actions for Your Rule section, click the Move It to the Specified Folder check box.

4. In the Rule Description section, click the Contains People link to open the Select People dialog box:

5. Enter a name and click Add or select a name from your Address Book, and click OK.

6. Click Specified to open the Move dialog box.

7. Select the folder where you want this person's messages to go, and click OK. If you need to create a folder, click New Folder.

8. Accept the name of the rule that Outlook Express proposes, or type a new name.

9. Click OK.

Now, when messages arrive from that person, you'll find them in their folder rather than in your Inbox.

TIP   To delete a rule, select it and click Remove in the Message Rules dialog box. To modify a rule, select it and click Modify.

To establish a rule that blocks unwanted messages, follow these steps:

1. In the main Outlook Express window, choose Tools ➤ Message Rules ➤ Blocked Senders List to open the Message Rules dialog box at the Blocked Senders tab.

2. Click Add to open the Add Sender dialog box:

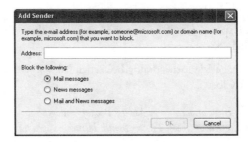

3. Enter the e-mail address that you want to block, specify whether you want to block mail, news, or both from this person, and click OK.

4. Click OK again in the Message Rules dialog box.

Now, mail from that address will go immediately to the Deleted Items folder. News from that person will simply not be displayed. (More on news in the last part of this chapter.) To change or delete this rule, open the Message Rules box, select the address, and click Modify or click Remove.

Adding and Managing Identities

If several people use the same computer either at home, at the office, or elsewhere, and thus also use Outlook Express, you'll probably want to take advantage of the Identities feature, which lets each person view their own mail and have individualized settings and contacts. Once you set up Identities, you can switch between them without shutting down the computer or disconnecting from and reconnecting to the Internet.

When you install Windows XP Professional, you are set up in Outlook Express as the Main Identity. To set up other identities in Outlook Express, follow these steps:

1. In the main Outlook Express window, choose File ➤ Identities ➤ Add New Identity to open the New Identity dialog box:

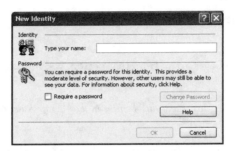

2. Enter the name of the identity you want to establish.

3. If you want to password protect this identity, click the Require a Password check box. Enter the password twice—once in the New Password box, and again in the Confirm New Password box. Click OK twice.

4. Outlook Express asks if you want to switch to this new identify now. If you do, click Yes; otherwise, click No.

5. In the Manage Identities dialog box, click New if you want to set up another identity; otherwise, click Close.

NOTE *You can also create an identity in Address Book if you open it by choosing Start ➤ All Programs ➤ Accessories ➤ Address Book. In Address Book, choose File ➤ Switch Identity to open the Switch Identities dialog box, and then click Manage Identities to open the Manage Identities dialog box. Now click New to open the New Identity dialog box and follow steps 2 through 5 just shown.*

The first time you log on as a new identity, you will be asked for some information about your Internet connection. To switch from one identity to another, choose File ➤ Switch Identity to open the Switch Identities dialog box. Select the identity, and click OK. To log off from an identity, choose File ➤ Identities ➤ Logoff Identity.

To delete an identity, select the identity in the Manage Identities dialog box, and click Remove.

Using Outlook Express As Your Newsreader

A newsgroup is a collection of articles about a particular subject. A newsgroup is similar to e-mail in that you can reply to what someone else has written (the newsgroup term for this is *posted*), and you can send a question or a response either to the whole group or to individuals.

The primary (but not sole) source of newsgroups is Usenet, which is a worldwide distributed discussion system consisting of newsgroups that have names which are classified hierarchically by subject. For example, `rec.crafts.metalworking` is a recreational group devoted to the craft of metalworking.

The leftmost portion represents the largest hierarchical category, and the name gets more specific from left to right. Table 14.1 lists the major top-level newsgroup categories and explains what topics each discusses. Currently, there are thousands and thousands of newsgroups on every conceivable topic. For an extensive listing of them, go to `www.ibiblio.org/usenet-i/hier-s/master.html`.

TABLE 14.1: THE MAJOR NEWSGROUPS

NEWSGROUP	WHAT IT DISCUSSES
alt	Newsgroups outside the main structure outlined in this table
biz	Business products, services, reviews, and so on
comp	Computer science and related topics, including operating systems, hardware, artificial intelligence, and graphics
humanities	Fine art, literature, philosophy, and the like
misc	Anything that does not fit into one of the other categories
news	Information on Usenet and newsgroups
rec	Recreational activities such as hobbies, the arts, movies, and books
sci	Scientific topics such as math, physics, and biology
soc	Social issues and cultures
talk	Controversial subjects such as gun control, abortion, religion, and politics

You access newsgroups by accessing the server on which they are stored. Not all servers store the same newsgroups. The network administrator or the owner of the site determines what to store, but if you request a particular newsgroup from your ISP, the ISP can forward that request to another server that does provide the newsgroup. Almost all news servers "expire" articles after a few days or, at most, a few weeks because of the tremendous volume. Although they might be archived at the site, these articles are no longer available to be viewed by users.

NOTE *Newsgroups are uncensored. You can find just about anything at any time anywhere. Nobody has authority over newsgroups as a whole. If you find certain groups, certain articles, or certain people offensive, don't go there, or use the Rules Editor that I talked about earlier to prevent certain articles from even being displayed. But remember, anarchy reigns in newsgroups, and you never know what you might stumble upon in the least likely places.*

Setting Up a Newsgroup Account

Before you can read newsgroups, you must set up a newsgroups account. Before you start, get the name of your news server from your ISP, and then follow these steps:

1. In the main Outlook Express window, select the Outlook Express folder, and in the pane on the right, click Set Up a Newsgroups Account to start the Internet Connection Wizard.

2. Supply the information that the Wizard requests, and click Finish when you are done. You'll now see a folder in the Folders list for your news server.

Connecting to Newsgroups

The next task is to download the list of newsgroups from your server. When Outlook Express asks if you want to do this, click Yes. This may take a while if you have a slow connection, but notice the incrementing number of newsgroups in the Downloading Newsgroups dialog box. In the process of writing this section, I downloaded a list of more than 30,000 newsgroups.

TIP   Only the names of the newsgroups are downloaded to your computer; their contents remain on the news server. Periodically, you can update this list by clicking Reset List.

When the list has finished downloading, you'll see the Newsgroup Subscriptions dialog box, as shown in Figure 14.4.

FIGURE 14.4

Use this dialog box to search for and subscribe to newsgroups.

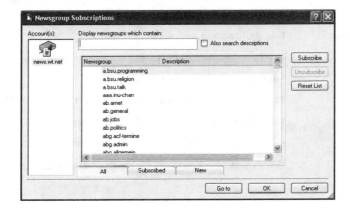

Finding a Newsgroup of Interest

You can select a newsgroup to read in two ways:

◆   You can scroll through the list (this will take a lot of time).

◆   You can search on a term.

Just for the sake of doing it, scroll the list a bit. As you can see, it's in alphabetic order by hierarchical categories. If you don't see anything right away that strikes your fancy, you can perform a search. Enter a term in the Display Newsgroups Which Contain text box, and then don't do anything! In a second, you'll see a list of newsgroups that contain articles about your topic.

Subscribing to a Newsgroup

Subscribing to a newsgroup doesn't involve a fee or any other transaction. Subscribing means simply creating a subfolder for a particular newsgroup in your news folder. Then, instead of selecting it from the Newsgroup Subscriptions dialog box, you can simply click the newsgroup's folder to see the list of articles in it.

Once you've located a newsgroup you want to read, you can select it, click Subscribe, and then click Go To to open it, or you can simply click Go To. To unsubscribe to a newsgroup, right-click its folder, and choose Unsubscribe.

Reading a Newsgroup

To read an article, simply click its header to display the message in the lower pane.

Outlook Express is a threaded newsreader in that it groups messages that respond to a subject line. If you see a plus sign to the left of a newsgroup header, you can click the plus sign to display a list of related messages. The more up-to-date term for threads is *conversation*. Newsgroup articles are grouped by conversations by default.

TIP *You can also organize mail messages by conversations. With your Inbox selected, choose View ➤ Current View ➤ Group Messages by Conversation.*

To read the articles from another newsgroup or to search for another newsgroup, double-click your main news folder, and then click Newsgroups to open the Newsgroup Subscriptions dialog box.

Posting to a Newsgroup

Replying to a newsgroup article or sending a message to a newsgroup is known as posting. You post to a newsgroup in much the same way that you compose and send e-mail. To send an original message to a newsgroup, open the newsgroup and click the New Post button. The New Message window will open with the group's name in the To line.

To reply to an individual article, click the Reply button, and to reply to the entire newsgroup, click the Reply Group button.

TIP *You can also access newsgroups on the Internet at* `http://groups.google.com/googlegroups/deja_announcement.html`*, and doing so is much easier than using Outlook Express.*

Customizing Outlook Express

Throughout this chapter, I've mentioned from time to time ways that you can specify how Outlook Express handles certain features, such as signatures. In most cases, you do this through the Options dialog box (shown in Figure 14.5), which you open by choosing Tools ➤ Options. Here's a quick rundown of what to use each tab for in the Options dialog box:

General Use this tab to specify settings for how Outlook Express starts and for sending and receiving messages.

Read Use this tab to set options for reading news and mail. For example, you can specify a maximum number of news article headers to download at one time.

Receipts Use this tab if you want to verify that your message has been read by the recipient.

Send Use this tab to set, among other things, the format (HTML or Plain Text) in which you will send all messages and the format you'll use to reply to messages. You can also specify whether copies of sent messages will be stored and whether you want Outlook Express to put the names and addresses of people you reply to in your Address Book.

Compose   Use this tab to specify the font and font size for mail messages and news articles that you create and to select stationery fonts for HTML messages.

Signatures   Use to create a signature, as discussed earlier in this chapter.

Security   Use this tab to specify your desired Internet Security zone and to get a digital ID.

Connection   Use this tab to specify how Outlook Express handles your dial-up connection.

Maintenance   Use this tab to specify what Outlook Express does with deleted items and to clean up downloaded messages, as well as to specify that all server commands are stored for troubleshooting purposes.

FIGURE 14.5

You use the Options dialog box to customize Outlook Express for the way you work.

NOTE   *If you have installed any of the Microsoft Office applications that include a spell checker, you will also see a Spelling tab in the Options dialog box.*

Summary

An e-mail program is arguably the most-used program in most businesses today. Though Outlook Express lacks the major features of its more robust sibling, Outlook, it contains everything you need to communicate over the Internet. And as you have seen in this chapter, it is extremely easy to use.

Part 3

Networking Windows XP Professional

In this section you will learn how to
- Understand Different Options for Networks
- Configure a Peer-to-Peer Network
- Connect to a Domain
- Use Windows XP Security to your Advantage
- Audit your Security Settings
- Telecommute Securely

Chapter 15

Windows XP Professional Networking and Network Design Primer

YOU'RE ON THE JOB, wondering what you can do to best take advantage of your network. Or you're at home, wondering if you should go through the trouble of connecting your computer with those of your spouse and children. Before you can know what to do, you need a basic lesson in networking.

This chapter is designed to show you what you need for a LAN. LANs can help you share software and hardware. LANs can help you work with others. Computers on a LAN can be set up in master/slave, peer-to-peer, and client-server relationships. With just a few tricks, LAN hardware is easy. Putting multiple LANs together is known as Internetworking, which is the basis for the TCP/IP protocol suite. This chapter covers the following topics:

◆ Overview of networking

◆ Networking vocabulary

◆ Theoretical networking concepts

◆ Types of networks

◆ Basic network connectivity

◆ Building your own network

What is a Network?

A network consists of two or more computers that communicate with each other. Larger organizations commonly connect their networks together. This process is known as *internetworking*. The largest internetwork is the Internet.

In most cases, when you connect your computer to the Internet, your computer joins a network that is set up by your ISP. Your ISP is then connected to the Internet. In Chapter 11, you learned about some of the settings you need to connect to the Internet. In this chapter, you'll see what you need to set up a Local Area Network (LAN).

Early Networking: Sneakernet

The oldest form of the computer network is commonly referred to as the *sneakernet*, an official-sounding name for a very unofficial way of doing business. In this popular networking arrangement, a user copied information to a floppy disk, put on a good pair of sneakers, and carried the file over to another computer or user. Not a very efficient method of sharing information by today's standards, but it got the job done. For some purposes, it may still be the best way to get information from one place to another.

Though wonderful for encouraging interoffice interaction, sneakernet poses a few serious disadvantages. Losing data is a big risk with this system because if you misplace or accidentally reformat the data disk, you lose the information. Making sure that everyone who's working on a document or worksheet has the same information is also cumbersome:

◆ What happens if you have a copy of the original disk and someone makes changes to the original without telling you?

◆ What happens if more than one person is working on a document and you need to incorporate everyone's changes into one copy?

◆ How do you keep people from leaving the building with disks full of sensitive information?

Obviously, if you want data integrity, security, and the best use of the creativity of all the people working on a document (and who doesn't?), sneakernet is not the way to go. What you need instead is some way of tying your network together other than having to rely on the trustworthiness and good will of your coworkers. What you need is a LAN.

LAN: The Alternative

LANs vary greatly in size—you can make a LAN out of two computers sitting across from each other in the same room or out of several thousand computers in the same building. The key parts to the definition of a LAN are that all the computers on the network are *grouped together in some fashion and are connected.*

NOTE *A network that extends over a larger area, such as a city block or a country, is known as a* wide area network (WAN). *These networks generally consist of two or more internetworked LANs.*

On most LANs, cables connect the LAN by linking the network cards that reside within each computer or printer on the network. Situations in which cable is *not* the means of connection will be discussed later in this chapter.

The preceding definition is the strict, textbook definition. However, in the real world, LANs are generally defined less by their physical characteristics and more by their function. In this sense, a LAN is a system in which linked computers and peripheral devices can share common information, software applications, printers, scanners, and fax services. LANs also enable the use of groupware for scheduling, shared databases and e-mail. The quick electronic dispersal of computer-generated information to people striving toward a common goal and existing in a single-user-per-computer environment truly defines a local area network.

Most of the functions of a LAN are based on using one or two computers as servers. With a LAN, you can do all the following:

◆ Share files through a file server

◆ Share applications from an application server

◆ Share printers through a print server

◆ Share schedules, transmit e-mail, and hold electronic meetings through a Groupware server such as Microsoft Exchange or IBM's Lotus Notes

◆ Share Internet connections and security

Other things that you can do on a LAN include sharing backup media such as Tape Drives and recordable CD and DVDs, playing multiuser games, and video conferencing with multiple users in a process known as *multicasting*.

FILE SHARING

One of the primary purposes of a LAN is to provide a common storage area so that several people can access the same files. File sharing can help ensure that anyone who uses that file is always working with the most recent version. Alternatively, if you don't want to share a file with the network but you need someone else to do some work on it, you can transfer the file to someone else—just move it from your folder to theirs or send it as an attachment to an e-mail message.

Note that the act of sharing a file with the network does *not* automatically give everyone on the network access to it. In many network operating systems, you can attach a password to your files so that only people who have the password can access them.

Alternatively, you can grant different levels of access to specific users, or a specific group of users. Access can be at levels such as read-only, read and change, and full control. This capability can prevent unauthorized users from seeing your work or making changes to your work. More information on this process is available in Chapter 18.

Sharing, transferring, and securing information between computers on a network is generally known as *file management*. You can share entire drives and folders. If you use a NTFS formatted drive, you can also share individual files.

NOTE   *As with individual files, you can restrict access to your shared resources (printers, CD-ROMs, scanners, tape drives, and so on) with passwords. Chapter 18 describes how you can restrict access to specific users.*

CONCURRENT USE OF APPLICATIONS

Many, but not all, software packages will work fine if you install them onto an *application server* and let people access them from their workstations. Here are a few of the advantages to locating software centrally (that is, on an application server):

◆ It frees disk space on individual computers. The bulk of the application is stored on one or two servers and not at each user's computer.

◆ Multiple users can use an application simultaneously (almost a necessity in many database applications).

◆ Upgrading software is easier because the application that needs to be updated is the copy of the software that is installed on the server.

NOTE   *When upgrading, some Windows applications have a certain number of files that need to be updated at each user's computer even though the major part of Windows is located on the application server. These files usually include configuration information that is specific to each computer system in your office.*

WARNING   *If you store applications on an application server and let users access them from their workstations, you are* still required to buy more than one license. *You should have proper software licensing for every user, even if you load only one copy of the software onto the server. Otherwise, you are committing software piracy—stealing from the developers of that software. Software piracy is a federal crime. One exception is software that uses one of the free licenses such as the Free Software Foundation's General Public License (*`http://www.fsf.org`*).*

LAN-dependent applications, such as e-mail, are usually licensed for a specific number of users. When you access the program from the server, a full-blown copy of the program is transported from the hard drive of the server to the memory of your computer. As you interact with the program, you are interacting with the copy that is stored in the memory of your computer. If you activate another program, such as a spell-check feature taken from a word processing program, that feature is transported from the hard drive of the file server to the memory of your computer. You need a license for every program and every computer that will store part of each program in its memory.

NOTE   *Application servers are often also known, inaccurately, as file servers. Since applications require CPU power, application servers require the fastest possible CPU(s). On the other hand, file servers work best with extra RAM. When a shared file is already available in RAM, file access speed is increased.*

PRINT SHARING

Printers are just one of a host of peripherals that you can share. A lot of people get confused about the nature of peripherals these days, but basically a peripheral device is anything that is external to the CPU and memory.

NOTE   *The words* peripheral device *and* peripheral *are just tech-speak for "a device that attaches to your computer system." Printers, scanners, sound cards, DVD players, fax modems, and keyboards are all peripheral devices.*

A LAN enables its users to share high-cost peripheral devices such as printers, and manage them so that two users do not attempt to use the devices simultaneously.

Print sharing saves network users time and money. Of course, even without a network, you don't have to buy printers for every workstation in the office. One or two devices will work just as well—if people don't mind standing in line to use them. However, if people must wait for a device to be free, you are spending the money you saved (by not buying the extra printer) on wasted time.

NOTE   You don't even need an extra computer to share a printer. Network print servers that are about the size of my hand are available. They have two connections: one to the network, the other to the printer. Once configured, a print server looks just like any other computer to a network.

As with file management, a network administrator can restrict access to the peripheral devices on a network so that only those people authorized to use them can access them. For example, you may not want people to print out rough drafts or family pictures on the $8,000 color printer. To set up Windows XP Professional as a print server, see Chapter 7.

GROUPWARE

Groupware is a type of application that supports group scheduling, e-mail, and possibly other functions such as database management and file sharing. This could be one of your office manager's favorite network features. Organizing departmental meetings can be an administrator's nightmare, as they try to sort through everyone's schedules to find a time when everyone can meet. Groupware can make this nightmarish task much more manageable.

Groupware keeps track of all users' schedules, either separately or together as one large calendar. Each person on the network keeps track of his or her own appointments in the virtual day planner. This information is automatically stored in a central database.

Now, let's say that you want to call a meeting of all the MIS people in your company. All you have to do is list the names of the people who should attend this meeting and then choose a date. The computer can tell you of any scheduling conflicts and let you modify the meeting time accordingly. Some scheduling software packages let you tell the computer to choose the first time that everyone is available, to save you the trouble of having to guess. After you've settled on a time, you can use the scheduling program to send "invitations" and ask people to confirm their attendance.

Groupware also supports input from multiple users to other applications, such as databases. For example, sales input from different stores can be merged on a database using the right kind of groupware. Some groupware packages such as Microsoft Exchange also include e-mail servers.

INTERNET CONNECTIONS AND SECURITY

The Internet can be a dangerous place for a computer. Every computer that connects to the Internet needs some form of security to protect it from attack. This means purchasing filters and virus scanners for every computer, and a firewall or proxy server for the whole network. Maintaining these systems can be a difficult and expensive enterprise.

However, if you set up a network with one shared connection to the Internet, it's easier to defend your computers. With the Internet Connection Sharing (ICS) techniques discussed in Chapter 11, only one computer from your network is seen on the Internet. With the Internet Connection Firewall (ICF), as described in Chapter 11, that computer is the only one at risk from Internet attacks.

Alternatively, you can use a hardware router to protect your network. As discussed later in this chapter, specialized routers can share one Internet connection and act as a firewall. With the right commands, the router can even block the communication ports used for specialty programs such as instant messaging and networked games. The router becomes the "computer" at risk; since there is no data on the hardware router, your risks are small.

Unfortunately, this does not protect you from risks inside your network. Malicious or poorly trained users can still download e-mail viruses or sabotage your data.

Networking Vocabulary

Like most other specialized fields, networking has its own jargon. This list is far from exhaustive—in the following chapters, more terms will be introduced—but it gives you a good starting place. Remember these definitions:

Client   Any computer with independent processing power (CPU and RAM) that can provide *input* to the network is a client. This definition includes personal computers, handheld scanners, and so on.

Server   A server is a computer that processes common requests from the network. For example, a print server queues and processes print jobs for a group of computers. The most common server is a file server. A file server is a computer that holds, manages, and secures access to files and data. It provides centralized control for and to your data and acts as a common location for your files for the purpose of centralized backup.

Workstation   Any computer physically operated by a user is a workstation. Most workstations are clients. Some workstations, especially in peer-to-peer networks, may also be configured as servers.

Terminal   A terminal is a computer-like device from which you can provide input to the network. While a terminal may include graphical processors, it may or may not have a processor or hard drive. Terminals are also known as slave computers.

Node   Each client, workstation, terminal, and server has a unique IP address on a TCP/IP network. Specialized hardware items such as routers and print servers also have their own unique IP address on a network. Each of these items is a *node*. Each node associates its IP address with the Network Interface Card.

Packet   A packet is the smallest unit of information that can be sent across a network. A packet contains the sending node's address, the receiving node's address, and the data being sent between the two nodes.

Ethernet   The trade name for the most common form of networking in use today. Ethernet is more formally known as IEEE standards 802.2 and 802.3. While there are several other types of networks available, current network equipment in most computer stores is based on some form of Ethernet. The basic Ethernet standards are listed in Table 15.1. As of this writing, all of these standards are commonly available in major computer stores, except 10-GB Ethernet.

Hub   A hub is a box that connects that the computers on a LAN. On an Ethernet network, messages are broadcast to all computers that are connected to that hub. This device can increase traffic on a LAN as a device (or node) broadcasts packets to all devices connected to the hub.

Switch   A switch is a box that connects some or all of the computers on a LAN. A switch can determine the destination node for a packet and can send the message directly to the node. Since other computers aren't bothered with that packet, a switch can reduce traffic on a LAN.

Router   A router connects a LAN to other networks such as another LAN or the Internet. If your router has enough connections, it can also connect all of the computers in your LAN. Closely related to *routing*, which is the transmission of data between networks.

TABLE 15.1: ETHERNET STANDARDS

COMMON NAME	STANDARD	SPEED
Ethernet	IEEE 802.3	10Mbps
Wireless Ethernet	IEEE 802.11	11Mbps
Fast Ethernet	IEEE 802.3u	100Mbps
Gigabit Ethernet	IEEE 802.3z	1000Mbps
10-GB Ethernet	IEEE 802.3ae	10,000Mbps

A Little Theory

In order to understand networks, you need to understand some theory. The OSI Model helps you understand the functionality of different types of network hardware and software.

The OSI Model provides the basis for organizing and classifying protocols into stacks. There are three major protocol stacks that Windows XP Professional can use for computer communication: NetBEUI, IPX/SPX, and TCP/IP.

OSI Model

The Open Systems Interconnect (OSI) model of networking provides the theoretical basis for all network hardware and software. It provides all of the functionality needed to translate the Word file that you're accessing from the server to the 1s and 0s that are transmitted over computer cables. The seven layers, from top to bottom, are as follows:

- Application (7)
- Presentation (6)
- Session (5)
- Transport (4)
- Network (3)
- Data Link (2)
- Physical (1)

NOTE *Some network designers refer to the numeric name for a layer; for example, the application layer is also known as layer 7.*

The following sections describe each of these layers in some detail. Perhaps the most important of these protocols form the basis for IP addressing, which is covered in some detail later in this chapter.

NOTE   One alternative to the seven-layer OSI model is the five-layer TCP/IP model of networking. The top three layers of the OSI model (5, 6, 7) approximately correspond to the top layer in the TCP/IP model. The bottom four layers in both models are for our purposes, the same thing. While purists may object, OSI layers are often used to describe the functionality of specific TCP/IP protocols, without reference to the TCP/IP model.

APPLICATION (7)

The OSI application layer includes the services and commands that users call to connect to a network. Common application layer protocols that you've seen earlier in this book include HTTP, FTP, and Telnet. One other important application layer protocol covered in Chapter 16 is the Domain Name Service (DNS), which contains a database of domain names such as www.mommabears.com and corresponding IP addresses such as 10.12.213.54.

OSI application layer protocols are different from regular applications. In fact, they translate the programs that you use such as Microsoft Word to a format usable by the OSI Presentation layer.

One example of application layer hardware is a computer that has direct connections to more than one kind of network. For example, a computer that is connected to a TCP/IP network on one end and an IPX/SPX network on the other end is a true application layer gateway. A more common example of a gateway is a computer configured for ICS/ICF as discussed in Chapter 11.

PRESENTATION (6)

The OSI presentation layer is a translator. It formats and encrypts data. For example, some presentation layer protocols can translate the words you type into computer codes such as ASCII.

SESSION (5)

The OSI session layer manages your time on a network. Computers exchange messages at the session layer to keep a connection open. If a user is not active, session layer messages may stop after a designated timeout period.

TRANSPORT (4)

The OSI transport layer drives the effort used by the network to insure that your message gets to the destination. Some transport layer protocols keep trying until the receiving computer confirms delivery. Others just use a *best effort*. One of the best effort protocols includes the Internet domain names that you're familiar with, such as www.mommabears.com.

NETWORK (3)

The OSI network layer includes the protocols that actually move data, in packets, from computer to computer, and from network to network. The most important network layer protocol is IP addressing.

Hardware routers work at the network layer. A router is installed as the interface between two or more networks. There are some hardware routers that are known as *router/gateways*, because they function at both layer 3 and layer 7.

DATA LINK (2)

The OSI data link layer translates packets to bits (1s and 0s). The data link layer includes two sublayers:

Logical Link Control (LLC): Supports synchronization and error checking.

Media Access Control (MAC): Allows computers to access a network. MAC addresses are the hardware addresses associated with a Network Interface Card.

Hardware components known as switches work at the data link layer. Normally, a switch divides a LAN into segments. One or more computers are located on each segment. A switch can regulate traffic in a LAN; messages within a segment are not sent to other segments, thereby reducing traffic on other parts of the LAN.

NOTE *Another name for a switch is a bridge. While* switch *is in more common use today,* switch *and* bridge *can be used interchangeably.*

NOTE *There are a number of hybrid switches on the market. For example, network salespeople may refer to a* Layer 4 switch *or a* Layer 7 switch. *These hybrids have some functionality at multiple layers. Since there is no standard for hybrid equipment, there is no true standard for what they do on a network.*

PHYSICAL (1)

The OSI physical layer sends the messages through cables, radio waves, light pulses, and so on, in the 1s and 0s of computer communication.

Protocol Stacks

With seven layers in the OSI model, you can imagine that there are a substantial number of protocols. In fact, there are three major groupings of protocols, organized in their own protocol stacks:

NetBEUI: The Network BIOS Enhanced User Interface (NetBEUI) was developed by IBM and adapted by Microsoft around 1990 for network communication. Because it is a relatively simple protocol, it is reliable and fast. However, it does not support routing data between networks. While NetBEUI is no longer officially supported in Windows XP, the files you need to install NetBEUI are available on the Windows XP CD-ROM. For more information see Microsoft Knowledge Base article Q301041.

IPX/SPX: Novell developed the Internetwork Packet Exchange/Sequenced Packet Exchange (IPX/SPX) protocol stack for use with the Novell network operating system (NOS). IPX and SPX are just two of the available protocols in this stack. IPX/SPX does support routing. Novell NOSes are still commonly used in larger corporations; however, IPX/SPX use is less common since Novell included TCP/IP as the preferred option in Novell 5.0, released several years ago. Some network administrators set up IPX/SPX on a LAN for security; because IPX/SPX is essentially a different language from TCP/IP, it is considerably more difficult for someone using the Internet to break into this type of network.

TCP/IP: The language of the Internet. Named for two of its component protocols, the Transport Control Protocol/Internet Protocol (TCP/IP) protocol stack. TCP/IP is routable. It is the preferred choice for modern networks. Since TCP/IP was developed concurrently with Unix, TCP/IP is native to any related operating system (Linux, BSD, Solaris). Specific TCP/IP protocols will be addressed in the next section.

TIP   *Microsoft Knowledge Base articles are readily available online. Navigate to* `http://support.Microsoft.com`, *and enter keywords or the article number as a search term. Alternatively, if you enter the article number in a comprehensive search engine such as Google (*`www.google.com`*), you'll probably find a direct link to the article. Articles begin with "Q" followed by a number.*

TCP/IP Network Protocols

There are a number of important TCP/IP protocols. Just a few are covered here, related to what you see in this book. They are listed with their associated OSI layer numbers.

Hypertext Transfer Protocol (HTTP) (7): Supports transmission of Web pages over the Internet. You can set up an HTTP server in Chapter 28.

File Transfer Protocol (FTP) (7): Enables uploads and downloads of files. You can set up a FTP server in Chapter 28.

Simple Mail Transfer Protocol (SMTP) (7): Allows users to send e-mail messages. You can set up a SMTP server in Chapter 28.

Post Office Protocol (POP) (7): Lets users receive e-mail messages. The most common POP in use today is known as POP3.

Transmission Control Protocol (TCP) (4): Sets up a connection between two different computers, with guaranteed data delivery.

User Datagram Protocol (UDP) (4): Sets up a connection between two different computers, with *best effort* (no guarantee) data delivery.

Internet Protocol (IP) (3): Allows for unique numeric addresses on a network. Discussed in more detail in the next section.

Internet Protocol Secure (IPsec) (3): Allows for encrypted IP messages. Requires an encryption key. Supports Virtual Private Networking (VPN), which is discussed in more detail in Chapter 20.

Dynamic Host Configuration Protocol (DHCP) (3): Leases one of a group of IP addresses to a computer. After a certain period of inactivity, the IP address can be reassigned to a different computer.

Ethernet (2): Allows the use of the network of the same name.

Point-to-Point Protocol (PPP) (2): Supports a connection to other networks such as the Internet. Most commonly used for dial-up connections through a telephone modem.

Point-to-Point Protocol over Ethernet (PPPoE) (2): Lets you use broadband connections such as DSL and cable modems to connect to your LAN to the Internet.

Point-to-Point Tunneling Protocol (PPTP) (2): Supports Virtual Private Networking (VPN). An option to IPsec.

IP Addressing

An IP address consists of four numbers between 0 and 255, such as 125.23.252.2. Every node on a network requires its own unique IP address. On a network, IP addresses can be divided into two portions: a network address and a host address. The network address is shared by all of the nodes on that network. The host address is unique to that node.

There are 32 bits in every IP address. This corresponds to a total of $2^{32} = 4,294,967,296$ possible addresses. One might think that 4 billion IP addresses would be enough for a world of just over 6 billion people. Although not all IP addresses are engaged at once, all available IP addresses are taken. See the IP version 6 sidebar for some details on the next generation of IP addressing.

There are five different categories of IP addresses available as described in Table 15.2.

TABLE 15.2: IP Address Classes

Class	Description
A	IP addresses between 1.0.0.0 and 126.255.255.255. Suitable for networks with millions of nodes.
B	IP addresses between 128.0.0.0 and 191.255.255.255. Suitable for networks with thousands of nodes.
C	IP addresses between 192.0.0.0 and 223.255.255.255. Suitable for networks of up to 254 computers.
D	IP addresses between 224.0.0.0 and 239.255.255.255 are reserved for multicast applications.
E	IP addresses between 240.0.0.0 and 255.255.255.254 are reserved for experimental use.

IP VERSION 6

The IP addressing described in this chapter is actually IP version 4 (IPv4). Because of the way IPv4 networks are assigned, all available IPv4 network addresses are taken. Many are taken by ISPs that can assign you one of these addresses when you connect to the Internet.

There is another type of IP addressing, known as IPv6. Instead of the 32 bits in an IPv4 address, an IPv6 address includes 128 bits. This corresponds to over 3.4×10^{38} addresses, or about 54,000,000,000,000,000,000,000,000,000 addresses for every human on earth. That should last for a few years!

While IPv6 is already in use in some countries, you still configure your computer with IPv4 addresses. Every IPv4 address is automatically translated to a unique IPv6 address for these more advanced networks.

DEFINING A SUBNET

When a browser looks for www.sybex.com, it's actually looking for the Web server that contains the files for the Sybex Web site. This is a specific computer. But your Windows XP computer doesn't know where the Sybex Web site is located. It needs an IP address. Chances are that it gets the IP address from your ISP's DNS server.

The next step is for your computer to determine if the IP address for the Sybex Web site is on your LAN.

A LAN recognizes computers with IP addresses on the *subnet* as being on the local network. A subnet is a group of IP addresses that can be used on a LAN. To define a specific subnet, you need a network address and a subnet mask.

All IP addresses that are not on the subnet are routed to outside networks. If your subnet is properly defined, a request for the Sybex Web site will be routed outside your LAN. (Unless you work for Sybex, of course.)

A standard network address is based in part on its address class. Class A network addresses are defined by the first number of the IP address. For example, the network address for 101.53.66.116 is 101. Class B network addresses are defined by the first two numbers of the IP address. For example, the network address for 145.23.53.123 is 145.23. Class C network addresses are defined by the first three numbers of the IP address. For example, the network address for 226.135.5.13 is 226.135.5.

In other words, if the first number of an IP address is between 1 and 126 (Class A), you can define its network address by replacing the last 3 numbers with 0s. If the first number of an IP address is between 128 and 191 (Class B), you can define its network address by replacing the last 2 numbers with 0s. If the first number of an IP address is between 192 and 223, you can define its network address by replacing the last number with a 0.

It's now easy to define the subnet mask. For our purposes, it's enough to just replace the numbers of the network address with 255s. Some examples are shown in Table 15.3.

TABLE 15.3: IP NETWORK ADDRESS EXAMPLES

IP ADDRESS	NETWORK ADDRESS	SUBNET MASK
2.51.33.185	2.0.0.0	255.0.0.0
118.53.63.183	118.0.0.0	255.0.0.0
163.13.215.231	163.13.0.0	255.255.0.0
199.213.2.55	199.213.2.0	255.255.255.0
213.254.186.2	213.254.186.0	255.255.255.0

NOTE *Subnet masks can actually be quite a bit more complex. For more information, see the book* TCP/IP Jump-Start *by Andrew Blank from Sybex (2002).*

USING THE SUBNET

Now you can define the IP addresses that you can use on a network. For example, take the first example from Table 15.3. That network address is 2.0.0.0. At first glance, you might think that you could assign all addresses between 2.0.0.0 and 2.255.255.255. But there are two more rules governing IP addresses:

◆ The first address in the subnet is the network address and cannot be assigned to any specific computer.

◆ The last address in the subnet is the broadcast address for that network and also cannot be assigned to any specific computer.

In other words, the assignable addresses on the 2.0.0.0 network start at 2.0.0.1, and end at 2.255.255.254. Some other examples are shown in Table 15.4.

TABLE 15.4: ASSIGNABLE IP ADDRESSES

NETWORK ADDRESS	SUBNET MASK	ASSIGNABLE IP ADDRESSES
12.0.0.0	255.0.0.0	12.0.0.1–12.255.255.254
135.52.0.0	255.255.0.0	135.52.0.1–135.52.255.254
206.35.153.0	255.255.255.0	206.35.153.1–206.35.153.254

SPECIAL IP ADDRESSES

If you've watched closely, you may have noticed that I left out a whole range of IP addresses. Some are reserved for special purposes; others are reserved for private IP networks. These addresses include:

0.0.0.0: Used by any computer on a TCP/IP network to refer to the local network.

127.0.0.0: Reserved for loopback purposes. Includes all addresses on this network, from 127.0.0.0 through 127.255.255.255. The loopback address, 127.0.0.1, is used in Chapter 16.

255.255.255.255: Used as a broadcast address to all computers on the local network.

PRIVATE IP ADDRESS RANGES

If you never connect your network to the Internet, you now have all the information that you need to assign an IP address to a specific computer. However, most people with networks do want to connect to the Internet. For your Internet connection, you need a unique IP address. But you don't need a unique IP address for every computer on your network. For the computers wholly inside your LAN, there are private IP addresses.

For example, when you set up ICS/ICF in Chapter 11, you assigned a unique public IP address to the NIC or telephone modem connection to the Internet. Now you can assign a private IP address on that computer's connection to your LAN.

There are a series of private IP addresses available for this purpose. These private IP addresses are never supposed to be used to connect to the Internet. There are four blocks of IP addresses officially reserved for private networks. The official private IP address ranges are shown in Table 15.5.

TABLE 15.5: PRIVATE IP ADDRESS RANGES

CLASS	PRIVATE NETWORK ADDRESS	ADDRESS RANGE
A	10.0.0.0	10.0.0.1–10.255.255.254
B	169.254.0.0	169.254.0.1–169.254.255.254
B	172.16.0.0	172.16.0.1–172.31.255.254
C	192.168.0.0–192.168.255.0	192.168.x.1–192.168.x.254

There are 256 available Class C private network addresses. With the standard Class C subnet mask of 255.255.255.0, you have to pick one of these network addresses. To get the corresponding address range, substitute the number you choose for x.

The 169.254.0.0 network address was originally assigned to Microsoft and has recently been adapted by the Internet Assigned Numbers Authority (IANA) as a private network address. If you have a network of computers where Windows 98 and later operating systems are installed, the Microsoft *Automatic Private IP Addressing* (APIPA) system automatically assigns an IP address from this range to the NIC.

SETTING UP A PRIVATE NETWORK

When you want to set up a LAN that's connected to the Internet, pick a private network address. Select from the list in Table 15.5. There are three basic ways to assign an IP address to different computers:

Static IP Addressing: Allows you to select an IP address and assign it directly to your NIC. For a NIC connected to your internal network, select an IP address from the range on your chosen private IP network. You can often get a static IP address from your ISP for your Internet connection, but you may have to pay more. Static IP addresses are a convenience for anyone who wants to connect to your computer from a remote location on the Internet.

DHCP Addressing: Lets a DHCP server assign the address. Hardware routers that connect a network to the Internet often include DHCP servers. You can often set up a hardware router with a range of IP addresses from your selected subnet. You can then set up each computer on your LAN to take an IP address from that router.

Automatic Private IP Addressing (APIPA): Assigns an IP address when no DHCP server is available. This is a Microsoft protocol, which uses the 169.254.0.0 network address.

To set up one of these addressing schemes for your NIC, go into its properties. Click Start ➢ Control Panel. In Control Panel, click the Network Connections applet. You should see the Network Connections window with a list of your NICs, similar to what is shown in Figure 15.1.

FIGURE 15.1

Windows XP Network Connections

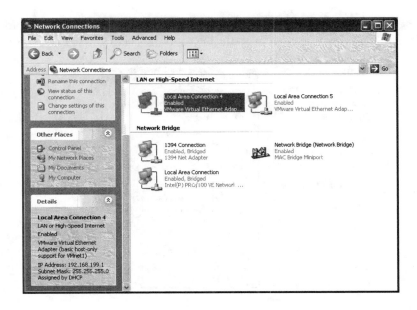

NOTE *For more information on the Network Bridge shown in Figure 15.1, see Chapter 16.*

In Figure 15.1, Local Area Connection 4 is highlighted. The essential properties for this NIC are displayed in the lower left corner under the Details heading. This lists the currently assigned IP address, subnet mask, and the way the address is assigned. If you want to make a change, right-click the NIC. In the shortcut menu that appears, click Properties to get the properties window for that NIC, similar to Figure 15.2.

FIGURE 15.2

Properties for a network connection

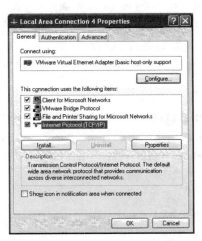

The properties window for the NIC should include "Internet Protocol (TCP/IP)." Highlight it and click Properties to get the Internet Protocol (TCP/IP) Properties window shown in Figure 15.3.

FIGURE 15.3

TCP/IP Properties for a network connection

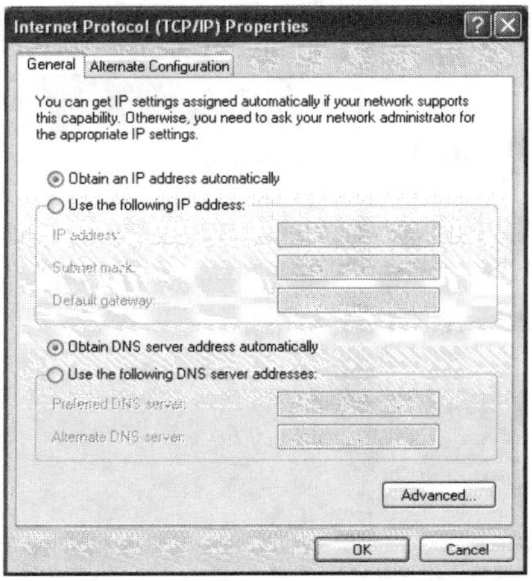

In this figure, the Obtain an IP Address Automatically option is selected. If you have a DHCP server on your network, this NIC gets its IP address from that server. Otherwise, the NIC gets its IP address through APIPA.

If you want to assign a static IP address, click Use the Following IP Address. Enter the IP address and subnet mask that you selected. For the Default gateway, enter the IP address of the computer or router on your network.

An assigned static IP address often means you also have to set the DNS server address. DNS servers translate names like www.sybex.com to their corresponding IP address such as 10.211.12.53. Internet DNS servers have unique IP addresses, which should be available from your ISP.

NOTE *If you have a NIC that supports Universal Plug and Play (UPnP), you may not have to bother with any of this. The UPnP standard supports automatic configuration of the NIC, including IP addressing, on the attached LAN. But for now, this is strictly theoretical. At the time of this writing, there are no UPnP devices available for sale.*

Network Relationships

Now that you see the advantages of a LAN, it's time to start thinking about organizing your computers. There are three basic ways to set up relationships between computers on a LAN:

- Master/slave
- Peer-to-peer
- Client-server

All of these networks depend on servers in some capacity.

Master/Slave

In the early days of computing, processing power and memory was relatively expensive. Many users had to share the same computer. The computers were the servers or the masters of the network. Users were stuck with the slaves, also known as terminals. Servers were configured with separate storage areas for every user.

Today, we may be coming full circle. With the development of the *Network Computer*, also known as the diskless workstation, it's possible to use Windows XP on a terminal in a master/slave network.

The Remote Desktop Connection discussed in Chapter 13 is one implementation of this kind of network. In that case, the *home computer* acts as a terminal, and *remote computer* acts as the master. All signals, including keystrokes and mouse clicks, are transmitted from the slave to the master computer.

Peer-to-Peer

Peer-to-peer networks represent an entirely different concept in networking. Rather than allocating every user on the network a central storage ground, peer-to-peer networking connects a group of totally independent computers. Each computer generally keeps its applications on its own hard disk so that if something happens to the network, it simply breaks down into a group of individual yet functional computers. If one workstation goes down, life can go on for the rest of the network if all users keep their needed files at their own workstation. In other words, a peer-to-peer network enables every workstation to lead a double life: to be a client *and* a server.

NOTE   *Chapter 16 goes into the details of using Windows XP Professional to connect a peer-to-peer network.*

Peer-to-peer networks give their users many of the same capabilities that client-server networks do. Each user decides what files, applications, and peripheral devices they will share with the rest of the network and then shares them. You can attach passwords to your resources so that unauthorized people can't access them. Alternatively, you can share things selectively, saying, perhaps, "Accounting gets to use the C drive, and Personnel gets to use the printer." In that case, Accounting and Personnel would need their own accounts on your Windows XP Professional computer.

On the subject of sharing resources, remember that because important information on a peer-to-peer LAN is distributed throughout the network, you'll have to leave networked computers on and connected to the network as long as anyone is working who needs the information on those computers.

How does a peer-to-peer network work? On a stand-alone computer, when you ask your operating system to access the drive, it can do it directly. The application talks directly to the operating system, which sends the information to the computer's disk. The operating system needs no go-between to help it access information and peripherals on its own computer.

If you're working on a network, however, the situation is a little different. The operating system needs help accessing information on other computers on the network. Its helper is called the *redirector* (or the *shell*, if you're a Novell user).

Client-Server

Client-server networks are similar in some ways to master/slave networks. In each, a central computer is in charge of the network and handles all requests. The main difference is that the client computers are able to compute on their own (assuming that they're PCs), unlike a regular terminal. These networks are most commonly used in larger companies.

However, client-server networks are like their peer-to-peer counterparts in a number of ways. Most importantly, each client can operate independently as a separate computer and can, by itself, function when the network stops.

Client-server networks are most commonly organized in domains, with a central database of users and profiles, as well as rights and permissions to specific files and folders.

NOTE   *Chapter 17 covers the details of connecting Windows XP Professional through a network to a domain.*

CONNECTING TO A DOMAIN

If you have access, joining a domain is easy. All you need is a domain username, password, and the name of the domain. This is your entrée into the world of resources connected to that domain. It requires a bit of a commitment, especially to store your files on servers managed through the domain.

But once committed, you can access your files and more from any workstation. For example, if you're working at another site, just log in to the domain from any workstation. If you're on another Windows XP Professional computer, you should get a desktop with the same icons and menus that you see on the computer at your desk. This is also known as a roving profile and is addressed in Chapter 16. If you've logged into the domain, it doesn't matter if you're across town or half way around the world. For more information on connecting to a domain, refer to Chapter 17.

Servers

The key to any of these networks is the server. It can be the start and end of all computing power in a master-slave network. It can be dedicated to certain purposes such as file storage and sharing in a client-server network. And workstations can be set up as non-dedicated servers in a peer-to-peer network.

A server can be installed on a computer with a different operating system. For example, you can set up a file or application server on a computer with one of the Unix style operating systems such as Linux or Solaris. Of course, you can also use any of the Windows Server operating systems as file or application servers. Whatever you use, the server operating system forms a shell around the disk operating system environment which filters out network commands and DOS commands, translating DOS commands to network commands, and vice versa.

A *dedicated server* is a separate computer whose only goal in life is to be a file or application server. By dedicating a computer as a server, you can configure its memory more efficiently. A *nondedicated server*, on the other hand, is a workstation that moonlights as a server—its memory is divided between its role as a workstation and as a server.

Why would you want a dedicated server? A dedicated server is faster, safer, and more efficient than one also being used as a workstation.

◆ It's faster because all of the server's memory and processing power are used to serve clients.

◆ It's safer because no one's using the computer as a workstation and possibly crashing it (everyone crashes *sometimes*). It's also safer because you can control security from one centralized location.

◆ It's more efficient because it does not have to divide its time between being a server (processing remote requests) and being a workstation (processing local requests).

In short, dedicating a computer as a server greatly improves your network's performance. Of course, the downside is cost, because you must buy a computer just to hold and maintain the integrity and security of your information. Because your server will have a lot of demands on it, you're going to want something fast with as much RAM as possible and a big hard disk, and that type of computer isn't cheap.

The expense of a dedicated server gives non-dedicated servers their place in life. A lower price tag is just about the only advantage you get from using your workstation as a server. Non-dedicated servers tend to be slower because any time the server/workstation is in use, the other workstations have to wait to access the server. This wait time can slow down your entire network.

Also, non-dedicated servers are much more likely to crash, increasing the risk of data loss all over your network. If you *must* use a server as a workstation, it's best to limit it to a less risky capacity such as a print or fax server. If one of those servers crash, it's a pain in the neck but probably won't stop access to Microsoft Word or allow the annual report to go down in flames.

What Type of Network is Best?

There is no "best" type of network. What's best for you depends on your needs and resources. If you're creating a network from scratch, some of the factors you should consider include:

Number of computers: If you have more than one computer, you don't want to have to purchase expensive peripherals for each system. All three types of networks permit you to connect a printer, for example, to one computer and share it on the network. Peer-to-peer networks of more than 10 or 15 computers are difficult to manage.

Number of users: If you have more than one user, you may have more than one person making changes to the files on your network. If you can afford it, a dedicated file server can ease the effort in maintaining a single copy of a file. Users who need access to client computers in different locations require a centralized database of users and passwords. Neither a dedicated file server nor a central database of users is possible in a peer-to-peer network.

Shared applications: If you have a substantial number of computers on your network, it can make sense to set up a dedicated application server. This is not an option in a standard peer-to-peer network.

Independent needs: If your users need the ability to work independently, even when the network is down, each user needs a separate computer. This is not possible in a master/slave network.

Centralized control: Domains in a client-server network provide a level of centralized control almost equal to that available with a master/slave network.

Cost: Dedicated file and application servers can be expensive, especially when applied to small numbers of users. An independent computer for every user creates a different kind of expense.

In most cases, the best choice is a client-server network. However, the facts associated with your particular network may lead you to a different conclusion.

The Look and Feel of a Network

The most common way to set up a LAN is with computers connected to a hub. The predominant choice for network technology is Ethernet. The nodes in most Ethernets are connected with twisted-pair cables. This type of cable includes eight wires and connects as easily as a telephone. This chapter covers the details later. But take a look at Figure 15.4, which gives you a feel for how a network is set up.

FIGURE 15.4

A typical network

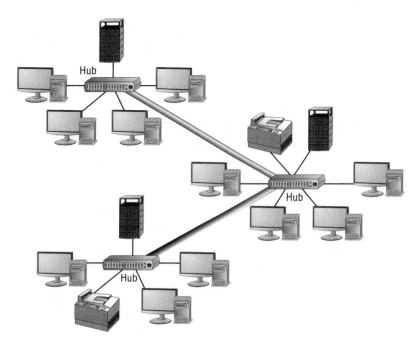

This is one LAN, organized into three different sets of computers. It could represent the setup of a LAN in a three-floor office. Assume that you install a hub in a wiring closet on each floor. You could then install cables between the hub and the computers on that floor. The cables between the hubs would run between floors.

The cable that is used to connect one hub to another hub (or a switch or a router) is generally referred to as a backbone. You always want to make sure that the cable that you use for the backbone is rated for speeds that meet or exceed the speed of the cable that you are using throughout the network (from hub to the nodes). The value of all this extra cable lies in your test instruments in the wiring closet. When someone complains that their workstation no longer works with the network, you can go straight to the wiring closet and test the particular cable. All the cables will be arranged in a nice, neat order, with clearly marked labels indicating which cable goes to what workstation.

Inside each wiring closet is a hub, the device that enables all the computers on a floor to interact as an Ethernet network. This hub connects to the next hub, thus connecting each hub to the computers on the network. You can test the hub by taking a portable computer to the hub, plugging it in, and trying to make a network connection. Some hubs (known as *smart hubs*, appropriately enough) can even assume diagnostic functions if they have SNMP (Simple Network Management Protocol) management capability. They monitor the amount and type of information being supplied by the client computers and detect errors on computers in the network.

You can also pay for software that will monitor the hubs from a central location. For example, I've said that on a LAN only one device can "talk" at a time. One particular type of hardware failure makes a computer chatter away endlessly; locking up the network, but a smart hub detects this failure and disconnects that malfunctioning computer from the network.

Alternatively, you could simply connect a portable computer to the hub—and then try to use the network. If the network is busy because of a chattering computer, disconnect one of the computers at the hub and try the portable again. Because all the connections are right at your fingertips, you need only a minute or two to test all the connections to find the chatterer.

NOTE   *You can connect a network like what is shown in Figure 15.4 to another network such as the Internet. Just connect one of the routers discussed earlier in this chapter to an available uplink port on one of the hubs.*

Building Your Own Network

Now that you've selected the software configuration for a network and have a general idea of the physical layout, you're ready for the hardware. To build a network, you need a Network Interface Card (NIC) for each computer. In most cases, you'll also need cables to connect to each NIC, and hardware such as hubs and routers to connect the NICs together.

All of the previously discussed network relationships—master/slave, client-server, peer-to-peer—work well with the various types of Ethernet networks. But before you can select a NIC, a cable, a hub, or a router, you need to know what type of Ethernet network you're going to build.

Selecting Ethernet Hardware

There are several types of Ethernet network equipment currently available at most larger computer stores. Decisions, decisions. Before you go out and purchase equipment, you have to make some choices. At minimum, you need to select the speed of your network. If you want a wireless Ethernet, you need to accept the associated higher costs and limited speeds. Whatever choice you make, you can then make sure that your components are consistent with that type (e.g. speed, wired or wireless) of network.

Ethernet networks can be built to capacities of 10Mbps, 100Mbps, or 1000Mbps. As illustrated in Table 15.1, these standards are sometimes known as regular Ethernet, Fast Ethernet, and Gigabit Ethernet. Full-duplex versions of each of these standards are available, with twice the speed. There's even a wireless Ethernet that operates at a capacity of 11Mbps.

The hardware that you select in the following sections, NICs, cables, hubs, and switches, routers, and so on, all need to support the characteristics that you select.

SPEED

Transmission speed is measured in millions of bits per second, or Mbps. A bit is short for a binary digit, the 1s and 0s associated with computers. NICs transmit bits of data through a network as a negative or positive electrical pulse.

Network Cards

The Network Interface Card (NIC), or the adapter card, is a card that you use to connect your computer to servers or other computers. The NIC you select should be consistent with the rest of your network. NICs are available which vary in the following characteristics:

Installation: Internal or External or PC Card

> **Internal NIC:** PCI or ISA
>
> **External NIC:** USB or IEEE 1394

Speed: 10Mbps, 100Mbps, 1000Mbps

Duplex: Full-duplex or half-duplex

Connection: Cabled or wireless

NIC INSTALLATION OPTIONS

A NIC can be internal or external to your computer. Internal NICs can fit into PCI or ISA expansion slots. Before you buy an internal NIC, make sure you have the right kind of slot free inside your computer. Some instructions for installing an internal NIC are available in Chapter 16.

Many internal NICs are older *legacy* components. For various reasons, legacy NICs don't always work with Windows Plug and Play. In those cases, you should note the I/O address, DMA channel, and IRQ ports used by your NIC. Some techniques for handling legacy NICs are available in Chapter 8.

NICs today are fairly inexpensive, unless you're setting up a Gigabit network. If you have a NIC that can't be configured through the Windows XP Professional Plug and Play system, it is often more cost effective to purchase a Plug and Play NIC. If you have a lot of peripherals, you may not be able to use the techniques described in Chapter 8 to find a free IRQ, and would otherwise have to uninstall a different component.

Windows XP Professional may not recognize all Plug and Play NICs. Other techniques to address this problem are described in Chapter 16.

WARNING   When installing any hardware inside your computer, be careful. Computers are sensitive to static electricity. Before touching any electronic components, touch a larger piece of metal, such as a computer case. While firm pressure can be required to install or remove a hardware card such as a NIC, never force a card into a slot. If it's the wrong slot, the crossed wires will likely destroy many of the circuits in your computer.

External NICs may connect to USB or IEEE 1394 enabled ports. Make sure your computers have the port that you want. Be especially careful if you want to get a USB NIC. There are two standards: USB 1.0 and USB 2.0. Be sure to match the NIC to the USB standard port available on your computer.

NOTE *If you see a FireWire or iLink NIC in your computer store, you should be able to use them with an IEEE 1394 connection on your computer. FireWire and iLink are trade names for components that meet IEEE 1394 standards.*

Credit card sized NICs are also available, primarily for laptop computers, which conform to the PC Card standards discussed in Chapter 10. They often come with separate adapters to connect to a cable or exchange signals with a wireless network.

NIC SPEED

Ethernet, Fast Ethernet, and Gigabit Ethernet NICs are readily available. Many NICs work at both Ethernet and Fast Ethernet speeds, which allows you to upgrade your network without changing your NIC. Some NICs are full-duplex, which essentially doubles the maximum data transfer speed. If you get a full-duplex NIC, make sure all of the other equipment that you get is also built for full-duplex data transmission.

NIC CONNECTIONS

NICs are available for regular twisted-pair connections that look like oversized telephone cables. With the latest advances in wiring, even Gigabit NICs can use the same cables. Wireless NICs are also available. Whatever your choice, make sure that your cables and other hardware are compatible.

NOTE *The terms* NIC, network card, *and* network adapter *all refer to the same thing—the Network Interface Card.*

Cables

Cables are the backbone of a regular computer network. All information runs through the cables, either in the form of electrical or light pulses through twisted-pair cable or fiber-optic cable. For your network to work well, information must pass through the cabling (or air) without electromagnetic or other interference. Interference generally won't corrupt the data, but it can slow down the network considerably. When you purchase a cable, you need to consider the following:

◆ Length

◆ Distance limits

◆ Interference

◆ Cable standards

◆ Connectors

NOTE *There are some network adapters that work with regular telephone or power lines. With these special adapters, you'd just plug them into a regular telephone jack or power outlet. As some of these systems can support 10Mbps Ethernet, this is a viable option in homes with extra telephone jacks or power outlets or small businesses. If you want 100Mbps Ethernet on regular telephone wires, you may have to wait until the third generation home phone line equipment is available, possibly by 2003.*

CABLE LENGTHS

When you calculate the distance between your computer and a hub, remember that you want to keep your cables out of the way. That probably means you'll be routing cables to walls, along baseboards, above ceilings, and more. For example, I use a 100-foot, Category 5 cable to connect two computers in adjacent rooms. This extra length allows me to route the cable along the far ends of walls and avoid doorways.

DISTANCE LIMITS

The rated speed on an Ethernet cable is limited to 100 meters, which corresponds to about 328 feet. If the distance between a computer and a hub is greater than 100 meters, don't use a longer cable. You may not like the result. Instead, get a repeater to maintain the strength of the signal over the extra distance.

INTERFERENCE

To avoid interference, keep your network cables away from anything that may create an electromagnetic field, including fluorescent lights, motors, and other cables or power lines.

Two alternate ways to avoid interference is by shielding your cable, such as with a metal conduit, or by running network cables at right angles to other cables or power lines. Another option is a fiber-optic based network, because light pulses are essentially impervious to electromagnetic interference.

Some judgment is required. For example, if you're using today's standard Ethernet cable for a 10Mbps Ethernet network, a little interference doesn't matter. The Category 5e (the "e" is for enhanced) cables available in most computer stores can handle near-Gigabit data transfer speeds. However, as your network speed requirements increase, you need to pay more attention to cabling and potential sources of interference.

STANDARDS

The standard for wiring regular Ethernet is known as Cat 5 UTP. This is short for Category 5 standard Unshielded Twisted-Pair cable, a standard of the Electronic Industries Association. While there are shielded cables, and lesser quality cables that support slower speeds, it is difficult to find these in most consumer computer stores today.

The latest version of this standard, Cat 5e, includes specially designed connectors that support speeds up to Gigabit Ethernet levels. These cables should be readily available in many computer stores, sometimes as Category 5 cable that complies with T568A or T568B standards.

However, if you need these speeds for high-performance applications such as broadband video, consider cables at Category 6 and Category 7 levels. However, these cables may be more difficult to get and are much more expensive.

NOTE   *There are regulations on the network cable that you can use in the workplace. If you install network cables in areas susceptible to fire such as ceilings, many governments require the use of* plenum *cables. These cables include special coatings that do not emit toxic fumes in a fire. Whatever you might think of government regulations, plenum cables are generally a good idea in any network installation.*

CONNECTORS

Most Category 5 UTP cable terminates using connectors that look like chunkier versions of the connectors used to plug your telephone into the wall, as shown in Figure 15.5. These are called RJ-45, whereas your telephone uses RJ-11 connectors. One end plugs into your computer's NIC, and the other plugs into a hub. While the connectors may be slightly different if you use Category 5e, 6 or 7 cables, they plug into hubs and NICs in the same way.

Many cables are sold with the connectors already attached. For larger networks, it may make more sense to purchase long lengths of cable, cut the cables to fit the physical layout of your office, and then attach a connector. Crimping tools are available for this purpose.

FIGURE 15.5

RJ-45 connector

Wireless Considerations

If you're going to create a wireless network, you don't need many cables. Wireless networks work through the air with radio signals, infrared, or even microwaves.

The most common wireless network is based on the IEEE 802.11b standard, colloquially known as *Wi-Fi*. It operates on an Ethernet-style network at up to 11Mbps. A number of other wireless networks are available, but as of this writing, they don't have the speed or the cost-effectiveness of a Wi-Fi network.

If you set up a wireless network, you need a wireless hub, switch, or router to send and receive the signals. These are radio style signals. In the frequencies used by IEEE 802.11b, (2.4GHz), you may get interference from microwave ovens, wireless phones, and other wireless devices such as PDAs and BlackBerry handhelds. A wireless network on a different subnet can also cause interference. If you're operating a wireless network, keep these sources away from the *Wireless Access Points*, where wireless devices send and receive signals.

Hubs

Computers on a standard LAN connect to a hub. A hub includes multiple ports to which you can connect RJ-45 or other types of cables. If you have more than two computers on your network, you need a hub. Different hubs are available for different speeds. As described earlier, smart hubs may also include diagnostic functionality. When you purchase a hub, check for the following:

Ports: You need a port for each computer that you want to connect. If your network might grow in the future, you may want additional ports. If you're using a wireless hub, each antenna serves as a port.

Uplink: If you want to connect your network to any other network such as the Internet, you should get a hub with an uplink port. Some hubs use a toggle to change a regular port to an uplink port. You can connect two hubs together by connecting the uplink port on one hub to the regular port on the second hub using a regular patch cable. Alternatively, you can connect two hubs together via regular ports using a crossover cable. A crossover cable is wired slightly different than a regular Ethernet cable and is used to connect some types of network devices in a daisy-chain fashion.

Speed: Ethernet hubs are available at all currently available speeds. But you need to make sure that the speed rating of your hub and NIC match. Some hubs can *autosense* or automatically detect the speed capabilities of a NIC, within limits.

Power: Remember, hubs are external and normally require a separate power supply.

NOTE   *If you have a network of two computers, you can connect them with a crossover cable, which is a standard UTP cable with the send and receive wires flipped on one end. This simulates what happens to a signal when going through the hub, and saves you the additional cost of purchasing a hub.*

Routers

Routers can serve the same function as a hub. With the right uplink port, it can also serve as a junction between networks, such as a small business network and the Internet. In fact, specialized routers are available. Some have embedded telephone modems. Others connect to external ISDN, DSL, satellite, or cable modems.

NOTE   *The only real "modem" is a telephone modem, because it can translate the 1s and 0s of computer talk to the sound waves transmitted through telephone wires. Broadband modems such as DSL, satellite, and cable modems are more closely related to Ethernet adapters. In fact, you can connect a NIC or the uplink port of a hub or router directly to most broadband modems. Consult your broadband modem manufacturer or ISP for more information.*

The ICS/ICF setup discussed in Chapter 11 assumes that you have a computer that is connected to your LAN and to the Internet. This requires two separate NICs, or a NIC and a telephone modem. Each connection requires its own IP address. Since this computer has a direct connection to the Internet, the ICF firewall may not always protect it from intruders. You can install a router in place of this computer. Since you don't store any data on the router (other than what's required to configure that router), this configuration is safer.

TIP   *The IP address on an ICS/ICF computer that's directly connected to the LAN is important. To other computers on the LAN, that's the default gateway address.*

Installation

If you use a cabled network, the biggest cost may be installation. In the workplace, bundles of network cables on the floor are often unsafe and unattractive. Many businesses treat the setup of a network just like the setup of telephones in the office.

If you're in the process of building, you may be able to set up the installation of network cables in the same conduits used for your telephone cables. You can then set up your network (RJ-45) and telephone (RJ-11) adapters in the same wall for every office.

However, if you already have an office, the time and expense associated with paying a contractor to set up your network can be daunting. If you're considering cut-rate cables, the thought of having a contractor tear up the walls in your office a *second* time should be sobering. In the long run, it may be more cost-effective to purchase Category 6 or Category 7 cables for your network installation.

Speed becomes a major consideration now and in the future. If your old cable can't keep up with the transfer rate of your new network, you'll need to replace it when you upgrade parts of the network, and that upgrade could be expensive. Clearly, the need for upgrades is yet another reason to plan your network ahead of time.

BUYING NETWORK EQUIPMENT

Purchasing the equipment for your first network does not need to be confusing or difficult. In fact, your choices for Ethernet networks are simple. They're based on speed and cabling, as required. The details are covered in previous sections. Here is a summary of your options:

Speed: 10Mbps, 100Mbps, 1000Mbps.

Duplex: Full-duplex

Cabling: Category 5 UTP can handle speeds up to 100Mbps. Category 5e UTP can handle 1000Mbps networks. If you're going to create custom lengths of cable, you also need a crimping tool to attach the RJ-45 style connectors. If you're using a wireless network, you don't need a cable.

Wireless Standard: Wi-Fi (IEEE 802.11b) or some other standard.

NIC: Internal, External, or PC Card.

Internal NIC: PCI or ISA

External NIC: USB 1.0, USB 2.0, or IEEE 1394 (iLink/FireWire)

Hub: Requires enough ports for each node on your LAN, an uplink port, and any additional computers that you may add in the future.

Switch: Can substitute for a hub. If you have a lot of traffic between several computers on your network, a switch can reduce traffic.

Router: Substitutes for a computer with a NIC on your LAN and a NIC or telephone modem that connects to another network such as the Internet.

Summary

In this chapter, we looked at the basics of networking. LANs help users share files, applications and more. We then covered some of the vocabulary and theory behind a network, and discussed various network relationships: master/slave, peer-to-peer, and client-server. Finally, we walked through the network components that you might get at your local computer store.

Chapter 16

Setting Up and Configuring a Peer-to-Peer Network

ONE OF THE MOST powerful features of Windows XP Professional is its capability to attach to and become part of a networking environment. In this chapter, we'll look at many of the decisions you will need to make in order to get the networking features to run reliably in that environment. You'll learn how to set up a simple peer-to-peer Ethernet network (including what to do if Windows XP doesn't detect your network interface card); how to configure your Windows 98/Me, Windows XP Professional, and Windows XP Home Edition machines using the Network Setup Wizard; how to manually configure your Windows 95 and NT Workstation machines; and how to set up your own IP addresses. You'll also learn how to allow users to share documents and printers and how to create profiles for users and hardware. For those of you working with more complex networking environments, this chapter covers how to connect Unix and Macintosh networks. Finally, the chapter wraps up with a section on troubleshooting your network.

In this chapter:

- ◆ Connecting your network
- ◆ Configuring your network
- ◆ Creating shares
- ◆ Attaching to network resources
- ◆ Understanding and using profiles
- ◆ Troubleshooting

Setting Up a Network

The whole idea of a network is to share things: space on a large disk drive, a particular file on that disk drive, a printer, and so on. Networks provide two major benefits. One, they can increase user productivity and collaboration. Two, they can save companies money on hardware and software. Imagine the cost difference of buying one color laser printer for the marketing department as opposed to buying one for each associate! As an example, let's consider a small office that needs to do some sharing.

In our office, Jennifer has more storage capacity on her machine than Joe does on his, but the office laser printer is attached to Joe's PC. Jennifer and Joe work on the office accounting system, so they need to share the accounting files—or they'll have to pass floppies back and forth via sneaker-net. Because Jennifer has more disk space, they put the accounting files on her machine. So, the network problems that we need to solve are as follows:

◆ Sharing Joe's printer with Jennifer

◆ Sharing Jennifer's disk with Joe

Let's solve their problem with a basic peer-to-peer network. Microsoft generally refers to peer-to-peer configurations as *workgroups* (as opposed to *domains*). With this type of network, Jennifer makes her hard disk available on the network, and Joe makes his printer available on the network. Assuming that both computers are running Windows XP Professional, here's how to get Joe onto Jennifer's disk and Jennifer onto Joe's printer:

1. Jennifer tells the Windows XP Professional networking software, "Offer the Acctng subfolder on my C drive to anyone who wants it. Call it Acctng." In Microsoft enterprise networking terminology, Acctng becomes the *share name* of that folder on Jennifer's machine (GTW09), and it's the name that others will use to access the resource over the network. In a few pages, I'll show you exactly how to share such a resource on the network so others can access it, but for now, remember this: a machine (named GTW09) is sharing a resource called Acctng with anyone on that network who's able to use it.

NOTE   *Here's an important concept in Microsoft networking: You must name each machine in the network, whether it is a server or a workstation. Often you will hear this name referred to as a NetBIOS name. You also must name each user (in our example, Joe and Jennifer). Because the PCs need names, we may as well name the PCs with their inventory numbers, which in this example are DELL05 and GTW09. Another common naming scheme is to name the computer based on the physical location within the company. A computer in the east wing, row L station 6 could be called EL06.*

WARNING   *Naming machines after their users is a bad idea, because PCs may be reassigned to other users.*

2. Joe then tells the networking software on his PC, "Attach me to the Acctng resource on Jennifer's machine."

3. Joe, meanwhile, tells his computer to share the printer on his LPT1 port, giving it a name—again, a share name—of JOLASER. Joe's machine is called DELL05, so the UNC name of that printer will be \\DELL05\JOLASER.

NOTE   *UNC stands for Universal Naming Convention. In the printer's UNC name, \\DELL05 is the machine name, and \JOLASER is the share name. UNCs are used all the time in networking and always follow a \\computer-name\sharename format.*

4. Jennifer then tells her networking software to make a network connection to JOLASER on Joe's machine, and to create it on her LPT1 port.

From now on, whenever Jennifer tells an application program to print to a laser printer on LPT1, the network software will intercept the printed output and will direct it over the network to Joe's machine. The networking software on Joe's machine will then print the information on Joe's printer. I've left out some of the "how do we do this?" information; it's coming right up.

WAYS TO CONNECT A PEER-TO-PEER NETWORK

In the next section of this chapter, I'll show you how to connect a network that uses an Ethernet hub, which I discussed in the previous chapter. You can, however, connect a peer-to-peer network in a couple of other ways:

◆ By using a special network adapter based on a home phone line network. In this system, a special network adapter with a converter is installed in each computer, and each computer is plugged in to a phone jack using a telephone cable.

◆ By using a wireless connection, which was described briefly in Chapter 15.

For some detailed information about these types of connections, open Help and Support Center, click the Networking and the Web link, click the Home and Small Office Networking link, and then click the Hardware Requirements for Home and Small Office Networking link. You'll also find some excellent information on this topic at www.homepna.com.

Windows XP Professional is designed to work in a variety of networking situations. XP makes the perfect network client for both home and office users. It doesn't matter if your network servers are running NetWare, Unix, or some other platform; Windows XP Professional will play nice with a variety of network operating systems. Windows XP Professional can also act as a server in a pinch—although you're better off going with a true server product for a long-term solution.

Connecting Your Ethernet Network

In the first part of this chapter, I'm going to show you how to set up a simple peer-to-peer Ethernet network that solves the problems of Joe and Jennifer that I just described. Using the information in the previous chapter, you first need to design your network, and then you probably need to go shopping—either on the Internet or at one of many computer centers that are springing up all over the place.

You need a Network Interface Card (NIC) for each computer on the network, a hub, and some cables. Many computers that you buy these days come with NICs already installed. If you have an older computer, though, you'll probably need to purchase a NIC. You can even buy a starter kit that contains everything you need—NICs, cables, and a hub—probably for less than $50. With that and a couple of screwdrivers, you're ready to get started. Follow these steps:

1. Turn off and unplug each computer that will be part of your network.

2. At each computer, open the case, and insert a NIC in an empty slot, screwing the card in securely so it won't come loose.

3. Replace the case.

4. Insert one end of the cable into the RJ-45 socket on the card and insert the other end of the cable into the hub. The hub number is not important as long as you don't plug it into a port labeled "Uplink" or "Crossover"—avoid those.

NOTE   *One way to avoid using a hub altogether is to buy a* crossover *cable. Plug one end of the crossover into one machine, and the other end into your second machine. The major drawback with this is that you can only have two computers on your network. While hubs are pretty inexpensive, this is an alternative if money is really an issue.*

5. Plug the hub into the power supply.

6. Turn on the hub and all connected computers. You'll see some lights start blinking on the hub. Most hubs will have a light for each port indicating whether it detects a connection, along with a power light and traffic indicators.

Because Windows XP Professional is Plug and Play, when you restart your computer after inserting the NICs, the system automatically loads the device drivers you need for the NICs. For the most part, Windows XP is very good about automatically detecting network cards after installing them and rebooting. In this respect, Windows XP is very user friendly. However, Windows XP is still a fairly new product. Not all network adapters have XP drivers available, and the NIC may not be detected. What do you do?

First of all, don't panic. Windows XP can sometimes use Windows 98 or Windows 2000 drivers. If your NIC came with a diskette or CD with drivers on it (it should have), try the 98 or 2000 drivers by using the Add Hardware Wizard. In Control Panel, click Add Hardware, and follow the on-screen prompts. If those drivers don't work, then look on the manufacturer's Web site to see if they have anything, be it advice or drivers, available for people in your situation. The absolute worst-case scenario is that you'll have to take the NIC back and get a different brand, but this is unlikely. Stick with name-brand parts, and you should never run into a problem that serious. Now you're ready to configure your network.

TIP   *Always check to make sure that the hardware you're purchasing is on the Hardware Compatibility List (HCL).*

Configuring Your Network

After successfully installing your network adapters, there are some common steps you need to take to get the network running properly. Among those steps are to name your computer and workgroup, add protocols necessary for communication (TCP/IP is installed by default, so you may not need to add more), and configure protocol parameters, like IP addresses. Using the Network Setup Wizard can help you simplify these configuration processes.

Using the Network Setup Wizard

Setting up a peer-to-peer network has never been easier than it is with Windows XP Professional. You simply follow the steps in the Network Setup Wizard, and in a very few minutes you're done.

The only catch is that the other computers on your network must be running one of the following operating systems:

◆ Windows 98 (First or Second Edition)

◆ Windows Millennium Edition

◆ Windows XP Professional

◆ Windows XP Home

If the other computers on your network are running some other operating system, you'll need to manually configure the network. This is because the Network Setup Wizard is only provided for the four operating systems listed above. Running the Network Setup Wizard not only will connect your computers to each other, but the Wizard will also configure all computers to access the Internet through one host computer.

WARNING *If you've already configured networking on your computer, the Network Setup Wizard overrides your current settings. In that case, look for the sections later in this chapter on manual configuration.*

I'll show you how to manually configure the network in the next section.

If your network hardware is installed and working properly, you're ready to begin. Log on as a Computer Administrator user on the host machine (the one that will share its Internet connection). (If you're not sure how to log on as a Computer Administrator user, find out how in the beginning of Chapter 3.) Once you're logged in, connect to the Internet, and then follow these steps:

1. Click Start ➤ All Programs ➤ Accessories ➤ Communications ➤ Network Setup Wizard to start the Wizard.

NOTE *If you see a "Cannot Complete the Network Setup Wizard" message, your computer already belongs to a domain. Instructions for setting up your computer on a domain, or converting it back to a workgroup member, are included in Chapter 17.*

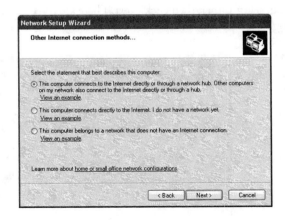

2. At the Welcome screen, click Next.

3. At the Before You Continue screen, look at the checklist, make sure you have completed your preparations, and then click Next to open the Select a Connection Method screen.

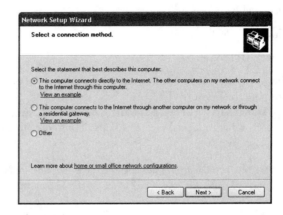

NOTE   *If you do not have two connections (one for the Internet and one for your local network), you will not be able to make this computer a router/gateway.*

4. Select the statement that best describes the setup of your system, and then click Next. What you do next depends on the configuration of your network. In this example, we've specified that this computer will connect directly to the Internet. For many small or home offices, where computers are connecting through a modem, DSL line, or cable modem, this is the appropriate choice. If you are participating on a large corporate network or otherwise have a proxy server, firewall, or hardware router/gateway between your computer and the Internet, you will need to choose the second option listed. If you're still not sure which option is right for you, select Other, then click Next. There are three other options that can be configured through the Network Setup Wizard, as shown in Figure 16.1.

FIGURE 16.1

The Network Setup Wizard is versatile.

Now you need to configure the other computers on your network. Running the Network Setup Wizard on the other computers will make them look for a host computer with a shared Internet connection. Therefore, your host computer will need to be up and running and connected to the Internet. Follow these steps at each computer:

1. Insert the Windows XP Professional CD in the CD-ROM drive.

2. At the opening screen, click Perform Additional Tasks.

3. At the next screen, click Set Up a Home or Small Office Network, and click Yes to continue.

4. The Wizard will give you some information on what it can do. Click Next on the next two screens to continue.

5. Select the network connection you wish to use. If your NIC is installed properly, it should be listed in the Connections box. Click Next to continue.

6. Since you have already set up your host computer, choose the option This Computer Connects to the Internet through Another Computer on My Network or through a Residential Gateway, and click Next.

7. Provide a description and name for this computer, and click Next.

8. Enter your workgroup name. Make sure that all computers on your network have the same workgroup name. Click Next to continue.

9. Click Next a few more times, and finally Finish. The Wizard will end and offer to reboot your machine for you.

NOTE *To run the Network Setup Wizard on a Windows 98, Windows Me, or Windows 2000 computer, you will need to have a Windows XP CD-ROM.*

Configuring Windows 95/NT Workstation Machines

If you're using Windows 95 or Windows NT Workstation on your other network computers, you'll need to configure those computers manually. If you prefer, you can also configure Windows 98/Me/2000 computers in nearly the same fashion. Follow these steps:

1. Right-click Network Neighborhood and choose Properties from the shortcut menu to open the Network dialog box.

2. In The Following Network Components Are Installed list in the Configuration tab, you need to see at least the following (you may see more, and that's OK):

   ◆ TCP/IP

   ◆ Identification

   ◆ File and Printer Sharing for Microsoft Networks

NOTE *For the remainder of this discussion, we are going to assume that this is a new installation and none of the required protocols are installed. We will begin by adding TCP/IP.*

3. Click Add to open the Select Network Component Type dialog box. Select Protocol and click Add again. Under Manufacturers, select Microsoft. In the right pane, scroll down and click TCP/IP. Click OK twice.

4. Insert the CD-ROM disk for your appropriate operating system. Click OK. At this point, you may have to provide the path to the operating system files. For Windows 95 it should be x:\Win95; for Windows 98, x:\Win98; for Windows 98 Second Edition, x:\Win98_SE; and for Windows NT, x:\i386. Replace x: with your CD-ROM drive letter; for example, if your CD-ROM drive is D, replace x: with **d:**.

5. Right-click Network Neighborhood and choose Properties from the shortcut menu to open the Network dialog box.

   In The Following Network Components Are Installed list in the Configuration tab, select TCP/IP *Your network adapter*. Click Properties.

You will see two choices: Obtain an IP Address Automatically or Specify an IP Address. Select one, depending on the criteria in the following sidebar:

CONFIGURING IP ADDRESSES ON A NETWORK

There are two basic ways to set up IP addresses for your peer-to-peer network. You can automate the process through DHCP or APIPA, or you can select and assign the IP addresses yourself. These techniques apply equally well to Windows 98/Me/2000 computers; you don't need the Network Setup Wizard.

OBTAIN AN IP ADDRESS AUTOMATICALLY

Use this setting if you have a Dynamic Host Configuration Protocol (DHCP) server (a server that automatically assigns IP addresses to client machines) or if this machine is connected to an Internet Connection Sharing host (Windows 9x, Windows 2000, or Windows XP).

SPECIFY AN IP ADDRESS

Enter your IP address and subnet mask. If you are designing a network that is not connected to the Internet, you can choose any IP address you want. For example,

```
IP address:     131.107.0.102
Subnet Mask:    255.255.0. 0
```

The numbers above the 255s in the subnet mask determine the network number. In this example, 131.107 is the network number. The network number *must* be the same for all the computers in the network. The number above the zero in the subnet mask is the host number, which must be *different* on each computer in the network.

On the other hand, if your network will be connected to the Internet, use one of the private network addresses described in Chapter 15. For example:

```
IP address:   10. X.  Y.  Z
Subnet Mask: 255.0.0.  0
```

Continued on next page

CONFIGURING IP ADDRESSES ON A NETWORK *(continued)*

or

```
IP address:  172. 16.  X.  Y
Subnet Mask: 255.255.0.  0
```

or

```
IP address:  192. 168.  56.  X
Subnet Mask: 255.255.255.  0
```

Of course, X, Y, and Z are not numbers. Substitute any number between 1 and 254 for X, Y, and Z, as long as each computer gets a unique number. Duplicate addresses on a network can cause a variety of communication problems. After you have made your selection and specified an IP address and subnet mask, click OK.

Identification

If you are going to connect your computers to share information, you must configure the Network Neighborhood properties' Identification tab. This tab sets the computer name for the computer and configures your computer in a workgroup (a group of computers that can share information). Follow these steps:

1. Select the Identification tab.

2. In the Computer Name text box, enter a name. This name can be up to 15 characters long and must be unique within your network.

3. In the Workgroup text box, enter a workgroup name. This name *must be the same* for each computer in the network. If you're at a loss for a name, use WORKGROUP or MSHOME.

NOTE *Capitalization of the workgroup name does not matter;* instructors *is identical to* Instructors, *which is identical to* INSTRUCTORS. *Also, do not give a machine the same name as any other machine in your environment.*

TIP *Don't just accept the defaults. The default workgroup name for Windows XP, MSHOME, differs from the default workgroup name for other Microsoft operating systems, WORKGROUP.*

Click OK.

Reboot the computer if prompted.

File and Printer Sharing for Microsoft Networks

File and Printer Sharing for Microsoft Networks does not need to be installed on Windows 95/98/Me machines for them to share resources on a network. Without it, Windows 95/98/Me machines can still be clients on a network; that is, retrieve files from and use printers on remote machines. However, they will not be able to host their own resources.

Windows NT machines also have the ability to share resources. However, Windows NT calls its server service "Server" and its client service "Workstation." These services are installed and configured by default on Windows NT machines.

Windows XP machines have the ability to share resources by default, and do not require additional configuration of File and Printer Sharing for Microsoft Networks.

Configuring Windows XP Manually

The previous section dealt with how to configure Windows 98 and NT machines to participate on your Windows XP network. If your network contains just Windows XP machines, there is no need to configure the networking parameters yourself. Simply use the Network Setup Wizard and have it take care of everything for you.

However, some people don't trust all of the automated features of computer and network setups. Although this may be obsessive, there's really nothing wrong with it. If you're one of those people who like to know everything that's going on in their machine, and therefore want to configure things manually in XP, here is some advice.

TIP   Double-checking your IP parameters and manually setting up your networking options are useful troubleshooting techniques if you are having communication problems on your network.

IP CONFIGURATION

Windows XP also has two options for configuring IP addresses, much like previous versions of Windows operating systems. The first option is to obtain an IP address automatically (through a DHCP server or APIPA), and the second option is to configure addresses manually. If you want to configure addresses manually, then the sidebar on IP addressing in the "Configuring Windows 95/NT Workstation Machines" section in this chapter will help you in XP.

Automatically obtaining an IP address can happen in one of two ways. First, if your network has a DHCP server, you will obtain an address from it. I'm guessing that if you have just a small office in your home, you don't have a DHCP server. That's okay. Let's say that you set your Windows XP machine to obtain an IP address automatically, but Windows XP cannot locate a DHCP server (which makes sense, because you don't have one). Windows XP will automatically assign an IP address and subnet mask to your machine. The address will be in the 169.254.X.X range, with a subnet mask of 255.255.0.0. This feature is called Automatic Private IP Addressing (APIPA).

NOTE   Windows 98, 2000, Me, and XP support APIPA.

You should be careful of one thing when using APIPA, though. Let's say that you have manually configured one computer with an address of 131.107.2.102 and a mask of 255.255.255.0. Another computer on the same network gets an APIPA-assigned address of 169.254.225.128, along with a mask of 255.255.0.0. Those two computers will not be able to talk to each other using TCP/IP. The reason for this is they have different network addresses, so they each think the other is physically somewhere else, when they're really on the same physical network. The computers will be confused, and won't talk.

To manually configure IP addresses on your Windows XP Professional computer, right-click My Network Places, and choose Properties. In the new window that opens, right-click Local Area

Connection, and click Properties again. Highlight TCP/IP, and choose Properties. Select the Use the Following IP Address radio button, and enter your IP address, subnet mask, and default gateway (if necessary). You can specify an address for a DNS server as well, or obtain that server's address automatically.

TIP *If you're configuring your network for an Internet connection and assigning IP addresses yourself, ask your ISP for their DNS server addresses. Enter these numbers in each of the computers on your network.*

IDENTIFICATION

Windows XP Professional does not have an Identification tab like Windows 95/98/Me and NT did. Instead, right-click My Computer, choose Properties, and then choose Computer Name. Here you will see your computer name, as well as the workgroup or domain name. You can also change that information here.

Page 91 in "Essential Skills for Windows XP Professional" also provides a visual guide to the Computer Name tab.

Network Bridging

If you have multiple NICs, you could set up a separate IP address for each NIC. Windows XP Professional looks at an IEEE 1394 adapter as a NIC. If you work with any virtual machine technology such as VMWare, that software also installs separate "virtual" NICs on your computer. Without Microsoft Windows XP Network Bridging technology, I would have to maintain four different NICs just on one computer. And managing a network can be difficult enough.

With a network bridge, I can easily manage four different NICs on the same computer, as shown in Figure 16.2.

Without the network bridge, I would need four different IP addresses. I would have to configure four sets of DNS addresses, reconfigure WINS as required, and so on. In addition, since the NICs could be connected to different networks, the computer would become a router, and I would then have to configure IP forwarding to get the NICs to talk to each other. Traffic from any one of these NICs could cause a traffic jam on the network.

With the network bridge, I need only one IP address. All of the NICs plug into my computer in the same way as they plug into a hub. But as a bridge (which is another name for a switch), it regulates traffic on the network. In other words, if I'm downloading a digital video through my IEEE 1394 port, that doesn't stop traffic that goes through my computer to a virtual machine or a USB device.

FIGURE 16.2

You can manage multiple NICs with one Network Bridge.

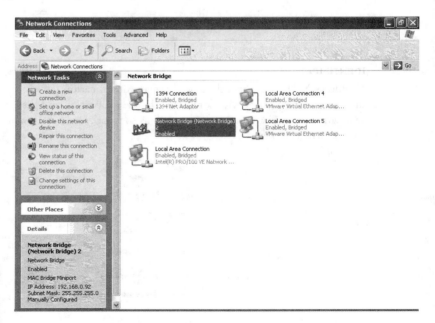

Sometimes you need separate IP addresses. For example, if you want two separate networks connected to your computer, it's easy to detach one of your NICs from the bridge. From the example shown in Figure 16.2, right-click the Network Bridge icon, then click Properties in the pop-up menu. In the Network Bridge properties window shown in Figure 16.3, the Adapters area includes the connections that are connected to the bridge. Deselect the connection of your choice and click OK.

FIGURE 16.3

Just deselect any connection that you want to detach from the properties of the Network Bridge.

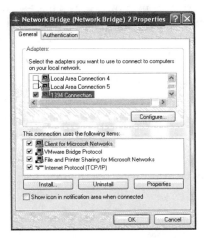

Now the Network Connections window is split between regular LAN connections and connections that are part of the Network Bridge, as shown in Figure 16.4. You can now configure the properties of the connections that you just decoupled from the bridge.

FIGURE 16.4

If you want to manage a NIC separately, just detach it from the Network Bridge.

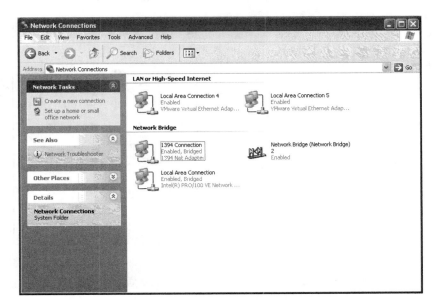

Creating Shares

When you configure your network using the Network Setup Wizard, the Shared Documents folder and any printer directly connected to your computer are shared automatically. Before users on your network can get to other resources on your computer, you must share those resources. To do this, you must be logged on as an administrator, or have a user account with local administrator privileges. You can create shares using Explorer or Computer Management. Using Explorer is simple and direct, so in this section that's what I'll use.

See page 72 in "Essential Skills" for a visual guide to sharing a folder on a network.

NOTE *To open Computer Management, in Control Panel click Administrative Tools and then click Computer Management. Alternatively, click Start ➤ All Programs ➤ Administrative Tools ➤ Computer Management.*

A share can be a folder, a drive, a program, a file—any resource on your computer that you want other people to be able to use over the network. For this example, I'm going to share a folder. Here are the steps:

NOTE *The file system that the shared resource is on is irrelevant in terms of operating system access, even though it may impact security. As an example, Windows 98 does not have the ability to read NTFS volumes locally. However, a Windows 98 machine can access a shared folder located on an NTFS partition elsewhere on the network.*

1. In Explorer, right-click the folder, and choose Sharing and Security from the shortcut menu to open the Properties dialog box for that folder at the Sharing tab:

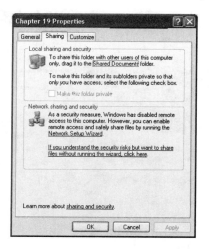

TIP *If you've already shared files without using the Network Setup Wizard, you're taken immediately to step 3.*

2. Before you can share the folder, you have to enable sharing. To do so, you can run the Network Setup Wizard by clicking that link in the Network Sharing and Security section, or you can click the If You Understand the Security Risks but Want to Share Files without Running the Wizard, Click Here link. Clicking this second link opens the Enable File Sharing dialog box:

Click the Just Enable File Sharing option, and then click OK.

3. Back in the Sharing tab, you'll see the following after you click the Share This Folder on the Network check box:

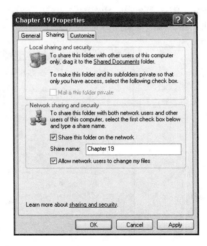

4. In the Share Name box, you can accept the name that Windows XP Professional suggests or enter another name.

5. If you want others on your network to be able to read the contents of the folder but not change them, clear the Allow Network Users to Change My Files check box.

6. Click OK.

7. Back in Explorer you'll see that the folder now has a hand under it to indicate that it is a shared folder.

Although Microsoft does not recommend sharing a drive, you can still do so. Follow these steps:

1. Choose Start ➤ My Computer to open the My Computer window.

2. Right-click the drive you want to share, and then select Sharing and Security from the short-cut menu to open the Properties dialog box for that drive at the Sharing tab:

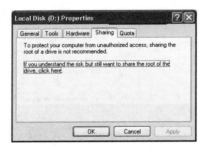

3. Click the If You Understand the Risk but Still Want to Share the Root of the Drive, Click Here link. You'll then see the following in the Sharing tab when you click the Share This Folder on the Network check box:

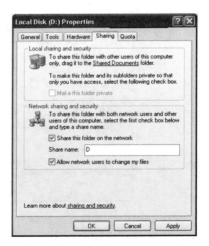

4. If you want others on your network to be able to read the contents of the drive but not change them, clear the Allow Network Users to Change My Files check box.

5. Click OK. The Setting Folder Permission dialog box will show the progress of sharing the drive.

6. Back in the My Computer window, you'll see that the drive now has a hand under it to indicate that it is shared.

Attaching to Network Resources

After your network is configured for sharing, one of the easiest ways to test your network connections is to attach to network resources. You can do so in the following ways:

- By browsing My Network Places
- By mapping a network drive
- By using UNCs to connect directly

See pages 73 and 74 in "Essentials Skills" for a visual guide to connecting a network drive.

Browsing My Network Places

To access My Network Places, click My Computer on the Start menu. Under Other Places, click My Network Places to open a window that displays the options on your network. Click View Workgroup Computers under Network Tasks to display other computers on your network. Then, double-click a computer to view and connect to its shared resources.

Mapping a Network Drive

Mapping a network drive involves assigning a drive letter to a network location. For example, if you frequently connect to another user's shared folder, you might assign it an unused drive letter on your computer.

When you frequently access particular network resources, mapping a drive to the network share is a great way to ensure that they're easily available. When you map a drive, you're telling your computer, "make the `docs` shared folder on `server1` my drive letter L." Drive L then appears in My Computer under Network Drives, and all you need to do to access it is to double-click it. Remember that the information is still physically stored on the other machine. All you've done is make a logical pointer on your machine pointing to the physical resource. It's purely for the sake of convenience. One of the benefits to networking is being able to back up your files and folders on another computer. You'll find that some applications won't recognize other network drives unless they are mapped—so that's another reason you need to know how to map network drives.

To map a drive, follow these steps:

1. On the Start menu, click My Computer. Under Other Places, right-click My Network Places, and choose Map Network Drive to open the Map Network Drive dialog box:

2. From the Drive drop-down list, select an unused drive letter.

3. From the Folder drop-down list, select the folder you want to map to, or click Browse to find the folder on your network.

4. If you want to use this mapping every time you log on, leave the Reconnect at Logon check box selected.

NOTE *Clicking the Connect Using a Different User Name link opens the Connect As dialog box. I'll discuss that option later in this chapter.*

5. Click Finish. The drive now appears in My Computer under Network Drives along with your local drives.

To disconnect a mapped drive, follow these steps:

1. In My Computer, choose Tools ➤ Disconnect Network Drive to open the Disconnect Network Drive dialog box.

2. Select the network drive you want to disconnect, and click OK.

TIP *If this process isn't working for some reason, the next section provides an alternative method for mapping network drives that is more reliable.*

Making a Direct Connection via a UNC

At the beginning of this chapter, I mentioned UNC names. Using UNC names is yet another way to attach to network resources. You do this in one of two ways. One way is to click the Start menu and choose Run. The other way is by executing `net use` statements at the command prompt. But before you can attach to resources on the network, you need to know which resources are available.

If you are using the `Run` command from the Start menu, type ***computername*** and it will show you the resources available on that machine. For example, if I knew that Joe had shared his printer but I could not remember the name, I could type in **\\DELL05**, hit Enter, and I would see what he has shared. To attach to a network resource using the `Run` command, use the full UNC name, like **\\GTW09\acctng**.

We already looked at how to use My Network Places and the `Run` command to locate network resources, but you can also do so at the command prompt using the `net view` command.

NOTE *So far in this chapter, I've been talking primarily about how to set up and configure a Windows XP Professional peer-to-peer network, although some of the information, such as mapping network drives, applies equally to a client-server network and domains, which I'll discuss in the next chapter. This section, however, contains information that sometimes applies to workgroups and sometimes applies to domains. You know which kind of network you have, so you'll know which instructions apply to your situation.*

NOTE *In environments with lots of shared resources, complex group and permission issues can arise. For information on groups and permissions, see Chapter 18.*

Here's how to use the `net view` command:

1. To display a list of the machines on your network, type **net view** at the command prompt.

2. To display a list of the resources on a particular machine, append the name of the machine. For example, if the machine name was spiritwolf, you'd enter **net view \\spiritwolf**.

3. To view the resources of a machine in another domain, for example, the server spiritwolf in the domain hq, you'd enter the following:

```
net view \\spiritwolf /domain:hq
```

4. To display a list of all the domains on the network, simply enter **net view /domain**.

USING NET USE: CONNECTING TO OTHER DRIVES AND PRINTERS

After you've browsed the network with the **net view** command, you can connect to all the available goodies (or disconnect from those you don't want) with the **net use** command. Use this command to connect to network resources as drives D through Z and printer ports LPT1 through LPT9.

WARNING *Drive letters can only be used once. So if your CD-ROM is drive D, you will only have drive letters E through Z available.*

To display information about the workstation's current connections, type **net use** without options, and you'll see something like this:

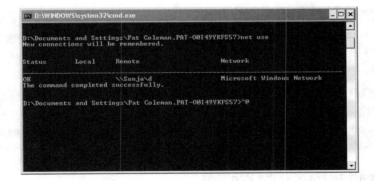

USING LONG FILENAMES IN UNCS

If you wanted to connect to a folder called Wpfiles on the spiritwolf server and make that your E drive, your command would be **net use E: \\spiritwolf\wpfiles**. You get to specify the port name or drive letter that you want to connect a resource to, but again, you're restricted to drive letters D through Z and ports LPT1 through LPT9. To connect to a printer instead of a folder, you would use a port—such as **lpt1:**—instead of a drive letter, and the printer name instead of the folder name. Your command may read **net use lpt1: \\spiritwolf\printer1**.

If the computer you're getting the resource from has a blank character in its name (that is, the computer name has two words in it), you must put the name in quotation marks, like this:

```
"\\eisa server"
```

If a password (let's say it's "artuser") is attached to the resource that you're trying to connect to, you need to include that in your connection command, like this:

```
net use lpt1: \\ted\hp4m artuser
```

Or, if you want the computer to prompt you for the password so that it isn't displayed on the screen, append an asterisk:

```
net use lpt1: \\ted\hp4m *
```

USING OTHER SWITCHES

No matter what kind of connection you make, you can make it persistent (that is, have it reconnect automatically every time you reboot your machine) by adding the switch `/persistent:yes` to the end of the command. If you don't want it to be persistent, use `/persistent:no` instead.

If you don't specify one or the other, the default is whatever you chose last. If you want to make all future connections persistent, type the following (or type `:no` if you want all future connections to be temporary):

```
net use /persistent:yes
```

Typing `/persistent` by itself at the end of the line won't do anything.

To disconnect from a resource, type the following:

```
net use devicename /delete
```

where *devicename* is the connection (such as D or LPT1). You don't have to provide a password or say anything about persistency to disconnect from a resource.

Using Profiles

Windows XP Professional uses two types of profiles: user and hardware. Although each serves a specific purpose, both types of profiles are used to customize the computing environment. In this section, we'll look at how to create and manage them.

Creating Hardware Profiles

If you use a laptop for business, you likely have encountered the following problem. When you bring your laptop into the office, you would like your computer to recognize the NIC and maybe an external monitor and keyboard. But when you take your laptop on the road, you want it to know that you do not currently have any of the "office" devices attached. Most laptops get their information by timing out on each device, which adds five minutes to the boot process and wastes time, not to mention wasting valuable battery life.

A feature of Windows XP Professional that is designed to alleviate this problem is a hardware profile. You can create a profile of the hardware that is attached to your machine when you are in the office and specify a different hardware profile for when you are on the road. And the fun doesn't stop there. You can create profiles for all the places in which you use your computer.

To create a hardware profile, follow these steps:

1. On the Start menu, right-click My Computer, and choose Properties from the shortcut menu to open the System Properties dialog box.

2. Select the Hardware tab, and click Hardware Profiles to open the Hardware Profiles dialog box:

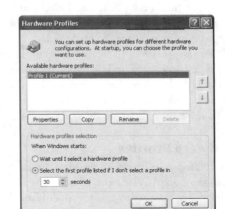

3. To create a new hardware profile, choose a configuration from the Available Hardware Profiles list, and then click Copy to open the Copy Profile dialog box.

4. Give the hardware profile a new name, and click OK. (I'll show you how to configure a profile a bit later in this section.)

TIP   *When naming hardware profiles, use an intuitive naming pattern. As an example, "Office" and "On the road" are certainly better alternatives than "Profile 1" and "Profile 2."*

5. To play with the docking properties of this profile, click Properties to open the Properties dialog box for the profile you are creating:

You can specify whether the system is going to be attached to a docking station when it is using this profile. A docking station is a box on your desk (usually at the office) that you plug your laptop into. You use docking stations because you can attach peripherals to them, such as a larger monitor, full-sized keyboard, and mouse. Then, when you come into the office, you simply plug your laptop into the dock, and you can use the larger monitor, keyboard, and mouse instead of the smaller ones on the laptop. However, when you do this, your laptop needs to know that sometimes it's using the laptop screen, whereas other times it's using the larger monitor. You tell the laptop this by configuring the docking properties.

If Windows XP Professional is not able to automatically detect the docking status of your laptop when in this profile, The Docking State Is Unknown option is selected. You can also strictly specify the state if it is always docked when using this profile or if it is *not* always docked when using this profile.

If this computer is a desktop, uncheck This Is a Portable Computer. When you've set your options, click OK to close the Properties dialog box, and then click OK twice more.

Managing Hardware Profiles

Now that you have created your hardware profile, you can begin to enable the services and devices that will be available through it. When you reboot your computer, choose a hardware profile. To enable or disable devices or services in this profile, follow these steps:

1. Click Start ➤ All Programs ➤ Administrative Tools ➤ Computer Management to open the Computer Management window.

2. Expand System Tools, and then select Device Manager to display the list of devices in the pane on the right.

3. Expand the device type you're interested in. Double-click the device that you want to enable or disable to open its Properties dialog box.

4. In the General tab, use the Device Usage drop-down list to enable or disable a device in the current hardware profile or in any (or all) hardware profiles, and then click OK.

5. To enable or disable services, expand Services and Applications, and then select Services to display the list of the services in the pane on the right:

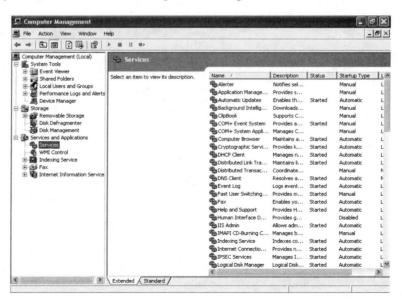

6. Double-click the service that you want to manage to open its Properties dialog box, and then click the Log On tab:

7. Select the specific hardware profile, click Enable or Disable, and then click OK.

NOTE *Services and the Service console are covered in detail in Chapter 27.*

Hardware profiles are included in Windows XP for convenience. They are intended to be a useful option for those who travel with laptops, not a security measure. In other words, if you have a user that you want to prohibit from using the modem, a hardware profile is not the answer. You will find that outside of the laptop realm, hardware profiles are rarely used.

Managing User Profiles

In Windows XP Professional, a user profile is a collection of environment settings that customize a user's interface. It can include display settings, network settings, printer settings, and so on. User profiles are of three types:

◆ Local

◆ Roaming

◆ Mandatory

User profiles are particularly useful when you have multiple users using the same workstation, or users that don't have an assigned desk location. If you and I use the same machine (you work days and I work the swing shift), you want to be able to have your settings (wallpaper, icons, printer, and network connections) every time you log in. So do I. User profiles is the answer.

The first time you log on to a computer, whether it's yours or that of someone else on your network, Windows XP Professional creates a *local user profile* for you that is specific to that machine. Since this is the first time you are logging on to this machine, Windows XP gives you what is called the *default user profile.* When you log off, any changes you've made to the environment during the sessions are saved in your local user profile. Local user profiles only apply to a local machine, hence their name.

NOTE *The* roaming user profile *and* mandatory user profile *configurations require a domain and will be covered in Chapter 17.*

To customize the default user profile so that each new user of the machine gets the same settings, follow these steps:

1. Log on to the computer as a new user.

2. Establish the desired settings, such as Start menu options, network connections, and so on, and then log off the computer.

3. Log back on to the computer as Administrator.

4. Right-click My Computer, and choose Properties from the shortcut menu to open the System Properties dialog box.

5. Click the Advanced tab, and then click Settings in the User Profiles section to open the User Profiles dialog box:

6. Highlight the profile that you want each new user to use, and then click Copy To to open the Copy To dialog box:

7. In the Copy Profile To box, enter the following path:

`%SYSTEMROOT%\Documents and Settings\Default User`

8. Click OK, and then click OK again.

If you should happen to delete a profile folder in the Documents and Settings folder, Windows XP Professional will react as if the user has never logged on to the system before. When the user logs on again, Windows will create a new profile folder for the user. This feature can be useful if the user has placed icons and information all over the Desktop and is now complaining that it keeps coming up as a mess. You can simply delete the profile folder, and a new one will be created the next time that user logs on. It will be the default environment as created in the Default User folder.

Connecting to Non-Microsoft Networks

Thinking that Microsoft-based operating systems are the only ones in existence on networks is short sighted. Although it's an oversight that Microsoft would surely allow you to maintain, now is a good time to discuss connecting to non-Microsoft operating systems and networks. This section specifically looks at connecting to Unix and Macintosh networks.

TIP *When working with multiple platforms, try to keep uniform usernames for all of your users. In other words, Sheila Sanders may have an easier time accessing resources if her account name is SSanders on all platforms, instead of Sheila on one and SSanders on another.*

Entering the Dark Place that Is Unix

Right now, you may be thinking, "But I don't know much about Unix, much less how it networks!" That's okay. By now, you have some knowledge of general networking principles, and the principles do not change from platform to platform. You still need to find a way to make the machines talk, and you still need to make resources available across the network.

Probably the biggest difference if you're using a Unix-based machine is the interface. Although there are some graphical interfaces for Unix (such as KDE and GNOME), most of the time Unix is run from a command prompt. Don't be scared of the dark place, just be able to type and you'll make it through. The good news is, accessing Unix-based resources from a Microsoft Windows XP Professional machine is incredibly similar to accessing Windows-based resources.

Microsoft offers two Unix interoperability products: Services for Unix 2.0 and Interix 2.2. The one you will be dealing with most is Services for Unix, which allows you to integrate your Windows XP Professional machine into a Unix environment. If you want to run Unix-based applications or logon scripts on your Windows XP Professional machine, you will need Interix.

NOTE *For purposes of this discussion, Unix, Solaris, and Linux support require the same configurations.*

The first thing you need to look at when trying to connect to a Unix-based machine is the network protocol. Unix uses TCP/IP by default, and so does Windows XP Professional. First problem solved. Just make sure the machines are configured properly.

NOTE *One of the great things about the TCP/IP protocol is that it's universal. Whether you're using Windows, Unix, or any other operating system, the rules for configuring addresses don't change. Therefore, if you're trying to communicate with a Unix machine, just make sure that all computers have the same network address, but a unique host address. If you've forgotten how this works, take a look at the "Configuring IP Addresses on a Network" sidebar earlier in this chapter.*

The next thing to look at is how the computers make requests. Windows XP Professional uses a protocol called Common Internet File System (CIFS) to make requests of the server. Unix uses the Network File System (NFS) protocol. Since the two are incompatible, we need to figure out a way to make the two platforms talk. Enter Services for Unix.

NOTE *Services for Unix is an umbrella term for four separate products: File Services for Unix, Client for NFS, Server for NFS, and Print Services for Unix. Only Print Services for Unix are automatically included with Windows XP Professional.*

Services for Unix contains many components—more than is necessary to cover here. Probably the most important ones are Client for NFS and Server for NFS. When you install Services for Unix on your Windows XP machine, these services allow you to not only request stuff from an NFS server but to host resources for NFS clients as well. Specifically, Services for Unix allows you to access files and printers on a Unix server, as well as have Unix machines access your files and printers. Services for Unix is a separate product that can be installed from its CD-ROM.

NOTE *Services for Unix is an optional add-on product that must be purchased from Microsoft.*

TIP *If you're planning to install Services for Unix 2.0, be aware of the telnet vulnerability described in Microsoft Knowledge Base article Q286043.*

Printing in Unix is also slightly different from Microsoft printing. Installing Services for Unix installs two critical printing components: Line Printer (lpr) and Line Printer Daemon (lpd). You can install Print Services for Unix from the Windows XP CD:

1. In Control Panel, click Network Connections.

2. Select the Advanced menu, then choose Optional Networking Components.

3. Place a check next to Other Network File and Print Services, and click Next.

4. Windows XP will copy the necessary files to your hard drive, and close the dialog box.

The lpr utility is what is used to send print jobs to the print service, which is lpd. Daemon, in Unix terms, simply refers to a service. If you wanted to, you could use lpr from a command prompt to send print jobs through lpd. It's easier to map to the printer, though. Here's how to add an LPT port:

1. Click Start, and choose Printers and Faxes.

2. Under Printer Tasks, select Add a Printer, which opens the Add Printer Wizard. Click Next.

3. Choose Local Printer Attached to This Computer, and clear the Automatically Detect check box.

4. Click Create a New Port, and for the Type of port, choose LPR Port. Click Next.

5. In the Name or Address of Server Providing lpd box, enter the DNS name or IP address of the host providing the lpd service (the Unix printer). You will also need to provide the name of the printer or print queue. Click Next.

6. The Wizard will finish the installation for you.

TIP   Services for Unix is not required for Unix and Windows to communicate. Samba is the Unix implementation of the Server Message Block format, which is the foundation of the NetBIOS protocol. If you install Samba on Unix (or Linux or Solaris), you don't need to make any changes to Windows XP. With Samba, shared Unix directories and printers work in a standard Microsoft Network Neighborhood or Domain.

Macintosh Networks

Networking professionals will tell you that the words "Macintosh" and "network" should never be used in the same sentence. Native Macintosh networking is horribly slow by today's standards, and creating Macintosh-accessible volumes on NT servers could cause crashes and headaches. Because of these issues, Macs don't have a good name in the PC-networking arena.

But for all the flak Macs get regarding networking, they make excellent graphics and design machines. Besides, most of the Macintosh networking components, including the NIC, are built-in.

Macintosh computers use the AppleTalk networking protocol by default. Fortunately, however, Macs also support TCP/IP. It's recommended that if you want to network with Macs, you should use the TCP/IP protocol. Windows XP Professional does not support the AppleTalk protocol.

Windows XP Professional does not come with any products or services to support Macs on a network. Windows 2000 Server comes with Services for Macintosh, which allows Mac users to save files on Windows 2000 servers. If you absolutely must get Windows XP Professional and Macs talking to each other, you will need a third-party solution. One such solution is PC MACLAN, by Miramar Systems.

NOTE *For more information about PC MACLAN, visit* `www.miramar.com/`.

Troubleshooting Windows XP Professional Networking

Because Windows XP Professional is a network operating system, it makes sense that you will probably encounter issues with your network from time to time. In most documentation you find today, the troubleshooting text tells you to perform "standard network troubleshooting" without ever telling you what that is. This section lets you in on that secret. Troubleshooting networking is one area in particular where my basic methodology will help you.

First, you start with any error message that Windows XP Professional gives you. This is always the first step in troubleshooting Windows XP Professional: Use whatever information it provides. Write the error message exactly as it appears because you can later use that to query the Knowledge Base in Help and Support Center. Next, you want to see what the Event Viewer can tell you. Event Viewer is probably the best friend you have in troubleshooting Windows XP Professional. It's not always clear and concise, but it will often tell you exactly what the problem is. It's always worth checking.

These things are true for any type of troubleshooting in Windows XP Professional. But basic network troubleshooting goes beyond Windows XP Professional's systems to encompass any network operating system. That's what we need to focus on in this section.

Is It Plugged In?

What do you need in order to have a conversation? You must have some kind of medium to carry the information from one person to another. You must also have some rules to determine how that conversation will take place. Imagine what happens when you meet someone on the street and strike up a conversation. You probably start by making eye contact, then smiling and speaking. If you both happen to speak at least one language in common, you can communicate easily. There may be a few failed attempts before you both find a language you can use, but eventually you will succeed.

A network is just like that. In its simplest form, a network can be two computers connected by a wire. When one wants to talk to the other, the first computer needs some kind of attention signal; then they both need to negotiate a common language and follow the rules of that language to communicate.

Networks can be simple systems or they can be complex. But however complicated they get, they all have certain things in common. They all have something connecting the nodes, and they all have at least one language. On most networks, the nodes are individual computers as well as intermediary systems such as routers, bridges, switches, and gateways. The language of a network is the protocol.

When troubleshooting any network system, keep these fundamental concepts in mind. Start with the communications medium. Is a proper cable plugged into the computer? Is the other end of the cable plugged into a hub or wall drop? If you are using coax cable, do you have a T-connector and possibly a terminator? Are the drivers for the network card installed and working? Do you have at least one protocol in common with the other computer?

These sound like simple questions, and they are, really. You might be surprised how often these simple questions will resolve your networking issues.

Configuration Testing

You will want to test your configuration if you can't connect to machines you think you should be able to. Keep the following principles in mind when troubleshooting networks:

◆ Isolate the problem before fixing it.

◆ Be familiar with the tools you have available.

◆ Always check the obvious things (i.e., connections) that could be wrong, no matter how silly it may seem.

When the system starts, you will know if Windows XP Professional can see the network during the logon procedure. You may see error messages, for example, if your TCP/IP address went awry or if the domain controller refuses to validate you into the domain. Even if no errors are immediately apparent, take a look in Event Viewer for potential conflicts. Event Viewer is a great tool for helping track down problems. To open Event Viewer, follow these steps:

1. Click Start ➣ All Programs ➣ Administrative Tools ➣ Computer Management to open the Computer Management window.

2. In the Computer Management pane, expand System Tools, and then expand Event Viewer.

3. Click System to display events in the pane on the right.

4. Look for red stop signs or yellow exclamation points. If you see one of these symbols, double-click it to open the Event Properties dialog box for that event, which will look similar to the following:

5. If the information in the Event Properties dialog box isn't sufficient to solve the problem, check the configuration of the component. In some cases, you may need to remove and reinstall it.

6. Click the Close button to close the Computer Management window.

TIP   When using Event Viewer to troubleshoot network problems, start at the top of the list and work down until you find event ID number 6005 with a source of eventlog. This represents the last time you booted the computer. The most likely source of your problems will be the event immediately above or immediately below the 6005 event. You should focus most of your efforts resolving these before moving on to the others.

Is Anybody Out There?

Most of the troubleshooting I've talked about so far has dealt with working on one computer at a time. Network troubleshooting often involves the connecting systems between the computers as much or more than the computers themselves. I've shown you many ways to work with problems on computers, but how do you see what's wrong with a whole network? That's what this section is about. Here I introduce you to some of the tools included in Windows XP Professional to troubleshoot the network.

The ultimate test of your configuration is being able to attach to all the resources you need. In Windows Explorer, look in My Network Places and click Entire Network; from there, clicking Microsoft Windows Network can give you insight into which parts of the network you can and cannot communicate with.

TIP   If you get an error message when viewing the Microsoft Windows Network or a workgroup, try viewing your computers and shares from the command line based on the Making a Direct Connection via UNC section earlier in this chapter.

TROUBLESHOOTING TCP/IP

The single most common network protocol today is TCP/IP. Its popularity is most likely due to the Internet, but it's also because TCP/IP is an industry standard suite of protocols. It is not just one protocol, but rather a group of them designed to perform specific tasks. The part that most people like is the industry standard part. That means that if you have Macs and NetWare and Unix computers on your network, your Windows XP Professional computer can communicate with all of them using TCP/IP. TCP/IP is also popular with support people because it has so many troubleshooting tools built into it.

Ping

The packet internetwork groper (Ping) is the most basic test of network communication over TCP/IP. What Ping does for you is bounce a series of packets off a remote host. You're essentially just saying "Hello?" over and over and (hopefully) getting a response each time. The basic syntax is `ping www.host.com` or `ping 10.1.0.44`.

So what does this tell you? Getting a response when pinging by IP address means that your network card is installed correctly, the driver is working, the TCP/IP protocol is working, Windows Sockets is working, the other computer is working, and everything in between is working. That's quite a lot of information for just one small command! When you ping by host name, you get all the previous information, plus you know that your hostname resolution is working.

You can also ping the address 127.0.0.1. This address is reserved for the local host (the local computer) and is a loop-back diagnostic test of your installed TCP/IP software. Successfully pinging the local host verifies that TCP/IP is successfully installed on the local computer.

With this in mind, follow this procedure to test your IP configuration and network connection:

NOTE *Some of these tests assume that your LAN is connected to the Internet.*

1. Test that you've installed the IP software by pinging the built-in IP loopback address. Type **ping 127.0.0.1**. If that fails, you know that you've done something wrong in the initial installation, so check that the software is installed on your system. This test does not put any messages out on the network; it just checks that the software is installed. By the way, the same thing happens if you ping your IP address, except that pinging your address also tests the network card.

   If that fails, your TCP/IP stack probably isn't installed correctly, or perhaps you mistyped the IP number (if it failed on your specific IP address but not on the loopback), or perhaps you gave the *same* IP number to another workstation.

2. Ping your default gateway to see that you can get to it, because it should be on your local subnet. For example, if your gateway were at 199.34.57.2, you would type **ping 199.34.57.2**, and you should get a response.

3. If you can't get to the gateway, check that the gateway is up and that your network connection is all right. Nothing is more embarrassing than calling in outside network support, only to find that your LAN cable fell out of the back of your computer.

4. Ping something on the other side of your gateway, such as an external DNS server. (Ping me, Mark Minasi, if you like: 199.34.57.1. I ought to be up just about all the time.) If you can't get there, it's likely that your gateway isn't working properly.

5. Next, test the name resolution on your system. Ping yourself *by name*. Instead of typing something such as **ping 199.34.57.35**, you'd type **ping test** (the machine you're on at the moment). That tests your DNS server, or your HOSTS file if you are using one instead of DNS.

6. Then, ping someone else on your subnet. Again, try using a fully qualified domain name on your local network, such as `mizar.Ursamajor.Edu`, rather than an IP address. If that doesn't work, use the IP address. If the IP address works, but the host name doesn't, you've got a problem with the HOSTS file or DNS.

7. Finally, ping someone outside your domain, such as `house.gov` (the U.S. House of Representatives), `www.yahoo.com`, or `orion01.Mmco.Com`. If that doesn't work but all the pings inside your network work, you've probably got a problem with your Internet provider.

WARNING *While pinging Web sites can help test connectivity, some Web sites do not allow pings in to their network. They block pings off as a security measure. So, the site may be up, but you won't get a response from a ping.* `Microsoft.com` *is a good example of this.*

If you're successful on all these tests, your TCP/IP connection should be set up properly.

Hostname

The hostname utility returns the hostname of the local computer. This can be helpful when you aren't exactly sure what it is.

IPConfig

IPConfig is right up there with ping when it comes to valuable TCP/IP utilities. This tool enables you to view some or all of your TCP/IP configuration (as the name might imply). To use it, type **ipconfig** at the command prompt to receive your IP address, subnet mask, and default gateway. If you type **ipconfig /all**, you will see a listing of every TCP/IP configuration for every interface on your computer. To give you some idea of the scope of information, Figure 16.5 shows the output of the `ipconfig /all` command.

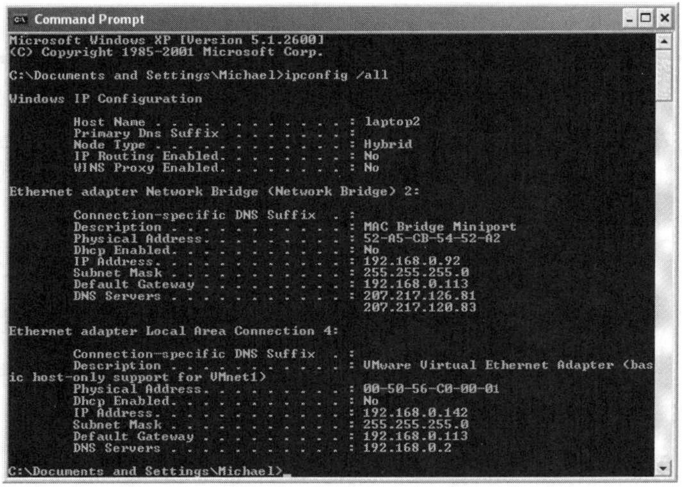

FIGURE 16.5

Output of the **ipconfig /all** command

If `ipconfig` reports an address that is unfamiliar to you, or reports no information at all, then you may have found your problem. IPConfig can also be used to release and renew IP addresses acquired through DHCP. The process for this is `ipconfig /release` then `ipconfig /renew`.

ARP

The ARP command views and modifies the Address Resolution Protocol (ARP) cache. ARP is used by TCP/IP to resolve an IP address such as 10.1.0.1 to a unique hardware address or MAC address.

The process that TCP/IP uses to communicate between two computers that are on the same subnet as the host server is shown in Figure 16.6. At the Application layer, the user types in a Universal Resource Locator (URL) to browse a favorite Web site. The user's computer is configured to use a certain Domain Name System (DNS) server that is responsible for resolving the name in the URL to an IP address. Then TCP/IP uses ARP to resolve that IP address to a unique physical address. Every network card has a unique hexadecimal number assigned to it when it is manufactured. That's the physical address or MAC address of the card.

FIGURE 16.6

Resolving a host name to a MAC address in TCP/IP networking

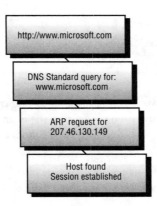

When ARP resolves an IP address to a unique hardware address, it stores the resolution in its cache. One thing you can do to improve the connection speed to a server that you use frequently is to make a static entry in the ARP cache. The command string below will add a static entry for a computer:

```
ARP -s 10.1.0.1 00-40-05-16-DA-8A
```

The -s switch tells the ARP command to make the entry permanent. You should be aware that *permanent* in this case means only until the computer is rebooted. If you want this entry to really be permanent, you must use the ARP command in a logon script or batch file in your Startup group.

TraceRT

The Trace Route (TraceRT) command is very much like Ping in that it bounces several packets of information off a remote computer. But TraceRT does more than that. It also shows a response from every router that the packets go through on their way to the remote computer.

This can be especially useful when dealing with communications issues with a remote host that is very far away (as in many routers away). TCP/IP uses a mechanism called a Time To Live (TTL) to determine how long a packet of data should be allowed on the network. If it didn't drop packets after a set period of time, packets would still be roaming the Internet from 20 years ago or more. The TTL is decremented automatically by at least one at each and every router it passes through (also called a *hop*). If a packet is forced to wait in a router due to network congestion, its TTL may be decremented by more than one.

TraceRT can reveal when the default TTL isn't high enough to allow for network congestion on the way to the remote host. The TTL setting can be adjusted in Windows XP Professional through the Registry at this location:

```
HKEY_LOCAL_MACHINE\System\CurrentControlSet\Services
\Tcpip\Parameters

Value name: DefaultTTL
```

The maximum setting for this value is 255.

The following troubleshooting scenario is a common support call in most networks. This time, imagine that you are the support person for a group of users on your company network and are attempting to correct a problem with network connectivity.

Scenario: Unable to "See" My Server

You have just received a call from a coworker, Mary, who is having trouble retrieving e-mail from her server. When you talk with her at her office, you learn that she is unable to open her e-mail application without receiving an error that the server could not be found. She is using TCP/IP as the only network protocol.

Has it ever worked before?   Mary tells you that she was able to get e-mail until yesterday when someone installed the latest version of the e-mail client. Ever since then, no luck.

Track possible approaches.   The problem could be the e-mail client but is more likely a simple configuration problem. You decide to do the following:

1. Verify IP address and configuration.

2. Test communication with the server.

3. Test communication with another computer other than the server.

The first thing to do is run `ipconfig /all` to verify the computer's current settings. You do this and find that the computer's IP address, subnet mask, and default gateway are all correct.

Next, you try pinging the server and get no response. You now try using Ping in a methodical process to determine where the failure is. You try pinging the default gateway (router) and you do receive a response. You don't know if there is another router between your default gateway and the e-mail server, but you can find out by using TraceRT. TraceRT returns success messages from three routers but fails to find the e-mail server.

You now know that the local computer's configuration is fine and that the default gateway is up and running. You know that at least three routers between the local computer and the e-mail server are functional. What you need to know is whether the last router is passing the information directly to the e-mail server and the e-mail server is down, or if there is another router beyond the third router that may be down.

When you pinged the e-mail server earlier, you did it by IP address. Now you try pinging by host name. The attempt fails, but it does resolve the name to an IP address, so you can tell that name resolution is happening correctly. Looking at the address of the e-mail server, you try another address that should be another server on that same section of the network. The Ping attempt to that address does respond.

NOTE   *Many network designers assign IP addresses in a set, predictable pattern. One common pattern is to assign all routers to the first 5 addresses on a subnet and servers to the last 20 addresses.*

What you know now is that the network is working correctly all the way to the remote subnet where the server is located, but the server itself is still not responding. This would be a great time to call the administrator of that server to see if the server is running. Another possible solution is that the server may have an incorrect TCP/IP configuration. If the server *is* running, you should verify the configuration on the server to see if it can communicate with any other computer.

TROUBLESHOOTING IPX/SPX

IPX/SPX used to be the protocol of choice on Novell networks, and it still is in many. It's a fine, routable protocol, relatively fast and easy to configure. So why is it being mentioned in a troubleshooting section? Because there are settings that are frequently misconfigured. The problems with the IPX/SPX protocol stem from those options for configuration that must be set correctly for two computers to hold a conversation. Most notable is the setting for frame type.

Frame type refers to the manner in which data is packaged when placed on the physical wire. It describes the header and addressing fields, the error correction, and the overall size of the data that can be sent at one time. IPX/SPX supports five frame types: 802.2, 802.3, Ethernet II, Ethernet SNAP, and Token Ring. The most common are 802.2 and 802.3. Windows XP Professional (like most operating systems) uses only one frame type at a time. Frame types are important because you must have the same frame type as the computer you are trying to communicate with. Mismatched frame types are probably the most common reason for failed communication over IPX/SPX.

In Microsoft networking, NWLink is called the IPX/SPX-compatible protocol even though it is fully compliant with all IPX/SPX standards. It is different only in that it provides a NetBIOS layer to facilitate name services on Microsoft network operating systems. For troubleshooting, that may or may not be important to know. What is important to know is that it is fully compliant with everyone else's IPX/SPX protocol.

Unlike TCP/IP in Windows XP Professional, NWLink doesn't ship with a bunch of troubleshooting utilities. That's usually not a problem because most issues will be resolved in the configuration. The primary tool for checking your NWLink configuration will be either the Network Connections applet in Control Panel or ipxroute.exe. Using ipxroute.exe enables you to view the current configuration of NWLink for each network adapter in the computer and to modify the IPX/SPX routing table if the computer has more than one network interface. Entering the command **ipxroute config** at the command prompt will display the current configuration of NWLink.

The properties dialog box for NWLink on Windows XP Professional covers the essentials—the adapter, the frame type, and the network number. The default setting for the frame type is Auto Detect. Microsoft tells us that this setting enables Windows XP Professional to scan the frame types being transmitted across the wire and then pick the most prevalent type. In fact, what appears to happen is that Windows XP Professional uses the very first frame type it comes across. Usually this will be correct. But on a network that utilizes multiple frame types, your Windows XP Professional computer may choose the wrong frame type when it starts up, causing you to be cut off from the servers you need.

The other important setting on this page is the network number. IPX/SPX handles routing of information by using these network numbers to identify each unique section of a network. Every segment (the section of network between two routers) must be assigned a unique network number. The default setting in Windows XP Professional takes care of that for you. When you are using Auto Detect for the frame type, it will also detect the local network number. If you change from Auto Detect to a specific frame type, you will need to enter a valid network number. Contact your network administrator if necessary.

How Do You Troubleshoot Windows XP Professional Network Architecture?

Although it's true that a good troubleshooting method can work you through almost any problem, at times you need to know more. In fact, I believe that the more you know about how something's put together, the easier it is to find what's wrong. That's certainly true of a complex system such as Windows XP Professional.

At the beginning of this chapter, I noted that troubleshooting is the process of going from a big-picture view of things to a small-detail view. Asking questions is the primary tool for accomplishing this, but knowledge is also a valuable tool. Figure 16.7 shows the overall network architecture of Windows XP Professional.

FIGURE 16.7

The network architecture of Windows XP Professional

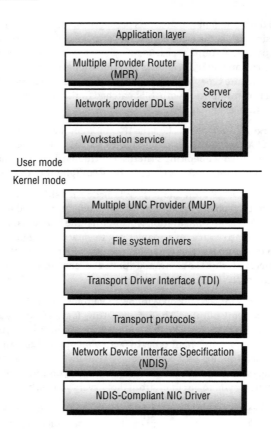

USER MODE COMPONENTS

The following are components of the user mode.

Application Layer

The Application layer is where your program is accepting your network requests. For example, when you type in the URL of your favorite Web site, you are interacting with the Application layer.

NOTE   This application layer is completely different from the OSI or TCP/IP application layers.

Multiple Provider Router

The Multiple Provider Router (MPR) is kind of like a traffic cop in that its job is to direct the flow of communication. Windows XP Professional uses the MPR only when you are mapping a network drive. Its task is to decide which of the installed network clients will do the best job in making the drive mapping.

The MPR is contained in the file `mpr.dll`.

Network Provider DLL

A DLL is a dynamic link library, which is basically a file that contains support functions for a program. In this case, the library of functions is part of a network client that is installed in Windows XP Professional.

There will be one provider DLL for each installed network client. The file for the native Windows XP Professional client, LanmanWorkstation, for example, is `ntlanman.dll`.

Workstation Service and Server Service

These are the user mode components of the Workstation and Server services. Essentially, these are "stubs" that provide user mode applications with access to the kernel mode Workstation and Server services of Windows XP Professional.

KERNEL MODE COMPONENTS

The following are components of the kernel mode.

Multiple UNC Provider

The Multiple UNC Provider (MUP) is a traffic cop like the MPR, except that instead of directing traffic when mapping drives, the MUP directs traffic when you are using a Universal Naming Convention (UNC) path.

You will be using the MUP's services whenever you click Start ➤ Run and type a path such as `\\Server5\Public`, or when your application connects to a server resource without mapping a drive letter first. An example is your e-mail program, which is configured to talk with one particular server to retrieve mail but doesn't require that you first map a drive to the share on the server.

When the MUP receives a request for service, its job is to decide which file system driver (which network client) can best answer the request, and then send the request to that driver.

The MUP is contained in the file `mup.sys`.

File System Drivers

File system drivers are the network redirectors and servers. When you install network support in Windows XP Professional, you always get two of these drivers by default. The first, `rdr.sys`, is the kernel mode component of the Workstation service, your native Windows XP Professional client. The second, `srv.sys`, is the kernel mode portion of the Server service.

There may be other file system drivers installed for other network clients. One common example is the `nwrdr.sys` driver for the Client Services for NetWare in Windows XP Professional.

Transport Driver Interface

Transport Driver Interface (TDI) doesn't actually exist as a file. It is what its name implies, an interface between the file system drivers and the transport protocols. The TDI is *exposed* by the two layers—that is to say that any file system driver for Windows XP Professional networking must support the functions used by TDI, and the same for the transport protocols.

This layered approach allows for portability and extensibility. Because of the TDI boundary layer, you can (in theory) install as many network clients and servers or as many protocols as you want on Windows XP Professional.

Transport Protocols

These are the protocols used to communicate on your network. The files for each should be easy to identify because they are usually just the name of the protocol with a SYS extension.

In theory, you can install an unlimited number of protocols in Windows XP Professional so long as they conform to the two boundaries in the network stack. Transport protocols must expose the TDI boundary on top and the NDIS layer on the bottom.

Network Device Interface Specification

Network Device Interface Specification (NDIS) is a boundary layer between the protocols and the adapter driver. But it has a more important job than that.

Years ago, when you wanted to develop a new driver for a network adapter card, you needed to think about details and settings like the media access scheme, error detection and correction, frame types, and so on, before you ever got to the part of the driver that just ran the card. NDIS was an effort by Microsoft, Intel, 3Com, and other companies to solve this problem. By conforming to a known standard, they could remove the common functions from the driver and load them into a library of functions that every network needs. Essentially, they wanted to stop reinventing the wheel every time they brought out another card.

NDIS, as it is implemented in Windows XP Professional, is an interesting component. It is both a file and a boundary layer. As a file, `ndis.sys` is a driver file that acts like a DLL in that it loads into memory and anybody who knows how to talk to it can ask NDIS for support. As a boundary, it defines a standard form of communication between the transport protocols and the network adapter card.

NDIS-Compliant Network Adapter Driver

At the bottom of the stack but certainly very important, the Network Interface Card (NIC) driver is responsible for error-free transmission and reception of data on the physical network medium.

Using the NDIS standard enables you to install as many NICs as you want in a computer (of course, you only have so many slots in your computer). As long as the drivers comply with the NDIS standard, you can bind multiple cards to one protocol or multiple protocols to one NIC.

The file containing the driver is named according to the naming convention of the manufacturer, but they all end with a SYS extension.

Quick Advice

As mentioned previously, troubleshooting is best learned by doing. There really is no good substitute for experience. To make things easier, though, there are some quick tips you can always keep in mind when troubleshooting a network:

- Always check your connections. Try another network cable if possible.

- Check and double-check your IP configuration, including IP address, subnet mask, default gateway, and DNS server addresses.

- Run `ipconfig` and `ping`. Make sure you're set up properly, and see what, if anything, you *can* connect to.

- Look in Event Viewer for any errors.

- Use your help and online resources.

- Delete and reinstall the network adapter if necessary.

Also, the Windows Help and Support center has a lot of good information, including Wizards, to assist in your troubleshooting. Take one step at a time, and if you make configuration changes, change one thing, test, and then change another if necessary. Don't change a bunch of stuff all at once, because you'll never know which change was the right one. One last thing—if you see someone troubleshooting a problem, and they say something like, "Huh, that's not supposed to happen," or "That's weird. . .," think about how silly a statement that *really* is. If everything was working as advertised, then why are they troubleshooting in the first place?

Summary

In this chapter, we've looked at how to set up and configure a network, create shares, attach to network resources, use user profiles and hardware profiles, and troubleshoot your network when things go awry. In the next chapter, we'll look at how to connect to a domain.

Chapter 17

Connecting to Domains

ALTHOUGH PEER-TO-PEER WORKGROUPS HAVE beauty in their simplicity, there are some limitations. As an example, did you know that with Windows XP Professional, Microsoft has limited workgroups to 10 computers? For larger networks, you will need to create a domain.

A Microsoft Windows domain is a network with a single database of usernames, passwords, profiles, and more. Once you get an account on a domain, you can log on through any computer on the network and have access to your files and preferences. You can even log on to the domain remotely from halfway around the world. Except for the limits you might encounter in network speed, everything else would be the same.

In Chapters 15 and 16, you learned to configure and install networks in a peer-to-peer relationship. Chapter 15 also described the client-server relationships that are associated with larger computer networks. The lessons of these chapters apply equally well here. For smaller networks, the required network hardware isn't significantly different between a peer-to-peer and a client-server domain based network.

Windows XP Professional is an excellent client on a network domain. In this chapter, we'll look at many of the decisions you will need to make in order to get the networking features to run reliably in that environment. You'll also learn how to connect documents and printers shared in the domain. To enable the consistent look and feel, you'll also create roving profiles for users and hardware. Finally, the chapter wraps up with a section on troubleshooting your domain.

In this chapter:

◆ Setting up a domain

◆ Requirements on the domain server

◆ Attaching to network resources

◆ Using profiles

◆ Troubleshooting

Setting Up a Domain

The basic reasons for a network are the same for peer-to-peer or client-server networks. It allows you to share files, printers, applications, and more. However, a domain can let you do more. With its centralized database of user names, you can use the same username and password on any computer on the domain.

As with peer-to-peer networks, domains increase user productivity. With their dedicated servers, domains are better at supporting collaboration. The following is an example of how this can work.

In our offices, Leslie is one of several engineers. The engineering office is 50 miles away from the manufacturing plant, but the engineers need to travel to the plant often to check on the product. Sydney is the manufacturing supervisor who is in constant need of engineering help. So, the network problems that we need to solve are as follows:

◆ Setting up workstations at the engineering and manufacturing facilities for all users

◆ Creating a common database for the engineers, accessible by manufacturing

Let's solve their problem with a client-server network on a Microsoft domain. With this type of network, Leslie can easily access her drawings from either facility, and Sydney can review the designs as they are developed. Assuming that both computers are running Windows XP Professional, here's how to get both users access to Leslie's files from any facility:

1. Using the user account, the computer account, and any folders that are set up for her on the domain controller, Leslie connects her Windows XP Professional workstation to the domain. She starts saving her engineering drawings on the domain server.

2. The network administrator sets up a roving profile on the server. Whenever Leslie logs on to the domain, she gets the same roving profile. It doesn't matter what workstation she uses.

3. The network administrator gives Sydney a different account on the domain controller. Sydney's username is included in a group with permissions to access Leslie's folder.

Now Leslie can access her drawings and files from either facility. Sydney can view Leslie's engineering drawings as required, so she can plan future manufacturing activity.

These actions apply on a server used as a domain controller. Domain controllers are by definition configured on computers with one of the Windows Server operating systems. Therefore, many of these steps are for the administrator responsible for the domain, and are beyond the scope of this book.

Windows XP Professional is designed to work in a variety of networking situations. XP makes the perfect network client for both home and office users. It doesn't matter if your network servers are running NetWare, Unix, or some other platform; Windows XP Professional will play nice with a variety of network operating systems. Windows XP Professional can also act as a server in a pinch—although you're better off going with a true server product for a long-term solution.

MICROSOFT DOMAINS AND INTERNET DOMAINS

Microsoft domains and Internet domains are related, but not identical concepts. A Microsoft domain includes a group of computers with a common database of users, groups, files, and so on. The Internet concept of a domain is based on a hierarchical organization of computers in a network, without any requirement for a common database of any sort. However, you can organize a Microsoft domain in the Internet hierarchical style.

For example, if you wanted to organize the Microsoft computers that belong to the mommabears.com network, you could give them the following names:

```
w95a.ms.mommabears.com
w98b.ms.mommabears.com
w2000c.ms.mommabears.com
wxpprod.ms.mommabears.com
wxpserver.ms.mommabears.com
```

All five computers (w95a, w98b, w2000c, wxpprod, wxpserver) would belong to the ms subdomain in the mommabears.com Internet domain. However, in a Microsoft domain, you don't have to follow Internet domain naming rules. Alternatively, you can follow the rules you used when you installed Windows XP Professional in Chapter 2, where the name of a computer is limited to 15 characters. This is also known as a NetBIOS name.

Requirements on the Domain Server

As a Windows XP Professional power user, you'll sometimes need to know the basics of what an administrator does on a domain server. The details of this process are beyond the scope of this book. You wouldn't want to see detailed information about configuring Windows NT or 2000 Server in a book on XP Professional, anyway.

A domain controller includes the information that you need to connect to that domain from a workstation. There are four basic steps that an administrator has to take on a properly configured domain controller.

- ◆ Create a User Account
- ◆ Create a Computer Account
- ◆ Set Up Appropriate Profiles
- ◆ Identify the New Computer

For more information on configuring a domain controller, refer to *Mastering Windows 2000 Server, Fourth Edition* from Sybex.

User Account

You need a user account on a domain controller in order to connect to a domain. By default, that account has a standard set of rights and privileges to certain folders on the server, including a data folder for your everyday work files. In addition, the user account of anyone who needs access to your work should be made a member of a group with appropriate rights to your data folder.

User accounts on a domain controller are different from user accounts in Windows XP Professional. They are kept on separate databases. Once your computer is configured for a domain, you can log in to either system through your Windows XP Professional computer.

When you start your computer, a domain-enabled XP Workstation makes you use the Ctrl-Alt-Del key combination to get to the Log On to Windows login screen. At the login screen, you can select where you want to log in.

1. At the login screen, if you don't already see the Log on to: drop down box, click Options.

2. Use the Log on to: drop down box to select whether you want to log on to the local computer or a domain.

3. Enter the username and password for the database you selected.

4. Click Start.

NOTE *If your XP Workstation hasn't been configured for a domain yet, continue to the "Connecting to a Domain" section later in this chapter for instructions.*

Computer Account

Before you can connect your Windows XP computer to a Microsoft domain, your computer also needs an account on the domain controller. Once created by your network administrator, you'll need to provide the computer account name and password to connect your XP Professional computer to that domain.

Alternatively, your administrator might give you temporary access to an administrative username on the domain, which you could use to create a computer account when you connect your XP Professional computer.

Profiles

In Chapter 16, I described the basics of user profiles on an XP Professional computer in a peer-to-peer network. There are two other profiles available: roaming and mandatory. Both require a domain and are discussed later in the chapter. However, to support access to your files and settings from any workstation on the domain, the domain administrator should set up a roaming or mandatory profile when he creates your user account on the domain.

Name of Domain

The final item you need to connect to a domain is the name. It could look like an Internet domain name such as `mommabears.com`, or it could be a NetBIOS style name such as DOMAIN-COMPANY.

Connecting to a Domain

To summarize the previous sections, you need to get the following information from your system administrator to connect to a domain:

◆ Your domain username

◆ Your domain password

◆ The name of the domain that you will join

◆ Your computer name (you may have to provide the computer name to the administrator, especially if you configured it in a workgroup)

◆ IP configuration details for the domain

NOTE *With the information shown above, you can set up your computer to join the domain during the Windows XP Professional installation process.*

Configuring Windows XP for a Domain

But you may not be able to just connect. First, you need to check to see if your IP configuration parameters are compatible.

When you get the configuration parameters you need from the domain administrator, remember that the domain probably includes a substantial number of computers. There may even be multiple LANs on the same domain. This means you'll probably have a DNS, DHCP, and possibly a WINS server on the domain. If you don't, or if you recognize a DNS server from an outside network, be skeptical.

IP CONFIGURATION

It's easier to configure your computer on a peer-to-peer network. As you read in Chapter 16, it's just a matter of selecting a group of IP addresses for your LAN, and typing them in with associated subnet masks, gateway addresses, and possibly the DNS addresses from your ISP.

TIP *Most domains include a DHCP server. If this applies to you, consult your network administrator. Depending on your domain's DHCP configuration, you may be able to skip some of the following steps.*

There is more to configure when you're getting XP Professional ready to connect to a domain. To see what I mean, open up the properties for your network adapter. Click Start ➤ All Programs ➤ Accessories ➤ Communications ➤ Network Connections. Right-click the connection that you're using and then click Properties in the shortcut menu. For example, Figure 17.1 shows the properties for my computer's Network Bridge.

FIGURE 17.1
Network Bridge
properties

Now highlight Internet Protocol (TCP/IP), and then click Properties. You'll see where you may already have configured your IP and DNS addresses. Figure 17.2 illustrates this window with static IP addresses, and DNS server IP addresses. Alternatively, you can select Obtain an IP Address Automatically. Your computer would first look to the DHCP server for an IP address assignment. If none were available, it would use the Automatic Private IP Addressing (APIPA) system. These systems are described in more detail in Chapter 16.

FIGURE 17.2
IP address properties

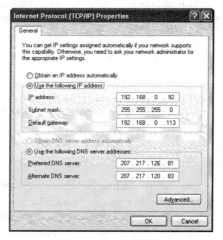

Additional IP and Gateway Addresses

Click Advanced to open the Advanced TCP/IP Settings window. It includes four tabs. You should see the IP Settings tab by default, as shown in Figure 17.3. You can assign additional IP addresses to your NIC. If there is more than one way for messages to leave your network, you can also assign additional Default Gateways. Just click the appropriate Add button. Finally, the automatic metric setting is checked by default. It's designed to optimize network traffic through your gateway(s).

FIGURE 17.3

You can add more
IP addresses and
gateways.

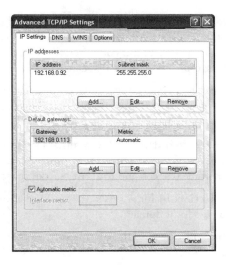

NOTE *Multiple default gateways are more common in a domain. While additional gateways can add to your security challenges, it also provides a backup if you need to ensure reliable connections to other networks and/or the Internet.*

Additional DNS Information

In a domain, your computers need a DNS server as an address book to figure out how to find other computers. Corporate domains include more than one DNS server. If one goes down or needs maintenance, backups keep a network going. If the domain is large, additional DNS servers help keep any one server from becoming overloaded.

Click the DNS tab. As you can see in Figure 17.4, you can add as many DNS addresses as you might need. The other options in this tab are as follows:

FIGURE 17.4

You can set up DNS
resolution in a num-
ber of ways.

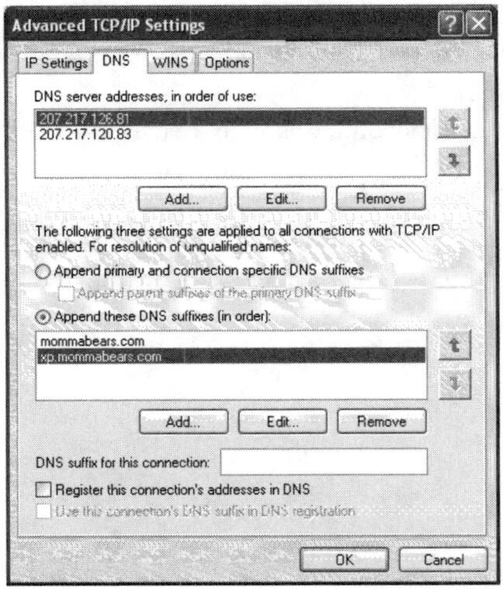

Append primary and connection specific DNS suffixes: Adds the name of your domain to the end of any specified computer name. For example, if you have a computer on the `xp.mommabears` `.com` network and searched for the laptop2 computer, this option assumes that you're really looking for the computer at `laptop2.xp.mommabears.com`.

Append parent suffixes of the primary DNS suffix: Uses parent suffixes. For example, the parent suffix of xp.mommabears.com is mommabears.com. Thus, if your computer can't find a `laptop2.xp.mommabears.com` computer, it would then look for `laptop2.mommabears.com`.

Append these DNS suffixes (in order): Adds the suffixes in the text box shown below. For the example shown in Figure 17.4, if you searched for a computer named bigshot, it would automatically look for `bigshot.mommabears.com` and `bigshot.xp.mommabears.com`, in that order.

DNS suffix for this connection: Includes this suffix if all other options fail. Normally, you should enter the name of the local domain.

Register this connection's addresses in DNS: Requests that your DNS server include the name of your computer in its records.

Use this connection's DNS suffix in DNS registration: Requests that your DNS server include the name of your domain in its database.

WARNING   *If you've specified DNS servers on the Internet, don't select either of the last two options under the DNS tab. At best, your ISP might get annoyed. It also provides an easy way for hackers to bypass your firewall. The exception is if you're using XP Professional as a server, with a "real" (not private) IP address on the Internet. But most ISPs charge more before they'll allow you to set up a server on their network.*

WINS

An alternative to DNS on Microsoft Windows networks is the Windows Internet Naming Service (WINS). Like DNS, WINS provides a database of computer names and IP addresses. The advantage is that WINS servers are automatically updated. However, Microsoft's relatively new Dynamic DNS service also provides for automatic updates. Therefore, you're more likely to use WINS on domains governed by older Microsoft servers such as NT 4.0. Click the WINS tab to review the information shown in Figure 17.5.

Because WINS will eventually become obsolete, I cover it in less detail. Under the WINS tab, you can include the IP addresses of WINS servers. Alternatively, LMHOSTS is a text file that you can substitute for a WINS server.

Generally on a Microsoft network, you want to enable NetBIOS over TCP/IP. However, this may already be set through your DHCP server. In any case, follow the instructions from your network administrator.

FIGURE 17.5

You can also set up WINS to help find computer names.

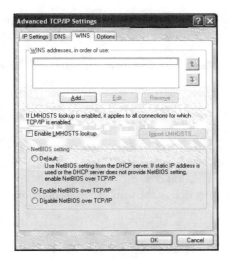

Options

Click the Options tab. The only default option available in XP Professional is IP filtering, which allows you to block some of the ports and protocols used in TCP/IP communication. This is a form of a firewall, which regulates traffic to and from a network. Under the Options tab, click Properties to get to the TCP/IP Filtering window shown in Figure 17.6.

FIGURE 17.6

You can filter a number of TCP/IP ports.

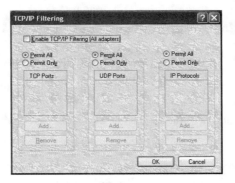

There are over 65,000 TCP/IP ports available. The first 1,024 ports are reserved for basic communication. For example, port 80 is reserved for HTTP, port 21 for FTP, and port 25 for sending mail (SMTP). It's common for a "hacker" to use one of these ports to get into a computer. The current list of TCP/IP port numbers is maintained by the Internet Assigned Numbers Authority at www.iana.org/assignments/port-numbers.

There are 255 IP protocol numbers available, which help define the purpose of each packet. For more information on IP protocol numbers, see www.iana.org/assignments/port-numbers.

Generally, you should limit port numbers and protocol numbers only on an Internet gateway. Creating these limits on a computer inside a LAN could limit what you can do on that network.

On most domains, Windows XP Professional computers are not used as gateways. If you want to set up an Internet gateway on an XP Professional computer, see Chapter 11. The ICS/ICF settings configured in that chapter are also an easier way to create a firewall.

IDENTIFICATION

Now you're ready to change the identification of your computer from a workgroup to a domain. Windows XP Professional does not have an Identification tab like Windows 98 and NT did. Instead, that information is associated with the properties for My Computer. To access these properties, right-click My Computer, choose Properties, and then choose Computer Name. As shown in Figure 17.7, you will see your computer name, as well as the workgroup or domain name. You can also change that information here.

FIGURE 17.7

The Computer Name tab shows if your computer is part of a workgroup or a domain.

See also page 91 in "Essential Skills for Windows XP Professional" also provides a visual guide to the Computer Name tab.

MAKING THE CONNECTION

Once you are armed with this information, you can join a domain using the Computer Name Changes dialog box in System Properties or the Network Identification Wizard. Since using the Wizard is more descriptive, I'll walk through the process using it next. If you want to use the Computer Name Changes dialog box, follow these steps to open it:

1. Click Start, right-click My Computer, and choose Properties from the shortcut menu to open the System Properties dialog box.

2. Click the Computer Name tab, and then click Change to open the Computer Name Changes dialog box.

3. In the Member Of section, click the Domain option, and then enter the name of the domain. Click OK to close the Computer Name Changes dialog box, and then click OK again to close the System Properties dialog box. If prompted, enter a username and password *on the domain* with the authority to add your computer.

See also pagees 91–92 in "Essential Skills" for a visual guide to connecting to a domain.

Now, let's step briskly through the Wizard:

1. In the System Properties dialog box, click the Computer Name tab, and then click Network ID to start the Network Identification Wizard.

2. At the Welcome screen, click Next to open the Connecting to the Network screen.

3. Click the option that tells Windows XP Professional this computer is part of a business network, and then click Next to open the next Connecting to the Network screen.

4. Click the My Company Uses a Network with a Domain option, and then click Next.

5. Be sure that you have all the information listed on the Network Information screen, and then click Next.

6. On the User Account and Domain Information screen, enter your domain username, your domain password, and your domain name. Click Next. If you see confirmation that your computer already has an account on the domain, click Yes.

7. On the Computer Domain screen, enter the name of your computer and your new domain, and click Next.

8. You'll see the Domain User Name and Password dialog box. Enter a domain username, password, and domain with sufficient permissions to add this Windows XP Professional machine to the domain (the account must have Administrator rights in the domain), and then click OK. At this point, Windows XP Professional creates a machine name within the domain. Depending on your network, this could take a few minutes. When Windows XP Professional has created the machine name, it will return you to the User Account dialog box. Click Next.

9. On the Access Level Wizard, select the type of access that you want for the local computer. You can choose from three radio buttons: Standard User, Restricted User, and Other. Standard users can modify the computer and install applications but have no rights to read files that do not belong to them. Restricted users can save documents but have no rights to modify the computer or add applications. The Other option allows you to insert the user into a different group, such as Administrators, which would grant complete rights to the entire Windows XP Professional computer. Select a radio button, and then click Next.

10. The final dialog box, Completing the Network Identification Wizard, will appear. Click Finish and then click OK to reboot.

After the computer reboots, follow these steps to log on to the domain:

1. At the Windows logon prompt, press Ctrl+Alt+Del as you normally would to log on to Windows XP Professional.

2. Enter a username to log on to the domain (this is not always the same name as the local user-name), enter a password, and select the appropriate domain. You can either type in the domain name or select it from the drop-down list that Windows XP Professional automatically builds for you. If your domain name does not appear, click the Options button.

3. Click the OK button to complete the domain authentication process.

One thing to keep in mind is that these steps work only if the computer and user accounts already exist on the domain. In addition, only domain administrator types have a username authorized to add your computer to the domain. It's not as though they want to give out the domain administrator password to everyone. If your user account does not have the necessary rights to join your computer to the domain, you may need some assistance from your network administrator.

REJOINING A WORKGROUP

It is easier to reconfigure your computer from a domain to a workgroup. First, make sure your IP address settings are consistent with other computers on your workgroup. For more information, see Chapter 16. Then return to the Computer Name tab shown in Figure 17.7. Click Change. Select the Workgroup option and then enter the name of your workgroup.

When you click OK, you'll be prompted for the username and password of an administrator on your computer (not on the domain). Once entered, XP Professional joins the workgroup of your choice.

Attaching to Network Resources

After your network is configured for sharing, one of the easiest ways to test your network connections is to attach to network resources. The process is nearly identical to that for a peer-to-peer network. In fact, if you've read Chapter 16, a lot of the following sections will seem familiar; they're just repackaged for domains. You can test your connections in the following ways:

◆ By browsing My Network Places

◆ By mapping a network drive

◆ By using UNCs to connect directly

See also pages 73–74 in "Essentials Skills" for a visual guide to connecting a network drive.

Browsing My Network Places

Open Windows Explorer. Click My Network Places to open a window that displays the options on your network. Double-click a computer to view and connect to its shared resources.

On a domain, this may not work if you didn't use the domain username and password. However, the other two methods can work, because they allow you to enter the domain username and password in order to make the connection.

Mapping a Network Drive

The basic process for mapping a network drive is essentially identical to that described for a peer-to-peer network in Chapter 16. If you're not logged in with a domain username and password, there are two differences:

Folder: Specify the name of the domain server and the associated share name in the Folder text box. In Figure 17.8, that would be net-server and inetpub.

User Name: Select different username. In the Connect As window that appears, type in a domain username and password. An example is shown in Figure 17.9.

FIGURE 17.8

Just specify the name of the domain server and shared directory.

FIGURE 17.9

If you're an authorized user on a domain, just specify your domain username and password.

ALTERNATE DOMAIN ACCOUNTS

But what if you are attaching to another server and you do not have an account on that server? This happens a lot to administrators.

If you have an administrator called Sheila Sanders, Sheila will have an account on her primary server that she logs on to. In addition, Sheila may need to attach to other servers that have resources she wants to use, even though she doesn't have an account on those servers. Another classic example would be that Sheila logs on to a Windows XP server as Sheila but has an account named SSanders on a NetWare server.

To resolve this issue, Sheila could log on to the Windows XP server as Sheila, but when she maps a drive to a Novell server, she could use the Connect As dialog box to connect to the NetWare server as SSanders. If the Sheila password on the Windows XP server and the SSanders account on NetWare are the same, Sheila gets direct access to the NetWare directory. If the passwords are different, Sheila will be prompted to enter a password for the NetWare server when she clicks OK to map the network drive.

Making a Direct Connection via a UNC

Alternatively, you can use various forms of the net command at the command line interface. Here's how to use the net view command:

1. To display a list of the computers on your network, type **net view** at the command prompt.

2. To display a list of the resources on a particular server, append the name of the machine. For example, if the server name was spiritwolf, you'd enter **net view \\spiritwolf**. This works even if spiritwolf is the server for your domain.

3. To view the resources of a machine in another domain, for example, the server spiritwolf in the domain hq, you'd enter the following:

   net view \\spiritwolf /domain:hq

4. To display a list of all the domains on the network, simply enter **net view /domain**.

USING NET USE: CONNECTING TO OTHER DRIVES AND PRINTERS

After you've browsed the network with the net view command, you can connect to all the available goodies (or disconnect from those you don't want) with the net use command. Use this command to connect to network resources as drives D through Z and printer ports LPT1 through LPT9.

WARNING *Drive letters can only be used once. So if your CD-ROM is drive D, you will only have drive letters E through Z available.*

To display information about the workstation's current connections, type **net use** without options, and you'll see something like this:

CONNECTING TO A RESOURCE IN THE LOCAL DOMAIN

To connect to a shared resource, such as a printer shared as lexmarko on server spiritwolf, type **net use lpt1: \\spiritwolf\lexmarko**. If you want to specify domain username mjang and password, type **net use lpt1:** \\spiritwolf\lexmarko * **/USER:mjang**, then you're prompted for a password.

USING LONG FILENAMES IN UNCS

If you wanted to connect to a folder called Wpfiles on the spiritwolf server and make that your E drive, you'd substitute **E:** for **lpt1:** and **Wpfiles** for **lexmarko** in the preceding example. Your command would be **net use E: \\spiritwolf\wpfiles**. You get to specify the port name or drive letter that you want to connect a resource to, but again, you're restricted to drive letters D through Z and ports LPT1 through LPT9.

If the computer you're getting the resource from has a blank character in its name (that is, the computer name has two words in it), you must put the name in quotation marks, like this:

```
"\\eisa server"
```

If a different username and password is attached to the resource that you're trying to connect to, such as on a domain server, you need to include that in your connection command, like this:

```
net use lpt1: \\ted\hp4m * USER:mjang
```

The asterisk tells the net command to prompt you for the password.

TIP   *When you use the* net *command to connect to a share, don't use more than one domain username.*

CREATING A DRIVE MAPPING FOR YOUR HOME FOLDER

To connect to your home folder (the folder on the server that has been assigned to you, assuming there is one), type the following:

```
net use /home
```

with the (optional) password and username on the end as just explained.

If you want to make the connection for another user, rather than for yourself, add the user's name (Frank) to the end of the line, like this:

```
net use lpt1: \\ted\hp4m * user:frank
```

The asterisk tells net to prompt you for a password. If the user for whom you are making the connection is in another domain, the user part of the statement looks like this:

```
user:domainname/frank
```

where domainname is the name of that user's home domain.

CONNECTING TO A RESOURCE IN ANOTHER DOMAIN

If you want to connect to a resource in a domain that is not your usual one, you must first log on to that domain. One way to do this is to have a user account for yourself in the second domain. Managing multiple accounts for one person can get extremely cumbersome, so it's not the best setup. Another way is to have a trust relationship between your domains. Trust relationships allow users in one domain the potential to access resources in the other domain. I say potential because we still have to deal with permissions.

Think of trust relationships in human terms. If I trust you, I may let you drive my car (my resource). However, you still can't drive my car until I give you the keys (permissions). But if I don't trust you, there's no way I am handing you my keys! After you've logged on to the proper domain, the process of connecting to resources is the same as described above.

NOTE   Trust relationships are set up between domains, not specific computers. Generally, the setting of trust relationships is a domain administrator's responsibility, and not something you will do from Windows XP Professional; however, it's important to talk about, since you may be part of a domain and need to access resources in another domain.

Using Profiles

Windows XP Professional uses two types of profiles: user and hardware. Although each serves a specific purpose, both types of profiles are used to customize the computing environment. In this section, we'll look at how to create and manage them.

Creating Hardware Profiles

Basic hardware profiles are addressed in Chapter 16. It makes no difference whether you're connecting a computer to a workgroup or a domain, the way you create and manage a different hardware profile remains the same.

User Profiles

In Windows XP Professional, a user profile is a collection of environment settings that customize a user's interface. It can include display settings, network settings, printer settings, and so on. User profiles are of three types:

- Local
- Roaming
- Mandatory

Local user profiles only apply to a local machine, hence their name. Since local user profiles apply to the local computer, they are covered in more detail in Chapter 16.

A *roaming user profile* can only be created by your system administrator and is stored on the server. A roaming user profile contains settings that are specific to you and is loaded whenever you log on to any computer on the network. Local user profiles and roaming user profiles contain the same types of information. The only differences are that a roaming profile is stored on a server (as opposed to the local machine), and roaming profiles follow you no matter where you log in. You must have a domain to use roaming user profiles.

TIP   If your network uses roaming user profiles, educate users to not store large files on their desktop, which is part of their profile. Every time they log on, the profile needs to be copied from the server it's stored on to the local machine. If there are large files as part of that profile, logging on to the network could take an excruciatingly long time.

A *mandatory user profile* specifies settings for an individual or a group of users and can only be created or modified by your system administrator. There is a major philosophical difference between mandatory user profiles and the other two we have discussed. With local and roaming profiles, users are allowed to customize their settings any way they choose. While this allows for freedom and personalization, people are known to abuse these types of privileges. With a mandatory user profile, the user gets a specified environment every time they log on. They are allowed to make changes, but every time they log off and back on, their settings are back to defaults. Most of the time, when users realize that their changes are not being kept, they will simply stop making changes at all.

NOTE *Mandatory user profiles will only work if you are implementing them across a network. They will not work locally.*

Please note that mandatory profiles do *not* keep users from making changes to their desktop settings. Mandatory profiles just don't save those changes that the user does make. If you want to keep people from changing desktop settings at all, you need to use either Local Security Policy (covered in Chapter 20), or Group Policies (which can affect an entire network).

Attaching to Network Resources Using Login Scripts

A very common way in which you will attach to network resources is through network drive mappings that the network administrator created in a login script. Often drive letters such as H and M are pointing to files on a file server on the network. The good news is, login scripts run automatically every time you log in (hence their name); therefore, they require no thinking on the part of the user.

You will be able to distinguish between network drives and local hard drives by the icon associated with the drive. Network drives have the little T connector and cable beneath the icon. From time to time, you may see a drive with a red X across it. This symbol indicates that you formerly had a drive mapped to this drive letter, but the system cannot find the network location at this time. This situation happens most frequently if you are accessing the network remotely via a modem, but could also be a sign of connectivity problems.

Troubleshooting Domains

Entire books have been written on the topic of troubleshooting networks. It's such a voluminous topic that it requires a lot of attention. To that end, there is no way this chapter can teach you everything you need to know to troubleshoot network problems. The best training for troubleshooting is simply hands-on experience. That said, this section will give you some pointers to get you started.

Receiving the Error Message "No Domain Server Was Available"

When logging on to the server, you may get an error message stating that no domain server is available to authorize you to log on to a domain. Often this error message will prevent you from seeing some resources in My Network Places and prevent you from accessing the network entirely.

NOTE *The title of this section is a good example of a specific error message. Whenever you receive specific error messages, write them down. They are invaluable to have when searching your resources for a solution. You're never going to know how to fix everything right away, but if you know where to look for help, you'll be a lot further ahead in the game.*

TIP   A good place to get started is Microsoft's Knowledge Base. It has a lot of articles about known error messages and may be able to help you. Go either to Microsoft's Web page (`www.Microsoft.com`) and click the Support link, or to `support .Microsoft.com`. You will be able to type in your error message and search through all of Microsoft's products, or choose the specific product you are interested in. The support page also provides a download area for patches, and newsgroups for you to post questions.

This message appears when the system is unable to contact a domain controller for the domain that you are logging on to. The obvious problem could be that the server is down. Another common cause of this error is that a switch, router, or gateway is malfunctioning in your environment; so check the hub and the bridges to make sure they are operating normally.

Easily the most common occurrence of this problem is when TCP/IP is the primary transport protocol in your environment. If the workstation is on one physical segment of the network and the domain controller is on another segment of the network, often the client machine is unable to see the server via NetBIOS. To test this situation, see if you can ping the server's address. If you can ping the server by using its IP address but are unable to contact the server for domain logon authentication, you have determined the cause of your dilemma.

One common solution is to install a Windows Internet Naming System Server (WINS Server) in your environment. It will handle the NetBIOS computer name to IP address name resolution (in much the same way that a DNS server handles IP host name to IP address conversions). Once the Windows Internet Naming Service is installed on a server, the Windows XP Professional computer must point to the WINS Server. To point the client to the WINS Server, follow these steps:

1. Click Start ➢ All Programs ➢ Accessories ➢ Communications ➢ Network Connections to open the Network Connections folder.

2. Right-click Local Area Connection (or Network Bridge if active) and select Properties to open the Properties dialog box for your connection.

3. Double-click Internet Protocol (TCP/IP) to open the Internet Protocol (TCP/IP) dialog box.

4. On the General tab, click the Advanced button to open the Advanced TCP/IP Settings dialog box. Select the WINS tab.

5. Click Add to open the TCP/IP WINS Server dialog box.

6. In the WINS Server box, enter the IP address of the WINS server, and click Add.

7. Click OK and then click OK twice more. Close Network Connections.

While installing WINS is a common solution to this problem, it has a few drawbacks. One, it means you must have an additional server available to run this service. Yes, WINS can be installed on a server that's already doing something else, like a file or print server, but why pile more work on that machine? Two, Microsoft is moving away from using WINS, and moving toward DNS for all name resolution situations.

That said, if your network has a DNS server (which it must if you are running a Windows 2000 or XP domain), configure your clients to use the DNS server. This should already be the case, and if the clients can find the DNS server, and the DNS server has the records it's supposed to have, you won't encounter this error message.

TIP   If your client computers are getting their IP configuration information from a DHCP server, the addresses of WINS and DNS servers can be supplied along with the IP address, subnet mask, and other parameters.

Identification

In a network with sufficient extra capacity, no extra work by the domain administrator should be required. However, if you have a problem connecting, have your administrator check the domain controller for the following issues:

Services: If the services related to networking such as DNS aren't running, they can't help your computer connect to the domain.

DNS Pointers: If the DNS server on your domain doesn't know about your computer, it can't find you when you try to log on. This includes reverse lookup zones.

DHCP Scope: If your domain uses DHCP to lease IP addresses, make sure you have enough available for the computers that are connected to your network.

Subnet: If you've manually assigned IP addresses, make sure each computer on the network belongs to the proper subnet. For examples of the range of IP addresses on a subnet, see Chapter 16.

Summary

In this chapter, we've looked at how to set up and configure an XP Workstation connection to a domain, attach to network resources, understand roaming and mandatory user profiles, and troubleshoot your network when things go awry. But an important aspect of networking is still missing: how to set up rights and permissions for shares and for files and folders. I'll discuss this in detail in the next chapter, because, as you well know by now, security is the main reason people migrate to Windows XP Professional in the first place.

Chapter 18

Living with Windows XP Professional Strict Security

IN CHAPTER 16, I walked you through the steps for creating and configuring a network, but one big piece of the networking pie is still missing: securing the resources on your network. From its inception, the NT family of operating systems was designed with security as a primary feature, and, of course, this architectural element is omnipresent in the Windows XP Professional.

Unlike some other operating systems, Windows XP Professional requires you to create a user account for yourself right on your PC before you can do anything on that PC. Yes, the idea that you must create your own user account on your personal PC before you can do anything with the PC is unusual—after all, most of us are accustomed to requiring network accounts, but not particular accounts on a workstation. But—as your father might say when you complain that something you don't like isn't fair—get used to it!

The user account is an integral part of Windows XP Professional and has some great benefits. For example, suppose you and Sue share a computer. You can set up the computer so that you own a folder on the hard disk and Sue owns another folder on the hard disk, and *it is completely impossible for Sue to access your data* (and vice versa) unless you give her permission.

In addition, you can restrict access to files and folders by setting permissions. As you may recall, in Windows XP Professional you can use the FAT, FAT32, or NTFS file system. If you use either FAT system, you can exercise only a limited amount of control over file and folder access, but if you use the NTFS system, you can exercise a great deal of control—whether the files are on your local computer or on your network.

In this chapter, we'll first look at how to set up user accounts, and then we'll look in detail at establishing permissions for shares, files, and folders. You will learn about the following topics:

- Understanding and creating accounts in Windows XP Professional
- Setting permissions
- Understanding ownership

Understanding User Accounts in Windows XP Professional

As you have just read, you must create separate user accounts on a Windows XP Professional machine before any user can log on to the workstation—and, unlike Windows 9x, Windows XP Professional won't let you get anywhere until you log on.

If your computer is part of a Windows XP Professional client-server network, two types of user accounts are available: domain accounts and local accounts. A domain account gives you access to the network and to the network resources for which you have permission. The manager of the server normally sets up domain accounts, which are stored in a directory on the server. The directory can either be Active Directory or a Windows NT domain directory.

A local user account is valid only on your local computer; local user accounts sit in a database called the *Security Accounts Manager*, or SAM. You create user accounts with the Users and Passwords applet, which you'll meet later in this chapter.

In this chapter, I'm going to talk about local user accounts only. If you happen to be the administrator of a domain on a network and you need help creating domain user accounts, take a look at *Mastering Windows 2000 Server, Fourth Edition* (Sybex, 2002).

Before I get into how you change or create an account, we need to look at the types of accounts in Windows XP Professional. The two broad categories are users and groups. A user account identifies a user on the basis of their user name and password. A group account contains other accounts, and these accounts share common privileges.

User accounts are of three types:

Computer Administrator   This account has full and complete rights to the computer and can do just about anything to the computer. The Computer Administrator account was created during installation and setup of Windows XP Professional. The Computer Administrator account cannot be deleted. You'll need to log on as Computer Administrator when you want to create new accounts, take ownership of files or other objects, install software that will be available to all users, and so on.

Limited   This account is intended for use by regular old users, those who should not be allowed to install software or hardware or change their user name. Someone with a limited account can change their password and logon picture.

Guest   This built-in account allows a user to log on to the computer even though the user does not have an account. No password is associated with the Guest account. It is disabled by default, and you should leave it that way. If you want to give a visitor or an occasional user access to the system, create an account for that person, and then delete the account when it is no longer needed.

As I said earlier, a group is an account that contains other accounts, and a group is defined by function. Using groups, an administrator can easily create collections of users who all have identical privileges. By default, every Windows XP Professional system contains the following built-in groups:

Administrators   Can do just about anything to the computer. The things that they can do that no other type of user can do include loading and unloading device drivers, managing security audit functions, and taking ownership of files and other objects.

Backup Operators   Can log on to the computer and run backups or perform restores. You might put someone in this group if you wanted them to be able to get on your system and run backups but not to have complete administrative control. Backup operators can also shut down the system but cannot change security settings.

Guests   Have minimal access to network resources. As I mentioned earlier, creating user accounts for occasional users is a much safer bet than using Guest accounts.

Network Configuration Operators   Can manage network configuration with administrative-type access. Although they do not have administrative access to your system, these users can modify network and dial-up connections.

Power Users   Can create new printer and file shares, change the system time, force the system to shut down from another system, and change priorities of processes in the system. They can't run backups, load or unload device drivers, or take ownership.

Remote Desktop Users   Have the right to log on remotely.

Replicator   Enables your computer to receive replicated files from a server machine.

Users   Can run programs and access data on a computer, shut it down, and access data on the computer from over the network. Users cannot share folders or create local printers.

HelpServicesGroup   A group of users for the Help and Support Center.

IIS_WPG   The Internet Information Services Worker Process Group; this group is available only if you have installed IIS. A member of this group can manage the IIS Web server (not content, just service).

Understanding User Rights

But what's this about shutting down the machine or loading and unloading drivers? Well, actually, the notion of a *user right* is an integral part of how Windows XP Professional security works. Basically, the difference between regular old users and administrators lies in the kinds of actions that they can perform; for example, administrators can create new user accounts but regular old users cannot. In Windows XP Professional terminology, the ability to perform a particular function is a user right.

To take a look at the user rights in Windows XP Professional and the types of users to whom they are assigned, follow these steps:

1. In Control Panel, click Performance and Maintenance, click Administrative Tools, and then click Local Security Policy to open the Local Security Settings window.

2. In the Security Settings pane, expand Local Policies, and then click User Rights Assignment to display a list of user rights in the pane on the right:

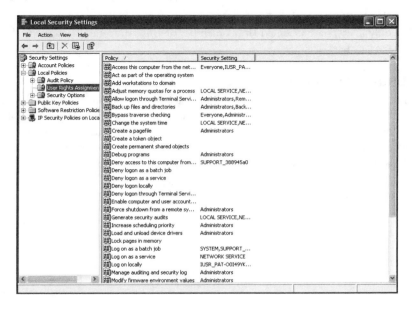

Most user rights are self-explanatory, but a few can use some clarification. Here's a list some of the rights and, where necessary, what they mean and what they're good for:

Back Up Files and Directories   Run backup utilities.

Change the System Time   Because the system time is important to the functioning of a network, not just anybody can change the system clock; it's a right. (Of course, you could always reboot the computer in DOS or go straight to the setup program in CMOS to reset the time, so it's not a very airtight security feature.)

Force Shutdown from a Remote System   Some utilities let you select a Windows XP Professional machine and force it to shut down, even though you're not logged on to that machine. (One such utility comes with the Resource Kit.) Because you wouldn't want just anybody doing a forced shutdown, Microsoft made this a right.

Load and Unload Device Drivers   A device driver is not only a video driver or SCSI driver; a device driver may be part of a software application or operating system subsystem. Without this right, you'll often be unable to install new software, and you'll usually be unable to change drivers or add and remove parts of the operating system.

Log on Locally   Sit down at the computer and log on.

Manage Auditing and Security Log   You can optionally turn on a Windows XP Security Log, which will report every single action that woke up any part of the security subsystems in Windows XP Professional. In general, I don't recommend using the Security Log because the output is quite cryptic and can be *huge*; logging all security events can fill up your hard disk quickly, and the CPU overhead of keeping track of the log will slow down your computer. You can't enable any security logging unless you have this right.

Restore Files and Directories   As the name states.

Take Ownership of Files or Other Objects   If you have this right, you can seize control of any file, folder, or other object even if you're not *supposed* to have access to it. This right is obviously quite powerful, which is why only administrators have it.

NOTE   *The user right to Take Ownership of Files or Other Objects is the secret to the administrator's power. You can do whatever you like to keep an administrator out of your data, but remember that the Computer Administrator can always take ownership of the file, and as owner, do whatever they want to the file including changing permissions. You cannot keep an administrator out; you can only make it difficult to get in.*

Creating a User Account

OK, now that you understand about the types of accounts and the concept of rights, let's create a new user account. You can do so in a couple of ways: using the Users and Passwords applet and using Computer Management. I'll start with the steps for creating a new user account with the Users Accounts applet:

   1. Log on as Computer Administrator.

2. Choose Start ➤ Control Panel to open Control Panel, and then click User Accounts to open User Accounts.

3. Click the Create a New Account link to open the Name the New Account screen:

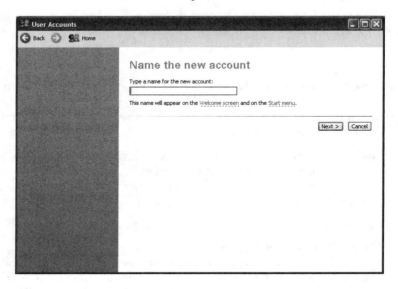

4. Enter a user name for the person, and then click Next.

NOTE   *In Windows XP Professional, a user name can be a maximum of 20 characters and is not case-sensitive.*

5. Specify the type of account you want this user to have, and then click Create Account.

6. Back in User Accounts, click Change an Account, click the account you just created, and then click Create Password to open the screen on which you can create a password for the account.

NOTE   *In Windows XP Professional, a password can be a maximum of 127 characters if you are in a pure Windows XP Professional environment. If you have Windows 9x machines on your network, keep the password to a maximum of 14 characters. Passwords are case sensitive.*

7. In the Type a New Password box, enter a password, and then enter it again in the Type the New Password Again to Confirm box. If you want, you can then type a hint (which can be seen by anyone using this computer) to trigger your remembrance of the password if you forget it.

8. Click Create Password to establish the password for the new user account.

See pages 75–76 of "Essential Skills for Windows XP Professional" for a visual guide to creating a user account.

To gain more control over the process of managing user accounts on Windows XP Professional, you will need to use the Local User Manager. In Control Panel, click Performance and Maintenance, click Administrative Tools, and then click Computer Management to open the Computer Management window. In the Computer Management (Local) pane, expand System Tools, expand Local Users and Groups, and then select Users to display a list of users in the right pane. Choose Action ➤ New User to open the New User dialog box, as shown in Figure 18.1.

FIGURE 18.1

Use the New User dialog box to add a new user to your system.

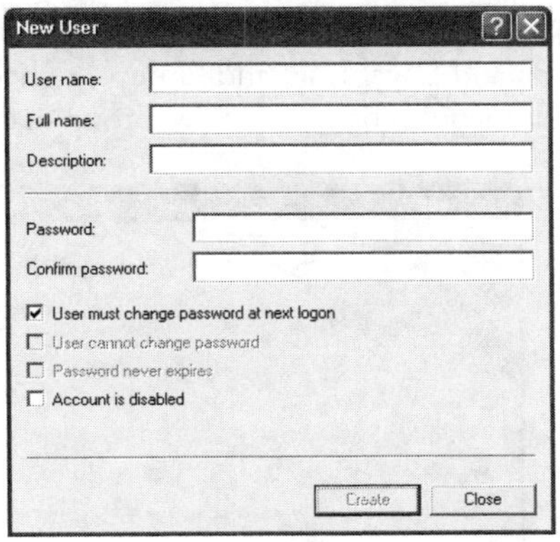

New User
User name:
Full name:
Description:
Password:
Confirm password:
☑ User must change password at next logon
☐ User cannot change password
☐ Password never expires
☐ Account is disabled
Create   Close

Now follow these steps:

1. Enter a user name for this new account.

2. Enter the person's full name.

3. Enter a description.

4. Enter and confirm a password.

5. Set the password options. The default option is User Must Change Password at Next Logon. This option means that only that user will know the password, which means better security. If you uncheck this option, the other two options become available. Select User Cannot Change Password if this account will be used for a service or for someone that you do not want to give the ability to change their own password. Select Password Never Expires if this password should be considered "permanent" and not have an automatic expiration.

6. The final option is to specify whether the account should be disabled. This is often a good idea if you want to change other properties of the account before it can be used, such as setting permissions on files and folders that this user will use. If this is the case, check the Account Is Disabled box.

7. When all options are selected, click Create to complete the process of making the new user account.

NOTE *To enable a disabled account, in the Local Users and Groups window, right-click the account, and choose Properties from the shortcut menu to open the Properties dialog box for that account. Clear the Account Is Disabled check box.*

Creating a Group Account

The process of creating a new group account is similar to creating a new user account. Local groups are useful for assigning permissions to resources. To create a new group account, follow these steps:

1. In Control Panel, click Performance and Maintenance, click Administrative Tools, and then click Computer Management to open the Computer Management window.

2. Expand System Tools, expand Local User and Groups, right-click Groups, and choose New Group from the shortcut menu to open the New Group dialog box:

3. Type a name for the group in the space provided. The name can contain any numbers or letters and can be a maximum of 256 characters. The name must be unique in the local database.

4. Enter some text in the Description field that will describe the membership and purpose of this group.

5. Click the Add button to open the Select Users dialog box:

6. In the Enter the Object Name to Select box, enter the name of the user you want to add to the group, and then click OK. Repeat step 5 and this step to add more users to the group.

7. Back in the New Group dialog box, click Close, and then close Computer Management.

See page 77 of "Essential Skills" for a visual guide to creating a group account.

Setting Permissions

The capability to restrict access to data is a really great feature of NT and Windows XP Professional. Prior to NT, my experience with operating systems of all kinds was that if you could gain physical access to a computer, you could get to its data; before NT, the only way to secure data with any confidence was to put the data on a server and put the server behind a locked door.

But network security is only as good as you make it. If a person can gain physical access to your machine, they can remove your hard disk and have all your data. Data security includes educating users to protect passwords and to apply permissions responsibly.

In this section, I'm going to show you how to set permissions at the share level and at the file and folder level. Remember, however, that you can establish file and folder security only if you are using the NTFS file system.

NOTE *To set permissions on a shared resource, you need to disable simple file sharing, which is enabled by default. In an Explorer window, choose Tools ➢ Folder Options to open the Folder Options dialog box. Click the View tab, and then in the Advanced Settings list, clear the Use Simple File Sharing (Recommended) check box.*

Setting Share-Level Permissions

In the previous chapter, I showed you how to share resources on your computer with others on your network. Now we need to look at what kind of access you want to give those who use your shared resources. To do this, you set the permissions.

To set share permissions, follow these steps:

1. In Explorer, right-click the shared resource, and choose Sharing and Security from the shortcut menu to open the Properties dialog box for the share at the Sharing tab.

2. Click the Permissions button to open the Permissions dialog box:

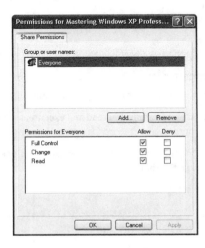

NOTE *The default shared permission in Windows XP Professional is for the Everyone group to have Full Control. In a secure environment, be sure to remove this permission before assigning specific permissions to users and groups.*

3. Click Add to open the Select Users or Groups dialog box, in which you can select which groups have access to a shared file or folder:

4. In the Enter the Object Name to Select box, enter the name of the user or group to whom you are granting permission, and click OK.

5. Back in the Permissions dialog box, you'll see that the user or group has been added to the Group or User Names list. In the Permissions section, click Allow or Deny to specify the type of permission you want to grant this user or group. Table 18.1 explains the choices.

6. When you've granted the permissions, click OK.

See page 78 of "Essential Skills" for a guide to setting share-level permissions.

TABLE 18.1: FILE PERMISSIONS

PERMISSION	DESCRIPTION
Full Control	The assigned group can perform any and all functions on all files and folders through the share.
Change	The assigned group can read and execute, as well as change and delete, files and folders through the share.
Read	The assigned group can read and execute files and folders but cannot modify or delete anything through the share.

Types of File and Folder Permissions

Share-level permissions determine who can access resources across the network and the type of access they will have. However, you can still assign more detailed permissions to the folders and files that can be accessed through the share. In addition, by using file- and folder-level permissions, you can restrict access to resources even if someone logs on to the system.

MULTIPLE GROUPS ACCUMULATE PERMISSIONS

You might have one group in your network called Accountants and another called Managers, and they might have different permission levels—for example, the Accountants might be able to only read the files, and the Managers might have Change access, which in NT was called Read and Write access. What about the manager of the Accounting department, who belongs to both the Managers and the Accountants groups—does he have Read access or does he have Change access?

In general, your permissions to a network resource *add up*—so if you have Read access from one group and Change from another group, you end up with Read *and* Change access. However, because Change access *includes* all the things that you can do with Read access, there's no practical difference between having Read and Change and having only Change access.

You've already seen that network shares have three types of permission levels: Read, Change, and Full Control. The permission types for files and folders are much more extensive, and each primary type includes still other types. Here are the primary types:

Read   Allows you to view the contents, permissions, and attributes associated with a resource. If the resource is a file, you can view the file. If the resource is an executable file, you can run it. If the resource is a folder, you can view the contents of the folder.

Write   Allows you to create a new file or subfolder within a folder if the resource is a folder. To change a file, you must also have Read permission, although you can append data to a file without opening the file if you have only Write permission.

Read & Execute   Allows you the permissions associated with Read and with Write and also allows you to traverse a folder, which means you can pass through a folder for which you have no access to get to a file or folder for which you do have access.

Modify   Allows you the permissions associated with Read & Execute and with Write, but also gives you Delete permission.

Full Control   Allows you the permissions associated with all the other permissions I've listed so far and lets you change permissions and take ownership of resources. In addition, you can delete subfolders and files even if you don't specifically have permission to do so.

List Folder Contents   Allows you to view the contents of folders.

If these levels of access are a bit coarse for your needs, you can fine-tune someone's access with what Microsoft calls *Special Access*. To modify the special access permissions for a file or folder, follow these steps:

1. In Explorer, right-click the resource whose permissions you want to modify, and choose Properties from the shortcut menu to open the Properties dialog box for that resource.

2. Click the Security tab, and then click Advanced to open the Advanced Security Settings dialog box:

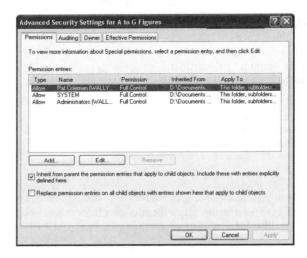

NOTE *If you don't see the Security tab in the Advanced Security Settings dialog box, in the Explorer view of My Computer choose Tools ➢ Folder Options to open the Folder Options dialog box. Click the View tab, and in the Advanced Settings list, clear the Use Simple File Sharing (Recommended) check box, and click OK.*

3. Click Edit to open the Permission Entry dialog box:

Here's a description of each of these permissions:

Full Control   As its name indicates and as discussed earlier in this chapter.

Traverse Folder/Execute File   You can change folders through this folder, and you can run this file.

List Folder/Read Data   You can read the contents of a file and display the contents of a folder.

Read Attributes   You can display the current attributes of a file or folder.

Read Extended Attributes   You can display the extended attributes of a file or folder, if there are any.

Create Files/Write Data   You can write data to a new file. When applied to a folder, this permission means you can write files into the folder, but you can't view what's already in the folder.

Create Folders/Append Data   You can create new folders in this location, and you can append data to existing files.

Write Attributes   You can modify the attributes of a file or folder.

Write Extended Attributes   You can create extended attributes for a file or folder.

Delete Subfolders and Files   You can remove folders contained within the folder you're working in, and you can remove the files contained in them.

Delete   You can delete files.

Read Permissions   You can display the current permissions list for the file or folder.

Change Permissions   You can modify the permissions for the file or folder. This permission is normally only included in Full Control.

Take Ownership   You can claim ownership of a file or folder.

These levels of granularity make security considerations more difficult to grasp initially, but they give a skilled administrator much finer control over how files and folders will be accessed.

To prevent someone from accessing a file or folder, you have two choices. The first, and usually the best, is to simply not grant the person access to the file or folder. That means, don't add their account to the list of permissions. The second method is to add the person's account to the permissions list, but check Deny for each permission. This creates an explicit No Access–type permission.

NOTE   *The special access items are all check boxes, not radio boxes, so you can mix and match as you like.*

Assigning File and Folder Permissions

Now that you know something about the types of permissions you can place on files and folders, let's walk though the steps to assign them:

1. In Explorer, right-click the file or folder for which you want to establish permissions, and choose Properties from the shortcut menu to open the Properties dialog box for that file or folder.

2. Click the Security tab:

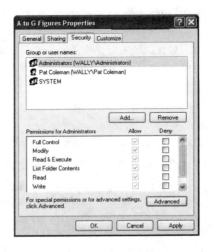

3. Click Add to open the Select Users or Groups dialog box.

4. In the Enter the Object Name to Select box, enter the name of the user or group to whom you are granting permission, and click OK.

5. Back in the Properties dialog box, you'll see that those groups or users have been added to the Group or User Names list. Click OK.

See page 79 of "Essential Skills" for a guide to setting file and folder permissions.

Auditing Files and Folders

In addition to assigning file and folder permissions, Windows XP Professional lets you keep track of who accessed a file and when. You can audit everyone or only specific users or groups. To enable, set up, and view auditing, you need to be logged on as an administrator. Enabling auditing is a bit of a pain, but you have to do it before you can set up auditing. Bear with me, and follow these steps:

1. At a command prompt, type **mmc /a** and press Enter to open the Microsoft Management Console.

2. Choose File ➤ Add/Remove Snap-In to open the Add/Remove Snap-In dialog box:

3. Click Add to open the Add Standalone Snap-In dialog box:

4. In the Snap-In list, select Group Policy, and then click Add to start the Group Policy Wizard:

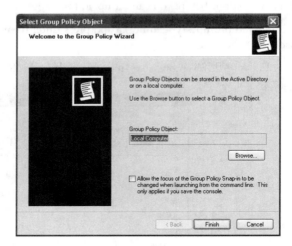

5. If Local Computer is not selected in the Group Policy Object box, browse for it, and then click Finish.

6. Back in the Add Standalone Snap-In dialog box, click Close.

7. Back in the Add/Remove Snap-In dialog box, click OK.

8. Now back in the MMC, expand Local Computer Policy, expand Computer Configuration, expand Windows Settings, expand Security Settings, expand Local Policies, and then click Audit Policy. You'll see the following:

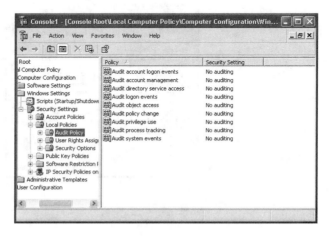

9. In the pane on the right, right-click Audit Object Access, and choose Properties from the shortcut menu to open the Audit Object Access Properties dialog box:

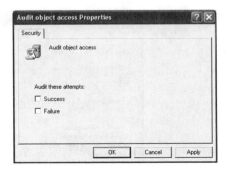

10. Click the check boxes to audit for success and failure, and then click OK.

11. Close the MMC.

Whew! Now you're ready to set up auditing. Follow these steps:

1. In Explorer, right-click the share you want to audit, and then choose Properties from the shortcut menu to open the Properties dialog box for that share.

2. Click the Security tab, click the Advanced button to open the Advanced Security Settings dialog box, and click the Auditing tab:

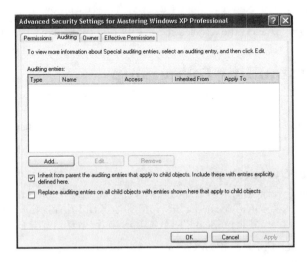

3. Click Add to open the Select User or Group dialog box.

4. In the Enter the Object Name to Select box, enter the name of a user or a group to audit, and then click OK to open the Auditing Entry dialog box:

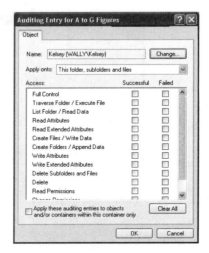

5. Select the entries that you want to audit, and then click OK three times.

To take a look at the events you've selected to audit, follow these steps:

1. In Control Panel, click Performance and Maintenance, click Administrative Tools, and then click Event Viewer to open the Event Viewer window.

2. In the pane on the left, select Security Log to display a list of audited events in the right pane.

Understanding Ownership

Ownership—what a confusing concept. *Ownership* is a process by which you can take exclusive control over a file or a folder; and you can do all of this with a click of a button. But before you get power drunk with the possibilities, let's take a closer look at what being the owner of a file really means.

Defining Ownership

Now, having worked with NT since its inception, I don't mind telling you that the whole idea of a folder or file's "owner" seemed a bit confusing until I finally figured out the definition. Here's a definition—and from this point on, let me shorten the term *file* or *folder* to *object*:

Minasi's Definition of an Owner An object's owner is a user who can *always* modify that object's permissions.

Ordinarily, only an administrator can control settings such as an object's permissions. But you want your users to be able to control objects in their own area, their own home folder, without having to involve you at every turn. For example, suppose you want to give another user access to a folder in your home folder. Rather than having to seek out an administrator and ask the administrator to extend access permissions to another user, you as the owner can change the permissions directly. Ownership lets users become mini-administrators, rulers of their small fiefdoms.

To find out who owns an object, follow these steps:

1. In Explorer, right-click an object, and choose Properties from the shortcut menu to open the Properties dialog box for that object.

2. Select the Security tab, and then click Advanced to open the Advanced Security Settings dialog box.

3. Select the Owner tab.

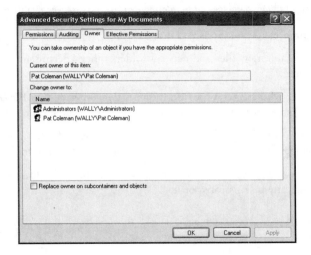

Taking Ownership

Users can't force themselves onto the permissions list for an object, but if they have the Take Ownership permission they *can* become the owner, and once they are the owner, *then* they can add themselves to the permissions list.

If you highlight your name in the Change Owner To list and click OK, you can become the owner of the object, but you can't see what's in the object because you are still not on the permissions list.

NOTE *Owners of files can't necessarily access those files. All that the owners of files can do is change the permissions on those files.*

Okay, then, how do you get to the object? Well, since you are an owner, you can change permissions. So you will add yourself to the permissions list and *then* gain access to the object.

Now, why were you able to do that? Because of a user right that all administrators have by default: Take Ownership. Perhaps if you were a more user-oriented than administrator-oriented company, you could remove the Administrators group from that right. By doing so, however, an administrator would be unable to poke around a user's area.

Further, users can always shore up their security just a bit by taking control of their home folder from the administrators. Recall that users have Full Control of their home folder, and Full Control includes the ability to take ownership of an object.

And if you're concerned about an administrator being able to take control at any time—where's the security in that?—consider that an administrator must *take* ownership in order to add themselves to the object's permissions list. In doing that, they leave fingerprints behind; if you log on one day and find that you're no longer the owner of something that you owned yesterday, you know that an administrator has been snooping—and if file auditing is in place, you can even find out who snooped.

NOTE *You can't give ownership; you can only exercise the permission to take ownership. If an administrator were to take ownership of a file, they could not edit the file and then give ownership back to the original owner.*

To summarize permissions and ownership:

◆ By default, new files and new subfolders inherit permissions from the folder in which they are created.

◆ A user who creates a file or a folder is the owner of that file or folder, and the owner can always control access to the file or folder by changing the permissions on it.

◆ When you change the permissions on an existing folder, you can choose whether those changes will apply to all files and subfolders within the folder.

◆ Users and groups can be denied access to a file or a folder simply by not granting the user or group any permissions for it.

WARNING *It is possible to lock out everyone including the operating system itself if you do not apply permissions correctly.*

Summary

In this chapter, we've looked at creating user and group accounts and at the rights that the various kinds of users and groups can have. I've also walked you through the steps involved in setting permissions for shares, files, and folders. Understanding and following these procedures is essential if you want the information on your Windows XP Professional system to be secure. And presumably that's one of the main reasons you're working with Windows XP Professional anyway, right?

Chapter 19

Auditing Security

IN THE LAST CHAPTER, we looked at how to deal with Windows XP security. If securing your computer is a primary concern to you, then the obvious first step is to know how to apply security settings. However, you can't just assume that since you set security up on your machine that all is well. There are many things you could have overlooked. Maybe you forgot to set security on a specific folder. Perhaps the security you set isn't as strict as it should be. Things like this happen, because, after all, we are human.

This is where auditing comes into play. After you have established security measures, auditing can help you check to make sure that no one is getting access to resources that they shouldn't. Auditing can act as a watchdog, if you will. In this chapter, we'll look at the many benefits of auditing, a few inconveniences of auditing, and how to set auditing up. We'll also look at

- ◆ Reasons to use and not to use auditing
- ◆ Implementing auditing through policies
- ◆ Auditing folders, files, and printers
- ◆ Monitoring audited events

Deciding What to Audit

Windows XP gives you a great deal of flexibility in auditing. You can decide to audit every time any user opens any file on your machine. You can also go to the other extreme, and choose no auditing whatsoever. But if you're like most people, you will choose a position somewhere in the middle.

Although there could be many factors that play into your decision to enable auditing, the most important consideration is the security of your computer. If you don't care about security and couldn't care less who sees your files or uses your printers, then auditing isn't for you. There's no sense in enabling it. However, if the files on your machine are confidential, then you'll likely want to know if someone is trying to get to them, or worse yet, has gotten to them.

Benefits of Auditing

Auditing provides increased security for your computer. No, auditing won't actually keep someone out of your files. That's what permissions are for. But, auditing is there to let you know about potential security breaches. For example, you can audit logon attempts to your computer. If someone has tried to log on to your machine a dozen times, using your username but the wrong password, auditing can track that. By reviewing your security logs, you will notice attempts to hack your machine. If you didn't have auditing, you might not know until it's too late.

You can use auditing to track almost everything that happens on your computer. You will know what happened (log on, file access, printer access), when it happened, and who did it. This way, if something bad does happen, you will have a culprit. In this way, auditing can be thought of as supplemental security. It won't keep a specific event from happening, but will leave a detailed electronic paper trail.

A discussion of the benefits of auditing wouldn't be complete unless you knew what types of things were available to audit. After all, how do you know it's good for you if you don't know exactly what it does? There are nine different types of events that can be audited in Windows XP. These events are listed in Table 19.1.

TABLE 19.1: WINDOWS XP AUDIT EVENTS

EVENT	DESCRIPTION
Account logon events	Audits when a user logs on to or off of another computer from this computer. This typically only happens in domains, so you won't likely use this event in Windows XP Professional.
Account management	Audits when changes are made to a user or group. These changes can include creation, deletion, renaming, disabling or enabling, and password changes.
Directory service access	Audits whenever a user accesses a directory services object other than a file, folder, or printer. Only used in Windows 2000 and Windows .NET domains.
Logon events	Audits whenever a user logs on or logs off of this computer. Very helpful.
Object access	Audits user's access to files, folders, and printers. Very helpful.
Policy change	Audits changes made to user rights policies, audit policies, and trust relationships.
Privilege use	Audits whenever a user executes a user right, other than logon, logoff, system shutdown, or network access events.
Process tracking	Tracks changes made by programs in Windows XP. Generally not very useful.
System events	Audits system shutdowns and restarts, or any attempted changes to the system's Security log. Sometimes useful.

Some of the events may seem redundant, and can be confusing as to their purpose. Let's try to clarify them now:

Account Logon Events vs. Logon Events   Account logon events is useful if someone uses your machine to log on to a Windows 2000 or Windows .NET domain. If you don't have a domain, you won't need to use this event. Logon events will track who logs on to your individual machine.

Directory Service Access vs. Object Access   Directory service access tracks whenever someone accesses a specific object in the Windows 2000 or Windows .NET directory. Object types include, but are not limited to, shared folder objects, user objects, and group objects. Once again, this is not generally useful for Windows XP Professional, because it implies that a domain is present. Object access tracks access to files, folders, and printer objects specifically. Implementing tracking on these three types objects is a two-step setup process, which we'll cover in the "Setting up Auditing" section of this chapter.

The events listed in Table 19.1 can be quite a lot to absorb. The two most commonly used audit events are Logon events and Object access. Account management, privilege use, and policy change are common in environments where there are multiple users with administrative privileges. Account logon events and Directory service access are used only when you have a domain. Process tracking and system events are rarely audited.

The Dark Side of Auditing

When deciding what to audit on your Windows XP computer, there are two negative aspects you will want to be aware of. The first one is performance overhead, and the second one is the volume of audited information.

Auditing adds overhead to your computer. Auditing is a process, much like an application, in that it performs a task based on a specific event happening on your computer. So if you have enabled auditing on every file on your machine, your computer needs to make a note of *who*, *what*, and *when* every time someone opens a file. This extra work slows down the machine. The more you audit, the more overhead you will have. Overhead becomes a more extensive issue when you are auditing servers, as they generally have more people accessing them than do workstations. Even so, overhead is still something to keep in mind when deciding what to audit on your XP workstation. Too much auditing can cripple your system's performance.

The sheer volume of audit records that your computer may generate can become overwhelming. Once again, the more you audit, the more you will have to deal with. With so many audit events to sort through, it can be difficult to find the specific piece of information you're looking for. Fortunately, Windows XP allows you to restrict your display to specific types of events through filtering. We'll look at how to filter events in the "Monitoring Security" section later in this chapter.

All in all, the benefits of auditing far outweigh the drawbacks. As long as you apply your auditing judiciously, you should be able to enjoy the benefits without causing any serious performance problems.

Setting up Auditing in Windows XP

Auditing is enabled in Windows XP Professional through the Local Security Settings console. Local Security Settings is part of Administrative Tools located in Control Panel. Figure 19.1 shows where Audit Policy is located within the security console. You must have administrative privileges to enable auditing.

NOTE   *Windows XP Home Edition does not come with a Local Security Settings console. Consequently, you cannot set up auditing from a Windows XP Home Edition computer.*

FIGURE 19.1

Local Security
Settings

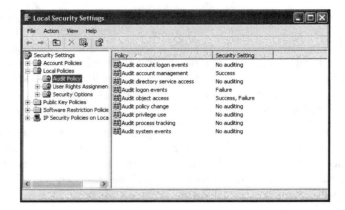

Notice in Figure 19.1, we have enabled a few of the more common auditing events. Also, when you enable auditing, you have the choice of auditing successes or failures of each type of event. Auditing logon failures could warn you about a potential hacker, whereas logon successes may just show you that you've indeed logged on every day for the last month. Once again, you have to decide on an appropriate auditing level for your computer. To set up auditing of an event, double-click it in the right pane, and check the Success and/or Failure box. An example is shown in Figure 19.2.

FIGURE 19.2

Auditing Object
Access

WARNING   *If you are part of a Windows 2000 or Windows .NET domain, domain-wide security policies set with Group Policy objects will override your local settings. Check with your domain administrator to see if this is going to be an issue.*

For most audit events, all you need to do is open up Local Security Settings, find the event you want to audit, and select the Success and/or Failure boxes. It's a relatively painless procedure. However, for object access, specifically auditing folders, files, and printers, you will need to perform an additional step.

The first step to auditing objects is just like auditing anything else. Open Local Security Settings and check Success and/or Failure for the Audit object access event. For object access, it's recommended that you always check both the Success and Failure boxes. By performing this first step, you have set up your machine to allow the auditing of folders, files, and printers. Now you have to tell your computer *which* folders, files, and printers you want to monitor.

There is logic in Microsoft making this a two-step process. If all you needed to do were to check the boxes in Local Security Settings, you would automatically enable auditing on *all* folders, files, and printers. In most cases, this is completely unnecessary—definite overkill. This two-step process lets you fine tune audit control over your machine.

NOTE   *In order to audit folders and files, the folders and files must be on an NTFS partition. FAT partitions do not support auditing. If you don't have a Security tab on your folder's Properties, check to make sure your partition is NTFS.*

For the second step, start by finding the folder, file, or printer you want to audit. Generally, it's best to audit folders rather than specific files, much like Microsoft recommends setting permissions at the folder level rather than the file level. Once you have found the folder that you want to audit, right-click it and choose Properties. In the Security tab, click the Advanced button, and then the Auditing tab. You will see a screen similar to the one shown in Figure 19.3.

FIGURE 19.3

The Auditing tab for the Docs folder

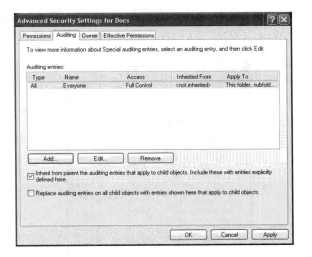

Unless you have set up auditing before, it's likely that your text box will be blank, as opposed to having the Everyone group in it like Figure 19.3 does. To add a group of people to audit, click the Add button. You will get a screen similar to Figure 19.4. Enter the group or user you want to watch in the Name box, and then check the boxes for which actions you would like to audit. Clicking the Full Control box will enable the whole column. If you want to be safe, choosing Full Control is the best option, but keep in mind this increases the amount of overhead for the workstation. In order to audit multiple groups, click the Add button in the Auditing tab again, and add the additional group. You can specify separate auditing policies for different groups.

FIGURE 19.4

Enabling audit entries for the Docs folder

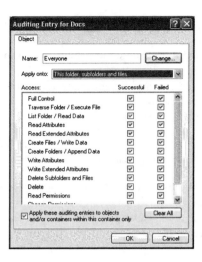

You can further customize your auditing preferences with the drop-down menu shown in Figure 19.5.

FIGURE 19.5

Fine-tuning audit entries

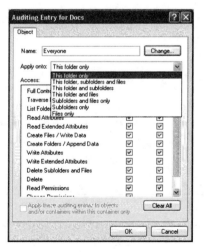

Auditing printers is done much the same way as auditing a folder. Go to the printer's Properties, click the Security tab, click the Advanced button, and then click the Auditing tab. Click the Add button to add a group, and you will get a display similar to Figure 19.6. Notice that printers give you less things to audit than do folders. From the Apply Onto drop-down menu, you can choose to audit the printer, documents sent to the printer, or both the printer and documents.

FIGURE 19.6

Auditing printers

For the most part, setting up auditing in Windows XP Professional is pretty simple. It does get more complex when you want to audit folders and printers, but if you remember to complete both steps, your auditing setup will turn out fine.

But now that you've enabled auditing, where do you go to see who has tripped audit events? Setting up auditing isn't enough. You need to periodically monitor your security logs to see if anything has gone awry.

Monitoring Security

The Event Viewer utility is used to monitor your security audits. Event Viewer is located in Administrative Tools in Control Panel. There are three logs in Event Viewer; the one we are interested in for auditing purposes is the Security log. Event Viewer's Security log is shown in Figure 19.7.

FIGURE 19.7

The Security log in Event Viewer

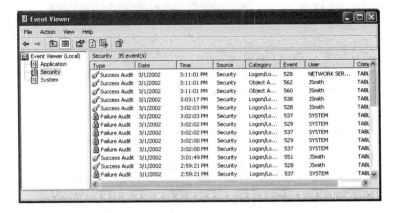

NOTE *In order to view the Security log, you must have administrative privileges.*

A quick look at the Security log will tell you whether the logged event was a success or failure, the date, time, category, event number, user performing the action, and the computer that it was performed on. It's an electronic paper trail of what's happened on your computer—at least what's happened in regards to what you've been auditing. To find out more details about a specific event, double-click it. You will get a screen similar to Figure 19.8.

FIGURE 19.8

Event detail

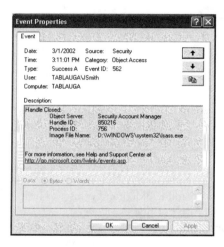

As I mentioned earlier, your security log can quickly acquire a large number of events. It can be difficult, if not impossible, to find the specific types of events you want to look at. Fortunately, Windows XP Professional Event Viewer comes with an ability to filter events based on almost any criteria you choose. As an example, if you wanted to find events that related to the user JSmith only, you could filter for the username JSmith. This is illustrated in Figure 19.9. To use filtering in Event Viewer, click View, and then Filter.

FIGURE 19.9

Filtering for Jsmith

Because the Security log can get quite large, Microsoft recommends that you periodically clear out the log. You can choose to delete all old security records, or save them for future reference. For details on how to do this, and more Event Viewer management topics, see Chapter 21.

Summary

Auditing allows you to monitor various security-based aspects of your computer. You can see if someone logged on or off, made changes to security settings, created or modified users, or accessed system resources.

Perhaps the biggest benefit of auditing is how it affords you the ability to check for potential system abuses. By enabling auditing of logon and logoff events, you can see if someone has been trying to hack your account. By auditing your folders, you can see who has accessed critical files. You can even audit your printers to see if someone in the Accounting department has been printing off high-quality glossy color photos of his family vacation on your printer at one in the morning.

Auditing is enabled through Local Security Settings in Administrative Tools in Control Panel. Once you have enabled auditing, you can check your Security log in Event Viewer to see if any events have happened. Although auditing itself will not keep people out of your resources—that's what permissions are for—auditing can tell you what actions were performed on your machine, allowing you to further control your security.

Chapter 20

Secure Telecommuting

IN THIS CHAPTER, WE'LL take a look at a common scenario—a corporate user who wants (or needs) to telecommute a portion of the time and needs to do so as securely as possible. We'll look at some of the common threats that a telecommuting user must face, along with what Windows XP Professional can do to protect against those threats.

In this chapter:

◆ Telecommuting overview: risks and rewards

◆ Protecting against the interception of data

◆ Protecting against the impersonation of a user

◆ Protecting against data abduction

Telecommuting Overview: Risks and Rewards

As telecommuting becomes more commonplace, the risks and rewards associated with it are becoming more apparent. The rewards are obvious: no dealing with traffic jams, being able to work in your bathrobe (if you want to), no office distractions, and so on. The risks, however, are a little less obvious. One of the biggest problems is the risk involved when corporate data is moved outside the corporation's walls.

The risks of telecommuting fall into three distinct areas:

◆ The interception of corporate data

◆ The impersonation of an authorized user

◆ The potential abduction of confidential data

It's interesting to look at the irony of the situation. Corporations are increasing their efforts to secure their data within their walls, but at the same time they are allowing more and more employees to telecommute. I can imagine that people who want to steal corporate data will eventually start to focus their efforts on telecommuting workers instead of the corporation's main systems, because most telecommuters make much easier targets.

The interception of data is an obvious threat: as data passes from your Windows XP Professional computer into your corporation's main systems, someone eavesdrops on the data transmission and reads the data. If your transmission is crossing the Internet, it will travel through many systems outside your company's control before it reaches its final destination. The same is true with dial-up modems, although the risks are slightly less as your traffic is being carried over the telephone network (a bit more secure). Still, risks do exist, and the main way to deal with the risk of data interception is through data encryption between the source and destination computers. I'll talk about some of the ways you can protect against data interception by encrypting transmissions leaving your Windows XP Professional computer.

The impersonation of a user is also a threat. If someone obtains your username and password, and if your account has dial-in access, that person can log in to your company's systems under your account, effectively impersonating you. Although the problem of account/password discovery happens within the corporation's walls as well (for example, users writing passwords on yellow sticky notes and attaching them to their monitors), it becomes more of a problem when a user's account is granted dial-in access. The pitfalls of this type of security breach are many—corruption of data, deletion of data, abduction of data, and the introduction of malicious viruses, just to name a few. You can take steps to prevent user impersonation. Some of them are built into Windows XP Professional, and others are security measures that your corporation must implement, and we'll take a look at a number of possible solutions later in this chapter.

Finally, the risk of having data abducted is also a threat. Corporate espionage is a significant problem in many large organizations (although corporations usually keep silent about it since reporting it would have a negative impact on the company's stock price). Again, although corporations are taking significant steps to increase the security of their data within the company's walls, they are allowing users to keep copies of some data on their own home computers or laptops. Instead of targeting a corporate network, it will eventually be easier for someone to target a telecommuting user if they want to obtain a copy of sensitive corporate data. After all, which would be more difficult—breaking into a company and trying to steal a computer, or breaking into someone's home and stealing their computer or laptop? We'll take a look at some of the utilities provided in Windows XP Professional that will allow you to secure data on your system so that even in the worst-case scenario—your computer is completely stolen—your company's sensitive data won't fall into the wrong hands.

Protecting Against the Interception of Data

If you are telecommuting, odds are you are connected to your corporation's network in one of three ways: directly—through some sort of wide-area network connection, indirectly—through an analog dial-up networking connection, or through a high-speed digital connection or possibly a virtual private network (VPN). No matter how you are connected, you can take steps to secure your communications.

Securing RAS Dial-In Sessions

The dial-in scenario is probably familiar if you've been using computers for any length of time. You install a modem, you define a dial-up networking entry to call into a remote network, and then your computer initiates a connection over your phone line. This is a relatively secure means of communicating with a remote network, but it still could be compromised: someone could tap into your phone line and record the data conversations traveling back and forth between your computer and the remote computer. Therefore, the primary means to protect RAS (remote access server) dial-in sessions is via encryption. Windows XP Professional makes it easy to implement (and require) encryption on any dial-up networking connection.

NOTE *Encryption is the process of encoding information so that it is secure from unauthorized access. Decryption is the reverse of this process.*

Assuming you have a working dial-up networking connection, setting up encryption is relatively easy. Follow these steps:

1. Choose Start ➤ Connect To ➤ Show All Connections to open the Network Connections folder.

2. Right-click the icon for your dial-up connection, and choose Properties from the shortcut menu to open the Properties dialog box for that connection.

3. Click the Security tab, click the Advanced (Custom Settings) option button, and then click the Settings button to open the Advanced Security Settings dialog box:

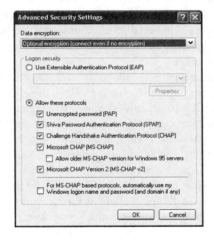

You'll notice that the very first item in the Advanced Security Settings dialog box is the Data Encryption drop-down list box. This option has four possible settings:

No Encryption Allowed   This setting will attempt to force your computer into a nonencrypted communication session. If the remote system that you are dialing into will allow any type of connection (encrypted or not), you will be able to connect. However, if the remote system will accept only encrypted connections, you will not be able to connect.

Optional Encryption   This setting will defer to whatever is required by the remote system you are calling into. If the remote system does not require encryption, this setting will let you connect. If the remote system does require encryption, this setting will also let you connect.

Require Encryption   Enabling this setting will implement a 40-bit encryption channel between your Windows XP Professional computer and the remote system. If the remote system cannot support encryption, your session will immediately disconnect, and you'll see a disconnection error message.

Maximum Strength Encryption   Enabling this setting will require a strong (128-bit) encryption channel between your Windows XP Professional computer and the remote system. You will see this option only if you purchased Windows XP Professional in the United States. If the remote system cannot support strong encryption, your session will immediately disconnect with an error message.

Enabling a data encryption option ensures that all your communications are kept private, even if someone is able to intercept them.

To enable encryption on your dial-up connection, select one of the protocols in the Logon Security section of the Advanced Security Settings dialog box.

See page 88 of "Essential Skills for Windows XP Professional" for a guide to securing a RAS dial-in session.

Virtual Private Networking Connections

Virtual private networking (VPN) connections are, by definition, meant to be private. VPNs were originally developed as a means to route confidential, private data across untrusted networks. As a result of the reach and popularity of the Internet, VPNs have enjoyed a considerable amount of success in the current market.

One of the better analogies I've found for explaining the concepts of a virtual private network is to refer to them as "pipes." To conceptualize VPNs, think of two pipes, one large and one small. Now, imagine that the small pipe actually runs *inside* the large one. It starts and ends at the same places the large pipe does, and it can carry materials on its own completely independently of whatever is happening in the large pipe. As a matter of fact, the only thing the small pipe is dependent on the large pipe for is the determination of the start and end points. Beyond that, the small pipe can operate independently of the large pipe in terms of direction of travel, materials it carries, and so on.

To add another layer to this analogy, let's assume that the large pipe is made of a transparent material and that the small pipe is made of metal. Anyone taking a look at the pipe-within-a-pipe would easily be able to see whatever is moving through the outside (large) pipe. However, whatever is traveling through the inside pipe would remain a mystery.

If this is starting to make sense, you should be thinking to yourself that the large pipe represents the unsecured network (that is, the Internet) and that the small pipe represents the virtual private network. VPN is a way of tunneling data packets through a connection that already exists but that can't be used on its own for privacy reasons. Obviously, the Internet is a perfect example of a network that often can't be used on its own for privacy reasons.

To establish a VPN connection to your corporate network, your company must have set up a VPN server capable of receiving those connections. (More information on setting up a virtual private networking server is available in *Mastering Windows 2000 Server, Fourth Edition,* Sybex, 2002.) If your company has set up a VPN server for you to dial in to, you will need to know the answers to the following questions:

◆ Which authentication type does it require?

◆ Which encryption strength does it require?

◆ What is the IP address or DNS (domain name service) name to connect to?

Once you know the answer to these questions, you can set up a VPN connection on your Windows XP Professional computer.

Since a VPN (typically) runs over the Internet, the first thing you must have on your system is a functional Internet connection. Whether your connection is a dial-up modem or a dedicated cable/xDSL connection is mostly irrelevant. Assuming you have an Internet connection in place, you can easily create a VPN connection. Follow these steps:

1. Choose Start ➢ Connect To ➢ Show All Connections to open the Network Connections folder.

2. In the Network Tasks bar, click the Create a New Connection link to start the New Connection Wizard.

3. Click Next to open the Network Connection Type screen:

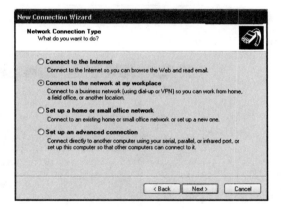

4. Select the Connect to the Network at My Workplace option, and then click Next to open the Network Connection screen:

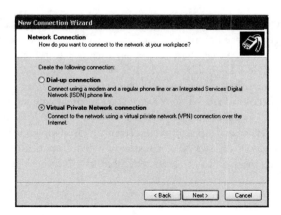

5. Click the Virtual Private Network Connection option, and then click Next to open the Connection Name screen:

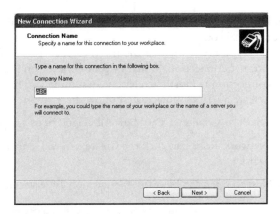

6. Enter a name for your connection, and then click Next to open the Public Network screen:

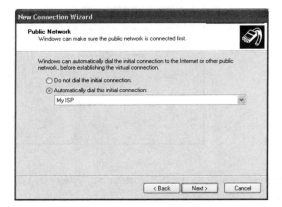

As I discussed earlier, connecting to a VPN (over the Internet) requires that a functional Internet connection be in place before establishing the VPN connection. Now, your connection to the Internet will most likely be one of two types—either a dial-up connection (such as a modem or an ISDN [Integrated Services Digital Network] line) or a dedicated connection that you do not need to dial (that is, it's always there, always on). If you are using a dial-up connection to connect to the Internet, you can instruct Windows XP Professional to automatically establish that connection first before initiating your VPN connection by selecting the Automatically Dial This Initial Connection option. Select your Internet dial-up connection from the drop-down list, and then any time you launch your VPN connection, Windows XP Professional will automatically log you in to the Internet. If you have a direct connection to the Internet (cable, xDSL, other), simply skip this step by selecting the

Do Not Dial the Initial Connection option. When you are finished with this step, click Next to open the VPN Server Selection screen:

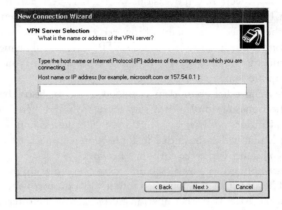

Since virtual private networks function over the Internet, you will connect to a VPN either via an IP address or a DNS name (which resolves into an IP address). Enter the name of your target VPN server, or enter the IP address of the destination system, and then click Next to finish your VPN connection.

In the final screen of the Wizard, specify whether you want a shortcut to this connection on your Desktop, and click Finish. You have now successfully created a VPN connection.

Now, if your corporation has implemented their VPN server correctly, it should be set up so that you can't connect unless your connection is encrypted. Assuming that is the case, you may need to set the appropriate encryption level for your VPN connection the same way you would set one for a RAS connection (as discussed earlier in the chapter).

Once you've got everything correctly defined on your system, you should be able to double-click your VPN icon on your Windows XP Professional system and get connected—securely—to your corporate network. Once you're connected, you should be able to navigate throughout your company's corporate network just as if you were sitting in the office.

See pages 89 and 90 of "Essential Skills" for a visual guide to setting up a VPN.

VPN Performance Considerations

Our look at virtual private networking wouldn't be complete without taking a bit of time to discuss performance issues. Although virtual private networking is a neat technology, some performance drawbacks are associated with it.

In the right set of circumstances, virtual private networking can provide fast, reliable, and secure connections to your company's network from across the Internet (or another unsecured network). However, in the wrong set of circumstances, virtual private networking can make an already slow dial-up connection seem even slower.

So what are the right circumstances? In my professional opinion, high-speed connectivity on the corporate side of your VPN, and preferably high-speed connectivity on both the corporate side and your personal connection. On occasions when I have been able to implement VPN circuits at locations with a T-1 or better available at both the company and client ends, performance has been wonderful and the connections reliable. However, due to the protocol overhead involved with PPTP (Point-to-Point Tunneling Protocol) and L2TP (Layer 2 Tunneling Protocol) and the inherent latency of the Internet, don't have high-performance expectations if you are planning to implement a VPN with a dial-up modem.

If you are using a dial-up modem, nothing will ever be faster than a direct dial-in connection. Period. Dial-in connections are simple. There's no encryption, and there's no VPN protocol overhead involved. Plus, your traffic does not have to cross through a countless number of routers before reaching its destination. Simply put, with a direct dial-in connection your packets go out of your computer, across the phone line, and directly into the corporate network.

If you are implementing a VPN connection over a dial-up modem, your packets must first be encrypted. They must then be bundled into a VPN protocol and then bundled again into another TCP/IP packet. After that, they are transmitted across the Internet, where they will probably pass through anywhere from 4 to 12 routers before reaching the VPN server at your corporation. Once the VPN server receives the packet, it must unpackage all the payload and then decrypt it. Although computers can do this quickly, it does add overhead to the process.

How much overhead? Well, there are no official numbers to go by, but I'd say you can expect a decrease in your performance ranging anywhere from 10 to 50 percent. Now, without getting into all the technical details, it is worthwhile to note that this isn't entirely Microsoft's fault; after all, they can't be blamed for the fact that the Internet can be inherently slow at times (or can they?). However, even with the worst-case scenario of a 50 percent reduction in performance, if there is 1Mb worth of bandwidth available on each side of the VPN, the effective speeds of the network are still roughly in the 500Kbps range—a very respectable amount. However, if you're using a 56K modem on your Windows XP Professional workstation (which probably won't connect much faster than 48Kbps), you can easily see how a 50 percent performance penalty can make a connection go from "slow" to "unusable."

Everything in life is a trade-off, and it will be up to you to decide if this will work adequately enough for your needs. After all, what is adequate to one person might be great to another and unacceptable to yet another. In either case, expect a performance penalty when implementing virtual private networking and plan accordingly.

Protecting Against the Impersonation of a User

Compromising a valid user's account name and password is a network administrator's worst nightmare. An unauthorized user—posing as a valid one—can steal, compromise, or sabotage data from the company's network. If that user has remote dial-in access capabilities as well, the problem is even worse as someone can dial in from anywhere in the world and make trouble for the network. Therefore, it is important to prevent your user ID and password from falling into the wrong hands.

Common Sense Guidelines

It still amazes me how many times I run into users who have written their usernames and passwords on a yellow sticky note and then stuck the note to their monitor. Talk about a security nightmare! Even if people don't stick their passwords on their monitors, users have a tendency to write them down on cards in their wallets or put them into an organizer such as a Palm. The first measure of good security is to never write your username and password down. If, for some reason, you must do so, at least write them on separate sheets of paper and store them in different places. Don't store them with each other.

Another common security problem is users who choose passwords that are easily guessed. For example, it's common for many people to use simple things for passwords, such as the type of car they drive, their favorite sport or a favorite athlete, their mother's maiden name, their middle name, and so on. All those types of passwords can be easily guessed if someone is determined enough.

The best types of passwords are complex combinations that have nothing whatsoever to do with you. You can make your passwords a bit more complex—but still easily remembered—by substituting letters, numbers, or symbols in place of actual words. This is the same type of logic that people use to spell out phrases on custom license plates. For example, you could use the phrase "No soup for you today!" as a password (with all due respect to the *Seinfeld* "Soup Nazi" episode) by using "nosoup4u2day". Such a password is still easy to remember, but is much more difficult to guess. Other suggestions for substitutions are

- Instead of the word "to" or "too," use the number 2.
- Instead of the word "for," use the number 4.
- Instead of the word "at," use the @ symbol.
- Instead of the word "and," use the & symbol.
- Instead of the word "you," use the letter U.
- Instead of the word "are," use the letter R.

I'm sure you get the point. The object is to keep the password something that you can remember while making it difficult to compromise. I've had good success using this formula.

Encrypted Authentication

If you are dialing into a remote network—either via a direct dial-in line or a VPN connection—Windows XP Professional must pass your user credentials (your username and password) to the remote system for authentication. The remote system will then check those credentials to determine if your account has been granted dial-in access. But how does Windows XP Professional send your credentials to the remote computer?

The answer can be found in the Advanced Security Settings dialog box. As you can see in that dialog box, Windows XP Professional can send your user credentials to the remote system in a number of ways, as long as the remote system is able to understand. Some of these authentication methods are encrypted, and some are not.

Extensible Authentication Protocol (EAP)   Since security and authentication is a constantly changing field, embedding authentication schemes into an operating system is impractical at times. To solve this problem, Microsoft has included support for Extensible Authentication Protocol, which is simply a means of "plugging in" new authentication schemes as needed. Presumably, any type of extensible authentication would be encrypted, but that could vary from one case to the next.

Unencrypted Password (PAP)   Password Authentication Protocol (PAP) is one of the first options and is also one of the least secure. It is no more secure than a simple conversation from your server saying "What is your name and password?" to the client, the client responding with "My name is Mark and my password is 'let-me-in.'" There is no encryption of authentication credentials whatsoever.

Shiva Password Authentication Protocol (SPAP)   SPAP is an encrypted password authentication method used by Shiva LAN Rover clients and servers. Windows XP Professional can provide SPAP authentication if needed.

Challenge Handshake Authentication Protocol (CHAP)   Defined in RFC (Request for Comments) 1334, and later revised in RFC 1994, CHAP is a means of encrypting authentication sessions between a client and server. Since this protocol is defined by an RFC, it enjoys a broad base of support among many operating systems and other devices.

Microsoft CHAP (v1 and v2) (MS-CHAP)   Microsoft's derivative of CHAP, or Challenge Handshake Authentication Protocol. An encrypted authentication method that also allows you to encrypt an entire dial-up session, not just the original authentication, which is important when it comes to setting up virtual private networking sessions.

Caller-ID/Callback Security

Although Caller-ID/callback security isn't an option for Windows XP Professional, it is worth discussing in terms of security. Simply put, let's assume that you have dial-in access to your corporate network, and the worst-case scenario comes true—someone obtains your user ID and password. Caller-ID and callback security can still provide your corporation with some level of protection. Both features work by verifying that you are actually calling from an authorized phone number—a phone number that has been predefined by the administrators of your corporate network.

Caller-ID Security   If the dial-in systems on your corporate network can support it, your account can be set up with a Caller-ID–based security option. In this scenario, when the computers on your corporate network receive your incoming call, they take note of the phone number. Once you provide a username and password authentication, your username is checked for an associated Caller-ID number. If the two numbers match, your call is granted. If the two numbers don't match, your call is denied. Therefore, even if someone has your username and password, this type of security can protect your corporation's computers. The drawback is that whenever you want to connect to your company's network, you must be calling in from the approved number.

Callback Security   This functions in a similar manner to Caller-ID security, but is a bit more secure (I've read that Caller-ID information can be spoofed with the correct equipment). With callback security enabled, your user account is associated with a call-back number. When you initiate a dial-in session to your company's network, you will provide your username and password.

The system that verifies your dial-in credentials will see that you have a call-back number associated with your account and immediately disconnect you. After it disconnects you, it will then initiate a call to your system and establish the connection. This is a very secure method of verifying a dial-in user; however, it comes at the price of having to always log in from the same phone number.

If you are concerned that your account credentials might fall into the wrong hands, talk to your network administrators to see if either of these options are available for your dial-in system. Windows 2000 Server supports both of them.

Third-Party Products: SecurID, SafeWord

Although this is a book about Windows XP Professional, I want to mention two products that fall into the "extremely cool" category of security products: SecurID from RSA Security and SafeWord from Secure Computing.

The nature of these two products is similar—they are what's known as a "second factor" authentication method. What that means is that your "first factor" of authentication—your username and password—is not good enough to obtain access to a resource; you must authenticate yourself in another (second) manner before access is granted. You can think of a second factor authentication as being similar to having two different locks on a door—a regular one and a deadbolt. You won't be granted access until you can provide the correct authentication (a key) for both.

How they work—from a user perspective—is quite simple. When you start a dial-up networking session, you are prompted for your username and password. That is your first authentication. After successfully negotiating a dial-in connection to your corporation's network, you are then prompted for a second authentication—a second "password," if you will. What's unique about this second password is that it's a different password every time.

SecurID works through a small key fob that has a digital readout on it. Every 60 seconds, a new number appears on the readout. The key fob is given to a user and must be used to gain access to the company's network. Let's take a look at a typical example.

Let's assume that a user named Wendy is trying to dial in to her company's network. Now, Wendy has a password for her account—let's assume that it's "arlington". Wendy also has a SecurID key fob that has been assigned to her. At the moment she is trying to sign in, her key fob is displaying the six-digit number 378265. As an added measure, Wendy also has a four-digit "pin" number assigned to her. Let's assume that she used 1234 for her pin number.

When Wendy dials in, she'll type in her username and password (wendy/arlington) just as in a normal dial-up connection. Her Windows XP Professional system will dial in to the company's network and negotiate a connection. Once the connection is negotiated, Wendy will be prompted for her SecurID passcode. At the moment she is logging in, the correct passcode for her will be "1234378265". Her passcode is validated by a SecurID server within the company's network, and if the passcode is correct, she is granted access to the network. The SafeWord system also functions on a similar, one-time password concept.

As you can see, this is an *extremely* secure means of authenticating a user. If someone manages to obtain Wendy's username and password, they are useless without her SecurID key fob. And even if someone were to obtain the key fob itself, it would still be useless without knowing Wendy's individual pin number.

Protecting Against the Abduction of Data

OK, I'll admit it, the word "abduction" sounds a bit too much like an *X-Files* episode, but the word just fits so well with the concept I am trying to get across. In any case, the abduction of data is simply someone without authorization copying corporate data off your system. You know, your typical corporate espionage stuff.

As I stated earlier in the chapter, I can imagine that this will become more and more of a problem as companies allow increasing amounts of data outside their corporate walls. After all, who is it more difficult to steal data from—the well-guarded and physically secured corporate network, or Joe the account executive walking out of the building late at night with his laptop? A quick bop on Joe's head and a grab of the laptop would compromise all the data stored on the laptop.

Or would it? Windows XP Professional contains encryption technologies that specifically address this type of situation. The encrypting file system (EFS) can ensure that no one other than you will be able to read your encrypted files if your computer is ever stolen.

The encryption capabilities available in Windows XP Professional (right out of the box) are very good. And with a few additional precautions, you can make sure that they are absolutely secure—that no one will be able to ever read your encrypted files.

NOTE *It goes without saying that if someone gets hold of your username and password, all bets are off. As far as Windows XP Professional is concerned, if someone logs in with your username and password, it must be you! Windows XP Professional will gladly decrypt all your files in that scenario. So, it's critical to make sure that your password is not discovered.*

Encrypting Files with EFS

Encrypting data is merely a matter of a few clicks of the mouse, and an entire folder or folder structure can be protected from prying eyes. Having said that, you should try to follow a few "best practices" principles when working with EFS:

Don't encrypt the Windows XP Professional folders. This would have a significant impact on your system—most likely it wouldn't boot. Fortunately, EFS will always try to prevent you from encrypting system files, but you probably shouldn't even try to in the first place.

Don't encrypt your My Documents folder. This runs 100 percent contrary to Microsoft's suggested practices. The reason I recommend that you *don't* encrypt your My Documents folder is because there are almost no visual clues in the Windows interface that a file or folder has been encrypted. I've already read a few accounts of users who were "playing around" with EFS and followed Microsoft's suggestions to encrypt the My Documents folder, but months later they forgot that they had done it. Because of some sort of failure (in one instance, a simple HAL [hardware abstraction layer] upgrade), the users reloaded Windows XP Professional. Guess what? Since they hadn't taken the additional step to back up their recovery keys, all their documents were irrecoverable. Gone. Personally, I like to make a folder called Encrypted Stuff, which gives me an obvious visual reminder that anything within that folder will be encrypted.

Encrypt your Temp folder.   Your temporary folder (which can usually be found by typing **SET** at a command prompt and looking for the TEMP= and TMP= folders) is often a repository for fragments of your data, documents, and so on. Sometimes programs don't properly clean up after themselves, and they leave fragments of your files in this folder. If this folder is encrypted, no leftover fragments can be used by anyone else.

Encrypt entire folders, not just files.   As I mentioned earlier, I like to make a special folder on my machine and call it Encrypted Stuff—then I just copy everything into it that I want protected. Encrypting files and folders is really quite simple. Follow these steps:

1. Click Start, right-click My Computer, and choose Explore from the shortcut menu to open an Explorer-type window.

2. Right-click the file or folder, and choose Properties from the shortcut menu to open the Properties dialog box for that item.

3. Click the Advanced button to open the Advanced Attributes dialog box:

Notice the two check boxes at the bottom of this dialog box: Compress Contents to Save Disk Space and Encrypt Contents to Secure Data. These two items are mutually exclusive, meaning that if you compress a file you can't encrypt it, and if you encrypt a file, you can't compress it.

4. If necessary, uncompress the file, and check the Encrypt Contents to Secure Data check box.

5. Click OK, and then click OK again to encrypt the file.

It almost seems too easy, doesn't it? Well, don't take my word for it—try logging in as someone else and see if you can read the file. You can't. Even if you have full access to the file under another user account, you won't be able to open the file, copy it, or do anything else with it. Only the user account that encrypted the file can decrypt it.

Summary

In this chapter, I talked about the security of corporate data once it moves outside your corporation's walls. I covered how to encrypt the data as it is transferred to your computer and even how to encrypt the data once it is stored on your computer. I talked about how to protect your account credentials and proposed solutions that you can provide to your corporate network administrators if an additional level of security is necessary.

Part 4

Diagnosing, Administering, Automating and Troubleshooting Windows XP

In this section you will learn how to:
- ◆ Manage Administrative and Diagnostic Tools
- ◆ Understand and Use the Registry
- ◆ Use Scripts to Automate Tasks
- ◆ Prevent Disasters and Recover From Them
- ◆ Use Advanced Troubleshooting Methodology

Chapter 21

Administrative and Diagnostic Tools

WINDOWS XP PROFESSIONAL COMES WITH administrative tools for you to use when you add new disk volumes and check on existing ones, track system events, watch system performance, and run general diagnostics. Let's take a look at these tools and how they can help you keep your system running smoothly.

- ◆ Running Disk Management
- ◆ Running Event Viewer
- ◆ Monitoring performance
- ◆ Running Task Manager

Running Disk Management

In Windows XP Professional, Disk Management is part of the Computer Management console in Administrative Tools. To open Disk Management, follow these steps:

1. Choose Start ➢ Control Panel to open Control Panel.

2. Click the Performance and Maintenance link, and then click Administrative Tools to open the Administrative Tools folder.

3. Click Computer Management to open the Computer Management window.

4. In the Computer Management pane, expand Storage, and then click Disk Management. You'll see something similar to the following.

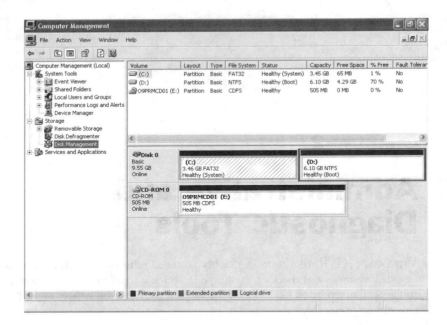

The Disk Management tool, which is displayed in the right pane of the Computer Management window, gives you a graphical representation of the hard disks and CD-ROM devices in your computer. You can, however, customize the way information is presented in a variety of ways.

The Disk Management window is in three parts. On the left is the Computer Management pane of the Computer Management console. The lower-right pane contains the information for all the physical disks installed in the computer, excluding floppy drives. The upper-right pane contains descriptions of those disks, including data on the amount of space used and free, the type of file system, and the health of that system.

To use Disk Management to create or delete partitions, format drives, and create stripe or volume sets, simply click the disk that you want to modify, and select the change that you want to make from the Action menu. Or you can right-click the drive that you want to modify, and then select the appropriate action from the shortcut menu.

Deciding Which File System Is Best

Windows XP Professional can use the File Allocation Table (FAT) file system supported by DOS and all versions of Windows, the File Allocation Table 32 (FAT32) file system supported by Windows 9*x* and Windows 2000, and the New Technology File System (NTFS) supported by Windows NT and Windows 2000. Each file system has its respective upsides and downsides. Here's a quick rundown.

FAT's main advantage is its backward compatibility with DOS and with Windows 9*x* systems using FAT. FAT's main disadvantage is that it's a 16-bit file system with a minimum cluster size of 32KB. The result is that FAT can address partitions only up to 2GB. If your drive is larger than this, you'll have to create two or more partitions to use FAT. Also, FAT has no security features. As a positive note, under Windows NT, the FAT file system has a maximum file and partition size of 4GB.

The FAT32 file system evolved from the traditional FAT file system used by DOS and Windows. Windows XP can format FAT32 partitions up to 32GB and can access FAT32 partitions up to the maximum size (although this is not recommended for partitions larger than 32GB). One downside to FAT32 is that, like FAT, it does not provide any local security.

In contrast, NTFS is a robust, 32-bit file system with many security features, including password protection for specific files, the capability to limit access to specific files, file compression, file recovery, and the capability to address very large partitions. Although a system using NTFS will run a bit slower than one using FAT in some cases, NTFS is your best bet if you want the additional features of Windows XP Professional.

To add another twist, Windows XP Professional provides support for usage quotas on NTFS partitions.

NOTE   *If you dual-boot Windows XP Professional formatted with NTFS and another operating system formatted with FAT or FAT32, Windows XP Professional can access the FAT and FAT32 files, but the other system will not be able to access NTFS files. The same is true of a network. If one machine uses NTFS and another uses FAT or FAT32, the NTFS machine will be able to access FAT and FAT32 files, but the FAT and FAT32 machine will not be able to access files on the NTFS machine.*

USING COMPRESSION IN NTFS

In Chapter 6, we looked at how to compress files and folders, but Windows XP Professional can also compress entire volumes. The compression ratio usually winds up being about 1.5:1, or 33 percent.

To compress an NTFS hard-disk volume, follow these steps:

1. Click Start, and then click My Computer.

2. Right-click the volume you want to compress, and choose Properties from the shortcut menu to open the Properties dialog box for that drive:

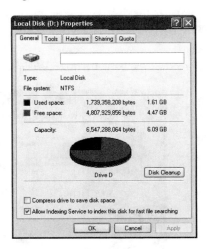

3. On the General tab, click the Compress Drive to Save Disk Space check box, and then click OK.

USING NTFS FILE SECURITY FEATURES

NTFS file security lets you change settings for disk drives, folders, and even files. These features can be useful if your machine stores many files that you share with other users on your network as well as your private files.

For information on how to set permissions for NTFS drives, folders, and files, see Chapter 18.

Setting Up a New Disk Drive in Windows XP Professional

If you've added a new disk drive to your system, Disk Management will be able to see it, but you'll need to create a partition and a volume on it before Windows XP Professional can use it.

NOTE   After you create a partition on a new disk and format it, you can use it in Windows XP Professional without rebooting. You can even change the size of a partition or extend it across several hard drives without rebooting.

Let's step through adding a new partition and creating a volume on a new disk:

1. In the Disk Management window, right-click the drive, and choose Initialize Disk from the shortcut menu to open the Initialize Disk dialog box:

2. Click OK to initialize the disk. When the initialization is complete, you'll see the Disk Management window again.

3. In the Disk Management window, select the new disk, and choose Action ➤ All Tasks ➤ New Partition to start the New Partition Wizard.

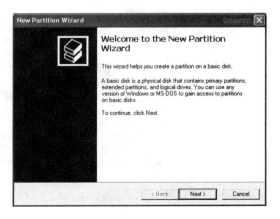

4. Click Next to open the Select Partition Type screen:

NOTE *Windows XP Professional supports a maximum of four primary partitions per hard drive or three primary partitions and one extended partition.*

5. Select the type of partition you want to create, either primary or extended, and click Next to open the Specify Partition Size screen:

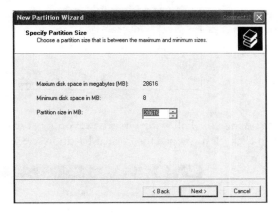

6. In the Partition Size in MB spin box, indicate the size of the partition, and then click Next to open the Completing the New Partition Wizard screen. Click Finish to close the Wizard and create the partition.

CREATING EXTENDED PARTITIONS AND LOGICAL DRIVES

The main difference between a primary partition and an extended partition is that you can create multiple logical drives only on an extended partition. So what's a logical drive? Simply put, a logical drive is a designated portion of a physical drive. Windows XP Professional is aware of two kinds of drives, physical and logical. A physical drive is the actual drive itself, and Windows XP Professional can create partitions on it and format it. You can create a logical drive on an extended partition that may be only part of a physical disk, but Windows XP Professional will see that logical drive as a separate unit, and you can map a drive letter to it.

NOTE   *Operating systems should be installed on and boot from primary partitions.*

NOTE   *Only extended partitions can contain logical disk volumes.*

To create a logical drive on an extended partition, follow these steps:

1. In the Disk Management window, right-click the partition, and choose New Logical Drive to open the New Partition Wizard.

2. At the Welcome screen, click Next to open the Select Partition Type screen, select the Logical Drive option, and click Next to open the Assign Drive Letter or Path screen:

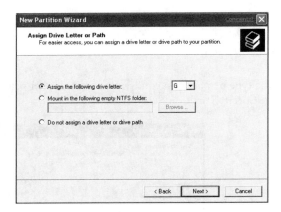

3. Click the Assign the Following Drive Letter option, use the spin box to select a drive letter, and then click Next to open the Format Partition screen:

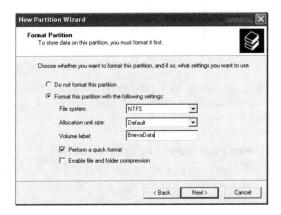

4. If necessary, click the Format This Partition with the Following Settings option, specify the file system you want to use and how to allocate the disk, and then give the volume a label. Tell the Wizard whether you want a quick format or to enable file and folder compression, and click Next.

NOTE *Remember, FAT will give you somewhat better speed performance but with limited volume size. NTFS enables you to use Windows XP Professional file compression, security features, and file recovery.*

NOTE *Disabling QuickFormat tells Windows XP Professional to first scan the partition for bad sectors. If you know the disk is free of bad sectors, go ahead and QuickFormat it. If you're not sure, it's better to have Windows XP Professional scan for bad sectors. It will take considerably longer than a QuickFormat but could save you trouble up the road.*

5. In the final screen of the Wizard, click Finish to format the drive.

USING DYNAMIC VOLUMES

Traditional partition types stored their information in a *partition table* that was located in the first physical sector of the hard disk. It was this location and its limited storage space for partition information that limited us to four partitions per physical disk. The partition table stores information for the size and location of each partition and is used to find the bootable partition during the startup procedure.

Dynamic volumes store their partition information in the data portion of the drive, and thus they are not limited in the amount of information they can store. To convert a basic disk to a dynamic disk, right-click the disk in the Disk Management tool, and select Dynamic from the shortcut menu. You will have to reboot to perform the conversion. After the restart, you will be able to create or modify dynamic volumes on the disk, including expanding the volume across multiple disks.

Dynamic volumes come in various flavors:

Simple A simple dynamic volume is similar to a traditional partition in that it exists on a single drive. It can be resized by extending the volume if it is on a dynamic disk that was created as a dynamic disk and not upgraded from a basic disk.

Spanned This dynamic volume spans two or more disks to create one logical volume, as its name implies, but it can be extended. Spanned volumes are the same as volume sets in NT 4, but in Windows XP Professional they are only available on dynamic disks.

Mirrored This volume type is only available on Windows 2000 Server. Mirrored volumes provide fault tolerance by keeping an exact mirror image of all data in the volume. If you lose one disk, you still have an exact copy of all the data.

Striped Striped volumes are the fastest type of dynamic volume and yield great benefits in performance. They are not fault tolerant, however. If you lose one disk, you lose all the data in the volume. They are the same as the traditional stripe sets available in NT, but stripe volumes are only available in Windows XP Professional on dynamic disks.

RAID 5 This type of dynamic volume is only available in Windows 2000 Server. RAID 5 is also known as striping with parity. RAID 5 allows the volume to lose one hard disk without failing. It does this by combining the remaining data with the parity information to recreate the data on-the-fly.

NOTE   *Dynamic volumes are not supported on portable computers, removable disks, detachable disks using Universal Serial Bus (USB) or IEEE 1394 (also called FireWire) interfaces, or on disks connected to shared SCSI buses.*

Running Event Viewer

One of Windows XP Professional's more handy tools is the Event Viewer, which can be helpful for troubleshooting a misbehaving PC or for getting a better handle on what Windows XP Professional is doing behind the scenes. To open Event Viewer, follow these steps:

1. Choose Start ➤ Control Panel to open Control Panel.

2. Click Performance and Maintenance, click Administrative Tools, and then click Event Viewer.

3. In the pane on the left, select Application, Security, or System. If you select System, you'll see something similar to the following:

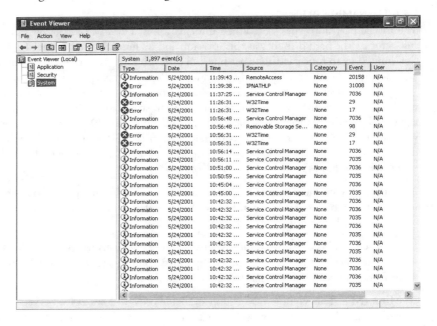

System events are logged by Windows XP Professional's system components, including hardware drivers. For example, if a driver fails to load, it will write a system event to the System log. Or if a Windows XP Professional service fails to initialize, the service reports its failure in the System log. There are three types of System log events:

Information   Logged when a driver or service starts successfully and indicated by the blue letter *i*. For example, each time you boot up Windows XP Professional, a system event is logged, indicating that the event log service was started.

Warning   Logged when a condition occurs that could mean future trouble, for example, a nearly full hard drive. Indicated by an exclamation point in a yellow triangle.

Error   Logged when a service or a driver fails to start or load and indicated by an X in a red circle. For example, if your network card driver fails, that error is logged, as is an error indicating that any network protocols communicating with that network card have failed.

Security events occur if you've enabled auditing on a shared disk, subfolder, or file. Audited events are written to the Security log when someone accesses your shared area and logs in. An administrator can specify which events are logged into the Security log. There are two types of Security log events:

Success   Logged when a user successfully logs on to one of your shared areas: a disk, a subfolder, or a file.

Failure   Logged when a user fails to log on to one of your shared areas.

Windows XP Professional applications write status and error messages in the Application log. If an application is crashing or behaving oddly, it's usually a good idea to check the Application log for error messages. The Application log uses the same three event types as the System log: Information, Warning, and Error. Application developers specify which events to log.

With Event Viewer, you can look at only one event log at a time. To change views, select the log you want to see.

TIP   When opening old log files, be careful not to confuse them with your system's actual logs. The system log files live in the `Winnt\System32\Config` *subfolder. If you open a log other than one of your system's three primary logs, its name will be displayed in the title bar of the Event Viewer window. Each time you open Event Viewer, it loads the system's three event logs.*

For any of your three logs, Event Viewer supports two viewing modes: All Records and Filter. The default view is the All Records view. In this view, you see all the events currently stored in a log. To view only specific events, follow these steps:

1. Choose View ➤ Filter to open the Properties dialog box for the log you are viewing.

2. Click the Filter tab:

3. Select the types of events, their source, category, and so on, and then click OK.

If a hardware device isn't loading or is behaving oddly, one of the first places to look for the cause is the Event Viewer because a misbehaving device will likely document its problems in the System log. And even though Warning and Error events are sometimes short on specifics, they can often be good indicators of where to begin looking. Here's what a troubleshooting session might look like.

On startup, the driver for a Sound Blaster card fails to initialize; the result is a lack of wave audio in Windows XP Professional. The first indicator you get is a message informing you that at least one Windows XP Professional service failed to start.

Upon opening Event Viewer, you'd see an Error event in the System log reported by Windows XP Professional's Service Control Manager. After clicking it, you'd see the message "The following boot-start or system-start driver(s) failed to load: sndblst." Although this somewhat terse message doesn't provide any specifics from Event Viewer, you could then check your Sound Blaster driver's status by following these steps:

1. Click Start, right-click My Computer, and choose Properties from the shortcut menu to open the System Properties dialog box.

2. Click the Hardware tab, and then click the Device Manager button to open Device Manager.

3. Expand Sound, Video and Game Controllers, right-click Sound Blaster, choose Properties from the shortcut menu to open the Properties dialog box, and check the settings.

Event Viewer has a few other handy features to check out. From the Action menu, you can clear all events from all three logs. Be careful here, however. Although Windows XP Professional will issue a warning, there's no Undo for clearing the logs. If you think you want to access event information contained in the logs, save them as backups in a different subfolder so that you can access them later if need be.

To change the size of a log or overwrite its settings, right-click the log, and choose Properties from the shortcut menu to open the log's Properties dialog box. Figure 21.1 shows the General tab for the System log's Properties dialog box.

FIGURE 21.1

You can change log settings in the log's Properties dialog box.

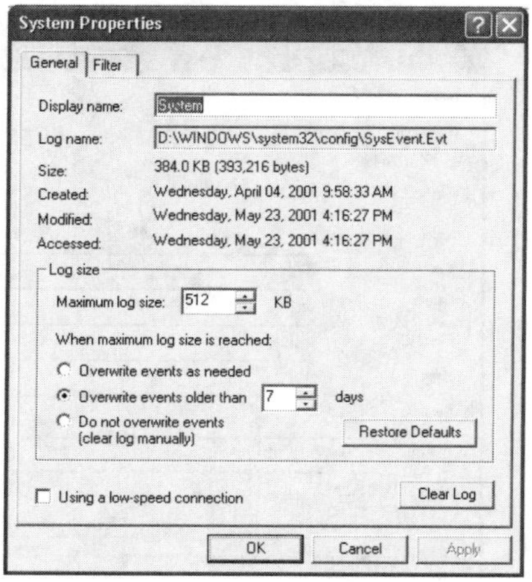

Log size can be anywhere from 64KB on up (the default is 512KB). Windows XP Professional defaults to overwriting events more than seven days old; so if your network administrator wants to back up your event logs weekly, all events will be cataloged. This can pose a problem only if your system is generating an unusually large amount of log events—for example, an application or device isn't working properly or a network protocol stack is continuously issuing warning events.

If you're getting event log information about other computers (or they're getting event log information about your computer) on your network and if you are connected to that network via a modem, click the Using a Low-Speed Connection check box.

NOTE *If you've set event overwriting to be cleared manually or have specified to overwrite events of a certain age, the Windows XP Professional System log can fill up and can no longer be updated until you make more room in the log. If your system is having problems and can't update the System log, diagnosing a problem may be more difficult. If your log file has filled, you can't re-enable event logging by increasing the logs' file sizes. You'll have to back up your logs, clear all events from them, and then increase the files' sizes.*

WARNING *Be careful to watch the size of logs as they grow. If you have set the logs to never overwrite and they fill up, Windows XP Professional may hang. If you are auditing for security events, the recommended setting is to never overwrite because security events should be documented over long periods of time. Clearing and archiving the log should be a part of routine maintenance.*

Using the View menu in Event Viewer, you can sort events chronologically, listing either the oldest or the newest events first. To find a specific event, choose View ➤ Find to open the Find in Local System dialog box:

This feature essentially duplicates the Filter function, except that Event Viewer's Find displays, one by one, events that fit a certain description rather than listing them all at once.

To modify the display in Event Viewer, choose View ➤ Customize to open the Customize View dialog box:

Click or clear a check box to show or hide an item.

Monitoring Performance

Windows XP Professional is designed to "self-tune" for optimal performance but also provides several tools for detecting possible performance bottlenecks. You can use the Windows XP Professional Performance console to monitor and log the performance of hundreds of variables, including some very esoteric ones intended to be used by developers and network administrators when tracking application and system behavior. In addition to tracking performance on your system, you can track performance counters on other Windows XP Professional machines on your network. We'll take a look at the Performance console and some of its components. Rather than cover every variable counter you can assign in Performance, we'll look at about a dozen or so key counters that deliver the most relevant system information.

NOTE *If you want only a quick read on Windows XP Professional "vitals," right-click the Taskbar and select Task Manager from the shortcut menu. Task Manager has a Performance tab that reports CPU usage and memory statistics. Task Manager also lists applications you have open, as well as processes that are running (those created by programs and Windows XP Professional services). Task Manager is discussed in detail at the end of this chapter.*

To open the Performance console, in Control Panel click the Performance and Maintenance link, click Administrative Tools, and then click Performance. Figure 21.2 shows the Performance console.

Performance provides three views of real-time data in System Monitor. To access one of these views, click the corresponding button on the toolbar. (To display a button's label, simply place the cursor over it.) The three views are simply different displays of the data that Performance can report. Here's a quick rundown:

View Graph Displays counters graphically. This is the view shown in Figure 21.2. You can add as many counters as you like, although more than about a half-dozen makes for a rather cluttered graph.

View Histogram   Displays bar graphs that dynamically update as the data changes.

View Report   Displays counters in real time (as Chart view does). Selected counters are listed and their values are updated at a specified rate.

FIGURE 21.2

The System Monitor in the Performance console delivers constantly updated information about the performance of subsystems, and it can update its display dozens of times a second.

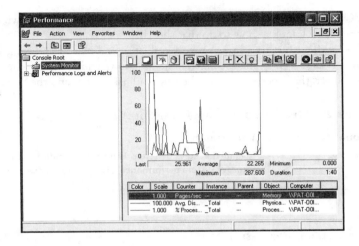

Before getting into detail about each of these views, let's look at some counters you're most likely to monitor.

Windows XP Professional classifies its subsystem components into objects, and each object has anywhere from two to more than a dozen counters that you can monitor. In addition, certain objects—such as processors, physical disks, and logical disks—also have instances because your Windows XP Professional system may have more than one of these types of hardware.

To display an explanation of what any counter monitors, follow these steps:

1. Click the Add button on the toolbar (it has a plus sign) to open the Add Counters dialog box:

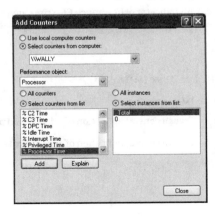

2. Select an object from the Performance Object drop-down list.

3. Select a counter from the Select Counters from List drop-down list.

4. Click the Explain button.

Obviously, you also use the Add Counters dialog box to specify which counters you want to monitor, and we'll look at how to do that shortly.

So without further ado, let's take a look at several objects and some of their counters. Tables 21.1 through 21.4 show you the counters, the functions, and the importance of four objects: the Paging File object, the Processor object, the PhysicalDisk object, and the Server object.

TABLE 21.1: THE PAGING FILE (SWAP FILE) OBJECT

COUNTER	IMPORTANCE
% Usage	A value that stays persistently high is one indicator that additional RAM would noticeably improve system performance, given the type of work you're doing.

TABLE 21.2: THE PROCESSOR OBJECT

COUNTER	IMPORTANCE
% Processor Time	May indicate that an application or a service is using the CPU excessively, cutting into overall system performance.
% Interrupt Time	Interrupts execute in Windows XP Professional's kernel mode; applications execute in user mode. Excessive hardware interrupts can hamper overall system performance.
% Privileged Time	Similar to % Interrupt Time; if your system is spending excessive amounts of time in Privileged mode, applications, which all run in user mode, have to wait for the CPU to return to user mode to access the CPU.
% User Time	An indicator of how much CPU time applications have available to them.

TABLE 21.3: THE PHYSICALDISK OBJECT

COUNTER	IMPORTANCE
Disk Read Bytes/sec	Gives a general indication of a disk's read performance.
Disk Write Bytes/sec	Gives a general indication of a disk's write performance.

TABLE 21.4: THE SERVER OBJECT

COUNTER	IMPORTANCE
Bytes Total/sec	Excessive network access of your system by other users can drag down your overall performance.
Errors Logon	Repeated failed logon attempts may mean a password-guessing program is trying to crack into your system.
Sessions Timed Out	Useful for setting idle time-out values. Each active peer connection to your system slightly diminishes overall system performance.

Adding a Counter in Graph View

Performance defaults to Graph view, which graphically displays any selected counters. Let's go through the steps to add the Processor object and % Processor Time counter and the Paging File object and % Usage counter:

1. In the Performance console, select System Monitor, and click the Add button to open the Add Counters dialog box.

2. In the Performance Object drop-down list, select Processor.

3. In the Select Counter from List drop-down list, select %Processor Time, and then click Add.

4. In the Performance Object drop-down list, select Paging File.

5. In the Select Counter from List drop-down list, select %Usage, and then click Add.

6. Click Close.

Back in the Performance console, you'll see something similar to the following:

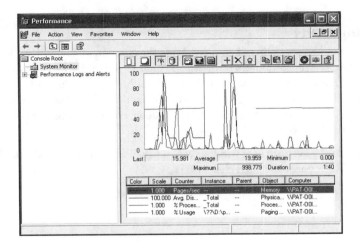

To save this view at any point in time, right-click the chart, choose Save As from the shortcut menu to open the Save As dialog box, give the file a name, and click Save. You can save the view as a Web page or as a report.

TIP To highlight a counter, select it at the bottom of the window and press Ctrl+H.

To customize the chart's colors, fonts, and other graphical elements, follow these steps:

1. Right-click the chart, and choose Properties from the shortcut menu to open the System Monitor Properties dialog box:

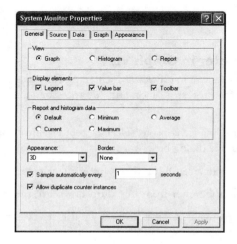

2. Click one of the five tabs, and then specify your options.

3. When you're finished, click OK.

Using Alerts

Alerts can be very useful when monitoring the computer system over a long period of time or when you have several computers to monitor. An alert is triggered when a condition you have selected occurs. For example, if you wanted to find out how often your CPU was being stressed by the normal level of activity throughout the day, you could make an alert that would trigger whenever the System object Processor Queue Length counter exceeded a count of two.

To set Alert counters, follow these steps:

1. In the Performance window, expand the Performance Logs and Alerts entry in the Console Root pane, and then click Alerts.

2. Right-click in the right pane, and choose New Alert Settings from the shortcut menu to open the New Alert Settings dialog box:

3. In the Name box, enter a name for this group of Alert settings, and then click OK to open the Properties dialog box for the new Alert group.

4. Enter a comment that describes the settings, and then click the Add button to open the Add Counters dialog box:

5. Select Use Local Computer Counters.

6. In the Performance Object drop-down list box, select an object.

7. In the Select Counters from List drop-down list box, select a counter, and then click Add.

8. When you're finished, click Close.

9. Back in the Properties dialog box, you can set a trigger using the Alert When the Value Is drop-down list box. Set a limit by entering a percentage in the Limit box.

10. Specify the frequency at which data is sampled using the Interval spin box and the Units drop-down list box.

11. Click OK.

To save this view of the Alert log, choose File ➤ Save As.

NOTE   *You cannot set an alert for both over and under conditions on the same counter.*

Using Counter Log View

Performance lets you track hundreds of counters in real time (as they happen), but often you may want to review system events one by one. To do this, you set Counter Logs to capture objects' counters to a file for later review. Let's step through logging Processor and Memory counters.

1. In the Console Root pane of the Performance console, expand Performance Logs and Alerts.

2. Select Counter Logs, right-click in the right pane, and choose New Log Settings from the shortcut menu to open the New Log Settings dialog box.

3. Enter a name that will describe this log, and click OK to open the Properties dialog box for this log.

4. Click the Add Counters button to open the Add Counters dialog box.

5. Click Use Local Computer Counters, and then select the Processor Performance object.

6. Click the All Counters button to add all the counters for this object.

7. Click the Add button.

8. Now repeat steps 5 through 7 using the Memory object.

9. Click the Close button.

10. Click OK to close the Properties dialog box and return to Performance.

11. Right-click the icon for the log settings you just created, and select Start from the shortcut menu to start the log. When you want to stop the log, right-click the icon again and select Stop from the shortcut menu.

WARNING *Carefully watch the size of the log file as it grows. It is easy to gather enough data to fill a hard drive if left unattended for too long. When monitoring performance over a long period of time, it is more common to set the time interval to several minutes to avoid gathering too much data.*

Viewing specific data points is a little tricky here because the timeframe "slider" controller works differently in each of the three views. Let's take a look at it. Follow these steps:

1. In the Performance console, select System Monitor, right-click in the right pane, and choose Properties from the shortcut menu to open the System Monitor Properties dialog box.

2. Click the Source tab.

3. Click the Time Range button, and then set the beginning and ending time to view using the end handles on the slider bar.

4. Click OK.

Because Log view shows only one data point at a time, you can change the data point by using the Time Range slider to change the start point. After you click OK, you'll see a data point for that time value. This view is useful for zeroing in on data at an exact time, but it isn't very useful for looking at multiple data points.

Using Report View

Similar to Graph view, Report view shows up-to-the minute statistics on object counters but displays them numerically rather than graphically. If you want to watch many counters simultaneously, Report view is your best bet because Graph view gets to be a cluttered mess when you try to display too many counters simultaneously. To display counters in Report view, click the View Report button. You'll see something similar to the following:

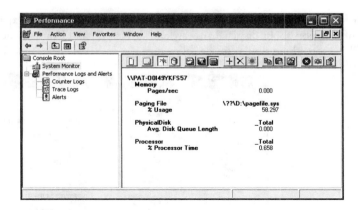

Running System Information

When everything on your system works, new devices install painlessly, and services work right the first time, life is good. If only it were always so. Alas, the general headaches of new hardware installation follow—cracking the box open, finding an available I/O slot, dealing with the mysterious force that makes your system's box much easier to rip open than it is to put back together. Then, after you restart the system, there may be I/O resource conflicts or services may fail for whatever reason. The fun never ends.

Fortunately, Windows XP Professional provides some tools to ease system troubleshooting. Chief among them is System Information, which you can use to display system information ranging from detailed display driver data to the services that are installed and the other services or devices on which they depend. To open System Information, click Start ➤ All Programs ➤ Accessories ➤ System Tools ➤ System Information.

The pane on the right displays the version and build of Windows XP Professional you're running, your CPU type, a serial number, and registration information, as well as information ranging from the manufacturer on your system and its model number to the amount of memory free or the amount of page file in use. Figure 21.3 shows information about my system.

FIGURE 21.3

The System Summary screen displays local configuration details.

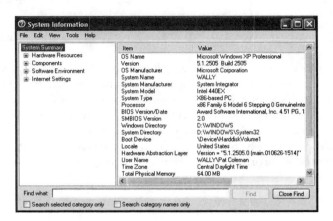

To view information on the hardware installed in your computer, expand Hardware Resources. For information about display hardware and drivers, expand Components, and then select Display. You'll see something similar to the following:

For information about the drives on your system, expand Storage under Components, and then select Drives. You'll see something similar to the following:

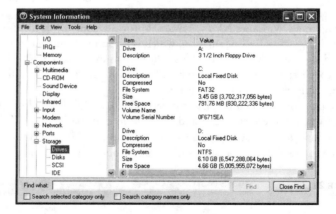

The Drives screen gives detailed information about local floppy, hard, and CD-ROM drives. Although there isn't really any diagnostic information available here per se, the Drives screen can indicate trouble with a drive simply by showing you that Windows XP Professional cannot see the drive. For example, say you have a second hard drive that is *not* displayed on this list. The drive's absence may indicate either a faulty data or power cable connection to the unit. If the drive is a SCSI device, the SCSI chain may be incorrectly terminated. If it's a second EIDE hard drive, there may be an incorrect master-slave configuration on the second drive. Before looking at more complicated problems, always check your physical connections. Often, the solution is simpler than you think.

TIP *You cannot get information about floppy, removable disk, or CD-ROM drives unless a disk is in the drive. With a disk present, you'll get information about that specific disk.*

For information about services, expand Software Environment, and click Services. You'll see something similar to the following:

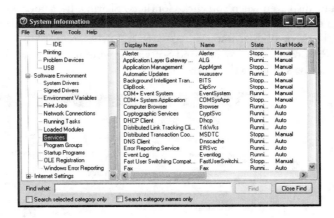

NOTE *You can't use the Services folder to start and stop services. For that, you use Services under Services and Applications in Computer Management.*

For information about system resources, expand Hardware Resources and select one of the sub-folders. Figure 21.4 shows the IRQs in use on my system, which I displayed by selecting the IRQs folder.

FIGURE 21.4

The IRQs in use on my system

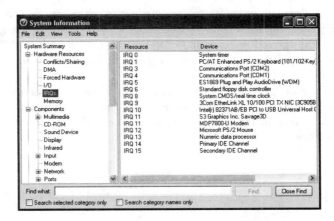

NOTE   *Windows XP Professional supports interrupt sharing by hardware devices to try to alleviate IRQ conflict problems. But older hardware devices that aren't aware of this feature frequently expect to be the sole possessors of a given IRQ and won't do very well sharing it with another device. The best plan of action is for each hardware device to have its own dedicated IRQ(s).*

Since Windows XP Professional is a Plug-and-Play operating system, the values contained in the System Information screen should be correct. But sometimes, a device won't be displayed here because its resources are in conflict with another device. In this case, the two devices in question should be displayed when you click Conflicts/Sharing. It's a good idea to check here before you install a new device so that you can figure out which resources are allocated and which are available. Be sure to check all three resource types: IRQs, DMA, and I/O.

For Registry information, expand Software Environment, and click Environment Variables. You'll see something similar to the following:

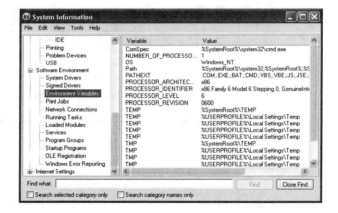

The Environment Variables folder is another view-only portion of the System Information screen; it displays Registry information about CPUs and system paths. You can't edit this information, but it may be valuable to a technical support engineer trying to troubleshoot your system. Windows applications, in addition to using the system's pagefile, will often write temporary files for storing less frequently used data rather than using system memory. It's a method of "cheating" on the amount of memory the application allocates or using allocated memory for more immediate or more frequently used tasks.

To create and print a report from any of the System Information screen items, select the item and choose File ➤ Print. Because so much information is generated, you might want to save the information in a file rather than printing it. To save the file, choose File ➤ Save to open the Save As dialog box.

Running Task Manager

Task Manager (see Figure 21.5) is a tool that lets you quickly monitor and troubleshoot Windows XP Professional, particularly in terms of the programs you are running.

NOTE *If multiple users are logged on to your computer, you will also see a Users tab in Task Manager.*

FIGURE 21.5

Use Task Manager to easily monitor programs you are running.

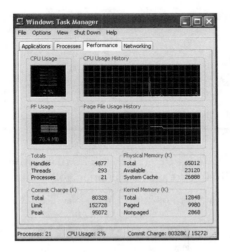

To run Task Manager, do one of the following:

◆ Right-click your Taskbar, and choose Task Manager from the shortcut menu.

◆ Choose Start ➤ Run, type **taskmgr** in the Open box, and click OK.

TIP *If your system is causing some difficulty that makes the above methods unavailable, press Ctrl+Alt+Delete to open Task Manager. Go ahead—try it.*

Figure 21.5 shows Task Manager open at the Performance tab. Regardless of which tab you are looking at, though, the bottom of Task Manager displays the number of processes being run, the percentage of CPU usage, and the amount of memory being used, including any virtual memory you may be using. This quick reference tells you everything you need to know in order to immediately understand the operating condition of your system.

TASK MANAGER APPLICATIONS

Task Manager's Applications tab lists all running applications and their current status (see Figure 21.6). An application's status will be either Running, if the program is behaving properly, or Not Responding, if the program is having problems.

FIGURE 21.6

The Applications tab of Task Manager

To close a running application, select it, and click End Task. To switch to a running application, select it, and click Switch To. To start a new application, follow these steps:

1. Click the New Task button to open the Create New Task dialog box:

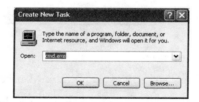

2. Type the name of the application in the Open box, and click OK.

TASK MANAGER PROCESSES

You can use the list on the Processes tab (see Figure 21.7) to monitor and halt any processes that are running on your computer. Processes are measured in all the separate executables that Windows XP Professional runs concurrently. This includes any applications you are running and all the background executables that Windows XP Professional runs automatically, including services. To terminate a running process, select it, and click the End Process button.

WARNING *Don't end a process unless it is marked as being errant. Ending a process that is running may crash other programs that are running correctly if they depend on that process.*

FIGURE 21.7

Task Manager lets
you monitor running
processes.

TASK MANAGER PERFORMANCE

You use the Performance tab to monitor your computer's usage of memory, processor time, and other resources. The two central graphs on the page measure the amount of memory used and the amount of processor time used. For multiple processors, you can choose to show one graph for each CPU or one graph for combined CPUs. The Performance tab also contains information on how much physical memory is being used and how much memory the Windows XP Professional kernel is using.

TIP   When you run Task Manager, a small green square appears on your Taskbar next to your clock. This is a CPU usage meter. Point to the usage meter to display the percentage of CPU usage at the current moment.

TASK MANAGER NETWORKING

You use the Networking tab (shown in Figure 21.8) to monitor Internet and local area network usage. At the bottom of this tab is information about the link speed and the number of bytes transferred for each adapter.

By default, Task Manager is always on top when you have multiple windows open on the Desktop. If you don't prefer this arrangement, choose Options ➤ Always on Top to clear the check mark. You can also use Task Manager to put your computer in hibernation, turn it off, restart it, log off, or switch users. Choose the appropriate item from the Shut Down menu.

FIGURE 21.8

The Networking tab
in Task Manager

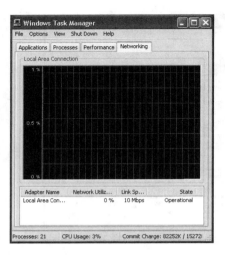

Summary

Windows XP Professional's suite of administrative tools covers the gamut of system functions, ranging from providing networking settings to detailed information about the operating system's main "plumbing."

   Most of the tools are intended to help troubleshoot system problems; using them in concert, you can gather sufficient information to remedy most system hiccups and even avert larger ones by catching them early. Although no set of tools is a panacea for all problems, those in Windows XP Professional will do a good job of helping you keep your system up and running.

Chapter 22

Understanding and Using the Registry

THIS CHAPTER COVERS HOW to work with one of the most mentioned but least understood components of Windows—the Registry, the giant repository of Windows' knowledge and wisdom about your computer. The chapter starts by discussing what the Registry is, what it does, why you might want to mess with it, and what the dangers are of doing so. It then details the step you *must* take before you make any changes to the Registry: backing up the Registry so that you can restore it if something goes wrong. After that, the chapter shows you how to use the Registry Editor to examine the contents of the Registry, find what you're looking for, and make changes.

In this chapter:

◆ Understanding the Registry and what it does

◆ Running Registry Editor

◆ Backing up your Registry

◆ Restoring the Registry from backup

◆ Registry subtrees and data types

◆ Finding and changing information in the Registry

What Is the Registry and What Does It Do?

Put simply, the Registry is a hierarchical database of all the settings required by your installation of Windows and the programs you've installed. These settings include information on the hardware installed on your computer and how it's configured; all the programs and their file associations; profiles for each user and group; and property settings for folders and files.

The Registry stores the information needed to keep your computer running. Windows itself stores a huge amount of information in the Registry, and each program you install stores information there too. You can store information in the Registry yourself if you want to, though unless you're creating programs, there's not much reason to do so.

The number of entries in the Registry depends on the number of users of the computer and the software installed, but between 50,000 and 100,000 entries is normal. This multitude of entries makes browsing through the Registry practical only for those with serious amounts of time weighing on their hands. Even searching through the Registry can be a slow process, because many of the entries contain similar information.

The Registry was introduced in Windows 95, and all 32-bit desktop versions of Windows have used it. In Windows 3.*x*, information was stored in initialization files—INI files for short. For example, Windows configuration information was stored in files such as WIN.INI and SYSTEM.INI. Most programs typically created configuration files of their own.

Centralizing all the information in the Registry has two main advantages. First, all the information is in one location. (Actually, it's in a couple of locations. More on this a little later in the chapter.) And second, you can back up the Registry (though most users forget or fail to do so) and restore it.

Not surprisingly, this centralization has the concomitant disadvantage that damage to the Registry can cripple Windows completely.

Why Work with the Registry?

Paradoxically enough, you *don't* work with the Registry—most of the time. In theory, you should never need to mess with the Registry.

That's why Windows provides no direct way from the user interface to view the Registry and change its contents. If you want to explore and change the Registry, you need to deliberately run the Registry Editor program, which is tucked away in a safe place where no casual user should stumble across it.

Most of the information that's stored in the Registry, you'll never need to change. Those relatively few pieces of information that Windows is happy for you to change are accessible through the Windows user interface, which provides you with an easier—if more restrictive—way of changing them than working in the Registry. For example, the settings in Control Panel applets store most of their information in the Registry, so you *could* edit the Registry and change the information there. But for all conventional purposes, you'll do better to work through those Control Panel applets and let them set the values in the Registry for you. Control Panel is designed to be easy to use, while the Registry isn't. Control Panel shows you your options in (mostly) intelligible ways; the information in the Registry is arcane when not incomprehensible. And Control Panel seldom screws up in translating your choices into hex and binary, whereas the Registry will happily accept input that will instruct Windows how to disable itself.

That said, sometimes you may need to access the Registry to change a vital piece of information that you cannot change through the user interface. Sometimes you'll need to access the Registry because something has gone wrong, and you need to change an entry manually. But more often, you'll hear about a cool tweak that you can perform by entering a new value in the Registry or by changing an existing value.

You can also use the Registry to store information of your own that you want to have available to Windows or to the programs you use. You might want to do this if you write your own programs, or if you use a macro language to create automated procedures in a program—for example, if you use VBA to automate tasks in Word, Excel, or Outlook. (You *could* also use the Registry to store odd information, such as names and addresses—but there are far better ways of spending your life.)

Preparing to Access the Registry

Before you do anything to the Registry, you need to understand this:

If you mess up the Registry, you may disable parts of Windows' functionality. You may even disable Windows itself so that it cannot boot.

So before you do *anything* to the Registry, back it up by exporting it as discussed later in this chapter. In fact, even if you don't make any changes to the Registry, it's a good idea to keep a backup of your Registry in case a program, Windows itself, or (more likely) a piece of malware makes a change for the worse.

Running Registry Editor

To work with the Registry, you use Registry Editor. Windows provides no Start menu item for Registry Editor, though you can of course create your own Start menu item if you want.

Unless you create a Start menu item or shortcut, the easiest way to run Registry Editor is to choose Start ➤ Run (or press Winkey+R), enter **regedit** in the Run dialog box, and click the OK button. Windows starts Registry Editor (shown in Figure 22.1).

FIGURE 22.1

Launch Registry Editor by choosing Start ➤ Run and entering **regedit** in the Run dialog box.

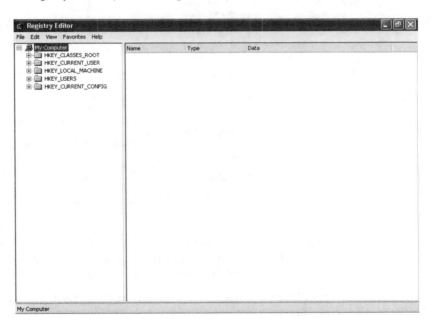

NOTE *If you've worked with the Registry in Windows 2000 or in Windows NT, you'll recall that those OSes included two Registry Editors—REGEDIT.EXE and REGEDT32.EXE. Both were functional, but REGEDT32.EXE offered a few more features than REGEDIT.EXE. Good news: Windows XP includes just one Registry Editor, REGEDIT.EXE, but there's a stub for REGEDT32.EXE, so you can start the same Registry Editor by using either name.*

Backing Up Your Registry

Before you do anything else with Registry Editor—and that includes exploring the subtrees and keys of the Registry, let alone changing any values—back up your Registry.

To back up the Registry, export it by taking the following steps from Registry Editor:

1. Select the My Computer item in Registry Editor.

TIP   If you want to back up only a subtree of the Registry, select the subtree instead of the My Computer item.

2. Choose File ➤ Export. Registry Editor displays the Export Registry File dialog box (shown in Figure 22.2). As you can see in the figure, this dialog box is a common Save As dialog box with an extra section tacked on at the bottom to house the Export Range box.

FIGURE 22.2

In the Export Registry File dialog box, specify that you want to export all of the Registry.

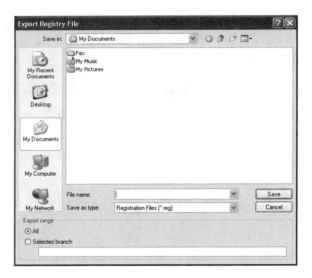

3. In the Export Range section, make sure the All option button is selected. If you chose a subtree in step 1, the Export Registry File dialog box appears with the Selected Branch option button selected and the subtree's name entered in the Selected Branch text box.

4. Specify the filename and location for the file as usual.

TIP   Registry files tend to be large—on the order of 20–30MB—so don't try to save yours to a floppy. If you have a CD recorder, save the Registry file to disk, and then burn it to CD.

5. Click the Save button. Windows saves the Registry file.

Restoring Your Registry

To restore your Registry (or part of it) from a Registry file you've exported, follow these steps:

1. From Registry Editor, choose File ➤ Import. Windows displays the Import Registry File dialog box, which is a renamed Open dialog box.

2. In the Files of Type drop-down list, select the Registration Files item or the Registry Hive Files item as appropriate.

3. Select the Registry file to import.

4. Click the Open button. Registry Editor imports the Registry file and adds it to the Registry.

Working in the Registry

Now that your Registry is safely backed up, it's time to examine how the Registry works and how you can change it.

As mentioned earlier in this chapter, the Registry is a hierarchical database. It's hierarchical in that its contents are arranged into a hierarchy of folders organized into five main areas called *subtrees* or *root keys*. You'll also sometimes hear them called *predefined keys*, though the term tends to be confusing because the Registry contains thousands of keys that are predefined. As you can see in Figure 22.1, the name of each subtree begins with the letters HKEY.

The Five Subtrees of the Registry

These are the five subtrees and the types of information they contain:

HKEY_CLASSES_ROOT This subtree contains an exhaustive list of the file types that Windows recognizes, the programs associated with them, and more.

HKEY_CURRENT_USER This subtree contains information on the current user and their setup. For example, when you're logged on, all your Desktop preferences are listed in this subtree.

HKEY_LOCAL_MACHINE This subtree contains information on the hardware and software setup of the computer.

HKEY_USERS This subtree contains information on the users who are set up to use the computer, together with a DEFAULT profile that's used when no user is logged onto the computer.

HKEY_CURRENT_CONFIG This subtree contains information on the current configuration of the computer—the hardware with which the computer booted.

Keys, Subkeys, and Value Entries

In Registry Editor, expand the HKEY_CURRENT_USER subtree by clicking the plus (+) sign next to it or by double-clicking its name. Registry Editor displays the items contained within the subtree—an apparently endless list of folder-like objects, many of them containing further objects. Figure 22.3 shows the HKEY_CURRENT_USER subtree and some of its subkeys expanded.

FIGURE 22.3

Each subtree contains keys, subkeys, and value entries.

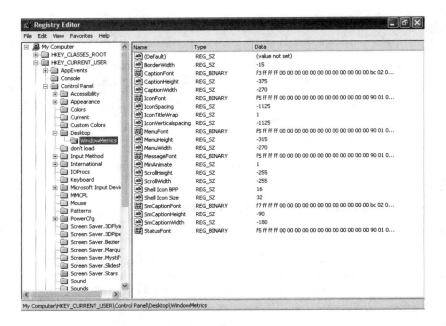

Within each subtree, there are keys, subkeys, and value entries. A *key* is (as it were) one of the folders within the subtree. Just as a subfolder is a folder within a folder, a *subkey* is a key within a key. Also as with "folder" and "subfolder," many people say "key" rather than "subkey" except when they need to be specific; this chapter does the same.

Each key or subkey can contain subkeys and value entries. The term *value entry* sounds like a management-consultant way of saying "value," but in fact it's not: a value entry is the current definition of a key and consists of a name, a data type, and the value assigned to the key.

For example, consider the MinAnimate key and value entry that you can see in Figure 22.3 in the HKEY_CURRENT_USER\Control Panel\Desktop\WindowMetrics subkey. As you can see in the Data column, the value of MinAnimate is 1. This value entry controls whether Windows animates windows when you minimize, maximize, or restore them. (The animation zooms the window from its displayed size and position down to its button on the Taskbar, and vice versa, instead of popping it off or back on the screen instantly.) A value of 0 indicates that the animation is off, a value of 1 that the animation is on.

MinAnimate is interesting in that it's an example of a key added to the Registry in Windows XP in order to implement functionality already in Windows. In earlier versions of Windows, including Windows NT and Windows 2000, this key wasn't included in the Registry, though its functionality was implemented in Windows. These versions of Windows automatically animated windows that you minimized, maximized, or restored.

This animation was (and remains) pure eye candy—and like much eye candy, this animation didn't appeal to everyone. On a slow computer, or one with an underpowered graphics card, it was particularly irritating, as Windows seemed to be running arthritically. To switch off this animation, you needed to create the `MinAnimate` value entry in the Registry, assign it the value 0, and then restart Windows. (You could also implement this change by using a utility such as TweakUI, which created and adjusted the `MinAnimate` value entry transparently for you.)

Windows XP lets you control this setting via the Animate Windows When Minimizing and Maximizing check box on the Visual Effects tab of the Performance Options dialog box. When this check box is selected, `MinAnimate` has the value 1; when the check box is cleared, `MinAnimate` has the value 0.

Registry Data Types

As you can see in Figure 22.3, the `MinAnimate` value entry is of type `REG_SZ`. REG means Registry, as you'd guess; SZ means string, indicating that the value entry contains a string of text (text characters, as opposed to, say, binary data). The `WindowMetrics` key also contains value entries of another data type, `REG_BINARY`. You get no prize for guessing that these are binary data.

Strings and binary data are the most widely used of the data types in the Registry. Next comes `REG_DWORD`, a double-word value entry. Figure 22.4 shows the `HKEY_CURRENT_USER\Control Panel\Desktop` key, which contains some double-word value entries as well as string and binary value entries.

The other two most widely used data types are `REG_MULTI_SZ`, multi-string entries, and `REG_EXPAND_SZ`, expandable strings. Table 22.1 provides a roundup of the five most widely used data types.

You can create and edit value entries with any of these data types. We'll get to that a bit later in the chapter, after discussing where the Registry is stored and how to find information in it.

FIGURE 22.4

The `HKEY_CURRENT_USER\Control Panel\Desktop` key contains a variety of data types.

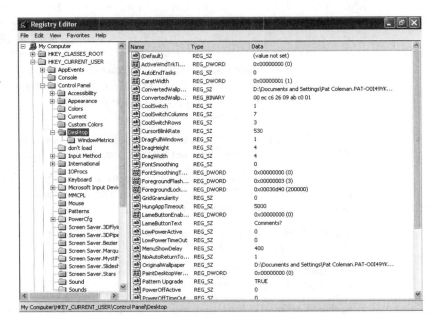

TABLE 22.1: THE FIVE MOST WIDELY USED REGISTRY DATA TYPES

TYPE	TYPE DISPLAYED	EXPLANATION
String	REG_SZ	Text.
Multi-String	REG_MULTI_SZ	Text, but with multiple text values.
Expandable String	REG_EXPAND_SZ	Text, but expandable.
Binary	REG_BINARY	A binary value, displayed as hexadecimal.
DWORD	REG_DWORD	Double-word: A 32-bit binary value displayed as an 8-digit hexa-decimal value.

NOTE   *Beyond these five widely used data types, the Registry can contain many different data types, such as* REG_DWORD_BIG_ENDIAN *(a value stored in reverse order of double-word value),* REG_DWORD_LITTLE_ENDIAN *(another type of double-word value),* REG_FULL_RESOURCE_DESCRIPTOR *(a hardware-resource list),* REG_QWORD *(a quadruple-word value), and* REG_FILE_NAME *(three guesses). You shouldn't need to mess with any of these unless you get into programming Windows—in which case, you'll need a book more specialized than this one.*

Where the Registry Is Stored

Most of the Registry is stored in several files on your hard drive. (Part of the Registry is created automatically when Windows boots and discovers which devices are attached to your computer.) These files are called *hives* (think bees, not allergies) or *hive files*. The hives are binary, but (as you'll see in the next section), if you're feeling curious, you can open them in a text editor and peek inside them.

Hive files containing computer-related information are stored in the `Windows\system32\config` folder, where `Windows` is your Windows folder. Hive files containing user-specific information are stored in the `Documents and Settings\`*`Username`* folder for each user.

These are the main hive files:

SYSTEM   This file contains information about the computer's hardware and about Windows. This information goes into the `HKEY_LOCAL_MACHINE\SYSTEM` key.

NTUSER.DAT   This file contains information about the user's preferences. Windows XP keeps an `NTUSER.DAT` file for each user in the `\Documents and Settings\`*`Username`* folder. This information goes into the `HKEY_CURRENT_USER` subtree.

SAM   This file contains the user database. This information goes into the `HKEY_LOCAL_MACHINE\SAM` key.

SECURITY   This file contains information on security settings. This information goes into the `HKEY_LOCALMACHINE\SECURITY` key.

SOFTWARE   This file contains information on the software installed on the computer. This information goes into the `HKEY_LOCAL_MACHINE\SOFTWARE` key.

DEFAULT   This file contains information about the default user setup. This information goes into the `HKEY_USERS\DEFAULT` key.

Each of the hive files has a log file named after it: DEFAULT.LOG, SOFTWARE.LOG, NTUSER.DAT.LOG, and so on. These log files note the changes to the hive files so that, if a change is applied that crashes the system, Windows can read the log, identify the problem change, and undo it.

Having read this, you're probably longing to lift the lid off a hive so you can see what's inside it. Perhaps if you use Notepad or another text editor, you can get a peek inside...

Don't.

Taking a text editor to a hive file would be like taking one of those old-fashioned can openers (you know, the ones that leave those nice jagged edges) to your favorite black box of electronic wizardry: clumsy, messy, and ultimately fruitless. In any case, Windows keeps the hive files open the whole time it's running so that it can write information to them and retrieve information from them whenever it needs, so they're locked. All you'll get for your pains is a message box telling you something like "The process cannot access the file because it is being used by another process." Translation: Windows needs this file. Hands off.

Let's look at what you *can* profitably do with the Registry: find keys and value entries or information in it, change values, and create (and delete) keys and value entries of your own.

Finding Information in the Registry

You can find information in the Registry in two ways: by digging through the Registry looking for it, or by using the Find function.

Digging through the Registry takes minimal explanation, because it's very similar to browsing in Explorer in Explore mode. You can expand and collapse keys as you would drives and folders in Explorer, and you can use type-down addressing to reach the next key or entry matching the letters you type. But because of the number of keys and value entries the Registry contains, you'll usually do better by searching through it than browsing.

If you know the name of a key, the name of a value entry, or the data contained in a value entry, you can search for it. For example, if you wanted to find where FTP sites were listed, you might search for FTP Sites. If you wanted to find out what the entry for the AutoCorrect file was called, you might search for .ACL, the extension of the AutoCorrect file. You can restrict the search by selecting only the check boxes for the items you're looking at—Keys, Values, or Data—in the Look At group section of the Find dialog box (shown in Figure 22.5). (Choose Edit ➤ Find to open the Find dialog box.) And you can search for only the entire string by selecting the Match Whole String Only check box. Selecting this check box prevents Find from finding the string you're looking for inside other strings—it makes Find find only whole strings that match the string in the Find What text box.

FIGURE 22.5

Use the Find dialog box in Registry Editor to find the keys, values, or data you want to manipulate.

Because of the volume of information that Windows stores in the Registry, the first match you find may not be the key (or value entry, or value) you need. For example, if you use your company's name as the Find item when looking for the `RegisteredOrganization` key for Windows, you may find another key, such as the registered organization for Internet Explorer. Close examination of the key will usually tell you whether you've found the key you were looking for. If not, press the F3 key or choose Edit ➤ Find Next to find the next instance.

Editing a Value Entry

To edit a value entry in the Registry, navigate to it and double-click it. (Alternatively, select it and choose Edit ➤ Modify.) Windows displays an Edit dialog box appropriate to the type of data the value entry contains.

String values and expandable string values are the easiest values to edit. In the Edit String dialog box (shown in Figure 22.6), enter the text of the string in the Value Data text box, and then click the OK button.

FIGURE 22.6

You can edit both string values and expandable string values in the Edit String dialog box.

Multi-string values are relatively simple to edit. In the Edit Multi-String dialog box (shown in Figure 22.7), enter all the data for the value entry on separate lines, and then click the OK button.

FIGURE 22.7

Editing a multi-string value in the Edit Multi-String dialog box

Double-word values are the next-easiest values to edit. In the Edit DWORD Value dialog box (shown in Figure 22.8), enter the data in the Value Data text box, and then choose the Hexadecimal option button or the Decimal option button as appropriate in the Base section. (When you're editing a built-in double-word value, you shouldn't need to change the existing Base setting.) Click the OK button.

FIGURE 22.8

Editing a double-word value in the Edit DWORD Value dialog box

Binary values are brutes to change, and you probably won't want to mess with them for fun. In the Edit Binary Value dialog box (shown in Figure 22.9), edit the data in the Value Data text box with great care, and then click the OK button.

FIGURE 22.9

Editing a binary value in the Edit Binary Value dialog box is hard work.

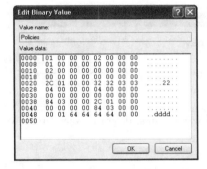

Adding a Key or a Value Entry

You can add a key or a value entry to the Registry either automatically or manually.

To add a key or value entry to the Registry automatically, double-click a REG file that you've received. For example, some programs sold via download use Registry keys to implement a license: you pay for the program and download it. The company then e-mails you a license and a REG file. To add the registration data to your Registry, double-click the REG file. Windows adds the necessary keys and value entries to the Registry.

To add a key or a value entry to the Registry manually, follow these steps:

1. Right-click the key in which you want to create the new key or value entry, choose New from the shortcut menu, and choose the appropriate item from the submenu: Key, String Value, Binary Value, DWORD Value, Multi-String Value, or Expandable String Value. Registry Editor creates a new key named `New Key #1` or `New Value #1` (or the next available number) and displays an edit box around it.

2. Type the name for the key or value entry.

3. Press the Enter key or click elsewhere in the Registry Editor window. Registry Editor assigns to the key or value entry the name you specified.

If you created a value entry, double-click it. Registry Editor displays the Edit dialog box appropriate to its type. Enter the data for the value entry as described in the previous section.

Deleting a Key or a Value Entry

Just as you can create keys and value entries, you can delete them. Generally speaking, it's a bad idea to delete any keys other than those you've created. Windows itself and Windows programs protect some keys in the Registry, but you'll find a surprising number that aren't deleted and that you can therefore delete freely.

To delete a value entry, right-click it and choose Delete from the shortcut menu. Registry Editor displays the Confirm Value Delete dialog box or the Confirm Key Delete check box (shown in Figure 22.10). Click the Yes button to confirm the deletion.

FIGURE 22.10

Confirm a deletion in the Confirm Key Delete dialog box (shown here) or the Confirm Value Delete dialog box.

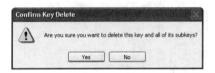

If the key or value entry is locked against deletion, Registry Editor displays an error message box.

Copying a Key Name

If you're describing to someone how to find particular information in the Registry, you'll need to get the key name right. But you don't need to type it painstakingly—you can copy it instead.

To copy a Registry key name, select it in the left-hand pane in Registry Editor and choose Edit ➢ Copy Key Name. You can then paste it from the Clipboard into a program.

An Example: Changing Your Windows Name and Organization

As mentioned at the beginning of the chapter, Microsoft reckons you should seldom (or preferably never) need to make changes to the Registry directly. But you'll probably run into tips and tweaks, online or in magazines, that promise to improve Windows' performance, compatibility, or behavior with a judicious change or two.

For example, say you misspelled your name or your organization's name during setup. Or perhaps you've bought a computer loaded with Windows from someone else. Either way, when you display the General tab of the System Properties dialog box, there's the misspelling or the wrong name laughing at you.

You'll want to change the name or organization name so that they're correct. There's no way to do so through the Windows user interface, but by navigating to the HKEY_LOCAL_MACHINE\SOFTWARE\ Microsoft\WindowsNT\CurrentVersion key and changing the RegisteredOwner and Registered-Organization value entries as appropriate, you can fix the problem in a minute or two.

Using Registry Favorites to Quickly Access Keys

If you find yourself using the Registry a lot, there's another feature you should know about: Registry favorites. To access the keys you need to work with frequently, you can create favorites in Registry Editor much as you can in Explorer and Internet Explorer.

To create a favorite, follow these steps:

1. Select the key to which you want the favorite to refer.

2. Choose Favorites ➤ Add to Favorites. Registry Editor displays the Add to Favorites dialog box:

3. In the Favorite Name text box, enter the name for the favorite. (By default, Registry Editor suggests the key name, but you may well want to change this to more descriptive text.)

4. Click the OK button. Registry Editor adds the favorite to your Favorites menu.

To access a favorite, display the Favorites menu and choose the favorite from the list.

To remove a favorite from the Favorites menu, choose Favorites ➤ Remove Favorite. Windows displays the Remove Favorites dialog box. Choose the favorite in the Select Favorite list box and click the OK button.

Summary

This chapter has discussed what the Registry is; what it does; why you *must* back it up before messing with it; how to mess with it; and why you shouldn't mess with it most of the time.

Chapter 23

Using Scripts to Automate Windows XP

VIRTUALLY EVERY TASK WE'VE performed so far has, in one way or another, involved utilizing Windows' many GUI tools such as the MMC, System Applet, Network Applet, and the like. Microsoft has gone to great pains to ensure that we have a variety of tools at our disposal for performing administrative functions. However, certain tasks—particularly common, repetitive tasks—can become quite tedious when executed one at a time using the GUI tools. It is in these instances that leveraging scripts can be advantageous. Not only does scripting save time, it can also allow you to accomplish certain tasks that are difficult, or even impossible, with the standard GUI tools. This chapter covers the following topics:

- Brief overview of scripting
- Writing shell scripts
- The Windows Script Host
- Advanced scripting concepts
- Sample scripts for common tasks

What Is Scripting?

Quite simply, *scripting* is the process of arranging individual commands such that they follow a logical course and produce a desired result. These commands can be DOS commands (shell scripting) or commands specific to a particular scripting engine (Windows Script Host [WSH] scripting). Scripting is a form of computer programming. Notice I didn't say "simple form" or "small form" of programming. Indeed, while most scripts are comparatively small and designed to perform quite specific, limited tasks, the differences between scripts and fully functioning computer programs have more to do with how they are deployed, rather than what they do. Here's a brief comparison.

Scripts are interpreted. In the XP world, scripts must be interpreted by a script engine during execution. Computer programs are generally pre-compiled into the bytecode of the target platform.

Scripts provide limited functionality. Most of the available scripting engines are subsets of larger programming languages. VBScript, for example, is based on Microsoft's more powerful Visual Basic language. While there are some things that it simply cannot do, there are ways to give your scripts power that rivals "professional" development languages. We'll discuss these techniques in the "Advanced Concepts" section.

Scripts are "clear text." Once a computer program is compiled to bytecode, it is very difficult (but not impossible) to view the original code. Scripts are stored as ANSI text so the script engine can parse the file and translate each command into the appropriate operation. For security reasons, scripts should be kept in a secure location on an NTFS partition with limited access. The script files themselves can also be encoded to make deciphering contents somewhat more troublesome.

Even with these limitations, scripting can be a powerful weapon in your administrative arsenal. The rest of this chapter will cover some of the basic concepts of scripting and will include sample scripts to help you apply this knowledge.

Shell Scripting with BAT and CMD Files

Many people look at shell scripting as a basic entry point into scripting—something to use to get their feet wet until they graduate to the more advanced scripting available with the Windows Script Host. While it is true that the WSH does provide a more powerful scripting environment, I tend to view the differences between the two based on the task I am trying to accomplish at the time. I believe it was Confucius who said, "Don't use a cannon to kill a mosquito." If the task at hand can be completed with a batch script, then there's no reason not to use one.

NOTE *It doesn't matter whether you use the extension* `.bat` *or* `.cmd`—*there's no difference. I use the* `.cmd` *extension for the scripts in this section.*

A *shell script* (also known as a *batch file*) is essentially a group of shell commands encapsulated into a file and executed in sequence. Shell commands are those commands that are typed directly at the Windows XP command prompt. These can include standard DOS commands such as `copy`, `dir`, `mkdir`, etc., as well as any executable applications that are capable of receiving command-line arguments, such as `cacls` and `net`.

In addition to OS commands and programs, shell scripts can contain additional code to aid in executing the script, including commands to perform script logic such as comparisons, loops, etc. Shell scripts have the extension of either `.bat` or `.cmd` and can be executed simply by typing the name of the script (with or without the extension) on the command line.

Tools for Scripting

Before you can begin creating scripts, you'll need an editor to get your code into the computer. The perennial favorite for creating batch scripts (and scripts for the Windows Script Host, for that matter) is Notepad. Veteran scripters refer to this simple text editor as "Visual Notepad," as in *Visual* Basic or *Visual* Studio—Microsoft's integrated development environment. While this sarcasm may be justified (Notepad does not perform any syntax checking, error handling, or even simple text formatting) virtually every scripter I've met relies on Notepad almost exclusively.

There are many third-party script editors available, as well. Feel free to experiment with them. Some are shareware and some are "Professional" products. Each has its own distinct advantages and disadvantages. I'm sure you'll find one that suits you just fine.

WARNING   *Notepad always tries to save a new script as a .TXT file. You have to remember to Save As ➤ Save As Type ➤ All Files (*.*), and then type the filename along with proper extension.*

For creating XML-based WSH scripts, an XML editor comes in handy. I like to use FrontPage, because it came with my Office XP software. I don't much fancy buying software when a tool I already have will work just fine. We'll discuss this in further detail in "XML-based Scripts" later in this chapter.

Your First Shell Script

There is an unwritten law of computer programming that states that your first application in any environment must be "Hello World!" Let's write a batch script to print "Hello World!" on the screen. (See Figure 23.1.)

```
rem HelloWorld.cmd
rem Displays "Hello World!" on the command line
echo off
echo Hello World!
```

FIGURE 23.1

Output from
`HelloWorld.cmd`

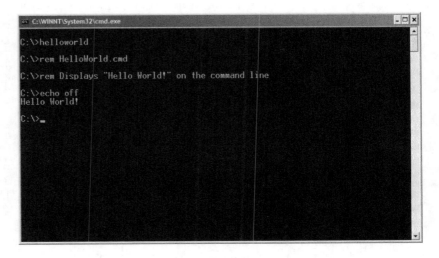

This simple script shows us some very important features of shell scripting. First, we can include remarks to help us understand what the script does. The `rem` keyword causes the rest of the line to be ignored, allowing you to comment your code.

Text is displayed using the echo function. Echo is also used to turn automatic echoing on or off. By default, the command interpreter automatically echoes each command to the screen, thus allowing you to follow the execution of the script. Sometimes this is advantageous, but it can quickly get out of hand. Turning this feature off allows you to limit output to only the text that you specify, so that important information doesn't get lost in a sea of echoes.

Adding Logic to Shell Scripts

While printing "Hello World!" on the screen can be a great deal of fun, let's see if perhaps we can write a batch script to do something a bit more productive. At the same time, we'll learn some of the advanced logic available to batch scripts.

Since batch scripts can include any shell command, the possibilities are limitless. Don't believe me? Go to a command prompt and, after the C:\, simply type **help**. Quite a list, no? And that's just the tip of the iceberg. The Windows XP Resource kit contains a wealth of utilities that can be used in batch scripts (as well as sample VBScripts, too.)

Any and all of these commands can be placed in a batch file to be invoked whenever necessary. That alone is worth the price of admission, in my opinion! May I enthrall you with a personal example? I have a batch file called Connect.cmd that stays on my desktop. Although small (it contains only two lines), it really comes in handy:

```
nbtstat -R
ping myinternalserver
```

I use this script every time I travel and need to tunnel into my private network over the Internet. The first line purges and reloads my remote cache name table (causing my LMHOSTS file to be parsed, which contains the IP addresses of computers in my internal network). The second line attempts to make a connection based on an internal name (invoking my firewall-security login screen). It sure is a lot easier to simply double-click this file on my desktop than to open a command-prompt window and type both lines.

The real power of scripting, however, is its ability to perform repetitive operations. In order to do this effectively, you need to be able to pass arguments to the script, store data in variables, perform comparisons and loops on this data, and control the flow of the script. Actually, there's quite a bit more involved in order to fully realize the capabilities of shell scripts, but the following list should get you off to a good start.

ARGUMENTS

Command-line arguments are automatically passed to your script when you run it. All that is required is that you include the code to capture these arguments. These arguments are stored, in the order entered, in the numbered variables *%1*, *%2*, *%3*, etc. The arguments on the command line are separated by a space. Here's an example:

```
C:\ShowArgs arg1 arg2 arg3
```

If you need to include more than one word as an argument, enclose the whole thing in quotes (just remember that the quotes themselves become part of the argument). You can strip out the quotes by referring to the variable as *%~x*:

```
C:\ShowArgs2 arg1 arg2 "This is argument 3"
```

Figure 23.2 shows these arguments being displayed in a script, both with and without the quotation marks removed.

FIGURE 23.2

Passing arguments to
batch scripts

FIGURE 23.2

Passing arguments to
batch scripts

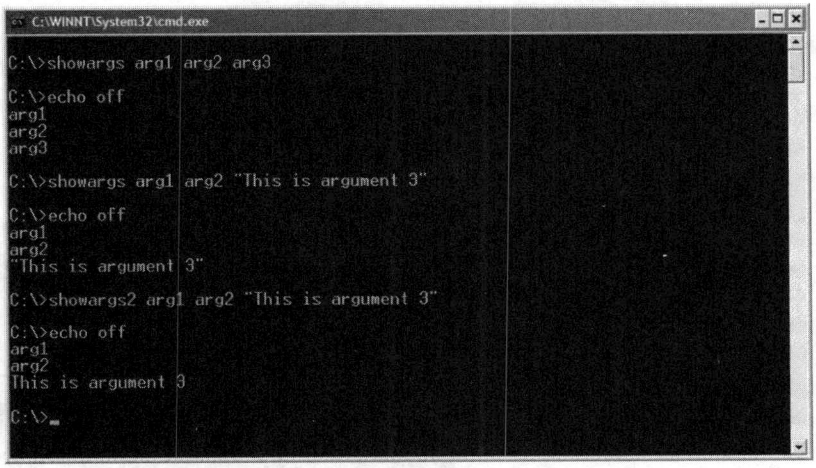

VARIABLES (THE *set* COMMAND)

Quite often the need arises to create variables to store additional data. This can be accomplished by using the **set** command to create an environment variable. Just remember to reset the variable back to empty before the script terminates.

```
rem The following line creates an environment variable
rem named 'var1' and assigns it the value of 'MyData'
set var1=MyData
rem the following line resets the environment variable to nothing
set var1=
```

The **set** command can also solve numerical expressions and assign the data to a variable. The expression can include both real numbers and/or other variables. This is accomplished using the /A flag.

```
echo off
rem The following line adds the two command-line
rem arguments together and multiplies them by 10
set /A var1=10*(%1 + %2)
echo %var1%
Set var1=
```

When I run this script as C:\ShowSet 5 4, the script echoes 90 to the screen, just as it should. In addition to "standard" math, these numerical expressions can include logical shift; bitwise AND, OR, and XOR; and more.

You can even use the set command to take user input from the command line. The /P flag allows you to prompt the user for input.

```
echo off
rem The following line prompts the user to enter their name
set /P var1=Enter your first name:
echo %var1%
Set var1=
```

Figure 23.3 shows the output from both of the previous scripts.

FIGURE 23.3

Output from the
set command

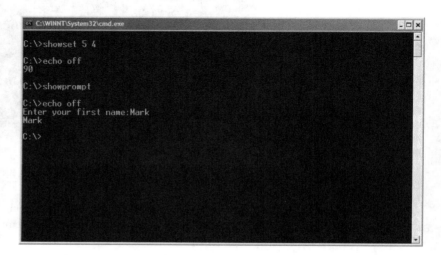

```
C:\>showset 5 4

C:\>echo off
90

C:\>showprompt

C:\>echo off
Enter your first name:Mark
Mark

C:\>
```

COMPARISONS AND LOOPS (THE *if* AND *for* COMMANDS)

The real "logic" of a script is found in the ability to perform operations selectively. The if and for commands allow you to perform two very important logical operations:

- ◆ Ensure that a particular criterion has been met prior to executing a section of the script (if)

- ◆ Execute the same operation over and over using different criteria (for)

The if command allows you to check for the existence of a file, compare the values of two strings or sets of numbers, and more. This is particularly useful when you have several subroutines set up to perform different operations. Depending upon the result of the if comparison, a particular subroutine can be called. When checking for files, the process is simple.

```
If exist file.tmp del file.tmp
```

Or you can use variables.

```
If exist %1 del %1
```

If necessary, you can specify the path, drive, etc. The `if` command also evaluates a variable and determines script flow.

```
If %1==delete goto :DeleteFiles
```

The `for` command enables you to perform operations on each file in a set of files.

```
For %%i in (*.txt) do copy /a All.txt+%%i All.txt
```

I said earlier in this chapter that scripts allow you to do some things that are impossible to do using GUI tools; this is one of those times. The above code takes every TXT file in the current directory and copies them all into one big file called `All.txt`. You can't do that in Explorer!

The `/R` option allows you to specify a root directory and perform the specified operation on every file in that directory and all subdirectories.

The `/D` option performs the command specified on all directories (rather than files) in the current directory.

Finally, as with the **set** command, you can strip the quotes out of the variable ($%%~i$), expand it to a path only ($%%~pi$), and expand it to a file extension ($%%~xi$).

FLOW CONTROL (THE *call* AND *goto* COMMANDS)

As your scripts become more complex, you need to maintain control over script execution. Remember, doing the same things over and over are what scripts do best. If you find yourself using the same code again and again, you can use **call** and/or **goto** to save a *lot* of typing. The **goto** command is pretty straightforward: It simply causes the script to jump to the specified label.

```
rem Just a hop, skip, and a goto
echo Hello There!
goto :goodbye
echo How are you?
:goodbye
echo Goodbye
```

In this script, `Hello There!` and `Goodbye` are the only things echoed to the screen. The **goto** statement caused us to skip over the line to echo `How are you?` When using **goto**, each jump is final. If you want to get back to where you were, you have to use another **goto** (and another label).

The **call** command allows you to either run another script (complete with arguments), or jump to a label in the current script and execute it as if it were a separate script. Once the code has executed to the end of the script (or the command `goto :EOF` has been executed), control is passed back to the line directly following the initial **call** command. Figure 23.4 shows the output from using **call...goto** for flow control.

```
echo off
rem The following "calls" several subroutines
echo Hello!
call :labl1
call :labl2
echo Nice seeing you!
goto :EOF
```

```
:lab1
echo How are you?
goto :EOF
:lab2
echo Goodbye
goto :EOF
```

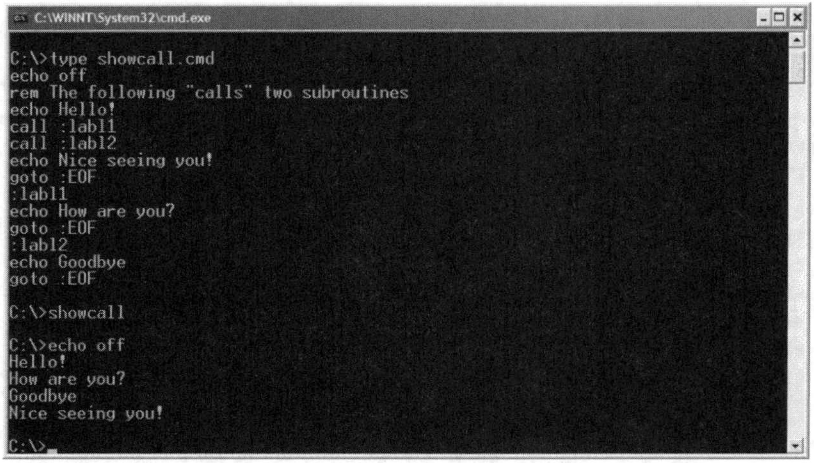

FIGURE 23.4

Using
`call...goto` for
flow control

Using `call...goto :EOF` in this manner is very similar to subs and functions in VBScript, which we discuss a bit later. It allows you to create procedures you can call over and over. To ensure proper execution, you merely need to place these subroutines at the end of your script and place a `goto :EOF` on the line just prior to the first routine.

Introduction to the Windows Script Host

While batch scripts can be very effective, there's no substitute for the power and flexibility of the Windows Script Host (WSH). The WSH is a COM-aware scripting environment (COM is Microsoft's Component Object Model) that not only allows you to create scripts in various languages, such as VBScript or JScript, it also enables you to extend the functionality of your scripts by directly accessing external COM components. (More on this topic in the "Advanced Concepts" section.)

The WScript and CScript Executables

A significant difference between shell scripts and WSH scripts is that the latter must be executed by passing the script as an argument to one of two engines: CScript.exe or WScript.exe. CScript.exe executes at the command line. The output of the script is similar to that of shell scripts (although the underlying code is quite different). WScript.exe executes the script within the Windows XP GUI. As such, all output is Window-based, in the form of a message box.

NOTE   *Because the* `WScript.exe` *engine displays all text in the form of a message box, you are required to click OK or press Enter every single time text is displayed before script execution will continue. For this reason alone, we will be using CScript to run the scripts we write for the rest of this chapter.*

You pass the desired script to the engine as an argument on the command line, along with any other required information such as flags or arguments required by your script: `cscript helloworld.wsf`

Scripts can also be started directly, either by typing their names at the command prompt or by double-clicking the script file from Windows Explorer.

WARNING   *Directly executing scripts causes them to run under* `WScript.exe` *(i.e., in the GUI). The only way to invoke scripts with CScript is to explicitly specify it when running the script.*

Script File Languages

A key advantage to writing scripts for use in the WSH is the choice of scripting languages available. Windows XP includes scripting engines (not to be confused with the script host engines `WScript.exe` and `CScript.exe`) for the VBScript and JScript languages. Additional ActiveX scripting engines, created by third-party vendors, are available for other languages. For the purpose of consistency, we'll stick to VBScript for the scripts we feature here.

VBSCRIPT

As I've mentioned, VBScript is a subset of Visual Basic. While it derives its functionality from a full-featured development language, there are quite a few limitations. Rather than discuss them here, I'll highlight them as they become apparent in our scripts. However, I try to follow these rules religiously when writing scripts in VBScript:

Option Explicit: This command should be placed at the beginning of the `<script>` section of every script you write. It forces you to declare variables before you use them. Variables are declared using the `dim` statement. This helps immensely when debugging. You'd be surprised how many times I've spent hours trying to figure out why a script isn't working properly, only to find that I misspelled a variable name at a critical stage.

Hungarian Notation: When you declare a variable, it is customary to have the variable name include a prefix that indicates the type of data it will hold. While VBScript does not allow you to specify the data type of variables, using Hungarian Notation will help keep your scripts more readable and less confusing.

strMyVariable: Indicates that the variable will hold a string of text.

intMyVariable or *iMyVariable*: Indicates an integer (whole number) value.

bMyVariable: Indicates a Boolean (True/False or Yes/No) value.

objMyVariable: Indicates that the variable will contain an object. We discuss objects in the "Advanced Concepts" section.

There are others, but these will pretty much cover the variables we will be using in our scripts.

XML-based Scripts

WSH 2.0 introduced the capability to write scripts in XML format. Prior to this, all scripts were single-language, with the scripts file extension indicating the language: `.vbs` for VBScript, `.js` for JScript, etc. By contrast, all WSH 2.0 scripts have the extension `.wsf`; they can contain multiple scripts, with each script having the capability of being in a different language. WSH 2.0 scripts offer some rather unique features not found in their WSH 1.0 counterparts.

Multiple Jobs: WSH 2.0 scripts can contain several jobs, each identified by a particular job ID. When a job is specified at runtime, only that job executes. If no job is specified, the first job is executed and the script terminates.

Multiple Scripts: Each job can contain multiple scripts, specified by the `<script>` tag. The language of the script is also determined by this tag, allowing a single script job to utilize scripts in any (or all) of the supported languages.

Objects: A significant XML tag is `<object>`. It allows you to specify an object that will be used by the entire job. This allows you (among other things) to persist data between several scripts.

Runtime Tags: These XML tags allow you to specify the usage requirements of a script. They also allow you to name your command-line arguments, enabling you to enter them in random order when running the script. As your scripts become more complex, the ability to ask the script what it does and what data it is expecting becomes invaluable.

Editing: Since the scripts are in XML format, you can use a standard XML editor to create and edit them. Most editors of this type perform basic text formatting and color coding to make the scripts easier to debug. Microsoft's FrontPage has an HTML view that you can use for this purpose.

Your First WSH 2.0 Script

In Listing 23.1, we have modified the HelloWorld script for use in the WSH. Figure 23.5 shows the output from this script when each job is executed individually.

LISTING 23.1: *HelloWorld.wsf*

```
<?xml version="1.0" ?>
<package>
  <comment>
  Hello World.wsf
  This script contains two jobs:
  Hello and Goodbye
  </comment>
  <job id="hello">
    <script language="VBScript">
    <![CDATA[
    'This script prints "Hello World!"
    WScript.Echo "Hello World!"
    ]]>
    </script>
```

```
    </job>
    <job id="goodbye">
      <script language="VBScript">
      <![CDATA[
      'This script prints "Goodbye World!"
      WScript.Echo "Goodbye World!"
      ]]>
      </script>
    </job>
  </package>
```

Output from
HelloWorld.wsf

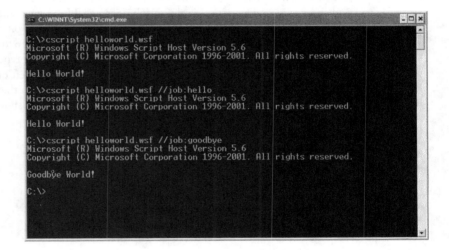

Listing 23.1 shows us quite a bit about XML-based scripts:

XML Version: The <?xml?> tag tells the script parser that this file needs to be strictly parsed (i.e., attribute names are case-sensitive, values are enclosed in quotes, etc.) By contrast, HTML files are loosely parsed. This tag is not required, but may be necessary for your scripts to be displayed properly, depending upon which XML editor you are using.

Package: The <package> tag tells WSH that one or more jobs follows. It is optional if your script only has one job.

Comments (XML): The <comment> tag allows you to include comments that pertain to the entire script. You can still comment individual lines of code, which we will see next.

Job Ids: The <job id="xxx"> tag specifies the name of each job in the script. The ID is optional if the script contains only one job. Figure 23.5 shows how this job is specified on the command line. If no job is specified, the first job in the script is executed.

CDATA: This tag causes the data contained within it to become opaque to the XML parser. It is only necessary when combined with the `<?xml?>` tag. Without this tag, logic from your script might "confuse" the XML parser. It might, for instance, read this script code: If `intA` < `intB` and think that the "is less than" comparator is actually the beginning of an XML tag.

Comments (Inline): You can add comments inline with your script code, as well. The keyword is the same as shell scripts: `rem`. However, VBScript provides a shortcut—a single quote mark (').

Adding Logic to Your Scripts

The XML tags I just listed notwithstanding, the real meat of the script is what resides inside the `<script>` tag. This is where you *get stuff done*. One of the best ways to get that stuff done in a structured, logical manner is through the use of procedures: subs and functions. The difference between the two is that a function may return a value, a sub does not. These are similar to the `call...goto :end` subroutines we used in our batch scripts, except that they are quite a bit more robust. For one thing, they don't execute unless they are called. You can place them anywhere in your script and rest assured they won't get in the way until you need them. Listing 23.2 uses both types of procedures to take a file name from the command line and display that file's properties. I've left out the "standard" XML in the interest of space. To use it in a `.wsf` file, simply place it between the `<script>...</script>` tags. It can also be saved as is to a `.vbs` file and used directly. Figure 23.6 shows the message box output by this script.

LISTING 23.2: *GetFileInfo.vbs*

```
'Use Subs and Functions to display file info
Option Explicit
Dim strArg, objFSO, objFile, strTxt
Set objFSO=CreateObject("Scripting.FileSystemObject")

strArg=GetArgs()
Display
Set objFSO=Nothing
WScript.Quit

Function GetArgs()
  If Wscript.Arguments.Count < 1 Then Wscript.Quit
  GetArgs=objFSO.GetAbsolutePathName (Wscript.Arguments(0))
End Function

Sub Display()
  'Display file information
  Set objFile = objFSO.GetFile(strArg)
  strTxt="Drive:" & objFile.Drive & vbCRLF
  strTxt=strTxt & "File name:" & objFile.Name & vbCRLF
  strTxt=strTxt & "Path:" & objFile.Path & vbCRLF
```

```
    strTxt=strTxt & "Size:" & objFile.Size & vbCRLF
    strTxt=strTxt & "Date created:" & objFile.DateCreated & vbCRLF
    strTxt=strTxt & "Date last modified:" & objFile.DateLastModified
    msgbox strTxt
End Sub
```

FIGURE 23.6

Detailed file information using the FileSystemObject

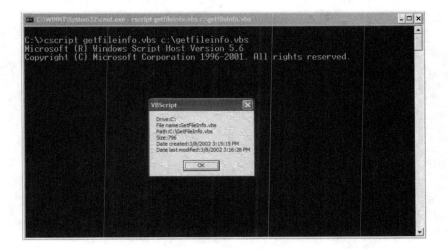

I threw a curve ball at you, did you notice? I used the FileSystemObject (FSO) to access information about the file specified on the command line. We discuss the FSO in more detail in the "Advanced Concepts" section. I included it in this script to give you a practical demonstration of subs and functions and, at the same time, show you how to perform a very useful task.

TIP   Indenting your code is important. Without it, tracing your logic can be a real pain! The general rule is to indent the code inside procedures, `If...Then` statements, and loops (`For...Next`, `Do...Loop`, etc.).

I also used another common technique designed to keep my code readable. You'll notice in both the `GetArgs` function and the `Display` sub, I have some long lines of code. When viewed in Notepad (with Word Wrap off, of course), the line can be as long as you want (but it can make it hard to follow the logic.) On a page in a book, there is limited width to work with. In either case, when you want to break a long line of code, simply type a space followed by an underscore (_) and a carriage return. This tells the VBScript parser that the following line of code is a continuation of the previous line. It's also customary to indent the following line so you know it is part of the previous line.

Structuring your code into subs and functions not only keeps things organized, it also aids in debugging your code (something we all have to deal with, no matter how long we've been scripting!)

Advanced Concepts

As discussed earlier, the WSH is a COM-aware scripting environment; COM provides a mechanism that allows for interoperability. It is the foundation of such things as object linking and embedding (OLE), a magic feature that allows you to drag a spreadsheet from Excel and drop it into a Word document. I could go into a bunch of boring details about the inner workings of COM, but space is limited and I'm sure you'd rather get to the good stuff. Suffice to say, COM allows us to access COM-enabled components (aka, objects) from our scripts. This section also discusses scheduling your scripts to run at a specified time.

Objects

Objects are COM-enabled components that can be accessed from within scripts. Components are a special kind of binary file. They are not executable on their own, but can provide their functionality to COM environments via exposed interfaces. There are two main interface types that pertain to scripting:

Properties: Properties hold data. This data can be as simple as a value that determines how the object works. A property may also store (persist) user data when necessary. Let's assume you have a component that allows you to perform symmetrical encryption on a file. This component would require a property, likely named "key," that specifies the key used to encrypt the file.

Methods: Methods perform a function. In the encryption example I just used, the component would likely have a method called *EncryptFile* that, when executed, uses the key specified in the "key" property to encrypt the file. There is an example of both properties and methods in the "Callable Objects" section later in this section.

INTRINSIC OBJECTS

Intrinsic objects are built in to the Windows Script Host. Every time you execute a script, these objects are created and sit waiting for you to use them. They can be referenced directly, without ever having to be assigned to variables or created. There are two intrinsic objects that you will likely use quite often:

The WScript Object: This object is used to print information on the screen (`WScript.Echo`), and to access command-line arguments (`WScript.Arguments`). Other methods include `Quit` and `Sleep`. Properties include `Name`, `ScriptName`, and `Version`. It also contains several child objects that are not intrinsic but can be called to perform other functions such as editing the Registry or mapping network drives.

The Err Object: This object allows you to trap errors in your scripts. Its main properties are `Number` and `Description`, which return the error number and a description of the error. It also has two methods: `Clear` and `Raise`. `Clear` resets the `Err` object. `Raise` actually allows you to cause an error to occur. This is invaluable when debugging your scripts. You want to make sure your error handling code works, don't you?

CALLABLE OBJECTS

In addition to intrinsic components, you can access external components, as well. To call a component, you simply create a variable to house it and execute the `CreateObject` method. Once this is done, the object is referenced via the assigned variable. Properties and methods are specified using a dot (`.`). For example, to call the `EncryptFile` method of the above discussed encryption component, I would simply execute the following code:

```
Dim objMyObject
Set objMyObject=CreateObject("MyEncrypt.Encryption")
objMyObject.File="C:\MyConfidentialData.mdb"
objMyObject.Key="secret"
objMyObject.EncryptFile
```

Many callable objects come built in to Windows XP. One such object that you are likely to use extensively is the FileSystemObject. The FSO actually consists of a parent object and several child objects. Once you have created the "main" component, additional components are called by executing specific methods. This is demonstrated in Listing 23.2. Once I created the FileSystemObject, I simply executed the `GetFile` method `Set objFile=objFSO.GetFile(strArg)` to create an instance of the `File` object (a child object of the FSO).

Another useful, built-in object is the Active Directory Services Interface. ADSI enables you to perform a gazillion useful tasks. Listing 23.3 in the next section demonstrates how to perform one very useful task with ADSI.

AUTOMATION

There are certain applications that can be utilized in the same manner as components. Indeed, the entire Office XP suite can be automated from within a script. In order to support automation, the application must have an exposed object model. This object model must be represented in a file called a *Type Library*. Type Libraries usually have the file extension of `.tlb` (the Office XP Type Libraries use `.olb` as their extension).

Utilizing the Type Library, you can, for example, start Word, create a new document, enter text, and save it. Or you can launch Internet Explorer and load a specified Web page! Or you can read information from an Excel spreadsheet and process it with your script! Or…well, you get the point.

Scheduling Scripts

A key advantage to using scripts is the ability to schedule them to run at any time. With the XP Task Scheduler, you can schedule a script to run every night, on a specific day every week, or on the next occurrence of a day and time. Scripts are scheduled using the `AT` command. You must remember to include all of the command-line arguments required by your script when scheduling it.

Scripts for Common Administrative Chores

No discussion of scripting would be complete without including a nice selection of sample scripts for you to use and learn from. The scripts included in this section cover different administrative tasks you are likely to perform quite frequently. Following each script, I've highlighted the salient code sections.

AddUser.wsf

This script (see Listing 23.3) uses the Active Directory Services Interface to automate adding users to your computer. It illustrates how useful ADSI can be even if you aren't part of a domain. You specify the username and password via the command-line arguments.

LISTING 23.3: *AddUser.wsf*

```
<?xml version="1.0" ?>
<package>
<comment>
AddUser.wsf
This script adds a user to the local computer
Using the ADSI interface
</comment>
  <job>
  <runtime>
    <description>
    Add a user to the local computer
    and place it in a group
    </description>

    <example>
    C:\cscript AddUser.wsf /uname:[username] /group:[group]
    </example>

    <named
      name="uname"
      helpstring="The username of the new user"
      type="string"
      required="true"
    />
    <named
      name="group"
      helpstring="The group in which to place the user"
      type="string"
      required="true"
    />
  </runtime>
  <script language="VBScript">
  <![CDATA[
  ' Add a user and place him/her into a group
  dim objADSI, objGroup, objUser, strUser, strGroup
  strGroup=WScript.Arguments.Named.Item("group")
  strUser=WScript.Arguments.Named.Item("uname")
  Set objADSI=GetObject("WinNT://mycomp,computer")
  Set objUser=objADSI.Create("User",strUser)
  objUser.SetInfo
```

```
    Set objGroup=GetObject("WinNT://mycomp/" & strGroup & ",group")
    objGroup.Add(objUser.ADsPath)
    objGroup.SetInfo
    ]]>
    </script>
    </job>
</package>
```

The only "hard coded" parameter in this script is mycomp, the name of the local computer. The script could be easily expanded to accept this information as an argument, as well, making it capable of adding a user to an NT domain. The usage of the <runtime> tags is explained following the next script.

You'll notice that once I create the user, I still have to execute the objUser.SetInfo method. This finalizes the deal. Once that's done, I can pass that user information to the objGroup.Add method to place the user into the group. Lots of possibilities exist using this script as a starting point. You could even use the application automation we discussed earlier to add a list of users from a spreadsheet.

ChangeRole.wsf

This script (see Listing 23.4) uses the WScript.Shell object to make a change to the registry—specifically, the Win32PrioritySeparation value. When you use the System applet to change your computer's performance option to adjust for Programs or Background Services, it utilizes this registry entry. It is this value that determines the role of your computer: Server or Workstation. No, it can't convert Windows XP Professional to Windows 2002 Server. What it does is determine how XP handles background processes in relation to foreground processes. If you are using XP Pro as, say, an intranet server in your organization, specifying a Server role will increase its performance in this capacity.

LISTING 23.4: *ChangeRole.wsf*

```
<?xml version="1.0" ?>
<package>
<comment>
ChangeRole.wsf
This script updates the Win32PrioritySeparation
key in the registry to change the performance
of applications running in the foreground
</comment>
  <job>
  <runtime>
    <description>
    This script allows you to change the
    performance role of your computer
    </description>
```

```
<example>
C:\CScript ChangeFGPerf.wsf /Role:[W/S]
</example>

<named
name="Role"
helpstring="The role for the computer"
type="string"
required="true"
/>
</runtime>

<object id="objShell" progid="WScript.Shell"/>

<script language="VBScript">
<![CDATA[
'Change foreground performance
Option Explicit
On Error Resume Next

Dim strRole, strKey, strDataType
strKey= _
   "HKLM\System\CurrentControlSet\Control\PriorityControl\Win32PrioritySeparation"
strDataType="REG_DWORD"
strRole=UCase(WScript.Arguments.Named.Item("Role"))

Select Case strRole
  Case "W"
  objShell.RegWrite strKey, 38, strDataType
  WScript.Echo "Priority Control has been set to optimize foreground applications."
  WScript.Quit

  Case "S"
  objShell.RegWrite strKey, 24, strDataType
  WScript.Echo "Priority Control has been set to optimize background services."
  WScript.Quit
End Select

WScript.Arguments.ShowUsage()
WScript.Quit
]]>
</script>
</job>
</package>
```

This script uses the `<object>` tag to create an instance of the `WScript.Shell` object. The computer's role is specified via a `<named>` argument. It also includes the `<runtime>` tags `<description>`

and `<example>`. These tags specify the information that is displayed whenever the script is run using incorrect (or no) arguments, or when it is run using the /? argument. Figure 23.7 shows this output.

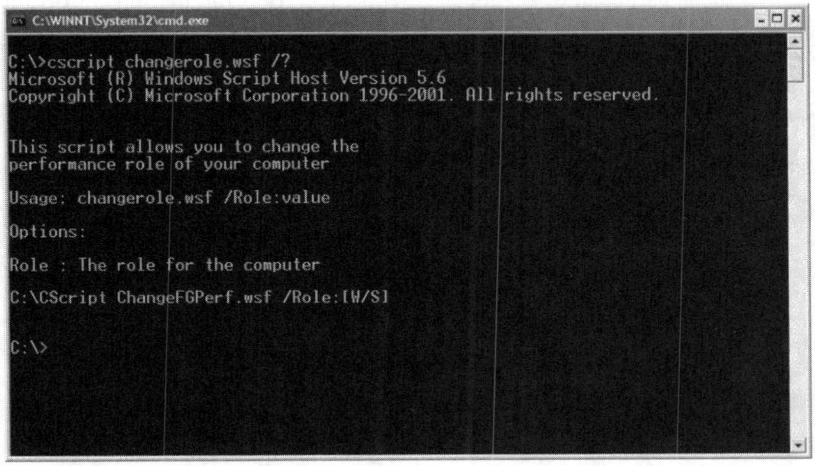

FIGURE 23.7

WSF scripts can display usage information describing how to run the script.

LogEvent.vbs

This script (see Listing 23.5) allows you to log an event to Windows XP's Application Event Log. While not terribly useful on its own, it can be invaluable when added to an existing script. As we discussed in the "Advanced Concepts" section, one of the joys of scripting is that you can schedule a script to run whenever you want it to. An event log entry noting whether or not the script completed successfully may be your only indication of potential trouble. Since you will likely add this code to an existing script, I have put the script in the .vbs file format.

LISTING 23.5: *LogEvent.vbs*

```
'Logs an event to the XP application log
Option Explicit
Dim objShell
Set objShell=CreateObject("WScript.Shell")
objShell.LogEvent 0, "Script: " & WScript.ScriptName & " Completed Successfully."
```

We use the WSHShell object to write the log entry. The LogEvent method requires two arguments, with a third optional argument:

Event Type: In this script, we logged an event type of 0, which is a "Success." Other types include: Error, Warning, Information, Audit_Success, and Audit_Failure.

Message: This is the text that is entered into the event log. If a script error happened to trigger the LogEvent method, you would want this text to include that error information.

Target (optional): This allows you to log an event to another computer. This is useful for aggregating all of the logged events on every computer in your organization to one central location.

Figure 23.8 shows this event viewed in the application log of the event viewer.

FIGURE 23.8

Log events to the application log

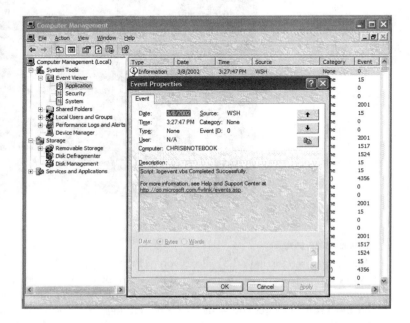

Summary

We've crammed quite a bit into this chapter. Hopefully it's given you a good foundation of knowledge to build upon, as well as provided some useful code that you can put to work right away.

Shell and WSH scripts allow you to automate some (or all!) of the redundant and not-so-redundant tasks that you face each day. Repetitive tasks can be accomplished much faster than is possible using the GUI tools. Scripts can be scheduled to run during off-hours, and through the use of COM objects, can perform some very powerful operations. For more information about WSH scripting, go to msdn .microsoft.com/scripting. It is my scripting home-away-from-home. You'll find downloads for the scripting engines, tutorials, a VBScript reference, and much more.

Chapter 24

Disaster Prevention And Recovery

DESPITE WINDOWS XP PROFESSIONAL'S RESILIENT nature, it still sometimes crashes. Some crashes are caused by random events: it really *is* possible for a cosmic ray to hit a critical part of a chip and freeze up a PC (and in that case there's not much to do other than to turn the machine off and then back on). But if you find Windows XP Professional crashing *regularly*, you have to do something about it, 'cause it's not supposed to. Of course, to do something effective about system crashes, you'll need a method, and that's what this chapter offers.

I'll avoid trotting out all the old an-ounce-of-prevention bromides (though there *is* a lot of truth to those old saws). I start off with a discussion of preventing trouble in the first place and then look at techniques you can use to gather the information needed to ascertain, attack, and fix problems that may sooner or later arise.

- ◆ Avoiding Windows XP Professional crashes
- ◆ Defragmenting files, cleaning up disks, and checking disks
- ◆ Restoring a configuration
- ◆ Installing and using the Recovery Console
- ◆ Using the Driver Verifier
- ◆ Using System File Checker
- ◆ Forcing a core dump
- ◆ Backing up and restoring

Avoiding Windows XP Professional Crashes

You can keep Windows XP Professional trouble at bay in a few basic ways:

◆ Buy reliable hardware, preferably hardware that is on the Windows XP Hardware Compatibility List.

◆ Protect the machine from environmental hazards, most notably substandard electric power.

◆ Install Windows XP Professional properly, or, in some cases, *re*install Windows XP Professional properly.

◆ Obtain the latest Microsoft-certified drivers for your hardware.

◆ Always shut down Windows XP Professional properly.

◆ Back up your hard disk.

◆ Be sure you have the proper security level for whatever function you're performing.

Let's look quickly at each of these.

Buy Reliable Hardware

One of the things that causes instability for *any* PC operating system is the hardware that the operating system must sit atop. PCs made by IBM were once the standard and, right or wrong, "PC-compatible" meant that they "did the same thing that the IBM machines did, including the bugs." Nowadays, there *is* no standard, and so no two brands of computers work exactly the same way.

A major point of difference between makes and models of computers is the expansion bus, the slots on a PC motherboard into which you plug expansion cards such as video boards, sound cards, and network boards. Because these slots must accommodate the connectors on the bottom of the expansion cards, the person who designs the motherboard and the person who designs the expansion card must agree on how that interface should work; the interface must be *standard*.

That's where the problem arises. A common PC interface standard is called the Industry Standard Architecture, or ISA, board. The *problem* with the ISA standard is that it's not really a standard; there is no carved-in-stone specification for it, just an informal industry consensus. The result is that if you take a "standard" ISA board and plug it into a "standard" ISA slot, it may not work perfectly 100 percent of the time. It'll probably work most of the time, but some small percentage of the time, data may get lost passing between the expansion card and the motherboard. If that data is crucial, the PC may lock up.

What can Windows XP Professional do about that? In other words, how can an operating system that wants to be stable work around an inherently unstable hardware platform? To a certain extent, there's nothing that the operating system can do, and some crashes are unavoidable. But some ISA boards are designed better than others, and only experimentation will separate the good from the bad. Further, the operating system can incorporate drivers for the hardware that are a bit more "forgiving." By forgiving, I mean that the driver is built to *anticipate* a certain number of hardware errors and to simply step around them.

"Aha!" you cry. "If they can make drivers 'forgiving,' why don't they *always* do that?" Well, for one thing, it's harder to write such drivers. For another, most driver authors resent writing drivers to support hardware that isn't really standard. Talk to them for a bit, and they start muttering about hitting moving targets and the like. Finally, and most important, adding forgiveness to a driver *slows it down*, and as all PC speed freaks know, slow is bad.

Again, what can you do about it? For one thing, stay as far away from ISA boards as you can. Yes, they're the most common and the cheapest boards, but there's usually a reason that cheap things are cheap.

TIP *Buy systems that have PCI slots (at least three slots), and use only PCI boards. Most of these systems also have ISA, but don't use them. Multiprocessor systems usually have a combination of PCI and EISA slots; both of those are fine to use because both are truly standard interfaces.*

The Peripheral Component Interconnect (PCI), Extended Industry Standard Architecture (EISA), and MicroChannel Architecture (MCA) buses were all designed by a central authority that published specifications, which, if followed, yield an expansion board that works predictably. That's why I strongly recommend staying with those three expansion slot types. In reality, however, you won't find many of today's systems with the MCA bus; it's about dead. Again, you'll find EISA slots on many multiprocessor systems, but not many EISA expansion boards are on the market. PCI has become more widespread, and FireWire (IEEE 1328) and USB are really on the move.

Guard Against Environmental Hazards

A decent number of PCs die each year because they get bad power. It's not something you can easily detect; it just happens. But you can prevent it.

PC power problems fall into three categories:

◆ Incorrect voltage—usually too low. Low voltage is called a voltage sag or brownout.

◆ Loss of power altogether.

◆ Extremely brief (under one 1/100 of a second) increases in voltage and power, called surges or spikes.

Low voltage causes your PC's power supply to try to compensate by drawing more current, which heats up the PC components and shortens their lives. You change voltage on an electrical circuit with a device called a transformer. A transformer that's smart enough to know whether to move the voltage up or down is called a *voltage regulator*, and for most PC applications, the name of the device that contains a voltage regulator is a *power conditioner*.

Loss of power altogether requires a battery of some kind. The two kinds of battery backup are *standby power supply (SPS)* and *uninterruptible power supply (UPS)*. An SPS has a battery that "wakes up," so to speak, when power to the PC is interrupted. Because an SPS doesn't always wake up fast enough, you need an SPS with a switching time (wake-up time) of 4 milliseconds or less. A UPS, in contrast, is always supplying power from the battery (while refilling it, of course) and so has no switching time. Clever marketers call their SPSs "UPSs." If in doubt, ask about the switching time.

Surges and spikes can be brushed aside by a power conditioner. Do *not* buy a surge protector, a cheap device that does little to protect you from power problems. A surge protector is based on a device called a Metal Oxide Varistor (MOV), which is a "kamikaze" device: After you get a little surge, the MOV stops the surge but dies in the process. The *next* surge goes through without trouble.

NOTE *To read more about PC power problems and solutions, pick up the latest edition of my book* The Complete PC Upgrade and Maintenance Guide, 2003 Edition *(Sybex, Inc.).*

Install Windows XP Professional Properly

A look back at Chapter 2 will remind you that you've got a lot of choices to make when you install Windows XP Professional. If you end up with a bad installation, reinstall Windows XP Professional or your Windows XP Professional applications. If you reinstall a piece of software, however, don't install it on top of an existing installation; that often doesn't wipe the old installation clean. Before reinstalling any software, remove it completely and check the Registry for any leftover pieces.

In Chapter 2, I tell you how to upgrade from an earlier version of Windows or NT, but the truth is, the most stable and reliable installations are built from the ground up. This usually means installing on a freshly formatted hard drive and then installing applications. If you simply must perform an upgrade, be sure to disable all third-party services. Heck, disable all the services you can easily live without for a while. The less that Setup has to worry about, the fewer things that can go wrong.

Obtain Tested, Certified Drivers for Your Hardware

Although Windows XP Professional was a solidly built system, it does have one fairly large Achilles' heel (or maybe a whole Achilles' foot): drivers. During the development of Windows XP Professional, Microsoft took a hard line with hardware vendors, insisting that they write "good" drivers that would pass Microsoft certification. In some cases, you may even see a warning message if you attempt to install new hardware or software with drivers that are not certified. Take this message to heart. A poorly functioning driver can be difficult to track down and can crash your system.

Always Shut Down Windows XP Professional Properly

Most people seem to know this by now, but it's worth repeating that you should *shut down Windows XP Professional properly*. Don't just turn off the computer; choose Start and then Turn Off Computer.

If you don't do that, you stand not only to lose data from your applications, but you may damage the operating system. If you are using only NTFS-formatted disks, the damage will be less than it would be with a FAT disk (NTFS incorporates fault-tolerant features), but you could lose data nevertheless.

Back Up Your Disk Regularly

I shouldn't have to say this, but...

The hard disks in most people's PCs aren't backed up. And there are as many excuses for this as there are PCs. But there's no reason for it, at least not any more. Iomega's Zip drives are a terrific way to quickly and easily save 100MB of data onto a thing that *looks* like a floppy but that stores much more data. Tape drives get cheaper all the time. And I just can't say enough about the value of CD-ROM burners for backups.

And Windows XP Professional even comes with a backup program, Backup, that I'll discuss later in this chapter.

Be Sure You're Authorized to Do Something Before Doing It

As you've read elsewhere in this book, living with Windows XP Professional means thinking differently because you're now living in a more secure world. That means that you may run into a kind of trouble fairly new to PC users—the inability to do a particular function on your system.

For example, imagine that when someone logs on to your network, they run a logon batch script that synchronizes their PC's clock with the time on the server; the command is `net time\\`*servername*`/ set/yes`. When you log on to a Windows XP Professional workstation as a simple domain user, you get an error indicating that you don't have the right to set the PC's clock.

Now, if you are a network techie, you would likely understand this error message and where it comes from—again, the account you used to log on is too low on the network's totem pole, so to speak. But for a regular, less-technical user, it could be somewhat disconcerting.

In general, remember that a Windows XP Professional computer runs different kinds of user accounts—administrators, users, power users, and so on. You'll make your life easiest if you remember to log on as an administrator for that particular workstation before trying to change permissions on files or do anything with the Administrative Tools.

An Ounce of Prevention

Before I get into what you can do to fix Windows XP Professional before it breaks, I want to point you toward some tools you can use from time to time that might well prevent some common, everyday problems: Disk Defragmenter, Disk Cleanup, and Check Disk.

Defragmenting Files

As files on your computer grow, they will not fit back into their original locations on your hard disk, so Windows XP Professional divides the files into pieces and spreads the files over several different disk locations. This is how Windows is designed to work and how the system juggles constantly changing file sizes. An unfortunate side-effect is that as a file is divided into more and more pieces it takes longer and longer for your system to find and retrieve the whole file when you open it. A disk defragmenter keeps your hard disk performance at its peak by finding fragmented files on your system and rewriting them into contiguous, continuous areas of your hard disk.

Disk Defragmenter works behind the scenes; although the files on your hard disk have actually been moved, you will still find them in the same folders. Follow these steps to use the Disk Defragmenter:

1. Choose Start ➢ All Programs ➢ Accessories ➢ System Tools ➢ Disk Defragmenter.

2. Choose the disk you want to defragment, and click the Analyze button. Disk Defragmenter looks at the drive and prepares a display and reports on the condition of the files on that drive; the Analysis Display box shows fragmented files, contiguous files, system files, and hard disk free space as stripes of different colors, as seen in Figure 24.1. Once the analysis is complete, Disk Defragmenter will display a message box that tells you whether you should defragment this disk. Click View Report to open the Analysis Report dialog box. At the top of the Analysis Report dialog box, you will see volume information, including the amount of fragmentation, free space, and file fragmentation. In the lower part of this dialog box, you will see

detailed information on specific files. Click the heading at the top of the columns to sort the data in that column.

3. Click Defragment to continue, or click Close to return to the main window.

FIGURE 24.1

Disk Defragmenter
Analysis Display for
a badly fragmented
drive

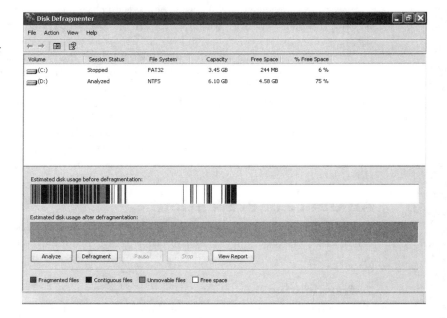

4. Once Disk Defragmenter starts working, you can click either the Pause or Stop buttons to pause or stop the process.

You can certainly perform other work on the computer while Disk Defragmenter is running, but the response time will be much slower, and Disk Defragmenter will start over each time you write a file to your hard disk. The best time to run Disk Defragmenter is while you are out for lunch or after you've finished your work for the day.

See pages 60–61 in "Essential Skills for Windows XP Professional" for a visual guide to defragmenting your hard disk.

Cleaning Up Disks

Have you ever wished there was some way you could just wave a magic wand and get rid of all the unused or temporary files that take up space on your hard disk? Well, there is such a tool, and it is called Disk Cleanup. Choose Start ➤ All Programs ➤ Accessories ➤ System Tools ➤ Disk Cleanup to open the Select Drive dialog box. Choose the drive you want to work with, and click OK to open the Disk Cleanup dialog box shown in Figure 24.2.

FIGURE 24.2

The Disk Cleanup dialog box

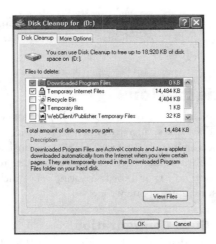

The Disk Cleanup dialog box has these tabs:

Disk Cleanup   Displays the amount of free space that could be recovered by deleting temporary files in certain categories or by emptying the Recycle Bin on your Desktop. As you check the boxes to delete files, a running counter tells you how much disk space will be recovered.

More Options   Lets you remove applications or Windows components that you don't use. In the Windows Components section, click the Clean Up button to start the Windows Components Wizard, which you can use to add or remove components. In the Installed Programs section, click the Clean Up button to open the Add or Remove Programs dialog box and change or remove a program. In the System Restore section, click the Clean Up button to remove all but the most recent restore point. I'll talk about System Restore later in this chapter.

See page 62 in "Essential Skills" for a visual guide to running Disk Cleanup.

Checking Disks for Errors

Another disk-management task you might have to perform from time to time is to check a hard disk for errors, and Windows XP Professional includes a tool for checking FAT32 volumes. All NTFS volumes log file transactions and replace bad clusters automatically. To check out a hard disk, open Explorer or My Computer, right-click the disk you want to work with, and then choose Properties from the shortcut menu. In the Tools tab, click the Check Now button to open the Check Disk dialog box, which contains these two options:

- Automatically Fix File System Errors
- Scan For and Attempt Recovery of Bad Sectors

Check the appropriate boxes, and then click Start to begin scanning the disk. A status bar across the bottom of the Check Disk dialog box indicates the progress of the tests, and you will see a message when the disk check is complete.

Restoring a Configuration

Sometimes, no matter how vigilant you've been, mistakes happen or something just goes wrong, and you need to fix your system. These fixes range from easy to horrific.

One thing that you *could* do is reinstall Windows XP Professional, a time-consuming process. But not only do you have to do the installation process itself, you have to set up all services and user accounts again, and this gets very boring and/or frustrating very quickly. Fortunately, there are other ways to fix your setup when something's gone wrong.

Using the Last Known Good Configuration

If you've changed your system so that it can't boot Windows XP Professional, one of these better solutions can be seen while you're rebooting. If you watch while your machine's booting up, you'll see a message on a black screen that says "For troubleshooting and advanced startup options for Windows XP Professional, press F8." If you press the F8 key, you'll see a menu with the following choices:

◆ Safe Mode

◆ Safe Mode with Networking

◆ Safe Mode with Command Prompt

◆ Enable Boot Logging

◆ Enable VGA Mode

◆ Last Known Good Configuration (Your Most Recent Settings That Worked)

◆ Directory Services Restore Mode (Windows Domain Controllers Only)

◆ Debugging Mode

◆ Start Windows Normally

◆ Reboot

◆ Return to OS Choices Menu

NOTE *You'll see this last choice only if you dual boot Windows XP Professional and some other operating system.*

These options cover most of the possible troubleshooting scenarios involving the boot process. If your machine won't boot, you probably don't want to use the current configuration; so choose the Last Known Good Configuration. This should make your machine bootable.

WHEN DOES (AND DOESN'T) IT WORK?

What are the criteria for a configuration being the Last Known Good one? To qualify, a configuration must not have produced any critical errors involving a driver or a system file, and a user must have been able to log on to the system at least once.

The Last Known Good Configuration can't always help you. If any of the following are true, you'll have to use another solution:

- You made a change more than one successful boot ago and want to restore things as they were before the change.

- The information that you want to change is not related to control-set information—user profiles and file permissions fall into the category of information that can't be changed with the Last Known Good Configuration item.

- The system boots, a user logs on, and then the system hangs.

- You change your video driver to an incompatible driver, restart the system, and then log on with the bad driver (you can still type, even if you can't see).

NOTE   *The key to getting Last Known Good to work is knowing what constitutes a successful logon. A successful logon occurs when you have entered your username and password and have been authenticated. Ever seen the message that a domain controller could not be found but you have been logged on with cached credentials? Windows XP Professional considers that a successful logon. If you suspect even for a moment that the change you made might not work, don't log on. Let the computer sit at the Ctrl+Alt+Del prompt for a couple of minutes. If you do not receive any messages about failed services, then log on.*

Using System Restore

If Windows XP Professional has been working correctly but you suddenly, inexplicably can't boot into Windows, you can use a feature that is new in Windows XP—System Restore. In a nutshell, System Restore creates restore points, such as the following:

- System checkpoints, which are scheduled and created by your computer

- Manual restore points, which you create

- Installation restore points, which are automatically created when you install certain programs

You use these restore points to revert to a system configuration that was working properly. (System Restore does not recover changes to personal data files.) You can change some System Restore settings, and we'll look at how to do that next. First, though, let's walk through a typical scenario.

You turn on your computer, Windows XP Professional starts to boot, but then just sits at the opening screen, doing nothing. You turn off your computer and turn it back on, and the same thing happens again. Turn your computer off again, turn it back on, and this time boot into Safe Mode, as described in the previous section.

After Safe Mode loads, you'll see a dialog box that gives you the choice of working in Safe Mode or using System Restore. Click No to use System Restore and to open System Restore at the Welcome screen. Click Next.

TIP   *Sometimes all you need to do to get your system back in shape is to boot into Safe Mode and then restart the system. Safe Mode loads only a minimal number of drivers, thus simplifying the boot process.*

In the Select a Restore Point screen, if no restore points have been created for the current day, click a boldface date on the calendar, and then, from the list on the right, select a time. Click Next to open the Confirm Restore Point Selection screen.

If you are ready to restore, click Next. When the restoration is complete, you'll see a message to that effect. Windows XP Professional will restart, using the settings in the restore point you selected. With a bit of luck, everything will be working properly.

NOTE   *During the restoration process, don't fiddle with your computer. Let Windows do its thing.*

See pages 68–69 in "Essential Skills" for a visual guide to restoring your system.

CREATING YOUR OWN RESTORE POINTS

You can also run System Restore from a working Windows XP Professional system and use System Restore to create your own restore point. To open System Restore, choose Start ➣ All Programs ➣ Accessories ➣ System Tools ➣ System Restore. You'll see the Welcome to System Restore screen:

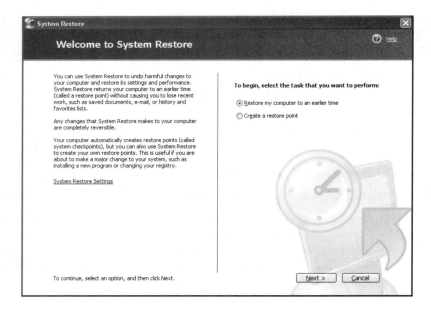

If you want to restore your computer to an earlier time, click that option. To create a restore point, click that option and then click Next to open the Create a Restore Point screen:

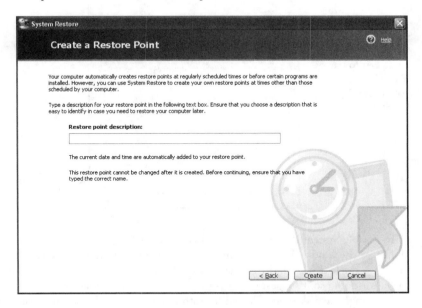

Enter a description for your restore point in the Restore Point Description box, and click Create. Windows creates the restore point and adds the current date and time to the description.

See pages 66–67 in "Essential Skills" for a visual guide to setting system restore points.

CHANGING SYSTEM RESTORE SETTINGS

To change the amount of disk space allotted to restore points or to disable System Restore, you use the System Restore tab in the System Properties dialog box (shown in Figure 24.3).

You can open this dialog box in the following ways:

◆ On the first System Restore screen, click the System Restore Settings link.

◆ Click Start, right-click My Computer, and then choose Properties from the shortcut menu.

◆ In Control Panel, click the Performance and Maintenance category, and then click System.

FIGURE 24.3

You can disable System Restore by clicking the Turn Off System Restore on All Drives check box, but it's best to leave System Restore enabled, as it is by default.

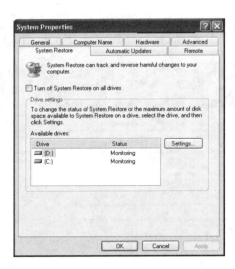

To disable System Restore (which is enabled by default), click the Turn Off System Restore on All Drives check box. (If you have multiple drives on your system, you can't turn off System Restore for only a single drive. All drives have System Restore disabled or enabled.) Unless you have a good reason for doing so, I suggest that you leave System Restore enabled.

To change the disk space allotted to restore points, click the Settings button to open the Settings dialog box:

Move the slider bar to change the amount of disk space.

Creating and Using the Automated System Recovery Disk

Every time you successfully edit your system's configuration, you should back the configuration up against the time when you unsuccessfully edit the settings. This backup is called the Automated System Recovery (ASR) disk.

TIP *Re-create the ASR after you have successfully booted with the new configuration information. This way, you'll know that the configuration you're backing up works.*

Versions of Windows NT and 2000 Professional used an Emergency Repair Disk (ERD) as a boot disk to run the repair tools on the CD. In Windows XP Professional, you create the Automated System Recovery Backup disk instead. It then contains only the files needed to start your system. You use the Automated System Recovery Backup disk and a backup of your system on some other medium to restore your system after a disk failure.

To create the Automated System Recovery Backup, follow these steps:

1. Choose Start ➢ All Programs ➢ Accessories ➢ System Tools ➢ Backup to start the Backup or Restore Wizard.

2. On the initial screen, click the Advanced Mode link to open the Backup Utility at the Welcome tab:

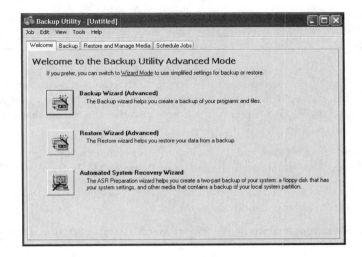

3. Click Automated System Recovery Wizard to start the Automated System Recovery Preparation Wizard:

4. Click Next to open the Backup Destination screen:

5. The Wizard assumes you are backing up to a floppy disk and gives it the name of `Backup.bkf`. Place a floppy in the drive, and click Next to open the last screen of the Wizard. Click Finish, and the Wizard copies to the floppy disk the system files that you'll need to restart after a failure.

To use the ASR disk and the backup of your system on another medium to recover from a system failure, have those two items and your Windows XP Professional CD available, and then follow these steps:

1. Place your installation CD in the drive.

2. Restart your computer. If you are asked to press a key to start the computer from the CD, do so.

3. During the text mode of Setup, press F2 when prompted.

4. Insert the ASR disk when prompted, and then follow the onscreen instructions.

The Recovery Console

Recovery Console is a command-line tool that you can use to start and stop services, format drives, and repair your system. To use Recovery Console, you really should be a power user, and you must be logged on as an administrator. This tool is not installed by default when you install Windows XP Professional, so the first order of business in this section is telling you how to install it.

Installing the Recovery Console

You install the Recovery Console from the Windows XP Professional installation CD. Insert your CD in the drive, and then click Exit when the installation options are displayed. Now, follow these steps:

1. At a command prompt, switch to your CD-ROM drive. If you have a 32-bit computer, type **\i386\winnt32.exe /cmdcons**, and press Enter. (Yes, there's a space between **exe** and the following slash.) If you have a 64-bit computer, type **\ia64\winnt32.exe /cmdcons**, and press Enter.

2. Windows now displays the Windows Setup dialog box, asking if you want to install the Recovery Console. Click Yes, and follow the on-screen instructions.

3. Windows XP Professional Setup will copy some files from the installation CD and then tell you that to use Recovery Console you'll need to restart the computer.

4. After you restart, the Recovery Console will be in the Startup menu (the text menu you see when you start up the computer), listed as Microsoft Windows XP Professional Command Console. To start it, just choose that option before the timeout to your default startup option expires.

Using the Recovery Console

When you choose to run the Recovery Console, select it from the list of available operating systems at startup. You can also run Recovery Console from your installation CD.

If the term "console" led you to expect some kind of GUI, you'll be surprised to see a simple command-line interface. Although it looks like an ordinary command prompt, the Recovery Console is not the command prompt that you can open from the Accessories menu. First, it supports only a few commands and only locally—this is not a network tool. Second, those commands are specialized for this interface and perform only a limited set of functions. The wildcard options in the copy command don't work in the console, you can only copy files from removable media to the system partition (but not the other way around—you can't use the console to back up files to other media), and although you can move to other logical drives on the hard disk, you can't read files on any partition other than the system partition—or even perform a dir function on them. If you try, you'll get an Access Denied error. The Recovery Console is not a command-line version of Windows XP Professional, cool as that would be.

NOTE *I'd expected that the Recovery Console would include a command-line version of RegEdit, as Windows 9x does. Sadly, it does not.*

You can't back up files. You can't read the contents of any folder not in the system root. You can't use wildcards. You can't edit security information. What *can* you do with the Recovery Console?

Mostly, you can fix your system partition to make it usable again. As you can see in Table 24.1, the Recovery Console is a set of commands that you can use to manipulate the files and structure of the system partition. There are a lot of functions with duplicate commands that use the same syntax; unless I specify otherwise, there's no difference between the two commands.

TABLE 24.1: SUPPORTED RECOVERY CONSOLE COMMANDS

COMMAND NAME	FUNCTION
attrib	Changes the attributes of a selected file or folder.
batch	Runs the commands specified in a text file so that you can complete many tasks in a single step.
cd or chdir	Displays the name of the current directory, or changes directories. Typing **cd..** closes the current directory and moves you up one in the tree.
chkdsk	Runs CheckDisk.
cls	Wipes the screen of any previous output, so you can see better.
copy	Copies files from removable media to the system folders on the hard disk (does not accept wildcards).
del or delete	Deletes one or more files (does not accept wildcards).
dir	Lists the contents of the current or selected directory.
disable	Disables the named service or driver.
enable	Enables the named service or driver.
diskpart	Replaces the FDISK tool you're probably familiar with. Creates or deletes disk partitions.
extract	Extracts a compressed installation file (one with a CAB extension) to the local fixed disk. Only works if you're running the Recovery Console from the installation disk.
fixboot	Writes a new partition boot sector on the system partition.
fixmbr	Writes a new Master Boot Record (MBR) for the partition boot sector.
format	Formats the selected disk.
help	Display a list of Recovery Console commands.
listsvc	Lists all the services and drivers running on the Windows XP Professional installation.
logon	Logs on to a Windows XP Professional installation.
map	Displays the drive letter mappings currently in place. Handy for getting the information you need to use diskpart.
md or mkdir	Creates a directory.
more, type	Displays the contents of the chosen text file.
rd or rmdir	Deletes a directory.
rename or ren	Renames a single file.
systemroot	Makes the current directory the system root of the drive you're logged into.

WARNING   *If you thought the Registry Editor was potentially dangerous, the Recovery Console is just as bad or worse. You can really screw up your system here, to the point that the only thing to do is reinstall and reload your backups. There's no Undo feature, not all the commands ask for confirmation, and there's no Read-Only setting like the one in* `regedt32`*. If you're not used to working from the command line, review what you want to do and the tools you need to do it before you open the console.*

Some of the commands shown in Table 24.1 will look familiar to old DOS hands, but many of them work a little differently from the way they did under DOS, using a slightly different syntax or only working under specific circumstances. Let's take a look at how you can use these commands to get things back up and running.

ENABLING AND DISABLING SERVICES

Why would you need to enable or disable services from the command line? Therein lies a tale.

A few years ago, I bought a new PC. Installed everything, ran the installation program for the 3Com network card in the server. Life was good.

Until I rebooted the computer.

You see, a diagnostic program was part of the setup for the NIC—an unavoidable part that you could not choose to not install. (Trust me: I tried, on several computers with the same set of hardware.) Whenever I started up the computer, this diagnostic program would scan the system and display a message that a newer version of my NIC's driver was available—did I want to use the new driver? Click OK or Cancel, and the message box would close for a second and then reopen, with the same message. Add to this that the searching and displaying was using up 100 percent of CPU time for a 350MHz Pentium II doing *nothing else but running the diagnostic*. Running the Task Manager (when I could get a spare cycle here or there to open it) didn't help, because the program wouldn't shut down even when I killed the process.

NOTE   *Worried about this happening to you? Although I've run into several people who've had the same problem with one version of the driver for the 3Com 3C905X Ethernet 10Base-T card, this issue seems to be fixed in the driver published in April 1999. Other than this glitch, I've been very happy with these NICs.*

OK, I figured—the problem is a runaway service, so if I can shut down the service I will resolve the problem. But shutting down the service is hard when you're clicking OK in a repeatedly reappearing dialog box and then frantically grabbing CPU cycles to open Control Panel and then Services before the dialog box opens and the CPU usage starts running at 100 percent again.

In this case, I was finally able to get to the Services applet, find the service (named 3Com Diagnostics, or some such, so identifying the problem child wasn't hard), and then stop and disable it. Problem solved. But it took a lot of time and mouse-clicking to get to that point. A tool that would enable me to boot to the command prompt and disable that service without having to work around the CPU-eating message box would have been nice. And that's where the services-related tools in the Recovery Console come in.

The first step to fixing a problem like this is running the `listsvc` utility from the Recovery Console. There are no arguments to this—just type **`listsvc`** at the command prompt, and Windows XP Professional will display a list of all the services and drivers currently installed for that installation of Windows XP Professional, a short description of what they are, and their start type (boot, automatic, manual, system, or disabled). Seeing all the services will probably take a few screens, but the services are listed alphabetically, so you can find the one you want fairly easily. Write down its name.

TIP *The names of services and drivers are not case sensitive.*

Once you've found the suspected problem child, it's time for the disable command. The syntax is simple: `disable servicename`. Windows XP Professional will then notify you that it found the Registry entry for this service (or tell you that it can't find an entry for this service, in which case you need to check your spelling and try again). It will also display the current start type and new start type for the service. Write down the current start type for the service in case you want to start it again.

To make the change take effect, type **exit** to leave the Recovery Console and restart the computer. See if disabling that service fixed the problem. If it did, you're home free. (Not sure how you'd know? Depends on what the problem was. In the case of the runaway 3Com Diagnostics, the fix was pretty immediate. As soon as I turned off the service, the problem disappeared.) If it didn't, you can return to the console, enable that service, and try something else.

You don't have to disable a service to keep it from running when Windows XP Professional starts, however. Instead, you could change its start type from automatic to manual. To do so, or to reenable a service you disabled, you'll need to use the enable command. Like disable, enable's syntax is simple: `enable servicename`. If run on a disabled service, this syntax will enable the service and restore it to whatever its start type was when it was disabled.

To change a service's start type without disabling it, add the new start type to the end of the enable command, like this:

```
enable servicename start_type
```

where `start_type` is one of the options in Table 24.2.

TABLE 24.2: START TYPES

START TYPE	MEANING
Service_boot_start	Boot
Service_system_start	System
Service_demand_start	Manual
Service_auto_start	Automatic

So, for example, instead of disabling the 3Com diagnostic service, I could have changed its start type from automatic to manual. That way, I could have started it at any time during the Windows XP Professional session, but it wouldn't start automatically.

REPLACING DAMAGED FILES

Perhaps the problem isn't a runaway driver or service, but a corrupted part of the operating system, as in error messages that say `Bad or Missing NTOSKRNL.EXE`. In such a case, you may need to replace all or part of your operating system. The tools most likely to apply to this scenario are the ones to create and delete folders, rename files, change attributes, and copy or extract files from other media.

Creating folders is simple. The command syntax is as follows:

```
md [drive:]path
mkdir [drive:]path
```

where *drive:* is the drive letter of the drive on which you want to create the folder, if it's not the current one, and *path* is the name of the folder you want to create. Just make sure that, if you don't spell out the location of the new folder, you're currently in the place where the new folder should be created.

The syntax for the rmdir and rd commands (for deleting folders) is the same as that for md. The only part of folder deletion that you have to watch is that you can't delete folders unless they're empty, with no subfolders. If you try, you'll get an error message telling you that the folder is not empty, and there's no switch to make rd act like deltree (an old DOS command that would delete subdirectories).

Before you delete a folder, run the dir command to check out its contents and make sure that you really do want to remove it. Conveniently, dir displays all files, hidden or not, and shows their attributes.

Rather than deleting entire folders, however, you're more likely to need to replace individual files. That's where **copy** and **extract** come in. The **copy** command is what it sounds like: a method for copying a file from one location to another, with the caveat I've mentioned before that you can only copy files *to* the system folder, not copy files *from* the system folder to removable media such as a Jaz drive. The syntax for copying files is simple:

```
copy source [destination]
```

where *source* is the name of the original file and *destination* is the folder where you're pasting the original (along with a new name, if you need it). If you don't specify a folder, the file will be copied to the folder from which you're running the command. The **extract** utility works the same way as **copy** and uses the same syntax, with one exception: you can only use **extract** if you started the Recovery Console from the Repair option in Setup. Neither copying utility supports wildcards (so you can't copy the entire contents of a folder very easily), but **copy** automatically decompresses compressed installation files for you. Both utilities will alert you if a file with the name of the one you're pasting already exists in that location.

If you're not sure that you want to replace an existing file, try renaming it and then copying the new file to the relevant location. The syntax for rename is as follows:

```
rename [drive:][path] filename1 filename2
```

This command works only on single files, and the renamed file must be in the same place as the original. That is, you can't use **rename** to move files. To do that, you'd need to use **copy**.

FIXING BOOT SECTORS AND BOOT RECORDS

Your computer uses a couple of pieces of information to navigate your hard disk. Those two pieces are the boot sector and the Master Boot Record (MBR). Most of the time, these pieces are pretty safe, but some things (such as some viruses) can target and infect them, or they can be lost. In such a case, you'll need a way to restore them.

First, a little background. The partition boot sector contains the information that the file system uses to access the volume. The Master Boot Record (discussed soon) examines the information in the boot sector to load the boot loader.

The Windows XP Professional boot sector contains the following information:

◆ A jump instruction

◆ The name and version of the operating system files (such as Windows XP Professional)

◆ A data structure called the BIOS Parameter Block, which describes the physical characteristics of the partition

◆ A data structure called the BIOS Extended Parameter Block, which describes the location of the Master File Table for NTFS volumes

◆ The bootstrap code

Most of the information in the boot sector describes the physical characteristics of the disk (for example, the number of sectors per track and clusters per sector), in addition to the location of the File Allocation Table (for FAT volumes) or the Master File Table (for NTFS volumes). The layout and exact information included in the boot sector depends on the disk format used.

Given that a disk may have more than one partition, how does the hard disk know where to find the different partitions? The first sector on every hard disk (whether the hard disk has an operating system on it or not) contains that disk's Master Boot Record (MBR). The MBR contains the partition table for that disk and a small amount of code used to read the partition table and find the system partition for that hard disk. Once it finds that partition, the MBR loads a copy of that partition's boot sector into memory. If the disk is not bootable (has no system partition), the code never gets used, and the boot sector is not loaded.

In short, a hard disk needs a functioning MBR to boot. The MBR is in the same place on every hard disk, so it's potentially an easy virus target.

OK—all that said, to write a new boot sector to a drive, type **fixboot**. This will write a new boot sector to the current boot drive. To create a new MBR, type **fixmbr**.

DELETING, CREATING, AND FORMATTING PARTITIONS

The Recovery Console includes tools not only for fixing Windows XP Professional, but also for completely wiping things out and starting over. With these tools you can repartition and reformat your hard disk. Partitioning is setting up logical drives on the disk; formatting is placing a file system on those drives so you can store data on them.

WARNING *You probably already know this, but just in case you've forgotten, repartitioning and formatting are destructive. Any data on the hard disk you've reformatted or repartitioned is history. Keep your backups.*

Before you start formatting or repartitioning, you might want to take a look at what you've already got in place. The Recovery Console's map command can help you do that. Type **map** at the command prompt, and you'll see output like the following:

```
?              0MB              Device\HardDisk0\Partition0
C:  FAT16  1028MB              Device\HardDisk0\Partition1
```

```
?            3310MB              Device\HardDisk0\Partition0
E:   NTFS    1028MB              Device\HardDisk0\Partition2
H:   NTFS    1028MB              Device\HardDisk0\Partition3
G:           1028MB              Device\HardDisk0\Partition4
?            227MB               Device\HardDisk0\Partition0
A:                               Device\Floppy0
D:                               Device\CDROM0
```

You can see from this that logical drive G on the hard disk hasn't been formatted, because it's not showing any file system. To format it, you would use the following syntax:

```
format g: [/q] [/fs:filesystem]
```

Here, /q tells **format** to do a quick format (not checking for bad sectors), and the /fs switch is for specifying the file system to use. You don't have to specify a file system (your options are NTFS, FAT32, and FAT), but if you don't, Windows XP Professional will format it to NTFS. When you run this command, Windows XP Professional will tell you that all data on that drive will be lost and ask you to confirm that the format should proceed. Do so, and a few seconds later you will have a newly formatted drive.

TIP *You can convert a FAT partition to NTFS, but you cannot convert an NTFS partition to FAT.*

You can format the G drive safely, or at least without affecting any other logical drives. What you can't do, even before formatting, is repartition to make the G drive bigger, perhaps giving it some of that space that isn't used on the disk.

When you're done with the Recovery Console, type **exit** and press Enter. The computer will reboot.

The Driver Verifier—a Babysitter for Your Drivers

It goes without saying that reliable hardware is the number one most important consideration when building reliable Windows XP Professional systems. However, equally as important is making sure that reliable drivers are used.

A hardware device—as far as Windows XP Professional is concerned—is only as good as its associated driver.

If you've been lucky, all the hardware on your system has well-behaved drivers that don't cause any problems. But what if you wanted to add an old, slightly outdated card to your system? How would that impact your system's stability? Or what if you found a new driver on the Internet for some existing hardware you have? Will the new driver be as stable on your system as your current driver? How can you be sure that updating to a new driver won't compromise your system stability in some way?

The Driver Verifier, first released in Windows 2000 Professional and included with Windows XP Professional, is the answer to all these questions and more. In reality, what the Driver Verifier does is quite simple. During normal Windows operations, all the drivers on your system reside in the kernel of the Windows XP Professional operating system and are supposed to play nicely together and with the operating system. Windows XP Professional doesn't really look at what they are doing. It more or less assumes that the drivers will be on their best behavior as long as they respond appropriately when called on. As an analogy, imagine a bunch of children playing around unsupervised in a back yard. Now, as long as they respond when you call to them, would you assume that they aren't doing anything they shouldn't be doing? I should hope not!

As anyone who has children knows, just because you don't find out that your kids are misbehaving doesn't mean that they're not causing trouble. Kids need supervision. Well, sometimes the drivers in your system need supervision. That's basically what the Driver Verifier does—it acts as a babysitter for your drivers. It puts them under a microscope and scrutinizes every single thing they do. Using our children analogy, imagine taking one of the children, putting them in their own private sandbox, and standing over them watching every single thing they do.

In effect, this is what the Driver Verifier does. By keeping an eye on how the drivers on your system utilize and access memory, your system will display a blue screen if a driver misbehaves. So, what does Windows XP Professional consider misbehaving? Well, the list is rather long—and *extremely* technical—to the point where addressing those issues would take up far more pages than are allocated to this book. Therefore, let's just take a look at the common circumstances in which you would want to use the Driver Verifier and how to use it.

Running the Driver Verifier

As I mentioned before, you will probably want to use the Driver Verifier if you want to add a new piece of hardware to your system or if you want to update an existing driver. In any case, if you are concerned about system stability, run the Driver Verifier in order to place the new (or updated) driver in its own private sandbox for the first few weeks.

WARNING   *During the course of writing this chapter, I placed the driver for my network adapter in the Driver Verifier to make sure it was behaving appropriately. For whatever reason, when I took the driver back out, my system would no longer access the Internet without causing a blue screen. Eventually, I figured out that this was due to a conflict with some personal firewall software that I was using. The personal firewall software worked fine before I started testing the Driver Verifier, but after I took my network adapter in and out of the Driver Verifier, my personal firewall would no longer work consistently. I'm sure that this was an atypical symptom of using the Driver Verifier program—and more likely a problem with my personal firewall software—but it does warrant a bit of caution. Even though this is a great diagnostic utility, unless you have something specific that you want to troubleshoot, it may not be wise to play around with it. And just in case you do want to use it, you might want to back up your system first.*

You can start the Driver Verifier in two ways:

◆   At the command prompt, type **verifier**.

◆   Choose Start ➤ Run to open the Run dialog box, and in the Open box, type **verifier**.

In either case, the Driver Verifier Manager opens , as shown in Figure 24.4.

On the first screen of the Driver Verifier Manager, you select the settings you want the program to use, create custom settings, delete existing settings, display existing settings, or display information about verified drivers. Unless you are the developer of a driver, click the Create Standard Settings option if you are ready to place a driver "in its sandbox," and click Next.

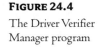

FIGURE 24.4

The Driver Verifier Manager program

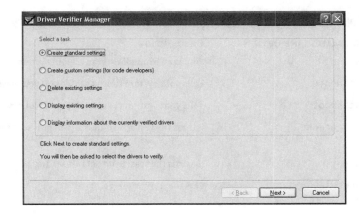

You can then select which driver or drivers you want to verify. Select an option to display a description of what that option will do at the bottom of the screen. If you select Automatically Select Unsigned Drivers, the Driver Verifier Manager will immediately search your system for any unsigned drivers and display a list of any it finds. Driver Verifier Manager will do the same if you select the Automatically Select Drivers Built for Older Versions of Windows option.

If you want to verify all drivers on your system, click that option, and then click Finish. If you just want to see a list of drivers, click Select Driver Names from a List. When you've made your choice, click Next, and Driver Verifier Manager will take care of the task.

System File Checker

One of the things that Microsoft has learned over the years is that more often than not, unreliable behavior in Windows can be directly attributed to missing, corrupted, or conflicting versions of critical system components. In an effort to resolve this problem, Microsoft has included a utility in Windows XP Professional called the System File Checker (SFC).

The System File Checker is a command-line utility that will scan the critical system files on your computer and replace any suspicious files with original copies either from your installation media or a special folder on your system. If you suspect that a Windows file on your system might have been damaged, run the System File Checker to find out for sure.

Running the SFC

The SFC will check approximately 2700 files on your system—namely most of the SYS, DLL, EXE, TTF, FON, and OCX files that were originally installed. When you run the SFC, you are in effect telling the utility to compare all the files on your system against the original installation media. Therefore, the SFC will need a copy of the original files to work from. Make sure that you have your original Windows XP Professional CD-ROM handy when you need to run this utility.

The SFC is a command-line utility, so you won't find it on any of the menus in your system. To launch the SFC, type **SFC** at a command prompt. If everything is working correctly, you should see a help screen giving you the available command options. The options are listed in Table 24.3.

TABLE 24.3: SFC COMMAND-LINE OPTIONS

COMMAND-LINE OPTIONS	DESCRIPTION
/scannow	Forces an immediate scan of your system
/scanonce	Tells your system to scan all files on your system at the next bootup
/scanboot	Tells your system to scan all files on your system at every bootup
/purgecache	Purges the Dllcache folder and begins scanning all protected system files immediately
revert	Returns the scan to its default setting
cachesize=x	Sets the file cache size

Since you're reading this chapter, you're most likely looking for troubleshooting information, either to repair a system that is currently experiencing problems or for future reference. For most troubleshooting purposes, a simple SFC /SCANNOW will suffice. This will begin checking each of the critical system files on your computer, comparing them against the original copies, and determining if any of the files have been corrupted.

As the tool is running, a status monitor will keep you informed as to how far the system has proceeded with its checking. If the SFC finds any files that are missing or corrupted (when compared with the Windows XP Professional source media), it will replace the file with the original version either from its cache on your hard drive or from the original media.

Just for giggles, I tested this capability on my system by overwriting one of the True-Type Font (TTF) files. Sure enough, once I ran the SFC, it saw that one of my files was corrupted and replaced it with an original copy of the file. I can definitely see where the SFC is useful in the case of corrupted files, virus infections, or just plain ol' human error. The SFC is a lifesaver!

The Registry Entry That Lets You Force a Blue Screen (Core Dump)

OK, so far in this chapter, I've been talking about ways to avoid blue screens or at least to minimize their impact. But what if you actually *want* to cause a blue screen?

Although unusual, on occasions you might want to force your system to crash via a blue screen. For example, you might want to test that Windows XP Professional will reboot itself properly and that all the necessary services on your system will start again. Or, you might want to see how well an application that is running on your system will perform in the event of a critical failure. For whatever the reasons, if you want to force your system to blue screen, you can do it.

All you need is one simple Registry modification. To modify the Registry in Windows XP Professional, you use RegEdit. As always, before making *any* modifications to your Registry, back it up.

After you back up your Registry, you will need to navigate to the HKEY_LOCAL_MACHINE\SYSTEM\CurrentControlSet\Services\i8042prt\Parameters. In there, you will create a create a key called CrashOnCtrlScroll as a DWORD type. Enter a value of 1 for the Registry key, and then reboot your system.

So what does this do? Well, the `i8042prt` service is responsible for handling your keyboard input. So this Registry entry allows you to force the system to crash through the use of a special keystroke. Useful for both diagnostic testing purposes and practical joking! Once you have this Registry key in your system, a simple Ctrl+ScrollLock+ScrollLock will cause your system to immediately blue screen (you must use the Ctrl key on the right side of the keyboard).

Backing Up and Restoring

A lot of what I've talked about in this chapter won't do you any good unless you've backed up your system. So, as I promised early on in this chapter, here are the steps for backing up and for restoring.

Making a Backup

The next thing you can do to make life easier for yourself is to back up important files. Yes, we know you have heard all this before; everybody's heard about making backups, but why should *you* make a backup?

To protect against hard disk failure A hard disk can fail at almost any time, but when it does, it is always at the most inconvenient moment.

To protect against accidental deletion of a file If you work on many projects, your chances of accidentally deleting a file are far higher than if you work on only one at a time.

To create an archive at the end of a project You can make a backup that contains all the files relating to a single project when the work is done; then if you need to refer to the files again, you know where to find them.

These are the main reasons to make a backup, but there are others. You might back up the files of a terminating employee in case the computer is reassigned within your department or is transferred to another department. In either case, the new user will likely clean up the hard disk—in other words, delete all the most important files. In addition, making a backup is one way to transfer a large number of files from one computer system to another. Finally, you should always back up before making a substantial change to your system such as installing new hardware, upgrading the operating system, or making a major configuration change to your application software.

Once you decide to make a backup, you need to plan your backup strategy and, most important, stick to it. With no plan, you will simply accumulate floppy disks or tapes haphazardly, you will waste tapes, and you will waste time looking for a file when you need to restore a file deleted by accident.

So how often should you make a backup? For an answer that fits the way you work, answer these questions:

♦ How often do your data files change? Every day? Every week? Every month?

♦ How important to your day-to-day operations are these files? Can you work without them? How long would it take you to re-create them?

♦ How much will it cost to replace lost files in terms of time spent and business lost?

In our computerized world, it takes hours to create an HTML page with just the right look or a budget spreadsheet that everyone agrees to, but either can be lost or destroyed in milliseconds. A hard-disk failure, a mistaken delete command, overwriting the file with an earlier version with the same name—these can destroy a file just as surely as fire, flood, or earthquake. You just have to lose one important file to become an instant convert for life to a program of regular, planned backups.

To start the Windows XP Professional backup program, choose Start ➢ All Programs ➢ Accessories ➢ System Tools ➢ Backup.

USING THE BACKUP OR RESTORE WIZARD

Using the Backup or Restore Wizard is a quick and easy way to learn about backups; it gets you going quickly with the minimum of technical knowledge. Later in this section, I'll walk you through the steps to do a manual backup.

To back up using the Wizard, follow these steps:

1. At the Welcome screen, click Next to open the Backup or Restore screen:

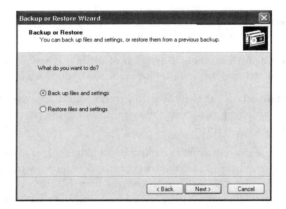

2. Click the Back Up Files and Settings option, and then click Next to open the What to Back Up screen:

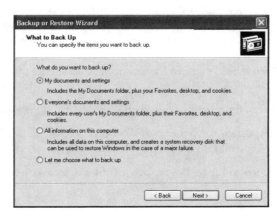

3. Select what you want to back up, and then click Next to open the Backup Type, Destination, and Name screen:

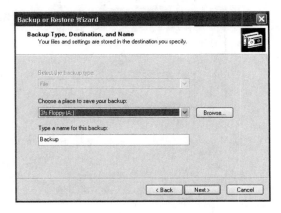

4. Select the type of medium to which you'll back up, give the backup a name, and then click Next to open the Completing the Backup or Restore Wizard screen.

5. Click Finish to start the backup.

NOTE *To select additional backup options, click the Advanced button on the final screen of the Wizard before you click Finish.*

A time will come when you want a little more control over your backups, and that is when you stop using the Wizard and take charge of the process yourself. At the Welcome dialog box, rather than invoking the Wizard, click the Advanced Mode button. Using the Backup Utility program involves essentially the same tasks that the Backup or Restore Wizard does for you—selecting the files, deciding where to put them, and specifying how the backup should actually be made. Let's take a look.

TIP *You must have the right permissions to make a backup or a restore. Make sure you are logged on as an administrator or as a backup operator if you are backing up files on a local computer. If you are not logged on as an administrator or backup operator, you must be the owner of the file or folders you want to back up, or you must have one or more of the following permissions: Read, Read and Execute, Modify, or Full Control.*

MAKING A MANUAL BACKUP

The Backup Utility dialog box opens at the Welcome tab, from which you can choose to use the Wizards. To make a manual backup, click the Backup tab, which is shown in Figure 24.5. If you have previously specified and saved a backup job, you can select it for use again using Job ➤ Load Selections. That done, all you have to do is click the Start Backup button to begin the backup.

FIGURE 24.5

The Backup tab in
the Backup Utility
program

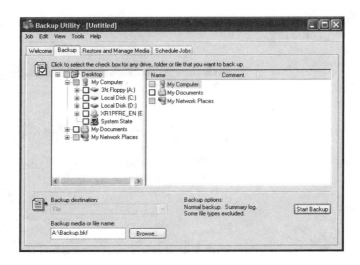

If you don't have a previously saved backup job or if you want to do things a little differently this time, the first task is to decide which files to back up. You can back up all the files and folders in the Backup tab, or you can back up only files that have changed, along with any new files never before backed up.

In the Backup tab, check the box next to the files and folders you want to back up. A blue checkmark indicates that the folder or file is selected for backup; a gray checkmark indicates that some of the files in the folder or on the drive have been selected for backup.

The next task is to select the destination device or drive for the backup and to name the backup file itself. Use the Backup Destination list below the main window to select the destination, and the Backup Media or File Name box to specify a name for this backup.

The last part of the process is to review the backup configuration settings. Choose Tools ➤ Options to open the Options dialog box shown in Figure 24.6.

FIGURE 24.6

The Options
dialog box

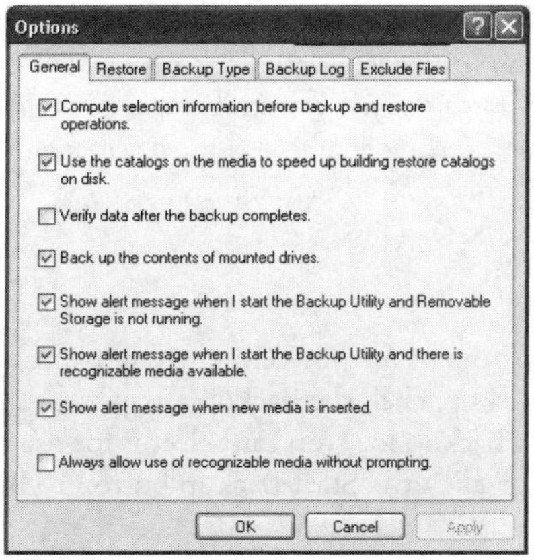

Across the top of the Options dialog box you will see the following tabs:

General   Lets you specify that the backed-up data are compared against the original files to ensure the data were properly backed up. You can also specify how data compression is performed and how you want the Backup program to respond if it finds that the medium (tape, disk, or CD) you are using already contains a backup.

Restore   Lets you specify what happens when duplicate files are found during a restore operation.

Backup Type   Lets you choose how the backup is made:

Normal   Backs up all the selected files and clears the archive bit.

Copy   Backs up all the selected files but does not clear the archive bit.

Differential   Backs up all the selected files that changed since the last Normal or Incremental backup. When the backup is complete, the archive bit for each file is left on.

Incremental   Backs up all the selected files that have changed since the last Incremental or Normal backup. When the backup is complete, the archive bit for each file is turned off.

Daily   Backs up all the files that have been modified today.

Backup Log   Lets you specify the elements you want to include in the backup log file.

Exclude Files   Lets you specify file types that you want to exclude from this backup; use the Add New and Remove buttons to select files for exclusion.

All that remains is to click the Start Backup button to begin the backup. Keep the backup in a safe place, preferably not next to your computer; if your computer is damaged by the sprinklers going off by accident, there is a very good chance that the backup will be destroyed at the same time.

TIP   Click the Schedule Jobs tab in the Backup Utility main window to specify the date for a backup.

Restoring a Backup

Most of the time, making a backup is a simple precaution, and you put it on the shelf along with the other tapes or Zip disks. But there will come a time, after a hard-disk controller failure perhaps, when you will need to restore a backup. Again, as when making the backup, you can use a Wizard, or you can do it manually.

USING THE RESTORE WIZARD

Using the Backup or Restore Wizard is a quick and easy way to learn about restoring backups; it gets you going quickly with the minimum of technical knowledge. To access this feature, click Restore Wizard in the Welcome tab of the Backup Utility dialog box. (You can also use the Backup or Restore Wizard described earlier.) If you would rather not use the Wizard, click the Restore and Manage Media tab, which is described in the next section.

The Wizard walks you through a sequence of dialog boxes that specify the following:

What to Restore   You can restore all files and folders in the backup set, or you can restore selected files and folders.

Restore From   Specify the type and location of the backup you want to restore.

Select Backup Sets   Select a backup set for the restore.

Where to Restore   Specify the target of the restore; most of the time, selecting Original Location to put the file back where it came from makes the most sense.

How to Restore   Specify whether existing files on your hard disk should be overwritten during the restore.

USING THE RESTORE AND MANAGE MEDIA TAB

Using the Restore and Manage Media tab in the Backup Utility dialog box involves essentially the same tasks that the Restore Wizard does for you—selecting the files, deciding where to put them, and specifying how the restore should actually be made. A checkmark in a gray check box means that only some of the files in a folder have been selected. A checkmark in a white box means that all files in a folder have been selected.

Summary

This chapter introduced you to some of the vital skills needed for troubleshooting Windows XP Professional when things go wrong. I discussed how to avoid Windows XP Professional crashes, which is the best troubleshooting technique of all, and how to restore a configuration. We then looked at System Restore, a new feature in Windows XP Professional, and at Recovery Console. Following that, we took a look at the Driver Verifier, the System File Checker, and the Registry entry that lets you force a core dump. Fixing Windows is no fun, but at least now you have an idea of how to go about it. You also know why it's important to back up your files, you know how to back up, and you know how to restore.

Chapter 25

Advanced Troubleshooting Methodology

EVER HAVE ONE OF those days? A day when nothing seems to go right with your computer? Unfortunately, an operating system such as Windows XP Professional is extremely complex, and any complex system will inevitably have those days. Just remember this quote from a favorite Scottish engineer: "The more they over-tink the plumbing, the easier it is to stop up the drains." With a system such as Windows XP Professional, things can go wrong in so many places that it's often difficult to find a place to start.

In this chapter, we take a look at the "how" of troubleshooting Windows XP Professional. I want to give you a workable method for finding your way through the maze. You will learn about the following:

- ◆ Troubleshooting principles and procedures
- ◆ Troubleshooting printing
- ◆ Troubleshooting Windows XP Professional setup
- ◆ Dealing with SCSI problems during setup
- ◆ Troubleshooting Stop errors

The Tao of Troubleshooting

At first it seems that troubleshooting mostly involves memorizing a lot of details about everything. When working with an experienced troubleshooter, you've probably even found yourself thinking, "How do they know that?" Truth is, most people never do well by simply trying to memorize everything. Human beings succeed best when working from their strengths; we all have problems when working from our weaknesses. To make troubleshooting a strength, you need to find the pattern in the chaos.

NOTE *The process of troubleshooting is the process of moving from big picture to small detail. Asking questions is the tool for breaking the big picture into small details.*

Consider this scenario: A friend tells you he is having trouble getting a vending machine to accept a dollar bill. If you happen to be a vending machine expert, you might know everything about how the dollar bill is drawn into the machine, every detail of the mechanisms that control the entire process. But you probably aren't a vending machine expert. Instead, being a good troubleshooter, you consider the directions on the machine. Then you start asking questions: "Has it ever worked before?" "Did you put the dollar in facing the right direction?" "Is the dollar bill folded?"

With this last question, your friend admits that the corners of the bill are a bit folded. So you try straightening them out. Then you test your solution by reinserting the bill. It works, and you are a hero. Of course, solving a problem like this has a low glory quotient, but it serves to illustrate the basics.

Define the Problem: "It's Broken."

The first step to successful troubleshooting is to define the problem accurately. Many times people will define a problem in very simple terms and expect you to know what they are talking about. Your job as a troubleshooter is to define the details of the problem: "So what *exactly* is broken?" This is a good question to start the conversation. (Incidentally, this may be a conversation with yourself if you are trying to solve your own problem.) Start by getting a clear description of what the person who is reporting the problem feels is the issue. It is often a good technique to take the time to write these points out on paper.

Try to get all the details that describe the problem as the user sees it. Ask questions like "Has it ever worked before?" or "When did you notice that it stopped working?"

Explore the Boundaries

This can be a painful lesson to learn. Often the person you are working with to solve a problem (yes, this can even be yourself) leaves out important details. This is almost never because they want you to fail, but rather because they don't think a particular detail is relevant. This is a painful lesson because you may spend a great deal of time pursuing irrelevant issues when the real problem is very simple. Consider the following illustration.

You are talking with a customer about their computer problem. The issue, as reported, is that the new modem isn't working. So right away you dig into the settings and configuration for the modem. You eventually discover that the customer has disabled the COM port in Device Manager because they didn't think they needed it!

Exploring the boundaries means finding out everything that may be wrong with the system. The extra information you get here *may* be unrelated to the problem, but it may be exactly the piece you need to solve the puzzle.

Brainstorm and Document

Now that you have a clue about where the problem lies, it's time to come up with some ideas to help focus on the real issue. While you are gathering your thoughts, write them down. It's a good idea to have at least three things to try before proceeding.

Writing down your ideas is important. You will be trying each possible approach, and this may take time. It may be difficult to remember each idea when you're in the heat of battle (figuratively speaking). Don't be afraid to add to this list as you go. Often you will discover the best approach while trying one of your initial ideas.

Test Your Ideas

This is a critical point: Test each approach—one at a time.

It is impossible to overemphasize this point. Many troubleshooters will try the "shotgun" approach, meaning they test every idea they can muster all at once. Most likely one of the ideas will work, but which one?

During the course of troubleshooting an operating system, you will frequently be disabling certain functionalities. If you try every idea at the same time, you may fix the problem, but you'll be left with an operating system that has been crippled by your actions. Worse yet, you won't know which areas to re-enable and which one to repair. So, test your ideas one at a time, and if the idea doesn't work, change your setting back to the way it was before trying your next fix. You don't want to cause more problems than necessary!

Testing each idea one at a time enables you to discover clearly what's broken and to easily find your way back through the maze of settings that have been changed.

Repair the Problem

This is the easy part—usually. Finding the problem can often be a time-consuming process, but repairing the broken portion of the system can be as simple as replacing a corrupt file. Perhaps the issue arises from bad hardware. This is easy to fix; just replace the hardware. (The hard part here is to find the money for the replacement.)

Clean Up After Yourself

Remember how I said earlier to test each possible solution individually? This is the phase where you undo some of the ideas that were unsuccessful, if you haven't already done so. Never leave the system worse than you found it. There are few support issues worse than a customer who is upset that the previous support person made their problems worse or caused new ones.

Again, it's helpful to have documented the approaches you tried—especially if you kept notes about what you did during the troubleshooting phase. If you did, it is simple to backtrack and turn features back on.

Provide Closure

If you are dealing with other people in your troubleshooting process, providing closure means informing them of what the problem was and what you did to resolve it. If you are going through this process to solve your own problem, it means reviewing what you did and understanding how to avoid this problem in the future.

Nearly every person you work with when supporting an operating system will want to know what the problem was and how to fix it. We all like to feel that we have been included in finding a solution, that we are part of a team effort. A word of advice here: If you are supporting people on Windows XP Professional as part of your job, always try to include the customer in the troubleshooting process. It helps them to feel better about the incident and about your presence. That, in turn, helps them to participate by giving you good information. And that makes everyone's day go better.

Now a moment for the darker side of support. If the problem was caused by the user's ignorance, getting closure is your opportunity to educate. If you do this with some sensitivity, you can turn this into a positive experience. If you give in to the temptation to tell the person that they're an idiot, you will be burning bridges that will be difficult to rebuild later. Your choice. If *you* are the customer, this is where you can ask advice or discover an opportunity for education.

Document the Situation

The problem is fixed, and the customer is happy. You have explained to them what went wrong, and they promised to never touch that button again. You're done, right? Not quite.

The last step, and one that most people often forget, is to document the situation. What was the problem? How did you fix it? It may even be helpful to leave brief notes about what you tried that didn't work. The question is, where do you document all of this? It really depends on your work situation. Some companies require server and workstation maintenance logs. They are generally stored in an easily accessible area so the network administrators can find them in a hurry.

If you work for a company that has multiple administrators (or network troubleshooters), keeping notes on a fixed problem is critical. If the problem happens again, you don't want to be the person that spends three hours trying stuff that someone else already tried to no avail. Nor do you want to be the person that has to look at your coworker who just spent three hours doing what didn't work for you last time either. Common logs are a great way to keep track of issues and expedite troubleshooting.

If you are the only troubleshooter, or if it's otherwise possible, keep your own log book of your activities, especially if you are new to troubleshooting. No one can possibly know or remember everything. The book can help your memory. Eventually, you may rely on it less and less, but when you need it, it's an invaluable tool.

No matter your situation, the documentation rule is simple. Document what you do, and do what you document. It will save everyone time and headaches in the long run.

Troubleshooting Printing

Printing is one of those areas that is most important to users of computer systems. Remember the promise of the "paperless office"? Anyone ever seen one? Printing is one of the highest causes of support calls, and it's one of the hardest areas to get good support in. This area in particular is one in which you need to think simple. Don't forget to ask yourself the easy questions, such as, "Is it plugged in?", "Is it turned on?", and "Is the correct driver properly installed?" If they are answered up front, these three questions can save you a lot of time troubleshooting printing issues. Just remember to ask diplomatically when troubleshooting someone else's printing problem. No one likes to feel dumb.

Let's work through a scenario to get a feel for how to apply the methodology to printing issues in Windows XP Professional. Here is your trouble ticket:

User:	Bob
Telephone:	12345
Problem:	Can't print
Description:	Nothing comes out when I try to print.
Priority:	URGENT!

As you can see, your user Bob is having trouble trying to print a document and feels it is urgent that this be resolved quickly. The first step is to define the problem, so you contact Bob at his cubicle. Bob informs you that the job he is trying to print is a monthly profit-and-loss report for The Boss. Sounds pretty important, so you get right to work on the problem.

Troubleshooting Scenario 1: Printer Is Unplugged

Simple questions first. Has it ever worked? Bob tells you that the printer worked fine the last time he tried to print, which was yesterday. What happened when he tried to print this time? He clicked Print in Word and got a message that the printer was offline or out of paper.

Test the approach. You look at the print device that is on Bob's desk, and you see that the lights are on. This indicates that the printer is plugged in and can access electricity. Next, you try toggling the online/offline switch and find that the print device is online. Still thinking simple, you next check the back of Bob's print device to make sure the parallel cable is firmly attached. It is. Bob's computer is a tower and is located under his desk. You crawl under the desk to check the parallel cable and find that it has fallen off the back of the computer. You reconnect the cable and try to print a test page. It works!

Provide closure. The closure comes with the determination that Bob may have accidentally kicked loose the cable when he stretched his feet out under his desk. One possible solution to avoid this is to be sure that the retaining clips of the parallel cable are correctly fastened on the computer's parallel port. Providing an explanation of the cause along with a solution gives the customer some closure on the issue.

This sounds ridiculously easy, right? You might be surprised to find out that this ticket, or a slight variation thereof, is a very common answer for help desks. Don't forget to document!

Troubleshooting Scenario 2: Nothing in the Print Queue Will Print

Explore the boundaries. When you contact Bob regarding his printing issue, he tells you that he has been trying to print for the last two hours but nothing is coming out of the printer. Bob tells you that there were no messages when he tried to print other than the pop-up message that the job was successfully printed. Windows XP Professional is accepting the print jobs when he submits them, but nothing is coming out.

Ask the simple questions. You investigate the simple issues first. The print device is connected and plugged in. It does display indicator lights, so you know that it is turned on and getting power. The cables are connected. Bob tells you that it printed fine yesterday, but it hasn't printed at all this morning. He insists that nothing has been changed on his computer, no software added, no hardware changed.

Track the possible approaches. You decide that some of the possibilities are that he might be printing to a different printer and doesn't realize it, or that something is wrong with the print queue.

Test the approaches. You check the Printers and Faxes folder on Bob's computer and verify the setting for his locally attached printer. Next, you verify that this printer is set as the default and that he has not redirected the output to another network printer. Opening the printer icon, you discover a long list of jobs that Bob submitted earlier today. Every job he has tried to print is listed, and the job on top of the list is a report from Excel.

You try checking to make sure that the printer has not been Paused. Everything looks fine, but no print jobs will process. You determine that the queue itself has become either corrupted or jammed.

Repair the problem.   After closing the Printers and Faxes folder, you open the Administrative Tools folder and double-click the Services icon. You scroll down the list to find the Print Spooler service and highlight it. You stop the service, wait a few seconds, then start it again.

TIP   *When the Print Spooler service becomes corrupt, or a job gets jammed in the queue, stopping and restarting the service may be enough to resolve the issue with no further effort.*

After restarting the Print Spooler service, you examine the queue and find that the jobs are unchanged. At this point, the most likely cause is a corrupted document stuck at the top of the queue. Make a note as to the document size and timestamp. Stop the Print Spooler again, and then open Explorer.

Using Explorer, open the WINNT folder and find the `system32\Spool\Printers` folder. Find the files with the approximate timestamp of the print job that was stuck at the top of the queue. There will be two files, one with the extension SPL, the other with the extension SHD. If you have trouble deleting the SPL file, you may still be able to fix the problem by renaming the SHD file and restarting the Print Spooler service.

NOTE   *Windows XP Professional uses two files for each print job submitted. The first is the actual spool file (`*.spl`), which contains the formatted data to be printed. The second is the shadow file (`*.shd`), which is basically a transaction file for the print job.*

After successfully deleting the two files, you restart the Print Spooler and immediately the print jobs begin to print.

Provide closure.   Talking with Bob, you describe the issue as a corrupted print job that acted like a cork in a bottle, plugging up the queue. This could have been caused by a problem with the printer settings, the queue itself being corrupt, or most likely the document being corrupt. In the last case, Bob could open the document in the original program and select Save As from the File menu to save a new copy of the document without the corruption. Once again, don't forget to document.

Other Print Troubleshooting Steps

There are several standard troubleshooting steps that you can add to your support toolbox. We have already discussed one of the most important—asking simple questions. Believe it or not, verifying that the print device is plugged in and turned on can solve many problems. This is no reflection on either the intelligence of the user or their knowledge of computing. Some *very* experienced people have called support with printing issues that were solved by either plugging in the print device or turning it on. We've all done it at some time.

Assuming that the print device is plugged in and turned on, and that you have verified the parallel cable as well, you need to test the print subsystem directly. To do so, follow these steps:

1. Choose Start ➢ Control Panel ➢ Printers and Faxes to open the Printers and Faxes folder (if you are using the Classic view of Control Panel, and as a system administrator or power user, I'm sure you are).

2. Right-click the icon for your printer, and choose Properties from the shortcut menu to open the Properties dialog box for your printer.

3. In the General tab, click Print Test Page.

If you are troubleshooting a non–PostScript print device that has been redirected to LPT1, you can try the following command at a command prompt:

Type dir > lpt1:

This copies the output of a `dir` command directly to the print device and bypasses the spooling provided by Windows XP Professional. If this fails or if the output is garbled, the issue may be a bad cable, faulty parallel port, or other hardware problem. If it works, you know the problem exists in Windows XP Professional or in the program.

NOTE   *Redirecting the output of a command to the port will not work if you are testing a PostScript device.*

If any devices are connected to the computer's parallel port between the computer and the print device, you should remove them and try printing again. Windows XP Professional is often not very forgiving about sharing ports with multiple devices.

Try a generic driver for the print device. If you are using a PostScript device, try installing the Apple LaserWriter driver. This is a very basic PostScript driver. If it works, you have identified the problem as a bad *.ppd driver for the PostScript print device. If it is a non-PostScript device, try the Generic-Text Only driver.

NOTE   *PostScript printers don't really have a printer driver. Instead they use a PostScript Printer Description file (*.ppd), which is essentially a text file that describes how to send print jobs to the print device.*

An issue that is often overlooked is the amount of space available for the spool file. Check to make sure that plenty of free space remains on the partition where Windows XP Professional is installed. If you run out of room for the spool file, one of two things will happen: Either the jobs won't print, giving you an error message about being out of memory; or the jobs will print, but the printing process will be incredibly slow. If you have multiple partitions on your hard drive, or multiple hard drives in your machine, you can move your print spooler to a location with more free space. To do this, open the Printers and Faxes window, and click the File menu ➢ Server Properties. In the Advanced tab, you will see a location for the spool folder. Type in an alternate folder location (on a different drive), and then click OK.

Another thing to try is printing from another operating system on the same computer if there is a dual-boot configuration. Or you could even try printing from the same application on a different computer.

One last possibility is that there is a problem with your document. It is possible that you will be able to print a less complex document from the same application. If this is the case, the problem is probably within the application.

Troubleshooting Windows XP Professional Setup

Many people encounter problems during the installation of Windows XP Professional, though most of the problems are minor and can be easily avoided. This section helps with troubleshooting the more difficult Setup issues.

In this section, we talk about troubleshooting Setup on the Intel and compatible platforms. The techniques work well for machines that are on the Hardware Compatibility List (HCL) and also for most machines that aren't on the list. Why would you want to install Windows XP Professional on a "noncompatible" system? Ever build your own computer? It wouldn't likely be on the HCL unless you want to pay Microsoft to test your computer and certify it for Windows XP Professional.

I've broken this section into parts that address problems you might encounter when planning for or during the text mode portion of Setup, during the transition to GUI mode, and during the final phase of rebooting.

Planning and Text Mode Setup

If you can restrain yourself from simply tearing the shrink-wrap from the box and whipping the CD-ROM out to start Setup, you should think about some things before you begin. Does your computer meet or exceed all the requirements? You may want to take the time to consult Chapter 2 again for setup guidance and hardware requirements. Assuming that you have done this and your computer meets all the requirements, there are some additional points you will want to document before starting.

What cards are installed in your computer? Do you have a network card? A sound card? What about a 3-D accelerator card? Do you have the settings for all these devices written down? Remember that Windows XP Professional is a Plug-and-Play operating system; it can find the settings for most of your hardware on its own, but you should still know what those settings are in case it can't find them. Do you have the latest, certified drivers for Windows XP Professional? Are the drivers on floppy disk or CD-ROM where you can get to them easily? Or are they on a network share? By the way, it won't do you any good to have your network card drivers out on a network server somewhere if you don't already have a functioning network card. Keep these handy on a floppy disk. Use Table 25.1 as a guide for the information you should have on hand prior to running Setup.

TABLE 25.1: USEFUL INFORMATION FOR SETUP

DEVICE	INFORMATION TO GATHER
Video display	Adapter brand and model, chip set
Network adapter	IRQ, I/O address, DMA, transceiver type
SCSI adapter	Manufacturer and model, chip set, IRQ, bus type
Mouse (pointing device)	Manufacturer and model, bus type, port
I/O ports	Serial, parallel, IRQ, I/O addresses
Internal modem	Port, IRQ, I/O address
Sound card	Manufacturer and model (or compatible model), IRQ, I/O address, DMA
Other devices	Hardware resources, device type, drivers

Now let's look at another troubleshooting scenario involving setup issues. In this situation, imagine you are the person responsible for installing Windows XP Professional and for providing general technical support to a group of users.

Troubleshooting Scenario 3: Drives Not Found

You are responsible for installing Windows XP Professional on a computer for one of the users in your department. You insert the installation CD and begin Setup. When Setup reaches the point where it displays your current disk and partition information, Setup displays the following error message:

```
Setup did not find any hard drives on your computer.
```

You know there are two hard disk drives in this computer and you can hear them spinning, so you know that they are receiving power. The first step in your troubleshooting methodology is to explore the boundaries of the problem.

You open the case of the computer to find out exactly what kind of hard disk drives are installed (after turning off the power, of course). You find that the drives are SCSI-2 2.1GB, and that they are attached to an Adaptec 2940 controller. No other SCSI devices are installed in this computer. When you investigate, you find that the computer had IDE drives and has recently been updated with a new SCSI controller and SCSI disks.

What you know and don't know at this point:

◆ The computer has never worked before in this configuration.

◆ The drives are SCSI, which require electronic termination and unique ID numbers on each bus.

◆ You do not know the state of the termination.

◆ You do not know the SCSI ID numbers for each drive.

Based on this information, you should already be suspecting that something is wrong with the hardware configuration. You reach into the case to ensure that the cables are tightly attached and find that they are. On these hard disks drives, the SCSI IDs are set by jumpers on the rear of the drive (you will probably have to remove the drives to get at them).

Your plan of attack:

1. Verify the SCSI ID numbers of the drives and controller.

2. Verify the termination of the drive chain.

3. Check the BIOS settings of the controller.

Before you go through the work to remove the hard disk drives to check their ID numbers, you boot the computer to run the SCSI BIOS program. This program enables you to view and modify the configuration of the devices, as well as run diagnostics and other utilities. This utility tells you that it sees both hard disk drives, one as SCSI ID #0, the other as SCSI ID #1. This means the ID numbers are not the issue. SCSI ID #0 and #1 are usually reserved for hard drives.

NOTE *SCSI ID numbers are important. Having a conflict between two or more devices on the same SCSI bus can cause Setup to fail to recognize installed hard disk drives. It can also cause the system to fail when booting or to hang after booting.*

The BIOS utility on the Adaptec controller also provides the capability to enable or disable termination on the controller card itself. You check and find that it is enabled correctly. Now you have verified the SCSI ID numbers, the controller settings, and half of the termination. The only thing left on your list is termination. To do this on older hardware, you have to pull out the last hard disk drive on the ribbon cable and check its termination. Newer drives are self-terminating, and normally the termination is on the ribbon cables.

Checking the last drive on the chain, you find that its terminator packs (resistors) are not set. This means that the SCSI bus is not terminated at one end. This may or may not be the problem, but it certainly needs to be fixed. You correct the termination and are ready to test the setup again. You start Setup, and this time everything runs fine.

Today, many SCSI drives are self-terminating, and you can also terminate on the ribbon cable instead of the drive. Today's SCSI is usually terminated on the SCSI controller and on the ribbon cable if building internal (to the PC) SCSI chains.

When you are troubleshooting problems on a SCSI-based system, always remember to check the termination. With SCSI, both ends of each drive chain must be terminated. Windows XP Professional is so sensitive about the stability of the hardware components that improper termination can be fatal to Setup. Even if you succeed with Setup, termination issues can result in hanging or even a blue-screen error. Even mismatched termination levels can cause this situation. If your controller has active termination and your hard disk has passive termination, you may have problems. Upgrading your SCSI chain to active termination or even forced-perfect termination at both ends can relieve the problem.

SCSI Troubleshooting

In the previous scenario, we looked at the possible importance of SCSI termination. In my experience, nearly 90 percent of the troubleshooting issues of Windows XP Professional Setup on SCSI-based computers involve termination problems. But there are other issues to be aware of as well. For instance, is the BIOS of the SCSI controller activated? This is another problem that would cause the preceding scenario.

A low-level format that is incorrect for the current drive geometry could cause file corruption, drives not being recognized by Setup, and system crashes. If you are installing a new SCSI drive or changing to a new make or model of SCSI controller, you should perform a low-level format of the drive to assure that the drive geometry will line up correctly.

In simpler terms, the drive controller performs a format of the disks within the drive so that the operating system will be able to write data to the individual sectors on the drive. In a way, sectors are like tiny boxes that are meant to contain information. Imagine trying to drop golf balls into small boxes. If you are lining them up correctly, it's easy. The balls simply drop right into place every time. But imagine now that you're slightly off your aim. The balls usually go in the boxes, but sometimes they bounce off the edges and roll away. That's what's happening when your drive isn't low-level formatted correctly for the specific controller. Each SCSI controller has its own geometry, its way of laying out those little boxes.

If multiple SCSI controllers are in the computer, does more than one of them have an active BIOS? If so, they may be competing for Int13 calls. This means that the "wrong" controller may be trying to boot the computer and therefore prevents the "right" controller from doing its job.

It's common today for people to try to mix SCSI device types—that is, to add 50-pin SCSI-2 devices to the same chain as SCSI-3 devices with 68 pins. That means that the cable has to change sizes from 68 wires to 50 wires. If you mix these devices, be certain that you buy the proper cable to make the conversion. If you don't, or if you try to convert from 68 to 50 wires and then back to 68, you will have wires that are not being terminated correctly. It is better by far to have only "wide" devices with 68 pins on one chain and "narrow" devices with 50 pins on a separate chain.

One other major factor with SCSI disks involves the controller. If the SCSI controller to which your drives are attached is not on the Windows XP HCL, you could run into major problems during installation. It's difficult, if not impossible, to install any operating system on a drive it refuses to acknowledge. To work around this, Windows XP will prompt you to press the F6 key early in setup (look at the messages at the bottom of the screen) to install third-party SCSI drivers. If you are having problems getting setup to recognize your SCSI controller, pressing F6 and providing a driver is certainly worth a shot.

Troubleshooting Text Mode to GUI Mode

The transition from the character-based portion of Setup to the graphical portion is the number one point where problems occur. This is a delicate time when Windows XP Professional (albeit a limited version of Windows XP Professional) is being booted for the first time. During this phase, Windows XP Professional is loading the kernel for the first time and initializing hardware and drivers. Some of the Setup specialists at Microsoft say that this is the toughest test of your computer hardware configuration that Windows XP Professional will ever make.

During this transition, Windows XP Professional is switching your CPU to a flat memory model and initiating multithreading. Windows XP Professional is also loading the hardware abstraction layer (HAL) at this time. If your computer requires a customized HAL, you may have severe problems here. Normally, it's only the top-of-the-line computer brands that take advantage of custom HALs. If you don't know, consult the manual for your system or contact the manufacturer.

This is the most likely point for blue screens, also called *Stop errors* because of the text at the top of the screen. Even though this may be the most likely point in which you'll encounter Stop errors, these errors can happen in other places, too. Because of their importance, I've set aside an entire section for Stop errors later in this chapter.

There is one critical error to talk about here:

```
Setup has encountered a fatal error that prevents it from continuing. Contact your
software representative for help. Status code (0x4, 0, 0, 0)
```

This error message is displayed on a blue screen but is not actually considered a blue screen because it does not display the typical Stop message. This indicates a problem with the Master Boot Record (MBR). Either the MBR has become corrupted or it's infected with a boot-sector virus. This usually happens only on dual-boot systems that use FAT as their primary boot partition, but it can also happen if you boot the computer with an infected floppy disk. Even though NTFS can become infected with viruses, NTFS is resistant to viruses in that Windows XP Professional doesn't allow any program to access the hardware directly. In theory, this should prevent any boot-sector virus.

Another possible MBR-related error message is this one:

```
Missing operating system. Insert a system diskette and restart the system.
```

It is possible to repair the MBR if you have a bootable floppy that you know is clean of any virus infection. (That's the hard part in getting rid of a virus.) An emergency boot disk from Windows 9x is especially helpful for this because you need `fdisk.exe`. After booting the infected computer with the boot floppy (you did write-protect the floppy, didn't you?), run `mem.exe` at the command prompt. The total bytes of memory (before anything is subtracted) should equal 640K. Next, run `chkdsk.exe` and look at the line for Total Bytes Memory (it's near the bottom), which should read 655,360. If either amount of memory is off, and especially if only *one* of them is off, you probably have a boot-sector virus loaded in memory. If both of these programs correctly report the amount of conventional memory, you can be reasonably certain that the virus is not in memory. If that's the case, you can type **FDISK/MBR** at the command prompt to rebuild the MBR. This command won't do anything else, provided the virus is not in memory. If the virus is in memory, this command may be fatal to your data.

WARNING   *The* `FDISK/MBR` *command is dangerous and should never be used without being absolutely positive that the boot-sector virus is not loaded in memory.* The result could be total data loss. *Most boot-sector viruses work by moving the MBR elsewhere on the disk, then replacing it with their own code. Anything that tries to scan the MBR is first infected by the virus, then redirected out to the real MBR in its new location.*

NOTE   *It's interesting to note that the Master Boot Record is operating system–independent. It's quite possible to rebuild the MBR for a Windows XP Professional computer using an emergency boot disk from Windows 98.*

MISCELLANEOUS SETUP ISSUES

If your computer hangs during the final reboot of Windows XP Setup, try removing the CD-ROM from the drive. Windows XP Professional supports the "El Torito" standard of bootable CD-ROMs using the No Emulation mode. If the BIOS of your computer supports bootable CD-ROMs but not the No Emulation mode, your system may hang. It may also give this error message:

```
BOOT: Couldn't find NTLDR
Please insert another disk.
```

This is fixed the same way—just remove the CD-ROM from the drive and reboot the computer. Setup should continue normally after booting.

NOTE   *If there are no CD-ROM's or floppy disks in your drives, and you are still getting the* `BOOT: Couldn't find NTLDR` *error message, you will need to boot to either a Windows XP boot disk or CD-ROM to continue. For more information on this, see the "Boot Process Troubleshooting" section later in this chapter.*

NOTE   El Torito *is the official name for a bootable CD-ROM name and is derived from the place of its creation—a restaurant where the engineers were having a few drinks.*

Addressing GUI Mode and Initial Boot Issues

During this phase of Setup, Windows XP Professional installs drivers and configures the system. Problems in this portion of Setup are typically fewer and generally related to configuration rather than failing hardware or drivers. This is also where Windows XP Professional will try to load the network for the first time in a full configuration.

It is possible to encounter video problems at this phase of Setup. On some computers the display will not reset correctly during a warm boot under Windows XP Professional. If this occurs, your display will be black or very distorted. Try turning off the power to the computer (yes, this is one of those rare cases where you power down without shutting down first), then restarting it. If this resolves the issue, you will have to power down the computer every time you reboot. This is a hardware issue related to the video and system BIOS and not a Windows XP Professional problem. If you've tried this and the display is still distorted, you will need to boot Windows XP Professional with the VGA option and change your display properties (and possibly the driver) to one that does work with your hardware.

Troubleshooting Stop Errors

As I mentioned earlier, Windows XP is an incredibly complex operating system. And with anything this complex, problems are bound to occasionally occur. The good news is that Windows XP is very stable. Problems are generally kept to a minimum, and the operating system itself should rarely crash. The bad news is, because of its stability, when a problem *is* serious enough to make it crash, Windows XP crashes hard.

Some people call Stop errors the "Blue Screen of Death," or BSOD, though you should be aware that there may be hundreds of possible blue-screen errors in Windows XP Professional. None of us will likely ever see them all; at least we can hope that we never see them all.

When you first see a Stop error, you may be overwhelmed with the information in front of you. Most of the time, the ominous blue background is a placemat for a horde of binary and hexadecimal information that is indecipherable to mere mortals. This information is provided for developers and debuggers. The first thing you want to look for is near the top of the message: the word STOP followed by a message. Depending on the Stop error, you may also find the name of the offending driver or application on the screen as well.

Stop errors can occur at almost any stage of Windows XP installation or operation. The errors can be broken into three categories, based on when they occur:

During Windows XP installation   If a Stop error happens here, it may indicate a BIOS incompatibility issue, failing hardware, or a faulty device driver. Make sure that all of your hardware is on the HCL.

During Windows XP startup   If Windows XP has been installed and working for some time, but an error occurs during startup, it could mean a couple of things. Generally, the culprit is a device driver or system service. If you just installed a new service, application, or driver and you get a BSOD upon reboot, the new software could be your problem.

During Windows XP operation   This is the most ambiguous time an error can happen. The error could be practically anything. A Stop error during operation can be caused by failing hardware (particularly memory and processor), system services, device drivers, and applications. The text of the Stop message will give you valuable information as to the cause of the problem.

Common Stop Errors

The title of this section, "Common Stop Errors," does not mean to imply in any way that Stop errors are common. In fact, it's quite the opposite. However, if you are one of the unlucky souls to encounter a Stop error, these are some of the more common ones that appear. They are listed in hexadecimal order for convenience.

```
STOP: 0x0000000A
IRQL_NOT_LESS_OR_EQUAL
```

This Stop message can appear at almost any time. Most of the time, this error points to a problem device driver, service, or application. On the Stop screen, it will usually tell you the name of the offending driver, service, or application. Be sure to write down the name of the offender, as this can be invaluable for troubleshooting.

```
STOP: 0x0000001E
KMODE_EXCEPTION_NOT_HANDLED
```

This Stop message occurs when the processor receives an instruction that it doesn't understand. Many times this is caused by invalid memory access violations. This Stop error often lists the name of the offending device driver.

```
STOP: 0x00000023
FAT32_FILE_SYSTEM
```

A problem has occurred with the FAT32 file system driver. This could indicate a hard disk connectivity problem, or a hard disk failure.

```
STOP: 0x00000024
NTFS_FILE_SYSTEM
```

This is the same as the 0x23 error, except it's for the NTFS file system.

```
STOP: 0x0000002E
DATA_BUS_ERROR
```

This is most often caused by failing physical memory (including video memory), but could also indicate a physical problem with the motherboard.

```
STOP: 0x00000077
KERNEL_STACK_INPAGE_ERROR
```

If Windows XP tries to read information from the page file and does not locate the information it expects, you will receive this error message. Failing physical memory, failing hard disks, corrupted data, and viruses can cause this error message. A very similar error message is the STOP: 0x7A KERNEL _DATA_INPAGE_ERROR message.

```
STOP: 0x0000007B
INACCESSIBLE_BOOT_DEVICE
```

This error almost speaks common English. Your computer can't find the boot device. Check your physical connections. This could also indicate a failing hard disk or disk controller.

One of the most interesting causes of the STOP: 0x7B is adding an IDE drive to a SCSI-based system. IDE controllers are enumerated before the SCSI controllers, meaning that the BIOS of the computer looks for them first. If you add an IDE drive to a computer that is already working fine with SCSI hard disks, you may very well see this blue screen. That situation can be fixed in the computer's BIOS. If your BIOS supports the option, set the boot order to go to the SCSI drives first, then the IDE.

```
STOP: 0x0000007F
UNEXPECTED_KERNEL_MODE_TRAP
```

Hardware failure generally causes this error message. If you are running an over-clocked processor, you can expect to see this Stop error at some point.

```
STOP: 0x000000D1
DRIVER_IRQL_NOT_LESS_OR_EQUAL
```

This cryptic message is actually one of the more common Stop errors. It happens when a device driver tries to access memory address that it's not supposed to. Poorly written drivers are generally the culprit, although software applications (particularly anti-virus programs or backup programs) can cause this error as well.

```
STOP: 0x000000D8
DRIVER_USED_EXCESSIVE_PTES
```

Once again, this is caused by a faulty driver. We can gather that from the error message, even if we have no idea what a PTE is. PTEs are page table entries, which Windows XP uses to keep track of memory information. Poorly written or corrupt drivers can cause this error. Another related error is STOP: 0x3F NO_MORE_SYSTEM_PTES.

```
STOP: 0xC000021A
STATUS_SYSTEM_PROCESS_TERMINATED
```

This error message usually indicates that a Windows XP user-mode subsystem has been compromised in some way. This is a serious problem. You may also see this error message if a backup has only been partially restored, or if permissions have been modified so that the System account no longer has access to required system files and folders.

```
STOP 0xC0000221
STATUS_IMAGE_CHECKSUM_MISMATCH
```

This error message usually points to a corrupted file or hard disk. You will usually see the name of the offending file on this blue screen.

This list is by no means intended to be complete. It's here to give you a general idea of what types of problems may cause your Windows XP machine to blue screen. As you can see, most Stop errors are caused by failing hardware, device drivers, services, or applications. If you encounter an error message not listed, or just want more information on blue screens, you can go to Microsoft's support site at www.microsoft.com/support and search for your specific error message.

One more thing to mention about blue screens applies more to upgrading Windows XP Professional from an earlier version than to a fresh installation. During an upgrade, Setup will notify you with a blue screen error that you must remove an application before you can continue. As soon as the application is removed, Setup will proceed normally.

Responding to Stop Errors

You can configure Windows XP Professional to respond in a variety of ways once it encounters a Stop error. To do this, you need to go to System Properties (either open the System icon in the Control Panel, or right-click the My Computer icon in your Start menu and choose Properties). Then in the Advanced tab, choose Startup and Recovery ➤Settings. You should see a screen similar to Figure 25.1.

FIGURE 25.1

Customizing Stop Error response

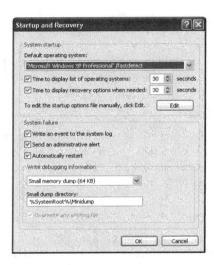

In Figure 25.1, take a look at the System failure section. In the event of a system failure, you can configure Windows XP to do any of the following three tasks: write an event to the System log, send an administrative alert, and automatically restart.

Writing an event to the System log will create an event for you to look at in Event Viewer, System log. While this event may not tell you everything you want to know, it will list the Stop error code so you have a point from which to start troubleshooting. Sending an administrative alert will do just that: send a popup alert to the administrator account. Automatically restarting is self-evident. If you do not choose this option, you will have to restart your computer manually after a Stop error occurs.

TIP   If you choose to have your system automatically restart, make sure to have Windows XP log an event in the system log as well. Otherwise, you may never know what went wrong, other than the fact that your computer just rebooted itself.

Within the System failure section, you also have the opportunity to customize the debugging information Windows XP writes when a Stop error happens. The debugging information is basically the contents of physical memory when the system crashed. Although the information may not be incredibly relevant for most of us, it can be useful to programmers or to the technicians at Microsoft's help desk.

Fixing Stop Errors

Fixing a Stop error is no different than troubleshooting any other problem with your computer. First and foremost, don't forget about your list of good troubleshooting procedures: define the problem, explore the boundaries, brainstorm, test your ideas, repair the problem, provide closure, clean up after yourself, and document the situation. Here are some general guidelines for fixing Stop errors:

◆ After you write down the message, reboot your computer. If the error doesn't come back, it's not a problem. This may sound cynical, but it's true. Sometimes the computer will "hiccup" and produce an error. Things happen. If the error keeps happening, then you have a problem.

◆ Suspect recent changes. If you just added hardware (including drivers) or software, it could be causing the problem. Try removing the hardware or application, or trying an alternate device driver.

◆ Check your system BIOS. Sometimes incorrect BIOS settings, especially with an ACPI-compliant BIOS, can cause blue screens. If possible, reset the settings to BIOS defaults.

◆ Search Microsoft's Knowledge Base. This site often has specific fixes for the problem you've just encountered. Remember, good troubleshooters don't necessarily know everything. They just know where to look to find answers.

Most of the time you can find a fix for your Stop error. The fix may be replacing hardware or installing different drivers or software. In more extreme cases, you may need to restore from a backup. In a worst-case scenario, you can always reinstall the operating system.

Boot Process Troubleshooting

The boot process is a common area where things can go wrong on your computer. There is a list of specific files that must be in a certain location on your hard disk and loaded in a certain order. If any of these files are missing or corrupt, your Windows XP machine will not boot.

Your system partition (generally your C drive) contains three required files, and two optional files for booting Windows XP. The required files are `ntldr`, `boot.ini`, and `ntdetect.com`. The optional files are `ntbootdd.sys` and `bootsect.dos`.

Here's a quick overview of the boot process. After the BIOS has completed its check, it looks for the `ntldr` file on your system partition. `Ntldr` loads the `boot.ini` file, which has two responsibilities: to point to the location on your hard disk(s) where your operating system files are located, and to provide you with a boot menu if you have multiple operating systems installed (or, in other words, you are dual-booting). If you boot into Windows XP, the `ntdetect.com` file performs a hardware detection and hands over to a file called `ntoskrnl.exe`, which is the executable to officially load Windows XP.

Let's say you are dual-booting Windows XP Professional and Windows 98. If you choose to load Windows 98 from your boot menu, the `bootsect.dos` file takes over instead of the `ntdetect.com` file. If the ARC paths in your `boot.ini` file use the SCSI option, you will need the `ntbootdd.sys` file. (Look in your `boot.ini`, and if you see the word SCSI followed by a bracketed number, you need the `ntbootdd.sys` file.)

If you receive an error message about any of these boot files, or a missing or corrupt `ntoskrnl.exe` file, there are two good ways to proceed. One is to boot to the Windows XP CD, which will start the setup program. When prompted, press R to begin the Recovery Console. Details on how to use the Recovery Console are located in Chapter 24.

The second method is to create a Windows XP boot disk. To do this, format a floppy disk in Windows XP, and then copy the `ntldr`, `boot.ini`, and `ntdetect.com` files to it (and the `bootsect.dos` and `ntbootdd.sys` files if you need them). This diskette is quite useful if you don't have your Windows XP Professional CD nearby. It doesn't start a fancy troubleshooting process like the Recovery Console, but it may get your computer up and running if one of your boot files is missing or corrupt.

The key to boot-process troubleshooting is to figure out how far the boot process gets, and then determine what you need to do to get your computer booted the rest of the way. In other words, if the `ntldr` file is working but it's the `boot.ini` causing the problem, how do you fix it? Just like troubleshooting anything else, narrow down the possibilities until you isolate the problem. Once the problem is isolated, it's a great deal easier to fix.

Summary

No matter what your interest is in Windows XP Professional, there will be times when understanding the process of troubleshooting will be helpful to you. Even if troubleshooting is never going to be part of your responsibility, things may go wrong. If you have even a basic understanding of the process, you will convey much more meaningful information to the person who *is* responsible for the troubleshooting.

Use the methods listed in this chapter when troubleshooting your own computer. Follow the guidelines for documenting the steps taken and the possible approaches to use. Always remember to think simple at first, and then move on to the more exotic as you eliminate basic possibilities.

Part 5

Advanced Topics

In this section you will learn how to:
- ◆ **Work with the Microsoft Management Console**
- ◆ **Manage Windows XP Services**
- ◆ **Configure IIS as a Web and FTP Server**

Chapter 26

The Microsoft Management Console

THIS CHAPTER ADDRESSES THE Microsoft Management Console, the Swiss Army knife of administrative tools for Microsoft Windows XP Professional.

Starting with Windows 2000, individual administrative tools—such as the User Manager, Server Manager, Event Viewer, and even Disk Administrator—were assimilated into the Microsoft Management Console (MMC). This all-in-one administrative tool can be set up to include everything that you need to administer Windows XP Professional, including Internet Information Server, which is covered in Chapter 28.

MMC is a framework for management applications, providing a unified interface for Microsoft and third-party management tools. MMC doesn't replace management applications; it integrates them into one single interface. (You can still access many tools through their original interfaces.) There are no inherent management functions in MMC at all. It uses component tools called snap-ins, which do all the work. MMC provides a user interface; it doesn't change how the snap-ins function.

To become a true power user, you must fully understand the MMC. This chapter covers the following topics:

- ◆ MMC Structure
- ◆ MMC Terminology
- ◆ Exploring MMC Snap-Ins
- ◆ Using the MMC
- ◆ The Computer Management Console

The Basic Features of MMC

The following benefits are associated with MMC:

- ◆ You only have to learn one interface to drive a whole mess of tools.
- ◆ Microsoft is encouraging software vendors to use MMC snap-ins.

◆ You can build your own consoles, which is practical and fun. Administrators can even create shortcuts on the console to non-MMC tools such as executables, URLs, Wizards, and scripts.

◆ By customizing MMC consoles, an administrator can delegate tasks to underlings without giving them access to all functions and without confusing them with a big, complicated tool.

◆ Help in MMC is context sensitive; it displays subjects for only the appropriate components. Okay, that's not really new, but it's still cool. Context sensitive menus are available through the Action and View menus, or by right-clicking the snap-in.

WHY ONLY ONE TOOL?

In the first years of Windows NT 4, administrators had to master multiple administration tools. A whole set of built-in tools, plus independent third-party tools, made administration sort of a mess. Although many administration tools functioned remotely, you had to install some of them separately (unless your desktop happened to include Windows NT server), and with third-party tools, you often had to jump through hoops to get them to work remotely, if at all. Even worse, with menus, buttons, toolbars, Wizards, tabs, HTML, Java (you get the picture), just learning how to navigate new software was a chore. Also, there was no simplified version of the User Manager that could be given to account operators and no way to hide menu items in administrative tools for those without full administrator rights.

So we complained. "As administrators, we need to be able to administer our networks from the comfort and luxury of our cubicles. And we don't want to waste time exploring all the windows, Wizards, and tabs in every new tool. And we need more flexible tools," we said. Behold, Microsoft heard our cries, and their response was the MMC. It's even available for Windows NT 4 if you've installed some of the later service packs.

The MMC turned out to be so popular that Microsoft expanded the number of available tools. Third-party vendors also create tools that can be installed in the MMC as snap-ins.

MMC Terms to Know

This section defines important terms you'll need to know when working with MMC.

A *console*, in MMC-speak, is one or more administrative tools in an MMC framework. The prebuilt admin tools, such as Active Directory Users and Computers, are console files. You can also make your own consoles without any programming tools—you needn't be a C++ or Visual Basic programmer, as I'll discuss a bit later. The saved console file is a *Microsoft saved console (MSC)* file and it carries the MSC extension.

NOTE   *It's important to distinguish between Microsoft Management Console and console tools. MMC provides a framework to create customized console-based tools.* MMC.EXE *is a program that presents administrators (and others creating console tools) with a blank console to work with. It might help to think of a new instance of* MMC.EXE *as providing the raw material for a tool. In that case, Microsoft Management Console provides the rules and guidelines for building the tool, and the new console you create is the finished product.*

Snap-ins are what we call administrative tools that can be added to the console. For example, the DHCP administration tool is a snap-in, and so is the Disk Defragmenter. Snap-ins can be made by Microsoft or by other software vendors. (You *do* need programming skills to make these, in other words.) A snap-in can contain components that allow us to manage various facets of our computer, like hard drives, users, and security. Although you can load multiple snap-ins in a single console, most of the prebuilt administrative tools contain only a single snap-in (except the Computer Management tool).

TIP   *By default, all MMC consoles, including the ones you create, are accessible through the Start menu. Click Start ➤ All Programs ➤ Administrative Tools and select the console of your choice.*

An *extension* is basically a snap-in that can't live by itself on the console but depends on a stand-alone snap-in. It adds some functionality to a snap-in. Some snap-ins work both ways. For example, the Event Viewer is a stand-alone snap-in, but it's also implemented as an extension to the Computer Management snap-in. The key point is that extensions are optional. You can choose not to load them. For example, Local Users and Groups is an extension to the Computer Management snap-in. If you remove the extension from the COMPMGMT.MSC file used by your support folk, or simply don't include it in a custom console that uses the snap-in, those who use the tool won't have the option to create or manage users and groups with the tool. They won't even see it. (Please note that this will not prevent them from creating users and groups by other means, if they have the correct administrative privileges.)

Administrators can create new MSC files by customizing an existing MSC file or by creating one from a blank console. The MMC.EXE plus the defined snap-ins create the tool interface. Also, it's possible to open multiple tools simultaneously, but each console runs one instance of MMC. Open an MSC file and look in Task Manager while it's running—you only see the MMC.EXE process running, not the MSC file, just as you see WINWORD.EXE running in Task Manager, but not the Word document's name.

The MMC Console

Microsoft Management Consoles (MMCs) can be configured and run in one four different modes:

Author mode: Allows you to create your own consoles with the snap-ins of your choice.

User mode—full access: Allows you almost total control of installed snap-ins, except you can't install or remove a snap-in.

User mode—limited access, multiple window: Allows you to use MMC with multiple embedded windows. However, you can't open a new window or close any of the preconfigured windows.

User mode—limited access, single window: Allows you to use MMC with one single embedded window.

Author mode is where you create and customize a console. But you shouldn't manage your system from any MMC author mode. Instead, you can save the console in one of the user modes. Different User modes are suitable for different types of users. The following sections describe the snap-ins and each mode in more detail.

What Are Snap-Ins?

Snap-ins include the essence of different Windows XP administrative utilities. You can add the snap-ins of your choice to the MMC. Some are already included with Windows XP Professional. More can be added through other applications such as Internet Information Server.

Many of the following snap-ins are the same as those used on Windows 2000. Some of these snap-ins can be used on local or remote computers. Successful remote access depends on configured rights and permissions on that computer. Available snap-ins include the following:

ActiveX Control: Allows control of the list of ActiveX objects that help Windows XP applications share information and more.

Certificates: Permits browsing of your computer's collection of digital signatures associated with applications, drivers, Web sites, and more.

Component Services: Allows configuration of COM components based on Microsoft's Component Object Model and related COM+ applications.

Computer Management: Installs the standard Computer Management Console, which is described later in this chapter. It can also be installed as a snap-in in a customized console.

Device Manager: Configures the manager of hardware devices as an MMC snap-in. This tool is covered in Chapter 8.

Disk Defragmenter: Installs the Disk Defragmenter discussed in Chapter 24 as an MMC snap-in.

Disk Management: Sets up Disk Management, which can help you manage the file systems and partitions on your drives. This tool is discussed in Chapter 21.

Event Viewer: Installs the Event Viewer, which is one of the key troubleshooting tools for Windows XP Professional. This tool is described in Chapter 21.

Folder: Installs the folder snap-in, which can help you organize your other snap-ins into different categories. Once installed, you can rename the Folder snap-in. When you add new snap-ins, you can select this folder before adding the new snap-in.

FrontPage Server Extensions: Sets up the snap-in that can help you administer FrontPage Server Extensions for Web servers.

Group Policy: Installs the Group Policy manager, which can help you administer XP policies for computer and user accounts on local or remote computers.

Indexing Service: Includes the Microsoft Indexing Service, which collects information from documents on local or remote computers in a separate database for quicker searches.

Internet Information Services (IIS): Add the management tool for IIS, which is the Microsoft server for Web, FTP, and mail services. IIS is addressed in more detail in Chapter 28.

IP Security Monitor: Allows you to monitor traffic on local or remote computers based on various IP Security Policies. Associated with the IPSec protocols that require encryption keys and can support Virtual Private Networking (VPN).

IP Security Policies: This allows you to set up specific policies for monitoring traffic on your network from a local or a remote computer.

Link to Web Address: Prompts you to enter a Web site or Web file. This allows you to use MMC as a browser based on the given location. You can also use this as a link to a specific e-mail address. For example, if there is a remote administrator who needs information from your console, you can set up his or her e-mail address in the following format: `mailto:administrator@abc.cba`.

Local Users and Groups: Lets you view and manage the users and groups on a local computer. With the right permissions, you can also set up users and groups on remote computers.

Performance Logs and Alerts: Allows you to configure counters, traces, and alerts. This snap-in can be used to manage the Performance console discussed in Chapter 21.

Removable Storage Management: Allows you to manage the information from removable media such as CDs, tape drives, and more. Can be configured for a local or a remote computer.

Resultant Set of Policy: Allows you to check or test the effect of multiple policies on specific users or computers. On a domain, you can use this to check the effect on remote computers.

Security Configuration and Analysis: Includes configuration and analysis tools to let you configure and analyze the effect of your security policies. This snap-in is covered in more detail in Chapter 18.

Security Templates: Includes the Windows XP Professional security templates that you can use in your security configuration and analysis. You can also set up the import (and export) of custom templates for your workgroup or domain. This snap-in is covered in more detail in Chapter 18.

Services: Permits you to monitor and manage services on local or remote computers. This snap-in is covered in more detail in Chapter 27.

Shared Folders: Allows you to monitor and manage shared files and folders on local or remote computers. As an administrator, you can disconnect users who are connecting to a share over a network. For more information on setting up a shared folder, see Chapter 16.

WMI Control: Installs the control tools for the Windows Management Instrumentation service, which includes VBScript objects that can further help you manage the Windows XP Professional Environment. For the latest information on WMI objects, use an Internet search engine such as `www.google.com` and use the following search phrase: "Managing Windows with WMI."

Working In Author Mode and Adding Snap-Ins

When you open the MMC without snap-ins, Windows XP Professional takes you to MMC Author mode to allow you to customize the administrative tool that you need. To start MMC, type **MMC.EXE** at a command prompt. Figure 26.1 shows MMC in Author mode.

FIGURE 26.1

MMC in
Author mode

FIGURE 26.1

MMC in
Author mode

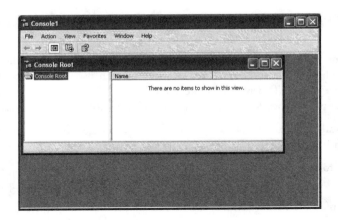

Start configuring your administrative tool. Add some of the available tools by following these steps:

1. Click File ➤ Add/Remove Snap-in to open the Add/Remove Snap-in window.

2. Click Add to open the Add Standalone Snap-in window (shown in Figure 26.2).

FIGURE 26.2

Available snap-ins

3. Select a snap-in of your choice. Click Add. Repeat with as many available snap-ins as desired. Click Close when you're finished.

4. The snap-ins that you selected are shown in the Standalone tab of the Add/Remove Snap-in window as shown in Figure 26.3. If you want to delete a snap-in, highlight it and click Remove. When you're ready, click OK to add these snap-ins to your console.

   Some snap-ins, such as Shared Folders and Computer Management, include extensions that are usually other snap-ins that are normally grouped together. Click the Extensions tab to see if the option is available for the snap-ins that you selected.

FIGURE 26.3

Selected snap-ins

5. Some of the available snap-ins allow you to easily access key utilities such as the Device Manager. Although the format is slightly different, the information shown in Figure 26.4 is identical to that shown in Chapter 8.

FIGURE 26.4

Snap-ins can help you access other tools.

6. Save the result under another name. Click File ➤ Save As. In the Save As window, enter a descriptive name such as Cert-Device and click Save. The console is saved with the .MSC extension by default.

Note that the titlebar now reflects the filename that you used. You can now close this window, for it is also saved in your Start menu. Click Start ➤ All Programs ➤ Administrative Tools ➤ Cert-Device.MSC (or the name that you used to save your console). Windows XP Professional opens the console that you've set up.

Once you're happy with your new administrative tool, you'll want to save it in one of the User modes to prevent further changes. Click File ➤ Options. The Console tab of the Options page opens, as shown in Figure 26.5.

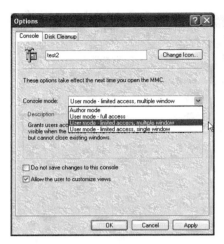

You can select from the four previously mentioned modes in the Console Modes drop-down box. The different user modes are discussed in following sections. For each mode, you can choose whether to allow the user to customize the tool with the other check boxes in the Options page:

◆ Do Not Save Changes to This Console: If checked, this option prevents users from making any permanent changes to this console.

◆ Allow the User to Customize Views: If checked, this option allows users to access the Customize View window.

Once you've created the options of your choice, click OK to exit the Options window. Click File ➤ Save As and enter the name of your choice.

Customizing MMC Views

If you set up a console that allows users to customize views, they can modify the look and feel of that console. To access the Customize View window shown in Figure 26.6, click View ➤ Customize. Each of the options are described below:

Console tree: Displays a list of snap-ins that are included in the console.

Standard menus: Includes the Action and View menus in the console toolbar. The Action menu allows you to see a context-sensitive list of options associated with the highlighted snap-in. Alternatively, you can just right-click the snap-in. The View menu allows you to customize the look and feel of the details associated with each tool.

Standard toolbar: Activates typical toolbar icons for navigation, help, and other context-sensitive options.

Status bar: Shows a message associated with the highlighted tool at the bottom of the console window.

Description bar: Provides information about the selected snap-in option in the details pane of the console.

Taskpad navigation tabs: Allows the user to use context-specific commands associated with snap-ins. See the Taskpad section for more information.

Snap-in Menus: Displays menus associated with a particular snap-in. Some snap-ins don't have individual menus.

Snap-in Toolbars: Includes toolbars associated with a particular snap-in. Some snap-ins don't have individual toolbars.

FIGURE 26.6

You can customize the look and feel of a MMC console.

User Mode-Full Access

By default, pre-built console tools such as Computer Management open in *User Mode-Full Access*. This is the best setup for junior system administrators or power users. Changes cannot be made to the console design. You can't add or remove snap-ins, for example. When a user is running a tool and not configuring it, it should be running in one of the User modes. The tool actually looks different in User mode than it does in Author mode.

The most prominent example of a pre-built console tool is the Computer Management console. To start it, click Start ➤ All Programs ➤ Administrative Tools ➤ Computer Management. Figure 26.7 shows the Computer Management console in User mode-Full Access.

In User mode, File menu options are limited. You can't add or remove snap-ins or change the mode of the console. But full access allows you to add windows and/or change the format of the console, such as the columns of data associated with a specific snap-in.

If you need to change a user mode tool, open `MMC.EXE` at the command line. Use the File menu to open the tool you want to change in Author mode. Console files are normally stored in either the `\Documents and Settings\username\Start Menu\Programs\Administrative Tools\` or the `\Windows\system32\` directories.

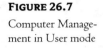

FIGURE 26.7

Computer Management in User mode

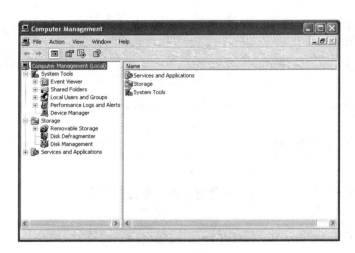

User Mode-Limited Access, Multiple Window

In author mode, you can restrict access further to different parts of the console. And you can set up limited access with multiple windows by default. This mode is known as *User Mode-Limited Access, Multiple Window*. As you can see in Figure 26.8, multiple windows are open by default, and the close button (the X in the upper right corner) in both windows is disabled. However, you can open additional windows. When you exit and return to this console, the changes are automatically saved.

FIGURE 26.8

Sample console in User Mode-Limited Access, Multiple Window.

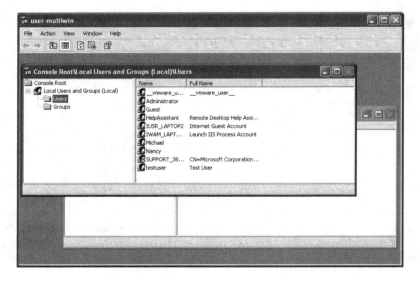

Limited Access, Multiple Window mode is best for users with specific dedicated tasks such as monitoring various print servers.

User Mode-Limited Access, Single Window

You can restrict console access to a single window. You can't open new windows in this type of console. The controls associated with multiple windows are disabled. Not surprisingly, this mode is known as *User Mode–Limited Access, Single Window*. An example of this mode is shown in Figure 26.9.

FIGURE 26.9

Sample console in User Mode-Limited Access, Multiple Window.

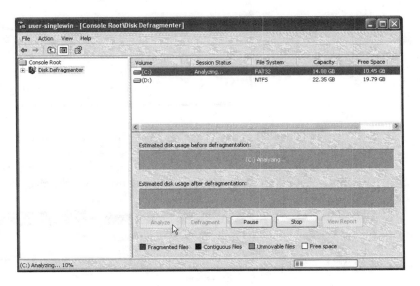

Limited Access Single Window mode is best for less experienced users. The limited flexibility associated with this type of console reduces the risk to your system.

The Computer Management Console

The most important pre-built MMC tool is the Computer Management console. The console tree includes: System Tools, Storage, and Services and Applications (see Figure 26.10). Notice that the focus is on the local machine by default; to connect to other computers on the network, right-click the Computer Management icon at the root of the tree (or click on the Action menu) and choose Connect to Another Computer from the shortcut menu.

The Computer Management console is *the* main tool for administering a single server, local or remote. If you only have one server on your network and you only want to use one admin tool, Computer Management fits the bill. To open the Computer Management console, click Start ➤ All Programs ➤ Administrative Tools ➤ Computer Management.

FIGURE 26.10

The Computer Management window

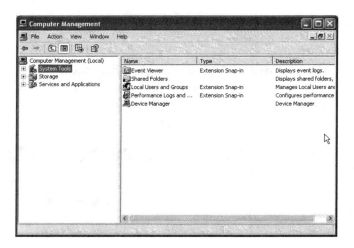

Expand the nodes in the Computer Management console tree to reveal the configuration tools and objects, as shown in Figure 26.11. Most of the core functions are under System Tools. Some functions even work remotely on NT 4 machines (you can view a remote machine's Event Logs, for example), but new features require the remote machine to be a Windows XP Professional box.

FIGURE 26.11

The expanded Computer Management window

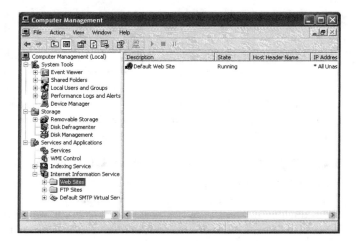

In the System Tools node, you can complete the following tasks:

◆ View events and manage the event logs. Basically the Event Viewer tool is turned into an MMC snap-in.

◆ Manage shared folders. View, create, and manage shares; view sessions and open files; and disconnect sessions.

- Manage devices. Device Manager is a great place to track down information about your hardware, update drivers, and troubleshoot resource conflicts.

- Configure Performance Logs and Alerts. You can create, configure, and monitor various performance settings.

- Create and manage local users and groups.

The Storage node includes options for managing removable storage, along with the Disk Defragmenter tool and the Disk Management tool, which is the equivalent of the Disk Administrator in NT 4. There is also a component to view logical drives, including network drive mappings, and their properties. This is useful if you want to quickly view free space or set NTFS security at the root of a partition, for example. Too bad you can't browse folders as you can in Explorer. Oh well, I guess we don't need *another* desktop shell program, do we?

The Services and Applications node includes telephony settings, services configuration, Windows Management Instrumentation (WMI), indexing, and IIS management stuff, the last of which is also available in the Administrative Tools group by itself (the tool is called Internet Services Manager, while the extension in Computer Management is called Internet Information Services). The components available in the Services and Applications node depend on what services are installed on your system. For instance, if Internet Information Services is not installed (and it isn't by default), you won't see that component.

It's easy to connect the Computer Management Console to a remote computer. Highlight Computer Management (Local), then click Action ➤ Connect to another computer. In the Select Computer window, enter the name of the other computer. The format depends on whether you've set up Windows XP Professional in a workgroup or a domain.

- Workgroup: Use the name of the workgroup and the computer in the format `workgroup-name\computername`.

- Domain: Use the fully qualified domain name for the computer, such as `\\xpcomp.windows.mommabears.com`.

What you can do on a remote computer depends on the applicable permissions and access rights associated with each tool. These concepts are explained in Chapter 18.

Additional Customization Options

Author mode in MMC is quite flexible. You can even use it to modify pre-built tools such as the Computer Management Console. To open up this tool in author mode, start the MMC. Type **MMC.EXE** at a command prompt. Click File ➤ Open and select `compmgmt.msc` from the `\Windows\system32` directory.

Whenever you change a standard tool, it's a good practice to make a backup before you begin. To backup the Computer Management Console, click File ➤ Save As and save it as another file such as `compmgmt-rev.msc`. Now you can experiment and still have the original Computer Management Console in reserve. The following sections address other available author mode options, menu by menu from the toolbar. The exceptions are the Window and Help menus, which you already know because they work in the same way as the Window and Help menus in other Microsoft applications.

File

The File menu should look familiar. You've already added snap-ins to other consoles and used the Options window to save customized consoles in one of the four different modes.

In any User mode, most File menu options are disabled. The File ➤ Options command opens the Options window. The Delete Files button in this window deletes the changes that you've made to other User mode consoles. For example, if you've opened new windows, they're normally saved. If you click Delete Files, the original console configuration is restored.

Action

Action menus in MMC are partially context sensitive. For example, in the console tree, navigate to Local Users and Groups ➤ Users and then select the Action menu. As you can see in Figure 26.12, you can set up new users from this menu. The options that you'll see in every Action menu (except a User Mode-Limited Access, Single Window console) are:

New Window from Here: Opens a new window within the available console.

Rename: Allows you to rename the top-level folder in the console tree.

Export List: Creates a text file with a list of plug-ins. You can share this information with other users for more standard consoles.

Help: Opens help topics on MMC and any plug-ins that you've installed.

Only context sensitive options are available in a User Mode-Limited Access, Single Window console.

FIGURE 26.12

The Computer Management Action window

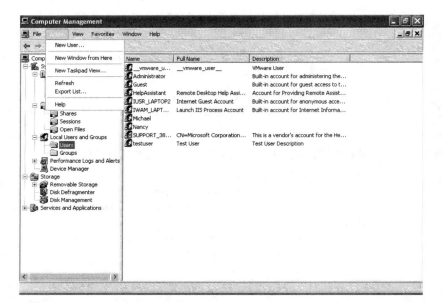

Taskpad

A *taskpad* is a graphical HTML window customized for a specific MMC plug-in. Taskpad options are available only in Author mode. To open a new console in Author Mode, type **MMC.EXE** at a command prompt. Use the File menu to open the console of your choice. Highlight the desired plug-in then click Action ➤ New Taskpad View. This starts the New Taskpad View Wizard. Click Next to start the Wizard and navigate to the Taskpad Display page shown in Figure 26.13.

FIGURE 26.13

The New Taskpad
View Wizard

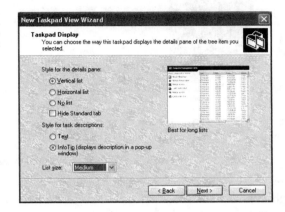

In the Taskpad Display page, you can set up the way the tasks are shown in the console. The options are divided into three categories:

Style for the details pane: Organizes the tasks and configured options for this snap-in. If you deselect Hide Standard tab, you can easily switch from the Taskpad display to the standard pane by clicking the appropriate tab near the bottom of the console window.

Style for task descriptions: Determines whether the descriptions are shown on the screen or in a pop-up window.

List size: Sets up the columns associated with each task. The Small, Medium, and Large options are associated with the number of columns shown in the Taskpad display.

Make your choices and click Next to continue. In the Taskpad Target page, you can set up whether this will apply to just the selected snap-in. Make your selection and click Next to continue.

In the Name and Description page, enter a name and description for the taskpad and then click Next to continue. This completes the New Taskpad View Wizard as shown in Figure 26.14. To continue, select the Start New Task Wizard and then click Finish.

FIGURE 26.14

Transition between
Wizards

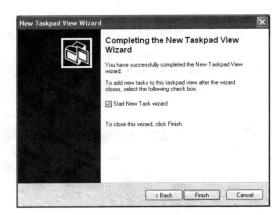

You're taken to the Welcome to the New Task Wizard page. Click Next to continue. As shown in Figure 26.15, there are three types of commands available:

Menu command: Allows you to select a task from the Action menu associated with the snap-in.

Shell command: Helps you configure a text command at the command-line interface based on what you might use at the MS-DOS style prompt. This is appropriate if you've set up a script such as for automated monitoring of disk activity.

Navigation: Allows you to select from a list of favorite snap-ins. The associated list of Favorites is different from any that you may have saved in your Web browser.

FIGURE 26.15

Select the right
Command type.

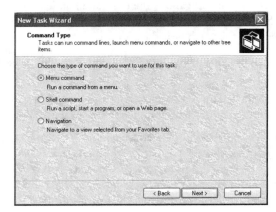

Click Next to continue. Depending on your selection, you'll need to choose a menu command, type in a shell command, or select a favorite.

Click Next to continue. Enter a Task name and description. If the tool is not familiar to your users, the description can be quite important.

Click Next to continue. Select an icon appropriate to your task.

Click Next to continue. You're shown a list of tasks that you've selected. If you need additional tasks, select the Run this Wizard again. Click Finish.

FIGURE 26.16

Selected Tasks are shown before you complete the New Task Wizard.

Now the tasks that you've selected are shown in the right-hand pane. As you can see in Figure 26.17, they do not have to be related to the task at hand. Now you can start the selected tasks by clicking them just like any link in a Web browser. Alternatively, you can return to the original view by clicking the Standard tab near the bottom of the console.

NOTE *If you don't see tabs at the bottom of the console, you selected Hide Standard Tab near the beginning of the New Taskpad Wizard as shown in Figure 26.13.*

FIGURE 26.17

A console with some tasks

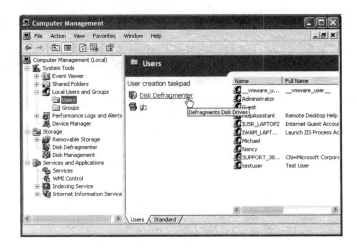

If you want to change the taskpad, click the Action Menu. You can now select Edit Taskpad View or Delete Taskpad View to edit or delete the task of your choice.

View

The View menu allows you to customize the look and feel of the options associated with each snap-in. The basic options (Large Icons, Small Icons, List, and Detail) work in the same way as from the Windows Explorer View menu. There are two other options unique to MMC:

◆ Add/Remove Columns: Allows you to customize the displayed columns for each snap-in.

◆ Customize View: See the Customizing MMC Views sidebar earlier in this chapter.

In many cases, you can also open a View menu by right-clicking the snap-in of your choice.

Favorites

You can set up Favorite tools in MMC the same way that you set up Favorite Web sites in Internet Explorer. (They are separate lists.) Select the snap-in of your choice then click Favorites ➤ Add to Favorites and follow the prompts in the windows which appear. You can then quickly navigate to Favorite snap-ins, or add a Favorite through the taskpad.

Summary

In this chapter, I've given you the basics of the Microsoft Management Console (MMC). It's a complex tool, so it's useful to recount the basic steps associated with creating or modifying a console:

◆ Open an existing console. Click Start ➤ All Programs ➤ Administrative Tools and select the console of your choice.

◆ Open a new console in Author Mode. Type **MMC.EXE** at a command prompt.

◆ Add a snap-in in Author Mode. Click File ➤ Add/Remove Snap-in.

◆ Add Taskpad views with links to other tools. Click Action ➤ New Taskpad View and follow the prompts.

◆ Set up a console in one of the four modes. Click File ➤ Options and select a Console mode with the settings of your choice.

◆ Save the console with the File ➤ Save As command. Saved consoles are accessible through the Start menu.

Chapter 27

Manage Windows XP Professional Services

A SERVICE IS A program that runs in the background to support basic activities; everything from automated updates through Web site connectivity. Everything important in Windows XP Professional depends on one or more services. As with many other critical systems, you can manage your services through the Microsoft Management Console that was covered in Chapter 26. Properly managed, many services allow Windows XP Professional to continue operating without reboots. Properly configured, you can make sure Windows XP turns on only the services that you need. This chapter covers the following topics:

◆ Why Services Exist

◆ Service Management Consoles

◆ Types of Services

◆ Managing and Configuring Windows XP Professional Services

◆ Troubleshooting Service Issues

The Purpose of a Service

Services run in the background. Most are started automatically when you start Windows XP Professional. Among other things, services provide the interfaces that allow you to connect to the Internet, manage interfaces to an Uninterruptible Power Supply (UPS), and more.

Windows XP Professional services are similar to *daemons* in the world of Unix and Linux. In either case, these are programs that run in the background and provide the interfaces required to run programs such as Internet connections and print servers.

You probably don't need to run every service. Each service takes up space in RAM and places demands on your CPU. Even if you have the fastest computer and Gigabytes of RAM, you generally do not want all services to run simultaneously. Some services have been known to conflict with each other.

In fact, if you have a relatively small amount of RAM (64MB–128MB), you'll want to disable as many services as possible. The following sections highlight several services that you may be able to disable, if you're not using the associated applications.

Specialized programs come with their own services that may cause problems. For example, some database programs explicitly state that you should turn off all but a few services on Windows XP Professional before starting the installation process.

The Service Management Console

Take a look at the installed services in Windows XP Professional. To open the Service Management Console shown in Figure 27.1, click Start ➢ All Programs ➢ Administrative Tools ➢ Services. By default, it opens this console in limited access, single window user mode, which means you can use it just for your services. It also opens with a taskpad that can allow you to start, stop, pause, or restart different services with a single click.

FIGURE 27.1

The Service Management console

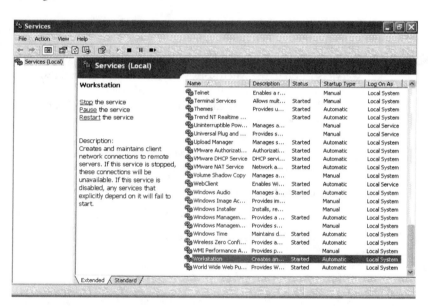

Note the two tabs at the bottom of Figure 27.1. The Extended tab is configured to allow you to manage the highlighted service. In contrast, the Standard tab includes no such feature.

NOTE   *This chapter assumes that you've read Chapter 26 and are comfortable with the basic operation of the Microsoft Management Console.*

TIP   *The Services snap-in is also available as part of the Computer Management console. Alternatively, click Start ➢ Run and type* **services.msc** *to start the Service Management Console.*

Click the Extended tab if required, and then click a service. Note the options for what you can do with this service. Repeat this with other services. Figure 27.1 shows the Workstation service selected, which allows you to connect to other computers on a LAN. The links allow you to quickly Stop, Pause, or Restart that service.

Windows XP Professional Services

There are a large number of services that are installed on Windows XP Professional. The following lists are based on a standard computer with IIS installed. I've divided these services into four categories:

◆ Services that are started automatically

◆ Services that you start manually

◆ Services that are disabled

◆ Services that you can add after installing Windows XP

Since required services vary with the hardware and software configuration of your computer, this may not be a complete list. Based on previous work on your computer, the service may be in a different category. Other services that you might see such as VMWare Authorization Service are associated with a particular program, in this case, with VMWare. New services are under constant development. If you don't see your service here, consult the developer of the associated application, or check the Microsoft Knowledge Base, available as of this writing at http://support.Microsoft.com.

In the following section on Configuring Services, you'll learn how to change the status of a service. Automatic services are started when you boot Windows XP. Specific programs often start manual services. Disabled services aren't available to support any programs that might need them. And other programs such as IIS and VMWare add additional services that fall into one of the other three categories.

Automatic Services

The following is a list of services that are started automatically when you boot Windows XP Professional. The list you see will vary by configuration.

While this is a long list, it can help you learn a lot about Windows XP Professional. If you're not using the applications associated with one of these services, you may be able to disable it and save resources for the programs that you need.

Automatic Updates: Permits automatic Windows XP updates as discussed in Chapter 2. You can safely disable this service and still run Windows Update manually. Keep it if you're configuring Windows XP Professional for users who would not run Windows Update on their own.

Computer Browser: Allows Windows XP to keep a list of computers on the LAN. If there are Windows servers on your network, they generally take on this task. A Windows XP Professional computer can take on a backup role for this service.

Cryptographic Services: Manages the certificates that you need to verify the authenticity of critical files and programs.

DHCP Client: Lets your computer get an IP address from a DHCP server. See Chapter 17 for more information on DHCP, which is the Dynamic Host Configuration Protocol. Don't disable this service unless you have a fixed IP address.

Distributed Link Tracking Client: Allows your computer to maintain the links between files on your computer or network. One example of a link is an Excel spreadsheet embedded in a Word document. If you don't have a NTFS partition, you can disable this service.

DNS Client: Permits contact between your computer and Domain Name Service (DNS) servers. This is almost always a requirement for computers on larger networks, or with a connection to the Internet. For more information, see Chapter 16.

Error Reporting Service: Allows error logs from non-standard applications. This service may not be necessary unless you need logs to help troubleshoot a specific application.

Event Log: Sends notification of major events and errors to the Event Viewer. This is a critical troubleshooting tool discussed in Chapter 26. Also required to support IIS, which is covered in Chapter 28.

Fax: Allows you to send and receive faxes. If you have trouble sending a fax, this service might be disabled and need restarting.

Help and Support: Lets you run the Help and Support center discussed in Chapter 3.

IPSEC Services: Manages security on TCP/IP networks. Required to support Virtual Private Networks.

Logical Disk Manager: Manages the status of disk drives automatically. This allows Windows XP Professional to see removable drives when they're installed.

Messenger: Allows administrative alerts. Not related to Windows Messenger. This is useful if you need to warn remote users about problems such as an impending reboot. Change the setting to match the Alerter service, which is addressed in the next section.

Net Logon: Supports sending usernames and passwords to a domain controller on a network. If you're not on a Domain as described in Chapter 17, you can disable this service.

Plug and Play: Supports most modern hardware on a plug and play operating system such as Windows XP.

Portable Media Serial Number: Retrieves the serial number of portable music players that are connected to your computer. If you're not using a portable digital music device such as a Rio player, deactivate this service.

Print Spooler: Loads files that are translated to your printer in memory. If you print, you need this service.

Protected Storage: Allows password protection for the files you specify.

Remote Procedure Call (RPC): Supports communication between applications on a Client/Server network. Many other services depend on RPC. If you plan to be on a network, you should always enable this service.

Remote Registry: Allows users with appropriate rights to modify the local registry from a remote computer. Disable this service unless you absolutely need to manage the registry from a remote computer.

Removable Storage: Permits different applications to share access to removable storage devices such as Tape drives. You can set this to Manual, activating it only as needed.

Secondary Logon: Allows users to logon more than once to the same system. This important security feature is described in more detail in Chapter 17.

Security Accounts Manager: Stores security information for local accounts. See Chapter 18 for more information.

Server: Permits access to the local computer as a server, typically for sharing files and printers.

Shell Hardware Detection: Allows the Autoplay feature to automatically run a CD that you've just inserted into a drive. Autoplay is described in Chapter 1.

SNMP Service: The Simple Network Management Protocol (SNMP) allows you to use services such as the Performance Console discussed in Chapter 21 to monitor network activity. It also supports network monitoring from other computers, even through other operating systems such as Linux.

System Event Notification: Supports connectivity for mobile devices. For example, this service allows you to enter e-mail on a laptop computer. Your mail is sent when you connect to a network.

System Restore Service: Allows you to restore systems to a predetermined configuration. This service is discussed in more detail in Chapter 24.

Task Scheduler: Permits you to schedule a task to run automatically on a specific time and date. For an example, see the Essential Skills section, page 63.

TCP/IP NetBIOS Helper: Allows Windows computers to communicate on a TCP/IP network. For more information on NetBIOS and TCP/IP, see Chapter 16.

Themes: Supports the basic themes and desktop backgrounds shown in Windows XP, including the ones shown in the Essential Skills section.

Upload Manager: Manages file transfer between clients and servers on a network.

Windows Audio: Supports sound. If you want sound, you need this service.

Windows Management Instrumentation: Sets up a common model for administering local and remote systems.

Windows Time: Synchronizes the time between computers.

Wireless Zero Configuration: Configures compatible wireless network adapters automatically.

Workstation: Manages network connections from a client computer on a network.

Manual Services

Manual services are not normally activated when you boot Windows XP Professional. However, associated programs and utilities can usually start these services on an "as needed" basis. The following list of services is usually set up for manual startup:

Alerter: Enables administrative alerts, such as a message from a System Administrator that the server is about to go down. Closely related to the Messenger service described in the last section.

Application Layer Gateway Service: Allows you to use the Internet Connection Sharing (ICS) and Internet Connection Firewall (ICF) features on the local computer. Don't let the Service console's reference to third party plug-ins confuse you; this is required for ICS/ICF. For more information on ICS/ICF, see Chapter 11.

Application Management: Allows for the installation and updating of certain types of applications. Required to support Windows XP fast booting through the `bootvis.exe` tool.

TIP *One tool that may reduce the time it takes for your system to start is* `bootvis.exe`*. You can download it as of this writing from* **www.microsoft.com/hwdev/fastboot***. Instructions are available in the White Paper associated with this utility, named* `fastboot-winxp.doc`*.*

Background Intelligent Transfer Service: Manages network file transfers through unused bandwidth; allows for interrupted file transfers.

Clipbook: Permits sharing of clipboard data. For more information, see Chapter 5.

COM+ Event System: Supports the System Event Notification service discussed in the previous section. In this case, COM is the Component Object Model, required for ActiveX programs.

COM+ System Application: Manages the configuration and tracking of COM+ based components. Closely related to the COM+ Event System service.

Distributed Transaction Coordinator: Allows resource communication between programs that manage databases, even on non-Windows operating systems.

Fast User Switching Compatibility: Supports multiple users on a Windows XP computer. Others may logon to your computer remotely through Terminal Services, even while you're logged on.

IMAPI CD-Burning COM Service: Allows recording onto CDs through the Image Mastering Applications Programming Interface (IMAPI).

Indexing Service: Allows the organization of the contents of local and remote files into a database. Supports the organization of data in Web searches. Required for the Fast Find feature associated with Microsoft Office. Since this uses a substantial amount of resources, do not use this feature unless your users need this level of access to data on your system.

Internet Connection Firewall (ICF)/Internet Connection Sharing (ICS): Supports the secure sharing of an Internet connection. For more information see Chapter 11.

Logical Disk Manager Administrative Service: Configures disks. Works with the Logical Disk Manager service. You do not need to start this to configure a new disk.

MS Software Shadow Copy Provider: Manages a special type of dynamic backup, known as a shadow copy. Closely related to the Volume Shadow Copy service.

NetMeeting Remote Desktop Sharing: Allows remote users access to your computer through the NetMeeting communication service described in Chapter 13. Unless you use NetMeeting, disable this service. Otherwise, this can be a security issue.

Network Connections: Supports network connectivity. Do not disable, unless your computer never connects to another network. Even Internet connections require this service.

Network DDE: Allows two applications to share the same data on a network. Supports Object Linking and Embedding (OLE) links as discussed in Chapter 5.

Network DDE DSDM: Enables sharing over a network. A prerequisite for the Network DDE service.

Network Location Awareness: Maintains information on connected logical networks. Required for ICS/ICF.

NT LM Security Support Provider: Provides security for some forms of network communication. Should be set at least to manual if you use Message Queuing, Telnet, or IIS.

Performance Logs and Alerts: Allows collection of performance data. If pre-configured benchmarks are met, this service triggers an alarm. If you're troubleshooting through the Performance Console, enable this service.

QoS RSVP: Allows configuration of messages to specific Quality of Service (QoS) parameters. In networking, messages are prioritized by a predetermined QoS.

Remote Access Auto Connection Manager: Supports network connections that require a search through a database of computer names based on a DNS server or NetBIOS names.

Remote Access Connection Manager: Supports Internet connections. Required for ICS.

Remote Desktop Help Session Manager: Allows the use of Remote Assistance. For more information on Remote Assistance, see Chapter 3.

Remote Procedure Call (RPC) Locator: Supports remote administration from the local computer.

Smart Card: Enables the use of smart card readers, which may become the standard for remote identification.

Smart Card Helper: Supports non-plug and play smart card readers.

SNMP Trap Service: Allows the receipt of messages through SNMP traps such as those associated with the Performance console.

SSDP Discovery Service: Allows the use of Universal Plug and Play (UPnP) devices such as those related to small business or home networks. As strange as it sounds, UPnP is not related to Plug and Play.

TCP/IP Print Server: Enables clients with Line Printer Daemon (LPD) software to print to the local computer. LPD is common in Unix/Linux systems as well as Windows NT computers that are connected through TCP/IP.

Telephony: Supports the Telephony Application Programming Interface (TAPI), which is required for communications programs such as Microsoft Fax and HyperTerminal. For more information on these programs, see Chapter 13.

Telnet: Allows remote access through Telnet clients on a TCP/IP network. For a description of the Remote Terminal (Telnet) service, see Chapter 12.

Terminal Services: Enables the use of Terminal Services Advanced Clients (TSAC) such as the Remote Desktop Connection discussed in Chapter 13.

Uninterruptible Power Supply (UPS): Supports the management of a UPS that is connected to and controlled by your computer. For more information, see Chapter 8.

Universal Plug and Play Device Host: Supports many home and small business network devices. Depends on the SSDP Discovery Service. This service is not related to Plug and Play.

Volume Shadow Copy: Supports the dynamic backups associated with the Microsoft Backup utility. Closely related to the MS Software Shadow Copy Provider. For more information on backups, see Chapter 24.

Windows Image Acquisition: Enables communication with some image devices such as scanners and digital cameras. Associated with the Scanners and Cameras Wizard in Control Panel.

Windows Installer: Supports the installation and maintenance of any application that uses instructions configured in MSI files such as Microsoft Office.

Windows Management Instrumentation Driver Extensions: Provides system management information for drivers. Related to the Windows Management Instrumentation Service described in the previous section.

WMI Performance Adapter: Enables the high-performance (HiPerf) class of data associated with the Performance Monitor discussed in Chapter 21.

Disabled Services

Disabled services are not activated when you boot Windows XP Professional. Unless you activate them in the Services console, associated programs and utilities cannot start these services. The following list of services is usually set up as disabled:

Human Interface Device Access: Associated with *hot buttons* on input devices such as keyboards and mice.

Routing and Remote Access: Enables configuration of the local computer as a Router, which acts as the interface between your network and another network such as the Internet. If you're using ICS/ICF, you don't need this service.

Additional Services

Additional services are added to the service console when you install the associated application. They can fall into any of the above categories (Automatic, Manual, Disabled). In preparation for Chapter 28, the services described here are associated with Internet Information Server (IIS):

FTP Publishing: Supports the configuration of an FTP site for sharing files with others. Information on accessing FTP sites is available in Chapter 12.

IIS Admin: Enables administration of IIS through the Microsoft Management Console.

Simple Mail Transfer Protocol: Allows the setup of a mail server through IIS. Do not confuse this with SNMP.

World Wide Web Publishing: Permits the setup of local Web site files, accessible through the network with IIS.

Configuring Services

You can modify how a service works on Windows XP Professional. The properties for each service include General Startup, Log On, and Recovery properties. The dependencies of each service are listed with the properties, as well. Finally, you can stop or start a service through the console or at the command line.

These are all tabs in the properties window associated with each service. A few services such as SNMP include other tabs that support the special configuration requirements of that service.

General Startup

In the Service console, highlight the service of your choice. Click Action ➤ Properties to open a properties window named for your service. The properties for the IIS Admin service are shown in Figure 27.2. If you don't have the IIS Admin service listed in your Service console, just select a different service. The basic information is consistent for all services.

FIGURE 27.2

Service properties

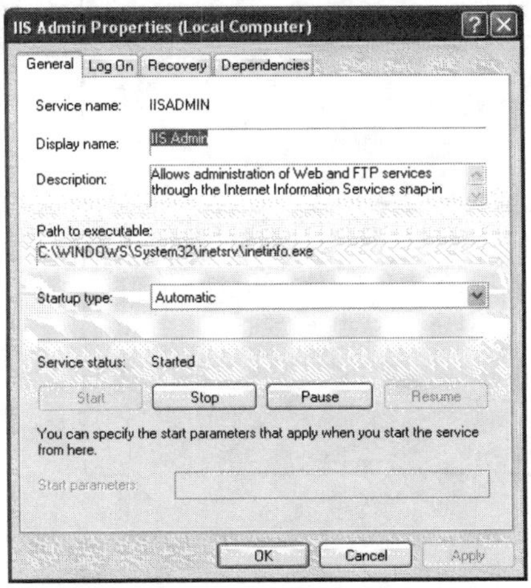

As you can see in Figure 27.2, this opens to the General tab by default. It lists the basic parameters of the service: the name, description, and the location of the associated executable file.

NOTE *Note the actual file associated with the service. It will come in handy later in the Service Commands section.*

The Startup type can be set to Automatic, Manual, or Disabled. As described earlier in this chapter, Automatic startup means this service starts when you boot Windows XP Professional. Manual startup leaves the service available for other programs or applications to start on an as-needed basis. Disabled startup means that service is unavailable for such programs.

As shown in the Service status section, you can Start, Stop, Pause, and Resume each service. When a service is stopped, you can specify Start parameters as you would at the command-line interface.

Log On

Every running service needs to log on before it starts. In the Properties window for your service, click the Log On tab, which is shown in Figure 27.3. Most services have their own generic account, known as the Local System account. The options are listed here:

Local System account: Allows most services to be set to log on to their own accounts, known generically as the Local System account. You won't find this account in the User management list.

Allow service to interact with desktop: Supports special configuration for services such as the Print Spooler. Alternatively, may allow some services to send messages to your desktop.

This account: Many services can be configured to use a different local or remote account. Some need special accounts, especially if network access to other computers is required. Two exceptions are the DNS and DHCP services.

Hardware Profile: Configured services can vary by the hardware profiles discussed in Chapter 16.

FIGURE 27.3

Log On properties

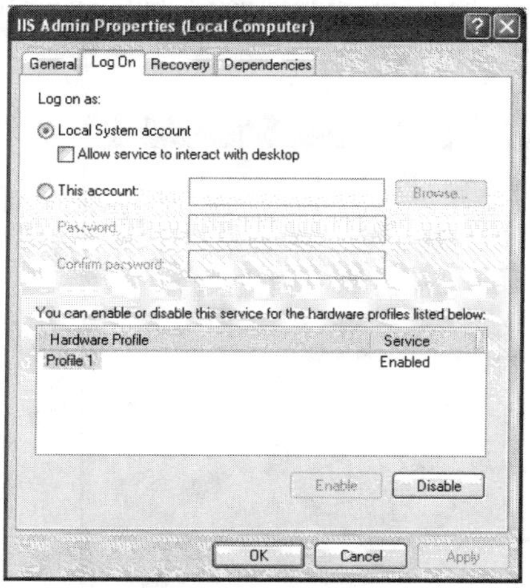

Recovery

If you install just a few applications, you may have over 100 configured services on your computer. Many services fail for "ordinary" reasons, such as a broken network connection or a modified configuration file. You don't want to have to restart the computer every time a service fails.

Click the Recovery tab on the properties window for a service. As you can see in Figure 27.4, you can set different actions for the first, second, and subsequent failures. You can set each service to take one of the following four actions in any of these cases:

FIGURE 27.4

Recovery properties

Take No Action: Allows a non-critical service to fail. Unless you use this option, some services such as IIS will automatically restart after a failure. If you're having a problem with IIS, you may want it to stop to give you a chance to maintain the associated Web or FTP server.

Restart the Service: Allows a service to be restarted, which is appropriate if the problem is temporary. For example, some network services fail if there is a temporary problem with the connections. Many of these services will work again if restarted.

Run a Program: Permits you to run the program of your choice, as shown in the Run program box. For example, you can automate a logging program to document the problem, or send a message to your users stating that a service is down.

Restart the Computer: Lets the failure of a service restart your computer. If you set this option, the configured service failure automatically restarts the computer based on the Restart service after: text box. Click the Restart Computer Options button. As you can see in Figure 27.5, the Restart Computer Options window allows you to send a message to computers on the network. The message shown in the figure appears when you select the Before Restart, Send This Message to Computers on the Network: check box. You can rewrite the message as desired.

FIGURE 27.5

You can warn remote users that you're about to restart your computer.

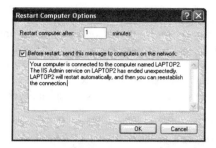

Dependencies

Many services depend on others. For example, you can't run a DNS Client service without TCP/IP. Click the dependencies tab in the properties window for your service. The Dependencies tab of the IIS Admin service is shown in Figure 27.6. The two text lists under this tab are described here:

FIGURE 27.6

Dependencies of a service

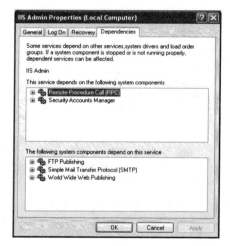

This Service Depends on the Following System Components: Lists the services required by the current service. You'll see in Figure 27.6 that the IIS Admin service depends on the Remote Procedure Call and Security Accounts Manager services.

The Following System Components Depend on This Service: Lists the services supported by the current service. You'll see in Figure 27.6 that the FTP Publishing, Simple Mail Transfer Protocol, and World Wide Web Publishing services won't run without the IIS Admin service.

Service Commands

You don't need the Service console to manage your services. In fact, you can use the net command at the command line to manage just about any Windows XP Professional service. The basic commands are fairly straightforward: net start *service* starts a service; other commands include net stop *service*, net pause *service*, and net continue *service*. The only twist is the net start command by itself, which lists currently running services.

As long as the Telnet service is started locally, you can even work from a remote computer. For example, open a Telnet session in HyperTerminal as described in Chapter 12. Enter the username and password that you use to administer the target Windows XP Professional computer, and Telnet takes you to a command prompt. Figure 27.7 shows this interface from a Windows 2000 Hyper-Terminal screen. The interface is nearly identical from just about any command line, including from a Windows 9x or a Unix/Linux computer.

FIGURE 27.7

You can use Hyper-Terminal to Telnet from a remote computer.

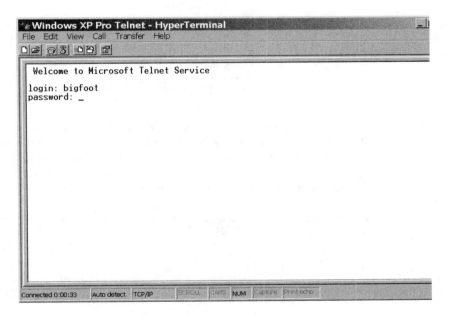

TIP *Don't connect to Telnet through the Windows 2000/XP command-line interface. There are limitations on Telnet connections through the command line that do not apply to HyperTerminal or even a Windows 9x command-line interface. If security is a concern, find and install a Secure Shell. There are many good options available online. Then disable the Telnet service so nobody can get in through that channel.*

Now try some of the net commands. If you want to see a list of open services, try net start | more. A partial list of open services is shown in the screen, similar to what you see in Figure 27.8. Press the spacebar to scroll through additional open services.

FIGURE 27.8

A Telnet view of
open services

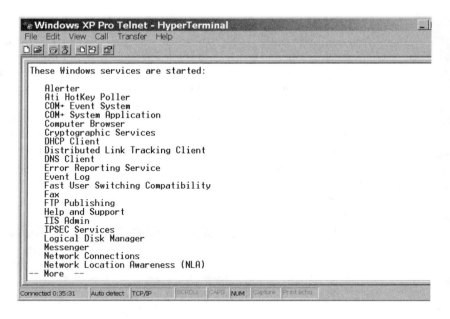

You can start, stop, pause, or resume any installed service. For example, if you wanted to stop the
IIS Admin service, type **net stop** "**iis admin**". The quotes apply if the name of the service is more
than one word. As you can see in Figure 27.9, Windows XP Professional warns you about any dependent services that must also be stopped, and gives you a chance to cancel the operation. If you continue,
messages are shown indicating the progress of the operation.

FIGURE 27.9

Remotely stopping a
service through the
command line

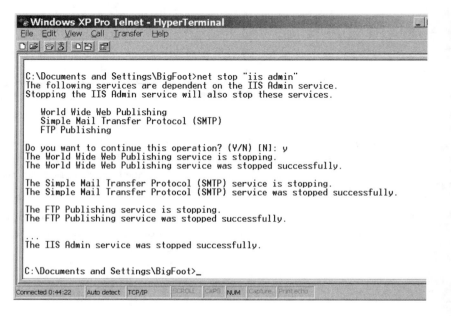

If you wanted to restart your Web server, just restart the World Wide Web Publishing service. Any dependent service, in this case, IIS Admin, is also started automatically.

TIP *When maintaining a service, you can use the Service name or the Display name. For example, since the service name for the World Wide Web Publishing service is W3SVC, the* `net start w3svc` *command has the same effect as* `net start "world wide web publishing"`.

Troubleshooting Service Issues

Managing services is like maintaining a network. If you have a problem with a service, you troubleshoot it. Based on the troubleshooting methodologies discussed in Chapter 25, it's best to check the simplest things first. On a network, you would check the connections between computers and power to the hubs, switches, and routers. Sometimes rebooting a computer or resetting a hub, switch, or router will address a problem on a network.

But if others are connected to your computer, they are depending on the connection. If your computer goes down, they can lose data. Therefore, you don't want to have to reboot it unless absolutely necessary.

This system applies equally well to services. For example, if you have a problem accessing Web pages on your Intranet, you may not have to reboot. First, you'll want to make sure your IIS Admin and World Wide Web Publishing services are actually active. Then you might try resetting these services by setting them to stop and then start again. The next step would be to check your connections and network as discussed in Chapter 16. You should also check other network-related services. For example, if the computers on your network rely on DNS to find each other, you need to make sure that the DNS service is active.

Other applications may have the same solution. If you're having problems printing, you can try stopping and restarting the Print Spooler service. If you're having problems printing from a Linux computer to a printer that's connected to a Windows XP computer, try stopping and restarting the TCP/IP Print Server service. If you can't connect from a remote computer via Telnet or Hyper-Terminal, try stopping and restarting the Telnet service.

Summary

The basic low-level programs that form the backbone of Windows XP Professional are also known as Services. There are many different kinds of Services that help you manage the basic functions of the operating system, as well as the way it interacts with a network. Some are started automatically when you start Windows XP Professional. Others can be manually started by specific applications. Still others are disabled by default. You can manage Windows XP Services either through the pre-configured MMC Service console. Alternatively, services can be managed at a command-line interface, even from a remote computer.

One of the first steps in troubleshooting many problems is to check the associated service. Sometimes you just need to turn it on. Sometimes resetting the service by turning it off and back on is sufficient.

Chapter 28

Hosting Web/FTP Servers

YOU CAN HOST A small Web site on your Windows XP Professional computer with Internet Information Server (IIS). While the number of connections is limited, IIS is easy to install and is highly configurable as a Microsoft Management Console snap-in. You can also use IIS to host a File Transfer Protocol (FTP) site for sharing files, and even a Simple Mail Transfer Protocol (SMTP) site for e-mail servers.

All three services are highly configurable. You can use the IIS console to manage these services locally or remotely. This chapter addresses the following configuration options in some detail:

- ◆ Installing Internet Information Server
- ◆ Understanding the limits of Windows XP Professional on IIS
- ◆ Configuring IIS as a Snap-in to the Microsoft Management Console
- ◆ Setting up a Web Server
- ◆ Setting up an FTP Server
- ◆ Setting up a Mail Server
- ◆ Troubleshooting IIS

Installing Internet Information Server

IIS is not installed by default. Unless you've upgraded from a Windows operating system with IIS or Personal Web Server, you need to install IIS to set up a Web, FTP, or SMTP site on your computer. This is a fairly easy process. Just use the Windows Components Wizard described in Chapter 5. Have your Windows XP Professional CD available and then follow these steps to install IIS:

1. Click Start ➢ Control Panel to open Control Panel.

2. Click the Add or Remove Programs link. Windows displays the Add or Remove Programs window.

3. Click the Add/Remove Windows Components button, and Windows will display the Windows Components Wizard.

4. Click the Internet Information Services (IIS) check box. By default, the check box is gray, which means that not all of the optional components are installed.

5. Click Details to open the Internet Information Services (IIS) window shown in Figure 28.1. As discussed in Chapter 5, you need to select desired components and click OK to continue. See the IIS Components sidebar for more information on the available choices.

FIGURE 28.1

There are many components available for IIS.

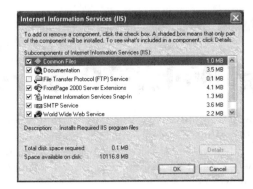

6. Click Next to continue. The Windows Components Wizard proceeds to install IIS on your computer.

7. When you see the Completing the Windows Components Wizard page, IIS is installed. Click Finish to complete the process.

IIS COMPONENTS—TO INSTALL OR NOT TO INSTALL?

You don't have to install all of the features associated with IIS. In fact, you should install just what you need. The more services you install, the more doors you open for hackers to get into your computer. For example, if you install the FTP service, some hackers may be able to get into your computer through the associated TCP/IP port. If you install FTP and don't use it, you may not even be paying attention when a hacker uses your computer for malicious purposes. With that in mind, the IIS components shown in Figure 28.1 have the following purposes:

Common Files: Includes the basic files required by all of the other components of IIS. If you delete this component, the Windows Components Wizard automatically deselects all other IIS components for you.

Documentation: Adds about 7MB of IIS help files and guides on your computer, in the \%System-Root%\Help\iisHelp directory, where %SystemRoot% is the directory with your basic operating system files, such as C:\Windows.

File Transfer Protocol Service: Configures the FTP service for file transfers. If you need to set up a FTP server, check this box. By default, this is deselected because FTP has often been a security problem in the past.

FrontPage 2000 Server Extensions: Includes the programs that allow you to use the full capabilities of the Microsoft FrontPage application for creating Web sites. The associated tools are fully compatible with FrontPage 2000 or FrontPage 2002.

Continued on next page

IIS COMPONENTS—TO INSTALL OR NOT TO INSTALL? *(continued)*

Internet Information Services Snap-in: Allows you to use an MMC console to administer FrontPage. It's more difficult to administer IIS without this snap-in.

SMTP Service: Adds outgoing mail service. The Simple Mail Transfer Protocol governs the TCP/IP service that allows you to set up an outgoing mail server. You probably already have SMTP service through your ISP, so this service shouldn't be necessary unless you want your e-mail to bypass your ISP's servers.

World Wide Web Service: Includes the Microsoft Web server service. Highlight this option and click Details. This service includes four subcomponents:

◆ **Printers virtual directory**: Allows remote users to access your Web server to print on your computers. Don't activate this unless absolutely necessary, as this can be a security hole.

◆ **Remote Desktop Web Connection**: Permits you to control this computer from a remote location through Internet Explorer. The basic requirements for Remote Desktop Connections are discussed in Chapter 13. Don't activate this unless absolutely necessary, as this can be a security hole.

◆ **Scripts virtual directory**: Sets up a directory with scripts for your Web site. If you have any complexity in your Web pages, such as database access, you need this subcomponent.

◆ **World Wide Web Service**: Add the Web server. This service is required to support any other Web service, the mail (SMTP) service, or to display IIS documentation.

If you want to remove one or more of these services, repeat the basic steps you used to install IIS. Just deselect the components you no longer need during the process.

Assuming that you've installed the World Wide Web service, IIS should now be installed and active on your computer. It's easy to verify successful installation. Open up Internet Explorer and enter `localhost` in the Address text box. Assuming you don't already have a Web page, you'll see the default shown in Figure 28.2. If you've installed the help files, you'll see those as well in a separate browser.

FIGURE 28.2

The IIS default Web page is visible only on the local computer.

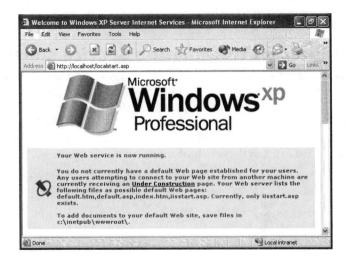

Windows XP Professional Limits on IIS

The IIS that you just installed on Windows XP Professional is essentially the same software that you can install on Windows .NET Server. However, Windows XP Professional limits access to 10 simultaneous TCP connections. That includes all connections made to your Web, FTP, and SMTP servers. Very few Internet Web or FTP sites would be practical with this limit.

NOTE   *In fact, some connections to a Web site open multiple pages that require more than one TCP connection. In other words, access to your Web site on a Windows XP Professional computer may be limited to fewer than 10 users.*

NOTE   *The version of IIS that comes with Windows XP Professional is 5.1. The version of IIS available with Windows .NET Server is 6.0. While Microsoft hasn't released Windows .NET Server at the time of this writing, the sites you create here should be easily transferable to the IIS that is available when Windows .NET Server is finally released.*

However, Windows XP Professional with IIS is still useful in the following ways:

◆ As a test bed: You can load a Web site on Windows XP Professional, and test its look and feel over your LAN. However, you won't be able to test the response of your Web site to any serious traffic. For that purpose, you need to test your Web site on an operating system such as Microsoft's .NET Web Server.

◆ With an Intranet: IIS on Windows XP Professional can be great if you're communicating with a small number of users, especially within a LAN or a Domain.

◆ For a small group: IIS on Windows XP Professional can be used to share information with a small group, such as for a project.

These are common uses on an Intranet. You can also connect IIS on Windows XP Professional to the Internet. Before you do this, talk to your ISP. Many ISPs, especially those that provide broadband service, may not even allow you to set up an Internet Web server on your home computer.

However, many ISPs do provide space for a small Web site with a limited amount of traffic with your ISP membership. If desired, you can pay your ISP (or another company) for more space and larger amounts of traffic.

The Internet Information Service Console

If you included the Internet Information Services snap-in when installing IIS, you have access to the IIS console. Click Start ➣ All Programs ➣ Administrative Tools ➣ Internet Information Services to open a console like what you see in Figure 28.3.

As with other MMC snap-ins discussed in Chapter 26, the IIS console allows for detailed configuration of each service. Just highlight the desired service and use the Action menu. Much of this chapter is dedicated to the details of this configuration process.

FIGURE 28.3

The Internet Information Services console allows you to manage Web sites, FTP sites, and SMTP mail servers.

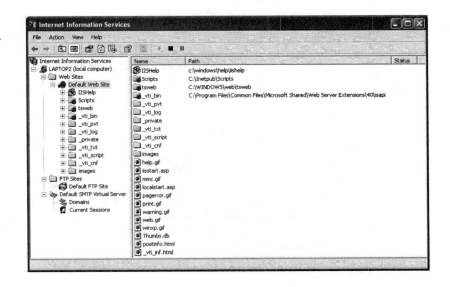

Connecting to Remote IIS Services

You can use the IIS console to administer remote computers that include IIS 4.0 and above. Highlight Internet Information Services, and then click Action ➤ Connect. In the Connect to Computer window shown in Figure 28.4, enter the name or IP address of the other computer. Assuming you want to administer the remote server, click Connect As. This allows you to enter the remote username and password you need to administer IIS on the remote computer.

FIGURE 28.4

Connecting to a remote IIS server

You can disconnect the IIS console from a remote or even the local IIS server. Just highlight the server of your choice, click Action ➤ Disconnect, and then confirm your selection.

Basic Configuration Management

Frequent backups are a good practice when you administer any computer. It's easy to back up your configuration that you set up through the IIS console. Highlight the server of your choice, and then click Action ➤ All Tasks ➤ Backup/Restore Configuration to open the Configuration Backup/Restore window shown in Figure 28.5.

FIGURE 28.5

Backing up an IIS
configuration

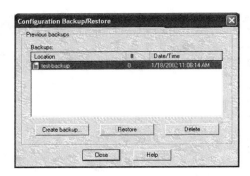

The options are fairly self-explanatory. If you want to create a backup, just click Create backup. If you want to restore a previously backed up configuration, highlight the name of the backup and click Restore. The default location for an IIS configuration backup file is the `%SystemRoot%\System32\inetsrv\MetaBack` directory.

NOTE *In IIS, the terms* directory *and* folder *are used interchangeably.*

Configuring the Web Server

It isn't practical to run a "real" Web site on Windows XP Professional. If you're setting up a Web site, you're eventually going to move the files you create to one of the Microsoft Windows server operating systems such as Windows .NET Server. IIS on Windows .NET Server and Windows 2000 Server allows you to configure multiple Web sites. Therefore, the following sections assume that there are multiple Web sites on the IIS Web server.

You can configure only one Web site on IIS for Windows XP Professional. But to understand the configuration process, it's easiest to assume that you can configure multiple Web sites on the same IIS Web server. Then, the configuration process for an IIS console becomes a simple exercise in configuring properties. There are four basic configuration levels in any IIS Web server:

Web Sites: Applies to all IIS Web sites configured on the local computer. The discussion throughout this section assumes that there are multiple Web sites.

Individual web site: Configures only one specific Web site. On Windows XP Professional, there is only one Web site. On current Microsoft Server operating systems, it's possible to install multiple Web sites, each with a unique configuration.

Folder: Allows you to configure each individual folder associated with a Web site.

Individual file: The configurable properties for individual files are identical to that for a folder.

Configuration is based on the properties at each level. Highlight the desired level in the left-hand pane of the IIS console and then click Action ➤ Properties.

Some of the properties tabs in the following sections look identical. Since they only affect one configuration level, the choices that you make will vary. This chapter addresses configuration at the

Web Sites and Default Web Site levels. After reading through the following sections, the configuration of folders and individual files in a Web server follow the same pattern.

Generic Web Site Configuration

You can configure a number of options associated with all of the Web sites on IIS. In the IIS console, highlight the Web Sites (not the Default Web Site) folder and click Action ➤ Properties to open the Web Sites Properties window shown in Figure 28.6. The ISAPI Filters tab should be open by default. Other tabs are described in the sections that follow.

FIGURE 28.6

Configuring ISAPI filters for all Web sites

ISAPI FILTERS

An ISAPI filter is a Dynamic Link Library in a DLL file that customizes the content of the Web page that is sent to a specific user. For example, if a cookie on a user's computer locates that computer in West Virginia, an ISAPI filter could send a Web page customized for that US State.

The ISAPI filters shown in Figure 28.6 apply to all Web sites configured on the server. The listed filters are processed on individual Web pages, based first on the priority (High or Low), then on the order shown in the tab.

You can adjust the processing order by highlighting the filter you want to change, and then clicking the up or down arrow on the left side of the ISAPI Filters tab. The first four of these default filters are located in the `%SystemRoot%\System32\inetsrv\` directory.

`sspifilt`: Allows for the transmission of secure Web sites. These are the Web pages associated with sensitive information such as bank accounts and credit card payments. Secure Web sites can be identified in a browser based on the letters in front of the address, `https` (which stands for secure HTTP).

`Compression`: Permits the compression of files such as pictures before sending them to the user.

`md5filt`: Lets IIS use digest authentication.

`pwsdata`: Supports the use of Web sites configured through Personal Web Server, which was included in older Microsoft operating systems for the home such as Windows 98.

`fpexed11.dll`: Allows the use of legacy Web pages created with FrontPage 1.x. If you use Microsoft proxy servers, you may need to delete these files before your users can access your Web site. Located in the `\Program Files\Common Files\Microsoft Shared\Web Server Extensions\40\bin\` directory.

HOME DIRECTORY

Click the Home Directory tab. This configures the home directory properties for all Web sites on this server. But since individual Web sites need their own home directories, you'll need to configure some details later, in the Home Directory section associated with a specific Web site. For this reason, details associated with a particular Web site are not available under the Web Site Properties window shown in Figure 28.7.

FIGURE 28.7

Web sites can share only some Home Directory properties.

However, wherever the directory is located, you can choose to set the same permissions for all Web sites on your implementation of IIS. The options associated with directory access include:

Script Source Access: Permits users to access the source code of a Web-based application, if Read or Write access is enabled.

Read: Allows users to read or download files from your Web sites.

Write: Lets users upload files to your Web sites' directories. Requires a browser that complies with the HTTP 1.1 standard, such as Internet Explorer 4.0 and above.

Directory Browsing: Allows users to read a list of files in the associated virtual directory. This option works only if there are no default documents, or that option is disabled under the Documents tab as discussed in the next section.

Log Visits: Enables logging for each user's visit to your Web site. As you'll see in the later sections on Logging, this can provide valuable data for anyone interested in the background of visitors to a specific site.

Applications can be associated with Web site home directories. In this case, an application is any executable file on a Web site. But since they are also associated with specific directory locations, the details are described in the Home Directory section associated with configuring a specific Web site.

DOCUMENTS

Click the Documents tab. Default documents are what you see when you just type in the name of a Web site. Based on the Documents shown in Figure 28.8, any Web site will search for a `default.htm`, `default.asp`, and an `index.htm` file in the home directory for a specific Web site. The first available file from this list is returned to the browser that's trying to connect to your site.

FIGURE 28.8

Web site default documents

Document footers are typically HTML formatted files that are added to the end of every Web page on a Web site.

DIRECTORY SECURITY

Click the Directory Security tab. At this level, only one option is available, to edit the authentication methods required for access to your Web site. Click Edit and review the Authentication Methods window shown in Figure 28.9.

By default, Web sites are set up for anonymous access. Anyone with a browser and the address of your Web site can access it if you make it available on the network. However, you can also set up Authenticated access, which requires a Web directory on a NTFS partition with associated user level security limits. For more information on NTFS based limits, see Chapter 18. The drawback of setting up such security at this level is that access passwords are sent in clear text. Anyone with the right network equipment can read the passwords as your users send them over the network.

FIGURE 28.9

Authentication methods

HTTP HEADERS

Click the HTTP Headers tab. The options shown in the tab are generally associated with specific Web sites and are therefore covered in detail in the HTTP Headers section associated with configuring a specific Web site.

CUSTOM ERRORS

Click the Custom Errors tab. Along with Web pages, browsers and Web servers exchange messages all of the time, based on HTTP. The Custom Errors tab is shown in Figure 28.10.

FIGURE 28.10

There are many types of HTTP errors.

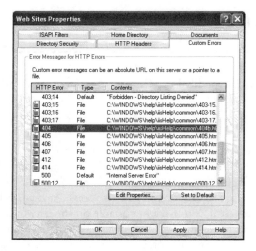

There are five basic categories of HTTP messages:

1xx: Messages between 100 and 199 are intermediate responses; communication is continuing between browser and server.

2xx: Messages between 200 and 299 tell the browser that the access request for the Web page and associated information was successful.

3xx: Messages between 300 and 399 are associated with redirection, such as a move to a different Web address.

4xx: Messages between 400 and 499 are error messages based on a problem at the browser such as "file not found."

5xx: Messages between 500 and 599 are error messages based on a problem from the Web server.

Microsoft provides standard error messages to send to user's browsers associated with each HTTP message. For example, Figure 28.11 shows a browser with the standard error page when a file is not found on the browser.

FIGURE 28.11

A standard file not found (404) error message

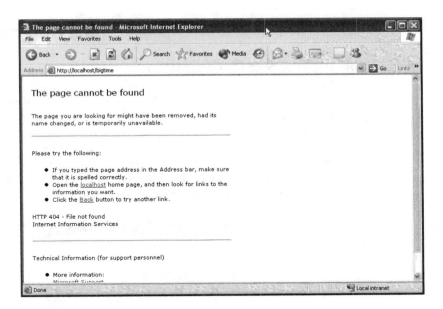

Alternatively, you could set up a different message. Under the Custom Errors tab, click 404 under the HTTP Error column, and then click Edit Properties. The Error Mapping Properties that opens gives you a chance to change the HTML file used for a 404 error. For example, if you try to access a non-existent page at www.minasi.com, you'll get the 404 error message shown in Figure 28.12, which provides additional helpful information for users.

FIGURE 28.12

A customized file not found (404) error message.

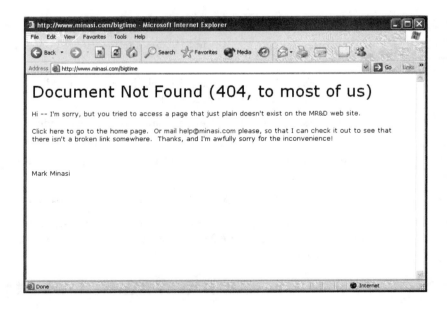

FIGURE 28.12

A customized file not found (404) error message.

Specific Web Site Configuration

Now that you have the basics, it's time to configure a specific Web site. In the IIS console, open the Web Sites folder and select a specific Web site. If you've just installed IIS, the Default Web Site is available for this purpose. Now click Action ➤ Properties. This opens the Properties window associated with your Web site.

As you can see in Figure 28.13, the Properties window for the specific Web site includes two additional tabs, Web Site and Server Extensions. But all tabs will be covered in the following sections, as there are detailed items that you can configure for a specific site. In some cases, a comparison of properties can help you learn more about configuring IIS.

FIGURE 28.13

There are many things to configure for a specific Web site.

WEB SITE

The Web Site tab as shown in Figure 28.13 should be open by default. As you can see, it includes three sections. The Web Site Identification section allows you to configure the following most basic parameters for the site:

Description: Identifies the Web site in the IIS console.

IP Address: Sets the IP address used to connect to this particular Web site. The Advanced button allows you to assign different TCP ports. For more information on TCP ports, see Chapter 16.

TCP Port: Fixes the default port for basic Web site communication. Port 80 is the default for HTTP.

SSL Port: Notes the default port for secure Web site communication. Port 443 is the default for HTTPS. You need a server certificate to allow IIS to serve Web pages through a secure port. If you have one, assign it through the Directory Security tab. Once a certificate is assigned, the SSL Port text box will become active.

The Connections section allows you to regulate how connections are maintained with users. The Connection Timeout sets a limit on idle time. As shown in Figure 28.13, the default is 900 seconds. If there were no communication between the server and browser for that period of time, the user would have to reconnect to the Web site. HTTP Keep-Alives are required for "complex" Web pages. Unless this is enabled, a browser may have to send new connection requests for each Web page element from a different file, such as pictures and icons.

NOTE *If you were configuring IIS on one of the Windows .NET Server operating systems, you would also see options for regulating the number of simultaneous connections.*

The Enable Logging section is important to any Web site. If you want to know anything about your users, you want to Enable Logging. Try a format, and then try connecting to the server from the local computer and a remote computer on your LAN. You can then review the log file in the %SystemRoot%\ System32\LogFiles directory. All provide a list of requests from the browser, which includes their IP address, username, time, requested file, and the amount of data transmitted. There are three log formats available for IIS:

Microsoft IIS Log File Format: Associated with a fixed ASCII format originally developed for older versions of IIS. Not in common use today.

NCSA Common Log File Format: Allows for log files in a format originally developed by the National Center for Supercomputing Applications (NCSA) in the 1980s. The NCSA developed the first viable Web servers at the University of Illinois. One of the developers of this Web server, Marc Andreeson, went on to develop the Netscape browser.

W3C Extended Log File Format: Configures the most current and flexible log file format, maintained by the World Wide Web consortium, which is also the IIS default format.

The W3C format is in most common use today. In the Active log format drop-down box, switch to W3C Extended Log File Format if it isn't already selected, and then click Properties. You'll see the Extended Logging Properties window, as shown in Figure 28.14.

NOTE   *Log files grow quickly. If you use the default Web site, your users call a single Web page. But since this calls up icons, banners, and more, it creates 19 log entries (based on the W3C Extended Log File Format). And this is a fairly simple Web site. Commercial Web sites are known to have daily log files in the hundreds of Megabytes. If you're administering a larger Web site, watch the size of your log files carefully.*

FIGURE 28.14

Setting up basic Web site logging

The General Properties tab should be open by default. There are a few options available, related to regulating the size of a log file:

New Log Time Period: New log files can be created on an hourly, daily, weekly, or monthly basis. Alternatively, you can set up a new log file after the current one reaches a specific size.

Use Local Time for File Naming and Rollover: If you deselect this option, IIS uses Greenwich Mean Time (GMT). Based on the settings shown in Figure 28.14, new daily log files would be created every day at 12 Midnight GMT.

Log File Directory: The location of your log files. If you have larger log files, you may want to select a directory on a less crowded drive.

Log File Name: The default shown indicates the subdirectory (W3SVC1) and a specific file format. The yymmdd part of the filename corresponds to the current date. For example, if this is a log file for December 25, 2002, the log filename will be ex021225.log.

TIP   *Although you can set log files to start based on local time or GMT, each entry in a log file is based on GMT. For example, if you see a log file entry at 02:30:43, and identify the user from the East Coast of the US, that user accessed your server at 9:30 P.M., Eastern Standard Time.*

Click the Extended Properties tab. As shown in Figure 28.15, there are a substantial number of details you can get about every request to your Web site. See the W3C Log File sidebar for more information on what you can configure. Log files can be useful for troubleshooting and are discussed in that section towards the end of this chapter.

FIGURE 28.15

There are a lot of
W3C Log File con-
figuration options.

W3C LOG FILES

There are a lot of options for data that you can collect in a W3C log file. The options shown below are just associated with IIS for Windows XP Professional. More log options are available with the Windows XP Server packages, especially if you use some form of the Microsoft Commerce Server. Some of these options are shown in Figure 28.15. They include the following list:

Date: Indicates the date of the request. If you keep daily log files, this information isn't necessary.

Time: Notes the time of the request. If you weren't limited by the Windows XP Professional 10 connection limit, this could help you measure the busy times for your Web site.

Extended Properties: Allows you to change the following other extended logging options, when selected:

Client IP Address: Add the IP address from the computer that the browser is using.

User Name: Includes the username, usually only from the LAN or local domain.

Service Name: Adds the name of the logging service, in this case, W3SVC1. This shouldn't change.

Server Name: Lists the computer name used to serve the Web pages. Useful for Web sites where user requests could go to different Web servers.

Server IP Address: Notes the IP address associated with the computer used to serve the Web pages.

Server Port: Includes the port number of the connection. For regular Web pages, the default TCP port is 80.

Method: Notes the command used by the browser (usually GET).

URI Stem: Lists the name of the file that is accessed, which can be the Web page, an ActiveX control page, an icon, and more.

URI Query: Includes a search term, such as through a search engine.

Protocol Status: Notes the HTTP message associated with the request.

Win32 Status: Notes the Windows message associated with the request.

Continued on next page

W3C LOG FILES *(continued)*

Bytes Sent: Includes the number of bytes sent by IIS to the client. Usually corresponds to the size of the requested file.

Bytes Received: Includes the number of bytes received by IIS.

Time Taken: Lists the amount of time on the server between when it gets the first packet of data from the client, and when it gets the acknowledgement from the client that it received the requested data.

Protocol Version: Notes the protocol, usually FTP, HTTP 1.0, or HTTP 1.1.

Host: Includes the name or IP address of the computer with the Web server.

User Agent: Notes the browser used on the client. Most browsers are compatible with some form of a protocol known as Mozilla or Gecko.

Cookie: Lists the content of a cookie sent to the client.

Referer: Notes the Web page or site where the subject file is used.

ISAPI FILTERS

Click the ISAPI Filters tab. The format is identical to that from Figure 28.6. The filters you configured there apply to all the Web sites on this installation of IIS. The filters that you add here apply only to this specific Web site. If desired, click Add to start the process of adding a filter.

HOME DIRECTORY

Click the Home Directory tab. While the format is identical to that shown in Figure 28.7, there is more that you can configure for a specific Web site. As you can see in Figure 28.16, you can specify the location of this Web site's files. At the top of the tab, there is one implied question. When connecting to this resource, the content should come from:

FIGURE 28.16

There is more to configure for a specific Web site's Home Directory.

A Directory Located on This Computer: Allows you to place the directory of your choice in the Local Path text box. This directory should contain the files you need for your Web site.

TIP *If you're setting up a real Web site directory on a Windows XP or .NET computer, this is your chance to set it up on a NTFS partition. Otherwise, if you configure Server Extensions to support the use of Microsoft FrontPage, it is possible for someone to upload malicious code to these less protected folders. For more information, see the Server Extensions section later in this chapter.*

A Share Located on Another Computer: Lets you use a directory on a remote computer. If you select this option, the Local Path text box changes to a Network Directory text box, where you can enter the path to the directory in the \\Server\Share format.

A Redirection to a URL: Permits you to send any browser that tries to connect to a Web site on your computer to a different network directory or a Web site such as www.mommabears.com. If you select this option, the Local Path text box changes to a Redirect to text box, where you can enter the name of the directory or Web site. As you would no longer be responsible for local scripts or applications, all such references are deleted, as shown in Figure 28.17. There are three other options:

The Exact URL Entered Above: Redirects all requests to your home page or subdirectories to the specified URL.

A Directory Below This One: Allows you to redirect requests to a child directory.

A Permanent Redirection for This Resource: Sends a message to the browser that the redirection is permanent, also known by its HTTP code, 301. Some browsers will use this code as a trigger to change associated bookmarks.

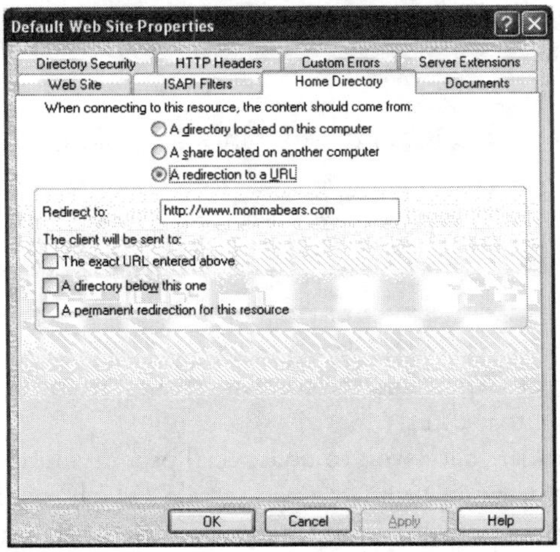

FIGURE 28.17

It's easy to redirect users to a different Web site.

DOCUMENTS

Click the Documents tab. The default settings appear identical to Figure 28.8, which identified default documents for all Web sites on the local IIS. You don't have to make any changes. However, unique default documents can help avoid confusion when you're running multiple Web sites on the same server. They can also improve security, if they are based on a name that a hacker wouldn't anticipate.

DIRECTORY SECURITY

Click the Directory Security tab. The default settings appear identical to Figure 28.9, which identified authentication and other security limits for all Web sites on the local IIS. You don't have to make any changes. However, any access controls or certificates that you add at this stage apply only to this specific Web site. If a hacker acquires the security key for one of your Web sites, individual certificates would protect any other Web sites on your server.

HTTP HEADERS

Click the HTTP Headers tab. This includes information related to the content of your Web site, and is therefore normally customized differently for each site. As you can see in Figure 28.18, this tab can be divided into four different sections.

FIGURE 28.18

HTTP headers help you classify the content of a Web site.

If you Enable Content Expiration, the content on the current Web site is not updated after the expiration date and time that you set.

Custom HTTP Headers allow you to use special programming instructions. For example, it's possible to force client browsers to refresh periodically, which can be useful for time-sensitive data such as the price of stocks or mutual funds that you own. More information on this topic can be found in the Microsoft Knowledge Base, article Q240774.

TIP   *Microsoft Knowledge Base articles are available online. Navigate to* `http://support.Microsoft.com`, *and enter keywords or the article number as a search term. Alternatively, if you enter the article number in a comprehensive search engine such as Google (`www.google.com`), you'll probably find a direct link to the article.*

Content ratings allow you to classify your Web site. General guidelines are available through the Internet Content Rating Association of the Recreational Software Advisory Council (RSAC), available online at `www.rsac.org`. The content that you configure for your Web site works with Internet Explorer's Content Advisor, described in Chapter 12. To set up a rating for your Web site, click Edit Ratings. You'll see the Content Ratings window in Figure 28.19.

FIGURE 28.19

You can configure RSAC Content Ratings for your Web site.

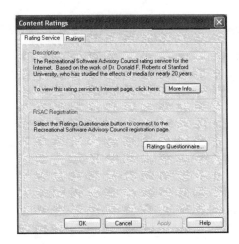

By default, you should see the Rating Service tab, which allows you to view the RSAC Web site and start a rating for your own Web site. Alternatively, you can set your own ratings for the level of Violence, Sex, Nudity, and Language associated with your Web site through the Ratings tab. Once you're finished setting up ratings, click OK to return to the HTTP Headers tab.

IIS 5.1 already configures all of the file types such as `.htm`, `.jpg`, and `.asp` that most users need for their Web servers. If you need an unusual file type for your Web site, click File Types and configure it in the File Types window that appears.

CUSTOM ERRORS

Click the Custom Errors tab. The default settings appear identical to Figure 28.10, which identified HTTP Error codes and associated Web pages for all Web sites on the local IIS. Any special Web pages that you configure for a HTTP error under this tab apply only to this specific Web site. While you don't have to make any changes, individualized error pages can help promote a unique look and feel for your Web site.

SERVER EXTENSIONS

Click the Server Extensions tab. This is found only with specific Web sites, as the properties that allow you and other Web page authors on your computer to use Microsoft FrontPage to edit your Web pages. As you can see in Figure 28.20, the information on this tab can be divided into three sections.

TIP   If you don't see any information under this tab, you haven't yet configured Server Extensions. To do so, return to the IIS console, highlight the Web site, and then click Action ➤ All Tasks ➤ Configure Server Extensions. This opens the Server Extensions Configuration Wizard, which allows you to configure the e-mail contact points for the author and administrator of the Web site. If your Web pages are not on a NTFS partition, the wizard warns you of potential security problems. You can change the location of your Web pages through the Home Directory tab associated with your Web site.

FIGURE 28.20

Server Extensions help you configure authoring and security options.

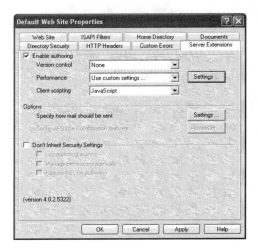

Enable Authoring: Allows the use of FrontPage to edit local Web pages. Version control allows you to have a historical record of changes. The Performance option and Settings button optimizes caches based on the size of your Web site. And there are two available types of Client scripting: JavaScript and VBScript.

Options: Lets you note how and where Web site related e-mail, such as to the administrator, should be sent. If the Microsoft Office Web Server is installed, you can also set up workgroup discussions through your Web site.

Don't Inherit Security Settings: Permits you to override any security settings that you created earlier for IIS. This includes logging of authors who change the Web site, overriding of Front-Page security settings to allow you to manage permissions manually, and the use of SSL to verify author identities before allowing them to change a Web page.

NEW VIRTUAL DIRECTORIES

You can create virtual directories for your Web site. These directories can help hide the real location of sensitive files. To create a new virtual directory, highlight the Web site in the IIS console. Click Action ➤ New ➤ Virtual Directory to start the Virtual Directory Creation Wizard. Click Next to go to the Virtual Directory Alias page shown in Figure 28.21.

FIGURE 28.21

You can use an alias that is different from the name of the directory you want to use.

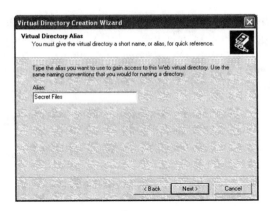

Enter an Alias of your choice and click Next to continue. On the next page, specify the path to the actual directory you want to use. Click Next to continue. You'll see the Access Permissions page shown in Figure 28.22. The permissions shown are fairly standard:

FIGURE 28.22

The default access permissions can help protect the files in your Virtual Directory.

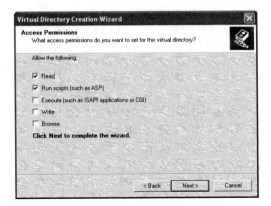

Read: Allows users to read Web site documents through their browsers.

Run Scripts: Permits users to run the basic scripts associated with many Web pages, such as Active Server Pages (ASP).

Execute: Lets users run applications through your Web pages.

Write: Allows users to upload new pages to your Web site.

Browse: Sets up the Web site to list files in the current directory, if the default documents shown under the Web site's Document tab have been disabled or do not exist.

Perhaps the most interesting of these options is Browse, which allows you to set up a FTP style interface for sharing files. For example, Figure 28.23 shows some of the files that I used to write this book in a Virtual directory named *Secret Directory*. Anyone with access to this page can download these files. But take care with the directories that you use; the wrong Virtual directory settings could also help a malicious user find the vulnerabilities in your system.

FIGURE 28.23

You can share files with a browser through your Web site.

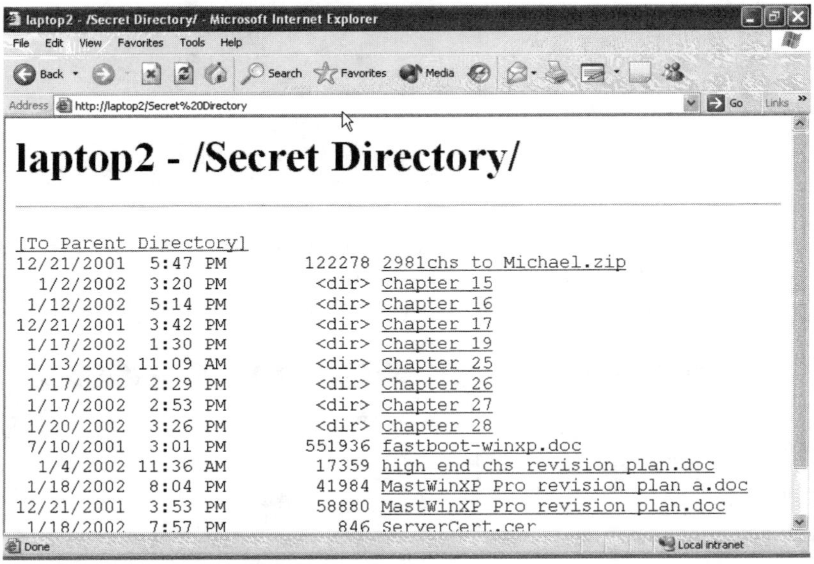

Configuring the FTP Server

When the first pre-Internet networks were developed in the 1970s, there was a lot of trust in the computer world. There was little need for computer security; few people made money from computer data. Most of the people working on this network were university researchers; they just wanted to exchange information. Anonymous connections allowed for the quickest possible exchange of data. The File Transfer Protocol was developed to help make this possible.

It's easier to configure an FTP server. Since multiple FTP sites on a single server are less common, you'll be configuring just the Default FTP Site. Return to the IIS console and highlight the Default FTP Site. Click Action ➤ Properties. This opens the Default FTP Site Properties window, as shown in Figure 28.24.

As you can see, there are four tabs shown in Figure 28.24 that address basic configuration (FTP Site), security (Security Accounts), messages to users (Messages), and the configuration of the FTP server home directory (Home Directory).

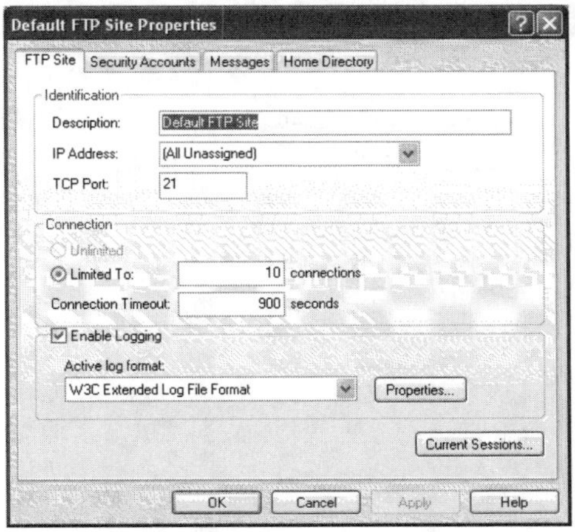

FIGURE 28.24

It's easier to set up a FTP site.

FTP Site

You should already see the information associated with the FTP Site tab. As shown in Figure 28.24, the information appears quite similar to the Web Site tab that you configured earlier in this chapter for the Default Web Site. There are four sections that you can configure:

Identification: Describes the name of the FTP site, the IP address used to connect, and the TCP Port. (The default TCP port for FTP communication is 21.)

Connection: Allows you to regulate the number of connections, as well as the amount of time the connection can be inactive before it's disconnected. Remember, for Windows XP Professional, the total number of connections is limited to 10. If you've configured a Web site as well, you may want to reduce this number further so your Web site is accessible by at least one user.

Enable Logging: Permits logging per W3C Extended Log File Format or the Microsoft IIS Log File Format, based on the general criteria described earlier in this chapter. The default directory with the actual FTP log files is slightly different from that for other servers.

Current Sessions: Lets you monitor currently connected users. Click this button, and you can disconnect currently logged on users in the FTP User Sessions window that appears.

Security Accounts

Click the Security Accounts tab. You see the options normally associated with FTP security, as shown in Figure 28.25. The default is to Allow Anonymous Connections. While people who log on to FTP anonymously get a generic username, passwords aren't even required.

If you deselect Allow Anonymous Connections, only people who have a username and password on your system can log onto your FTP server. Even if they're administrative users, they don't automatically have write access through your FTP server.

NOTE   *The FTP Site Operators section of the Security Accounts tab is not active and cannot be changed when you're configuring FTP on IIS 5.1 on Windows XP Professional.*

FIGURE 28.25

IIS uses standard
FTP security
requirements.

Messages

You can set up various messages for your FTP users. Click the Messages tab. The message boxes
shown in Figure 28.26 are fairly self-explanatory.

FIGURE 28.26

Creating messages
for your FTP users

Banner: Lists the message you see when you connect to the FTP server, before you log in.

Welcome: Sends a message to a user after a successful login.

Exit: Sends a message to a user after he or she exits from the server.

Maximum Connections: Sends a message to the user if there are already too many other connections to the server.

Figure 28.27 illustrates the effect of these messages on an FTP session: the banner upon connection, the welcome message after the password is accepted, an exit message after terminating the session, and the maximum connections message when the server is too busy.

FIGURE 28.27

The effect of FTP messages

Home Directory

There are a number of options available for the home directory for your FTP server. Click the Home Directory tab and you'll see that the options shown in Figure 28.28 are fairly straightforward.

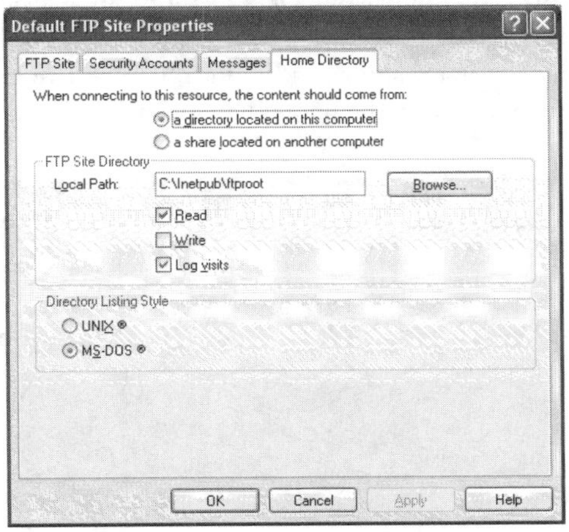

FIGURE 28.28

Setting up the FTP Home Directory

The first option is whether the files on your FTP server should come from the local or a remote computer. If you keep A Directory Located on This Computer selected, the FTP Site Directory allows you to type a path in the Local Path text box. If you select A Share Located on Another Computer, the Local Path text box turns into a Network Share text box, where you can enter the share in the \\Servername\sharename format. In that case, you'll also see a Connect As button, which you can use to let IIS log in to the remote computer.

In either case, there are three options associated with configuring a specific FTP Site Directory:

Read: Gives you read access to the home directory. Allows you to use various directory commands such as dir and ls to list the files in that directory. Read access is required at least on the home directory; otherwise, your users won't be able to log in to your FTP server.

Write: Permits you to upload files to the FTP server. Since users with write access can overwrite the files on your FTP server, this would create a security issue.

Log Visits: Data from visitors is collected in log files, as described earlier with the FTP Site tab and in related information discussed in configuring a Web server.

There are two different Directory Listing Styles, UNIX and MS-DOS. The style you select determines the FTP server response to the ls command, which is a FTP command from UNIX used to list the contents of directories. If UNIX style is selected, the ls (and dir) command gives you a file list with permissions, ownership, file size, file type, and creation date. If your users are more comfortable with a UNIX type operating system such as Linux, BSD, or Solaris, consider using a UNIX directory listing style. It does not change anything else related to your FTP site. For more information on FTP as a client, see Chapter 13.

Virtual Directories

If you want to share files in a specific directory, you don't have to copy them to the FTP server home directory. You can set it up a virtual directory. You won't have to move your files. To create a virtual directory in the IIS console, highlight your Default FTP Site. Click Action ➤ New ➤ Virtual Directory to start the Virtual Directory Creation Wizard, and then click Next to continue. This takes you to the Virtual Directory Alias page shown in Figure 28.29, where you can enter the virtual directory name of your choice. Just remember the name that you use.

FIGURE 28.29

Setting up a Virtual Directory alias

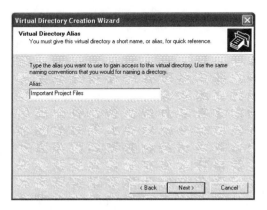

Click Next to continue. Enter the path to the directory to the files you want to put on the FTP server, and then click next to continue. This takes you to the Access Permissions page shown in Figure 28.30, where you can set Read and Write permissions on your new virtual directory.

FIGURE 28.30

Setting up permissions on a Virtual Directory

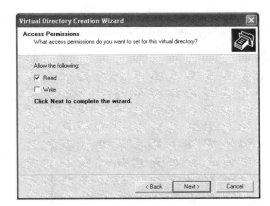

While you need to select Read permissions to let FTP users read the contents of your new virtual directory, remember that Write permissions may be a security risk. Click Next to continue, then click Finish to complete the Virtual Directory Creation Wizard.

Before you can use your new virtual directory, you need to create a "mirror" as a subdirectory of your FTP home directory. The default FTP home directory as shown in Figure 28.28 is C:\Inetpub\ ftproot. Navigate to this directory in Explorer and create a new folder with the same name as your virtual directory alias. Don't add any files to this folder. The FTP server automatically mirrors the files through your virtual directory.

Now you're ready to use the new virtual directory. Figure 28.31 illustrates a FTP session using the virtual directory shown in Figure 28.29 (Important Project Files).

FIGURE 28.31

Accessing a Virtual Directory

```
Command Prompt - ftp laptop2
Secret FTP Site
226 Transfer complete.
ftp: 129 bytes received in 0.00Seconds 129000.00Kbytes/sec.
ftp> cd "important project files"
250 CWD command successful.
ftp> ls
200 PORT command successful.
150 Opening ASCII mode data connection for file list.
2981chs to Michael.zip
Chapter 15
Chapter 16
Chapter 17
Chapter 19
Chapter 25
Chapter 26
Chapter 27
Chapter 28
fastboot-winxp.doc
high end chs revision plan a.doc
MastWinXP Pro revision plan a.doc
MastWinXP Pro revision plan.doc
snif.conf
226 Transfer complete.
ftp: 251 bytes received in 0.00Seconds 251000.00Kbytes/sec.
ftp>
```

Configuring the SMTP Server

Outgoing e-mail uses the Simple Mail Transfer Protocol (SMTP). Most home users send e-mail through the SMTP facilities provided by their ISP. However, the ISP's SMTP server may not always be available. The standard Microsoft application for large organizations that need an outgoing e-mail server is known as Microsoft Exchange.

However, with the SMTP server included with IIS, you may not need Microsoft Exchange to handle outgoing e-mail. This service already provides what you need for small-scale systems. Of course, if you're satisfied with the outgoing e-mail service provided by your ISP, you should uninstall or deactivate this service instead.

If you want to set up SMTP on your IIS console, highlight Default SMTP Virtual Server. Click Action ➤ Properties to open the Default SMTP Virtual Server Properties window shown in Figure 28.32.

FIGURE 28.32

Setting up a SMTP virtual server

NOTE   *Although it does support the SMTP Server service, Windows XP Professional is* not *designed to be a fully functional e-mail server. Use another product, such as Microsoft Exchange Server, for proper handling of e-mail.*

Basic SMTP Configuration

You should see the information associated with the General tab of the Default SMTP Virtual Server Properties window. If you've studied the properties associated with configuring a Web or FTP server, these settings should look familiar by now. Otherwise, here is a brief description of the settings associated with the General tab:

IP Address: Allows you to specify the IP address associated with the SMTP server. If you need to set a TCP port other than the default of 25, click Advanced.

Limit number of connections to: Permits you to limit the number of users who connect simultaneously to this SMTP server. Remember, this is also subject to the 10-connection limit associated with Windows XP Professional.

Connection time-out (minutes): Closes a connection after the specified period of inactivity.

Enable logging: Begins the logging process, based on the same log formats described earlier when configuring an IIS Web server. The Properties button allows you to configure details of what is actually logged.

Access

There are a number of ways to limit access to a SMTP server on IIS. Click the Access tab to view the four basic categories of controlling access as shown in Figure 28.33. The only item that you must configure to get SMTP to work for you is based on the Relay restrictions.

FIGURE 28.33

Controlling access to
a SMTP virtual
server

Access Control: Allows you to set up different forms of authentication for users who want access to your SMTP server. These include anonymous access, basic authentication with clear-text passwords, and access with some forms of encryption.

Secure Communication: Lets you add a server certificate to your SMTP server. If you click Certificate, you start the Web Server Certificate Wizard.

Connection Control: Permits you to set up a list of allowed (or prohibited) computers by their fully qualified domain names or IP addresses.

Relay Restrictions: Allows you to identify computers that are allowed to use this SMTP server. This is the only item under access which you must reconfigure to let users on your network use this server. Click Relay to open the Relay Restrictions window. Select the Only the List Below option, then click Add. This opens the Computer window shown in Figure 28.34. Click Single computer and add the IP address of your computer. Alternatively, click Group of computers and add the Subnet address and Subnet mask for your computer. Click OK. The result should be shown in the Relay Restrictions window, similar to what you see in Figure 28.35. For more information on IP addressing, see Chapter 16.

FIGURE 28.34

Adding computers
to a SMTP server

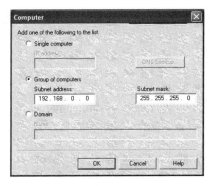

FIGURE 28.35

The list of comput-
ers allowed to use
your SMTP server

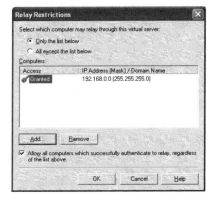

Messages

There are a number of ways to regulate messages on a SMTP server on IIS. Click the Messages tab
to view the message control options as shown in Figure 28.36. These options include:

FIGURE 28.36

Controlling message
information

Limit Message Size to (KB): Specifies the maximum allowed message size. The minimum limit is 1KB. If your users send HTML enabled e-mail or attachments of any size, you'll need much larger limits.

Limit Session Size to (KB): Notes the maximum amount of data that a user is allowed to send through the SMTP server during each connection.

Limit Number of Messages per Connection to: Creates a limit on the number of e-mails that can be sent per connection.

Limit Number of Recipients per Message to: Sets a maximum number of e-mail addresses for each message.

Send Copy of Non Delivery Report to: Specifies an additional e-mail address for undeliverable e-mails, such as those sent to an unavailable e-mail address.

Badmail Directory: Notes the directory with undeliverable e-mails, based on the limits shown under the Delivery tab.

Delivery

There are a number of ways to manage the delivery of messages on a SMTP server on IIS. Click the Delivery tab to view outbound and local options as shown in Figure 28.37. These options are required because not all attempts to deliver an e-mail actually work:

FIGURE 28.37

Controlling delivery methods

Outbound: Applies to e-mail addresses on external servers. If your SMTP server has trouble delivering a message, it will try again several times. By default, if a message is not delivered the first time, the server tries again in 15 minutes. If the message isn't delivered the second time, it tries again 30 minutes later, and so on, until the time specified as the Expiration timeout. The Delay notification specifies the wait time before the SMTP server tells the sender that there is a problem.

Local: Applies to e-mail addresses on a local server. The Delay notification and Expiration time-out settings work in the same way as for Outbound settings.

Outbound Security: Specifies authentication that is sent to external servers.

Outbound Connections: Limits the number of simultaneous external connections.

Advanced: Details the routing options for external messages.

LDAP Routing

The Lightweight Directory Assistance Protocol (LDAP) allows you to use a specific type of server to help identify e-mail recipients. Normally, LDAP isn't required to find an e-mail address, and therefore isn't enabled by default. Click the LDAP Routing tab to view relevant options, as shown in Figure 28.38.

FIGURE 28.38

Controlling message information

If you Enable LDAP routing, you can specify more information about the LDAP server:

Server: Notes the name of the server with the LDAP database.

Schema: Lists the type of directory service, which may be associated with an Active Directory domain, a Site Server/Commerce Server directory, or an Exchange mailbox service.

Binding: Specifies authentication method.

Domain: Lists the domain, if account and password information has to be sent to access the database.

User Name: Notes the name required to log into the database.

Password: Adds the authentication password for the database.

Base: Specifies a naming context.

Security

This is the simplest property associated with the SMTP virtual server. It establishes the list users allowed to act as SMTP virtual server operators. By default, the Administrators group is part of this list. If you need to add additional users, click the Security tab, then click Add to add users.

Troubleshooting IIS

As discussed in Chapter 25, troubleshooting is an exercise in checking the simplest causes first. You've read about the three services associated with IIS. If you have a problem with any of these services, the simplest causes relate to:

Installation: Make sure that the service in question is actually installed.

Activity: Check the service to make sure that it's actually started.

Implementation: Stop and start a service. That is often all that is required to implement any recent configuration changes to a particular service.

You can even go so far as to uninstall and reinstall a service. Assuming that you've backed up a good configuration, you can safely uninstall and reinstall a service. Then you can test the original setup, make any necessary changes, and restore the service. Restoring an existing configuration is fairly easy. In the IIS console, highlight the name of the server, and then click Action ➤ All Tasks ➤ Backup/Restore Configuration.

NOTE *For more information on backing up an IIS console configuration, see the section earlier in this chapter on Basic Configuration Management.*

Log Files

If a service is working, you can get more information on what is happening from the log file that you've set up for the service. Log files are available and are easily configurable for all of the IIS services.

For example, assume you're looking at a lot of activity on your network interfaces, and you know that nobody on your LAN is accessing your Intranet site. If you're collecting the right kind of data, log files can help you diagnose the problem. For example, look at the following excerpt from a Web log file:

```
00:29:12 10.39.52.112 - W3SVC1 MainServer GET /private.htm
```

This tells you that at 12:29 A.M., someone using IP address 10.39.52.112 and no defined username, accessed the server named `MainServer`, and accessed the `private.htm` file from your Web site home directory. Assume you don't expect users to access the `private.htm` file outside of regular work hours.

But remember, the entries in a log file are based on GMT. If the IP address is assigned to one of your offices on the West Coast of the US, the access attempt was made at 4:29 P.M. PST, which is probably just the end of their workday. In this case, your troubleshooting through your log files explained the unknown problem.

Remember, you can configure the IIS Web server to collect a lot of different kinds of information that can help you diagnose other problems.

Summary

This chapter addressed the three basic services that you can set up and configure with Internet Information Server (IIS): Web service, FTP service, and SMTP service. IIS and associated services are easy to install through the Add or Remove Programs link in Control Panel. Although Windows XP Professional limits the number of connections to your IIS services to 10, this is still a good test bed for these services.

It's easy to configure IIS through its own MMC snap-in, the IIS console. You can use it to monitor local or remote services. Once set, the configuration can be readily backed up and restored.

Web site configuration is a complex enterprise; the properties for the service affect the properties for the Web site. Configurable settings include ISAPI filters, directory locations, default documents, security, HTTP headers, custom HTTP error messages, logging, and server extensions.

FTP site configuration is a bit less complex. Configurable settings include connection control, logging, security, status messages, and directory settings. You can even customize the site for UNIX users.

You can even configure a mail server on Windows XP Professional, known as a SMTP server. As with FTP, you can configure connection control, logging, security, and directory settings. You can also manage the size of information sent by your users, manage delivery issues, and use LDAP access to identify some types of e-mail recipients.

Despite the complexity of IIS, troubleshooting is easy. Whenever you make a change, just restart the applicable server. Make sure all the components are there. And you can use the log files that you configured for each service to diagnose most problems.

Appendix A

Web Publishing with Windows XP Professional

THIS APPENDIX DISCUSSES HOW to publish information to the Web. The material isn't difficult (or even long), but there are three questions you need to consider: First, what will you publish? Second, where will you publish it? And third, how will you get it there?

This appendix covers the following topics:

◆ Understanding copyright issues involved in publishing to the Web

◆ Performing quality control

◆ Deciding where to publish your material

◆ Publishing material to the Web

What Will You Publish?

The first question is what you're going to publish. You'll have your own answer to this question, of course—anything from your family photos to your political opinions, from your company's employee directory to your company's compensation and benefits policies.

But before you publish anything, you *must* consider one issue: copyright. And you really ought to consider another issue: quality control. This section discusses those issues.

Understanding Copyright Issues

Before you publish any material to the Web, make sure you can legally do so. This means either understanding the basics of copyright law or consulting a lawyer. Three guesses as to which is less expensive.

Right. So here's an executive summary:

◆ If you created an original work yourself, you hold the copyright to it. For example, if you take an original digital photo, write an original story, or compose an original song, you hold the copyright to it. (If the work isn't original, you've probably infringed copyright. For example, taking a digital photo of someone else's work is unlikely to create an original work.) You can post that work to the Web if you want. (And you can try to defend your copyright against anyone who infringes it.)

◆ As the copyright holder, you have five main rights to the work:

  ◆ The Reproduction Right (making copies of the work)

  ◆ The Distribution Right (distributing it)

  ◆ The Modification Right or Derivative Works Right (creating other works based on the work)

  ◆ The Public Performance Right (performing or transmitting the work)

  ◆ The Public Display Right (displaying the work in a public place)

  You can exercise these rights yourself or grant them to other people. For example, the author of a book often grants to a publisher the Reproduction Right and the Distribution Right, so that the publisher can print copies of the book and distribute them.

◆ If someone else created the work, you probably need to get explicit permission to publish or distribute it.

◆ Some works are in the *public domain,* a notional area that contains all works that are not protected by copyright and which you can therefore publish and distribute freely. Some works are never protected by copyright, because they're not copyrightable due to their nature (for example, facts, URLs, and names are not copyrightable), because they're not copyrighted (for example, U.S. government publications under the authorship of the federal government are not copyrighted), or because the creator of the work has chosen to put it in the public domain. Other works go out of copyright because the copyright has expired or has been lost.

WARNING   *Some Web site hosting services use their Terms and Conditions to claim copyright of any original material you post. Read the small print before you post anything on these services.*

Those are the bare bones of what you need to know about copyright to avoid committing copyright violations left, right, and center. Here are some resources for understanding copyright:

◆ Brad Templeton's *10 Big Myths About Copyright Explained* site (`www.templetons.com/brad/copymyths.html`) debunks the biggest myths about copyright.

◆ The U.S. Copyright Office (`www.loc.gov/copyright`) offers a number of resources on copyright, including the Copyright FAQ (`www.loc.gov/copyright/faq.html`) and a Copyright Basics section (`www.loc.gov/copyright/circs/circ1.html`).

◆ The Copyright Clearance Center (`www.copyright.com`) provides a central location for getting permission to reproduce many copyrighted works. (For others, you may need to contact the creator of the work directly.)

◆ Chapter 2 of *Internet Piracy Exposed* by Guy Hart-Davis (Sybex, 2001) discusses copyright law in the context of what you can and cannot legally do with material on the Internet.

Controlling Quality

As you'll have noticed if you've spent more than a few hours surfing, the Web already suffers from a severe lack of quality control. You'll improve your karma if you don't add to this problem.

Historically, the high cost of publishing a work has acted as a strong incentive for the publisher to ensure the work is of a high enough quality that it will appeal to its intended audience. For example, if a publisher publishes a book that's so bad (or on so unappealing a topic) that nobody buys it, they lose money. If a record company issues an unlistenable CD, they're unlikely to achieve significant sales. And if an artist paints wretched pictures, the chances of their finding a market are slim.

By contrast, the Web is more or less a free-for-all. The cost of publishing to the Web can be extremely low (or can be nothing): you need do little more than create files and post them on a Web site, and anyone with an Internet connection and Web browser can access them. If they don't like what they find at your site, they probably won't return, but the cost to you remains minimal.

But if you want people to look at what you post, make sure that its quality is at least acceptable:

◆ Don't post just anything (or *everything*) you have. Select the best items and post them. If they draw acclaim (or rapture), consider posting more.

◆ Spell-check any text you post. If your grammar isn't the greatest, get someone competent to check it for you. Involve an editor or proofreader if you're looking to be professional and persuasive. (For editors and proofreaders, the unedited and unproofed content on the Web can be painful and gratifying in that it illustrates the need for their often unseen and unsung services.)

◆ Use graphics in moderation—and make sure they contribute to your site. Gratuitous graphics grate on the visitor nearly as badly as artless alliteration.

◆ Produce any audio material to a reasonable standard. Your band's live tapes might not make the cut unmixed; mixed, they might.

◆ Produce any video material to a higher standard. Because downloading video is a serious investment of time and bandwidth over any but the very fastest connections, you'll need to give people a good reason to download your video—and try not to disappoint them.

Above all, beware technologies that make it too easy to post material to the Web. Just because you *can* publish material directly to the Web doesn't mean that you should; in fact, it often means just about the opposite. For example, Windows XP's Scanner and Camera Wizard offers to copy pictures you download from a digital camera or images you acquire via a scanner directly to the Web. In most cases, this is a very bad idea:

◆ Even if you've edited the photos on the digital camera ruthlessly so that you're sure you're not downloading any duds, you may need to crop the pictures, change their size or resolution, or otherwise manipulate them before posting them to the Web.

◆ Unless you hold the copyright to the documents you are scanning, or the documents are in the public domain or otherwise not copyrighted, you will need to get permission before publishing them to the Web.

Similarly, Windows Movie Maker includes a feature for publishing a movie to a Web server. This feature is more reasonable, in that Windows Movie Maker lets you preview the movie before you publish it. All the same, think twice before uploading huge amounts of scantily reviewed material to the Web.

Where Will You Publish Your Content?

Once you've established that you've got content that you think is worth posting, you need somewhere to publish it. In most cases, your choice will be between your ISP and a free Web hosting service such as MSN.

One of the factors you should evaluate when choosing an ISP is how much Web space they give you and how much traffic they allow your site as part of your monthly fee (or free, as the case may be). Make sure that the ISP allows you plenty of space for as much material as you'll need to post at once (you can always delete some of the fatter files to make room for new material) and that they'll sell you more space and bandwidth for a modest fee should the need arise.

How Will You Publish Your Content?

Windows XP offers two ways of getting material onto your Web site: creating it offline and using FTP to transfer a copy of it, and using Web Digital Authoring and Versioning (WebDAV) to create the files directly online.

Using FTP

The standard way to get material onto your Web site is to create and assemble the material offline and then upload it to the Web site via FTP. If you're uploading a new version of a page, the upload overwrites the existing page. You can spend as long as you need creating and saving the content, and because the files you're working with are stored on a local drive, you can access them at full speed.

You can transfer material to and from an FTP site using three main methods:

◆ Create a network place for the site and access it via the My Network Places folder.

◆ Access the site from Internet Explorer and create a favorite for it.

◆ Use an FTP client to access the site.

We'll discuss these methods in a moment or two. But first, WebDAV.

Using WebDAV

If your ISP supports WebDAV, you can use the new and snappier method of getting material onto your Web site, which is to create it or edit it in situ by using any program that can save directly to a Web folder or to an FTP site.

This method can simplify the process of making minor edits to a page and seeing the effects of the changes. But there are two problems:

◆ First, because even the fastest residential Internet connection is hundreds of times slower than the data-transfer speeds inside even a modest PC, this method makes for painfully slow opening and saving of documents. If there's a problem with the Internet connection, the document you're working on can become corrupted. If this is the only copy you have of the document, you may lose everything in it. Figure A.1 shows the Windows—Delayed Write Failed dialog box, which gives an example of such unwelcome news.

FIGURE A.1

Saving files directly to your Web site doesn't always work—and when it fails, you can lose the document involved.

◆ Second, most ISPs cache Web pages so that they can deliver them more frequently. This means that changes you make to your site may not be propagated through the network until the cache is refreshed. This refresh may take anything from a few minutes to (in extreme cases) a day or two.

These two problems mean that the second way of adding content to a Web site is best left for intranet situations, where you can access the site at full network speeds and perhaps manipulate the refresh process yourself.

Because Windows XP implements WebDAV, XP-aware programs can save directly to FTP sites and Web folders. For example, the ability (mentioned earlier in this appendix) of the Scanner and Camera Wizard and Windows Movie Maker to save material directly to the Web comes courtesy of WebDAV. Similarly, Microsoft Office programs such as Word and Excel can save directly to Web folders—all you need do (in theory) is use the My Network Places list in the Save As dialog box to select the network place, and you're away.

Using Network Places to Access an FTP Site or Web Folder

Network places provides the easiest built-in way to access an FTP site or Web folder for transferring files. A network place essentially puts a pretty face on copying to an FTP site or a Web folder by disguising it to look like a folder on your hard drive. You'll notice the difference, because when you save or copy a file to a network folder, the operation takes place at the speed of the your Internet connection rather than at normal blazing computer speeds. But otherwise, the operation is seamless and almost effortless.

CREATING A NEW NETWORK PLACE

To create a new network place, you use the Add Network Place Wizard. Follow these steps:

1. Choose Start ➢ My Network Places to open the My Network Places folder.

TIP   If your Start menu doesn't include a My Network Places link, choose Start ➢ My Computer, and then click the My Network Places link in the Other Places list in the My Computer window.

2. Click the Add a Network Place link in the Network Tasks list to start the Add Network Place Wizard, which displays its Welcome screen.

NOTE   *You can also start the Add Network Place Wizard by clicking the Network Place or Site link in the Map Network Drive dialog box (choose Tools ➤ Map Network Drive).*

3. Click the Next button. The Wizard displays the Where Do You Want to Create This Network Place? screen (shown in Figure A.2).

FIGURE A.2

On the Where Do You Want to Create This Network Place? screen of the Add Network Place Wizard, choose the service you want to use.

4. In the list box, select the Web host or local network location you want to use. In the figure, your choices are limited to MSN Communities or Choose Another Network Location. The next sections discuss these choices.

Creating a Network Place on MSN

To create a network place on MSN, select the MSN Communities item on the Where Do You Want To Create This Network Place? screen of the Add Network Place Wizard. Click Next, and the Wizard walks you through the process of creating a place called My Communities on MSN. This place is linked to your Passport identity.

Creating a Network Place in Another Network Location

To create a network place in another network location, take the following steps:

1. On the Where Do You Want to Create This Network Place? screen of the Add Network Place Wizard, select the Choose Another Network Location item.

2. Click the Next button. The Wizard displays the What Is the Address of This Network Place? screen (shown in Figure A.3).

FIGURE A.3

On the What Is the Address of This Network Place? screen of the Add Network Place Wizard, specify the folder or FTP site containing the network place.

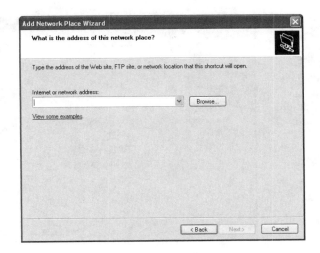

3. In the Internet or Network Address text box, enter the location of the network folder, Web folder, or FTP site. For most purposes, you'll want to use one of these three formats:

Network Place	Format
Shared folder on network	`\\server\folder`
Web folder	`http://server/folder`
FTP site	`ftp://ftp.domainname.domain`

4. Click the Next button. The Wizard checks the type of authentication required and displays the appropriate dialog box:

   ◆ For an FTP site, the Wizard displays the User Name and Password screen (shown in Figure A.4 with the Log On Anonymously check box cleared). If you log on anonymously to this network place, leave the Log On Anonymously check box selected, as it is by default. If you need to supply a username and password (as is more likely), clear the Log On Anonymously check box and enter your username in the User Name text box. Click the Next button.

   ◆ For a Web folder, the Wizard displays the Enter Network Password dialog box (shown in Figure A.5). Enter your username and password. Select the Save This Password in Your Password List check box if you think it advisable. Then click the OK button.

5. The Wizard displays the What Do You Want to Name This Place? screen (shown in Figure A.6).

6. Enter the name for the network place. This name is for your benefit, so make it descriptive. By default, Windows suggests a variation on the address for the network place, so you'll often want to change it.

FIGURE A.4

On the User Name and Password screen of the Add Network Place Wizard, choose whether to log on anonymously or specify your username.

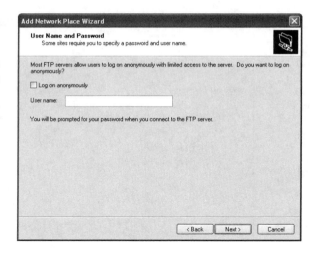

FIGURE A.5

In the Enter Network Password dialog box, enter your username and password for the Web folder.

FIGURE A.6

On the What Do You Want to Name This Place? screen of the Add Network Place Wizard, specify the name you want to use for the network place.

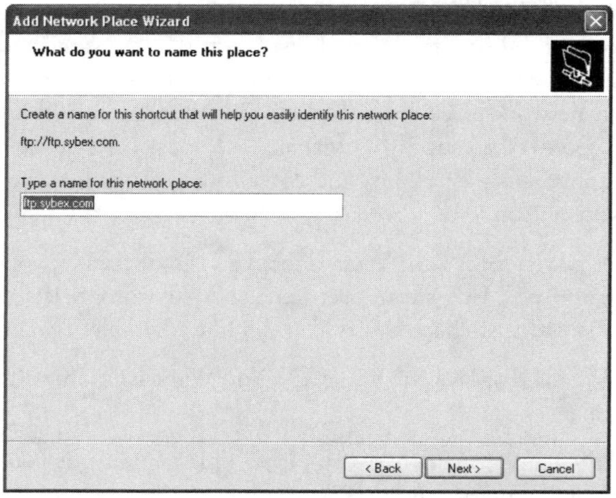

7. Click the Next button. The Wizard displays the Completing the Add Network Place Wizard screen.

8. If you want to open the network place immediately, leave the Open This Network Place When I Click Finish check box selected. Otherwise, clear this check box.

9. Click the Finish button. The Add Network Place Wizard closes itself and creates the network place.

ACCESSING A NETWORK PLACE

Once you've created a network place, you can access it from Explorer by using the My Network Places window (choose Start ➤ My Network Places).

To open a network place, double-click it. If you saved your password for the network place, Windows opens the network place at the full speed of your Internet connection. If the network place is on MSN, Windows automatically logs you in to the network place using your .NET Passport.

If the network place is an FTP site, Windows displays the Log On As dialog box (shown in Figure A.7). Enter the password. Select the Save Password check box if you want Windows to store your password so that you can access this network place without interruption next time. (Remember that storing a password compromises your security.) Then click the Log On button.

FIGURE A.7

For an FTP site, you need to enter your password in the Log On As dialog box.

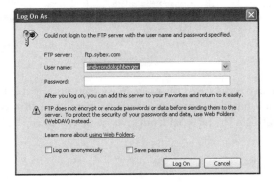

You can add files to the network place by using regular Explorer techniques. For example, you can drag files from another folder and drop them on the icon for a network place to copy them to that network place.

FTP via Internet Explorer

You can also use Internet Explorer for FTP. There's no particular advantage to using Internet Explorer when you can use a network place instead, but Internet Explorer works well enough to be worth considering as an alternative.

To transfer files via FTP using Internet Explorer, take the following steps:

1. Choose Start ➤ Internet. Windows launches Internet Explorer.

2. In the Address bar, enter the FTP address, username, and password (if you choose) using the following format:

```
ftp://username[:password]@ftpserver/url
```

3. Click the Go button or press the Enter key. If you specified your password (and got it right), Windows connects to the FTP server and displays the folder. If you chose not to specify your password, Windows displays the Log On As dialog box, in which you can enter your password and choose whether to save it.

TIP   Once you've connected to the FTP site, create a favorite for it so that you can access it quickly in the future.

FTP via an FTP Client

Network places provide smooth access to Web folders and FTP sites, but for more powerful FTP capabilities, you may want to invest in a graphical FTP client such as WS_FTP Pro (`www.ipswitch.com`) or CuteFTP (`www.globalscape.com`).

NOTE   Windows includes an FTP client built in—but unfortunately it's a command-line client, which means that in order to use it, you need to use Unix-style commands. If you know these commands, launch the FTP client by choosing Start ➢ Run, entering ftp in the Open text box in the resulting Run dialog box, and clicking the OK button. If you don't know these commands and don't want to learn them, stick with Internet Explorer or a graphical FTP client.

Summary

This short appendix has discussed the main considerations in publishing material to the Web: what you can legally publish and the importance of performing quality control; where to publish your material; and how to get the material from your computer to the Web host.

Appendix B

Connecting to Novell NetWare Networks

NOVELL'S NETWARE RETAINS ITS popularity mainly because of its Novell Directory Services (NDS). NDS is a redundant, scalable, mature distributed directory service that eases administrative tasks and provides unified authentication. Microsoft provides a NetWare client to connect Windows XP Professional to NetWare servers—albeit a very basic client. In this appendix, I'll discuss the capabilities of Microsoft's Client Service for NetWare (CSNW) and show you how to install it.

- ◆ Understanding the difference between NDS and bindery-based services

- ◆ Using Novell administration utilities

- ◆ Running NetWare and Windows XP Professional together

- ◆ Printing to Novell printers

- ◆ Enabling long filename support on the Novell server

- ◆ Choosing a Novell client solution

- ◆ Installing the Novell client

- ◆ Configuring the Novell client

CSNW Features

CSNW provides the following features:

Novell script processing   CSNW processes the system and individual login scripts created by the network administrator of the Novell network.

Seamless File and Print Services   Drive letters can be mapped to NetWare volumes either through login scripts or by using any of the mapping utilities in Windows XP Professional. These volumes appear just like a local drive, and you can continue using long filenames on

NetWare mapped drives since NetWare supports long filenames. You can print to NetWare print queues using conventional UNC naming, or you can capture a queue to an LPT port using standard Windows XP Professional tools. NetWare servers are *browsable* via the Network Explorer views, which makes it even easier to find NetWare resources, map network drives, or use printer resources.

Bindery and/or NDS authentication   Versions of NetWare prior to 4.*x* used a server-centric database, called the *bindery*, for authentication. NetWare versions 4.*x* and later still provide bindery emulation; however, the preferred method is to authenticate with NDS. CSNW can use either of these methods to connect to a NetWare file server.

WARNING   *As mentioned earlier, CSNW is a very basic client for connections to NetWare servers. Microsoft has not made a strong effort to update CSNW since it was first released for Windows NT 4. A major drawback of CSNW is its lack of IP support. NetWare administrators will be forced to load the IPX protocol on servers that contain replicas or partitions of the NDS database and any other server providing services to a Windows XP Professional using CSNW. Additionally, Windows XP for 64-bit processors will not support the Client Service for NetWare because of its dependency on the IPX protocol. If you must use IP as the protocol or if you need a feature-rich client to connect to NetWare, Novell will provide a 32/64-bit client. As of this writing, the Novell client for Windows XP is not available. However, version 4.8 for Windows 2000 can be installed on a Windows XP system, and I used and tested it to write this appendix.*

Before we look at the procedure for installing the Client Service for NetWare, let's look at the versions of NetWare to which you may have to connect—NetWare 3, 4, and 5. Much of our focus will be on versions 4 and beyond since Netware 3.*x* is no longer a mainstream network operating system and was discontinued by Novell in October 2000. I'll also discuss how you can use printer resources on NetWare servers, and then I'll talk about utilizing login scripts and mapping drives to NetWare servers.

Novell Directory Services Versus Bindery-Based Servers

NDS and bindery services are both directory services. All network operating systems contain a directory that stores user IDs, passwords, and rights to folders at a minimum. The NDS Directory is much more complicated than the Bindery directory and will be the subject of most of this section, which will serve as only a primer. Having an overview of NDS will help you understand the parameters you'll need to enter to connect to NDS later when you install CSNW or a Novell-supplied client.

The hierarchy of NDS is similar to that of Windows 2000 Server's Active Directory (AD). The NDS hierarchy or directory tree consists of network resources known as NDS *objects*. NDS can be compared to the directory structure on your PC's hard disk. On your PCs, you organize your data by creating folders off the root directory, and you insert data files into folders. NDS is organized similarly into *containers* and *leaf* objects, respectively. NDS containers can contain other container objects, or they can contain leaf objects that represent network resources, such as servers, printers, users, and groups. All objects within NDS contain attributes or properties. The combination of all of these attributes within the directory tree is called the *schema*. The schema can be extended, so third-party application developers can extend object attributes and create completely new objects. Therefore, NDS can be more than just a directory for authentication and permissions. It can also be used to provide applications and network services. For example, it can be used to distribute applications, control hardware inventory, and monitor applications that require tight security such as a VPN (Virtual Private Network) and e-commerce applications.

NDS containers are organizational folders that are frequently designed to look like company locations and business units. At the top is the root object. Typically the root contains only a few organizational objects called the Country (C) or Organization (O) objects. The Country object is optional, but every tree must contain an Organization object, which is typically the company name. Beneath the Organization object are containers known as organizational units (OUs). An OU can contain other OUs or it can contain leaf objects. A leaf object is often referred to by its *common name* (CN). It is important to know these objects and their abbreviations when you configure CSNW and the Novell client.

Copies of the NDS database, called replicas, are usually distributed between multiple file servers to load balance and for redundancy purposes. Replicas are synchronized so that every server contains an up-to-date version of the same informational database. Furthermore, NDS can be partitioned at various layers of the tree, so a server might contain only a portion of the database or a part of the tree. This capability is important for file servers in remote locations across wide area networks that need to conserve bandwidth and preserve CPU usage. In organizations that have many servers, some are usually dedicated to NDS. NDS can burn quite a number of processing cycles since it provides authentication services and runs a number of processes including replication.

When you install the first NetWare NDS server, you need to think through the NDS design and implementation carefully. Scrutinize all logistics, including standards-based naming conventions for all objects and the placement of OUs within the directory. A directory that has not been thought out often contains random authentication problems, and replication performance will suffer. Fortunately, Novell provides plenty of tools to resolve these issues.

A NetWare 3 server holds its security information in a security database called the *bindery*. The bindery method of security views each server as an individual entity, and the security that you assign to various directories is kept independently on each server. The bindery is a flat database, meaning it has no hierarchy and is not graphically viewed.

To illustrate the difference, assume that you have to build 100 user accounts on 5 NetWare servers and that each of the 100 users needs access to the 5 NetWare servers. In a NetWare 3 environment, you have to build 500 user accounts—one for each of the 100 users on each of the 5 servers. In a NetWare 4 or 5 environment, you have to build only 100 user accounts because all 5 servers are part of the same NDS tree; you have to log on to an NDS tree only once.

This difference is important to you at the Windows XP Professional level because the information you'll provide to configure CSNW is different for bindery servers than it is for NDS. You'll need this information for troubleshooting purposes, and you will need to understand what it is you are configuring!

Using Novell Administration Utilities

NetWare 3.*x* used various DOS-based utilities for administration. The primary utilities are called SYSCON and Pconsole. SYSCON, short for system configuration utility, is a DOS-based menu-driven program for creating users, groups, and login scripts and for managing accounting, setting directory permissions, and setting user restrictions. Pconsole, short for Printer Console, is also a DOS-based menu-driven program that allows you to create print queues and printers. You can also use a handful of other administrative utilities and many powerful command-line tools instead of these menu-driven applications. The following list shows them in simple alphabetic order:

Chkvol	Help	rconsole	settts
Colorpal	listdir	remove	slist
Dspace	Map	revoke	syscon
Fconsole	Ncopy	rights	tlist
Filer	Ndir	security	userlist
Flag	pconsole	send	volinfo
Flagdir	Psc	session	whoami
Grant	Pstat	setpass	

You must map a drive to the NetWare volume where these utilities are located in order to run them. Windows XP Professional will not run them correctly from a UNC path.

Most administrative tasks in NDS require just one tool, the NetWare Administrator (NWADMIN). NWADMIN is a graphical view of NDS that allows you to create organizational units; create users, printers, and groups; modify login scripts; and more. NWADMIN is similar to Windows XP's Microsoft Management Console (MMC) in that you can extend the capabilities of NWADMIN by "snapping-in" new administration tools. For example, you can snap-in Symantec's Norton AntiVirus (NAV) to administrate NAV on all your NetWare servers. You can launch NWADMIN only from a workstation (running Windows 9x, Windows NT, Windows 2000 Professional, or Windows XP Professional) attached to a NetWare server. However, Novell has released a new administration utility called ConsoleOne (see Figure B.1) that has many of the same features of NWADMIN and more.

ConsoleOne is a graphical tool for administering network resources, including NDS objects, schema, partitions, replicas, and NetWare servers. The real beauty of ConsoleOne is that it can be launched on the console of a Netware 5.x server or from a workstation. In the past, NetWare servers always required a workstation to begin administrative tasks. Now, you can walk right up to a server and begin adding users and setting permissions. This is particularly helpful in first time installations and smaller networks.

Another cool feature of ConsoleOne is its Web portal to NetWare servers that allows you to use some utilities and view the status of your NetWare file server as shown in Figure B.2. ConsoleOne is not fully baked, especially when running from a NetWare server. This means that not all of the utilities have been blended into ConsoleOne and you must use legacy tools, but it is Novell's intent that ConsoleOne be the complete tool for all administrative tasks, and it does show a lot of promise.

The bad news for people who want to use Windows XP Professional to manage their NetWare 5 network is that NWADMIN and ConsoleOne will not work with CSNW. NWADMIN and ConsoleOne require several Novell dynamic link libraries (DLLs) that are installed only when using Novell's client software. If you are serious about managing your NetWare environment from within Windows XP Professional, you should strongly consider downloading Novell's Client version 4.8 for Windows 2000 and Windows NT. Later in this appendix, I'll get into the special installation for this client that is required for Windows XP.

FIGURE B.1

ConsoleOne will be the one-stop administration tool for Netware 5 servers and beyond.

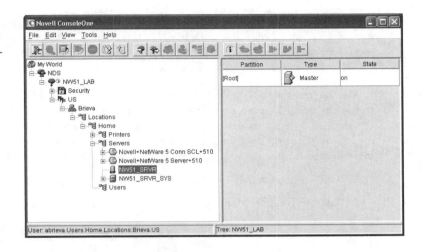

FIGURE B.2

The NetWare Web Portal accessible though ConsoleOne

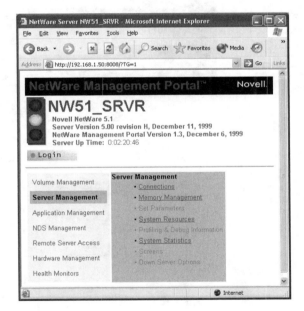

Accessing a NetWare Server

After you install the Client Service for NetWare (discussed in the "Configuring Windows XP Professional to Run in Parallel with NetWare" section of this appendix), you can access the resources of a NetWare 3 server as well as a NetWare 4 or 5 servers, as long as you have a valid login ID and password. The login scripts that reside on the Novell server will run even on your Windows XP Professional workstation, mapping your drives and capturing your printer ports.

NOTE *When Windows XP Professional starts up and the CSNW is installed, you will first be prompted for the standard Windows login ID and password. The user ID and password you enter are passed along to the CSNW. Therefore, the user ID that you enter must match the ID that has been created on the NetWare file server. This is another weakness of the CSNW and a reason for using the Novell client instead of CSNW.*

You can browse for NetWare servers, map network drives, and browse for network resources within the tree. Mapping a network drive is an easy way to use the same drive letter for common applications or to access shared data every time you log in to the network. You can map drives using the Map a Network Drive command that's available in every Explorer Window, or you can browse through the list of server volumes on any given server. To map a network drive, follow these steps:

1. Choose Start ➢ My Network Places to open the My Network Places window.

2. Choose Tools ➢ Map Network Drive to open the Map Network Drive dialog box:

3. Click Browse to open the Browse for Folder dialog box and view a list of network resources:

4. Double-click NetWare or Compatible Network to view all NetWare servers and NDS trees.

5. Double-click a server that you want to map a network drive to.

6. You can map a drive directly to a volume or you can expand a volume to map directly to a folder on the server. Select a folder and then click OK.

7. To make this a permanent mapped drive, click the Reconnect at Logon check box, and then click Finish.

Running NetWare and Windows Networking Together

The idea here is simple: Your office contains both a Windows server or servers (Windows NT, Windows 2000, and in the future, Windows .NET Server) and a NetWare server or servers. Many NetWare servers are still using the IPX/SPX protocol, and in most cases, Windows servers will be using TCP/IP. Windows XP Professional can easily resolve this problem because it can handle network clients and run multiple protocol stacks at the same time.

NOTE *A common belief in the networking world is that Microsoft operating systems use only NetBEUI and that NetWare uses only IPX/SPX. Today you will typically find that both are coexisting quite well using TCP/IP to communicate. To communicate, matching protocols must be running on the server and on your Windows XP Professional client configurations.*

WARNING *Although both operating systems can use TCP/IP to communicate over the network, the Microsoft Client Services for NetWare will work only with the NWLink IPX/SPX protocol installed. Here again, Microsoft is fostering the belief that NetWare only uses IPX/SPX for network communication.*

Configuring Windows XP Professional to Run in Parallel with NetWare

Running Windows XP Professional in parallel with NetWare requires that the Client Service for NetWare be installed on the Windows XP Professional machine. Installing the Client Service for NetWare is a straightforward procedure. Follow these steps:

1. Choose Start, right-click My Network Places, and choose Properties from the shortcut menu to open the Network Connections window.

2. Select Local Area Connection, and then in the Network Tasks bar, click the Change Settings of This Connection link to open the Local Area Connection Properties dialog box.

3. Click the Install button to open the Select Network Component Type dialog box.

4. Select Client from the list, and click Add to open the Select Network Client dialog box.

5. Double-click Client Service for NetWare to open the Local Area Connection Properties dialog box.

6. Click Install. Windows XP Professional copies the appropriate drivers to your system and makes changes to your Registry that enable the Client Service for NetWare to load the next time you start your system.

If you are loading the Client Service for NetWare and have not previously loaded the NWLink IPX/SPX–Compatible Transport protocol, this protocol will load automatically as you install the service. The Client Services for NetWare will not work at all without NWLink installed. If you disable NWLink, Windows XP Professional will automatically disable the Client Services for NetWare.

Normally, you do not need to modify the properties of NWLink. However, if there are multiple frame types on the same network, you may need to adjust the properties of NWLink. To change the properties of NWLink, follow these steps:

1. Select NWLINK IPX/SPX/NetBIOS Compatible Transport, and click the Properties button to open the Properties dialog box for this protocol:

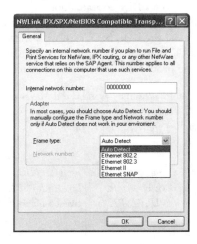

2. Select your preferred frame type from the Frame Type drop-down list.

3. Click OK to save your settings.

WARNING   *It is highly recommended that you not alter any other settings in the NWLink Properties dialog box. These refer to prior releases of Windows that were capable of emulating NetWare servers. Microsoft removed this capability in Windows 2000 and has not updated CSNW in quite some time.*

After you reboot the system, Windows XP Professional attempts to log on to Novell for the first time, as shown in Figure B.3.

FIGURE B.3

CSNW will prompt you to insert information the first time you attempt to log in to NetWare.

With the client software provided by Microsoft, you can either log on to a Novell 3 bindery by clicking the Preferred Server button or log on to an NDS tree by clicking the Default Tree and Context button. If you are going to log on to an NDS tree, you need to provide the context of your user object within the directory tree. Your context is a path to where your user login ID resides in the tree. You need to enter the path, beginning from where the user ID resides in the tree, all the way up the tree. The path is a series of container objects separated by periods. You should not provide the parameter codes before each option (that is, omit the o= and the cn=). This is where it becomes helpful to understand NDS as explained in the previous section, "NDS Versus Bindery-Based Services."

An example of entering context into CSNW is supplied in Figure B.4. In this case, the user ID ABRIEVA is a user object that resides in the organizational unit called *users*. Working your way up the tree, you can see that the OU=users is a child of OU=home, which is a child of OU=locations, which is a child of OU=Brieva, which is a child of OU=US.

FIGURE B.4

Configuring the
Client Service for
NetWare

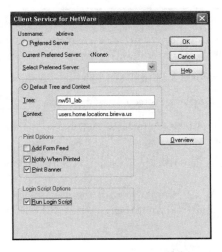

Figure B.5 displays the NetWare NDS administration tool, NWADMIN, and shows where the user object resides within the tree for this example. If you enter the context information incorrectly, you will get a dialog box telling you that you've entered the context wrong or it can't find a server. If you receive this message, you have not entered the correct context or the protocols on your Windows XP Professional do not match the protocols on the server. You can try to either re-enter the correct context or abandon the NDS authentication and continue logging in to Windows XP Professional.

The nature of being a client in a networked environment is that you can log on to one server one day and log on to another server on another day. If you are an administrator, you can switch between servers more frequently. You can change the NetWare server that you log on to with great ease. In Control Panel, you will notice the CSNW icon. By clicking this icon, you can adjust your settings and the NetWare servers or tree that you log on to. The dialog box is identical to that shown earlier in Figure B.4.

FIGURE B.5

A visual representation of where the user ID resides in this example

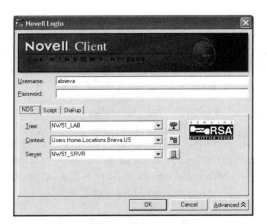

From this dialog box, you can specify or change the server, or you can log on to a NetWare NDS tree. In addition, you can set the print settings. The three options are as follows:

Add Form Feed   Adds a form feed to the end of each print job

Notify When Printed   Displays a screen message when your print job finishes printing

Print Banner   Adds a cover page to the beginning of each print job, specifying who printed the job and the date and time

Any settings that you make here will apply to any Novell print queue that this Windows XP Professional computer accesses.

The final option in CSNW determines whether the system login script that resides on the NetWare server will run. This feature will run either a NetWare 3.*x* login script or an NDS login script.

Printing to Novell Printers

You can connect to Novell printers in Windows XP Professional in a number of ways. I'll go over the two most common.

This first option may be necessary if you want to print directly to the printer. That is, this option does not perform a redirect to an LPT port and uses UNC conventions to find printer resources.

To connect to a NetWare print queue, follow these steps:

1. Choose Start ➤ Printers and Faxes to open the Printers and Faxes folder.

2. In the Printer Tasks bar, click the Add a Printer link to start the Add Printer Wizard.

3. At the Welcome screen, click Next to open the Local or Network Printer screen.

4. Click the A Network Printer or a Printer Attached to Another Computer option, and then click Next to open the Specify a Printer screen.

5. Click the Browse for a Printer option, and then click Next to open the Browse for Printer screen:

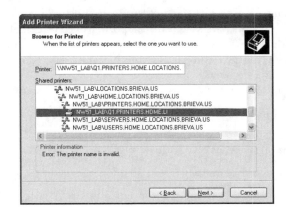

6. Double-click NetWare or Compatible Network to view a list of servers and NDS trees. Queues that reside in NDS require that you browse the NDS tree and know the location of the queue object within the tree. Bindery queues require you to know which server the queues reside on. In either case, work your way down the server or the NDS tree to locate the queue, and then click Next to open the Printer Selection screen.

7. Select the printer manufacturer and printer model.

8. Have the appropriate driver CD or disk ready, or know the location where the driver is stored. At the Printer Driver screen, insert the disk that contains the driver when prompted, and click OK.

9. Click Finish to complete the printer installation.

Alternatively, you can capture or redirect output that is destined for an LPT to a network printer. This option is easier, but it's not for everyone. Here's what you need to do:

1. Install your printer drivers as if they were being installed to your LPT1 port. Follow the instructions above to install the printer locally. Be sure that in the Local or Network Printer screen you choose the Local Printer Attached to This Computer option, and check the Automatically Detect and Install My Plug-and-Play check box.

2. Choose Start ➤ My Network Places to open the My Network Places folder.

3. From the Network Tasks bar, choose View Network Connections.

4. Double-click Netware or Compatible Network to display Netware Servers and NDS trees.

5. Double-click the Server icon to display a list of server resources, including print queues and server volumes.

6. Right-click the print queue, and select Capture Printer Port from the shortcut menu. Choose an LPT port to connect to, for example LPT1.

Enabling Long Filename Support on the Novell Server

NetWare requires you to enable long filename support on the NetWare servers prior to revision 5. NetWare 5 file servers have long name support enabled by default. Different revisions of NetWare require slightly different commands. It is not necessary to restart the server after entering these commands; however, this process will slow your NetWare server down dramatically. Make sure you perform these tasks after hours.

For versions of NetWare earlier than 4.10, follow these steps:

1. At the NetWare server prompt, type the following:

```
Load os2
add name space os2 to volume sys
```

(and to every volume where you want long name support)

2. Add the following to the startup.ncf file:

```
load os2
```

For versions of NetWare 4.11 and later, follow these steps:

1. At the NetWare server prompt, type the following:

```
Load long
add name space long to volume sys
```

(and to every volume where you want long name support)

2. Add the following to the startup.ncf file:

```
load long
```

Choosing a Novell Client Solution

I've already mentioned that the Novell 32-bit client solution has more features than CSNW and that it will resolve problems with TCP/IP connectivity and using NDS administration tools. Novell's client is a true 32-bit client, and eventually we will see a 64-bit version of the client.

NOTE *As of this writing, the Novell client is not available for Windows XP. However, version 4.8 of the Novell client for Windows NT/Windows 2000 can be used with Windows XP. In fact, if you've upgraded to Windows XP Professional and had a prior release of the Windows NT/Windows 2000 client already loaded, the Windows XP Professional will also upgrade your Novell client to version 4.8. If you performed a fresh installation of Windows XP Professional or you are just adding the NetWare client now, you'll need to use the special instructions in the following paragraphs to load the Novell Client to Windows XP Professional.*

Novell has a package of network tools called Zero Effort Networking, or *Z.E.N.works*. Z.E.N.works gives you complete control over desktop and user management from the NetWare 4 and 5 environments. It's actually similar in many ways to Microsoft's Zero Administration Windows (ZAW) initiative in that it uses policies and login scripts to manage users and computers. But in the case of Z.E.N.works, the policies are being applied based on NDS objects across all client platforms, not just one version of Windows.

The full version of Z.E.N.works provides several useful help desk functions as well, including a ticketing system for reporting problems and remote control ability. The version that is supplied with NetWare 5 is the "light" version, which includes everything except the help desk tools and is supported by all the current Novell client platforms.

Installing the Novell Client

Before you even think about installing the Novell Client, make sure that CSNW is not already installed on your Windows XP Professional setup. Such an installation causes horrible instability in Windows XP and should be avoided at all costs. If CSNW is installed, remove it and reboot your computer.

NOTE *Always look for the latest Novell client available. By the time you read this, the Novell client for Windows XP may have become available. Windows clients are available on Novell's website at* `www.novell.com/download`.

The Novell client for Windows NT/Windows 2000 requires a slightly modified installation. If you attempt to use Novell's conventional method of installing the client, using NWSetup, Windows XP Professional will warn you that the client is not compatible with Windows XP and abort the installation. To get around this, follow these steps:

1. After downloading the client, double-click the executable and extract the contents to a subdirectory on your computer.

2. Click Start, right-click My Network Places, and choose Properties from the shortcut menu to open the Network Connections window.

3. Select Local Area Network, and then in the Network Tasks bar, click the Change Settings of This Connection link to open the Local Area Connection Properties dialog box.

4. Click Install to open the Select Network Component Type dialog box.

5. Select Client, and then click Add to open the Select Network Client dialog box:

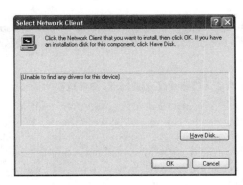

6. Click Have Disk to open the Install from Disk dialog box. Browse to the location where you've extracted the contents of the Novell client, and work your way down to this path: `novell\english\winnt\i386\NLS\ENGLISH`. Select `OEMSETUP.INF` and then click OK to display the Select Network Client dialog box again, but with the Novell Client for Windows 2000 in the Window:

7. Click OK to copy the installation files. When the copy is complete, you'll see a dialog box asking you to reboot your computer.

If you are using Novell in a pure IP environment, you have completed the installation. If you require the IPX protocol, do not reboot. Add the NWLink IPX/SPX protocol. Follow these steps:

1. In the Local Area Connection Properties dialog box, click Install to open the Select Network Component Type dialog box.

2. Select Protocol, and then click Add to open the Select Network Protocol dialog box.

3. Choose Microsoft from the list of manufactures in the left pane, and then select NWLink IPX/SPX NetBIOS Compatible Transport Protocol from the list of available protocols. Click OK.

4. When this installation of the protocol is complete, you'll return to the Local Area Connection Properties dialog box. Click Close, and then reboot your computer.

Configuring the Novell Client

Once the Novell client is installed, it integrates very well with Windows XP Professional, offering multiple logins that can be configured between the NetWare and Windows XP Professional environments with a single click.

When you reboot the workstation, you'll notice immediately that the Novell client has been installed. The Microsoft three-finger login has now been replaced with a Novell dialog box requesting you to press Ctrl+Alt+Del. When you do, you'll see a Novell login dialog box that displays a location in which to enter your username and password. There's also a Workstation Only check box. When this check box is selected, the Novell client will bypass a Novell login and log in to the local workstation or the domain of your choice.

Clicking the Advanced button extends the view of the Novell login client to display the NDS, Script, Windows NT/Windows 2000, and Dial-up tabs. The Novell client allows you to log in to servers after you've logged in to Windows XP, and this is the dialog box being shown. On the NDS tab, you can select to browse for NDS trees, browse NDS to easily insert the correct context, and browse to find a preferred server. These options alone are a world of difference in comparison with CSNW in which you had to know exactly where your login object was created within the tree. While you still need to have an idea of where your object is, a well-designed tree will help you find your user ID quickly.

The Scripts tab allows you to run NetWare scripts and/or run your own login scripts. On the Windows NT/Windows 2000 tab, you can enter a login name, either a different name or the same login name, for Windows authentication, and you can select whether to log on locally or log in to a Windows domain. You use the Dial-up tab to dial in to any connections you have already preconfigured.

Summary

That's it for the relatively simple task of connecting to an existing NetWare network with Windows XP Professional. In this appendix, I've introduced you to NetWare terminology, showed you how to connect to a NetWare printer, and how to log on to a NetWare system.

Appendix C

Active Directory Essentials

IF YOU'RE USING WINDOWS XP Professional in a corporate environment, chances are good that your XP box is networked, and that the network is based either on servers running Windows NT 4, Windows 2000 Server, or, if you're reading this after mid-2002, Windows .NET Server.

If that's true and if you're networked with Windows NT 4, you have what is (not surprisingly) called an "NT 4 domain." (For details about an NT 4 domain, see my book *Mastering NT Server 4*, Seventh Edition, published by Sybex.) But if your networks are based on Windows 2000 Server and/or Windows .NET Server, you probably have what is called an "Active Directory" domain. Although I can't make you an Active Directory (AD) expert in one day, I'll introduce you to the basics of AD here.

Not that long ago, networks were small (remember when the only "networks" you cared about were CBS, NBC, and ABC?), and so were their problems. But nowadays it's not unusual to see worldwide networks connecting hundreds of thousands of PCs and users. Managing that kind of complexity brings up big problems—oops, we're supposed to call them challenges; I always forget. One of the answers to the obvious question "Why bother with Windows 2000 and .NET Server, anyway?" is that they were designed with some of those challenges in mind. That's important because NT 4 *didn't* address many of those problems.

You'll notice that, for most of this appendix, I'll be talking about Windows 2000 Server. And, yes, I realize that this book is about Windows XP Professional. If you're using Windows XP Professional on a stand-alone computer or a small peer-to-peer network that connects Windows XP Professional, Windows 2000, NT, and Windows 9x machines, you don't need to know anything about Active Directory. But if you're part of a large client-server network, and your Windows XP Professional workstation is connected to a Windows 2000 Server machine, you do need to understand Active Directory, and the information in this appendix is important to you. After I explain what the hoopla is all about, I'll give you step-by-step instructions for connecting to an AD domain.

So let's start out by examining why we bother with networks in the first place.

◆ Keeping track of who can use the network

◆ Finding stuff on the network

◆ Creating new types of subadministrators

◆ Subdividing control over a domain

◆ Dealing with connectivity and replication issues

◆ Building big networks

Security: Keeping Track of Who's Allowed to Use the Network and Who Isn't

A network's first job is

◆ To provide central places to store simple things such as files or more complex things such as databases, shared printing, or fax services

◆ To make it possible for people to communicate by means of e-mail, videoconferencing, or whatever technology comes up in the future

◆ More recently, to make it easier for people to buy things

Fast on the heels of that first job, however, is the second job of every network: to provide security. Once, most computer networks were unsecured or lightly secured, but human nature has forced a change, and there's no going back. Just as businesses have locks on their doors, file cabinets, and cash registers to protect their physical assets, so also do most modern firms protect their information assets. And no matter which vendor's network software you're using, computer security typically boils down to two parts: authentication and authorization. To see why, consider the following example.

Acme Industries sells pest control devices. They've got a sales manager named Wilma Wolf; Wilma wants to see how the sales of a new product, Instant Hole, is doing. Acme's got it set up so that Wilma can review sales information through her Web browser—she just surfs over to a particular location on one of the company's internal Web servers, and the report appears on her screen.

Of course, Acme management wouldn't be happy about just *anybody* getting to these sales report pages, so the pages are secured. Between the time that Wilma asked for the pages and the time that she got them, two things happened:

Authentication The Web server containing the sales reports asked her workstation, "Who's asking for this data?" The workstation replied, "Wilma." The server then said, "Prove it." So the workstation popped up a dialog box on Wilma's screen asking for her username and password. She types in her name and password, and assuming that she types them in correctly, the server then checks that name and password against a list of known users and passwords and finds that she is indeed Wilma.

Authorization The mere fact that she's proven that she's Wilma may not be sufficient reason for the Web server to give her access to the sales pages. The Web server then looks at another list sometimes known as the Access Control List, a list of people and access levels—"Joe can look at this page but can't change it," "Sue can look at this page and can change it," "Larry can't look at this page at all." Presuming Wilma's on the "can look" list, the server sends the requested pages to her browser.

Now, the foregoing example may not seem to contain any deep insights—after all, everyone's logged into a system, tried to access something, and either been successful or rejected—but understanding how Windows 2000/.NET Server and in particular AD is new requires examining these everyday things a bit. Here's a closer look at some of the administrative mechanics of logins.

Maintaining a "Directory" of Users and Other Network Objects

Every secure system has a file or files that make up a database of known user accounts. NT 4 only used a single file named SAM, short for the less-than-illuminating Security Accounts Manager. It contained a user's username (the logon name), the user's full name, password, allowed logon hours, account expiration date, description, primary group name, and profile information. Of course, the file was encrypted; copy a SAM from an existing NT 4 system and pull it up in Notepad, and you'll see only garbage.

Windows 2000 Server/Windows .NET Server store most of their user information in a file called `ntds.dit`, but `ntds.dit` is different from SAM in a couple of ways:

◆ First, `ntds.dit` is a modified Access database, and Windows 2000 Server/Windows .NET Server actually contain a variant of Access's database engine in their machinery. (Microsoft used to call the Access database engine JET, which stood for Joint Engine Technology—no, the meaning isn't obvious to me either, I think they just liked the acronym—but now it's called ESE, pronounced "easy," which stands for the equally useful name Extensible Storage Engine.)

◆ Second, as you'll see demonstrated over and over again, `ntds.dit` stores a much wider variety of information about users than the SAM ever did.

The information in `ntds.dit` and the program that manages `ntds.dit` are together called the *directory service* (DS). (As a matter of fact, most folks will never say "ntds.dit"; they'll say "directory service.") Which leads to a question: What exactly is a "directory"?

It would seem (to me, anyway) that what we've got here is a database of users and user information. So why not call it a database? No compelling reasons; mostly convention, but there *is* one interesting insight. According to some, databases of users tend to get *read* far more often than they get *written*. That allows a certain amount of database engine tweaking for higher performance. This subset of the class of databases gets a name—*directories*. I guess it makes sense, as we're used to using lists of people called office directories or phone directories. I just wish the folks in power had come up with some other name; ask most PC users what a directory is, and they start thinking of hard disk structures: C:\Windows—isn't that a directory?

Centralizing the Directory and Directories: a "Logon Server"

"Please, can't we set things up so I only need to remember *one* password?"

Consider for a moment when Windows 2000 Server/Windows .NET Server will use that user information located in AD. When you try to access a file share or print share, AD will validate you. But there's more at work here. When fully implemented, AD can save you a fair amount of administrative work in other network functions as well.

For example, suppose your network requires SQL database services. You'll then run a database product such as SQL Server or Oracle on the network. But adding another server-based program to your network can introduce more administrative headaches because, like the file and print servers, a database server needs authentication and authorization support. That's because you usually don't want to just plunk some valuable database on the network and then let the world in general at it—you want to control who gets access.

So the database program needs a method for authentication and authorization. And *here's* where it gets ugly: in the past, many database programs required their administrators to keep and maintain a list of users and passwords. The database programs required you to duplicate all that work of typing in names and passwords, to redo the work you'd already done to get your Novell, Banyan, NT, or whatever type LAN up and running. Yuk. But it gets worse. Consider what you'd have to do if you ran both NT as a network operating system *and* Novell NetWare as a network operating system: yup, you're typing in names and passwords yet again. Now add Lotus Notes for your e-mail and group-ware stuff, another list of users, and hey, how about a mainframe or an AS/400? More accounts.

Let's see—with a network incorporating NT, Oracle, NetWare, and Notes, you've got each user owning *four* user accounts. Which means each user has *four* passwords to remember. And, every few months, four passwords to remember to change.

This seems dumb; why can't you just type those names and passwords once into your Windows 2000 Server/Windows .NET Server and then tell Oracle, NetWare, and Notes to just ask the local Windows 2000 Server/Windows .NET Server machine to check that you are indeed who you say you are rather than making Oracle, NetWare, and Notes duplicate all that security stuff? Put another way, you have a centralized computer that acts as a database server, another that acts as a centralized e-mail server, another as a print server—why not have a centralized "logon" server, a centralized "authentication" server? Then your users would have to remember (and change) only one password and account name rather than four.

Centralized logons would be a great benefit, but there's a problem with it: how would Notes actually *ask* the Windows 2000 Server/Windows .NET Server to authenticate? What programming commands would an Oracle database server use to ask a Microsoft "logon server" (the actual term is *domain controller*, as you'll learn later) if a particular user should be able to access a particular piece of data?

Well, if that domain controller were running NT 4, the programming interface wouldn't have been a particularly well-documented one. And third parties such as Oracle, Lotus, and Novell would have been reluctant to write programs depending on that barely documented security interface because they'd be justifiably concerned that when the *next* version of NT appeared (Windows 2000 Server, and then Windows .NET Server), Microsoft would have changed the programming interface, leaving Lotus, Novell, and Oracle scrambling to learn and implement this new interface. And some of the more cynical among us would even suggest that Lotus and Oracle might fear that Microsoft's Exchange and SQL Server would be able to come out in Windows 2000 Server/Windows .NET Server–friendly versions nearly immediately after Windows 2000 Server/Windows .NET Server's release.

Instead, Microsoft opted to put an industry standard interface on its AD, an interface called the Lightweight Directory Access Protocol (LDAP). Now, LDAP may initially sound like just another geeky acronym, but it's more than that—what Microsoft's done by putting an LDAP interface on Active Directory is to open a doorway for outside developers. And here's how important it is: yes, LDAP will make Oracle's or Lotus's job easier should they decide to integrate their products' security with Windows 2000 Server/Windows .NET Server's built-in security. But LDAP also means that it's (theoretically, at least) possible to build tools that create Active Directory structures—domains, trees, forests, organizational units, user accounts, all of the components. It means that if Windows 2000 Server/Windows .NET Server gets popular but Microsoft's Active Directory control programs turn out to be hard to work with, some clever third party can just swoop in and offer a complete replacement, built atop LDAP commands.

Which, after you spend a bit of time with the Microsoft Management Console (MMC), may not seem like a bad idea—but I'll leave you to make your own judgment about that.

Searching: Finding Things on the Network

Thus far, I've been talking about the directory service as if it only contains user accounts. But that's not true—the DS not only includes directory entries for people, it also contains directory entries describing servers and workstations. And that turns out to be essential, for a few reasons.

Finding Servers: "Client-Server Rendezvous"

Client-server computing is how work gets done nowadays. You check your e-mail with Outlook (the client), which gets that mail from the Exchange machine down the hall (the server). You're at your PC (the client) accessing files on a file server (the server). You buy a shirt at L.L. Bean's Web server (the server) from your PC using Internet Explorer (the client).

In those three cases, the copy of Outlook on your desktop had to somehow know where to find your local Exchange server, you couldn't get files from your file server until you knew which file server to look in, and you couldn't order that shirt until you'd found the address of the L.L. Bean Web server, www.llbean.com.

In every case, client-server doesn't work unless you can help the client find the server; hence, the phrase "client-server rendezvous." In the Outlook case, your mail client knows where your mail server is probably because someone (perhaps you) in your networking group set it up, feeding the name of the Exchange server into some setup screen in Outlook. You may have found the correct file server for the desired files by poking around in Network Neighborhood in Windows 9x or in My Network Places if your workstation is running Windows XP Professional, or perhaps someone told you where to find the files. You might have guessed L.L. Bean's address, seen it in a magazine ad, or used a search engine such as Yahoo! or AltaVista.

Those are three examples of client-server rendezvous; many more happen in the process of daily network use. When your workstation seeks to log you in, the workstation must find a domain controller, or to put it differently, your "logon client" seeks a "logon server." Want to print something in color and wonder which networked color printers are nearby? More client-server rendezvous.

In every case, AD can simplify the process. Your workstation will be able to ask AD for the names of nearby domain controllers. You can search the AD for keywords relevant to particular file shares and printers.

Name Resolution and DNS

But merely getting the name of a particular mail, Web, print, or file server (or domain controller) isn't the whole story. From the network software's point of view, www.llbean.com isn't much help. To get you connected to the Bean Web server, the network software needs to know the *IP address* of that server, a four-number combination looking something like 208.7.129.82. That's the second part of client-server rendezvous.

In the case of a public Web site such as Bean's, your computer can look up a Web server by querying a huge network of publicly available Internet servers called the Domain Name System, or DNS. The public DNS contains the names of many machines you'll need to access, but chances are good that your company's internal network doesn't advertise many of its machines' names on the Internet; rather, your internal network probably runs a set of private DNS servers.

After its inception in 1984, DNS didn't change much. But RFC 2052 (introduced in October 1996) and RFC 2136 (introduced in April 1997), transformed DNS into a naming system that's good not only for the worldwide Internet but also for internal intranets. Many of the pieces of DNS software out in the corporate world don't yet support 2052 and 2136, so it's a great convenience that Windows 2000 Server/Windows .NET Server's DNS server supports those features.

NOTE *RFC stands for Request for Comments, which is a document or a set of documents in which proposed Internet standards are described or defined.*

Creating New Types of Subadministrators

The next network challenge becomes apparent after a network has grown a bit. When a network is small or new, a small group of people do everything, from running the cables and installing the LAN adapter boards to creating the user accounts and backing up the system. As time goes on and the network gets larger and more important to the organization, two things happen:

◆ First, the organization hires more people—*has* to hire more people, because there are more servers to tend and user accounts to look after—to handle all the different parts of keeping a network running.

◆ Second, networks get political: all of a sudden, some of the higher-ups get clued to the fact that *what those network geeks do affects our ability to retain our power in this organization.*

Both of those things mean that your firm will soon start hiring more network helpers. In some organizations, these newly created positions get to do much of the scut work of network administration, stuff that is (a) pretty simple to train people to do and (b) of no interest to the old-timer network types. Examples of the I-don't-want-it-you-can-have-it jobs in a network include:

Resetting passwords For security's sake, we network administrators usually require users to change their passwords every couple months or so. We also inveigh against the evils of writing those passwords down, so it's common for users to forget what they set their most recent passwords to. Resetting passwords to some innocuous value is something that really needs to be done quickly—the natives get restless when you take a week to let them back on the network—and it's a relatively simple task, so it's perfect for the newly hired, minimum-wage network assistant.

Tending the backups For tediousness, nothing matches the sheer irritation of backups. Most of us who manage large networks are forced to use tape drives for backups, and, well, some days it seems like tape drives were invented by someone who was abused by network administrators as a small child. They're balky and prone to taking vacations at random times, and you never can predict exactly how much data you can get on 'em—eight gigs one day, three the next, and as a result, *someone's* got to be around ready to feed in another blank tape. And somebody's got to label them and keep track of them; ask most network admin types what job they'd most like to give someone else to worry about, and backups are likely to be at the top of their wish list.

Hiring a few low-wage backup watchers and password fixers also gives a firm a sort of a "farm team," a place to try out folks to see if they're capable of learning to eventually become network analysts with more responsibilities (and, they hope, more salary).

But regular old users can't do things such as resetting passwords and running backups—you need at least some administrative powers to do those things. Recall that we'd like to hire this "network scut work" person or persons at a pretty low hourly rate, and that's troublesome from a security point of view. If they can leave this job and go off to one with the same pay level whose main challenge is in remembering to say, "Would you like fries with that, sir?" it might not be the brightest idea to give them full administrative control over the network. Is there a way to create a sort of partial administrator?

NT 4 gave us *some* of that, as there was a prebuilt group called Backup Operators, but there wasn't a Reset Password Operators group, and besides, all NT 4 offered was a small set of prebuilt groups of types of administrators—the groups were called Server Operators, Account Operators, and Backup Operators—with different levels. There wasn't a way to create a new type of group with a tailor-made set of powers. Windows 2000 Server/Windows .NET Server changes that, offering a sometimes bewildering array of security options.

Delegation: Subdividing Control over a Domain

In the last section, I offered two examples of things that might motivate changing how the network works—a growing set of network duties that require some division of labor (which I covered in that section) and growing attention from upper management as it becomes increasingly aware of the importance of the network in the organization. That second force in network evolution is perhaps better known as "politics." Despite the fact that it's something of a bad word, we can't ignore politics—so how does Windows 2000 Server/Windows .NET Server address an organization's political needs?

To see how, consider the following scenario. Some fictitious part of the U.S. Navy is spread across naval facilities across the world, but perhaps (to keep the example simple) its biggest offices are in Washington, DC; San Diego, CA; and Norfolk, VA. There are servers in DC, San Diego, and Norfolk, all tended by different groups. For all the usual reasons, the officers in charge of the Norfolk facility don't want administrators from DC or San Diego messing with the Norfolk servers; the DC folks and the San Diego folks have similar feelings, with the result that the Navy technology brass wants to be able to say, "Here's a group of servers we'll call Norfolk and a group of users we'll call Norfolk Admins. We want to be able to say that only the users in Norfolk Admins can control the servers in Norfolk." They want to do similar things for San Diego and DC. How to do this?

Well, under NT 4, they could do it only by creating three separate security entities called *domains*. Creating three different domains would solve the problem because separate domains are like separate *universes*—they're not aware of each other at all. With a DC domain, a Norfolk domain, and a San Diego domain, they could separate their admins into three groups that couldn't meddle with one another. It's a perfectly acceptable answer and indeed many organizations around the world use NT 4 in that manner—but it's a solution with a few problems.

For one thing, enterprises usually want *some* level of communication between domains, and to accomplish that, the enterprises must put in place connections between domains called *trust relationships*. Unfortunately, trust relationships are a quirky and unreliable necessity of any multidomain enterprise using NT 4. With Windows 2000 Server/Windows .NET Server, in contrast, the Navy need only create *one* domain and then divide it using a new-to-NT notion called *organizational units*, usually abbreviated *OUs*.

More specifically, the Navy would solve their problem in this way:

◆ They'd create one domain named (for example) NAVY.

◆ Inside NAVY, they'd create an organizational unit named Norfolk, another called DC, and a third named San Diego. They would set up their servers and then place each server into the proper OU.

◆ Also inside NAVY, they'd create a user group named Norfolk Admins, and two others named San Diego Admins and DC Admins. They'd create accounts for their users and place any administrators into their proper group, depending on whether they were based in DC, San Diego, or Norfolk.

At this point, understand that the San Diego Admins (kinda sounds like a baseball team, doesn't it?) don't yet have any power: there's no magic in Windows 2000 Server/Windows .NET Server that says, "Well, there's an OU named San Diego and a group named San Diego Admins, I guess that must mean I should let these Admin guys have total control over the servers in the San Diego OU." You have to create that link by *delegating control* of the San Diego OU to the user group San Diego Admins. (Windows 2000 Server/Windows .NET Server has a Wizard that assists in doing this.) OUs are an excellent tool for building large and useful domains.

Satisfying Political Needs

"That's *my* data, so I want it on *my* servers!" As information has become the most important asset of many firms—for example, I once heard someone comment that the majority of Microsoft's assets resided in the crania of their employees—some firms have been reluctant to yield control of that information to a central IT group. Nor is that an irrational perspective: if you were the person in charge of maintaining a five-million-person mailing list, and if that list generated one half of your firm's sales leads, you might well want to see that data housed on a machine or machines run by people who report directly to you.

Of course, on the other side of the story there is the IT director who wants Total Control of all servers in the building, and her reasoning is just as valid. You see, if a badly run server goes down and that failure affects the rest of the network, it's *her* head on the chopping block.

So on the one hand, the department head or VP wants to control the iron and silicon that happen to be where his data lives, and on the other hand, the IT director who's concerned with making sure that all data is safe and that everything on the network plays well with others wants to control said data and network pieces. Who wins? It depends—and that's the "politics" part.

What do Windows 2000 Server/Windows .NET Server do to ameliorate the political problems? Well, not as much as would be nice—there is no "make the vice presidents get along well" Wizard—

but Windows 2000 Server/Windows .NET Server's variety of options for domain design gives the network designers the flexibility to build whatever kind of network structure they want.

Got a relatively small organization that would fit nicely into a single domain, but one VP with server ownership lust? No problem, give the VP an OU of their own within the domain. Got a firm with two moderately large offices separated by a few hundred miles? Under NT 4, two domains and a trust relationship would be the answer, and you could choose to do that under Windows 2000 Server/Windows .NET Server, but that's not the only answer. As Windows 2000 Server/Windows .NET Server is extremely parsimonious with WAN bandwidth in comparison with NT 4, you might find that a single domain makes sense as it's easier to administer than two domains, but not impossible from a network bandwidth point of view. And bandwidth utilization is our next topic.

Connectivity and Replication Issues

More and more companies don't live in only one place. They've purchased another firm across the country, and what once were two separate *local* area networks are now one firm with a wide area network need. If that WAN link is fast, there's no network design headache at all: hook the two offices up with a T1 link, and you can essentially treat them as one office.

That's beneficial because each site will usually contain a domain controller—one of those servers that hosts the AD database and that acts as a machine to accomplish logins. But those domain controllers must communicate whenever something changes, as when a user's password changes or when an administrator creates a new user account. This is called *AD replication*. The same thing happened with NT 4, as NT 4 also allowed you to put multiple domain controllers in an enterprise.

In NT 4, suppose you've got two offices connected by a slow WAN link. Suppose further that you've got a domain controller in each of these offices. They need to replicate their SAM database between domain controllers (recall that NT 4 used a user database named SAM; the Windows 2000 Server/Windows .NET Server database is called AD). NT 4's domain controller updates happened every five minutes. That means that a domain controller might try to replicate changes to another domain controller every five minutes, even if they're only connected with a very slow link. All that chatter could well choke a WAN link and keep other, more important traffic from getting through.

Windows 2000 Server/Windows .NET Server improves upon that by allowing you to tell domain controllers about how well they're connected. The idea is that you describe your enterprise in terms of *sites*, which are basically just groups of servers with fast connections—groups of servers living on the same local area network, basically. You can then define how fast (or probably, slow) the connections *between* those sites are, and Windows 2000 Server/Windows .NET Server will then be a bit smarter about using those connections.

In particular, Windows 2000 Server/Windows .NET Server AD servers compress data before sending it over slow WAN links. Taking the time to compress data requires a certain amount of CPU power, but it's well worth it, as AD is capable of a 10 percent compression ratio!

Not only do you often face slow links, you often must live with *unreliable* links, ones that are up and down or perhaps only up for a short period of time every day. Windows 2000 Server/Windows .NET Server lets you define not only a WAN link's speed but also the times that it is up.

NT 4's directory replications require a real-time connection called a Remote Procedure Call (RPC). RPCs are like telephone calls—the domain controller programs on each side must be up and running and actively communicating simultaneously. Inasmuch as domain controllers can be more or less busy as the day wears on, requiring this kind of shared concentration in order to get a simple directory replication accomplished is a bit demanding. It might be nicer if replications could work less like a telephone call and more like a mailing—and to a certain extent, Windows 2000 Server/ Windows .NET Server allows this, or rather points to a day in the future when it'll be possible.

It's possible for one domain controller to simply *mail* part of its replication data to another domain controller. Then, even if the receiving domain controller is not currently online, the mail message is still waiting for it, ready to be read when the receiving domain controller is again awake. Sounds good, but unfortunately, not *all* of the directory replication can happen over mail. Microsoft said when they released Windows 2000 Server that they would change that in a future release, but they haven't in Windows .NET Server.

Site control will make life considerably easier for those managing multilocation networks.

Scalability: Building Big Networks

Large enterprise networks found NT 4 lacking in the number of users that its SAM database could accommodate. Although you could theoretically create millions of user accounts on an NT domain, it's not practical to create more than about 5,000 to perhaps 10,000 user accounts in a domain. (If you took the MCSE exam for NT Server and are looking at that number oddly, it's because they made you memorize 40,000 as the answer to the question "How many user accounts can you put on an NT domain?" In my experience, that's just not realistic, hence my 5,000 to 10,000 number.)

Five thousand user accounts are more than most companies would ever need. But some large firms need to incorporate more user accounts into their enterprise, forcing them to divide their company's network into multiple domains—and multiple domains were to be avoided at all costs under NT 4 because of the extra trouble in maintaining them.

AD can accommodate many more user accounts than NT's SAM. Furthermore, AD allows you to build larger networks by making the process of building and maintaining multidomain networks easier. Whereas once an administrator of a multidomain network had to build and maintain a complex system of interdomain security relationships—the *trust relationships* I've already referred to—now Windows 2000 Server/.NET Server will let you build a system of domains called a *forest*. A forest's main strength is that once a group of domains has been built into a forest, the trusts are automatically created and maintained. There are additionally smaller multidomain structures called trees that also feature automatic trusts.

Simplifying Computer Names or Unifying the Namespace

Devices on a network mainly identify themselves by some long and unique number. On an intranet or the Internet, it's a unique 32-bit number called an *IP address*. Networks also commonly exploit a 48-bit address burned into each network interface card called a *MAC* (Media Access Control) *address*. Any Ethernet, Token Ring, ATM (Asynchronous Transfer Mode), or other network interface has one of these addresses, and some conventions that network manufacturers have agreed upon have ensured that no matter whom you buy a NIC (Network Interface Card) from, the NIC will have a 48-bit address that no other NIC has. Some parts of NT identify PCs by their IP address (or addresses—

a machine with multiple NICs will have an IP address and MAC address for each NIC), others by the PC's MAC address or addresses.

But people don't relate well to long strings of numbers—telling you that you can send me mail at `mark@11001110111101101111110011001000` is technically accurate (presuming that you can find a mail client that will accept network addresses in binary) but not very helpful. It's far more preferable to be able to instead tell your mail program to send mail to `help@minasi.com`, which you can do. Somehow, however, your mail client must be able to look up `minasi.com` and from there find out where to send mail for `minasi.com`. In the same way, pointing your Web browser to `www.microsoft` `.com` forces the browser to convert `www.microsoft.com` into the particular IP address or addresses that constitute Microsoft's Web site. This process of converting from human-friendly names such as `minasi.com` to computer-friendly addresses such as 11001110111101101111110011001000 is called *name resolution*. It's something every network must do.

So why is name resolution a problem with NT? Because most of the networking world uses *one* approach to name resolution, and up through version 4, NT used a different one.

Most every firm is on the Internet, has an internal intranet, or both. Intranets and the Internet use the DNS form of name resolution. DNS names are the familiar Internet names such as `www.microsoft` `.com`. PCs resolve DNS names by consulting a group of servers around the world called, not surprisingly, DNS servers. Your company or Internet Service Provider operates one or more DNS servers, and your Internet software uses these nearby DNS servers to resolve (for example) `www.minasi.com` to the Internet address 206.246.253.200.

NT-based networks using Internet software don't use DNS for much of their work. Instead, Microsoft invented its own name servers somewhat like DNS but using NetBIOS names; they called these name servers Windows Internet Name Service, or WINS, servers. The NetBIOS naming systems is incompatible with DNS; NetBIOS names are simpler—no more than 15 characters, no periods.

That leads to this problem: nearly every firm is on the Internet—*has* to be on the Internet—and so every firm must give DNS names to their computers. But if they're also using NT, they need to give their systems NetBIOS names. That in and of itself *is* not a great burden; what *is* a burden is that these names are important to the programs that use them, and programs typically can need one of the two names and can't use the other of the two.

Let's take an example. Suppose someone wants to log on to an NT 4 domain at Acme Technologies. To accomplish that, this person's workstation must find a domain controller for that domain. The workstation does that by searching for a machine with a particular NetBIOS name. Let's say that Acme does indeed have a domain controller around named LOGMEIN (its NetBIOS name) which *also* acts as a Web server with the DNS name `reptiles.pictures.animalworld.com`, as it hosts pages of pictures of local reptiles. Let's also suppose that for some reason ACME has no WINS servers but has a great network of DNS servers.

DNS names are of no value to the workstation looking for a logon. You could have the finest set of DNS servers in the world, but it would make no difference—without a functioning WINS server, that workstation would probably be unable to locate a domain controller to log you in. On the other hand, if someone sitting at that very same workstation sought to view the reptile pictures on `http://` `www.reptiles.pictures.animalworld.com`, they'd just fire up Internet Explorer and point it at that URL. Internet Explorer is, of course, uninterested in NetBIOS names, relying mainly on DNS names.

The workstation would quickly locate the Web server and browse its pages, even as that same workstation was unable to detect that the very same server could perform logins.

Windows 2000 Server/Windows .NET Server solves this problem by largely doing away with WINS, using DNS for all its name resolution needs. Unfortunately, however, Windows 2000 Server/Windows .NET Server uses DNS for all *its* name resolution needs—older Windows 9*x* and Windows NT 4 systems still rely on WINS. So while WINS' role is diminished, it'll still be around until you've pulled the plug on the last Windows 9*x* and NT machines.

Satisfying the Lust for Power and Control

Well, okay, maybe it's not *lust*, but it's certainly *need*. Put simply, there just plain aren't enough support people around, and there is no shortage of users to support. In 1987, many firms retained one support person for every 100 users; in many companies nowadays, that ratio is more like one support person for every 2,000 users.

Although it was once possible for a support person to physically visit every user's PC to perform support tasks, it's just not reasonable to expect that anymore. Support people need tools that allow them to get their work done from a central location as much as is possible. And, although not every user is all that happy about it, one way to simplify a support person's job is to standardize each PC's desktop. In some cases, support staffs need software tools to allow them to *enforce* that standard desktop. (As you can imagine, it's a very political issue for many firms.)

In NT 4, Microsoft started helping support staffs centralize their desktop control with something called *system policies*. But system policies were lacking in a few ways. AD improves upon system policies with a kind of "system policies version 2" called *group policies*.

Better security, more flexible administration options, wiser use of bandwidth, and providing godlike control to administrators: that's basically what AD is trying to accomplish.

Connecting a Windows XP Professional Machine to an AD Domain

So now that you know all about Active Directory and what it's for, let's take a look at how you can connect your Windows XP Professional workstation to an Active Directory domain. The steps are actually quite easy, and if you work along with the examples that follow, you should be connected to an Active Directory domain in no time.

Checklist

First, there are a number of things that you should make sure you know in advance before trying to connect to an Active Directory domain. Specifically, be sure you have the following information available before starting:

- The name of the AD domain you will be joining.

- Your username and password, as they are defined in the AD.

◆ Whether an account has already been added to the AD for your machine (each machine has an account, as does each a user).

◆ If an account has not been added for your machine, you will need a login and password in the Active Directory that has the rights to create an account for your machine.

Connecting to AD

Once you have verified all of the items on the checklist, you've got what it takes to add your machine to an Active Directory domain. The next step is to verify that the correct components are installed on your Windows XP Professional computer (and to install them if they're not) and then to add your machine to the Active Directory domain.

VERIFY OPERATING SYSTEM PREREQUISITES

In order to connect to an Active Directory domain, two networking components must be in place on your system:

◆ Client for Microsoft Networks

◆ An appropriate communications protocol (NWLink IPX/SPX or TCP/IP)

Both components are necessary for any Microsoft operating systems to talk to each other, so it is important to make sure they are properly installed before trying to join an Active Directory domain. To verify that both components are installed, follow these steps:

1. Choose Start ➤ Connect To ➤ Show All Connections to open the Network Connections folder.

2. Right-click the icon that represents your network (Local Area Connection), and choose Properties from the shortcut menu to open the Properties dialog box for your network.

3. In the list of configured components you should see the Client for Microsoft Networks and Internet Protocol (TCP/IP). Make sure that both items are enabled (the check box next to the item is selected).

You now have everything you need to connect to a domain. You just need to tell Windows XP Professional to do it.

CHANGE YOUR COMPUTER NAME

To tell Windows XP Professional to join an Active Directory domain, you change the network identification information on your system. However, the configuration for doing so is a bit hidden. Instead of being with the other networking items, the Active Directory domain items are configuration parameters in My Computer. To change network identification, follow these steps:

1. Click Start, right-click My Computer, and choose Properties from the shortcut menu to open the System Properties dialog box.

2. Click the Computer Name tab, and you will see the current identification of your system consisting of a machine name and the current domain or workgroup your system is configured to use.

3. To change this configuration, click the Change button to open the Computer Name Changes dialog box:

As you can see, the name of my machine is douglaptop, and it was originally a member of a workgroup called WORKGROUP. I've told Windows XP Professional to join an Active Directory domain called ACTIVEDIR by clicking the Domain radio button and entering the name of the domain that my system should join. After you make the necessary changes to your system, click OK. Either one of two things will happen.

First, you might see a dialog box welcoming you to the domain you specified. What that means is that someone—an administrator or someone else—has already set up an account for the name of your computer within the Active Directory. If this is the case, all you will need to do is reboot to complete your changes. You can now proceed to the "Logging In to Active Directory" section of this appendix.

However, more often than not there won't be an account for your computer within the Active Directory, so you'll need to add one. You'll know this is the case if you get prompted for a username and password.

Active Directory doesn't let just anyone add machine accounts to its database; you need an Active Directory user account that has the right to do so. The Administrator account will work for these purposes, but depending on your circumstances, you may not have been provided with the administrative password to the Active Directory. There are also ways to create special accounts for one purpose—to add machines to domains—but ultimately if you don't know of an account to use at this point, you will need to contact an administrator for the Active Directory in order to complete this process (that's why this information was listed in the prerequisites).

Assuming you have the correct username and password to use (or that someone has entered it for you), the next thing you should see is a dialog box welcoming you to the domain you've joined.

Your machine will need to be rebooted for the changes to take effect, so go ahead and reboot your system.

LOGGING IN TO ACTIVE DIRECTORY

The next time your computer boots up, it probably won't look much different. You'll be presented with the same login box that you've always seen. However, if you click the Options button on the main login screen, you will see a drop-down list of domains to choose from. By default, your system will continue to use its own local accounts database for logging in, so you will need to click the drop-down list and choose the domain you just joined. Select the appropriate domain, and then enter your Active Directory username and password in the appropriate fields. If everything is configured correctly, you should end up logging in to the Active Directory domain. Congratulations!

Summary

The purpose of this appendix was to introduce you to AD. As you can tell from even these few pages, AD is a complicated topic. If you're interested in learning more, I recommend that you take a look at *Mastering Windows 2000 Server,* Fourth Edition (Minasi, Anderson, Smith, Toombs; Sybex, 2002) and *Mastering Active Directory, for Windows .NET Server,* by Robert R. King (Sybex, 2002).

Index

Note to the Reader: Throughout this index **boldfaced** page numbers indicate primary discussions of a topic. *Italicized* page numbers indicate illustrations.

A

acceleration
hardware, 349, 385
video, 373
Accept All Cookies option, 478
Access Control option, 869
Access Level Wizard, 92, 641
Access Permissions page, 861, *861*, 866–867, *867*
Access Rights of Internet Sites section, **363**
Access Rights of Other Applications section, **363**
Access tab, **869**, *869*
Accessibility dialog box, 475
accessibility options, **222–223**
Accessibility Wizard for, **223**, *223*
for all users, **226**, *227*
for hearing-impaired users, **224–225**, *225*
in Internet Explorer, 475
Magnifier, **227**, *227*
for mobility-impaired users, **225–226**, *226*
Narrator, **228**, *228*
On-Screen Keyboard, **228**, *228*
in setup, 138, *138*
Utility Manager, **228–229**, *229*
for visually-impaired users, **224**, *224*
Accessibility Options dialog box, 138, *138*, **223–226**, *224–227*
Accessibility Wizard, **223**, *223*
Account Is Disabled option, 657–658
Account logon events, auditing, 672
Account management events, auditing, 672
accounts
group, **77**, *77*, **658**, *658*
for newsgroups, **557**
user, **652–653**
creating, **75–76**, *75–76*, **146**, **655–658**, *656–657*

for domain servers, **634**
rights in, **653–655**, *654*
ACPI (Advanced Configuration and Power Interface), 404, 418–419
Action menu in MMC, **820**, *820*
activating Windows, **146–147**
Active Directory, **901–902**
computer names in, **910–915**, *914*
connecting to, **912–915**, *914*
connectivity and replication issues in, **909–910**
delegation in, **907–908**
policies in, **912**
political issues in, **908–909**
scalability of, **910**
searching in, **905–906**
security in, **902–905**
subadministrators for, **906–907**
active users, 103, 160, **166**
ActiveX Control snap-in, 810
adapter requirements, **125**
Adapter tab, 202
Add a Contact Wizard, **520–522**, *521*
Add a File dialog box, 130
Add a File Type dialog box, 130–131, *131*
Add a Setting dialog box, 130
Add a Shortcut to This Connection to My Desktop option, 35
Add Counters dialog box, 709–711, *709*, 713–714
Add Favorite dialog box, 461–462, *461*
Add Fonts dialog box, 320, *320*
Add Form Feed option, 894
Add Hardware Wizard, **336–338**, *337–338*, 351
Add Input Language dialog box, 141
Add Network Place Wizard, 879–883, *880–882*
Add New Programs screen, 39, 236
Add or Remove Programs window, 39, 41, 149, **236–239**, *238*

Add Printer Driver Wizard, 53
Add Printer Wizard, **44–47**, 49
    for local printers, 301–305, *302, 304–305*
    for Novell printers, 894–895, *895*
    for remote printers, 309–311, *309–310*
    for Unix printers, 616
Add/Remove Columns command, 824
Add/Remove Snap-in dialog box, 665, *665*, 812
Add Scheduled Task icon, 63
Add Sender dialog box, 555, *555*
Add Standalone Snap-in dialog box, 665–666, *665,*
    812–813, *812*
Add Standard TCP/IP Printer Port Wizard, 310
Add to Favorites dialog box, 735, *735*
Additional Drivers dialog box, 308, *308*
address bars on taskbars, **30**, *30*
Address Resolution Protocol (ARP), **486**,
    622–623, *623*
Address toolbar, 8–9
addresses
    gateway, **636–637**, *637*
    IP. *See* IP addresses
AddUser.wsf script, **752–753**
administration utilities for Novell networks, **887–891**,
    889–890
Administrative Tools, 697
    for Event Viewer, 704
    for performance, 708
Administrator Password screen, 155
Administrators group, 653
ADSL (Asymmetric DSL), 432
Advanced Appearance dialog box, 214, *215*, 325, *325*
Advanced Attributes dialog box
    for compression, 284, *284*
    for encryption, 58–59, 287, 693
Advanced Audio Properties dialog box, 385–386, *386*
Advanced Configuration and Power Interface (ACPI),
    404, 418–419
Advanced Controls dialog box, 388, *388*
Advanced Options dialog box, **137–139**, *137*
Advanced Port settings for modems, 345
Advanced Power Management (APM), 404, 418–419
Advanced Privacy Settings dialog box, 479, *479*

Advanced Search dialog box, 375, *375*
Advanced section for SMTP servers, 872
Advanced Security Settings dialog box
    for auditing, 667, 675, *675*
    for authentication, 689
    for dial-in sessions, 683–684, *683*
    for ownership, 669
    for permissions, 662, *662*
    for RAS dial-in sessions, 88
Advanced Settings dialog box
    for ICS, 452–454, *452–453*
    for modems, 345, *345*
Advanced Signature Settings dialog box, 553
Advanced tab
    for battery monitoring, **407–409**, *408*
    for favorites, 462
    for firewalls, 436, *436*
    for ICS, 450–452, *450*, 454
    for Internet Connection Firewall, 87
    for Internet Explorer, **482**, *482*
    for modems, 344, *344*
    for printer servers, 53, 318
    for printing, 51, 306, *307*, **313–314**, *314*, 468
    for Start menu, 11, 219, *219*
    for Stop errors, 802
    for USB hubs, 350
    for user profiles, 614
    for Web content, 480
Advanced TCP/IP Settings dialog box, 144, 636–639,
    637, 639, 648
AGP graphics cards, 351
alarms, power, **405–406**, *406*
Alarms tab, 405, *406*
Alerter service, 830
alerts, **712–713**, *713*
All Files and Folders link, 27
All Programs list, **263–264**, *264*
All Records view, 705
Allow Anonymous Connections option, 863
Allow Network Users to Change My Files option, 72
Allow service to interact with desktop option, 834
Allow the User to Customize Views option, 814

Allow This Program to Run in the Background option, 515

Allow Users to Connect Remotely to this Computer option, 85

alt newsgroups, 557

Always Ask Me for My Password When Checking Hotmail ... option, 514

Always Hide option, 13

Always Show option, 13

Always Show Icon on the Taskbar option, 408

Amount of Disk Space to Use for Temporary Offline Files setting, 412

analog modems
    configuring, **342–345**, *342–345*
    in installation, **141**
    for Internet connections, **424–427**, *424–427*
    setting up, **144–145**
    troubleshooting, **455–456**

Analysis Report dialog box, 60–61, 761

animation for windows, 728

anonymous access
    for FTP, 486–487, 881
    for Web sites, 849, 863

answer files, **152–157**

antivirus programs
    compatibility of, 247
    in installation, **131**

Anyone Who Uses This Computer option, 36

APIPA (Automatic Private IP Addressing), 576, 600, 636

APM (Advanced Power Management), 404, 418–419

apmstat.exe utility, 419

AppCompat database, 248

Appearance tab, 213–214, *213*, 325

Append parent suffixes of the primary DNS suffix option, 638

Append primary and connection specific DNS suffixes option, 638

Append these DNS suffixes (in order) setting, 638

AppleTalk networking protocol, 617

Application layer, **570**, **626–627**

Application Layer Gateway Service, 830

Application log, 705

Application Management service, 830

application servers, 565–566

applications. *See* programs

Applications tab, 168, 243, *243*, 719–720, *720*

Apply All Settings to Defaults for New Users option, 226

Apply All Settings to Logon Desktop option, 226

Approved Sites tab, 480

arguments in scripts, **740–741**, *741*

ARP (Address Resolution Protocol), **486**, **622–623**, *623*

ASR (Automated System Recovery), 114, **768–770**, *769–770*

Assign Drive Letter or Path screen, 702, *702*

associations for files, **291–292**, *292*

asterisks (*) in searches, 282

Asymmetric DSL (ADSL), 432

AT command, 751

at signs (@) for separator pages, 317

attaching to network resources, **642**
    login scripts for, **647**
    mapping network drives for, **643**, *643*, **645**
    My Network Places for, **642**
    UNCs for, **644–646**

attachments, e-mail
    including, **553**, *554*
    rules for, **554–555**, *554–555*
    saving, **545–546**, *546*

attrib command, 772

audio. *See* sound

Audio and Video Tuning Wizard
    for Messenger, **517–519**, *517–519*
    for Remote Assistance, 190

Audio Tuning Wizard, 508

Audit Object Access Properties dialog box, 667, *667*

auditing, **671**
    benefits of, **672–673**
    disadvantages of, **673**
    Event Viewer in, **677–679**, *677–678*
    files and folders, **664–668**, *665–668*
    setting up, **673–677**, *674–677*

Auditing Entry dialog box, 668, *668*, 675–677, *676–677*

Auditing tab, 667, *667*, 675–676, *675*
authentication
 in Active Directory, 902–904
 encrypted, **689–690**
 for Web sites, 849
Author mode in MMC, **811–814**, *812–814*
authorization in Active Directory, 902–904
AutoHide the Taskbar option, 216
Automated System Recovery (ASR), 114, **768–770**, *769–770*
Automated System Recovery Wizard, 769–770, *769–770*
Automatic Private IP Addressing (APIPA), 576, 600, 636
Automatic Reset option, 226
automatic services, **827–829**
Automatic Update section, 382
Automatic Updates service, 827
Automatic Updates tab, 150, *151*
Automatically Detect and Install My Plug and Play Printer option, 45
Automatically Dial This Initial Connection option, 90
automation
 installation, **152–157**
 scheduling tasks, **63–65**, *63–65*
 with scripts. *See* scripts
AutoPlay feature, **108**, 132, 135
availability of programs, **233**

B

B (bearer) channels, 437
Back Up Files and Directories right, 655
backbones, 582
background
 Desktop, 165, **208–209**, *209*
 in e-mail, **551–552**
 in Remote Desktop Connection, 535
Background Intelligent Transfer Service, 830
Background Picture dialog box, 551
Background Sound dialog box, 551–552
backslashes (\) for separator pages, 317–318
Backup Destination screen, 770, *770*

Backup Log tab, 785
Backup Operators group, 653
Backup or Restore screen, 782, *782*
Backup or Restore Wizard, **782–783**, *782–783*
Backup tab, 784, *784*
Backup Type, Destination, and Name screen, 783, *783*
Backup Type tab, 785
Backup Utility program, 114
 for ASR, 769, *769*
 for backups, **783–784**, *784*
 for restores, 785–786
backups
 CDs for, **293**
 for certificates, **56–57**, *56–57*, **285–286**, *286*
 creating, **781–785**, *782–784*
 for disaster prevention, **760**
 for installation, **128**
 for licenses, **379–380**, *379–380*
 for Registry, **726**, *726*
 restoring, **785–786**
 subadministrators for, 906–907
"Bad or Missing NTOSKRNL.EXE" message, 774
Badmail Directory option, 871
bandwidth-throttling technology, 150
Banner section for FTP servers, 864, *865*
Base setting in LDAP, 872
basic disks, converting, 703
.bat files, **738**
batch command, 772
batteries for notebooks, 400, **404**
 advanced options for, **407–408**, *408*
 hibernation for, **408–409**, *409*
 power alarms for, **405–406**, *406*
 power meters for, **406–407**, *407*
 power schemes for, **404–405**, *405*
battery power, UPSs for, **352**
 choosing, **352–353**
 installing, **353–356**, *353–355*
bearer (B) channels, 437
Before You Continue screen, 440, *440*, 445, 596
binary data in Registry, 729–730
bindery, **886–887**
Binding setting in LDAP, 872

BIOS settings, Stop errors from, 803
Bitmap Caching option, 535–536
biz newsgroups, 557
Block All Cookies option, 477
Blocked Senders tab, 555
blocking chat users, **525–526**, *526*
Blue Screen of Death (BSOD)
 forcing, **780–781**
 from Stop errors, **799**
  common, **800–801**
  fixing, **802–803**
  responding to, **802**, *802*
bookmark lists, 462
"BOOT: Couldn't find NTLDR" message, 798
boot disks, 804
boot.ini file, 803–804
boot process, **798–799**, **803–804**
boot records and sectors, fixing, **775–776**
bootsect.dos file, 803–804
boundaries in troubleshooting, **788**
brainstorming in troubleshooting, **788**
branches in Explorer, **267**
bridges, **112**, 571, **602–603**, *602–603*
Briefcase feature, 288, 411
 copying files for, **414–415**, *415*
 creating files for, **414**
 synchronizing files for, **415–416**, *415*
broadband connectivity, 424
Browse Dialog box, 40
Browse for Computers dialog box, 532
Browse for Folder dialog box
 for file and setting transfer, 129–130
 for license backups, 379
 for network drives, 73
 for network resources, 890, *890*
 for shortcuts, 31
Browse for Printer screen, 49, 895, *895*
Browse permission, 861–862
browsing
 in Help and Support Center, **178–181**, *179–180*
 on Web
  with Internet Explorer. *See* Internet Explorer

 with MSN Explorer, **484–486**, *484–485*
 utilities for, **486–491**, *487, 489*
BSOD (Blue Screen of Death)
 forcing, **780–781**
 from Stop errors, **799**
  common, **800–801**
  fixing, **802–803**
  responding to, **802**, *802*
built-in groups, **653**
built-in monitors, **400–401**
burning CDs, **293**
 problems in, **296–297**
 storage area for
  checking files in, **294**
  clearing files in, **297**, *297*
  copying files to, **293–294**, *294*
button appearance, 214
Buttons tab, 221
Bytes Total/sec counter, 711

C

cable modems
 advantages of, **429–430**
 connections for, **431–432**
 disadvantages of, **430**
 hooking up, **430–431**
 operation of, **428**
 setting up, **145–146**
 speed of, **428–429**
 troubleshooting, **456**
cables
 network, 582, **585–587**, *587*
 SCSI, 797
Cache Manager, 120
call command, **743–744**, *744*
callable objects, **751**
Called Subscriber Identification (CSID) screen, 496, *496*
caller-ID/callback security, **690–691**
Calling Call tab, 410
cameras for still images, **395**
Cancel command for printing, 316

Cancel All Documents command, 315

Cannot Complete the CD Writing Wizard screen, 296, *296*

Cannot Continue the Add Hardware Wizard screen, 337

Cannot Install This Hardware screen, 332, *333*, 336

card services, 401

cartridges, printer, 324

Cascade Windows command, 5–6

Cat 5 UTP cable, 586

cataloging media files, **359**, *359*

Category view, **104–105**, *104*, 198–199, *198*

CD Audio page, 367

cd command, 772

CD drives

    adding, **345–346**, *346*

    requirements for, **126**

CD Writing Wizard, 24, 294–297, *295–296*

CDDB online database, 364–365

CDs

    for backups, **293**

    burning, **294–297**, *294*, *296–297*

    copying, **365–372**, *365*, *367–368*, *371*

    copying files to, **23–24**, *23–24*

    listening to, **38**, *38*

    playing, **364–365**

Certificate Export Wizard, 56, 286

Certificate Import Wizard, 288

certificates

    backing up, **56–57**, *56–57*, **285–286**, *286*

    for Web content, 480

Certificates dialog box, 56–57, 285, *286*

Certificates snap-in, 810

Challenge Handshake Authentication Protocol (CHAP), 690

Change Default Preferences settings, 345

Change Font option, 514

Change Icon dialog box, 210

Change My Message Font dialog box, 524

Change or Remove Programs page, 41, 238

Change permission, 660

Change Permissions permission, 663

Change the System Time right, 655

ChangeRole.wsf script, **753–755**, *755*

changing drivers, **80–83**, *80–83*, **340–341**, *340*

CHAP (Challenge Handshake Authentication Protocol), 690

character sets in Internet Explorer, 475

chatting

    in NetMeeting, **510–511**, *510*

    in Remote Assistance, **190**, **192–193**

    in Windows Messenger, **522–523**, *523*

        adding people to conversations, **524**

        blocking users, **525–526**, *526*

        text settings for, **524**

        video in, **525**, *525*

        voice in, **524**, *524*

chdir command, 772

Check Disk dialog box, 763–764

checking

    disks, **763–764**

    files in CD storage area, **294**

chkdisk command, 772

CIFS (Common Internet File System), 616

Classic Start menu, 220, *220*

Classic view, 198–199, *198*

clean installations, 127, **139**

    adding services in, **143**

    computer name in, **141**

    converting partitions for, **140**

    date and time in, **141**

    display settings in, **144**

    hard disk partitions for, **139–140**

    modem dialing information in, **141**

    name and organization in, **142**

    networking settings in, **142–143**

    product key in, **141**

    regional and language options in, **140–141**, *141*

    TCP/IP configuration in, **143–144**

    uninstalling services in, **143**

cleaning up

    desktop, **210**, *211*

    disks, **62**, *62*, **762–763**, *763*

cleanup utilities, compatibility of, 247

clearing

    CD storage area files, **297**, *297*

    log files, 706

ClearType feature, 109, **325**
client-server networks, **579–580**
Client Service for NetWare (CSNW) features, **885–886**
clients in networks, 568
    Novell NetWare
        configuring, **898–899**
        installing, **897–898**, *897–898*
        selecting, **896–897**
Clipboard, **256**, *257*
Clipbook service, 830
ClipBook Viewer, **257**, *258*
clipbrd.exe program, 257
Close command, 6
closing windows, 6
closure in troubleshooting, **789–790**
cls command, 772
.cmd files, **738**
collaboration, domains for, 632
Collection in Progress screen, 131, *131*
collections for Windows Movie Maker, **392**, *392*
color
    for chatting, **524**
    in e-mail, **551–552**
    options for, **213–214**, *213–215*
    for printers, **315**
    in Remote Desktop Connection, 533
    for Web pages, 475
color depth, **203–205**, *205*
Color Management tab, **315**
color schemes, 214
Colors dialog box, 475
COM, 750
COM+ Event System service, 830
COM+ System Application service, 830
Command Type screen, 822, *822*
commands for services, **837–839**, *837–838*
Commit Charge counter, 167
Common Files in IIS, 842
Common Internet File System (CIFS), 616
communications programs. *See* NetMeeting; Remote Desktop Connection; Windows Messenger
comp newsgroups, 557

compact privacy policies, 477
comparisons in scripts, **742–743**
compatibility
    hardware, 336
    as installation consideration, **126–127**
    program, **245–248**, *248*
Compatibility mode, **93–94**, *93–94*, **115–116**, 245–247
    formal setup, **248–254**, *249–254*
    problems in, **255**, *255*
    quick setup, **254–255**, *254*
Compatibility tab, 254–255, *254*
Compatible Hardware and Software page, **179**, *179*
Completing the Add Hardware Wizard screen, 338
Completing the Add Network Place Wizard screen, 883
Completing the Add Printer Wizard page, 46
Completing the Backup or Restore Wizard screen, 783
Completing the CD Writing Wizard screen, 24, 296, *296*
Completing the Collection Phase screen, 131
Completing the Found New Hardware Wizard screen, 334, 336
Completing the Network Identification Wizard, 641
Completing the Network Setup Wizard screen, 444, 447
Completing the Program Compatibility Wizard page, 253
Completing the Send Fax Wizard screen, 500
Completing the Windows Components Wizard page, 842
Component Services snap-in, 810
components, adding and removing, **240–241**, *240*
Compose tab, 560
compression
    for CDs, 369–370
    and encryption, 693
    for files and folders, **108**, **283–285**, *284*, **699**, *699*
Compression filter, 847
computer accounts for domain servers, **634**
Computer Administrator privilege, 75
Computer Administrators, 160, 652
Computer Browser service, 827
Computer Domain screen, 92, 641

Computer Management console, **817–819**, *818*
    for Disk Management, 697–698, *698*
    for groups, 77
    for hardware profiles, 612, *612*
    for peer-to-peer networks, 619
    for shares, 604
Computer Management snap-in, 810
Computer Name Changes dialog box
    for Active Directory, 914, *914*
    for domains, 640–641
Computer Name tab
    for Active Directory, 914
    for domains, 91, 640–641, *640*
    for peer-to-peer networks, 601, *601*
computer names
    in Active Directory, **910–915**, *914*
    in domains, 91, 640–641, *640*
    in installation, **141**, 155
    in peer-to-peer networks, 601, *601*
Computer Names screen, 155
Computer window, 869, *870*
computers
    locking, **165**
    notebook. *See* notebook computers
    roles for, **753–755**, *755*
Configuration Backup/Restore window, 845–846, *846*
Configuration tab, 598
Configure Port option, 53
Confirm Delete dialog box, 297, *297*
Confirm Device Removal dialog box, 339
Confirm File Delete dialog box, 25
Confirm Folder Delete dialog box, 25
Confirm Multiple File Delete dialog box, 26
Confirm Offline Subfolders dialog box, 55, 290, *290*,
    413, *413*
Confirm Restore Point Selection screen, 68, 766
Confirm Skin Delete dialog box, 376
Confirm Value Delete dialog box, 734, *734*
conflicts, IRQ, 718
Congratulations screen, 145
Connect dialog box
    for dial-up connections, 35–36

    for HyperTerminal, 505
    for VPNs, 90
Connect As dialog box, 74, 608, 643, *643*
Connect Password Required dialog box, 165
Connect to Computer window, 845, *845*
Connect To dialog box, 505
Connect to the Internet option, 34
Connect to the Network at My Workplace option, 89
Connect Using a Dial-Up Modem option, 34
Connect Using a Different User Name link, 74
Connecting to the Network screen, 92, 641
Connection Control option, 869
Connection Description dialog box, 505
Connection Name screen, 89, 426, *426*, 686, *686*
Connection section for FTP sites, 863
Connection Settings section, 532
Connection tab
    in Outlook Express, 560
    in Windows Messenger, **517**
Connection time-out (minutes) setting, 868
connections
    Active Directory, **912–915**, *914*
    dial-up Internet, **33–37**, *33–37*
    domains, 580, **631**, **635**, **640–642**
    firewalls for, **87**, *87*
    IIS services, **845**, *845*
    Internet. *See* Internet connections
    network drives, **73–74**, *73–74*
    newsgroups, **558**, *558*
    NIC, 585
    peer-to-peer networks, **593–594**, **608–610**, *609*,
        615–618, *617*
    radio stations, **374**
    remote. *See* Remote Desktop Connection
    shared printers, **49**, *49*
    UNCs for, **608–610**, *609*, **644–646**
    VPN, **89–90**, *89–90*
    Web sites, 853
Connections tab, **481**, *481*
connectivity
    in Active Directory, **909–910**
    Internet, **112–113**

connectors, cable, 587
Console tab, 813
Console tree option, 814
ConsoleOne utility, 888, *889*
consoles
    IIS, **844–846**, *845–846*
    MMC. *See* MMC (Microsoft Management
      Console)
contacts in Windows Messenger
    adding, **520–522**, *520–521*
    listing, **522**, *522*
    removing, **522**
Contacts pane, **543**, 548
containers, 886
content
    searching for files by, 28
    Web, **211–213**, *211–212*, **479–480**, *480*
    for Windows Movie Maker
      importing, **392–393**, *393*
      for projects, **395–396**, *395*
      recording, **393–395**, *394*
Content Advisor dialog box, 479–480
Content Ratings window, 859, *859*
Content Scrambling System (CSS), 378
Content tab
    for certificates, 56
    in Internet Explorer, **479–480**, *480*
Control Panel, **197–198**, 677
    for accessibility options, **223–226**, *224–227*
    for auditing, 673
    categories in, **104–105**, *104*, 198–199, *198*
    for certificates, 56
    for dialing rules, 410
    for disk management, 697
    for Event Viewer, 704
    for Internet connections, 33
    for performance, 708
    for printers, 44
    for program installation, 39
    for uninstalling, 149
    for volume control, 383–384
Control Panel applets, Registry information for, 724
controllers, SCSI, 797

convergence in monitors, 206
Conversation window
    in Remote Assistance, 192, *192*
    in Windows Messenger, 522–523, *523–524*,
      525–528, *527*
converting
    basic disks to dynamic disks, 703
    to NTFS, **140**
    Sound Recorder files, **390–391**, *391*
    WAV files, 390
cookies, **477–479**, *478–479*
Cookies folder, 276
Copy All Installation Files from the Setup CD
    option, **137**
Copy backup type, 785
copy commands, **21**, *21*, 256, 772, 775
Copy from CD tab, 367
Copy Here option, 273
Copy Items dialog box, 20, 70
Copy Music tab, 365, 367, *367*, 369
Copy Music to This Location option, 368
Copy Profile dialog box, 611
Copy Settings option, 368–369
Copy This File link, 20, 70
Copy This Folder link, 20, 70
Copy to CD or Device tab, 380–382
Copy To dialog box, 614–615
copying
    CDs, **365–372**, *365*, *367–368*, *371*
    files, **20–24**, *20–24*, **273**
      audio, **381–382**, *382*
      for Briefcase, **414–415**, *415*
      to CD storage area, **293–294**, *294*
      in recovery, 775
      from remote computers, 490, **538**
    folders, **20–24**, *20–24*, **273**
    Registry key names, **734**
Copyright Clearance Center, 876
copyright issues, 377
    in copying CDs, 365–366
    in Web publishing, **875–876**
core dumps, **780–781**
corrupted files, 780

Counter Log view, **713–714**
counters, **708–710**
cover pages for faxes, **500–504**, *500–502*
crashes
    avoiding, **758–761**
    shutting down after, **173**
Create a New Account link, 75
Create a New Connection link, 89
Create a New Connection Wizard, 33
Create a Password for Your Account screen, 71
Create a Restore Point screen, 67, 767, *767*
Create Account option, 75
Create Files/Write Data permission, 663
Create Folder dialog box, 545, *545*
Create Folders/Append Data permission, 663
Create from File tab, 259–260, *260*
Create New tab, 260–261, *260*
Create New Task dialog box, 720, *720*
Create Offline Files Shortcut on the Desktop
    option, 412
Create Password option, 76
Create Shortcut Wizard, 31–32
Create Shortcuts Here command, 9
Create Shortcut(s) Here option, 273
CreateObject method, 751
Critical Alarms section, 355
Critical Battery Actions dialog box, 406, *406*
Critical Battery threshold, 405
crossover cables, 594
Cryptographic Services, 827
CScript.exe file, **744–745**
CSNW (Client Service for NetWare) features, **885–886**
CSS (Content Scrambling System), 378
Current Sessions section, 863
cursor blink rate, 221
Custom Errors tab, **850–851**, *850*, **859**
Custom HTTP Headers option, 858
Custom Notifications dialog box, 217–218, *217*
Customize Classic Start Menu dialog box, 220, *220*
Customize Notifications dialog box, 13
Customize Regional Options dialog box, 140
Customize Start Menu dialog box, 11–12, 218–219,
    219, 263, *263*

Customize tab for folders, 279, *279*, 281
Customize the Software screen, 155
Customize Toolbar dialog box, 280, *280*, 482–483, *482*
Customize View dialog box, 708, *708*, 814–815, *815*
Customize View option, 824
Cut command, **21**, *21*, 256
CuteFTP client, 884
cutting with Remote Desktop, **538**

D

D (data) channels, 437
daemons, 825
Daily backup type, 785
damaged files, replacing, **774–775**
"DATA_BUS_ERROR" message, 800
data (D) channels, 437
Data Link layer, **571**
data types in Registry, **729–730**, *729*
database records, 233–234
date
    changing, **199–200**, *199–200*
    in installation, **141**
    searching for files by, 28
Date and Time Settings screen, 142
DDE (Dynamic Data Exchange), 258
deaf users, accessibility options for, **224–225**, *225*
decrypting files and folders, **58**, *58*, **286–287**
DeCSS utility, 378
dedicated servers, 580–581
Default FTP Site Properties window, 862–866,
    863–865
DEFAULT hive file, 730
DEFAULT.LOG file, 731
Default Preferences dialog box, 345, *345*
DEFAULT.RDP file, 533
Default SMTP Virtual Server Properties window,
    868, *868*
defaults
    gateways, 144, 146
    for printers, 51
    user profiles, 614
    Web site documents, 849
defragmenting hard disks, **60–61**, *60–61*, **761–762**, *762*

del command, 772
delegation in Active Directory, **907–908**
delete command, 772
Delete permission, 663
Delete Subfolders and Files permission, 663
Delete This File link, 25
Delete This Folder link, 25
Deleted Items folder, 543, 547, 555
deleting and removing
    audio clips, 382
    components, **240–241**, *240*
    contacts, **522**
    e-mail, **547**
    favorites, 181, 462
    files and folders, **25**, *25*, **274–275**, 775
    fonts, 321
    History list items, 464
    hot-pluggable devices, 331
    message rules, 555
    offline files, 54
    partitions, 140, **776–777**
    printer drivers, **311**
    programs, **41**, *41*, **237–240**, *238–239*
    radio stations, 375
    Registry favorites, 735
    Registry items, **734**
    Start menu items, 10–11
    Windows Media Player skins, 376
Delivery tab, **871–872**, *871*
Dependencies tab, **836**, *836*
Description bar option, 815
Description setting, 853
descriptions
    for groups, 77
    for tasks, 821
    for Web sites, 853
Desktop
    background for, 165, **208–209**, *209*
    cleaning up, **210**, *211*
    icons on, **209–210**, *210*
    parts of, **163–165**, *164*
    in Remote Desktop Connection, 535

    saving files and folders to, **273**
    toolbars on, **8–9**, *8–9*
    Web content on, **211–212**, *211–212*
Desktop Cleanup Wizard, **210**, *211*
Desktop (Create Shortcut) command, 32
Desktop folder, 276
Desktop Items dialog box
    for Desktop Cleanup Wizard, 211
    for icons, 210, *210*
    for Web content, 211, *211*
Desktop tab
    for background, 209, *209*
    for icons, 209
    for Web images, 467
Details dialog box, 238, *238*
details pane in MMC, 821
Details view
    in Briefcase, 415, *415*
    in Explorer, 17, *17*, 270–271, *270*
device drivers. *See* drivers
Device Manager
    for drivers, 81–83
    for hardware profiles, 612
    for hardware properties, 339, *340*
    for USB hubs, 349, *349*
Device Manager snap-in, 810
Device Settings tab
    for fonts, 322–324, *324*
    for printers, 51, **314**, *314*
devices. *See* hardware
Devices tab
    for CDs, 370, *371*
    for Windows Media Player, 381
DHCP (Dynamic Host Configuration Protocol),
    572, 600
    for domains, 635–636
    for private networks, 576, 578
    scope issues in, 649
    setting for, 145–146, 598
DHCP Client service, 828
Diagnostics tab, 343, *344*
Dial Control setting, 343

dial-in sessions
    Remote Desktop Connection for. *See* Remote
        Desktop Connection
    security for, **88**, *88*, **682–684**, *683*
dial-up Internet connections
    setting up, **33–35**, *33–35*
    using, **36–37**, *36–37*
dialing locations for notebook computers,
    409–410, *410*
Dialing Rules tab, 410
Did the Program Work Correctly? screen, 252, *253*
Differential backup type, 785
digital certificates
    backing up, **56–57**, *56–57*, **285–286**, *286*
    for Web content, 480
digital licenses, 378
Digital Subscriber Line. *See* DSL (Digital Subscriber
    Line)
Digital Subscriber Line (DSL) or Cable Modem
    option, 144
dir command, 775
Direct Cable Connection, 410
direct connections, UNCs for, **608–610**, *609*, **644–646**
Directory Below This One option, 857
Directory Browsing access, 848
Directory Located on This Computer option, 857
Directory Security tab, **849**, *850*, **858**
directory servers, **511**
directory service access
    auditing, 672
    vs. object access, **673**
directory services, **886–887**, 903
DirectX Diagnostics Tool, 207, *207*
disable command, 772, 774
disabled services, **832**
disabling
    hardware, **338–339**, *339*
    services, **773–774**
disaster prevention and recovery, **757**
    backups in
        creating, **781–785**, *782–784*
        restoring, **785–786**
    blue screens, **780–781**

checking disks, **763–764**
cleaning up disks, **762–763**, *763*
crash avoidance, **758–761**
defragmenting files, **761–762**, *762*
driver verifier for, **777–779**, *779*
Recovery Console for, **770–777**
restoring configuration, **764–770**, *766–770*
System File Checker for, **779–780**
Disconnect Network Drive dialog box, 608
Disconnect Windows dialog box, 539, *539*
Disconnect Windows session dialog box, 539, *539*
disconnected users, 103, 160
disconnecting
    in Remote Assistance, **191**, **193**
    in Remote Desktop Connection, **539**, *539*
Disk Cleanup feature, **62**, *62*, 762–763, *763*
Disk Defragmenter, **60–61**, *60–61*
Disk Defragmenter snap-in, 810
Disk Management, **697–698**
    for drive setup, **700–701**
    for dynamic volumes, **703–704**
    for file systems, **698–700**
    for partitions, **701–703**, *702*
Disk Management snap-in, 810
Disk Read Bytes/sec counter, 710
Disk Write Bytes/sec counter, 710
diskless workstations, 579
diskpart command, 772
disks
    checking, **763–764**
    cleaning up, **62**, *62*, **762–763**, *763*
    converting to NTFS, **140**
    copying files to, **22**, *22*
    defragmenting, **60–61**, *60–61*, **761–762**, *762*
    dynamic volumes, **703–704**
    file systems on, **698–700**
    floppy, **22**, *22*, **414–416**, *416*
    mapping, 73–74
        in domains, **643**, *643*, **645**
        in Novell NetWare networks, **890–891**
        in peer-to-peer networks, **607–608**, *607*
    partitions for. *See* partitions
    removable, **22**, *22*, **347–348**, *348*

space requirements for, **125**
utilities for, **131**, 247
display
    color and appearance options, **213–214**, *213–215*
    desktop, **208–212**, *209–212*
    installation settings for, **144**
    screen savers, **213**
    themes for, **208**
Display a Reminder Every setting, 412
Display Alerts Near the Taskbar When an Instant
    Message Is Received option, 515
Display Alerts Near the Taskbar When Contacts Come
    Online option, 515
display fonts, **324–325**, *325*
Display Properties dialog box
    for background, 209, *209*
    for monitors, 351
    for power options, 404
    for resolution, 205, *205*
    for video cards, 348
    for wallpaper, 467
Display Settings dialog box, 144, 155
Display subroutine, 748–749
Display tab
    for Remote Desktop Connection, 86, 533, *533*
    for visually-impaired users, 224, *224*
Display the Connection Bar When in Full Screen Mode
    option, 533
Display Troubleshooter feature, 207, *207*
distances with network cables, **586**
Distributed Link Tracking Client service, 828
Distributed Transaction Coordinator service, 830
Distribution Folder screen, 154
DLLs (dynamic link libraries), **627**
DMA channels, **330**
DNS Client service, 828
DNS information
    for domains, **637–638**
    pointer issues with, 649
DNS suffix for this connection setting, 638
DNS tab, 637, *637*
Do Not Dial the Initial Connection option, 90

Do Not Save Changes to This Console option, 814
Do You Have a Windows XP CD? screen, 147
Do You Use a Username and Password to Connect to
    the Internet? screen, 145
Do You Want Help Finding an Internet Service
    Provider? screen, 145
Do You Want to Set Up Internet Access Now?
    screen, 145
Do You Want to Use the Shared Connection? screen,
    445, *445*
docking stations, 400, 611–612
Documentation component in IIS, 842
documentation in troubleshooting, **788**, **790**
Documents folder, 276
Documents tab, **849**, *849*, **858**
Domain setting in LDAP, 872
Domain User Name and Password dialog box, 92, 641
domains
    alternate accounts for, 643
    connecting to, 580, **631**, **635**, **640–642**
    identification for, **640**, *640*, **649**
    IP configuration for, **635–640**, *636–637*, *639*
    joining, **91–92**, *91–92*
    logging on to, **163**
    Microsoft vs. Internet, **633**
    network resources for, **642–647**, *643–644*
    profiles for, **646–647**
    in Remote Desktop Connection, 532
    servers for, **633–634**
    setting up, **632**
    troubleshooting, **647–649**
Don't Inherit Security Settings option, 860
Don't Prompt Me Again to Install This Software
    option, 333
Don't Search. I Will choose the Driver to Install
    option, 82
Don't Show Me This Message Again option, *526*
DOS programs
    compatibility of, 245–246
    uninstalling, **239–240**
double-word data in Registry, 729–730
Download Complete dialog box, 473, *473*

Download tab, 469
Download the Updates Automatically and Notify Me
   When They Are Ready to Be Installed option, 151
downloading files
     with FTP, **486–488**, *487*
     with Internet Explorer, **473**, *473*
Downloading Newsgroups dialog box, 558
Drafts folder, 543
dragging files, **273**
drive letters, mapping, 73–74
     in domains, **643**, *643*, **645**
     in Novell NetWare networks, 890–891
     in peer-to-peer networks, **607–608**, *607*
DriveImage package, 127
Driver.cab file, 328
"DRIVER_IRQL_NOT_LESS_OR_EQUAL" mes-
   sage, 801
Driver tab
     for monitors, 203
     for rolling back drivers, 84
     for video, 202
"DRIVER_USED_EXCESSIVE_PTES" message, 801
Driver Verifier, **777–779**, *779*
drivers, **102**, **327–328**
     changing, **80–83**, *80–83*, **340–341**, *340*
     file system, **627–628**
     forgiving, 758–759
     I/O manager for, 120
     .INF files, **328–329**, *329*
     installing, **330–331**, **333–336**, *334–335*
     for monitors, **203**, *203*
     for NICs, **628–629**
     for printers, **300–305**, *302, 304*, **311**
     problems from, **760**
     referral site for, **111**
     rolling back, **84**, *84*, **115**
     searching for, 336
     signing, **328**
     verifier for, **777–779**, *779*
     versions, **329**
     for video, **201–202**, *201–202*
     viewing, **340–341**, *340*

Drivers tab
     for print servers, 53, 318
     for viewing and changing drivers, 340, *340*
drives
   CD
     adding, **345–346**, *346*
     requirements for, **126**
   disk. *See* disks
   DVD
     adding, **346–347**
     requirements, **126**
   network. *See* network drives
   in setup, **795–799**
Drives screen, 716, *716*
DS (directory service), **886–887**, 903
DSL (Digital Subscriber Line), **432**
     advantages and disadvantages of, **433**
     hooking up, **433–434**
     operation of, **432**
     setting up, **145–146**
     speed of, **432–433**
     troubleshooting, **456**
DualView feature, 350, **400–401**
DVD drives
     adding, **346–347**
     requirements for, **126**
DVD tab, 372–373, *372*
DVD Region tab, 346
DVDs, playing, **372–373**, *372–373*
Dynamic Data Exchange (DDE), 258
Dynamic Host Configuration Protocol (DHCP),
   572, 600
     for domains, 635–636
     for private networks, 576, 578
     scope issues in, 649
     setting for, 145–146, 598
dynamic link libraries (DLLs), **627**
Dynamic Update
     for compatibility, 126
     in installation, 133–134, 139
dynamic volumes, **703–704**

E

e-mail
   in Internet Explorer, **465**, *465*
   in Outlook Express. *See* Outlook Express
   for Remote Assistance, 183
      receiving, **189**, *189*
      responding to, **191**, *191*
      sending, **185–187**, *185–187*
   SMTP servers for. *See* SMTP servers
e-mail addresses for Messenger contacts,
   520–521, *521*
EAP (Extensible Authentication Protocol), 689–690
echo function, 740
Edit Binary Value dialog box, 733, *733*
Edit DWORD Value dialog box, 732, *733*
Edit Multi-String dialog box, 732, *732*
Edit String dialog box, 732, *732*
editing
   embedded objects, 261
   fax cover pages, **501–504**, *501–502*
   Internet radio presets, **375**
   Registry. *See* Registry Editor
   scripts, 746
   Start menu, **263–264**, *263–264*
   Windows Media Player tags, **361–362**, *362*
Effects dialog box, 214, *214*
EFS (Encrypting File System), 58, **285**
   backing up certificates for, **285–286**, *286*
   encrypting and decrypting in, **286**
   for telecommuting, **692–693**, *693*
embedded objects, editing, 261
embedding in OLE, 258
emoticons, 514
emptying Recycle Bin, 26, **275**
Enable Advanced Printing Features option, 314
Enable Authoring option, 860
enable command, 772, 774
Enable Digital CD Audio for This CD-ROM Device
   option, 346
Enable File Sharing dialog box, 605, *605*
Enable Logging section
   for FTP sites, 863

   for SMTP servers, 869
   for Web sites, 853
Enable Offline Files option, 54
encoding regions, **346–347**
Encrypt Offline Files to Secure Data option, 412
Encrypt the File and Parent Folder option, 58
Encrypt the File Only option, 58
encrypted files
   sharing, **59**, *59*, **287**
   transferring, **288**
Encrypting File System (EFS), 58, **285**
   backing up certificates for, **285–286**, *286*
   encrypting and decrypting in, **286**
   for telecommuting, **692–693**, *693*
encryption, **58**, *58*, **286–287**
   for authentication, **689–690**
   certificates for, 56
   for copyright protection, 378
   for dial-in sessions, 88, **683–684**
   in telecommuting, **692–693**, *693*
End Program dialog box, 244, *244*
Enter Network Password dialog box, 881–882
Environment Variables folder, 718, *718*
environmental hazards, guarding against, **759–760**
Err object, **750**
error correction for CDs, 371
Error events, 705
Error Mapping Properties dialog box, 851
Error Reporting Service, 828
Errors Logon counter, 711
Ethernet networks, 568, 572, 582
   connecting, **593–594**
   hardware for, **583–584**
Event Log service, 828
Event Properties dialog box, 619, *619*, 678, *678*
Event Viewer, 668, **704–708**, *704–708*
   in auditing, **677–679**, *677–678*
   for peer-to-peer networks, 619–620
Event Viewer snap-in, 810
events in Windows Messenger, 515
Exact URL Entered Above option, 857
exchanging data between programs, **255–256**
   Clipboard for, **256**, *257*

ClipBook Viewer for, **257**, *258*
OLE for, **258–261**, *259–261*
Exclude Files tab, 785
Execute permission, 861
Executive services, 118–119
exit command, 774
Exit section for FTP servers, 864
expandable strings in Registry, 729–730
Experience tab, 86, 535, *535*
Explorer, **266**
    branches in, **267**
    folders in
        customizing, **279–280**, *279*
        managing, **272–275**
        options for, **277–279**
    Internet. *See* Internet Explorer
    navigating in, **14–15**, *14–15*
    opening vs. exploring in, **266**, *266–267*
    saving e-mail in, **544–545**, *544*
    toolbars in, **280**, *280*
    views in, **16–17**, *16–17*, **267–271**, *268–270*
Export List command, 820
Export Registry File dialog box, 726, *726*
exporting Windows Movie Maker projects, **396–397**, *397*
extended partitions, **701–703**, *702*
Extended tab, 826–827
Extended Properties tab, 854, *855*
Extensible Authentication Protocol (EAP), 689–690
extensions
    file associations for, **291–292**, *292*
    snap-ins as, 809
Extensions tab, 812
external monitors, **400–401**
external NICs, 585
Extra initialization settings for modems, 344
extract command, 772, 775
eye candy, **105**

F

Failure events
    auditing, 674–675
    logging, 705
Fast User Switching Compatibility service, 830

Fast User Switching feature, 54, **288**, **411**
FAT file system
    vs. NTFS, **698–700**
    partitions for, 139–140
FAT32 file system, 699
"FAT32_FILE_SYSTEM" message, 800
favorites
    in Help and Support Center, **181**
    Internet Explorer sites, **460–462**, *461*, *463*, **468**
    in MMC, **824**
    offline, **468–470**, *469–470*
    in Registry Editor, **735**, *735*
Favorites folder, 276
Fax Configuration Wizard, 95–96, 495–497, *495–497*
Fax Console, 96, **504–505**, *504*
Fax Cover Page Editor, 501–504, *501–502*
Fax Monitor dialog box, 505
Fax Properties dialog box, 505
Fax service, **95–96**, *95–96*, **109**, **493–494**, 828
    configuring, **494–497**, *494–497*
    cover pages in, **500–504**, *500–502*
    Fax Console, 96, **504–505**, *504*
    installing, **494**
    sending faxes in, **498–500**, *498–499*
fdisk.exe program, 798
File and Folder Tasks list, 15
File and Printer Sharing for Microsoft Networks, **599–600**
File Download dialog box, 473, *473*
File In Use dialog box, 234
file management, 565
File menu in MMC, **820**
File Name Options dialog box, 368, *368*
File Services for Unix product, 616
file systems
    drivers for, **627–628**
    FAT vs. NTFS, **698–700**
    I/O manager for, 120
File Transfer Protocol. *See* FTP (File Transfer Protocol) and FTP servers
File Transfer Protocol Service, 842
File Types tab
    for associations, 291–292, *292*

for folders, 278
for Media Library, 363
filenames
 on Novell NetWare networks, **896**
 renaming, **19**, *19*, **274**, 775
 in UNCs, **645**
files
 associating, **291–292**, *292*
 auditing, **664–668**, *665–668*
 in CD storage area
  checking, **294**
  clearing, **297**, *297*
  copying to, **293–294**, *294*
  writing from, **294–296**, *295–296*
 compressed, **108**, **283–285**, *284*, **699**, *699*
 copying, **20–24**, *20–24*, **273**
  audio, **381–382**, *382*
  for Briefcase, **414–415**, *415*
  to CD storage area, **293–294**, *294*
  in recovery, 775
  from remote computers, 490, **538**
 corrupted, 780
 defragmenting, **60–61**, *60–61*, **761–762**, *762*
 deleting, **25**, *25*, **274–275**
 dragging, **273**
 encrypted, **59**, *59*, **287=288**
 encrypting and decrypting, **58**, *58*, **286–287**,
  692–693, *693*
 Explorer for. *See* Explorer
 moving, **20–24**, *20–24*, **272**
 with multiple users, **161**, **233–234**
 offline. *See* offline files
 permissions for, **661–664**, *662*, *664*
 properties for, **280–281**
 recovering, **26**, *26*, **275**
 for Remote Assistance invitations, 183, **188**, **192**
 saving to Desktop, **273**
 searching for, **27–29**, *27–29*, **281–282**,
  281–282
 sharing, **70**, *70*, **565**
 synchronizing, **410–411**, **414–416**, *415–416*
 transferring, 102
  encrypted, **288**

 with FTP, **486–488**, *487*
 in HyperTerminal, **506**
 in Internet Explorer, **473**, *473*
 in Remote Assistance, **193**
 in Windows Messenger, **526–528**, *527–528*
Files and Settings Transfer Wizard, **102**, 127
 for restoring, **147–148**, *148*
 for saving, **128–131**, *129–131*
Filmstrip view, 17, *17*, 268, *269*
Filter tab, 705, *705*
Filter view, 705
filtering
 events, 705, *705*
 IP, **639–640**, *639*
 for Web servers, **847–848**, *847*, **856**
FilterKeys feature, 225
Find in Local System dialog box, 707, *707*
finding. *See* searching
finger program, **488**
firewalls, **87**, *87*, **112**, **435–436**, *436*
first-party cookies, 477
fixboot command, 772
Fixing a Problem tool, 111
fixmbr command, 772
floppy disks
 for Briefcase operations, **414–416**, *416*
 copying files to, **22**, *22*
flow control in scripts, **743–744**, *744*
Fn key on notebooks, 399, *400*
Folder Options dialog box, **277–279**
 for associations, **291–292**
 for hidden folders, 276
 for offline files, 289, *289*, **411–412**
Folder snap-in, 810
folders
 auditing, **664–668**, *665–668*
 compressed, **107**, **283–285**, *284*, **699**, *699*
 copying, **20–24**, *20–24*, **273**
 creating, **18**, *18*, **272**, 775
 deleting, **25**, *25*, **274–275**, 775
 drive mapping for, 643, **645**
 encrypting and decrypting, **58**, *58*, **286–287**,
  692–693

Explorer for
  customizing, **279–280**, *279*
  managing, **272–275**
  options for, **277–279**
moving, **20–24**, *20–24*, **272**
names for, **18–19**, *19*, **274**
offline. *See* offline files
permissions for, **661–664**, *662*, *664*
private, **71**, *71*
properties for, **280–281**
recovering, **26**, *26*, **275**
saving
  to Desktop, **273**
  e-mail in, **545**, *545*
sharing, **70**, *70*, **72**, *72*
in Windows Messenger, 516, 528
Folders list in Outlook Express, **542–543**
Folders pane in Explorer, 267–268
Following System Components Depend on This
  Service option, 836
Font Size Used for Help Content list, 178
fonts, **319**
  for chatting, **524**
  ClearType feature, **325**
  installing, **320**, *320*
  managing, **320–321**, *321–322*
  printer-resident, **323–324**
  selecting, **324–325**, *325*
  size of, 214
  substitution tables for, **324**, *324*
  types of, **322–324**, *323*
  for Web pages, 475
  in Windows Messenger, 514
Fonts dialog box, 319, 475
for command, **742–743**
Force Shutdown from a Remote System right, 655
forests, 910
format command, 772
Format Partition screen, 702, *702*
formatting partitions, 140, **776–777**
Forms tab, 318
Forums tab, 52
forwarding e-mail, **547**

Found New Hardware Wizard
  for drivers, **331–336**, *332–335*
  for monitors, 351
fpexedll.dll filter, 848
frame types in IPX/SPX, **625**
FrontPage 2000 Server Extensions, 842
FrontPage Server Extensions snap-in, 810
FTP (File Transfer Protocol) and FTP servers,
  486–488, *487*, 572
  configuring, **862**
  FTP Site tab for, **863**, *863*
  Home Directory tab for, **865–866**, *865*
  Messages tab for, **864–865**, *865*
  Security Accounts tab for, **863**, *864*
  virtual directories for, **866–867**, *866–867*
  for Web publishing, **878**, **881**, **883–884**
FTP Publishing service, 833
FTP Site tab, **863**, *863*
Full Control permission, 660–661, 663
Full mode in Windows Media Player, 358, *358*
Full-Text Search Matches option, 175, 177
function keys on notebooks, 399, *400*

G

games, 108
gateway addresses for domains, **636–637**, *637*
GDI (Graphics Device Interface), **121**
General Properties tab, 854
General Public License, 566
General tab
  accessibility options, 226, *227*
  backups, 785
  compression, 284, 699
  Desktop Cleanup Wizard, 211
  dialing rules, 410, *410*
  encryption, 58–59, 286–287
  folders, 277
  hardware profiles, 612
  History list, 463–464
  Internet Explorer, **474–475**, *474*
  ISDN, 439
  log settings, 706
  network bridges, 603, *603*

Outlook Express, 543, 559
peer-to-peer networks, 601, *601*
printers, 50, **312**, *312*, 793
properties, 280–281
RAM, 124
Remote Desktop Connection, 86, 532–533, *532*, 536
services, **833–834**, *833*
SMTP servers, **868–869**, *868*
Start menu, 11, 218–219, 263, *263*
System Configuration Utility, 237
TCP/IP, 143–144
Web content, 480
Get Names feature, 367
Get Updated Setup Files screen, 133–134, *134*, 138, *138*
GetArgs function, 748–749
GetFile method, 751
GetFileInfo.vbs script, 748–749, *749*
Getting Ready screen, 425, *425*
Ghost package, 127
Give This Computer a Description and Name screen, 441, *441*, 447
Give Warning Message When Turning a Feature On option, 226
goto command, **743–744**, *744*
Graph view, 708, *709*, **711–712**
graphic equalizers, **360–361**, *361*
graphics
    acquiring and handling, **107**
    in e-mail, **551**
    Web, **467**
Graphics Device Interface (GDI), **121**
grid view for fax cover pages, 501, *501*
group policies, Active Directory for, 912
Group Policy snap-in, 810
Group Policy Wizard, 665, *665*
Group Similar Taskbar Buttons option, 216
groups
    accounts for, **77**, *77*, **658**, *658*
    built-in, **653**
    Taskbar button, **105–106**
groupware, 567

Guest account, 160, 652
Guest privilege, 75
Guests group, 653
GUI mode issues, **797–799**

H
HAL (Hardware Abstraction Layer)
    for compatibility, 245
    and kernel, **119**
hard disks. *See* disks
hardware, **327**
    Add Hardware Wizard for, **336–338**, *337–338*
    adding
        CD drives, **345–346**, *346*
        DVD drives, **346–347**
        removable drives, **347–348**, *348*
        video cards, **348–349**, *349*
    for crash avoidance, **758–759**
    disabling, **338–339**, *339*
    drivers for. *See* drivers
    Found New Hardware Wizard for
        for drivers, **331–336**, *332–335*
        for monitors, 351
    hot-pluggable devices, **331–332**
    in installation, **128**
    multiple monitors, **350–351**
    properties for
        for drivers, **340–341**, *340*
        for modems, **342–345**, *342–345*
        for resource assignments, **341–342**, *341–342*
        viewing, **339**, *340*
    system resources for, **329–330**
    uninstalling, **339**
    USB hub usage, **349–350**, *349–350*
Hardware Abstraction Layer (HAL)
    for compatibility, 245
    and kernel, **119**
hardware acceleration, 349, 385
Hardware Acceleration setting, 385
hardware compatibility list (HCL), 351
hardware profiles
    creating, **610–613**, *611–613*
    for domains, **646**

managing, **612–613**, *612–613*
for notebook computers, **402–404**, *403*
for services, 834
Hardware Profiles dialog box, 403, *403*, 611, *611*
Hardware tab
for disabling hardware, 339
for drivers, 81
for mouse, 222
for profiles, 611
for properties, 339
Hardware Type screen, 334, *334*
Hardware Update Wizard, 81–83
for drivers, 340
for monitors, 203, *203*
for video, 202, *202*, 348
HCL (hardware compatibility list), 351
hearing-impaired users, accessibility options for, **224–225**, *225*
HelloWorld.cmd script, 739–740, *739*
HelloWorld.wsf script, 746–747, *747*
help, **110–111**
Help and Support Center. *See* Help and Support Center
Microsoft Online Support, **194**
newsgroups for, **194**, 196
Remote Assistance. *See* Remote Assistance
troubleshooters for, **194–195**, *195*
on Web, **196**
Help and Support Center, **110–111**, **173**
browsing in, **178–181**, *179–180*
for Compatibility mode, **248–254**, *249–254*
favorites in, **181**
history in, **182**, *182*
for NetMeeting, 507
for newsgroups, 194
options in, **178**
printing in, **182–183**
searching in, **175–178**, *175, 177*
starting, **173–174**, *174*
for troubleshooters, **194–195**, *195*
views in, **182**
Help and Support service, 828
help command, 772, 820

HelpServicesGroup group, 653
Hibernate tab, 409, *409*
Hibernation
enabling and disabling, **408–409**, *409*
troubleshooting, **418–419**
hidden components, removing, **241**
hidden folders, 276
Hide Inactive Icons option, 13
Hide when Inactive option, 13
hiding
font variations, 321
icons, 13
Taskbar, 216
high contrast display, 224
High option for cookies, 477
High security level, 476
Histogram view, 709
history and History lists
in Help and Support Center, **182**, *182*
in Internet Explorer, **463–464**, *463*
settings for, **474–475**
hive files, 727, 730
HKEY_ subtrees, 727
Hold Mismatched Documents option, 313
home computers, Remote Desktop Connections to, **86**, *86*, 529
Home Directory tab
for FTP servers, **865–866**, *865*
for Web servers, **848–849**, *848*, **856–857**, *856–857*
home folders, drive mapping for, **645**
Home page
in Help and Support Center, **173–174**, *174*
in Internet Explorer, **474**
Host a Meeting dialog box, 511, *511*
hosting NetMeeting meetings, **511**, *511*
hosting servers, **841**
FTP. *See* FTP (File Transfer Protocol) and FTP servers
IIS for
installation and setup, **841–846**, *842–843, 845–846*
troubleshooting, **873**

SMTP. *See* SMTP servers
Web. *See* Web servers
hostname utility, 622
hot-pluggable devices, **331–332**
How Do You Want to Add a Contact? screen, 520, *521*
How Do You Want to Locate the Program That You Would Like to Run with Compatibility Settings? screen, 248–249, *249*
How to Restore dialog box, 786
How Will This Computer Connect to the Internet? screen, 144
HTML (Hypertext Markup Language)
  for e-mail, **549–553**, *550*, *552*
  viewing pages in, 459
HTTP (Hypertext Transfer Protocol), 572
HTTP Headers tab, **850**, **858–859**, *858*
hubs, 568, 583, **587–588**
  in peer-to-peer networks, 594
  USB, **349–350**, *349–350*
Human Interface Device Access service, 832
humanities newsgroups, 557
Hungarian notation, 745
hybrid switches, 571
Hyperlink dialog box, 552
hyperlinks, **552**
HyperTerminal program, **505–506**, *506*
Hypertext Markup Language (HTML)
  for e-mail, **549–553**, *550*, *552*
  viewing pages in, 459
Hypertext Transfer Protocol (HTTP), 572

I

I/O addresses, **330**
I/O Manager, **119–120**, *119*
i386 folder, 139
IANA (Internet Assigned Numbers Authority), 576
IASPI tab, **847–848**, *847*, **856**
ICF (Internet Connection Firewall), **87**, *87*, **112**, 435–436, *436*
ICMP (Internet Control Message Protocol) echo packets, 489, *489*
ICMP tab, 453–454, *453*

icons
  on desktop, **209–210**, *210*
  in notification area, 13
  size of, 11
Icons view, 17, *17*, 268
ICS (Internet Connection Sharing), **112**, **439**
  alternatives to, **449–450**
  computer setup for
    client computer, **444–447**, *445–447*
    sharing computer, **440–444**, *440–444*
  configuring, **450–451**, *450*
  IP addresses for, **454**
  NAT in, **448–449**, *449*
  operation of, **448**
  programs and services for, **451–454**, *452–454*
  turning off, **454**
  working with, **455**
ID numbers, SCSI, 795
identification and identities
  for domains, **640**, *640*, **649**
  in e-mail, **555–556**, *556*
  in FTP sites, 863
  in peer-to-peer networks, **599**, **601**, *601*
Identification tab, 599
if command, **742–743**
IIS (Internet Information Services)
  console for, **844–846**, *845–846*
  installing, **841–843**, *842–843*
  limits on, **844**
  troubleshooting, **873**
IIS Admin service, 833
IIS_WPG group, 653
IM (instant messaging), 512
images
  acquiring and handling, **107**
  in e-mail, **551**
  Web, **467**
IMAPI CD-Burning COM Service, 830
impersonation, user
  caller-ID/callback for, **690–691**
  encrypted authentication for, **689–690**
  guidelines for, **688–689**
  third-party products, **691**

Import Registry File dialog box, 727
importing Windows Movie Maker content,
    392–393, *393*
"INACCESSIBLE_BOOT_DEVICE" message, 800
Inbox folder
    for faxes, 504
    in Outlook Express, 542
Incoming folder, 504
incompatible programs, **247–248**, *248*
Incorrect Operating System dialog box, 248, *248*
Incremental backup type, 785
Indexing Service, 830
Indexing Service snap-in, 810
Industry Standard Architecture (ISA) boards, 758
.INF files, **328–329**, *329*
Information events, 704
INI files, 724
Initialize Disk dialog box, 700, *700*
Insert Attachment dialog box, 553, *553*
Insert Object command, **259–261**, *260*
Insert the Disk You Want to Use screen, 444, *444*
Install from a List or Specific Location option, 81, 332
Install from Disk dialog box, 82–83, 143, 334–336, 898
Install Printer Software screen, 45, 304, *304*
Install Program As Other User dialog box, 232, *232*
Install Program from Floppy Disk or CD-ROM
    screen, 40
Install Programs on Your New Computer screen, 131
Install the Software Automatically option, 332
Install Windows XP link, 132, *132*, 135, *135*
Installation Complete screen, 43
installing, **123**
    automating, **152–157**
    clean. *See* clean installations
    compatibility checking in, **126–127**
    drivers, **330–331**, **333–336**, *334–335*
    Fax service, **494**
    fonts, **320**, *320*
    hot-pluggable devices, **331–332**
    IIS, **841–843**, *842–843*
    Internet connections, **144–146**
    methods, **127**
    NetMeeting, **507–508**, *507–508*

networks, **589**
new installations, **135–139**, *135–138*
Novell clients, **897–898**, *897–898*
old Windows version removal in, **149**
order of, **124**
preparation for
    antivirus software, **131**
    backups, **128**
    hardware, **128**
    Internet connection information, **128**
    settings transfer, **128–131**, *129–131*
printers, **44–47**, *44–47*, **301–305**, *302, 304*
problems from, **760**
programs, **39–40**, *39–40*, **232**, *232*, **235–237**
Recovery Console, **771**
remote printers, **309–311**, *309–310*
requirements
    adapters and monitors, **125**
    CD drives, **126**
    disk space, **125**
    processor, **124**
    RAM, **124–125**
settings transfer in
    restoring, **147–148**, *148*
    saving, **128–131**, *129–131*
Stop errors in, 799
uninstalling, **149**, *149*
updating, **149–152**, *151*
upgrading, **132–134**, *132–135*
UPSs, **353–356**, *353–355*
user accounts, **146**
Windows activation, **146–147**
Windows registration, **147**
instant messaging (IM), 512
Integrated Services Digital Network (ISDN), **436–437**
    advantages and disadvantages of, **437–438**
    hooking up, **438–439**
    operation of, **437**
interface
    accessibility options. *See* accessibility options
    Control Panel, **197–199**, *198*
    date and time, **199–200**, *199–200*
    display, **208–214**, *209–215*

keyboard and mouse, **220–222**
Start Menu, **218–220**, *218–220*
system sounds, **222**, *222*
Taskbar, **215–218**, *215–217*
video settings, **201–207**, *201–203, 205–207*
interference with network cables, **586**
Interix 2.2 product, 615
Internet Account Information screen, 427, *427*, 431
Internet Assigned Numbers Authority (IANA), 576
Internet connection command, 36
Internet Connection Firewall (ICF), **87**, *87*, **112**, 435–436, *436*
Internet Connection Firewall (ICF)/Internet Connection Sharing (ICS) service, 830
Internet Connection screen, 425, *425*, 431
Internet Connection Sharing. *See* ICS (Internet Connection Sharing)
Internet Connection Wizard, 557
Internet connections, **144**, **423**
    with analog modems, **144–145**, **424–427**, *424–427*
    with cable modems, **145–146**, **428–432**
    with DSL, **145–146**, **432–434**
    features for, **112–113**
    in installation, **128**
    Internet Explorer. *See* Internet Explorer
    with ISDN, **436–439**
    with LANs, **146**
    with satellite, **434–435**
    security for, **435–436**, *436*
    setting up, **33–35**, *33–35*
    sharing. *See* ICS (Internet Connection Sharing)
    troubleshooting, **455–456**
    types of, **424**
    using, **36–37**, *36–37*
Internet Control Message Protocol (ICMP) echo packets, 489, *489*
Internet Explorer, **113**, **457**
    customizing, **473–474**
        Advanced tab, **482**, *482*
        Connections tab, **481**, *481*
        Content tab, **479–480**, *480*

        General tab, **474–475**, *474*
        Privacy tab, **477–479**, *478–479*
        Programs tab, **481**, *481*
        Security tab, **475–476**, *476*
    downloading files with, **473**, *473*
    e-mail in, **465**, *465*
    favorite sites in, **460–462**, *461, 463*, **468**
    History list in, **463–464**, *463*
    Links bar in, **460**, *460*
    Media bar in, 113, **464–465**, *464*
    navigating Web with, **458–460**, *459*
    newsgroups in, **465**
    offline favorites in, **468–470**, *469–470*
    printing Web pages in, **467–468**, *467*
    saving Web pages in, **466–467**
    searching with, **470–472**, *471–472*
    starting, **457–458**, *458*
    text size in, **483**, *483*
    toolbar in, **482–483**, *482*
    for Web publishing, **883–884**
Internet Information Services (IIS)
    console for, **844–846**, *845–846*
    installing, **841–843**, *842–843*
    limits on, **844**
    troubleshooting, **873**
Internet Information Services (IIS) snap-in, 810, 843
Internet Information Services (IIS) window, 842, *842*
Internet Options dialog box, **473–474**
    Advanced tab, **482**, *482*
    for certificates, 285
    Connections tab, **481**, *481*
    Content tab, **479–480**, *480*
    for favorites, 462
    General tab, **474–475**, *474*
    for History list, 463–464
    for Internet Explorer, 458
    for printing, 468
    Privacy tab, **477–479**, *478–479*
    Programs tab, **481**, *481*
    Security tab, **475–476**, *476*
Internet Properties dialog box, 56–57, 473
Internet Protocol (IP), 572

Internet Protocol (TCP/IP) dialog box, 648
Internet Protocol (TCP/IP) Properties dialog box,
    143–144, 578, *578*, 636, *636*
Internet Protocol Secure (IPSec), 572
Internet radio, 373, *374*
    connecting to stations, **374**
    presets for, **375**
    searching for stations, **375**, *375*
Internet Settings for Windows Media Player, **382**
Internet Time tab, 200, *200*
Internet Web browsing
    with Internet Explorer. *See* Internet Explorer
    with MSN Explorer, **484–486**, *484–485*
    utilities for, **486–491**, *487*, *489*
Internet zone, 475
Internetwork Packet Exchange/Sequenced Packet
    Exchange (IPX/SPX) protocol
    overview, 571
    troubleshooting, **625**
internetworking, 563
interpreted scripts, 737
interrupt request lines (IRQs), **329–330**
    conflicts in, 718
    with PC Cards, 417
% Interrupt Time counter, 710
intrinsic objects, **750–751**
invitations in Remote Assistance, 183–185
    e-mail, **185–187**, *185–187*, **189**, *189*, **191**, *191*
    file, **188**
    status of, **188–189**, *188*
    Windows Messenger, **187–189**, **192**, *192*
Invite to This Conversation dialog box, 524
IP (Internet Protocol), 572
IP addresses, **573**
    for ICS, 451, **454**
    for LPD, 617
    name resolution for, **905–906**
    for NetMeeting, 510
    for peer-to-peer networks, **598–601**, *601*
    for private networks, **576–578**, *577–578*
    private ranges, **575–576**
    for SMTP servers, 868

special addresses, **575**
subnets in, **574–575**
for TCP/IP, 143–144
for virtual NICs, **602–603**, *602–603*
for VPN, 687
for Web sites, 853
IP configuration for domains, **635–640**,
    636–637, *639*
IP filtering, **639–640**, *639*
IP masquerading, **448–449**, *449*
IP Security Monitor snap-in, 810
IP Security Policies snap-in, 811
IP Settings tab, 636, *637*
IP version 6, 573
ipconfig utility, 510, **622**, *622*
IPSec (Internet Protocol Secure), 572
IPSEC Services, 828
IPX/SPX (Internetwork Packet Exchange/Sequenced
    Packet Exchange) protocol
    overview, 571
    troubleshooting, **625**
"IRQL_NOT_LESS_OR_EQUAL" message, 800
IRQs (interrupt request lines), **329–330**
    conflicts in, 718
    with PC Cards, 417
IRQs screen, 717, *717*
Is the Hardware Connected? screen, 337
ISA (Industry Standard Architecture) boards, 758
ISDN (Integrated Services Digital Network),
    436–437
    advantages and disadvantages of, **437–438**
    hooking up, **438–439**
    operation of, **437**
ISPs
    for DSL, 433–434
    for ICS, 450
    for Internet connections, 425
    for ISDN, **438**
    for satellite service, 434
    for Web publishing, 878–879
Items to Synchronize dialog box, 291, *291*, 413, *414*,
    470, *470*

J

joining domains, **91–92**, *91–92*

K

Keep Printed Documents option, 313
Keep Taskbar on Top of Other Windows option, 216
kernel mode, **118–121**, **627–629**
"KERNEL_STACK_INPAGE_ERROR" message, 800
Keyboard tab, 225–226, *226*
keyboards
    language support for, 141
    for mobility-impaired users, 225–226, *226*
    on notebooks, 399, *400*
    On-Screen Keyboard, **228**, *228*
    options for, **220–221**
    in Remote Desktop Connection, 534
keys
    encryption, 56
    Registry, **727–729**, *728*, **733–734**
"KMODE_EXCEPTION_NOT_HANDLED" message, 800
Knowledge Base, **175–176**, 178
    for error messages, 648
    for Stop errors, 803

L

L2TP (Layer 2 Tunneling Protocol), 688
Language Preferences dialog box, 475
Language Settings section, 372
languages
    for DVDs, 372
    in installation, 136, **140–141**, *141*
    in Internet Explorer, 475
    keyboard layout for, 141
LANs, **564–565**
    application use on, **565–566**
    file sharing on, **565**
    groupware on, **567**
    print sharing on, **566–567**
    security on, **567**
    setting up, **146**
laptop computers. *See* notebook computers

Last Known Good Configuration, **764–765**
latency in VPN, 688
Layer 2 Tunneling Protocol (L2TP), 688
LCD screens, 400
LDAP (Lightweight Directory Access Protocol), **872**, 904–905
LDAP Routing tab, **872**, *872*
leaf objects, 886–887
legacy applications, Compatibility mode for, **115–116**
length of network cables, **586**
Let's Get on the Internet screen, 145
Let's Set Up Your Internet Account screen, 145
License Management dialog box, 379–380, *379–380*
licenses and license agreements, 132, 136, 140, 154
    for audio and digital files, **377–379**
    backing up, **379–380**, *379–380*
    for networks, 566
    restoring, **380**, *380*
    for Windows Update, 43
Lightweight Directory Access Protocol (LDAP), **872**, 904–905
Limit Message Size to (KB) option, 871
Limit number of connections option, 868
Limit Number of Messages per Connection option, 871
Limit Number of Recipients per Message option, 871
Limit Session Size to (KB) option, 871
Limited account, 652
Limited users, 160
limits for Remote Assistance, **184–185**, *184*
Line Printer (LPR), 617
Line Printer Daemon (LPD), 616–617
line voltage indicators, 352
Link to Web Address snap-in, 811
linked objects in OLE, **261**, *261*
linking in OLE, 258
Links bar in Internet Explorer, **460**, *460*
Links dialog box, 261, *261*
links in Internet Explorer, **465**
Links toolbar, 8–9
Linux operating system, networks using, 615
List Folder Contents permission type, 661
List Folder/Read Data permission, 663
List My Most Recently Opened Documents option, 12

List view, 17, *17*, 269, *270*
listening to audio CDs, **38**, *38*
listsvc command, 772–773
LLC (Logical Link Control) layer, 571
LMHOSTS file, 638
Load and Unload Device Drivers right, 655
Load Settings folder, 276
Local Area Connection Properties dialog box, 891, 897–898
Local Devices section, 534
Local Drive dialog box, 347
Local Intranet zone, 475
Local or Network Printer screen, 45, 49, 302, *302*, 894
Local Printer Attached to This Computer option, 45
local printers
    drivers for, **301–305**, *302*, *304*
    sharing, **305–308**, *306–308*
Local Procedure Call facility, **120**
Local Resources tab, 86, 534, *534*
Local section for SMTP servers, 872
Local Security Settings console, 654, *654*, 673–675, *674*
Local System account option, 834
Local User and Groups, 77
Local User Manager, 657
local user profiles, 613, 646
Local Users and Groups snap-in, 811
Locate File dialog box, 82, 335
Lock the Taskbar option, 7, 216
locking
    computers, **165**
    files, **233–234**
    Taskbar, 7, 105, 216
lockups from power management, **419**
Log File Directory setting, 854
Log File Name setting, 854
log files
    for FTP servers, 866
    for IIS, **873**
    for Registry, 731
    scripts for, **755–756**, *756*
    size of, 707

    for SMTP servers, 869
    for Web sites, 849, **853–856**, *854*
Log Off button, 103
Log Off Windows dialog box, 162, 165, *539*, 540
Log On As dialog box, 883, *883*
Log on Locally right, 655
Log On tab, 613, *613*, **834**, *834*
Log On to Windows dialog box, 165, 536, *536*, 634
Log Visits option, 849, 866
LogEvent.wsf script, **755–756**, *756*
logged on users, displaying, **166**, *166*
logging. *See* log files
logging off, **162**, *163*
    other users, **169–170**, *170*
    Remote Desktop Connection remote sessions, **540**, *540*
logging on, **160–162**, *162*
    to Active Directory, **915**
    to domains, **163**
Logical Disk Manager service, 828
Logical Disk Manager Administrative Service, 830
logical drives, **701–703**, *702*
Logical Link Control (LLC) layer, 571
login scripts, **647**
logon command, 772
Logon events, auditing, 672–673
Logon Message dialog box, *536*, 537
logs. *See* log files
long filenames
    on Novell NetWare networks, **896**
    in UNCs, **609–610**, **645**
loopback addresses, 575, 621
loops in scripts, **742–743**
lossless compression, 369
lossy compression, 369–370
Lotus SmartSuite 96, **255**, *255*
Low Battery threshold, 405
Low option for cookies, 478
Low security level, 476
low voltage conditions, 759
LPD (Line Printer Daemon), 616–617
LPR (Line Printer), 617

M

MAC (Media Access Control) address, 910–911
MAC (Media Access Control) layer, 571
Macintosh networks, **617–618**
Macintosh OS vs. Windows XP, **118**
Magnifier, 138, **227**, *227*
Magnifier Settings dialog box, 227, *227*
mail. *See* e-mail
Maintenance tab, 547, 560
Make a New Folder link, 18
Make a Sound When Turning a Feature On or Off
    option, 226
Make Available Offline option, 55
Make This Folder Private option, 71
Manage Auditing and Security Log right, 655
Manage Documents permission, 307
Manage Identities dialog box, 556
Manage Printers permission, 307
mandatory user profiles, 614, 647
manual services, **830–832**
map command, 772, 776–777
Map Network Drive dialog box, 73–74, 607–608, *607*
mapping drives, 73–74
    in domains, **643**, *643*, **645**
    in Novell NetWare networks, 890–891
    in peer-to-peer networks, **607–608**, *607*
marking e-mail, **544**
Master Boot Record (MBR), 775–776, 797–798
master/slave networks, **579**
Maximize option, 6
Maximum Connections setting, 864
Maximum Port Speed setting, 343
Maximum Strength Encryption setting, 684
MBR (Master Boot Record), 775–776, 797–798
md command, 772, 775
md5filt filter, 847
Me Only option, 36
measurements for forms, 52
Media Access Control (MAC) address, 910–911
Media Access Control (MAC) layer, 571
Media bar, 113, **464–465**, *464*
Media Files section, **363**

Media Guide tab, **357–358**
Media Library, **359**, *359*, **362–363**, *363–364*
Media Player. *See* Windows Media Player
Medium option for cookies, 478
Medium-High option for cookies, 478
Medium security level, 476
Medium-Low security level, 476
memory
    managing, **114–115**
    requirements for, **124–125**
    for services, 825–826
    video, 204
    virtual, 120, 125
Menu and Window Animation option, 535
Menu commands in Taskpad, 822
Message field for fax cover pages, 502
Message Rules dialog box, 555
messages
    e-mail. *See* e-mail
    Messenger. *See* Windows Messenger
    Task Manager for, **170–171**, *171*
Messages tab
    for FTP servers, **864–865**, *865*
    for SMTP servers, **870–871**, *870*
Messenger. *See* Windows Messenger
Messenger service, 828
meters, power, **406–407**, *407*
methods in WSH, **750**
Microphone Mute option, 524, *524*
microphones for Windows Messenger, **518–519**
Microsoft Challenge Handshake Authentication
    Protocol (MS-CHAP), 690
Microsoft IIS Log File Format, 853
Microsoft Internet Directory service, 511
Microsoft Knowledge Base, **175–176**, 178
    for error messages, 648
    for Stop errors, 803
Microsoft Management Console. *See* MMC (Microsoft
    Management Console)
Microsoft Online Support, **194**
Microsoft saved console (MSC) files, 808
mirrored dynamic volumes, 703
misc newsgroups, 557

"Missing operating system" message, 797
mkdir command, 772
MMC (Microsoft Management Console), **807**
    Author mode in, **811–814**, *812–814*
    Computer Management console, **817–819**, *818*
    customization options for, **819–824**, *820–823*
    features of, **807–808**
    modes for, **809**
    snap-ins for, **810–814**, *812–814*
    terminology for, **808–809**
    User Mode-Full Access in, **815**, *816*
    User Mode-Limited Access, Multiple Window in,
        816–817, *816*
    User Mode-Limited Access, Single Window in,
        817, *817*
    views in, **814–815**, *814–815*
MMC.EXE program, 808–809, 811
mobility-impaired users, accessibility options for,
    225–226, *226*
modal dialog boxes, 243
Modem Configurations dialog box, 439
Modem Dialing Information screen, 142
modems
    analog
        configuring, **342–345**, *342–345*
        in installation, **141**
        for Internet connections, **424–427**, *424–427*
        setting up, **144–145**
        troubleshooting, **455–456**
    cable. *See* cable modems
    ISDN, **438–439**
Modems tab, 343
Modify permission type, 661
Monitor and Graphics Card Properties dialog box,
    348–349, *349*
Monitor Settings dialog box, 144
Monitor tab, 203, 205, *206*
monitors
    configuring, **348–349**
    controls for, **206**
    drivers for, **203**, *203*
    multiple, **113**, **350–351**
    for notebook computers, **400–401**

requirements, **125**
resolution of, 144
more command, 772
More Options tab, 763
mouse
    for notebook computers, 400
    options for, **220–222**
    troubleshooting, **417**
MouseKeys feature, 226
Move dialog box, 555
Move Here option, 273
Move Items dialog box, 20
Move This File link, 20
Move This Folder link, 20
movies. *See* Windows Movie Maker
moving
    e-mail, **544**
    files and folders, **20–24**, *20–24*, **272**
    taskbar, **7**, *7*
MP3 file format, 369–370
MP3 tags, editing, **361–362**, *362*
mp3PRO, 370
MPRs (Multiple Provider Routers), **627**
MS-CHAP (Microsoft Challenge Handshake
    Authentication Protocol), 690
MS Software Shadow Copy Provider service, 831
MSC (Microsoft saved console) files, 808
MSN Explorer, 113, **484–486**, *484–485*
multi-string entries in Registry, 729–730
multifunction devices, **102**
multihomed computers, 491
multimedia files in Internet Explorer, 464
multiple dialing locations, **409–410**, *410*
multiple drivers for printers, **303–305**, *304*
multiple monitors, **113**, **350–351**
Multiple Provider Routers (MPRs), **627**
Multiple UNC Providers (MUPs), **627**
multiuser considerations, **103**, **232**, **276**
    availability of programs, **233**
    folders, **276–277**
    installing programs, **232**, *232*
    open files, **233–234**
    running programs, **234–235**

MUPs (Multiple UNC Providers), **627**
music
 audio CDs, **38**, *38*
 in Internet Explorer, 464
 Windows Media Player for. *See* Windows Media
  Player
Mute option, 387
Mute Video Soundtrack option, 396
My Computer link, 15
My Documents folder, 14, 18, 692
My Music folder, 14–15, **106–107**
My Network Drive dialog box, 890, *890*
My Network Places, **607**, **642**, **879–883**,
 880–883, 890
My Pictures folder, 14, 17, **106–107**
My Pictures Slideshow screen saver, 105
My Recent Documents folder, 277
My Videos folder, 14

N

Name and Description screen, 821
name resolution in Active Directory, **905–906**
Name the New Account screen, 75, *656*
Name Your Network screen, 442, *442*
Name Your Printer screen, 46
names
 in Active Directory, **905–906**, **910–915**, *914*
 CDs, 24, 295
 computers
  in installation, **141**, 155
  in peer-to-peer networks, 601, *601*
 in copying CDs, 368
 domain servers, **634**
 Favorite sites, 462
 files, **19**, *19*, **274**, 775
 folders, **18–19**, *19*, **274**
 groups, 77, 658
 hardware profiles, 611
 in installation, **141**
 Internet connections, 35
 in Novell NetWare networks, **896**
 in peer-to-peer networks, 592–593, 601, *601*

printer, 46
 in Remote Desktop Connection, 532
 share, 592, 605
 shortcuts, 32
 VPN connections, 90
narration in Windows Movie Maker, **396**
Narrator, 138, **228**, *228*
NAT (Network Address Translation), **448–449**, *449*
navigating
 Desktop, 164
 in Explorer, **14–15**, *14–15*
 in Help and Support Center, **174**
 in Taskpad, 822
NCSA Common Log File Format, 853
NDIS (Network Device Interface Specification),
 628–629
net continue command, 837
Net Logon service, 828
.NET Messenger Service dialog box, 520, *520*
.NET Passport Wizard, 513
net pause command, 837
net start command, 837
net stop command, 837–838
net use command, **609–610**, *609*, 644–645, *644*
net view command, 608–609, 644
NetBEUI (Network BIOS Enhanced User Interface)
 protocol, 571
NetBIOS names, 592
NetDDE driver, 258
NetHood folder, 276
NetMeeting, **507**
 Chat for, **510–511**, *510*
 directory servers for, **511**
 hosting meetings, **511**, *511*
 installing, **507–508**, *507–508*
 making calls in, **509**, *509*
 sharing documents in, **512**
 video for, **512**, *512*
NetMeeting Remote Desktop Sharing service, 831
netstat program, **489**, *489*
NetWare Administrator (NWADMIN) utility, 888, 893
NetWare networks. *See* Novell NetWare networks
Network Address Translation (NAT), **448–449**, *449*

Network and Internet Connections screen, 33
Network BIOS Enhanced User Interface (NetBEUI)
   protocol, 571
Network Bridge, 603, *603*, 635–636, *636*
Network Computers, 579
Network Configuration Operators group, 653
Network Connection screen, 685, *685*
Network Connection Type screen
   for analog modems, 424
   for cable modems, 431
   for VPNs, 89, 685, *685*
Network Connections dialog box, 454, *454*
Network Connections folder, 87–89, 648, 683, 685, 913
Network Connections service, 831
Network Connections window
   for dial-up connections, 33
   for ICS, 450
   for Network Bridge, 603, *603*
   for Novell NetWare networks, 891, 897
   for private networks, 576, *577*
   for VPN, 89
network connectivity, **112**
Network DDE service, 831
Network DDE DSDM service, 831
Network Device Interface Specification (NDIS),
   628–629
Network dialog box, 597–598
network drives
   connecting to, **73–74**, *73–74*
   mapping, 73–74
      in domains, **643**, *643*, **645**
      in Novell NetWare networks, 890–891
      in peer-to-peer networks, **607–608**, *607*
Network File System (NFS) protocol, 616
Network Identification Wizard, 91–92, 641
Network Information screen, 92, 641
Network Interface Cards (NICs), **584–585**, 594
   drivers for, **628–629**
   virtual, **602–603**, *602–603*
Network layer, **570**
Network Location Awareness service, 831
network resources, attaching to, **642**
   login scripts for, **647**

mapping network drives for, **643**, *643*, **645**
My Network Places for, **642**
UNCs for, **644–646**
Network Settings screen, 142
Network Setup Wizard, 112
   for ICS
      clients, **444–447**, *445–447*
      computers, **440–444**, *440–444*
   for peer-to-peer networks, **594–597**, *595–596*,
      600, 604–605
Networking Components screen, 143, 155
networking settings in installation, **142–143**
Networking tab, 721, *722*
networks, **563–564**
   bridges in, **112**, 571, **602–603**, *602–603*
   for Briefcase operations, **415–416**
   cables for, **585–587**, *587*
   Ethernet hardware for, **583–584**
   hubs for, 568, 583, **587–588**, 594
   installing, **589**
   IP addressing in, **573–578**, *577–578*
   LANs, **564–567**
   look and feel of, **582–583**, *582*
   network cards for, **584–585**
   Novell. *See* Novell NetWare networks
   OSI model, **569–572**
   peer-to-peer. *See* peer-to-peer networks
   printers on, 49
   relationships in, **578–581**
   routers for, **588**
   sharing folders on, **72**, *72*
   sneakernet, **564**
   Task Manager for, **721**, *722*
   TCP/IP protocols, **572–573**
   vocabulary for, **568–569**
   wireless, **587**
New Alert Settings dialog box, 713, *713*
New Connection Wizard
   for analog modems, 424–428, *425–427*
   for cable modems, 431–432
   for dial-up connections, 33–34
   for VPNs, 89, **685–687**, *685–687*
New Desktop Item dialog box, 212

New Group dialog box, 658, *658*
New Group option, 77
New Identity dialog box, 556, *556*
new installations, 127, **135–139**, *135–138*
New Location dialog box, 410, *410*
New Log Settings dialog box, 713
New Log Time Period option, 854
New Mail Rule dialog box, 554, *554*
New Message window, 465, 548–549, 551–552, 559
New or Existing Answer File screen, 153
New Partition Wizard, 700–703, *700–702*
New Playlist dialog box, 360
New Task Wizard, 822–823, *822–823*
New Taskpad View Wizard, 821–822, *821–822*
New User dialog box, 657, *657*
New Window from Here command, 820
news newsgroups, 557
Newsgroup Subscriptions dialog box, 558–559, *558*
newsgroups
    for help, **194**, 196
    in Internet Explorer, **465**
    in Outlook Express. *See* Outlook Express
NFS (Network File System) protocol, 616
NICs (Network Interface Cards), **584–585**, 594
    drivers for, **628–629**
    virtual, **602–603**, *602–603*
No, Refine This Search And... links, 29
No, Try Different Compatibility Settings option, 94
No Access permission, 663
"No Domain Server Was Available" message, **647–649**
No Emulation mode, 798
No Encryption Allowed setting, 683
nodes in networks, 568
nohiber.txt file, 420
non-Microsoft network connections, **615**
    Macintosh, **617–618**
    Unix, **615–617**, *617*
non-scaleable fonts, **322–323**, *323*
nondedicated servers, 580–581
Normal backup type, 785
notebook computers, **399**
    battery monitoring in, **404–409**, *405–409*
    vs. desktop, **399–400**, *400*

    features for, **109**
    hardware profiles for, **402–404**, *403*
    monitors for, **400–401**
    multiple dialing locations for, **409–410**, *410*
    PC cards for, **401–402**, *402*
    synchronizing files on, **410–411**
        Briefcase for, **414–416**, *415–416*
        offline files for, **411–413**, *412–414*
    troubleshooting
        mouse, **417**
        PC Cards, **417**
        power management, **418–420**
notification area, 106
    customizing, **13**, *13*, **217–218**, *217*
    volume settings in, **383–384**, *384*
Notify Me Before Downloading Any Updates and
    Notify Me Again before Installing Them on My
    Computer option, 151
Notify When Printed option, 894
Novell NetWare networks, **885**
    administration utilities for, **887–891**, *889–890*
    clients for
        configuring, **898–899**
        installing, **897–898**, *897–898*
        selecting, **896–897**
    directory services in, **886–887**
    long filenames in, **896**
    printing in, 886, **894–895**, *895*
    with Windows networks, **891–894**, *892–894*
NT LM Security Support Provider service, 831
ntbootdd.sys file, 803–804
ntdetect.com file, 803–804
ntds.dit file, 903
NTFS (NT File System)
    auditing files in, 675
    compression in, **283–285**, *284*
    converting partitions to, **140**
    vs. FAT, **698–700**
    selecting partitions for, 139–140
"NTFS_FILE_SYSTEM" message, 800
ntldr file, 803–804
NTUSER.DAT hive file, 730
NTUSER.LOG file, 731

NWADMIN (NetWare Administrator) utility, 888, 893

NWLink protocol, **625**

O

object access
   auditing events for, 672–673
   vs. directory service access, **673**
Object Linking and Embedding (OLE), **258**
   embedded objects in, 261
   Insert Object command, **259–261**, *260*
   linked objects in, **261**, *261*
   Paste Special command, **258–259**, *259*
Object Manager, **120**
objects
   in Active Directory, **903**
   counters for, **709–711**
   in Novell NetWare networks, 886–887
   in WSH, **750–751**
Obtain IP Automatically (DHCP) option, 145–146
Office Clipboard, **256**, *257*
Offline Favorite Wizard, 468–469, *469*
offline favorites, **468–470**, *469–470*
offline files, 114, **288**
   configuring, **289–290**, *289*, **411–412**, *412*
   Fast User Switching feature with, **288**, **411**
   selecting, **55**, *55*, **290**, *290*, **413**, *413*
   synchronizing, **54**, *54*, **290–291**, *291*, **411–413**, *412–414*
   working with, **290**, **413**
Offline Files tab, 54, 278, 289–290, *289*, 411–412, *412*
Offline Files Wizard, 289–290, 413
OLE (Object Linking and Embedding), **258**
   embedded objects in, 261
   Insert Object command, **259–261**, *260*
   linked objects in, **261**, *261*
   Paste Special command, **258–259**, *259*
On-Screen Keyboard, **228**, *228*
Online Assisted Support, **110**
online support, **194**
Open Advanced Properties for This Task when I Click Finish option, 65

Open Attachment Warning dialog box, 191
Open dialog box
   for answer files, 153
   for visualizations, 376
   in Windows Media Player, 360
open files with multiple users, **233–234**
Open Folder command, 9
Open the Folder That Contains This Item link, 29
Open With dialog box, 292, *292*
opening items in Explorer, **266**, *266–267*
OpenType fonts, 319
operating systems
   compatibility of, 247
   for shared printers, **308**, *308*
   support for UPSs, 352
optimizing. *See* performance
Option Explicit command, 745
Optional Encryption setting, 683
Optional Networking Components option, 616
Options dialog box
   for Backup Utility, 784–785, *784*
   for copying CDs, 365–367, *367*, 369–370, *371*
   for DVDs, 372–373, *372*
   for Internet radio, 374
   for Media Library, 362–363, *363–364*
   for MMC consoles, 813–814, *814*
   in NetMeeting, 512
   in Outlook Express, 543, 547, 552, *552*, **559–560**, *560*
   for visualizations, 376, *377*
   for Windows Media Player, 381, 383, *383*
   in Windows Messenger, **513**
      Connection tab, **517**
      Personal tab, **514**, *514*
      Phone tab, **514**, *515*
      Preferences tab, **514–516**, *516*, 528
      Privacy tab, **516–517**, *516*
Options for Icons in the Navigation Bar list, 178
Options screen, 177
Options section for server extensions, 860
Options tab
   for IP filtering, 639
   for printing, 183, 468

organization name in installation, **142**
Organize Favorites dialog box, 462, *463*, 469
OS/2 operating system vs. Windows XP, **117**
OS/2 subsystem, 121
OS X, compatibility of, 246
OSI model, **569–572**
Other Places list, 15
Outbound section for SMTP servers, 871
Outbound Connections section for SMTP
  servers, 872
Outbound Security section for SMTP servers, 872
Outbox folder
  for faxes, 504
  in Outlook Express, 542
outlets for UPSs, 353
Outlook Express, 465
  customizing, **559–560**, *560*
  for e-mail, **541–542**
    attaching files to, **553**, *554*
    creating and sending, **548–549**, *548*
    HTML for, **549–553**, *550, 552*
    identities in, **555–556**, *556*
    reading and processing, **543–547**,
      544–546
    retrieving, **543**, *543*
    rules for, **554–555**, *554–555*
  for newsgroups, **556–557**
    accounts for, **557**
    connecting to, **558**, *558*
    posting to, **559**
    reading, **559**
    searching for, **558**
    subscribing to, **558–559**
  tour of, **542–543**, *542*
overhead
  in auditing, 673
  in VPN, 688
overwriting log events, 707
Owner tab, 669, *669*
ownership, **668**
  defining, **668–669**, *669*
  taking, **669–670**

P
packets in networks, 568
Paging File object, 710
PAP (Password Authentication Protocol) authentication, 690
Parental Control option, 372
partition tables, 703
partitions
  converting to NTFS, **140**
  creating, **701–703**, *702*
  deleting, 140, **776–777**
  for installation, **139–140**
  in recovery, **776–777**
Passport sign-in, **520–521**, *521*
Password Authentication Protocol (PAP) authentication, 690
passwords
  Administrator, 155
  for cable modem connections, 431
  for certificates, 57
  for directories, 904
  for domains, 92, 580, 635, 641–642
  for folders, 71
  for FTP sites, 487, 881, 883–884
  good, **689**
  for identities, 556
  for Internet connections, 35–36, 427
  in LDAP, 872
  for network drives, 643, 645
  for Novell clients, 899
  for peer-to-peer networks, 610
  in Remote Assistance, 183, 186
  in Remote Desktop Connection, 532
  for scheduled tasks, 64
  for screen savers, 213
  subadministrators for, 906–907
  in telecommuting, 691
  for user accounts, 76, 656–657
  for Web sites, 863
  for Windows Messenger, 520
Paste command, **21**, *21*, 256
Paste Special command, **258–259**, *259*

Paste Special dialog box, 259, *259*
pasting with Remote Desktop, **538**
Pause command, 316
Pause Printing command, 315
Pause Printing link, 47
pausing
    defragmentation, 61
    printing, 47, 315–316
PC Cards
    for notebook computers, **400–402**, *402*
    troubleshooting, **417**
PC MACLAN product, 618
PCI (Peripheral Component Interface) bus, 759
PCI graphics cards, 351
PCL.sep file, 316
Pcmcia.sys driver, 417
Pconsole utility, 887
peer-to-peer networks, **579**, **591**
    bridging in, **602–603**, *602–603*
    configuring, **594**
        File and Printer Sharing for Microsoft
            Networks, **599–600**
        identification, **599**, **601**, *601*
        IP, **600–601**, *601*
        Network Setup Wizard for, **594–597**,
            595–596
        Windows95/NT workstation machines,
            597–598
    connecting
        direct connections, **608–610**, *609*
        to non-Microsoft networks, **615–618**, *617*
        steps in, **593–594**
    network resources for, **607**
        direct connections, **608–610**, *609*
        mapping drives, **607–608**
        My Network Places for, **607**
    profiles in
        hardware, **610–613**, *611–613*
        user, **613–615**, *614*
    setting up, **591–593**
    shares in, **604–606**, *604–606*
    troubleshooting, **618–619**
        architecture in, **626–629**, *626*

configuration testing, **619–620**, *619*
    IPX/SPX, **625**
    TCP/IP, **620–625**, *622–623*
    tips, **629**
Per Site Privacy Actions dialog box, 479, *479*
performance
    with auditing, 673
    with multiple users, 161
    in Remote Desktop Connection, 535
    System Information for, **715–718**, *715–718*
    Task Manager for, **721**
    in VPN, **687–688**
Performance and Maintenance screen, 80, 83
Performance console, **708–711**, *709*, *711*
    alerts in, **712–713**, *713*
    Counter Log view in, **713–714**
    Report view in, **714**, *715*
Performance Logs and Alerts service, 831
Performance Logs and Alerts snap-in, 811
Performance Options dialog box, 729
Performance tab
    for audio, 385, *386*
    for Internet radio, 374
    for Task Manager, 721
Peripheral Component Interface (PCI) bus, 759
peripheral devices, 566
Permanent Redirection for This Resource option, 857
permissions, **79**, *79*, **659**
    for files and folders, **661–664**, *662*, *664*
    groups for, 77
    for printers, **306–308**, *307*
    problems from, **761**
    share-level, **78**, *78*, **659–660**, *659–660*
    for user accounts, **653–655**, *654*
Permissions dialog box, 78, 659–660, *659*
persistent connections, 610
persistent cookies, 477
Personal Cover Pages dialog box, 500, *500*
personal information numbers (PINs), 147
Personal Information section for Web content, 480
Personal tab
    for certificates, 56, 285, *286*
    in Windows Messenger, **514**, *514*

Personalize Your Software screen, 142
phase for monitors, 206
Phone and Modem Options dialog box, 505
Phone Number to Dial screen, 426, *426*
Phone tab, **514**, *515*
PhysicalDisk object, 710
Pick How You Want to Contact Your Assistant screen, 185, *185*
Picture dialog box, 551
picture-in-picture option, 525
pictures
    acquiring and handling, **107**
    in e-mail, **551**
    Web, **467**
Pin to Start Menu command, 10
pincushioning in monitors, 206
ping program, **488–489**, *489*, **620–621**
pinned shortcuts
    editing, **263**, *263*
    on Start menu, 10–11, **263**, *263*
PINs (personal information numbers), 147
piracy, 566
Place a Call dialog box, 509, *509*
planning setup, **794–795**
Platform screen, 153, *153*
Play Control, **387–388**, *387–388*
Play Control dialog box, 384, 387
Play Sound When Contacts Sign in or Send a Message option, 515
Player Settings, **383**, *383*
Player tab, 383, *383*
playlists, **360**
Please Choose Your Search and Installation Option screens, 81, 333
Please Select Application dialog box, 250
Please Type Your Contact's Complete E-mail Address screen, 521
Please Wait screen, 443, *443*, 447
Plug and Play service, 828
Point-to-Point Protocol (PPP), 572
Point-to-Point Protocol over Ethernet (PPPoE), 573
Point-to-Point Tunneling Protocol (PPTP), 573, 688
Pointer Options tab, 221

Pointers tab, 221
policies, Active Directory for, **912**
Policy change events, auditing, 672
political issues in Active Directory, **908–909**
POP (Post Office Protocol), 572
portable computers. *See* notebook computers
portable devices, Windows Media Player for, **380–382**, *382*
Portable Media Serial Number service, 828
ports
    for hubs, 588
    for printer servers, 53, 318
    for printers, 45, 304, *304*, 310, *310*, **312–313**, *313*, 316, 617
    for UPSs, 352
    for Web sites, 853
Ports tab
    for printer servers, 53, 318
    for printers, **312–313**, *313*, 316
POSIX subsystem, 121
Post Office Protocol (POP), 572
posting to newsgroups, **559**
PostScript printers, 793
power alarms, **405–406**, *406*
power and power management
    for hubs, 588
    problems in, 759
    troubleshooting, **418–420**
    UPSs for, **352**
        choosing, **352–353**
        installing, **353–356**, *353–355*
Power Meter dialog box, 407, *407*
Power Meter tab, 406–407, *407*
power meters, **406–407**, *407*
Power Options Properties dialog box
    Advanced tab, 407–408, *408*
    for hibernation, 408–409, *409*
    for power alarms, 405–406, *406*
    for power meters, 406–407, *407*
    for power schemes, 404–405, *405*
    for UPSs, 353–356, *353*
power schemes, **404–405**, *405*
Power Schemes tab, 404–405, *405*

Power tab, 350, *350*
Power Users group, 653
PPP (Point-to-Point Protocol), 572
PPPoE (Point-to-Point Protocol over Ethernet), 573
PPTP (Point-to-Point Tunneling Protocol), 573, 688
predefined Registry keys, 727
Preferences tab, **514–516**, *516*, 528
Preparing the Cover Page screen, 499, *499*
Presentation layer, **570**
presets for Internet radio, **375**
Preview pane in Outlook Express, 542
previewing in Windows Movie Maker, **396**
primary partitions, 701–702
Print Banner option, 894
Print dialog box
    for faxes, 498
    for Help and Support Center, 183
    for Internet Explorer, 467–468, *467*
Print permission, 307
Print Server Properties dialog box, 318–319
print servers, properties for, **52–53**, *52–53*,
    318–319
Print Services for Unix product, 616
Print Spooled Documents First option, 313
Print Spooler service, 828
Print Test Page option, 50, 793
Print Test Page screen, 46
Printer and Faxes folder, 50
Printer Attached to Another Computer option, 49
printer-resident fonts, **323–324**
Printer Sharing screen, 46, 305, *305*
printers
    auditing, 676, *677*
    connecting to, 49, *49*, **644**
    installing, **44–47**, *44–47*
    local
        drivers for, **301–305**, *302, 304*
        sharing, **305–308**, *306–308*
    properties for, **50–51**, *50–51*, **311**
        Advanced, **313–314**, *314*
        Color Management, **315**
        Device Settings, **314**, *314*
        General, **312**, *312*

        Ports, **312–313**, *313*
        Utilities, **315**
    remote, **309–311**, *309–310*
    removing drivers for, **311**
    sharing, **48–49**, *48–49*, **305–308**, *306–308*,
        566–567
Printers and Faxes folder, 52, 494, *494*
Printers and Faxes screen, 48, 315
Printers and Other Hardware screen, 44, 48, 336
Printers folder, 792
Printers virtual directory, 843
PrintHood folder, 276
printing, **299–301**
    Disk Defragmenter analysis report, 61
    e-mail, **544**
    in Help and Support Center, **182–183**
    on Novell NetWare networks, 886,
        894–895, *895*
    queues for, **315–316**, *315*, **791–792**
    with Remote Desktop, **538**
    separator pages for, **316–318**, *317*
    transferring print jobs, **316**
    troubleshooting, **790–793**
    Web pages, **467–468**, *467*
Printing Preferences dialog box, 312, *312*
priority for e-mail, 549
Privacy Import dialog box, 478
Privacy tab
    in Internet Explorer, **477–479**, *478–479*
    Windows Messenger, **516–517**, *516*
private folders, **71**, *71*
private keys, 56
private networks, **576–578**, *577–578*
% Privileged Time counter, 710
Privilege use events, auditing, 672
problem definition in troubleshooting, **788**
Process Manager, 120
Process tracking events, auditing, 672
processes, displaying, **166–169**, *167, 169*, **720**, *721*
Processes tab, **166–169**, *167, 169*, 720, *721*
Processor object, 710
processor requirements, **124**
% Processor Time counter, 710

product keys, 101, 132, 136, 142, 155
Product to Install screen, 153, *153*
productivity, domains for, 632
profiles
    creating, **610–613**, *611–613*
    for domain servers, **634**
    for domains, **646–647**
    managing, **612–613**, *612–613*
    for notebook computers, **402–404**, *403*
    for services, 834
    user, **613–615**, *614*
Program Compatibility Data screen, 252, *253*
Program Compatibility Wizard, 93–94
Program Files folder, 233
programs, **719–720**, *720*
    availability of, **233**
    exchanging data between, **255–256**
        Clipboard for, **256**, *257*
        ClipBook Viewer for, **257**, *258*
        OLE for, **258–261**, *259–261*
    for ICS, **451–454**, *452–454*
    installing, **39–40**, *39–40*, **232**, *232*, **235–237**
    on LANs, **565–566**
    removing, **41**, *41*, **237–240**, *238–239*
    running, **242**
        in Compatibility mode, **248–253**, *249–255*
        displaying, **166–169**, *167–169*
        with multiple users, **234–235**
        at startup, **236–237**
    switching, 243, *243*
    unresponsive, **242–245**, *243*
Programs Compatibility Wizard, 249, *249*
Programs tab
    for Internet Explorer, 458, **481**, *481*
    for Remote Desktop Connection, 86, 534, *535*
projects in Windows Movie Maker, **395–397**, *395*, *397*
Prompt for Password When Computer Resumes from Standby option, 408
properties
    for files and folders, **280–281**
    for print servers, **52–53**, *52–53*
    for printers, **50–51**, *50–51*
    in WSH, **750**
Properties dialog box
    Active Directory, 913
    alerts, 713
    CD drives, 346, *346*, 370
    CDs, 371, *371*
    Compatibility mode, 254–255, *254*
    compression, 699
    counter logs, 713
    DVD drives, 346
    encryption, 693
    folders, 279, *279*
    hardware profiles, 611–612, *611*
    ICS, 450–454, *450*
    permissions, 664, *664*
    sharing, 659, *659*
    from shortcut menus, 271
    volume control, 388–389, *388*
    Web sites, 852, *852*
Properties tab
    CD drives, 346, *346*
    DVD drives, 346
protected memory management, **114–115**
Protected Storage service, 828
protocols
    in OSI model, **571–572**
    statistics for, **489**, *489*
Provide Contact Information screen, 186, *186*
Providing the Product Key screen, 155
Pscript.sep file, 317
public domain works, 876
public keys, 56
Public Network screen, 686, *686*
publishing, Web. *See* Web publishing
pwsdata filter, 848

Q

QoS RSVP service, 831
quality control in Web publishing, **877–878**
Quality of Service Packet Scheduler, 112
Query modem setting, 343

question marks (?) in searches, 282
queues
    for printing, 301, **315–316**, *315*
    troubleshooting, **791–792**
Quick Launch toolbar, 8–9, **216–217**, *217*
QuickFormat feature, 703

R

R2 cards, 417
radio
    Internet, **373**, *374*
        connecting to stations, **374**
        presets for, **375**
        searching for stations, **375**, *375*
    in Internet Explorer, 464
Radio Tuner page, 373, *373*
RAID 5 dynamic volumes, 703
RAM. *See* memory
RAS dial-in sessions, **88**, *88*, **682–684**, *683*
raster fonts, 322
Rating Service tab, 859
Ratings tab, 480, 859
raw partitions, 139
RCP (remote file copy), **490**
rd command, 772, 775
rdr.sys file, 627
Read permission, 660–661
    for FTP servers, 866
    in IIS, 848
    for Web sites, 861
Read Attributes permission, 663
Read & Execute permission, 661
Read Extended Attributes permission, 663
Read Permissions permission, 663
Read tab, 559
reading newsgroups, **559**
Ready to Activate Windows? screen, 144–146
Ready to Apply Network Settings screen, 442, *442*, 447, *447*
Ready to Get an Internet Account? screen, 145
rebooting after Stop errors, 803
rec newsgroups, 557

Receipts tab, 559
Receive File dialog box, 506
receiving files in Windows Messenger, **528**, *528*
Recipient field for fax cover pages, 502
Recipient Information screen, 498, *498*
Reconnect at Logon option, 74
Record Control, **389**, *389*
Record dialog box, 394–395, *394*
Record Narration Track dialog box, 396
recording
    audio files, **389–391**, *389*, *391*
    CDs. *See* burning CDs
    Windows Movie Maker content, **393–395**, *394*
records, database, 233–234
recovering
    from disasters. *See* disaster prevention and recovery
    files and folders, **26**, *26*, **275**
Recovery Console, **770**
    for boot sectors and boot records, **775–776**
    for damaged files, **774–775**
    enabling and disabling services in, **773–774**
    installing, **771**
    for partitions, **776–777**
    working with, **771–773**
Recovery tab, **835**, *835*
Recreational Software Advisory Council (RSAC), 859
Recycle Bin
    emptying, 26, **275**
    recovering items from, **26**, *26*, **275**
    sending items to, 25, **275**
Redirection to a URL option, 857
redirectors, 579
refresh rate, **203–206**, *205–206*
regedit program. *See* Registry Editor
REGEDT32.EXE editor, 725
Regional and Language Options dialog box, 140–141, *141*
Regional Options screen, 140–141, *141*
regions for DVD drives, **346–347**
Register this connection's addresses in DNS option, 638
registering Windows, **147**
Registration IDs, 147

Registry, **723–724**
accessing, **725**
for blue screens, **780–781**
data types in, **729–730**, *729*
editing. *See* Registry Editor
hives in, 727, 730
keys in, **727–729**, *728*, **733–734**
location of, **730–731**
for multiple users, 235
searching, **731–732**, *731*
subkeys in, **727–729**, *728*
subtrees in, **727**
value entries in, **727–729**, *728*, **732–734**, *732–733*
working with, **724**
Registry Editor, **724–725**, *725*
for adding items, 733–734
for backing up items, **726**, *726*
for deleting items, 734
favorites in, **735**, *735*
for restoring items, **727**
Relay Restrictions option, 869
Relay Restrictions window, 869, *870*
rem keyword, 739
Remote Access Auto Connection Manager service, 831
Remote Access Connection Manager service, 831
Remote Assistance, **110–111**, **183**
enabling, **184**, *184*
invitations in
e-mail, **185–187**, *185–187*, **189**, *189*, **191**, *191*
file, **188**
responding to, **191–193**, *191–192*
status of, **188–189**, *188*
Windows Messenger, **187–189**, **192**, *192*
limits for, **184–185**, *184*
receiving assistance in, **189–191**, *189–191*
security in, **183**
Remote Assistance screen, 189–190, *189–191*
Remote Assistance Settings dialog box, *184*, 185, 190
Remote Desktop, 114
Remote Desktop Connection, **85–86**, *85–86*, 109, **528–529**
connecting with, **536–537**, *536–538*

disconnecting with, **539**, *539*
logging off with, **540**, *540*
returning to local desktop, **539**
settings for, **531**, *532*
Display tab, 533, *533*
Experience tab, 535, *535*
General tab, 532–533, *532*, 536
Local Resources tab, 534, *534*
Programs tab, 534, *535*
remote computer, **530–531**, *530–531*
terminology, **529–530**
working with, **538**
Remote Desktop Disconnected dialog box, 537–538, *538*, 540, *540*
Remote Desktop Help Session Manager service, 831
Remote Desktop Users dialog box, 85, 530–531, *531*
Remote Desktop Users group, 653
Remote Desktop Web Connection, 843
remote file copy (RCP), **490**
remote printers, **309–311**, *309–310*
Remote Procedure Call (RPC) service, 828
Remote Procedure Call (RPC) Locator service, 831
Remote Procedure Calls (RPCs), 909–910
remote program execution, **490**
Remote Registry service, 829
remote shell program, **490**
Remote tab, 85, 184, *184*, 530, *530*
Removable Disk dialog box, 347–348, *348*
removable disks, **22**, *22*, **347–348**, *348*
Removable Storage Management snap-in, 811
Removable Storage service, 829
Remove Favorites dialog box, 735
Remove from This List command, 10
remove terminal program, **490**
removing. *See* deleting and removing
ren command, 772
Rename command in MMC, 820
rename command in Recovery Consoles, 772, 775
Rename from command, 19
Rename This File link, 19
Rename This Folder link, 19
renaming files and folders, **19**, *19*, **274**, 775
repair in troubleshooting, **789**

repeat delay, keyboard, 221
repeat rate, keyboard, 221
replacing damaged files, **774–775**
replication
    in Active Directory, **909–910**
    in Novell NetWare networks, 887
Replicator group, 653
replying to e-mail, **546–547**
Report view, 709, **714**, *715*
Request for Connection dialog box, 537, *537*
Require Encryption setting, 683–684
resizing taskbar, **7**, *7*
resolution, setting, **203–205**, *205*
resource assignments, viewing and changing, **341–342**, *341–342*
Resources tab, **341–342**, *341–342*, 349
Restart Computer Options window, 835, *836*
Restart the Computer option, 835
Restart the Service option, 835
Restoration Complete screen, 69
Restore All Items link, 26
Restore and Manage Media tab, **785–786**
Restore Declined Updates option, 151
Restore Files and Directories right, 655
Restore From dialog box, 786
Restore My Computer to an Earlier Time option, 68
restore points
    creating, **66–67**, *66–67*, **766–767**, *766–767*
    selecting, **68–69**, *68–69*, **765–766**
Restore tab, 785
Restore This Item link, 26
Restore Wizard, **785–786**
restoring
    backups, **785–786**
    configuration, **764**
        Automated System Recovery disk for, **768–770**, *769–770*
        Last Known Good Configuration for, **764–765**
        system, **68–69**, *68–69*, **765–768**, *766–768*
    licenses, **380**, *380*
    Registry, **727**

Restricted Sites zone, 475
Resultant Set of Policy snap-in, 811
Resume command, 316
Resume Printing link, 47
resuming printing, 47, 316
reverting to Windows ME and Windows 98, **149**, *149*
Review and Install Updates link, 42
REXEC program, **490**
right-clicking
    dragging files with, **273**
    for shortcut menus, 271
rights. *See* permissions
ripping CDs, **365–372**, *365, 367–368, 371*
RJ-11 connectors, 587
RJ-45 connectors, 587
rmdir command, 772, 775
roaming user profiles, 614, 646
roles, computer, **753–755**, *755*
Roll Back Driver option, 84
rolling back drivers, **84**, *84*, **115**
root object, 887
route program, **491**
routers, 568, **588**
Routing and Remote Access service, 832
Routing Options screen, 96, **497**, *497*
RPCs (Remote Procedure Calls), 909–910
RSAC (Recreational Software Advisory Council), 859
RSH program, **490**
rules
    for dialing, 410, *410*
    for e-mail, **554–555**, *554–555*
Run a Program option, 835
Run dialog box, 242
Run Installation Program dialog box, 40
Run Scripts permission, 861
Run This Program When Windows Starts option, 514
running programs, **242**
    in Compatibility mode, **248–253**, *249–255*
    displaying, **166–169**, *167–169*
    with multiple users, **234–235**
    at startup, **236–237**

S

Safe Mode, 765–766
Safely Remove Hardware feature, 331, 401–402, *402*
SafeWord product, **691**
SAM (Security Accounts Manager), 652
SAM hive file, 730
Sample Rate Conversion Quality setting, 385
satellite connections, **434–435**, **456**
Save As dialog box
    for files, 273
    for Performance views, 712
    for sound files, 390–391
    for System Information, 718
    for Web pages, 466
    for Windows Movie Maker projects, 397
Save Attachments dialog box, 546, *546*
Save File dialog box, 188
Save Message As dialog box, 544–545, *544*
Save Movie dialog box, 397, *397*
Save My Password option, 532
Save Photo dialog box, 395
Save Picture dialog box, 467
Save Scheme dialog box, 405
Save This User Name and Password for the Following
    Users option, 36
Save Web Page dialog box, 466
saving
    Alert log views, 713
    e-mail, **544–546**, *544–545*
    files and folders to Desktop, **273**
    Performance views, 712
    settings, **128–131**, *129–131*
    sound files, 390–391
    System Information reports, 718
    Web pages, **466–467**
    Windows Movie Maker projects, 397
scalability of Active Directory, **910**
scaling Remote Assistance display, **193**
Scan for Updates link, 42
Schedule screen, 499–500, *499*
Schedule tab, 65
Scheduled Task Wizard, 63–65

Scheduled Tasks folder, 63
schedules
    for faxes, 499–500, *499*
    groupware for, 567
    for scripts, **751**
    for tasks, **63–65**, *63–65*
Schema setting, 872
schemas
    in LDAP, 872
    in Novell NetWare networks, 886
sci newsgroups, 557
screen appearance, Desktop. *See* Desktop
Screen Saver tab, 213, 404
screen savers, 162, **213**
Script Source Access option, 848
scripts, **737–738**
    for adding users, **752–753**
    arguments in, **740–741**, *741*
    comparisons and loops in, **742–743**
    for computer roles, **753–755**, *755*
    example, **739–740**, *739*
    flow control in, **743–744**, *744*
    logic in, **740**
    for logs, **755–756**, *756*
    for network resources, **647**
    on Novell networks, 885
    tools for, **738–739**
    variables in, **741–742**, *742*
    with WSH. *See* WSH (Windows Script Host)
Scripts tab, 899
Scripts virtual directory, 843
scrolling Taskbar, 105
SCSI devices, **795–797**
SDSL (Symmetric DSL), 432
Search bar, 174
Search Companion, **27–29**, *27–29*, **108**, **281–282**,
    281–282
Search Companion bar, 470–472, *471–472*
Search for Media Files dialog box, 359, *359*
Search Results screen, 27, 522
search services, 470
searching
    in Active Directory, **905–906**

for contacts, **521–522**, *521*
for drivers, 336
for files, **27–29**, *27–29*, **281–282**, *281–282*
in Help and Support Center, **175–178**, *175*, *177*
with Internet Explorer, **470–472**, *471–472*
for Internet radio stations, **375**, *375*
for newsgroups, **558**
Registry, **731–732**, *731*
Secondary Logon service, 829
sectors, boot, **775–776**
Secure Communication option, 869
securID product, **691**
security, **651**
    in Active Directory, **902–905**
    auditing in, **664–668**, *665–668*
    for dial-in sessions, **88**, *88*, **682–684**, *683*
    in FAT, 698–699
    for Internet connections, **435–436**, *436*
    on LANs, **567**
    in Novell NetWare networks, 887
    in NTFS, 140, 700
    ownership in, **668–670**, *669*
    permissions in. *See* permissions
    in Remote Assistance, **183**
    for scripts, 738
    for SMTP servers, 873
    in telecommuting. *See* telecommuting
    user accounts for, **652–653**
        creating, **146**, **655–658**, *656–657*
        group accounts, **658**, *658*
        rights in, **653–655**, *654*
    for Web servers, **849**, *850*, **858**
Security Accounts Manager (SAM), 652
Security Accounts Manager service, 829
Security Accounts tab, **863**, *864*
Security Configuration and Analysis snap-in, 811
SECURITY hive file, 730
Security log, 677–679, *677*
Security Logging tab, 453, *453*
Security Properties dialog box, 678, *678*
Security Reference Monitor, 120
Security Settings dialog box, 476, *476*

Security Settings pane, 654, *654*
Security subsystem, 121
Security tab
    for auditing, 667, *667*, 675–676
    for dial-in sessions, 88, 683
    for Internet Explorer, **475–476**, *476*
    for Outlook Express, 560
    for ownership, 669
    for permissions, 79, 662, 664, *664*
    for printers, 306, *307*
    for SMTP servers, **873**
Security templates snap-in, 811
Security Warning dialog box, 42, 374
Select a Compatibility Mode for the Program screen,
    93, 250–252, *251*
Select a Connection Method screen, 440, *440*, 445,
    596, *596*
Select a Printer Port screen, 45, 304, *304*, 310, *310*
Select a Restore Point screen, 68, 766
Select a Title for the Program screen, 32
Select a Transfer Method screen, 129, *129*
Select Backup Sets dialog box, 786
Select Certificate Store dialog box, 288
Select Columns dialog box, 168–169, *168*
Select Custom Files and Settings screen, 130–131, *130*
Select Device for Sending or Receiving Faxes screen,
    95, 495, *495*
Select Display Settings for the Program screen, 94,
    250–252, *251*
Select Drive dialog box, 62
Select Logon and Logoff Options screen, 163
Select NetWare Logon dialog box, 892, *892*
Select Network Client dialog box, 143, 891, 897–898,
    897–898
Select Network Component Type dialog box, 143, 598,
    891, 897
Select Network Protocol dialog box, 143, 898
Select Partition Type screen, 701–702, *701*
Select People dialog box, 554, *554*
Select Program to Schedule dialog box, 64
Select Recipients dialog box, 548
Select Remote Users option, 85

Select Stationery dialog box, 550
Select the Connections to Bridge screen, 446, *446*
Select the Device Driver You Want to Install for This
    Hardware screen, 82–83, 334–336, *335*, 338, *338*
Select the File to Import dialog box, 392–393, *393*
Select User dialog box, 287
Select User or Group dialog box, 667–668
Select Users dialog box
    for groups, 77, 658
    for Remote Desktop Connection, 85, 530
Select Users or Groups dialog box
    for groups, 660, *660*
    for permissions, 78–79, 664
Select Your Internet Connection screen, 441, *441*
Send a File dialog box, 526–527, *527*
Send an Invitation dialog box, 188
Send Copy of Non Delivery Report option, 871
Send Fax Wizard, 498–500, *498–499*
Send File dialog box, 506
Send Message dialog box, 171, *171*
Send tab, 547, 559–560
Send To command, 22–23
Send To folder, 277, 500
Sender field for fax cover pages, 502
Sender Information screen, 95, 495, *495*
sending
    e-mail, **548–549**, *548*
    faxes, **498–500**, *498–499*
    files in Windows Messenger, **526–527**, *527*
    messages to users, **170–171**, *171*
Sent Items folder, 504, 542
.sep file extension, 316
Separator Page dialog box, 317, *317*
separator pages for printing, **316–318**, *317*
SerialKeys feature, 225
Server Extensions tab, **859–860**, *860*
Server Properties option, 52
Server service, 627, 829
servers, **580–581**
    application, 565–566
    counters for, 711
    directory, **511**
    domain, **633–634**

hosting, **841**
    FTP. *See* FTP (File Transfer Protocol) and FTP
      servers
    IIS for, **841–846**, *842–843*, *845–846*, **873**
    SMTP. *See* SMTP servers
    Web. *See* Web servers
    in LDAP, 872
    in networks, 568
    print, **52–53**, *52–53*, **318–319**
    time, **200**
Service Management Console, **826–827**, *826*
Service Settings dialog box, 452, *452*
services, **825**
    adding, **143**
    additional, **833**
    automatic, **827–829**
    commands for, **837–839**, *837–838*
    configuring
        Dependencies tab for, **836**, *836*
        General tab for, **833–834**, *833*
        Log On tab for, **834**, *834*
        Recovery tab for, **835**, *835*
    disabled, **832**
    enabling and disabling, **773–774**
    for ICS, **451–454**, *452–454*
    issues with, 649
    manual, **830–832**
    purpose of, **825–826**
    Service Management Console for, **826–827**, *826*
    troubleshooting, **839**
    uninstalling, **143**
Services for Unix product, 615–617
Services screen, 717, *717*
Services snap-in, 811
Services tab, 452, *452*
Session layer, **570**
Sessions Timed Out counter, 711
Set As Default Printer command, 47
set command, **741–742**, *742*
Set My Message Font dialog box, 514
Set Search Options screen, 177–178, *177*
Set the Invitation to Expire screen, 186–187, *187*
Set Up My Connection Manually option, 34

SetInfo method, 753
Setting Folder Permission dialog box, 606
Setting Up a High Speed Connection screen, 145
settings
    with multiple users, 235
    transferring, 127
        restoring in, **147–148**, *148*
        saving in, **128–131**, *129–131*
Settings dialog box, 768, *768*
Settings tab
    for DualView, 401
    for monitors, 203, 351
    for refresh rate, 205
    for resolution, 205, *205*
    for scheduled tasks, 65
    for video, 201–202, *201*, 348
"Setup did not find any hard drives on your computer"
    message, 795
"Setup has encountered a fatal error that prevents it
    from continuing" message, 797
Setup Manager Help file, 155
Setup Options screen, 136–139, *136*
Setup program, **144–147**
    for clean installations, **139–144**
    for new installations, **135–139**, *136, 138*
    troubleshooting, **794–799**
    for upgrading, **132–134**, *133–135*
SFC (System File Checker), **779–780**
share-level permissions, **78**, *78*, **659–660**, *659–660*
Share Located on Another Computer option, 857
Share Name option, 46
share names, 592, 605
Share This Folder link, 72
Share This Folder on the Network option, 72
Share This Printer option, 48, 51
Shared Documents folder, 70, 604
Shared Folders snap-in, 811
Shared Music folder, 70
Shared Pictures folder, 17, 70
Shared Videos folder, 70
sharing
    documents, **512**
    encrypted files, **59**, *59*, **287**

files, **70**, *70*, **565**
folders, **70**, *70*, **72**, 72
Internet connections. *See* ICS (Internet Connection
    Sharing)
in peer-to-peer networks, **604–606**, *604–606*
printers, **48–49**, *48–49*, **305–308**, *306–308*,
    566–567
between programs, **255–256**
    Clipboard for, **256**, *257*
    ClipBook Viewer for, **257**, *258*
    OLE for, **258–261**, *259–261*
Sharing and Security option, 71
Sharing dialog box
    for folders, 71
    in NetMeeting, 512
Sharing tab
    for folders, 71–72, 281
    for peer-to-peer networks, 604–606, *604, 606*
    for permissions, 78, 659, *659*
    for printers, 48, 51, 306, 308
SHD extension, 792
Shell commands in Taskpad, 822
Shell Hardware Detection service, 829
shielding, cable, 586
Shiva Password Authentication Protocol (SPAP), 690
shortcut menus, **271**
shortcuts
    cleaning up, 211
    on Desktop, **31–32**, *31–32*, 164
    editing, **263**, *263*
    on Quick Launch toolbar, 8–9
    on Start menu, 242
Show Contents of Window While Dragging option, 535
Show Favorites on the Navigation Bar option, 178
Show Graphics (Emoticons) in Instant Messages
    option, 514
Show History on the Navigation Bar option, 178
Show Me as "Away" When I'm Inactive for NN
    Minutes option, 515
Show Open Window command, 5
Show the Clock option, 13
Show the Desktop command, 5
ShowSounds feature, 225

shutting down Windows
options for, **172–173**, *173*
problems from, **760**
signatures in e-mail, **552–553**, *552*
Signatures tab, 552, *552*, 560
signed drivers, **328**
signing out and back in with Windows Messenger, **520**, *520*
simple dynamic volumes, 703
Simple Mail Transfer Protocol (SMTP), 572
Simple Mail Transfer Protocol servers. *See* SMTP servers
Simple Mail Transfer Protocol service, 833
Simple Network Management Protocol (SNMP), 583
16-bit programs
vs. 32-bit, **246–247**
uninstalling, **239–240**
64-bit programs, 246
size
font, 214
icons, 11
Internet Explorer text, **483**, *483*
logs, 707
partitions, 701
searching for files by, 28
taskbar, **7**, *7*
Skin Chooser page, 375–376
Skin mode, 358, *358*
skins for Windows Media Player, 358, *358*, **375–376**
Smart Card service, 831
Smart Card Helper service, 831
smart hubs, 583
SmartSuite 96, **255**, *255*
SMTP (Simple Mail Transfer Protocol), 572
SMTP servers, **867–868**
Access tab for, **869**, *869*
Delivery tab for, **871–872**, *871*
General tab for, **868–869**, *868*
LDAP Routing tab for, **872**, *872*
Messages tab for, **870–871**, *870*
Security tab for, **873**
SMTP Service, 843
Snap-in Menus option, 815

Snap-in Toolbars option, 815
snap-ins for MMC, **809–814**, *812–814*
sneakernet, **564**
SNMP (Simple Network Management Protocol), 583
SNMP Service, 829
SNMP Trap Service, 831
soc newsgroups, 557
socket services, 401
software. *See* programs
Software Environment section, 718
SOFTWARE hive file, 730
SOFTWARE.LOG file, 731
sorting
in Explorer, 271
fonts, 321
programs, 238
sound, **106–107**
audio CDs, **38**, *38*
audio clips, **360**
in e-mail, **551–552**
recording, **389–391**, *389*, *391*
in Remote Desktop Connection, 534
system, **222**, *222*
in Windows Movie Maker, **395–396**
sound effects, **360–361**, *361*
Sound Recorder, **389–391**, *389*, *391*
Sound Retrieval System WOW (SRS WOW), 372
Sound Selection dialog box, 391, *391*
Sound tab, 225, *225*
Sounds and Audio Devices Properties dialog box
for Messenger, 515
for system sounds, 222, *222*
for volume, **384–385**, *384*, 387
Sounds tab, 222, *222*
SoundSentry feature, 225
soundtracks, **396**
spanned dynamic volumes, 703
SPAP (Shiva Password Authentication Protocol), 690
speaker balance, **385**, *385*
Speaker Volume dialog box, 385, *385*
Speaker Volume setting for modems, 343
speakers for Windows Messenger, 518–519
Speakers tab, 385, *386*

Special Access, 662
Specify a Printer screen, 894
Specify an IP Address option, **598–599**
Specify Partition Size screen, 701, *701*
speed
    cable modems, **428–429**
    DSL, **432–433**
    hubs, 588
    ISDN, 437
    networks, 584
    NICs, 585
    satellite service, 434
SpeedStep feature, 109
spikes, power, 759
SPL extension, 792
spool files, 793
Spool folder, 318
spoolers
    for printing, 301, **315–316**, *315*
    troubleshooting, **791–792**
Spooling option, 313
SPSs (standby power supplies), 352, 759
SRS WOW (Sound Retrieval System WOW), 372
SRS WOW Effects panel, 361, *361*
srv.sys file, 627
SSDP Discovery Service, 831
SSL Port setting, 853
sspifilt filter, 847
Standalone tab, 812
Standard menus option, 814
Standard tab, 826
Standard toolbar option, 814
standards
    for hardware, 758
    for network cables, **586–587**
Standby mode, troubleshooting, **418–420**
standby power supplies (SPSs), 352, 759
Start menu, **262**, *262*
    classic, **220**, *220*
    customizing, **10–12**, *10–12*, **218–219**, *219*
    editing, **263–264**, *263–264*
    for navigating, 164

    new features of, **103**, *104*
    shortcuts on, 242
Start Menu Folder, 277
Start Menu tab, 11, 218, *218*
starting
    Help and Support Center, **173–174**, *174*
    Internet Explorer, **457–458**, *458*
    Sound Recorder, **389**, *389*
    Windows Media Player, **357–358**
    Windows Messenger, **513**, *513*
startup
    running programs at, **236–237**
    stop errors in, 799
Startup and Recovery dialog box, 802, *802*
Startup folder, 236–237
startup.ncf file, 896
Startup tab, 237, *237*
Startup type for services, 834
static IP addressing, 576
static with analog modems, 455
stationery for e-mail, **550–551**
Stationery Setup Wizard, 551
status
    of Remote Assistance invitations, **188–189**, *188*
    in Windows Messenger, **526**
Status bar option, 814
Status dialog box, 37
"STATUS_IMAGE_CHECKSUM_MISMATCH"
    message, 801
"STATUS_SYSTEM_PROCESS_TERMINATED"
    message, 801
StickyKeys feature, 225
Stop errors, **799**
    common, **800–801**
    fixing, **802–803**
    responding to, **802**, *802*
storage area for CDs
    checking files in, **294**
    clearing files in, **297**, *297*
    copying files to, **293–294**, *294*
Storage node in Computer Management, 819
Storyboard view, 395, *395*

strings in Registry, 729–730
striped dynamic volumes, 703
styles for chatting, **524**
subkeys in Registry, **727–729**, *728*
submenus, 12
subnets and subnet masks
    in IP addressing, **574–575**
    issues with, 649
    for LANs, 146
    for TCP/IP, 143
subscribing to newsgroups, **558–559**
substitution tables for fonts, **324**, *324*
subtrees in Registry, **727**
Success events
    auditing, 674–675
    logging, 705
Suggested Topics, 175, 177
Summary tab
    for MP3 files, 362
    for properties, 281
Support page
    in Help and Support Center, **179**, *179*
    for newsgroups, 194
surges, power, 759
SVGA adapters, **125**
Swap File object, counter for, 710
switches, 568, 571
switching
    programs, 243, *243*
    users, **165**
Symmetric DSL (SDSL), 432
Synchronize All Offline Files Before Logging Off
    option, 412
Synchronize All Offline Files When Logging On
    option, 412
Synchronize dialog box, 55
synchronizing files, **410–411**
    Briefcase for, **414–416**, *415–416*
    offline files, **54**, *54*, **290–291**, *291*, **411–413**,
    412–414
.sys extension, 327
SYSCON utility, 887

SYSPREP tool, 114
Sysprint.sep file, 316
Sysprtj.sep file, 317
system, restoring, **68–69**, *68–69*, **765–768**, *766–768*
System Configuration Utility, 237, *237*
System Event Notification service, 829
System events, auditing, 672
System File Checker (SFC), **779–780**
System File Protection, **115**
SYSTEM hive file, 730
System Information, **715–718**, *715–718*
System log, **704–706**, 802
system management ports, 352
system modal dialog boxes, 243
System Monitor, 708–709, *709*, 712
System Monitor Properties dialog box, 712
system policies, 912
System Properties dialog box
    for Active Directory, 913
    for disabling hardware, 339
    for domains, 91, 640–641
    for drivers, 80–83
    for hardware profiles, 611
    for log settings, 706
    for RAM, 124
    for Remote Assistance, 184, *184*
    for Remote Desktop Connection, 85, 530–531, *530*
    for restore points, 66–67
    for Stop errors, 802
    for System restore, 767, *768*
    for user profiles, 614
    for Windows Update, 150, *151*
system resources for hardware, **329–330**
System Restore feature, 68–69, **115**, **765–768**,
    766–768
system restore points
    creating, **66–67**, *66–67*, **766–767**, *766–767*
    selecting, **68–69**, *68–69*, **765–766**
System Restore Service, 829
System Restore tab, 66–67, 767–768, *768*
System Settings Change dialog box, 447
system sounds, **222**, *222*

System Summary screen, 715, *715*
System Tools node, 818–819
System Tray, 13
systemroot command, *772*

T

Take No Action option, 835
Take Ownership permission, 663, 669
Take Ownership of Files or Other Objects permission, 655
talk newsgroups, 557
TAPI (Telephony Application Programming Interface), **427–428**
task descriptions in MMC, 821
Task Manager, 165, **719**, *719*
    for logged on users, 166, *166*
    for networking, **721**, *722*
    for performance, **721**
    for processes, **720**, *721*
    for programs, **719–720**, *720*
        running, **166–169**, *167–169*
        switching, *243*
        unresponsive, 243
Task Scheduler service, 829
Taskbar, **105–106**
    address bars on, **30**, *30*
    arranging windows with, **5–6**, *5–6*
    locking, 7, 105, 216
    for logging off other users, 169–170, *170*
    for navigating, 164
    notification area on, **217–218**, *217*
    options for, **215–216**, *215–216*
    resizing and moving, **7**, *7*
    for sending messages, 171
    toolbars on, **216–217**, *216–217*
Taskbar and Start Menu Properties dialog box
    for notification area, 13
    for Start menu, 11–12, 218, *218*
    for Taskbar, 215, *215*
Taskbar tab, 215–216, *215*
Taskpad Display page, 821, *821*
Taskpad navigation tabs option, 815

Taskpad Target page, 821
taskpads in MMC, **821–823**, *821–823*
tasks, scheduling, **63–65**, *63–65*
TCP (Transmission Control Protocol), 572
TCP/IP (Transmission Control Protocol/Internet Protocol), **572–573**, 617
    alternate configuration, 112
    in installation, **143–144**
    printer ports in, **310**, *310*
    troubleshooting, **620–625**, *622–623*
TCP/IP Filtering window, 639–640, *639*
TCP/IP NetBIOS Helper service, 829
TCP/IP Print Server service, 832
TCP/IP WINS Server dialog box, 648
TCP Port setting, 853
TDI (Transport Driver Interface), **628**
telecommuting, **681**
    risks and rewards in, **681–682**
    security in
        authentication, **689–690**
        caller-ID/callback, **690–691**
        file encryption, **692–693**, *693*
        guidelines, **689**
        RAS dial-in sessions, **682–684**, *683*
        third-party products, **691**
        VPN, **684–688**, *685–687*
Telephony Application Programming Interface (TAPI), **427–428**
Telephony service, 832
Telnet program, **490**
Telnet service, 832, 837–838, *837–838*
Temp folder, encrypting, 693
Templates folder, 277
Templeton, Brad, 876
temporary cookies, 477
temporary Internet files, **474**
10 Big Myths About Copyright Explained, 876
terminal emulation software, 505
Terminal Services service, 832
terminals in networks, 568
termination, SCSI, 796
Test Your Compatibility Settings screen, 94, 252, *252*
testing in troubleshooting, **789**

text
    for chatting, **524**
    in Internet Explorer, **483**, *483*
text mode setup, **794–795**
Text Services and Input Languages dialog box,
    141, *141*
TFTP (Trivial File Transfer Protocol), **488**
The Following Hardware Is Already Installed on Your
    Computer screen, 336–337, *337*
The Wizard Can Help You Install Other Hardware
    screen, 337, *337*
The Wizard Is Ready to Install Your Hardware
    screen, 338
themes
    for display, **208**
    in Remote Desktop Connection, 535
Themes service, 829
Themes tab, 208
third-party cookies, 477
32-bit programs vs. 16-bit, **246–247**
This account option, 834
This Service Depends on the Following System
    Components option, 836
Thumbnails view, 16, *16*, 268, *269*
thunking, 246
Tile Window Vertically command, 5–6
Tile Windows Horizontally command, 5–6
time
    changing, **199–200**, *199–200*
    in installation, **141**
time servers, **200**
Time To Live (TTL) mechanism, 623
Time Zone screen, 155
Time Zone tab, 199–200
Timeline view, 395, *395*
Titles view, 268
To Run the Wizard with the Network Setup Disk
    screen, 444
To This Folder on My Hard Drive setting, **137**
ToggleKeys feature, 226
toolbars
    customizing, **280**, *280*
    displaying and using, **8–9**, *8–9*

    in Internet Explorer, **482–483**, *482*
    on Taskbar, **216–217**, *216–217*
Tools, help for, 111
Tools page, **181**, *181*
tracert program, **491**, **623–624**
Transfer in Progress screen, 148, *148*
transferring files, 102
    encrypted, **288**
    Files and Settings Transfer Wizard for,
        102, 127
        for restoring, **147–148**, *148*
        for saving, **128–131**, *129–131*
    with FTP, **486–488**, *487*
    in HyperTerminal, **506**
    in Internet Explorer, **473**, *473*
    in Remote Assistance, **193**
    in Windows Messenger, **526–528**, *527–528*
transferring print jobs, **316**
Transmission Control Protocol (TCP), 572
Transmission Control Protocol/Internet Protocol
    (TCP/IP), **572–573**, 617
    alternate configuration, 112
    in installation, **143–144**
    printer ports in, **310**, *310*
    troubleshooting, **620–625**, *622–623*
Transmitting Subscriber Identification (TSID) screen,
    496, *496*
Transport Driver Interface (TDI), **628**
Transport layer, **570**
transport protocols, **628**
Traverse Folder/Execute File permission, 663
Trivial File Transfer Protocol (TFTP), **488**
Troubleshoot tab, 349, *349*
troubleshooters, **194–195**, *195*
troubleshooting
    boot process, **798–799**, **803–804**
    CD writing, **296–297**, *296*
    domains, **647–649**
    hardware, 349, *349*
    IIS, **873**
    Internet connections, **455–456**
    notebook computers
        mouse, **417**

PC Cards, **417**
    power management, **418–420**
peer-to-peer networks, **618–619**
    architecture in, **626–629**, *626*
    configuration testing, **619–620**, *619*
    IPX/SPX, **625**
    TCP/IP, **620–625**, *622–623*
    tips for, **629**
    printing, **790–793**
    SCSI devices, **795–797**
    services, **839**
    setup, **794–799**
    steps in, **787–790**
    Stop errors, **799–803**
    uninstalling programs, **239–240**
    video problems, **207**, *207*
troubleshooting utilities, compatibility of, 248
TrueType fonts, 301, 319
trust relationships, 645–646, 910
Trusted Sites zone, 475
TTL (Time To Live) mechanism, 623
Turn Off Automatic Updating. I Want to Update My Computer Manually option, 151
Turn Off Computer option, 103, 172–173
Turn Off Computer screen, 172–173, *173*
Turn Off System Restore option, 67
Turn Off System Restore on All Drives option, 67
Turn On Internet Connection Firewall for This Connection option, 35
two-click renaming technique, 19
two-way satellite, 434–435
Type 1 fonts, **322**
type command, 772
Type Libraries, 751
Type Your Contact's First and Last Name screen, 521, *521*
Typical Settings option, 142

U

U.S. Copyright Office, 876
UDP (User Datagram Protocol), 572
unblocking chat users, **525–526**, *526*

UNC (Universal Naming Convention), 592
    for direct connections, **608–610**, *609*, **644–646**
    long filenames in, **609–610**, **645**
Undo Cascade command, 5–6
Undo Tile command, 5–6
Unencrypted Password authentication, 690
"UNEXPECTED_KERNEL_MODE_TRAP" message, 801
Unimodems, 342
Uninstall Windows XP dialog box, 149, *149*
uninstalling
    hardware, **339**
    programs, **237–240**, *238–239*
    services, **143**
    Windows XP, **103**, **149**, *149*
unInstallShield, 239, *239*
uninterruptible power supplies (UPSs), **352**, 759
    choosing, **352–353**
    installing, **353–356**, *353–355*
Uninterruptible Power Supply (UPS) service, 832
Universal Naming Convention (UNC), 592
    for direct connections, **608–610**, *609*, **644–646**
    long filenames in, **609–610**, **645**
Universal Plug and Play Device Host service, 832
Unix hosts, installing printers through, **311**
Unix networks, **615–617**, *617*
Unix vs. Windows XP, **117–118**
Unlock Computer dialog box, 165
unlocking taskbar, **7**, *7*
Unpin from Start Menu command, 10
unresponsive programs, **242–245**, *243*
unsatisfactory cookies, 477
Unused Desktop Shortcuts folder, 211
Update Driver option, 81
Update Driver Warning dialog box, 335
updating
    monitor drivers, **203**
    video card drivers, **201–202**, *202*
    with Windows Update, **149–152**, *151*
    Windows XP, **42–43**, *42–43*, 101
Upgrade Advisor program, 126–127
Upgrade Report screen, 126, *126*, 133–134, *133*, *135*

upgrading
    considerations in, **116–117**
    steps in, **132–134**, *132–135*
uplink ports, 588
Upload Manager service, 829
UPS Configuration dialog box, 355–356, *355*
UPS Interface Configuration dialog box, 354, *354*
UPS Selection dialog box, 354, *354*
UPS tab, 353–354, *353*
UPSs (uninterruptible power supplies), **352**, 759
    choosing, **352–353**
    installing, **353–356**, *353–355*
URLs with Internet Explorer, 458–459
% Usage counter, 710
USB hub usage, **349–350**, *349–350*
Use Local Time for File Naming and Rollover
    option, 854
Use Printer Offline command, 316
Use Simple Sharing (Recommended) option, 78
Use this connection's DNS suffix in DNS registration
    option, 638
User Account and Domain Information screen, 92, 641
User Account dialog box, 641
User Accounts screen, 163
User Datagram Protocol (UDP), 572
User Interaction Level screen, 154, *154*
user interface
    Control Panel, **104–105**, *104*
    eye candy, **105**
    notification area, 106
    Start menu, **103**, *104*
    Taskbar, **105–106**
user mode, **121–122**, **626–627**
User Mode-Full Access in MMC, **815**, *816*
User Mode-Limited Access, Multiple Window in
    MMC, **816–817**, *816*
User Mode-Limited Access, Single Window in MMC,
    817, *817*
User Name and Password screen, 881, *882*
user profiles
    for domains, **646–647**
    managing, **613–615**, *614*
User Profiles dialog box, 614, *614*
% User Time counter, 710

usernames
    for cable modem connections, 431
    for domains, 92, 580, 635, 641–642
    for FTP sites, 487, 881, 884
    for Internet connections, 35–36, 427
    in LDAP, 872
    for network drives, 643
    for Novell clients, 899
    in peer-to-peer networks, 592
    in Remote Desktop Connection, 532
    for scheduled tasks, 64
    in telecommuting, 691
    for user accounts, 75, 657
    for Web sites, 863
users
    accounts for, **652–653**
        creating, **75–76**, *75–76*, **146**, **655–658**,
            656–657
        for domain servers, **634**
        rights in, **653–655**, *654*
    active, 103, 160, **166**
    in Active Directory, **903**
    adding, **752–753**
    disconnected, 103, 160
    impersonation of
        caller-ID/callback for, **690–691**
        encrypted authentication for, **689–690**
        guidelines for, **688–689**
        third-party products, **691**
    logged on, **166**, *166*
    logging off, **169–170**, *170*
    in multiuser environments, **276–277**
    sending messages to, **170–171**, *171*
    switching, **165**
Users and Passwords applet, 652
Users group, 653
Users tab
    for logged on users, 166, *166*
    for logging off other users, 170, *170*
    for sending messages, 171
    for switching users, 165
Using NetMeeting screen, 507
Utilities tab, **315**
Utility Manager, **228–229**, *229*

V

value entries in Registry, **727–729**, *728*, **732–734**, *732–733*

variables in scripts, **741–742**, *742*

VBScript language, **745**

VDMs (video display metafiles), 121

vector fonts, 322

VGA video drivers, 419

Video Acceleration Settings dialog box, 373, *373*

video and video cards, **106–107**

    acceleration settings for, 373

    in chatting, **525**, *525*

    drivers for, **201–202**, *201–202*

    in Internet Explorer, 464

    movies. *See* Windows Movie Maker

    for NetMeeting, **512**, *512*

    playing, **360**

    resolution, color depth, and refresh rate, **203–206**, *205–206*

    Windows Media Player for. *See* Windows Media Player

    in Windows Messenger, **517–519**

video display metafiles (VDMs), 121

Video Display Troubleshooter, 207, *207*

Video tab, 512

View Graph view, 708, *709*, **711–712**

View Histogram view, 709

View Installed Printers or Fax Printers link, 48

View menu

    in Explorer, 16, 267

    in MMC, **824**

View or Change Your Invitation screen, 188, *188*

View Report view, 709

View tab

    for Control Panel, 197

    for folders, 278–279

views

    in Explorer, **16–17**, *16–17*, **267–271**, *268–270*

    in Help and Support Center, **182**

    in MMC, **814–815**, *814–815*

virtual directories

    for FTP servers, **866–867**, *866–867*

    for Web servers, **860–862**, *861–862*

Virtual Directory Alias page, 860, *861*, 866, *866*

Virtual Directory Creation Wizard, 860, *861*, 866–867, *866–867*

virtual memory and Virtual Memory Manager, 120, 125, 169

Virtual Memory Size option, 169

virtual NICs, **602–603**, *602–603*

Virtual Private Networking (VPN)

    operation of, **684–687**, *685–687*

    performance of, **687–688**

    setting up, **89–90**, *89–90*

Visual Effects tab, 729

visualizations for Windows Media Player, **376–377**, *377*

Visualizations tab, 376–377, *377*

visually-impaired users, accessibility options for, **224**, *224*

voice in Windows Messenger, **517–519**, *517–519*, **524**, *524*

Volume Control program, **386–389**, *387–389*

volume settings

    for CD drives, 346

    for Windows Media Player

        advanced, **385–386**, *386*

        displaying, **383–384**, *384*

        program for, **386–389**, *387–389*

        Sounds and Audio Devices Properties for, **384–385**, *384*

        speaker balance, **385**, *385*

    for Windows Messenger, 519

Volume Shadow Copy service, 832

Volume tab, 384–385, *384*, 387

VPN (Virtual Private Networking)

    operation of, **684–687**, *685–687*

    performance of, **687–688**

    setting up, **89–90**, *89–90*

VPN Server Selection screen, 687, *687*

W

W3C Extended Log File Format, 853

W3C log files, 855

wallpaper, **208–209**, *209*, 467

WANs (wide area networks), 564

Warning dialog box, 238–239

Warning events, 704

WAV files, converting, 390
Web, help on, **196**
Web browsing, **112–113**
  with Internet Explorer. *See* Internet Explorer
  with MSN Explorer, **484–486**, *484–485*
  utilities for, **486–491**, *487*, *489*
Web content on desktop, **211–212**, *211–212*
Web pages, saving, **466–467**
Web portals in Novell NetWare networks, 888, *889*
Web publishing, **108**, **875**
  copyright issues in, **875–876**
  FTP for, **878**, 881, **883–884**
  location of, **878**
  Network Places for, **879–883**, *880–883*
  quality control in, **877–878**
  WebDAV for, **878–879**, *879*
Web servers, **846–847**
  Custom Errors tab for, **850–851**, *850*, **859**
  Directory Security tab for, **849**, *850*, **858**
  Documents tab for, **849**, *849*, **858**
  Home Directory tab for, **848–849**, *848*,
    856–857, *856–857*
  HTTP Headers tab for, **850**, **858–859**, *858*
  IASPI tab for, **847–848**, *847*, **856**
  Server Extensions tab for, **859–860**, *860*
  virtual directories for, **860–862**, *861–862*
  Web Site tab for, **852–856**, *852*
Web Site Identification section, 853
Web tab, 211, *211*
Web Site tab, **852–856**, *852*
WebDAV, **878–879**, *879*
Welcome screen, 161, *162*, 165
Welcome section for FTP servers, 864
Welcome tab, 769, *769*, 783
Welcome to Microsoft Windows screen, 144
Welcome to Microsoft Windows XP screen, 128
Welcome to Setup screen, 139
Welcome to System Restore screen, 766, *766*
Welcome to the Add Hardware Wizard screen, 336
Welcome to the Network Setup Wizard screen, 444–445
Welcome to the New Task Wizard screen, 822
Welcome to the Programs Compatibility Wizard
  screen, 248

Welcome to Windows Setup screen, 132–133, *133*,
    136, *136*
What Do You Want to Name This Place? screen,
    881–882, *882*
What Do You Want to Transfer? screen, 129–130, *129*
What is The Address of This Network Place? screen,
    880–881, *881*
What to Back Up screen, 782, *782*
What to Restore dialog box, 786
What's Your Computer's Name? screen, 142
wheel-style mouse, **417**
Wheel tab, 222
When I Press the Power Button on My Computer
    list, 408
When I Press the Sleep Button on My Computer
    list, 408
Where Are the Files and Settings? screen, 147, *148*
Where Do You Want to Create This Network Place?
    screen, 880, *880*
Where to Restore dialog box, 786
Which Computer Is This? screen, 129, 147
Which Program Do You Want to Run with
    Compatibility Settings? screen, 250, *250*
Which Users Have Added You? dialog box, 517
Who Will Use This Computer? screen, 146
Wi-Fi networks, 587
wide area networks (WANs), 564
wildcards in searches, 282
Win16 on Win32 (WOW) environment, 121–122
Win32 subsystem, **121**
windows (objects)
  appearance settings for, 214
  arranging, **5–6**, *5–6*
Windows (operating system)
  activating, **146–147**
  old version removal, **149**
  registering, **147**
  shutting down, **172–173**, *173*
  upgrading from, **116–117**, **132–134**, *132–135*
Windows Audio service, 829
Windows Classic theme, 208
Windows Components Wizard, 240–241, *240*,
    841–842

Windows - Delayed Write Failed dialog box, 879, *879*
Windows Driver Protection feature, 328
Windows Explorer. *See* Explorer
Windows Image Acquisition service, 832
Windows Installer service, 832
Windows Internet Naming Service (WINS), **638**, *639*, 648
Windows Layout Properties dialog box, 542
Windows Log On screen, 163
Windows Logo testing, 336
Windows Management Instrumentation service, 829
Windows Management Instrumentation Driver service, 832
Windows Media Audio (WMA) files, 38, 365, 369–370
Windows Media Player, **106**, **357**
   for CDs
      audio, 38
      copying, **365–372**, *365*, *367–368*, *371*
      playing, **364–365**
   controls on, **358–359**, *359*
   for DVDs, **372–373**, *372–373*
   editing tags in, **361–362**, *362*
   graphic equalizer and sound effects in, **360–361**, *361*
   for Internet radio, **373–375**, *374–375*
   for licenses, **377–380**, *379–380*
   Media Guide tab, **358**
   Media Library for, **359**, *359*, **362–363**, *363–364*
   options for, **382–383**, *383*
   playing files in, **360**
   playlists in, **360**
   for portable devices, **380–382**, *382*
   skins for, **375–376**
   starting, **357–358**
   visualizations for, **376–377**, *377*
   volume settings for
      advanced, **385–386**, *386*
      displaying, **383–384**, *384*
      program for, **386–389**, *387–389*
      Sounds and Audio Devices Properties for, **384–385**, *384*
      speaker balance, **385**, *385*

Windows Media Player Software Development Kit, 376
Windows Messenger, **512**
   chatting in, **522–523**, *523*
      adding people to conversations, **524**
      blocking users, **525–526**, *526*
      text settings for, **524**
      video in, **525**, *525*
      voice in, **524**, *524*
   configuring
      Connection tab, **517**
      Personal tab, **514**, *514*
      Phone tab, **514**, *515*
      Preferences tab, **514–516**, *516*, 528
      Privacy tab, **516–517**, *516*
      voice calls, **517–519**, *517–519*
   contacts in
      adding, **520–522**, *520–521*
      removing, **522**
   for Remote Assistance invitations, **187–189**, **192**, *192*
   signing out and back in with, **520**, *520*
   starting, **513**, *513*
   status in, **526**
   transferring files in, **526**
      receiving, **528**, *528*
      sending, **526–527**, *527*
Windows Movie Maker, **107**, **391–392**
   collections for, **392**, *392*
   importing content for, **392–393**, *393*
   projects in, **395–397**, *395*, *397*
   recording content for, **393–395**, *394*
Windows Product Activation (WPA) feature, **101**
Windows Script Host. *See* WSH (Windows Script Host)
Windows Setup Manager window, 154–156, *154–155*
Windows Setup Manager Wizard, **152–157**, *152–155*
Windows Task Manager dialog box, 170, *170*
Windows Time service, 829
Windows Update, **42–43**, *42–43*, 101, **149–150**
   configuring, **150–151**, *151*
   in Help and Support Center, **179**
   manual operation, **151–152**
   running, **150**

Windows Update screen, **179**
Windows Upgrade Advisor program, 126–127, *126*
Windows XP Setup dialog box, 134, *134*
Windows XP theme, 208
Windows95/NT workstation machines, **597–598**
WindowsMedia.com database, 364
winipcfg utility, 510
Winkey, **109**, **171–172**
WINS (Windows Internet Naming Service), **638**, *639*, 648
WINS tab, 638, *639*, 648
WinZip utility, 283
Wireless Access Points, 587
wireless networks, **587**
Wireless Zero Configuration service, 829
wiring closets, 582–583
wizards, **102**
WMA (Windows Media Audio) files, 38, 365, 369–370
WMA tags, editing, **361–362**, *362*
WMI Control snap-in, 811
WMI Performance Adapter service, 832
Workgroup or Domain screen, 155
workgroups, 592
    joining, 642
    for peer-to-peer networks, 597, 599
Workstation service, 627, 829
workstations in networks, 568
World Wide Web Service, 843
World Wide Web Publishing service, 833
WOW (Win16 on Win32) environment, 121–122
WPA (Windows Product Activation) feature, **101**
Write Attributes permission, 663
write combining method, 349
Write permission, 661
    for FTP servers, 866
    for IIS, 848
    for Web sites, 861

Write Extended Attributes permission, 663
Write These Files to CD link, 24
writing CDs, **293**
    problems in, **296–297**
    storage area for
        checking files in, **294**
        clearing files in, **297**, *297*
        copying files to, **293–294**, *294*
WS_FTP Pro client, 884
WScript.exe file, **744–745**
WScript object, **750**
WSH (Windows Script Host), **744**
    example script in, **746–748**, *747*
    executables for, **744–745**
    languages for, **745**
    logic in, **748–749**, *749*
    objects in, **750–751**
    XML-based scripts in, **746**

X

XML-based scripts, **746**

Y

Yes, Export Private Key option, 57
Yes, Finished Searching link, 29
Yes, Write These Files to Another CD, 24
Your Computer Has Multiple Connections screen, 446, *446*
Your Product Key screen, 132, 136, 142
You're Almost Done screen, 443, *443*, 447

Z

Zero Administration Windows (ZAW), 896
Zero Effort Networking (Z.E.N.works), 896–897
Zip compression, **283**
zones in Internet Explorer, **475–476**, *476*

WHAT YOU THINK!

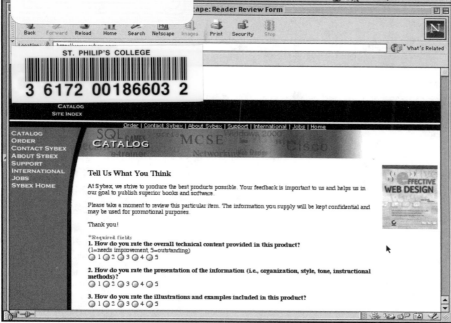

Your feedback is critical to our efforts to provide you with the best books and software on the market. Tell us what you think about the products you've purchased. It's simple:

1. Visit the Sybex website
2. Go to the product page
3. Click on **Submit a Review**
4. Fill out the questionnaire and comments
5. Click **Submit**

With your feedback, we can continue to publish the highest quality computer books and software products that today's busy IT professionals deserve.

www.sybex.com

SYBEX Inc. • 1151 Marina Village Parkway, Alameda, CA 94501 • 510-523-8233

Master These Fundamentals

Install Windows XP Professional		Chapter 2
Set Up and Use Dual Operating Systems		Chapter 2
✳ Switch from One User to Another **NEW!**		Chapter 3
✳ Get Remote Assistance **NEW!**		Chapter 3
✳ Use the Improved Control Panel to Customize Your Desktop **NEW!**		Chapter 4
Install and Remove Programs		Chapter 5, pp. 39–41
✳ Customize the Improved Start Menu and Taskbar **NEW!**		Chapter 5, pp. 10–12
✳ Learn How to Use the Explorer Bar **NEW!**		Chapter 5, pp. 14–17
Organize Files and Folders		Chapter 6
✳ Enable Compatibility Mode **NEW!**		Chapter 5, pp. 93–94
✳ Burn a CD **NEW!**		Chapter 6
✳ Compress Files and Folders **NEW!**		Chapter 6
Encrypt Files and Folders		Chapter 6, p. 58
Add a New Printer		Chapter 7, pp. 44–47
Install and Configure Hardware		Chapter 8
✳ Roll Back a Driver **NEW!**		p. 84
✳ Run Windows Media Player 8 **NEW!**		Chapter 9
Run Windows XP Professional on a Laptop		Chapter 10
✳ Use the Connection Wizard **NEW!**		Chapter 11
✳ Connect to the Internet via Broadband **NEW!**		Chapter 11
✳ Enable Internet Connection Firewall **NEW!**		Chapter 11, p. 87
Share an Internet Connection		Chapter 11
✳ Browse the Web with Internet Explorer 6 **NEW!**		Chapter 12
Use NetMeeting to Conference, Chat, and Collaborate		Chapter 13
✳ Instant Message with Windows Messenger **NEW!**		Chapter 13
✳ Set Up Remote Desktop Connection **NEW!**		Chapter 13, pp. 85–86
Use Outlook Express as a Mail and News Reader		Chapter 14

✳ **NEW!** *to Windows XP Professional*